Illinois Highways, Volumes 2-4

ILLINOIS HIGHWAYS
OFFICIAL PUBLICATION
STATE HIGHWAY DEPARTMENT

| VOL. 2 | SPRINGFIELD, ILLINOIS, JANUARY, 1915 | No. 1 |

AN OLD GRAVEL ROAD AT OREGON, ILLINOIS, RE-SURFACED WITH STONE WHICH IS PENETRATED WITH A HEAVY ASPHALTIC BINDER.

A WATERBOUND MACADAM ROAD AT COLLINSVILLE, ILLINOIS, MAINTAINED BY APPLYING A SURFACE TREATMENT OF HEAVY ASPHALTIC OIL.

ILLINOIS HIGHWAYS.

Published Monthly by the
State Highway Department.

ILLINOIS HIGHWAY COMMISSION.

A. D. Gash, President.
S. E. Bradt, Secretary.
James P. Wilson.

Wm. W. Marr, *Chief State Highway Engineer.*
P. C. McArdle, *Assistant State Highway Engineer.*

H. E. Bilger, *Road Engineer, Springfield, Illinois.*
C. Older, *Bridge Engineer, Springfield, Illinois.*
B. H. Piepmeier, *Assistant Engineer, Springfield, Illinois.*
G. F. Burch, *Assistant Engineer, Springfield, Illinois.*
F. L. Roman, *Testing Engineer, Springfield, Illinois.*

DIVISION ENGINEERS.

H. B. Bushnell..............Aurora
R. L. Bell...................Paris
H. E. Surman............Rock Island
A. H. Hunter...............Peoria
Fred Tarrant............Springfield
C. M. Slaymaker.......E. St. Louis
J. E. Huber...............Marion

CONTENTS.

This number of the Illinois Highways on "The Maintenance Of Gravel and Macadam Roads," has been prepared and arranged by B. H. Piepmeier, Assoc. M., Am. Soc. of Civil Engineers, Asst. Eng. State Highway Department.

APPOINTMENT OF CHIEF STATE HIGHWAY ENGINEER.

Mr. William W. Marr, of Chicago, was appointed Chief State Highway Engineer by Governor Edward F. Dunne, effective December 16, 1914. This position was filled temporarily, since the resignation of Mr. A. N. Johnson, by Mr. P. C. McArdle, Assistant State Highway Engineer.

Mr. Marr is a graduate of the University of Notre Dame, a member of the American Society of Civil Engineers and of the Illinois Society of Engineers and Surveyors.

He was for nine years in charge of the construction of pavements and highways in Chicago, Cook County, and at the time of his appointment was a member of the firm of Aetna Engineering Bureau, Consulting Engineers for a score of Cities in the Middle West.

DEPARTMENTAL WORK.

STATE HIGHWAY COMMISSION.   January 1, 1915.

Gentlemen:

I submit the following report on the present condition of the work being done by the State Highway Department.

STATE AID ROAD WORK.

The last work for the construction season on State aid roads ended December 31, 1914, at which time there had been entirely completed about sixty-four (64) miles of concrete and brick roads with thirty-three (33) additional miles being under contract.

It is quite probable that construction work will not be resumed until about the middle of next April. This matter being governed entirely by weather conditions at the time.

State aid road in Sangamon County, designated as Section D, on route No. 6, enjoys the unique distinction of being the first public highway to be taken over for perpetual maintenance by the State of Illinois. The taking over and maintenance of this particular road by the State dates from November 27, 1914, at which time final payment for the construction of the road was made to the contractor, Mr. John Bretz, of Springfield, Illinois. This event really opens up a new chapter in the history of rural highway maintenance in the State.

As other roads are accepted and taken over from time to time, there will be accumulating upon the State the obligation for the maintenance and repair of these roads to meet the continually changing traffic conditions. It is evident that the maintenance of a large number of very short sections of road, distributed over the length and breadth of the entire State cannot be handled as economically as it could be if the mileage in each county were greater.

As the mileage of roads to be maintained by the State increases from year to year, the expense for maintenance and repairs on these roads will be considerably reduced per square yard of pavement. For the first few years, while the mileage is small and widely distributed, the proportional part of the total expenses for maintenance and repairs chargeable to administration expenses will be somewhat high. With an increasing mileage to be maintained, however, the administration expenses per square yard of pavement treated will decrease from time to time.

The many features of our State aid roads will be observed and studied carefully under actual service conditions. It is anticipated that minor modifications will be made from time to time in many of the features that go to make up the road, with a view of eventually evolving the particular type and method of construction that will be of the most service to each particular community of the State.

TOWNSHIP ROADWORK.

All the township roadwork that was under way this season has been completed or closed down until next spring.

The total amount of road completed last season with State machinery and State supervision was 239,803 square yards, or thirty-three miles in length, of which 3.5 miles are concrete, 3.2 miles are bitumin-

V.4 no 7 last issue pub.
See p.72 v. no.7

ous macadam, 22.7 miles are water-bound macadam and 3.6 miles of re-surfacing.

The macadam road outfits Nos. 1, 2, 3, 4, 5, 7, 8, 9 and 11, the tractor hauling outfit, the concrete mixers, No. 1 and 2, and the oil outfits Nos. 1, 2 and 3 are now stored at the State Fair Grounds and are being over-hauled. Roller outfit No. 10 is stored at Beecher, Ill. Roller No. 6 with oil outfit No. 4 and two heating kettles are stored at Oregon, Ill. Roller No. 2 and concrete outfit No. 3 are stored at Petrolia, Ill. Oil outfit No. 5 with three heating kettles is stored at Peoria, Ill. Oil outfit No. 6 is enroute to Springfield.

Mr. Chamberlin and Mr. Little, roller operators, are stationed at the State Fair Grounds, making the necessary repairs on all road equipment.

There are several jobs that will be ready for work next spring. The equipment that is stored at the points above mentioned, will be used on work at these places next season.

BRIDGE WORK.

During the month of December, plans and specifications for thirty-four bridges, (twenty-nine concrete and five steel) were prepared and sent to County Superintendents of Highways; total estimated cost $63,425.00.

Contracts were awarded for three steel and two concrete bridges, at average cost of 85 per cent of the estimates; total estimated cost, $35,490.00.

The date of letting was set for six bridges, having a total estimated cost of $14,500.00.

Blue prints of thirty-five standard bridge plans were sent upon request to County Superintendents.

Three bridge plans, prepared by County Superintendents were checked and approved.

On January 1, 1915, there were nine bridge inspection reports on hand ready for work. Unless a large amount of bridge work is received before the publication of this bulletin, the department will be in very good shape to turn out plans on short order.

BLUE PRINTING.

During the month of December, 1914, 35 blue prints were made of our bridge standards for County Superintendents of Highways, as well as prints for 3 foreign bridge plans, averaging two sheets, 6 prints being made of each sheet, or about 36 prints. Prints were made of 7 bridges designed by this department, 15 sets each, as well as 3 preliminary sets being sent to the various counties for their use in letting said bridges, totaling 242 prints. Preliminary prints were also made of 5 bridges designed by this department for use of county boards, 3 sets being made of each, or 30 prints.

Preliminary prints were made for 2 sections of roads in 2 counties for county boards to pass on, official prints then being made for county clerks, county superintendents and this office. Each road section averages about 12 sheets, making a total of 96 prints. Copies of plans for 3 sections of roads were made and sent to contractors. These also average 12 sheets each, making 36 prints.

Miscellaneous prints, (about 400) made for office use, make a grand total for the month of December of 875 prints.

Very truly yours,
WM. W. MARR,
Chief State Highway Engineer.

THE MAINTENANCE OF GRAVEL AND MACADAM ROADS.

The problem of economically maintaining gravel and macadam roads is commanding considerable attention in many sections of the country. Correspondence is received continually by the State Highway Department, relating to the proper methods and materials to be employed in the maintenance of these roads that were constructed at a time and under conditions when there was little occasion for maintenance work.

New traffic requirements have brought about conditions demanding efficient maintenance methods and materials. Highway officials, therefore, are seeking advice from those whose entire time and study are devoted to the construction and maintenance of public highways.

Hence, it has been decided to devote considerable space in this issue of the "Illinois Highways" to the maintenance of the gravel and macadam road, in the belief that the suggestions offered will be useful in the adoption of methods and materials in road maintenance that will be in keeping with modern requirements.

More than 90 per cent of the existing hard roads in Illinois are constructed of either gravel or crushed stone. It is estimated that 50 per cent of the hard road surfaces that will be constructed in the next five years will be either gravel or crushed stone.

While people realize that there is a heavy maintenance expense connected with the construction of such roads, yet their low first cost makes them very popular. There are many sections in Illinois that have little or no hard surfaced roads, and the prevailing desire to secure mileage, under any hard road improvement plan, favors gravel or macadam road construction.

It is evident that careful study and consideration must be given to the proper methods and materials to be employed in the maintenance of such roads.

The purpose of this issue will be to outline in a general way the materials that are ordinarily used and the various methods followed in the repairing and maintaining of gravel and macadam roads.

It is also expeced to offer some suggestions for maintenance and to give sufficient cost data on repair work to guide the road officials that are contemplating such improvements.

On account of the large number of gravel and macadam roads that have already been constructed and the rapid deteriorating effects that modern traffic has upon them, it is urged that a definite plan of maintenance be inaugurated and put into operation before the repair work becomes unduly expensive.

ROAD DRAG FOR MAINTAINING GRAVEL AND MACADAM ROADS.

The light road drag may be effectively used in maintaining gravel or macadam roads that have been built without the use of a roller, or on newly constructed roads where some of the material has been displaced by traffic. Where the road grader would necessarily disturb the surface, the road drag simply serves to smooth over the road, fill in the hollows and maintain the crown.

Many of the gravel roads in Illinois are constructed by hauling the bank run gravel and dumping it directly on the road, expecting the traffic to smooth it down and make a hard and lasting surface. Much credit is given to the quality of the gravel, to say that such work has made many very desirable roads. However, an occasional dragging of the roads that are constructed in this way will assure much longer and better service. The dragging will fill all wheel ruts and depressions and allow the desired cross-section to be maintained. The occasional filling of ruts, wheel marks and depressions will shift traffic to different parts of the road surface. The shifting of traffic compacts the road more uniformly and this very materially increases the life of the wearing surface.

THE ROAD DRAG FILLING DEPRESSIONS AND RUTS AND RENEWING THE CROSS-SECTION ON AN OLD GRAVEL ROAD.

Dragging should be more frequent for the first year after the road is completed than at any later time, and, as is the case of all road dragging, the work should be done when the surface is in a moist and soft condition. As the road ages and becomes set, the road drag will have little effect on it unless a prolonged period of rain has made the road very soft.

The ordinary light drag is very effective in maintaining newly built macadam roads, where power rollers have not been used in their construction. Such roads often have many loose stones on the surface that have worked out of the road, and this material can be brought back to place by means of the light drag. Where the light drag is used on the stone road during the first year all the loose material will usually compact with the macadam road and give no further trouble. If the loose stones are allowed to remain on the surface of a well bonded and compacted macadam road, they become a nuisance to traffic and often an injury to the road. In this case, the drag may be used in dragging the loose stones to the edge of the road.

Macadam or gravel roads that are subjected to heavy automobile traffic are often thereby swept clean of all fine bonding material. Much of the old bonding material can be restored to the road surface if the drag is used at the proper time. The occasional use of the road drag on the side roads will also bring some surplus earth next to the metal surface which will aid in holding the material in place and permit traffic to pass on and off the hard road with more ease.

As to the best time for dragging roads, experience proves that more satisfactory results can be secured early in the spring, or after the road has become thoroughly saturated with water. The new material that is brought upon the surface of the road will unite with the old surface and be compacted by the traffic. The small ruts and slight depressions can be filled in this way, and the road will last much longer, besides being more desirable for the traffic. A light dragging of a gravel or macadam road, immediately following a rain, will often prove beneficial, as it will place material into the ruts and depressions that are holding water, thereby forcing the water to the sides and allowing the surface to compact more uniformly. Where the water is allowed to stand upon the surface of a gravel or macadam road, the surface soon becomes softened and the traffic will grind the material out much faster than on other parts of the road surface.

There are many miles of gravel and macadam roads that have been maintained, to a reasonable degree of satisfaction, by means of a road drag and at a cost from 5 to 10 dollars per year per mile.

PATCHING GRAVEL AND MACADAM ROADS.

Gravel or macadam roads that have formed ruts or deep depressions may be satisfactorily repaired by filling such depressions with material similar to that of which the road is constructed. Where the ruts or depressions are of such size that they cannot be readily filled by the drag, as previously referred to in this issue, they can be benefited by filling the depressions with a good bonding gravel or crushed stone and screenings.

Gravel roads may be patched or repaired by dumping a good quality of bonding gravel into the depressions,

MACADAM ROAD, SHOWING NEED OF REPAIRS BY PATCHING.

smoothing off the surface and allowing the traffic to compact same. The bonding gravel, however, should be graded from about 1 inch down to sand, and contain from 15 to 20 per cent clay. The material should also be damp when placed in the depressions so that traffic will compact it more readily. A dry or clean gravel is usually very hard to keep in the depressions. The most favorable time for repairing depressions in old gravel roads is early in the spring, when the surface of the road is soft and when there will not be an excessive amount of dry weather to permit the traffic to grind out the new material before it has had time to throughly set.

In repairing macadam roads, it is often necessary to make the sides of the depressions vertical by means of a scarifier or a hand pick. The depressions are then filled with a coarse stone and thoroughly compacted into place by means of a hand tamper or roller. The surface is then covered with limestone screenings or a fine quality of bonding gravel, after which the surface should be thoroughly soaked with water to insure that all cavities in the stone are filled with the bonding material.

Where a macadam or gravel road has been pitted or worn in holes as shown above, it is not economy to neglect repairs until the entire surface is destroyed. Roads that are patched promptly with a suitable material will have the original surface restored and this will often eliminate the necessity for reconstruction. Holes that are not filled promptly will collect water and the road will disintegrate rapidly.

SURFACE DRESSING FOR GRAVEL AND MACADAM ROADS.

Gravel and macadam roads that are subjected to heavy traffic and that have received no attention in the way of maintenance soon require a new wearing or bonding surface. The usual method of repairing gravel and macadam roads, is to wait until the surface is in such shape that there is required from 3 to 5 inches of new material to resurface the road. This application is of course expensive and it may in many cases be avoided entirely if a light treatment of the best bonding material is applied, as soon as there is any indication of the surface stones becoming loose or depressions and ruts forming.

A MACADAM ROAD SWEPT FREE OF ITS BONDING MATERIAL BY AUTO TRAFFIC. THE SURFACE SHOULD HAVE A LIGHT APPLICATION OF BONDING GRAVEL OR A SURFACE TREATMENT OF OIL AND SAND.

Gravel or macadam roads that have been subjected to heavy automobile traffic are soon swept clean of all surface bonding material and require a surface treatment of some kind to prevent destruction. Roads in this condition present a mosaic surface, and if they are given no attention, traffic will soon loosen some of the stone and the road will start to ravel.

A light dressing of good bonding gravel or limestone screenings to the surface of the road as soon as indica-

tions of raveling appear will often prevent destruction of the road. The application of the bonding material will smooth over the surface and make it more satisfactory for traffic. The surface dressing is applied primarily to supply a bonding material. It will therefore be applied at various intervals and not to exceed about one inch in thickness.

A WELL CONSTRUCTED MACADAM ROAD, FOUR YEARS OLD, RESURFACED WITH TWO INCHES OF COARSE STONE, IMPROPERLY BONDED. MONEY AND MATERIAL PRACTICALLY WASTED.

The size of the material best suited for the light surface treatments should be graded from about ½ inch down. A good bonding gravel containing 15 to 25 per cent of clay gives the best results. If stone screenings are used, about 50 per cent of the material should pass a ⅛ inch screen, and where possible, the screenings should be from a quarry that is known to produce good bonding material. A small amount of clay, not to exceed 10 percent., will often assist the screenings to compact more readily. After the bonding material has been spread evenly over the road, it should be thoroughly soaked with water to assist it in bonding to the old surface.

On roads that receive very heavily loaded wagons and where steel tires predominate, a coarser material will give the desired results. The steel tires grind up the coarser stones and furnish the necessary binder. However, where the road is subjected to considerable automobile traffic, much more care must be taken in selecting the bonding material to insure satisfactory results.

The gravel or macadam road that has become worn or dug out in holes cannot be satisfactorily repaired by the light surface dressing, but requires an application of at least three inches of coarse material. In this case the road may be considered as requiring resurfacing and this method will be explained more fully under that heading.

The picture shown above is of a well built macadam road constructed four years ago. This last season the Highway Commissioners attempted to resurface the road by applying only 2 inches of coarse stone ranging from 1 to 2 inches in size. The coarse stone was spread evenly over the surface of the road and then covered with stone screenings. The stones were too coarse to adhere to the old road surface and the application was not sufficient to permit the new material to bond together. As soon as traffic came upon the road therefore, the stones were displaced.

On account of the size of the material and the thickness of the application, the repairs are considered a failure. It only proved to be a waste of time and material and a menace to traffic for several months. The repairs referred to were estimated at $980.00 for the one mile of road 12 feet wide.

There are many other cases however, where a light surface dressing of gravel or stone screenings has been applied and has proven to be a lasting benefit to the road, where the cost was very much less than the one referred to above.

THE USE OF THE SCARIFIER IN MAINTAINING GRAVEL AND MACADAM ROADS.

When gravel or macadam roads become so badly worn that it is impossible to keep them in good condition by the ordinary methods of maintenance, resurfacing becomes necessary. When resurfacing without the use of a scarifier is done, on a road that has become badly worn, it usually requires from three to ten inches of new material to cover the high places sufficiently to insure a good bond and to fill the low places to the required cross-section. The varied thickness of the new material will not compact uniformly under the traffic and will often cause the road to wear uneven again.

Roads that are resurfaced by applying new material on a compacted road surface will soon build the hard road so high that it will be dangerous to traffic in passing or in driving from the hard road to the earth side roads. It also takes much more material to resurface an old hard road where it has not been loosened and leveled. To insure effective results and economy in resurfacing an old gravel or macadam road, the surface should be picked up or scarified so that all new material will be more uniformly distributed and keyed into the surface of the old road.

A THREE AND ONE-HALF TON SCARIFIER LOOSENING AN OLD MACADAM ROAD, PREPATORY TO RESURFACING WITH NEW MATERIAL.

The wheels of an ordinary three wheeled road roller are so made that it is possible to insert spikes in the rear wheels and spike up the surface of the road. In connection with the spiking, there is usually a heavy harrow that follows the roller to aid in loosening up the spots that are not broken by the wheel spikes. The heavy harrow also aids in sifting the finer stone and dirt to the bottom of the road. There are some objections to loosening a macadam road by means of spikes in the roller wheels as the spikes crush many of the stones.

Scarifiers are commonly used in resurfacing old gravel or macadam roads. Some scarifiers are made so they can be attached to the roller direct, in which case the weight of the roller is used to force the spikes into the surface of the road. There are many advantages in this type of scarifier as the machine can be carried with the roller and instantly put into operation when the roller is traveling in any direction. The most common type

A MACADAM ROAD AFTER IT HAS BEEN THOROUGHLY SCARIFIED AND HARROWED.

used, however, is the one that is built separately and weighs from three to four tons. This machine can be attached behind a roller or tractor as desired. Most types of scarifiers are designed so that it is not necessary to turn them around. This is accomplished by having two sets of picks, one set to be used when the machine is going forward and the other when in the opposite direction. With either type of scarifier the spikes may be set so that practically any depth from one to six inches can be loosened. The scarifier tends to bring the stones to the surface and to shake the smaller stones and dirt down beneath. After the surface is thoroughly scarified a heavy harrow is dragged over the road several times to further assist in sifting the dirt to the bottom.

After being thoroughly scarified and harrowed, some roads may be shaped and re-rolled without adding any new material. However the usual method of repairing is to add about three inches of new material then harrow and roll. After the road is thoroughly rolled, it may be surfaced with a bonding gravel or puddled with stone screenings and water.

There will be less material used in resurfacing a gravel or macadam road where the road has been loosened by the use of the scarifier. The material will also be more uniformly distributed, making it possible to secure a much smoother surface. The saving in material alone will often pay for a scarifier if a district has a number of gravel and macadam roads to resurface.

The cost of loosening the ordinary gravel or macadam road in Illinois, where a tractor or roller is used in connection with a scarifier, will average from ½ to ¾ cents per square yard.

Where the road surface is loosened by means of spikes in the roller wheels and afterwards followed with a heavy harrow, the cost will be from 1½ to 2 cents per square yard.

The average cost of resurfacing gravel or macadam roads, where material has to be shipped in, is about 10 cents per square yard for each inch of new material that is to be added.

BITUMINOUS SURFACES FOR MAINTAINING GRAVEL AND MACADAM ROADS.

Light road oils were first used in this country about twenty years ago in the State of California. About ten years later oil was used to a slight extent in many other parts of the country for the suppression of dust. The oils proved to be very satisfactory in keeping down the dust and preserving the road, so their use rapidly increased until today nearly all towns and cities of any size use the material in some form.

Generally, most oils used were light in character and could be applied cold. At present, however, the use of the light oils is diminishing and a heavier asphaltic oil and refined tar are being used for surface treatment, which not only keep down the dust, but also serves as a protection to the road surface.

There has been much light oil used for suppressing the dust on earth roads. However, a growing objection has been noticed against many such surface treatments, as some require from two to six weeks for the oil to set up, so that tracking will not occur. Many of the lighter oils are very greasy and are found to be of little benefit to the road besides they volatilize very rapidly and a new application is required about the time the previous treatment begins to set up. In recent years, the refined tars and asphaltic oils have been used and have given much better satisfaction.

It has been found that well built gravel or macadam roads that have been treated with about one-half gallon of refined tar or asphaltic oil per square yard, and have received a thin covering of coarse sand or stone chips, have set up promptly, so that no tracking is noticeable, and that the mat surface gives satisfactory protection to the road for at least one year, and in many cases two or three years, depending upon the traffic conditions and the quality of the material applied.

A careful inspection of many bituminous macadam roads constructed in Illinois, has indicated a deterioration of the road as soon as the mat surface of bituminous material has been worn through. This may be explained by the breaking down of the comparatively soft limestone that is necessarily used in many of the Illinois roads. The bituminous mat surface into which has been incorporated a good coarse quartz sand will resist the wear better than the ordinary stone road. It therefore seems advisable to occasionally apply a small quantity of a good bituminous material to the old road, to protect same from excessive wear.

If newly built gravel or macadam roads are inspected carefully during the first year and are not allowed to become rutted or raveled, they may be surface-treated with a heavy asphaltic oil or refined tar and made to last longer, as well as become much more satisfactory for traffic.

Gravel or macadam roads that receive a preponderance of auto traffic are soon whipped bare of all the bonding material and will begin raveling if not attended to. The application of a good bituminous material to the amount of one-half gallon per square yard, and then treated with sand or stone, will furnish a carpet or mat that will prevent dust and excessive wear on the body of the road. While the surface treatment may have to be applied each year, or every other year, it is worthy of careful consideration by all road officials who have gravel or macadam roads that are subjected to much auto traffic. It is also well to consider bituminous treatments on all new gravel or macadam roads that are constructed on heavily traveled routes.

CONSTRUCTION OF BITUMINOUS SURFACES.

Before constructing a bituminous surface of heavy asphaltic oil or refined tar on a gravel or macadam road, all depressions, ruts, pot holes and other irregularities should be completely eliminated by proper repairs, so that the entire road surface is even. All surplus dust must be removed from the surface, preferably by the ordinary street sweeper. However, hand brooms may be used, but this method is very slow and expensive. The surface should be swept so clean that the crushed stone and pebbles are well exposed. Care should be taken, however, to not loosen the bond on the road surface. Should any spots on the road surface show signs of being loose or contain a surplus of fine material, it is often necessary to replace them with new material or to bond them thoroughly by applying a small amount of the hot bituminous material before the surface treatment is applied.

Where surface treatments are applied on newly built roads, care should be taken to insure that all surface stones are well bonded and all voids in the surface filled with a road material before the oil is applied.

There are three things that should be watched very closely in applying bituminous surfaces: first, that the road surface is uniform and thoroughly bonded; second, that there is no dust on the road surface and third, that the road surface and all material used is dry.

APPLYING BITUMINOUS MATERIAL BY HAND.

The application of the bituminous material may be made either by hand or by mechanical methods. When applied by hand, the ordinary pouring can is used and is filled from a large supply tank that is driven along beside the work. It is very difficult to apply the bituminous material evenly from the pouring can and where such a method is used it is necessary to immediately follow the application with a heavy brush broom and keep sweeping the surplus oil ahead. This method of applying the material is very slow and expensive and is rarely used today except on small jobs and on patch work.

There are a great many different types of mechanical distributors on the market, and it is not difficult to secure the necessary apparatus for applying the hot bituminous material, if a mile or more of road is to be constructed.

The apparatus which is used by the State Highway Department has been designed so that it will apply either light or heavy bituminous material, and in any quantities desired. The apparatus is a steel tank of about 600 gallon capacity, mounted on a heavy truck. The steel tank is air tight and is designed to withstand an internal pressure of 100 pounds per square inch. At the rear end of the distributor is a furnace which will burn either wood or coal for heating the tank. A Westinghouse air pump is attached to the front end of the distributor and

barrels or in metal drums. The barrels or drums are then emptied into auxiliary kettles having a capacity of about 450 gallons each. The auxiliary kettles are filled and heated while the pressure tank is being emptied. The practice several years ago was to deliver the bituminous material in railroad tank cars to a convenient

PRESSURE DISTRIBUTOR APPLYING ASPHALT ON A MACADAM ROAD. EQUIPMENT OWNED BY STATE HIGHWAY DEPARTMENT.

this is connected with the steam roller, so that a pressure or vacuum can be secured in the tank very quickly. A guage is placed at the top of the distributor for regulating the pressure.

A thermometer is attached at the rear end to indicate the temperature of the binder. The bituminous material is carried from the tank to the spray by a flexible metal hose which can be carried by one man and permits the operator to apply either large or small quantities as desired. Attached to the end of the metal hose is a spraying nozzle as shown below.

Steam is conducted from the steam roller to the nozzle by a ⅜-inch pipe, as shown in the above cut. The arrangement of the apparatus is such that the binder is forced through the 1½-inch hose and pipe and as it is discharged from the nozzle a jet of steam blows into the binder breaking it into a fine spray. This makes it possible to apply the bituminous material uniformly over the surface of the road.

The apparatus has proven to be very satisfactory as it will apply any grade of binder and in any quantities desired. The force with which the binder leaves the nozzle aids it in penetrating all interstices in the road as well as freeing the stones of the dust coating that they may have.

With the equipment referred to above, it is convenient to have the binder delivered alongside the road in

siding where the material was heated and pumped directly into the distributing wagon and carried to the road. This system may be used to some advantages when light road oils are used, but with the heavier products the expense connected with heating the railroad tank cars; the time required to empty same and the distance the heating plant is from the work; also the difficulty of having sufficient road surface prepared ready to receive the entire 8,000 or 10,000 gallons, which is the capacity of the steel tank cars, makes this system very impractical and it has accordingly given way to the use of auxiliary heating kettles alongside the road. With the auxiliary heating kettles, the bituminous material may be delivered in wooden barrels or metal drums and used as needed.

As soon as the hot bituminous material is applied, it should be covered lightly with torpedo gravel or stone chips, free from dust, and which range in size from ⅛ to ⅜ inch. The gravel or chips should be broomed over the surface of the road to such thickness only as to prevent the bituminous material from adhering to wheels. On heavily traveled roads and where the road receives its first treatment better results can be secured by applying the bituminous surface in two courses; the first treatment should have about ¼ gallon of material per square yard after which it is sprinkled with torpedo gravel or chips and rolled. The second application of ¼ gallon per square yard is applied and the surface again treated with sand or stone chips, after which it may be rolled and thrown open to traffic.

gravel roads at a very much lower figure than we have been doing heretofore. The present system of maintenance allows the surface of a gravel or macadam road

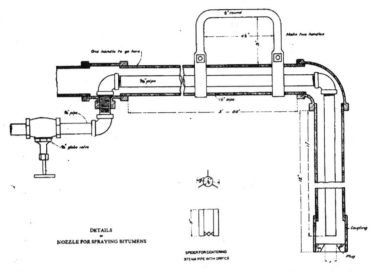

DETAILS
of
NOZZLE FOR SPRAYING BITUMENS

SPIDER FOR CENTERING
STEAM PIPE WITH ORIFICE

DETAILS OF NOZZLE FOR SPRAYING BITUMINOUS MATERIALS. USED BY THE STATE HIGHWAY DEPARTMENT.

The entire surface treatment should not receive over one-half gallon per square yard and should be from ¼ to ⅜ inches thick when completed. It will require about one cubic yard of torpedo gravel or chips for every 125 to 150 square yards of surface to be treated. Excessive thickness in the mat surface should be avoided to secure the best results. For this reason, the machine method of applying bituminous material is much preferred, as it can be applied thinner and more uniformly.

The State Highway Department now owns six complete oiling outfits and it will be glad to loan them to any township upon receipt of proper application forms. On account of the demand for this machinery, it is well for townships to plan their work far enough ahead that proper arrangements can be made by this department for handling the work. It is expected that the only charge connected with securing such equipment will be the freight from shipping point to the nearest siding.

The State Highway Department stands ready to assist all townships and districts in the proper maintenance of gravel or macadam roads. The testing department is equipped to make the tests on all road materials, and it will gladly furnish advice to road officials, free of charge, in regard to the quality of binder which they propose to use. The department will also furnish expert engineering supervision over the construction of such roads, providing proper arrangement can be made with the officials in charge.

If it were possible to inaugurate a system of maintenance on surface oiled macadam roads, whereby they might receive regular and frequent inspection and repairs, it would be possible to maintain the macadam and

or oiled surface to be completely destroyed before the road officials are forced to make the necessary repairs. This is very clearly brought out in the picture below. A supply of torpedo gravel or stone chips and oil should be kept constantly on hand in the vicinity of such roads and

A BITUMINOUS SURFACE ON AN OLD MACADAM ROAD. SURFACE TREATMENT WORN AWAY IN SPOTS SHOWING DISREGARD OF PROPER MAINTENANCE.

the holes and ruts repaired as rapidly as they develop and usually before they become large enough to hold water or to be noticeable to traffic.

APPLICATION OF LIGHTER OILS.

Where light oils are applied on earth roads or on gravel or crushed stone roads for the purpose of suppressing the dust, it is not necessary to heat the oil or to be so careful in the removal of all dust before applying same. However, should the road have a heavy covering of dust, the surplus should be scraped or broomed to one side and the oil applied upon the road surface. Soon after the oil is distributed it should be covered with some of the dust, or preferably a coarse sand after which it may be thrown open to traffic. Where light oils are used for laying the dust, it is necessary to make one or two applications each year. The applications should be repeated rather than to apply a surplus at any one time. A surplus of the light oil will usually make a very undesirable surface and it becomes a nuisance to traffic. From ¼ to ½ gallon per square yard is usually sufficient. Many of the light oils may be applied cold, and they can usually be delivered in railroad tank cars, then pumped from the car into an ordinary street sprinkling wagon, or a similar distributing equipment.

This method of suppressing the dust appeals to many road officials, as it can be applied very quickly and the first cost is very small. However, as it gives but very little protection to the road and the application must be repeated once or twice each year, the cost will often equal or exceed the application of the heavier products, besides it will not give the satisfaction to the traffic as will the heavier products that are applied hot.

A WELL CONSTRUCTED MACADAM ROAD TREATED WITH A LIGHT OIL FOR SUPPRESSING THE DUST.

The light road oils can usually be purchased for 3 to 6 cents per gallon, but an oil having a good asphaltic base will cost from 4½ to 10 cents per gallon. It is recommended that the heavier asphaltic oils and refined tars be used where possible, as their use will give more lasting results.

SOME MISCELLANEOUS MATERIALS FOR GRAVEL AND MACADAM ROADS.

Besides light oils and tars, there are dust preventatives used that require applications with more or less frequency, such as water, sea water, salt solutions, calcium chlorides, gluterin, etc. The application of water is the most common method of laying the dust, but on account of its scarcity in many sections of the state and the numerous applications that are necessary

to keep down the dust, it is an expensive treatment. While the cost of sprinkling under economic management may not exceed 3 cents per square yard, per season, yet the public often demands a more lasting surface treatment if it can be secured at a reasonable cost.

The use of calcium chloride, which is a bi-product in the manufacture of common washing soda, has been used by many localities and found to be very satisfactory for keeping down the dust. Its action in the surface of the road is to keep it moist, it has the property of absorbing moisture from the air and retaining it in the surface of the road for several weeks. It is ordinarily shipped in granulated form in air-tight steel drums. It may be used on the road in two ways; first by sprinkling the dry powder uniformly upon the surface of the road and second by making a solution with water and sprinkling it upon the road, the same as water. When applied dry, it will require from 1 to 1½ pounds to the square yard and when applied in solution, it should be dissolved at the rate of 1 lb. to 1 gallon of water. To secure freedom from dust about one application should be used each month during the dusty season. The cost of such treatments will average about 3 cents per square yard per season. The powdered form may be purchased in metal drums, of about 350 pounds each, for from $14 to $18 per ton, f. o. b. at points of manufacture.

Glurtin which is the water lyes from the woodpulp factories, is often used as a road binder and dust layer. The objection to this material, as with all such dust layers, is that the material dissolves readily in water and for this reason the applications have to be repeated often.

However, on account of the binding properties of glutrin, an application of such material on a newly constructed road will assist the surface bonding material in holding the stones in place, as well as to prevent dust for a considerable time after its application.

The glutrin can be purchased for about 14 cents per gallon and it can be diluted one half or more before application. To use the material as a dust layer, it may be diluted 3 to 4 times, but where it is to be used as a binder, it should be diluted about one-half. About two applications are required each season to insure the best results.

PROTECTING GRAVEL AND MACADAM ROADS FROM EXCESSIVE WEAR.

On account of the comparatively soft limestone that is necessarily used in Illinois for road construction and the character of the gravel that is used, it is quite important that the construction be carried out according to standard practice and all precautions taken to prolong the life of such roads.

While space has not been taken in this issue for outlining standard methods to be followed in constructing gravel or macadam roads, a few fundamental principles will be suggested that should be observed to assist in reducing maintenance to a minimum.

All crushed stone or gravel roads should be constructed on a well drained subgrade. Soft places in the subgrade readily show up in the surface of the road and maintenance becomes heavy from the start. Stone laid upon a dusty or muddy subgrade will not give the best results as, the dust or mud works up through the stone, leaving an uneven wearing surface. Soft, disintegrated stones or pebbles should be avoided as they will rapidly grind to dust, leaving holes in the road and a dusty surface that will be a menace to traffic. Gravel and macadam roads should be constructed of well graded stones of uniform and fairly good size, and yet not so large as to form a rough surface. Large pockets of fine gravel or stone screenings will produce not only a dusty road, but also one that will rapidly form pockets. All roads should be thoroughly rolled where possible and only sufficient bonding material added to fill the voids and hold the stones in place.

A SURFACE DRESSING AT THE RIGHT TIME WOULD HAVE SHIFTED THE TRAFFIC TO DIFFERENT PARTS OF THE ROAD AND PREVENTED THE RUTS. ROAD SHOULD NOW BE SCARI- FIED AND RESURFACED.

Where a road surface is covered heavily with dust or screenings or where the surface is allowed to wear uneven, the traffic will be confined to a single track and nothing will destroy a road quicker. The rutting evil is the most difficult to eliminate on this type of road. To prevent ruts, it is necessary to have an adequate system of maintenance; that is, where the drag may be used, the surface patched or redressed with screenings, or a bituminous material applied when necessary. The shifting of the traffic to all parts of the hard road surface will aid not only in keeping down the dust, but will prolong the life of the road.

The following suggestions are offered to assist in reducing to a minimum the ruts caused by tracking:

Construct all roads of as hard a material as can be secured and compact them with a roller. Use large stones and only sufficient screenings or bonding material to hold the stones in place.

Build a road with a minimum crown. The flatter the crown the less tendency there will be for traffic to concentrate in the center of the road.

Build a wide road. The wider the paved surface, the more traffic will distribute itself over the surface of the road. Construct a road with a wide berm so traffic may readily drive on and off the metal surface.

Educate the public to the importance of distributing the traffic as uniformly as possible over the road. This may be done by bringing the matter before automobile associations and teamsters' unions, etc; also by erecting "ANTI RUT" signs along the road and in public places, and by newspaper articles and special bill posters.

By obstructing the road at intervals by placing timbers or stones in the beaten track. The obstacles laid across alternate wheel tracks and occasionally shifted to the opposite side will force the traffic to distribute the wear more uniformly over the surface of the road and prevent serious rutting. This, however, may be objectionable from the standpoint of endangering and interfering with traffic.

Any of the above methods will assist in preventing ruts and will reduce maintenance to a minimum. However, the surest way to prevent ruts and to maintain the road is to treat it with a heavy bituminous material that will make it hard, dustless and smooth.

SPECIFICATIONS FOR BITUMINOUS SURFACES.

The following specifications are given as a guide in selecting the better grades of asphaltic oils and coal tar products that may be used in surfacing gravel and macadam roads. The specifications are drawn to cover the heavier bituminous products and are not to be considered as being applicable to all conditions.

In the selection of a bituminous material or a dust preventative, there are many things to be taken into consideration. Chief among these are the type of road under consideration, the condition of the surface, the character of traffic, the requirements of the public and the amount of money available. All these things should be taken into consideration before deciding upon the method of improvement or the quality of material that is to be used. After this has been done materials should be purchased under a well drawn set of specifications and be applied according to standard practice.

SPECIFICATIONS FOR BITIUMINOUS BINDER H. O. TO BE USED IN THE SURFACE TREATMENT OF MACADAM ROADS.

1. The material shall be free from water.

2. SPECIFIC GRAVITY—The specific gravity at 25°C (77°F) shall not be less than 0.98 per cent.

3. TOTAL BITUMEN.—The bituminous material shall be soluble in chemically pure cold carbon bisulphide to the extent of at least 99.5 per cent.

4. NAPHTHA INSOLUBLE BITUMEN.—Of the total bitumen not less than 10 nor more than 25 per cent by weight shall be insoluble in 86°B paraffine naphtha at air temperature. On evaporation of the naphtha solution, the residue obtained shall be adhesive and sticky and not oily.

5. LOSS ON EVAPORATION.—When 20 grams (in a tin dish 2⅜ inches in diameter and ¾ inches deep with vertical sides) are maintained at a temperature of 163°C (325°F) for 5 hours in a N. Y. testing labratory oven, the loss shall not exceed 20 per cent by weight.

6. PENETRATION.—The penetration of the bituminous material as determined with a Dow penetration machine, using a No. 2 needle, 100 grams weight, 5 seconds time and a temperature of 25°C (77°F) shall not be less than 30 mm.

7. When evaporated in the open air at a temperature not exceeding 260°C (500°F) until 25 per cent has been lost on evaporation, the penetration of the residue as determined with a Dow penetration machine, using a No. 2 needle, 100 grams weight, 5 seconds time and a temperature of 25°C (77°F) shall not be more than 10 mm.

8. FIXED CARBON.—The fixed carbon shall not be less than 5.0 per cent nor more than 13.0 per cent.

9. The bituminous material shall not contain more than 2.0 per cent by weight of paraffine scale.

SPECIFICATIONS FOR COAL TAR PRODUCTS USED FOR THE SURFACE TREATMENT OF MACADAM ROADS.

SPECIFIC GRAVITY.—The specific gravity at 25°C shall not be less than 1.18 nor more than 1.24.

FREE CARBON.—The free carbon content shall not be less than 12 nor more than 22 per cent. In determining the free carbon, the coal tar product will be dissolved in chemically pure carbon bisulphide and the residue filtered on Gooch crucible. The per cent residue minus the per cent of ash will be taken as the per cent of free carbon. No centrifuge is to be used in these tests.

CONSISTENCY.—The consistency as determined by Howard & Morse float apparatus at a temperature of 50°C shall not be less than 20 seconds nor more than one minute.

DISTILLATION.—Fractional distillation shall give results within the following limits, all measurements being by volume at 25°C.

Up to 110°C the distillate shall not exceed 2 per cent and shall be free of ammoniacal water.

Up to 170°C the distillate shall not exceed 10 per per cent.

The total distillate up to 315°C shall be at least 25 per cent.

MODERN ROAD EQUIPMENT FOR COUNTIES AND TOWNSHIPS.

There are comparatively few kinds of construction work that are being done today in the manner in which they were done 20 years ago, nor are the same tools being used. Recent requirements for constructing and maintaining the modern highways have brought many new machines on the market. It is not the purpose of this paper to discuss the merits of any particular make of machinery, but rather to enumerate the more important road machinery and give briefly their field of usefulness.

On account of labor conditions existing in rural territory, it has been necessary for road officials to seek the most modern equipment for doing their work. The over-desire of road officials to procure equipment that would construct and maintain the modern roads at the minium of cost has in many cases led the Highway Commissioners to purchase labor saving equipment that was not commensurate with the amount of work they had to do. In the intelligent use of the modern equipment lies one of the principles making for efficiency. But this is true only when there is sufficient use to be made of it to justify the expenditure.

The business man of today is reducing to a minimum the equipment that can be used but a few days each year. He realizes that machinery not in use is earning nothing and is depreciating almost the same as the machine that is in constant use. It is evident that there are many road machines on the market today that would very materially reduce the annual cost of roadwork, but on account of the limited means or use that any one township may have for the machine, makes the owning of such equipment prohibitive.

While the road law of Illinois makes it possible for the Counties to assist in road improvement, yet the prevailing unit is the township and road district, which ordinarily averages 6 miles square.

The average township with from 1 to 3 commissioners has an annual income of about $4,000.00;

it also has about 70 miles of road, with the necessary culverts and bridges to construct and maintain. There are many townships that have some of their roads improved and are out of debt, while others have no improved roads, many bad culverts and bridges and are in debt. This is often the result of the geographical location of the township. The township or road district that by chance includes a city, will of course, have an opporunity to make more improvements and to own more equipment than the township that by chance lays between two wealthy townships or in a very rough and unsettled district.

It is therefore evident that before the proper equipment could be recommended for any one township, it would require a detailed study of its conditions. On account of the limited use that townships have for many modern machines, even though they may be used to a great advantage, it is recommended that counties look forward to the owning of all modern equipment, which may be effectively used by its townships or road districts, and to loan it to the road officials at actual cost of operation.

There are very few townships that have sufficient work to justify the installation of a stone crusher, though there may be abundance of good road material at hand. The limited means of the ordinary townships permits it to construct but very few hard roads each year. It is therefore cheaper for the township to ship materials in and pay the extra cost for the small amount of work they are able to do. Many counties, if equipped with a portable crushing plant, under the direct supervision of the County Superintendent of Highways, could no doubt supply the needs of its townships and do it in many cases at a much lower figure than they could purchase the material in the open market.

There are many efficient hauling outfits such as tractors, motor trucks, industrial railroad outfits, dump wagons, etc., that would very materially aid the average township in its improvement work, but on account of its limited use, it would in the majority of cases, be an extravagant expenditure. However, the amount of work that is done in any one year in the average county would justify the expenditure.

There are many modern machines used for constructing and maintaining gravel and macadam roads, such as road rollers, scarifiers, elevating graders, tractor graders, sprinkling wagons and special oiling outfits that would greatly simplify the work of the average township, but the work they have to do along this line, in many cases does in no way justify the township in owning such equipment.

On account of the condition referred to above, many townships have been hindered from making improvements that were possible, and also from properly maintaining the work they have been able to do. Many townships, by the judicious management of their officials, have been able to build a number of very creditable gravel and macadam roads. However, in the last few years, the change in traffic conditions have made these same townships seek new methods of construction and maintenance and the requirements have come so rapidly that the average township cannot adjust itself to the needs of the modern traffic. Their delay in maintenance may be attributed to the officials not having the opportunity to keep in touch with modern methods of maintenance work, and the inability of the township to procure the proper equipment for doing the work.

The equipment owned by the average township consists of a few drags, a few old slip scrapers, possibly a few wheel scrapers and three or four old graders. It is readily seen that while the above named articles may be in keeping with the amount of work that is done, it cannot be expected that efficient results in construction or in maintenance can be expected with such equipment.

It is strongly urged and recommended by the State Highway Department that the county as a unit take up the matter of assisting the townships and road districts in constructing and maintaining all roadwork and especially have possession of the most modern road equipment that is needed for the various kinds of work that its townships may have to do, and to place the machinery under the general supervision of the County Superintendent of Highways, that he may loan it to the various townships that are in need of such equipment.

On account of the numerous small jobs that the townships are forced to do by day labor and their inability to purchase modern road equipment, it has led the State Highway Department to furnish many townships in the State with expert engineering supervision and modern road equipment for doing the work they have had to do. The State Highway Department now owns eleven 10-ton road rollers, one 30-horse tractor with four 7-ton dump wagon trailers, six complete oiling outfits, 3 large concrete mixers, two scarifiers, two street sweepers, and other incidental equipment, such as sprinkling wagons, pumps, pipe, wheel scrapers, tool boxes and incidental tools, all of which may be loaned to any township without charge, excepting the freight from shipping point to destination. However, it will readily be seen that with the large amount of road improvement that is being considered by the townships in Illinois, that it will be impossible as well as impractical, for the State Highway Department to furnish the necessary equipment. It is further urged, therefore, that the County Superintendents of Highways make a more thorough study of he needs of the various townships in their respective Counties and impress upon the County officials the importance of owning equipment that will be in keeping with the requirements of the work the townships have under consideration.

1914 MACADAM ROAD CONSTRUCTION, WASHINGTON TOWNSHIP, WILL CO., AT BEECHER, ILLINOIS.

(CONVICT LABOR.)

By C. M. Hathaway, Assistant Engineer, Illinois State Highway Department.

On December 15, the last section of the macadam road at Beecher was thrown open to traffic, thus giving to Washington Township 14 miles of water-bound macadam road; 12½ miles of which have been constructed since June, 1914. By the completion of this work there is now (except for ½ mile in Crete Township and 1 mile near Momence) an unbroken system of hard roads extending from Chicago south to Kankakee.

In 1913 the township first levied a special hard roads tax of $1.00 on a hundred dollars valuation, this tax to run five years, and late in the fall of the same year, the proceeds of this tax together with the regular road and bridge fund were used in the construction of the first mile and one-half of macadam road. This work was done by the local commissioners with day labor. Early in the spring of 1914 it was decided to build 10 or 12 miles of road during the year and accordingly bonds for $35,000.00 were voted at the spring election. The money thus derived together with the 1914 hard road tax levy and the road and bridge assessment gave a fund amounting to about $53,000.00 for the 1914 construction and $2,000.00 for road and bridge purposes.

The system laid out was ideal in several respects; it leads from four directions into Beecher, the railroad and business center of the township; it embraces the Chicago Road, the main line road from Chicago to Danville and intermediate points; and it practically cuts the township in half both east and west and north and south, thereby accruing some benefit to every taxpayer in the township.

As outlined in the August issue of "Illinois Highways," the State Highway Department was called upon to make plans and furnish machinery and superintendence for this work, while it was arranged with the Joliet Penitentiary to furnish about 50 convicts. The State Highway Department arranged to furnish as needed, several more men, the local commissioners paying their salaries and expenses. The final organization from the State Highway Department was as follows:

C. M. Hathaway, Supt. in Charge.

Floyd Little, in charge of the hauling outfit.

Fred Thatcher, } Foremen.
D. S. James, }

Carl Little, } Roller Operators.
John Riley, }

In July a second steam roller was added to the equipment and in September a third roller and scarifier was sent from the Highway Department. It was largely due to these additional rollers and their excellent operation that the work was completed this season. The full quota of equipment from the State Highway Department comprised: Six 7-yard hauling wagons, the traction hauling engine, four road plows, six large wheel scrapers, three 10 ton steam rollers, three sprinkling wagons and one large water-hauling wagon, one gasoline engine and a scarifier. In addition, there was leased for four months from the Orenstein-Arthur Koppel, Co., one 30 H. P. steam locomotive, sixty 1½ yard dump cars and 4½ miles of 24 inch guage track, 20 pound rails, including curves, frogs and switches.

Due to the great amount of grading work involved, it was deemed advisable to organize a separate grading gang of local teams and men. Road Commissioner, Fred Erikson, was placed in charge of this work, and with 10 to 12 teams and 4 to 6 men carried on the grading in advance and independently of the other organization.

Grading was commenced June 1st, on the East Road. Four deep cuts and several fills were made besides the cutting off of the many knobs and filling of hollows, to give a uniform and unbroken grade line. Wherever practical the standard 30 foot roadway was maintained. On the Chicago Road, still greater attention was given to the grading, as this road, will be subjected to a heavy through auto traffic. The south section, especially, was a succession of hills and hollows. except on the south mile, where there was a low swampy area. Hills were cut from 3-7 feet and the material used for fill. The resulting grade was rolling, but greatly reduced and uniform. By cutting out 3 foot side ditches, using the waste as fill, and putting in two new culverts, the swampy section was raised to a satisfactory grade. On the north section the profile was more uniform, so that the chief grading was to secure the standard width and provide good deep side ditches.

There were no bridges constructed or replaced on either of these roads, but several old tile culverts were replaced with cast-iron pipe, usually to give a greater area, and new cast-iron pipe culverts were laid wherever needed. All old culverts were lengthened to 36 feet and all new ones laid to the same length; no head walls were needed in any instance.

The use of cast-iron pipe instead of concrete was due to the fact that the township had a large supply of this particular pipe already bought.

As the convict camp was not well established until June 18, the hauling was delayed later than was anticipated, it being July 1st before the hauling outfit was unloaded and enough track laid on the East Road to start hauling. As the operation of the unloading chute for stone was fully described in the August issue of "Illinois Highways" it will not be detailed again except to note that, considering the local conditions and class of labor employed, its operation was entirely satisfactory from the standpoint of efficiency and economy.

The system of track-laying and placing the stone was essentially as follows:

After the sub-grade had been cut out with the road machine to a very nearly finished shape, the rail sections were laid down the middle, taking pains to keep them about 5 feet from one shoulder and well balanced up from dips and kinks. (After a heavy rain it was usually necessary to haul out 6 to 8 yards of stone and ballast up all soft places to keep the track from slumping or sliding). Due to the amount of work in moving track, the stone was all laid in one full 8" course which required two dumps to the car length for a 12-foot road and correspondingly less for a 10-foot road. This was accomplished by throwing the track 2 feet toward the shoulder after the first dump, after which the second load could be dumped or scattered, as desired. The track was then thrown well up on the shoulder and screenings hauled and dumped in proper amount outside the rail, on the shoulder. Thus spreading and rolling could begin as soon as the last dump of stone was made. Two men could easily handle this track work under ordinary circumstances, while if one or two extra men were needed, they could be taken off the sub-grade trimming gang, which was usually only about 1,000 feet ahead. These track-men were also of assistance and practically a necessity in dumping.

Four or five men usually handled the sub-grade trimming, which consisted chiefly in getting shoulders to accurate lines and smoothing out any irregularities in the surface. These men also put in the lateral drains.

Hauling on the East Road was completed about September 1, and the track was shifted to the south section of the Chicago Road, this work being accomplished at the rate of about one mile a day, requiring about 12 men unbolting and picking up track and the

same number laying and bolting up ahead. By this time an increase in the convict force made a double shift train crew possible, so that the outfit was kept in operation from 4 a. m. to 8 p. m., in which time 10 to 12 trainloads of about 28 cars each could be hauled. The unloading chute made this work possible without using an extra crew loading, although at the latter end of the work an extra crew was kept busy loading, these crews being made up of such men from the convict camp as wanted this work. Whenever possible, such labor was paid for on a piece work basis, and when not 20c per hour was allowed. Due to this extra work, aided by a much better organization, the hauling on the south section was completed by October 1st, and that on the north section (Chicago Road) by November 1, which was the time limit on the lease of the hauling outfit. Due to the inability of the Penitentiary to furnish stone fast enough, 1,500 feet on the south end of the Chicago Road was constructed of Thornton stone, this material being hauled by teams about ¾ mile. The same lack of screenings made it necessary to haul about 500 tons of screenings on the north section by teams.

In spreading stone and screenings and rolling, there was little if any variation from the usual methods. As one convict gang of picked men was put on this work, and kept there from start to finish, this phase of the work doubtless proceeded with the most efficiency, and its organization was about the best of any of the convict gangs.

Realizing the necessity of using some bonding material with the Joliet screenings, especially during the hot, dry weather, the Commissioners decided to use bonding gravel and commercial bonding screenings on the East Road. The Road was first finished with Joliet screenings and puddled in the usual manner, after which a ¾ inch wearing course of bonding gravel or bonding screenings (½" to dust) was applied. The screenings were puddled and the gravel was rolled dry, then wet down and thoroughly rolled again as soon as the surface was sufficiently dry to prevent sticking to the wheels. As this work was practically completed by September 1st, the results may be noted as follows on December 15th:

Station 0-72, bonding gravel; road well bonded and required absolutely no repairs.

Station 72-124, bonding screenings; this section ravelled considerably at first due to dry weather and 8 to 10 loads of screenings were needed to put it in shape again. Traffic and a little rolling after a rain put the surface in excellent shape after a short time.

Station 124-210, bonding gravel; this section was badly rutted due to heavy hauling, but there was practically no ravelling. By raking the excess gravel into the ruts and later re-rolling, this section was repaired with very little cost.

Station 210-222, bonding screenings; same results as from Station 72-124.

On the south section of the Chicago Road a bonding gravel was used from Station 333-280. Up to December 15, this section was in good shape and required practically no repairs. On the rest of the south section the road was finished with Joliet screenings and opened to traffic. This was done to let all ravelling occur before using any bonding material. After four weeks, about 1¼ miles at the south end showed some very bad ravelling and accordingly this stretch was re-rolled and a bonding gravel applied. On the remainder of this section, the ravelling was so slight that all spots were touched up with screenings and the road again opened to traffic.

From Station 0-105 on the north section of the Chicago Road, the road was finished without any bonding material, it being hoped that the fall and spring rains together with traffic would produce the desired bonding. From Station 105-160, the first coat of screenings was spread, wet and rolled, after which about ¾″ of bonding gravel was spread and wet down and then rolled as soon as it had dried out enough not to stick. These two sections have not been down long enough to show any results.

On the south section of the Chicago Road, just after crossing Indiana Street, a 500 foot stretch was constructed with a preparation of silicate of soda, this material being donated and the construction supervised by the Philadelphia Quartz Co., manufacturers of the silicate.

There was also consructed on the south end of the Chicago Road about 1,800 feet of 9 foot macadam in Yellowhead Township, Kankakee County. This stretch filled in the gap between the two townships. The labor for this section was practically all done by the Commissioners of Yellowhead Township, the State furnishing superintendence and machinery.

Construction on these three sections was completed about December 6, and about ten days was spent in touching up and putting in shape all places which showed any signs of rutting or ravelling. It is intended to leave one roller at Beecher this winter in order that one of the State roller operators may go over all these roads next Spring and put them in first-class condition.

It was also intended to go over the 1913 sections as some re-shaping and touching up was needed, but the setting in of cold weather put a stop to any efforts in this direction.

As the West Road was only one mile in length and over two miles from the leading station, and since crossing the main line of the C. & E. I. R. R. with the industrial outfit was out of the question, it was decided to do the hauling with teams, using the grading gang for this work as soon as available. Practically no convict labor was used on this road. The grading on this road was the most costly of any mile encountered, chiefly because over two-thirds of it was located through a low swampy area and had a very flat roadway. By using the waste material from one deep cut and cutting 3′ ditches on each side, a very good elevation was secured for the new roadway. One steel leg bridge was replaced with an 18″ cast iron pipe culvert, which will carry all ordinary flow, while the deepening of the side-ditch allows additional waterway to the bridge 800 feet beyond. There were no special features of construction on this section except the one course construction. A glance at the cost data given below will show the economy with which the hauling was done, especially since it was done at intermittent stages due to irregular stone shipments. Thornton screenings were used exclusively as a binder on the first half mile and Joliet screenings on the last. The latter required some rolling and touching up after three weeks traffic while very few repairs were needed on the former. A 150 foot stretch of concrete 9 feet wide, with 3 feet stone shoulders was constructed on the west end as a protection against mud from the adjoining earth roads. As the west end of the 1913 section

was badly ravelled and out of shape, about 600′ was scarified, re-shaped, given a 3″ course of 2½″ stone and finished in the usual manner. The results were enirely satisfactory.

The Indiana Street Section, 3,600 feet in length, is the main travelled street through Beecher. The existing grade was followed and enough dirt was graded off the road surface to make all necessary shoulders. To leave the old foundation, which was an old 12 inch macadam, intact and still get the proper crown, the macadam was made 3 inches to 4 inches thick at the sides and 6 inches at the center. Hauling was done entirely with teams, the maximum haul being only ⅓ mile. No convict labor was used on this section, except in levelling stone. The macadam was 20 feet wide, except 600 feet on both sides of the C. & E. I. R. R., where it was narrowed to 12 feet. Thornton screenings were used entirely as binder.

The convict camp and its organization was described in the August issue of this bulletin and there were no changes of importance. An average working force of 46 men was kept. Camp was broken November 21, as the practical completion of the work made it impossible to keep this large force of men at work.

In arranging the cost data given below the East Road and the south and north sections of the Chicago Road are taken as one, due to similar hauling conditions and the use of convict labor, while the West Road and Indiana Street are considered separate.

While it may be noted that the cost of haul with the Koppel outfit runs high, it must be borne in mind that the rental on this equipment amounted to $7,850 on an equipment whose first cost was only $17,500. Moreover, the heavy grade just before reaching the Chicago Road necessitated cutting the trains in two, which lost 10 to 15 minutes on each trip. As the maximum haul over this hill was 14 cars, all trains were limited to 28 cars, whereas 35 cars might have been handled on level ground. The actual cost per ton mile for hauling with this outfit figured 19.4c. In contrast to this, the haul on the West Road with teams figured at 23.4c per ton mile.

With these figures still showing an advantage of 4 cents per ton mile in favor of the hauling outfit, it would be well to note several other important features which made an industrial outfit of this type most valuable on a job of this magnitude.

It had a distinct advantage over teams, auto trucks or traction outfits during wet weather since all hauling was done over dirt roads. Six to eight cubic yards of ballast would put three miles of track in good shape in two or three hours after a rain.

It would have been impossible to organize enough teams in a farming community of this kind to have handled 250 yards of stone per day.

The industrial outfit was operated as a unit by one man of known ability with a force of 7 to 8 men while a team organization would have comprised 40 to 50 units of uncertain quantity scattered over 3 to 4 miles of road.

The outfit worked 12 to 14 hours per day and with increased unloading facilities could have made longer hours.

Hot weather did not affect efficiency of operation.

The ease with which track was handled kept the sub-grade in perfect condition without ruts or broken down shoulders.

With a convict gang working, the two main gangs were centralized at the loading station and dumping point which prevented mixing of local teamsters with convicts, a thing which is not desirable.

The 1½ yard unit car at the loading chute was handled with ease and efficiency.

As a feature of comparison for other jobs, the rental cost should be replaced with a logical depreciation charge of $3,500 (on $17,500) which, with less adverse hauling conditions would bring the cost per ton mile down to ½ that of team haul, an item well worth considering when the hauling of 28,000 tons of stone is involved.

The cost of unloading stone for the hauling outfit was 10.3c per ton, using convict labor, while that on the West Road was 8.9c per ton with local labor.

The cost of spreading stone where the hauling outfit was used was considerably increased, due to the fact that the screenings could not always be dumped just where needed, thus involving some rehandling with teams. Some allowance must be made for this fact in comparing the cost of spreading stone on the several roads. Extreme difficulty in securing water for puddling also increased the cost of rolling. Two pumps operated by gas engines were usually in operation for this work, one being moved from point to point, the water supply at Beecher and the windmills of generous farmers were also called into play whenever available. The haul on all water for puddling averaged about 1 mile.

MACADAM ROADS.

FINAL COST REPORTS.

Chicago Road and East (State Line) Road; Washington Township; Will County.

CONDITIONS.

(All work except grading done with convict labor).
Amount of road laid, 55,494 feet; 69,424 square yards.
Width of road, 10 and 12 feet; thickness, 8 inches.
Average length of haul, 2.18 miles.
Work began, June 1, 1914; work completed, Dec. 12, 1914.
Rate of pay for men, 22½c per hour; teams, 50c per hour.
Convict labor @ 50c per day, (straight time).

COST OF LABOR AND SUPPLIES.

	Total cost	Cost per sq. yd.
Engineering and inspection	$ *	$ *
Superintendence	1,407.59	0.020
Excavation	4,756.55	0.069
Stone, f. o. b. siding	13,845.48	0.199
Loading and hauling stone or gravel including bonding material	15,680.09	0.226
Cost bonding gravel and screenings f. o. b. siding	2,825.34	0.041
Shaping and rolling sub-grade and side-roads	2,261.36	0.033
Spreading stone and screenings	3,017.27	0.044
Rolling and sprinkling	2,216.94	0.032
Cost of culverts and bridges	631.87	0.009
Depreciation or rental on State equipment	*	*

Total cost $46,642.49
Total cost per square yard 0.671
Cost excluding excavation, culverts and bridges........0.595
*Indicates paid or furnished by the State Highway Department.

West Road;   Washingtown Township;   Will County.
CONDITIONS.
(All work done with local labor).
Amount of road laid, 5,300 ft, (600 ft. resurfaced); 6,555 sq. yds.

Width of road, 10 feet; thickness, 8 inches.
Average length of haul, 1.5 miles.
Work began, Aug. 10, 1914; work completed, Dec. 11, 1914.
Rate of pay for men, 22½c per hour; teams, 50c per hour.

COST OF LABOR AND SUPPLIES.

	Total cost	Cost per sq. yd.
Engineering and inspection	$	$
Superintendence	.....	.....
Excavation	793.42	0.121
Stone, f. o. b. siding	1,221.70	0.186
Loading and hauling stone or gravel including bonding material	1,107.58	0.169
Bonding screenings, f. o. b. siding	211.43	0.032
Cost cement	28.80	0.004
Shaping and rolling sub-grade and side roads	142.17	0.022
Spreading stone and screenings	163.46	0.025
Rolling and sprinkling	188.70	0.029
Depreciation or rental on State equipment	*	*

Total cost $3,857.26
Total cost per square yard 0.588
Cost excluding excavation...........................0.467
*Indicates paid by the State Highway Department.

Indiana Street Road; Washington Township; Will County.
CONDITIONS.
(All work done with local labor).
Amount of road laid, 3,591 feet; 7582 sq. yds.
Width of road, 12 and 20 feet; thickness, 5 inches.
Average length of haul, ¼ miles.
Work began, Nov. 3, 1914; work completed, Nov. 28, 1914.
Rate of pay for men, 22½c per hour; teams, 50c per hour.

COST OF LABOR AND SUPPLIES.

	Total cost	Cost per sq. yd.
Engineering and inspection	$	$
Superintendence	31.25	0.004
Excavation	.....	.....
Stone, f. o. b. siding	746.16	0.098
Loading and hauling stone or gravel including bonding material	456.52	0.060
Bonding screenings, f. o. b. siding	326.06	0.043
Shaping and rolling sub-grade and side-roads	28.78	0.004
Spreading stone and screenings	117.56	0.016
Rolling and sprinkling	168.02	0.022
Depreciation or rental on State equipment	*	*

Total cost $1,874.75   0.247
Total cost per sq. yd...........................0.247
Cost excluding excavation 0.247
*Indicates paid or furnished by the State Highway Department.

EXAMINATION
FOR
JUNIOR ENGINEERS FOR THE STATE HIGHWAY DEPARTMENT

Will be held by the State Civil Service Commission at the following named points, on

MARCH 6, 1915

Anna.	Jacksonville.	Marion.	Quincy.
Urbana.	Kankakee.	Mt. Vernon.	E. St. Louis.
Chicago.	Lincoln.	Murphysboro.	Watertown.
Elgin.	Macomb.	Peoria.	Springfield.

Application blanks may be secured upon request to the State Civil Service Commission, Springfield, Ill.

All applications must be on file in Springfield by February 27, 1915.

No restrictions as to residence.

Minimum age, 21 years.

The salary to start will be $75.00 per month with field subsistence.

The maximum salary of Junior Engineers is $100.00 per month.

SCHNEPP & BARNES, PRINTERS, SPRINGFIELD, ILL.

ILLINOIS HIGHWAYS
OFFICIAL PUBLICATION
STATE HIGHWAY DEPARTMENT

| VOL. 2 | SPRINGFIELD, ILLINOIS, FEBRUARY, 1915 | No. 2 |

CONCRETE SUB-FLOOR.
Ready for Wearing Surface.

CONCRETE SUB-FLOOR.
Macadam Wearing Surface.
See Article, Floors for Steel Highway Bridges, page 20.

ILLINOIS HIGHWAYS.
Published Monthly by the
State Highway Department.

ILLINOIS HIGHWAY COMMISSION.
A. D. Gash, President.
S. E. Bradt, Secretary.
James P. Wilson.

Wm. W. Marr, *Chief State Highway Engineer.*
P. C. McArdle, *Assistant State Highway Engineer.*

H. E. Bilger, *Road Engineer, Springfield, Illinois.*
C. Older, *Bridge Engineer, Springfield, Illinois.*
B. H. Piepmeier, *Assistant Engineer, Springfield, Illinois.*
G. F. Burch, *Assistant Engineer, Springfield, Illinois.*
F. L. Roman, *Testing Engineer, Springfield, Illinois.*

DIVISION ENGINEERS.
H. B. Bushnell..............Aurora
R. L. Bell.....................Paris
H. E. Surman.........Rock Island
A. H. Hunter...............Peoria
Fred Tarrant...........Springfield
C. M. Slaymaker........E. St. Louis
J. E. Huber................Marion

CONTENTS.

SHORT COURSE CANCELLATION.

The short course in Highway Engineering, scheduled to be given at the University of Illinois from
February 11 to 23, was postponed on account of the
fear of the spread of the hoof and mouth disease.

The meeting of last year. resulted in much good to
all those who attended and the indications were that
the meeting this year would have been larger and better than ever.

It' is regretted that it was necessary to postpone
this meeting, but it is hoped that arrangements can be
made to hold it at a later time.

The "Illinois Highways" will contain, from month
to month, different articles and papers which were to
be presented at this meeting and as these articles are
concerning the practical side of road making, we feel
that they will be, not only interesting, but also instructive.

RE-ALLOTMENTS.

The State Highway Commission will, during the
month of February, make re-allotments of that portion
of the State Road and Bridge Fund, which was alloted
to different counties, for the building of State aid roads,
but not accepted by them.

Fourteen counties did not accept their allotments,
and this money, amounting to about $120,000 will be
re-alloted to the other eighty-eight counties which accepted their original allotments, and are either doing,
or have made arrangements to do, State aid road work.
This re-allotment will be 12% of the total allotments
for the fiscal years, 1913-14 and 1914-15.

It is expected and desired that this additional
money will be used in making extensions to the roads
now under contract or to be contracted, although in a
few counties, where the road work under contract in
1914 has been completed, and enough money is not on
hand to build an economical length of road, this money
may be used in building bridges on State Aid Routes.

The State Highway Commission regret that
arrangements could not be made to use this money in
the counties to which it was originally alloted, but
realize that a few of the counties, at the present time,
do not intend to take advantage of the provisions of
the State Aid law, hence this money will be used to
increase the mileage of hard roads in those counties
which realize the value of good roads.

CONTRACT FOR CEMENT.

On February 23, 1915, proposals will be received
by the State Highway Commission for the furnishing
of cement, for the construction of State aid roads,
within the State. The proposals will cover the furnishing of about 235,500 barrels and separate prices will be
received for the cement delivered, in each county.

It is estimated that over $25,000, was saved to the
people of the State during the past year by the State
furnishing the cement for all State aid work, and as
more work is to be done this year than last, the saving
should be proportionately larger.

DEPARTMENTAL REPORT.

February 1, 1915.

STATE HIGHWAY COMMISSION.

Gentlemen: I submit the following report on the
present condition of the work being done by the State
Highway Department.

STATE AID ROAD WORK.

During the month of January surveys for State
Aid Road work were made in the following counties:
Henry, Bureau, JoDaviess, Mercer, Pike, Morgan,
Piatt, Massac and Clinton. Plans for this work are now
under way and will be completed in time for action by
the county boards at their next quarterly meeting.

During the month, several other counties have
been visited by the respective division engineers with
the idea of obtaining an advance preliminary resolution
so as to have surveys made and plans completed in
time for the next regular meeting of the county board.

The standard cross-sections for both concrete and
brick roads have been revised and redrawn. Experience from last season seemed to indicate that these
sections would bear revision in many details, to the
end that the completed road will not only be more
satisfactory, but that it can be constructed at a somewhat lower cost.

In the specifications for both the concrete and the brick roads, such changes have been found necessary as to necessitate the issuance of an entirely new edition. The revision embodies many points that have confronted the division engineers during the recent construction season. In general, the modifications that have been made in the specifications will make for a somewhat less expensive construction without appreciably lowering the quality of the work. The most economical adjustment of the requirements of the specifications to the varied physical conditions encountered throughout the state, can be effected only by successive revisions of the specifications in the light of experience gotten from their operation in practical road construction. Consequently, it is anticipated that from time to time there will arise suggestions that indicate additional modifications in the specifications.

BRIDGE WORK.

During the month of January plans and specifications for 17 bridges were prepared and sent to county superintendents; total estimated cost, $17,610.

Contracts were awarded for 2 steel and 10 concrete bridges, at an average cost of 86% of the estimates; total estimated cost $23,380.

The date of letting was set for 18 bridges, having a total estimated cost of $41,610.

Blue-prints of 70 standard bridge plans were sent upon request to county superintendents.

Eighteen bridge plans, prepared by county superintendents were checked and approved.

On February 1, 1915, there were 25 bridge inspection reports on hand ready for work.

LABORATORY WORK.

During the month of January, 1915, twenty-four samples of miscellaneous materials were tested. Experiments were undertaken with a water-proofing compound and blocks of slag concrete were prepared for compression tests. A test to determine the hardness of gravels has been devised and 13 samples of miscellaneous gravels were submitted to this test.

BLUE PRINTING.

During the month of January, 1914, 70 blue prints were made of our bridge standards for county superintendents of highways, as well as prints for nine foreign bridge plans averaging two sheets, six prints being made of each sheet, or about 108 prints. Prints were made of four bridges designed by this department, 20 sets each, as well as three preliminary sets being sent to the various counties for their use in letting said bridges, totaling 184 prints. Preliminary prints were also made of seven bridges designed by this department for use of county boards, three sets being made of each, or 42 prints.

Preliminary prints were made for one section of road for the county board to pass on, official prints then being made for county clerk, county superintendent, and this office. This road section averages about 12 sheets, making a total of 48 prints.

Miscellaneous prints, about 600 made for office use, make a grand total for the month of January of 1052 prints.

Very truly yours,

W. W. MARR,
Chief State Highway Engineer.

STATE AID ROADS.

All hard roads, constructed in the State of Illinois with State Aid money, under the provisions of the revised Road and Bridge law of 1913, become State Aid Roads as soon as they are completed and are accepted by the State Highway Commission. The State is required to maintain these roads forever, and no part of their upkeep is paid by the county in which they are constructed.

The following table shows in detail the location of all roads, which have been accepted by the State previous to February 1, 1915. These roads represent 23 separate sections of road improvement, totaling 24.1 miles in length, in 15 different counties.

It is expected that every month some sections of roads will be accepted until the whole system of State Aid Roads is under the control of the State.

STATE AID ROADS.

County.	Sec.	Type.	Length.	Mileage.	Date accepted.	Total cost.	Unit cost per mile.	Remarks.
Sangamon	B	Concrete...	3,320'	0.63	11-27-14	$ 7,536.92	....	Includes 940' Co. Ext.
Sangamon	D	Concrete...	3,268'	0.62	11-27-14	6,651.30	....	Includes 1,068' Co. Ext.
Champaign	C	Brick......	7,050'	1.33	12-4-14	18,539.32	$13,930	
Edgar	A	Brick......	5,192'	0.98	12-4-14	14,895.94	15,200	
Cass	A	Concrete...	3,900'	0.74	12-16-14	6,901.10	9,330	
Iroquois	B	Concrete...	13,306'	2.52	12-16-14	22,785.08	9,050	
Sangamon	C	Concrete...	2,400'	0.45	12-16-14	6,663.90	14,810	
Tazewell	A	Concrete...	4,280'	0.81	12-16-14	9,824.84	12,130	
Will	A	Concrete...	9,900'	1.87	12-16-14	19,902.74	10,640	
Bond	A	Brick	2,000'	0.38	12-24-14	9,684.88	25,500	
Cook	A	Concrete...	2,623'	0.50	12-24-14	6,916.78	13,830	
Cook	B	Concrete...	7,111'	1.34	12-24-14	19,500.62	14,550	
McHenry	A	Concrete...	2,600'	0.49	12-24-14	5,963.28	12,170	
Sangamon	E	Concrete...	3,318'	0.63	12-24-14	7,705.50	....	Includes 968' Co. Ext.
McHenry	B	Concrete...	1,500'	0.28	12-31-14	3,571.38	12,800	
Livingston	A	Concrete...	12,485'	2.37	1-8-15	26,239.76	11,080	
Sangamon	A	Concrete...	3,300'	0.63	1-8-15	6,493.04	....	Includes 1,100' Co. Ext.
Tazewell	C	Concrete...	2,300'	0.44	1-8-15	4,151.54	9,440	
Clay	A	Concrete...	3,700'	0.70	1-22-15	6,288.70	9,000	
Douglas	B	Brick	2,520'	0.48	1-22-15	6,007.70	12,500	
Cook	E	Concrete...	19,442'	3.68	1-27-15	65,808.40	17,880	
Kankakee	A	Concrete...	9,450'	1.79	1-27-15	22,682.05	12,670	
Menard	A	Concrete...	2,300'	0.44	1-27-15	6,206.99	14,110	
Total.............			127,265'	24.10				

FLOORS FOR STEEL HIGHWAY BRIDGES.

By Clifford Older, Assoc. M. Am. Soc. C. E. Bridge Engr. Ill. Highway Department.

Definite statistics in regard to the number and length of highway bridges for any considerable mileage of highways are difficult to obtain and are not at present available. In some states, however, we are able to ascertain the amount of the total expenditure for bridge-work of all kinds. Available information of this kind seems to indicate that approximately one-half of the funds raised for ordinary road and bridge purposes are expended in the renewal and maintenance of bridges.

It is evident therefore that if maintenance expenditures are to be reduced to the minimum, highway bridges and bridge floors should receive careful consideration.

Judging from conditions in Illinois, it is probable that at least 90% of all existing highway bridges are provided with nothing better than plank floors, and that the maintenance of these floors costs approximately 15% of the total expenditure for road and bridge maintenance, or about $10.00 per mile of road per annum.

FLOORS FOR NEW BRIDGES.

It is a simple matter to provide sufficient strength in the design of a new bridge, to accommodate any of the various modern types of floors or wearing surfaces.

It seems desirable to select a type of floor which will permit the use of a wearing surface of the same kind as that on the adjacent highway, so that the same method of maintenance may be used on the bridge floor as elsewhere.

The difference in weight of various types of floors has but little effect on the design and cost of concrete bridges. Steel bridges, however, are materially affected in both design and cost, by a comparatively small variation in the weight of the floor.

The bridge floor should then preferably consist of two elements.

The sub-floor, which should be as permanent as the bridge superstructure and should provide the necessary strength to transmit the highway loads to the floor supports, and a wearing surface of such character as to permit of economical maintenance.

In considering construction materials for both these elements, the matter of weight increases in importance with the length of span.

For sub-floors of the more permanent type, buckle plates with concrete covering, reinforced concrete, and creosoted plank cover the field.

For wearing surfaces, brick, concrete, creosoted blocks, macadam, gravel, mixtures of bituminous materials with sand, gravel or stone, plank, ordinary soil and practically all other varieties of surfacing materials have been used.

In comparing costs, it is necessary to consider not only the cost of the floor and its maintenance, but also the effect of the weight of floor selected on the design and cost of the remainder of the bridge.

CLASSIFICATION OF FLOORS WITH RESPECT TO WEIGHT.

For the purpose of considering the effect of the weight of the floor on the design of the superstructure, the various types of floors are herein grouped in four classes.

Class A Floors. Floors which weigh approximately 100 lbs. per sq. ft. of roadway surface are included in Class A. Floors consisting of a reinforced concrete sub-floor, assumed to weigh 50 lbs. per square foot, on which is placed a wearing surface of concrete, brick, macadam or gravel, are of this class. The wearing surface is assumed also to weigh fifty lbs. per ft. of roadway surface.

CREOSOTED PLANK SUB-FLOOR.

The saving in the weight and cost of the steel in the trusses and floor system for the lighter floors may outweigh the advantage of having the same wearing surface on the bridge as elsewhere on the highway.

Floors for steel bridges only will be considered in this discussion.

It is desirable to provide an independent wearing surface so that although the pavement may be worn practically through, the bridge may still carry traffic with safety.

Class B. Floors. Floors which weight approximately 65 lbs. per sq. ft. of roadway surface are included in Class B. Floors consisting of a concrete sub-floor, with a creosoted block wearing surface and floors consisting of creosoted plank sub-floors with a brick wearing surface, are of this class.

Class C. Floors. Floors which weigh approximately 32 lbs. per sq. ft. are included in Class C. Floors consisting of a creosoted plank sub-floor with a creosoted block wearing surface, are included in this class.

Class D. Floors. Floors which weigh approximately 26 lbs. per sq. ft. are included in Class D. Floors consisting of a creosoted plank sub-floor with a wearing surface about three-fourths of an inch thick, composed of a mixture of gravel and bituminous material are of this class.

weight of steel for a variation of ten lbs. per sq. ft. in the weight of the floor.

Figure IV shows the average contract price for the

CREOSOTED PLANK SUB-FLOOR.
Bituminous Gravel Wearing Surface.

Buckle plate floors are not considered, as they weigh as much and cost more than concrete sub-floors.

DESCRIPTION OF FLOORS ILLUSTRATED.

Figure 1 shows standard designs used by the Illinois Highway Department for the floors above mentioned.

The creosoted plank sub-floors, (Floor C and Floor D) are crowned by bending the plank over the stringers and anchoring the ends to the nailers by means of lag screws.

The creosoted blocks, (Floor B and Floor C) are laid on a ¼ inch bituminous felt cushion, which is coated with asphalt immediately before laying the blocks.

Ship-lap sub-plank are used for floors having a bituminous gravel wearing surface. The use of this form of sub-plank has been found to be the cheapest and most effective method of preventing the leakage of the bituminous material.

EXPLANATION OF CURVES.

The curves (Figure 11) show the weight of the structural steel in bridge superstructures as a per cent of the weight of the steel in superstructures having Class A floors. That is, the weight of superstructure steel in bridges having floors weighing 100 lbs. per sq. ft. is taken as 100%, and the weight of steel required for the lighter floors expressed as a percentage of this weight.

These curves are based on the weight of steel in spans which conform to the standard designs of the Illinois Highway Department. The designs used provide for 16 foot roadways. The curves were checked at a number of points, however, for 18 foot roadway designs and were found to conform very closely. These curves are sufficiently accurate to enable a designer to determine the relative cost of steel superstructures having floors of various types and weights.

The curve (Figure III) is based on the curves (Figure II) and shows the average per cent variation in

Illinois Highway Department standard 16 foot roadway steel spans with floor complete.

For spans up to 80 feet inclusive, riveted pony

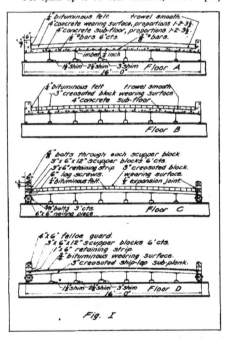

Fig. I

trusses are used. For spans from 90 to 160 feet, riveted Pratt trusses are used. This rate of span length covers at least 90% of the highway bridges in Illinois.

The average contract price of materials is as follows:

Structural steel complete in place........$ .03½ per lb.
Concrete sub-floors, including reinforcing
   steel .... 12.00 per cu. yard
Concrete wearing surface, 4 inches thick. .90 per sq. yard
Creosoted sub-plank (12 lb treatment)
   complete in place, $70.00 per thousand
   feet board measure.
Creosoted block wearing surface......... 1.80 per sq. yard
Bituminous gravel wearing surface....... .60 per sq. yard

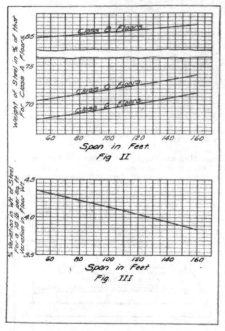

Fig II

Fig. III

The average cost of sub-floor and wearing surface per foot of 16 feet wide roadway (1.78 sq. yds. including curbs), is as follows:

Concrete sub-floor with concrete wear-
   ing surface (wt. 100lb per sq. ft.).$4.25 per ft. of bridge
Concrete sub-floor with creosoted block
   wearing surface (wt. 65lb per
   sq. ft.)........................... 5.80 per ft. of bridge
Creosoted plank sub-floor with creo-
   soted block wearing surface (wt.
   32lb per sq. ft.).................. 7.30 per ft. of bridge
Creosoted plank sub-floor with bitu-
   minous gravel wearing surface
   (wt. 26lb per sq. ft.)............. 5.15 per ft. of bridge

It seems probable that under average conditions the length of life of the floors represented by the upper three full line curves may equal that of the remainder of the superstructure and that the cost of maintenance for this period would be small.

The experience of the Illinois Highway Department seems to indicate that under average conditions, the bituminous wearing surface requires a light treatment of oil and stone chips or screened gravel, at intervals of about

four years at a cost of about ten cents per square yard and a probable complete resurfacing once in about twelve years at a cost of approximately 60 cents per square yard. This amounts to 7½ cents per square yard, per annum. Adding to the first cost of the bridge, the maintenance charge capitalized at 6%, Curve D₁, Figure IV results. The position of this curve indicates that it would be preferable to use creosoted block or other floor in building new structures.

Probably 95% of existing steel highway bridges were originally designed for ordinary plank floors. Under average conditions and at the present price of yellow pine, which is the material now quite generally used, the annual cost of maintaining such floors is about 35c per square yard. The first cost, plus the maintenance charge capitalized at 6% results in curve E. Figure IV.

CONCLUSION.

It is evident that ordinary plank floors having an average life of not more than three and one-half years are to be avoided when possible.

It is to be noted that with the exception of the floor with the bituminous surface, the cost of the floor increases as the weight decreases, and yet the cost of the entire superstructure decreases as the weight of floor decreases.

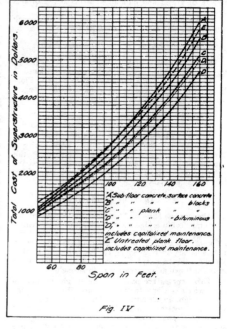

"A" Sub-floor concrete, surface concrete
"B" " " " " blocks
"C" " " plank
"D" " " " bituminous
"D₁". " " "
includes capitalized maintenance.
"E" Untreated plank floor.
includes capitalized maintenance.

Fig. IV

The saving in cost for the lighter floors increases with an increase in the unit cost of structural steel in place, and decreases with an increase in the cost of the materials used in such floors.

In reflooring old steel bridges of satisfactory design, a creosoted sub-plank with bituminous wearing surface has been found to give reasonable service. The weight is somewhat greater than that of a plank floor, but the effect of the added weight is probably offset by the reduction of impact, due to the comparatively smooth and yielding surface.

The cost of maintaining the bituminous surface is only about 20% of that of an ordinary plank floor.

There seems to be no place in the economic design of new highway bridges, for floors consisting of a creosoted plank sub-floor with a brick wearing surface as the life of such a floor could hardly be greater than that of floor C, Figure 1, while the cost of the complete superstructure would be greater than that represented by curves B and C, Figure IV.

The floors listed under Class A seem hardly to be justifiable, except for short spans, unless other considerations outweigh first cost.

SOME FEATURES OF BRICK ROAD CONSTRUCTION.

[By Rodney L. Bell.]

In the December issue of "Dependable Highways," there is a picture of a brick road in Holland that was constructed one hundred years ago. This picture was taken by an official of the Bureau of Public Roads. Brick has been used for paving purposes in England about as long, but the first information we have of its use in the United States as a paving material was at Charleston, W. Va., in 1870. The idea was conceived by Dr. J. P. Hale of that city and was laid according to his plans and at his own expense.

The foundation for this pavement was composed of a layer of planks covered with sand, on which the bricks were laid on edge in zig-zag courses, the interstices being filled with sand. The bricks were the ordinary building bricks of that time, except that they were burned somewhat harder than usual.

In 1871, N. B. Heafer, a building brick manufacturer of Bloomington, Illinois, constructed a brick pavement on Center Street opposite the Court House in that city. The base of this pavement was composed of four inches of cinders covered with a layer of sand, upon which a course of brick was laid flatwise. This course of brick was covered with a layer of sand and another course of brick was laid edgewise and the interstices filled with sand. The bricks used were the ordinary building bricks of that time.

The method used in the construction of this old Bloomington road became known as two course construction and was used very extensively during the earlier days of brick pavement construction. Considering the quality of the materials used, it gave reasonably good results, but now it has for the most part been superseded by more advanced types of construction. There are some places, however, where brick are laid on the natural soil without any foundation other than the sand cushion. This, of course, is a cheaper construction and on some soils may give a fair amount of wear. Personally, I feel that it is absolutely folly to put as good a wearing surface as brick on a natural soil foundation.

Bricks are also laid on gravel, macadam, shale, slag and concrete foundations. Where there is an old macadam or gravel road sufficiently true to grade to permit resurfacing and covering with a brick wearing surface, it will probably pay for ordinary traffic, but to start on new construction with anything but a concrete base appears to be a penny-wise, pound-foolish policy, as the cost of the concrete base is so very little. I firmly believe that a brick road with gravel or macadam base should have either a bituminous or sand filler. The bituminous filler will increase the cost almost enough to put in a concrete base, while a sand filler allows the brick to chip, causing them to wear rapidly at the corners and produce a rough riding pavement.

I do not believe that anyone will deny that the best type of brick pavement is laid on a concrete base with grout filler, a longitudinal expansion joint on one side for roads and narrow streets and on both sides for wide streets, and with no cross expansion joints, and it is of this sort of pavement that I desire to speak.

In a road of this kind, use is made of the best two materials as yet discovered for roadwork. There may be differences of opinion about concrete as a wearing surface, but as a foundation, it is the best that can be obtained. It is monolithic and no other foundation material even approaches it in effectiveness.

I do not care to give a detailed account of the construction of brick roads, for you are no doubt familiar with that, but there are a few things dealing with each part of the work that may be worth mentioning.

In a brick road, as well as any other type of construction, you cannot expect to get any better work than your specifications call for, but assuming that your specifications are all that are to be desired, the perfect job is obtained only by careful, sensible attention to the little points in construction. This sort of inspection not only assures a good durable pavement, but a nice looking piece of work as well, and when we pay the price necessary to obtain a good brick pavement, it is worth some care and money to see that it is presentable. A good job is worth what it costs, while a sloppy job has no excuse for its existence.

SUB-GRADE.

I believe that, all things considered, the subgrade should be parallel to the finished road, giving a uniform thickness of concrete base under the entire pavement, rather than make the base thinner at the edges, to secure the required crown. This latter method is wasteful of base concrete, as it makes the center excessively heavy in order that the edges be not weakened. When we are using a concrete base only four inches or four and one-half inches thick, it is necessary that the subgrade be reasonably true. The only way that I know to insure a uniform thickness of concrete base is to go over the subgrade with a template after the side forms are set and men will dress just as much subgrade, using a crowned template as a flat one. Most contractors realize that it is the economical thing to do. No engineer wants less concrete than the plans call for and no contractor can afford to fill up depressions with gravel and sand and cement, with earth at the present price.

We generally set grade stakes at twenty-five foot intervals on each side of the road and I have noticed that a gang of men using these stakes will not leave a subgrade flat but always crowned a little for a flat subgrade looks hollow to the eye.

COMBINED CONCRETE BASE AND CURB.

The concrete for the base must be laid between the side forms and struck off with a template before the inside form for the curb can be placed. In making a template for this work, it should be cut true to the crown of the finished road and the cutting edge shod with metal.

The ends of the template that rest on the side forms should be raised at least one-quarter inch to allow for settlement when the base is floated. Where crushed stone is used as the coarse aggregate, the template may have to be raised to three-eighths inch.

The base should be finished so as not to vary more than one-quarter inch and if the template is properly made, this will work no hardship on a contractor. The entire purpose of the inspection is to secure as nearly a perfect surface as possible and care is needed at all stages. To get this surface, a road doesn't have to be sandpapered, on the other hand, a job which has all its parts thrown together, can't expect to be very presentable.

The inside forms for the curbs rest on the concrete and are held by clamps and dividers, the dividers being removed as soon as the concrete is placed. The outside of the curb is rounded with an ordinary sidewalk edger, but the inside is left square, thus securing a better joint between the curb and the brick. The inside form is likely to settle slightly in the soft base, so it is often necessary to remove the small ridge of concrete with a pick before the sand cushion is placed.

One of the first difficulties met when starting the concrete base is to get the proportions adjusted, so that you are getting the proper amount of cement. No matter how willing the contractor may be, it is necessary to keep a close watch on the men until they get used to the proper charge. This is especially true when changing to a different mixture from that with which they have been accustomed. Using the graded material required under the specifications of the Illinois Highway Department, I have no hesitancy in saying that in calculating the amount of cement required, allowance should not be made for more than forty per cent voids.

The specifications of the Illinois Highway Department for a concrete base now call for one part cement, three parts fine aggregate and five parts coarse aggregate. It is probable that these will be changed the coming year to one part cement, three and one-half parts fine aggregate and six parts of coarse aggregate, as the feeling is fairly general that our present base is unnecessarily rich. I expect the majority of concrete base laid is made from pit run material. This practice tends to cheapen the construction both as to cost and to quality, and personally I feel that it cheapens the quality of the work faster than it does the cost. There are only a comparatively few places where a suitable pit run material can be obtained. and by suitable I mean having the proper proportions of fine and coarse aggregate. Assuming that we have a pit run material such that when your specifications for one part cement to three or three and one-half parts of sand are complied with, it still is an economical material to use. You may ask, what is the objection to using it? My objection to pit run material is that it is impossible to get a uniform base. Material when loaded in the cars, tends to separate into coarse and fine aggregate and when dumped from the wagons, the coarse aggregate runs to the edges so that part of the time most of the charge is fine aggregate and at other times it is mostly coarse aggregate. A mixture of this kind can be handled in a bridge abutment where you have a sufficient depth of concrete to spade but a four inch layer spread out on the ground is not conducive to spading and a batch of cement and coarse aggregate means a porous place in the base. When using fine aggregate and coarse aggregate from separate piles, each batch is the same as every other batch, which insures a uniform mixture throughout the base.

SAND CUSHION.

The specifications of the Illinois Highway Department require an inch sand cushion under the brick as finished. This means about one and one-half inches of compacted sand when the brick are laid. After the brick are rolled, they are left practically flush with the curb and the sand cushion will not be rolled up between the courses of brick more than one-half inch. One might say that the sand cushion absorbs the little irregularities in the brick and the concrete base, assuring us of a more nearly perfect surface than we would otherwise secure. If this is the purpose of the sand cushion, I feel that the tendency should be for a less rather than a greater thickness of sand cushion. The thicker the cushion, the more likelihood of securing an uneven surface. Then again, the thicker the sand cushion, the more chances of rolling the sand up between the courses of brick. I firmly believe that if there is more than one-half inch of sand between the courses of brick, they should be taken up and relaid ; if this is not done where a grout filler is used, a pavement is almost sure to buckle. A brick pavement will take care of the compression if it has a chance, but it hasn't a fair chance with a yielding filler like sand for the lower portion and a solid filler like grout for the top portion.

LAYING BRICK.

When using a grout filler, all brick should have some sort of lug or raised letters and these should always be laid the same way. If this is done, you are assured that the grout will reach to the sand cushion at all places. If this is not done, there are certain to be some places that will not be grouted.

The longitudinal expansion joint should be placed on the side from which the laying starts.

Brick should be carried onto the road on pallets, instead of wheeling in barrows and dumping on the brick already laid.

Enough men should follow the laying gang to keep the brick culled up ahead of the men who do the batting. A large portion of the brick that are rejected are plainly culls, that the ordinary laborer can detect as well as an inspector. Most of these are misshaped or badly chipped brick which can be used for bats on the unfinished side. Incidentally this saves a considerable amount of work for the inspector.

GROUT FILLER.

An otherwise good pavement may be ruined by poor grouting and a good job of grouting may insure a fair pavement out of what was in other ways an inferior piece of work. One of my inspectors told a contractor this summer that he admitted that a good filler, like charity, covered a multitude of sins.

One of the main things in grouting is to get the first application so thin that it can't help but penetrate to the bottom of each and every course. Fool proof in other words. If there is any place that perfect work is required, the placing of the grout filler is that place. The Illinois Highway Department specifies the use of rattan brooms to brush in the first application and squeegees for the subsequent application. Three applications may finish the job and it may take five. The grouting must be continued until the filler is brought flush with the top of the brick and just as little surplus grout on top of the brick as possible. In ending a day's work, care should be taken to end with a square joint. This can be accomplished by the use of tin headers, five inches wide by twenty-four inches long. These headers can be placed between two courses of brick and removed after the grout has had a chance to stiffen but not set.

CROSS EXPANSION JOINTS.

I realize that some engineers still believe in the cross expansion joint, but experience generally seems to show that they are not only a useless but a detrimental appendage. The belief is prevalent now, that instead of preventing buckling, they encourage it and you know that within two years from the time the road is finished, there will be a low place at each joint.

In the eastern division, no state aid brick roads have been constructed with cross expansion joints. If you ask me the reason, I will say that the theory is that they are not needed and experience has proven the theory to be correct.

The brick road between Buffalo and Niagara Falls, seventeen miles long and eighteen feet wide, has no cross expansion joints. There is a brick road leading east from Livingston, New York, along the south bank of the St. Lawrence river, seven miles in length, that has no cross expansion joints. All of the better work around Cleveland, Ohio, was and is being constructed without cross joints. At Paris, Illinois, we have one road, two and one-half miles long, with no cross joints and it is in perfect condition.

The main objection to the brick road is the cost and any means of reducing the cost of construction without impairing the quality is much to be desired. It seems to me that a brick wearing surface should last forty years on our country highways and to put that sort of wearing surface on an inferior foundation is not only poor judgment but borders on the foolish.

Many engineers doubt the advisability of curbs for country highways, and considerable work has been constructed without them, but forty years is a long time for a brick edge to stand the turning on and off of the traffic and the additional cost of the curb is so small that I do not see how we can afford to leave it off. A road without a curb might be in perfect condition after twenty-five years and then if the brick on the edge started to loosen, it would cost more to keep them replaced than the original cost of the curb. If the concrete curb should wear out completely in twenty-five years, you would then be just where you started with the other type of construction.

Any sort of construction work develops along two lines:

First. To improve the quality.

Second. To cheapen the cost.

Brick roads have been developed to a high point, and the tendency now seems to be to try and cheapen the cost to compete with concrete and to me it seems to be a step in the wrong direction. I never heard anybody claim that a natural soil foundation, a macadam foundation, or a gravel foundation was as good as a concrete foundation. I never heard anybody say that pit run gravel was better than separated aggregate. I never heard anybody say that a road without a curb was better than one with a curb. Neither did you. The only argument is that it is cheaper, and to my mind, when cheapness takes the place of quality, it ceases to be a virtue. "The satisfaction in the quality remains long after the price is forgotten."

Everything else being equal, the life of the pavement depends directly upon the quality of the brick that makes up the wearing surface. Brick are manufactured at a large number of places and from many different kinds of shale. The shale from these different deposits

requires different amounts of burning and the resulting brick are of different colors and of varying hardnesses. I believe that our present method of applying the rattler test leaves something to be desired. I believe that each shale deposit should be made the basis of scientific investigation as to the burning required to produce the best results with that material. After this is determined, each plant would know exactly what was expected of it. I believe this is a step in advance of anything yet attempted, but I believe it is feasible and would work no hardship on the manufacturer. A maximum average loss would need to be required just as now, but I believe that brick made from one shale that will show an average loss of twenty-two per cent in the rattler, might be better than brick from another plant that only shows a loss of twenty per cent, because the first were properly burned and the latter were under burned. A common standard for all is the easy but not the scientific way.

ROAD WORK IN SCHUYLER COUNTY.

By W. S. Henderson, County Superintendent of Highways.

I want to review briefly but comprehensively the operations of this office, and take up in a general manner at least some of the work that has been done during the past year. I say, I think with a pardonable degree of pride, that our undertaking has been largely successful. Much of which success I attribute not only to the fact of my never trying to see how little I could do and discharge my duty under the law, but of ever being willing, as the township officials and private citizens who have sought my advice will attest to, to do anything in my power, to go the limit for the good of the people, always trying to secure for them value received for any and all money spent under my supervision: also to the hearty co-operation of all officials with whom I have labored.

It has indeed been a pleasure to aid township officials in carrying out the provisions of the new road and bridge law; and with the cooperation of the commissioners we have been able to solve many problems. I have settled many disputes over new roads, altering roads, line and hedge fences, and drainage difficulties which have been very annoying to the commissioners. It is my purpose to be of service wherever I may be, and I welcome good-natured criticism from anyone, and especially from members of the board of supervisors. It is my supreme desire to make the highways of Schuyler County better; but it is only possible for them to reach the highest state of perfection through and by the hearty cooperation of everyone interested. Cooperation is the key-note; therefore if our roads are to be made better and at the minimum cost, we must pull and work together.

The new road law, commonly known as the Tice law, practically revolutionized the manner of conducting work on roads and bridges. And after a year under its operation I am thoroughly convinced that it is much the best road law we have ever had. It is true there is some opposition to it, but I sincerely believe that it is largely because of the hard-road, state-aid feature that is a part of it. Aside from that, the law in general put into practice, most assuredly and without question, means better roads and bridges at a smaller cost. Some dishonest salesman, whose crooked business has reecived its just dues, might attempt to tell you differently.

The good road movement is nation-wide. Illinois has been slow in taking hold, being quite a bit behind a large number of states which she completely outranks in other ways. We have had merely a beginning this year; yet it is impossible to place a value in dollars and cents upon the movement. In this matter a great deal of authority and power is vested in the board of supervisors, and as their actions will be guided largely by the wishes of their constituents, it behooves every citizen of this county to make a very careful study of the situation, and then use his influence for the best interests of everybody. The aiding or retarding of the good road movement rests entirely with the people, and I firmly believe it will have your support. People everywhere are clamoring for better roads and a more permanent type of culverts and bridges. They are tired of seeing their money continually spent on repair and piece work. I believe many of us will live to see the time when repair on culverts and bridges will, in a manner, be a thing of the past. This will be brought about by the erection of permanent structures, large enough to do the work intended. The rains of last September damaged the roads of Schuyler County fully ten thousand ($10,000.00) dollars. At least seventy-five per cent of this damage was due to improperly constructed or insufficient culverts. Many times culverts have been constructed without any regard for the amount of water they might be called upon to carry. I have actually seen an 8-inch corrugated culvert placed in the bottom of a draw that was expected to carry the water from at least thirty acres, and it is a very common thing to find 12, 15, or 18 inch pipes attempting to carry the water from forty acres to a quarter-section. I do not say this in a spirit of condemnation of anyone but rather the system under which we have been working. Men without any special training or experience have been expected to do the work of an experienced engineer.

Let us now go to a consideration of the type and costs of culverts. The type in this county most in use is the corrugated metal. In many cases I fear these will prove to be expensive luxuries, I say luxuries because from a utility standpoint they are not worth considering. The galvanized steel will not last an average of ten years in our soils, which are more or less acid. My attention has been called to such pipe this year, which I was told were in the ground just seven years and they were practically eaten up. Many of the culverts have been and are being sold throughout the county at the price of pure iron. Galvanized iron will last, according to a bulletin of the U. S. Department of Agriculture, from eighteen to twenty-five years. But how are you going to tell whether you are getting steel or iron? There is practically no difference in the weight. You can not tell any difference by looking at them. In fact a real difference can only be determined by a laboratory test. Now as to price, let us see what they cost. The prevailing prices are about as follows: 12-inch, 80 cents to 90 cents per foot; 36-inch, $3.50 per foot; 60-inch, $6 to $7 per foot. All intermediate sizes in proportion. These prices are for guaranteed iron, and are what the commissioners are paying for local shipments. Figuring the same price on a pound basis it means 12 cents to 14 cents per pound. I want to ask what else in galvanized iron you are paying that price for besides culvert pipe? At the first public letting under my supervision, in which the county was interested, we bought $369.25 worth of guaranteed pure iron culverts at a fraction under six cents a pound. To determine exactly what we got, a sample was cut from one of these culverts and sent to the State Laboratory and a test came back of 99.75% pure iron. Figuring from the local prices prevalent the people were saved on this one deal at least $375.00. But I do not want to go on record as favoring

even iron culverts. I believe there is a cheaper and more permanent culvert. To say nothing about longevity, let us compare the costs of metal and good concrete culverts. For example, take a 36-inch corrugated iron culvert 24 feet long; you have for its cost laid down at your railroad station and not installed, $75.60 to $84.00; and the very cheapest steel would cost you $45.00. An all reinforced concrete box culvert 2½ feet by 3 feet can be furnished and finished by day labor for less than $40 and be let by contract under $50. This is figuring good clean gravel, a mixture of 1-4 and heavily reinforced. I have not figured headwalls in either case, which are essential to any type of culvert.

Going a little farther into the value of the purchasing ability of one who knows the worth of materials, I will say that at this first letting, referred to above, there was also purchased two steel bridges, one a 22-foot span and the other a 24-foot span. Price, $340. I know of a township that last year bought a 24-foot span almost identical with the one mentioned and paid for it $375. So on the face of those figures the people are ahead $35 in money and got a steel bridge, 22-foot span, for nothing. At a subsequent letting in which the county was interested, a bridge was contracted for and afterwards erected. It was a 47-foot span with two 20-foot approaches; price, $554. And only last year there was one erected in the county 40 feet long, without any approaches, for which was paid $750. I will allow you to figure the gain for the people.

On the Buenavista and Littleton township road, for which the Board of Supervisors appropriated one-third of a $5,000 cost, I helped arrange all the work and supervised the letting of all contracts. The total amount expended on the entire work was $2,115.71, which was $2,884.29 less than the appropriation. In one township I settled a squabble over a new road by a compromise between the parties. The road contended for would have cost the people $2,500, the compromise actually cost $398. I might go on and enumerate many other money-saving instances but space forbids, and I fear the report would grow tiresome. But as to whether your superintendent has earned his salary I can secure the affidavit of one board of commissioners which will state that in dollars and cents alone I have saved my salary in their township. So if I have been of any value anywhere else I must conclude that the county as a whole is ahead.

During the year I have gotten out plans and specifications for some twenty concrete structures, varying in price from $130 to $600. I think this speaks well for the men in charge of the township road work, when we consider that at the beginning of the year more than one-half of the townships of the county did not have a permanent structure in them and very few in the remaining ones. These progressive commissioners should receive your praise.

Because of the fair, square business methods of some salesmen of road supplies it has been a pleasure to recommend them to the commissioners; but I have had some trouble with dishonest ones. Men who use all kinds of schemes to evade the law. Men who offer the commissioners money on the ground "to show my appreciation for your business." Men who only want to sell $190, $195, and in some instances $199.50 worth, but attempts have been made to sell each of the three commissioners that amount. Now there is a reason for this. They know that the superintendent knows, or at least should know, the price of material, and also the quality, and when they do not want the superintendent to O. K.

the order there is something manifestly wrong. I will leave it to your own conclusions as to whether somebody is getting hum-bugged, whether there is graft behind the machine, or some other reason for it.

I want to go on record as being opposed to the practise of township and county officials, for that matter, making trips at another's expense to these so-called factories, where you usually see only a blacksmith shop where they rivet culvert pipe and punch bridge steel. Hundreds of commissioners have been tolled away on these trips really expectiing to see something worth while. Some return thoroughly disgusted, but others continue to go. If these companies were actually paying the expenses of these trips I would not be heard to say one word against anyone going who cared to make the trip. A salesmen recently said to me, "I have taken many on these larks and the average cost per trip has been around $50, but I never figured I lost anything by so doing." Just recently the commissioners of a certain township in this county took one of these trips innocently, without any intention of buying, but after they were there they were induced to buy. Their bill amounted to $203.50, but the agent said: "Rather than bother your superintendent (or words to that effect) I will discount your bill $4, making it $199.50." Upon receipt of the bill by the supervisor he discovered some irregularities, refused payment of the same and the matter was taken up with me. In my office the commissioners gave the history of the deal. The material had been shipped and upon investigation we found it to be the poorest kind of quality and we further found that the price had been advanced 30c per foot over what had been agreed upon and one slip scraper had not been shipped at all. Figuring up, we found that they had tacked on that bill $61.75 for the people to pay as the expenses of that trip. The material was left on the company's hands and it is needless to say these commissioners will not take a similar trip soon. I have had many invitations during the last year to take such excursions with all expenses paid, but I have not taken advantage of any because I believe it to be morally wrong; and if I am ever guilty I would deserve to be fired by the county. Bear in mind that the taxpayers directly or indirectly stand every cent of the expense. Now I am not stepping on anybody's toes purposely, but I am certainly earnest in my contention. Whenever the selling interests put up the expenses it gives them an undue leverage on the purchaser. It is an attempt to "make friends." There is an old maxim that has been the guiding principle of successful business men for ages: "There are no friends in business; buy where you can buy cheapest, all things well considered." I think we should follow that rule in public affairs. I have confidence enough in the road officials of Schuyler county as men to believe, that when this thing is presented and opened up in the proper light that our minds will be of one accord.

Fully 90% of the roads of the State are earth roads, and 100% in Schuyler county. My opinion is that the per cent will remain high for many years to come. The big problem before us, then, is to improve that class of roads. I find that people everywhere are demanding an earth road that is passable every day of the year, and I believe such a condition is possible. But we must proceed logically and follow up our work by maintaining them the year around. I believe the various commissioners are doing the very best possible with the funds alloted to their care. They realize that the taxpayer is demanding value received for every dollar levied for road and bridge purposes. It is my aim and duty to

see that this is done, insofar as I am authorized by law to do so. I am proud of the work that has been done the past year. It is not up to what we hope to accomplish another year, but when we consider that on the first day of last April only six townships out of the thirteen had any money to work with, except their poll tax, we are amazed at the amount of good work that has actually been done.

I desire to thank each member of the Board of Supervisors and all others who have so kindly given me their support during the trying times of the past year. It has indeed been a pleasure to hear of your appreciation, to know of your good will, and to see your self-sacrifices for the betterment of road conditions.

May the good work go on!

HIGHWAY MATTERS IN FORD COUNTY.

[By C. F. Helman, County Superintendent of Highways.]

Formed out of the somewhat misshaped remnants of the State of Illinois after the boundary lines of all the other counties had been traced and defined "little Ford" is, as this name indicates, one of the smaller counties in the state; but it is nevertheless not the least.

Sixty-three counties have smaller acreage than Ford, twenty three have less inhabitants, and from the swamps, producing at the time of the formation of this county nothing more valuable than bulrushes and bullfrogs, a large acreage of its lands has climbed up to a productiveness equal to that possessed by any farmlands in the state, or any other state for that matter.

The "Blue-Book of Illinois" having reminded me of the true standing of Ford county as to size and population in comparison with the other counties of the state, I fully realize, that I have hardly done my county justice in not bringing it before the readers of the "Illinois Highways" until this late date, and begging leave to offer my humble apology for this negligence I will endeavor to give a brief outline of the conditions prevailing here as to matters connected with my office.

Three of the townships in the south part of the county, namely, Patton, Button and Drummer have built gravel roads during the past few years, making a total mileage of about 79 miles for the county of this type of hard roads, and one mile of macadam was built under the supervision of the State Highway Department in Sullivant Township three years ago. All other roads in the county are earth roads.

Patton township takes the lead in mileage of gravel roads; having 59 miles to its credit. Nearly all the gravel roads in Patton township have been built of local bank gravel, more or less well adapted for the work . Lacking in wearing quality much of the gravel had to be renewed frequently, and while serviceable roads were thus obtained, the economy of using such material unless it can be bought and placed at a very low figure, I doubt.

Accepting for part of the work of gravel road building done last year, only the very best gravel obtainable from local banks, we shipped in considerable of good bonding road gravel, and selecting for its use roads favorably located for shortest possible haul from railway station, the additional cost of these roads per mile became comparatively small and fully justified by the much improved lasting quality of the work.

Button Township shipped in all the gravel used last season. Drummer township has for years shipped in nearly all its gravel so that a renewal of the gravel coating has been required less frequently.

The manner of constructing the gravel roads in the past has merely consisted in smoothing off the road bed a little, setting two parallel guage planks 10 or 12 feet apart and the placing of sufficient gravel between the planks to make a uniform layer 12 inches deep. The packing of the gravel has been left to the traffic.

The work of placing the gravel obtained from local pits or banks, has often been done by farmers, living near by, who hauled gravel for only a few days in succession, making the hauling so irregular that it has been difficult for the Commissioners to guard against the placing of unfit material and avoid other undesirable features in connection with the work. Non uniformity of material and some of it placed so late in the season that it was dumped on the road in big frozen lumps could result in nothing but a wavy road.

The commissioners, as well as the traveling public, are well aware of the disadvantages connected with such uneven roadbeds, and we will all do our best to straighten out the kinks the minute the frost goes out of the ground in the spring.

The gravel roads built last year were completed before November 1st, the work being given careful inspection in all respects, and the commissioners endeavored to keep the gravel well shaped up and smooth until heavy freezing took place, which causes us to anticipate better results than heretofore have been obtained.

Appointed late in the spring most of the spring work had been done before I had opportunity to examine the work and make any suggestions in connection with it.

On most of the roads in the county I found some work done in the form of grading, leveling, or dragging, with the main roads having received the most attention.

There has been a tendency in some localities to throw up a high rolling grade every fourth or even sixth year, and leaving such grades to practically take care of themselves during the intervening years with exception of an occasional and rare dragging, and that this idea of road maintenance still prevailed in some localities of my county was made evident to me by the extremely high, narrow and unsuited grades often found, especially in townships which were the owners of road-levelers.

It seems that at least some of the agents for these road-levelers cause the commissioners to believe that earth roads can be built swiftly and effectively with this machine alone, and that consequently a desperate attempt to accomplish this in a hurry is made by the man handling the leveler. Great quantities of large clods entangled with weeds and grasses were scraped up to the center of the road and in most cases given no further attention, making the crudest form of road improvement imaginable and confining the traficable road to a dangerously slanting strip of road on each side of the "sweet potato ridge."

In some sections of the county, however, the ridges formed by the leveler were pulverized and harrowed to much advantage and I think that all my commissioners agree with me now that, while the road leveler is a very useful machine for leveling earth roads, it is not well adapted for the building of roads and does not and can not successfully take the place of the blade grader.

Considerable road grading and leveling was done during the fall, and the piling up of high ridges in the middle of the road grade was largely avoided.

The commencement of the heavy road work in the spring, as soon as the roads become fit for it and before weeds and grasses have attained any appreciable growth, has been agreed upon, and organized and systematic dragging of the roads at all seasons, when needed, has been planned for the whole county and is in operation in some townships.

The drainage of the Ford County roads, I believe, can be generally classed up to the standard of the best counties in this respect.

Only a few roads are lacking in drainage of some form and while I am unable at the present time to give the actual mileage of the tile drains along the roads, I can safely state that all the more important roads, have one or two strings of tile, where needed.

I do not mean to give the impression that we are done with the tiling of the roads in Ford county. It is my aim to induce the commissioners of each township to set aside, out of the yearly levy, a specific sum for the tiling of the roads, and not let one year go by without being able to add a sizeable length to their mileage of road drains.

Everybody can quickly detect the benefits derived from the under-drainage of the roads and this feature of road improvement is one which if judiciously done meets with unqualified approval from the public.

Considerable road drainage was done in some townships last year and I do not anticipate meeting any great obstacles in my endeavor to make a good showing in this respect for the whole county this year.

CONVICT LABOR IN ROAD BUILDING.

Governor Edward F. Dunne has signified his desire to have the convicts at Joliet, who can be trusted, made useful to themselves as well as the public.

The prisoners themselves crave to be rehabilitated as citizens and become useful members of society instead of a detriment to humanity.

Warden Allen and the State Highway Commission call on the various counties, cities and communities of the State to enter a friendly contest for their services.

At a conference held at Springfield, in the office of the Governor, between Edward F. Dunne, Governor, Edmund Allen, warden of the Penitentiary at Joliet, and the three members of the State Highway Commission, it was shown by the warden that there were two hundred and fifty trusty prisoners who could be relied on for faithful services and good deportment if permitted to work on the public highways in different parts of the State.

It was first determined that the chief benefits to the commonwealth to be derived by using the convicts outside of the prison walls would be to rehabilitate the men themselves in their own manhood, thus preparing them again for citizenship before leaving the penal institution.

It was then shown that the men to be selected were not vicious characters at heart and would not require much guarding, and that therefore their keep outside of the penal institution would not exceed fifty cents each day. It was therefore decided to only charge the communities who should call for their services that amount per day and that this should cover every expense that the communities would incur from the time the convicts left the penitentiary until their return.

It was also decided that it would not be very profitable to the localities to take them to any community for the purpose of constructing less than five miles of highway.

It was further shown that the greatest saving to the locality employing them, would be to have them construct macadam roads, and that the State could furnish the crushed stone for making such roads by the community paying the freight on the stone from the prison to the railroad station nearest the scene of the improvement to be made and furnishing teams to haul the stone from the station or stations and scatter it along the route to be improved.

It was further shown that the only added expense to the communities employing the labor would be the freight on the steam rollers, tools and machinery necessary to carry forward the work to completion, and pay the expenses of the engineers from the Highway Department while supervising the work.

Therefore it was determined that for the city or cities, community or communities who would first provide a fund to meet the expense necessary under the provisions above stated for the construction of not less than five miles of highway, provided the local highway commissioners call for the prisoners, as required by law, the State Highway Commission will at once undertake the construction of such highway or highways. Said road, however, not to be taken over as a state aid road, but to be left to the maintenance of the community or communities where it is located.

It will not be necessary for any community to employ more than fifty convicts at any one time to entitle them to this service. This would enable five different localities to work in the manner above provided at the same time.

The construction work may be done on any road under the jurisdiction of the local highway commissioners, which would include any state aid road not under actual construction by the State and county.

All of the cities, counties and communities of the State are hereby given the opportunity to compete for this improvement and to the first community or communities complying with the terms above mentioned, the services will be rendered. Estimates of cost for construction per mile will be given as soon as the location of the road is ascertained.

EDMUND M. ALLEN,
Warden, State Penitentiary, Joliet, Ill.

STATE HIGHWAY COMMISSION,
By A. D. GASH,
S. E. BRADT,
JAS. P. WILSON.

RULES FOR ROAD DRAGGING.

Make a light drag.
Drive the team at a walk.
Ride on the drag, don't walk.
Don't drag a dry road.
Drag when the road is muddy
Drag, if possible, immediately before a freeze.

Begin at one side of the road, returning on the opposite side.

Always drag a little earth towards the center of the road until it is raised ten or twelve inches above he edge of the roadway.

Do not attempt to move very much material at one time with a drag.

If the drag cuts in too much shorten the hitch.

The amount of earth the drag will carry can be regulated by the driver, according as he stands near the cutting end or away from it.

When the roads are first dragged after a very muddy spell, vehicles should drive, if possible, to one side until the road has had a chance to freeze or partially dry out. The exercise of a very little care on the part of the users of the road will do quite as much as the drag towards securing a smoother road. The law provides a penalty for anyone who wilfully ruts or cuts up a dragged road.

PRESS COMMENTS.

HIGHWAY BURDENS OF SOME TOWNSHIPS.

While at the court house Saturday, we dropped into the office of County Superintendent Of Highways, in the basement of the court house and found Mr. O. B. Conlee at work on reports to be filed with the State Highway Commission. As he went along with his reports he discovered the burdens some townships had to carry and he wrote the following article:

"The poorer the township, as a rule, the more roads and bridges it has to provide and maintain. There are fewer creeks to cross and fewer hills to run around in road construction through the level prairie township, where the land is high priced and a comparatively low tax levy brings in ample funds. Two townships in Macoupin county with only 58 miles of road and no bridges to maintain that would cost over $1,000, have an assessed valuation of $1,800,000, while five of our poorer townships with a number of bridges from 60 to 140 feet in length and 303 miles of road to maintain have a combined assessed valuation of only $1,804,000.

"Ten townships with 589 miles of road, making a levy of 61 cents, have only $22,624 or $38.00 per mile for maintenance. These townships average three bridges to the mile.

"Ten townships with 471 miles of road, with an average levy of 60 cents have $48,823 or $103.00 per mile for maintenance, with a fraction less than two bridges to the mile.

"Two townships with 91 miles of road with an average levy of 43½ have $15,260, or $167 per mile for maintenance, with less than two bridges to the mile.

"It can readily be seen from the above figures, that the revenue for road and bridge purposes is not distributed as it should be, in order to get uniform results for the public. I can see only two ways for these conditions to be remedied, one is for the county to build the bridges in the townships, the other to have a unit of taxation for each county with a 61 cent rate on the total assessed valuation of the county."
—Carlinville Democrat.

POOR ROADS.

When the people can be made to understand that it actually costs more in time and money to travel over a poor road than it does to travel over a good one, they will be less inclined to begrudge the expense of good roads, and what is more important still, will be willing and anxious to put the business of road making into the hands of intelligent men who understand the business. Poor roads are the expensive thing that curse a country district—Franklin Grove Reporter.

HARD ROADS.

About the only way that there will ever be hard roads in the State of Illinois is to pass a law compelling each county to build a certain number of miles of hard roads each year. We know that the farmers would set up a terrible howl against such a law but there never was a law passed that was worth a tinker's darn, that there was not a howl about. This howl would not last long, and when the farmer found that he could take his produce to town any time of the year over good roads, he would soon get in line with a whoop. The building of hard roads has to be started some time and the sooner such a law is enacted the sooner we will have good roads.—Gillespie News.

MAKING A GOOD BEGINNING.

Many miles of hard roads were built in Illinois last year under the Tice Law's provision.

Enough work was done to make the State aid law a permanency. There is left no ground for either fears or hopes of its repeal.

In every county where the building of permanent roads was started, continuance will be demanded until every township has been reached.

The State's automobile license fund, growing larger every year, will continue to be devoted to improvement of the highways; and more, not less, will be appropriated from the general fund for application to this purpose.

The state wil do more, and not less, in future years. And every county, will meet State aid's conditions and receive the share allotted to it out of funds to which it must contribute whether it refuses or accepts the benefits at its disposal.

A start has been made that assures no stop until the roads of Illinois become a credit to the state instead of a reproach. Nothing is at all in doubt excepting the rapidity of progress.

The rate of road construction may be presently much more than five miles a year in Fulton county. Townships and landowners are not forbidden to assist the state and county nor prohibited from paving intersecting roads while state and county pave the main highways. The Federal Government, concerned in the condition of the rural mail routes, may soon extend a powerful helping hand.

Illnois including twenty-six townships in Fulton county, is coming out of the mud. And the date of complete emergement may be nearer than any citizen of Kerton, Cass or Waterford, any citizen of Putnam, Joshua or Lewistown, or even any citizen of Buckheart, Farmington or Canton now supposes.—Canton Register.

OPINIONS OF THE ATTORNEY GENERAL.

WIDTH OF ROADS—HOW REDUCED.

January 23, 1915.

Mr. C. J. JOHNSON,
　Highway Commissioner, Kinsman, Illinois.

DEAR SIR: I am in receipt of your favor of the 21st inst., concerning the matter of reducing the width of public roads.

I infer from your letter that some farmers are rearranging their fence lines in such manner as to reduce the width of certain roads without having presented a petition for such reduction, as provided by section 74 of the Revised Road and Bridge Act.

Roads established under the Road and Bridge Act of 1883 were required, under section 30 of said act, to be of a width of not less than forty feet nor more than sixty feet. Section 73 of the revised Road and Bridge Act provides as follows:

"All public roads established under the provisions of this act shall be of the standard width of forty feet."

However, the above provision does not mean that a road established under the act of 1883, sixty feet in width, is reduced to a width of forty feet under the revised act. A road that was sixty feet in width under the act of 1883 continues to remain sixty feet in width under the revised act unless the width of such road is reduced by an order of the highway commissioners acting upon a petition, as provided by section 74 of the revised act, which provides as follows:

"The commissioners of highways of any town or road district may reduce the width of any existing public road within any town or road district to a width of forty feet when the same is petitioned for by a majority of the land owners along the line of said road, within said town or district. When possible the land so vacated by reducing the width of the road shall be taken equally from both sides of the public highway. In cases of natural obstructions on one side of the public highway or where the said road extends along the right-of-way of any railroad, river or canal, the commissioners are authorized to reduce the width of the road on one side only."

You will note that a petition to reduce the width of a road must be signed by a majority of the land owners along the line of said road, within the town. It would seem that a petition to reduce the width of a road must apply to the entire length of such road within the town. Under section 31 of the Act of 1883, a petition might be presented to high-

way commissioners to reduce the width of a portion of a road within a town; but the intent of the revised act is that roads shall be of a uniform width along their entire distance within the town. The provision in section 31 of the act of 1883, authorizing the reduction of a portion of a road, was omitted from the revised act. All roads established under the revised act are required to be of a width of forty feet; and highway commissioners, acting upon petitions to reduce the width of roads heretofore established, should fix the width of such roads at forty feet as specified in section 74.

Concerning the matter of a town meeting voting by acclamation that the highway commissioner apply a certain part of the road funds in a particular manner will say, clause 6, subdivision (B), section 50, provides that highway commissioners shall have general charge of the roads and bridges in their town, and make it their duty to keep the same in repair and to improve them so far as practicable. There is no provision of the statute which authorizes the voters at a town meeting to specify the character of improvements to be made on roads or the kind of material to be used in making repairs and improvements; such matters come within the exercise of the discretion which the statute vests in highway commissioners.

I note, too, your statement that last spring it was voted at the town meeting that the highway commissioners levy an additional tax of nineteen cents under section 58 to be used for the purpose of grading roads.

Section 58 provides as follows:

"When damages have been agreed upon, allowed or awarded for laying out, widening, altering or vacating roads or for ditching to drain roads, the amounts of such damages, not to exceed for any one year twenty cents on each one hundred dollars of the taxable property of the town or district shall be included in the first succeeding tax levy provided for in section 56 of this Act and be in addition to the levy for road and bridge purposes; and when collected, shall constitute and be held by the treasurer of the road and bridge fund as a separate fund to be paid out to the parties entitled to receive the same. It shall be the duty of the commissioners of highways at the time of certifying the general tax levy for road and bridge purposes within their town or district to include and separately specify in such certificate the amount necessary to be raised by taxation for the purpose of paying such damages. Upon the approval by the county board of the amount so certified, as provided in the preceding section, the county clerk shall extend the same against the taxable property of said town or district, provided the amount thus approved shall not be in excess of twenty cents on each one hundred dollars of the taxable property therein."

You will note that section 58 does not authorize the levying of a tax for the purpose of grading roads. A tax can only be levied under section 58, for the purpose of paying damages that have been agreed upon, allowed or awarded, for laying out, widening, altering or vacating roads or for damages agreed upon, allowed or awarded for ditching to drain roads. A tax cannot legally be levied under section 58 for any purpose except to pay damages that have been agreed upon or allowed for the purposes therein specified. Said section is similar to section 15 of the Act of 1883. The Supreme Court, in construing section 15 of the Act of 1883, in the case of *The People v. The Chicago, Burlington & Quincy Railroad Co.*, 252 Ill. 482, holds, in substance, that a tax levy could not legally be made under that section unless damages had been agreed upon or awarded for some of the purposes specified. The construction put upon said section 15 by the court is applicable to section 58 of the revised act.

Very respectfully,

352—B.　　　　　　　　P. J. LUCEY, *Attorney General.*

BRIDGES ON COUNTY LINES BUILT AT EXPENSE OF ADJOINING COUNTIES.

September 14, 1915.

Hon. HARRY EDWARDS,
　State's Attorney, Dixon, Illinois.

DEAR SIR: I am in receipt of your favor of the 11th instant, in which you inquire, in substance, whether a bridge costing $300, on a county line road, should be built at the expense of the adjoining counties, under section 36 of the revised Road and Bridge Act, or at the expense of adjoining towns under sections 63 and 64.

In reply, will say, section 36 provides, in part, as follows:

"Bridges over streams which divide counties, and bridges on roads on county lines, and bridges within eighty rods of county lines shall be built and repaired at the expense of such counties. And all such bridges over streams which form the boundary line between two counties, and all such bridges with eighty rods of such boundary line, when the cost of constructing the same shall be $5,000 or over, shall be built by such counties respectively in the proportion that the taxable property in each county respectively bears to each other according to its assessed value as equalized at the time of constructing such bridge. * * * * * * * *: *Provided*, that for the building and maintaining of bridges over streams near county lines in which both are interested and where the cost thereof is less than $5,000, the expense of building and maintaining any such bridge shall be borne by both counties in such proportion as shall be just and equitable between the counties, taking into consideration the taxable property in each, the location of the bridge, and the advantage of each, to be determined by the commissioner in making contracts for the same, as provided for in section 37 of this act."

Section 37 provides:

"For the purpose of building or keeping in repair such bridge or bridges, it shall be lawful for the County Boards of such adjoining counties, to enter into joint contracts, and such contracts may be enforced in law or equity against such County Boards, and such County Boards may be proceeded against jointly, by any parties interested in such bridge or bridges, for any neglect of duty in reference to such bridge or bridges, for any damage growing out of such neglect."

It will be noted that section 36 provides two methods of apportioning the cost of bridges on county line roads. If the cost of such bridge is $5,000, or over, it is apportioned between the counties in the proportion that the taxable property in each county bears to such cost. If the cost of such bridge is less than $5,000, the cost is to be apportioned between the counties taking into consideration the taxable property in each, the location of such bridge and advantage to be derived by each county from such bridge. The reasonable construction of section 36 would seem to be that adjoining counties are liable for the construction of bridges on county line roads irrespective of the cost of same.

Sections 63 and 64 would seem to have reference only to bridges on or near town lines within a county; they are not applicable to bridges built on county line roads or over streams that divide counties.

Very respectfully,

P. J. Lucey, *Attorney General.*

THE LETTING OF CONTRACT FOR BRIDGE BUILT BY COUNTY AID.

October 30. 1915.

James L. Kirkpatrick, Esq.,
Supervisor, Tiskilwa, Illinois.

Dear Sir: I am in receipt of your favor of the 6th instant, in which you inquire whether, in letting a contract for the construction of a bridge built by county aid, it is necessary to advertise the letting of such contract in a newspaper.

Section 35 of the revised Road and Bridge Act provides in part:

"When it is determined by the county board to grant the prayer of the highway commissioners asking aid for the construction of such bridge * * * * *, the county board shall thereupon enter an order directing the county superintendent of highways to prepare plans and specifications for such improvement. The contract for such improvement shall thereupon be let in the manner authorized by said county board, subject to the provisions of the law relating to the letting of contracts: * * *."

Section 26 contains a provision in part as follows:

"In letting contracts for the building of bridges, or culverts, wherein the county alone is interested, * * *, or the county and township or road district are interested, it shall be the duty of the officials in letting said contract to invite, receive and consider proposals on any other plan other than the one prepared by the county superintendent of highways, * * * * * * * *."

Neither section 26 nor 35 specifically require that notice of the letting of a contract for a bridge built by county aid shall be published in a newspaper; and so far as any express provision of the act is concerned, the manner of giving notice of such letting may be said to rest in the discretion of the county board. I am, however, inclined to the opinion that, as a matter of public policy, the better method would be to give notice of the letting of such contracts by publication in a newspaper.

Very respectfully,

253—AL. P. J. Lucey, *Attorney General.*

CONSENT OF ABUTTING PROPERTY OWNER DOES NOT GIVE A CORPORATION THE RIGHT TO ERECT POLES IN PUBLIC HIGHWAY.

October 7, 1915.

Hon. John M. Wilson,
State's Attorney, Aledo, Illinois.

Dear Sir: I am in receipt of your favor of the third instant, in which you submit the following proposition:

"If a public service corporation, like an electric company, has the consent of the owners of land adjoining a public highway, to erect poles in the highway, on which to string wires carrying a high voltage current, have the highway commissioners, any power to prevent the same, or have the highway commissioners any duty of any kind in the matter? (Said electric company, not having the consent of any municipal authority, township or County)."

Under clause 6, subdivision "B," section 50, of the revised Road and Bridge Act, commissioners of highways have general charge of the roads and bridges of their town or district. The control of highways in this State is by statute vested in highway commissioners. It is a rule of law, that an abutting owner, who owns the fee, may make such reasonable use of a highway as does not interfere with the public easement; but the abutting owner has not the right to place any obstructions in a public highway; nor will his consent give any person or corporation the right to place an obstruction in a public highway; nor can he exercise any control over such highway, for the reason, as noted, that the control of highways is, by statute, vested in the board of highway commissioners.

Under the rule announced by the Supreme Court, in the case of *Inter-State Telephone and Telegraph Co. v. Town of Towanda*, 221 Ill., 299, the placing of poles in a public highway, where such right is not given by statute, without the consent of the highway commissioners, would amount to an obstruction of such highway.

Very respectfully,

P. J. Lucey, *Attorney General.*

QUESTIONS AND ANSWERS.

CONCERNING THE MAINTENANCE OF GRAVEL AND MACADAM ROADS.

The following answers will be made as brief as possible and serve to fit the majority of conditions that exist on Illinois roads.

Q. What should be done with a newly built waterbound macadam road that shows signs of raveling in spots?

A. Cover spots lightly with a good bonding gravel or stone screenings. A very light application of clay will often stop the raveling.

Q. How may macadam roads adjacent to earth roads be protected?

A. Dump cinders or loose stone on the earth roads for a few hundred feet adjacent to the macadam road.

Q. What should be done with a gravel or macadam road that is badly rutted?

A. Loosen the rutted surface with a scarifier, add a little new material and re-roll.

Q. What should be done with a road that shows signs of sinking at places?

A. Put in under drains.

Q. What is a desirable thickness for ordinary gravel or macadam roads?

A. Ten or twelve inches, measured loose, if road is well drained.

Q. What is the best scheme for keeping down dust on gravel and macadam roads?

A. Remove all dust from the road, then apply a hot asphaltic oil or tar and then sand the surface lightly.

Q. Can oil or tar be applied cold to the surface of a road?

A. Yes, the lighter grades. Such treatments are suitable for laying the dust.

Q. Can oil or tar be applied to the road by means of the ordinary street sprinkling wagon?

A. Yes, the lighter grades that need not be heated before applying. It is better to apply all bituminous material by means of a specially prepared distributing wagon.

Q. What will be the total cost, including labor and materials, for applying ½ gallon of heavy asphaltic oil or tar per square yard?

A. From 8 to 12 cents per square yard, on first application.

Q. What is the cost of applying the lighter oils, including labor and materials?

A. From 3 to 6 cents per square yard.

Q. What is the average price of light oils used for suppressing the dust? Heavy oils and tars?

A. Dust laying oils, 3 to 6 cents per gallon; heavy oils and tars, 6 to 9 cents per gallon; heavy road binders, (Mexican and California products, 9 to 15 cents per gallon. Light oils may be delivered in steel tank cars or wooden barrels. The heavy products in steel drums.

Q. What grade of oil should be used for laying the dust on earth roads?

A. The very best asphaltic oil that can be applied without heating is the cheapest. It will contain from 30 to 40 percent. asphaltic residue. Oils containing from 50 to 70 percent. asphaltic residue will be more lasting but will require heating before applying.

Q. How may road surfaces be treated to prevent discoloration?

A. Apply silicate of soda, glutrin or calcium chloride.

Q. What is a desirable crown for a 12 foot bituminous macadam road? A waterbound macadam or gravel road?

A. A 12 foot bituminous macadam road about 3 inches. and a 12 foot gravel or waterbound macadam road about 1½ inches.

APPOINTMENTS OF COUNTY SUPERINTENDENTS TO FEBRUARY 1, 1915.

County.	Name.	Address.
Adams		
Alexander	W. N. Moyers	Mound City, Ill.
Bond	R. O. Young	Sorento, Ill.
Boone	Thos. W. Humphrey	Belvidere, Ill.
Brown	W. O. Grover	Mt. Sterling, Ill.
Bureau	Frank R. Bryant	Princeton, Ill.
Calhoun	Jno. A. Earley	Batchtown, Ill.
Carroll	L. P. Scott, (Temporary)	Mt. Carroll, Ill.
Cass	John Goodell	Beardstown, Ill.
Champaign	Geo. C. Fairclo	Court House, Urbana, Ill.
Christian	C. A. Pennington	Taylorville, Ill.
Clark	Zane Arbuckle	Marshall, Ill.
Clay	Howard Anderson	Louisville, Ill.
Clinton	Jno. T. Goldsmith	R. F. D. No. 3, Carlyle, Ill.
Coles	Harry Shinn	Mattoon, Ill.
Cook	Geo. A. Quinlan	Chicago, Ill.
Crawford	J. P. Lyon	Robinson, Ill.
Cumberland	Jno. A. Decker	Toledo, Ill.
DeKalb	Wm. C. Miller	Sycamore, Ill.
DeWitt	E. F. Campbell (Temporary)	Clinton, Ill.
Douglas	L. O. Hackett	Tuscola, Ill.
DuPage	Eugene L. Gates	Wheaton, Ill.
Edgar	Karl J. Barr	Paris, Ill.
Edwards	Chas. C. Rice	Albion, Ill.
Effingham	Geo. T. Austin	Effingham, Ill.
Fayette	P. E. Fletcher	St. Elmo, Ill.
Ford	C. F. Helman	Paxton, Ill.
Franklin	Geo. F. Hampton	Benton, Ill.
Fulton	E. F. Motsinger	Canton, Ill
Gallatin	Victor Pearce	Equality, Ill.
Greene	Irving Wetzel	Carrollton, Ill.
Grundy	Fred W. Stine	Morris, Ill.
Hamilton	Gregg Garrison	Garrison, Ill.
Hancock	Wm. Burgner	Carthage, Ill.
Hardin	W. M. Ball	Elizabethtown, Ill.
Henderson	C. R. A. Marshall	Stronghurst, Ill.
Henry	Jas. H. Reed	Cambridge, Ill.
Iroquois	Benj. Jordan	Watseka, Ill.
Jackson	Thos. G. Dunn	Gorham, Ill.
Jasper	S. A. Conner	Newton, Ill.
Jefferson	Tony C. Pitchford	Mt. Vernon, Ill.
Jersey	Chas. E. Warren	Jerseyville, Ill.
JoDaviess	Geo. E. Schroeder	Stockton, Ill.
Johnson	Chas. A. Hook	Vienna, Ill.
Kane	Geo. N. Lamb	St. Charles, Ill.
Kankakee	Frank M. Enos	Kankakee, Ill.
Kendall	Jno. D. Russell	Oswego, Ill.
Knox	Harley M. Butt	Galesburg, Ill.
Lake	Chas. E Russell	Waukegan, Ill.
LaSalle	Geo. Farnsworth	Ottawa, Ill.
Lawrence	R. J. Benefield	Lawrenceville, Ill.
Lee	L. B. Neighbour	Dixon, Ill.

County.	Name.	Address.
Livingston	R. W. Osborn	Pontiac, Ill.
Logan	Thos. S. Davy	Lincoln, Ill.
McDonough		
McHenry	C. L. Tryon	Woodstock, Ill.
McLean	Ralph O. Edwards	Bellflower, Ill.
Macon	Preston T. Hicks	Decatur, Ill.
Macoupin	O. B. Conlee	Carlinville, Ill.
Madison	W. E. Howden	Edwardsville, Ill.
Marion	Lee S. Trainor	Centralia, Ill.
Marshall	L. H. Eldridge	Lacon, Ill.
Mason	H. V. Schoonover	Havana, Ill.
Massac	J. Thrift Corlis	Metropolis, Ill.
Menard	C. M. Buckley	Petersburg, Ill.
Mercer	J. E. Russell	Aledo, Ill.
Monroe	Albert R. Gardner	Waterloo, Ill.
Montgomery	P. M. Bandy	Barnett, Ill.
Morgan	Lawrence V. Baldwin	Jacksonville, Ill.
Moultrie	T. C. Fleming	Sullivan, Ill.
Ogle	Alex Anderson	Polo, Ill.
Peoria	W. E. Emery	512 N. Glendale Ave., Peoria, Ill.
Perry	Frank House	St. Johns, Ill.
Piatt	Thos. J. Anderson	Monticello, Ill.
Pike	H. H. Hardy	Hull, Ill.
Pope	W. T. S. Hopkins	Dixon Springs, Ill.
Pulaski	W. N. Moyers	Mound City, Ill.
Putnam	Mason Wilson (Temporary)	McNabb, Ill.
Randolph	Henry I. Barbeau	Prairie du Rocher, Ill.
Richland		
Rock Island	Wallace Treichler	Rock Island, Ill.
St. Clair	David O. Thomas	Belleville, Ill.
Saline	Jno. P. Upchurch	Harrisburg, Ill.
Sangamon	Edwin White	Springfield, Ill.
Schuyler	W. S. Henderson	Rushville, Ill.
Scott	Geo. H. Vannier	Bluffs, Ill.
Shelby	N. A. Baxter	Shelbyville, Ill.
Stark	Wm. Slater	Wyoming, Ill.
Stephenson	O G. Hively	Freeport, Ill.
Tazewell	Frank S. Cook	Mackinaw, Ill.
Union	Jos. F. Howenstein	Anna, Ill.
Vermilion	Wm. S. Dillon	Danville, Ill.
Wabash	Guy W. Courter	Mt. Carmel, Ill.
Warren	C. L. McClanahan	Monmouth, Ill.
Washington	Jno. A. Davenport, Jr.	Nashville, Ill.
Wayne	Griff Koontz	R. F. D., Barnhill, Ill.
White	Geo. H. Brown	Carmi, Ill.
Whiteside	V. N. Taggett	Morrison, Ill.
Will	Will H. Smith	204 W. Allen, Joliet, Ill
Williamson	P. B. Wilson	Marion, Ill.
Winnebago	Albertus R. Carter	Rockford Ill.
Woodford	A. H Hurd	El Paso, Ill.

ILLINOIS HIGHWAYS
OFFICIAL PUBLICATION
STATE HIGHWAY DEPARTMENT

| VOL. 2 | SPRINGFIELD, ILLINOIS, MARCH, 1915 | No. 3 |

SECTION A. STATE-AID ROUTE 9A, TAZEWELL COUNTY.
Ten-foot Concrete Road, with Four-foot Macadam Shoulders; Length 4,280 Feet; Completed 1914. Picture Taken Before Shoulders Were Finished.

SECTION A. STATE-AID ROUTE 3, JEFFERSON COUNTY.
Ten-foot Concrete Road with Four-foot Macadam Shoulders; Length 3,822 Feet; Completed 1914.

ILLINOIS HIGHWAYS.

Published Monthly by the
State Highway Department.

ILLINOIS HIGHWAY COMMISSION.

A. D. Gash, President.
S. E. Bradt, Secretary.
James P. Wilson.

Wm. W. Marr, *Chief State Highway Engineer.*
P. C. McArdle, *Assistant State Highway Engineer.*

H. E. Bilger, *Road Engineer, Springfield, Illinois.*
C. Older, *Bridge Engineer, Springfield, Illinois.*
B. H. Piepmeier, *Assistant Engineer, Springfield, Illinois.*
G. F. Burch, *Assistant Engineer, Springfield, Illinois.*
F. L. Roman, *Testing Engineer, Springfield, Illinois.*
J. M. McCoy, *Chief Clerk, Springfield, Illinois.*

DIVISION ENGINEERS.

H. B. Bushnell..............Aurora
R. L. Bell.....................Paris
H. E. Surman..........Rock Island
A. H. Hunter...............Peoria
Fred Tarrant...........Springfield
C. M. Slaymaker........E. St. Louis
J. E. Huber................Marion

CONTENTS.

THE USE OF CONCRETE AND BRICK AS PAVING MATERIALS ON ILLINOIS HIGHWAYS.

By H. E. Bilger, *Road Engineer, Illinois State Highway Department.*

The rural highway problem in Illinois is receiving increased attention each year. People are coming to realize that the improvement of the highways has not, up until this time, been commensurate with the development and the commercial importance of the State. In this connection it is interesting to recall that among the states of the Union, Illinois ranks second in value of mining products, third in value of its manufactures, third in population, tenth in density of population, twenty-third in size and twenty-third in the percentage of its improved roads. As for density of population, Illinois has 101 persons per square mile, as compared with 31 persons per square mile for the United States as a whole. An idea

as to the unequal distribution of this population throughout the 102 counties of the State can be gotten from the fact that Cook County, having the highest density of population, has 2,578 persons per square mile; while Henderson County, having the lowest density of population, has only 26 persons per square mile.

The variation in the trend of the population is as marked as that of the density. Between the last two census reports, the population of Chicago increased 29 per cent, while the population of the State increased only 17 per cent, and during the same period the rural population in 68 counties actually decreased. Of the counties that increased in population, the extremes are found in Fayette County, which increased only 1 per cent, and in Williamson County, which increased 62 per cent; while of the counties that decreased, DeWitt decreased 1 per cent and Pope 17 per cent.

No less marked than the unequal distribution of the Illinois population is the stage of development throughout the several counties. In the light of this fact, it is evident that the intelligent development of the rural highway problem requires a full appreciation of the local condition in each county of the State. It is only by such an appreciation that methods and types of road improvement can be worked out to adequately satisfy the needs of the local communities with expenditures within their comfortable reach.

Pursuant to the new road law, which went into effect July 1, 1913, there has been designated by the several counties some fifteen thousand miles of rural public highway for state-aid improvement. Without entering into a discussion of the economical types of construction to fit the wide variation of conditions, the following will be confined to a consideration of the types that have up to this time been contracted for. This new road law provides for rural road improvement with state-aid to the amount of 50 per cent of the total cost; the remaining portion being paid by the counties. The work up to this time has been let on the lump sum contract basis.

During the latter half of the year 1914, the Illinois Highway Commission entered into contract for the construction of 75 separate state-aid roads, of which 18 were vitrified brick and 57 Portland cement concrete. These roads are almost invariably of either ten or eighteen foot widths. The 18 brick roads aggregated 114,188 square yards in 17.7 miles, and are located in eleven counties The 57 concrete roads aggregated 539,933 square yards in 75 miles and are located in 37 counties. The surface of the brick roads is made up of four-inch vitrified paving bricks, with a six-inch flush concrete curb on each side. The bricks are grouted with a 1 to 1 Portland cement filler and are cushioned on 1 inch of compacted sand. The foundation consists of a 1-3-5 concrete base supported upon the natural soil. The thickness of the base at the edges is 4 inches, but on the center line it is 5 inches for ten-foot roads, and 6 inches for eighteen-foot roads The concrete roads are of a 1-2-3½ mixture of one course construction. The thickness of the slab at the edges is 6 inches, but on the center line it is 7 inches for ten-foot roads, and 8 inches for eighteen-foot roads. The slab is supported upon the natural soil.

The average amount of excavation on all 75 jobs was 3,800 cubic yards per mile. Nearly all of the jobs were awarded practically at the estimate of the State Highway Department. From the actual cost record of constructing these roads, we are assured that the itemized estimates were reasonably well balanced with respect to the value of the several items of work entering to make up the total job. By excluding all rough grading, drainage structures, and the like, and prorating the estimated value of the pavement proper to the contractor's bid, we are enabled to get not only relative figures, but almost absolute prices on the concrete or brick pavement proper. From the experience gotten from the award of these 75 contracts, it would appear that where the haul does not exceed 2 miles, the brick pavement proper has been built at a cost to the taxpayers of $2.00 per square yard; and the concrete pavement proper at a cost of $1.20 per square yard. The greatest variation from these averaged figures is not great, and they may be taken as substantially correct, save that with slight changes in the specifications, the price of the brick pavement proper, including the concrete curb, could have been $1.90. Having those two figures in mind, $1.90 for brick and $1.20 for concrete, it will be interesting to consider some economic features with regard to these two modern types of pavements.

Economic considerations with regard to all features of the highway problem can be worked out only in the light of local conditions in the particular community, so for the purpose at hand there will be considered some of the general features relating to the use of concrete and brick as pavements on main traveled county roads in Illinois. Next only to the states of Louisiana and Delaware. Illinois is the most level state in the Union. This topographic condition admits of the free use of both concrete and brick for public highway paving materials. It is quite probable that of the public highways designated for state-aid improvement, as much as 70 per cent of the total mileage will economically admit of grades not to exceed 3 per cent. From this fact, it is plain that the relative extent to which these two types of modern pavement will be employed must hinge upon considerations other than topographic. Nor are there any traffic or climatic conditions generally in the rural districts of Illinois that would materially invite the adoption of either of these types of pavement to the exclusion of the other. Generally, it can be stated that the consideration that should measure the relative magnitude of the adoption of these pavements are, first, their intrinsic merits, and, second, their total cost to the taxpayers.

THE CONCRETE PAVEMENT.

In all highway improvement the consideration of first cost bears tremendous weight with the taxpayers. Available funds almost invariably fall short of being sufficient to carry out the proposed improvement. Because of this condition, the public looks with great favor upon the types of construction that are less expensive in first cost. In view of our rapidly changing traffic conditions, with the consequent development of road-types to meet them, it is quite probable that in order to meet future traffic conditions there will be developed some economical form of re-surfacing for the concrete pavement. There is to be considered also the fact that with a given amount of money available, the mileage of highways to be improved with a concrete pavement is somewhat greater than the mileage that could be improved were the brick pavement to be adopted.

In the construction of a concrete pavement, homogeneity of the concrete is the prime requisite. Uniformity of wear on the pavement is not possible when the concrete is not homogeneous throughout its exposed surface. The quality of the coarse aggregate commercially available is a vital governing condition in concrete road construction. While it would be highly advisable that the French co-efficient of wear of this material be not less than ten, yet there are extremely few quarries in Illinois

that can comply with this requirement. Inasmuch as the requirements of the specifications must be in harmony with commercial practicabilities, it becomes necessary at times to admit such material in road construction as the laboratory pronounces not to be of the first-class. In the light of these conditions, there are many sections in Illinois where the available material is hardly satisfactory for concrete roads, but entirely so for the concrete base for brick roads. In these particular sections the taxpayers would do well to look deeply in the real economics of the concrete and the brick roads before adopting the type less expensive in first cost. The possible development for the concrete road is very promising, and because of the extent to which the availability of local materials govern its cost, these developments will probably take the form of a relatively temporary surfacing with an adequate system of maintenance.

When a satisfactory method of surfacing the concrete pavement has been worked out, the troubles now arising from joints and cracks will have been reduced to a minimum. With regard to the spacing of transverse joints in a concrete pavement, our experience has been that the matter is not yet susceptible of mathematical analysis. True it is that computations have been made involving such factors as physical properties of the concrete, and friction coefficient between the concrete and sub-grade, but experience seems to indicate that the behavior of the pavement in actual service is not such as to be predicted by mathematical computations. The occurrence of transverse cracks has been almost as erratic in pavements with joints spaced 50 feet apart as in those spaced 100 feet apart. Past experience now points to the advisability of building concrete pavements with no transverse joints whatever, except that at the end of each day's work the end of the slab might be faced with a piece of wool felt, possibly one-eighth inch in thickness. This would permit concreting to be resumed the next day with the least disturbance to the concrete previously placed. It is not to be expected that a slab of concrete some seven inches in thickness and several hundred or several thousand feet in length can undergo the process of setting up hard without yielding to the shrinkage stresses necessarily introduced by the high consistency of the concrete. I believe that the occurrence of transverse cracks cannot be entirely forestalled by any considerations of the subgrade when a concrete of high consistency is used, and that the occurrence would be almost equally probable and erratic if the concrete pavement were uniformly supported upon a liquid bearing throughout its entire length. It would seem that the difficulties are inherent in the nature of the material, but in all probability can be reduced by using a lower consistency, and by the addition to the cement of a percentage of inert material, as hydrated lime, for the purpose of reducing the voids in the concrete, without affecting its physical qualities.

The degree of homogeneity required in a concrete road is difficult to get under actual construction conditions It is evident that the prevailing practice of shoveling the fine and the coarse aggregates directly from the earth sub-grade, is such as to permit lumps of foreign material to enter the concrete. While a high degree of inspection can reduce the probability of this occurrence considerably, yet it cannot wholly eliminate it.

The concrete pavement should welcome our rapidly changing traffic conditions. While the design of motor vehicles continues the use of rubber or some similar material for tires, the increasing popularity of the concrete pavement will be commensurate with the increase in traffic of this character.

THE BRICK PAVEMENT.

As a construction proposition in the way of providing a serviceable pavement with low expenses for its up-keep, the merits of vitrified brick have become established by many years of experience. It would seem that were it possible to reduce the first cost of brick construction by some 30 per cent, the extent of the near future adoption of this pavement for Illinois roadwork would be limited only by the capacity of the brick plants to furnish the material.

By the provision of a slightly higher percentage of the construction for engineering services, a more detailed study of the local conditions would be made, to the end that the requirements of the specifications would be better adjusted to meet the varied physical conditions encountered. Without a detailed study of the actual conditions

ment construction job, and consequently the close study of details during construction, as well as while making the survey, will enable exceptional conditions to be provided for by increasing the thickness of the base, or by some other means.

It is believed that a concrete mixture of 1-3½-6 for the base will in the end prove more economical than the 1-3-5 mixture which has heretofore been used. In the light of our requirements as to the fine and the coarse aggregate, the practice of specifying a very rich concrete throughout the entire length of the pavement, in order to care for possible weak spots in the sub-grade, is not economical. All isolated weak spots in the sub-grade should be treated as individual matters, and should be taken care of by special treatment. With proper and practicable workmanship in striking off the surface of the

SECTION A. ROUTE 3, OGLE COUNTY.
Showing Concrete Base for Ten-foot Brick Road.

of each particular piece of work, and the arbitrary requirement of such dimensions and materials as will almost certainly provide so-called fool-proof construction, expenditures for highway improvement cannot be conducted along the most economical lines. It would seem that by the present revision of our specifications for brick pavement construction, such economy will be brought about as will promote a somewhat more general adoption of this type of pavement.

With due consideration having been given to the sub-grade, there appears no necessity for the concrete base having other than uniform four-inch thickness for ten-foot pavements, and 4½ inches for eighteen-foot pavements. For pavements of no greater width than some eighteen feet, practicability and economy provides the pavement crown by crowning the sub-grade, rather than by increasing the thickness of the concrete base at the center. It is not to be expected that sub-grade conditions will be uniform throughout the length of any pave-

concrete base, there appears no reason why the sand cushion after compaction should have a thickness of more than one inch. A greater thickness of sand cushion and failure to compact it are conditions that permit the sand to enter the spaces between the bricks and thereby seriously reduce the efficiency of the grout filler.

With respect to the bricks themselves, it would seem that the first opportunity for lowering the construction cost would concern their quality rather than their size. For average rural traffic requirements, it is not always economical to require the hardest bricks commercially available for this purpose. A condition that makes for a serviceable brick pavement is not the absolute hardness of the brick, but rather the uniformity of quality. For most all rural traffic conditions in Illinois, bricks that are satisfactory in other respects should provide a serviceable and economical pavement, providing the loss by abrasion does not exceed an average of 22 per cent, and on any individual brick 26 per cent.

There is every reason to believe that without noticeably reducing the quality of the pavement, our revised specifications will permit the construction of brick pavements at a figure some 15 or 20 cents per square yard lower than the prices gotten in 1914. It is not apparent that under the conditions in question the first cost of the brick pavement can be reduced materially below $1.80 per square yard. The pavement in its very nature has certain items in its construction cost practically fixed, and aside from what has heretofore been mentioned, further reductions in its first cost must be brought about by the adoption of more economical means and methods of handling and transporting the materials.

However, even with the present cost of construction, expenditures for brick pavements to be built in accordance with modern specifications are amply justified by the assured serviceability inherent in the very make-up of the pavement.

ACCIDENT REPORTS.

For the purpose of obtaining information to aid in promoting the movement for better and safer road and bridge construction, the State Highway Commission desires to obtain data in regard to accidents which occur on our public highways and which result in the loss of property, injury to persons, or loss of life.

Report blanks have been sent to each county superintendent of highways, which should be used for any accident which may occur in his county. The report should be forwarded to the State Highway Department as promptly as possible after the necessary information has been obtained.

It is not intended that the site of the accident be visited in each case. It should ordinarily be sufficient to obtain the information by telephone interview with parties familiar with the circumstances. When convenient, it would be desirable to submit with the report, photographs, particularly when the accident is due to a defect in road or bridge construction, dangerous railroad crossings, etc.

In order that our records may be complete, we would appreciate it if people, generally, would notify the county superintendent of highways whenever an accident occurs in their vicinity.

DEPARTMENTAL REPORT.

March 1, 1915.

STATE HIGHWAY COMMISSION.

Gentlemen: I submit the following report on the present condition of the work being done by the State Highway Department:

STATE-AID ROAD WORK.

During the month of February plans for the following state-aid work were sent to respective county clerks:

County.	Section.
Bureau	A
Bureau	B
Bureau	C
Bureau	D
Morgan	A
Johnson	A
Piatt	A
Peoria	B
Edwards	A
Mercer	A
Mercer	B

Plans for the following state-aid work are in preparation and will be sent to the county clerks during the first week of March, in order that action may be had upon same at the March meeting of the county boards:

County.	Section.
White	A
St. Clair	A
Clinton	A
Effingham	A
McHenry	C
McHenry	D
McHenry	E
McHenry	F
Kendall	A
Sangamon	F
Pike	A

The status of all state-aid road and bridge work now under contract is indicated by the following table:

CONDITION OF STATE-AID ROAD WORK MARCH 1, 1915.

County.	Sec.	Per cent completed.	Note.	Contractor.	Resident Engineer.
Adams	A	85%	N. P. I.	Cameron, Joyce & Co., Keokuk, Iowa.	
Alexander	A	Not begun.		Bland & Fitzgerald, Cairo, Ill.	
Bond	A	Final settlement.		Robert Curdie, Alton, Ill.	Greenville, Ill.
Boone	B	95%	P. C.	Frank Taylor, Belvidere, Ill.	Belvidere, Ill.
Carroll	A	00%	W. N. B.	Gund-Graham Co., Freeport, Ill.	
Cass	A	Final settlement.		Beardstown Conc. Const. Co., Beardstown, Ill.	Beardstown, Ill.
Champaign	A	90%	P. C.	C. A. Michael, Mattoon, Ill.	Champaign, Ill.
Champaign	B	100%		C. A. Michael, Mattoon, Ill.	Champaign, Ill.
Champaign	C	Final settlement.		Stipes & Pilcher, Champaign, Ill.	
Clark	A	85%	P. C.	Robert Thompson, Marshall, Ill.	Martinsville, Ill.
Clay	A	Ready for final.	P. C.	F. S. Nichols, Flora, Ill.	Clay City, Ill.
Coles	A	Final.		Edw. M. Laing Co., Highland Park, Ill.	Champaign, Ill.
Cook	B	100% Final.		Bloodgood & Summerville, Harvey, Ill.	Harvey, Ill.
Cook	A	100% Final.		Bloodgood & Summerville, Harvey, Ill.	Harvey, Ill.
Cook	C	80%		W. J. Walter, Glencoe, Ill.	Park Ridge, Ill.

CONDITION OF STATE-AID ROAD WORK—Continued.

County.	Sec.	Per cent completed.	Note.	Contractor.	Resident Engineer.
Cook......	D	90%	P. C.	E. J. Mahony Co., 526 Reaper blk., Chicago.	Summitt, Ill.
Cook......	E	100% Final.	....	Ill. Hydraulic Stone & Const. Co., Elgin, Ill	
Cook......	F	10%	....	Cullen-Freistedt Co., Tribune bldg., Chicago.	Harvey, Ill.
Cook......	G	Not begun.	....	Walter & Windes, Glencoe, Ill.	
Crawford..	A	40%	....	F. W. McElroy, Robinson, Ill.	Palestine, Ill.
Crawford..	B	50%	....	F. W. McElroy, Robinson, Ill.	Palestine, Ill.
DeKalb....	A	100%	....	C.W.Jensen & Co., 133 W. Wash. st., Chicago.	
DeKalb....	C	97%	P. C.	C.W.Jensen & Co., 133 W. Wash. st., Chicago.	DeKalb, Ill.
Douglas...	A	30%	....	Goggin Const. Co., Arcola, Ill.	
Douglas...	B	Final settlement.	....	Goggin Const. Co., Arcola, Ill.	Hindsboro, Ill.
DuPage...	A	70%	....	E. J. Mahony Co., 526 Reaper blk., Chicago.	Elmhurst, Ill.
Edgar.....	A	Final settlement.	....	Allan J. Parrish, Paris, Ill.	
Edgar.....	B	Final settlement.	....	Allan J. Parrish, Paris, Ill.	
Fayette....	A	Work not begun.	....	P. M. Johnston & Co., St. Elmo, Ill.	
Franklin...	A	Ready for final.	....	J. L. Dorris Const. Co., Harrisburg, Ill.	Whittington, Ill.
Fulton....	A} B} C}	Work not begun.	....	Carpenter Const. Co., Cloverland, Ind	
Grundy....	A	Work not begun.	W. N. B.	A. L. Booth and Wm. Gilchrist, Gardner. Ill.	
Hardin....	A	Bridges.	....	Williams & Townsend, Marion, Ill.	
Iroquois...	A	95%	....	Davis Ewing Concrete Co., Bloomington, Ill.	
Iroquois...	B	Final settlement.	....	Davis Ewing Concrete Co., Bloomington, Ill.	Watseka, Ill.
Jackson...	A	80%	....	Alex.N.Todd, 179 W.Washington st., Chicago.	Murphysboro. Ill
Jefferson..	A	Ready for final.	....	Collins & Co., Mt. Vernon, Ill.	Mt. Vernon, Ill.
Jersey.....	A	90%	P. C.	C. M. Hanes, Jerseyville. Ill.	Jerseyville. Ill
Kane......	A	76%	....	C.W.Jensen & Co. 133 W. Wash. st., Chicago.	Aurora, Ill.
Kankakee..	A	Final.	P. C.	Andrew Ward & Son, Chicago Heights.	Kankakee, Ill
Lake......	A	60%	....	H. G. Goelitz Co., Oak Park, Ill.	Lake Villa, Ill.
LaSalle....	A	Not let yet.	....		
LaSalle...	C	29%	....	W. J. Brennan, LaSalle, Ill.	LaSalle, Ill.
Lawrence..	A	95%	P. C.	A. M. Shattuck, Brazil, Ind.	Bridgeport. Ill.
Lee.......	A	55%	Concrete stopped Oct. 31.	Edw. M. Laing Co., Highland Park. Ill.	
Livingston.	A	Final settlement.	....	Booth & Nicholson, Pontiac, Ill.	Pontiac, Ill.
Logan.....	A	90%	P. C.	John Awe, Lincoln, Ill.	Lincoln, Ill.
Logan.....	B	3%	N. P. L	John Awe, Lincoln, Ill.	Lincoln, Ill.
Logan.....	C	None.	W. N. B.	W. D. Alexander Co., Normal, Ill.	
Logan... .	D	90%	P. C.	John Awe, Lincoln, Ill.	Lincoln, Ill.
McHenry..	A	Final.	....	Logan & Giertz, Elgin, Ill.	
McHenry..	B	Final.	....	Logan & Giertz, Elgin, Ill.	
Macoupin..	A	45%	....	McBride & Wargenstedt, Carlinville, Ill.	Carlinville, Ill.
Madison...	A	Not begun.	....	Charles H. Degenhardt, Alton, Ill.	
Marshall...	A				
Menard....	A	Final settlement.	....	E. E. Brass, Petersburg, Ill.	Petersburg, Ill.
Monroe....	A	(Not awarded.)			
Moultrie...	A	35%	....	Edw. M. Laing Co., Highland Park. Ill.	Sullivan, Ill.
Ogle......	A	45%	Work closed down Nov. 10.	Gund-Graham Co.. Freeport. Ill.	
Peoria....	A	90%	P C.	Canterbury Bros., Peoria, Ill.	Peoria, Ill.
Randolph..	A				
Rock Island	A	Finished Dec. 5.	....	McCarthy Imp. Co., Davenport, Iowa.	Taylor Ridge, Ill.
Rock Island	B	....	....	McCarthy Imp. Co.. Davenport, Iowa.	
Sangamon.	A	Final settlement.	....	R. F. Egan, Springfield, Ill.	
Sangamon.	B	Final settlement.	....	Henry Nelch & Son. Springfield, Ill.	
Sangamon.	C	Final settlement.	....	Henry Nelch & Son. Springfield, Ill.	
Sangamon.	D	Final settlement.	....	Jno. E. Bretz, Springfield. Ill.	
Sangamon.	E	Final settlement.	....	R. F. Egan, Springfield. Ill.	
Schuyler...	A	None.	W. N. B.	F. E. Ball, Hampshire, Ill.	
Scott......	A	(Not awarded.)			
Stark......	A	(Not awarded.)			
Stephenson	A	Ready for final.	....	Gund-Graham Co., Freeport, Ill.	Freeport, Ill.
Tazewell..	A	Final settlement.	....	H. K. Rhoades & Co.. Lincoln, Ill.	Tremont, Ill.

CONDITION OF STATE-AID ROAD WORK—Concluded.

County.	Sec.	Per cent completed.	Note.	Contractor.	Resident Engineer.
Tazewell...	C	Final settlement.		W. D. Alexander & Co., Normal, Ill.	Tremont, Ill.
Tazewell...	D		W. N. B.	W. D. Alexander & Co., Normal, Ill.	
Vermilion..	A	41%		Edw. M. Laing Co., Highland Park, Ill.	Champaign, Ill.
Warren....	A	95%	P. C.	Merrifield Const. Co., Monmouth, Ill.	Monmouth, Ill.
Warren....	B	65%		Merrifield Const. Co., Monmouth, Ill.	Monmouth, Ill.
Whiteside..	A	85%		Shugart & Munsen, Nevada, Iowa	Morrison, Ill.
Whiteside..	B	Not begun.		Walter & Windes, Glencoe, Ill.	
Whiteside..	C	Not begun.		Walter & Windes, Glencoe, Ill.	
Will.......	A	Final.	P. C.	Chicago Heights Coal Co., Chicago Heights, Ill.	Joliet, Ill.
Will......	B			Chicago Heights Coal Co., Chicago Heights, Ill.	Joliet, Ill.
Williamson	A	90%	P. C.	Cameron, Joyce & Co., Keokuk, Iowa	Marion, Ill.
Winnebago.	A	Not begun.		Walter & Windes, Glencoe, Ill.	
Winnebago.	B	Not begun.		Connelly & Dunning, Chicago, Ill.	
Woodford.	A	90%	P. C.	W. D. Alexander & Co., Normal, Ill.	Eureka, Ill.

LEGEND :
   N. P. L. =No pavement laid.
   P. C.   =Pavement completed.
   W. N. B.=Work not begun.

REPORT OF TOWNSHIP ROAD CONSTRUCTION.

Following is a list of the points at which we have township work under consideration for 1915 construction:

Petrolia Road, Petty Township, Lawrence County, about 1½ miles of concrete pavement, ten feet in width. Work will be started about May 1.

Aurora Road, Aurora Township, Kane County, about 1¼ miles of eighteen foot concrete pavement. Work will be started about April 15.

Tuscola Road, Tuscola Township, Douglas County, about 2 miles of sixteen-foot concrete pavement. Work will be started about April 15.

Eldorado Road, East Eldorado Township, Saline County, about 1¼ miles of ten-foot concrete pavement. Work will be started about June 1. Concrete outfit will be shipped from Petrolia Road to this point.

Reading Road, Reading Township, Livingston County, about 20 miles of nine, ten and twelve-foot water-bound macadam roads. It is expected that work will start about April 1. Convict labor will be used on this work.

Lawrenceville Road, Lawrenceville Township, Lawrence County, 3½ miles of resurfacing on gravel road. Work will be started about April 1.

Jerseyville Road, English Township, Jersey County, 1¼ miles of possibly brick pavement, 10 feet in width. Work will likely start about May 1.

Sand Ridge Road, Sand Ridge Township, Jackson County, 3 miles of ten-foot waterbound macadam. Work will start about April 15.

Joliet Road, Joliet Township, Will County, 25 miles of surface oiling on macadam roads, width varying between 12 feet and 18 feet. It is expected that work will start about April 15.

Effingham Road, Douglas Township, Effingham County, 1 mile of resurfacing on an old macadam road. Work will probably start about May 1.

Anna Road, Road District No. 5, Union County, consisting of possibly 7 miles of gravel and macadam

roads 10 feet wide. Work will likely start the latter part of April.

Pontiac Road, Pontiac Township, Livingston County, 2 miles of resurfacing on an eighteen-foot gravel road. Work will start probably in April.

The Beecher Roads, Washington Township, Will County, will require some attention about April 1. There were 13 miles built at this place last year and it will be necessary to go over the entire mileage and make the necessary repairs to those places showing signs of rutting or raveling. About 30 days will be required to complete this work.

Oregon Road, Oregon Township, Ogle County. There is one complete bituminous outfit stored at this point awaiting further action by the local authorities in regard to determining the amount of road they will build this season.

The above listed townships will take all of the machinery that we have available for constructing concrete, brick, macadam and oil macadam roads. There are one or two points that will have to wait until about June or July to receive equipment.

We have a number of other inquiries concerning engineering assistance and equipment for 1915 construction, but no definite arrangements have been made or formal applications for same filed to date.

To date arrangements have been partially made for the construction of 70 miles.

CONTRACTS AWARDED FOR STATE-AID ROADS.

On February 23, bids were received and opened and contracts awarded for the construction of approximately 8 miles of state-aid roads.

Engineers' estimates and bids received are exclusive of cement and other material to be furnished by the State.

The following tabulation will show the names and also bids received on the several sections, together with the name of the successful bidder:

COOK COUNTY, SECTION G, ROUTE 3.

Length, 12,957 feet; width, 18 feet; type, concrete; engineer's estimate, $34,470.64; date of letting, February 23, 1915.

Name of bidder.	Amount of bid
Standard Paving Co., Chicago, Ill.	$31,086 00
Cullen, Friestedt Co., Chicago, Ill.	35,900 00
C. W. Jensen Co., Chicago, Ill.	31,298 00
Walter & Windes, Glencoe, Ill.	27,069 78
The Fred R. Jones Co., Chicago, Ill.	33,610 59
Bloodgood & Summerville, Harvey, Ill.	32,800 00
Gary Construction Co., Gary, Ind.	29,250 00
Yeagy & Cutler, Gary, Ind.	30,750 00
Ill. Hydraulic Stone & Const. Co., Elgin, Ill.	27,800 00
Davis Ewing Concrete Co., Bloomington, Ill.	30,480 00
Connelly & Dunning, Chicago, Ill.	29,850 00
Ajax Const. and Eng. Co., Gary, Ind.	29,780 00
Andrew Ward & Son, Oak Glen, Ill.	33,270 00

Contract awarded to Walter & Windes, Glencoe, Ill.

MADISON COUNTY, SECTION A, ROUTES 1 AND 11.

Length, 9,000 feet; width, 18 feet; type, brick; engineer's estimate, $33,366.70; date of letting, February 23, 1915.

Name of bidder.	Amount of bid.
Dunlap & Dippold Co., Edwardsville, Ill.	$32,981 00
Herrick Construction Co., Carlinville, Ill.	31,397 00
Charles H. Degenhardt, Alton, Ill.	29,982 50
Meyer & Thomas Construction Co., East St. Louis, Ill.	33,300 00
P. M. Johnson & Co., St. Elmo, Ill.	30,980 00
Hanes & Nelson, Jerseyville, Ill.	30,195 00
Robert Curdie, Alton, Ill.	32,666 72
Granite City Lime and Cement Co., Granite City, Ill.	32,100 00
Walter Coonan, East St. Louis, Ill.	33,100 00

Contract awarded to Charles H. Degenhardt, Alton, Ill.

WINNEBAGO COUNTY, SECTION B, ROUTE 11.

Length, 6,200 feet; width, 10 feet; type, concrete; engineer's estimate, $18,582.70; date of letting, February 23, 1915.

Name of bidder.	Amount of bid
Hart & Page, Rockford, Ill.	$18,413 65
C. W. Jensen Co., Chicago, Ill.	16,989 00
Johnson, Dobler Co., Rockford, Ill.	16,747 00
Walter & Windes, Glencoe, Ill.	16,766 00
Fair & Taylor, Belvidere, Ill.	18,036 71
The Fred R. Jones Co., Chicago, Ill.	17,434 00
Cameron, Joyce & Co., Keokuk, Iowa	18,082 00
Metz & McVay, Gary, Ind.	17,043 00
Ill. Hydraulic Stone & Const. Co., Elgin, Ill.	18,500 00
Davis Ewing Concrete Co., Bloomington, Ill.	16,980 00
A. E. Rutledge, Rockford, Ill.	16,400 00
Connelly & Dunning, Chicago, Ill.	14,400 00
Andrew Ward & Son, Oak Glen, Ill.	18,102 00

Contract awarded to Connelly & Dunning, Chicago, Ill.

WINNEBAGO COUNTY, SECTION A, ROUTE 10.

Length, 5,280 feet; width, 18 feet; type, concrete; engineer's estimate, $15,563.00; date of letting, February 23, 1915.

Name of bidder.	Amount of bid.
Hart & Page, Rockford, Ill.	$14,881 20
C. W. Jensen Co., Chicago, Ill.	13,589 00
Johnson Dobler Co., Chicago, Ill.	13,819 00

Name of bidder.	Amount of bid.
Walter & Windes, Glencoe, Ill.	10,947 00
Fair & Taylor, Belvidere, Ill.	14,981 30
The Fred R. Jones Co., Chicago, Ill.	14,850 60
Cameron, Joyce & Co., Keokuk, Iowa.	14,750 00
Metz & McVay, Gary, Ind.	13,900 00
Ill. Hydraulic Stone & Const. Co., Elgin, Ill.	13,200 00
Davis-Ewing Concrete Co., Bloomington, Ill.	12,350 00
A. E. Rutledge, Rockford, Ill.	13,590 00
Connelly & Dunning, Chicago, Ill.	11,740 00
Andrew Ward & Son, Oak Glen, Ill.	14,863 00
F. E. Ball & Co., Hampshire, Ill.	15,200 00

Contract awarded to Walter & Windes, Glencoe, Ill.

WHITESIDE COUNTY, SECTIONS B AND C, ROUTE 1

Length, 6,400 feet; width, 10 feet; type, concrete; engineer's estimate, $12,968.00; date of letting, February 23, 1915.

Name of bidder.	Amount of bid.
Grohne Contracting Co., Joliet, Ill.	$12,600 00
Walter & Windes, Glencoe, Ill.	10,887 68
Ernest Berns, Terre Haute, Ind.	12,430 00
F. E. Ball & Co., Hampshire, Ill.	12,947 00
W. J. Brennan, LaSalle, Ill.	12,767 00

Contract awarded to Walter & Windes, Glencoe, Ill.

ALEXANDER COUNTY, SECTION A, ROUTE 1.

Length, 5,100 feet; width, 15 feet; type, gravel; engineer's estimate, $5,992.00; date of letting February 23, 1915.

Name of bidder.	Amount of bid.
Bland & Fitzgerald, Cairo, Ill.	$5,448 00
C. M. Hanes & Co., Cairo, Ill.	5,699 00
B. I. Britton, Mounds, Ill.	5,879 00

Contract awarded to Bland & Fitzgerald, Cairo, Ill.

TABLE SHOWING ALLOTMENTS, ACCEPTANCES OF ALLOTMENTS, AMOUNTS FORFEITED AND RE-ALLOTMENTS OF STATE-AID APPROPRIATION.

County.	1913-1914 State allotment.	Acceptance by county board.	Forfeited.	Reallotment.
Adams	$9,856 00	$9,856 00		$1,182 00
Alexander	3,253 00	3,253 00		890 00
Bond	5,099 00	5,099 00		611 00
Boone	4,617 00	4,617 00		554 00
Brown	2,632 00		$2,632 00	
Bureau	21,258 00	21,258 00		2,550 00
Calhoun	1,070 00	1,070 00		128 00
Carroll	7,777 00	7,777 00		933 00
Cass	3,529 00	3,529 00		423 00
Champaign	25,867 00	25,867 00		3,104 00
Christian	14,842 00		14,842 00	
Clark	5,294 00	5,294 00		635 00
Clay	3,297 00	3,297 00		395 00
Clinton	6,088 00	6,088 00		730 00
Coles	8,423 00	8,423 00		1,010 00
Cook	120,320 00	120,320 00		14,438 00
Crawford	18,106 00	18,106 00		2,172 00
Cumberland	3,099 00	2,254 00	845 00	
DeKalb	16,662 00	16,662 00		1,999 00
Douglas	9,444 00	9,444 00		1,133 00
DuPage	14,839 00	14,839 00		1,780 00
Edgar	13,175 00	13,175 00		1,581 00
Edwards	1,312 00	1,312 00		157 00
Effingham	5,772 00	5,772 00		692 00

TABLE OF STATE-AID APPROPRIATION—Continued.

County.	1913-1914 State allotment.	Acceptance by county board.	Forfeited.	Reallotment.
Fayette.........	7,686 00	7,686 00	....	922 00
Ford...........	7,862 00	7,862 00	....	943 00
Franklin........	5,082 00	5,082 00	....	609 00
Fulton..........	19,310 00	19,310 00	....	2,317 00
Gallatin....	2,612 00	2,612 00	....	313 00
Greene..........	7,895 00	2,871 00	5,024 00	....
Grundy.........	10,585 00	10,585 00	....	1,270 00
Hamilton........	3,825 00	3,825 00	....	459 00
Hancock..	12,069 00	5,000 00	7,069 00	....
Hardin.........	412 00	412 00	....	49 00
Henderson......	5,753 00	....	5,753 00	....
Henry..........	15,433 00	15,433 00	....	1,851 00
Iroquois........	27,544 00	27,544 00	....	3,305 00
Jackson.........	6,039 00	6,039 00	....	724 00
Jasper..........	3,569 00	3,569 00	....	428 00
Jefferson.......	4,180 00	4,180 00	....	501 00
Jersey..........	3,168 00	3,168 00	....	380 00
JoDaviess......	7,489 00	7,489 00	....	898 00
Johnson........	1,413 00	1,413 00	....	169 00
Kane...........	26,400 00	26,400 00	....	3,168 00
Kankakee.......	11,385 00	11,385 00	....	1,366 00
Kendall.........	8,338 00	8,338 00	....	1,000 00
Knox...........	12,182 00	....	12,182 00	....
Lake...........	15,505 00	15,505 00	....	1,860 00
LaSalle........	34,081 00	34,081 00	....	4,089 00
Lawrence.......	6,484 00	6,484 00	....	778 00
Lee............	11,577 00	11,577 00	....	1,889 00
Livingston......	14,897 00	14,897 00	....	1,787 00
Logan..........	14,099 00	14,099 00	....	1,691 00
McDonough.....	7,529 00	7,529 00	....	903 00
McHenry........	14,283 00	14,283 00	....	1,713 00
McLean.........	26,150 00	....	26,150 00	....
Macon..........	18,295 00	....	18,295 00	....
Macoupin.......	11,709 00	11,709 00	....	1,405 00
Madison........	20,218 00	20,218 00	....	2,426 00
Marion.........	6,325 00	6,325 00	....	759 00
Marshall.......	6,564 00	6,564 00	....	787 00
Mason..........	6,960 00	....	6,960 00	....
Massac.........	1,480 00	1,480 00	....	177 00
Menard.........	3,177 00	3,177 00	....	381 00
Mercer.........	10,169 00	10,169 00	....	1,220 00
Monroe.........	2,368 00	2,368 00	....	284 00
Montgomery....	12,523 00	5,000 00	7,523 00	....
Morgan.........	7,156 00	7,156 00	....	858 00
Moultrie........	5,744 00	5,744 00	....	689 00
Ogle...........	14,294 00	14,294 00	....	1,715 00
Peoria.........	26,265 00	26,265 00	....	3,151 00
Perry..........	2,305 00	2,305 00	....	276 00
Piatt..........	8,434 00	8,434 00	....	1,012 00
Pike...........	7,870 00	7,870 00	....	944 00
Pope..........	990 00	990 00	....	118 00
Pulaski........	1,496 00	1,496 00	....	179 00
Putnam........	2,865 00	2,865 00	....	343 00
Randolph.......	2,838 00	2,838 00	....	340 00
Rock Island....	7,153 00	7,153 00	....	858 00
St. Clair.......	14,061 00	14,061 00	....	1,687 00
Saline.........	7,254 00	7,254 00	....	870 00
Sangamon......	18,403 00	18,403 00	....	2,208 00
Schuyler	5,789 00	5,789 00	....	694 00
Scott..........	2,081 00	2,081 00	....	249 00
Shelby.........	9,779 00	9,779 00	....	1,173 00
Stark..........	5,503 00	5,503 00	....	660 00
Stephenson.....	7,857 00	7,857 00	....	942 00
Tazewell........	11,819 00	11,819 00	....	1,418 00
Union..........	1,620 00	1,620 00	....	194 00
Vermilion.......	30,476 00	30,476 00	....	3,657 00
Wabash........	2,995 00	2,995 00	....	359 00
Warren.........	12,865 00	12,865 00	....	1,543 00
Washington.....	5,357 00	1,800 00	3,557 00	....
Wayne.........	4,983 00	4,983 00	....	597 00
White.........	8,189 00	8,189 00	....	982 00
Whiteside......	13,145 00	13,145 00	....	1,577 00
Will...........	22,874 00	22,874 00	....	2,744 00
Williamson.....	6,765 00	6,765 00	....	811 00
Winnebago......	20,897 00	20,897 00	....	2,507 00
Woodford.......	8,068 00	8,068 00	....	968 00

BRIDGE WORK.

During the month of February, plans and specifications for 15 bridges were prepared and sent to county superintendents; total estimated cost $14,855.00. The small number of plans prepared during the month was due to the fact that nearly all of the draftsmen in the department were employed on plans for State aid roads; also three large bridges were designed which consumed a large amount of time.

Contracts were awarded for one steel and seven concrete bridges, at an average cost of 81.5% of the estimates; total estimated cost, $17,720.00.

The date of letting was set for 8 bridges, having a total estimated cost of $13,230.00.

Ten bridge plans, prepared by county superintendents were checked and approved.

On March 1, 1915, there were 83 bridge inspection reports on hand ready for work, of which 47 were for bridges to be built as State aid work.

LABORATORY WORK.

During February, 35 samples of various materials comprising sands, gravels, rocks, asphalts and paving bricks were tested. A test to determine the wearing qualities of the sands was devised and 23 samples of sand were submitted to this test.

BLUE PRINTING.

During the month of February, 1915, 104 blue prints were made of our bridge standards for county superintendents of highways, as well as prints for 8 foreign bridge plans averaging two sheets, 6 prints being made of each sheet, or about 96 prints. Prints were made of 13 bridges designed by this department, 20 sets each, as well as 3 preliminary sets being sent to the various counties for their use in letting said bridges, totaling 598 prints. Preliminary prints were also made of 6 bridges designed by this department for use of county boards, 3 sets being made of each, or 36 prints.

Preliminary prints were made for 7 sections of road for the county board to pass on, official prints then being made for county clerk, county superintendent, and this office. (This road section averages about 12 sheets, making a total of 336 prints.)

Miscellaneous prints, about 600 made for office use, make a grand total for the month of February of 1,770 prints.

Very truly yours,

W. W. MARR,
Chief State Highway Engineer.

SUPERVISING OF CONTRACT WORK.

By H. B. BUSHNELL, *Assoc. M. Am. Soc. C. E., Division Engineer, State Highway Department.*

The writer shall limit his paper to a general discussion of this subject as it applies to highway construction.

The supervision of Contract Work under the State Highway Department is in direct charge of the Division Engineer. He has under him one or more resident engineers or inspectors on each job. These men report directly to the Division Engineer, who handles all matters pertaining to construction.

The average County Superintendent in the more progressive counties has a somewhat similar organization, but on a smaller scale. He has his inspectors on the more important work and they report directly to him. He is able to give a general supervision to all the work in conjunction with his other duties.

The use of concrete for highway roads and bridges has grown rapidly in the past few years. The personal equation enters into the quality of concrete to a greater extent than in nearly any other form of construction.

Good concrete is dependent upon good cement, clean and well graded, fine and coarse aggregate, clean water, proper proportions, thorough mixing and proper placing. If any one of these points is neglected, the resultant product is imperfect.

Concrete work is ordinarily done by common laborers and therefore the personal equation is large. Naturally, a man working with a shovel for $2.00 per day is not expected to have a comprehensive knowledge of concrete. It is hard to impress upon him the fact that he must not shovel dust and dirt with his sand, gravel or stone. It is also hard to impress upon him the fact that in order to get a uniform mixture, he must load his wheel-barrow the same every time, that he must put in the same amount of water and cement and that he must keep each batch in the machine until it is thoroughly mixed.

The personal equation of the laborer enters into each one of these items.

Our factor of safety takes care of some of these defects, due to the fact that our assumed working stress is based upon conditions such as one ordinarily gets in actual construction under careful supervision, but it is certainly not safe, or good practice to permit carelessness on the part of the laborer, with the idea that the factor of safety is a cure-all for all defects. The best and only satisfactory safe-guard in keeping the personal element within proper limits is careful supervision.

The dangers of improper construction in highway work, are magnified by the fact that we must often deal with contractors and foremen that are unable to read a set of plans.

One of the most important points in reinforced concrete construction is the proper spacing of the steel, yet it is not an uncommon occurrence to find a contractor with his steel wired in place on the compression side of his wall instead of the tension side.

Such errors are not deliberate on the part of the contractor, as he effects no saving in cost, but are due solely to carelessness or ignorance and inability to read the plans. If reinforced concrete is to be an effective material, the steel must be placed in the location for which it is designed.

The writer recalls an instance that came under his observation a few years ago in Rock Island County. In checking up an abutment for which the footing and part of the wall had been built, he found that the footing had been excavated about one foot narrower than called for on the plans. The foreman claimed he had made a mistake in measuring. The footing was reinforced by transverse bars the same length as the width of the footing and upon questioning, the foreman admitted that he could not place these bars transversely because his excavation was not wide enough, so he put them longitudinally. Naturally the footing was rebuilt. We have here an example of where the steel was deliberately misplaced and in such a manner that it did absolutely no good.

The examination of bridge foundations cannot be given too great care and wherever possible, should be made by the engineer himself rather than left to an inspector.

In steel construction, the field riveting and painting are the principal items for inspection. This inspection should be made wherever possible before the riveting and painting gang leave the job, in order that imperfect work may be corrected at a minimum of cost to the contractor.

In concrete, brick or bituminous road construction, inspection is absolutely necessary every day that the metaled surface is being placed. The details of construction, demanding special attention, will be covered in other papers, so no attempt will be made to do so in this one.

The necessity for careful inspection and supervision is evident and cannot be handled safely on work of any importance without reliable resident engineers or inspectors.

You County Superintendents, should use all your influence on your County Boards to secure efficient inspectors on your more important work. You assume a certain responsibility when you accept a piece of work built in accordance with our present road and bridge law and for your own protection, as well as the protection of the general public, you should insist that this work be given proper supervision.

The most common method for providing this resident inspection on bridge work is for the joint bridge committee to vote to pay for such services.

In case the bridge is built by one township and the county, each pays one-half. In case there are two townships and the county involved, each township would pay one-fourth, and the county one-half.

In some cases, the cost of supervision is included in the contract price. This has one good feature. It furnishes an incentive to the contractor to hasten the completion of his work in order to reduce the cost of supervision.

Either method is good and should be encouraged.

Probably the greatest problem with the majority of County Superintendents is that of convincing your County Board that a resident inspector is a necessity, but this is not logically the first point pertaining to the proper supervision of contract work.

The first and fundamental feature relating to the supervision of contract work of any kind is the preparation of an adequate set of plans and specifications.

There is nothing more liable to cause dissatisfaction on the part of the contractor, and consequent friction between him and the engineer, than an incomplete plan or overlapping, ambiguous or misleading clauses in the specifications.

The plans should be complete even to the smallest detail.

The specifications should be not only complete, but plain. They should leave nothing to be inferred or presumed, and above all, should not be misleading.

We have all had experiences with both good and bad contractors. If we could always pick our contractors, we might be able to make our plans and specifications less bulky, but in public work, where general competition is invited, such a procedure is impossible.

The high-grade and honest contractor is entitled to, and appreciates the benefits of a good set of specifications. It enables him to bid in an intelligent manner and with the knowledge that all his competitors are bidding on the same class of work.

In dealing with the dishonest contractor, definite and complete specifications are absolutely a necessity.

Assuming that our plans and specifications are complete, the next important step affecting the work is the engineer's estimate. Unless this estimate is reasonable, the experienced contractor is discouraged from bidding and the competition limited to an inexperienced and inferior class of men.

There are men in the contracting business who have not the experience or training to enable them to intelligently estimate the cost of a piece of work. These men often take for granted that the engineer's estimate is on the safe side and blindly cut this slightly, trusting to luck that they will come out with a profit. Although, strictly speaking, such a contractor has no one to blame but himself, yet he will invariably feel that the engineer misled him by making his estimate unreasonably low. Such conditions as this do not facilitate good work and will eventually reflect to the discredit of the engineer. We now have suitable plans and specifications with a reasonable estimate.

The next step is the awarding of the contract. All of these points have a vital effect on the finished work and should therefore logically be included under supervision.

If we were building a house for our own use, we would not consider it a good investment to award a contract to an inexperienced and unreliable man for $5,000.00, if we could get an experienced and thoroughly reliable man to take the job for $5,100.00. Why then, should this same kind of an investment be considered good just because public funds are involved.

In general, the law relating to the letting of contracts for public work is to the effect that the contract shall be awarded to the lowest responsible bidder. This word responsible should be weighed carefully. We, as public officials, are often too afraid of censure and the popular cry of graft, to reject the low bidder, when we know that he is incompetent, inexperienced, irresponsible and dishonest. By such actions, we show ourselves to be poor trustees of public funds.

Any engineer of experience knows that it is impossible to get first-class work from a third-class contractor who is losing money on the job.

Unfortunately for contractors as a whole, a small percentage of dishonest men have wedged their way into this line of business and as a result have created in the minds of many, the idea that in general, contractors are crooked. This is not true. The average contractor has as high a degree of honesty as the average man in other lines of business. A contractor is entitled to certain rights and privileges just the same as a man in any other line of work.

The writer has found that the most satisfactory way to deal with contractors is to assume that they are honest until they prove themselves to be otherwise.

Do not go onto a job with a chip on your shoulder. Do not be arbitrary and do not lead the contractor or his representative to believe that you think he is dishonest. Give him to understand that you and your inspectors are on the job to assist him in every way possible and not simply there as a watchdog.

Nearly every man has a certain amount of pride in his work, even though this may appear to be of very limited extent in some cases. You can absolutely kill this sense of pride where any exists by a domineering and fault-finding attitude.

It is regrettable, but I suppose unavoidable that the average graduate from our technical schools has very little conception of the relation between the inspector and the contractor. An inspector should never become too familiar with either the contractor or his foreman, but he must not go to the other extreme of holding himself entirely aloof. He must maintain a certain amount

of reserve in order that he may command a proper respect for his instructions. No definite rules can be laid down to cover the relations between contractor and inspector. The personnel of both parties must be considered. The inspector must study the man with whom he is dealing and adapt himself to existing conditions.

In highway work, we always have been and probably will be burdened to a certain extent with contractors inexperienced in this particular class of work. The writer has often noticed in visiting a job of road or bridge construction that the work was not being handled economically, and under these conditions, has made it a practice to advise with the contractor and to assist him in any way possible to organize his work to effect the greatest economy. The average contractor appreciates this disposition on the part of the engineer to assist him, and you not only facilitate the speed of the job, but the quality as well. The engineer may also protect the quality of the work and at the same time protect the contractor against possible loss by cautioning him against taking too great risks.

Assume a concrete bridge, built upon false work that you know to be weak. Instead of calling the contractor's attention to the matter—you assume the attitude that if the superstructure sags, that you will order it torn out and replaced. The sag may be only slight, not enough to justify you in tearing it out, yet enough to spoil an otherwise perfect job, in which case the quality of the work has suffered. On the other hand, the sag may necessitate the rebuilding of the entire superstructure, and in this case, the contractor has a loss forced upon him that could have been avoided by proper coordination on the part of the engineer.

Where possible, the design of false work should be taken up with the contractor before the material is ordered, thereby insuring a safe design at a minimum cost. Do not allow a man to go ahead and spend money on a design that you know will not be safe, and then compel him at a great cost to tear it down and rebuild. Never wait until the last minute to call the contractor's attention to impending dangers, lack of materials or mismanagement that will eventually tie up his work. Help him plan his work so as to secure greatest safety, speed and efficiency.

Whenever possible, make tests on materials at the shipping point, thereby protecting the contractor in a degree, against delays, due to rejected materials. In all such cases, however, never waive the right to rejection in the field, if the material delivered falls below specifications.

Inspection at shipping point reduces the field rejection to a minimum but does not in any sense guarantee that all material delivered from said shipping point will be accepted.

Complaints relative to defective or unsatisfactory work, material, rate of progress or any feature of the job that could possibly later be of importance in the final settlement of the contract, should be made in writing.

Whenever important orders or complaints, changes in specifications or plans are given in the field, they should be verified by letter. Do not do this with the expectation that any trouble will arise, but as a safeguard in case of dispute.

The average contractor in highway work is not so heavily burdened with money but that he is continually clamoring for an estimate. Where the law permits, reasonable estimates every thirty days have a tendency to reduce the cost of the work by increasing the competition.

Some engineers are very arbitrary regarding the granting of estimates, but this practice is to be condemned. The man who does satisfactory work is entitled to and should receive a reasonable estimate promptly. Whenever possible, this estimate should be made to be of greatest benefit to the contractor. There are times when the engineer may materially assist the contractor by withholding the estimate a week or ten days, and at the same time not inconvenience himself. In the majority of cases, this consideration of the contractor is reflected in the quality of the work.

To what extent should we back up the inspector on the job? This is a question that is continually before us and one that offers rather difficult solutions at times. If he is right, the problem is easy for we will back him to the limit. If he is actually wrong, he should not be upheld. If he is working an injustice on the contractor, yet is really within the terms of the contract, the solution is more difficult and becomes a personal problem. We must consider the object for which this man is placed upon the job, the attitude of the contractor toward the inspector's instructions and his job in general. If the contractor attempts to override the inspector and bluff the matter through, the engineer, in order to preserve the respect for the inspector, must uphold him, but if the contractor, after being unable to agree with the inspector, takes the matter up with the engineer in conjunction with the inspector, the dispute may be settled without destroying any of the respect for the inspector and without imposing an injustice on the contractor.

If we allow the contractor or his foreman to override the inspector, we had just as well remove him from the job, for his prestige has been destroyed and his efficiency, so far as that job is concerned, greatly weakened.

These facts are generally understood by the better class of contractors, yet we all occasionally have experiences with the man who attempts to bulldoze and override everyone who opposes his ideas or methods. In such cases, the engineer must stand by his inspectors and the rights granted him in the contract, or turn over the inspection, as well as the actual construction of the work, to the contractor.

There is a certain amount of elasticity in any set of specifications, which means that the engineer must give and take, to a certain extent, in his dealings with the contractor.

In order to avoid disputes between the inspector and contractor, make it a practice to never make concessions or agreements of any kind without notifying the resident engineer.

There may be times when the engineer, with his broader experience, is satisfied that he can deviate slightly from the specifications, thereby materially aiding the progress of the work, yet at the same time, in no way affecting its quality.

We do not, as a rule, permit an inspector to assume such responsibilities, yet, if the engineer does not keep the inspector fully informed, he is courting disputes with the contractor and is encouraging him to override the inspector's instructions.

Careful observation of these details will reduce the troubles of supervision of all kinds of contract work to a minimum, and, as a general rule, the less the friction, the better the quality of the finished work, which is the ultimate aim of any kind of supervision.

EARTH ROAD CONSTRUCTION AND MAINTENANCE.

(By JNO. A. DECKER, *County Superintendent of Highways, Cumberland County.*)

The economical building and caring for dirt roads is one of the leading topics of the day. There should be correct construction, and there must be a clear distinction between what constitutes reconstruction and what may be termed maintenance. It should also be remembered that economy assumes the use of the proper tools at hand, in other words—although the drag might be used in building earth roads, it is more properly a tool for maintaining them. By the same line of reasoning we can readily see the folly of wearing out expensive grading machinery doing work that could be better done with the drag. There are two systems of earth road repair, the annual reconstruction and the continuous or drag system.

The first method and one that has been practised for years in my county, permits the roadway to go to pieces under traffic for one or more years and then regrade it at a cost of that which approximates its first construction.

The second method assumes that the maintenance should begin immediately upon the completion of the first construction and the road kept in good condition at all times. There can be no argument as to the proper system. Any one who has traveled over the dirt road before and after its maintenance with the road drag is a competent witness and good advisor.

Not only is the method of periodic rebuilding costly, but the results are rarely satisfactory, the road so treated is never in first-class condition.

The road grader is one of the most valuable road tools used, but its injudicious use has spoiled more roads than any other.

Road building should be done in the early spring and thus avoid having a windrow of grass and weeds in the center of the road, driving the traffic to the sides, which seriously interferes with the side ditches.

Improved roads and modern machinery for maintenance of same are just as essential to up-to-date road improvement as modern machinery is to the farmer who farms on a scientific principle, and as the time has come when our earth roads must be worked on a more systematic plan than in the past, and at a time when the people are calling for better roads it is necessary and advisable to use machinery of modern construction that will do the work, both speedily and economically. Road work at the present time must of necessity be done by engine power on account of scarcity of good grader teams. It is also a loss of time and money to purchase light machinery. We find it necessary to have machines of such dimensions and weight as will not only level the road, but will pare off bumps and ridges, and move the dirt after the ditches have been opened up with a grader at the sides to the center of the road, also filling up the low places.

The engine can thus travel in the center of the road and keep packing the traveled part of the road, and does not cost any more to move the earth from both sides than it does from one.

My plan of building dirt roads is to make them 24 feet from ditch to ditch and that the center of the crown should be 24 inches higher than the drains on either side. Then we have from center of the crown to the drains on either side a distance of 12 feet, a fall of 24 inches as water shed for the road.

It appears to be a feasible idea that some system of road dragging should be inaugurated in each locality, contracts should be made with residents adjacent to the road to be maintained. Such contracts should provide for the operation of a road drag at a definite rate per mile traveled. The drag to be used when instructed by the official in charge. This dragging work should for the most part be purely maintenance, and there should be a special fund in each township set apart as a dragging fund.

Good dragging is the main factor in road building. Roads should be raised above the level of the adjacent land in order that the water may readily get away. The side drains of dirt roads present quite a few difficulties well known to those connected with road building. The main thing is getting frequent outlets, and not allowing the water to flow for long distances by the road side.

SMALL BRIDGES AND CULVERTS.

(By V. N. TAGGETT, *County Superintendent of Highways, Whiteside County.*

I have often thought how pleasant would be the job of highway commissioners and county superintendents if all of the funds available for road work could be used in building roads, instead of being divided to build and repair bridges, and build and repair roads. I have in mind a two-mile strip of the Lincoln Highway in Whiteside County that has 15 bridges and culverts, varying from 12 inches to 16 feet, to say nothing of six or eight private entrances. In a number of our townships we have had to spend more money in replacing old bridges and culverts this year than we have had to put into actual road repair and construction. It is readily seen, therefore, that small bridges and culverts form an extremely important part of highway work.

In the early days of road building, most of the culverts and small bridges were constructed with logs for stringers and plank for the floor; and there is no doubt that in most cases they were good bridges; that is, they were cheap to build and the maintenance cost was small, for good plank could be obtained for from $8 to $15 per thousand. Now with white oak $40 to $50 per thousand and "A No. 1" stuff hard to get at that price, in most cases it is out of the question even to consider any wood construction, except for maintenance.

The problem that commissioners face now is entirely different than it was 15 or 20 years ago. Now there are so many types of culverts recommended that one hardly knows just what type to use. We have vitrified sewer pipe, cast iron pipe, reinforced concrete pipe, steel or boiler pipe, corrugated iron pipe and monolithic concrete, and each sort has its supporters. The sewer tile are quite apt to break, if they are not more than a couple of feet below the track; then, too, they and the reinforced concrete tile are very likely to get out of line and the joints open up, letting the dirt into the tile, thus stopping it up. Cast iron is excellent, but the cost is exceedingly high. We have a number installed in our county and they are giving splendid satisfaction. Steel or old boiler pipe are very common and seem to last fairly well, but in a number of cases I have seen them collapse; also, they rust rather rapidly.

Of the corrugated iron pipe, I hardly know what to say. According to agents, there are two kinds, the kind we sell, which is good, and the kind the other fellow sells, which is bad. A. R. Hirst, State Highway Engineer

of Wisconsin, when asked his opinion of the "tin-horn culvert," as he called it, said that the state was using it on state roads—on about 130 miles they had one corrugated iron pipe. He went on to explain that he considers them all right in soft ground, where a heavier culvert will bury itself, and also in a few locations where the culvert must be installed without delay. Here, I believe, is the field for this sort of culvert. If a variety of sizes are kept on hand, they can be installed at once where old culverts fail, and then at a more convenient time, they can be removed and a permanent concrete culvert built. My observation has been that in the majority of cases a concrete box culvert can be built just as cheaply as you can put in an 18, 24 or 30 inch tube and construct the necessary head walls. In Whiteside County some commissioners have encased their tubes in concrete, although I would hardly recommend that as an economical procedure.

The type of culvert which I consider best is a reinforced box of the proper size. It will be better to build the culverts a little larger than is absolutely demanded, for the increased cost is negligible. For spans up to 7 feet, a six-inch floor will suffice, if reinforced with one-half-inch square rods at six-inch centers to carry the load, and one-half-inch square rods at twelve-inch centers placed longitudinally to take care of temperature stresses. The short bars which in reality carry the load are very essential, and care should be exercised in placing them. Always get them within an inch of the tension side of the concrete; in the case of floors, it is the lower side. On a six-inch floor with the steel imbedded 1 inch, the effective or net depth of the floor is 5 inches. Now, if by accident or through carelessness the steel is placed 2½ inches from the bottom, the effective or net depth is reduced to 3½ inches and the strength of the floor is reduced by the ratio of five squared to three and one-half squared, or twenty-five to twelve, or two to one. Thus we see that the strength of the floor is reduced one-half by changing the location of the steel just 1½ inches.

Probably the limiting span of box culverts in most cases is 8 to 10 feet. Here is where small bridges enter.

As I said a while ago, the first bridges were made of logs for stringers, and plank for floors. The logs were replaced, first with plank, later with I-beams. Now as we get tired of buying plank for floors, we replace the plank with concrete. The arch plates offer a very convenient and economical method of construction, for after the beams are in position, all one has to do is to get the arch plates, put them into place between the beams and pour in the concrete. After the concrete has set up for a few days, a few inches of dirt is hauled in, and the bridge is ready for traffic. The one thing about this style of floor which appeals to a person is its convenience. However, after a few years, the plates rust out, and so are of little use to assist in supporting the floor. They are, in fact, of a temporary nature. I much prefer, if I-beams are used, to build a flat slab and let the concrete extend down between the beams a half-inch or so, just about to the under side of the upper flange, using the lower flange to support the forms. In this way, the reinforcing can be laid across the beams and wired in place before starting to pour concrete. This style uses less concrete, and thus is lighter, and will carry a heavier load than the arch plate type. One objection to each of these types is that the most important part of the I-beam is left exposed to the action of the weather, and will in time rust enough to materially weaken the bridge. Some advocated imbedding the entire beam in concrete, although it is far from economical. There is two or three times the amount of concrete used, and this in turn increases the weight of the floor, and we have to buy more I-beams to carry it.

May I say a word right here in regard to the size and spacing of I-beams? The old plank floors weigh about 16 pounds per square foot, and are supposed to be designed to carry a live load of 100 pounds per square foot, or the average threshing engine, which in the past has been about 8 or 10 tons. Today we have 10 and 12, and even 15 ton engines, tractors, and ditchers using our roads. The four-inch floor will weigh 50 pound per square foot and 6 inches of dirt on top of this will make another 50 pounds, but more often the concrete is 5 or 6 inches. thick, making the total weight of the floor and covering at least 115 pounds per square foot. This amounts to as much as our old bridges were designed to carry. It is true that there was a factor of safety used in designing the old bridges, or rather there was supposed to be, but I know of places where it was neglected entirely, for reasons best known to the bridge company. It is a fact that a concrete floor will spread a concentrated load over more stringers than will the plank floor, and, being smoother, will do away with much of the vibration, but the added strength is very slight, while the weight of the floor and covering is six or seven times that of the wood one. I know there are places where concrete has been placed on I-beams designed only for a plank floor, no additional steel being used. It is hard to tell just how some of these carry the traffic without falling, but as someone has expressed it, they stand up from force of habit.

To my mind the ideal floor for small bridges is the flat slab, reinforced with steel rods. In this type, the steel and concrete are made to act together, all the steel being placed where it will take tension, while the concrete supplies the strength in the compression side, in addition to forming a protective covering for the steel, thus utilizing each material to the best advantage. One objection, and practically the only one, to the reinforced slab, is that false work must be built to carry the slab during construction. This extra cost, however, is more than balanced by the saving in the amount of steel used. The steel rods are easily handled by one or two men, and there is not the danger of accidents that there is in handling I-beams. Of the greatest importance, however, is the fact that the steel is entirely surrounded by concrete and thus protected from the elements. We know that the quality of exposed concrete improves with age, and exposed steel begins to deteriorate at once. We have every reason to believe that in twenty-five, fifty, or one hundred years hence our reinforced concrete slab bridges will be in a better condition than they are six months after construction.

In locating new bridges, it is well to consider carefully the location in connection with the road and the present and future course of the stream. Natural creeks have a way, over in Whiteside County, of twisting around in figure eights, etc., cutting in at one bend and straightening out at others, especially so as they approach our roads. The provision in the law whereby commissioners may enter lands to change water courses is surely a good one. In a number of cases this year we have arranged with land owners to cut new channels, giving the water a straight chute to the bridge.

The time has come when the public is calling for permanent construction work. We must build for the next generation as well as for the present. If we put in a bridge today that must be continually repaired, or perhaps replaced in the course of ten or fifteen years, we are imposing an unnecessary burden on those who pay the taxes. I know that there are some who object to anything more than the bare necessities in bridge work, but they are few, the majority demanding good work. It is by far the best to enjoy the satisfaction of having used the people's money for something of which the whole community will be proud. It is only in so doing that we can be true to the trust reposed in us.

PRESS COMMENT.

HARD ROADS GOOD SO FAR.

People who have to travel over the state-aid roads east and west of town are not finding any fault so far with the sort of travel accommodations furnished to them. The surface is, of course, practically as smooth as a floor and there has been no giving away of the soil at the sides as it was claimed would be the case by those who commenced before they were finished to find fault with them. It is true, however, that there has been no really muddy weather as yet and that the hardest test is yet to come. If these roads get through the spring thaws without the imperfections so freely prophesied by their opponents, it is very likely that a more favorable public opinion will develop than has been the case heretofore. The farmers along the routes and the traveling public that have to use them are not just now inclined to be captious.

—*Watseka Republican.*

HARD ROADS NOT DEAD.

The "hard roads" question has been given a long sleep. It has slumbered since last September. At that time the board of supervisors administered an anesthetic. The board, in effect, said that the question of hard roads was one with which the people could not be trusted to deal—that they were not competent to judge whether they wanted hard roads or not. That was the blow that killed hard roads.

But the question is not dead. It will be like "Banquo's ghost"—bob up serenely. No great, prosperous, advancing community will "waddle" around in the mud for long.

Vermilion County voted its bonds, $1,500,000 of them. Rock Island County was in the front line at that time. It has dropped back. Vermilion County will have the advantage of being the first county in the State to make the move. Rock Island could have had the same advantage.

The time to get busy on the road question is now. The spring will elect a new board of supervisors. They should be pledged to do that which the present board was afraid to do.

—*Rock Island Union.*

COUNTY TO BUY ROAD-BUILDING OUTFITS.

The Kane County Good Roads Association will ask the supervisors of Kane County to appropriate $15,000 for the purchase and operation of road-building outfits, which may be operated in each of the county's sixteen townships. This was determined at the annual meeting of the association held in the Geneva court house. It is proposed to use the outfits in the construction of gravel roads.

—*Bloomington Pantagraph.*

OPINIONS OF THE ATTORNEY GENERAL.

DAMAGES AGREED UPON OR ALLOWED FOR LAYING OUT A ROAD—HOW PAID.

September 10, 1914.

Hon. Louis A. Busch,
    State's Attorney, Urbana, Illinois.

Dear Sir: I am in receipt of your favor of the 4th instant, concerning the matter of payment of damages in opening a road, and citing in that connection sections 95 and 58 of the Revised Road and Bridge Act.

You inquire whether in case Highway Commissioners advance the payment of damages out of the General Road and Bridge Fund, they may subsequently make a levy under section 58 to cover damages so advanced.

Section 95 provides, in part, that if damages resulting from the establishing of roads shall not be paid within ninety days from the time of the final determination to open same, such new road shall be deemed to be vacated.

Section 58 provides:

"When damages have been agreed upon, allowed or awarded for laying out, widening altering or vacating roads or for ditching to drain roads, the amounts of such damages, not to exceed for any one year twenty cents on each one hundred dollars of the taxable property of the town or district shall be included in the first succeeding tax levy, provided for in section 56 of this Act, and be in addition to the levy for road and bridge purposes; and when collected, shall constitute and be held by the treasurer of the Road and Bridge Fund as a separate fund to be paid out to the parties entitled to receive the same. It shall be the duty of the Commissioners of Highways at the time of certifying the general tax levy for road and bridge purposes within their town or district to include and separately specify in such certificate the amount necessary to be raised by taxation for the purpose of paying such damages. Upon the approval by the County Board of the amount so certified, as provided in the preceding section, the County Clerk shall extend the same against the taxable property of said town or district, provided the amount thus approved shall not be in excess of twenty cents on each one hundred dollars of the taxable property therein."

Section 60 provides:

"Whenever damages have been allowed for roads and ditches, the Commissioner of Highways may draw orders on the treasurer, payable only out of the tax to be levied for such roads or ditches, when the money shall be collected or received, to be given to persons damaged."

This section is identical with section 17 of the Act of 1883. There would seem to be no way of avoiding the limitation of time fixed by section 95 for the payment of damages resulting from establishing a road.

However, under the rule announced by the Appellate Court in the case of *Commissioners of Highways v. Deboe*, 43 App. 25, Commissioners would have the power, under section 60, when damages have been allowed, to issue orders for same to be paid out of a tax to be subsequently levied under section 58.

It is entirely optional with the landowner whether he will accept an order, to be paid out of a tax to be subsequently levied, in payment of damages.

The Supreme Court, in the case of *Caldwell v. Highway Commissioners*, 249 Ill. 366, holds, in substance, that the owner of land taken for a highway may refuse to accept such orders in lieu of money, and may enjoin the opening of the road until damages are paid or tendered.

Where the owners refuse to accept orders issued by Highway Commissioners, under section 50, it would seem that their damages must be paid or tendered in money within the time limit fixed in section 95.

Concerning the right of Highway Commissioners to levy a tax to pay damages advanced by them, out of the general Road and Bridge Funds, will say, the Supreme Court, in the case of *The People v. The Cairo, Vincennes and Chicago Railway Co.*, 256 Ill., 286, held that under section 15 of the act of 1883, Highway Commissioners had the power to levy a tax to pay damages advanced by them out of the general Road and Bridge Funds. Holding of the Court in that case would apply to section 58 of the revised act.

Very respectfully,

P. J. LUCEY, *Attorney General.*

ELECTION TO AUTHORIZE ISSUING BONDS TO BUILD BRIDGE. HOW HELD.

September 26, 1914.

JAMES W. MOORE, ESQ.,
Town Clerk, Sumner, Illinois.

DEAR SIR: I am in receipt of your favor of the 23d instant, in which you make inquiry concerning the manner of holding an election to vote on the proposition of issuing bonds for the purpose of building a bridge.

I assume that your inquiry has reference to an election held under section 61 of the revised Road and Bridge act, which provides as follows:

"When the highway commissioners desire to expend on any bridge or other distinct and expensive work on the road, a greater sum of money than is available to them by other means, the said commissioners may call a special town or district election to vote on the proposition, which

shall be clearly stated in the petition substantially as follows: 'To borrow $............. to construct or repair (describe the bridge or other work).' Upon determining to call such election the highway commissioners shall order the town or district clerk, by an instrument in writing to be signed by them, to post up in ten of the most public places in said town or district, notices of such special town or district meeting; which notice shall state the object, time and place of meeting, the maximum sum to be borrowed, and the manner in which the voting is to be had, which shall invariably be by ballot, and shall be 'For borrowing money to (here define the purpose)'; or 'Against borrowing money to (here define the purpose).' The special town or district election shall be held at the place of the last annual town or district meeting or election by giving at least ten days' notice, and returns thereof made in the same manner as other special town or district elections are now, or may hereafter be provided by law; and if it shall appear that a majority of the legal voters voting at said election shall be in favor of said proposition the said commissioners of highways and town or district clerk, as the case may be, shall issue from time to time, as the work progresses, a sufficient amount in the aggregate of the bonds of said town or district for the purpose of building such bridge, or other distinct and expensive work; said bonds to be of such denominations, bear such rate of interest, not exceeding six per cent, upon such time, and be disposed of as the necessities and convenience of said town or district require: *Provided*, that said bonds shall not be sold or disposed of for less than their par value, and such town or district shall provide for the payment of such bonds by appropriate taxation."

It will be noted that the above section provides for the calling of a special town meeting by the clerk, upon the order of the highway commissioners, and further provides that such special town election shall be held at the place of the last annual town meeting, etc. This section is similar to section 20 of the Road and Bridge act of 1883.

Paragraph 53, chapter 139, Hurd's Statutes 1913, provides: "Each town shall for the purpose of town meetings constitute an election precinct."

Paragraph 56 of said chapter provides:

"The supervisor, assessor and collector of the town shall be ex-officio judges of all elections in their town except as otherwise provided by law."

The Appellate Court, in construing section 20 of the act of 1883, in the case of *Frantz v. Patterson*, 123 App. 13, held, in substance, that the supervisor, assessor and collector were the proper persons to serve as judges of a special town meeting called for the purpose of holding an election to vote on the proposition of borrowing money to build a bridge; and that such election should be conducted in the same manner in which general elections are conducted. The rule, announced by the court in the above cited case, would seem to apply to a special town meeting called, under section 61 of the revised act, to vote on the proposition of issuing bonds for the purpose of building a bridge.

Very respectfully,

P. J. LUCEY. *Attorney General.*

TAXES FOR ROADS AND BRIDGES—HOW LEVIED. SECTIONS 50 AND 56 OF ACT CONSTRUED.

January 4, 1915.

Hon. HARRY EDWARDS,
State's Attorney, Dixon, Ill.

DEAR SIR: I am in receipt of your favor of the thirtieth ultimo, and note statement to the effect that certain commissioners of highways in your county held a meeting between the first Tuesday in August and the first Tuesday in September, in 1914, pursuant to section 50 of the road and bridge act, and determined upon a tax rate for roads and bridges of 61 cents on the hundred dollars, which they certified to the county clerk; that later, at their meeting held on the first Tuesday in September, they certified to the board of supervisors, as prescribed by section 56, the sum of $1,500 as the amount necessary to be raised by taxation for road and bridge purposes, which amount, so certified, was approved by the county board at its September meeting; that a tax rate of 61 cents on the hundred dollars assessed valuation of the town would produce a fund in excess of $3,000. You further say that the county clerk is uncertain whether he should extend the rate of 61 cents on the collectors' books, or a rate on the basis of $1,500, the amount of levy approved by the county board. You call attention to an apparent conflict between section 50 and section 56, regarding the time fixed for making a levy by highway commissioners, and ask to be advised whether the county clerk should extend a rate of 61 cents on the hundred as determined by the commissioners at their meeting held between the first Tuesday in August and the first Tuesday in September in pursuance of the provision in section 50, or extend a rate that will produce the sum of $1,500, the amount certified by the commission as prescribed by section 56, at their meeting held on the first Tuesday in September.

It will be noted that section 50 relates principally to prescribing in a general way the powers and duties of highway commissioners; and among others is a provision requiring them to hold a regular semi-annual meeting between the first Tuesday in August and the first Tuesday in September of each year, at a time to be named by their president, for the purpose of determining the tax rate to be certified by them to the county board, as in the act thereafter provided. And under paragraph 3, subdivision "B" of said section, highway commissioners are to determine the taxes necessary to be levied for road and bridge purposes, subject to limitations in the act thereinafter provided. Both of these provisions in section 50, relating to the levy of a tax, are general, and do not specifically fix the time nor the manner of making a levy, nor prescribe the rate that may be levied.

Section 56 fixes definitely the meeting at which highway commissioners are required to make the levy for roads and bridges, prescribes for the filing of a certificate of the amount levied with the county clerks, requires the amount of such levy to be approved by the county board, and prohibits the county clerk from extending a rate in excess of 61 cents on the hundred dollars valuation. There is no provision in section 50 for the filing of any certificate of the rate determined upon by the commissioners, with the county clerk. And, as will be noted, under section 56, highway commissioners do not, in fact, determine the rate; they certify the amount necessary for road and bridge purposes, and, if approved by the county board, the county clerk extends a rate that will produce such amount.

It is the holding of this department that the levy made by highway commissioners should be made at the time and in the manner prescribed by section 56.

In the case mentioned by you, the county clerk should extend a rate that will produce the sum of $1,500, being the amount approved by the county board, and, according to your statement, an amount that will come within a rate of 61 cents on the hundred dollars valuation.

Very respectfully,

P. J. Lucey, *Attorney General*

APPOINTMENTS OF COUNTY SUPERINTENDENTS TO MARCH 1, 1915.

COUNTY.	NAME.	ADDRESS.
Adams	Lewis L. Boyer	Liberty, Ill.
Alexander	W. N. Moyers	Mound City, Ill.
Bond	R. O. Young	Sorento, Ill.
Boone	Thos. W. Humphrey	Belvidere, Ill.
Brown	W. O. Grover	Mt. Sterling, Ill.
Bureau	Frank R. Bryant	Princeton, Ill.
Calhoun	Jno. A. Earley	Batchtown, Ill.
Carroll	L. P. Scott, (Temporary)	Mt. Carroll, Ill.
Cass	John Goodell	Beardstown, Ill.
Champaign	Geo. C. Fairclo	Court House, Urbana, Ill.
Christian	C. A. Pennington	Taylorville, Ill.
Clark	Zane Arbuckle	Marshall, Ill.
Clay	Howard Anderson	Louisville, Ill.
Clinton	Jno. T. Goldsmith	R. F. D. No. 3, Carlyle, Ill.
Coles	Harry Shinn	Mattoon, Ill.
Cook	Geo. A. Quinlan	Chicago, Ill.
Crawford	J. P. Lyon	Robinson, Ill.
Cumberland	Jno. A. Decker	Toledo, Ill.
DeKalb	Wm. C. Miller	Sycamore, Ill.
DeWitt	E. F. Campbell (Temporary)	Clinton, Ill.
Douglas	L. O. Hackett	Tuscola, Ill.
DuPage	Eugene L. Gates	Wheaton, Ill.
Edgar	Karl J. Barr	Paris, Ill.
Edwards	Chas. C. Rice	Albion, Ill.
Effingham	Geo. T. Austin	Effingham, Ill.
Fayette	P. E. Fletcher	St. Elmo, Ill.
Ford	C. F. Helman	Paxton, Ill.
Franklin	Geo. F. Hampton	Benton, Ill.
Fulton	E. F. Motsinger	Canton, Ill.
Gallatin	Victor Pearce	Equality, Ill.
Greene	Irving Wetzel	Carrollton, Ill.
Grundy	Fred W. Stine	Morris, Ill.
Hamilton	Gregg Garrison	Garrison, Ill.
Hancock	Wm. Burgner	Carthage, Ill.
Hardin	W. M. Ball	Elizabethtown, Ill.
Henderson	C. R. A. Marshall	Stronghurst, Ill.
Henry	Jas. H. Reed	Cambridge, Ill.
Iroquois	Benj. Jordan	Watseka, Ill.
Jackson	Thos. G. Dunn	Gorham, Ill.
Jasper	S. A. Conner	Newton, Ill.
Jefferson	Tony C. Pitchford	Mt. Vernon, Ill.
Jersey	Chas. E. Warren	Jerseyville, Ill
JoDaviess	Geo. E. Schroeder	Stockton, Ill.
Johnson	Chas. A. Hook	Vienna, Ill.
Kane	Geo. N. Lamb	St. Charles, Ill.
Kankakee	Frank M. Enos	Kankakee, Ill
Kendall	Jno. D. Russell	Oswego, Ill.
Knox	Harley M. Butt	Galesburg, Ill.
Lake	Chas. E. Russell	Waukegan, Ill.
LaSalle	Geo. Farnsworth	Ottawa, Ill.
Lawrence	R. J. Benefield	Lawrenceville, Ill
Lee	L. B. Neighbour	Dixon, Ill.

COUNTY.	NAME.	ADDRESS.
Livingston	R. W. Osborn	Pontiac, Ill.
Logan	Thos. S. Davy	Lincoln, Ill.
McDonough		
McHenry	C. L. Tryon	Woodstock, Ill.
McLean	Ralph O. Edwards	Bellflower, Ill.
Macon	Preston T. Hicks	Decatur, Ill.
Macoupin	O. B. Conlee	Carlinville, Ill.
Madison	W. E. Howden	Edwardsville, Ill.
Marion	Lee S. Trainor	Centralia, Ill.
Marshall	L. H. Eldridge	Lacon, Ill.
Mason	H. V. Schoonover	Havana, Ill.
Massac	J. Thrift Corlis	Metropolis, Ill.
Menard	C. M. Buckley	Petersburg, Ill.
Mercer	J. E. Russell	Aledo, Ill.
Monroe	Albert R. Gardner	Waterloo, Ill.
Montgomery	P. M. Bandy	Barnett, Ill.
Morgan	Lawrence V. Baldwin	Jacksonville, Ill.
Moultrie	T. C. Fleming	Sullivan, Ill.
Ogle	Alex Anderson	Polo, Ill.
Peoria	W. E. Emery	512 N. Glendale Ave., Peoria, Ill.
Perry	Frank House	St. Johns, Ill.
Piatt	Thos. J. Anderson	Monticello, Ill.
Pike	H. H. Hardy	Hull, Ill.
Pope	W. T. S. Hopkins	Dixon Springs, Ill.
Pulaski	W. N. Moyers	Mound City, Ill.
Putnam	Mason Wilson (Temporary)	McNabb, Ill.
Randolph	Henry I. Barbeau	Prairie du Rocher, Ill.
Richland		
Rock Island	Wallace Treichler	Rock Island, Ill.
St. Clair	David O. Thomas	Belleville, Ill.
Saline	Jno. P. Upchurch	Harrisburg, Ill.
Sangamon	Edwin White	Springfield, Ill
Schuyler	W. S. Henderson	Rushville, Ill.
Scott	Geo. H. Vannier	Bluffs, Ill.
Shelby	N. A. Baxter	Shelbyville, Ill
Stark	Wm. Slater	Wyoming, Ill.
Stephenson	O. G. Hively	Freeport, Ill.
Tazewell	Frank S. Cook	Mackinaw, Ill
Union	Jos. F. Howenstein	Anna, Ill.
Vermilion	Wm. S. Dillon	Danville, Ill.
Wabash	Guy W. Courter	Mt. Carmel, Ill.
Warren	C. L. McClanahan	Monmouth, Ill.
Washington	Jno. A. Davenport, Jr.	Nashville, Ill.
Wayne	Griff Koontz	R. F. D., Barnhill, Ill
White	Geo. H. Brown	Carmi, Ill.
Whiteside	V. N. Taggett	Morrison, Ill.
Will	Will H. Smith	204 W. Allen, Joliet, Ill.
Williamson	P. B. Wilson	Marion, Ill.
Winnebago	Albertus R. Carter	Rockford Ill.
Woodford	A. B Hurd	El Paso, Ill.

ILLINOIS HIGHWAYS

OFFICIAL PUBLICATION
STATE HIGHWAY DEPARTMENT

| VOL. 2 | SPRINGFIELD, ILLINOIS, APRIL, 1915 | No. 4 |

DEKALB COUNTY—SECTION A—ROUTE 1.
Ten Foot Concrete State Aid Road—Length 6009 Feet. Completed 1914.

SANGAMON COUNTY—SECTION B—ROUTE 3C.
Eighteen Foot Concrete State Aid Road—Completed 1914.

ILLINOIS HIGHWAYS.

Published Monthly by the
State Highway Department.

ILLINOIS HIGHWAY COMMISSION.

A. D. Gash, President.

S. E. Bradt, Secretary.

James P. Wilson.

Wm. W. Marr, *Chief State Highway Engineer.*

P. C. McArdle, *Assistant State Highway Engineer.*

H. E. Bilder, *Road Engineer, Springfield, Illinois.*

C. Older, *Bridge Engineer, Springfield, Illinois.*

B. H. Piepmeier, *Assistant Engineer, Springfield, Illinois.*

G. F. Burch, *Assistant Engineer, Springfield, Illinois.*

F. L. Roman, *Testing Engineer, Springfield, Illinois.*

J. M. McCoy, *Chief Clerk, Springfield, Illinois.*

DIVISION ENGINEERS.

H. B. Bushnell..............Aurora

R. L. Bell....................Paris

H. E. Surman..........Rock Island

A. H. Hunter...............Peoria

Fred Tarrant...........Springfield

C. M. Slaymaker........E. St. Louis

J. E. Huber................Marion

CONTENTS.

PROCLAMATION—ROAD DAY.

To the People of the State of Illinois:

Again it becomes my pleasure, as well as a duty, to call the attention of the people of the State of Illinois to the question of the need of improving our public highways.

The advancement made under the new road law during the last year has been pronounced when we take into consideration that the constitutionality of the law was tested in the Courts, necessitating delay until the Court of last resort could definitely determine that question. The people are to be congratulated that the legislature did its part of the work so well that the Supreme Court sustained every section of the law by a unanimous decision. We can now move forward with the work of making better roads with steadiness and in a systematic manner.

The need for better highways is so pressing that every citizen, highway official and good roads organization should participate in some way in the active work. With this end in view, I have deemed it wise again to set aside a day to be known as "ROAD DAY," upon which all of our citizens should be invited to devote their time to actual road construction, such as grading, draining, dragging, hauling, placing earth, gravel, stone and other materials.

I recommend also that a Good Roads program be arranged in each of the schools of the State, which program should embrace the reading of this proclamation, together with such other good roads literature as is deemed appropriate, and insofar as it is possible, to have a Good Roads address delivered by someone who is competent to talk upon the subject of constructing and maintaining our public highways.

NOW, THEREFORE, I, EDWARD F. DUNNE, Governor of the State of Illinois, hereby proclaim Tuesday, April 22, 1915, as "ROAD DAY" for this year, and call upon all of the citizens to set it apart as a day of work upon the public highways of the State and study of the best means of bringing about better roads for the State of Illinois. And I respectfully call upon all highway officials and Good Roads organizations throughout the commonwealth to assist in directing the work on that day into systematic and practical channels.

IN WITNESS WHEREOF, I, EDWARD F. DUNNE, Governor of the State of Illinois, do hereby set my hand and cause to be affixed the Great Seal of State, this Twentieth Day of March, A. D. 1915.

E. F. DUNNE,
Governor.

By the Governor:

LEWIS G. STEVENSON,
Secretary of State.

DEPARTMENTAL REPORT.

April 1, 1915.

STATE HIGHWAY COMMISSION.

GENTLEMEN: I submit the following report on the present condition of the work being done by the State Highway Department:

STATE-AID ROAD WORK.

During the month of March surveys were made for state-aid work in the following counties:

Hamilton	Calhoun
Marion	Randolph
Gallatin	Logan
Ford	Sangamon
LaSalle	

During March plans for state-aid work were sent to the county boards in the following counties:

County.	Section.
White	A
St. Clair	A
Clinton	A

County.	Section.
Effingham	A
McHenry	C
McHenry	D
McHenry	E
McHenry	F
Kendall	A
Sangamon	F
Shelby	A
Pike	A
Massac	
Saline	A
Kankakee	B
Henry	B
JoDaviess	A
JoDaviess	B
Edgar	C
Marshall	C

The status of all state-aid road and bridge work now under contract is indicated by the following table:

CONDITION OF STATE-AID ROAD WORK APRIL 1, 1915.

County.	Sec.	Per cent completed.	Note.	Contractor.	Resident Engineer.
Adams....	A	35%	N. P. L.	Cameron, Joyce & Co., Keokuk, Iowa.	
Alexander.	A	Not begun.	....	Bland & Fitzgerald, Cairo, Ill.	E. A. Kane.
Bureau....	A	Not begun.	....	Grohne Construction Co., Joilet, Ill.	W.L.Schwaderer.
Bureau....	B	Not begun.	....	Grohne Construction Co., Joilet, Ill.	
Carroll....	A	00%	W. N. B.	Gund-Graham Co., Freeport, Ill.	
Champaign.	A	90%	P. C.	C. A. Michael, Mattoon, Ill.	C. H. Apple, 207 S. Cross st., Champaign, Ill.
Champaign.	B	100%	....	C. A. Michael, Mattoon, Ill.	C. H. Apple, 207 S. Cross st., Champaign, Ill.
Clark......	A	85%	P. C.	Robert Thompson, Marshall, Ill.	Martinsville, Ill.
Cook......	C	80%	....	W. J. Walter, Glencoe, Ill.	Park Ridge, Ill.
Cook......	D	90%	P. C.	E. J. Mahony & Co., 526 Reaper Blk., Chicago.	Summitt, Ill.
Cook......	F	10%	....	Cullen-Friestedt Co., Tribune Bldg., Chicago.	O. B. Kercher.
Cook......	G	Not begun.	....	Walter & Windes, Glencoe, Ill.	A. F. Keehner.
Crawford..	A	40%	....	F. W. McElroy, Robinson, Ill.	Palestine, Ill.
Crawford..	B	50%	....	F. W. McElroy, Robinson, Ill.	Palestine, Ill.
DeKalb....	A	100%	....	C. W. Jensen & Co., 133 W. Wash. st., Chicago.	DeKalb, Ill.
DeKalb....	C	97%	P. C.	C. W. Jensen & Co., 133 W. Wash. st., Chicago.	DeKalb, Ill.
Douglas...	A	30%	....	Goggin Construction Co.,˙ Arcola, Ill.	
DuPage...	A	70%	....	E. J. Mahony & Co., 526 Reaper Blk., Chicago.	Elmhurst, Ill.
Fayette....	A	Work not begun.	....	P. M. Johnston & Co., St. Elmo, Ill.	
Franklin...	A	Ready for final.	....	J. L. Dorris Const. Co., Harrisburg, Ill.	
Fulton....	A B C	Work not begun.	....	Carpenter Const. Co., Cloverland, Ind.	E. B. Blough, 316 N. Main st., Canton, Ill.
Grundy....	A	Work not begun.	....	A. L. Booth & Wm. Gilchrist, Gardner, Ill.	G.E.Schopmeyer, Morris, Ill.
Hardin....	A	Bridges.	....	Williams & Townsend, Marion, Ill.	
Iroquois...	A	95%	....	Davis-Ewing Concrete Co., Bloomington, Ill.	F. C. Feutz, R. F. D. No. 6, Watseka, Ill.
Jackson....	A	80%	....	Alex N. Todd, 179 W. Wash. st., Chicago....	M. J. Fleming, care Logan hotel, Murphysboro, Ill.
Jefferson..	A	Ready for final.	....	Collins & Co., Mt. Vernon, Ill.	

CONDITION OF STATE-AID ROAD WORK—Continued.

County.	Sec.	Per cent completed.	Note.	Contractor.	Resident Engineer.
Jersey.....	A	90%	P. C.	C. M. Hanes, Jerseyville, Ill.	
Kane......	A	76%	....	C. W. Jensen & Co., 133 W. Wash. st., Chicago.	
Lake......	A	60%	....	H. G. Goelitz Co., Oak Park, Ill...........	Lake Villa, Ill.
LaSalle....	A	Not let yet.			
LaSalle....	C	29%	....	W. J. Brennan, LaSalle	Geo. H. Baker LaSalle, Ill.
Lawrence..	A	95%	P. C.	A. M. Shattuck, Brazil, Ind...............	Bridgeport, Ill.
Lee.......	A	55%	Concrete stopped Oct. 31, 1914.	Edw. M. Laing Co. (Inc.), Highland Park, Ill.	
Logan.....	A	90%	P. C.	John Awe, Lincoln, Ill....................	C. A. Clark, Lincoln, Ill.
Logan.....	B	3%	N. P. L.	John Awe, Lincoln, Ill....................	C. A. Clark, Lincoln, Ill.
Logan.....	C	None.	W. N. B.	W. D. Alexander & Co., Normal, Ill.........	C. S. McArdle, Lincoln, Ill.
Logan.....	D	90%	P. C.	John Awe, Lincoln, Ill....................	C. A. Clark, Lincoln, Ill.
Macoupin..	A	45%	....	McBride & Wargensted, Carlinville, Ill......	Carlinville, Ill.
Madison...	A		W. N. B.	Chas. H. Degenhardt, Alton, Ill............	C. I. Burggraf, care Illini hotel, Alton, Ill.
Marshall...	A				
Monroe....	A	(Concrete.)	W. N. B.	Renkel Const. Co., St. Louis, Mo	
Moultrie...	A	35%	....	Edw. M. Laing Co. (Inc.), Highland Park, Ill.	Sullivan, Ill.
Ogle......	A	45%	Work closed down Nov. 10.	Gund-Graham Co., Freeport, Ill.	
Peoria.....	A	90%	P. C.	Canterbury Bros., Peoria.................	Peoria, Ill.
Randolph..	A				
Rock Island	A	Finished Dec. 5.	....	McCarthy Improvement Co., Davenport, Iowa.	
Rock Island	B		....	McCarthy Improvement Co., Davenport, Iowa.	
Schuyler...	A	None.	W. N. B.	F. E. Ball, Hampshire, Ill.	
Scott......	A	Not awarded.			
Stark......	A	Not awarded.			
Stephenson	A	Ready for final.	....	Gund-Graham Co., Freeport, Ill.	
Tazewell...	D		W. N. B.	Gund-Graham Co., Freeport, Ill.	
Vermilion..	A	41%	....	Edw. M. Laing Co., Highland Park, Ill.	P. J. Jervis, 205 N. Walnut st., Danville, Ill.
Warren....	A	95%	P. C.	Merrifield Const. Co., Monmouth, Ill.	Monmouth, Ill.
Warren....	B	65%	....	Merrifield Const. Co., Monmouth, Ill.	
Whiteside..	A	85%	....	Shugart & Munsen, Nevada, Iowa..........	Morrison, Ill.
Whiteside..	B	Not begun.	....	Walter & Windes, Glencoe, Ill.	
Whiteside..	C	Not begun.	....	Walter & Windes, Glencoe, Ill.	
Will......	B		W. N. B.	Walter & Windes, Glencoe, Ill.	
Williamson	A	90%	P. C.	Cameron, Joyce & Co., Keokuk, Iowa.......	L. Schwartz, 301 S. Market st., Marion, Ill.
Winnebago	A	20%	W. N. B.	Walter & Windes, Glencoe, Ill.	
Winnebago	B		W. N. B.	Connelly & Dunning, 164 W. Wash., Chicago.	
Woodford.	A	90%	P. C.	W. D. Alexander & Co., Normal, Ill........	Eureka, Ill.

LEGEND:
N. P. L. =No pavement laid.
P. C. =Pavement completed.
W. N. B.=Work not begun.

TOWNSHIP ROAD CONSTRUCTION.

The following is a detailed report of the condition of the township road work to date:

PETTY TOWNSHIP, LAWRENCE COUNTY.

1½ miles of concrete pavement to be constructed beginning about May 1. Equipment stored at Petrolia.

AURORA TOWNSHIP, KANE COUNTY.

1½ miles of 18 ft. concrete pavement, construction to start about the middle of April. Machinery will be shipped from Springfield within ten days.

READING TOWNSHIP, LIVINGSTON COUNTY.

About 20 miles of 9 and 10 ft. macadam road to be built with convict labor. Work to start about April 5.

TUSCOLA TOWNSHIP, DOUGLAS COUNTY.

2 miles of 16 ft. concrete pavement, construction will start about April 15. Machinery will be shipped within ten days.

ELDORADO TOWNSHIP, SALINE COUNTY.

1¼ miles of concrete pavement 10 ft. wide, construction to start when work in Petty township, Lawrence county is completed, which should be about June 1.

LAWRENCEVILLE TOWNSHIP, LAWRENCE COUNTY.

About 3½ miles of resurfacing gravel road work. Is now under way, Mr. Roy Stover in charge of equipment. All work will be completed latter part of April.

ENGLISH TOWNSHIP, JERSEY COUNTY.

1⅛ miles of 10 ft. brick to be used in resurfacing old macadam road. Work will probably start latter part of April.

SAND RIDGE TOWNSHIP, JACKSON COUNTY.

3 miles of macadam road. Work will start about April 15.

JOLIET TOWNSHIP, WILL COUNTY.

About 25 miles of 12 to 16 ft. macadam roads to be resurfaced with oil. Work will start about April 15.

DOUGLAS TOWNSHIP, EFFINGHAM COUNTY.

About 1 mile of 12 ft. macadam road to be resurfaced. Work will start about the first of May.

ROAD DISTRICT NO. 5, UNION COUNTY.

7 miles of macadam road. Work will start sometime in April.

PONTIAC TOWNSHIP, LIVINGSTON COUNTY.

2 miles of gravel road to be resurfaced. Work will probably start the first of May.

WASHINGTON TOWNSHIP, WILL COUNTY.

Rerolling roads built at this point in 1914. Machinery working at this point, Mr. D. S. James in charge of same. Work will be completed latter part of April.

OREGON TOWNSHIP, OGLE COUNTY.

There is now stored at this point one roller and one complete oiling outfit. There are several miles of road anticipated at this point on which work will likely start sometime in April.

SHILOH VALLEY TOWNSHIP, ST. CLAIR COUNTY.

1 mile of 16 ft. bituminous macadam road, construction to start possibly in June.

DEKALB TOWNSHIP, DEKALB COUNTY.

About 3 miles of macadam road to be resurfaced. Work will likely start sometime in May when equipment is available.

YELLOWHEAD TOWNSHIP, KANKAKEE COUNTY.

3 or 4 miles of resurfacing work on macadam roads. There is likely very little rolling and it is expected that Mr. D. S. James can do this work sometime in May after the Beecher road is completed.

ROAD DISTRICT NO. 7, ALEXANDER COUNTY.

3 miles of macadam road construction and surface oiling. Work to start probably in June.

SEVEN HICKORY TOWNSHIP, COLES CO.

4 miles macadam road, construction will likely start in July.

We have one outfit ready to ship to the contractor of the state-aid road in Alexander county for the work that is to be built at this point. We are holding one outfit pending the awarding of the contract in Union county.

We have formal applications on file for all of the above named roads which aggregate to date about 75 miles of roads. We have had correspondence with a number of townships that are anticipating road improvement and who wish some assistance from this department in the way of equipment and engineering services.

There are a number of township roads being constructed at the present time under the direct supervision of the highway commissioners using penitentiary stone. The Joliet penitentiary is now shipping about 15 cars daily and the Southern penitentiary about 4 cars per day. At this rate, it is expected that the majority of the requests for such material will be filled.

We have on file an application for convict labor in Livingston county. We expect an application from Putnam county within a few days. There are a few other places that have made some inquiry in regard to convict labor but no definite arrangements have been made to date.

All repairs on machinery owned by this department will be completed within the next two weeks and be ready for shipment to the various townships that have made requests for assistance.

The small auto truck for maintenance work has been completed and will be started out within the next ten days for maintenance on state-aid routes.

CONTRACTS AWARDED FOR STATE-AID ROADS.

During the month of March, bids were received and contracts awarded for the construction of approximately 8.70 miles of state-aid roads.

Engineers' estimates and bids received are exclusive of cement and other material to be furnished by the State.

The following tabulation will show the names of bidders and amount of bid on the several sections, together with the name of the successful bidder:

MONROE COUNTY, SECTION A, ROUTE 1.

Length, 1,900 feet; width, 10 feet; type, concrete; engineer's estimate, $2,978.94; date of letting March 10, 1915.

Name of bidder.	Amount of bid.
Renkel Const. Co., St. Louis, Mo.	$2,300 00
St. Clair Engr. & Cons. Co., Belleville, Ill.	2,976 00

Contract awarded to Renkel Const. Co.

BUREAU COUNTY, SECTIONS A AND B, ROUTES 7 AND 4.

Length, 7,928 feet; width, 15 feet; type, concrete; engineer's estimate, $15,955.00; date of letting March 10, 1915.

Name of bidder.	Amount of bid.
Empire Cons. Co., Des Moines, Iowa	$14,997 00
Ernest Burns, Terre Haute, Ind.	14,500 00
Davis Ewing Conc. Co., Bloomington, Ill.	13,490 00
Cameron Joyce & Co., Keokuk, Iowa	14,777 00

Name of bidder.	Amount of bid.
Herrick Const. Co., Carlinville, Ill.	13,473 00
Grohne Const. Co., Joliet, Ill.	12,866 00
C. A. Williston, Chicago, Ill.	12,978 00
Andrew Ward & Son, Oak Glen, Ill.	14,676 00
Metz & McVay, Gary, Ind.	14,420 00
Bloodgood & Summerville, Harvey, Ill.	14,500 00
W. J. Brennan, LaSalle, Ill.	12,924 00
C. W. Jensen & Co., Chicago, Ill.	13,992 00
Connelly & Dunning, Chicago, Ill.	13,249 00
F. E. Ball & Co., Hampshire, Ill.	15,190 00
McLain Bros. & Chas. R. McLain, Moline, Ill.	15,923 00
Ill. Hy. Stone & Cons. Co., Elgin, Ill.	14,210 00

Contract was awarded to Grohne Cons. Co.

MORGAN COUNTY, SECTION A, ROUTE 4.

Length, 4,468 feet; width, 18 feet; type, concrete; engineer's estimate, $10,529.21; date of letting March 31, 1915.

Name of bidder.	Amount of bid.
Herrick Cons. Co., Carlinville, Ill.	$ 8,073 00
Davis Ewing Concrete Co., Bloomington, Ill.	9,545 00
C. W. Jensen & Co., Chicago, Ill.	8,985 00
Ernest Burns, Terre Haute, Ind.	9,900 00
Lastross & Lashnett, Jacksonville, Ill.	10,096 00
John E. Bretz, Springfield, Ill.	10,300 00
Cameron Joyce & Co., Keokuk, Iowa	10,300 00
F. S. Nichols, Flora, Ill.	10,495 00
Andrew Ward & Son, Oak Glen, Ill.	9,612 00
P. M. Johnston & Co., St. Elmo, Ill.	8,490 00
Thos. H. Cutler & Co., Gary, Ind.	8,590 00

Contract awarded to Herrick Cons. Co.

CLINTON COUNTY, SECTION A, ROUTE 11.

Length, 5,550 feet; width, 15 feet; type, concrete; engineer's estimate, $9,597.60; date of letting March 31, 1915.

Name of bidder.	Amount of bid.
Parham Cons. Co., East St. Louis, Ill.	$9,296 00
C. W. Jensen & Co., Chicago, Ill.	9,498 00
H. H. Hall, Alton, Ill.	9,100 00
Townsend B. Smith, Evanton, Ill.	8,844 00
F. S. Nichols, Flora, Ill.	9,240 00
P. M. Johnston & Co., St. Elmo, Ill.	8,570 00
St. Clair Engr. & Cons. Co., Belleville, Ill.	9,547 60

Contract awarded to P. M. Johnston & Co.

EFFINGHAM COUNTY, SECTION A, ROUTE 7.

Length, 7,560 feet; width, 10 feet; type, concrete; engineer's estimate, $9,275.84; date of letting March 31, 1915.

Name of bidder.	Amount of bid.
Harry O. Fizenmeyer, Jr., Terre Haute, Ind.	$9,160 00
C. W. Jensen & Co., Chicago, Ill.	9,198 00
Ernest Burns, Terre Haute, Ind.	8,200 00
Candy & McElroy, Robinson, Ill.	8,790 00
H. H. Hall, Alton, Ill.	9,100 00
Townsend B. Smith, Evanston, Ill.	8,740 00
Cameron Joyce & Co., Keokuk, Iowa	8,874 84
F. S. Nichols, Flora, Ill.	8,965 00
P. M. Johnston & Co., St. Elmo, Ill.	7,740 00

Contract was awarded to P. M. Johnston & Co.

PIATT COUNTY, SECTION A, ROUTE 2.

Length, 5,000 feet; width, 9 feet; type, brick; (with 3 ft. macadam shoulders); engineer's estimate, $13,106.33; date of letting March 31, 1915.

Name of bidder.	Amount of bid.
Goggin Const. Co., Arcola, Ill.	$12,995 00
W. F. Lodge, Monticello, Ill.	12,765 00
Metz & McVay, Gary, Ind.	11,475 00

Contract awarded to Metz & McVay.

PEORIA COUNTY, SECTION B, ROUTE 4.

Length, 10,452 feet; width, 18 feet; type, concrete; engineer's estimate, $30,457.64; date of letting. March 31, 1915.

Name of bidder.	Amount of Bid.
Canterbury Bros., Peoria, Ill.	$28,956 00
Herrick Construction Co., Carlinville, Ill.	28,193 00
C. W. Jensen & Co., Chicago, Ill.	27,795 00
Carpenter Construction Co., Brazil, Ind.	28,400 00
D. A. Meyers, Peoria, Ill.	26,800 00
A. D. Thompson Co., Peoria, Ill.	29,200 00
Miner & Korsno, Guthrie, Ill.	25,732 42
Andrew Ward & Son, Oak Glen, Ill.	26,969 00
Barnewolt Construction Co., Peoria, Ill.	27,900 00
Gary Construction Co., Gary, Ind.	25,885 00
C. A. Williston, Chicago, Ill.	26,662 00
Ajax Const. and Eng. Co., Gary, Ind.	24,745 00
F. E. Ball & Co., Hampshire, Ill.	29,576 00

Contract awarded to Ajax Const. and Eng. Co.

UNION COUNTY, SECTION A, ROUTE 1.

Length, 3,200 feet; width, 15 feet; type, gravel; engineer's estimate, $3,130.00; date of letting March 31, 1915.

Name of bidder.	Amount of bid.
Meyer & Thomas Construction Co., East St. Louis, Ill.	$3,045 00

Contract awarded to Meyer & Thomas Construction Co.

BRIDGE WORK.

During the month of March, 1915, plans and specifications for 25 bridges were prepared and sent to county superintendents; plans for 22 state-aid bridges were sent to county clerks; total estimated cost, $127,120.

Without having complete information from county superintendents in regard to results of lettings, our records show that contracts were awarded for eight concrete bridges and one steel bridge, at an average cost of 84 per cent of the estimates; total estimated cost, $23,285.

The date of letting was set for 30 bridges, having a total estimated cost of $65,845.

Twenty-two bridge plans prepared by county superintendents were checked and approved.

On April 1, 1915, there were 166 bridge inspection reports on hand ready for work, 110 of these being practically completed and ready to send out.

LABORATORY WORK.

During the month of March 58 samples of miscellaneous materials comprising 17 asphalts and road oils, 5 tars and tar products, 5 samples of paving bricks, 8 sands, 14 gravels, 6 samples of rocks and crushed stone, 2 paints and 1 cement were tested.

A bulletin on dust prevention, including specifications for oils and tars used in the surface treatment of various types of roads, has been prepared and will be issued in a short time.

BLUE PRINTING.

During the month of March, 1913, 107 blue prints were made of our bridge standards for county superintendents of highways, as well as prints for 14 foreign bridge plans averaging two sheets, six prints being made of each sheet, or about 168 prints. Prints were made of 21 bridges designed by this department, 20 sets each, as well as three preliminary sets being sent to the various counties for their use in letting said bridges, totaling 966 prints. Preliminary prints were also made of 11 bridges designed by this department for use of county boards, three sets being made of each, or 66 prints.

Preliminary prints were made for 20 sections of road for the county board to pass on, official prints then being made for county clerk, county superintendent and this office. Each road section averages about 12 sheets, making a total of 960 prints.

Miscellaneous prints, about 600 made for office use, make a grand total for the month of March of 2,867 prints.

Very truly yours,

WM. W. MARR,
Chief State Highway Engineer.

SUGGESTIONS FOR ROAD DAY.

Attention is called to the Governor's Proclamation, setting aside April 22, to be observed as "Road Day."

It is desirable that this day be observed by inaugurating work of a systematic character to be carried on throughout the year, and these suggestions are made to help in formulating a more complete plan, suitable for the conditions encountered.

In order to make "Road Day" a success it is essential to secure the cooperation of all citizens, highway officials and good roads organizations, and it is suggested, therefore, that each county superintendent of highways call a meeting of good roads enthusiasts immediately after the town election so that the new commissioners may be present. The different features of the work for "Road Day" should be presented and the commissioners should outline the work which they have to do. The county superintendent should go into each township with the commissioners and arrange in some detail exactly the work to be taken up during the coming season, having in mind the accommodation of the greatest number of people, together with the funds available for the work.

All good roads clubs, commercial associations, civic and highway organizations should arrange with the local highway officials to do their work at places where it is the most needed.

The work on Road Day should include grading, cutting down hills and filling low places; grading and widening approaches to bridges; widening and grading approaches at railroad crossings.

Ditches should be opened; broken culverts should be repaired and plans made for building permanent culverts as fast as possible.

Rubbish should be removed from the roadsides, hedges trimmed and obstructions at corners removed. Trees should be preserved and, in general, endeavor to have the roadside made more attractive.

In some localities it may be practical to haul gravel or crushed stone. If this is done the roadbed should be properly prepared. See that the gravel or stone is well spread and not left in heaps for traffic to do the spreading.

Whenever possible, all earth roads should be dragged systematically. It is estimated that last year at least 10,000 miles of earth roads were dragged, and if conditions are favorable this year, a much larger number of miles should be dragged.

Some organized effort should be made to have the principal roads in each town first put in condition. These would include naturally all those indicated as state-aid routes, and any other main roads that have not been so designated.

The exact nature of the work on "Road Day" will depend on weather conditions and locality. In some instances it may be possible to start grading crews; in others, to start dragging; others to clean the ditches; and in others to pile the rubbish preparatory to burning.

All road officials should endeavor to interest as many people as possible in the work, and have them come out prepared to do actual work.

Let us cooperate, one with another, to inaugurate a new era of efficient work in the State and swell the enthusiasm for better roads.

DON'TS FOR ROAD DAY.

Don't try to do too much.

Don't start more than you can finish.

Don't haul stone or gravel onto roads that have not been properly graded and drained.

Don't grade roads that have not been properly staked out on correct lines.

Don't plow long stretches of road and leave them impassable.

Don't scrape sods onto the traveled roadway and leave them for passing vehicles to smooth down.

Don't fail to come out on "Road Day" and do your share of the work.

HAULING ROAD SURFACING MATERIALS WITH INDUSTRIAL EQUIPMENT.

By FRED TARRANT, *Division Engineer, Illinois Highway Department.*

Road construction a few years ago was conducted on a much smaller scale than at present, requiring only a small amount of equipment and very little capital. With the increasing demand for hard roads, the methods of construction have gradually changed until the equipment required is much larger.

One of the principal operations in the construction of roads and pavement, (and by no means a small item) is the hauling of materials. Each and every contract is a special hauling proposition which confronts the engineer or contractor, and the solution requires a careful consideration of the particular conditions involved.

Equipment that can be used successfully on one job may have its draw-backs on another, and failure cannot always be held against the equipment. The ability of the superintendent has a great deal to do with the success or failure of the proposition. In some cases a superintendent will handle an equipment successfully, while another with the same equipment under similar conditions will make an utter failure, largely due to lack of ability.

The amount of work handled per year and the profit derived therefrom depend largely upon the contractor's facilities for handling the work promptly and economically.

TEAM HAULING. The use of teams is one of the oldest methods of hauling materials in the construction of roads and pavements, and from all indications will continue to be used for some time to come.

The cost of team hauling varies greatly in different localities, influenced largely by local conditions. On country roads, 40 cents per cubic yard for the first mile and 20 cents for each additional mile is a fair estimate.

SOIL CONDITIONS. Soil conditions greatly affect the cost of team hauling, and, due to this fact, there are many instances in which this method does not prove as economical and satisfactory as some others.

SCARCITY OF TEAMS. Another very serious problem that often confronts the contractor is the scarcity of teams at certain seasons of the year, the general demand for teams being so great that they are difficult to secure at reasonable prices. I well remember one job on which I was compelled to depend upon farm teams. Before starting the job I was assured by the township commissioners that after the corn was laid by they would secure for me upon a few days' notice all the teams I could use, but no sooner was the corn laid by than harvest time was at hand, then fall plowing, wheat sowing, and, last but not least, came corn husking and with it winter.

A few contractors are well supplied with teams and do not depend upon outside help, but the majority of the contractors with whom we have dealings in this State depend upon such outside help.

WEATHER CONDITIONS. During the long, hot days of July and August, the efficiency of team hauling is greatly reduced.

NEW DEVELOPMENTS. New developments in machinery, however, have placed at the disposal of the contractor other methods of hauling, which, under favorable conditions, are much more economical and faster than hauling by teams. Steam and gasoline tractors, motor trucks and industrial railways each have a definite field in which their use results in a big saving over the team method.

SELECTION OF EQUIPMENT. First. In the selection of equipment due consideration must be given to first cost, as some machinery will pay for itself in a comparatively short time, and one can readily foresee whether he has enough work ahead to make the investment profitable, while others require an enormous outlay and must be used a number of years before first cost is realized. In any event, there must be the assurance that sufficient work can be secured.

Second. The depreciation which is often figured too low.

Third. The maintenance, which not only includes repair work, but cost of delays due to the idle time of machine.

Fourth. Cost of operation, which should be taken under average and normal conditions.

Fifth. The speed with which a machine performs its work.

It is advisable to use a machine that is suitable for different classes of work than one which is highly suitable for a certain class of work, but which, on account of lack of adaptability, may be idle a large percentage of the time.

No two factors play more important parts in the success or faliure of a contractor than, first, purchasing of proper equipment, and, second, perfecting a smooth running organization in which the labor cost is under constant observation and control.

TRACTOR HAULING. The success attained by hauling with tractors in a large measure depends upon natural conditions. Soil, as well as weather conditions must be favorable in order to accomplish the best results. A small amount of rainfall makes the roads slippery and often causes the tractor to go into the ditch to remain until the road dries. This is partly due to the construction of the wheels of the tractor, which should be built to conform to the curvature of the road and thereby provide an equal distribution of the weight over the entire bearing surface of the wheel.

COMPARING TRACTOR AND TEAM HAULING. In comparing the cost per ton mile of hauling with the tractor with that of teams, I am convinced that the tractor is the cheaper.

On the Fieldon Road in Jersey County, a tractor was used in hauling part of the material used in the construction of a waterbound macadam road. The tractor outfit consisted of a steam engine and four, seven-yard wagons. The average haul for the tractor was 3 miles, while that of the teams was $1\frac{1}{2}$ miles. The cost per ton mile for the tractor, not taking into consideration interest and depreciation, was 15 cents; while for the teams under similar conditions was 33 cents.

In my opinion, tractor hauling would be much more economical if smaller wagons were used, thus enabling one tractor to haul a greater number of wagons and increasing the tonnage and lowering the cost per ton mile.

With the heavy units, one is very often delayed on account of soft or bad places in the road, thus requiring one to split his load, which requires a great loss of time.

With the smaller units, in all probability a smaller amount of the load would be confined to the bad place, thus enabling the engine to pull the load through without any trouble. In case of stalling, it is always much easier to pull a small load out than a heavier unit.

Consideration should be given to the question of damage to roads by heavy outfits. If heavy equipment is to be used in hauling, the roads will have to be designed to take care of that kind of traffic, otherwise the maintenance of these roads will be something enormous.

INDUSTRIAL EQUIPMENT. The building of roads with the aid of industrial railway equipment was given careful consideration by the township commissioners of Embarras Township, Edgar County, and Sargent Township, Douglas County, in 1913, and the commissioners of Washington Township, Will County, in 1914. The work in each instance was under the supervision of an engineer from the State Highway Department, and the industrial railway equipment was decided upon.

On the Embarrass and Sargent Township work, the equipment was used in the construction of 12½ miles of waterbound macadam road 10 feet wide. The equipment consisted of two twenty-horsepower locomotives, 6 miles of portable track and 60 cars.

The rails and ties were made up into 15-foot sections, each section weighing 225 pounds and capable of being handled by two men. The switch and curved sections were in 15-foot lengths and were easily and quickly fitted into main track in case a switch or turnout was desired. The steel ties and angle joints were all bolted securely, and, in laying the track the sections were shoved together with a pinch bar, and two bolts held the sections securely.

In this equipment we received two flat cars upon which to haul steel, but I found I had much better success by removing the beds from the stone cars and hanging 16 or 18 sections on each car, coupling the cars together by using a six-foot coupling pole. Later, upon moving this entire equipment six miles overland to another job, it was a very common occurrence to see one of these engines pushing or pulling 15 to 18 of these trucks each loaded with 16 or 18 sections, or about three-fourths mile of track.

TRACK LAYING. In laying this track, a crew generally consisted of four men, as the best efficiency was secured from this number. The amount these four men would lay depended largely upon natural conditions. After becoming thoroughly acquainted with the work and knowing how to take advantage of it, an average of 2,000 feet could easily be laid and lined up in one day.

The track was usually laid the full length of the road and near the side of the prepared subgrade. The construction of the road was started at the far end, and, as the work was completed, the track was pulled up and relaid on the next route, or brought into the yard and stacked in a pile ready for shipment.

TRACK UPKEEP. In order to keep the track in good alignment, one man was required to go over the track continually, watching for low joints and loose connections. This is very important in case there are any steep grades, as it is absolutely necessary that the track be kept in first class shape in such places. Care in this matter greatly increases the efficiency of the engine. In places of this character, it is often necessary to increase the speed of the engine in order to climb the grade with the load.

The train load was made up by placing ten or twelve loaded cars ahead of the engine and from twelve to sixteen loads behind the engine, depending upon the grade. This arrangement proves most satisfactory in dumping and also in ascending the steep grades.

Where grades are 4 per cent or over, it is necessary for the train crew to drop the rear end of the train, push the cars in front of the engine to the top of the hill, and then back up for the rear end. This requires but little extra time and makes it possible to haul 30 to 40 cubic yards at a trip.

The cars were steel dump cars, weighing about 1,000 pounds, capable of dumping on either side and carrying a yard and a half of material each.

The dumping of the stone was handled by a brakeman and a helper. The train was stopped at the proper place and eight to ten cars were tipped over, dumping the stone about the center of the prepared subgrade. After the stone was dumped, the empties were pulled out and the track thrown over on the earth shoulder and realigned. By uniform loading, the proper amount of stone was dumped from each car to make the desired thickness of stone in the road.

A very economical way to handle the switching in the yard is by means of a mule, thus increasing the efficiency of the engine. The watering plant should consist of a gasoline engine and an elevated tank with coal bins handy, so coal and water can be taken at the same time, thus utilizing all the time possible and greatly increasing the efficiency of the engine. A small amount of time wasted on each trip due to poor organization and switching in the yard with the engine, however small it may seem, soon counts up, and, in the course of a day, one or more trips may be lost which would add greatly to the cost of hauling.

Some of the advantages in favor of the industrial railway for hauling materials on roads are:

First. Cheap hauling.

. Second. Quicker hauling.

Third. Hauling under almost any weather conditions, independent of muddy or sandy roads, or hot weather.

Fourth. Independence of labor strikes.

Fifth. Reduction of men on the pay roll.

Sixth. No expense for resurfacing of subgrade, as this outfit does not leave a noticeable impression on the ground. This is very often quite an item where teams or traction outfits are used.

Seventh. Light weight of the outfit, making it possible to cross light country bridges.

Eighth. Small amount of space required for operation.

WEATHER CONDITIONS. Weather conditions had very little effect on the hauling with this equipment on these jobs, as only two days in the entire season were lost, and that was due to the fact that one-quarter mile of the track was laid on very low ground and the water was above the rails. After the water had gone down, the track was moved to higher ground and hauling was resumed.

SOIL CONDITIONS. The soil was of a heavy, black, mucky nature and one in which hauling by means of teams or tractors would have been greatly handicapped in wet weather. The only way in which it affected the industrial railway was that it made the shifting of the track much harder than in dry weather.

NATURAL CONDITIONS. On the Brocton job no serious natural conditions were encountered, as the greater amount of the hauling was over practically level ground with the exception of three hills which were a little better than 4 per cent grades.

Upon the completion of hauling the stone for 8½ miles of this road, our central loading station, together with the entire equipment, was transferred 6 miles overland to a new station. This was accomplished in six days by picking up the track in the rear and hauling and placing it ahead continuously. In this manner we were not only able to move the entire equipment much quicker, but cheaper than if it had all been picked up and loaded on railroad cars. This movement, including picking up and relaying track to the new location, cost $329.

LOADING OUTFIT. One of the very essential things in the hauling of material, which is often overlooked, is the loading. There are several different methods which have been used very successfully, but which is the fastest, cheapest and the best, I am unable to say.

With any equipment, it is very essential that the least time possible be spent in loading.

On one of these jobs, a pit was dug under the railroad track and a loader consisting of a belt conveyor propelled by a gasoline engine was installed. The stone was dumped from the railroad cars into the pit and elevated into the one and one-half yard. cars. It was the intention to keep 20 cars at the loading plant, while each engine was on the road with 20 loaded cars each.

The loading was placed in charge of a good foreman who devoted all of his attention to the loading and very seldom the engines had to wait for the cars to be loaded.

QUICK HAULING. The equipment was leased for six months, but owing to the fact that it was delayed in transit, it cut down our time limit on the hauling. A little less than five months were consumed in hauling 25,473 cubic yards of stone with an average haul of 3.17 miles, which included unloading and reloading of equipment.

COST OF HAULING. The cost of hauling this stone on the rental basis, which included all expenses incurred in the hauling, as well as the freight both ways from Koppel, Pa., was 14.8 cents per ton miles. Included in this hauling also was the necessary expense to put the equipment back in first class shape.

The comparative cost of team haul on this job would, at least calculations, be 28 or 30 cents per ton mile, regardless of the fact that it would have been impossible to have secured a sufficient number of teams to have completed the work in a year. In this instance, if the township had owned the equipment, the cost per ton mile would have been much lower.

Figuring on 20 per cent for depreciation, also the necessary repairs to put the equipment in first class working condition after use, the cost per ton mile would have been 11 cents.

FORMS FOR ANNUAL REPORTS.

. We are printing in this issue of "Illinois Highways" complete forms, condensed, for annual reports of both the township treasurer of the road and bridge funds and the township highway commissioners.

There are a number of different forms being used at the present time, but we have failed to find a form for either of these reports which contains all the information that should be contained in a report of this kind. In view of this fact we are printing these forms for the purpose of having a uniform system of reports in use throughout the entire State.

We would therefore suggest that in the future when making annual reports that blanks be used that conform with the forms printed herein.

TREASURER'S ANNUAL STATEMENT OF FUNDS RE-CEIVED AND DISBURSED FOR THE FISCAL YEAR ENDING ...., 191..

STATE OF ILLINOIS,
COUNTY OF .... } ss.
TOWN OF ....

OFFICE OF TREASURER OF
THE ROAD AND BRIDGE
FUND OF SAID TOWN.

To the Highway Commissioners, Town of ....,
County of ...., State of Illinois.
I, ..., treasurer of the road and bridge funds for the Town of ....,

County of ...., State of Illinois, being duly sworn, depose and say that the following statement by me subscribed is a correct statement of the amount of road and bridge funds on hand at the beginning of the fiscal year above stated; the amount of road and bridge funds received; the sources from which received; the amount expended, and the purpose for which expended as set forth in said statement.

....

Treasurer.

Subscribed and sworn to before me this .... day of ...., A. D. 19..

....

RECEIPTS.

Date.	Funds Received And From What Sources Received.	Am't.
....	Amount of Road & Bridge Funds on hand at the beginning of the year.....	.... ..
.... ..		.... ..
.... ..		.... ..
.... ..		.... ..
.... ..		.... ..

FINANCIAL STATEMENT.

Date.		Dr.	Cr.
....	To balance received from....	.... ..	.... ..
....	Acct. road and bridge fund..	.... ..	.... ..
....	To receipts from all sources..	.... ..	.... ..
....	By orders paid...............	.... ..	.... ..
....	To balance on hand..........	.... ..	.... ..
	SPECIAL FUNDS		
.... ..	....	.... ..	.... ..
.... ..	....	.... ..	.... ..
.... ..	....	.... ..	.... ..
.... ..	....	.... ..	.... ..

DISBURSEMENTS.

Ord. No.	Date.	To Whom Paid.	What For.	Am't.
.... ..	..	....	....	..
.... ..	..	....	....	..
.... ..	..	....	....	..
.... ..	..	....	....	..
.... ..	..	....	....	..

SUMMARY OF EXPENDITURES AND FOR WHAT PURPOSE EXPENDED.

EARTH ROADS:
 Grading ....
 Dragging ....
 ....

HARD ROADS:
 Construction ....
 Repairs ....
 ....

BRIDGES:
 Bridges and Culverts......................
 Repairs ....
 ....

SUPPLIES:
 Machinery ....
 Repairs ....
 ....

NEW ROADS:
 Damages ....
 ....

MISCELLANEOUS:
 ....
 ....
 ....
 ....

Total must agree with Total Disbursements.

HIGHWAY COMMISSIONERS' ANNUAL REPORT.

*To the Board of Town Auditors, Town of ....,
County of ...., State of Illinois.*

The commissioners of highways of the town of
..............., County of ...., State
of Illinois, present the following report for the fiscal
year ending ...., 191..

POLL TAX.

Poll tax assessed, $......; amount paid, $......;
amount delinquent, $......

ROAD AND BRIDGE FUND.

Balance on hand at beginning of year, $......;
received from tax levy, $......; received from other
sources, $......; orders paid, $......; balance on
hand, $......; orders drawn and unpaid, $......;
liabilities incurred and not paid, $...... (on account
of ....)

ROAD DAMAGES.

Paid for damages in laying out, altering, widening, or vacating roads and right of way for ditches, the
sum of $......

SUGGESTIONS ON FUTURE WORK.

....
....
....
....

FINANCIAL STATEMENT.

Date.	Road and Bridge Fund.	Debit.	Credit.
......	To balance on hand...........	.....	.....
......	Received from all sources....	.....	.....
......	By orders paid...............	.....	.....
......	To balance on hand...........	.....	.....

SPECIAL FUNDS.

.....	....	..	.....
.....	....	..	.....
.....	....	..	.....
.....	....	..	.....

RECEIPTS FROM ALL SOURCES.

Date.	From Whom.	What For.	Am't.
....	....	....	....
....	....	....	....
....	....	....	....
....	....	....	....

DISBURSEMENTS.

Ord. No.	Date.	Whom Paid.	What For.	Am't.
....	..	....	....	..
....	..	....	....	..
....	..	....	....	..

....
....
....

Highway Commissioners.

BRIDGE WORK IN FORD COUNTY.

By C. F. HELMAN, *County Superintendent of Highways.*

Bridge work done in Ford County last year was
not of very great magnitude, and consisted mainly in
such work as had to be done.

One new 65-foot span steel bridge on concrete
abutments was completed shortly before I got in office,
and contracts for two 60-foot span steel bridges on
concrete abutments were let soon after, and were built
during the fore part of the summer. Several pairs of
concrete abutments under steel bridges were built; repairing of old steel bridges undertaken where required,
and seven reinforced concrete bridges of spans from 6
to 10 feet were constructed.

My commissioners all agree with me that it is
proper and the best practice to gradually replace as
many as possible of the old bridges with structures of
reinforced concrete, and in case the necessary money

were available, I believe Ford County in a short time would make a good showing in reinforced concrete bridge work. As conditions are now, we have to go a little slow and confine ourselves to the replacing only of such bridges which cannot safely be trusted to bear up under the traffic. I am preparing plans for a number of reinforced bridges and expect to have at least 25 new bridges of this type constructed during the summer.

Quite a number of concrete bridges have been built in Ford County during the last eight or ten years, and particularly in Patton Township which adopted years ago concrete as the material for practically all the bridges which were to be renewed, and did not span dredge ditches.

Most of the concrete bridges in this township were designed by the State Highway Department and built under its supervision, and the commissioners who took the necessary steps to accomplish this may well feel proud over this progressive achievement, the justification of which is so conclusively proven by the fact that all the bridges so built are in excellent condition today, and, judging from all indications, will so remain.

And it is furthermore a fact that Patton Township by the efforts of these commissioners now has the distinction of possessing more concrete bridges constructed under the supervision of the State Highway Department than any other township in Illinois.

It is not necessary nowadays to employ lengthy arguments to convince the people of Patton Township of the durability and safety of those reinforced structures which have only slender steel rods bedded in a comparatively thin layer of concrete to bear up the traffic in place of more substantial and reliable looking steel beams, but a few years ago there was required not only a good deal of effort on the highway commissioners' part to set at rest the doubts which naturally would arise in their own minds as to the advisability of adopting a type of bridge construction with which they were not at all acquainted, but a good, stiff backbone to stand up against and overcome the suspicions with which the public regarded the matter and not to be moved by the persistent calamity predictions freely and apparently well meaningly voiced by those who had figured on the old wooden bridges being replaced by steel structures and had such for sale.

The example set by Patton Township has already had a beneficial effect on the bridge work in other townships and has also in a large measure helped to give the people of the community the true conception of the valuable work done by the State Highway Department.

Now a few words in regard to the sentiment in my county as to the Tice road law and the hard road proposition.

The highway commissioners, while not feeling very enthusiastic over the new conditions created by the Tice law, or entirely in accord with all of its provisions, have, however, adjusted themselves to the new regime with commendable promptness and have at all times with courtesy and apparent cheerfulness given me such assistance in my work as I have found necessary to request.

The supervisors have appropriated for hard roads more than the amount required to meet the present allotments to Ford County of State funds for the building of state-aid roads, and the first section of state-aid roads to be built in the county was selected at the March meeting of the board and this road will be constructed during the coming summer.

While the citizens of Ford County all believe in and advocate good roads, they feel, however, a little dubious as to the advisability of undertaking the construction of hard roads on a large scale and prefer to wait for some little time with the view of ascertaining how this procedure, which is just about to be launched in Vermilion County, will work out before arriving at definite conclusions in the matter.

However, I predict that "little Ford," which in progressive enterprise never has taken a back seat, will after due deliberation and a careful weighing of all matters pertaining to the hard roads question, come in line with, and soon thereafter march ahead of, most of the counties of its size in the State in hard road building.

I figure that the building of the first section of state-aid road is of great importance as an educational factor and will be a valuable and much needed illustration of what a state-aid road in this locality really looks like. Many a "doubting Thomas" will inspect it and from the inspection draw the conclusion that good, durable hard roads can be built on the mucky highways of Ford County, after all.

A good roads club, in which all the townships of the county are to be represented, is now under formation and I anticipate much valuable help from this organization.

AN OPEN LETTER TO THE GENERAL PUBLIC.

By J. A. Decker, County Superintendent of Highways, Cumberland County.

Road building is a serious public business, and its importance should not be underestimated, for upon it depends the development of our great agricultural districts. Publicity is just as essential to successful operation of a public bureau engaged in the study of roads, as it is in the prosecution of your private affairs. The greatest good to the greatest number of people, is our motto and is only possible where the system of public improvements under contemplation permits the free and full discussion of all subjects pertaining to road building and road maintainence on a systematic and economical plan. Illinois educational campaign has resulted in a system of perfect cooperation between township and county and state and nation, and what is more to the point, the man who foots the bill knows what is going on. Public office is a public trust and we owe to the public our devotion and we expect to give our best thought, judgment and action to the betterment of the public highways, tempered in an economical manner to the taxpayers of the county. We call upon the general public not to look upon public improvement with an eye singly to your own interest; remember there are others. Remember there are more roads in your township than you can see from your own door steps. Allow your commissioner to first improve the mail routes and general traveled roads and then the secondary one be looked after. Cumberland county has 704 miles of public highways, over 1600 bridges and culverts comprising a total length of 20,000 lineal feet, equal to one continuous bridge almost four miles long. Think of the great expense the public has been to in building them and we are at a great expense in maintaining them, so don't expect too much in the way of public improvement, for it takes money and time to make our public highways what they should be.

We make a personal appeal to each land owner, taxpayer and the general public to lend a hand in this much needed improvement. Each person of Cumberland county can do something toward lessening the expense of road improvement and better conditions without much trouble to themselves. You can cut the brush along your farms and remove obstructions in drain ditches that might save your township many dollars. Sometimes people in an unthoughtful way throw brush, tin cans, wire and dead poultry in ditches. It is not only unlawful but is a great inconvenience to road workers to make the ditches depositories for such. There will be a force of men in each township this spring, grading the highways and if you have been guilty of these unthoughtful acts, please rectify them so that it will not cost the public for your carelessness.

No one man can improve the highways of a neighborhood. All must act together in behalf of their common interests. They will in the end, by intelligent cooperation and systematic methods be the recipients of benefits far beyond any possible results arising from discordant and uncompromising individual demands.

We insist that you yield your individual interest to a wider range of road improvement than to a single system wider than the horizon as seen from your own doorstep.

We earnestly ask your hearty cooperation in the great task before us and hope that Cumberland county will be lifted out of the mud.

OPINIONS OF THE ATTORNEY GENERAL.

ROADS ON TOWN LINES—HOW LAID OUT.

December 22, 1914.

J. J. FALKNER, Esq.,
   Highway Commissioner, Jerseyville, Ill.

DEAR SIR: In reply to your favor of the nineteenth instant, relative to laying out a road on town lines, will say, section 99 of the revised road and bridge act provides as follows:

"Public roads may be established, altered, widened or vacated on county or township or district lines, or from one township or district to another, and in case a railroad right of way or stream of water joins the boundary line of such county line, then along the line of such railroad right of way or stream of water, in the same manner as other public roads, except that in such cases, a copy of the petition shall be posted up in and presented to the commissioners of each town or district interested; said petition to be as in other cases, and signed by not less than twelve, or two-thirds of the owners of land residing thereon, in either township or district or county within two miles of the road to be so altered, widened, vacated, located or laid out. Whereupon it shall be the duty of the commissioners of the several towns or districts to meet and act together, in the same time and manner as in other cases, in considering the petition, viewing the premises, adjusting damages,, and making all orders in reference to such proposed road, alteration, widening or vacation, and a copy of all final orders and plats and papers shall be filed and recorded in each of the counties and towns or districts interested. In case the said commissioners are unable to agree, the county superintendent of highways shall act as arbitrator between them in case the towns or districts shall lie within the same county, and if in different counties the State Highway Commission or any person designated by him, shall so act. All appeals hereinbefore provided for may likewise to be taken to the county superintendent of highways, or in case the towns

or districts shall lie in two or more counties, to the State Highway Commission."

The above provision is similar to section 57 of the road and bridge act of 1883. The Supreme Court, in construing section 57 of the act of 1883, in the case of *Wright* vs. *Commissioners of Highways et al*, 145 Ill., 48, involving the proceedings of highway commissioners in laying out a road on a county line and in three towns, held, in substance, that the correct practice was to prepare three petitions addressed to the joint board of commissioners of highways, one for each town, and on each petition being signed by not less than twelve land owners residing in the town for which it is prepared, to be delivered to board of commissioners of such town.

And the Appellate Court, in construing said section 57, in the case of *The People* vs. *Spangler*, 150 Ill., App. 509, held, in substance, that a petition presented to the highway commissioners of two towns asking for the laying out of a road on a line between two towns would not confer jurisdiction, unless signed by not less than twelve or two-thirds of the owners of land residing thereon, within two miles of such road, in either town.

You will note that section 99 of the revised act requires a petition for the laying out of a road on town lines, to be signed by not less than twelve, or two-thirds of the owners of land residing thereon, in either township within two miles of the road to be laid out.

You say in your letter, the road petitioned for affects four towns. Applying the rule announced by the Supreme and Appellate Courts in the cases above cited, there should be a petition for each town, addressed to the joint board of commissioners, and the petition prepared for each town should be signed by not less than twelve, or two-thirds of the owners of land of such town residing thereon, within two miles of the proposed road. You will note, too, that said section makes it the duty of the commissioners of the several towns to meet and act together. And in order to constitute a valid meeting it would seem that a majority of the commissioners of each town should participate in such meeting. The proceedings and orders of such joint meeting are similar to the proceedings and orders of a board of commissioners in laying out a road in a single town.

I would suggest that where a petition for a road affects several towns, and the commissioners are not clear as to the correct procedure in the matter, it would be advisable to consult local counsel for the purpose of avoiding complications.

Very respectfully,
        P. J. LUCEY, *Attorney General.*

WHETHER MANDAMUS WILL LIE TO COMPEL ONE OF ADJOINING TOWNS TO JOIN IN CONSTRUCTING BRIDGE UNDER SECTION 63 OF REVISED ACT.

November 11, 1914.

Hon. J. N. THOMAS,
   State's Attorney, Monmouth, Ill.

DEAR SIR: I am in receipt of your favor of the sixth instant, in which you state, in substance, that it is necessary to build a new bridge within 80 rods of a line of adjoining townships over a stream on a road crossing town lines, as provided by section 63 of the revised road and bridge act; that the highway commissioners of one of the towns refuse to join the commissioners of the town within which such bridge will be located in building same.

You inquire, in effect, whether mandamus will lie to compel the objecting commissioners to join in building such bridge, or whether the question of building the same by the town within which such bridge will be located should be submitted to a vote under the provisions of Section 66.

Section 63 provides as follows:

"Bridges over streams which divide towns or districts and bridges over streams on roads on town or district lines, and bridges within 80 rods of town or district lines over streams on roads extending from one town or district into another town or district and crossing town or district lines shall be built and repaired at the expense of such towns or districts. *Provided*, that the expense of building and maintaining any bridge over a stream near town or district lines in which both are interested and where the cost thereof is less than $5,000, shall be bourne by both towns or districts in such portion as shall be just and equitable between said towns or districts, taking into consideration the taxable property in each, the location of the bridge, and the advantage of each, to be determined by the commissioners in making contracts for the same, as provided for in Section 64 of this act."

The above provision of the revised act is identical with Section 21 of the road and bridge act of 1883, as amended by act of June 5, 1909, in so far as that act related to bridges required to be built by adjoining towns.

Section 64 of the revised act provides:

"For the purpose of building or keeping in repair such bridge or bridges, it shall be lawful for the commissioners of such adjoining towns, or districts, whether they be in the same or different counties to enter into joint contracts, and such contracts may be enforced in law or equity against such commissioners jointly, the same as if entered into by individuals, and such commissioners may be proceeded against jointly by any parties interested 'n such bridge or bridges, for any neglect of duty in reference to such bridge or bridges, or for any damage growing out of such neglect."

Section 66 provides, in part, as follows:

"Whenever the commissioners of either of such adjoining towns * * * shall refuse to enter into such joint contracts to build and maintain such bridge or bridges, the commissioners of the other town * * * may submit such question to the annual * * * town meeting or call a special * * * town meeting to vote upon the proposition as to whether such * * * town shall proceed to build and maintain such bridge or bridges at its own expense. * * *"

Sections 64 and 66 of the revised act are respectively identical with Sections 22 and 23 of the act of 1883.

The question as to whether mandamus would lie to compel the commissioners of a town, who refused to join in a contract with the commissioners of an adjoining town, for the construction of a bridge under Section 21 of the act of 1883, to join in constructing such bridge, was considered by the Appellate Court in the case of *The People ex rel* vs. *Commissioners of Highways*, 53 App. 442. The Appellate Court affirmed the decision of the circuit court in sustaining a demurrer to the petition for mandamus, and held, in effect, that the writ of mandamus would not lie to compel the commissioners of one town to join with the commissioners of an adjoining town, in a contract for the construction of a bridge over streams between adjoining towns. The case was appealed to the Supreme Court and is reported in 158 Ill., 197. The Supreme Court reversed the judgments of the circuit and Appellate Courts, on the ground that the petition for the writ of mandamus showed that some years previous a contract had been entered into between the towns under which a bridge had been built, but had decayed and been washed away; holding, in effect, that such contract was a continuing one, and that upon the destruction of the first bridge, it became the duty of the adjoining towns, in accordance with the contract between them under which such bridge was built, to replace it with a new bridge. As noted, the opinion of the Supreme Court was based upon the fact of a contract between the two towns. The Court, in its opinion, page 208, says:

"It is the law of this State that no town is legally liable, without its assent, to aid in the construction or repair of bridges over streams on town-line roads, or for bridges across a stream constituting a part of its boundary; but it is equally a part of the law that any town may voluntarily assume such liability by contract or agreement, express or implied."

The effect of the Court's ruling is, that the writ of mandamus will not lie to compel one town to join with an adjoining town in building a town-line bridge, unless there is a contract between them, either express or implied, to build such bridge.

In the matter of county-line bridges, required to be built by adjoining counties, section 35 of the revised act contains a specific provision, whereby a county may be compelled to join in building such bridges, but such provision is not contained in section 63, which relates to town-line bridges.

Concerning any action brought against highway commissioners under section 64, it would seem that such action would have to be against the commissioners of both towns jointly, and be based upon a contract, either express or implied, between the two towns.

Very respectfully,

P. J. LUCEY, *Attorney General.*

THE COUNTY BOARD MAY LEVY A TAX FOR STATE AID ROADS WITHOUT SUBMITTING SUCH TAX TO A VOTE WHEN THE AMOUNT OF SUCH LEVY WILL COME WITHIN THE RATE WHICH THE COUNTY BOARD IS AUTHORIZING TO LEVY FOR COUNTY PURPOSES.

September 25, 1914.

HON. H. E. POND,
State's Attorney, Petersburg, Illinois.

DEAR SIR: I am in receipt of your favor of the 22d instant, in which you inquire, in effect, whether the County Board the right to levy a tax for State Aid roads, independently of a vote of the people, when there are no available funds in the treasury that may be appropriated to that purpose.

Section 15c of the revised Road and Bridge Act provides:

"It shall be considered sufficient acceptance of the allotment to a county of the State appropriation for the construction of State Aid Roads, if a County Board shall give notice to the State Highway Commission that it has assessed a tax to raise its portion of the cost, or that it has passed an order submitting to a vote of the people the question of raising an additional tax for this purpose, or that it has passed an order submitting to a vote of the people the question of issuing bonds for this purpose. Otherwise, a county's allotment shall be considered forfeited, as provided in section 15b of this Act."

This section would seem to provide three methods by which a county may raise funds to meet the amount allotted to it by the State Highway Commission for the construction of State Aid Roads, as provided by section 15a; one is the levy of a tax by the County Board, a second is by submitting to a vote of the people the question of raising an additional tax, and a third is by submitting to a vote of the people the question of issuing bonds for such purpose. Clause 6, section 25, chapter 34, Hurd's Revised Statutes, 1913, confers upon County Boards the power:

"To cause to be annually levied and collected for county purposes, including all purposes for which money may be raised by the county by taxation, not exceeding 75 cents on the one hundred dollars valuation, and in addition thereto an annual tax not exceeding one hundred cents on the one hundred dollars for the purpose of paying the interest and principal of indebtedness which existed at the time of the adoption of the constitution."

Section 121, chapter 120, provides, in part:

"The County Board of the respective counties shall, annually, at the September session, determine the amount of all county taxes to be raised for all purposes. The aggregate amount shall not exceed the rate of seventy-five cents on the one hundred dollars valuation, except for the payment of indebtedness existing at the adoption of the present State Constitution, unless authorized by a vote of the people of the county. When for several purposes, the amount of each purpose shall be stated separately: etc."

The provision in the sections of the statutes above cited, which prohibits the County Board levying a tax for county purposes in excess of a rate of seventy-five cents on the hundred dollars valuation, except for the payment of indebtedness existing at the time of the adoption of the constitution, unless authorized by a vote of the people, is in conformity with section 8, article 9 of the constitution of 1870. A tax levied by the County Board for State Aid Roads would come within the designation of a tax for county purposes.

It is the duty of the County Board, as provided by section 121, chapter 120, in making a levy for several purposes, to specify separately the amount for each purpose. It would be necessary therefore for the County Board, in making a levy of a tax for State aid roads, to specify definitely the amount of such levy. If all the amounts levied by the board for the various county purposes, including the amount levied for State Aid Roads, do not exceed a rate of seventy-five cents on the hundred dollars valuation, then the levy for State Aid Roads may be made a part of the levy made for county purposes, without submitting the question of such levy to a vote of the people; but if the amount to be levied for State Aid Roads, added to the various other amounts levied for county purposes, will exceed a rate of seventy-five cents on the hundred dollars valuation, then in that case the amount to be levied for State Aid Roads should be submitted to a vote in accordance with the provisions of section 27, chapter 34.

Very respectfully,

P. J. LUCEY, Attorney General.

DAMAGES FOR OPENING ROAD—HOW PAID.

September 10, 1914.

HON. LOUIS A. BUSCH,
State's Attorney, Urbana, Illinois.

DEAR SIR: I am in receipt of your favor of the 4th instant concerning the matter of payment of damages in opening a road, and citing in that connection sections 95 and 58 of the revised Road and Bridge act.

You inquire whether in case highway commissioners advance the payment of damages out of the general road and bridge fund, they may subsequently make a levy under section 58 to cover damages so advanced.

Section 95 provides, in part, that if damages resulting from the establishing of roads shall not be paid within ninety days from the time of the final determination to open same, such new road shall be deemed to be vacated.

Section 58 provides:

"When damages have been agreed upon, allowed or awarded for laying out, widening, altering or vacating roads or for ditching to drain roads, the amounts of such damages, not to exceed for any one year twenty cents on each one hundred dollars of the taxable property of the town or district shall be included in the first succeeding tax levy, provided for in section 56 of this Act, and be in addition to the levy for road and bridge purposes; and when collected, shall constitute and be held by the treasurer of the road and bridge fund as a separate fund to be paid out to the parties entitled to receive the same. It shall be the duty of the commissioners of highways at the time of certifying the general tax levy for road and bridge purposes within their town or district to include and separately specify in such certificate the amount necessary to be raised by taxation for the purpose of paying such damages. Upon the approval by the county board of the amount so certified, as provided in the preceding section, the county clerk shall extend the same against the taxable property of said town or district, provided the amount thus approved shall not be in excess of twenty cents on each one hundred dollars of the taxable property therein."

Section 60 provides:

"Whenever damages have been allowed for roads or ditches, the commissioner of highways may draw orders on the treasurer, payable only out of the tax to be levied for such roads or ditches, when the money shall be collected or received, to be given to persons damaged."

This section is identical with section 17 of the act of 1883. There would seem to be no way of avoiding the limitation of time fixed by section 95 for the payment of damages resulting from establishing a road.

However, under the rule announced by the Appellate Court in the case of *Commissioners of Highways* v. *Deboe*, 43 App. 25, commissioners would have the power, under section 60, when damages have been allowed, to issue orders for same to be paid out of a tax to be subsequently levied under section 58.

It is entirely optional with the landowner whether he will accept an order, to be paid out of a tax to be subsequently levied, in payment of damages.

The Supreme Court, in the case of *Caldwell* v. *Highway Commissioners*, 249 Ill. 366, holds, in substance, that the owner of land taken for a highway may refuse to accept such orders in lieu of money, and may enjoin the opening of the road until damages are paid or tendered.

Where the owners refuse to accept orders, issued by highway commissioners, under section 60, it would seem that their damages must be paid or tendered in money within the time limit fixed in section 95.

Concerning the right of the highway commissioners to levy a tax to pay damages advanced by them, out of the general road and bridge funds, will say, the Supreme Court, in the case of *The People* v. *The Cairo, Vincennes and Chicago Railway Co.*, 256 Ill. 286, held that under section 15 of the act of 1883, highway commissioners had the power to levy a tax to pay damages advanced by them out of the general road and bridge funds. The holding of the Court in that case would apply to section 58 of the revised act.

Very respectfully,

P. J. LUCEY, *Attorney General.*

QUESTION AND ANSWERS.

Are Commissioners liable for damages when the water has washed the banks in a cut in the road until the farmer's fence has fallen into the road?

O. B. CONLEE.

I would refer you to an opinion of the Attorney General published in "Illinois Highways" Vol. 1, No. 1, page 8, which says, in part, as follows:

"'The Supreme Court, ...holds, in effect that townships are not liable in their corporate capacity for damages for injury resulting from the negligence of Highway Commissioners. Whether the party injured would have a right of action against the commissioners, personally, is a matter which would depend upon the particular facts in the case, and concerning which this Department would have no authority to render an opinion."

We voted at the 1914 spring election to abolish the payment of a poll tax. Since that time we have begun to see things in a different light, and would like to know how soon we can vote on this question again.

GEO. W. BAKER,
West York, Ill.

The Revised Road and Bridge Law of 1913, in Article 6, Subdivision 3, Section 55, outlines the method to be employed in withdrawing from the payment of a poll tax. There is no provision in the law, however, which authorizes a township or road district, after once voting to do away with the poll tax, to reconsider the question.

We believe that your original vote on this question was final and that you have no legal right to vote on this question again.

I wish to know if it is not the duty of the Highway Commissioners of the townships to keep the culverts cleaned out and the water running in the ditches at the side of public highways.

JOHN W. RANDOLPH,
Elmhurst, Ill.

The general powers and duties of highway commissioners are given under Paragraph 50, Subdivision B of the Revised Road and Bridge Law of 1913, among which are the following:

(B) GENERAL POWERS AND DUTIES—The Highway Commissioners of each town or road district shall have power and it shall be their duty.

(4) To direct the expenditure of all moneys collected in the town or district for road and bridge purposes and draw their warrants on the town or district treasurer therefor.

(5) To direct the construction and repair of roads and bridges within the town or district, to let contracts, employ labor, and purchase material and machinery therefor, subject to the limitation herein provided, etc.

(6) To have general charge of the roads and bridges of their town or district, to keep the same in repair and to improve them as far as practicable.

You will note that, under the law quoted, the repair and maintenance of roads and bridges in a township or road district is under the control of the highway commissioners.

It is their duty to keep culverts cleaned and ditches open, in so far as the funds, at their command, allow them to do so.

Is it necessary for the Supervisors to publish their reports as Treasurers of Road and Bridge funds?

K. J. BARR,
County Supt. of Highways, Edgar Co.

We would refer you to the opinion of the Attorney General on "Financial Statement of Treasurer," as published on page 37 of Vol. 1, No. 2 "Illinois Highway." You will please note that paragraph 9, Chapter 102, Hurd's Statute 1913, to which he refers, provides that such statements shall be published if there is a newspaper in the county, unless the rate of publication exceeds one dollar per hundred words, in which case it is unnecessary.

Have Highway Commissioners the power to enter land to open a ditch, which drains a road, if the land-owner objects?

O. L. HUDDLESTON,
Plymouth, Ill.

Paragraph 133 of the Revised Road and Bridge Law of 1913 gives Highway Commissioners the power to contract with land owners for opening ditches across their land which drain roads, and also defines the method to be employed in case the land owner does not consent to the cutting of such ditch, which is substantially as follows:

"The Highway Commissioners apply to any Justice of the Peace of the county for a summons, to be served on said owner, commanding him to appear before the said Justice for the purpose of having the damages assessed which such owner may sustain by reason of the digging or opening of such ditch or drain. The case shall be tried, by jury, before the justice and damages assessed. Either party may appeal in case they feel themselves aggrieved. If no appeal is taken within five days, the highway commissioners must pay the amount awarded before entering upon such lands to open the ditch. The highway commissioners are authorized to use the poll tax and road money of their town or district for the payment of such judgment."

Can we compel telephone companies to remove brush and limbs of trees, which they trim and throw onto the highway, or must these be removed at township expenses?

O. L. HUDDLESTON,
Plymouth, Ill.

"Telephone companies have no right to trim trees and brush on the public highway, unless such power is given them by an agreement or contract with the townships, or by the highway commissioners. In case a telephone company has trimmed trees and brush on the highway and have left the trimmings so that they are a hindrance or obstruction to the highway, the company should be notified to remove the same as authorized in paragraph 151 of the Revised Road and Bridge Law of 1913 and if the obstruction is not removed in a reasonable length of time, the highway commissioners should have the same removed and bring action to recover the necessary cost of such removal from the company."

APPOINTMENTS OF COUNTY SUPERINTENDENTS TO APRIL 1, 1915.

COUNTY.	NAME.	ADDRESS.
Adams	Lewis L. Boyer	Liberty, Ill.
Alexander	W. N. Moyers	Mound City, Ill.
Bond	R. O. Young	Sorento, Ill.
Boone	Thos. W. Humphrey	Belvidere, Ill.
Brown	W. O. Grover	Mt. Sterling, Ill.
Bureau	Frank R. Bryant	Princeton, Ill.
Calhoun	Jno. A. Earley	Batchtown, Ill.
Carroll	L. P. Scott, (Temporary)	Mt. Carroll, Ill.
Cass	John Goodell	Beardstown, Ill.
Champaign	Geo. C. Fairclo	Court House, Urbana, Ill.
Christian	C. A. Pennington	Taylorville, Ill.
Clark	Zane Arbuckle	Marshall, Ill.
Clay	Howard Anderson	Louisville, Ill.
Clinton	Jno. T. Goldsmith	R. F. D. No. 3, Carlyle, Ill.
Coles	Harry Shinn	Mattoon, Ill.
Cook	Geo. A. Quinlan	Chicago, Ill.
Crawford	J. P. Lyon	Robinson, Ill.
Cumberland	Jno. A. Decker	Toledo, Ill.
DeKalb	Wm. C. Miller	Sycamore, Ill.
DeWitt	Melvin Tuggle	Clinton, Ill.
Douglas	L. O. Hackett	Tuscola, Ill.
DuPage	Eugene L. Gates	Wheaton, Ill.
Edgar	Karl J. Barr	Paris, Ill.
Edwards	Chas. C. Rice	Albion, Ill.
Effingham	Geo. T. Austin	Effingham, Ill.
Fayette	P. E. Fletcher	St. Elmo, Ill.
Ford	C. F. Helman	Paxton, Ill.
Franklin	Geo. F. Hampton	Benton, Ill.
Fulton	E. F. Motsinger	Canton, Ill.
Gallatin	Victor Pearce	Equality, Ill.
Greene	Irving Wetzel	Carrollton, Ill.
Grundy	Fred W. Stine	Morris, Ill.
Hamilton	Gregg Garrison	Garrison, Ill.
Hancock	Wm. Burgner	Carthage, Ill.
Hardin	W. M. Ball	Elizabethtown, Ill.
Henderson	C. R. A. Marshall	Stronghurst, Ill.
Henry	Jas. H. Reed	Cambridge, Ill.
Iroquois	Benj. Jordan	Watseka, Ill.
Jackson	Thos. G. Dunn	Gorham, Ill.
Jasper	S. A. Conner	Newton, Ill.
Jefferson	Tony C. Pitchford	Mt. Vernon, Ill.
Jersey	Chas. E. Warren	Jerseyville, Ill.
JoDaviess	Geo. E. Schroeder	Stockton, Ill.
Johnson	Chas. A. Hook	Vienna, Ill.
Kane	Geo. N. Lamb	St. Charles, Ill.
Kankakee	Frank M. Enos	Kankakee, Ill.
Kendall	Jno. D. Russell	Oswego, Ill.
Knox	Harley M. Butt	Galesburg, Ill.
Lake	Chas. E. Russell	Waukegan, Ill.
LaSalle	Geo. Farnsworth	Ottawa, Ill.
Lawrence	R. J. Benefield	Lawrenceville, Ill.
Lee	L. B. Neighbour	Dixon, Ill.
Livingston	R. W. Osborn	Pontiac, Ill.
Logan	Thos. S Davy	Lincoln, Ill.
McDonough		
McHenry	C. L. Tryon	Woodstock, Ill.
McLean	Ralph O. Edwards	Bellflower, Ill.
Macon	Preston T. Hicks	Decatur, Ill.
Macoupin	O B. Conlee	Carlinville, Ill.
Madison	W. E. Howden	Edwardsville, Ill.
Marion	Lee S. Trainor	Centralia, Ill.
Marshall	L. H. Eldridge	Lacon, Ill.
Mason	H. V. Schoonover	Havana, Ill.
Massac	J. Thrift Corlis	Metropolis, Ill.
Menard	C. M. Buckley	Petersburg, Ill.
Mercer	J. E. Russell	Aledo, Ill.
Monroe	Albert R. Gardner	Waterloo, Ill.
Montgomery	P. M. Bandy	Barnett, Ill.
Morgan	Lawrence V. Baldwin	Jacksonville, Ill.
Moultrie	T. C. Fleming	Sullivan, Ill.
Ogle	Alex Anderson	Polo, Ill.
Peoria	W. E. Emery	512 N. Glendale Ave., Peoria, Ill.
Perry	Frank House	St. Johns, Ill.
Piatt	Thos. J. Anderson	Monticello, Ill.
Pike	H. H. Hardy	Hull, Ill.
Pope	W. T. S. Hopkins	Dixon Springs, Ill.
Pulaski	W. N. Moyers	Mound City, Ill.
Putnam	Mason Wilson (Temporary)	McNabb, Ill.
Randolph	Henry I. Barbeau	Prairie du Rocher, Ill.
Richland		
Rock Island	Wallace Treichler	Rock Island, Ill.
St. Clair	David O. Thomas	Belleville, Ill.
Saline	Jno. P. Upchurch	Harrisburg, Ill.
Sangamon	Edwin White	Springfield, Ill.
Schuyler	W. S. Henderson	Rushville, Ill.
Scott	Geo. H. Vannier	Bluffs, Ill.
Shelby	N. A. Baxter	Shelbyville, Ill.
Stark	Wm. Slater	Wyoming, Ill.
Stephenson	O. G. Hively	Freeport, Ill.
Tazewell	Frank S. Cook	Mackinaw, Ill.
Union	Jos. F. Howenstein	Anna, Ill.
Vermilion	Wm. S. Dillon	Danville, Ill.
Wabash	Guy W. Courter	Mt. Carmel, Ill.
Warren	C. L. McClanahan	Monmouth, Ill.
Washington	Jno. A. Davenport, Jr.	Nashville, Ill.
Wayne	Griff Koontz	R. F. D., Barnhill, Ill.
White	Geo. H. Brown	Carmi, Ill.
Whiteside	V. N. Taggett	Morrison, Ill.
Will	Will H. Smith	204 W. Allen, Joliet, Ill.
Williamson	P. B. Wilson	Marion, Ill.
Winnebago	Albertus R. Carter	Rockford Ill.
Woodford	A. B. Hurd	El Paso, Ill.

ILLINOIS HIGHWAYS
OFFICIAL PUBLICATION
STATE HIGHWAY DEPARTMENT

| VOL. 2 | SPRINGFIELD, ILLINOIS, MAY, 1915 | No. 5 |

CHAMPAIGN TOWNSHIP—CHAMPAIGN COUNTY.
Working on Arthur Road at Big Four Crossing on "Road Day."

CHAMPAIGN TOWNSHIP—CHAMPAIGN COUNTY.
Extensive Grading Being Done by Group of Workers on "Road Day."

ILLINOIS HIGHWAYS.

Published Monthly by the

State Highway Department.

. ILLINOIS HIGHWAY COMMISSION.

A. D. Gash, President.

S. E. Bradt, Secretary.

James P. Wilson.

WM. W. MARR, *Chief State Highway Engineer.*

P. C. McARDLE, *Assistant State Highway Engineer.*

H. E. BILGER, *Road Engineer, Springfield, Illinois.*

C. OLDER, *Bridge Engineer, Springfield, Illinois.*

B. H. PIEPMEIER, *Assistant Engineer, Springfield, Illinois.*

M. W. WATSON, *Assistant Engineer, Springfield, Illinois.*

G. F. BURCH, *Assistant Engineer, Springfield, Illinois.*

F. L. ROMAN, *Testing Engineer, Springfield, Illinois.*

J. M. McCOY, *Chief Clerk, Springfield, Illinois.*

DIVISION ENGINEERS.

H. B. Bushnell..............Aurora

R. L. Bell....................Paris

H. E. Surman..........Rock Island

A. H. Hunter...............Peoria

Fred Tarrant...........Springfield

C. M. Slaymaker........E. St. Louis

J. E. Huber................Marion

CONTENTS.

ROAD DAY.

Extensive plans had been made in nearly every section of Illinois to observe "Road Day" this year in a more thorough manner than ever before. In most of the State these plans could not be carried out because of the very heavy rain which fell during "Road Day" and the day previous, making most of the dirt highways in the State too muddy to travel or work on.

In some sections of the State so much enthusiasm had been aroused that the people carried out their "Road Day" plans, regardless of the extremely unfavorable weather conditions and much actual roadwork was done.

Some communities, rather than be deprived of a chance to do actual work on "Road Day," postponed the day until weather conditions were more favorable.

The Governor's trip along the "Lincoln Trail", from East St. Louis to Salem, was marked by many enthusiastic meetings, where short stops and informal addresses were made by Governor E. F. Dunne and members of his party. Informal discussion of the best methods of roadwork on Southern Illinois soils and other conditions featured the stops in the different cities. "State-aid" hard roadwork, which has been undertaken by many of the Southern Counties was encouraged, and the counties advised to build these hard roads as fast as their finances would allow.

The innovation started this year, of having a good roads address delivered to school children, was very general all over the State, and much good will eventually come by educating our future citizens concerning better road matters.

While the actual work done on "Road Day" this year was not as large as it would have been had weather conditions been more favorable, still the good that it has done in bringing to the attention of the people the need for better roads, cannot be measured in dollars and cents.

As a result of "Road Day", good road making, in many parts of the State is expected to be greatly stimulated.

SUPREME COURT OPINIONS.

Elsewhere in this issue will be found two decisions by the Supreme Court which directly affect the workings of road officials. The first decision was in regard to a contract let by the State Highway Commission for the furnishing of cement to be used in State-aid road construction. The Supreme Court held that, as the State Highway Commission was empowered to furnish any tools, machinery or materials to the contractors and charge them a reasonable compensation therefor, or in case it was impossible to get a contractor to do the work within the estimated cost, the Commission by law was empowered to build the road themselves, it was necessary that the Commission use their judgment in the purchasing of whatever material they felt was necessary in order to do the most effective work.

The State Highway Commission, believing that it was better for all concerned, that all cement be purchased and tested at one central point, rather than at several, had gone ahead and let a contract for this cement, which not only saved to the people of the State at least $25,000, but also permitted all cement which is used in State-aid Roadwork to be tested, to see that it conformed to the specifications.

The Second Decision was in regard to the payment of a poll tax and the Supreme Court held that the Poll Tax requirement, in the revised Road and Bridge Law of 1913, was unconstitutional.

It was held that the tax was not equal and uniform throughout all the townships and road districts, as it excluded the payment of a poll tax by the residents of incorporated cities and villages, which is a part of the corporate township and made an unequal distinction against those residing in the township outside of the corporate cities and villages.

Many townships and Road Districts had decided by an election to do away with the payment of a poll tax, and the Supreme Court's decision will not affect them. There are many other townships and Road Districts, however, which had decided to retain the payment of a poll tax, as they felt it necessary to raise this additional money to be expended on their road and Bridge work.

Section 55 of the Revised Road and Bridge Law of 1913 is therefore unconstitutional and void.

ROAD DAY TRIP BY GOVERNOR DUNNE AND PARTY

"Road Day" celebrated throughout Illinois by meetings of various kinds for road improvements, was of especially high interest in Southern Illinois because

The first meeing was held at East St. Louis on the evening of April 21, when the Good Roads party was entertained at a banquet at the Elks Club, given by the East St. Louis Commercial Association, at which meeting addresses were made by Governor Dunne, Lieutenant-Governor O'Hara, Messrs. Gash and Wilson of the State Highway Commission, Senator Barr and Adjutant General Dickson.

The trip on "Road Day" was started at 6:30 A. M. from the Illinois Hotel, East St. Louis, in a driving rain. After traveling through miles of mud Belleville was reached at 8:00 A. M., where a stop of fifteen minutes was made. From Belleville, the party proceeded toward Shiloh, but before reaching this place the Governor's car and one other, had skidded into the ditch, from which they had to be extricated; luckily, no one being hurt.

From Shiloh to O'Fallon the party proceeded over an asphalt macadam road, which had been built under

ROAD DAY PARTY.
At Elks Club East St. Louis, Illinois.
Lower line left to right—Fred Kern, A. D. Gash, Mayor Chamberlin, Governor Dunne, Senator Barr, Senator Womack, Senator Compton.

of the presence of Governor Dunne, Members of the State Highway Commission, and other Good Road boosters who toured the Lincoln Trail running eastward from East St. Louis across "Egypt."

the supervision of the State Highway Department and this stretch of road was in fine condition.

Shortly before reaching Lebanon the party was met by a procession of autos which preceded them to the city where they were welcomed by school children waving flags. Here brief addresses were made by Governor Dunne, Senator Barr, Mr. Gash and Mr. Wilson.

Proceeding into Trenton the street was lined on both sides with school children, welcoming the party, where a short meeting was held.

Thence through Breese. Beckemeyer, Carlyle, Odin and into Salem where they were met by a monstrous crowd. The houses were all decorated with flags and bunting, the city presenting a gala-day appearance. A short meeting was held at the court house steps.

Proceeding eastward from Salem, the party encountered the worst road of any on the trip, the seventeen miles to Xenia, the home of Senator Campbell, being made in one hour and fifteen minutes. This road, being typical of many in Illinois, showed how bad a road could become and what an improvement could be made if proper attention was given to dragging, grading and drainage.

After a short stop at Xenia the party traveled back over the same bad road to Salem, thence over the C. & E. I. R. R. to Mt. Vernon, the home of Senator Piercy, where the day was closed by a large meeting in the Court House, which was addressed by Governor Dunne, Lieutenant-Governor O'Hara, Senator Barr, Mr. Gash and Mr. Wilson.

The party was ably guided and cared for by the Vincennes-St. Louis Good Roads Association in charge of Ex-Senator C. E. Hull, Salem. Hon. Robt. S. Jones, Flora, D. M. Morris, Salem, and H. J. C. Beckemeyer, Carlyle.

The party was delayed, on account of bad roads, from one-half to two hours, but every point in the schedule was made. The patience of the people, who waited in large numbers, to hear the Governor and his party, was splendid.

Much enthusiasm was shown all along the route for better roads and the need of them was quite apparent.

Better roads would have been appreciated by the members of the Governor's party on "Road Day."

DEPARTMENTAL REPORT.

May 1, 1915.

STATE HIGHWAY COMMISSION:

GENTLEMEN: I submit the following report on the present condition of the work being done by the State Highway Department:

STATE-AID ROAD WORK.

During the month of April plans were sent to the County Board for the following work:

County.	Section.
Kankakee	B
Calhoun	A
Ford	A
Jasper	A, B & C
Shelby	B, C & D
Marion	A, B & C
Marshall	B
Tazewell	E
Bond	B
Edwards	A
Schuyler	B

Plans and specifications for the following are about ready to be sent to the County Board:

County.	Section.
Menard	B
Kane	B & C
Hamilton	A & B
Pulaski	A
Gallatin	A & B

Surveys for work in the folowing counties will be made within the next ten days:

Macoupin
Montgomery
Putnam
Scott
Washington

TOWNSHIP ROAD CONSTRUCTION.

The following is a detailed report of the condition of the township road work to May 1, 1915:

Petty Township, Lawrence County—1½ miles of concrete pavement to be constructed this season. Work started April 28. F. C. Feutz, of this Department, is in charge of work.

Aurora Township, Kane County—1½ miles of 18 ft. concrete pavement, construction started April 20. H. N. Kleizer, of this Department, is in charge of the work.

Reading Township, Livingston County—About 20 miles of 9 inch macadam road to be built with convict labor. Work started April 1. Convicts will be on the work about May 10. Mr. F. L. Little, of this Department, is in charge of the work.

Tuscola Township, Douglas County—2 miles of 16 ft. concrete pavement will be constructed under lump sum contract. No supervision or machinery required from this Department.

Eldorado Township, Saline County—1¼ miles of concrete pavement 10 ft. wide, construction to start when work in Petty Township, Lawrence County is completed, which should be about June 1.

Lawrenceville Township, Lawrence County—The 2½ miles of gravel road resurfacing was completed April 15. Mr. Roy Stover was in charge of equipment.

English Township, Jersey County—The proposed 1½ miles of 10 ft. brick road at this point was voted down by the people on April 6.

Sand Ridge Township, Jackson County—3½ miles of macadam road. Work started April 28. I. E. Scott, from this Department, is in charge of work.

Joliet Township, Will County—About 25 miles of 12 to 16 ft. macadam roads to be surface oiled. Work may be done without supervision from this Department.

Douglas Township, Effingham County—About 1 mile of 12 ft. macadam road to be resurfaced. Work will start about May 15.

Road District No. 5, Union County—7 miles of macadam road. Work will start sometime in May.

Pontiac Township, Livingston County—2 miles of gravel road to be resurfaced. Work started April 29. Mr. C. Gray, of this Department is in charge of work.

Washington Township, Will County—Re-rolling roads built at this point in 1914. Machinery working at this point. Mr. D. S. James in charge of same. Work will be completed about May 10.

Oregon Township, Ogle County—There is now stored at this point one roller and one complete oiling outfit. There are several miles of road anticipated at this point on which work may start sometime in May.

Shiloh Valley Township, St. Clair County—1 mile of 16 ft. bituminous macadam road, construction to start possibly in June.

DeKalb Township, DeKalb County—About 3 miles of macadam road to be resurfaced. Work will likely start the first of May. Equipment is shipped.

Yellowhead Township, Kankakee County—3 or 4 miles of resurfacing work on macadam roads. There is likely very little rolling and it is expected that Mr. D. S. James can do this work sometime in May after the Beecher road is completed.

Bridgeport Township, Lawrence County—¾ miles of macadam road resurfaced. Work completed April 26. Roy Stover in charge of work.

There are a number of township roads being constructed at the present time under the direct supervision of the highway commissioners, using penitentiary stone. The Joliet penitentiary is now shipping about 15 cars daily and the Southern penitentiary about 3 cars per day. Considering the amount of crushed stone it will take to supply the convict camp at Reading, Illinois, and the machinery that we have working at other points, it seems that it will be impossible for the penitentiary to supply the demand.

STATE AID ROAD MAINTENANCE.

We now have four portable heating kettles stationed in various districts in the State that are being used in connection with maintaining cracks and joints in concrete and brick pavements.

The small auto truck has been out since April 15,

BREESE—CLINTON COUNTY.
Governor Dunne Addressing Audience.

Road District No. 7, Alexander County—3 miles of macadam road construction and surface oiling. Work to start probably in June.

Seven Hickory Township, Coles County—4 miles of macadam road construction. Will likely start latter part of May.

We have one outfit ready to ship to the contractor of the state aid road in Alexander County for the work that is to be built at this point. We are holding one outfit pending the awarding of the contract in Union County.

We have formal applications on file for all of the above named roads which aggregate to date about 75 miles of roads. We have had correspondence with a number of townships that are anticipating road improvement and who wish some assistance from this department in the way of equipment and engineering services.

maintaining the cracks and joints in pavements in the northern part of the State.

All joints and cracks in State-aid roads in the following named counties have been maintained to date: Iroquois, Cass, Logan, Livingston and Kankakee.

BRIDGE WORK.

During the month of April, 1915, plans and specifications for 53 bridges were prepared and sent to the County Superintendents; plans for 64 State-aid Bridges were sent to County Clerks; total estimated cost $128,566.

Contracts were awarded for 28 concrete bridges and two steel bridges, at an average cost of 82½ per cent of the estimates; total estimated cost $30,585.

The date of letting was set for 69 bridges, having a total estimated cost of $80,639.

Eight bridge plans, prepared by County Superintendents were checked and approved.

On May 1, 1915, there were 84 bridge inspection reports on hand ready for work; 38 of these being practically completed and ready to send out.

LABORATORY REPORT.

One hundred sixty-one (161) samples of miscellaneous materials were tested during the month of April. A bulletin on dust prevention has been issued and may be obtained from the State Highway Department, by requesting bulletin No. 6.

CONTRACTS AWARDED FOR STATE-AID ROADS.

During the month of April, bids were received and contracts awarded for the construction of approximately 1.70 miles of state-aid roads.

Engineers' estimates and bids received are exclusive of cement and other material to be furnished by the State.

The following tabulation will show the names of bidders and amount of bid on the several sections, together with the name of the successful bidder:

KENDALL COUNTY—SECTION A—ROUTE 1.

Length, 7,300 feet; width, 15 feet; type, concrete; engineer's estimate, $13,334.80; date of letting, April 7, 1915.

Name of Bidder.	Amount of Bid.
Thos. H. Cutler & Co., Gary, Ind	$11,470 00
Connelly & Dunning, Chicago, Ill	12,240 00
Chicago Heights Coal Co., Chi. Heights, Ill.	12,490 00
Andrew Ward & Son, Oak Glen, Ill	11,200 00
Ajax Cons. & Engineering Co., Gary, Ind	12,485 00
H. H. Eulady, Oswego, Ill	11,998 80
C. W. Jensen & Co., Chicago, Ill	12,195 00
F. E. Ball, Hampshire, Ill	11,342 00
Miner & Korsmo, Chicago, Ill	11,780 00
Booth, Nicholson & Gilchrist, Gardner, Ill.	11,189 00
Ill. Hy. Stone & Cons. Co., Elgin, Ill	11,900 00

The contract was awarded to Booth, Nicholson & Gilchrist.

SANGAMON COUNTY—SECTION F—ROUTE 4.

Length, 1,700 feet; width, 18 feet; type, brick; engineer's estimate, $5,362.57; date of letting, April 7, 1915.

Name of Bidder.	Amount of Bid.
Jno. E. Bretz, Springfield, Ill	$5,350 00
H. Nelch & Son, Springfield, Ill	5,340 00
R. F. Egan, Springfield, Ill	5,300 00

The contract was awarded to R. F Egan.

MASSAC COUNTY—SECTION A—BRIDGES.

Engineer's estimate, $2,925.00; date of letting, April 14, 1915.

Name of Bidder.	Amount of Bid.
The Parham Cons. Co, East St. Louis, Ill	$2,898 00
W. H. Hoffman, LaFayette, Ind	2,588 00
Townsend B. Smith, Evanston, Ill	2,916 00

MASSAC COUNTY—SECTION A—Concluded.

Name of Bidder.	Amount of Bid.
Vincennes Bridge Co., Vincennes, Ind	2,844 85
Montgomery Parker Co., Rockport, Ind	2,621 00
W. J. Cox, Metropolis, Ill	2,685 00

The contract was awarded to W. H. Hoffman.

JOHNSON COUNTY—SECTION A—BRIDGES.

Engineer's estimate, $2,760.00; date of letting, April 14, 1915.

Name of Bidder.	Amount of Bid.
Wm. Lough & Son, Marion, Ill	$2,613 75
Henry Six, Vienna, Ill	2,356 00
The Parham Cons. Co., East St. Louis, Ill	2,649 00
Williams & Townsend, Marion, Ill	2,725 00
W. H. Hoffman, LaFayette, Ind	2,389 00
Townsend B. Smith, Evanston, Ill	2,638 00
Montgomery Parker Co., Rockport, Ind	2,353 00

The contract was awarded to Montgomery Parker Company.

BLUE PRINTING.

During the month of April 1915, 113 blue prints were made of our bridge standards for county superintendents of highways, as well as prints for 11 foreign bridge plans averaging two sheets, six prints being made of each sheet, or about 132 prints. Prints were made of 26 bridges designed by this department, 20 sets each, as well as three preliminary sets being sent to the various counties for their use in letting said bridges, totaling 1196 prints. Preliminary prints were also made of nine bridges designed by this department for use of county boards, three sets being made of each, or 54 prints.

There was also printed six prints each of the various townships (averaging 14) in eight counties of the State, or about 672 prints.

Preliminary prints were made for 17 sections of road for the county board to pass on, official prints then being made for county clerk, county superintendent, and this office. Each road section averages about 12 sheets, making a total of 816 prints.

Miscellaneous prints, about 600 made for office use, made a grand total for the month of April of 3583 prints.

Very truly yours,

Wm. W. Marr,
Chief State Highway Engineer.

TOWNSHIP ROAD REPAIRS.

Lawrence Township, Lawrence County.

The following cost data was taken from road repairs made in Lawrence Township, Lawrence County, under the direction of Wm. Philbert, Highway Commissioner of Lawrence Township and R. J. Benefield, Superintendent of Highways and Mr. Roy Stover, in charge of State equipment.

The old gravel roads were badly worn and very irregular in shape. It was necessary to scarify the entire road about 6 inches deep and re-shape and level same, after which a very light application of bonding gravel was applied and the entire road rolled. It will be noted that the cost of such repairs is very light. The scarifying of the old gravel road brings new material to the surface and puts a new surface on the old road that makes it possibly better than it was in the beginning.

FINAL COST REPORT ON REPAIRS.

State road, Lawrence Township, Lawrence County.

CONDITIONS.

Contractors profit and overhead charges not included; amount of road repairs, 5,280 feet; 5,280 square yards. Width of road, 9 feet; width of repairs, 9 feet. Length of haul on materials, 4 miles. Total material used, 191 cubic yards. Rate of pay, men 22 cents, teams

yards. Width of road, 9 feet; width of repairs, 9 feet. Length of haul on materials, average 3½ miles. Total material used, 317 cubic yards. Rate of pay, men 22 cents per hour; teams, 75 cents per yard. Work began March 25; work completed April 7.

COST OF LABOR AND MATERIALS.

	Total.	Sq. yd.
Scarifying old road................	$ 16 18	$ .0020
Gravel, 317 cubic yards @ $1.05 per cubic yard, delivered...........	332 85	.0420
Incidental hauling.................	18 00	.0023

TRENTON—CLINTON COUNTY.
School Children Welcoming Governors' Party on "Road Day."

.333 cents per hour. Work began April 8, 1915; work completed April 15, 1915.

COST OF LABOR AND MATERIALS.

	Total.	Sq. yd.
Scarifying old road................	$ 8 72	$ .0016
Gravel, 191 cubic yards @ $1.05 per cubic yard, delivered...........	200 55	.0380
Incidental hauling.................	21 00	.0040
Spreading gravel..................	17 50	.0033
Rolling and sprinkling.............	16 49	.0031
Total cost....................	$264 26	$ .0500

Mt. Carmel road, Lawrence Township, Lawrence County.

CONDITIONS.

Contractors profit and overhead charges not included. Amount of road repairs, 7,920 feet; 7,920 square

Spreading gravel..................	17 50	.0022
Rolling and sprinkling.............	41 34	.0052
Total cost....................	$425.87	$ .0537

REPORTS—COUNTY SUPERINTENDENTS.

ADAMS COUNTY.

[By L. L. BOYER, *County Superintendent of Highways.*]

Plans had been adopted and a campaign for better highways was all but carried out "Road Day," when the rain fell and the work was postponed until the next day.

In Camp Point the commercial club members, public-spirited citizens, farmers, etc., were all at work, making a clean sweep of the township.

Thomas Gooding, highway commissioner of the northern district in Gilmer township, reports work of grading, dragging, placing of culverts, cutting brush and cleaning roadsides, cutting down hills and grading up to bridges and culverts. Nearly everyone in the village of Fowler helped with the work.

There were 24 workers out from Liberty and many more from the surrounding country.

Many who had promised to work a day on the highways and were kept away by the rain on "Road Day" offered their services free to the commissioners, even several days afterwards.

We figure that somewhere near \$1,000 worth of work was done in Adams County.

CLAY COUNTY.

[By HOWARD ANDERSON, *County Superintendent of Highways.*]

Rain and threatening weather stopped regular road-work in this county on "Road Day," hence nothing in the way of extras was undertaken.

Most regrettable is the weather interference with the Xenia meeting. Much interest was shown in the meeting, and much good could have been accomplished under fair weather conditions.

CHAMPAIGN COUNTY.

[By GEO. C. FAIRCLO, *County Superintendent of Highways.*]

With a week of sunshine before and with four days of sunshine since, it almost seems that the elements were against "Road Day" in Champaign County, but the rain, which was a handicap to "Road Day," was a boon to the farmers, the sun smiled on "Road Day" in the afternoon, and everyone went home happy at night.

"Road Day" this year in Champaign County, in spite of the rain, was a decided success in comparison to last year, when very little was done on account of the backward season.

Champaign Township had the best celebration of any township in the county. With John Lowman, Frank Miller, N. R. Hammersmith, highway commissioners, taking a lively interest and stirring up enthusiasm, the farmers of Champaign Township, the merchants, contractors and people of Champaign and the Chamber of Commerce of Champaign became interested, and, with the cooperation of all, the day was quite a success. Thirty teams had been promised for the day, and on the morning of "Road Day" every team that had been promised was on the job.

The Champaign Chamber of Commerce had called a special meeting of the board of directors, which had passed the following resolution:

"Whereas Governor Edward F. Dunne has proclaimed Thursday, April 22, 1915, as Good Roads Day in the State of Illinois and urges every citizen to observe that day in a manner to improve the public highways of the State, and,

"Whereas a special meeting of the board of directors of the Chamber of Commerce of Champaign, Illinois, was called for the purpose of taking proper action to insure the success of this movement for better roads in Champaign Township: Be it

"*Resolved*, That this board, in the name of the Chamber of Commerce of Champaign, Illinois, hereby endorses Good Roads Day and expresses a desire that members of the association offer such assistance as they can, and be it further

"*Resolved*, That the sum of \$100.00 be appropriated from the lot fund to be paid out for labor on that day, under the direction of the board of highway commissioners of the Town of Champaign.

"Dated at Champaign, Illinois, this 20th day of April, 1915."

With the appropriation provided in the resolution men were hired to shovel dirt into dump wagons, which was hauled 1,300 feet to the intersection of the Illinois Central Railroad and the Arthur Road to make an approach grade on each side. In this crew were 14 teams and drivers with dump wagons, two plow teams and drivers and 56 laborers, under the able direction of Frank Miller, our 350-pound highway commissioner and the largest highway commissioner in the State.

Crew No. 2, working at the intersection of the Big Four crossing and the Arthur Road, consisted of nine teams and drivers, with slip scrapers, who were making an approach grade to the Big Four tracks.

Crew No. 3 consisted of seven teams and drivers, with slip scrapers, working on the Springfield Road, filling the low ground between the Illinois Central and Illinois Traction Company's tracks. This crew was driven in at 9 o'clock by the rain and finished their work on the next day.

The highway commissioners are now finishing the work started by Crews 1 and 2.

Mayor-elect E. S. Swigart of Champaign had solicited the merchants of Champaign for food for the dinner, which was to be served on the lawn of the Arthur farm by six young ladies of Champaign to all who worked on the roads of Champaign Township on "Road Day."

The different crews were to have driven in autos to the east, but on account of the rain, Crew No. 3 was unable to be present. The rain preventing the dinner being held on the lawn, it was served in the Bonner Factory—the manager having kindly consented to make room for the tables. The menu was as follows:

Roast beef, brown potatoes and gravy, green onions, dill pickles, bread and butter, pie, ice cream, coffee and cigars, and was thoroughly enjoyed by all.

The members of the board of directors of the Champaign Chamber of Commerce took dinner with us, and spent most of the afternoon overseeing the work. Wm. Sullivan, secretary, and C. W. Murphy, managing secretary of the Chamber of Commerce, acted as paymasters at night.

Contractor J. W. Stipes, for his part of "Road Day," proposed to drag and put in condition the earth road at each side of the brick state-aid road on the Bloomington Road, and is doing the work today.

In Urbana Township, the commissioners had interested the mayor and street department of the city of Urbana in the grading of the Cunningham Road, which is partly inside of the city limits of Urbana, and which, I believe, is the worst road in Champaign County. It was expected that this road, for a length of about a mile, would be regraded, dragged and put in good condition. This work was postponed on account of the rain, but has now been completed.

Rantoul Township had planned to make a grade between the Illinois Central and K. C. T. tracks, where they intersect the highway, and to have a picnic dinner at noon. Seven men, with teams and slip scrapers, reported for work, and there would have been twelve if it had been a bright day. These seven worked until it rained, got soaked and went home happy. The commissioners are now completing the work.

Scott Township had 30 men and teams on the road on the morning of "Road Day," grading bridge and railroad approaches, filling low places. cutting down high places and dragging, but all were driven in by the rain. Many of the other townships had planned to do many things on "Road Day," but were prevented by the rain; but everybody was happy and predicted a great day next year.

DEWITT COUNTY.

[By Melvin Tuggle, *County Superintendent of Highways.*]

The Governor's proclamation and "Road Day" suggestions were mailed out to the commissioners of highways. All the daily papers in the county printed suggestions and proclamation, and endeavored to push the work along.

interest in the day by traveling in one body over about 100 miles of our roads, picking up loose rocks from the gravel roads, filling up a few culvert approaches and doing such other minor repair work as the time allowed.

The trip was finished by a meeting held at Piper City in the northern part of the county. Short speeches were given by several of the party, and, before the meeting adjourned a permanent "Good Roads Association" for Ford County was organized.

The work on the postponed Good Roads Day amounted to the dragging of 110 miles of road, the grading of 12 miles, of which the work on three miles was very heavy; one bridge approach, requiring remodeling for 200 feet, was graded, and two concrete culverts were built. The total estimated value of the work done being $380.00.

SALEM—MARION COUNTY.
"Road Day" Meeting on the Courthouse Steps.

Rain fell part of the day and not much except dragging was done, and not any more than the usual amount of that.

I hope for a better organization next year.

FORD COUNTY.

[By C. F. Helman, *County Superintendent of Highways.*]

Heavy rains fell all over Ford County during the night preceding the twenty-second of April, and it became necessary to postpone the "Road Day" for a week.

This delay proved unfortunate, inasmuch as the farmers on the twenty-ninth, when the Road Day was held, were in the fields planting corn, and only a few could be induced to take part in the road work.

Approximately 170 business and professional men from the cities and towns of the county manifested their

Much interest in the good roads movement was manifested throughout the whole county; everybody seemed delighted with "Road Day" and predicted much good to result by its observance.

FULTON COUNTY.

[By E. F. Motsinger, *County Superintendent of Highways.*]

We accomplished the following work on "Road Day":

Miles of roads dragged.................. 100
Miles graded........................... 25
Cubic yards of stone and gravel hauled.... 500
Total mileage improved................. 150

Two railroad approaches were graded and five culverts were repaired or built. The total estimated amount of work done was $1,000.00.

The attention of the people was called to "Good Roads Day" through the newspapers of the county. A special request was sent to each highway commissioner, urging him to interest his people on this day. We had planned to do a large amount of work, but the inclement weather made this impossible. In this county, in various sections, much work has been done prior to April 22. in which the idea of "Good Roads Day" has been carried out. Several hills have been cut down, reducing grades from 8 per cent to 10 per cent to 3 per cent or 4 per cent. The estimated value of this work is $700.00. Considerable brush was cut on the twenty-second.

We have the pledges of work at the value of $500.00 for the purpose of cutting down a hill in Orion Township. Much interest has been displayed in behalf of "Good Roads Day," and this county would have done a tremendous amount of work, had the weather permitted.

We do not confine ourselves to this day, but expect to have another "Good Roads Day" in the near future.

HAMILTON COUNTY.

[By GREGG GARRISON, *County Superintendent of Highways.*]

The highway commissioners met at the county seat Saturday, April 17, and discussed various methods of getting the people of their townships interested in doing something on the roads April 22. The roads of this county are all earth roads, so dragging, grading and cleaning the road right of way was what we arranged to do on "Good Roads Day; but, when April 22 came, a rain came also. Still there was some work done in Crouch Township, where several miles of roads were dragged, and trees and stumps were cleared from the road right of way. In Mayberry Township, more than forty men were at work with teams, shovels and axes upon their roads. In Dahlgren Township alone, $150 was made up to be expended on their roads, when weather conditions would permit. The banks and rural free delivery carriers going out from that town gave $5 each. In Broughton, the business houses were all closed, and the men worked the roads as best they could.

HENDERSON COUNTY.

[By C. R. A. MARSHALL, *County Superintendent of Highways.*]

Henderson County reports 130 miles of roads improved, in connection with "Road Day." Ninety-seven miles were dragged and 33 miles were graded. Eighteen culverts were repaired or built. The estimated value of this work being $1,005.00.

The grading and dragging reported was the mileage completed by "Good Roads Day" and includes work done prior to, but not after April 22, 1915.

I might also add that the steel bridges in our county will soon have their second coat of paint, the supervisors providing 600 gallons of blue lead paint for the purpose, and the townships applying same.

Bridge contracts nearing completion amount to $872.00, and bridge contracts beginning work amount to $3,155.00.

KANKAKEE COUNTY.

[By F. M. ENOS, *County Superintendent of Highways.*]

In connection with "Good Roads Day" I desire to report that the following work was accomplished: Five

hundred and four miles of roads were dragged; 14 miles were graded, and 840 yards of stone and 80 yards of cinders were hauled, making a total of 519 miles of road improved; 10 bridges were painted, and 51 culverts repaired or built. The total value of work done was $4,425.40, of which the donated labor amounted to $538.00.

This is road work which was done between April 15 and 22, as I had written a letter to each road commissioner in the county on February 25, advising them that "Good Roads Day" would be on April 15, and asking that they would get their roads dragged and graded, ditches and roadsides cleaned, holes filled, culverts and bridges repaired, etc.

Owing to the heavy rain during the night before "Road Day", some of this road-dragging work and a part of the stone work was not finished during the day, but the commissioners of the different townships completed it the next day, and also dragged and levelled many more miles of road.

In addition to the work done on "Good Roads Day," the commissioners of Kankakee, Ganier, Momence and Bourbonnais Townships are arranging to oil about thirty miles of macadam road in the near future. Kankakee Township is also arranging to scarify, redress and bond five miles of macadam within the next few days.

I wish to add to this report that the roads are in better condition than ever before at this time of the year, and that all the township commissioners are enthused and ready to boost the good roads proposition, as are also the landowners and citizens in general, in our county, and we are not going to stop on "Good Roads Day", but we are going to keep the good work moving.

KNOX COUNTY.

[By H. M. BUTT, *County Superintendent of Highways.*]

"Road Day" was observed in Knox County this year for the first time, and I feel pleased with the results obtained. Our plans for April 22 were not carried out, on account of rain on that date, but on the following day the citizens did good work. The work included 475 miles of road dragged and 36 miles of road graded, including the grading of 12 bridge approaches and 10 railroad approaches. Three bridges were painted and 20 culverts repaired or built. The total estimated value of the work done being $1,500.00.

A "Tag Day" had been planned in Galesburg, which was to enable the city people to aid in making better roads. Tags were to be sold to automobile owners and the money received to be used for oiling the highways leading into the city. The rain spoiled this, but, since that time, soliciting has been done and about $1,500.00 is now subscribed for the oiling.

Although I have not received a report from every commissioner, I am satisfied that a great deal of benefit was derived for the "Road Day."

We hope for better results next year, with a much better organization.

MARSHALL COUNTY.

[By L. H. ELDRIDGE, *County Superintendent of Highways.*]

A county meeting of highway officials was held at the court house on Monday previous to "Good Roads Day."

A good attendance and much interest was shown in the better roads movement. The weather had been extra fine for some time previous to "Good Roads Day," so consequently much dragging was done before that date.

This day, coming at the time when farming operations were being rushed and help for road work hard to get in some of our rural townships, the result was that there was no work reported in about one-half of the townships. Those townships having tractor outfits made the best showing.

From reports at hand, Bennington Township made the best showing with 9¾ miles graded, leveled and improved, 2 bridge approaches graded, 1 railroad crossing graded, 1 bridge painted, 3 bridges repaired, 4 culverts installed for a total value of $200.00.

Most of our roads had been dragged before "Road Day," and many townships had been grading since April 1.

A rain in the county prevented much work on April 22.

Our roads, for dirt roads, are in very good condition.

MONROE COUNTY.

[By ALBERT R. GARDNER, *County Superintendent of Highways.*]

In regard to the road work done in this county on "Road Day," all of the work here was done on earth

CHAMPAIGN TOWNSHIP—CHAMPAIGN COUNTY.
Arthur Road North of Illinois Central Crossing on "Road Day."

The total amount of work done in connection with "Road Day" was the dragging of 332 miles of road, the grading of 9¾ miles, 4 bridge approaches graded, 4 railroad approaches graded, 1 bridge painted, 5 culverts repaired or built, the estimated value of all work done being $775.00.

I consider this a very good showing, considering the busy season.

The county superintendent of schools also fully cooperated in the movement of circularizing every school in the county, so that the children were told something as to the advantages of good roads.

MERCER COUNTY.

[By J. E. RUSSELL, *County Superintendent of Highways.*]

"Road Day" was celebrated in Mercer County by the dragging of 20 miles of roads and the grading of 12 miles. The approaches to three railroad crossings were also graded.

roads. It consisted in grading hills and a general widening of the roads all over the county, especially good work being done in Road Districts Nos. 6 and 8.

MOULTRIE COUNTY.

[By T. C. FLEMING, *County Superintendent of Highways.*]

Preparations were made for grading, dragging roads, hauling gravel and building concrete culverts, but, on account of heavy rains, no work was accomplished.

However, this work will be done as soon as weather permits.

PIATT COUNTY.

[By T. J. ANDERSON, *County Superintendent of Highways.*]

We had heavy rains on "Road Day," and the day preceding, and our plans were not carried out as planned. However, as each township in Piatt County owns a large gasoline tractor and road leveler, our roads, to my personal knowledge, have all been graded or levelled prior to "Road Day."

One township has painted all the bridges in the township.

Our roads have been in fine shape all spring, as every day is "Road Day" with Piatt's up-to-date highway commissioners.

We will expend about $60,000 on brick roads this summer, and have about $65,000 in the eight townships for regular road and bridge work.

While the rain on "Road Day" was a great boon to the farmers, it also dampened our road work, but not our enthusiasm for good roads.

POPE COUNTY.

[By W. T. S. Hopkins, *County Superintendent of Highways*.]

On account of the bad weather, not much good work was accomplished on "Road Day."

However, we dragged and graded about five miles of road and repaired or built six culverts.

The total estimated value of the work done being about $75.00.

STEPHENSON COUNTY.

[By O. G. Hiveley, *County Superintendent of Highways*.]

On "Road Day" we had eight large engine graders and two road machines or levelers working, and graded 15 miles of road.

Approaches were graded to six bridges and altogether 20 miles of roads were improved.

Two bridges were painted and five culverts were built or repaired.

The estimated value of the work done was $1,500.00.

TAZEWELL COUNTY.

[By F. S. Cook, *County Superintendent of Highways*.]

There was too much rain shortly before "Road Day" to allow much work being done in Tazewell County.

However, about thirty miles of roads were dragged and, in the afternoon, some dragging contests were decided.

WOODFORD COUNTY.

[By A. B. Hurd, *County Sperintendent of Highways*.]

In regard to work done on "Road Day," will say that a rain in this locality prevented any active work being done in this county.

We have in Woodford County, eleven townships which own road machinery, suitable for tractor power. Three of these townships own their own tractors, the others hire tractors to pull their grader outfits. Some of our townships did grade all of their roads prior to "Road Day," others were working upon theirs at that time, and those not having power graders were at work upon their roads early this year. I think I am safe in saying that more miles of roads have been graded in Woodford County this year than ever before, and the commissioners all over the county are awake to the advantages of a well-graded road. They are spending a portion of their money for grading.

It is hard to work up any enthusiasm among the communities for doing work "free gratis." It is not quite so hard to get the work done when they see the money ahead to pay them for their services.

The time may come when the good roads problem will have reached the stage when we can call for work on certain days, but it has not reached that state at the present time, in Woodford County.

SELLING ON RECOMMENDATIONS.

[By J. A. Davenport, *County Superintendent of Highways, Washington County*.]

A good recommendation from one official to another concerning an article which the one has used undoubtedly carries weight, the value of which depends on the recommending official.

It is the custom nowadays for material and supply firms to circularize heavily with opinions, reports and articles concerning the materials they have for sale. Some groups publish small magazines for this purpose. However, the culling of quotations and short passages from reports and letters is a much-abused practice. In many cases the idea to be conveyed by the writer is sidetracked, or negatived, and an altogether false impression is given. In many cases, these opinions seem to be against the best practice. Direct communication with the author will usually give valuable sidelights on the subject matter as presented, if such information is needed, or communication with the State Highway Department will usually furnish all the necessary information.

Apparently fair and innocent quotations are many times found to be twisted, and more harmful than the most lurid assertions. The old quotation that "Liars will figure" still applies in too many cases.

POLL TAX UNCONSTITUTIONAL.

Mr. Justice Dunn delivered the opinion of the Court:

Section 55 of the Road and Bridge Law of 1913 (Hurd's Stat. 1913, p. 2128,) provides for the assessment of a poll tax for highway purposes upon able-bodied men between the ages of 21 and 50 years. Seymour Ide, a resident of the Town of Dixon, in Lee County, refused to pay the tax, and the commissioners of highways sued him for it in the name of the town. Upon the appeal to the circuit court a jury was waived, the case was tried by the court upon a stipulation as to the facts, there was a judgment for the defendant, and the Town of Dixon appealed directly to this Court upon the ground that the constitutionality of said section 55 is involved. The Court held, as a proposition of law, that the section is unconstitutional. There was another question in the case, but it is not necessary to consider it.

The provisions of section 55 necessary to be considered in this case are as follows: "At their annual meeting to be held on the second Tuesday after the annual town meeting or district election in each year, each board of highway commissioners shall make out a list of able-bodied men in their town or district between the ages of twenty-one (21) and fifty (50) years, and deliver the same to the town or district treasurer on or before the first day of May in each year, and assess at such meeting against each person upon such list a sum of not less than one (1) nor more than three (3) dollars, as a poll tax for highway purposes, to be paid in cash to such treasurer by the first Monday of June of each year. *Provided*, that paupers, idiots, lunatics and such others as are exempt by law shall not bé compelled to pay a poll tax for highway purposes. *Provided*, also, that this list shall not include persons within the limits of cities or incorporated villages." Then follow directions as to the method of proceeding to collect the tax.

It was stipulated that the Township of Dixon includes the City of Dixon, which comprises about one-third of the township; that the commissioners of highways of the township assessed a poll tax of $2 upon all

cept as to his place of residence, does not have to pay it. A resident of the city of Dixon is as much a resident of the town of Dixon as a resident of the town outside the city. The territory of the city of Dixon is a part of the town of Dixon and for township purposes is a part of the latter municipality. The corporate authorities of this municipality, can only assess a tax uniform in respect to persons within the territory of the municipality.

The commissioners of highways are corporate authorities of the town, and any tax assessed by them must be uniform as to all persons in the town. The exemption of residents of the city by the proviso to section

"ROAD DAY" IN HENDERSON COUNTY.
Ironing Out the Rough Places.

able-bodied men over 21 and under 50 years of age, but assessed it only upon those residing outside of the City of Dixon; that Seymour Ide was an able-bodied man between the ages of 21 and 50 years, residing in the Township of Dixon and the City of Dixon, not falling within any exemption from the payment of the tax, and that the notice required by the statute was duly served upon him.

One objection made to the tax is that it is not equal and uniform throughout the township. Section 9 of article 9 of the constitution authorizes the General Assembly to vest municipal corporations with authority to assess and collect taxes for corporate purposes, but requires that such taxes shall be uniform in respect to persons and property within the jurisdiction of the body imposing the same. This imposes upon the right of highway commissioners to assess and collect a tax the condition that it shall be uniform in respect to persons and property within their jurisdiction—that is, within the township. A tax cannot be said to be uniform as to persons within the jurisdiction when one person within the jurisdiction has to pay the tax and another person within the jurisdiction in prescisely the same circumstances, ex-

55 is repugnant to the constitution, and the section is therefore inoperative and void.

The commissioners were without authority to assess the poll tax, and the judgment of the circuit court must be affirmed.

Judgment affirmed.

SUPREME COURT OPINION.

State Highway Commission Has Power to Purchase Cement for State Aid Roads.

Mr. Justice Watson delivered the opinion of the court:

On June 20, 1914, the appellant filed his bill in the circuit court of DeKalb county praying the annulment of a certain contract made by and between the State Highway Commissioners and the Marquette Cement Manufacturing Company, and also praying for an injunction against said highway commissioners restraining them, and each of them, from purchasing cement or other material for the construction of State aid roads, and also from issuing any order or in any other manner directing the Auditor of Public Accounts to draw his warrants upon the State Treasurer for the payment of any public moneys on account of cement furnished under said contract, or otherwise, for the construction of State aid roads, and that upon final hearing the injunction be made permanent.

Later an amended bill was filed by agreement of the parties, and it will be hereinafter called the bill. A demurrer was filed to the bill, and a stipulation was made to the effect the decision of the court on demurrer should be final and be followed by a decree granting the relief prayed or dismissing the bill for want of equity. The demurrer, which was general, was sustained, and thereupon the appellant declined to plead further, and the court entered its decree dismissing the bill for want of equity and giving judgment against the appellant for the costs of suit. An appeal was allowed and perfected and the case taken to the Appellate Court for the Second District. Objection being made that the real party in interest is the State of Illinois and not the highway commissioners, the Appellate Court held the State is a party in interest and ordered the cause transferred to this court, as is provided by law.

But one question is presented for decision, says appellant, and in his brief he thus states the question: Have the State Highway Commissioners the power to purchase materials for the construction of State-aid roads? The theory of appellant's bill is the commissioners do not have this power. The circuit court held otherwise. By four assignments of error appellant challenges the correctness of the holding.

Briefly stated, the bill alleges appellant is a citizen and a resident tax-payer of DeKalb county and as such brings this suit; that the appellees, A. D. Gash, S. E. Bradt, and James Wilson are the State Highway Commissioners; that said commissioners, assuming to act under and by virtue of the act approved June 27, 1913, commonly known as the Tice Road law, advertised for bids to be submitted to them for the furnishing of the cement required in the construction of all State aid roads in the State during the year 1914; that on April 1, 1914, numerous bids were submitted to said commissioners for the furnishing of said cement, and on April 8 said commissioners without any authority attempted to, and did, award the Marquette Cement Manufacturing Company the contract for the furnishing of the cement required in the construction of State aid roads in ninety-four counties in the State during the year 1914; that subsequent thereto said commissioners executed an instrument in writing purporting to be a contract, obligating the State of Illinois and said commissioners to purchase from said company all the cement required in the construction of State aid roads in said ninety-four counties; that said commissioners have directed the preparation of specifications for the construction of State aid roads, providing therein that the cement required will be furnished by the State at certain prices therein specified, and inviting bids for the construction of State aid roads and for the furnishing of all materials, except cement, required therefor; that the necessary steps have been taken in many of the counties, as provided in said act, for the construction of State aid roads, and that large quantities of cement will be required for the construction of said roads; that said commissioners have publicly advertised in a number of counties in the State for bids to be submitted to them on July 1, 1914, for the construction of State aid roads in said counties, and that on said date said bids will be opened and the contracts awarded for the construction of State aid roads in said counties; that under the specifications for the construction of said roads for which bids are to be submitted large quantities of cement will be required, and it is the purpose of said commissioners to let contracts for and require the construction of State aid roads in numerous counties throughout the State as soon after July 1, as said contracts can be let and the work of construction begun; that the value of the cement required for the construction of State aid roads in said ninety-four counties in the year 1914, will be about $400,000; that it is the purpose of said commissioners to purchase, on behalf of the State, all of the cement required in the construction of State aid roads during the year 1914 and to require the use of the same; that complainant is advised the said Tice Road law does not authorize, or purport to authorize, said commissioners to purchase cement or any other material to be used in the construction of State aid roads, and the instrument in writing purporting to be a contract entered into by said commissioners is null and void by reason of the lack of power and authority of the commissioners to enter into said contract, and said commissioners have no power or authority to purchase cement or bind the State of Illinois to purchase cement or other material required in the construction of State aid roads; that said commissioners have stated they propose to purchase all of the cement required for the construction of State aid roads in the State during the year 1914, and they will, in conformity with the provisions of the instrument in writing between the commissioners and the Marquette Cement Manufacturing Company, issue orders to the Auditor of Public

Accounts authorizing and directing him to draw warrants upon the State Treasurer for the payment of all cement so furnished by said Marquette Cement Manufacturing Company out of the funds of the State which are derived by taxation on the property of your orator and of all other tax-payers; that if such orders are issued and warrants are drawn upon the treasurer, the same will constitute an illegal and unlawful expenditure of the public funds of the State, to the damage of your orator and of all other tax-payers of the State.

The appellees filed a general demurrer. The grounds of demurrer were: (1) Complainant's bill fails to allege the facts necessary to entitle him to sue in this cause; (2) the commissioners, who are made defendants, are agents of the State, and the State is the real defendant therein and is wrongfully made a defendant thereto; (3) the commissioners have the express power, by virtue of law, to make and enter into the contract alleged in complainant's bill to be null and void; and (4) the bill of complaint is not sufficient, in law or equity, upon which to be granted the relief prayed for.

For a reversal of the decree appellant relies upon the provisions of section 19 of article 4 of the constitution, which, so far as it is to be considered here, reads as follows: "The General Assembly shall never * * * authorize the payment of any claim, or part thereof, hereafter created against the State under any agreement or contract made without express authority of law; and all such unauthorized agreements or contracts shall be null and void." Emphasis is laid upon the word "express," as distinguished from and excluding any implied authority of law. The view of this court is, the distinction between express and implied authority of law is too clearly drawn in the adjudicated cases cited to permit of any confusion, and there is no reason to doubt the sense in which the word "express" is used in the constitutional clause quoted. The power must be express or it does not exist. United States v. C., St. P. M. & O. Ry. Co., 151 Fed. Rep. 84.

On the one hand it is claimed the Tice Road Law does not constitute "express authority of law" for the acts of the commissioners questioned in this case. By the name used is meant the act of the General Assembly approved June 27, 1913, (the new Road law) and it is pointed out by appellant that while that act, in terms, authorizes the State Highway Commissioners (hereinafter referred to as the commissioners) to purchase materials for the repair of roads, it does not explicitly say, if it does at all say, they may purchase materials for the construction of roads; also, that in the preparation of plans, specifications and estimates for the construction of roads the commissioners are authorized to include therein the value of any materials and the fair rental value of any implements, apparatus and machinery, suitable for road construction which the commissioners desire should be furnished or supplied by the State. In this connection our attention is called to three enactments of the General Assembly in 1905, being the act creating a State Highway Commission, since superseded by the present commission; the act authorizing the employment of convicts in the manufacture of drain tile, road tile, road tools, vehicles and machinery and preparing materials for building and ballasting roads; and the amendment to the act regulating the employment of convicts so as to provide for furnishing the crushed rock or other road materials manufactured by them, free at the penal or reformatory institution, upon the requisition of the State Highway Commission.

The three acts mentioned are claimed to be constituent part of a general plan, in connection with the State Highway Commission, whereby the State would have at all times certain road building materials and tools for local use on the order of the commissioners, and that upon the adoption and approval of the Tice Road law the General Assembly had in its consideration such materials and tools rather than such as might be acquired by purchase; also, it is contended that since by the terms of the Tice Road law the commission is given power to acquire lands containing materials suitable for road construction or road repair, the inference it might buy construction materials upon the market is necessarily excluded. It is also pointed out that by direct use of effective words the commission is by the Tice Road law authorized to purchase materials for repairing and maintaining State aid roads, the conclusion of the appellant being that language equally direct would have been employed if the commission, by any intention of the General Assembly, had been empowered to purchase materials for construction of such roads.

Section 32 of the act (Hurd's Stat. 1913, p. 2120) is the section giving authority to purchase materials, supplies, etc., for the purpose of keeping State-aid roads in repair, and section 134 of the act gives the power of eminent domain for the purpose aforementioned. The legal maxim, *expressio unius exclusio alterius* is well supported, if support were needed, by 19 Cyc. 23, and authorities there cited, and it is elementary that highway officers have, in general, only such powers as are conferred by statute. (Ohio and Mississippi Railway Co. v. People, 123 Ill. 648.) Many other authorities are brought to our attention and might be cited here to establish and buttress the principles of law and of legal construction laid down in appellant's brief did space permit, but practically the sole question before the trial court and this court was and is, does the law expressly authorize what the commission has done and is doing?—and that question must be determined from a consideration of the law itself, according to the established rules of construction.

The section of the constitution herein above quoted, being section 19 of article 4, declares null and void all contracts and agreements which create a liability against the State without express authority of law. The constitution is the organic law, but it nevertheless is law, and like all other laws it must have both a reasonable and practical interpretation. (Knickerbocker v. People, 102. Ill. 218.) An express grant of power or duty to do a particular thing includes the express grant of power to do all that is reasonably necessary to execute that power or duty. Lewis v. Colgan, 115 Cal. 529; City of Chicago v. Stratton, 162 Ill. 494; People v. Drainage Comrs. 143 id. 417; Field v. People, 2 Scam. 79.

Three laws were enacted by the Forty-eighth General Assembly appropriating to the commissioners a total sum of $1,100,000 for building and maintaining State aid roads in the several counties, being, respectively, House Bills 608, 679 and 894, each providing for the Auditor of Public Accounts to draw warrants upon the State Treasurer for the disbursement of the money upon the order of the commission, accompanied by a detailed statement showing the amount expended and the purpose of the expenditure, clearly distinguishing amounts expended for the building from those of maintaining such roads. (Laws of 1913, pp. 41-43.)

The Tice Road law, adopted also by the Forty-eighth General Assembly, is in practical effect a revision of the road laws of the State and is divided into ten articles, 168 sections and many sub-sections. Its title is, "An Act to Revise the Law in Relation to Roads and Bridges." (Hurd's Stat. 1913, p. 2110.) By article 2 of the act a State highway department is created, with commissioners and other officers and agents, and the general powers and duties of the commission are enumerated in twelve sub-sections. We here quote two of them: "(10) Let all contracts for the construction or improvement of State aid roads." "(12) Perform all other duties prescribed in this act or reasonably inferable therefrom." Section 9 of article 4 of the act provides for the payment of State aid roads one-half by the county and one-half by the State, and for the same to be laid out, constructed and improved as is in the act afterwards directed. Section 18 of the same article provides for including in the estimates the value of any materials and the fair rental value of any implements, apparatus and machinery the State may furnish. Section 30 authorizes the commission to construct State aid roads directly, if, under conditions specified, it cannot contract for the same within the estimate.

We should allow the three appropriation bills above referred to, and the clauses selected from the Road law, to speak for themselves upon the question of express power but for the extended and able argument presented by the appellant upon the exclusion doctrine above referred to, and upon the further contention that sub-section 12, above quoted, is meaningless and without force and adds nothing to the eleven preceding sub-sections—the appellees, of course, contending for the opposite view.

We are of the view that the statutes appropriating funds to the commission for the building of State aid roads, together with the statute giving the commission power to let all contracts for the construction of such roads, or in a certain event to construct the same through its own agencies, and to perform all other duties prescribed in the act or reasonably inferable therefrom, confer upon the commission full and express power to purchase such road building materials, tools, implements and machinery as may from time to time be needed for the purposes aforesaid, and in their discretion to estimate and anticipate the needs and prepare therefor, as the bill here under consideration shows was done, and to the same extent as if the methods of its procedure in the premises were as definitely prescribed as the same are prescribed in relation to letting contracts for highway construction.

We do not attach controlling importance to the contention of appellant to the effect the commission's powers in regard to supplying road building materials, tools and machinery are limited to those acquired by virtue of the three enactments of 1905, *supra*, and to those acquired by and through the power of eminent domain conferred by the Tice law, because it is conceivable that many varieties of materials, tools and machinery useful in building State aid roads might not be produced at the penal and reformatory institutions of the State and might not be found obtainable by and through the exercise of the power of eminent domain.

We hold, also, the power to purchase materials for road construction is not excluded by the grant of power to purchase materials for repair of roads or the grant of power to obtain materials by the condemnation of real estate, because to hold otherwise would bring us to the unreasonable conclusion that the commission, by determining, by and thr̶█████████ estimates, the kind of road to be made and ███████ rials to be used therein would find itself under a duty to construct the road in the event a contract therefor could not be secured within the estimate and yet be unable to perform that duty for want of power to purchase the specific materials, assuming the State did not produce the same at its penal and reformatory institutions and that said materials could not be found through the process of the power of eminent domain.

We would not be understood as limiting the right of purchase to those comparatively rare instances in which the commission will be under a duty to construct the State aid roads directly, for the Tice law in authorizing the State, in the discretion of the commission, to furnish materials for the construction of State aid roads and fix the price to be charged therefore, is without limit and is not confined to materials already on hand. The determination of the kind of materials and the method of their acquirement are by the act confided to the discretion of the commission. There is no contention in the bill that such discretion has been abused or misused.

For the reasons indicated, the decree of the circuit court of DeKalb county must be and is affirmed.

Decree affirmed.

OPINIONS OF THE ATTORNEY GENERAL.

MONEY ALLOTTED A COUNTY BY THE STATE HIGHWAY COMMISSION IS EXPENDED UNDER THE DIRECTION OF THE COMMISSION.

March 19, 1915.

Hon. J. H. Lane,
    State's Attorney, McLeansboro, Ill.

Dear Sir: I am in receipt of your favor of the 15th instant, and quote therefrom as follows:

"As I understand it, under the appropriation of the Automobile fund, there was $1,800 appropriated to this county, and our county raised an equal sum by taxation of $1,800. I am informed by one of the supervisors that they passed an order of the board distributing this $3,600 equally among the nine townships of the county for the purpose of building bridges."

You inquire:

"Is this division of this money equally among the townships of the county a legal division of it?"

I assume that your statement and inquiry has reference to the allotment made to counties by the State Highway Commission in accordance with section 15a of the revised Road and Bridge act. The county board has no control or jurisdiction over the allotment of State Aid funds which the State Highway Commission makes. Both the allotment made by the State Highway Commission and the amount raised by the county to meet such allotment, can be expended only on State Aid roads; and only under contracts let by the State Highway Commission. The county board may initiate proceedings under section 16 for the construction of a State Aid road along a route previously designated, as provided by section 10, to be improved as a State Aid road. When the State Highway Commission and the county board have finally determined upon the improvement of a designated road, as provided by sections 21 and 22; contracts for such improvement are let by the State Highway Commission in accordance with section 26. The county is required to raise one-half the amount to be expended in making such improvement. But, as stated, both the amount raised by the county and the amount of the allotment made to a county by the State Highway Commission are expended upon contracts let by the Commission, and the county board has nothing to do with the expenditure of such funds or the letting of such contracts.

There is no provision of the act which authorizes the county board to apportion to the various towns the allotment made to a county by the State Highway Commission, and the amount raised by the county to meet such allotment.

The allotment made by the State Highway Commission is not paid into the county treasury, but remains in the State treasury and is paid out on warrants drawn by the Auditor of Public Accounts upon the order of the State Highway Commission.

Very respectfully,

P. J. LUCEY, *Attorney General.*

TOWN AND TOWNSHIP OFFICERS.

May 6, 1915.

HON. C. N. HOLLERICH,
State's Attorney, Princeton, Illinois.

DEAR SIR: I am in receipt of your favor of the 3d instant, in which you inquire whether the compensation of highway commissioners for services in attending meetings of the board is payable from the road and bridge fund or from the town funds.

In reply, I will call your attention to section 53 of the revised Road and Bridge act, which provides in part as follows:

"The commissioners shall each receive for each day necessarily employed in the discharge of their duties the sum of two dollars ($2.00) upon a sworn statement to be filed by such commissioner in the office of the town clerk, showing the number of days he was employed and the kind of employment, and giving the dates thereof."

You will note that the basis of the compensation to be paid highway commissioners is the affidavit required to be filed with the town clerk. The statute draws no distinction between services performed in attending meetings of the board and other services performed in the discharge of their duties.

Paragraph 121, chapter 139, Hurd's Revised Statutes, 1913, makes it the duty of the board of town auditors to examine and audit all charges and claims against their town, and the compensation of all town officers except the compensation of supervisors for county services.

"The following shall be deemed town charges:
1. The compensation of town officers for services rendered their respective towns."

It is the holding of this department that highway commissioners in counties under township organization are town officers; and except where the statute specifically provides otherwise, their compensation for any services performed by them in the discharge of the duties of their office, is a town charge to be audited as other claims against the town and is payable out of the town fund and not out of the road and bridge fund.

Very respectfully,

P. J. LUCEY, *Attorney General.*

APPOINTMENTS OF COUNTY SUPERINTENDENTS TO MAY 1, 1915.

COUNTY.	NAME.	ADDRESS.
Adams	Lewis L. Boyer	Liberty, Ill.
Alexander	W. N. Moyers	Mound City, Ill.
Bond	R. O. Young	Sorento, Ill.
Boone	Thos. W. Humphrey	Belvidere, Ill.
Brown	W. O. Grover	Mt. Sterling, Ill.
Bureau	Frank R. Bryant	Princeton, Ill.
Calhoun	Jno. A. Earley	Batchtown, Ill.
Carroll	L. P. Scott, (Temp.)	Mt. Carroll, Ill.
Cass	John Goodell	Beardstown, Ill.
Champaign	Geo. C. Fairclo	Court House, Urbana, Ill.
Christian	C. A. Penington	Taylorville, Ill.
Clark	Zane Arbuckle	Marshall, Ill.
Clay	Howard Anderson	Louisville, Ill.
Clinton	Jno. T. Goldsmith	R. F. D. No. 3. Carlyle, Ill.
Coles	Harry Shinn	Mattoon, Ill.
Cook	Geo. A. Quinlan	Chicago, Ill.
Crawford	J. P. Lyon	Robinson, Ill.
Cumberland	Jno. A. Decker	Toledo, Ill.
DeKalb	Wm. C. Miller	Sycamore, Ill.
DeWitt	Melvin Tuggle	Clinton, Ill.
Douglas	L. O. Hackett	Tuscola, Ill.
DuPage	Eugene L. Gates	Wheaton, Ill.
Edgar	Karl J. Barr	Paris, Ill.
Edwards	Chas. C. Rice	Albion, Ill.
Effingham	Geo. T. Austin	Effingham, Ill.
Fayette	P. E. Fletcher	St. Elmo, Ill.
Ford	C. F. Helman	Paxton, Ill.
Franklin	Geo. F. Hampton	Benton, Ill.
Fulton	E. F. Motsinger	Canton, Ill.
Gallatin	Victor Pearce	Equality, Ill.
Greene	Irving Wetzel	Carrollton, Ill.
Grundy	Fred W. Stine	Morris, Ill.
Hamilton	Gregg Garrison	Garrison, Ill.
Hancock	Wm. Burgner	Carthage, Ill.
Hardin	W. M. Ball	Elizabethtown, Ill.
Henderson	C. R. A. Marshall	Stronghurst, Ill.
Henry	Jas. H. Reed	Cambridge, Ill.
Iroquois	Benj. Jordan	Watseka, Ill.
Jackson	Thos. G. Dunn	Gorham, Ill.
Jasper	S. A. Conner	Newton, Ill.
Jefferson	Tony C. Pitchford	Mt. Vernon, Ill.
Jersey	Chas. E. Warren	Jerseyville, Ill.
JoDaviess	Geo. E. Schroeder	Stockton, Ill.
Johson	Chas. A. Hook	Vienna, Ill.
Kane	Geo. N. Lamb	St. Charles, Ill.
Kankakee	Frank M. Enos	Kankakee, Ill.
Kendall	Jno. D. Russell	Oswego, Ill.
Knox	Harley M. Butt	Galesburg, Ill.
Lake	Chas. E. Russell	Waukegan, Ill.
LaSalle	Geo. Farnsworth	Ottawa, Ill.
Lawerence	R. J. Benefield	Lawrenceville, Ill.
Lee	L. B. Neighbour	Dixon, Ill.
Livingston	R. W. Osborn	Pontiac, Ill.
Logan	Thos. S. Davy	Lincoln, Ill.
McDonough	W M. Bonham	Macomb, Ill.
McHenry	C. L. Tryon	Woodstock, Ill.
McLean	Ralph O. Edwards	Bellflower, Ill.
Macon	Preston T. Hicks	Decatur, Ill.
Macoupin	O. B. Conlee	Carlinville, Ill.
Madison	W. E. Howden	Edwardsville, Ill.
Marion	Lee S. Trainor	Centralia, Ill.
Marshall	L. H. Eldridge	Lacon, Ill.
Mason	H. V. Schoonover	Havana, Ill.
Massac	J. Thrift Corlis	Metropolis, Ill.
Menard	C. M. Buckley	Petersburg, Ill.
Mercer	J. E. Russell	Aledo, Ill.
Monroe	Albert R. Gardner	Waterloo, Ill.
Montgomery	P. M. Bandy	Barnett, Ill.
Morgan	Lawrence V. Baldwin	Jacksonville, Ill.
Moultrie	T. C. Fleming	Sullivan, Ill.
Ogle	Alex Anderson	Polo, Ill.
Peoria	W. E. Emery	512 N. Glendale av., Peoria, Ill.
Perry	Frank House	St. Johns, Ill.
Piatt	Thos. J. Anderson	Monticello, Ill.
Pike	H. H. Hardy	Hull, Ill.
Pope	W T. S. Hopkins	Dixon Springs. Ill.
Pulaski	W. N. Moyers	Mound City, Ill.
Putnam	Mason Wilson	McNabb, Ill.
Randolph	Henry I. Barbeau	Prairie du Rocher, Ill.
Richland		
Rock Island	Wallace Treichler	Rock Island, Ill.
St. Clair	David O. Thomas	Belleville, Ill.
Saline	Jno. P. Upchurch	Harrisburg, Ill.
Sangamon	Edwin White	Springfield, Ill.
Schuyler	W. S. Henderson	Rushville, Ill.
Scott	Geo. H. Vannier	Bluffs, Ill.
Shelby	N. A. Baxter	Shelbyville, Ill.
Stark	Wm. Slater	Wyoming, Ill.
Stephenson	O. G. Hively	Freeport, Ill.
Tazewell	Frank S. Cook	Mackinaw, Ill.
Union	Jos. F. Howenstein	Anna, Ill.
Vermilion	Wm. S. Dillon	Danville, Ill.
Wabash	Guy W. Courter	Mt. Carmel, Ill.
Warren	C. L. McClanahan	Monmouth, Ill.
Washington	Jno. A. Davenport, Jr	Nashville, Ill.
Wayne	Griff Koontz	Fairfield, Ill.
White	Geo. H. Brown	Carmi, Ill.
Whiteside	V. N. Taggett	Morrison, Ill.
Will	Will H. Smith	204 W. Allen, Joliet, Ill.
Williamson	P. B. Wilson	Marion, Ill.
Winnebago	Albertus R. Carter	Rockford, Ill.
Woodford	A. B. Hurd	El Paso, Ill.

ILLINOIS HIGHWAYS

OFFICIAL PUBLICATION
STATE HIGHWAY DEPARTMENT

| VOL. 2 | SPRINGFIELD, ILLINOIS, JUNE, 1915 | No. 6 |

HARVEY ROAD, COOK COUNTY.
oot Concrete State-aid Road, Built During 1914 by Illinois Hydraulic Stone and Construction Co., Elgin, Ill. Total Length 19,442 Feet; Total Cost, $66,023.10.

WEST JEFFERSON ROAD, SANGAMON COUNTY.
18-foot Concrete State-aid Road. Total Length 3,318 Feet. Built During 1914 by R. F. Egan, Springfield, Ill.

ILLINOIS HIGHWAYS.

Published Monthly by the

State Highway Department.

ILLINOIS HIGHWAY COMMISSION.

A. D. Gash, President.

S. E. Bradt, Secretary.

James P. Wilson.

Wm. W. Marr, *Chief State Highway Engineer.*

P. C. McArdle, *Assistant State Highway Engineer.*

H. E. Bilger, *Road Engineer, Springfield, Illinois.*

C. Older, *Bridge Engineer, Springfield, Illinois.*

B. H. Piepmeier, *Assistant Engineer, Springfield, Illinois.*

G. F. Burch, *Assistant Engineer, Springfield, Illinois.*

M. W. Watson, *Assistant Engineer, Springfield, Illinois.*

F. L. Roman, *Testing Engineer, Springfield, Illinois.*

J. M. McCoy, *Chief Clerk, Springfield, Illinois.*

DIVISION ENGINEERS.

H. B. Bushnell..............Aurora

R. L. Bell.....................Paris

H. E. Surman..........Rock Island

A. H. Hunter................Peoria

Fred Tarrant............Springfield

C. M. Slaymaker........E. St. Louis

J. E. Huber.................Marion

CONTENTS.

BUSINESS RELATION BETWEEN CONTRACTOR AND ENGINEER.

[By H. B. Bushnell, Associate Member American Society Civil Engineers, Division Engineer State Highway Department.]

There is a more or less prevalent idea among many taxpayers and some few engineers that contractors as a class are dishonest. This opinion is generally formed by a very limited experience in dealing with contractors and contract work.

The nature of a contractor's work, especially when he is engaged on public work, readily yields itself to criticism. Quite often we hear a contractor condemned for a poor piece of work when the blame properly belonged on the engineer. There have been instances of bridge failures and examples of unsatisfactory roads and pavements when the contractor was entirely innocent and yet received the majority of the blame. The contractor may build his work in strict accordance with the specifications furnished and yet be blamed by the general public if the work is not satisfactory.

The mistakes of engineers are frequently shouldered by the contractor. The general public is a peculiar and fickle party to deal with. It is easily influenced and very seldom investigates carefully into the true merits of a case.

During the past year the writer had charge of a piece of work built by a contractor who was a stranger to him. Before the work started he made inquiry of an engineer who had had some business dealings with the contractor as to his reputation. He reported that all he knew about the man was that he had built a job in his town that had not yet been accepted, and the general impression was that the work was improperly done. The writer found from his experience with this same contractor that he was strictly square and honest, and that his work was excellent. As a matter of curiosity he made an investigation of the piece of work that was the basis of the local engineer's opinion and found that the reason the work had not been accepted was because of a technical error in the legal proceedings involved. The legal talent should have shouldered the blame, yet the contractor in reality had thrust upon him an unsavory local reputation through no fault of his own.

Another instance occurred in a small municipality in the southeastern part of this State a few years ago. Specifications were drawn for a gravel road. The mayor of the town had seen some gravel roads built in Indiana without the use of a roller, the road being compacted by traffic and partially bonded by the clay tracked on from the side roads. He conceived the idea that if a little clay was good, more would be better, so he had a clause incorporated in the specifications that the gravel should be covered with a 6-inch layer of yellow clay. The contractor persuaded the mayor that 6 inches was excessive and finally had the depth reduced to 3 inches. The road was built as specified. The writer happened to visit this town shortly after the road was completed and the mayor asked him to investigate the work. As you would imagine, the clay had caused the gravel to ball up, leaving the surface a series of humps and holes.

The property owners had gotten out an injunction to stop payment for the work. The mayor would not admit that the specifications were at fault and was making an effort to prove the contractor was to blame. In slang terms the contractor was being made the "goat". He was eventually paid, but was compelled to go to court for a settlement and to subject himself to unjust criticism. It is such incidents as these that have had much to do with creating in the mind of the general public the idea that contractors are dishonest.

There is a contractor in this state who so firmly believes that the contractor is ultimately blamed for the success or failure of a finished piece of work that he refuses to bid on work where the specifications do not meet with his approval. He claims that it has been his experience that the general public soon forgets the specifications and the engineer that made them, but that they do not forget the contractor. If the work is satisfactory, he gets the credit, and if it is unsatisfactory he gets the blame. In so much as he depends upon his finished work for his reputation, he contends that he cannot afford to take any chances on questionable specifications. He carries the point so far that he will not bid on a pitch or asphalt filled brick pavement, because, in his estimation, the only proper method to construct a brick pavement is with a cement grout filler.

Do not infer that the writer thinks that all contractors are perfectly honest, or that they should be classed as philanthropists. There are dishonest and crooked contractors, the same as there are dishonest men in other lines of business activity. All of them will bear watching, yet the crooked and really dishonest contractor is the exception and not the rule.

We, as engineers, should be careful that our experiences with these exceptional cases do not prejudice us so that we impose unnecessary hardships and restrictions upon the men who are endeavoring to do good, conscientious work.

The contractor is a party to a contract the same as the State, county, or any other party of the first part, and is entitled to certain rights and privileges. He is not an undesirable citizen, or a necessary evil, but is a very necessary and important factor in the development of improvements of all kinds.

One of the most difficult problems confronting the engineer in the preparation of his specifications is that of making them rigid enough to control the refractory and bad contractor, and yet, at the same time, not handicap the man who is sincere and straightforward in his work.

The specifications should be so drawn as to insure good and satisfactory work in every detail, and yet at a cost that is not excessive. If the cost were not a consideration it would be an easy matter to prepare specifications that would absolutely hold almost any contractor.

The cost, however, is a very important factor and must be carefully considered. Any unnecessary restrictions upon the work increases the cost to the contractor which, in turn, increases the cost to the party of the first part.

Many engineers and county superintendents fail to appreciate the effect that an extremely short specified period of time for the completion of a piece of work has upon the cost. In some cases the difference in cost might be small, yet, in general, it is considerable. Any time that you specify a time for completion so limited that it necessitates starting work immediately upon the awarding of the contract, you limit the competition to contractors who have outfits that are idle, or those that are willing to buy an outfit at hurry-up prices, in which case the increased cost is charged to the job. There are times in public, as well as private work, where the advantages of an early completion of a given piece of work more than offset any increased cost. As public officials, we must weigh carefully all of these points, and, if it is found to be good judgment to require special restrictions, provision for the added cost should be made in the estimate.

The engineer and the contractor, while representing the two sides of a contract, should work with the same ultimate end in view, that is, the completion of a satisfactory piece of work. Naturally the contractor endeavors to secure this end with the least cost to himself.

This tendency is not to be condemned, as it is simply a case of good business ability, unless carried to such an extent that it infringes upon the specifications and the quality of the work. If the latter case exists, the engineer must then exert the powers vested in him and see that the work is properly done.

An engineer may assist or retard a contractor in many ways. If he cooperates with him, the quality of the work, as a rule, is improved, for most contractors are human and appreciate this attitude on the part of the engineer. The party of the first part benefits not only in having a better finished product, but in future work; benefits in price, for when a contractor knows that the engineer is disposed to treat him fairly and not impose unnecessary hardships upon him, he is in a better position to figure closely on his job.

Some engineers assume the attitude that, if the work is not done properly they will not accept it and deliberately let the contractor go ahead and do things that are not in accordance with specifications, without making any effort to correct the faults. This method is to be condemned. Often infringements are the result of ignorance, and in such a case, failure of correction is an injustice to the contractor and poor business policy for the party of the first part. If the work is allowed to continue in an unsatisfactory manner to completion, one of two things is sure to happen, either the work is accepted or rejected. If accepted, the party of the first part is not getting what it is entitled to get, under the provisions of the contract. If it is rejected and the work torn out and replaced, the party of the first part is obliged to undergo delay and the inconvenience that always results from such conditions. A compromised job is rarely satisfactory to anybody concerned and on public work is food for gossip that is almost invariably grossly exaggerated, no matter how carefully and fairly the settlement was adjusted. Compromise settlements for inferior work have been made in the past and will, of necessity, be made in the future, but every effort should be made to avoid them. The occasion is rare when the contractor will deliberately disobey the instructions of the engineer. There are occasionally cases on public work where the contractor, through some political connections, or friendship, figures that he can override the engineer and secure an acceptance through what is commonly called "pull." Such occurrences were much more common in the past than they are at present, although there are yet some few contractors that are not educated up to this point.

The engineer should exert every effort to secure, for the party of the first part, a satisfactory piece of work and all that can reasonably be expected under the specifications. He should not, however, abuse the powers vested in him to impose useless hardships upon the contractor. There are times where it becomes the duty of the engineer to protect the contractor from unjust demands, made by the party of the first part. An occasion of this kind happened in Henry County some three or four years ago. A bridge company had contracted to build a structure within a given period, which appeared to everybody concerned a very reasonable time. Work started very shortly after the contract was awarded. Quicksand was encountered in the footing, the river rose twice, flooding the cofferdams and the canal broke, cutting off, for the time being, transportation facilities for material. As a result of these unforseen difficulties the work was not completed within the time limit required in the contract. It was, however, completed in a very satisfactory manner and at a big loss to the contractor, yet in spite of these facts, the bridge committee endeavored to enforce a penalty on the contractor because the work was not completed within the specified time and produced a written opinion from a local attorney in which the claim was made that acts of God, labor difficulties, strikes, etc., were afforded no excuse in the sight of the law for a contractor. It was the very unpleasant duty of the writer to attempt to persuade this committee that they had no moral or legal right to the penalty, as the contractor had done everything within his power to complete the work and that, if they did withhold any of the money due the contractor that they were actually stealing it. It is much easier, at such times, to follow the lines of least resistance and stay out of controversies of this kind, but a man does not deserve the name of engineer that has not the backbone to stand up for what he knows to be right, no matter whether he is acting in the interest of the contractor or the public.

The old saying, "If you don't expect to enforce the law take it off the statutes," holds good with a set of specifications and any instructions you may give to a contractor. Disobedience of one law breeds contempt for all law and the same is true as regards orders given to a contractor that are not enforced. Do not be arbitrary and do not give orders unless they are necessary, and then see that they are obeyed.

In starting a job give the contractor to understand exactly what you will expect of him and that you stand ready to assist him in any way possible to carry on his work in an efficient and economical manner, but that in turn you insist that he build the work as specified. Such an understanding, at the start of a job, will often obviate later controversies and insure a better finished product for, as a rule, the fewer the controversies the better the completed work.

DEPARTMENTAL REPORT.

June 1, 1915.

I submit the following report on the present condition of the work being done by the State Highway Department:

STATE-AID ROAD WORK.

During the month of May, plans for State-aid work were sent to the county clerks, as indicated by the following tabulation:

County.	Section.
Kane	B & C
Hamilton	A & B
Pulaski	A
Gallatin	A & B
Wabash	A
Jackson	B
Randolph	B
LaSalle	D & A
Williamson	B & C
DuPage	B
Fayette	B
Livingston	B
Greene	A
Perry	A
Jersey	B
McDonough	A, B, C & D
Scott	B
Fulton	D
Macoupin	B
Putnam	A & B
Washington	A

The status of all State-aid road and bridge work now under contract is indicated by the following table:

CONDITION OF STATE-AID WORK JUNE 1, 1915.

County.	Sec.	Per cent completed.	Note.	Contractor.	Resident engineer.
Adams	A	48%		Cameron, Joyce & Co., Keokuk, Iowa	C. A. Clark, 426 N. 7th st., Quincy, Ill. Phone 3817-W.
Alexander	A	22%		Bland & Fitzgerald, Cairo, Ill.	E. A. Kane, Unity, Ill.
Bureau	A	70%		Grohne Construction Co., Joliet, Ill.	E. L. Schwaderer, 205 E. Peru st., Princeton, Ill.
Bureau	B	2%		Grohne Contracting Co., Joliet, Ill.	E. L. Schwaderer, 205 E. Peru st., Princeton, Ill.
Bureau	C		W. N. B.	C.W.Jensen & Co., 133 W. Wash. st., Chicago	
Bureau	D		W. N. B.	C.W.Jensen & Co., 133 W. Wash. st., Chicago	
Calhoun	A		W. N. B.	Rees Bros., Quincy, Ill.	
Carroll	A	2%	N. P. L.	Gund Graham Co., Freeport, Ill.	S. C. Campbell, Box 216, Mt. Carroll, Ill.
Clark	A	85%		Robert Thompson, Marshall, Ill.	M.W.Parrish, Martinsville, Ill
Clinton	A		W. N. B.	P. M. Johnston & Co., St. Elmo, Ill.	
Coles	A	100%		Edw. M. Laing Co. Inc., Highland Park, Ill.	H. B. Sennott, 1605 Wabash Ave., Mattoon, Ill., Phone 281.
Cook	D	90%	P. C.	E. J. Mahony Co., 526 Reaper Block, Chicago	
Cook	F			Cullen-Friestedt Co., Tribune bldg., Chicago	O. B. Kercher, 25 Elmwood pl., LaGrange, Ill. Phone 1096-R
Cook	G	35%		Walter & Windes, Glencoe, Ill.	A. F. Keehner, Desplaines. Ill.
Crawford	A	40%		F. W. McElroy, Robinson, Ill.	M.M.Small, 204 S. Howard st., Robinson, Ill. Phone 323-3.
Crawford	B	82%		F. W. McElroy, Robinson, Ill.	Chas. H. Apple, Box 171, Robinson, Ill. Phone 12608.
Douglas	A	88%		Goggin Construction Co., Arcola, Ill.	Geo. H. Baker, 25 E. Doggy st., Tuscola, Ill.

CONDITION OF STATE-AID WORK—Continued.

County.	Sec.	Per cent completed.	Note.	Contractor.	Resident engineer.
DuPage....	A	70%	....	E. J. Mahony & Co., 526 Reaper blk., Chicago	
Edgar.....	C	....	W. N. B.	Alan Jay Parrish, Paris, Ill.	
Edwards...	A	....	W. N. B.	G. W. and G. C. Morgan, Carmi, Ill.	
Effingham..	A	....	W. N. B.	P. M. Johnston & Co., St. Elmo, Ill.	
Fayette....	A	70%	....	P. M. Johnston & Co., St. Elmo, Ill..........	S.H.Phinney, care M. F. Houston, 628 Gallitan st., Vandalia, Ill.
Ford......	A	....	W. N. B.	Metz & McVay, Gary, Ind.	
Fulton.....	A	24%	....	Carpenter Construction Co., Cloverland, Ind.	R. L. Hufford, 316 N. Main st., Canton, Ill. Phone 116-R.
Fulton.....	B	75%	....	Carpenter Construction Co., Cloverland, Ind.	E. B. Blough, 316 N. Main st., Canton, Ill. Phone 116-R.
Fulton.....	C	30%	....	Carpenter Construction Co., Cloverland, Ind.	E. B. Blough, 316 N. Main st., Canton, Ill. Phone 116-R.
Grundy....	A	80%	....	A. L. Booth and Wm. Gilchrist, Gardner, Ill.	Geo. E. Schopmeyer, 113 W. North st., Morris, Ill.
Hardin....	A	(Bridges.)	....	Williams & Townsend, Marion, Ill.	
Henry.....	A	....	W. N. B.	Grohne Contracting Co., Joliet, Ill.	
Henry.....	B	....	W. N. B.	Grohne Contracting Co., Joliet, Ill.	
Iroquois...	A	98%	P. C.	Davis-Ewing Concrete Co., Bloomington, Ill.	R. P. Devine, Box 406, Watseka, Ill.
Johnson...	A	(Bridges.)	W. N. B.	Montgomery, Parker Co., Hatfield, Ill.	
Kane......	A	94%	....	C.W.Jensen & Co., 133 W. Wash. st., Chicago	L. R. Wheeler, Geneva, Ill.
Kane......	B	....	W. N. B.	W. E. Cummings, Geneva, Ill.	
Kankakee..	B	....	W. N. B.	Bloodgood & Summerville, Harvey, Ill.	
Kendall....	A	3%	....	Booth, Nicholson & Gilchrist, Gardner, Ill...	Ezra C. Wenger, 18 S. Lincoln st., Aurora, Ill.
Lake......	A	90%	....	H. G. Goëlitz Co., Oak Park..............	J. R. Goetzman, care W. H. Miller, Lake Villa, Ill.
LaSalle....	C	45%	....	W. J. Brennan, LaSalle, Ill..............	W.C.Locke, LaSalle, Ill. Phone 725 Utica Exchange.
Lee........	A	55%	....	Edw. M. Laing Co. Inc., Highland Park, Ill.	
Logan.....	B	50%	....	John Awe, Lincoln, Ill.................	J.T.Child, 222 McLean st., Lincoln, Ill. Box 304. Phone 559.
Logan.....	C	90%	....	W. D. Alexander & Co., Normal, Ill.	
McHenry...	C	....	W. N. B.	C. A. Williston, 343 S. Dearborn st., Chicago	
McHenry...	D	....	W. N. B.	C. A. Williston, 343 S. Dearborn st., Chicago	
McHenry...	E	....	W. N. B.	C. A. Williston, 343 S. Dearborn st., Chicago	
McHenry...	F	....	W. N. B.	C. A. Williston, 343 S. Dearborn st., Chicago	
Macoupin..	A	53%	....	McBride & Wargensted, Carlinville, Ill......	W. T. Page, Carlinville, Ill.
Madison...	A	80%	....	Chas. H. Degenhardt, Alton, Ill...........	C. I. Burggraf, care Y. M. C. A., Alton, Ill.
Marion....	A	(Bridges.)	W. N. B.	F. S. Nichols, Flora, Ill.	
Marion....	B	....	W. N. B.	H. H. Hall Const. Co., East St. Louis, Ill.	
Marion....	C	(Bridges.)	W. N. B.	M. R. McCall, Sandoval, Ill.	
Marshall...	B	....	W. N. B.	Ajax Const. & Eng. Co., Gary, Ind.	
Marshall...	C	(Bridges.)	W. N. B.	Capperune & Dayo, Bradford, Ill.	
Massac....	A	5%	....	W. H. Hoffman, Lafayette, Ind...........	J. P. Murphy, Rose Hotel, Metropolis, Ill.
Monroe....	A	60%	....	Renkel Const. Co., Maplewood, Mo........	B. C. McCurdy, Illmo Hotel, East St. Louis, Ill. Phone working hours 245, Millstadt, Ill.
Morgan....	A	40%	....	Herrick Construction Co., Carlinville, Ill....	C. S. McArdle, 335 W. Court st., Jacksonville, Ill. Phone 613 Ill. phone.
Moultrie...	A	70%	P. C.	Edw. M. Laing Co. Inc., Highland Park, Ill..	C. C. Hinsdale, 1610 Harrison st., Sullivan, Ill.
Ogle......	A	87%	P. C.	Gund-Graham Co., Freeport, Ill...........	John Johnson, R. F. D. No. 3, Oregon, Ill.
Peoria.....	A	99%	P. C.	Canterbury Bros., Peoria, Ill.............	Fred Beyer, Mayer Hotel, Peoria, Ill.

CONDITION OF STATE-AID WORK—Concluded.

County.	Sec.	Per cent completed.	Note.	Contractor.	Resident engineer.
Peoria.....	B	....	W. N. B.	Ajax Const. & Eng. Co., Gary, Ind..........	Simon Garbulsky.
Piatt......	A	27%	....	Metz & McVay, Mansfield, Ill..............	E. B. Gordon, Box 31, Mansfield, Ill.
Pike.......	A	....	W. N. B.	Cameron, Joyce & Co., Keokuk, Iowa	
Pope......	A	....	W. N. B.	Chas. Gullett, Golconda, Ill.	
Rock Island	B	75%	....	McCarthy Improvement Co., Davenport, Iowa	
St. Clair....	A	....	W. N. B.	H. H. Hall Const. Co., East St. Louis, Ill.	
Saline.....	A	....	W. N. B.	Ernest Berns. Terre Haute, Ind..	
Sangamon..	F	....	....	R. F. Egan, Springfield, Ill.	
Schuyler...	A	32%	....	F. E. Ball, Hampshire, Ill...............	J. J. O'Loughlin, Box 151, Rushville, Ill.
Schuyler...	B	....	W. N. B.	Zastrow & Lashmet, Jacksonville, Ill.	
Shelby....	A	....	W. N. B.	Herrick Construction Co., Carlinville, Ill.	
Shelby.....	B	....	....	Townsend B. Smith, Evanston, Ill.........	H. W. Wilkison, care Neel Hotel, Shelbyville, Ill.
Shelby.....	C	....	....	Townsend B. Smith, Evanston, Ill.........	H. W. Wilkison, care Neel Hotel, Shelbyville, Ill.
Shelby.....	D	....	....	Tressler & True, Tower Hill, Ill............	L. A. Doan, Shelbyville, Ill.
Tazewell...	D	....	W. N. B.	W. D. Alexander & Co., Normal, Ill.	
Vermilion..	A	53%	....	Edw. M. Laing Co. Inc., Highland Park, Ill..	P. F. Jervis, 205 N. Walnut st., Danville, Ill.
Warren....	B	80%	....	Merrifield Const. Co., Monmouth, Ill.......	Clyde B. Ross, 525 S. 11th st., Monmouth, Ill. Phone 1339.
Whiteside..	B	....	....	Walter & Windes, Glencoe, Ill.............	O. F. Goeke, Morrison, Ill.
Whiteside..	C	....	....	Walter & Windes, Glencoe, Ill.............	O. F. Goeke, Morrison, Ill.
Will.......	B	44%	....	Chicago Heights Coal Co., Chicago Heights, Ill.	Geo. L. Judson, 408 Scott st., Joliet, Ill. Phone Chicago phone 1778-J.
Winnebago.	A	....	....	Walter & Windes, Glencoe, Ill.	
Winnebago.	B	7%	....	Connelly & Dunning, 161 W.Wash.st., Chicago	S. F. Wilson, Route 8, Rockford, Ill. Phone 947-3. Wire, Rockford, Ill.
Woodford..	A	90%	P. C.	W. D. Alexander & Co., Normal, Ill.........	C. W. Ellsworth.

LEGEND:
    N. P. L.—No pavement laid.
    P. C.—Pavement completed.
    W. N. B.—Work not begun.

TOWNSHIP ROAD CONSTRUCTION.

The following is a detailed report of the condition of the township road work to June 1. 1915:

Petty Township, Lawrence County—1½ miles of concrete pavement under construction at Petrolia. Work 20 per cent completed. F. C. Feutz of this Department is in charge of work.

Aurora Township, Kane County—1¼ miles of 18-foot concrete pavement under construction. Work 75 per cent completed. H. N. Kleiser of this Department is in charge of the work at Aurora.

Reading Township, Livingston County—About 20 miles of 9-foot macadam road to be built with convict labor. Work started April 1. Convict camp is now established and work is under way. Mr. F. L. Little of this Department is in charge of the work.

Eldorado Township, Saline County—1¼ miles of brick pavement 10 feet wide to be constructed near Eldorado. Work will start about June 15.

Sand Ridge Township, Jackson County—3½ miles of macadam road. Work started April 28. I. E. Scott from this Department is in charge of work. Work is about 20 per cent completed.

Douglas Township, Effingham County—About 1 mile of 12-foot macadam road to be resurfaced. Work may start about July 1.

Road District No. 5, Union County—7 miles of macadam road. Work may start some time in June.

Pontiac Township, Livingston County—2 miles of gravel road to be resurfaced with bituminous macadam. Construction started April 29. Mr. C. Gray of this Department is in charge. Work about 20 per cent completed.

Washington Township, Will County—Rerolled roads built at this point in 1914. Mr. D. S. James was in charge of work. Completed rolling May 15.

Oregon Township, Ogle County—There are several miles of road anticipated at this point on which work may start some time in June.

Shiloh Valley Township, St. Clair County—1 mile of 16-foot bituminous macadam road, construction to start about June 15.

DeKalb Township, DeKalb County—About 3 miles of macadam road being resurfaced at this point. State machinery being used.

Yellowhead Township, Kankakee County—½ mile of road resurfaced at this point. Mr. D. S. James was in charge of State equipment. Work completed May 20.

Road District No. 7, Alexander County—3 miles of macadam road construction and surface oiling. Work to start about July 1.

Seven Hickory Township, Coles County—4 miles of macadam road construction. Will start about June 15.

We have one outfit working on the State-aid road in Alexander County. Mr. Frank Nelson is in charge of equipment.

We are holding one outfit pending the awarding of the State-aid contract in Union County.

We have formal applications on file for all of the above named roads which aggregate to date about 60 miles of roads. We have had correspondence with a number of townships that are anticipating road improvement and who wish some assistance from this Department in the way of equipment and engineering services.

There are a number of township roads being constructed at the present time under the direct supervision of the highway commissioners, using penitentiary stone. The Joliet penitentiary is now shipping about 15 cars daily, and the Southern penitentiary about three cars per day. Considering the amount of crushed stone it will take to supply the convict camp at Reading, Illinois, and the machinery that we have working at other points, it seems that it will be impossible for the penitentiary to supply the demand for the material.

STATE-AID ROAD MAINTENANCE.

We now have four portable heating kettles stationed in various districts in the State that are being used in connection with maintaining concrete and brick pavements by filling cracks and joints with bituminous material.

The small auto truck has been working in the northeast division, filling cracks and joints in concrete pavements. The truck will finish in the northeast division about July 1.

All joints and cracks in State-aid roads in the following named counties have been filled with a bituminous material:

Iroquois.	Cook.
Cass.	Lawrence.
Logan.	Sangamon.
Livingston.	Jefferson.
Kankakee.	Williamson.
Will.	Franklin.

CONTRACTS AWARDED FOR STATE-AID ROADS.

During the month of May, bids were received and contracts awarded for the construction of approximately 12.00 miles of State-aid roads.

Engineers' estimates and bids received are exclusive of cement and other material to be furnished by the State.

The following tabulation will show the names of bidders and amount of bid on the several sections, together with the name of the successful bidder:

FORD COUNTY—SECTION A—ROUTE 1.

Length, 5,900 feet; width 10 feet; type, brick; engineer's estimate, $15,917.00; date of letting, May 5, 1915.

Name of bidder.	Amount of bid.
Miner & Korsmo, Chicago, Ill	$15,760 00
Chicago Heights Coal Co., Chicago Heights	15,685 00

Name of bidder.	Amount of bid.
Chas. S. Upham, Odell, Illinois	15,150 00
John E. Bretz, Springfield, Ill	14,886 00
Metz & McVay, Gary, Ind	14,845 00
Rees Brothers, Quincy, Ill	15,650 00

The contract was awarded to Metz & McVay.

PIKE COUNTY—SECTION A—ROUTE 6.

Length, 7,800 feet; width, 10 feet; type, concrete; engineer's estimate, $12,241.48; date of letting, May 5, 1915.

Name of bidder.	Amount of bid.
F. E. Ball & Company, Hampshire, Ill	$12,200 00
Henry Nelch & Son, Springfield, Ill	11,989 70
Cameron, Joyce & Co., Keokuk, Iowa	11,469 26
Ajax Const. & Eng. Co., Gary, Ind	11,777 00
C. M. Hanes, Jerseyville, Ill	12,000 00
Rees Bros., Quincy, Ill	11,949 00
Thos. H. Cutler, Gary, Ind	11,589 00
Ernest Berns, Terre Haute, Ind	12,000 00

The contract was awarded to Cameron, Joyce & Co.

SHELBY COUNTY—SECTION A—ROUTE 15.

Length, 4,800 feet; width, 10 feet; type, concrete; engineer's estimate, $7,142.64; date of letting, May 5, 1915.

Name of bidder.	Amount of bid.
A. C. Loomis, Mattoon, Ill	$7,142 00
Sell & Collar, Pana, Ill	7,142 64
Cameron, Joyce & Co., Keokuk, Iowa	6,763 00
Herrick Const. Co., Carlinville, Ill	6,263 00
Bloodgood & Summerville, Harvey, Ill	6,635 00
Ernest Berns, Terre Haute, Ind	6,342 00

The contract was awarded to Herrick Const. Co.

KANKAKEE COUNTY—SECTION B—ROUTE 1—6.

Length 1,200 feet; width, 10 feet; type, concrete; engineer's estimate, $2,049.00; date of letting, May 5, 1915.

Name of bidder.	Amount of bid.
Bloodgood & Summerville, Harvey, Ill	$1,990 00

The contract was awarded to Bloodgood & Summerville.

BUREAU COUNTY—SECTIONS C AND D—ROUTES 3 AND 1.

Length, 8,200 feet; width. 15 feet; type, concrete; engineer's estimate, $15,590.00; date of letting. May 5, 1915.

Name of bidder.	Amount of bid.
Miner & Korsmo, Chicago, Ill	$12,317 00
Grohne Contracting Co., Joliet, Ill	12,770 00
Connelly & Dunning, Chicago, Ill	12,269 00
C. W. Jensen & Co., Chicago, Ill	11,840 00
F. E. Ball & Co., Hampshire, Ill	14,585 00
Chas. I. Upham, Odell, Ill	14,400 00
W. J. Brennan, LaSalle, Ill	13,989 20
Ajax Cons. & Eng. Co., Gary, Ind	12,798 00
Thos. H. Cutler, Gary, Ind	12,670 00
E. A. Coates, Chicago, Ill	13,090 00

The contract was awarded to C. W. Jensen & Co.

SHELBY COUNTY—SECTION B—BRIDGES.

Engineer's estimate, $3,726.00; date of letting. May 5, 1915.

Name of bidder.	Amount of bid.
Zastrow & Lashmet, Jacksonville, Ill	$3,430 00
Jno. H. Baker, Sullivan, Ill	3,650 00
Townsend B. Smith, Evanston, Ill	3,298 00
L. C. Kesler, Herrick, Ill	3,697 00

Name of bidder.	Amount of bid.
Amos Culbertson, Oconee, Ill	3,840 00
Herrick Construction Co., Carlinville, Ill	3,501 00
Parham Construction Co., East St. Louis, Ill	3,524 00

The contract was awarded to Townsend B. Smith.

SHELBY COUNTY—SECTION C—BRIDGES.

Engineer's estimate, $3,585.00; date of letting, May 5, 1915.

Name of bidder.	Amount of bid.
Zastrow & Lashmet, Jacksonville, Ill	$3,327 00
John H. Baker, Sullivan, Ill	3,450 00
Townsend B. Smith, Evanston, Ill	3,248 00
L. C. Kesler, Herrick, Ill	3,565 00
Herrick Construction Co., Carlinville, Ill	3,359 00
Parham Construction Co., East St. Louis, Ill	3,298 00

The contract was awarded to Townsend B. Smith.

SHELBY COUNTY—SECTION D—BRIDGES.

Engineer's estimate, $3,063.00; date of letting, May, 5, 1915.

Name of bidder.	Amount of bid.
Zastrow & Lashmet, Jacksonville, Ill	$2,923 00
John H. Baker, Sullivan, Ill	2,950 00
Townsend B. Smith, Evanston, Ill	2,898 00
L. C. Kesler, Herrick, Ill	3,047 00
Blackerby Bros., Herrick, Ill	3,099 00
Amos Culberson, Oconee, Ill	3,142 00
Herrick Construction Co., Carlinville, Ill	2,844 00
Parham Construction Co., Carlinville, Ill	2,970 00
Tressler & True, Tower Hill, Ill	2,843 00

The contract was awarded to Tressler & True.

SALINE COUNTY—SECTION A—ROUTE 1.

Length, 7,500 feet; width, 10 feet; type, concrete; engineer's estimate, $10,710.00; date of letting, May 20, 1915.

Name of bidder.	Amount of bid.
J. L. Dorris Const. Co., Harrisburg, Ill	$10,599 90
Herrin Construction Co., Herrin, Ill	10,471 66
Grohne Contracting Co., Joliet, Ill	9,744 00
Ernest Berns, Terre Haute, Ind	9,000 00
Rees Bros., Quincy, Ill	10,670 00
Louis Rich, East St. Louis, Ill	10,650 00

The contract was awarded to Ernest Berns.

EDGAR COUNTY—SECTION C—ROUTE 1.

Length, 1,300 feet; width, 10 feet; type, brick; engineer's estimate, $2,838.92; date of letting, May 20, 1915.

Name of bidder.	Amount of bid.
Alan J. Parrish, Paris, Ill	$2,780 00

The contract was awarded to Alan J. Parrish.

POPE COUNTY—SECTION A—BRIDGES.

Engineer's estimate, $1,735.00; date of letting, May 20, 1915.

Name of bidder.	Amount of bid.
Charles Gullett, Golconda, Ill	$1,205 00

The contract was awarded to Chas. Gullett.

HENRY COUNTY—SECTIONS A AND B—ROUTE 1.

Length, 10,866 feet; width, 10 feet; type, concrete; engineer's estimate, $24,214.00; date of letting, May 20, 1915.

Name of bidder.	Amount of bid.
Bloodgood and Summerville, Harvey, Ill	$21,950 00
Gary Construction Co., Gary, Ind	19,600 00

Name of bidder.	Amount of bid.
J. E. Bretz, Springfield, Ill	$22,300 00
Chas. Winn, Muscatine, Iowa	23,265 00
Shugart & Munsen, Nevada, Iowa	22,680 00
Ajax Const. & Eng. Co., Gary, Ind	20,881 00
C. A. Williston, Chicago, Ill	21,700 00
C. W. Jensen & Co., Chicago, Ill	20,690 00
Chicago Heights Coal Co., Chicago H'ghts, Ill	23,295 00
Joseph H. Campbell, Bloomington, Ill	23,490 00
Cameron, Joyce & Co., Keokuk, Iowa	22,949 00
Grohne Contracting Co., Joliet, Ill	19,330 00
Chas. H. Hammann, Geneseo, Ill	23,500 00
Rees Bros., Quincy, Ill	23,112 00
Porter, McCully Const. Co., Mackinaw, Ill	22,400 00
McCarthy Imp. Co., Davenport, Iowa	22,400 00

The contract was awarded to Grohne Contracting Company.

MCHENRY COUNTY—SECTIONS C, D, E, AND F—ROUTES 11, 3, 15 AND 12.

Length, 9,000 feet; width, 15 feet; type, concrete; engineer's estimate, $14,836.00; date of letting, May 20, 1915.

Name of bidder.	Amount of bid.
Bloodgood & Summerville, Harvey, Ill	$12,220 00
Thos. H. Cutler & Company, Gary, Ind	12,100 00
Cullen, Friestedt & Co., Chicago, Ill	14,742 00
F. E. Ball & Co., Hampshire, Ill	13,500 00
Ajax Const. & Engr. Co., Gary, Ind	14,320 00
C. A. Williston, Chicago, Ill	11,370 00
Booth, Nicholson & Gilchrist, Gardner, Ill	13,979 00
C. W. Jensen & Co., Chicago, Illinois	13,485 00
Ill. Hydraulic Stone & Const. Co., Elgin, Ill.	13,733 00
Rees Bros., Quincy, Ill	12,676 00
Logan Giertz Const. Co., Elgin, Ill	14,250 00

The contract was awarded to C. A. Williston.

EDWARDS COUNTY—SECTION A—ROUTE 1.

Length, 2,100 feet; width, 10 feet; type, gravel; engineer's estimate, $2,767.00; date of letting, May 20, 1915.

Name of bidder.	Amount of bid.
G. W. & G. C. Morgan, Carmi, Ill	$2,724 00

The contract was awarded to G. W. & G. C. Morgan.

MARION COUNTY—SECTION A—BRIDGES.

Engineer's estimate, $5,950.00; date of letting, May 20, 1915.

Name of bidder.	Amount of bid.
H. H. Linder, Centralia, Ill	$6,370 00
L. C. Kesler, Herrick, Ill	5,736 00
F. S. Nichols, Flora, Ill	5,650 00

The contract was awarded to F. S. Nichols.

MARION COUNTY—SECTION C—BRIDGES.

Engineer's estimate, $1,200.00; date of letting, May 20, 1915.

Name of bidder.	Amount of bid.
Parham Const. Co., East St. Louis, Ill	$1,143 00
H. H. Linder, Centralia, Ill	1,094 00
L. C. Kesler, Herrick, Ill	1,180 00
M. R. McCall, Sandoval, Ill	970 00
R. A. Medaris Const. Co., Springfield, Ill	1,150 00

The contract was awarded to M. R. McCall.

MARION COUNTY—SECTION B—ROUTE 7.

Length, 4,600 feet, width, 10 feet; type, concrete; engineer's estimate, $5,661.00; date of letting, May 20, 1915.

Name of bidder.	Amount of bid.
Voght Concrete Co., Salem, Ill.	$5,552 00
Collins & Pavey, Mt. Vernon, Ill.	5,445 00
P. M. Johnston & Co., St. Elmo, Ill.	4,940 00
H. H. Hall Const. Co., East St. Louis, Ill.	4,890 00

The contract was awarded to H. H. Hall Const. Co.

SCHUYLER COUNTY—SECTION B—ROAD AND BRIDGE.

Length, 100 feet; width, 10 feet; type, concrete; engineer's estimate, $1,154.36; date of letting, May 20, 1915.

Name of bidder.	Amount of bid.
Zastrow & Lashmet, Jacksonville, Ill.	$1,054 00

The contract was awarded to Zastrow & Lashmet.

ST. CLAIR COUNTY—SECTION A—ROUTE 14.

Length, 9,000 feet; width, 15 feet; type, concrete; engineer's estimate, $20,942.00; date of letting, May 26, 1915.

Name of bidder.	Amount of bid.
Rees Bros., Quincy, Ill.	$18,249 00
H. H. Hall Const. Co., East St. Louis, Ill.	16,900 00
Cameron, Joyce & Co., Keokuk, Iowa	20,126 00
Walter Coonan, East St. Louis, Ill.	20,295 00
Hoeffken Bros., Belleville, Ill.	20,418 50
Bloodgood & Summerville, Harvey, Ill.	18,990 00
Renkel Construction Co., St. Louis, Mo.	18,887 00
Thos. H. Cutler Co., Gary, Ind.	17,333 00
Candy & McElroy, Robinson, Ill.	18,990 00
Gass Bros., Belleville, Ill.	19,950 00
Dunlap, Dippold Co., Edwardsville, Ill.	19,800 00
Meyer & Thomas Con. Co., East St. Louis, Ill.	19,965 00
Hiram Lloyd Bldg. & Con. Co., St. Louis, Mo.	20,500 00
Louie Rich, East St. Louis, Ill.	17,548 00

The contract was awarded to H. H. Hall Construction Company.

MARSHALL COUNTY—SECTION B—ROUTE 2.

Length, 2,600 feet, width, 10 feet; type, concrete; engineer's estimate, $5,380.56; date of letting, May 26, 1915.

Name of bidder.	Amount of bid.
Rees Bros., Quincy, Ill.	$5,200 00
Ajax Const. & Eng. Co., Gary, Ind.	4,395 00
Frank Burke, Chicago, Ill.	5,190 00
Bloodgood & Summerville, Harvey, Ill.	4,881 00
Gary Construction Co., Gary, Ind.	4,747 00

The contract was awarded to Ajax Construction & Engineering Company.

CALHOUN COUNTY—SECTION A—ROUTE 1.

Length, 1,920 feet; width, 12 feet; type, macadam; engineer's estimate, $2,340.00; date of letting, May 26, 1915.

Name of bidder.	Amount of bid.
Rees Bros., Quincy, Ill.	$2,000 00

The contract was awarded to Rees Bros.

MARSHALL COUNTY—SECTION C—BRIDGES.

Engineer's estimate, $6,490.00; date of letting, May 26, 1915.

Name of bidder.	Amount of bid.
Capperune & Deyo, Bradford, Ill.	$5,972 00
R. A. Culliman, Tremont, Ill.	6,258 00

Name of bidder.	Amount of bid.
R. A. Medaris Const. Co., Springfield, Ill.	$6,400 00
D. M. Dean, Lacon, Ill.	6,200 00

The contract was awarded to Capperune & Deyo.

KANE COUNTY—SECTION B—ROUTE 1.

Length, 96 feet; width, 18 feet; type, concrete and bridge; engineer's estimate, $2,436.58; date of letting, May 26, 1915.

Name of bidder.	Amount of bid.
W. E. Cummings, Geneva, Ill.	$2,237 00

The contract was awarded to W. E. Cummings.

BRIDGE WORK.

During the month of May, 1915, plans and specifications for 135 bridges were prepared and sent to County Superintendents of Highways or to County Clerks; total estimated cost $115,457.00.

Contracts were awarded for eighty-five (85) concrete bridges and four (4) steel bridges, at an average cost of 89½ per cent of the estimates; total estimated cost, $58,284.00.

The date of letting was set for ninety-eight (98) bridges, having a total estimated cost of $68,141.00.

Thirty-five (35) bridge plans, prepared by County Superintendents, were checked and approved.

On June 1, 1915, there were 137 bridge inspection reports on hand ready for work; 63 of these being practically completed and ready to send out.

LABORATORY WORK.

During the month of May, 306 samples of miscellaneous materials were submitted to the laboratory for testing purposes, and a large number of requests were received in regard to the quality and suitability of various materials which have been tested in the past. Owing to the large amount of work on hand, it has been impossible to examine all the materials submitted up to date, but with a few exceptions all tests have been reported within ten days or two weeks after the samples were received. As a general rule, the samples are tested in the order received, and whenever possible, samples should be forwarded in time to allow two (2) weeks for testing purposes.

BLUE PRINTING.

During the month of May, 1915, 79 blue prints were made of our bridge standards for county superintendents of highways, as well as prints for three foreign bridge plans averaging two sheets, six prints being made of each sheet, or about 36 prints. Prints were made of 15 bridges designed by this department, 20 sets each, as well as three preliminary sets being sent to the various counties for their use in letting said bridges, totaling 690 prints. Preliminary prints were also made of 19 bridges designed by this department for use of county boards, three sets being made of each, or 115 prints.

There was also printed six prints each of the various townships (averaging 14) in four counties of the State, or about 336 prints.

Preliminary prints were made for 15 sections of State-aid work for the county board to pass on, official prints then being made for county clerk, county superintendent, and this office. Each section averages about 12 sheets, making a total of 720 prints.

Miscellaneous prints, about 600 made for office use, made a grand total for the month of May of 2,576 prints.

Very truly yours,

WM. W. MARR.
Chief State Highway Engineer.

ESTIMATING CURVES FOR HIGHWAY BRIDGES.

[By G. F. BURCH, *Assistant Bridge Engineer, Illinois Highway Department.*]

In any organized system of bridge work, it is found that the major part of the work lies between certain limits. The range of the work, and the determination of the limits within which the great bulk of the work is confined is dependent upon the organization and the class of work handled.

In highway bridge work, the length of spans required ranges from a lower limit of about six feet to an upper limit of perhaps one hundred fifty to one hundred

Plate No. 1.

A TYPICAL RIVETED PONY TRUSS WITH CONCRETE FLOOR.

sixty feet. Abutments of several different types are required, ranging in height from eight to thirty feet. There are of course many bridges having a total length of more than one hundred sixty feet, but most of them are made up of a number of spans which fall within the limits before mentioned.

A number of modern highway organizations have adopted so-called standard plans of bridges, and, so far as possible, have plans for all span lengths and heights of abutments ordinarily required within the range of work undertaken.

The adoption of standard plans greatly facilitates the process of preparing estimates. Having a standard basis upon which to work, the field man and the office man work more closely in harmony with each other, and the personal equation, which is always to be reckoned with when many men are working on one project, is controlled to such an extent that uniform results are obtained.

The preparation of estimates is of equal importance to both the field man and the office man, but it is the field man who most needs convenient and reasonably accurate data upon which to base his estimates. He also is often called upon to prepare an estimate on short notice, upon the accuracy of which a great deal may depend. On the other hand, the office man usually has more leisure in preparing his estimates, and he has the office files at hand upon which to base his judgment.

The cost of labor and materials must be determined for each and every job and cannot be estimated by any set rule. But the quantities of materials required for any job can be estimated very closely by means of tables or curves, especially if plans are standardized.

The curves given in this paper deal with quantities only, and are intended primarily for use in the field. The data on which these curves are based was compiled from

the bridge plans prepared by the Illinois Highway Department during the past eight years. Some four hundred and fifty plotted points were used in determining the curves, each point representing a standard plan, or a plan based on a standard type of construction. When these curves are used for plans based on the Illinois Highway Department standards, the maximum error for superstructures is only about three and one-half per cent, and for substructures about five per cent.

SUPERSTRUCTURES.

In all of the superstructure curves, the span length is plotted directly against the weight of steel and cubic yards of concrete.

Steel Trusses.—The steel truss superstructures are of the ordinary Pratt truss type with parallel chords. All connections are riveted and the designs provide for a four-inch concrete floor, with a wearing surface or pavement assumed to weigh not less than fifty pounds per square foot. On account of the weight and rigidity of the concrete floor, no allowance is made for impact. Floor systems are designed to carry a 15 ton traction engine in addition to the dead load. Trusses are designed to carry a uniform live load of one hundred pounds per square foot of roadway surface for spans of from fifty to one hundred and fifty feet, and a uniform load of eighty-five pounds for spans over one hundred and fifty feet. Tension members are designed for a stress of sixteen thousand pounds per square inch. Compression members are designed for a stress of sixteen thousand—70 1/r pounds per square inch, but not to exceed fourteen thousand pounds per square inch. Pony trusses are used for spans from fifty to eighty-five feet and through trusses for spans from ninety to one hundred and sixty feet. (Plate No. 1 illustrates a typical pony truss with concrete floor on reinforced concrete abutments. Plate No. 2 illustrates a through Pratt truss having a span of one hundred and fifty feet.) Figure I gives the curves for the weight of structural steel, and cubic yards of con-

Plate No. 2.

RIVETED THROUGH PRATT TRUSS WITH CONCRETE FLOOR.

crete in floors for sixteen and eighteen-foot roadways. The break in the steel curves is at the point where the change is made from low trusses to high trusses.

Reinforced Concrete Through Girders.—Reinforced concrete through girders are used for spans from thirty to sixty feet. This type of structure is designed to carry either a uniform load of one hundred and twenty-five pounds per square foot or an engine load of twenty-four tons. The design provides for a wearing surface weighing fifty pounds per square foot.

As free expansion and contraction are allowed by the cast iron rockers placed under each girder at one end of the span, the allowable unit stresses used are quite high. Designs are figured for a steel stress of sixteen thousand pounds per square inch and a compression stress of approximately one thousand pounds per square inch in concrete. A maximum unit shear of one hundred twenty pounds per square inch is allowed. Stirrups are provided for all shear in excess of forty pounds per square inch. Figure II shows curves giving the quanti-

Plate No. 3.

REINFORCED CONCRETE THROUGH GIRDER BRIDGE—SPAN 60 FEET—ROADWAY 18 FEET.

ties of concrete and reinforcing steel for sixteen, eighteen and twenty-foot roadways.

Reinforced Concrete Slabs.—For spans less than thirty feet, the slab type of construction has been found to be somewhat cheaper than the girder type. This is due to the fact that the arrangment of the steel is much simpler and less steel is used per cubic yard of concrete. It has not been found practicable to make provision for free expansion of slabs. Accordingly, a stress of twelve thousand pounds per square inch of reinforcing steel is allowed for dead and live load stresses. The concrete stress is eight hundred pounds per square inch. Slabs are designed for the same live loads as girders.

Figure III gives the quantities of concrete and steel in slabs having clear roadways of sixteen, eighteen, twenty and twenty-four feet, for spans from five to thirty feet.

SUBSTRUCTURES.

In preparing curves to show the quantities in abutments, it was found that there were many variables which might be considered, but which, if used, would produce so complex a formula as to make the curves of little use in the field. It was found that curves giving reliable results might be obtained by plotting cubic yards of concrete in two abutments against a formula which represents a measure of the quantities desired. The variables in this formula are H, the height of abutments from bottom of foundations to top of roadway; R, the clear width of roadway on the superstructure; W, the length of the average wing wall. For plain concrete abutments, the best results were obtained by using the formula $H^2 (R + 2W)$ and for reinforced abutments the formula $H (R + 2W)$.

Plain Concrete Abutments.—Plain concrete abutments for steel bridges are designed with a footing width of one-third of the height over all. The thickness of the footing is usually 18 to 24 inches. The width of the base of the abutment and wing walls at the top of the footing is made approximately one-quarter of the height of the walls. The back of the abutment wall is vertical and the

face of the wall is battered to a top width of thirty to thirty-eight inches. The wing walls are battered on both sides and have a top width of twelve inches. Figure IV shows the curves from which the yardage of plain concrete abutments for steel bridges may be obtained. When field measurements are made to determine the necessary height of abutments, and the width of roadway is decided upon, it is an easy matter to estimate the length of wing-walls which will be required. These figures are used in the formula $H^2 (R + 2W)$ and the yardage of concrete is read directly from the curve.

The design of plain concrete abutments for girder bridges, is similar to the design for steel bridges, except that the wing walls are battered on the face side only, and the top width of the abutment wall is eighteen inches. Figure V presents the curve from which quantities for this type of abutment are obtained.

Plain concrete abutments for slab bridges differ slightly from the design given before. The width of footing on the abutment wall is limited only by the safe bearing capacity of the soil, with a minimum of three feet. This width may sometimes be less than one-third of the height over all. This is deemed to be safe on account of the restraining effect of the superstructure. The top width of the abutment wall is twelve inches. The curve for estimating yardage is shown in Figure VI.

Reinforced Concrete Abutments.—In reinforced concrete abutments for steel bridges the abutment walls and wing walls are designed as self-supporting walls of the cantilever type. An equivalent fluid pressure of fifteen pounds per cubic foot is assumed in designing and to correspond with the fluid pressure the width of footings is made one-third of the height over all. The thickness of footings is made the same as the thickness of the walls at the top of the footings with a minimum of eighteen inches. Abutment and wing walls are constructed with

Plate No. 4.

TYPICAL REINFORCED CONCRETE SLAB BRIDGE WITH TIED-BACK WINGS.

a vertical back, the bottom thickness varies from fifteen to twenty-four inches, and the face of the wall is battered uniformly to a top width of twelve inches on wing walls and ten inches on abutments. The allowable stress in reinforcing steel is sixteen thousand pounds per square inch. On account of the difficulty of placing steel in substructure work, the percentage of steel used is very low, varying from three to five-tenths of one per cent, with a correspondingly low concrete stress.

To provide sufficient bearing area for the shoes of the steel span, the thickness of the wall at the juncture of the wing and abutment is increased to give a post effect. Between the posts on which the shoes rest, and

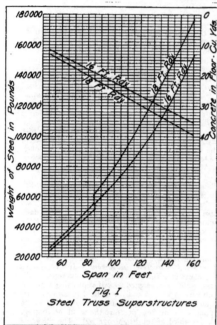

Fig. I
Steel Truss Superstructures

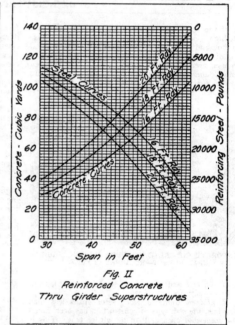

Fig. II
Reinforced Concrete
Thru Girder Superstructures

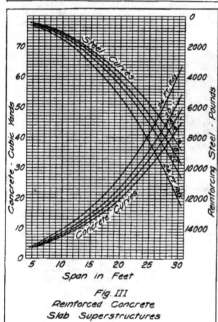

Fig. III
Reinforced Concrete
Slab Superstructures

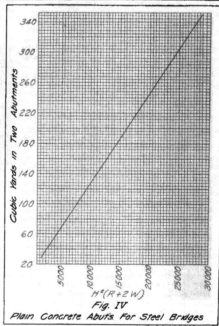

Fig. IV
Plain Concrete Abuts. For Steel Bridges

at the proper elevation, is constructed a reinforced slab on which the end joists of the span are supported. As in all other reinforced abutments, horizontal steel is provided in the walls to take temperature stresses and to insure mutual support between wing walls and the abutment. One-half inch square bars spaced twelve inches centers are provided for this purpose. Figure VII shows the curve for obtaining the cubic yards of concrete in two abutments, the yardage being plotted against the formula H (R + 2W).

For girder bridges, two new types of reinforced abutments have been developed in the last few years. In both types, the abutment wall is designed as a horizontal slab supported by the wings. The main reinforcement is placed horizontally near the stream side of the wall, and is securely anchored in the wings. The temperature steel in this case in placed vertically. The thickness of the wall varies with the height and width of roadway, and ranges from twelve to eighteen inches. The width of footing is proportional to the load supported. Pockets are built in one abutment wall to receive the rockers which allow free movement of the superstructure. In one type of construction, the wing walls are designed as self-supporting cantilevers to withstand a fluid pressure of fifteen pounds. The main reinforcement is placed vertically near the back side of the walls and also near the top of the footings.

In the other type of reinforced abutments for girder bridges, the wing walls, which make only a slight angle with the axis of the road are designed as vertical slabs. The bottom of the wall is restrained by the earth and the top of the wall is restrained by the struts which connect one wing wall to the other across the roadway. The principal reinforcement is vertical and is placed near the side of the wall opposite to the fill. Stress is transmitted from the vertical slab to the struts through a horizontal T beam in the wing wall at the elevation of the struts. The steel in the struts is hooked around the T beam steel. The thickness of the wing walls ranges from twelve to twenty-four inches according to the height. Figure VIII shows the curves for estimating the yardage in these two types of abutments, the upper curve being for the cantilevered wing wall type, and the lower curve for the tied-back type. In comparing the amount of concrete required in these two types of abutments, it must be remembered that for any particular case, the length of wing walls required for the tied-back type is greater than is required for the cantilever type of wing, on account of the fact that the earth slope is all on the outside of the wing.

For slab bridges, there are also two distinct types of reinforced abutments. The wing walls are of the same construction as those just described for girder bridges. As no provision is made for movement between the superstructure and the substructure of slab bridges, due to temperature changes, the restraining effect of the superstructure load is taken into account in the design of the abutment wall. The wall is designed as a vertical slab with the main reinforcement placed near the stream face of the wall. The thickness of wall ranges from twelve to twenty-four inches. The footing is designed to distribute the load over the foundation without exceeding the safe bearing capacity of the soil. Figure IX shows the curves for obtaining the cubic yards of concrete in each of the two types of abutments.

To illustrate the use of the estimating curves, suppose that upon measuring up the site for a new bridge, it is found that a clear span of fifty feet will provide adequate waterway. The height from finished roadway to bed of stream is eight feet, and by carrying the footings four feet below the bed of stream, good foundation material is encountered. This makes the height over all, from finished roadway to bottom of footings, twelve feet. Also assume that the traffic on the road demands a twenty-foot roadway, and that good gravel may be obtained at reasonable cost one-half mile from the site. Referring to Figure II, we see that a reinforced concrete through girder superstructure having a span of fifty feet and twenty-foot roadway contains about ninety-six cubic yards of concrete and twenty-three thousand pounds of steel. The abutments being comparatively low and the

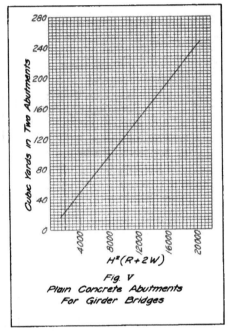

Fig. V
Plain Concrete Abutments
For Girder Bridges

cost of gravel very reasonable, it is probably safe to assume that plain concrete abutments will be cheaper than reinforced. Referring to Figure V, in order to use the curve we must determine the value of the formula $H^2 (R + 2W)$. H, the height over all, is known to be twelve feet and R, the roadway is twenty feet. We will assume that the wings should make an angle of 45 degrees with the face of the abutment; also that the toe of the earth slope around the wing must stop at the elevation of the stream bed and in line with the face of the abutment. As the height from finished roadway to bed of stream is 8 feet, a wing wall 8 feet long will be sufficient to protect the roadway with an earth slope of 1½ to 1. Substituting these values for H, R and W, we find that $H^2 (R + 2W)$ equals 5,184. Entering the curve we find that there are about 62 cubic yards in the abutments. Adding, we find that the job

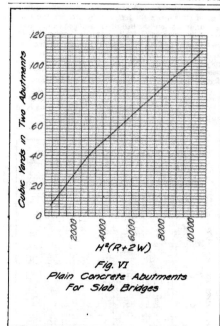

Fig. VI
Plain Concrete Abutments
For Slab Bridges

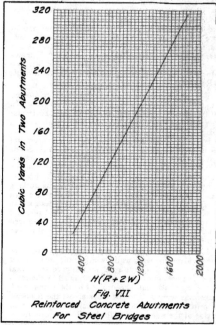

Fig. VII
Reinforced Concrete Abutments
For Steel Bridges

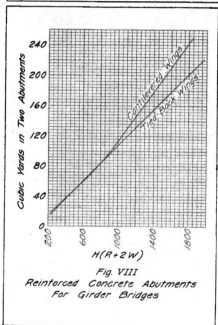

Fig. VIII
Reinforced Concrete Abutments
For Girder Bridges

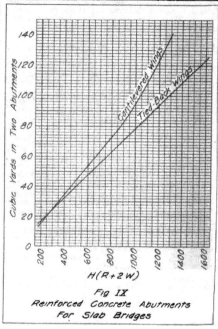

Fig IX
Reinforced Concrete Abutments
For Slab Bridges

has a total of 158 cubic yards of concrete and 23,000 pounds of steel. Upon ascertaining the local prices for labor and materials, an estimate can be made of the cost of the job which will compare very favorably with an estimate made after the complete plans are prepared.

The object of this paper has been to show what can be done by way of giving the field engineer definite information from which he can prepare reliable estimates. Curves of this nature have been in use by the Illinois Highway Department for a number of years, and the idea can easily be applied to any system of bridge work in which standard plans are employed.

BETTER ROADS.

[Address Delivered Before the Rural Letter Carriers of Whiteside County, Illinois, by V. N. TAGGETT, County Superintendent of Highways.]

I know that you are all good roads boosters, for anyone who travels 25 or 30 miles on country roads six days every week in the year cannot help but be a good road advocate; so I shall not try to arouse your interest in the movement. I could cite data and figures showing you how much bad roads cost the people of Illinois by adding to the wear and tear on wagons, buggies, horses, harnesses and automobiles, to say nothing of the additional time that is lost in getting through bad roads, but you know all those costs from experience. The thing that you are interested in is not "Do good roads pay?" for you already know that they do, but the all-important question is "How are we going to get them?" and "What can I do to help in the work?" The only way to bring about an improvement of any sort is to keep agitating it. There are some people in this county who do not know what good roads are. I do not mean that they have not seen improved roads, and, in fact, used them, but what I mean is that they cannot conceive of having a good road from their home to market. All of their good road ideas are abstract and have to do with some improvement miles away from their home. When every one in a certain locality is alive to the movement, then that locality will get better roads. Of course, we can hardly hope that every crossroad will ever be a boulevard, paved with some hard surface, but all of our main market roads will soon be improved so that they will be 365-day roads; that is, good the year round, while all public roads will be maintained in a decent condition.

One criticism that is often heard of the present tendency in Illinois is that we are spending too much of the money in very limited areas. Possibly it is a just one; I am not prepared to say at this time, although I could have answered a year ago. It is true that there are always certain bad places in remote locations that demand attention and repair from time to time, but the logical and natural method of improving roads is to commence at the centers of population and market places, and gradually work out in all directions. In this way the greatest number of people are served, for ten to twenty rigs will use the road near town for every one that uses the road out six or eight miles from town. The plan of the State Highway Department is to have all State-aid roads paved within the next 15 years. These State-aid roads, by the way, are the market roads of the county, constituting one-fifth of all our roads. These roads were selected by our county board of supervisors, after a careful study of all our roads.

It is hardly probable that any of our townships will do any extensive so-called permanent road construction, so here is the field for grading and dragging dirt roads, and using gravel freely. Here, too, is the chance for you rural carriers to do some missionary work. You, who are on the roads every day, know what consistent dragging will do with a common dirt road, and you also readily observe the difference when you strike a piece of gravel. As you go over your route and meet your patrons, just remind them of the excellent piece of road up by the schoolhouse or drop the information that Mr. So-and-so has been out with his split-log drag. It will not be very long, in most cases, until they all fall into line and boost for better roads.

Another way in which you carriers can cooperate in bettering the road conditions is to notify the highway commissioners or myself of bad places, holes, washouts, rough places and of improper or careless dragging, as you observe them along your routes from day to day. I am sure that every commissioner will appreciate your letting him know these conditions that need his attention, for these men are all primarily interested in serving the people by getting results. As I said before, the only way to get these results is by cooperation. A community can only progress by the united effort of all. Perhaps we cannot always agree as to the best method of procedure, but, of course, these differences will have to be settled as they arise.

Now, in order to get better roads for Whiteside County, I want you rural mail carriers to always feel free to call my attention to any conditions which you believe need to be remedied. In fact, I want you to feel that it is your duty to do it.

TOWNSHIP ROAD REPAIRS.

Bridgeport Township; Lawrence County.

The following cost data was taken from road repairs made in Bridgeport Township, Lawrence County, on an old macadam road that was constructed five years ago.

The old macadam road had worn down into ruts, and it was necessary to scarify the surface for a depth of about 6 inches, reshape the old stone and apply a light application of bonding gravel. After this was done, the road was rolled and thrown open to traffic.

FINAL COST REPORT ON REPAIRS.

Bridgeport road, Bridgeport Township, Lawrence County.

CONDITIONS.

Contractor's profit and overhead charges not included; amount of road repaired, 3,900 feet, 5,200 square yards. Width of road, 12 feet; width of repairs, 12 feet. Length of haul on materials, ½ mile. Total material used, 288 cubic yards. Rate of pay, men, 20 cents; teams, 40 cents per hour. Work began, April 16; work completed, April 26, 1915.

COST OF LABOR AND MATERIALS.

	Total.	Square yard.
Scarifying old road	$ 15 43	$.003
Gravel, 288 cubic yards @ $.975 F. O. B.	281 15	.054
Hauling gravel, 288 cubic yards @ $.50	144 00	.027
Incidental hauling	6 75	.002
Spreading stone and screenings	94 00	.018
Rolling and sprinkling	30 36	.006
Total cost	$571 69	$.110

BEECHER ROAD—WASHINGTON TOWNSHIP—WILL COUNTY.

The following cost data was taken from work done on the Beecher roads, Washington Township, Will County.

About 13 miles of waterbound macadam road were constructed at Beecher during the year 1914, under the supervision of this Department, using convict labor. On account of having to construct the macadam roads as one course construction ten inches thick, it was impossible to get them thoroughly rolled. The work was finished during freezing weather, which also prevented additional rolling that was intended. There was also a shortage in the supply of water during the summer of 1914, that prevented proper flushing. For the above reasons, together with the poor bonding screenings that were used, it was expected that considerable raveling of the surface would take place and that additional rolling and screenings would be required this spring.

The last two miles that were constructed at this point showed a few ruts this spring, the balance of the road had a few loose stones scattered her and there over the surface, with occasional places raveling out and the entire surface loosened.

The entire road, excepting about four miles, was thoroughly rolled and the necessary bonding screenings added to make a tight and uniform surface.

It will be noted that the cost of the repairs was very light. The rolling that was done on the road this spring has, without question, proved to be of as much, if not more, benefit than if the same amount of work had been done on the roads last fall.

FINAL COST REPORT ON REPAIRS.

CONDITIONS.

Contractor's profit and overhead charges not included; amount of road repaired, 50,160 feet, 59,708 square yards. Width of road, 10 feet, 15 feet and 20 feet; width of repairs, 10 feet, 15 feet and 20 feet. Average length of haul on materials, 2 miles. Total material used, 278 cubic yards. Rate of pay, men, 20 cents; teams 50 cents per hour. Work began, March 26; work completed, May 8, 1915.

COST OF LABOR AND MATERIALS.

	Total.	Square yard
Stone or gravel, 278 cubic yards @ $1.05 F. O. B. Beecher	$291 90	$.0049
Hauling stone	271 80	.0045
Spreading stone and screenings	107 80	.0018
Rolling and sprinkling	166 00	.0028
Total cost	$837 50	$.0140

NARROWING OF OUR COUNTRY HIGHWAYS.

[By A. B. Hurd, County Superintendent of Highways, Woodford County.]

Highway commissioners are asking to narrow certain roads to a width of 40 feet. Is it a wise thing to do, and, if so, why?

If these requests had been made 50 years ago, when we were driving the old ox teams, or 25 years ago, when all traffic upon our highways was horsedrawn, moving at six to ten miles per hour, it might have been wise; but today, with the automobile dashing along the highways at 40 miles per hour, driven many times by one whose entire mind is fixed upon his destination, is it not a different proposition? Do you like the nerve shock when an auto goes thundering by with just a hair's breadth between you? What does the horsedrawn vehicle have? They are fortunate if they have a level road and can give the car wide berth. Many people, who have been in favor of narrow roads, change their minds after having one of these heart throbs, caused by a frightened horse, or having been hit by a careless driver.

A member of the State Highway Department said that they regretted beyond measure, that this law was ever placed upon our statutes, and on July 1, 1914, they passed the following resolution:

"Resolved, that it is the sense of this Commission that the standard width of the right-of-way of State-aid roads be at least fifty (50) feet, and that no State-aid road be reduced to a less width. We trust you will be governed by the spirit of this resolution."

The width of our finished hard road is 30 feet, viz., 10 feet of concrete in the center, 4 feet of crushed rock on either side, and 6 feet of earth shoulders outside of the crushed rock. On each side of this we have the ditches and sidewalks.

In order that a ditch may be economically maintained, its width at top should be four times its depth at center. The law for grading roads requires that one-tenth of width of road be left on each fence line for a walk. Now, see how this figures out for a 40-foot road. Thirty feet of road, four feet on each side for a walk and one foot on each side for a ditch. This would allow a ditch 12 inches wide and 3 inches deep. Is this ditch all that is required at any point along the road?

To narrow a 66-foot road to 40 feet is giving away three and one-eighth acres of land per mile. At $250 per acre, $780 per mile, $9,360 on the twelve miles narrowed last year, and $10,920 on the fourteen miles now petitioned for. What does the township, what do the taxpayers not fronting on the roads to be narrowed, what do the unborn generations receive for this present? All they can justly claim is that they do not have to mow weeds on the road given away, provided all move their fences out. At the September meeting of the Illinois State Association of Highway Commissioners, held at Joliet, they passed a resolution, which, if it becomes a law, will do away with the weed nuisance. It reads as follows:

"Be it resolved, that a law be enacted which will absolutely require all land owners to cut all grass and weeds, grub all willows and remove all rubbish from the road abutting their land, and along fences adjoining the highway opposite such land."

With this law upon our statute books, there is no benefit to be claimed for the township and there are many reasons why they should not be narrowed.

Most of the townships road tile and open road ditches are more than 20 feet from the center of the road. If a farmer builds his fence outside the open ditch, he will allow the ditch to fill as fast as possible and the township will have to grade a new ditch outside the new fence line, an expense which all taxpayers must bear alike. The township must also bear the expense of surveying the road narrowed, unless arrangements are made otherwise.

Sum up these points and answer the question:
"Is it wise to narrow our roads to 40 feet?"

SCHNEPP & BARNES, STATE PRINTERS—ILLINOIS, 1915.

ILLINOIS HIGHWAYS

[Printed by authority of the State of Illinois.]

STATE HIGHWAY DEPARTMENT

| VOL. 2 | SPRINGFIELD, ILLINOIS, JULY, 1915 | No. 7 |

CHURCH STREET ROAD—GIBSON CITY, ILLINOIS.
Bituminous Macadam Road Built 1911. Picture Taken Spring 1915. Entire Surface in Good Condition, with no Maintenance to Date.

ROCKFORD TOWNSHIP—WINNEBAGO COUNTY.
Macadam Road 15 Years Old. Surface Oiled With Montezuma Crude Oil.

ILLINOIS HIGHWAYS.

Published Monthly by the

State Highway Department.

ILLINOIS HIGHWAY COMMISSION.

A. D. GASH, *President*.

S. E. BRADT, *Secretary*.

JAMES P. WILSON.

WM. W. MARR, *Chief State Highway Engineer*.
P. C. McARDLE, *Assistant State Highway Engineer*.

H. E. BILGER, *Road Engineer, Springfield, Illinois*.
C. OLDER, *Bridge Engineer, Springfield, Illinois*.
B. H. PIEPMEIER, *Assistant Engineer, Springfield, Illinois*.
G. F. BURCH, *Assistant Engineer, Springfield, Illinois*.
M. W. WATSON, *Assistant Engineer, Springfield, Illinois*.
F. L. ROMAN, *Testing Engineer, Springfield, Illinois*.
J. M. McCOY, *Chief Clerk, Springfield, Illinois*.

DIVISION ENGINEERS.

H. B. Bushnell..............Aurora
R. L. Bell....................Paris
H. E. Surman..........Rock Island
A. H. Hunter..............Peoria
Fred Tarrant............Springfield
C. M. Slaymaker........E. St. Louis
J. E. Huber................Marion

CONTENTS.

ROAD APPROPRIATIONS—CHANGES IN THE ROAD LAW—GOOD WORK DONE BY THE LEGISLATURE JUST ADJOURNED.

[By S. E. BRADT, Secretary, State Highway Commission.]

That the people of this State are back of the good roads movement and are determined to "pull Illinois out of the mud" is again evidenced by the work of the Forty-ninth General Assembly.

The Tice Road Law as originally passed was fundamentally sound and laid the foundation for the great improvement that is sure to come; nevertheless it has been broadened and strengthened by the work of this Legislature. This, together with the increased appropriations, will result in the greatest progress in road construction that has ever been seen in Illinois.

COUNTY BOARD DETERMINES TYPE OF ROAD.

Section 9 was amended by placing with the county boards of the various counties the duty of determining the type of road to be constructed in their respective counties, i. e., whether an earth road, a gravel, macadam, concrete or brick road. This is the only feature in connection with road legislation passed by this General Assembly that is looked upon by the advocates of economic road construction as being out of line with progressive road work.

The State Highway Department, with its force of technically-trained men, its experience and the information at its command, is better equipped than any county can be to determine the most economical type of road to be built to meet the requirements of the local traffic. In general, a central authority is necessary to prevent the recurrence of the same mistakes in many different counties, which inevitably result when the counties act independently and without the benefit of the knowledge gained by experience elsewhere.

Because of the urgent demand for the immediate improvement of the roads, the county boards in some counties will be obliged to construct a large mileage of cheaper first-cost roads regardless of future maintenance cost, rather than a less mileage of more permanent roads economically adapted to the traffic which they will be called upon to carry. While this will result in a financial loss, because of heavy maintenance and rebuilding costs, it has a large measure of compensation in serving a greater number of people. As these roads wear out, demand will come for a more permanent type of construction at which time we will have had a larger experience, both in traffic requirements and the ability of different road materials, to withstand that traffic.

COUNTY MUST PUBLISH COST OF DIFFERENT TYPES.

The amendment provides for giving the public full information as to the cost of the different types of construction before the county board decides that question, and further requires that all State aid roads shall be built according to the plans and specifications and under the supervision of the State Highway Department.

COUNTY PAYS FOR MAINTENANCE OF EARTH ROADS.

This amendment provides further that where an earth road is constructed the county shall pay the cost of maintenance, and that where a gravel or macadam road is constructed the county shall pay one-half the cost of maintenance and the State one-half. This change in the maintenance feature of the law removes the only objection raised by the State Highway Commission to the building of earth roads with permanent culverts and proper drainage under the law as originally passed. Had the 1913 law contained this same maintenance provision, which will permit the construction of earth roads, every one of the 102 counties of the State would have accepted State aid, instead of only 92 counties.

COOK COUNTY MAY BUILD STATE AID ROADS THROUGH CITIES AND VILLAGES.

Section 9 was also amended at the request of Cook County, permitting the construction of State aid roads through cities and villages of 20,000 or fewer inhabitants. This will relieve the situation in Cook County where villages, often financially unable to improve their roads, are found at intervals of every few miles.

MAY CALL SPECIAL ELECTION TO VOTE ON BOND ISSUES.

The next important change is the addition of a new section, known as 15 (D). Under the original Tice Law, counties were empowered to issue bonds upon an affirmative vote of the people of the county, but this vote could be taken only at a general county election which occurred every second year. The new section provides for the calling of a special election where so desired, also requires that the bonds shall mature serially and all within 20 years; further, that the roads shall be built according to the plans and specifications and under the supervision of the State Highway Department and when completed shall become State aid roads to be maintained by the State.

COUNTIES MAY USE STATE ALLOTMENT TO PAY OFF BONDS.

One of the most important provisions of this amendment is that where any county has constructed all or part of its system of State aid roads at its own cost that county may use its allotment of State funds toward liquidating any unpaid indebtedness incurred in the construction of said road, but not exceeding one-half of the cost of the same.

One of the criticisms of the State aid feature of the law has been that it works too slowly. Many of the people say they want the roads now rather than wait 20 or 25 years for the completion of the system. This amendment offers the counties where the people are willing to vote bonds the opportunity of building all or part of their State aid roads in three or four years, and then using the State allotment to repay a part of the bonds. In other words, the counties may advance the money to build the roads and pay the interest on the bonds for the privilege of having the roads to use now.

There is no question as to the equity of improving roads through a bond issue, provided the bonds mature serially and all within the life of the improvement. If the correct type of construction is used to meet the traffic requirements, then the taxpayer who assists in paying off the bonds gets value received each year for all he pays and is entitled to assist in paying for the improvement. This is considered to be one of the most valuable changes made in the present law.

COUNTY BOARDS MAY BUY HEAVY ROAD MACHINERY AND LEASE TO TOWNSHIPS.

To section 32 has been added sub-section (A). This change was made in the interest of the township roads and permits the county boards to take over the maintenance of the proposed system of State aid roads; also to purchase the high-priced machinery, such as tractors, levelers, steam rollers, etc., and lease them to the townships for the improvement of the township roads. It is apparent that but few townships can afford to own this class of machinery, but under this provision the county can own it and all of the townships can receive the benefit.

COUNTY BOARDS MAY ACCEPT DONATIONS AND PAY MORE THAN ONE-HALF THE COST.

Section 29 (A) has been added by this Legislature and permits county boards to accept donations from cities, villages, corporations and individuals for the purpose of improving the State aid road system, and through this donation or otherwise to elect to pay more than one-half the cost of improvement of any section of State aid road.

The law formerly held rigidly to the payment of one-half of the cost of any improvement by the State and one-half by the county, and although many donations were offered they could not be included in the State aid contract, except where they applied upon the county's share of the fund.

Under the amendment a donation can be accepted by the county and used in the contract to extend the road.

POLL TAX SECTION CHANGED.

The decision of the Supreme Court finding the poll tax section unconstitutional caused the re-enactment of that section (55). It was changed by leaving out the provision that the poll tax list "shall not include persons within the limits of cities or incorporated villages" and thus making it apply to residents of cities and villages as well as the residents of the county. The new section also provides that one-half of the poll tax collected from residents of a city or village shall be paid to the city or village treasurer.

ROAD DRAGGING MADE COMPULSORY.

Section 62 has been amended by requiring that $3.00 to $5.00 per mile for each mile of earth road in a township shall be set aside for road dragging purposes, and providing that this fund shall be used for that purpose and no other. The law previously provided for road dragging, but this change makes it mandatory.

LARGE SUM APPROPRIATED.

The foregoing constitute the principal changes made by the Legislature in the law. In addition, however, a very liberal appropriation was made for carrying on the work. The previous General Assembly appropriated a total of $1,100,000 of which $800,000 was from the automobile license fund and $300,000 from the general fund. This was an initial appropriation none of which was used until July, 1914. This General Assembly has appropriated $2,000,000 from the automobile license fees. This will permit us to allot to each county each year almost as much as was allotted to them for the two previous years, and means that there will be expended upon our system of State aid roads during the next two years $4,000,000.

WORK WILL BE DONE MAINLY IN 1916 AND 1917.

While allotments will be made soon after July 1, 1915, work will not begin in most counties till the spring of 1916, for the reason that the counties will not have the money available from which to appropriate an amount equal to the allotment until after the collection of the taxes next year.

WORK OF LEGISLATURE TO BE COMMENDED.

The people of Illinois want good roads and are only waiting to be told how they can get them. Every step taken by this Legislature has been along the line of increasing the facilities for carrying on this work. The people of Illinois are to be congratulated upon the good work of this General Assembly in road legislation and the members are entitled to the commendation of all believers in good roads. Special mention should be made of the work of Homer J. Tice, author of the Tice Law and chairman of the House Road and Bridge Committee, and of Adam C. Cliffe, chairman of the Senate Committee on Roads and Bridges; also Edward J. Smejkal and Edward C. Curtis, chairmen of the appropriation committees of the House and Senate, respectively.

DEPARTMENTAL REPORT.

July 1, 1915.

I submit the following report on the present condition of the work being done by the State Highway Department:

STATE AID ROAD WORK.

During the month of June, plans for State aid work were sent to the county clerks, as indicated by the following tabulation:

County.	Section.
Menard	B
LaSalle	D
Vermilion	B
Mercer	C, D & E
Saline	B
Stephenson	B
Cass	B
White	A
Stark	B & C
Woodford	B
Cumberland	A & B
Fulton	E
Wayne	A & B
Montgomery	A & B

The status of all State aid road and bridge work now under contract is indicated by the following table:

CONDITION OF STATE AID WORK JULY 1, 1915.

County.	Sec.	Per cent completed.	Note.	Contractor.	Resident engineer.
Adams.....	A	86%	....	Cameron, Joyce & Co., Keokuk, Iowa.......	C. A. Clark, 426 N. 7th st., Quincy, Ill. Phone 3817-W.
Alexander..	A	42%	....	Bland & Fitzgerald, Cairo, Ill.............	E. A. Kane, Unity, Ill.
Bond......	B	....	W. N. B.	Renkel Construction Co., Maplewood, Mo.	
Bureau....	A	81%	....	Grohne Contracting Co., Joliet, Ill........	E. L. Schwaderer, 205 E. Peru st., Princeton, Ill.
Bureau....	B	47%	....	Grohne Contracting Co., Joliet, Ill........	E. L. Schwaderer, 205 E. Peru st., Princeton, Ill.
Bureau....	C	....	....	C.W.Jensen & Co., 133 W. Wash. st., Chicago	C. W. Ross, gen. del., Princeton, Ill.
Bureau....	D	....	....	C.W.Jensen & Co., 133 W. Wash. st., Chicago	C. W. Ross, gen. del., Princeton, Ill.
Calhoun...	A	5%	....	Rees Bros., Quincy, Ill...................	Jno. A. Earley, Batchtown, Ill.
Carroll....	A	8%	N. P. L.	Gund-Graham Co., Freeport, Ill...........	S. C. Campbell, Box 216, Mt. Carroll, Ill.
Cass.......	B	....	....	John G. Pratt, Virginia, Ill.	
Clark......	A	90%	....	Robert Thompson, Marshall, Ill...........	M.W. Parrish, Martinsville, Ill.
Clinton....	A	....	W. N. B.	P. M. Johnston & Co., St. Elmo, Ill.	
Cook......	D	90%	P. C.	E. J. Mahony & Co., 526 Reaper blk., Chicago	H. M. Kleiser, 1710 Mich. av., Chicago. Phone Calumet 428.
Cook......	F	55%	....	Cullen-Friestedt Co., Tribune bldg., Chicago	O. B. Kercher, 25 Elmwood pl., LaGrange, Ill. Phone 1096-R.
Cook......	G	40%	....	Walter & Windes, Glencoe, Ill...........	A. F. Keehner, Desplaines, Ill.
Cumberland	A	(Bridges.)	W. N. B.	Candy & McElroy, Robinson, Ill.	
Cumberland	B	(Bridges.)	W. N. B.	Candy & McElroy, Robinson, Ill.	
Crawford..	A	41%	....	F. W. McElroy, Robinson, Ill.............	M.M.Small, 204 S. Howard st., Robinson, Ill. Phone 323-3.
Crawford..	B	96%	....	F. W. McElroy, Robinson, Ill.............	R. P. Devine, Box 171, Robinson, Ill.
DeKalb Ext	C	34%	....	C.W.Jensen & Co., 133 W. Wash. st., Chicago	Geo. E. Schopmeyer, 423 N. 3d st., DeKalb, Ill.
DuPage....	A	70%	....	E. J. Mahony & Co., 526 Reaper blk., Chicago.	
DuPage....	B	....	W. N. B.	Thos. H. Cutler, Gary, Ind.	
Edgar.....	C	100%	....	Allan J. Parrish, Paris, Ill.	
Edwards...	A	2%	....	G. W. & G. C. Morgan, Carmi, Ill.........	A.B.Brower, care Mrs. Harris, Albion, Ill. Phone-Albion. Wire Southern R. R. Sta.
Effingham..	A	26%	....	P. M. Johnston & Co., St. Elmo, Ill........	W. V. Cruse, 919 Park av., Effingham, Ill.

CONDITION OF STATE AID WORK—Concluded.

County.	Sec.	Per cent completed.	Note.	Contractor.	Resident engineer.
Fayette....	A	90%	....	P. M. Johnston & Co., St. Elmo, Ill.........	S. H. Phinney, care M. F. Houston, 628 Gallitan st., Vandalia, Ill.
Franklin....	B	(Bridges.)	W. N. B.	Wm. Lough & Son, Marion, Ill.	
Ford......	A	19%	....	Metz & McVay, Gary, Ind................	P. W. Freark, Roberts Hotel, Roberts, Ill.
Fulton.....	A	81%	....	Carpenter Construction Co., Cloverland, Ind.	A. K. Fogg, Canton, Ill.
Fulton.....	B	100%	....	Carpenter Construction Co., Cloverland, Ind.	E. B. Blough, 255 W. Walnut st., Canton, Ill.
Fulton.....	C	37%	....	Carpenter Construction Co., Cloverland, Ind.	E. B. Blough, 255 W. Walnut st., Canton, Ill.
Fulton.....	D	(Bridges.)	W. N. B.	Central States Bridge Co., Indianapolis, Ind.	
Fulton.....	E	(Bridges.)	W. N. B.	M. R. VanHouten, Canton, Ill.	
Gallatin....	A	(Bridges.)	W. N. B.	Wm. Lough & Son, Marion, Ill.	
Gallatin....	B	(Bridges.)	W. N. B.	Wm. Lough & Son, Marion, Ill.	
Greene....	A	(Bridges.)	W. N. B.	C. M. Hanes, Jerseyville, Ill.	
Hamilton..	A	(Bridges.)	W. N. B.	W. T. Bland, Cairo, Ill.	
Hamilton..	B	(Bridges.)	W. N. B.	W. T. Bland, Cairo, Ill.	
Hardin....	A	(Bridges.)	W. N. B.	Williams & Townsend, Marion, Ill.	
Henry.....	A	....	....	Grohne Contracting Co., Joliet, Ill.	
Henry.....	B	....	....	Grohne Contracting Co., Joliet, Ill.	
Jackson....	B	....	W. N. B.	Meyer & Thomas Const. Co., E. St. Louis, Ill.	
Jasper.....	A	(Bridges.)	W. N. B.	Candy & McElroy, Robinson, Ill.	
Jasper.....	B	(Bridges.)	W. N. B.	Candy & McElroy, Robinson, Ill.	
Jasper.....	C	(Bridges.)	W. N. B.	Candy & McElroy, Robinson, Ill.	
Jersey.....	B	(Bridges.)	W. N. B.	Herrick Construction Co., Carlinville, Ill.	
Johnson....	A	(Bridges.)	....	Montgomery, Parker Co., Hatfield, Ind......	J. P. Murphy, care C. A. Cooper, R. F. D. No. 2, Bumcombe. Ill.
JoDaviess..	A	....	W. N. B.	Empire Construction Co., DesMoines, Iowa.	
JoDaviess..	B	....	W. N. B.	Empire Construction Co., DesMoines, Iowa.	
Kane......	A	94%	....	C.W.Jensen & Co., 133 W. Wash. st., Chicago	L. R. Wheeler, Geneva, Ill
Kane......	B	....	W. N. B.	W. E. Cummings, Geneva, Ill.	
Kane......	C	....	W. N. B.	Thos. H. Cutler & Co., Gary, Ind.	
Kankakee..	B	....	W. N. B.	Bloodgood & Summerville, Harvey, Ill.	
Kendall....	A	14%	....	Booth, Nicholson & Gilchrist, Gardner, Ill...	Ezra C. Wenger, 293 N. Y. st., Aurora, Ill.
Lake......	A	90%	....	H. G. Goelitz Co., Oak Park, Ill...........	J. R. Goetzman, care W. H. Miller, Lake Villa, Ill.
LaSalle....	A	....	W. N. B.	W. J. Brennan, LaSalle, Ill.	
LaSalle....	B	....	W. N. B.	F. E. Ball, Hampshire, Ill.	
LaSalle....	C	86%	....	W. J. Brennan, LaSalle, Ill...............	W. C. Locke, LaSalle, Ill. Phone 725, Utica Exchange.
LaSalle....	D	....	W. N. B.	W. J. Brennan, LaSalle, Ill.	
Lee.......	A	74%	....	Edw. M. Laing Co., Inc., Highland Park, Ill..	Abram Ackert, 1223 3d st., Dixon, Ill.
Livingston.	B	....	W. N. B.	Jno. E. Bretz, Springfield, Ill.	
Logan.....	B	90%	....	John Awe, Lincoln, Ill.	
Logan.....	C	90%	....	W. D. Alexander & Co., Normal, Ill.........	J. T. Child, care J.N. Vaughan, Latham, Ill.
McDonough	A & B	(Bridges.)	W. N. B.	Electric Wheel Co., Quincy, Ill.	
McDonough	C	(Bridges.)	W. N. B.	Electric Wheel Co., Quincy, Ill.	
McDonough	D	(Bridges.)	W. N. B.	Electric Wheel Co., Quincy, Ill.	
McHenry..	C	....	....	C. A. Williston, 343 S. Dearborn st., Chicago	H. C. Petersen, 331 S. Jefferson st., Woodstock, Ill.
McHenry..	D	....	....	C. A. Williston, 343 S. Dearborn st., Chicago	H. C. Petersen, 331 S. Jefferson st., Woodstock, Ill.
McHenry..	E	6%	....	C. A. Williston, 343 S. Dearborn st., Chicago	H. C. Petersen, 331 S. Jefferson st., Woodstock, Ill.
McHenry..	F	....	....	C. A. Williston, 343 S. Dearborn st., Chicago	H. C. Petersen, 331 S. Jefferson st., Woodstock, Ill.

CONDITION OF STATE AID WORK—Continued.

County.	Sec.	Per cent completed.	Note.	Contractor.	Resident engineer.
Macoupin..	A	77%	....	McBride & Wargensted, Carlinville, Ill......	W. T. Page, Carlinville, Ill.
Macoupin..	B	(Bridges.)	W. N. B.	Zastrow & Lashmet, Jacksonville, Ill.	
Madison...	A	78%	....	Charles H. Degenhardt, Alton, Ill.........	C. I. Burggraf, care, Y. M. C. A., Alton, Ill.
Marion....	A	(Bridges.)	W. N. B.	F. S. Nichols, Flora, Ill.	
Marion....	B	....	W. N. B.	H. H. Hall Const. Co., East St. Louis, Ill.	
Marion....	C	(Bridges.)	W. N. B.	M. R. McCall, Sandoval, Ill.	
Marshall...	B	....	W. N. B.	Ajax Const. and Eng. Co., Gary, Ind.	
Marshall...	C	(Bridges.)	....	Capperune & Deyo, Bradford, Ill..........	Louis Simon, Lacon, Ill. Bell phone No. 8.
Massac..	A	5%	....	W. H. Hoffman, Lafayette, Ind...........	Fred Larson.
Menard....	B	(Bridges.)	W. N. B.	Zastrow & Lashmet, Jacksonville, Ill.	
Mercer....	C	(Bridges.)	W. N. B.	Connelly & Dunning, Chicago.	
Mercer....	D	(Bridges.)	W. N. B.	Porter-McCully Const. Co., Mackinaw, Ill.	
Mercer....	E	(Bridges.)	W. N. B.	Porter-McCully Const. Co., Mackinaw, Ill.	
Monroe....	A	86%	....	Renkel Construction Co , Maplewood, Mo...	B. C. McCurdy, Illmo Hotel, E. St. Louis, Ill. Phone working hours, 245 Millstadt, Ill.
Montg'mery	A	(Bridges.)	W. N. B.	Herrick Construction Co., Carlinville, Ill.	
Montg'mery	B	(Bridges.)	W. N. B.	Herrick Construction Co., Carlinville, Ill.	
Morgan....	A	55%	....	Herrick Construction Co., Carlinville, Ill....	C. S. McArdle, 335 W. Court st., Jacksonville, Ill. Phone 613 Ill.
Ogle......	A	99%	....	Gund-Graham Co., Freeport, Ill...........	John Johnson, R. F. D. No. 3, Oregon, Ill.
Ogle......	B	....	W. N. B.	B. F. Davis, Oregon, Ill.	
Peoria.....	B	1%	....	Ajax Const. and Eng. Co., Gary, Ind.......	Simon Garbulsky, care F. H. Apple, R.F.D. No. 2, Peoria.
Perry.....	A	(Bridges.)	W. N. B.	Renkel Construction Co., Maplewood, Mo.	
Piatt......	A	46%	....	Metz & McVey, Mansfield, Ill..............	E. B. Gordon, Box 31, Mansfield, Ill.
Pike.......	A	10%	....	Cameron, Joyce & Co., Keokuk, Iowa......	C. C. Hinsdale. Pittsfield, Ill.
Pope......	A	....	W. N. B.	Charles Gullett, Golconda, Ill.	
Putnam....	A	(Bridges.)	W. N. B.	Renkel Construction Co., Maplewood, Mo.	
Putnam....	B	(Bridges.)	W. N. B.	Renkel Construction Co., Maplewood, Mo.	
Pulaski....	A	(Bridges.)	W. N. B.	Bland & Fitzgerald, Cairo, Ill.	
Rock Island	B	90%	....	McCarthy Improvement Co., Davenport, Iowa.	
Randolph..	B	(Bridges.)	W. N. B.	Wm. Lough & Son., Marion, Ill.	
St. Clair...	A	8%	....	H. H. Hall Const. Co., East St. Louis, Ill....	G. C. Geraty, Belleville, Ill., care D. O. Thomas.
Saline.....	A	3%	....	Ernest Berns, Terre Haute, Ind...........	M. J. Fleming, 212 E. Walnut st., Harrisburg, Ill.
Saline.....	B	(Bridges.)	W. N. B.	J. L. Dorris Construction Co., Harrisburg, Ill.	
Sangamon..	F	87%	....	R. F. Egan, Springfield, Ill...............	C. H. Apple.
Schuyler...	A	76%	....	F. E. Ball, Hampshire, Ill................	J. J. O'Laughlin, Box 151. Rushville. Ill.
Schuyler...	B	....	W. N. B.	Zastrow & Lashmet, Jacksonville, Ill.	
Scott......	B	(Bridges.)	....	C. A. Wever & Son, Clayton. Ill.	B. C. McCurdy (Tem), Exeter, Ill. Tel. call Exeter through Jacksonville.
Shelby.....	A	(Bridges.)	....	Herrick Construction Co., Carlinville, Ill....	N. T. Ashkins, care Neal Hotel, Shelbyville, Ill.
Shelby.....	B	(Bridges.)	....	Townsend B. Smith, Evanston, Ill.........	Theo. Plack, care Neal Hotel, Shelbyville, Ill.
Shelby.....	C	(Bridges.)	....	Townsend B. Smith, Evanston, Ill.........	Theo. Plack, care Neal Hotel, Shelbyville, Ill.
Shelby.....	D	(Bridges.)	....	Tressler & True, Tower Hill, Ill.........	L. A. Doan, Shelbyville. Ill.
Stark......	B	(Bridges.)	W. N. B.	Connelly & Dunning, Chicago.	
Stark......	C	(Bridges.)	W. N. B.	Connelly & Dunning, Chicago.	
Stephenson.	B	(Bridges.)	W. N. B.	W. H. Shons, Freeport, Ill.	
Tazewell...	D	36%	....	W. D. Alexander & Co., Normal, Ill.........	C. W. Ellsworth, 313 S. Capitol, Pekin, Ill.

CONDITION OF STATE AID WORK—Concluded.

County.	Sec.	Per cent completed.	Note.	Contractor.	Resident engineer.
Tazewell...	E	18%	....	R. A. Medaris Const. Co., Springfield, Ill....	Jno. D. Mattison, gen. del., Tremont. Wire and phone care F. A. Blue.
Union.....	A	....	W. N. B.	Meyer & Thomas Const. Co., E. St. Louis, Ill.	
Vermilion..	A	67%	....	Edw. M. Laing Co., Inc., Highland Park, Ill..	P. F. Jervis, 205 N. Walnut st., Danville, Ill.
Vermilion..	B	....	W. N. B.	Cameron, Joyce & Co., Keokuk, Iowa.......	Danville, Ill.
Wabash....	A	....	....	Hoffman, Townsend & Parks, Mt. Carmel, Ill.	H. W. Wilkison, Mt. Carmel, Ill.
Warren....	B	100%	....	Merrifield Construction Co., Monmouth, Ill.	
Washington	A	(Bridges.)	W. N. B.	H. E. Haun, Richview, Ill.	
Wayne.....	A	(Bridges.)	W. N. B.	Wayne Co. Concrete Const. Co., Fairfield, Ill.	
Wayne.....	B	(Bridges.)	W. N. B.	Wayne Co. Concrete Const. Co., Fairfield, Ill.	
White.....	A	....	W. N. B.	Morgan, Morgan & Mossberger, Carmi, Ill.	
Whiteside..	B	15%	....	Walter & Windes, Glencoe, Ill.............	O. F. Goeke, 109 E. Morris st., Morrison, Ill.
Whiteside..	C	30%	....	Walter & Windes, Glencoe, Ill.............	O. F. Goeke, 109 E. Morris st., Morrison, Ill.
Will.......	B	76%	....	Chicago Heights Coal Co., Chicago Heights, Ill.	Geo. L. Judson, 408 Scott st., Joliet, Ill. Phone, Chicago Heights 1778-J.
Williamson.	B	....	W. N. B.	Wm. Lough & Son, Marion, Ill.	
Williamson.	C	....	W. N. B.	Wm. Lough & Son, Marion, Ill.	
Winnebago.	A	....	....	Walter & Windes, Glencoe, Ill.............	L. Schwartz, care Illinois Hotel, Rockford, Ill.
Winnebago.	B	13%	....	Connelly & Dunning, 164 W. Wash. st., Chicago	S. F. Wilson, Route 8, Rockford, Ill. Phone 947-3, Wire Rockford, Ill.
Woodford..	B	(Bridges.)	W. N. B.	Davis & Widmer, Deer Creek, Ill.	

LEGEND: W. N. B.—Work not begun.   N. P. L.—No pavement laid.   P. C.—Pavement completed.

TOWNSHIP ROAD CONSTRUCTION.

The following shows the location of road equipment and the condition of all township road work under construction and anticipated, July 1, 1915:

Location.	Amt. of Road.	Type of Road.	Per cent completed.	State equipment.	Men in charge.	Remarks.
Reading......	20 mi.	9′ macadam....	20%	2 rollers, 1 BP engine, 6 wheelers.....	F. H. Little............	Convict labor.
Rockford.....	8 mi.	Surface oil work.	80%	1 roller, 3 distributors, 2 cookers.......	D. S. James.	
Sand Ridge...	3½ mi.	10′ macadam....	10%	1 roller........	I. E. Scott.	
Petrolia......	2 mi.	10′ concrete.....	50%	1 roller, 1 mixer........	F. C. Feutz.	
Fair Grange..	4 mi.	10′ macadam....	5%	1 roller........	H. B. Sennit.	
Aurora.......	1¼ mi.	18′ concrete.....	100%	1 mixer........	H. M. Kleizer.	
Eldorado.....	1¼ mi.	10′ brick........	5%	1 roller, 1 mixer........	Latimer, roller operator.	
Matteson.....	3 mi.	Macadam.......	15%	1 roller, 1 router.......	Fred Thatcher.	
Pontiac......	½ mi.	Asphalt.........	100%	1 scarifier, 1 harrow.......	C. Gray.	Completed June 15.
Hodges Park.	......	Gravel..........	75%	1 roller.........	Nelson, roller operator...	State aid.
Tremont......	......	Concrete.......	5%	1 roller 1 mixer........	Hickman, roller operator.	State aid
DeKalb......	3 mi.	Macadam.......	20%	1 roller........	Muzzy, roller operator.	

TOWNSHIP ROAD CONSTRUCTION—Concluded.

Location.	Amt. of Road.	Type of Road.	Percent completed.	State equipment.	Men in charge.	Remarks.
Cairo........	2½ mi.	Macadam.				
Oregon.......	3 mi.	Oil work.				
Pekin........	2 mi.	Oil work.				
Woosung.....	3 mi.	Macadam....		1 scarifier, 1 harrow.		
Anna.......·.	7 mi.	Macadam.				
Shiloh.......	1 mi.	Asphalt.				
Peoria.......	......	....		1 oiler, 3 heaters stored near Peoria.		
Effingham....	1 mi.	Macadam.				

MAINTENANCE WORK.

All State aid roads in the following named counties have had maintenance to the extent of having all cracks and joints filled with bituminous material.

Iroquois.	Cook.	DeKalb.
Cass.	Lawrence.	Boone.
Logan.	Sangamon.	Lake.
Livingston.	Jefferson.	Kane.
Kankakee.	Williamson.	
Will.	Franklin.	

Additional work was done on the macadam shoulders in Jefferson County.

All weeds on State aid roads will be cut in July, if possible.

LABORATORY WORK.

During the month of June, 1915, one hundred sixty-three (163) sample of miscellaneous materials comprising cements, sands, gravels, crushed stones, bricks, paints, road oils, asphalt, tars, waters, creosote oils and linseed oils, were tested. There were also three mill and plant inspections, and two field inspections.

CONTRACTS AWARDED FOR STATE AID ROADS.

During the month of June, contracts were awarded for State aid road work as follows:

County.	Route.	Sec.	Type of road.	L'gth feet.	Date awarded.	*Contract price.	Name of Contractor.
Tazewell.....	11	E	Concrete.....	1,500	June 2, 1915	$ 1,937.00	R. A. Medaris Const. Co.
Wabash......	2	A	Gravel......	8,860	June 2, 1915	6,300.00	Hoffman, Townsend & Parks.
LaSalle......	9	A	Brick......	4,040	June 2, 1915	23,991.00	W. J. Brennan.
Union........	1	A	Macadam....	2,200	June 9, 1915	3,050.00	Meyer & Thomas Const. Co.
Bond........	7	B	Brick.......	600	June 9, 1915	1,250.00	Renkel Const. Co.
Livingston....	2a	B	Brick......	2,800	June 9, 1915	5,340.00	John E. Bretz.
Kane........	1	C	Concrete....	2,700	June 9, 1915	3,980.00	Thos. H. Cutler & Co.
Franklin......	1	B	Bridges.....	......	June 9, 1915	1,200.00	W. Lough & Son.
Pulaski......	2	A	Bridges.....	......	June 9, 1915	2,922.00	Bland & Fitzgerald.
Jasper.......	....	A	Bridges.....	......	June 9, 1912	2,240.00	Caudy & McElroy.
Jasper.......	....	B	Bridges.....	......	June 9, 1915	2,000.00	Caudy & McElroy.
Jasper.......	....	C	Bridges.....	......	June 9, 1915	2,465.00	Caudy & McElroy.
Scott........	1	B	Bridges.....	......	June 9, 1915	4,300.00	C. A. Wever & Son.
Gallatin......	1-2-4	A	Bridges.....	......	June 16, 1915	2,636.00	Wm. Lough & Son.
Gallatin......	3-5-6	B	Bridges.....	......	June 16, 1915	1,780.00	Wm. Lough & Son.
Randolph....	1-2-4-6	B	Bridges.....	......	June 16, 1915	5,627.00	Wm. Lough & Son.
Menard......	4	B	Bridges.....	......	June 23, 1915	805.00	Zastrow & Lashmet.
Macoupin....		B	Bridges.....	......	June 23, 1915	2,564.00	Zastrow & Lashmet.
McDonough..	....	A	Bridges.....	......	June 23, 1915	3,760.00	Electric Wheel Co.
McDonough..	4	B	Bridges.....	......	June 23, 1915	3,498.00	Electric Wheel Co.
McDonough..	· 1-2-3	C	Bridges.....	......	June 23, 1915	3,625.00	C. D. Stratton.
McDonough..	15	D	Bridges.....	......	June 23, 1915	3,836.00	Central States Bridge Co.
Williamson...	10	C	Bridges.....	......	June 23, 1915	740.00	W. Lough & Son.
Jo Daviess...	1	A	Concrete....	}7,100	June 30, 1915	9,989.00	Empire Const. Co.
Jo Daviess...	1	B	Brk. & Conc.				
Hamilton....	....	A	Bridges.....	......	June 30, 1915	4,005.00	W. T. Bland.
Hamilton....	....	B	Bridges.....	......	June 30, 1915	4,114.00	W. T. Bland.
Jackson......	4	B	Macadam shoulders.	3,400	June 30, 1915	1,725.00	Meyer & Thomas Const. Co.

CONTRACTS AWARDED FOR STATE AID ROADS—Concluded.

County.	Route.	Sec.	Type of road.	L'gth feet.	Date awarded.	*Contract price.	Name of Contractor.
LaSalle......	11	D	Brick......	1,600	June 30, 1915	9,027.00	W. J. Brennan.
DuPage......	1	B	Concrete....	2,225	June 30, 1915	4,480.00	Thos. H. Cutler.
Cass........	7	B	Concrete....	445	June 30, 1915	637.00	John G. Pratt.
Cumberland..	3-5-6-7	A	Bridges....	.....	June 30, 1915	2,075.00	Caudy & McElroy.
Cumberland..	1-1a-5-7	B	Bridges....	.....	June 30, 1915	2,240.00	Caudy & McElroy.
Fulton.......	2	D	Bridges....	.....	June 30, 1915	2,588.00	Central States Bridge Co.
Fulton.......	....	E	Bridges....	.....	June 30, 1915	1,902.50	M. R. Van Houten.
Greene.......	1-3-8	A	Bridges....	.....	June 30, 1915	5,150.00	C. M. Hanes.
Jersey.......	4-8	B	Bridges....	.....	June 30, 1915	984.00	Herrick Const. Co.
LaSalle......	1	B	Brick......	2,640	June 30, 1915	8,800.00	F. E. Ball.
Mercer.......	3-4-5-6	C	Bridges....	.....	June 30, 1915	4,548.00	Connelly & Dunning.
Mercer.......	1	D	Bridges....	.....	June 30, 1915	7,740.00	Porter McCully Con. Co.
Mercer.......	2-7-8	E	Bridges....	.....	June 30, 1915	4,510.00	Porter McCully Con. Co.
Montgomery..	....	A	Bridges....	.....	June 30, 1915	4,547.00	Herrick Const. Co.
Montgomery..	....	B	Bridges....	.....	June 30, 1915	4,497.00	Herrick Const. Co.
Ogle........	2-5	B	Bit. surf....	19,192	June 30, 1915	1,500.00	E. F. Davis.
Perry........	2-10	A	Bridges....	.....	June 30, 1915	4,950.00	Renkel Const. Co.
Putnam......	1-3-4	A	Bridges....	.....	June 30, 1915	3,311.00	Renkel Const. Co.
Putnam......	1-4-6-44	B	Bridges....	.....	June 30, 1915	3,104.00	Renkel Const. Co.
Saline........	8-10	B	Bridges....	.....	June 30, 1915	1,720.00	J. L. Dorris Const. Co.
Stark........	1-2-3-3a-5	B	Bridges....	.....	June 30, 1915	6,280.00	Connelly & Dunning.
Stark........	1-5-7-8	C	Bridges....	.....	June 30, 1915	5,910.00	Connelly & Dunning.
Stephenson...	6-7-8-14	B	Bridges....	.....	June 30, 1915	2,088.00	W. H. Shons.
Vermilion....	2	B	Earth work and culverts	2,550	June 30, 1915	7,063.78	Cameron, Joyce & Co.
Washington...	2-3-13	A	Bridges....	.....	June 30, 1915	3,194.00	H. E. Haun.
Wayne.......	9-10-12-12a	A	Bridges....	.....	June 30, 1915	3,657.88	Wayne Co. Con. Const. Co.
Wayne.......	1-2-13-16	B	Bridges....	.....	June 30, 1915	4,072.35	Wayne Co. Con. Const. Co.
White........	11	A	Gravel......	11,746	June 30, 1915	13,600.00	Morgan, Morgan & Massberger.
Woodford....	7	B	Bridges....	.....	June 30, 1915	1,520.00	Davis & Widmer.

* Does not include cost of cement in road work.

BRIDGE WORK.

During the month of June, 1915, plans and specifications for 160 bridges were prepared and sent to county superintendents of highways or to county clerks; total estimated cost $112,361.00.

Contracts were awarded for 249 concrete bridges and 9 steel bridges, at an average cost of 92.7 per cent of the estimates; total estimated cost $169,914.00.

The date of letting was set for 228 bridges, having a total estimated cost of $163,548.00.

Thirty-two bridge plans, prepared by county superintendents, were checked and approved.

On July 1, 1915, there were 37 bridge inspection reports on hand ready for work; plans for all of these except one being practically completed.

BLUE PRINTING.

During the month of June, 1915, 98 blue prints were made of our bridge standards for county superintendents of highways, as well as prints for 6 foreign bridge plans averaging 2 sheets, 6 prints being made of each sheet, or about 72 prints. Prints were made of 19 bridges designed by this department, 20 sets each, as well as 3 preliminary sets being sent to the various counties for their use in letting said bridges, totaling 874 prints. Preliminary prints were also made of 32 bridges designed by this department for use of county boards, 3 sets being made of each, or 192 prints.

There was also printed 6 prints each of the various townships (averaging 14) in 3 counties of the State, or about 252 prints.

Preliminary prints were made for 26 sections of State aid work for the county board to pass on, official prints then being made for county clerk, county superintendent, and this office. Each section averages about 12 sheets, making a total of 1,248 prints.

Miscellaneous prints, about 600 made for office use, made a grand total for the month of June of 3,336 prints.

Very truly yours,

Wm. W. Marr,
Chief State Highway Engineer.

DIXIE HIGHWAY ROUTED THROUGH ILLINOIS.

[*By* L. M. Vaughn, *Secretary Illinois Dixie Association, and Secretary of the Danville Industrial Club.*]

One hundred and thirty miles of the great Dixie Highway which stretches from the Gulf of Mexico to the Great Lakes is to be constructed through this State.

Through the efforts of her State executive, two energetic commissioners, the Illinois Dixie Association organized to boost the movement and the enthusiastic support of practically every citizen in every city, town and hamlet along the line, Illinois entered the race to win this great north and south roadway—entered as a dark horse months after other states had organized to build it—and captured the prize.

This highway will be built a solid pavement from

Chicago to the gulf. It will stretch south to Danville and then into Indiana to Indianapolis and there divide, one branch going to Cincinnati and the other to Louisville, Ky. Illinois State Highway Engineer W. W. Marr, secretary of the commission, and R. J. Finnegan, of the Chicago Journal, represented this State and stood pat for a maximum of the roadway through Illinois.

Provision is now being made in each county for construction of the road. The supervisors in practically every county through which it will pass have taken up the matter and before fall construction will without doubt be underway.

The road will connect the great north middle west metropolis with the southern summer resorts. It will furnish to autoists a most desirable touring route and when completed it is believed will be used by hundreds of autoists daily.

ROAD CONSTRUCTION IN READING TOWNSHIP, LIVINGSTON COUNTY, WITH CONVICT LABOR.

[By B. H. PIEPMEIER, *Engineer in Charge of Maintenance and Township Road Construction.*]

Reading Township, Livingston County, is a rich agricultural township, lying just south of Streator, Illinois. There are but two small villages in the township, which together have a total population of about 400. The township, which is six miles square, has an assessed valuation of $1,275,000.

For the past few years many arguments have been presented to the taxpayers in favor of hard roads. The township officials and a number of interested farmers became enthusiastic for better roads and proceeded to draw up a petition to vote bonds in the township to the extent of $63,500, ($1.00 on the $100.00 assessed valuation for five years) for constructing some 15 to 20 miles of crushed stone roads nine feet wide. The petition was presented before the taxpayers at the April election last spring and it carried by a large majority.

After the bond issue had carried, the commissioners communicated with the State Highway Commission for its assistance. The State Highway Commission agreed to furnish them with an engineer to superintend the construction, three macadam road outfits and the necessary crushed stone from the penitentiary, providing convict labor could be used in constructing the road.

The writer made a very careful study of the system of proposed roads in the township and decided that it was entirely practical to construct a majority of the roads during this season, and to handle all the work from one central point, where a convict camp might be established.

Surveys were ordered and all detailed arrangements made for starting the work within 30 days after the bonds were voted.

On April 7, Mr. Floyd Little, of the State Highway Department, was placed in direct charge of all the improvement.

On May 13, 46 convicts were sent out to Reading and a camp was established.

During the months of April and May there was very little work done on account of delays in disposing of bonds and on account of the general condition of the weather. However, by the 1st of June, all preliminary arrangements had been made and actual construction started.

Mr. Floyd Little, superintendent, is in direct charge of all work. He is supplied with a small auto truck that is used in shifting men to and from different points on the job. The car also enables him to keep in close touch with all divisions of work, namely, the unloading plant, the hauling system, the excavation, subgrade work, the spreading and the finishing. The work is scattered over some 20 miles of road and even with the car, it keeps the superintendent very busy.

EQUIPMENT.

To build the number of miles desired in one season and in the most economical manner with convict labor, it was decided that all the crushed stone should be hauled with an industrial railroad outfit. The commissioners accordingly arranged to rent a complete outfit, which consists of one 30-horsepower locomotive, 65 one and one-half yard dump cars, five and one-half miles of 24-inch gauge, 20-pound steel rail, and accessories from the Orenstein, Arthur Koppel Company of Chicago. The railroad equipment was delivered on the ground and ready to work May 20.

The industrial railroad was decided upon for hauling the material for several reasons, namely: The material could be delivered rapidly and by one unit, which could be easily supervised and depended upon. It could haul a load over the black earth roads even when water soaked, or in a condition that no other practical method of hauling could be used. It could be easily handled by convict labor and it could be worked overtime when desired.

The principal grading on the proposed system of roads was to prepare a subgrade or roadbed for the crushed stone. An elevating grader and heavy road grader was therefore purchased by the township and put in use preparing the roads for the hard surfacing material.

Three 10-ton steam rollers were furnished by the State Highway Department, together with the necessary accessories, such as sprinkling wagons, plows, harrows, tool boxes, etc.

A 30-horsepower steam tractor pulling engine for the graders was furnished by the State Highway Department; also six large wheel scrapers.

Because of the difficulty in securing teams in a farming community of this kind, team work was reduced to a minimum. A gasoline engine and pump and two miles of pipe line were installed for pumping water onto the road for supplying the boilers of the steam rollers and for flushing the screenings into the macadam surface in preference to hauling the water by teams. Small creeks are so located over the township that two miles of pipe line will deliver water to any portion of the roads to be improved.

UNLOADING DEVICE.

On account of the quantity of stone that has to be handled from one central plant and the necessity of having some device that would load the industrial train rapidly, it was decided to construct an unloading bin, as shown in the picture below, and to use a belt and bucket elevator for carrying the material from the pit beneath the track, to the bin. The Santa Fe Railroad agreed to furnish the Roger Center Dump Cars on all shipments to this point.

The bin has a capacity of about 80 cubic yards, and is constructed so as to permit the dinky cars to pass under the center of the bin for loading. There are four trapdoors in the bottom of the bin, and the one and one-half cubic yard cars can be filled in about five seconds. With the unloader, a minimum number of men are used at the unloading plant. The train of material is always made up quickly so there are no un-

Unloading Plant, Material In Cars Are Dumped Into Pit Under Track and Elevated to Bin by Belt and Buckets.

necessary delays for the locomotive, which insures efficiency in hauling. A secondhand 16-horsepower traction engine was purchased for driving the belt and for working the drum that spots the railroad cars over the pit.

With the device shown, 10 to 15 cars of stone may be unloaded daily, which will readily supply the one hauling outfit on the two and one-half mile average haul. The locomotive hauls about 40 dump cars or 60 cubic yards per trip, and makes from 6 to 10 trips per day.

YARDS.

The industrial tracks in the yards are laid so that there is but one move for the locomotive in the yards, and that one is to uncouple the empty train and to couple up with the loaded cars. On the first stop, the engine is supplied with water, coal and oil, which takes about five minutes.

The switching in the yards is done with a horse. The empty cars are spotted and the loaded cars made up into a train for the locomotive. This arrangement

Material Yards and Unloading Plant.

saves time for the locomotive to the extent of an extra trip or two each day. The horse was purchased by the township, so the cost of the switching will be small.

EXCAVATION.

The excavation is handled by a large traction engine, elevating grader, an ordinary engine grader and

six wheel scrapers. All of this equipment is placed in charge of one man, who reports directly to the superintendent. The grading is completed as far in advance of the improvement as possible.

SUBGRADE.

The subgrade work is handled by one man, who has use of the tractor, grader and team leveller. He also has a squad of men for doing the necessary handwork.

HAULING.

All hauling is done with the locomotive and dump cars as shown in the accompanying pictures. The train crew consists of an engineer, front and rear flagman. The steel track is first placed a little to one side of the center of the subgrade, and as soon as one dumping of stone has been made, the track is shifted to the edge of the subgrade, where another dump is made to make up the required amount of material. The track is then shifted to the earth shoulder, and the necessary screenings and bonding materials dumped on the earth shoulder. When all material is dumped for about a mile of road, the track is picked up and extended on another route. Two or three men, known as trackwalkers, are required to patrol the track and

Preparing Subgrade for Crushed Stone.

keep it lined up so that a maximum speed may be maintained by the locomotive.

SPREADING AND FINISHING.

All spreading, shaping and finishing of the macadam is under the direct charge of one man, who reports to the superintendent. The stone which has been dumped upon the subgrade is first spread by means of a team grader. After the material is evenly distributed over the subgrade, a heavy harrow is driven over the road, to distribute the material more uniformly, and to shift the dirt and fine particles of stone to the bottom of the crushed material. After this is done, the earth shoulders are drawn up properly to the stone road and the finishing touches are made by men with stone forks and shovels. The road is rolled with the 10-ton rollers and if any depressions are formed, they are immediately filled with additional stone. The road is then thoroughly rolled until no depressions are formed by the roller wheels and the stone is thoroughly compacted and keyed. The screenings are then whipped over the road from shovels and broomed and rolled in dry until all voids between the stones are filled, after which it is flushed with water, and puddled with the roller.

BRIDGE WORK.

All bridge and culvert work on this system of roads is handled by a contractor, under the county superintendent of highways and superintendent in charge.

CONVICT CAMP.

The prison camp is officially known as "Camp Dunne." Mr. T. G. Keegan is directly in charge of all prison camps. He is assisted at the camp at Reading

All Stone is Delivered by Industrial Railroad Equipment.

by Wm. Mahony, who looks after the men during the day, and Lewis Falkie, who acts as watchman at night. The law permitting convicts to work upon the public highways has been in effect since 1913. "Camp Dunne" is recognized as the sixth road camp that has been established since that time.

Location:—The camp is located on a two-acre lot within one block of the postoffice at Reading, Illinois, and within three blocks of Moon Station on the Santa Fe Railroad. The camp ground is adjacent to a small creek which affords good drainage.

Equipment:—The camp consists of the following: One plain building 18 by 60 feet, as shown in the cut above. This building is partitioned off for a kitchen, dining room and officer's dining room. Adjacent to the kitchen is a good well, equipped with a small gasoline pump which supplies the washhouse and kitchen with an abundance of water.

An old building on the ground was utilized for a combination washroom and laundry. The washroom

Industrial Hauling Outfit.

is supplied at all times with hot and cold water. Two convicts work in the laundry. Everything washable is washed each week.

There is a barber chair adjacent to the washhouse, where the convicts may receive the necessary haircut and shave as desired.

Two large tents 14 by 14 feet are located near the entrance to the camp ground. One is used by the officers and the other for a commissary.

On the highest portion of the grounds there are located thirty 9 by 9 feet sleeping tents, each tent accommodating two men. All the tents are floored with lumber. Each man has his own bed and bedding, consisting of an iron bedstead, wire springs, mattress, a pillow, blanket and linen. During cold weather the tents are supplied with small coal stoves so the camp may remain in use during severe weather, if needed.

Sanitation:—The entire camp is kept clean. No convict is permitted to commit any act which may cause filth. All garbage is carted away from the camp. The kitchen, dining room and outhouses are all screened to keep out insects. Precautions are taken to prevent the breeding of flies and mosquitoes.

Each convict is required to take a bath at least once each week. He is permitted to take as many other baths as he chooses. The camp, as a whole, looks much better than the ordinary construction camp, in fact, it compares favorably with the best kept home with respect to sanitation.

Clothing:—An expert tailor, having a good equipment, is kept constantly at work repairing, altering

Building Erected for Dining Room and Kitchen for a Convict Labor Camp.

and making garments. All garments are inspected at least once each week, and buttonholes, tears and weak spots are repaired without delay.

The convicts are permitted to wear ordinary citizen's clothes, so it is very hard to distinguish prison labor from free labor. Most of the convicts dress up on Sunday in madeover secondhand clothing, which has been given to them by their friends or donated to the camp. Donations are always welcomed by the prisoners.

Rules and Privileges:—The camp rules are simple, but strict obedience to them is required. No convict is permitted to indulge in any form of disorderly conduct. Gambling and drinking are barred from the camp. The men must be either in the camp or on their work and are not permitted to loiter about the community. They are required to arise at 5:30 a. m., be ready for breakfast at 6.00 a. m., and on their work at 6.45 a. m. Their dinner hour is from 11.45 to 12.45. Quitting time is 5.00 p. m. Supper is served at 6.00 and all lights out at 9.30 p. m.

No road work is required of the men on Saturday afternoon, Sundays and holidays.

During leisure hours they are permitted to enter into any beneficial form of recreation. Each person is permitted to write only one letter per day and to receive visitors every Saturday afternoon. There is no limit on the mail the convicts may receive.

The convicts are permitted to earn money when there is an occasion to work overtime on the road. They also make small amounts selling souvenirs to visitors. They are not permitted to have any money in their possession. Each convict is furnished with a pass book in which credit and debit are entered as fast as money is earned or expended. His balance is turned over to him on the completion of his sentence.

Supplies:—The convicts are supplied with three good meals each day. Practically all their food is prepared at the camp.

The State furnishes the convicts with all the chewing and smoking tobacco they care to use. Those who prefer not to use tobacco furnished by the State are permitted to purchase tobacco and cigars at cost from the commissary.

Convict Work:—The road camps that are sent out from the penitentiary have selected men for the various divisions of work in the road camps. They are assigned to various divisions of work and kept at that one thing as much as possible, which always insures the best results.

View of Dining Room in Convict Labor Camp.

In the camp at Reading there are 46 convicts. Ten are assigned to camp duties and 36 to actual work on the road.

The 10 men at the camp are assigned as follows: There being first and second cook in the kitchen and four assistants, who look after the dining room, the delivery of field dinners, and many other small details about the camp. There are two men in charge of the laundry, one in charge of the tailoring department and one general clerk.

Of the 36 men that are on the road, eight are assigned to the unloading plant, about six to the hauling gang, four to subgrade work and the balance to spreading and shaping stone and screenings. The men on road work are not definitely assigned, but are shifted from one division of work to another as the superintendent may see they are needed.

The men are at their work nine hours each day and any part of rainy days that it is possible to work. Where the men are working several miles from camp, meals are carted to them by one of the dining room

assistants, so there is no loss of time in reporting back to camp for meals.

There are two crews for the industrial railroad hauling system. One crew goes on at daylight and works until noon. The other crew runs the equipment until dark. The crews relieve one another at meal time so there is no loss of time hauling material during meal hours or when it is light enough to handle the equipment.

Sleeping Tents for Men at Convict Labor Camp.

There are no guards over the men at any time. They are merely counted twice a day to make sure they are all on the job. The men are permitted to work with free labor, by themselves, or in groups, as the superintendent may see fit. So far the road camps have been handled in such a way that it would be difficult for an outsider to determine a prison camp from the ordinary free labor camp.

Any township or county officials in Illinois that are particularly interested in convict labor on the public highways, will undoubtedly be benefited by visiting the camp at Moon, the first station south of Streator on the Sante Fe Railroad. The State Highway Commission will be glad to meet any party at Moon and go over the work with them or explain more in detail concerning convict labor camps upon receipt of inquiry.

TOWNSHIP ROAD CONSTRUCTION.

Pontiac Township, Livingston County.

The following cost data were taken from work done in resurfacing an old gravel road with bituminous macadam.

The old gravel road was first scarified, reshaped and harrowed, after which it was rolled to a true cross-section. Crushed limestone, ranging in size from 1 inch to 2½ inches, was spread uniformly to a depth of about 4 inches. The stone was harrowed and rolled once.

Bermudez road binder asphalt was applied at the rate of one and one-half gallons per square yard. The asphalt surface was then covered with stone chips, after which a squeegee coat of asphalt, about one-fourth gallon per square yard, was applied and covered with stone chips, as before.

The asphalt was applied by the "Climax Distributor" which was furnished by the Good Roads Machinery Company, of Fort Wayne, Ind., for demonstrating purposes. The distributor proved to be a very efficient machine for applying the heavy asphaltic material.

Mr. R. W. Osborne, county superintendent of highways, was instrumental in getting this work done. Mr. C. Gray, of this department, was directly in charge of the work and Mr. Smith, of Albany, N. Y., was present to demonstrate the use of the distributor.

FINAL COST REPORT ON BITUMINOUS MACADAM ROADS.

Pontiac Road, Pontiac Township, Livingston County.

CONDITIONS.

(No allowance made for contractors profit and overhead charges.)

Amount of road laid, 2,640 feet; 4,693 square yards. Amount of road treated with bitumen, 4,693 square yards. Amount of bituminous material used per square yard, 1.7 gallons. Width of road, 16 feet; thickness, 4 inches. Average length of haul, one-half mile. Work began April 27, 1915; work completed June 14, 1915. Rate of pay for men, 25 cents per hour; teams, 40 cents per hour.

COST OF LABOR AND SUPPLIES.

	Total cost.	Cost per sq. yd.
Engineering and inspection		
Superintendence	$ *186.22	$ *0.040
Excavation		
Scarifying	67.45	.016
Stone and chips F. O. B. siding, 1,242 cubic yds. at $0.646 per cu. yd.	803.50	.171
Gravel or sand, F. O. B. siding		
Unloading stone to storage or loading direct	126.40	.027
Hauling stone or gravel, including bonding materials	270.30	.052
Incidental hauling		
Shaping and rolling subgrade and side roads	56.61	.012
Bituminous binder, 8,030 gal. at 13.6 F. O. B. siding, 10% 10 days	1,097.66	.233
Heating and applying binder, coal, labor, spreading screenings, etc.	150.20	.032
Spreading stone	84.30	.015
Rolling, including incidental repairs, coal, etc.	11.20	.002
Cost of culverts and bridges		
Freight on equipment	11.92	.002
Depreciation or rental on equipment.		
Total cost	$2,865.76	$0.608

* Indicates paid or furnished by the State Highway Department.

TOWNSHIP ROAD REPAIRS.

The following is a detailed statement of the cost of surface-oiling a novaculite gravel road that had been in use for about 10 years. The surface of the road had worn down approximately two inches, becoming rough and bare in spots, while in other places the surface was very tight and slightly caked with fine material. The entire surface was swept as clean as possible with the ordinary rotary broom. It was impossible to get the road entirely free from dust, as the heavy sweeping would loosen the surface stones.

The asphalt was applied at the rate of about four-tenth gallons per square yard of surface, from the standard spraying machine owned by the department. Five to 24 hours after the oil was poured, it was covered with a light treatment of river sand. The sand was considered entirely too fine for oil work, but it was preferred by the local authorities.

FINAL COST REPORT ON REPAIRS.

Hawthorne Place, Woodside Township, Sangamon County.

CONDITIONS.

(Contractors profit and overhead charges excluded.)

Amount of road repaired, ... feet; 18,450 square yards. Width of road, 24 and 30 feet. Length of haul on materials, one-fourth mile. Total bituminous material used, 7,850 gallons (Montezuma crude). Rate of pay, men, 22 cents; teams, 56 cents per hour. Work began May 23, 1915; work completed June 9, 1915.

COST OF LABOR AND MATERIALS.

	Total.	Per sq. yd.
Engineering and inspection		
Superintendence	$ *67.96	$ *0.00369
Sweeping old road	100.01	.00543
Sand, 109 cu. yds. at 90c F. O. B.	98.10	.00532
Hauling sand, 109 cu. yds. at 45c.	48.90	.00265
Bitumen, 8,040 gallons at .0484 F. O. B. Springfield	389.14	.02109
Spreading sand and screenings	61.28	.00332
Rolling and sprinkling		
Heating and applying bituminous material, including hauling	235.34	.01275
Total cost	$1,000.73	$0.0542

* Indicates paid or furnished by the State Highway Department.

The cost of heating and applying bituminous material is a little high, due to delays on account of rain, extra switching, demurrage and a fire, which all together amounted to about $100.00.

CARMI, ILLINOIS—BRIDGE FAILURE.

[By G. H. Brown, *County Superintendent of Highways, White County.*]

Herewith are shown some pictures of the bridge over the Little Wabash River at Carmi, Illinois. The first bridge at this site was a wooden superstructure boxed

Carmi, Ill., Bridge, Showing Failure of One Span.

up on the sides, with solid roof, and gave an appearance somewhat like a tunnel, and rested on a stone substructure. It was built in 1840 and at the time was supposed to be above high water, but the August freshet in 1875 passed all previous high waters and got over the floor, which made it necessary to tear off some of the siding to get the driftwood past.

Carml, Ill., Bridge at Low Water.

This bridge was replaced in 1878 by the iron structure shown in the accompanying pictures. It consisted of two spans each 136 feet in length. One of these pictures shows the bridge at low water, such as we have every summer.

One shows it at high water, such as we had in the springs of 1897, 1898, and 1913. The other views show it as it looks today.

When the iron structure was erected the west abutment and middle pier were thought to be good and were used for the iron structure, but were built up some three feet higher in order to be above any new high water mark that might be established. This increased height in the middle pier can be seen in the picture. The east abutment was built new.

The weakness of the west abutment was the cause of the bridge being in the river. It was built of sandstone and supposed to rest on a shale foundation. The street west from the bridge was paved a few years ago. There is a sharp decline towards the bridge in the street for several hundred feet and water coming down here was poured onto this abutment and the embankment in front of it. This caused excessive pres-

Carml, Ill., Bridge During High Water.

sure and continued moisture on the abutment, and it soon developed cracks from top to bottom under each truss. The recent rains caused such an additional amount of pressure that the strain could not be resisted and the result can be seen.

This bridge was city property and under the law we had until today (July 1, 1915) the county had no

voice about it and could not assist in its maintenance. I recently wrote an article for one of our local papers and advised people not to cross this bridge unless it was necessary, and then to go slowly and carefully. Many took the advice and did not cross when it could be avoided, yet about 800 vehicles crossed it on the last Saturday it was used, and although it was a rainy night, there were 80 vehicles crossed between 6.00 and 9.00 o'clock p. m. on Sunday before it went down at 4.30 a. m. the next morning.

Carml, Ill., Bridge After High Water.

The iron in this structure was treated with a good coat of paint when it was erected and had another about 20 years ago.

KANE COUNTY—PRIZE ESSAYS.

During the spring of 1915, the Kane County Good Roads Association offered prizes of $5.00 and $2.50 to each high school; and $5.00 and $2.50 to the grade and district schools of each township for the best and second best essays on the subject of good roads.

The offer met with a very hearty response on the part of the pupils, the teachers, and County Superintendent of Schools, E. A. Ellis, who states that no subject has ever been introduced in the schools of this county which brought out a more general response from the pupils as was evident by the manner in which they looked up the material, from many sources, organized it and then reproduced it as their own work. Over 600 essays were submitted. Eleven first prizes and 10 second prizes were awarded to the winners from the high schools; and 15 first prizes and 15 second prizes were awarded to the winners from the grade and district schools, the prizes amounting in all to $192.50.

The Kane County Federation of Woman's Club then offered a first and second prize for the best and second best essay selected from the entire county. The federation held a good roads basket picnic celebration at Riverbank Villa on June 5, when the essays were read by their respective authors.

The following essay was awarded the grand prize:

FIRST PRIZE ESSAY.

[RACENE MARTIN, *136 North Prairie Street, Batavia, Illinois, Grade 12, District No. 10.*]

GOOD ROADS.

The benefits of good roads have been estimated in many of their divisions. Although some of these divisions are more important than others, each promotes or is the result of the other.

When good roads reduce the cost of hauling, adjacent land becomes more valuable; there is a corresponding tendency for population to increase, and, in its turn this tendency strengthens the demand for more and better roads. Good roads are a decided benefit to both rural and urban districts, but the country, inhabited by the burden bearers of our land, find that their's is the greatest need. It seems that the economic value of good roads is their greatest asset.

Modern improved roads have three decided advantages over those which are not improved; they have a better surface, reduced grades, and shortened distances. The increased speed, the greater land, and the fact that on roads with improved surface, hauling becomes, to a great extent, independent of the weather conditions, means a considerable saving on the cost of hauling.

Since roads shorten the distance and lessen the cost of hauling they are beneficial to farmers. Towns also receive a direct financial boost from improved roads. They become a market for a greater scope of products and more producers take away supplies. They bring the country and city into closer touch with each other's wants.

· The cost of hauling farm produce to market is probably not so much increased by the presence of excessive grades as it is by the bad conditions of the road surface. Almost all roads are fairly hard at certain times of the year, but in the spring they are not dependable. When the speed is the same a horse can haul from three to five times as many tons a day on a macadam road as upon a moderately muddy one. This is because the effective radius of travel from a given point on a macadam road is from three to five times the radius of travel from that point on a moderately muddy road.

There is no question that poor roads cause an economic waste. In 1906 the Bureau of Statistics of the Department of Agriculture deduced an average cost per ton-mile of 22.7 cents, based upon inquiries sent to nearly 3,000 county superintendents. Since, in that year, less than 8 per cent of the roads in this country were improved, these figures are an average cost of hauling on unimproved roads.

Farmers sooner or later come to realize the value of diversified farming. Perhaps no cause limits farming of this description as bad roads do, and on the other hand, nothing makes it possible to the extent that improved roads do. In the case of fruit growers and truck gardeners, whose products must be moved away from the farm immediately, good roads are essential that the producer get full value for his produce. It is reasonable to say, then, that good roads mean that diversified farming will be encouraged, the area of profitable production increased, and the opportunity for favorable marketing improved, and a more uniform distribution of farm products secured.

Good roads make for a decided increase in the value of land about them. When his road is improved the land owner appreciates the greater earning power of the better site his land offers and accordingly raises the price. The buyer also appreciates these added facilities and is willing to pay for them. The cost of road improvement is generally met by taxation of some form, which in many instances causes the landowners to add to the selling price of their land the amount which the roads have cost them. Landowners are becoming more and more aware of the fact that the money spent for road improvement is an investment of capital and a paying one.

The price of farm land, like that of any other commodity, is ruled by the relation between supply and demand. The increased price of land marks a readjustment between the supply and demand which, in some cases, is sharp and immediate.

A distinct item of increased value is becoming more evident each year; that is, immigration into the rural districts where the road conditions are favorable.

The common cry "back to the soil," is made an inviting one when the road conditions and their subsequent advantages make the rural districts attractive. In this respect the sections where the roads are improved have their greatest influence upon motorists.

The benefit of good roads to tourist travel is one which cannot be overlooked from the economic standpoint. It is estimated that thirty thousand tourists have visited Switzerland each year and many of these are Americans. This little country has built up her roads as an investment and now depends largely upon the expenditure of these tourists as a source of revenue. This money is a sufficient amount to make it worth while to keep it in our own country. Figures from the Denver Chamber of Commerce show that six thousand automobilists visiting Colorado, spent two million seven hundred thousand dollars in that state alone.

Motorists are making more effort than any other class of people to secure improvement of public highways. They have attended public gatherings, have perfected organizations, published magazines and even subscribed to funds for improvement of highways. The State Automobile Association, of Idaho, raised fifteen thousand dollars to complete the Ross Ford road by popular subscription. No one has helped more materially to make the Lincoln Highway possible than the tourists. It is obvious then, that, in reckoning the benefits of good roads, the possibility and probability of increased tourist travel must be included as an economic factor.

Considering everything then, it can be said that the economic value of good roads as a means of communication and transportation are well worth the effort and capital used in building them.

OILING ROADS.

From inquiries received it is apparent that some county boards desire to expend part of their State aid funds in the oiling of dirt roads. While we know and appreciate the benefits that accrue from the oiling of highways, still there is no provision of the law, which permits the State Highway Commission to use State funds for the oiling of earth roads.

The suggestion has been made, that when the State and county jointly improve a dirt road by grading, leveling and crowning, including surface or sub-surface drainage, the highway commissioners of the township or road district in which the road is located should appreciate the improvement enough to do the initial oiling of the road. In fact the commissioners should gladly agree to do the initial oiling in order to get the road improved, for thereafter the maintenance of such a road is by law required to be done by the county.

An amendment to the road law passed by the legislature just adjourned, permits townships to vote to raise a tax or issue bonds for grading and oiling earth roads, but this will not affect the State aid roads as constructed or improved by the State and county.

ILLINOIS HIGHWAYS

[Printed by authority of the State of Illinois.]

STATE HIGHWAY DEPARTMENT

VOL. 2	SPRINGFIELD, ILLINOIS, AUGUST, 1915	No. 8

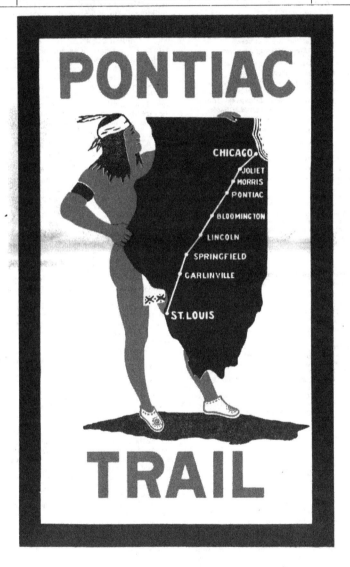

ILLINOIS HIGHWAYS.

Published Monthly by the
State Highway Department.

ILLINOIS HIGHWAY COMMISSION.

A. D. Gash, *President.*
S. E. Bradt, *Secretary.*
James P. Wilson.

Wm. W. Marr, *Chief State Highway Engineer.*
P. C. McArdle, *Assistant State Highway Engineer.*

H. E. Bilger, *Road Engineer, Springfield, Illinois.*
C. Older, *Bridge Engineer, Springfield, Illinois.*
B. H. Piepmeier, *Assistant Engineer, Springfield, Illinois.*
G. F. Burch, *Assistant Engineer, Springfield, Illinois.*
M. W. Watson, *Assistant Engineer, Springfield, Illinois.*
F. L. Roman, *Testing Engineer, Springfield, Illinois.*
J. M. McCoy, *Chief Clerk, Springfield, Illinois.*

DIVISION ENGINEERS.
H. B. Bushnell..............Aurora
R. L. Bell.....................Paris
H. E. Surman..........Rock Island
A. H. Hunter................Peoria
Fred Tarrant............Springfield
C. M. Slaymaker........E. St. Louis
J. E. Huber.................Marion

Address all communications in regard to "Illinois Highways," to State Highway Department, Springfield, Illinois. Attention of K. N. Evans, Department Editor.

CONTENTS.

MR. McARDLE GRANTED LEAVE OF ABSENCE.

Mr. P. C. McArdle, who for the past year and a half has been Assistant Chief State Highway Engineer, has been granted a leave. of absence from his State work to take charge of the hard road work in Vermilion County.

The people of Vermilion County, at the fall election in 1914, voted to issue bonds in the sum of $1,500,000 for the purpose of constructing hard roads. In order that the construction work should be handled successfully, the county board determined to secure the services of a thoroughly competent highway engineer, and, after a country-wide investigation, the position was offered to Mr. McArdle.

As Mr. McArdle was acting Chief State Highway Engineer from July 1, 1914, to December, 1914, during which time he organized and perfected the work of building State aid roads throughout the State, there can be no doubt but that he will be even more successful in this county work.

Vermilion County is to be congratulated upon securing the services of an engineer, who by his proven ability, will complete a system of hard roads in that county, which will be second to none in the State.

The State Highway Department regrets losing the services of Mr. McArdle during his leave of absence, but appreciates the good that he will do in his new field, and knows that the cause of good roads will be greatly benefited in this State on account of the manner in which he will manage this work.

STATE AID ALLOTMENTS FOR 1915-16.

The following statement shows the amount of money which was apportioned for State aid road work by the State Highway Commission to the different counties in the State for the fiscal year 1915-16. The total amount appropriated for State aid road work for the next two years was $2,000,000 of which $1,000,000 was available July 1, 1915, and $1,000,000 will be available July 1, 1916.

From the amount available July 1, 1915, $10,000 was set aside as a fund for the maintenance of State aid roads, and the remaining $990,000 was apportioned to the different counties for construction work. Another apportionment will be made after July 1, 1916, of the funds then available, which should give to each county an amount approximately the same as allotted to them this year.

The apportionment for each county, except Cook County, is in the direct proportion that the amount of road tax paid by each county bears to the total amount paid in all counties. Cook County, being the only county in the State which pays over 40 per cent of the State's money, is entitled to receive 25 per cent of the money it paid in, which is appropriated for road work.

In the last published report of the State Auditor dated 1914, in statement No. 23 will be found the amount paid by each county for road and bridge tax for the year 1913, the last year for which the figures are now available. Reference to this table will make it possible for anyone to check the allotment made to any particular county.

The attention of county boards should be called to the fact that another allotment of State funds will be made after July 1, 1916, at which time each county should receive approximately the same amount as allotted for this fiscal year, although each may receive a slightly greater amount, if for any reason some counties do not take advantage of their allotments for this year. Some counties may desire to have constructed next year, the amount of road that would take up their entire allotments for the two years and it will be necessary for them to make provision therefor at their September meeting when county levies are made, if they do not already have funds on hand, which can be appropriated to meet the State allotments.

It should be noted in this connection that the increase in the road and bridge tax for the State during the two years from 1911 to 1913 was over 24 per cent. If the allotment made to any county for this year seems out of proportion to the amount which they received for the two-year period 1913-14-15, it is to be explained by the fact that their road and bridge tax has varied at a different rate than that of the State as a whole.

In order to receive their fair share of the State allotments, each county should see that their road and bridge tax was in proportion to that which the other counties in the State were raising. As an illustration of what an increase in the road and bridge tax of the townships would mean, it should be noted that for every $8 collected as road and bridge tax in 1913, $1 is returned this year as State aid and another dollar will be returned next year, or a total amount returned of $2. If the amount of road and bridge tax in any township for 1913 had been $800 less, the county in which that township is located would have received $100 less on this year's State aid allotment, and also $100 less on next year's allotment and conversely if their tax had been $800 greater they would have received $100 more this year and another $100 more next year. Hence, the advantage of having the individual township's levy as high a rate for road and bridge work as possible, for they would not only get the advantage from having more money to keep up their roads and bridges, but also they would help their county by making it possible to have their State aid fund increased.

There are very few townships or road districts in this State which should not raise their full amount of road and bridge tax, or 61 cents on the $100 valuation.

The amount of State aid that each county will receive for the year 1915-16 is shown in the following table:

Counties.	Allotment 1915-16.	Counties.	Allotment 1915-16.
Adams	$ 9,591	Grundy	$ 8,841
Alexander	10,390	Hamilton	3,489
Bond	4,334	Hancock	9,719
Boone	5,808	Hardin	661
Brown	2,799	Henderson	5,107
Bureau	19,764	Henry	13,027
Calhoun	1,596	Iroquois	19,294
Carroll	7,407	Jackson	7,880
Cass	6,893	Jasper	4,052
Champaign	20,676	Jefferson	5,124
Christian	12,912	Jersey	3,808
Clark	5,446	JoDaviess	6,285
Clay	3,487	Johnson	984
Clinton	4,851	Kane	23,582
Coles	8,905	Kankakee	10,394
Cook	108,994	Kendall	6,050
Crawford	4,904	Knox	11,624
Cumberland	3,220	Lake	11,953
DeKalb	15,482	LaSalle	28,384
DeWitt	7,920	Lawrence	6,647
Douglas	7,951	Lee	10,461
Dupage	11,266	Livingston	15,880
Edgar	13,529	Logan	10,936
Edwards	1,552	Macon	16,683
Effingham	3,904	Macoupin	11,027
Fayette	7,253	Madison	15,469
Ford	8,503	Marion	6,042
Franklin	6,185	Marshall	6,118
Fulton	11,811	Mason	5,336
Gallatin	2,267	Massac	1,552
Greene	7,049	McDonough ...	7,987

Counties.	Allotment 1915-16.	Counties.	Allotment 1915-16.
McHenry	$ 12,956	Schuyler	$ 4,587
McLean	24,196	Scott	3,370
Menard	3,657	Shelby	11,904
Mercer	9,085	Stark	5,097
Monroe	2,896	St. Clair	10,085
Montgomery ...	10,818	Stephenson	10,348
Morgan	9,304	Tazewell	9,240
Moultrie	5,626	Union	2,526
Ogle	12,949	Vermilion	29,482
Peoria	21,744	Wabash	2,846
Perry	2,618	Warren	9,069
Piatt	7,223	Washington ...	4,356
Pike	8,664	Wayne	5,844
Pope	1,243	White	4,531
Pulaski	1,987	Whiteside	13,741
Putnam	2,585	Will	17,772
Randolph	3,615	Williamson	5,440
Richland	3,337	Winnebago	14,042
Rock Island ...	6,285	Woodford	8,415
Saline	8,462		
Sangamon	17,010	Total	$990,000

ACCIDENT REPORTS.

During the month of July we received 11 accident reports from different county superintendents throughout the State. Of these reports three were caused by autos being struck on railroad crossings and seven were caused by careless driving of automobiles, such as attempting to turn out of a rut while going at a high rate of speed, racing after night, two automobiles running into each other at crossroads, and one team being forced into the ditch by a machine which refused to share a part of the traveled road. One accident was caused by a thrashing engine falling through a wooden bridge.

There were 25 persons seriously injured, of whom only one was killed, the others receiving injuries such as broken arms, legs, hips, ribs, collar bones, etc., while nearly all were badly cut and bruised.

The property damage as reported amounted to $8,975.

It is apparent that careless and fast driving of automobiles on country roads is the cause of many accidents which should be avoided. Too many drivers "take a chance," either to beat a railroad train over a crossing or to travel at a rate of speed much in excess of that allowed by law or that which the roadbed over which they are traveling is in condition for.

We know that many accidents happen on our highways which the county superintendents forget to advise us concerning, but enough are reported to indicate that accidents are very general all over the State, and that in order to reduce their number it will be necessary to devise some scheme to check the inefficient drivers.

ROAD AND BRIDGE TAXES.

Many townships throughout the State have been deprived of a part of their road and bridge taxes during the past few years because their highway commissioners did not hold a meeting, as required by law, for the purpose of determining the tax rate which they were to certify to the county board.

The law on this point is very explicit and must be followed. Section 50 of the Revised Road Law, among other things, states:

"They (highway commissioners) shall also hold a regular semi-annual meeting between the first Tuesday in August and the first Tuesday in September of each year at a time to be named by their president, for the purpose of determining the tax rate to be certified by them to their respective county boards, as hereinafter provided."

Section 56, in defining general tax levy for road and bridge purposes, says in part:

"At a regular meeting to be held on the first Tuesday in September, the board of highway commissioners in each town or road district shall annually determine and certify to the board of supervisors or board of county commissioners the amount necessary to be raised by taxation for the proper construction, maintenance and repair of roads and bridges in such town or road district. Such certificate shall be filed in the office of the county clerk, and by that official presented to the county board at their regular September meeting for their consideration."

Highway commissioners should realize that they must follow the law in regard to making this road and bridge tax, and that, if they do not, they are liable to loose a portion of this tax, which generally is badly needed. It is an easy matter to make this tax levy correctly and highway commissioners should be careful to comply with the law.

NAMING THE TRAILS.

Another great automobile road has been officially christened and opened to travel, the name plates marking the course of the *Pontiac Trail*, the connecting highway between Chicago and St. Louis, having been placed in position on the guide posts which were erected at intervals of a mile along this highway by the Goodrich Tire Co., showing the mileage to Chicago and St. Louis, and the nearest local towns.

These name plates bear, in addition to the name, "Pontiac Trail," the full-length figure of an Indian upholding a map of the State of Illinois. The significance will be grasped at once, for this trail will inevitably become the great thoroughfare of the State, connecting as it does, its largest city with the metropolis of its western border, and passing through its capital as well as so many other prosperous cities and villages, and the heart of the corn belt.

The appropriateness of the Indian figure to the name is likewise at once apparent, and for this great highway the name is doubly significant, for the famous chief whose name it bears, in the later years of his life, often crossed its course, since near its southern terminus he spent his last years and met his death, and three quarters of a century ago his name was commemorated by the christening of one of the prettiest, most prosperous and energetic of the many towns, through which the trail will pass.

It is but justice to say that these name plates are paid for and put up at the expense of the live business men of the city of Pontiac, who are appreciative of the compliment paid their city by the naming of the trail, and who are also appreciative of the benefit their town will derive from being on the line of this splendid highway.

The naming of the trail after Pontiac, the great Indian, who was able by his genius and the power of his personality to league all the tribes of the Northwest in one great confederacy against the English, was most appropriate, for while the scene of his great conspiracy and his warlike achievements was the region of the Great Lakes, his later life was spent in the country at the foot of the trail, and here he met his death by assassination at the hands of an Indian spy of the British in 1772.

The story of Pontiac, of his great confederacy of warring and hostile tribes, which he formed and held together at the close of the French and Indian war, of his great conspiracy against the English, and his plan to capture every frontier fort on May 6, 1763, a plan which only failed of complete success by the narrow margin of Fort Pitt, Niagara and Detroit, has been told at length by Francis Parkman in "The Conspiracy of Pontiac," and the career of the great chief has figured in history, legend, song and story.

Indeed, his whole career was a romantic one, and the story of the capture of Mackinac by the stratagem of an Indian ball game, of the saving of Detroit by the fondness of an Indian girl for Major Gladwyn, its commandant, and the many other incidents of its long siege, and of the whole war, have been immortalized by such authors as Mary Hartwell Catherwood and Gilbert Parker. The name should throw a glamour of romance about the trail which now further honors the memory of this mighty aboriginal statesman and warrior.

The course of the trail, after leaving Chicago, passes down the beautiful Desplaines Valley on the south side of that river, and of the Illinois and Michigan and Drainage Canals, in general paralleling the two latter.

Passing Summit, the traveler on the highway can, by a short detour, pass the monument of boulders marking the spot where Father Marquette camped, and where he first saw the Desplaines River on his voyage of exploration to the Mississippi. From Summit the road leads by Argo, with its mammoth corn products plant, by the stone quarries of Lemont and Lockport to the bustling industrial city of Joliet, the site of the Northern Illinois Penitentiary, one of the largest and most noted prisons in the world, and the home of numerous iron and steel plants and other manufactures.

Here the Pontiac Trail intersects the famous Lincoln Highway from coast to coast. Hereafter the two highways will undoubtedly, to all practical intents, monopolize automobile traffic between St. Louis and eastern points on the Lincoln Highway, to the everlasting benefit of Joliet garages and hotels.

From Joliet the trail crosses the Desplaines and proceeds down the north side of that river and of the Illinois to Morris, county seat of Grundy County and a prosperous agricultural town of 4,000 souls. Morris is the nearest point on the trail to the State park at Starved Rock, with its scenic and historic interest, and the trail thus far is the shortest and best road between Chicago and the park, and here will flow a heavy and rapidly increasing motor traffic.

From Morris the way turns south, across the Illinois River and through a fine farming country, and a mile north of Dwight enters Livingston County, the second agricultural county of Illinois. Here it may be well to state parenthetically that the trail crosses the very mid region of McLean and Livingston Counties, and that McLean and Livingston Counties are respectively first and second in the banner farming State of Illinois in the value of farm products, and that for oats and corn they have no rivals in the United States or even in the world.

Dwight is a handsome, well-built and exceptionally well-paved town, whose chief point of interest is the attractive buildings of the Leslie E. Keeley Co. From Dwight the road turns southwesterly, in the main paralleling the Alton Railroad, through Odell to Pontiac, the capital town of Livingston County, and the namesake of the trail.

Pontiac has also the distinction of being one of the most attractive cities of its size and class to be found within many a day's journey, with miles of pavement arched over by spreading trees, and the pleasant Vermilion River winding through its midst and almost encircling the grounds of its famous chautauqua, probably second in importance only to the parent institution in New York. Pontiac is primarily a city of homes and has infinite attractions as a residence town, although it also is celebrated for its shoes and is the site of the Illinois State Reformatory.

From Pontiac the trail pursues its way through the world's garden to Chenoa, just across the line in McLean County, where it intersects another newly named and established road, "The Corn Belt Route," from Logansport, Indiana, to Peoria.

Beyond Chenoa the trail passes between beautiful waving fields of oats and corn, through the prosperous agricultural towns of Lexington and Towanda, to Normal and Bloomington, contiguous cities, the former the seat of two State institutions, the Illinois Soldiers' Orphans' Home and the Illinois State Normal University, the latter especially, with its wide and beautifully shaded campus, being well worth visiting.

Bloomington is the queen of the corn belt. Devastated by a great fire on June 12, 1900, which burned over 10 acres of its business district, including the courthouse, with a loss of more than $2,000,000, the city has come to regard the fire as its greatest blessing, and to-day, its business district is devoid of those ramshackle, prehistoric structures which disfigure most cities, and Bloomington has no competition in the matter of looks among cities even twice its size.

At Bloomington are located the great car shops of the Alton Railroad, and here also is the Illinois Wesleyan University, a Methodist school of importance. Bloomington, with the adjoining town of Normal, also boasts many beautiful residences, miles of perfect pavement and some beautiful parks, and is well worthy of a special visit, and a day or two's stopover by the motoring tourist.

Leaving Bloomington, the trail still continues through the heart of the corn belt, and a short distance south passes through the famous Funk farms near Funk's Grove, with their thousands of acres of perfectly tilled land and model farm buildings and farm methods.

Pioneers in progressive farming, the Funk family were also early and firm believers in good roads, and at the present time do all the road work in their township at actual cost, making use of their farm tractors for the purpose.

Still southwestward, the trail takes its way through McLean, and Atlanta, and Lawndale to Lincoln, county seat of Logan County, a busy city of 10,000 people, and an important railroad center, having important mining interests. Lincoln also has the State School and Colony, an institution for the feebleminded, and the Illinois State Odd Fellows' Orphans' Home, and a Presbyterian College, and it also has a chautauqua, situated near the trail, and about two miles southwest of the city.

After Lincoln, the next large town on the trail is Springfield, the State capital, whose historic associations with the personality of Lincoln are too well known to need enlargement. His homestead and his grave are here, and the streets he walked in life, and here came at one time or another every conspicuous figure in the public life of Illinois. Here are the State House and many other public buildings, and here is located the State Fair, past whose grounds the trail enters Springfield, also passing the mammoth plant of the Illinois Watch Co.

At Springfield the trail is crossed by the Pike's Peak Ocean to Ocean Highway, and here another interchange of travel will eventually be developed.

From Springfield, still in the main following the Alton Railroad, the trail leads to the historic old town of Carlinville, capital of Macoupin County, named after a former governor. From Springfield, south, fields of corn and oats have largely given place to wheat, and the towers of coal mines frequently break the horizon, for here the trail passes through an important coal-producing region, and here it has reached the ancient hunting grounds of the chief whose name it bears.

From Carlinville the road bears nearly due south, and at the important mining and manufacturing town of Collinsville, turns nearly west into East St. Louis and across the Mississippi to its destination.

The shortest route for motor travel between Chicago and St. Louis, with so many large and important towns on its course, and intersecting, as it does, so many important east and west thoroughfares, its rapid development as a highway is easily forecasted. Already it is a well-cared-for highway, and following, as it does, State aid roads every inch of its length, its permanent improvement will be rapid and certain. At the present time, the trail follows stone roads the entire distance from Chicago to Morris, a distance of about 60 miles, and at Morris there are about 2½ miles of concrete road. South of Pontiac, there are 5 miles of asphalt, stone and concrete road, and about 4 miles of concrete and crushed stone through Funk's Grove. At Lincoln there are 2½ miles of concrete road, and at Springfield 3 or 4 miles of the same.

It is planned to form the Pontiac Trail Association, with a vice president in each township and an officer in each county through which the trail passes, for the purpose of improving the dirt roads along the route, and of hastening the coming of a permanent highway.

The Goodrich Tire Co., in addition to erecting the guideposts above referred to, are preparing a road log of the route, copies of which can be had, when completed, from the company at Akron, Ohio, from the garages at the towns along the road, and from the superintendents of highways of the counties through which it passes.

And so the christening of the trails goes merrily on, thanks to the gasoline engine, which has carried road building in Illinois further in five years than in the preceding century.

DEPARTMENTAL REPORT.

August 1, 1915.

STATE HIGHWAY COMMISSION:

GENTEMEN: I submit the following report on the present condition of the work being done by the State Highway Department:

BRIDGE WORK.

During the month of July, 1915, plans and specifications for 52 bridges were prepared and sent to county superintendents of highways; total estimated cost, $99,440.

Contracts were awarded for 28 concrete bridges and 2 steel bridges, at an average cost of 88 per cent of the estimates; total estimated cost, $26,860.

Twenty-three bridge plans, prepared by county superintendents, were checked and approved.

On August 1, 1915, there were 36 bridge-inspection reports on hand ready for work.

LABORATORY WORK.

During the month of July, 1915, 181 samples of miscellaneous materials comprising cements, sands, gravels, crushed stones, bricks, road oils, asphalts, tars, creosote oil and creosoted lumber were tested. There were also eight field inspections.

CONTRACTS AWARDED.

During the month of July, bids were received and contracts awarded on two sections of roads in Kankakee County, this being the first work started during this fiscal year. It was necessary for the county board to hold a meeting to accept their State aid allotment, after which the work was advertised and bids received on July 27.

It is not expected that many county boards will hold a meeting to accept State aid until their September meeting, so that few contracts will be awarded until after that time.

Engineer's estimates and bids received are exclusive of cement, which is furnished by the State.

The following tabulation will show the names of bidders and amount of bid on the several sections, together with the name of the successful bidder:

Kankakee County, Section C, Route 1-G; length, 3,560 feet; width, 10 feet; type, *concrete;* engineer's estimate, $6,047; date of letting, July 28, 1915.

Name of bidder.	Amount of bid.
Frank L. Shidler, Kankakee, Ill.	$5,900 00
Carpenter & Weaver, Terre Haute, Ind.	5,647 00
R. A. Medaris Const. Co., Springfield, Ill.	6,000 00
Andrew Ward & Son, Oak Glen, Ill.	4,900 00
John Moroff & Son, Kankakee, Ill.	5,696 00
G. H. Summerville, Chicago Heights, Ill.	5,453 00
Goggin Construction Co., Arcola, Ill.	5,716 80

Contract awarded to Andrew Ward & Son.

Kankakee County, Section D, Route 1; length, 5,000 feet; width, 15 feet; type, *concrete;* engineer's estimate, $9,159; date of letting, July 28, 1915.

Name of bidder.	Amount of bid.
Carpenter & Weaver, Terre Haute, Ind.	$8,459 00
R. A. Medaris Const. Co., Springfield, Ill.	9,000 00
Andrew Ward & Son, Oak Glen, Ill.	7,300 00
John Moroff & Son, Kankakee, Ill.	8,500 00
C. W. Jensen & Co., Chicago, Ill.	9,475 00
G. H. Summerville, Chicago Heights, Ill.	8,523 00
Goggin Construction Co., Arcola, Ill.	7,880 40

Contract awarded to Andrew Ward & Son.

BLUE PRINTING.

During the month of July, 1915, 78 blue prints were made of our bridge standards for county superintendents of highways, as well as prints for 4 foreign bridge plans averaging 2 sheets, 6 prints being made of each sheet, or about 48 prints. Prints were made of 21 bridges designed by this department, 20 sets each, as well as three preliminary sets being sent to the various counties for their use in letting said bridges, totaling 966 prints. Preliminary prints were also made of 16 bridges designed by this department for use of county boards, 3 sets being made of each, or 96 prints.

Preliminary prints were made for 6 sections of State aid work for the county board to pass on, official prints then being made for county clerk, county superintendent and this office. Each section averages about 12 sheets, making a total of 288 prints.

Miscellaneous prints, about 600 made for office use, made a grand total for the month of July of 2,078 prints.

Very truly yours,

WM. W. MARR,
Chief State Highway Engineer.

MAINTENANCE OF STATE AID ROADS IN ILLINOIS.

[By B. H. PIEPMEIER, *Associate Member American Society Civil Engineers, Maintenance Engineer, State Highway Department, Springfield, Ill.*]

(A portion of the following article is a reprint from the Engineering News of August 12, 1915.)

The 1913 session of the Legislature enacted a Road Law in Illinois creating State aid to the extent of fifty per cent (50%) of the cost of construction on a system of State aid routes, aggregating about 16,000 miles, or about seventeen per cent (17%) of the total road mileage of the State.

The law requires that "whenever a State aid road shall be constructed or improved in any county, the State shall thereafter keep all such roads in proper repair and the total cost of such maintenance shall be paid out of the State Road and Bridge Fund."

Inasmuch as the law requires the State to stand the upkeep cost on the State aid roads after construction, the State Highway Commission has deemed it advisable in the majority of cases to have the roads constructed of some of the more durable types of pavements, such as concrete and brick. It is well recognized that the State aid routes are the main traveled thoroughfares and necessarily require considerable attention, even when constructed of the higher types of pavements.

While the law has been in effect but two years and there has been, in round numbers, only about one hundred miles of road constructed under State supervision and State aid, it would seem at first thought that the upkeep cost on these roads would be almost negligible at this time. While it is expected that the maintenance cost will be very light the first few years, it is quite important that they receive attention as needed. The saying, "A stitch in time saves nine," is vitally true when applied to the maintenance of roads.

Inasmuch as a majority of the roads have been constructed of concrete and brick, particular attention has been directed along the line of inaugurating a system of maintenance that will properly care for these types of pavements. Particular attention, therefore, will be given to the maintenance equipment and methods adopted for filling the joints and cracks in concrete and brick pavements that have been constructed under State aid.

CONDITIONS.

The one hundred miles of pavements that have been constructed are widely separated in a great many different counties of the State. However, about 50 per cent of the concrete pavements constructed are within a radius of 75 miles of Chicago, or within the northeast division. The other six divisions of the State have both concrete and brick pavements, widely scattered over their divisions.

EQUIPMENT.

On account of the present small mileage of improved roads, as well as their wide distribution throughout the State, it was thought expedient, at this time, to furnish a small portable heating kettle, steel broom, heavy barn broom, a scratching tool and pouring can, to four of the seven divisions; two of the divisions being able to borrow from their adjoining divisions and take care of the necessary work of filling the cracks and joints in the State aid pavements for the next two years.

Portable Hand Kettle and Equipment For Heating Bituminous Material to Fill Joints and Cracks in Concrete and Brick Pavements.

The northeast division, which has about 50 per cent of the State aid concrete pavements within a radius of 75 miles, is provided with a small maintenance truck. The principal use of the truck is to transport from place to place the necessary heating apparatus, bituminous filler and sand. The maximum load that is transported to different sections of roads does not exceed 1,000 pounds. The light truck, which could be easily converted into a car that might be used by the division engineer, when not in use on maintenance work, was, therefore, considered to be most satisfactory.

A Ford runabout was equipped by removing the rear hood and constructing a 42-inch by 36-inch demountable body on the back. In the lower corners of the body were placed 3 by 3 by ⅜-inch angles, which projected in the rear sufficient to support a 32 by 30 by 16-inch heating kettle. In one corner of the body a socket was provided for holding a light derrick equipped with a differential chain block for hoisting drums and barrels of bituminous material into the truck and for dismounting the heating kettle when

other use of the car is desired. The derrick was made so that one man could handle any load that he wished to put into the truck. The derrick pole could also be removed easily and carried at a suitable place under the body of the car when not in use. On account of the load, the car was required to carry the oversize tires 31 by 4 inches, with demountable rims.

A rectangular heating kettle 32 by 30 by 16 inches was constructed with a tight-fitting lid and mounted on the rear of the truck. Beneath the heating kettle were mounted six standard cup gasoline burners, which are supplied with gasoline from the auto gas tank.

Gas was used for heating the bituminous material in preference to other fuel, largely on account of its weight, cleanliness and convenience.

Ford Maintenance Truck, With Heating Kettle and Derrick For Loading Barrels. Used For Maintaining State Aid Concrete and Brick Pavements.

It has been found that about 1 gallon of gasoline will supply sufficient heat for one day's work. The gas burners may be started quickly and when the bituminous material is once hot, one burner will keep it at the proper temperature throughout the day. The gasoline burners work satisfactorily while the car is enroute to place, so there is practically no time lost in getting the material heated. When the car is needed for other use, the kettle is dismounted and a small gasoline can hooked onto the side of the kettle, which is connected with the burners by a short hose. This arrangement enables the operator to keep a constant fire under the kettle when he has the car elsewhere on the road, looking after work.

OPERATION.

A great deal of dependence can be put in the truck maintenance, as an expert can be placed in charge of it and this insures efficiency. The expert is the only one that goes with the truck from place to place. He hires all help required upon any particular job. If there were more than one with the truck there would be many days in which they could not all work on account of weather conditions. Bad weather, under the present system, causes but little loss of time, as there are usually a number of things that can be done by the man in charge, such as cleaning out ditches, clearing culverts, fixing up the side roads, etc.

Where the portable heating kettle is used, one is required to depend upon the average laborer to do and supervise a majority of the work. On account of the delays in shipping the kettle from place to place, it is not always convenient to have an expert follow it.

The division engineer therefore directs the shipping of the equipment from place to place and arranges with some local party to do the work in accordance with his directions. However, under this scheme the division engineer is required to give considerable of his time to the maintenance work.

It was first estimated that the truck would be consigned to the northeast division, but on account of its efficiency and convenience it is now being considered to have it, or a similar truck, for use on all State aid roads, even though many of them are separated by long stretches of earth roads.

MATERIALS.

The State Highway Department for the last four years has used and investigated various materials that may be used in filling cracks and joints in concrete pavements. It is evident that a well-selected bituminous material and clean, coarse sand meets the requirements, if properly applied. The Mexican, Texas and California asphalts and refined tars have been used. The proper grade of refined tar seems to give the best results. However, with any of the bituminous materials it seems necessary to cover all cracks and joints twice each year, once in the spring and again late in the fall.

FUTURE WORK.

While the small truck referred to above has been very dependable and has fulfilled most of the require-ments imposed upon it in the way of upkeep on the macadam and earth shoulders, side roads, ditches, etc., yet it was not designed for this purpose. It is expected that in the near future a much larger truck, operated in the same manner, will have to be equipped to handle the upkeep on all gravel and macadam roads, macadam and earth shoulders, side roads, ditches, etc.

REPORTS.

The truck operator is required to make a daily report on postal card to the maintenance engineer at the head office, giving the date of arrival on the job, the amount of road covered each day, the approximate time of finishing work and other remarks pertaining to the road.

He also sends such postal card reports to the division engineer, that will keep him advised about when the road will be completed and when he will arrive at the next point. This is required that the division engineer may know what progress is being made in his division and arrange to visit the respective jobs if he finds it possible.

Upon the completion of a route or section of a State aid road, the operator, or man in charge of the work, makes out a detailed report of all expenditures on the form accompanying this paper. This report is checked by the division engineer, if possible, and then forwarded to the head office, where the maintenance engineer makes final check on all items of expenditure.

UPKEEP COST ON STATE AID ROADS   Year.................. ...

County.............. .. .. Sec......... .. ... Route ....   Local Name of Road. ....
Nearest R. R. Station ....

DESCRIPTION

PAVEMENT	MACADAM SHOULDERS	CONDITION OF PAVEMENT
Type.......................	Length...............	Total Length Long't Cracks.. ....ft.
Length..................	Width	Total Length Trans. Cracks ....ft.
Width	Sq. Yds....	Total Length of Joints. . . ..ft.
Sq. Yds. (b)......	Condition.........	Total Length all Cracks and Joints (a).........ft.
		Discontinuity a-b............ ....

MATERIALS

BITUMINOUS MATERIAL USED	DESCRIPTION OF OTHER MATERIALS USED
Quantity Ordered........... gallons at............f. o. b. Station	Sand. ....
Quantity Used ... ... gallons at.......... .f. o. b. Station..........	Stone or Gravel.. . ...
Brand...	
Unused material in care of....................	....
Remarks	....

MAINTENANCE ON SLAB

Date.	COST OF MATERIALS USED					COST OF LABOR		COST OF TRANSPORTATION						Total
	Sand.	Bitumen.	Coal.	Gas for heating.	Hardware.	Skilled.	Common.	Storage.	Teaming.	Freight.	Gas, oil, repairs	Labor.	Dep. on Equip't.	
.. ..						....								
....	....	....	...	..	....			....		....		....		
....	....	.... .	....	...	...	....						...		
... .						...				.....		...		
... .	....	... ..	....	...	.. ...	......		....	..		...	....		
Total cost...	....	......	......	....	.....	....		....	..	... ..	..	.... ..		
Cost per sq.yd.	... . ..	....	... ...	....	... ..	....		....		... ..		....		

Fig. 1. Showing Form For Record of Maintenance on Slab.

COST OF UPKEEP ON ROADSIDES AND DITCHES.

Date.	MACADAM SHOULDERS.				EARTH SHOULDERS.				DITCHES AND DRAINS.				VEGETATION.			
	Skilled Labor.	Labor and Teaming.	Mat'-rials.	Eq't.	Skilled Labor.	Labor and Teaming.	Mat'-rials.	Eq't.	Skilled Labor.	Labor and Teaming.	Mat'-rials.	Eq't.	Skilled Labor.	Labor and Teaming.	Mat'-rials.	Eq't.
Total Cost																

Date.	CLEANING.				CULVERTS.				BRIDGES.				SUMMATION OF COST.	
	Skilled Labor.	Labor and Teaming.	Mat'-rials.	Eq't.	Skilled Labor.	Labor and Teaming.	Mat'-rials.	Eq't.	Skilled Labor.	Labor and Teaming.	Mat'-rials.	Eq't.	Mainten'ce on Slab.	
													Macad'm Shoulders.	
													Earth Shoulders.	
													Ditches and Drains.	
													Vegetation.	
													Cleaning.	
													Culverts.	
													Bridges.	
Total Cost														

* Charged to State Road and Bridge Fund. "Fill this card out complete in ink." Fix depreciation on Ford truck—2.00 per mile of pavement maintained and portable heating kettles—1.00 per mile of pavement maintained.

Supervision.

Grand Total Cost.

Remarks:

Approved.

Work done by......................................

In charge.

Maintenance Engineer.

Fig. 2. Showing Form For Record of Cost of Upkeep on Roadsides and Ditches.

STATE OF ILLINOIS
STATE HIGHWAY DEPARTMENT
Detail Statement of Expenditures from Special Maintenance Fund for Month of .... 191.........

ITEMIZED STATEMENT OF EXPENDITURES.	EXPENDED					RECEIVED		
	County	Section	$	cts.	Receipt Number	Date	$	cts.
						On hands 1st		
Total expended								
Balance on hand								
Total						Total		

....
Engineer.

Fig. 3. Form for monthly report of division engineers and maintenance engineer on expenditures from maintenance fund.

The forms referred to are made up into books for the division engineers. Every other leaf in the book is detachable. The division engineer records all information and items of expenditure on the detachable leaf. This is transferred to similar printed sheets in the book by carbon paper. The detachable leaf is printed on both sides. The division engineer's book, therefore, has Figure 1 recorded on the left-hand page and Figure 2 on the right-hand page.

All leaves in the book are of the standard 5 by 8 inches, tab-card size. This permits the original copy to be conveniently filed at the head office as a permanent record of the cost of upkeep on each individual section of State aid road. The division engineers also have a permanent and convenient record of expenditures made.

In the back of the upkeep cost record book, there are a number of blank leaves, as shown in Figure 3. These are used for making up monthly statements to the Chief State Highway Engineer, of all money received and expended on the upkeep of all State aid roads during the month. These reports are used in accounting to the State Highway Commission and State Auditor.

COST DATA.

The following cost data has been taken from some work recently done with the portable heating kettle and automobile truck. Only cost data in maintaining the slab or pavement proper is given at this time. The upkeep cost on macadam and earth shoulders, side roads and ditches will be reported when more complete cost data will be available.

supervision is recorded and the time required for doing the work is taken into consideration. The division engineer must necessarily give considerable of his time to maintenance work, where the portable hand kettle is used. However, he has the opportunity to select good weather for all work done with the outfit and accordingly does not have any men charged against maintenance work when they are not able to work on the roads, as has been the case with the truck.

It will be noted from the table above that the cost of filling cracks and joints varies from $0.0010 to $0.0057 per square yard of pavement, the cost usually varying in proportion to the discontinuity of the pavement. Discontinuity is represented by the figure found by dividing the total length of all cracks and joints, in feet, by the square yards of pavement. The expression of discontinuity is figured for each road on which work is done, as it serves as a guide to compare the cost of maintenance work. It also gives a basis for comparing the condition of surfaces on various pavements.

The specifications under which the State aid roads were constructed required a ¼-inch felt joint to be placed at an angle of 75 degrees with the center line of the pavement and at intervals of 100 feet; joints were also required at the close of each day's work, but in no case were they to be spaced less than 10 feet unless specified by the engineer. The 10 and 18-foot pavements, when constructed under these specifications, have, under normal conditions, a discontinuity of from .090 to .100. If joints had been placed at 50-foot intervals instead of 100-foot the discontin-

---

FIG. NO. 6.

Some Cost Data Showing the Relative Efficiency of Different Methods of Maintaining Concrete Pavements by Filling Cracks and Joints with Bituminous Material.

PORTABLE HEATING KETTLE USED.

County.	Section.	Built.	Width.	Sq. Yds. (a)	Total length in ft. of cracks and joints. (b).	Expression of discontinuity of pavement. b/a.	COST OF LABOR.			MATERIALS.		*Dep. on equipment.	†Supervision.	Total cost.	Cost per Sq. Yd.
							Skilled.	Common.	Teams, Freight, Storage, Transportation.	Bituminous material.	Sand and stone.				
Cass	A	1914	10	7,279	917	.126	$11 00	$ 3 50	$ 9 95	$ 1 92	$ 60	$1 25		$28 22	$ .0039
Iroquois	A	1914	10	13,433	1,753	.130	3 90	4 80	8 85	5 17	2 30			25 42	.0019
Iroquois	B	1914	10	14,784	1,980	.134	3 30	4 40	10 60	4 63	42	2 60		25 95	.0017
Sangamon	B	1912	18	13,600	2,240	.172	10 00	17 67	11 25	20 87	2 00	1 21		63 00	.0060
Sangamon	B	1914	18	4,400	854	.194	5 00	7 30	8 75	3 75		40		25 20	.0057
Sangamon	C	1914	18	4,400	577	.131	3 00	1 22	1 25	1 87	20	40		7 94	.0018
Sangamon	D	1914	18	4,000	774	.193	3 00	1 22	1 25	1 87	20	40		7 94	.0020
Sangamon	E	1914	18	4,700	690	.147	5 00	4 12	3 75	1 87	30	45		15 49	.0033
Menard	A	1914	10	2,667	290	.108	3 85	70	3 61	1 25	25	45		10 11	.0038

Average cost per square yard—$.0039

AUTO TRUCK USED.

County.	Section.	Built.	Width.	Sq. Yds. (a)	Total length in ft. of cracks and joints. (b).	Expression of discontinuity of pavement. b/a.	Skilled.	Common.	Teams, Freight, Storage, Transportation.	Bituminous material.	Sand and stone.	*Dep. on equipment.	†Supervision.	Total cost.	Cost per Sq. Yd.
Logan	A	1914	10	4,000	458	.115	3 00	2 00	56	1 74	10	1 40		8 80	.0022
Logan	D	1914	10	4,000	503	.126	3 00	2 00	70	2 17	10	1 40		9 37	.0034
Livingston	A	1914	10	13,810	2,240	.162	12 00	3 75	2 80	5 57	50	4 70		29 32	.0021
Kankakee	A	1914	10	10,500	1,711	.163	14 00	4 00	1 80	5 30	1 00	3 60		29 20	.0028
Will	A	1914	10	10,666	2,000	.184	18 00	4 60	4 89	4 62	30	3 60		35 91	.0034
Cook	E	1914	18	38,884	5,488	.141	21 00	8 00	4 54	8 92	40	7 40		50 88	.0013
Cook	B	1914	18	14,222	1,821	.128	4 50	3 00	1 26	5 72	10	2 75		17 33	.0012
Cook	A	1914	18	5,240	708	.135	1 50	1 00	57	1 11		1 00		5 18	.0010

Average cost per square yard $ .0022

* Under depreciation one dollar per mile of pavement maintained is charged against the portable heating kettle equipment and two dollars per mile for the auto truck.
† The cost of supervision is prorated against the maintenance and upkeep at the close of the season.

It will be noted from the cost data given above that the average cost of maintenance where the truck was used was about one-third less than where the portable hand kettle was used. This will be offset considerably more in favor of the truck when the cost of

uity of the surface on the normal 10 and 18-foot pavements would have been from .180 to .200. From a maintenance standpoint, therefore, it would be an advantage to have as few joints as possible. Four years' experience in maintaining concrete pavements in

Illinois indicates that joints, even though protected with armor plates, require about the same attention as do the ordinary cracks.

TERMS USED.

It is evident that the term "maintenance" has been greatly misused, or at least used to express two or three widely different things connected with the taking care of roads. Some have divided the term, using "strict maintenance," "partial maintenance," "total maintenance," etc. It would seem proper to confine the term "maintenance" to the wearing surface or traveled portion of the road and to use it in connection with those operations necessary to keep the traveled portion of the road true to its original type and to use the term "upkeep" in its broader sense and to connect it with those operations necessary to keep or restore the entire road to its original type. The upkeep should apply particularly to the side roads, ditches, etc.

The term "repairs" should be used to denote all operations necessary to restore the traveled portion of the public highway to its original condition.

KANE COUNTY PRIZE ESSAY CONTEST.

SECOND PRIZE ESSAY.

[JANET JOHNSON, *Hampshire, Ill., Hampshire Junior H. H. S., District No. 26.*]

GOOD ROADS.

One of the most important movements of the present day is that of good roads. Many bills and resolutions have been introduced into congress to provide, in one way or another, for Federal participation in road building. In general, this is not a new question to the civilized nation, but never before in the history of our country has it's immediate need presented itself so emphatically as now. This problem not only includes their construction, but their maintenance as well and requires the cooperation of every progressive individual with that of the county, State, and Federal Government.

The value of improved roads has been recognized by all prosperous nations ever since civilization began. Commerce, travel, military control, and warfare depend largely upon the quantity and quality of the world's road systems. The word itself comes down to us from the German phrase, to ride, and is closely connected with the Gallic word meaning wagon. Of the earlier tribes, the Romans were the most skillful in the art of road building. One of the best known roads of that period was the Appian Way, begun by Appius Claudius in 312 B. C. As the road movement became more significant to the public, laws were passed concerning them. England took up the construction of macadamized roads, and France, following the former's example, now has one of the most envied road systems in the world.

The work of organized road making in the United States has flourished, chiefly, within the last century. During recent years the states have taken up this matter and as a result, local laws have been passed, old roads reconstructed, and new ones made. Enormous sums of money are being expended each year on the improvement of public roads, but of the 2,226,842 miles of road in the United States, only ten per cent are classed as improved. State aid is of the most importance, not because of its financial help, but in giving the best supervision of the construction, gaining the best methods, and in stirring up every individual to do his best to make this undertaking a success in his locality.

It is rather difficult to demonstrate in dollars and cents just how valuable good roads are to a community. In the first place, improved highways help business, stimulate trade, facilitate transportation, put money in circulation, and increase values.

Everything we eat or wear must be hauled over wagon roads. It is therefore necessary for this means of transportation to be improved, thereby cheapening the hauling, the goods, and lowering the cost of living. The enthusiasm for good roads is now widespread among all classes of society. The farmers realize their benefit to them, in decreasing their cost of transportation, in increasing the value of their farms and adding to the general convenience and comfort of their homes. Their families can easily communicate with the church, town and neighbors at all times, and consequently, will be contented to remain on the farm. The residents of the town or city are also included in these benefits, for improved roads will give them a more regular supply of farm products, will open up to them a source of enjoyment and will bring the town and country in close relationship, therefore leading to greater business activity everywhere.

The great road epoch of the United States has just begun. It is therefore necessary to find the best aid, material, and methods of construction, in order to make road improvement a success. Back in the early nineties some of the states introduced plans for state aid in the construction of roads and few people realized then, that within two decades this movement for government improved roads would sweep the entire land. National aid is not the solution for the building of roads. Many counties have borrowed large sums of money, on from thirty to fifty years bonds for the construction of roads, only to let them fall into disuse within four or five years, from neglect of maintenance. Before experimenting with Federal aid in any form, it would be much wiser to reform and modernize our present State, county, and township systems. Experience has proved that State aid is much better than either the county or township system, but State road building cannot progress at any considerable rate until it is removed from politics and apportioned according to the merit system.

In the counties and townships, the present system of road maintenance consists in the appointment, every year or two, of several petty officials without knowledge and experience. The qualification for the appointment of road supervisor is almost entirely political and not according to merit. However, we have maintained this system throughout the greater portion of the country, with the result that not a county in the United States has obtained a good road system under this obsolete plan. If instead of employing this vast army of incompetent officials, one or more counties or townships would secure an experienced highway engineer and allow him to select his own laborers, a great transformation would take place in the condition of our highways.

The benefits derived from improved roads are probably of endless value, if the best drainage, material, and methods have been chosen. By having better transportation facilities all products are cheapened and the prosperity of the county is thereby increased. As I have stated before the epoch for improved roads in the United States, has just opened. The interest of the people has just awakened and will no doubt rise to a climax within the next few years. Let us, therefore, work together, each doing his share, in order to bring about the success of this movement in our country. If we do so, it is very probable that within the next twenty years the United States will have passed through one of the greatest periods in her history.

THE SOUTHERN ILLINOIS GROUP OF COUNTIES HOLDS QUARTERLY MEETING OF ASSOCIATION OF COUNTY SUPERINTENDENTS OF HIGHWAYS.

The counties in the southern end of the State held their regular meeting of county superintendents of highways at Marion on July 27. This group of counties, of which J. E. Huber, of Marion, is division engineer of the State Highway Department, was organized and held its first meeting at Mt. Vernon about three months ago.

Those present at Marion were:

Howard Anderson, Louisville, Clay County.
Geo. F. Hampton, Benton, Franklin County.
Gregg Garrison, Garrison, Hamilton County.
Lee S. Trainor, Centralia, Marion County.
J. Thrift Corlis, Metropolis, Massac County.
W. T. S. Hopkins, Dixon Springs, Pope County.
Henry I. Barbeau, Prairie du Rocher, Randolph County.
Jno. P. Upchurch, Harrisburg, Saline County.
Jos. F. Howenstein, Anna, Union County.
Geo. H. Brown, Carmi, White County.
Chas. C. Rice, Albion, Edwards County.
P. B. Wilson, Marion, Williamson County.
J. E. Huber, Division Engineer, Marion, Ill.

The sessions were held at the Williamson County courthouse, the time being devoted to a "round table" discussion of road problems peculiar to the territory represented.

The revisions and amendments to the Road and Bridge Laws passed by the Legislature were read and discussed.

After adjournment a trip of inspection was made over the State aid road in West Marion Township and to the new concrete bridges now in course of construction on the Marion-Carbondale Road.

The association accepted the invitation of Massac County to meet in Metropolis on October 28 and 29, and in addition to the regular meeting to visit the new Ohio River bridge now under construction.

CONCRETE ROAD CONSTRUCTION IN AURORA TOWNSHIP, KANE COUNTY.

[By B. H. PIEPMEIER, *Maintenance Engineer, Illinois State Highway Department, Springfield, Ill.*]

Aurora Township has a great many gravel roads, all of which proved to be very economical until the last few years. The increased auto traffic and heavy auto-trucking near the city of Aurora, which has a population of from 30,000 to 40,000, has, however, compelled the highway commissioners to spend excess money and time in maintaining such roads.

The commissioners of this township have, therefore, started out to construct a mile or more each year of the more permanent types of pavement, particularly near the city, where the roads must receive the excessive traffic. Mr. G. N. Lamb, county superintendent of highways, and Phillip Konen, Peter Altringer and John N. Reckinger, highway commissioners of Aurora Township, wished to build this year a concrete pavement, using a few different materials and methods of construction to investigate their respective advantages. They wished to make the investigation for the benefit of future work they anticipated.

They communicated with the State Highway Commission for assistance in furnishing the necessary machinery and supervision for the work they had under consideration. Their request was granted and the machinery was shipped and on the ground ready

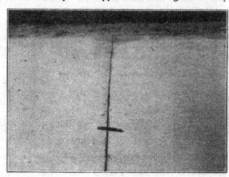

Texture of Surface on Concrete Road, Aurora Township, Kane County, Showing ¼ Inch Felt Joint. The Right Side Shows the Beginning of the Continuous Slab, Where 10% Hydrated Lime Was Added to the Portland Cement.

for work April 15. Mr. H. N. Kleizer, an experienced junior engineer of the State Highway Department, was assigned to this work to have direct charge of all construction, under Mr. H. B. Bushnell, division engineer, of the Illinois State Highway Department.

The first part of the road was constructed in the usual way, placing transverse joints at intervals of 100 feet at right angles to the center line of the road. In the center of the one mile stretch of road the pavement was constructed as a continuous slab for a distance of about 1,100 feet. The butt joint that was formed at the close of each day's work was reinforced by eighteen 3-foot ½-inch square twisted bars placed 12 inches center to center near the center of the concrete slab. The reinforcing was used at the close of each day's work, to insure a perfectly tight joint and a continuous slab over the required distance.

18 Foot Concrete Road, Aurora Township, Kane County. 1,100 Feet Built Without Transverse Joints. Hydrated Lime Used in a Portion of the Road. The Road is in First Class Condition.

One hundred and seventy-five barrels of hydrated lime was donated f. o. b. Marblehead, Ill., by the Marblehead Lime Co., for the road referred to.

While it is not possible at this time to pass judgment upon the portion of the pavement that contains no joints or on the portion that received the hydrated lime, it can be said from a construction standpoint both are very desirable.

The elimination of transverse joints is not expected to give any trouble, and it makes quite a saving in the cost of the road and insures a more uniform surface on the finished pavement. It is expected that there will be transverse cracks at from 30 to 50-foot intervals, but these may be maintained at less expense than the first cost of installing any form of joint. Besides, where joints are used, there is about the same amount of maintenance expense required.

18 Foot Concrete Road, Aurora Township, Kane County. Built by Day Labor Under Supervision of State Highway Department.

While the use of hydrated lime in addition to the Portland cement adds a little to the cost for materials, the cost is more than offset by the ease with which the concrete is handled and finished. Indications, at present, are that the hydrated lime is going to add to the life of concrete pavements.

The following is an itemized statement of the cost of the work referred to above:

FINAL COST REPORT ON CONCRETE ROADS.

Jericho Road—Aurora Township—Kane County.

CONDITIONS.

(Excluding contractor's profit and overhead charges.)

Amount of pavement laid 5,300 feet, 10,600 square yards; width of pavement laid, 18 feet; width of shoulders, 5 feet; length of pavement constructed without transverse joints, 1,100 feet; spacing of transverse joints in 4,200 feet of pavement, 100 feet; length of haul for sand and cement, ¾ mile; length of haul for gravel and hydrated lime, 1½ miles; cost of cement per barrel f. o. b. siding, $1.11; cost of sand per cubic yard f. o. b. siding, 90 cents; cost of gravel per cubic yard f. o. b. siding, 90 cents; cost of hydrated lime per barrel f. o. b siding (freight only), 14 cents; cost of labor per hour, 30 cents; cost of teams per hour, 60 cents; amount of cement used per square yard of pavement, 0.328; amount of hydrated lime used 10 per cent of cement in addition to cement, 175 barrels; work started April 15; completed June 15, 1915.

COST OF LABOR AND SUPPLIES.

	Total cost.	Cost per sq. yd.
Engineering, inspection and superintendence	$ 370 00	$.0349
Excavation	2,213 13	.2080
Hauling gravel	1,146 18	.1080

	Total cost.	Cost per sq. yd.
Hauling sand	$ 372 75	$.0351
Hauling cement	333 60	.0315
Hauling hydrated lime	10 50	.0010
Gravel, 1,630.3 cu. yds. @ 90¢ f. o. b. siding	1,467 27	.1382
Sand, 1,028.1 cu. yds. @ 90¢ f. o. b. siding	925 29	.0873
Cement, 3,456 bbls. @ $1.11 f. o. b. siding	3,836 16	.3620
Shaping and rolling subgrade and side roads	719 10	.0677
Mixing and placing concrete, handling forms and joints	2,209 61	.2082
Covering, seasoning and cleaning concrete	160 00	.0151
Cost of culverts	183 30	.0173
Depreciation on equipment	420 00	.0396
Total cost	$14,366 89	$1.3539
Total cost excluding excavation and culverts	11,970 46	1.1300

Indicates paid by the State Highway Department.

BITUMINOUS SURFACE ON OLD MACADAM ROADS, ROCKFORD TOWNSHIP, WINNEBAGO COUNTY.

[By B. H. PIEPMEIER, *Maintenance Engineer, Illinois State Highway Department, Springfield, Ill.*]

Rockford is one of the richest townships in Illinois. It has a very large road and bridge income from taxes. It is also abundantly supplied with a fair grade of limestone and gravel that is used for improving the roads. These conditions have made it possible for the township to improve a large number of the public highways.

The bulk of the material used, however, has been a soft, light, spongy limestone, with streaks of clay and sandstone throughout the formation. While a large per cent of the limestone is too soft for concrete work of any kind, or for first-class macadam road construction, it has been delivered on the road very cheaply and has given very good satisfaction for the traffic it has had to carry.

Rockford Township, Winnebago County. Bituminous Surface on Old Macadam Road.

The limestone is recognized as one of the best bonding materials in the State, and it is for this reason, perhaps, that the roads that have been built with it have stood up so well.

The increased automobiling and heavy trucking in the vicinity, however, led one of the commissioners to investigate the use of some form of surface treatment that would hold down the dust and prevent excessive wear on the old macadam roads.

Applying Bituminous Material Under Pressure. Pressure Secured by Steam Pump Driven From Roller.

The highway commissioner, Mr. T. G. Levings, and the county superintendent of highways, Mr. A. R. Carter, got in communication with the State Highway Department, concerning advice in the application of a bituminous surface.

After the writer had made a very careful investigation of the condition of the roads and the character of the materials of which they were constructed, it was recommended that all flat and uneven roads be first reshaped with a bituminous macadam surface, or water-bound macadam, then the surface maintained by the application of a good grade of bituminous material and sand as it was required.

A comparatively light asphalt oil and tar was recommended for use on the roads, on account of the tight surface and the clay content of the surface bonding material.

Among the bituminous products recommended, the township officials selected the three following named materials: Montezuma crude, "Mexican asphalt," which cost 4.88 cents per gallon delivered; Aztec liquid asphalt, "Mexican product," which cost 4.67 cents per gallon, tank cars, delivered; Tarvia B, which cost 5.56 cents per gallon, tank cars, delivered.

Rockford Township, Winnebago County. Montezuma Crude Asphalt Used in Surface Oiling.

The Montezuma crude asphalt had to be heated to 150 to 200 degrees F. before applying. The other materials were applied cold.

The roads were prepared first by thoroughly sweeping the surface with a horse-driven rotary steel broom. The bituminous material was then applied at the rate of about one-fourth gallon per square yard of surface, after which it was sanded lightly with torpedo gravel or stone chips, ranging in size from one-eighth to three-eighths inch. After 12 hours the second application of bituminous material was applied at the rate of approximately one-fourth gallon per square yard and the surface again sanded.

After the road had about 12 hours' time to set, it was thrown open to traffic.

The bituminous material was applied with equipment furnished by the State Highway Department. A tank wagon as shown on page 126 is air-tight and holds about 600 gallons. It is equipped with a Westinghouse air pump, and special spraying device, designed by the writer. The material was applied under pressure of from 15 to 30 pounds per square inch.

All work was carried out under the direct supervision of Mr. D. S. James, construction superintendent of the State Highway Department.

Rockford Township, Winnebago County. Aztec Liquid Asphalt on Old Macadam Road.

The following is an itemized statement of the cost of the work referred to above:

COST OF APPLYING BITUMINOUS SURFACES ON MACADAM ROADS.

River Road—Rockford Township—Winnebago County.

CONDITIONS.

(The following figures do not include contractor's profit or overhead expenses.)

Total length of road treated, 10,997 feet; total square yards of road treated, 21,994 square yards; condition of old macadam road, very tight and dirty; kind of bituminous material used, Montezuma crude asphalt; amount of bituminous material used, 0.36 gallon per square yard; amount of torpedo gravel or stone chips, 103.5 cubic yards; average length of haul on materials, 3½ miles; general condition of weather, very rainy most of time; rate of pay for labor, 25 cents per hour; teams, 50 cents per hour.

ITEMIZED COST OF WORK.

	Total cost.	Cost per sq. yd.
Engineering and inspection........	[1]......	[1]......
Superintendence	$158 40	$[1].0071
Bituminous material, 7,926 gal. @ 8.0488 f. o. b. siding..........	387 58	.0176
Torpedo gravel and stone chips 103.5 cu.yds. @ 85¢ f.o.b. siding	88 02	.0040

	Total cost.	Cost per sq. yd.
Hauling bituminous material.....	$ 57 50	$.0026
Hauling torpedo gravel and stone chips	194 50	.0089
Heating and applying bituminous material, demurrage, etc.......	[2]57 50	[2].0027
Spreading torpedo gravel and stone chips	93 37	.0042
Sweeping and cleaning old road.	67 06	.0030
Depreciation on equipment......	[1].......	[1].......
Freight on equipment..........	56 00	.0026
Incidental expense	49 90	.0023
Total cost	$1,209 83	$.0550

[1]Indicates paid or furnished by the State Highway Department.
[2]Steam for heating was supplied without cost to the township.

Auto Club Road—Rockford Township—Winnebago County.

CONDITIONS.

(The following figures do not include contractor's profit or overhead expenses.)

Total length of road treated, 9,484 feet; total square yards of road treated, 12,645 square yards; condition of old macadam road, very tight and dirty; kind of bituminous material used, Aztec liquid asphalt; amount of bituminous material used, 0.60 gallon per square yard; amount of torpedo gravel or stone chips, 104 cubic yards; average length of haul on materials, 3 miles; general condition of weather, good; rate of pay for labor, 25 cents per hour; teams, 50 cents per hour.

ITEMIZED COST OF WORK.

	Total cost.	Cost per sq. yd.
Engineering and inspection.....	[1].......	[1].......
Superintendence	[1]$ 35 00	[1]$.0027
Bituminous material, 8,035 gal. @ $.0487 f. o. b. siding.........	[2]391 30	[2].0309
Torpedo gravel and stone chips, 104 cu. yds. @ 45¢ f. o. b siding	46 80	.0037
Hauling bituminous material....	25 00	.0019
Hauling torpedo gravel and stone chips	78 50	.0062
Applying bituminous material, demurrage, etc.	23 20	.0019
Spreading torpedo gravel and stone chips	31 35	.0025
Sweeping and cleaning old road.	23 48	.0018
Depreciation on equipment......	[1].......	[1].......
Freight on equipment (booked against River Road)..........	....	....
Incidental expense	....	....
Total cost	$654 63	$.0516

[1]Indicates paid or furnished by the State Highway Department.
[2]About 500 gallons of oil were held in storage for future repair work.

Auto Club Road—Rockford Township—Winnebago County.

CONDITIONS.

(The following figures do not include contractor's profit or overhead expenses.)

Total length of road treated, 16,764 feet; total square yards of road treated, 18,627 square yards; condition of old macadam road, very tight and dirty; kind of bituminous material used, Tarvia B; amount of bituminous material used, 0.55 gallon per square yard; amount of torpedo gravel or stone chips, 77.5 cubic yards; average length of haul on materials, 3½

miles; general condition of weather, very rainy most of the time; rate of pay for labor, 25 cents per hour; teams, 50 cents per hour.

ITEMIZED COST OF WORK.

	Total cost.	Cost per sq. yd.
Engineering and inspection......	[1].......	[1].......
Superintendence	[1]$ 35 00	[1]$.0019
Bituminous material, 10,037 gal. @ $.0575 f. o. b. siding........	577 00	.0310
Torpedo gravel and stone chips, 77.5 cu. yds. @ 45¢ f.o.b. siding	34 27	.0018
Hauling bituminous material	111 00	.0059
Hauling torpedo gravel and stone chips	140 00	.0075
Applying bituminous material, demurrage, etc.	31 43	.0018
Spreading torpedo gravel and stone chips	88 00	.0047
Sweeping and cleaning old road..	30 54	.0016
Depreciation on equipment......	[1].......	[1].......
Freight on equipment (booked against River Road)..........	....	....
Incidental expense	61 00	.0033
Total cost	$1,111 94	$.0595

[1]Indicates paid or furnished by the State Highway Department.

THE PRACTICABILITY OF A COUNTY ROAD EQUIPMENT.

[*By* THOS. W. HUMPHRIES, *County Superintendent of Highways, Boone County.*]

The practicability of any equipment depends upon the amount of service that can be secured by the parties owning the same, in proportion to the importance of the work to be done, the amount invested in the outfit, and the expense of maintaining the same.

To properly and economically build and maintain roads and bridges, either townships or counties must supply the necessary equipment for this purpose. The amount that either of these units can profitably invest in equipment therefor, depends upon the available funds to keep the different machines in operation in the hands of suitable operators and under competent superintendency the greatest number of days throughout the season. Considering the very limited amount of money which is available for road and bridge work in the ordinary rural township, it would seem impracticable, if not impossible to provide each township with but a very meager equipment, and if a suitable equipment were available even by a special tax to provide payment for the same the interest and depreciation would be too great to be economical considering the limited use that could be made by the individual township.

Traction engines and suitable graders, rollers, rockcrushers, large mixers and other heavy machinery have usually proven poor investments for townships that have tried it, and the hiring usually expensive and unsatisfactory. But I think the county might economically provide such machinery and bridge equipment, build and equip suitable buildings for the shelter and care of same when not in use. A matter that is usually entirely neglected by townships even with the meager equipment now owned by them. They should secure reliable and experienced operators for the same and should cooperate with the different townships throughout the county.

More and better work is demanded upon our highways at the present time than can justly be expected of the rural townships. All of the taxpayers of the county are benefited, to some extent, by the good roads of the county and therefore might rightfully be expected to assist in their building and maintainance. Even if the townships paid the expense of operating the various outfits while in use by them, they would be relieved of all interest, risk and depreciation.

These outfits, if properly handled, would do much better and cheaper work and could be used throughout the season, thereby doing the work of several townships each year.

If the townships do not have funds enough to keep the equipment busy all the time, funds should then be provided by the county and the outfits be kept at some needed work, thereby giving steady employment to the operators. The work done for the townships would be much more uniform than would usually be done by the various townships without properly experienced help which in most cases cannot be obtained for short periods, and the county would not be heavily burdened by this method.

In Boone county we have a steam grading outfit which was provided with an engineer, operator for grader, oil and repairs furnished by county, townships paying fifteen dollars ($15.00) per day for use of same.

Building Gravel and Earth Roads, Kane County. Equipment Owned by the County and is Under the Direct Control of County Superintendent of Highways.

This outfit did nearly all the grading for three (3) townships the past year at from one-half (½) to one-third (⅓) of the cost usually paid for this work according to the statements of the commissioners of these townships, and all grades were uniform in width, crown and ditches and much more compact than when done with the usual horse-drawn outfits.

This outfit was idle a good deal of the time for lack of funds but that will not occur this season as the townships are reserving more money for this work and four (4) townships have already made application to have their grading done.

I feel sure we will need to purchase or hire another outfit or it will not be possible to do all the work for these townships.

Where the roller is used to drag and roll either for repair or new work, ten dollars ($10.00) per day is charged, the county furnishing operator, coal and oil for this work. The county appropriated fifteen hundred dollars ($1,500.00) so that the county superintendent might go forward with this work somewhere in the county,

even after the townships had used their available funds and we expect to place "Little Boone" right up towards the front in 1915.

OPINIONS OF THE ATTORNEY GENERAL.

HARD ROADS—CONTRACTS TO BE LET FOR.

Mr. G. L. Krans,   *April 23, 1915.*

Highway Commissioner, Belvidere, Illinois.

Dear Sir: I am in receipt of your favor of the 20th instant, and note that your town has voted a special tax for the construction of hard roads. You inquire, in substance, whether the highway commissioners, without advertising for bids as the statute requires, may not divide such tax between them to be expended by them in constructing such roads.

I assume that such tax was authorized by a vote had under section 108 of the revised Road and Bridge Act, which provides as follows:

"On the petition of twenty-five per cent of the land owners who are legal voters of any township to the town clerk thereof, in counties under township organization or road districts in counties not under township organization, to the district clerk, he shall, when giving notice of the the time and place for holding the next annual town meeting or road district election, also give notice that a vote will be taken at said election or meeting for or against an annual tax not to exceed one dollar on each one hundred dollars assessed valuation of all the taxable property, including railroads in the township or road district, for the purpose of constructing and maintaining gravel, rock, macadam or other hard roads. Said petition shall state the location and route of the proposed road or roads, and shall also state the annual rate per cent not exceeding one dollar on each one hundred dollars, and the number of years not exceeding five, for which said tax shall be levied. If in any such petition a special election shall be requested for such purposes it shall be called in the manner provided for calling special elections in section 112 of this Act."

Section 115 of said act provides:

"Whenever it shall be voted to construct gravel, rock, macadam or other hard roads in any township or district it shall be the duty of the county superintendent of highways of the county in which said township so voted is located to at once survey (or cause to be surveyed) the route of the road thus to be improved, and to prepare suitable maps, plans, specifications, and estimates of the cost of the proposed improvement. The county superintendent of highways shall divide the same into convenient sections, each of which shall be numbered. The county superintendent of highways, upon the completion of said maps, plans, specifications and estimates, shall file one copy of the same with the town or district clerk of the township wherein the proposed road is to be constructed and one copy with the commissioners of highways of said township."

Section 116 provides as follows:

"When the plans and specifications are completed, the commissioners shall advertise for sealed bids for said work, by publishing a notice thereof for at least three weeks in some newspaper published in said township or road district. If there is no newspaper published therein, then in the newspaper published nearest said township or road district, and also by posting notices in at least ten of the most public places in said town or road district."

You will note that Section 115 very specifically provides that where a town votes a special tax for the construction of hard roads, that it shall be the duty of the county superintendent of highways to cause the route of such roads to be surveyed and prepare suitable maps, plans, specifications and estimates of the cost of such proposed improvement. And section 116 just as definitely makes it the duty of the highway commissioners upon the completion of such plans and specifications, to advertise for sealed bids for such work; and it is their duty to open such bids and let contracts in the manner specified by section 118. There is no provision of the statute which authorizes the highway commissioners to apportion a special hard road tax between them to be used by them without advertising for bids for the work proposed to be done.

Where the statute provides for public improvement and prescribes the manner of making same, such improvements cannot legally be made in a manner different to that which the statute prescribes.

Very respectfully,

P. J. Lucey, *Attorney General.*

Schnepp & Barnes, State Printers Springfield, Ill. 1915.

ILLINOIS HIGHWAYS

[Printed by authority of the State of Illinois.]

STATE HIGHWAY DEPARTMENT

| VOL. 2 | SPRINGFIELD, ILLINOIS, SEPTEMBER, 1915 | No. 9 |

SCENES ALONG SECTION A, ROUTE 1, KENDALL COUNTY STATE AID ROAD.

ILLINOIS HIGHWAYS.
Published Monthly by the
State Highway Department.

ILLINOIS HIGHWAY COMMISSION.
A. D. GASH, *President.*
S. E. BRADT, *Secretary.*
JAMES P. WILSON.

WM. W. MARR, *Chief State Highway Engineer.*

BUREAU CHIEFS.
H. E. BILGER, *Road Engineer, Springfield, Illinois.*
C. OLDER, *Bridge Engineer, Springfield, Illinois.*
B. H. PIEPMEIER, *Maintenance Engineer, Springfield, Illinois.*
F. L. ROMAN, *Testing Engineer, Springfield, Illinois.*
J. M. McCOY, *Chief Clerk, Springfield, Illinois.*
G. F. BURCH, *Assistant Bridge Engineer, Springfield, Illinois.*
M. W. WATSON, *Assistant Road Engineer, Springfield, Illinois.*

DIVISION ENGINEERS.
H. B. Bushnell..............Aurora
R. L. Bell.....................Paris
H. E. Surman..........Rock Island
A. H. Hunter...............Peoria
Fred Tarrant............Springfield
C. M. Slaymaker........E. St. Louis
J. E. Huber.................Marion

Address all communications in regard to "Illinois Highways," to State Highway Department, Springfield, Illinois. Attention of T. W. Dieckmann, Department Editor.

CONTENTS.

USE OF STATE AID FUNDS.

September 1, 1915.

To COUNTY BOARD:

Because of the many inquiries reaching this department, the State Highway Commission has deemed it advisable to formulate and define as clearly as may be, its policy regarding the use of State aid funds for the construction and maintenance of earth roads and bridges in accordance with the amended law and thereby answer at once most of the questions asked.

Under the Tice Law as amended, the county board has the privilege of designating the type of road to be built with State aid, that is, whether an earth, gravel, macadam, concrete or brick road shall be constructed and the State Highway Commission is charged with the duty of preparing plans and specifications and supervising the construction of the work, which involves passing upon suitableness of material. Whatever type of road may be selected it is the duty of the State Highway Commission to draw specifications for the best known form of construction of the type chosen and through competent inspection and supervision turn over to the taxpayers the best results possible under the conditions for the money expended.

It should be kept clearly in mind, however, that the durability of a road surface has a very distinct relation to the amount and character of the traffic it bears as well as to the quality and intelligent use of the material from which it is constructed and that to overburden a road results as disastrously as overloading a bridge so far as economy is concerned. Experience and judgment are necessary to determine the economic type of road under a given set of conditions and the State Highway Commission places its forces of practical, experienced, and technical men at the disposal of the various county boards whenever requested to aid in the solution of this most difficult and troublesome problem.

The law provides for the construction of roads and bridges and for the repair and maintenance of roads and bridges that have been constructed with State aid.

The maintenance feature as changed by the last Legislature requires the State to pay the entire cost of maintenance of all roads, except earth roads, the maintenance of which is to be paid by the county, and gravel and macadam roads, the maintenance of which is to be paid equally by the State and county.

The question has been asked, "Will the State Highway Commission permit the use of State aid funds for the purchase and application of oil for oiling existing earth roads?" Such is not the intent of the law. This is distinctly a maintenance proposition and it should be clearly understood that the oiling of earth roads is a temporary expedient and at best its usefulness is short lived. The Commission will, however, in view of the fact that the application of a properly prepared oil is an improvement to an earth road, use oil in the construction of State aid earth roads, when requested by the County Boards, but will require thereafter that the county shall pay for re-oiling, from year to year, or oftener if required, as a part of the maintenance of such State aid roads, which, as we have indicated above, devolves upon the county. An earth road is defined to be a road properly graded and drained, that is, the hills cut, the hollows filled, necessary ditches, bridges and culverts built and the whole surface brought to such condition that if it has been properly maintained, a durable wearing surface may be laid thereon without repeating any of the work already done.

Concerning the use of the State aid funds in building bridges and culverts, that it is the judgment of the Commission that it is not contemplated by the law that all of the State aid money in a county shall be expended, from year to year, on bridges and culverts, but that the building of these bridges and culverts shall be taken up as a part of the road construction, as shall from time to time be determined. In most counties there are sufficient funds available in the township treasuries, with county aid, to take care of this work satisfactorily. However, in counties where there is evidence of a lack of funds for this work, the Commission will determine how much, if any, of the State aid fund may be used for that purpose, but will require that the bridges and culverts be limited to such sizes and such localities as will enable the department to carry on the work economically, both as to cost of construction and cost of supervision.

The State Highway Commission earnestly desires to cooperate with the various county boards to the end that the funds available for road improvement shall be wisely and economically expended for the greatest benefit to the tax paying public and will place all its resources at the disposal of those who seek its aid within the provisions of the law. Experienced men from this department will on request attend the meetings of the county board and render such assistance as lies within their power.

ILLINOIS STATE HIGHWAY COMMISSION,
A. D. Gash, *President.*
S. E. Bradt, *Secretary.*
James P. Wilson.
By Wm. W. Marr,
  Chief State Highway Engineer.

THE DESIGN OF CROSS-SECTIONS FOR STEEP GRADES ON PUBLIC HIGHWAYS

[*By* B. H. Piepmeier, *Maintenance Engineer, State Highway Department, Springfield, Illinois.*]
(Published in "Engineering and Contracting." Issue of Sept. 8, 1915.)

Roads on steep grades, improperly designed or located, often result in expensive upkeep.

The most important problem connected with the design of a modern highway is that of properly providing for all drainage. Good drainage insures that the upkeep cost will be reduced to a minimum.

Yet in view of this well-established principle of construction it is common to find many pavements in use where drainage has not been properly provided. This is especially true on steep grades and on soils that wash badly.

Fig. 1—18-Foot Concrete Pavement With Vertical Curb, on Grade of Six Per Cent. Built 1912.

Earth in some localities erodes more readily than in others, so necessarily needs more attention. The tendency in construction is to reduce the first cost of

the road. In doing so important features of the pavement that make for more permanent and safer highways are often neglected.

The writer has examined a number of pavements constructed on long, steep grades and on soils that erode easily and it is evident that some form of cross-section that will confine the water on the pavement or within a paved gutter is usually necessary on long grades that exceed about five per cent, and particularly on soils that are inclined to wash badly.

Fig. 2—Concrete Pavement With Sloping Curb, Constructed on Sandy Soil on Grade of Six Per Cent. 20 Feet Between Curbs.

A number of concrete and brick pavements with macadam, gravel and earth shoulders constructed on grades varying from four to ten per cent have been inspected and in nearly every case the side ditches were unnecessarily deep and the macadam, gravel or earth shoulders gullied out until the road was unsafe.

Occasionally a road is constructed on a tight soil which does not wash badly even on the steep grades. There are also times when the earth side roads and ditches sod rapidly and in such cases the formation of sod prevents excessive erosion for several years. However, in a majority of cases the entire road is loosened up during construction and before it becomes thoroughly compacted and set, rains will cause trouble.

A steep crown on a cross section carries the surface water to the side ditches more rapidly and gives much better results on steep grades than the ordinary flat crown. The steep crown sheds the surface water quickly and more uniformly which prevents a great many side gullies. But with the rapidly moving traffic it is not always safe to construct a steep crown without endangering traffic during wet slippery weather. It is evident, therefore, that some other form of section is necessary in many cases to provide for the surface water, and afford safety to traffic.

From the results of a careful study of the various cross-sections in use on steep grades, the writer has concluded that some form of section shown in Fig. 1, 2, 3, or 4, where there is an integral curb or concrete gutter, in connection with the pavement, is the safest and most economical cross section for a majority of roads on steep grades.

Where the pavement is constructed with a curb as shown in Fig. 1, it should not be less than about eighteen feet, between curbs, and as much more as traffic may require. This form of pavement acts as a gutter for carrying the water down the hill. The slight crown in the pavement forces small volumes of water next to the curb and leaves the center of the pavement free of water. Excessive rain may of course fill the pavement to the top of the curb but such rains are of short duration and cause no inconvenience.

Fig. 3—Concrete Pavement, 20 Feet Between Curbs, Constructed With Sloping Integral Curb, on Grade of Seven Per Cent. Soil Very Sandy.

The section of pavement shown in Fig. 2, where the integral curb slopes back at an angle of about forty-five degrees, has preference over that in Fig. 1, as it presents a better appearance and is safer for traffic. Should a team become frightened and turn around quickly on such a pavement the sloping curb permits the wheel to climb over the curb without turning over the vehicle or breaking the wheel. The vertical curb often prevents the wheel from climbing and the result is a breakdown.

Fig. 4—15-Foot Concrete Pavement, Showing Concrete Gutters at Top of Hill. Soil Very Sandy. Gutters Prevent Wash and Reduce Upkeep Cost to a Minimum.

From the top of the curb back to the embankment the earth slope should be about four to one for a distance of at least four feet. The side cut presents a good appearance and permits one to see around slight curves more readily and will also act as a table to catch any earth slides that may come down from the side cut.

Where the above sections are used there is no chance for the gutters to become clogged and serious damage be done by washouts. This means a great deal on the average country highway as there is no opportunity to clean the gutters, catch basins, etc., on the country roads as there is on city streets. To reduce the upkeep cost to a minimum, therefore, it is necessary to design a pavement or section, so to say, "fool proof". In a majority of cases the small repairs that

are necessary on the average country road often require a greater expense in getting someone on the job to do the work than the cost of doing the work.

Where pavements are constructed with earth, macadam or gravel shoulders there is a tendency for heavily loaded wagons to pull one wheel against the side of the pavement to help hold back the load in going down the grade. This practice in nearly every case will soon result in forming ruts, which will permit water to accumulate, making them larger and more serious.

Fig. 5—Open Down Spout Conducting Water From Concrete Gutters to Side Ditches at Foot of Hill.

A number of pavements have been examined where large tile were embedded two or three feet below the side ditches and catch-basins constructed at intervals to carry the surface water into the tile. This method of providing for surface and underground water is in first cost somewhat cheaper than other methods but there is always some unexpected heavy rain that is sure to clog the tile inlet with earth or debris of some kind and it refuses to carry the water with the result that quite often the entire tile is washed out and a good portion of the earth shoulder washed away. Such construction should be avoided as it is sure to mean expensive upkeep for the road.

Fig. 6—15-Foot Brick Pavement With Concrete Gutters Through the Cut. Wing Walls Constructed at End of Gutters to Turn Water to Side Ditches. Gutters Should Have Extended Farther Down the Grade Before Turning Off.

The writer has also examined many other devices for protecting the side road and ditches from washing. In Fig. 7 are shown curtain walls constructed at intervals of from 20 to 50 feet depending upon the grade of the ditch.

The curtain walls are of concrete and constructed to reach from the traveled portion of the road across the side ditch and into the side cut. They are constructed at such intervals and made of such depth that the bottom of one wall is level with or below the top of the one next below it. The tops of the walls are depressed so the water is confined to one place in following down the side ditch.

This method of preventing excessive wash is not always satisfactory. If the walls are properly constructed they prevent the side ditch from getting unnecessarily deep, but there is usually a very unsightly waterfall just below each cross wall and in a great many cases rip-rap or some form of protection is necessary just below each wall to prevent serious washouts. While in first cost this method may be attractive, yet considering the results and the unsightly appearance and danger to traffic it can not always be recommended.

Where the water is confined between two curbs on the pavement there is no possible chance for excess wash, and the water upon reaching the bottom of the hill may be carried off to the side ditch as shown in Fig. 5. The side ditch at the bottom of the grade should have a natural slope for carrying the water so there will be no excessive washing from turning the water into the side ditches. When conducting the water from the side gutters, at the bottom of the hill, to the side ditch the flume should deflect from the pavement at an angle of not more than about 30 degrees. If a greater angle is used the water will not make the turn on account of its velocity and some form of additional protection as shown in Fig. 6 is necessary to prevent the water from washing out the earth shoulder just beyond the end of the gutter.

Any abrupt waterfall as shown in Fig. 5 should have the bank thoroughly protected with concrete or similar material to prevent the water from cutting back up the hill.

There has been some objection offered to turning a concrete or brick pavement into a ditch and permitting the surface water to be carried upon the surface of the pavement from the standpoint that ice will form in the winter months and the road become impassable. This objection is not serious in Illinois, as there are very few days in the year that such a condition will exist.

Fig. 7—10-Foot Brick Pavement With 4 Foot Macadam Shoulders Constructed on Grade of Seven Per Cent. Concrete Wing Walls Constructed Across the Side Ditch at Intervals of 30 Feet to Prevent Excessive Wash.

Pavements as shown in Figures 1, 2, 3, and 4, have been in use three and four winters and there have been

practically no objections to them, but, on the contrary many very favorable comments.

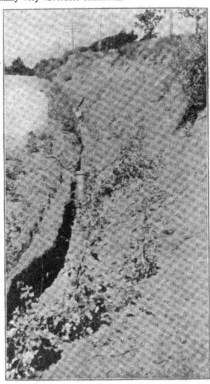

Fig. 8—An Improved Road Constructed on Sandy Soil, Six Per Cent Grade. Side Ditches Provided With 10-inch Tile, With Catch Basins at Intervals of 50 Feet. Note Tile and Catch Basins About Washed Out.

The above investigation was made and this report is published with the permission of Wm. W. Marr, Chief State Highway Engineer of Illinois.

SUPERELEVATION OF CURVES ON HIGHWAYS, ILLINOIS PRACTICE.

[By H. E. BILGER, Road Engineer, State Highway Department.]

[Reprinted from Engineering News of July 8, 1915.]

The advent of the motor vehicle upon our rural public highways, with the consequent stimulus that has been given to the adoption of types of highway improvement best suited to withstand this new character of traffic, presents to the engineer many details of design and construction that heretofore have not required much consideration.

One of these details that is demanding more and more attention each year is the matter of providing the proper crown, cross-slope or super-elevation of the portion of the pavement on curves. As in most other matters of engineering design or construction, there can be no one best solution of the problem, inasmuch as the governing conditions on different pieces of work may bear relatively different weights.

Generally speaking, I would say that the treatment to be administered should vary with the type of the pavement and with the relative amounts of motor and horse-drawn traffic, and should depend upon such minor considerations as the radius of the curve and the climatic conditions.

This matter is receiving especial consideration in Illinois, inasmuch as for practically all State aid road construction vitrified brick and Portland cement concrete alone have been adopted up to this time. The employment of these costly types of pavement requires for the development of their merits, that all matters relating to the horizontal and the vertical alignment of the pavement be cared for just as accurately as though the work were on a city street.

In Illinois, the popular widths of brick and concrete pavements are 10 and 18 feet, though the 15-foot width is destined soon to surpass these in point of mileage. For other types of construction the prevailing widths are 10, 12 and 15 feet, but the 12-foot width is losing in popularity. On tangents, the brick and the concrete types are designed with a one-inch crown for the 10-foot widths, and with a two-inch crown for the 18-foot widths.

From past experience it would seem that, all matters considered, the most satisfactory treatment of these types on curves is to carry the profile of the center line and of the inner edge of the pavement around the curve without a break, but to elevate the outer longitudinal half of the slab two inches for the 10-foot pavements and four inches for the 18-foot ones. On the inner as well as on the outer longitudinal half of the slab the convexity of the surface should be avoided, to the end that the entire portion of the slab that comes upon the curve may be a surface having a straight-line top on any cross-section.

Gravel and macadam road surfaces should be similarly treated on curves, that is, by elevating the outer longitudinal half of the metaled-way by an amount

STATE AID ROADS.

The following table shows the location of all roads which have been constructed under the joint expense of the State and County, and have been accepted by the State Highway Commission, since Feb. 1, 1915.

The State Highway Commission has formally accepted 49 sections of roads, in 32 different counties, totaling 55.61 miles in length. The State is required to maintain these roads forever at its own expense.

STATE AID ROADS.

County.	Section	Type.	Length.	Mileage.	Date accepted.	Total cost.	Unit cost per mile.	Remarks.
Accepted prior to Feb. 1, 1915			127,265'	24.10		$311,290 00		
Boone	B	Conc. 10'	4,276'	0.81	2– 3–15	$ 9,107 86	$11,240	
Dekalb	A	Conc. 10'	6,009'	1.14	4– 8–15	11,155 12	9,790	
Dekalb	C	Conc. 10'	15,723'	2.98	4– 8–15	26,887 01	9,020	
Stephenson	A	Brick 18'	3,286'	0.62	4–14–15	15,452 74	24,920	
Logan	A	Conc. 10'	3,700'	0.70	5–26–15	6,117 31	8,740	
Logan	D	Conc. 10'	3,700'	0.70	5–26–15	7,233 36	10,330	
Whiteside	A	Conc. 10'	3,100'	0.59	6– 2–15	9,464 08	16,040	
Cook	C	Conc. 18'	24,000'	4.55	6– 2–15	63,315 26	13,695	
Warren	A	Brick 10'	5,500'	1.04	6– 2–15	14,734 74	14,170	
Rock Island	A	Conc. 10'	4,969'	0.94	6– 2–15	9,301 08	9,894	
Jackson	A	Brick 10'	3,630'	0.69	6– 9–15	11,819 85	17,140	
Williamson	A	Conc. 10'	6,630'	1.26	6– 9–15	13,029 29	10,340	
Champaign	A	Brick 10'	7,700'	1.46	6– 9–15	19,691 21	13,490	
Champaign	B	Brick 10'	7,810'	1.48	6– 9–15	19,180 71	12,700	
Jersey	A	Conc. 10'	3,100'	0.59	6– 9–15	5,861 44	9,930	
Franklin	A	Conc. 10'	4,878'	0.92	6–23–15	9,992 35	10,860	
Douglas	A	Brick 10'	6,300'	1.19	6–30–15	15,015 96	12,620	
Lawrence	A	Conc. 10'	5,680'	1.08	6–30–15	14,473 04	13,400	
Coles	A	Brick 10'	6,900'	1.31	7–15–15	18,302 82	13,970	
Moultrie	A	Conc. 10'	7,100'	1.34	7–15–15	12,607 78	9,408	
Woodford	A	Conc. 10'	7,300'	1.38	7–15–15	16,955 77	12,290	
Grundy	A	Conc. 10'	9,400'	1.80	7–27–15	20,314 51	11,290	
Peoria	A	Conc. 10'	6,159'	1.17	7–27–15	19,932 89	17,040	
Rock Island	B	Conc. 10'	3,000'	0.57	7–27–15	6,059 64	10,630	
Warren	B	Brick 10'	5,000'	0.95	7–27–15	13,714 30	14,436	
Edgar	C	Brick 10'	1,300'	0.25	7–27–15	3,154 40	12,620	
Total to Sept. 1, 1915			293,435'	55.61		$704,164 52		

equal to twice the crown on tangents for the particular type in question.

Where the central angle of the curve is more than about 30 degrees, the width of the pavement around the curve should be increased by some 30 or 40 per cent, and the pavement's position should be such as to bring its inner edge within some four feet of the fence corner, necessitating the inner ditch being converted into an underground waterway.

When such pressure is brought to bear by the taxpaying public as to require the engineer to construct a brick or concrete pavement to one side of the center line of the highway, the upper surface of the pavement should be flat and, of course, should drain to the nearest side ditch.

Occasionally theoretical arguments are advanced for crowning, or rather convexing, the upper surface of the pavement that drains to one side only. The argument usually put forth is that if the completed surface is not convex it will present the unsightly appearance of being concave. This is merely a matter of construction. If the design of the template is such as to assure against deflection, I have not yet heard advanced a worthy argument for a brick or concrete "offcenter" pavement with a convex surface.

In anticipation of a deflection of the template it would, of course, be only the part of wisdom to use a template curved convexly by at least the amount of the expected deflection, but the use of a template of questionable rigidity is clearly not in accord with the other construction requirements of good brick and concrete pavements.

CONVICT LABOR IS MAKING GOOD.
ON
TOWNSHIP WORK IN READING TOWNSHIP, LIVINGSTON COUNTY.

The macadam road work at Reading is progressing nicely considering the weather conditions. About twelve of the twenty miles have been graded and the subgrade prepared for the stone. The stone for about nine miles of nine-foot macadam road has been hauled and is in place ready to roll. The wet weather has delayed the rolling and finishing but about 5 miles have been finished to date.

Stone Elevator and Storage Bin on the 20 Mile Macadam Road Job, Reading Township, Livingston County.

Very accurate figures have been kept of the cost of unloading stone by means of the elevator and bin as shown above. Accounting for the expense of constructing the pit and bin together with depreciation

on equipment and the rental on the steam engine that furnishes the power, the cost to date has been less than 5 cents per cu. yd. This price also includes the expense of unloading about 60 cars of screenings that have been unloaded by hand directly into the dinkey cars or on the ground.

The convicts do all the work connected with unloading the cars, filling the bin, and loading the industrial hauling outfit. They take much pride in keeping the bin full so there are no delays in loading out the dinkey train.

The device as shown in the above photograph has proven to be very satisfactory for work of this kind.

A more complete description of the Reading Township Convict camp may be found in the July issue of *Illinois Highways*.

B. H. PIEPMEIER, *Maintenance Engineer.*
Aug. 30, 1915.

BUILDING CONCRETE ROADS BY DAY LABOR.

[*By A. H. HUNTER, Division Engineer, Illinois Highway Department.*]

The State Highway Commission was created by an act of the Illinois General Assembly in February 1905. One of the duties imposed by this Act was that an investigation of road building should be made in which different methods of construction, kinds of material and systems of drainage should be employed in order to determine, if possible, the character of road best suited to the various sections and soil conditions of the State. It was also required that a complete record of all cost should be kept and that standards for the construction of highways should be developed. Even under the law enacted two years ago, this condition remains much the same as in the original bill. Money was necessary to carry out such an undertaking as this and each session of the legislature has seen fit to make appropriations ranging from $25,000 per year in 1905, to $100,000 per year in 1913 and 1914. However, in the construction of experimental roads, the cost has been borne largely by the local authorities, either directly through appropriations of the road authorities or by private subscriptions, or a combination of the two.

The construction of experimental concrete roads was undertaken by the Illinois Highway Commission, first in the summer of 1912. From that time until the present, more than 60,000 square yards of concrete surface have been laid under our plans and supervision, not to mention several pieces let by contract, for which we furnished plans and inspection only. The work handled by contractors will not be considered in this article.

Before entering into a discussion of concrete roads built by day labor under the supervision of the Illinois Highway Department, I wish to call your attention to the many large subjects which may be included under this heading. The subjects of excavation, drainage, aggregate, mixture and expansion, with perhaps others, are each sufficiently large to supply material for an article of considerable length. However, I will give only an outline of our method of handling this work and devote some space to the vital points of concrete road construction.

Upon receipt of application for an experimental road from the local authorities and the selection of the road, a survey is made by engineers from our office. A transit line is run, usually in the center of the old road, and all angles and turns noted, with stakes set every 100 feet in the fence line. Cross sections are taken at each station, bench marks established and checked. Care is taken to provide good drainage and inspection is made of all bridges and culverts included in the work. The notes are plotted on return to the office, the grade line established, quantities computed and balanced, allowing about 25 per cent excess of cuts over fills to provide for waste and shrinkage. This percentage of excess is an average value for Illinois conditions, but in very heavy cuts, it can be reduced to 15 per cent. In light excavation, an excess as high as 35 per cent has worked well. It must be kept in mind that construction stakes are required on concrete roads and guessing at the grade is not permitted.

The question of grade for concrete roads in Illinois is not serious, due to the nature of the land. However, concrete surfaces have been placed on seven per cent grades and are proving very satisfactory.

On commencing construction, a Resident Engineer from the office of the State Highway Department is given complete charge of the work. He is assisted by one or more foremen, a timekeeper, and such other assistants as may be required. In many instances, one of the local highway commissioners is employed as foreman, for it has been found that local men are better acquainted with the local conditions and their assistance in securing labor and materials has been valuable. The State supplies a 10-ton roller, a concrete mixer, and incidental equipment. In some instances, a scarifier, car dumps, and wheel scrapers have been furnished. To operate concrete machinery to advantage, experienced men are required. To secure such help, it has been the policy of our department to supply two machinery operators. These men are on the pay roll of the State and the local people are at no expense for their services. In the early period of construction, the operators are busy in assembling the machinery and rolling the subgrade, while later they are employed in operating the concrete mixer.

The excavation is carried on well in advance of the placing of materials, so as to permit the proper rolling and surfacing of the subgrade. In a level country where there is light excavation, the center can be shaped with a grader, the sides and ditches being left until after the construction of the improved roadway. Heavy cuts may be handled by slips, wheelers or wagons, depending on the length of haul. The large fills must be deposited in thin layers and thoroughly rolled, so as to prevent settlement. Experience has proven that no amount of rolling can compact dry or slightly moist earth, so water should be applied to such places or the fill remain exposed to the weather for a long time previous to the placing of the concrete slab. The safest method for heavy fills is to place the earth one season and withhold the road surface until the following year. Very little rock excavation has been encountered, and on only one road constructed in 1914, did the excavation of rock reach 1,200 cubic yards.

The advantages of concrete roads, their thickness, character of the mixture, and their length of service are questions attracting the attention of many road engineers to-day. The success of a concrete road depends largely upon the closely related questions of subgrade and drainage. No concrete road of whatever mix and economic thickness of concrete can ever prove ultimately successful unless the subgrade has

been properly constructed and provision made for disposal of the surface water.

It seems that each individual has his own idea as to what comprises the subgrade. To secure uniformity in our cost data, the subgrade has been defined as that work required to shape the last three inches of earth material necessary to produce the required elevation of the earth base. In all cost data hereinafter referred to, the above meaning of subgrade shall be understood. In some experimental roads, the subgrade was completed by hand in order to secure a uniform base, care being taken not to permit any excavation or furrows below the plane of the base. In concrete roads, it is highly desirable to have the earth sub-base uniform, as soft spots and hard lumps are equally harmful. When the hand work has been completed, the earth should be rolled until firm. As a matter of economy, the subgrade should conform to the cross section and grades so that additional concrete, which is expensive, may be avoided. As a detail of construction, it is equally important that thin places in the concrete be avoided for such places give conditions sure to develop cracks. Cracks are undesirable in a concrete road so every effort should be made to eliminate them or at least reduce their number to a minimum.

In the standard cross section used in the construction of the earlier concrete roads the subgrade was crowned 3 inches in roads 16 feet wide, while in nine or ten foot roads, it was crowned one inch. Drainage was provided by means of two sets of ditches, filled with coarse aggregate, namely: longitudinal and lateral drains. The former consists of a 6 by 8-inch trench under the outer edge of the concrete continuing for the entire length of the road. The latter extends from the longitudinal drain to the side ditch and is of the same manner of construction as the first. They are usually placed opposite the end of each expansion joint, and at such other places as the character of the soil seems to warrant. The purpose of such drains is to prevent water collecting underneath the slab. This water, if not removed, makes possible serious frost action resulting in longitudinal cracks. The efficiency of these drains has been much questioned but they were employed in the season of 1914. In the next cross section used, the subgrade was made flat. In explanation of this change I will say that it has been found that a longitudinal crack developed in many of the slabs of concrete road that had been made according to the first cross section, this crack almost always appearing well within the middle third. Since these cracks, very undesirable, were common, it seemed probable to us that they could be eliminated by strengthening this portion of the road. This was readily accomplished by a reduction of the crown of the earth sub-base and a corresponding increase in thickness of the concrete. In addition, these cracks were found to widen rapidly, much increasing the seriousness of their occurrence. We reasoned that the action of gravity would slowly separate one section from the other, and these sections of slab once cracked longitudinally, acted as separate units contracting and expanding in proportion to the change in temperature, permitting the refuse and earth on the road surface to drop into the opening and eventually prevent the return of the section to the original position. How much of this theory is practical, we can not yet say, as this section was employed only during 1914.

Your attention is called to the fact that the crown of the pavement has been changed from three to two inches. Assuming that a flat subgrade was desired, it would be necessary to make the thickness of the concrete at the center 9 in. in order to maintain a thickness of 6 in. at the edges. We did not feel that a thickness of 9 in. was required at the center, but were convinced that 6 in. was the minimum thickness for the concrete at the edge.

Attention should be given to the selection of the aggregate. In our first experimental construction, it was specified that the coarse aggregate should be hard, durable material, passing a one-inch screen and should include all sizes down to sand grains. From this it would seem that a well-graded pit-run gravel would be highly satisfactory. In practice, however, it was found that such material of ideal mixture could scarcely be obtained. In our later specifications, the material is separated into coarse and fine aggregate with the per cent of material passing several screens given.

Previous to the time of our first concrete road, several concrete roads had been constructed and we endeavored to profit by the experience of those before us. It has been established that lean mixtures such as 1-2½-5, 1-3-5 or 1-3-6 are unsuited to concrete pavement work. The past and present practice of the Illinois Highway Commission has been to use a mixture of 1-2-3½. This proportion of material insures a slight excess of mortar. Failures of many concrete road surfaces are probably due to a lack of mortar in the concrete as much as to the lack of cement in the mortar.

Water is employed in constructing the earth sub-base, the concrete slab, and to effect the proper curing of the concrete slab after it is laid. Probably a fair amount of water required to construct and cure a cubic yard of concrete when placed in a road, would amount to 75 gallons. Although in the dry fall or summer more is required. The problem that confronted our resident engineers was to deliver this water in sufficient quantity to the desired place. When a road adjoined a city having a water system, good results were obtained by joining a pipe line to a hydrant and placing T's at frequent intervals in the line so that connection could be made to the mixer or to a sprinkling hose. In sections of isolated country road, a pressure pump operated by a gasoline engine was employed. On one road water was secured from a temporary reservoir formed by damming a stream, while in another, it was secured from a nearby river.

It has been our practice to mix in a batch mixer, having a capacity of 12 cubic feet, the material per batch being measured by volume, two sacks of cement being taken as the unit.

The materials are dumped into the mixer and water added in sufficient quantity to produce a plastic mass. The amount of water necessary to obtain the desired consistency can be secured only by experiment. Any variation in the quality of aggregate, the amount of moisture it contains, makes necessary a variation in the amount of water required. The mixed batch should have only sufficient water to give a plastic mass from which the cement and sand will not separate when placed in the road. Any mixture which shows a marked separation of coarse aggregate, is too wet. It was found that wet concrete possessed two disadvantages. First, that the separated coarse aggregate collected in pockets and was frequently lacking in mortar to fill its voids. Second, as a consequence of pockets of coarse aggregate, other pockets of mortar existed. The disadvantage of this condition was

that such spots, when exposed to heavy traffic were rapidly resulting in a wavy surface.

The concrete placed between the forms was cut off to the desired crown by means of a steel shod template, cut to the crown of the road. This template was pulled along the side forms with a combined pulling and sawing motion.

The surface of all roads was not finished smooth, but left slightly rough. A wood float was found to give good results and in a few instances, the surface after being brought to grade was brushed lightly with a street broom. One or two finishing devices have been employed but have not given satisfaction, so the finishing remains to be done by hand. On the concrete roads constructed in Wayne County, Michigan, some experiments were conducted with mechanical finishing devices in the summer of 1914, but these do not seem to have proven satisfactory. A novel method of concrete road finishing has recently been employed in the state of Oregon. A machine was designed to perform the two duties of striking off and compacting the newly-placed concrete. This machine is self-propelling and consists of a roller and a cutting edge set in a frame, supported at the ends by the side forms. It seems to have been successful in striking off and compacting the concrete but the finish seemingly remained imperfect, for men with wood floats were still required to secure the desired surface. This method of rolling, while entirely new, may be of considerable importance and seems worthy of investigation in the future.

Many inferior concrete pavements result from the improper curing of the concrete slab.

Shrinkage cracks occur if the concrete has not been covered and kept thoroughly moist for a period of ten days. The writer recalls one instance on a concrete road when many cracks appeared while the concrete was still so soft that it could be dented with the finger. As prevention for such damage, a canvas is placed on the newly constructed road as soon as the concrete has set sufficiently. This canvas is kept moist until the concrete is hard enough to permit of an earth covering. This earth covering is kept thoroughly wet for a period of ten days.

A concrete pavement presents may characteristics totally unlike any other form of pavement in general use. It is practically a monolithic surface, rigid and entirely lacking in any resilient qualities. Owing to the action of temperature, there is a tendency for the concrete to lengthen on a hot day and shorten on a cold day. It is evident that cracks appear on cold days, while at the other extreme of temperature, the concrete will be stressed under compression. If the formation of haphazard contraction cracks are to be prevented, it would seem necessary to provide joints close enough together that there will be sufficient strength in the concrete to drag one half its length between joints. In the first expansion joints constructed, the length of slab between joints was taken as 50 feet. On the basis of the assumption that each slab must drag one-half its length between joints and assuming the coefficient of friction of concrete and sub-soil as one, the tensile strength developed would be approximately 25 pounds per square inch. However, many contraction cracks have occurred even when the above precautions were taken.

Many different joints have been used, a few of which are as follows:

A section of joint was used, made of two 2x6-inch planks on edge held apart by wedges while the concrete was being placed. When the concrete had set slightly, the wedges were loosened and the two planks removed. The lower part of this slot was then filled with gravel, while the top was closed by placing creosoted wood blocks on edge. The blocks were carefully placed, thoroughly tamped and left with their upper surface about one-fourth inch above the concrete surface. This joint was employed on the first concrete road built. However, it is not proving up to expectations as the gravel or sand slowly settled permitting the wood blocks to sink below the concrete surface.

Another section of expansion joint was used in which the concrete edges were protected by means of standard Baker plates. The three-eighth inch space between plates was filled with a bituminous filler. To obtain this space, sections of steel plates were used which separated the pavement for its entire depth. The protection plates and the plates for making the expansion joint were held in place by a patented holder, shaped to the crown of the pavement and supported at the ends by the side forms. The concrete was then poured and struck off with the template. The concrete was permitted to take an initial set, the holder loosened and removed, and the steel plates removed, leaving the space to be filled with tar or asphalt later. This joint was employed in the latter part of 1912 and the season of 1913. It has not proven entirely satisfactory. In the first place, its cost is 12 cents per foot of joint, exclusive of labor. In the second place, it was found difficult to place on a very wide roadway, resulting in slight lumps or depressions. To relieve the jolt thus occurring to a wagon, it was decided to place the joint at an angle of 60 degrees with the center line of the roadway. By placing the joint at this angle, only one wheel was jolted at a time and the body of the carriage not so much disturbed. Again it was found desirable not to place successive joints parallel; that is, one joint should be swung 60 degrees in one direction and the succeeding joint swung 60 degrees in the opposite direction. It was found that vibrations caused by joints so placed were compensating rather than accumulating. The most recent joint construction is at right angles to the pavement proper, and spaced 100 feet apart. Expansion is provided in the one-fourth inch of tar felt.

The concrete road built by day labor has served a triple purpose. First, to determine what modifications were necessary in the methods of concrete road construction to adapt it to conditions encountered in Illinois. In other words, they were experimental. Second, they have served the more important purpose of demonstrating in many places in this State, the economic value of improved highways. Third, they have supplied data valuable for the preparation of estimates for contract work.

TOWNSHIP CONCRETE ROAD CONSTRUCTION.

[By B. H. PIEPMEIER, Maintenance Engineer.]

Petty Township, Lawrence County, has completed another mile of first-class concrete pavement.

A great deal of credit is due Mr. Havill, Highway Commissioner, Mr. Benefeld the County Superintendent of Highways, and Mr. F. C. Feutz, Assistant Engineer of the State Highway Department who was in direct charge of the work.

Petty Township is not a rich agricultural community but it is abundantly supplied with oil wells. The oil work creates a very large amount of heavy traffic. It was found in adjacent townships that the ordinary gravel or macadam roads failed under the heavy loads usually hauled by the oil refinery companies. The road officials therefore wisely selected a more permanent surface for their township road work.

10 Foot Concrete Road, Petty Township, Lawrence County. Showing Oil Wells in Back-ground.

Last year about 1½ miles of 10-ft. concrete road with 2-ft. gravel shoulders were constructed by the township under the direct supervision of this Department.

There remains another mile of concrete road to be completed yet this fall. The taxpayers are apparently very enthusiastic over this type of road and are continually urging their highway commissioners to build more of such roads.

The following gives an itemized statement of expenditures for the Spring Hill Road.

FINAL COST REPORT ON CONCRETE ROAD.
(Excluding Contractor's profit and overhead charges.)
SPRINGHILL ROAD—PETTY TOWNSHIP—LAWRENCE COUNTY.

CONDITIONS.

Amount of pavement laid 5,345.0 feet, 5,938.9 sq. yards; width of pavement 10 feet; length of pavement constructed with transverse joints 5,345.0 feet; spacing of transverse joints in 5,345.0 feet of pavement average 100 feet; length of haul for materials, average 4.0 miles; cost of cement per barrel f. o. b. siding $1.23; cost of sand per cubic yard f. o. b. siding $1.12; cost of stone per cubic yard f. o. b. siding $1.12; amount of cement used per square yard of pavement, 0.287 barrels; rate of pay for labor 20c per hour; teams 40c per hour.

COST OF LABOR AND SUPPLIES.	Cost per
	Total cost.	sq. yd.
Engineering and general supervision. [1]	[1] ....
Superintendence and Inspection.....	[1]$345 00	[1]$0.058
Excavation	661 54	0.112
Gravel, 1285.5 ton @ 80¢ f. o. b. siding	1,030 40	0.174
Unloading to storage or loading sand and stone direct	60 00	0.010
Hauling stone or gravel..........	872 85	0.148
Sand, 707.5 ton @ 80¢ f. o. b. siding.	566 00	0.095
Hauling sand	503 70	0.084
Cement, 1704½ bbls. @ $1.23 f. o. b. siding	2,096 54	0.353
Hauling cement	301 25	0.051
Incidental hauling	42 00	0.007

[1] Indicates paid by State Highway Department.

	Total cost.	Cost per sq. yd.
Hauling and placing macadam shoulders and stone drain..............	25 00	0.004
Shaping and rolling subgrade and side roads	321 87	0.054
Mixing and placing concrete, handling forms and joints...........	735 93	0.124
Covering, seasoning and cleaning concrete	82 00	0.014
Cost of culverts and bridges........	340 00	0.057
Freight on equipment.............	32 16	0.005
Depreciation or rental on equipment [1]	[1]	
Insurance, printing and incidental supplies	221 72	0.037
Total cost	$8,237 96	$1.390
Cost, excluding excavation, culverts and bridges	$7,236 42	1.220

[1] Indicates paid by the State Highway Department.

HARD ROAD BUILDING IN KANKAKEE COUNTY.

[By F. M. Enos, *County Superintendent of Highways.*]

Our county completed during the year of 1914 about two miles of concrete State Aid Road under the supervision of the State Highway Department, consisting of a concrete pavement ten feet wide with four foot macadam shoulders on either side. It has been subject to a very severe test on account of exceptionally heavy and almost continuous rains during the spring and summer. Our concrete pavement, barring a few small cross cracks that were anticipated, is in perfect condition. The macadam shoulders are in like condition.

Section A—Kankakee County.
State Aid Road Beside the Kankakee River.

Our entire two miles of concrete road skirts the beautiful Kankakee River and a trip over it takes one past not only exceptionally fine farming land, but some of the most beautiful scenery in this part of Illinois.

The farm owners adjoining our State aid road are progressive and very enthusiastic and take pride in keeping all brush, weeds and grass cut the full length of the road, thus materially adding to the beauty of the road as well as improving sanitary conditions.

We expect to construct nearly two miles of additional concrete road this year which when completed will give a continuous hard road from Kankakee City to Chicago.

Section A—Kankakee County.
State-aid Road Showing Improved Farm Entrance.

Our people very much regret that the last Legislature saw fit to amend the Tice Road Law in such a way that it takes from the State Highway Department the power of naming the type of State aid road, thus destroying the original object of the Tice Road Law that contemplated uniform and permanent roads throughout Illinois.

There is a universial feeling in our county that permanent hard roads are beneficial to the business and professional men as well as the farmer and our whole people are hopefully looking forward to the day when hard roads will be constructed throughout Kankakee County. We realize that in order to secure the best results all interests must cooperate, carefully study all phases of the question and determine how to secure the best and most roads for the least money. By keeping *everlastingly at it* there is no question but what in a few years impassable mudholes in our main roads will be ancient history and entirely forgotten.

10-Foot Concrete State Aid Road With 4-Foot Macadam Shoulders.

REPORT FROM DEWITT COUNTY.

[By Melvin Tuggle, *County Superintendent of Highways.*]

I have been County Superintendent of Highways for so short a period, and have necessarily accomplished so little that it seems inopportune to submit a report, yet I feel that the county board, and the people whom they represent have a right and may care to know what has been undertaken. If the superintendent has taken steps in the wrong direction, he should receive the criticism of this board that he may have a better guide to the future; and so far as his steps have been in the right direction, he would appreciate and believes should have the encouragement of every member of the board. Therefore, that I may be able to cooperate with the county board, the Commissioners of Highways, and the whole people of Dewitt County in furthering the cause of better earth roads, which now seems to be one of the foremost questions in the minds of the people, I therefore most respectfully submit to you this report.

The complaints that come to this office would indicate that the people are demanding better roads, and also that in many cases they do not realize how small an amount of money there is at the disposal of the road officials to build and maintain the highways.

It would seem then, that whatever is done in improving our highways should not be done hastily. Time should be taken to work out some efficient and economic system of maintenance and repair that will at least give us the best service for the amount of money we can afford to expend.

An inspector is in charge of the construction of the county line bridge, between McLean and Dewitt Counties has been secured for a consideration of $75.00 per month to be paid by the two counties in the ratio of their assessed valuation. No work has yet been done.

In Texas Township a steel leg bridge which we failed to visit on our inspection tour has since been reported in immediate need of repair. Plans for rebuilding with concrete abutments and floor were suggested by the highway commissioners. With suggestions for added strength, the construction was approved by me, and its being reported an emergency, the commissioners of highways are to build the improvements by day labor, the work to be in charge of one of the commissioners. (Estimated cost about $300.00.)

Plans have been secured for five concrete bridges. To date, but one has been accepted by the commissioners, it being the Carl Swigart Bridge in Harp Township. A plan was secured for a concrete bridge in Wilson Township, having an 8-foot span and 20-foot roadway. A majority of the commissioners not favoring a concrete bridge, bought a steel leg bridge with a roadway two foot smaller and at a cost of $25.00 more than the estimated cost of the concrete bridge.

The steel bridge was approved by me (though less efficient and of greater cost) because the commissioners of Wilson Township were unwilling to put in a concrete bridge, and taking into consideration that they were among the heavy taxpayers of the township and having served several terms as commissioners of highways, their expression no doubt, was the expression of the taxpayers whom they represented. I also found in the township some concrete culverts of poor design and faulty construction, which have proven failures and no doubt have prejudiced the people against the use of concrete. In all the other cases where concrete plans were at hand and were not used, a lack of funds made it necessary to abandon the improvement or secure county aid.

In designing or recommending bridges or culverts it has been my policy to ask for a roadway of from 18 to 24 feet according to the amount and kind of traffic on the designated road. A wider roadway than has been the custom proves more economical, when the repairs that must be put on narrow culverts and approaches are considered; also the "Safety First" slogan should not be overlooked.

In every case, the concrete culverts and small bridges designed have been of a more efficient character and usually of less cost than a steel structure of the same or smaller design.

It is also noticeable that where corrugated pipes are used, and concrete headwalls needed, an all-concrete culvert could be planned for the same, and in some cases less money than the pipe culverts.

I have found many corrugated pipe culverts above 12 inches or 15 inches in diameter in bad condition. It is my opinion, that they are about the most expensive type of culvert construction in our county.

I would recommend, generally, for the greatest economy and efficiency, cast iron for culverts up to two feet, and for larger ones, concrete. However, there are some places where corrugated culverts can be used to advantage.

I have sent four specimens of gravel to the State Laboratory for test. It is my plan to find, if possible, local material that dependable concrete can be made from in order to eliminate the higher cost of shipping in material.

In most cases of road and bridge inspection, the supervisor as well as the commissioners of highways have been able to accompany me some of the time and I am sure that much good has come from their efforts thus expended. Since the supervisor is ex officio treasurer of the Road and Bridge Fund, and the representative of his township on the county board, there is perhaps no one in his township who should be more conversant with the highways and their condition. Therefore, it is my desire that they accompany me on inspection work when possible and especially on the initial trip. I believe that we can thus jointly learn facts that will enable us to cooperate more closely.

In justice to the commissioners of highways throughout the county, I wish to say I find them generally trying to serve their township as best they can within the means at their disposal, and along the lines they deem most efficient and economical.

Some of the commissioners of highways had not been supplied with a copy of the Revised Road and Bridge Law, and while they may not have followed the law they have been governed by what they believed the law to be, and were under the delusion that all their powers had been taken from them. I have supplied a copy of the law to all with whom I have come in contact, and pointed out their powers and duties, which are about the same as those delegated by the old law.

I believe the commissioners of highways are as anxious as myself to serve the people in the fullest capacity. Personally I invite the criticisms and suggestions of every citizen in the county upon road problems.

It is my opinion that with a full road and bridge levy it will take ten years of careful expenditure of money to supply all the permanent culverts needed, keep the roads in a passable condition and take care of the drainage.

It would seem then that if we would get out of the mud without increased taxation, the gratuitous use of the split-log drag should be encouraged.

ROAD OILING.

[By B. H. Piepmeier, *Maintenance Engineer.*]

A considerable mileage of oiled earth roads is contemplated in Illinois and for the benefit of those contemplating such work, the following is written:

Where earth roads are properly drained and oiled, they will undoubtedly improve traffic conditions in many localities. It should be kept in mind, however, that the oiling alone of earth roads will not make the "permanent earth road." This term we understand to mean a road properly graded and drained and so located and constructed that none of the work done will have to be repeated preparatory to laying a hard surface. The oil is used to shed the water and lay the dust. The combined oiling and dragging of earth roads will very materially improve them.

Where a road is subjected to exceptionally heavy traffic, it is not always advisable to spend each year $250 to $500 per mile of road to keep it oiled. Such expenditures will soon pay the large per cent of the cost of some form of hard surfacing material for the road, which will undoubtedly make the road more nearly meet the requirements of heavy traffic. However, there are a great many earth roads in the average community that can be economically maintained by the proper use of road oils and such work should be encouraged.

There are many officials that use road oil regardless of the condition of the road or the quality of the oil. Such practice should be condemned. The misuse of road oils can in a great many cases, be laid at the door of the over-anxious salesman. This salesman through competition often submits a very low price and will sell an inferior oil. The use of an inferior grade of oil on a road that is improperly prepared only results in discouraging the taxpayers.

There are a number of principles that should be observed in the application of a road oil. First, the earth road should be well drained and properly shaped and compacted before the oil is applied. The road should be graded so there is no possible chance for any surface water to stand on the road, all ruts should be filled following a rain and the surface should be perfectly smooth and free from dust. The oil should, if possible, be applied under pressure and from nozzles that will permit the oil to be spread uniformly over the surface of the road. It is not good practice to apply a surplus of oil; it had better be applied at intervals of 3 or 4 months rather than to have the road flooded with a single treatment. One-quarter to three-eighths gallons per square yard of surface will usually be sufficient, though some earth roads may take slightly more.

Where it is possible to sand an earth road immediately following the application of oil, a slightly heavier oil may be used and considerable better results may be expected.

It is advisable to apply first a light oil which will penetrate to a depth of four or five inches and then to apply a heavier oil that more lasting results may be secured. The semi-asphaltic or paraffin oils, having an asphaltic residue of from 50 to 60 per cent according to spec. No. 2 or 4 of Bulletin No. 6, of the State Highway Department may be applied to earth roads with excellent results. However, such products must usually be heated before applying. The heating may be accomplished by connecting an ordinary steam traction engine with the heating coils in the bottom of the railroad tank car. About 24 hours time is required for the steam heat to raise the temperature of the oil in the tank car to a point where it is in proper condition to apply on the road.

Such road oils as referred to can usually be purchased from a number of companies at prices ranging from 3 to 3½ cents per gallon delivered in tank cars of 6, 8 or 10,000-gallon capacity.

The lighter semi-asphaltic or paraffin oils having an asphaltic residue of 30 to 40 per cent may be applied cold, but will not usually give as good results as the heavier products. Such oils lay the dust for a short while but do not protect the roads as do heavier products.

The natural asphaltic oils or fluxed asphalts that come from the Trinidad Islands, Mexico and California fields, have more binding and lasting qualities than the semi-asphaltic or paraffin oils usually purchased in Illinois. The natural or fluxed asphaltic oils may be purchased at prices ranging from 4½ cents to 7 cents per gallon, tank cars, delivered. Such oils containing from 50 to 60 per cent pure asphalt may be applied to earth roads without heating. The saving in the cost of heating on the natural asphaltic or fluxed products will often reduce their cost of application to that of applying the semi-asphaltic or paraffin oils that ordinarily must be heated before applying.

There are always a great many questions asked concerning how to purchase road oil and how to determine its quality after it is delivered. Here it is necessary to urge that all road oil be purchased under a well-drawn set of specifications. It should be tested by a reputable chemist after delivery, to make sure that the quality of the material is known. There are a number of short field methods often recommended for determining the quality of bituminous materials but such methods cannot be relied upon.

The testing of the material may cause three or four days' delay but this is justified if it will assure first class material. The Chemist of the State Highway Department will make all such tests for road officials in Illinois, if the material is purchased under specifications published by the Department. The Department, upon request from road officials, will be glad to furnish such information as it may have concerning various bituminous products together with their approximate cost.

The practice of buying road oil under a guarantee of 40 to 50 per cent asphalt, without any further specifications means but very little and should be discouraged. A requirement of this kind will permit such a wide variation in the material that an inferior as well as a good grade of oil may comply with it.

The semi-asphaltic or paraffin oils may contain 40 or 50 per cent asphaltic residue but at the same time contain a large per cent of light oils that have a greasy paraffin base which tend to make the road slippery. In some cases such oil actually disturbs the bond in the earth road, and makes it worse than if the oil had never been applied. The light paraffin oils sometimes fail to hold down the dust and the oiled dust, which is much more disagreeable than ordinary dust, begins to fly. It is well to lay emphasis on the quality of oil used as much depends on it to accomplish the best results.

In oiling gravel or macadam roads, more care should be taken in the selection of the proper grade of asphaltic oils or refined tars. If the gravel road is very dirty, natural asphaltic or fluxed oils containing from 50 to 70 per cent asphalt, or a light coal tar product that may be applied cold will give the best results. If the gravel or macadam road is in good shape and clean, a somewhat heavier product may be used. In oiling gravel or macadam roads of any character, arrangements should be made to sand the surface lightly after the oil or tar is applied.

The State Highway Department will be glad to furnish any of its engineers to advise with road officials concerning the application of the proper grades of oil and tar to use for any specific road that may be under consideration. Also to furnish oiling equipment if same is available.

BRIDGE FAILURE, EDGAR TOWNSHIP, EDGAR COUNTY.
12 Ton Traction Engine Fell Through one 16 Foot Bent of 80 Foot Steel Truss Built in 1895. Unfastened Floor Beams Slipped off of Joist Allowing Floor to Fall through.

SCENE OF ACCIDENT AT WOOD STREET, PARIS, ILL., AUG. 8, 1915.
Automobile Collided With Paris-Terre Haute Interurban Car, Seriously Injuring Four Persons. Corner Obscured by Young Orchard. Parties in Auto Were Familiar With Turn, But Did Not Approach With Due Caution.

OPINIONS OF THE ATTORNEY GENERAL.

POLL TAX.

August 28, 1915.

Hon. J. PAUL CARTER, *State's Attorney, Nashville, Ill.*

DEAR SIR: I am in receipt of your favor of the 26th instant and note statement to the effect that a certain township in your county voted, under the road and bridge act of 1913, to abolish the poll tax provided for by section 55 of said act; that subsequently the Supreme Court held said section 55 to be invalid. You further state said township now wishes to levy a poll tax.

You inquire, in substance, whether the fact that the township voted to abolish the poll tax provided for by said section 55, which the Supreme Court in the case of *Town of Dixon v. Seymour Ide,* 267 Ill. 445 held to be unconstitutional, has any bearing upon the rights of the highway commissioners of said town to assess a poll tax in accordance with an act of the Forty-ninth General Assembly, which provides for the assessment of a poll tax, and which acts as a substitute for the act of 1913.

The fact that the town voted *to abolish* a poll tax provided for under section 55 of the act of 1913, has no bearing upon, and in no way affects the assessment of the poll tax provided for by the act of 1915.

The Supreme Court in the case of *Highway Commissioners v. Bloomington,* 253 Ill., 164, holds in substance that where an act is declared to be unconstitutional, the situation in legal contemplation is as though no statute had ever been passed. It follows, therefore, that the opinion of the Suupreme Court holding the poll tax provided for by section 55 of the act of 1913, invalid, has the same effect, as though said act contained no provision for the levy of a poll tax. Under the act of 1915, which created a new section 55, it becomes the duty of highway commissioners at their meeting to be held the second Tuesday after the annual town meeting in 1916, to assess a poll tax, unless upon a petition as therein prescribed the voters, at the town meeting to be held on the first Tuesday of April, 1916, vote to abolish such tax.

Very respectfully,

P. J. LUCEY, *Attorney General.*

COMMISSIONERS OF HIGHWAYS—POWERS OF.

April 8, 1915.

MR. JOHN FINNEY,
Attorney at Law, Joliet, Illinois.

DEAR SIR: I am in receipt of your favor of which, as attorney for the board of highway commissioners of the town of Joliet, you inquire whether the commissioners have the authority to contract for the purchase of a motor truck valued at $4,000.00 without the approval of the county superintendent of highways.

Replying, I will call your attention to sub-division (B), Section 50 of the Revised Road and Bridge Act, which provides in part as follows:

"The highway commissioners of each town * * * * shall have power and it shall be their duty: * * * * * * (5) To direct the construction and repair of roads and bridges within the town * * * * to let contracts, employ labor and purchase material and machinery therefor, subject to the limitations herein provided: *Provided, however,* that no contract shall be let for the construction or repair of any road or bridge or part thereof in excess of the amount of $200.00, nor shall any machinery or other appliances to be used in road construction in excess of such amount be purchased without the approval of the county superintendent of highways."

Highway commissioners are statutory officers; they are created by statute and can exercise only such powers as the statute confers upon them. The Supreme Court, in the case of *The Ohio and Mississippi Railway Company v. The People,* 123 Ill. at page 650, says:

"It is a plain proposition that the highway commissioners have no powers except those conferred by the statute, and that they can perform no acts or impose no burdens except those plainly authorized by the statute; and when they undertake to perform any act which the statute does not say they may do, that act will be void."

You will note that clause 5, subdivision (B), section 50, above quoted, expressly prohibits the purchase by highway commissioners of any machinery or other appliances for road purposes, in excess of the sum of two hundred dollars, without the approval of the county superintendent of highways.

Very respectfully,

P. J. LUCEY, *Attorney General.*

TOWNSHIP OFFICIALS HAVE NO RIGHT TO LEVY AN ADDITIONAL TAX TO PAY A DEBT.

April 1, 1915.

MR. JAMES W. MOORE,
Town Clerk, Sumner, Illinois.

DEAR SIR: I am in receipt of your favor of the 23d ultimo from which it appears that your town is in debt on account of roads and bridges to an amount approximating $2,000; that a levy of sixty-one cents (the highest rate that can be levied for road and bridge purposes) does not produce sufficient funds to keep up the roads and bridges. You inquire whether the town board of auditors may audit the claims which go to make up such road and bridge indebtedness, upon which audit a town tax may be extended for payment of same.

Your inquiry is, in effect, whether the town may levy a tax for general road and bridge purposes.

In reply will say the Supreme Court, in the case of *Robinson v. McKenney,* 239 Ill. 343, holds in substance that the power to levy taxes for general road and bridge purposes rests in the commissioners of highways; that such tax, in order to be valid, must be levied by the commissioners of highways in the manner prescribed by statute; and the Appellate Court, in the case of *Challacombs* v. *Anderson*, 173 App. 144, holds in substance that the board of town auditors can not be compelled to cause a general town tax to be levied to pay a judgment rendered against the highway commissioners for labor and material furnished. The court, at page 149, says:

"The town fund is entirely distinct and levied for purposes wholly different from those to which the funds of the highway commissioners can be devoted. The law will not permit a town tax to be levied and a town fund raised for the purpose of discharging a debt, which the town as a corporation has not incurred."

There is no provision of the statute which authorizes the board of town auditors to audit and allow, as charges against the town, claims that are payable out of the road and bridge fund.

The Supreme Court, in the case of *Sullivan* v. *Commissioners of Highways*, 114 Ill. 262, holds that highway commissioners have no authority of law to contract an indebtedness in respect to roads and bridges, unless the money to pay such debt is in the treasury, or unless a levy out of which it may be paid has been actually levied.

If highway commissioners would follow the rule laid down by the court in the above cited case, they would avoid incurring an indebtedness beyond their ability to meet.

Very respectfully,

P. J. LUCEY, *Attorney General.*

A BRIDGE BUILT BY ADJOINING TOWNS UNDER A CONTRACT UNDER SECTION 22 OF THE ACT OF 1883, IS TO BE KEPT IN REPAIR BY THE ADJOINING TOWNS AS PROVIDED IN SUCH CONTRACT.

HON. C. N. HOLLERICH,   *March* 8, 1915.
State's Attorney, Spring Valley, Illinois..

DEAR SIR: I am in receipt of your favor of the 2d instant, citing section 63 of the revised Road and Bridge act, which provides as follows:

"Bridges over streams which divide towns or districts and bridges over streams on town or district lines, and bridges within eighty rods of town or district lines over streams on roads extending from one town or district into another town or district and crossing town or district lines, shall be built and repaired at the expense of such towns or districts: *Provided*, that the expense of building and maintaining any bridge over a stream near town or district lines in which both are interested and where the cost thereof is less than $5,000, shall be borne by both towns or districts in such portion as shall be just and equitable between said towns or districts, taking into consideration the taxable property in each, the location of the bridge, and the advantage to each, to be determined by the commissioners in making contracts for the same, as provided for in section 64 of this Act."

I quote from your letter as follows:

"The Commissioners of two adjoining townships in this county entered into a contract twenty years ago whereby one of the said townships agreed to pay 40 per cent and the other 60 per cent of the expense of the construction and repair of a bridge coming within the provisions of the foregoing section, and the county superintendent of highways has requested me to obtain your opinion as to whether such contract was affected in any way by the adoption of the road and bridge law of 1913."

I am assuming that the contract in question was properly entered into and made a matter of record in both towns; that the bridge to which said contract relates is still standing and that your inquiry has reference to, whether the liability of the adjoining towns for the maintenance and repair of such bridge is to be determined by said contract or by the provisions of section 63 of the Road and Bridge act.

Section 21 of the Road and Bridge act of 1883, applicable to counties under township organization, provided, in part, as follows:

"Bridges over streams which divide towns or counties, and bridges over streams on roads on county or town lines, and bridges within eighty rods of county or town lines over streams on roads extending from one county or town into another county or town and crossing county or town lines, shall be built and repaired at the expense of such towns or counties.

Provided, that for the building and maintaining of bridges over streams near county or town lines in which both are interested and where the cost thereof is less than $5,000, the expense of building and maintaining any

such bridge shall be borne by both counties or towns in such portion as shall be just and equitable between said towns or counties, taking into consideration the taxable property in each, the location of the bridge, and the advantage to each, to be determined by the commissioners in making contracts for the same, etc."

Section 22 of said act (chapter 121, Hurd's Revised Statutes, 1911) provided as follows:

"For the purpose of building or keeping in repair such bridge or bridges, it shall be lawful for the commissioners of such adjoining towns, whether they be in the same or different counties or county boards of such adjoining counties, to enter into joint contracts, and such contracts may be enforced in law or equity against such commissioners jointly, the same as if entered into by individuals, and such commissioners or county boards may be proceeded against jointly, by any parties interested in such bridge or bridges, or for any damage growing out of such neglect."

It will be noted that section 21 of the act of 1883 imposed upon adjoining towns the duty to build and repair certain bridges; and section 22 of said act authorized and empowered highway commissioners of adjoining towns to enter into joint contracts for building and keeping in repair such bridges.

Where a bridge has been built by highway commissioners of adjoining towns, under a contract for the building and keeping in repair of same, in accordance with the provisions of section 22 of the act of 1883, the liability of said towns to keep such bridge in repair, is to be determined by such contract, and not by the provisions of section 63 of the revised act. The provisions of section 63 of the revised act does not have the effect to change or alter the terms of a valid contract, respecting the keeping in repair a bridge, entered into as provided by said section 22 of the act of 1883, prior to the enactment of the revised act. Such contract would be an existing obligation, at the time the revised act went into effect, which the revised act could not impair.

Section 14, article 2 of the Constitution, expressly provides that no law impairing the obligation of an existing contract shall be passed.

Very respectfully,

P. J. LUCEY, *Attorney General.*

COMMISSIONERS OF HIGHWAYS NOT TO HAVE, DIRECTLY OR INDIRECTLY, ANY PERSONAL PECUNIARY INTEREST IN THE EMPLOYMENT OF LABOR.

E. MARSHALL, Esq., ·   *October* 29, 1914.
Supervisor, Whittington, Ill.

DEAR SIR: I am in receipt of your favor of the twenty-fifth instant, in which you inquire, in substance, whether, when a commissioner of highways employs his team in working the roads, he is to be paid for such labor out of the town funds or out of the road and bridge fund.

In reply, I will call your attention to section 72 of the revised road and bridge act, which provides as follows:

"In letting contracts, employing labor, or in purchasing tools, machinery or materials, neither the highway commissioners nor the county superintendent of highways shall have, directly or indirectly, any personal pecuniary interest therewith."

The section quoted above would seem to deny to one holding the office of commissioner of highways, the right to employ his team in working roads. By section 53, the compensation of highway commissioners is fixed at the sum of $2 per day, upon a sworn statement to be filed in the office of the town clerk, showing the number of days he was employed and the kind of employment, and giving the dates. It is the holding of this department that the compensation of highway commissioners fixed by statute is payable out of the town funds.

By section 52, the road and bridge fund is subject to the commissioners of highways, and is paid out on orders issued by them.

Section 72, which prohibits highway commissioners having directly or indirectly any personal pecuniary interest in the employment of labor, is based upon the principle, that it is against public policy for one who holds a public office to be interested in performing labor to be paid for out of funds, which are controlled by him by virtue of his office.

Under the rule announced by the Appellate Court, in the case of *Houseweart* v. *Doocy*, 164 App., 331, it would seem that any compensation to which highway commissioners may be entitled is payable out of the town funds.

Very respectfully,

P. J. LUCEY, *Attorney General.*

HARD ROADS—MONEY BORROWED—HOW APPLIED.

April 17, 1915.

Mr. C. E. CLAYTON,

Town Clerk, Ancona, Illinois.

DEAR SIR: I am in receipt of your favor of the 10th instant enclosing what purports to be a copy of a petition by the highway commissioners in their official capacity, and one hundred freeholders, of the town of Reading in Livingston County for a special election for the purpose of voting on the proposition to borrow $63,500 to be used in the construction of gravel, rock, macadam or other hard roads in said township. Attached to said petition is a letter designating the roads to be improved, which you state was circulated at the same time as the petition and shown to the signers thereof that they might the more thoroughly understand the proposition.

You further state, in effect, that the amount voted may not be sufficient to improve all the roads designated and that if the construction is carried on as specified in the letter attached to the petition, the north side of the town will have the greater part of the improved roads.

You inquire whether the commissioners are bound to follow the order of construction outlined in the letter attached to the petition, or whether the freeholders on the south side of the township can compel an equal amount of improvement.

It is apparent that the proposition mentioned was submitted to a vote under section 112 of the revised Road and Bridge Act which provides as follows:

"On the petition of the commissioners of highways, in his official capacity, and of one hundred of the freeholders of any town or district (or where there may be less than two hundred such freeholders, then a majority of them) to the town or district clerk requesting him, when giving notice of the time and place for holding the next annual town meeting or road district election, to also give notice that a vote will be taken at said election or meeting on the proposition, 'For borrowing $........ (to construct or maintain gravel, rock, macadam or other roads, or to construct or repair any bridge or bridges, or to construct or repair any other distinctive work on the road),' he shall, when giving notice of the time and place for holding the next annual town meeting or road district election, also give notice, that a vote will be taken at said election or meeting upon the proposition, "For borrowing $...... (to construct or maintain gravel, rock, macadam or other roads, or to construct or repair any bridge or bridges, or to construct or repair any other distinctive work on the road).'

"If in any such petition a special election shall be requested for such purpose, it shall be called as follows:

"Upon the filing of such petition the town or district clerk shall call such special town or district election by posting up in ten of the most public places in said town or district, at least ten days prior to the day fixed for said special town or district election, notice of such special town or district election, which notices shall state the filing of said petition, the time and place of said special election, and that a vote will be taken at said election or meeting upon the proposition, 'For borrowing $........ (to construct or maintain gravel, rock, macadam, or other roads, or to construct or repair any bridge or bridges, or to construct or repair any other distinctive work on the road),' and the manner in which the voting is to be had.

"Such special election shall be held at the place of the last annual town or district election, and returns thereof shall be made in the same manner as other special or district elections are now or may hereafter be provided by law.

"The vote at such regular or special election shall invariably be by a separate ballot and shall be in the following form:

| For borrowing $........ to construct or maintain gravel, rock, macadam or other roads. | Yes. |
| | No. |

"And if it shall appear that a majority of the legal voters voting at said election on said proposition voted in favor of said proposition, the commissioners of highways and the town or district clerk, as the case may be, shall - issue (from time to time as the work progresses) a sufficient amount, in the aggregate, of the bonds of said town or district for the purpose of building and maintaining gravel, rock, macadam or other roads, or for the purpose of constructing or repairing such bridge or bridges, or for the purpose of constructing or repairing such other distinctive work on the road as the case may be. Said bonds to be of such denominations, bear such rate of interest, not exceeding five per cent, upon such time, and be disposed of as necessities and convenience of said town or district may require: *Provided,* that said bonds shall not be sold or disposed of either by sale or by payment to contractors for labor and materials for less than their par value; such bonds to be issued in not more than ten annual series; the first series of which shall mature not more than five years from the date thereof and each succeeding series in succeeding years thereafter. A register of all issues of said bonds shall be kept in the office of the county clerk of the county in which said township or district is located, showing the date, amount, rate of interest, maturity, and the purpose for which said bonds were issued, which information shall be furnished to the county clerk in writing by the town or district clerk, and it shall be the duty of such county clerk to extend annually against the property in said township or road district a tax sufficient to pay the interest of said bonds in each year prior to the maturity of such first series and thereafter he shall extend the tax in each year sufficient to pay each series as it matures, together with interest thereon and with the interest upon the unmatured bonds outstanding. Such bonds may be lithographed and the interest for each year evidenced by interest coupons thereto attached, which shall be signed by the same officers who executed by original or *fac-simile* signatures, the bonds: *Provided, however,* that the amount, including the principal and interest to be voted upon, shall not exceed the amount which can be raised during a period of five years by a levy of one dollar per year on each one hundred dollars of taxable property as taken for assessment purposes in such town or district; the proceeds of said bonds to be paid to the treasurer and to be disbursed by him upon the order of the commissioners of highways."

The above quoted provision is in substance identical with paragraph 248a, chapter 121, Hurd's Statutes, 1911, same being section 4a of the Hard Roads Act of 1883 as subsequently amended.

It will be noted that neither in section 4a of the Hard Roads Act of 1883 nor in section 112 of the revised act is there any provision which requires the petition for a vote on a proposition to borrow money for the construction of hard roads to describe the roads to be improved. Paragraph 245 of said chapter 121, Hurd's Statutes, 1911, being section 1 of the Hard Roads Act of 1883, did require that a petition for a vote on the proposition to levy a special tax for the construction of hard roads should describe the roads to be improved, and the same requirement is contained in section 108 of the revised act where the vote is had on a petition to levy a special tax.

The Supreme Court, in construing section 4a of the Hard Roads Act of 1883, in the case of *The People* v. *The Toledo, Peoria and Western Railway Co.,* 248 Ill. 105, held in substance that it was within the discretion of the commissioners to determine upon what roads the money authorized to be borrowed should be applied; and it would seem that where the voters with a knowledge of the roads to be improved vote to borrow money, they can not afterwards insist upon the money so borrowed being applied to the improvement of other roads. Whether the court might hold that the commissioners having seen fit to annex to the petition a description of the roads to be improved waived by so doing their power to exercise a discretion, and that the only use they could make of such fund would be the improvement of the roads described, I am unable to say; but the voters having voted with a knowledge of the fact of what roads were proposed to be improved, can not afterwards insist on the improvement of different roads.

Very respectfully,

P. J. LUCEY, *Attorney General.*

ILLINOIS HIGHWAYS ✓

[Printed by authority of the State of Illinois.]

OFFICIAL PUBLICATION OF THE

STATE HIGHWAY DEPARTMENT

| VOL. 2 | SPRINGFIELD, ILLINOIS, OCTOBER-NOVEMBER, 1915 | No. 10 |

MAINTAINING GRAVEL AND MACADAM ROADS BY APPLYING TAR.

MONOLITHIC BRICK PAVING CONSTRUCTION—LAYING BRICK.
FOR DETAILS OF THIS CONSTRUCTION SEE PAGE 155.

ILLINOIS HIGHWAYS.

Published Monthly by the
State Highway Department.

ILLINOIS HIGHWAY COMMISSION.
A. D. GASH, *President.*
S. E. BRADT, *Secretary.*
JAMES P. WILSON.

WM. W. MARR, *Chief State Highway Engineer.*

BUREAU CHIEFS.
H. E. BILGER, *Road Engineer, Springfield, Illinois.*
C. OLDER, *Bridge Engineer, Springfield, Illinois.*
B. H. PIEPMEIER, *Maintenance Engineer, Springfield, Illinois.*
F. L. ROMAN, *Testing Engineer, Springfield, Illinois.*
J. M. McCOY, *Chief Clerk, Springfield, Illinois.*
G. E. BURCH, *Assistant Bridge Engineer, Springfield, Illinois.*
M. W. WATSON, *Assistant Road Engineer, Springfield, Illinois.*

DIVISION ENGINEERS.
H. B. Bushnell..............Aurora
R. L. Bell.....................Paris
H. E. Surman...............Moline
A. H. Hunter...............Peoria
Fred Tarrant............Springfield
C. M. Slaymaker.......E. St. Louis
J. E. Huber.........Mount Vernon

Address all communications in regard to "Illinois Highways," to State Highway Department, Springfield, Illinois. Attention of T. W. Dieckmann, Department Editor.

CONTENTS.

THE BENEFITS AND BURDENS OF BETTER ROADS.

Paper Presented at the Pan-American Road Congress by S. E. Bradt, Secretary of the Illinois Highway Commission.

Without doubt the great majority of the people are in favor of better roads; the disagreement comes when they consider the degree of betterment, which is the determining factor in the amount of the burden it will impose upon the community. It is my purpose in this paper to show that if we have the correct type of road con-

struction and if the cost is properly distributed, the burden will rest lightly upon all and will be small in comparison to the benefits.

GOOD ROADS CONCERN OF ALL.

Road improvement is fundamentally an economic problem and affects either directly or indirectly our entire citizenship, regardless of whether they live in the country, the town or the crowded city; regardless of whether they drive a pleasure car, a lumber wagon, or walk the streets of the tenement district. The greatest direct benefits will come to the users of the road; but in each instance there are indirect benefits reaching a greater number of people, and hence of greater importance finally than the direct benefits.

AN 18-FOOT CONCRETE ROAD, AURORA TOWNSHIP, KANE COUNTY. BUILT BY DAY LABOR, UNDER SUPERVISION OF STATE HIGHWAY DEPARTMENT.

For our purpose we will classify the users of the road as follows:

I. The Farmer:
   (a) in hauling his surplus products to the shipping point, or direct to the consumer. (This traffic at the present time is largely horse drawn, but, with a better road system, will gradually change to motor drawn.)
   (b) in carrying his children to school, his family to church or to the city entertainment.

II. The Lumberman or the Mine Owner:
   (a) in hauling his product to the shipping point. (This traffic is decreasing, as competition forces the elimination of the expense of hauling by bringing the railroad nearer.)

III. The Business Man:
   (a) in saving his time.
   (b) in lessening upkeep. (This traffic is now largely motor-driven.)

IV. The Tourist:
   interpreted here to mean all travelers for recreation, whether to the adjacent town or across the continent. (This traffic is mainly motor-driven.)

Let us look at some of the benefits to these four classes more in detail, and also note some of their indirect influences.

BENEFIT TO THE FARMER, LUMBERMAN, AND MINE OWNER, IN HAULING PRODUCTS.

The entire surplus production of the farm and many of the products of the forest and mine must first be hauled over our country roads to the shipping point. The office of Public Roads estimates the cost of this hauling at not less than $500,000,000 annually. It further estimates that improved roads would reduce this cost one-half; which would result in a saving of $250,000,000 annually.

Indirect Gain to All People.—While this gain of $250,000,000 would be a direct benefit to the farmer, the lumberman, and the mine owner, it would be an indirect gain to the entire people. The carrying of these products to the shipping point is as much a factor in distribution as is carrying it from the shipping point to the consumer. The people are quick to recognize that any increase in freight rates means an increase in the price of commodities, but have failed to realize that the cost of hauling to the railway station is equally a factor in their cost and hence in the cost of living. Freight rates have been reduced since 1837 nearly 90 per cent; but during that time there has been practically no reduction in the cost of highway transportation. The reason for this is that railroads have been constructed and operated from the standpoint of paying interest and dividends, which has forced systematic and economic management; whereas our highways, because of our failure to appreciate their economic importance, have been neglected and the limited amount of work expended upon them has been unsystematic, uneconomic and without satisfactory returns.

Benefit to City Residents.—An indirect benefit of no small consequence accrues hereby to the resident of the city in the delivery of the products of the farm and truck garden direct from producer to consumer. This means not only more palatable food, but food that is more sanitary as well.

Benefit to the Farmer's Family Educationally.—The inaccessibility of the country schools for several months of the year due to impassable roads is one of the great drawbacks to country life. Another drawback is the small school district supported by a few farmers and with a small number of children and a small assessed valuation from which to collect taxes for its support. This results in a low-salaried teacher, conducting a poor school with poorer surroundings.

Consolidated Schools.—The solution of this problem lies in the consolidated rural school, specializing in the agricultural branches which will give the pupils an insight into the problems of the farm and inspire them with the wonderful opportunity for the improvement of farm life financially, socially and mentally. Better roads will mean more consolidated schools and larger units of consolidation which will give more funds and greater school facilities, or will mean access to the city schools without leaving the farm.

Social Advantages.—Again, the farmer will receive a direct benefit from good roads in the increase of social and religious advantages. The lack of these is felt most keenly by the wife and children and is often the determining factor in the decision of the boy and the girl to leave the farm. This is traceable directly to road conditions which generally keep them at home for several months during the winter and spring and can be overcome only through improving the roads so that the country church and the city entertainments are accessible at all seasons.

Dependence Upon Farmer.—Both educationally and socially the farmer would receive the greatest direct advantage from road improvement, but it must be remembered that no one class of our citizens can improve themselves financially, educationally, socially or religiously without indirectly benefiting every other class of our citizens. This is doubly true of the farmer. People have lived without the merchant, the manufacturer or the banker and could do so again, but the failure of the farmer to produce his annual crop would mean starvation. A partial failure would mean higher prices and unsatisfied hunger for some. As population increases we must have a constantly increasing food supply. Adding to the educational and social advantages of farm life means more attractive farms, more farmers, greater efficiency, as well as more permanency in production, a larger and hence a cheaper food supply.

Improved Surroundings.—Outside of the tangible benefits to the farmer already enumerated there are others not so evident. As a man tears down the old house and builds in its place a modern one, not that he will make money by the transaction, but that he will add to the comfort, the pleasure and satisfaction of himself and his family, so will he for the same reason advocate and stand ready to pay his share of the cost of a better road. The better road and the automobile combined with the modern house, the telephone and the free delivery of mail, the consolidated school, the resuscitated country church, will make the farm home an attractive place for the boy and the girl, for the father and the mother. This combination will not only check the farm to city movement, but will make the "back to the farm movement" a practical possibility.

THE BUSINESS MAN.

We have considered the benefit to the farmer, the lumberman, and the mine owner as users of the road. Now let us look at the benefit to the business man from the same standpoint. In these days we have come to measure distance more by minutes and hours than by miles. The saving of time to the business man is often the difference between success and failure. In this saving of time the automobile is one of his most useful agents, and the better the road the greater is its usefulness to him.

THE TOURIST.

The benefit of road improvement to the tourist as a user of the road is self-evident; and to attract and hold the tourist we must have good roads. We have the expanse of territory, the scenic effects and the historic spots. We lack only the improved roads to make this country the mecca for the tourists of the world.

The indirect benefit of this traffic to the United States is the expenditure of millions of dollars at home rather than in foreign countries.

The Automobile Owner.—To convey some idea of the direct benefit of improved roads to automobile owners I would call attention to the fact that there are over 2 000 000 autos in use in the United States to-day and they are being manufactured at the rate of over 500 000 annually. It is a conservative estimate to say that a system of improved roads would mean a saving to the owners in tires, repairs, and gasoline of not less than $50 per car per year, or a total of $100 000 000 annually on the cars now in use.

Let us summarize some of the benefits. Better roads will mean:

Better farmers.
Greater farm efficiency.
Less tenancy.
Larger production.
Higher land values.
Cheaper distribution.
Cheaper commodities.
Purer milk.
Fresher vegetables.
More work accomplished by business men.
More time for pleasure.
More tourists.
More money spent at home.
Less gasoline.
Less tire trouble.
Better rural schools.
Better school attendance.
Better social conditions.
Better rural churches.
More attractive rural homes.
More boys staying on the farm.
More girls marrying farmer boys.
More sociability.
Better citizenship.

THE BURDENS OF BETTER ROADS.

The question now arises, are the benefits worth the cost. Fortunately, the answer to this question has not been left to us. The American people have already answered it in the affirmative. The people as a whole stand for progress and, without doubt, road improvement is to be one of the greatest factors in national progress. In some sections of the country, however, owing to the fact that local legislation fails to place the burden of taxation in the proper place, or does not afford facilities for the equitable financing of the burden, the work is advancing slowly.

In discussing the burdens I shall consider:
1. The size of the burdens.
2. Who shall carry them?
3. How can they be carried?

Mileage to Be Improved.—We have in the United States approximately 2 200 000 miles of highways. By relocation and eliminating the unnecessary sections this would be easily reduced to less than 2 000 000 miles. Of this 2 000 000 miles some 240 000 are already improved, leaving 1 760 000 miles to be improved.

Cost Depending on Conditions.—What it will cost to improve this 1 760 000 miles depends chiefly upon the type. This in turn should be determined by the amount and kind of traffic. Investigation has shown that 20 per cent of our roads carry approximately 80 per cent of the traffic. It, therefore, follows that this 20 per cent should be built of a more permanent, hence more costly type, than the remaining 80 per cent. It is also true that there is a large variation of traffic on the different sections of this 20 per cent of the system, which would mean a considerable variation in type and width, hence in cost of construction. From the foregoing it will be seen that to determine the cost of a system of roads over a given area, there should be a study of the local conditions in each section of the area. This survey should include a count showing the number and kind of vehicles with approximate loads, the population of the tributary territory, the industries of the locality and available road-building material. I have no knowledge of any large section where such a survey has been made, and, hence, in order to give any figures that would indicate the approximate burdens of better roads, it is necessary to rely upon estimates.

Illinois as an Illustration.—For this purpose I shall take the State of Illinois. Many of the states having State Aid in road work have laid out a system of through routes, and main market roads comprising from 10 to 20 per cent of their total mileage. Illinois has such a system which includes about 16 000 miles (17 per cent of the total 94 000 miles). Local officials report that of the 94 000 miles 9 000 are improved. We will assume that 3 000 miles of the improved roads are included in our State Aid system of 16 000 miles, thus leaving still to be improved 13 000 miles of the said system. Our estimate of the cost of improving this 13 000 miles is as follows:

3 000 miles @ $15 000 ....$ 45 000 000
6 000 miles @   10 000 .... 60 000 000
4 000 miles @   6 000 .... 24 000 000

Total $129 000 000

Cost to Taxpayer.—As before stated, the different estimates of costs arise from different widths of the roads as well as different types of construction, depending upon traffic, and are purely estimates, as we have taken no traffic census. There will be a variation both as to the number of miles in each class and the cost, but we assume that the entire system can be adequately improved within the estimate. This sum of $129 000 000 spread over a period of 20 years would require $6 450 000 annually. On the assumption that the average equalized assessed valuation for the State for the next 20 years will amount to $3 000 000 000, the above $6 450 000 would cost the taxpayer an average of 21¼c per $100 of assessed valuation. This would mean that the man owning a home valued at $1 500, assessed at $500, would pay $1.07 per year.

Cost to Farmer.—Under our State aid system by which the State and the county each pay one-half the cost of the State aid roads, the farms of the State on the average pay 40 per cent of the cost of the improvement, the balance of 60 per cent being paid by personal property, cities, villages and corporations. Forty per cent of the $6 450 000 required annually would be $2 580 000, which would be the proportion paid by the farmer. This, divided among the 34 000 000 acres of farm land in Illinois, would mean a cost of seven cents per acre annually for a period of 20 years to the farms of Illinois for the improvement of this system of 13 000 miles of roads. This is assuming that all of the money is provided by a direct tax with no assistance from any special tax, or from the Federal Government. Even on this basis the burden when spread over the entire State, is small.

Improvement of Connecting Roads.—You will say that we have provided for only 20 per cent of our mileage, which is true; but we have provided for 80 per cent of the traffic. Further, our townships are levying at this time a tax from which they realize over $7 000 000 annually which will be applied to the improvement of the remaining 80 per cent of the roads. Again, inasmuch as these roads receive only 20 per cent of the traffic, it follows that they should be improved at a very much less cost per mile, and that upon a large part of the mileage, because of light traffic, the economical type of construction will be a well-graded and drained earth road with systematic dragging. Illinois with a little less than the average of improved roads should be fairly typical of the general average.

Distribution of Burden.—Another feature that has a very important bearing upon this question of how burdensome the cost of better roads will prove to be is the matter of its distribution among the different taxing bodies.

Burden Concern of All.—We have shown that road improvement is no longer a matter of purely local concern, but of benefit to all. It is also evident from all the estimates of cost given for Illinois that the cost in the aggregate involves a sum comparable only to the cost of our railway systems, from which it follows that we must have assistance from all possible sources. These sources are: The Federal Government, which derives its income mainly from customs and internal revenue, thus drawing indirectly from all classes; the State tax, reaching all property within the State and including all the larger cities and corporations, as well as many fees and special taxes; the county and township taxes, more localized in their scope and nearer the source of the benefits; and in addition to the above the automobile and kindred license fees, collected from a certain part of those benefited. All of these channels are utilized at the present time except that no aid is received from the Federal Government.

Federal Aid.—If our statement is true that all the people are benefited by good roads, then all the people should share the burdens. There are in the United States many millions of people who pay no town, county or State taxes, and who can only aid in this work through indirect taxes which they pay to the Federal Government.

Hence, only through Federal aid can these millions be called upon to share their part of the burden.

The Government has, in recent years, taken a considerable amount from the revenue contributed at home and expended it in improving the highway systems of Cuba and our island possessions, but has steadfastly declined to assist in improving the roads at home. It is committed to the principle of aiding and fostering internal improvements along other lines, having expended many millions for public buildings, rivers and harbors and other similar improvements. It has even gone to the extent of purchasing foreign territory for the purpose of constructing a world waterway upon which it has expended 300 to 350 millions of dollars. Many of these improvements were needed, and all are beneficial to a restricted number of people, but no one will say that these benefits are at all comparable to the benefits which would have been derived from the expenditure of an equal amount of money in road improvement. That this same amount of money would reach a vastly greater number of people and cause a much greater development of the resources of the country, if expended on roads, does not admit of successful contradiction.

Roads Important to National Defense.—To look at the matter of Federal aid from another standpoint, we hear much in these days about our lack of preparedness for defense, in the case of attack, and the indications are that public sentiment favors the strengthening of our army and navy and our coast defense; but no preparation for defense will be complete without the proper improvement of our highways.

The war now in progress is a conflict in which the machinery of war is playing the most important part; and no part of the machinery is more important in its general utility than the motor-driven vehicle. As an illustration of the part it is taking, I would call attention to the fact that in the year ending June 1, we shipped to Europe 13 432 trucks, saying nothing of the unfilled orders, and that we are now sending to the war zone an average of over 100 trucks per day. Trucks without roads would be useless. And if the government is to prepare any adequate plans for defense it can not overlook the improvement of our highways.

Amount of Federal Aid.—The extent to which the government should assist in road improvement should be commensurate with the importance of the project and with the amount of money required to carry it on. We are now expending annually over $200 000 000. It would appear that assistance to the extent of $50 000 000 would not be out of place. We have been expending about that amount annually on the Panama Canal, which is now completed. This amount of money could be profitably expended in furthering road development. Whether the government shall construct a system of government roads, or assist the states in the improvement of rural mail routes is not so important, as enlisting the government in the work. The economic advantages undoubtedly lie in a cooperation of the State and Federal departments; but it is not my purpose to discuss this matter.

Cost, How Provided.—The next question that arises, is, how shall the money be raised; shall we proceed on the "pay as you go" plan, or shall we borrow the money? I have shown that to build these roads over a period of 20 to 25 years would not be burdensome to the people, but public sentiment is rapidly working toward the point of demanding immediate improvement of a fair proportion of this mileage, especially the main roads. In other words, they want them now. There can be no argument against the "pay as you go" system, if you have the money, or are willing to wait for the improvement until you can raise the money; but if you haven't the money and do not want to wait you will be obliged to borrow.

Issuing Bonds.—There are certain rules which should govern in issuing bonds for road improvement.

1. Bonds should not be issued so as to place any burden upon the future taxpayer for which he does not receive full value.

2. Bonds should be issued to mature serially.

Under these rules it follows that bonds should not be issued for temporary work. It also follows that the durability of the improvement should be one of the important factors in determining the rapidity with which the bonds should be retired.

The issuing of bonds maturing serially has the advantage of avoiding the necessity for providing a sinking fund to retire them at some future date; and what is equally important, the taxpayer is paying for the improvement at the same time that he is wearing it out. Under these rules paying for road improvements through the issuing of bonds is the most equitable system of financing. As an illustration, instead of paying this year the entire cost of improving a small piece of road, would it not be better to use the same amount of money in paying one installment upon the cost of improving the entire road? In the first instance, the community would pay the entire cost of the small part and drive through the mud on the balance of the road; while in the second instance they would have the entire road improved, and the taxpayers using the road each year thereafter would pay a share of the cost.

Automobile License Fees.—Another source of revenue for road construction and maintenance outside of taxation and bond issues is the automobile and kindred license fees. These fees are reaching as much as a million dollars annually in some states and are a decided help in carrying on the work. They are paid very willingly by owners of automobiles when the money is being economically used in improving the highways.

Economy and Efficiency in Construction.—Finally, the burdens will be materially decreased by a careful, systematic and economic expenditure of the people's money. Not only that, but the people will cheerfully pay for improvements that give them value received. In many states we are still struggling with the small unit of control which is sure to give unsystematic work and uneconomic results. Only to the extent that road construction is systematized and connected from the State Department to the district organization, with trained and efficient road builders in charge, shall we be able to give to the people the proper returns for the money expended.

CONCLUSION.

I have already summarized the benefits to be derived from better roads. I have endeavored to show that, while the burden is large in the aggregate, if properly distributed over a series of years, it will be comparatively small to each individual, and that the direct saving through the use of the road over a period of years will pay for the improvement; that the Federal Government should join with the State, the county, and the township in carrying this burden; that the issuance of bonds for this improvement is equitable if under proper restrictions; that we should conserve all road funds by systematic work under competent direction.

A prominent writer has said that the era just passed is the steam age and that we are now entering the gasoline age, also that the steam age is responsible for the development of the great railway systems of the country and that the gasoline age will bring about a like development of the highways; further that the result of the steam age has been the concentration of the people as well as capital in large centers, whereas the tendency of the gasoline age, both as to people and capital, will be from the city toward the country. This statement is unquestioned as regards the past and its prophecy as to the future is in harmony with the trend of the times.

NOTES ON THE CONSTRUCTION AND CARE OF EARTH, GRAVEL AND MACADAM ROADS.*

[By H. E. BILGER, *Road Engineer, Illinois State Highway Department.*]

In seeking advisable methods of procedure in the construction and care of earth, gravel, and macadam roads in rural territory in Illinois, it is necessary to disregard largely the practice that heretofore has been prevailing, and to keep very closely in mind the actual requirements of present traffic. Inasmuch as there was a time when this practice was duly warranted, it will be well to recall briefly the former conditions that fostered the old methods of constructing and maintaining these roads, in order to appreciate more clearly the changed conditions now existing.

When these methods were first inaugurated the country was but sparsely settled and the land unimproved. The people had but little occasion for traveling more than just a few miles from their homes, and even when such occasion did arise the financial conditions were such as to prohibit any considerable amount of traveling on the public highways. Owing to the fact that ready cash was not freely in circulation for the payment of debts, the labor system grew up and became almost universally adopted as the system whereby the roads were constructed and maintained. This labor system, then, of paying road taxes has grown up from the condition that labor was plentiful and not readily exchangeable for cash.

In addition to this, vehicle facilities for travel on the highway were as necessarily to confine this travel within a comparatively small radius from the home. Because of there being so little inter-communication among the people, their knowledge of affairs in general remained limited almost by their own individual experiences. These experiences make for the accumulation of general knowledge at but a very slow rate indeed, for the repetition of error, due to the absence of opportunity to profit by the experience of others, fosters a condition that is practically stagnant. It is striking how these conditions harmonize with the idea of the small political township being the governmental unit for the administration, construction, and maintenance of the principal public highways.

Instituted by these early conditions and continuing up until even recent years, the rural road improvement that has been carried on in Illinois has been of such a character as to attempt to satisfy the needs of only the immediate present and within a very small local community. Year after year the annual tax levy, both labor and cash, has been expended in an ill-directed and piecemeal fashion in perfect harmony with the original

* Paper presented at sixth annual convention of Illinois State Association of Highway Commissioners, at Peoria, Illinois, September 10, 1915.

practice of working the roads, and almost to the utter disregard of the requirements of traffic. The work has been so light, so scattered, and of such a temporary character that no small portion of the total funds expended has gone for administrative purposes.

In many cases creditable attempts have been made locally toward the proper improvement of the highways, but owing to the insufficiency of funds to carry out the work economically, and also to the small size of the township as the administrative unit, the results have been anything but what would represent work that was directed in a systematic manner and in accordance with a well-conceived plan. It could not be expected, of course, that modern ideas and methods of solving the road problem would be inaugurated under conditions that were not conducive toward their practical application.

In contrast with these earlier conditions let us briefly consider the ones existing to-day. In the first place, both the urban and the rural population have become comparatively dense, and consequently there has come about a corresponding increase in the price of real estate. Instead of there being ample farm labor for road work as formerly, such labor has become very scarce and the taxpayer, as a rule, prefers to pay his road taxes with cash and to convert his labor to more profitable fields of activity.

Money has come into circulation more freely than heretofore, and as a result people have been afforded more or less opportunity for traveling within a larger circle in their neighborhood, and thereby accumulating such knowledge about modern improvements as can be obtained in practically no other way. In addition to this, it must be appreciated that vehicle facilities for travel on the highways have become entirely revolutionized within recent years. These facilities broaden still more the range of general knowledge of the community at large.

The situation presented by these new conditions is that the general public is no longer concerned with the material welfare of merely the one township in which they reside, but their interest extends as well throughout the adjoining townships and, in many cases, even the adjoining counties. While there still remain many lines of activity that are matters strictly local to the township, and consequently should be administered by township officials, yet public improvements have become of such a character as to concern most vitally those living entirely without and at some considerable distance from the township immediately concerned. The improvement of the public highway, for example, represents a constructive problem that much concerns a great portion of the residents of one or more counties.

There having recently sprung up such demand for highway travel facilities as can not economically be satisfied by the old system, it is but logical that the township should no longer have jurisdiction over the administration, construction or maintenance of the principal highways. As the plane on which we live and the methods by which we travel are changed from time to time, there must come about a corresponding change in all matters relating to the public highway.

Legislators have recently appreciated this fact and have accordingly enacted laws whereby the county as the administrative unit shall have jurisdiction over such of the highways as appear to be of most concern to the public at large. With the county as the governmental unit there is offered such opportunity for road improvement as to upset entirely the old-time practice, and to

provide at a reasonable expense modern roads of a quality that will adequately satisfy the needs of public travel throughout the entire year.

In constructing either a gravel or a macadam road it is necessary to construct properly an earth road first, and consequently the earth road will be considered. The distinct features that should inhere in earth-road improvement are practically identical with those that now characterize our practice in the construction of hard-surfaced State aid roads. These features collectively constitute the fact that a properly constructed earth road needs only the addition of the metal surface to be converted into a quality of construction that will satisfactorily meet the requirements of modern traffic.

Earth road improvement consists of three operations, viz., bettering the horizontal alignment, building the drainage structures, and doing the necessary grading. These three items of work are done in the order named, and for all practical purposes they may properly be termed permanent improvements. The completed earth road should conform with respect to alignment, drainage, etc., to the corresponding features of the most modern hard-surfaced roads now being built in Illinois. In other words, the only additional expenditure to convert the earth road into a modern hard-surfaced road is the amount necessary to provide in place the 10, 12, 15, or 18-foot width of road metal or wearing surface.

In the recent revision of the Illinois Tice Road Law the legislature has seen fit to speak of permanent earth roads, while to the various types of surfacing material for the earth roadbed there has not been made any mention regarding the probable life of the work. This matter has been the occasion of provoking some rather humorous comment upon the part of those familiar with the behavior of the Illinois soils when saturated with water. Upon a second thought, however, it will be appreciated that the term "permanent" can more properly be applied to an earth road than to any other type that has yet been devised. With whatever materials we may choose to construct the wearing surface on the earth road, the fact remains that the life of this surface is of but a temporary character as compared with the life of the roadbed formed by old Mother Earth underneath.

In considering the life of an earth road it would be very superficial, indeed, to consider only the physical condition of the upper few inches of the road surface. With satisfactory original construction the condition of this surface is dependent upon faithful maintenance, while the earth road as a type in itself consists more properly of the horizontal and the vertical alignment, the width of graded roadway, and the angle of side slopes for cuts and fills. As the improvement in these respects is made to conform to the requirements of both the traffic and the action of the elements, it will be appreciated that in no other character of work does there prevail the inherent permanency as when a volume of earth is taken from where it will never be needed and put where it will always be needed.

Once the earth roadway is practically completed, the operation of applying the gravel or macadam-wearing surface requires a serious consideration of the traffic conditions, the availability and the character of the materials, and the funds available for the work. The metal wearing surface usually represents the greater portion of the total expenditure, and also the portion of the improvement that is susceptible to changes in either the character, volume or distribution of the traffic. For this reason, the cost of the wearing surface should be considered in terms of the construction cost, the interest cost, the maintenance cost, and the depreciation cost. Both the absolute and the relative weights to be assigned to each of these four costs are so dependent upon the local conditions that a complete analysis is required for each individual case.

The adoption of the gravel surface is usually prompted by considerations of lower construction cost, due to the supply of material being readily available nearby. The ease of handling, spreading, and rolling this material also contributes to this lower cost with the result, that as the total construction cost is kept low, the interest cost is kept proportionately so. The advantages of a low construction cost are numerous. Should the type not have been selected with wisdom, or should a new and unforeseen traffic condition have developed, the lower the original construction cost, as a rule, the better prepared will the community be to build to satisfy the new requirements. This lower cost also tends to meet the ever-pressing public demand that the length of the improvement be extended to reach at least the next farmer's property.

In the maintenance cost also does the gravel road usually rank ahead of the macadam, due not only to the lower cost of additional materials, but also to the fact that the labor item is smaller. Practically all of the rural conditions prevailing where gravel roads are economical are more favorable toward the maintenance of these roads with teams and road drags than they are toward the maintenance of macadam roads by hand labor and the use of small tools. For this reason, the labor is usually less expensive per unit area for gravel road maintenance than for macadam.

In prolonged periods of hot and dry weather the gravel road will nearly always prove to be more serviceable than the macadam road. On the other hand, it will often rupture and disintegrate under the stress of external forces while the macadam road will be preserved in its integrity by the mechanical bond. However, where the cost per unit volume of the gravel at the job is lower by any appreciable figure than the cost of crushed rock, the relative merits of the two types can be disregarded and the gravel type should under usual conditions be adopted.

The advisability of either gravel or macadam road construction varies with factors other than construction cost and the relation of the traffic features to the serviceability of the type. Whether the improvement is the first of the general character in the community, or merely an addition to a system of hard roads already existing, figures largely in the maintenance cost of the road. Under the latter conditions, the burden coming upon the improvement would in all probability be no greater than the road could withstand; while under the former, the volume of traffic to which the road would be subjected might in a few months reach a figure that would warrant concrete or even brick construction.

The general character of the soil for the shoulders and on the nearby roads may also have a bearing upon the virtual cost of the type constructed. Sticky and gummy soils on shoulders and side roads seriously increase maintenance costs on gravel and macadam roads. These costs are further increased as the number of private entrances to farms and fields is increased.

The proper improvement of a highway necessarily requires that there be constructed many small culverts and bridges that at present are either worn out or are improperly located. These drainage structures, as well as the provision for underdrainage, should be cared for at the time and in conjunction with the other improvements. Under Illinois conditions all culverts, and also all reasonably small bridges, should be built of concrete. The cross culverts should be designed with a clear roadway varying from about 24 to 30 feet, depending upon the importance of the road being improved.

All side culverts leading to side roads should be provided with a clear roadway varying from about 20 to 40 feet, and those leading to private farm entrances should have a roadway of not less than 16 feet. For these latter structures it has been learned from field experience that generally the most economical procedure is to imbed ordinary farm-drain tile in a 4-inch concrete base, and then surround the tile with about 4 inches of concrete. The cost of farm tile for this purpose is considerably more than offset by the saving that results from doing away with the necessity for building forms for the concrete, and for the subsequent removal of these forms.

MAINTENANCE.

The fact of road construction being completed does not mean that the problem is solved. Gravel, macadam and all other types of hard roads, as well as earth roads require maintenance, the difference being chiefly a matter of degree and of character of work required. The three distinct systems of maintenance usually recognized are the intermittent, the patrol, and the gang systems. For each of these systems there is a proper field, and no one of them alone is perfectly applicable under all conditions for a given type of road.

Under the intermittent system the work on a given section of road is done by one or more men only at such times as the condition of the road requires. That is, no periodical schedule for doing the work is adhered to; but instead, the labor forces are called into action at any time the condition of the road requires that the work be done. This system exclusively is applicable only for more or less unimproved roads upon which there is a comparatively small amount of travel. Some conditions that foster the use of the intermittent system are a sparse population, a low type of road, and the availability of ordinary labor. It will be noted that from the very earliest times this system of road maintenance has been in vogue in Illinois.

Up until recently the conditions in general have been such as to warrant the use of this system, but as these conditions gradually pass away it is necessary that the system give way to the adoption of one that is designed to meet the new conditions. The intermittent system will not be abandoned entirely, however, for the third-class roads of almost every township constitute such a large mileage and accomodate so little traffic that even under our modern conditions this system, if properly administered, will undoubtedly continue to prove economical.

The application of this system of maintenance to the earth road consists almost entirely in keeping the weeds cut down and in dragging the traveled portion of the road; provided, however, that in the original construction adequate provision was made for surface and underground drainage. Efficient earth road maintenance requires that the entire length of the work be divided into comparatively short sections, each section being in charge of some individual with ample authority and corresponding responsibility. It is usually uneconomical to maintain earth roads by any system other than the intermittent one. The very detail and frequent character of

· the work required is such as to necessitate that attention be concentrated when needed upon small sections of the road. Where higher types of road improvement are adopted correspondingly larger sections should be put in charge of an individual for maintenance, and, on the other hand, the lower the type of the improvement the smaller should be the sections into which the work is divided.

The patrol system is the recognized practice of maintaining roads by dividing the work into comparatively short sections and having each section in charge of a man who devotes his entire time to the work. This system is especially applicable to the lower types of hard roads, inasmuch as the maintenance work is of such a character as to require one of experience. The system applies especially where the work is rather heavy and where, as is so frequently the case, the traffic requirements are rather beyond the type of road.

The patrol system lends itself naturally to gravel and macadam roads on account of the peculiar character of work that is continually occuring and requiring immediate attention. The use of the drag is very effective for maintaining gravel roads, for the ruts and holes can readily be filled by dragging the displaced gravel into them. A road drag properly used will generally maintain a well-constructed gravel road more economically than almost any other instrument. For macadam roads, however, the drag is not equally efficient. Macadam road maintenance requires detailed attention in the defective spots rather than merely a general smoothing over of the entire surface of the road. It is usually necessary to keep supplying fresh material instead of merely reshaping with the drag the material with which the road was originally constructed.

The gang system is the method of road maintenance whereby a large mileage is cared for by two or more men who devote their entire time to the work. This system is especially applicable to the higher types of roads, as vitrified brick and Portland cement concrete, for the reason that the character of the maintenance work is such as to demand that it be done by experienced hands. The amount of maintenance required on the pavement proper per mile of road is in fact very small, but the work must be of a comparatively high order.

Since the amount of work per mile is so small, it will be seen how under the gang system a large mileage of road can be included in one section. The gang and the intermittent systems combined usually make for more economical results than the gang system alone. The work of the gang is confined to the pavement proper, while the periodical work on the roadsides and ditches is done under the intermittent system.

The governing conditions that affect road maintenance are so varied that no one of these three systems can economically be applied to all of the roads in any one county. All of the conditions attending each particular road must be analyzed, and then the particular system or combination of systems adopted that will most satisfactorily meet the requirements of the case. On the third-class roads of the county this work can usually be done most economically by the intermittent system, unless the county is in one of the highest developed parts of the State.

The real road maintenance problem in Illinois for many years to come will consist in dealing with the earth road which constitutes more than 90 per cent of the entire rural mileage. Without maintenance, it almost ceases to perform the functions of a public highway, but with proper maintenance no other road responds so effectively to the real needs of the traveling public as does the ordinary earth road. Between the present condition of our earth roads and the condition to which they could be brought and maintained by just a little intelligent effort, there exists a gap that is far beyond the realization of the general public. The earth road has never been given even half a chance to make good. With the same opportunity to make good that has been afforded other types of roads, I am satisfied that for a selected 70 per cent of our total rural mileage, the humble earth road would show up for true serviceability far beyond any type of hard road feasible for Illinois.

SELECTION OF MATERIALS FOR USE IN THE CONSTRUCTION OF MAIN RURAL ROADS IN ILLINOIS.

[By W. W. Marr, Chief State Highway Engineer.]

In order to select the economic type of improvement for main rural highways through the State of Illinois, it is necessary to consider the most important factors entering into the cost of such improvements, namely, the first cost, the interest on the investment, and the maintenance cost.

Generally speaking, pavements of high first cost are low in maintenance cost, but will, of course, be high in interest on the investment. Pavements of low first cost are, on the other hand, low in interest on investment and higher in maintenance cost.

The whole problem may be viewed as one of public service, and is in a great many respects directly comparable with the cost of service in railroad transportation, in electric lighting, telephone and telegraph service, etc. In other words, the problem is primarily to transport passengers and commercial packages over the rural highways for the social and commercial advantages of the people. With this view in mind it becomes apparent that where traffic is excessive some means of sustaining that traffic economically must be devised and a sufficiently durable improvement made to produce the desired result. It may be taken as a general rule that the stronger a pavement and the more capable its material to resist the wear of traffic, the greater will be its cost of construction.

Inasmuch as the wear and tear on road surfaces is almost directly proportional to the amount and kind of traffic, it follows that where traffic is light, a comparatively inexpensive type of improvement may economically sustain it. In other words, a gravel road may be as economical and permanent as a brick road if each is sustaining only the traffic it is designed for or is capable of carrying. The maintenance cost varies with the load burden imposed upon the pavement by the traffic and the interest on the investment will be less as its first cost is reduced. It must not be understood, however, that this is an argument for cheaper pavements regardless of conditions. The reduction of first cost can be justified economically only with due consideration of several important limiting factors, and it should be kept in mind that in most instances the first roads built under the State aid system will be those which carry the greatest traffic, and also that these roads will be called upon immediately after completion to bear additional traffic, which will later be diverted over other roads.

In this connection the meaning of the term "permanency" should be clearly understood. There is no permanent wearing surface in the narrow sense of the term. In some sections in Illinois, such as Milwaukee Avenue, north of Chicago limits, the Lincoln Highway, near any of the larger cities, etc., only the most durable and consequently expensive construction can at all approach real permanency.

When a road is prepared for a wearing surface by grading, bridging and draining, the most truly permanent part of the work has been done. This usually represents from 20 to 40 per cent of the cost of the road. If operations are carried no further, we call the product an earth road. Earth roads consist of the material found naturally in place in the particular locality, or may be formed by the artificial mixture of sand and clay.

Following this, in the order of cost and ability to resist the action of traffic, comes what is generally known as the gravel road. This road consists of gravel either naturally in place along the line of improvement, or hauled in, and may be made in several degrees of strength and durability. There are many miles of good gravel roads in northern Illinois, some of which could be economically maintained for several years without any new construction.

Next in order comes the water-bound macadam road, which consists of broken stone bonded together with such material as stone chips or bonding gravel, by means of water and rolling. This also can be made in several different types or degrees of strength and ability to resist the action of traffic.

Possibly the next type in order would be the same road treated with oil or some bituminous binder, which would tend to waterproof and otherwise strengthen the road and thereby increase its usefulness.

Then follows the bituminous macadam, in which the essential difference from the water-bound macadam lies in the use of a bituminous binder to hold together the pieces of broken stone of which the road metal is composed.

Bituminous concrete, Portland cement concrete, vitrified brick, sheet asphalt and other types of paving follow, and are, as respects permanency, more or less the same, depending largely upon whether or not the character and amount of traffic are suited to their powers of resistance and to various construction features which involve the strength and durability of the finished product. It is a grave economical error to limit the term "permanent" to one or two types of wearing surfaces.

In general it may be said that if the traffic and type of road are properly suited to each other, the cost of service for hard roads is approximately *constant* for all types of wearing surfaces. Cost of service in this connection is understood to mean the total cost per unit of area per unit of time per unit of load, and to be constant for an indefinite period of time.

It should be kept in mind that the cost of the first improvement bears directly upon this cost of service, for money at 3½ per cent compound interest doubles in twenty years, and at 5 per cent in fourteen years. So as the first cost becomes less, the saving on money invested may be an appreciable item in providing a fund for the purpose of maintaining the roads to a desired standard of excellence and usefulness. In this way, where the lighter types of improvement are sufficient to meet the demands of traffic, it is wasteful to invest money where it serves no purpose. Later on, the amount so saved might be used for the purpose of resurfacing the road to meet the increased demands of a greater volume and a changed character of traffic.

Another important factor that should not be overlooked is that the more roads built the easier, and consequently the cheaper it is to build them. This has a double significance, in that the sooner hard roads are in service, the sooner and more generally will their advantages be felt, and also in that the cost of reconstruction will be less proportionately than the cost of first construction, because of the increased facilities for handling materials over better roads.

The durability of different types of roads varies in general with the burden of traffic, although in some types, notably those involving bituminous materials, the life of the pavement may not exceed fifteen or twenty years, even though the traffic is not in itself sufficient to wear the pavement out. In fact, bituminous pavements as a rule, require traffic in reasonable quantities to get the greatest use in length of life out of them.

The Massachusetts Highway Commission states in its 1914 report, that from their observations "a good gravel road will wear reasonably well and be economical with fifty to seventy-five light teams, carriages and wagons; twenty-five to thirty heavy one-horse wagons; ten to fifteen heavy two or more horse wagons, and fifty to seventy-five automobiles per day. Water-bound macadam will stand with one hundred and seventy-five to two hundred light teams, carriages and wagons; one hundred and seventy-five to two hundred heavy one-horse wagons; sixty to eighty heavy two or more horse wagons, and not over fifty automobiles at high speed. Standard width of roadway, 15 feet." With various modifications, the amount of traffic which can be carried may be increased. So each type of road surface will sustain some certain amount of traffic without serious wear or maintenance cost as compared with its first cost and the interest on the investment.

No absolute length of life can be assigned to any of the commonly used materials for road construction, as the life of a pavement varies widely with the amount and character of the traffic, as well as the quality of the materials and the degree of perfection attained in handling them to the best advantage.

In regard to recommendation as to the type of road which the State could assume the burden of maintaining, it naturally follows from the foregoing that no one, two or three types could possibly meet economically the wide range of conditions to be found on the sixteen thousand miles of designated State aid roads in Illinois.

In order to solve this problem, it is necessary to take into consideration all the local conditions, such as amount and character of traffic, probable future development, availability of local materials and various items of cost, both of construction and maintenance. In fact, it may be said that in a large number of cases any one of two or three and possibly even more types of construction could economically meet the requirements, and the choice as to which one of these types should be used would be a matter of local preference. In my opinion, therefore, the State Highway Commission should gather such information as may be necessary to determine the economic type or types of pavement in each locality. This information would be of great value to the local authorities and also to the State, in the determination of the economical types and in designating limits beyond which it would be unwise, as a matter of scientific economy, to go.

In other words, it appears that the central authority, the State Highway Commission, should place itself in a position to render all possible assistance to local authorities for the solution of the technical and economic sides of the problem, with a view to preventing as far as possible, the recurrence of mistakes made by other authorities in the pursuit of the best road. As a matter of fact, there is no such thing as a best pavement, and any number of different types may be designed which will have a good and economical place in the scheme of road improvement contemplated in such a large area as the State of Illinois. In many specific instances, several types may be of practically equal ultimate cost on a unit basis of service.

Certain items of work, such as locating, grading, draining, building bridges and culverts, etc., are common to all types of road construction and may be considered the most permanent part of road improvement. Thus an earth road, properly constructed, represents the highest percentage of permanency in the amount invested. It would seem, however, that the maintenance of earth roads could not reasonably be undertaken by the State, especially in view of the uncertainty existing as to what constitutes proper maintenance. Hard roads may be maintained at a fairly well-defined standard of excellence and usefulness, but the essential difference between hard roads and earth roads is not in the amount, kind, or weight of traffic they respectively carry, but in the relative percentage of the total time that each will be in service.

When so-called semi-permanent roads, such as gravel and macadam, are built, the maintenance might be undertaken by the State on a sliding scale and a proportionate cost paid by the State, ranging from nothing to one hundred per cent, in accordance with the economic cost of service in the particular case involved.

For State aid roads which are to be maintained wholly by the State after construction, it would seem that in justice to all, a fair distribution of the maintenance fund should be made, and this is only possible by means of several types of pavements, inasmuch as the wear and tear varies between wide limits and may in some instances be less on gravel roads than it is in other instances on concrete or brick roads.

In determining the life of a pavement from examples of the type known to have been in place for a certain number of years, it must be borne in mind that many pavements now existing do not bear the traffic they would bear if in good and serviceable condition, and that some of them have long since outlived their usefulness and exist only because the means or proper incentive to replace them does not exist.

In other words, many pavements are not giving adequate or desirable service, and in this discussion all conclusions are drawn on the assumption that the particular pavement in question is maintained in first-class condition and to a reasonably constant standard of excellence in order that satisfactory service may be afforded.

Of course, there are other factors than those previously mentioned, entering into the cost of service in connection with rural highway improvement, such for instance, as the salvage value at the end of the period when reconstruction becomes more economical than continued repairs.

All the conclusions in the foregoing discussion are based upon the assumption that the cost of service on a unit basis includes the total cost of all the various items involved over an indefinite period and including reconstruction when necessary.

To summarize, the types of pavements which might properly be adopted for main rural highways in the State of Illinois cover a wide range and depend upon *cost*, which varies with availability of materials; *traffic*, which varies in amount and kind with different locations; and *local preference*, which changes largely with popular sentiment.

The State might reasonably assume the burden of maintaining a pavement regardless of type, if the traffic is proportioned to the ability of the particular type in question to resist the wear occasioned by the traffic burden which will be placed upon it.

The State might cooperate with the county to share a portion of the cost of maintenance where the type of pavement selected is only partially able to withstand economically the burden of traffic which will come upon it. The State should not assume any portion of the cost of maintaining earth roads unless the partnership between the State and county were extended to cover the entire item of maintenance, in which case an equitable solution of the problem would appear to be an equal division of the cost of maintenance between the State and county, regardless of type of improvement.

I would recommend that the State adopt some comprehensive scheme for taking a census of traffic and gathering such other information, previously outlined, as is necessary for the proper scientific solution of the problem of determining upon its economic types of roads for the various localities and conditions to be met in the State of Illinois. This may be accomplished in part through the Highway Department directly and in part through the cooperation of the County Superintendent of Highways.

BRICK MONOLITHIC CONSTRUCTION OF COUNTY HIGHWAYS.

[*By* R. L. BELL, *Division Engineer, Illinois State Highway Department.*]

(*A Paper Read Before the Northwestern Road Congress. Reprinted from* ENGINEERING AND CONTRACTING.)

The dictionary gives the meaning of monolithic as "something which is constructed all in one piece," and while the road which is to be described has a concrete base with a brick-wearing surface, the brick are placed directly on the concrete while it is still green, so that to all intents and purposes the road is made up of one solid slab.

Fig. 1. VIEW SHOWING END OF ONE DAY'S WORK AND BEGINNING OF ANOTHER.

Since the first monolithic brick road was laid, April 1 and 2, 1915, at Paris, Illinois, our common enemy, the so-called cushion, has found some very strong and able defenders. The writer was of the opinion that every one conceded that the only reason for the layer of sand between the concrete base and the brick-wearing surface was to take up the irregularities in the concrete base and the paving block, but it seems there are those who believe that it acts as a cushion. With the old type of construction, when sand or asphalt filler was used and each brick might act, at least partially independent of the other, this might have been true, but if sand acts as a cushion it must give or move and this is fatal to a cement grout-filled brick road.

Many engineers have aimed at the elimination of the sand cushion and a brief account of such work as the writer has been able to find a record of might not be out of place.

Baltimore constructed a street some four or five years ago and in place of using the ordinary sand cushion, a dry mortar cushion, one part cement to five parts sand, was used. This cushion was spread on the concrete base, struck off to a thickness of one inch as in ordinary construction. The brick were then laid and rolled, after which water was applied on the top of the brick in sufficient quantity to set the cushion. I believe that Baltimore is doing more work along this same line at the present time.

The city of St. Louis is putting in some of the same kind of work this year, except a 1½-inch dry-mortar cushion is used, said cushion being made up of one part cement to four parts sand. In 1914 there was laid in Cleveland, Ohio, a strip of pavement which was along the same line as the work we have done in Paris. The 6-inch concrete base was laid and 5-inch brick were immediately placed on the green concrete, rolled by a light roller and grouted. This was put in by a cold storage company, but the name of the company or the exact location is not a matter of record. In the Pennsylvania Railway Station in New York there is an example of this work which was laid on a dry mortar cushion. The brick were only 2½ inches thick and were fire-clay brick. The writer has been told, but has been unable to verify it, that paving of the same kind has been laid in Springfield, Missouri, along the street car tracks. It is very probable that other work has been done along these same lines of which there is no record.

Where grout filler is used the sand cushion is not so much a convenience as a constant source of annoyance and worry, if the work is to be properly constructed.

FIG. 2. VIEW SHOWING EDGE OF ROAD. NOTE THAT THE GROUT FILLER EXTENDS TO THE BOTTOM OF THE BRICK.

One specification is, that sand must not be rolled up between the brick more than one-half inch. This means that any brick pavement that receives a rain before the brick have been rolled is very apt to need to be taken up and relaid. It makes inspection exceedingly difficult in that it is hard to tell just where to draw the line, And then, again, we know that the sand does not need to be rolled up over the entire length of the road but if it occurs at any place it is liable to cause trouble where no cross-expansion joints are used. We do not use cross-expansion joints and are firm believers in not only their uselessness, but their destructiveness to brick roads. The cross-expansion joints provide that which we are trying to avoid, that is, a chance for the pavement to give. A pavement without cross-expansion joints does not move in expansion if it is properly confined but only tends to move. The force is always there, however, to move it when the restraints are removed. A good illustration of this was seen at Paris, Illinois, this summer. A brick road, with no cross-expansion joints, 4500 feet long and 17 feet wide, terminating at one end against an 80-foot steel bridge, was laid on a 1-inch sand cushion. Due to the construction of a new dam it became necessary to remove this bridge and put in a new one some 8 feet higher than the old structure. This necessitated the removing of some 400 or 500 feet of the above described road. Just as soon as these brick were removed the pavement began to creep and has moved some 3 or 4 inches since the restraint was removed.

During the past summer the writer inspected at Chrisman, Illinois, a pavement that had blown up. This pavement was constructed in 1914, the brick being on a 2-inch sand cushion and rolled with an 8-ton roller. When an examination was made of the brick that had blown up it was found that in a majority of the cases the sand had been rolled up between the brick at least one-half the depth of the brick, or 2 inches. To anyone familiar with what brick will do under such conditions it is no wonder at all that this pavement refused to stay in place.

FIG. 3. A CLOSE VIEW OF THE TEMPLATE. NOTE THE DRY MORTAR MIX BETWEEN THE TWO EDGES OF THE TEMPLATE. THE TEMPLATE IS NOW READY TO MOVE AHEAD. THE WOODEN GUIDE IS SHOWN JUST IN FRONT OF THE TEMPLATE.

In order to get away from the constant worry of how the sand cushion was acting this type of pavement was developed. Mr. Blackburn, of Paris, Illinois, made the first sample of this work and the details of the construction have been worked out by Alan J. Parrish, a contractor of Paris, Illinois.

When the weather stopped the State aid work in Edgar County in 1914, we had enough donated money left to build 400 feet of 10-foot brick road. When this construction was brought to the writer's attention, he immediately secured the consent of the State Engineer to build this 400 feet, using this type of construction. The work was started April 1, 1915, and 200 feet laid; the remaining 200 feet being laid April 2. Since that time we have constructed in and near Paris 13 150 square yards of this type of brick road and have under contract at the present time 11 780 square yards of State aid work which will be constructed this year. Before starting work this spring, we were wondering as to how it would work out in practice. We found that it not only worked out completely satisfactorily but it is an easier type of construction in every way than if we were using the old methods.

In the preparation of the subgrade the rough work is generally done with a traction engine and a grader, the engine thoroughly compacting the subgrade. The subgrade is dressed up by hand after which a 5-ton self-propelling roller is kept constantly at work while the material is being hauled. Steel forms 8 inches in depth and 12 feet long are then set true to line and grade. The concrete base is 4 inches thick and the brick are 4 inches in depth making when completed an 8-inch monolithic pavement. Steel forms, while not absolutely essential, are a great convenience in this type of construction.

Fig. 4. View Showing a Strip of the Concrete Base Covered With a Thin Film of Dry Mortar. Note the Plank That is Used by the Carriers to Walk Upon as They Come Onto the Pavement. The Man Who is Doing the Batting is Seen About Six Feet Behind the Brick Layers.

LAYING THE BASE.

The concrete for the base was a 1 to 6 mixture of cement and washed gravel. The gravel tested very close to 50 per cent through a ¼-inch square mesh. The base for the State aid work now under contract will be 1 part cement, 3½ parts fine aggregate and 6 parts coarse aggregate. Enough water is used so that the concrete is of a quaky consistency but will not flow.

It was found that an excess of water caused no trouble in keeping the brick up to a true surface. In order to get approximately the right thickness of concrete before cutting it with the template, a small wooden guide is used.

The steel template used is necessary in order to secure accurate results on this type of work. This template, (see Fig. 8) is made of a 6-inch I-beam in front and a 6-inch channel behind. They are placed 2 feet apart and supported by four rollers, one at each end of each member. The rear edge of the template is set exactly 4 inches below the top of the forms and the front edge is set 4-3/16 inches below the top of the form. The hopper like space between the two edges is kept filled with a dry mix consisting of 1 part cement

to 5 parts sand. The template is drawn forward by means of a cable and a friction clutch on the mixer. As the template is drawn forward, the front edge cuts the concrete 3/16 inches below the grade and a thin film of dry mortar is spread over the concrete, filling all the little depressions in the surface. Theoretically, the dry-mortar coat should be exactly 3/16 inches in thickness. In reality it does not have any noticeable thickness but is sufficient to give a perfectly smooth surface on which to lay the brick.

Fig. 5. Brick Ready to be Grouted.

LAYING THE BRICK.

Practically the only place where more care must be taken with this type of construction than where a sand cushion is used, is in the laying of the brick. It is essential to have the brick rolled within 20 to 30 minutes after the concrete base is laid and to do this culling must be reduced to a minimum. The carriers are required to deliver the brick to the setter so that he can easily lay them in the road with the good face up and the lugs all one way. In this way the most of the culling is done by the carriers and but very few brick need be turned after they are placed in the road. It is necessary for the setter to use a little more care than where a sand cushion is used, but he is the only man in the gang who does not work at top speed. It is advisable to have two planks 1 by 12 inches and of a length equal to the width of the pavement for the carriers to use when coming on the pavement. This saves tracking dirt onto the brick and also prevents uneven places in the pavement, due to the fact that the carriers will all come on the pavement at about the same place.

Fig. 6. Finished Subgrade Showing Steel Forms in Place.

As soon as the brick are laid the necessary culling and batting is done, the pavement swept and rolled. A two-section roller 30 inches long and 24 inches in diameter and weighing about 750 pounds is used. This roller is easily handled by one man and leaves a much better surface than it is possible to secure using the old type of construction. The brick are not imbedded more than ¼-inch in the base.

A 1 to 1 mix of cement and sand is used for the grout filler. This is mixed dry in a small batch mixer and then conveyed to the grout boxes on the pavement by means of wheelbarrows.

FIG. 7. VIEW SHOWING ROLLER USED.

The maximum size of batch allowed in the boxes is 2 cubic feet of the mixture. Water is added slowly and the mortar built up gradually, after which it is thinned to a consistency that will flow readily into the joints. The grout is stirred constantly while being removed from the boxes with scoop shovels. The joints are filled completely full at the first application but after settling the top of the grout is about ½ inch below the top of the brick. Before the first application has taken its initial set the joints are filled a second time. The second application of the grout is mixed to a consistency of thick cream. In making this second application enough surplus is left on the road so that the surface can be gone over again without bringing the boxes back. The surface is finished with a squeegee, the joints being left entirely filled.

FIG. 8. THE TEMPLATE.

In order to secure the best obtainable surface the squeegees are pulled over the road at an angle of 45

degrees with the joints. This prevents the squeegee from dragging mortar out of the joints and leaving them lower than the surface of the brick.

The pavement is covered the following day with one-half inch sand or earth which is kept wet at least five days. The side forms are removed the second day. The pavement is allowed to set 10 days before the side roads are graded, three weeks before being opened to traffic.

FIG. 9. ONE BRICK REMOVED SHOWING FILM OF WATER WHICH HAS BEEN ROLLED UP TO TOP OF THE CONCRETE BASE.

ADVANTAGES OF NEW TYPE.

(1) A better surface can be obtained.

(2) The work is easier on both contractor and inspector.

(3) There is no guess work at any point of the construction.

(4) Under similar conditions it represents a saving of from 10 to 12 cents per square yard over the old method.

(5) Eliminates the breaking down of the filler at a construction crack, as each brick has a rigid support.

(6) Opens the field for experiment with thinner brick.

(7) The filler is sure to reach the bottom of the paving block.

(8) Removes need of a flush curbing.

(9) Eliminates the rumbling in brick pavements.

Some 200 engineers and contractors have visited the work at Paris and, without exception, they have been very enthusiastic over the possibilities of this type of construction.

DEDICATION OF NEW CONCRETE PAVEMENT ON FAMOUS THOROFARE A SOCIETY EVENT.

Highway officials and good road boosters from Chicago, Cook County and the Illinois Highway Department left the Art Institute, Chicago, at 1:00 p. m., Saturday, October 16, to dedicate the new State Aid concrete pavement on Milwaukee Avenue, Cook County, Illinois. When several of the contemplated pavements from Evanston, Wilmette and other North Shore suburbs of Chicago are completed, and when the concrete section on Milwauukee Avenue has been extended to the county line, as is now planned, there will be a direct good roads route from Chicago and the

North Shore suburbs to the attractive lake region of Northern Illinois and Southern Wisconsin. It is hoped that this road will soon be paved all the way from Chicago to Milwaukee, Wis.

Milwaukee Avenue is one of the most important thorofares in the State. It is the artery of a large system of county roads and an outlet from the extensive truck gardening district tributary to Chicago. In the height of the season hundreds of farmers travel the road daily, hauling tons of garden produce to the city. When Milwaukee Avenue has been completed for its entire length there will never be any occasion for delay on account of bad roads, as a concrete pavement is serviceable in all kinds of weather.

Nor is travel on this highway limited to farmers. The traffic census shows that the average travel during week days is 1,500 cars and on Saturdays, Sundays and other holidays as many as 4,000 cars traverse this thorofare. Milwaukee Avenue also offers a popular road over which merchants deliver goods to outlying portions of Chicago and suburbs beyond.

On the way to the dedication a long string of automobiles from Chicago was met at Niles by the Niles Improvement Club with many more machines, and escorted by them from Niles over Milwaukee Avenue to "The House that Jack Built" where over 500 listened to the addresses of A. D. Gash, president of the Illinois Highway Commission, who stated that the concrete pavement on Milwaukee Avenue was one of the best roads in the State, and J. M. Fitzgerald, Chairman of the Roads and Bridge Committee of the County Commissioners. George Melzer of Glenview gave an address of welcome and recited some interesting facts about the old toll and plank roads on Milwaukee Avenue. Wm. G. Edens, President of the Associated Roads Organization of Chicago and Cook County was chairman of the meeting and accepted the road on behalf of the public, and Robert Redfield of Kennicott's Grove told how much the property owners along Milwaukee Avenue appreciated the work of the State in building this highway. He declared it was a pleasure to travel over this road, the longest stretch of concrete pavement in the State.

At the conclusion of the speeches the scene shifted to the road proper, where H. B. Bushnell, Division Engineer for the State Highway Department, and George A. Quinlan, County Superintendent of Highways, removed the barricade across the last stretch of pavement. Then Mr. Fitzgerald, handling a gold and silver shovel in a manner which showed him to be an expert cleared from the pavement the last remnant of dirt covering, and Miss Louise Redfield, daughter of Robert Redfield assisted by Miss Ardath Walter, daughter of Wm. J. Walter, the contractor who built the road, christened it with a perfectly good bottle of champagne and the words, "I christen thee Milwaukee Avenue."

Dedications of newly constructed concrete pavements in Cook County and vicinity have become quite notable society events. At this ceremony, Miss Redfield was further assisted by Miss Laura Kennedy, the sponsor of Sheridan Road in Highland Park, Mrs. Helquist, of Western Avenue, Blue Island, Miss Virginia Poehlmann and Miss Sullivan of the 1914 work on Milwaukee Avenue, Niles, Miss Hazel Leigh, who represented "Miss Dixie," and Miss Margaret West who represented "Miss Chicago" at the Dixie Highway pageant the week previous.

A large number of women were in attendance at the ceremony and all joined in a jollification in the dining room and on the dance floor at "The House That Jack Built" after the christening.

The above sign is being used in Cook County by Superintendent George A. Quinlan to direct traffic around a road that is blocked for repairs or construction. These signs are placed all along the detour in both directions. They are of wood, 18 by 24 inches, with black letters on a yellow background.

THE OILED EARTH ROADS OF CALIFORNIA.

[By AUSTIN B. FLETCHER, *Highway Engineer, California Highway Commission.*]

In California the first use of light crude asphaltic oil as a dust preventive and surface protector of earth roads was made in the early nineties. From 1899 to 1904 the county and city governments in all parts of the state made quite extensive use of crude oil on the earth roads. In 1904 a total of over 2,200 miles of county roads and over 500 miles of city streets had been laid in about forty of the counties of the state.

For this work many different kinds of oil were used and experiments were made with a great variety of different methods of road construction and oil application. Oils containing as low as 10 per cent asphalt were used and in gravity as high as 16° Baume.

The greater portion of the oil used contained from 30 to 60 per cent asphalt and was from 12 to 14° Baume in gravity. A more useful and practical test of the oil would have been a determination of the viscosity of the oil but the records of this work do not give data on this property of the oils used.

By 1906 there were very few sections of oiled road that were satisfactory for the traveling public and only in a few localities could the oiled earth road be called a success. The publication of many articles, reports and bulletins favorable in their criticism of this construction has given the oiled earth roads of California an unmerited reputation as to their length of satisfactory service, their simplicity of construction and their adaptability to all sorts of soils, weather conditions and character of traffic.

The crude asphaltic oils and the light road oils manufactured for the oiling of earth roads in this State usually contain rather high percentages of very volatile oils that evaporate early in the life of the road. The loss of the lighter material results in a hardening of the oiled earth surface.

Very likely the greater portion of the oiled earth roads that have become very objectionable to the traveling public, due to their wavy surface, have been constructed with an excessive amount of oil.

In sheet asphalt construction it has been found that for a given mineral aggregate the desirable percentage of bituminous binder must be kept within very narrow limits. This is true to a slightly less degree with the bitumen used in the oiled earth surface. Coarse sandy soils require less road oil for a given thickness of surfacing than the fine silty soils. The allowable amount of oil that can be used with certain soil is fixed between very narrow limits.

Road surfaces that are overoiled are not firm under traffic and there is generally a tendency for the surface material to slowly flow to lower elevations. The shoulders of such roads, after a few months, show a very deep thickness of wavy, somewhat spongy, oiled earth and the crown of the road is protected by an oil surfacing that is rapidly ironed out by traffic and becomes so thin that it breaks under traffic. Once the surface is cut through to the underlying soil base, a bad chuck hole is rapidly formed.

Throughout the valley and coast counties of California there are miles of oiled earth roads that are so objectionable to the traffic that the traveled way is on the sides of the road and not at all on the oiled section.

The failures of oiled earth roads may be due to one or more of many mistakes, the more common ones being the use of too much oil per square yard of road surface, the lack of properly incorporating the oil in the road surface, and the use of an oil not suited to the work.

Doubtless a proper maintenance would have saved many of the oiled earth roads from such marked failures. It is difficult to find many sections of this type of road that have proved satisfactory over a period of more than a few years. There are a few oiled earth roads that have given satisfaction and have required but little maintenance over periods of from three to eight years. These roads are not subject to very heavy traffic.

The California Highway Commission has made but little use of this type of road construction. In a few places in the state where the road had very deep fills it has been inadvisable to build a concrete pavement until the fills have had sufficient time to settle thoroughly. In such cases the road surface has been wet and rolled and then the surface of the road broken up for a depth of about an inch and a coat of light asphaltic oil applied. This was regarded only as a temporary expedient to protect the road surface from excessive cutting during the heavy rains of winter and as a dust preventive during the dry months.

There were used or this construction oils varying in specific viscosity (Engler test) from 5 to 15. The oil contained from 75 to 90 per cent of 80 penetration asphalt. The oil was applied on the road under pressure and at a temperature of about 250° Fahr. A very light oil also has been used which contained from 30 to 60 per cent of asphalt of 80 penetration. This oil was applied by gravity at the rate of 1.5 gallons per square yard.

As has been stated above, the oiling of earth roads by this commission has been done only as a temporary measure to carry the road through a year or two while the fills were settling.

OPINIONS OF THE ATTORNEY GENERAL.

COMPENSATION OF HIGHWAY COMMISSIONERS, EXCEPT WHERE STATUTE SPECIFICALLY PRESCRIBES OTHERWISE, IS A TOWN CHARGE, AND IS PAYABLE OUT OF TOWN FUNDS.

October 5, 1915.

STATE HIGHWAY DEPARTMENT,
Springfield, Illinois.

GENTLEMEN: I am in receipt of your favor of the 30th ult., enclosing copy of letter of Mr. A. R. Carter, who, for some county not specified, holds the office of county superintendent of highways.

It appears from Mr. Carter's letter that in some of the towns in his county there are no funds in the town treasury available for the payment of the compensation of highway commissioners. He inquires what action may be taken to compel the payment of the compensation of highway commissioners.

It appears, also, that in some of the towns in his county, the practice is to pay the compensation of highway commissioners out of the road and bridge fund, and he inquires what action should be taken by him in the matter.

Section 53 of the revised Road and Bridge Act of 1913 provides in part:

"The commissioners shall each receive for each day necessarily employed in the discharge of their duties the sum of two dollars ($2.00) upon a sworn statement to be filed by such commissioner in the office of the town * * * clerk showing the number of days he was employed and the kind of employment, and giving the dates thereof."

It will be noted that the basis for the payment of the compensation of highway commissioners is the sworn statement of their services which they are required to file with the town clerk.

Paragraph 120, chapter 139, Hurd's Statutes, 1913, provides that the board of town auditors shall meet at the town clerk's office for the purpose of examining and auditing the town accounts, semiannually, on the Tuesday next preceding the annual meeting of the county board and on the Tuesday next preceding the annual town meeting.

Paragraph 121 of said chapter makes it the duty of the board of auditors at the time and place of the meeting prescribed by said paragraph 120, to examine and audit all charges and claims against their town and the compensation of all town officers, except the compensation of supervisors for county services.

Paragraph 125 of said chapter provides in part:

"The following shall be deemed town charges:

1. The compensation of town officers for services rendered their respective towns."

It is the holding of this department that the compensation of highway commissioners, except where the statute specifically prescribes otherwise, is a town charge, to be audited by the board of town auditors as other claims against the town are audited, and is payable out of the town funds and not out of the road and bridge fund.

Such compensation when audited and allowed by the board of auditors should be included in the certificate of claims allowed, which the board of auditors files with the town clerk, and included in the amount which the town clerk certifies to the county clerk to be levied for town purposes. In case the board of auditors should refuse to audit the claim of highway commissioners and include same in the certificate filed by them with the town clerk, a writ of mandamus to compel action by the board of auditors.

Officially, the county superintendent of highways has no duty to perform concerning the matter of the compensation of highway commissioners; officially, he has nothing to do, either with approving or allowing such compensation.

I will add in this connection that the county superintendent of highways is a county officer, and I suggest that you call Mr. Carter's attention to clause 7, of section 5, chapter 14, Hurd's Statutes 1913, which makes the State's Attorney the legal adviser of county officers.

Very respectfully,

P. J. LUCEY, *Attorney General.*

ILLINOIS HIGHWAYS

[Printed by authority of the State of Illinois.]

OFFICIAL PUBLICATION OF THE

STATE HIGHWAY DEPARTMENT

| VOL. 2 | SPRINGFIELD, ILLINOIS, DECEMBER, 1915 | No. 11 |

COUNTY AND STATE PULLING TOGETHER ON THE RIGHT ROAD.

ILLINOIS HIGHWAYS.
Published Monthly by the
State Highway Department,
Springfield, Illinois.

ILLINOIS HIGHWAY COMMISSION.
A. D. GASH, *President.*
S. E. BRADT, *Secretary.*
JAMES P. WILSON.

WM. W. MARR, *Chief State Highway Engineer.*

BUREAU OF ROADS.
H. E. BILGER, *Road Engineer.*
M. W. WATSON, *Assistant Road Engineer.*
C. M. HATHAWAY, *Office Engineer.*
L. P. SCOTT, *Chief Draftsman.*

BUREAU OF BRIDGES.
CLIFFORD OLDER, *Bridge Engineer.*
G. F. BURCH, *Assistant Bridge Engineer.*
A. W. CONSOER, *Office Engineer.*

BUREAU OF MAINTENANCE.
B. H. PIEPMEIER, *Maintenance Engineer.*
F. T. SHEETS, *Assistant Maintenance Engineer.*

BUREAU OF TESTS.
F. L. ROMAN, *Testing Engineer.*
W. C. ADAMS, *Chemist.*

BUREAU OF AUDITS.
J. M. McCOY, *Chief Clerk.*
T. W. DIECKMANN, *Department Editor.*
R. R. McLEOD, *General Bookkeeper.*
G. E. HOPKINS, *Property Clerk.*

DIVISION ENGINEERS.
R. L. Bell, Buchanan-Link Bldg., Paris, Ill.
H. B. Bushnell, 144 Fox St., Aurora, Ill.
J. E. Huber, Wise Building, Mt. Vernon, Ill.
A. H. Hunter, 302 Apollo Theater Bldg., Peoria, Ill.
C. M. Slaymaker, 510 Metropolitan Bldg., E. St. Louis, Ill.
H. E. Surman, 614 People's Bank Bldg., Moline, Ill.
Fred Tarrant, State Highway Department, Springfield, Ill.

Address all communications in regard to "Illinois Highways," to State Highway Department, Springfield, Illinois. Attention of T. W. Dieckmann, Department Editor.

CONTENTS.

VERMILION COUNTY BOND ISSUE VALIDATED.

Justice Dunn of the Illinois Supreme Court in a decision just handed down, has validated the $1,500,000 bond issue of Vermilion County which was voted for the purpose of constructing hard roads in that county.

This decision is very important at this time when many counties are contemplating similar bond issues, as it clears up any doubt which might have existed concerning the right of the counties to issue such bonds. The decision is also valuable because it shows the powers of action that are possessed by the supervisors.

The opinion is printed below, and everyone interested in any way in the road question is urged to read through it carefully. It is well worth reading.

JOHN GOODWINE ET AL., APPELLANTS,

v.

COUNTY OF VERMILION ET AL., APPELLEES.

Mr. Justice Dunn delivered the opinion of the court:

John Goodwine and other residents, property owners and taxpayers of the county of Vermilion filed in the Circuit Court a bill against the county, the chairman of the board of supervisors and the county clerk, the purpose of was to enjoin the issue and sale of bonds amounting to $1,500,000 and the collection of a tax for the payment of them. An answer was filed, the cause was heard and a decree was rendered dismissing the bill for want of equity, from which the complainants have appealed.

The proposed bond issue purported to be for the purpose of aiding in the construction of roads and bridges in the county, and it appears from the pleading, the exhibits and a stipulation in regard to the facts upon which the cause was heard, that in May, 1914, a committee of the county board was appointed to consult with the State Highway Commission and its engineers relative to building a system of hard roads in the county to connect all the towns of the county with the county seat. The committee reported recommending the appropriation of funds to the amount of $1,500,000 to aid in the construction of roads and bridges in the county, the levy of necessary taxes for their payment, and the submission to the voters of the county, at the election in November, of the question of issuing county bonds for the purpose. The board of supervisors thereupon adopted a resolution that the sum of $1,500,000 be raised by the issuing of county bonds to that amount for the purpose of aiding in the construction of roads and bridges in the county in accordance with the provisions of the report of the committee; that such sum of money be appropriated from time to time, as needed, in the manner provided by law, for the purpose of aiding in the construction of such roads and bridges in the county; that the necessary taxes required to pay off the principal and interest of such bond issue be levied, assessed and collected from time to time in the manner required by law, and that the question of issuing said county bonds be submitted to the legal voters of the county at the election in November, 1914. A majority of the votes at the election having been cast in favor of the issue of the bonds, a committee of the county board was authorized to advertise for bids on them, to be received on May 17, 1915. Before that date the bill for an injunction in this case was filed. After the filing of the bill a curative act was passed by the Legislature for the purpose of legalizing all elections where the people have voted in favor of issuing bonds for the purpose of aiding in the construction of roads and bridges in any county or other municipality and the bonds issued in pursuance of such elections. (Laws of 1915, p. 581.)

The appellants contend that the proposed bond issue was in violation of that provision of the Constitution which prohibits any county from becoming indebted to an amount exceeding five per centum of the value of the taxable property therein; that the board of supervisors had no authority to call the election or issue bonds for the purpose of aiding in the construction of roads and bridges in the county; that the bonds were not issued for the purpose of aiding any township in the construction of roads and bridges in the county but as an independent work of the county, and that the curative act just referred to is inoperative and of no effect.

The assessed value of the real and personal property of the county was $36,402,538, 5 per cent of which is $1,820,000. It is stipulated that the aggregate amount of interest on the bonds during the period of twenty years to be paid by the county would amount to $570,000. While the principal of the bonds is less than the limit of indebtedness which the county may incur, if the interest is to be considered in determining the amount of such indebtedness that amount will exceed the constitutional limit by $250,000. The appellants insist that the liability of the county for the interest is the same as its liability for the principal of the debt; that the amount of the indebtedness to be incurred by the issue of the bonds will be the full amount of the principal and interest for the time the bonds have to run, and that the whole amount of such indebtedness will be incurred at the time the bonds are issued. The appellees contend that interest is a mere incident of the principal and can not be regarded as a part of the indebtedness until it has accrued. We have held that accrued interest is a debt within the constitutional limitations (*Stone* v. *City of Chicago*, 207 Ill., 492), but the question in regard to accuring interest has never been decided by this court. The doctrine is stated in McQuillin on Municipal Corporations, (Vol. 5, Sec. 2224), that "interest is not a debt, within the meaning of debt-limit provisions, until it is earned and becomes due, and in determining whether an indebtedness will be created in excess of the debt limit, unearned interest can not be added to the principal. The authority granted by the constitution or statute to contract a debt refers to the amount of the debt at the date at which it is created and has no reference to the amounts of interest which accrue thereafter. On the other hand, interest which has become due and payable is a part of the existing indebtedness in figuring the total amount of municipal indebtedness." The cases of *Ashland* v. *Culbertson*, 103 Ky., 161, *Finleyson* v. *Vaughn*, 54 Minn., 331, and *Herman* v. *City of Oconto*, 110 Wis., 660, sustain this statement. In the last case it is said: "Interest is not a debt, within the meaning of the constitution, until it is earned and becomes due." This is in accordance with the ordinary view, which in estimating the liabilities of individuals or corporations, does not take into consideration interest to accrue on unmatured obligations. Such interest is not to be regarded as a part of the indebtedness of municipal corporations within the constitutional prohibition.

The appellees claim that the action of the supervisors was in accordance with the power conferred by sections 56 and 40 of the act in relation to counties, while the appellants contend that those sections confer no authority on the board of supervisors to call an election for the voting of bonds to build hard roads. The sections are as follows:

"Section 56. Said board shall have power to appropriate funds to aid in the construction of roads and bridges in any part of the county, whenever a majority of the whole board of the county may deem it proper and expedient."

"Section 40. When the county board of any county shall deem it necessary to issue county bonds to enable them to perform any of the duties imposed upon them by law, they may, by an order, entered of record, specifying the amount of bonds required, and the object for which they are to be issued, submit to the legal voters of their county, at any general election, the question of issuing such county bonds. The amount of the bonds so issued shall not exceed, including the then existing indebtedness of the county, five per centum on the value of such taxable property of such county, as ascertained by the assessment for the State and county tax for the preceding year. Said vote shall be by ballot, on which shall be written or printed 'For county bonds,' or 'Against county bonds,' and if a majority of the votes at such election on that question shall be 'For county bonds,' such county board shall be authorized to issue such bonds of not less than twenty-five dollars ($25), nor more than one thousand dollars ($1,000) each, payable respectively, in not less than one nor more than twenty years, with interest payable annually or semiannually, at the rate of not more than 8 per cent per annum."

Section 56 was not repealed by the passage of the Road and Bridge law of 1913 but is still in force and confers upon the county board power to levy a tax to aid in the construction of roads in the county. (*People* v. *Jacksonville and St. Louis Railway Co.*, 265 Ill., 550; *People* v. *Wabash Railroad Co.*, id. 530). This provision gives the county board a discretion to aid any town in the construction of roads and bridges. Section 40 authorizes the board of supervisors to submit to the legal voters of the county the question of issuing bonds whenever they shall deem it necessary to issue bonds to enable them to perform any of the duties imposed upon them by law.

The appellants argue that a difference is recognized in the statute between duties imposed by law and powers conferred upon the county board; that the powers conferred by section 25 on the county board are to be exercised in the discretion of the county board, and that the duties referred to in section 40 are only those specified in section 26 of the act, stating that it shall be the duty of the county board of each county to do certain things. In our judgment there is no such distinction. The duties imposed upon the county board by law include not only those things which the county board is directed to do by the express mandate of the Legislature, but also those things for the performance of which the Legislature has conferred power upon the county board when the public interest requires that those things should be done. The county board has no powers except those expressly conferred upon it by statute or necessary for the performance of the powers which are expressly conferred. Whatever duty it owes is necessarily a duty imposed by law. Whenever the public interest requires that an act which the county board is authorized to do should be done and it is within the power of the county board to do it, then it is the duty of the county board to do that act. The duty may be one which can not be enforced by mandamus. It may not be absolute but relative, dependent upon time, place, manner or condition. The financial condition of the county may make impossible what would otherwise be a pressing duty, and several urgent demands may require the postponement of one or more in favor of another. When the county board, however, deems it necessary, to enable it to perform any of its duties, to issue county bonds, it may submit the question to the legal voters of the county. When the board arrived at the determination that the public interest of the county demanded that it should aid in the construction of roads and bridges, then it was the duty of the county board to aid in their construction, and that duty was imposed upon it by law. Under those circumstances section 40 expressly authorized the submission to the people of the question of issuing bonds for the purpose of raising money.

Sections 27 and 28, to which the appellants refer, have no application to this situation. Those sections refer only to a case where the county board shall deem it necessary to assess taxes the aggregate of which shall exceed the rate of 75 cents on each $100 valuation. No such excessive rate is necessary in the present case. The yearly installment of the bonds, together with interest on the whole amount is only half of 75 cents on each $100 valuation, as shown by the record.

The appellants contend that the bonds are proposed to be issued, not for the purpose of merely aiding in building roads and bridges, but for the purpose of building a complete and comprehensive system of hard roads connecting practically all the cities and villages of the county with the county seat, consisting of approximately 170 miles of roads; that it is no part of the scheme that the villages or townships shall contribute or pay, in their corporate capacity, any of the cost of said roads but that all are to be built at the expense of the county; that the purpose of the county is to completely build the roads and pay for them, including the cost of engineering, excavating, paving, furnishing material, work and labor, making a complete highway without any of the cost thereof being assessed against or paid by the townships, and that although the words "for the purpose of aiding in the construction of roads and bridges" are used in the proceedings, their use is merely a pretext and device to make it a legal duty imposed upon the county board to call an election to authorize said bonds.

It appears from the record that there are eighteen townships in Vermilion county and about 1,558 miles of public roads; that it is intended to construct about 175 miles of highway by improving less than one-half of their width and building a few bridges; that the part of said roads which the county proposes to improve is a strip 16 feet wide; that there will be constructed in each township from two to eighteen miles of public highway, except in the town of Danville, in which there will be a little over one mile of road outside the city of Danville; that the roads are to be constructed of concrete or brick, 10 feet wide, with gravel or rock shoulders 3 feet wide on each side; that the

old bridges are to be used and that all the roads are to be improved according to the plans and specifications approved by the State Highway Commission. It is averred in the answer that the towns will provide a large part of the grading and drainage for said system, and that some of the towns will furnish and pay for some of the gravel to be used in the shoulders of a part of the roads. It is manifest that the work is being done according to a plan or scheme for the systematic improvement of the roads in such a way as to connect all parts of the county with the county seat; that the scheme was adopted by the county board of its own initiative, without the action or petition of the commissioners of highways of the various towns or of any of them, and that the work is to be done under the authority of the board of supervisors and the supervision of its agents according to plans and specifications to be approved by the State Highway Commission, but it does not follow that the funds are not appropriated to aid in the construction of roads and bridges in the county. Section 56 of the act in relation to counties has been, in substantially its present form, a part of the statute since 1851, when it appeared in the act to provide for township organization. (Laws of 1851, p. 51.) Prior to 1849 the counties in the State had exclusive charge and control of all the roads within their respective boundaries, and the public highways were laid out, constructed, altered, maintained and repaired under the direction of the county commissioners' court. In 1849 a township organization law was passed which placed the roads within each town under the jurisdiction of commissioners of highways. (Laws of 1849, p. 190.) A new law on the same subject took its place in 1851, containing the provision which is now section 56 of the act in relation to counties. In the revision of the statute, in 1874, this section was transferred to the act in relation to counties. Since the first township organization act the care of the roads in counties under township organization has been a charge upon the townships in which they were situated and not on the counties, and the highway commissioners of the towns have had jurisdiction over them. The section of the statute which authorized county boards to appropriate funds to aid in the construction of roads and bridges in the county made no provision as to how, when, where, why, to what extent, under what circumstances or on whose request they should give aid. It did not require that the aid should be upon the application of the town, or of the highway commissioners, or the petition of individuals. The matter was left entirely to the discretion of the board as to when it would aid, where, to what extent and in what manner. The board had a right, if in the judgment of a majority of its members the public interest required it to do so, to offer aid without being asked, and to aid in one township or more and not in others. If the county board, acting in good faith, according to the best judgment of its members as to the requirements of the public interest, should undertake to aid all the towns in the county in a systematic manner, so as to bring about the building of a connected system of highways through every township leading to the county seat, no valid objection could be taken to such action. It may help any township. It may help each township. It may help all the townships. Why may it not help all the townships at the same time and in such a way as to produce a connected system of roads? The 175 miles of roads proposed to be constructed are slightly more than 11 per cent of the roads in the county. The proportion in each township, no doubt, varies, in some cases being more and in others less than 11 per cent. The form which the aid has taken is the construction by the county of a part of the highways which the townships were required to maintain. In fact, the part proposed to be constructed by the county is less than half the width of the road. Why may not the county, under the statute, assist in the construction of the roads in a township by assuming the exclusive burden of building a definite portion of the roads of the township as well as by assuming the burden of paying a portion of the cost of all the roads? It might well be that the county would be willing to assist in the building of roads in all the townships according to a systematic plan, under one management and direction, when it would not be willing to contribute to any township without such plan. It can not be said that the plan was not to aid the townships in the construction of roads because the plan originated with the county. It relieved the townships of the cost of construction of so much road. If the county did the whole of the work it was an aid to the township in relieving it of so much of its municipal burdens. It might be that the consent of the township authorities would be necessary to the construction of the particular road desired to be improved, but it is not necessary that any contract should have been entered into by the authorities of the town and the county, or any consent procured, before the county undertook to raise the money to carry out the scheme which it had determined upon. If the county board had, by agreement with the commissioners of highways of any township, agreed to assist the commissioners by the construction of a certain road in the township, it would hardly be contended that it was not within the power conferred by the Legislature in doing so. If it might assist one township in this way then certainly it could assist every other township in the same way. If in so assisting, the roads were selected so as to make a connected system of highways, connecting the townships with one another and with the county seat, this circumstance would constitute no valid objection to the aid furnished any township or all of them. The essential thing is that the county board had the right to aid in the construction of highways in any township in the county or all of them, and it is not a valid objection to such aid that it took the form of concentrating the expenditure in the complete construction of a definite portion of road in each township, that the aid was offered by the county and not requested by the township or that it was done under the supervision of the county and by its agents.

Section 126 of the Road and Bridge act is as follows:

"Section 126. The several county boards of counties are hereby vested with the same powers for constructing, repairing and maintaining gravel, rock, macadam or other hard roads in their respective counties as the commissioners of highways acting severally or together or with the several county superintendents of highways according to the provisions of this act. The county board of any county may also assist any town or road district therein in the construction of a hard road under the provisions of this act, to the extent of 25 per cent of the cost thereof: *Provided, however,* that the question of raising a special permanent road tax or of issuing bonds for the purposes set forth in this act, shall first be submitted to the legal voters of the county, at any regular election for county officers, on the petition of one hundred land owners who are legal voters in said county, to the county clerk, previous to time of posting the notices for said county elections said petition and notices to designate the road or roads to be improved and number of years, not to exceed five, for which the tax shall be continued."

The powers granted by this section refer only to the constructing, repairing and maintaining of gravel, rock, macadam or other hard roads according to the provisions of the Road and Bridge act. The limitations imposed apply only to proceedings under that act, and the section does not repeal, limit or modify section 56 of the County act. It is not necessary to consider the effect or validity of the curative act.

The action of the board of supervisors was within the power conferred upon them by the statute.

The decree of the Circuit Court was right, and it will be affirmed.

Decree affirmed.

THE GOOD ROADS MOVEMENT IN LAKE COUNTY.

The picture below tells an interesting story. It is significant of the fact that the value of good roads has been recognized. The people are fast becoming aware that the matter is one which has been allowed to remain too long under cover and that the time has come when the potential power of the highways must be used in aiding the development of our State.

Lake County furnishes an excellent example of the spirit which is manifesting itself in nearly all the counties in the State. On October 18, the county superintendents

[Courtesy of Waukegan Gazette.]

of the "northeast group" held their regular meeting at Waukegan, Illinois. Nearly all the members of the twelve counties constituting the group were in attendance, also a number of county supervisors and other good roads enthusiasts.

During the morning a number of papers were read and discussed in accordance with a program that had been previously prepared by the chairman, G. N. Lamb, county superintendent of Kane County. At 12.30 the meeting adjourned and those in attendance were entertained at luncheon as guests of the Waukegan Commercial Association. After the luncheon several brief talks were made by Messrs. McArdle, Bushnell, Quinlan, Lamb, Russell and others. After these talks were concluded a tour of inspection was made in automobiles tendered by the Commercial Association. The harbor at Waukegan was first visited, then the party started southward along the north shore. The first stop was made at the new Waukegan Terminal; from there the party motored to the naval training station, where a short time was devoted to a casual inspection of the buildings and the work being done in training young men. The tour was continued south through Lake Forest and Highland Park over a number of different types of permanent road construction. From Highland Park the tour was westward to Deerfield, stopping on the way to witness the operation of the Lake County Roller Road outfit.

The enthusiasm of this meeting and the interest aroused resulted in the Business Men's Association backing a movement for organizing a "Good Roads" Association. About ten days later this association held a meeting and smoker at which a number of talks were given on the subject of good roads. County Superintendent Russell explained the features of the law which permits the counties to bond themselves for the purpose of constructing their designated State aid roads.

At this meeting Mr. R. W. Dunn, of the Good Roads Association of Chicago, gave an enthusiastic and well-received talk on the benefit of road organization. The result of this meeting was that a resolution was passed calling for a meeting to be held at Libertyville in Lake County for the purpose of organizing a Lake County Good Roads Association. Temporary committeemen were appointed to prepare for this meeting, which was held at Libertyville, November 15. Mr. A. D. Gash, of the State Highway Commission, was the principal speaker. His talk on the history, value, benefits, etc., of good roads was enthusiastically received by the approximately ninety delegates from the different sections of the county, who were present.

The afternoon session of this meeting was devoted to organization, and Mr. R. B. Swift, a prominent business farmer near Libertyville was elected president; R. W. Kend, vice president; James H. King, treasurer, and Mr. McGill, of Waukegan, secretary.

Further details of organization and arrangements for committee making were made, and those present signed up as charter members of the association.

At the September meeting of the board of supervisors, a tentative proposition for a bond issue of a million dollars and additional tax levies for the purpose of constructing State aid and county aid roads was presented by the county superintendent of highways. A special committee was appointed by the board to consider the proposition and to report back at the December meeting with their recommendations.

That the county is alive with interest in this matter is evidenced by the fact that a number of meetings have been called in the smaller cities and villages, and more are being arranged for the purpose of discussing good

roads, and ways and means, and a lively interest is being taken in the subject.

That the spirit of road improvement in Lake County is making itself felt in a material way is evidenced by a letter from L. J. Wicks, of Avon Township, Lake County, who says:

"I would like to let you hear from Lake County and Avon Township concerning the spirit of good roads in our township. We have been doing some graveling on certain roads specified in a special tax levied for the purpose, and also have been working on several other important roads. With the cooperation of the citizens of the village and parts of the township, we were able to gravel one mile of road without any expense to the township, excepting the cost of the gravel. This was accomplished through the medium of a "Road Day." The arrangements were made by a special committee and the commissioners. At 7 o'clock in the morning of the designated day, the teams and men began to arrive. In all forty-three teams were on hand, besides about twenty men. The work of graveling the road went forward with a fine spirit. Lunch was served at noon, and then the work was resumed. By evening the work was completed and those who had participated in Avon Township's Good Roads Day felt well repaid for their work."

This is the spirit which is manifesting itself all over Illinois, and it is such spirit and determination which is making the people realize the importance and value of improved highways.

HIGHWAYS AND BRIDGES IN OGLE COUNTY.

By ALEX. ANDERSON,
County Superintendent of Highways, Ogle County.

The county of Ogle lying in the second tier of counties from the north and west sides of the State contains a variety of roads and road materials. The accompanying report of the superintendent of highways on the roads and bridges of the county will, if examined, maintain this assertion. All of the materials used for surfacing the improved roads have been taken from the immediate vicinity of roads improved, with the exception of the asphalt and brick. The surfacing material has been largely stone or gravel, and during the past year several miles of earth roads have been oiled.

STATE AID ROAD CONSTRUCTED IN OGLE COUNTY.

The brick State aid road constructed during the past summer, a section of which is shown in the accompanying cut, is 9 feet in width and two miles in length, one-half of which has a 6-inch concrete curb, made by extending the base. Macadam shoulders of 3½ feet in width are constructed on each side along the entire length, making a road 16 feet wide. The brick surface was placed one-half of its width to the side of the center line of the highway, thus leaving room for an earth track. The total cost of the road was about $15,000 per mile with an average haul for all materials, except stone, of about four miles.

Type of Concrete Bridges Built in Ogle County.

The bridges built in the county during the recent past have been largely of concrete of a type which is shown in the accompanying cut. The width of roadway has been increased in most cases until 20 feet is common for the larger bridges, unless of extra length, and of 24 and 28 feet for all culverts. The commissioners are convinced that the greater roadway is much to be preferred and they could not be persuaded to return to the narrower widths. The cut shows a concrete slab, built askew, 16-foot span, and 20-foot roadway, finished with white waterproofing.

A number of the townships have done some very good work grading roads during the past season, especially the ones that have been fortunate enough to own or hire a tractor, although it was a very bad year to do grading. The county board offered an inducement for some better road work during the coming year by appropriating an amount sufficient to pay 25 per cent of the cost, not to exceed $500, in any one township, and the total cost where aid is to be given to be not less than $1,000. Practically all of the townships expect to avail themselves of the offer during the coming spring and summer. The type of road and kind of work to be done is to have the approval of the superintendent of highways.

The statistics included in the above-mentioned report were obtained by the county superintendent largely from reports made to him by the highway commissioners on blanks prepared for the purpose. Each bridge and culvert and road in the township were inspected, and the information about each was tabulated on the blanks opposite a number or letter designating the same. Maps of each township have been prepared on which the location of the bridges are given and the number designating the same and the roads are also indicated by a letter.

Report on the Highway Bridges and Public Highways of Ogle County by the Superintendent of Highways.

HIGHWAY BRIDGES, OGLE COUNTY, JUNE 1, 1915.

Township.	Bridges more than 60 feet long.						Bridges 9 to 60 feet long, inclusive.									Bridges, culverts and farm entrances 8-ft. span or less.												Summary.				
	Steel on stone or concrete abutments.	Steel on steel tube or leg foundations.	Wood on concrete or stone abutments.	Total No. of bridges more than 60 ft. long.	Total length of bridges more than 60 ft. long.	Needing repairs.	Concrete or stone.	Steel on stone or concrete abutments.	Steel on steel legs, posts or tubes.	Wood on concrete or stone abutments.	Wood throughout.	Total No. of bridges 9 to 60 ft. long.	Total length of bridges 9 to 60 ft. long.	Needing repairs.	Needing replacement.	Concrete or stone.	Steel on stone or concrete abutments.	Steel on steel legs, posts or tubes.	Wood on concrete or stone abutments.	Wood throughout.	Corrugated pipe.	Plain steel pipe.	Vitrified tile pipe.	Total No. of bridges 8 ft. span or less.	Total length of openings 8 ft. span or less.	Needing repairs.	Needing replacement.	Grand total of all bridges and culverts.	Total length of all bridges.	Road mileage of township.	No. of bridges per mile of road.	Length of bridge per mile of road.
Brookville	....	1	....	1	74	..	7	4	18	....	8	37	946	2	..	2	....	....	....	32	1	....	1	36	168	6	....	74	1,188	40½	1.8	29.5
Buffalo	....	....	....	....	......	..	2	20	....	18	..	40	574	4	..	15	14	....	13	16	74	....	8	140	360	13	....	180	934	65	2.8	14.4
Byron	3	....	....	3	771	..	...	35	3	6	4	48	987	1	2	3	3	1	6	12	22	1	....	47	132	2	4	98	1,820	61	1.6	31.0
Dement	1	1	....	2	147	..	...	10	23	1	2	36	394	..	1	10	....	4	1	50	89	21	5	180	404	....	10	218	1,145	53½	4.1	21.5
Eagle Point	....	....	....	....	......	..	4	12	1	....	..	17	324	3	..	20	12	....	1	11	7	5	4	60	198	8	5	77	522	45½	1.7	11.5
Flagg	3	....	....	3	244	1	...	21	2	....	..	23	505	2	..	1	2	2	....	19	46	3	45	118	182	10	23	144	1,034	62½	2.3	16.5
Forreston	....	....	....	....	......	..	14	12	6	....	1	33	761	5	3	114	....	1	....	60	27	....	....	202	600	4	16	235	1,361	68	3.5	20.0
Grand Detour	....	1	1	3	176	..	1	7	7	2	1	18	261	4	1	2	....	....	2	3	7	3	10	27	72	1	....	47	609	17½	2.8	34.8
Lafayette	....	....	....	....	......	..	1	7	2	1	..	11	209	..	..	....	1	1	1	10	25	22	2	63	206	....	5	74	507	28½	2.6	17.9
Leaf River	2	....	....	2	135	2	2	22	....	6	3	33	705	3	2	8	....	....	1	14	13	5	3	45	127	7	3	80	967	61	1.3	15.9
Lincoln	....	....	....	....	......	..	15	6	17	4	10	52	1,141	..	1	2	....	....	....	98	65	2	13	176	486	10	12	228	1,627	68	3.3	23.9
Lynnville	2	3	....	5	366	..	1	25	13	1	..	40	940	3	..	3	2	....	....	80	57	2	23	107	208	1	21	152	1,512	57	2.7	26.5
Marion	1	1	....	2	130	..	...	10	6	....	..	16	452	2	..	39	1	....	1	78	17	5	13	159	452	25	5	177	1,034	73½	2.4	14.1
Maryland	....	....	....	....	......	..	11	27	1	....	10	49	1,348	2	7	12	2	....	....	73	5	3	14	108	443	5	25	157	1,781	58½	2.7	30.4
Monroe	3	....	....	3	503	1	3	13	3	3	11	35	531	3	9	11	6	....	....	70	53	11	14	165	474	7	41	203	1,508	64½	3.1	23.4
Mt. Morris	....	1	....	1	78	..	10	20	12	2	3	47	969	3	4	21	17	2	1	73	....	35	20	169	510	11	34	217	1,547	61	3.5	25.3
Nashua	2	....	....	2	375	..	3	4	1	....	..	8	180	..	..	6	9	....	4	2	1	....	6	28	109	....	4	38	644	27½	1.4	23.4
Oregon	1	....	....	1	962	..	2	6	11	1	5	25	444	5	9	10	5	6	3	11	22	....	46	102	256	8	9	128	1,662	37	3.5	19.0
Pine Creek	2	3	....	7	589	2	4	12	18	4	9	48	835	1	7	4	3	2	5	40	70	....	32	149	393	8	29	204	1,817	75	2.8	24.2
Pine Rock	1	2	....	3	317	..	7	10	3	....	5	25	492	..	..	12	....	....	....	65	43	....	12	132	323	....	....	160	1,132	64	2.5	17.7
Rockvale	2	1	4	7	720	..	11	7	16	3	10	49	884	6	2	40	3	....	3	14	19	....	7	88	263	10	5	144	1,807	64¾	2.2	27.9
Scott	1	1	....	2	137	..	7	2	11	9	4	33	600	1	3	18	....	....	1	98	....	2	12	132	428	1	4	167	1,165	64	2.6	18.2
Taylor	....	....	....	....	......	..	1	6	5	....	..	12	240	5	..	4	1	2	3	4	21	4	13	52	120	3	2	64	360	24	2.5	15.0
White Rock	....	....	....	....	......	..	3	16	8	....	1	28	560	3	2	19	2	1	....	85	23	....	25	155	412	9	34	183	972	60½	3.0	16.0
Woosung	....	....	....	....	......	..	1	14	9	1	1	26	525	10	2	9	8	1	12	8	28	10	21	97	252	9	6	123	777	34¼	3.6	22.5
Totals	24	17	5	46	5,824	6	110	339	198	64	88	780	16,027	68	48	398	92	22	58	905	735	134	355	2,737	7,081	158	297	3,572	29,503	1,335	2.7	22.1

PUBLIC HIGHWAYS, JUNE 1, 1915.

Township.	Sand roads.	Clay roads.	Loam roads.	Gravel roads.	Stone roads.	Asphalt road.	Brick road.	Total miles.	Road and bridge fund.	Special fund.
Brookville	.....	40½	.....	.....	.....	.....	.....	40½	$ 1,175	$ 1,020
Buffalo	.....	16	19	.....	30	.....	.....	65	8,800	.....
Byron	.....	14	37¼	.....	9¾	.....	.....	61	5,795	.....
Dement	.....	.....	42¼	9¾	1¼	.....	.....	53¼	5,785	6,640
Eagle Point	.....	24¾	12½	2¼	6	.....	.....	45½	2,660	2,770
Flagg	21½	½	23	4	13	1	.....	62¾	13,225	500
Forreston	.....	18	43¾	6½	.....	.....	.....	68	8,000	.....
Grand Detour	4	10¼	.....	1	2	.....	.....	17¼	1,000	725
Lafayette	1	7¼	17½	.....	2¼	.....	.....	28¾	1,900	1 465
Leaf River	.....	32	10½	.....	18½	.....	.....	61	5,320	.....
Lincoln	.....	15¼	52¾	.....	.....	.....	.....	68	5,500	.....
Lynnville	.....	.....	57	.....	.....	.....	.....	57	4,800	.....
Marion	6¼	32½	16¼	4¾	11¼	.....	.....	72¼	7,000	.....
Maryland	1	28¾	21	7¾	.....	.....	.....	58½	5,000	.....
Monroe	.....	2	46	13	3¼	.....	.....	64¼	5,600	.....
Mt. Morris	.....	57	3	.....	¼	.....	.....	60¼	8,500	.....
Nashua	5¼	9½	1¾	3¼	6	1¼	.....	27¼	2,400	2,180
Oregon	7¾	13		2	12¼	1¼	.....	37	7,500	6,000
Pine Creek	.....	66¾	6¾	1¼	.....	.....	.....	75	4,500	.....
Pine Rock	22¼	6¼	28¾	4½	.....	.....	2	64	4,200	.....
Rockvale	6	48¾	2	.....	8	.....	.....	64¾	2,700	3,450
Scott	1¼	.....	31¼	31	.....	.....	.....	64	6,940	.....
Taylor	6¼	7¼	3	6¼	¼	.....	.....	24	1,300	.....
White Rock	.....	.....	49¼	11	.....	.....	.....	60¼	3,500	.....
Woosung	.....	7	9	.....	18¼	.....	.....	34¼	2,500	3,440
Totals	83	459	535	108	144	4	2	1,335	$125,630	$28,190

SURFACE OILING AN OLD NOVACULITE GRAVEL ROAD.

ROAD DISTRICT NO. 5, ALEXANDER COUNTY, ILLINOIS.

By **B. H. PIEPMEIER,** ***Maintenance Engineer.***

There are a number of gravel roads in and about Cairo. They have been built of what is locally known as hill gravel and novaculite gravel. The novaculite gravel may be found in most of the small streams; it is mined extensively, however, from the hills near Tamms, Illinois. It is an excellent bonding gravel and is accordingly used considerably for road construction and for patching existing gravel roads. The gravel packs readily without rolling, and wears about the same as an ordinary macadam road, but washes badly in the early spring and wet seasons.

The Mound City Road, leading out of Cairo, was constructed of this gravel a number of years ago, and each year had a few repairs. About every third year it was necessary to apply an entire new surface dressing. This became expensive and very inconvenient to traffic. The Mound City Road was one of the heaviest-traveled roads leading out of Cairo, so the road district commissioners were very anxious to try some surface treatments that would eliminate the dust and prevent the road from wearing so rapidly. Upon the advice of the State Highway Department, they ordered one tank of Mexican asphaltic oil, containing from 60 to 65 per cent asphalt, and applied it to the surface as indicated below. The oil was applied cold and within twelve hours after the application a light dressing of river sand was applied and the road opened to traffic.

The oiled surface to date has given entire satisfaction, and similar work will be continued next season.

The following gives the itemized cost of the work, as recorded by Mr. Theodore Plack, engineer in charge for the State Highway Department.

COST OF APPLYING BITUMINOUS SURFACES ON MACADAM ROADS.

CAIRO ROAD, R. D. NO. 5, ALEXANDER COUNTY.

CONDITIONS.

The following figures do not include contractor's profit or overhead expenses.

Total length of road treated, 8,200 feet; total square yards of road treated, 16,400; condition of old macadam road, fair; kind of bituminous material used, Aztec liquid asphalt; amount of bituminous material used, one-half gallon per square yard; amount of torpedo gravel or stone chips, sand, .006 tons per square yard; average length of haul, one-half mile; general condition of weather, fair; rate of pay for labor, 15 cents per hour; teams, 40 cents per hour.

ITEMIZED COST OF WORK.

	Total cost.	Cost per sq. yd.
*Superintendence, engineering and inspection	$ 34 20	$0.0021
Bituminous material, 8,184 gal. @ 0.047 f.o.b siding..............	384 85	.0034
Torpedo gravel and stone chips, 66½ cu. yds. @ 0.59 f.o.b siding.	39 25	.0024
Heating and applying bituminous material, demurrage, etc........	51 85	.0032
Spreading torpedo gravel and stone chips, sand	51 55	.0031
Sweeping and cleaning old road....	5 60	.00034
Depreciation on equipment........	*	*
Freight on equipment............	88 20	.0054
Total cost	$655 30	$0.0399

* Indicates paid or furnished by the State Highway Department.

COOK COUNTY COMMISSIONERS INSPECT STATE AID ROADS.

On November 26, the board of county commissioners were the guests of the associated roads organizations of Chicago and Cook County on the first annual inspection of State aid roads laid in Cook County, Illinois. The trip covered 100 miles of good and bad roads entirely within the limits of Cook County, except one short excursion into Dupage County to see the concrete pavement laid by the Dupage county board on Wheaton Road, an extension of the Twelfth Street Concrete Road of Cook County. In several towns along the way the citizens extended enthusiastic receptions to the county board, and the good roads sentiment in Cook County sustained a remarkable impetus.

The trip was so arranged as to cover typical improved highways, as well as some of the unimproved roads. The rainy weather which prevailed, served to call forcibly to the attention of the commissioners the contrast between muddy, unimproved highways and the concrete roads built by State aid.

Under the law as originally framed, the county was not permitted to build roads within village limits. The error of this was excellently shown on the Twelfth Street Road, where alternate good and bad stretches were encountered. The good stretches were those built under State aid and the bad spots were unimproved stretches on the same road within village limits. There was a sigh of relief each time a good road was reached. By an amendment to the Tice Law of Illinois, the county is empowered to pave the bad stretches through villages with a population of 20,000 or less.

Citizens of Riverdale, Harvey, Blue Island, Lyons and Riverside met the county board to express to them their appreciation of the work done in Cook County and to bring to their attention the necessity for additional improvement on other main-traveled highways. These receptions showed the desire of the several villages that the highways connecting them with Chicago be improved.

The seven-mile stretch of concrete road on Milwaukee Avenue, one of the principal thoroughfares leading to Chicago and used largely by automobilists and truck farmers, was included in the trip. This is the longest continuous stretch of concrete highway in Illinois.

The associated roads organization acted as host at a luncheon served at the Chauteau Desplaines in Lyons, at a reception at the "House that Jack Built" on the Milwaukee Avenue Concrete Road, and at a dinner at the Sherman House, following the trip.

President Reingberg and the other members of the county board expressed themselves as greatly pleased with what they had seen, and extended their hearty cooperation to the citizens of the county in continuing the good work already done to pull Cook County out of the mud.

VERMILION COUNTY—REPORT OF COUNTY SUPERINTENDENT.

By W. S. DILLON,
County Superintendent of Highways, Vermilion County.

On the ninth of December, 1914, I presented my first report to the board of supervisors as superintendent of highways of Vermilion County.

In my previous report, I spoke of two county aid contracts being let—one for the Gordon Fill Culvert at a cost of $4,189.90, and one for the Wallace Chapel Bridge at $4,198. These two structures are now in use and are giving complete satisfaction. Gordon Fill has been giving trouble for years and has cost the township a considerable sum of money. After some study, the present design was adopted as the most economical, and, after six months or more of service, is acknowledged to be a permanent structure. County aid will probably be asked for at least two structures in the coming year, one costing approximately $15,000 and one $3,000.

BOND ROADS.

In January, 1914, the road improvement committee employed a competent civil engineer to superintend the building of the bond roads, and also other necessary engineers, under the supervision of the superintendent of highways. Three engineering corps, one level party and an office force were organized, consisting of twenty-two men. Drawing-room furniture, field instruments, office and laboratory fixtures were bought at a cost of $1,475.81. Three weeks' time was required in perfecting this organization and more than 200 applications were received for positions.

By the twentieth of January, the third engineering corps entered the field, and by the first of May the 174.2 miles, besides 20 miles additional of cut-offs and resurveys, making a total of 194.2 miles, were surveyed. January, February, and a part of March of this time was very bad weather, and it was only by the remarkable perseverence of the men in the field that such a showing was possible. Maps, plans, preliminary estimates and specifications were prepared by the office force for the letting on May 17, the field force assisting them after the first of May. In the meantime an injunction suit had been filed and the road improvement committee ordered that all contractors and bondsmen be notified that no bids would be opened on May 17. This was done, some seventy-five notices being sent out. Up to this time correspondence had been carried on with con-

tractors and material men all over the country; there was an average of two material men, transportation men or contractors in the office every day during this time. The total cost of the bond road work from January 1 to May 17, was $12,096.78, including the $1,475.81 mentioned above; an average cost per mile of $54.50 for field and office expenses. After the May meeting, the forces were cut down and the work virtually stopped.

STATE AID ROADS.

Vermilion County will soon have a considerable mileage of State aid roads. Section A, route 2, extending from the north city limits to the Kenley Place, one-fourth mile north of Newell Road, has been completed at a cost of $48,171.10 plus the cost of cement, $5,915.04 and extra work, $779.68, a total of $54,865.82, the work being done by E. M. Laing & Co., of Highland Park, Ill. The total length of this road is 16,100 feet, 6,100 feet being of brick 18 feet wide, and the balance 10 feet of brick; the width of the traveled way being 30 feet for the whole road.

Section B, route 2, has been let to Cameron, Joyce & Co., Keokuk, Iowa, for $7,063.78. In addition to this, extra work to the amount of $4,908.80 was ordered, making a total of $11,972.58. This work extends from the Kenley Place north a distance of 4,053 feet to the top of the hill north of the North Fork River, and consists of the grading and straightening of the road for this distance. There will be no greater improvement in Vermilion County than on this stretch of road. The contract for the surface of this stretch will be let later. This grading is now practically complete.

Section C, on the twenty-seventh of August, was let to the Central States Bridge Co., of Indianapolis, Ind., for the sum of $11,498.00. This contract is for a 160-foot span steel bridge with concrete abutments and a wood block floor over the North Fork. The excavation for the south abutment is finished and ready for the concrete.

Section D, in August, was let to the McCalman Construction Co., of Decatur, Ill., for the sum of $34,900, excluding the cost of the cement. This work consists of the grading, draining, bridging and paving of 15,600 feet north of the top of the hill north of the North Fork River. In addition to this, they have been awarded extra work, consisting of grading, draining and bridging from the north end of section D to the Bismark Road. The grading on the original contract is finished and most of the culverts and bridges. The State would not allow the contractors to pave any on this stretch until spring.

Section D, which covers about 3½ miles of the proposed bond system, has been let according to the surveys prepared from this office.

When the contracts under way are completed Vermilion County will have 6 miles of completed pavement and 1.2 additional miles of completed grade, reaching from the city limits to the Bismark Road, and costing, not including the 2,221 feet to Bismark Coroner, approximately $118,483.36, as follows:

Vermilion County has had three allotments for State aid roads, as follows: 1913–14, $11,082; 1914–15, $19,394.00; 1915–16, $29,482.00; 1916–17, $29,482.00, which will be available July 1, 1916; a reallotment of $3,657.00, making a total of $93,097.00 from the State.

On July next the 1916–17 allotment of $29,482.00 will be available from the State, making the sum of $58,964.00, plus any balance unexpended and any reallotment for State aid work in Vermilion County.

The property owners along the line of this improvement have aided in many ways, giving time, and money, and land in order to get the best possible road. It would have been impossible to make the changes, which consisted of straightening and widening the road, without this aid.

Quite a number of complaints have been made to this office as the work progressed, but to date all of them have been satisfactorily arranged.

TOWNSHIPS.

Commissioners have reported eight permanent bridges built according to State highway standards and plans furnished from this office, costing from $250.00 to $450.00 each; four concrete culverts, costing from $80.00 to $100.00 each; three repair jobs, costing from $250.00 to $500.00 each, and numerous small culverts, costing less than $200.00.

They have also placed 20,000 yards of gravel on the roads; graded several miles, and dragged approximately 100 miles.

Blount Township has placed more good tiling than any township outside of Danville. This is an improvement that can be recommended very strongly. In Elwood Township, two miles of road were scarified, leveled and rolled at a cost of $100.00 per mile. This work was a success and is a good example for other townships to follow who have rough macadam or gravel roads.

Very few of the townships have places for keeping their machinery under cover, as the law requires. Several are arranging to build, and it would be wise if all would arrange to do the same.

Georgetown Township voted bonds for 5¼ miles of hard roads through Westville and Georgetown. Surveys, plans, estimates and specifications were made by the superintendent at a cost to the township of $461.71. The money from the sale of bonds is in the bank, but is tied up by an injunction.

Elwood Township voted bonds for two miles of hard roads, which we are working on at the present time.

MEETINGS.

In the last year the superintendent of highways has attended thirty-three road improvement committees in which he acted as secretary of the committee and has kept the minutes of the meetings; a National good roads convention in Chicago, December 14, 1914, at his own expense; a short course in highway engineering at Springfield, Ill., March 29 to April 3, under the auspices of the State Highway Department; a final hearing of the Carter road case at Rossville, Ill., on June 15; a meeting of road commissioners, town clerks and supervisors of Vermilion County; a Dixie Highway celebration in Danville, October 9, 1915; the Northwestern Road Congress in Cedar Rapids, Iowa, October 4 to 7, with Mr. P. C. McArdle and Mr. John Olmsted, as per resolution of the county board, September 14, 1915; in October the opening of Milwaukee Avenue in Cook County, Chicago, with Mr. P. C. McArdle, assistant State highway engineer. This road is the longest stretch of State aid work in the State. The superintendent made, on May 12 and 13, an inspection trip to Chicago, with the road improvement committee to view different types of pavement; four inspection trips to Paris to see the new Monolithic type of brick pavement; one trip with the State Highway Commission, one trip with members of the Vermilion County board and township commissioners, the other with contractors, four trips with P. C. McArdle to visit gravel pits at Terre Haute and Clinton, Ind., Hillary, Bismark, Grape Creek,

and one trip to the Casparas stone quarry at Fairmount, Ill., fifteen or twenty trips with P. C. McArdle covering the entire system of bond roads, making several trips to places needing special study and also to confer with commissioners as to what they might be willing to help on bridges, right of ways, widening roads, etc.; three trips with members of the road improvement committee covering the entire system of bond roads; on June 22, District 5 of the Illinois Association of County Superintendents of Highways, consisting of thirteen counties, met in the superintendent's office at Danville, Ill. G. C. Fairclo, of Champaign County, was made president, and Wm. S. Dillon, of Vermilion County, secretary. On September 4, a second meeting of the district was held in Danville, at which eight of the thirteen counties were represented and three representatives of the State Highway Department were present.

The superintendent has made an average of two bridge inspections and four road inspections a month with the different commissioners in the past year. There has been on on average one commissioner a day, two supervisors a week, one State official a week, one contractor or material man a day and one person on miscellaneous business a day in the office.

APPLYING A LIGHT BITUMINOUS SURFACE ON THE LOWDEN ROAD AT OREGON.

By B. H. PIEPMEIER, Maintenance Engineer.

The Lowden Road was constructed as a bituminous macadam road in 1914. The original road was constructed of local stone which is very soft. The road was badly rutted and out of shape in many places, yet it was considered good enough to use as a foundation course for some surfacing material.

On account of the low rate at which local stone could be placed on the road, it was decided to use this stone in connection with some bituminous material. The road was therefore reshaped and surfaced with local stone at a depth of from 3 to 10 inches and then penetrated with Aztec Road Binder at the rate of approximately 2 gallons per square yard of surface.

SIXTY-FOOT BRIDGE ON LOWDEN ROAD,

repaired by adding two new steel stringers and shimming all stringers to a 3-inch crown, then flooring bridge with creosoted lumber, calking all cracks with oakum and applying a 1-inch surface of asphalt and torpedo gravel. The surface on the road and bridge is the same, so it is impossible to detect any jar when going over the structure.

The road was in excellent condition and was very satisfactory to the local people, but it was decided that, on account of the soft stone that was used and which was beginning to show through the asphalt surface in places, to treat the entire surface with a light application of a high-grade asphaltic material and a very hard, coarse sand.

The following gives an itemized cost of the surface work:

COST OF APPLYING BITUMINOUS SURFACES ON MACADAM ROADS.

LOWDEN ROAD, SECTION B, OGLE COUNTY.

CONDITIONS.

The following figures do not include contractor's profit or overhead expenses.

Total length of road, 16,222 feet; total square yards of road treated, 30,906; condition of old bituminous macadam road, good; kind of bituminous material used, Trinidad "B"; amount of bituminous material used, ⅓ gallon per square yard; amount of torpedo gravel, or stone chips, 0.016 + tons per square yard; average length of haul of materials, 1½ miles; general condition of weather, rainy; rate of pay—labor, 25 cents per hour; teams, 50 cents per hour; work started August 15, 1915; completed September 20, 1915.

ITEMIZED COST OF WORK.

	Total cost.	Cost per sq. yd.
Engineering and inspection.......	[1].......	[1].......
Superintendence	[1]$107 33	[1]$0.0035
Bituminous material, 9,617 gal. @ 7.7¢ f. o. b. siding.............	[1]738 51	[1].0239
Torpedo gravel and stone chips, 484 tons, stone $1.40; gravel, $1.82½ f. o. b. siding................ {	[1]37 50 786 46	[1].0012 .0255
Hauling torpedo gravel and stone chips	261 00	.0084
Heating and applying bituminous material, demurrage, etc........	321 00	.0104
Spreading torpedo gravel and stone chips	[1]172 63	[1].0056
Sweeping and cleaning old road...	16 44	.0005
New equipment (pump)	22 75	[1].0007
Freight on equipment............	46 90	.0015
Incidental expense	68 20	.0022
Culverts and patching holes......	82 82	.0027
	$2,661 54	$0.0861

[1] Indicates paid by the State Highway Department from maintenance fund.

BUREAU COUNTY SUPERINTENDENT PUBLISHES A MONTHLY ROAD BULLETIN.

In order to keep closely in touch with road officials and workers of his county, County Superintendent Bryant of Bureau County publishes monthly a neat four page multigraphed pamphlet which deals with the various questions concerning the roads of his county.

The heading of this pamphlet reads "Issued every month from the office of the office of the County Superintendent of Highways in the interest of mutual cooperation and knowledge of current affairs of all road officials and workers of Bureau County."

The columns of this little paper are open to the people of Bureau County for a discussion of the various road problems which come up from time to time. Much good certainly has been and is being done in the way of obtaining the necessary publicity on road problems,

which is so essential for the cooperation needed in road work.

Mr. Bryant is certainly to be commended for his progressive spirit in establishing this paper, especially as he personally paid for the multigraph outfit which is used in printing the bulletin. This meant an expenditure of $250.00 out of his own pocket but he says that he is more than satisfied with his investment.

RELATION OF COUNTY SUPERINTENDENTS TO TOWNSHIP HIGHWAY COMMISSIONERS.

By L. B. NEIGHBOUR,
Superintendent of Highways, Lee County.

I shall write from observations and experiences of considerably less than a year, and I remind you, at the outset, that my work has been in a county of the first class. Experience in a county of the second or third class might have resulted in quite a different paper.

The topic has suggested to my mind the following heads for treatment:

(a) Relations growing out of the County Superintendent's duties specifically enumerated in the law.

(b) Those growing out of work ordered by the State Highway Department, in conformity with the provision that the County Superintendent is a deputy of the State Highway Engineer, being the local man of the State Highway Department.

(c) Those inferable from the general spirit of helpfulness of the law, and the express provision that the superintendent shall "advise and direct the Highway Commissioners of the several towns and districts of his county as to the best methods of repair, maintenance and improvement of highways and bridges."

(d) Means that the superintendent may take of getting his ideas before his commissioners.

(e) Measures the superintendent may adopt for winning for his office the approval, cooperation, and support of the commissioners.

(a) Under the statutory duties of the superintendent we may first consider the annual inspection of roads and bridges. There is no one to whom his findings can well be of greater interest than to the commissioners. The inspection is as profitable to them, before outlining their season's work, as it can be to him, for any of his uses. I suspect that the underlying purpose of this whole inspection business is really to help the local road authorities in their work.

It seems to me to follow that the superintendent and the commissioners should form a party and go over the roads together. This work will be done as early in the spring as may be practicable, the dates being set by the superintendent, according to some feasible schedule of his own. The commissioners, acting as they will be, for the welfare of the highways of the town, will look to the town for their compensation for the time so spent in its service, and will so feel the more ready to go.

The automobile will be found the most satisfactory vehicle for use on most of these trips.

Our counties will average, I judge, not far from 20 townships each. These will each have, say, 60 miles of road, so your average superintendent has a distance of 1200 miles to ride on this errand alone. It is evident that if he relies on horseflesh, either the horse must "go some" or the superintendent will have an all-summer conference with his commissioners, in the performance of this one duty.

These inspection trips furnish an ideal opportunity for the "advising" mentioned in the statute. For we must realize that there are many features of the road work, the cost of which does not reach the $200 limit, and yet call for expert knowledge and make good advice desirable. Some such features are the smaller culverts, their material and mode of construction; concrete floors for bridges and culverts needing repair, with the question of whether the structures are strong enough to support such a floor; the character of the gravel near at hand and most likely to be used in such work; the drainage of the road, etc.

The law makes all bridges and culverts built by the town and for which the town alone is responsible, subject to the approval of the county superintendent. The commissioners are accordingly ready enough to turn over to him the work of designing, drawing the plans, and preparing specifications for these. He meets with the commissioners for the necessary inspection of the sites; again when he has the plans ready for them to pass upon; then sees to the advertising for the bids, attends the lettings, and approves the contracts. Moreover, he will, in all likelihood, be asked to pass upon the completed work, and to make the final estimate.

The provision of the law that all purchases and contracts in an amount exceeding $200 must have the approval of the superintendent is the one most likely to be viewed with suspicion, if I may not say with active antagonism, by the commissioners. Neither is it a feature of the law that contributes to the convenience or pleasure of the superintendent. He becomes much sought after by the agents of machinery concerns, even to the extent of being routed out of bed at nights to answer their telephone calls and make appointments with them. The superintendent can scarcely be expected to be present at every township meeting at which a $200 purchase may be made or a $200 improvement decided upon. Then, no direction has been given the commissioners as to the steps to be taken by them in submitting their contracts to the superintendent for his approval.

In so far as Lee County is concerned, I am free to confess the meeting of this requirement of the law has not been well systematized as yet. In some cases, the superintendent has really O. K.'d the written contract. In others, he has advised or approved the improvement, and then the commissioners have gone ahead, made any necessary contract and carried things through. The orders on the town treasurer, in payment for such work, have then been sent to the superintendent for his indorsement, as a protection to the contractor and the treasurer.

It is the opinion of the writer that blank forms should be prepared, on which to write all such Highway Commissioners' contracts; that these contracts should be made out in triplicate; that the town clerk should mail or otherwise deliver them to the county superintendent for his O. K.; and then that one copy, each, should be returned to the parties to the contract, and one retained in the county superintendent's office.

The county aid bridge provisions of the law bring many points of contact between superintendent and commissioners. The initial steps in such cases, however, will probably be taken by the commissioners. To begin with, the need of a new bridge will usually be obvious. Towns are not unduly anxious to pay for a new bridge, or even

to pay half the cost. The first step will probably be to ask the superintendent to go out to look over the site and see what he thinks of the project for a new bridge. He sets a date to meet with them, looks over the situation, assures himself of the need for the bridge, and hears the various suggestions of the commissioners. Then he gives them a rough and approximate estimate of the probable cost, to be incorporated in their petition to the supervisors.

A service he may then perform, before the next meeting of the county board, is to investigate, in the records of the county clerk, the credentials of the town for securing county aid, namely, whether its road and bridge tax for the past two years has been the maximum allowable, and whether the estimated cost of the bridge exceeds 12c. per $100 on the assessed valuation of the town.

If aid is granted, the superintendent is then automatically ordered to prepare or secure the necessary plans and specifications. Thus far, in my practice, I have applied to the State Highway Department for the plans for all county bridges. We have thus, for one thing, gained the advantage of the department's wide advertising of the work, as well as had the assurance of competent designing. As in case of bridges built by the town, I have done the local advertising, attended the lettings, put my name to the contracts, passed upon the completed work, and certified the cost of same, duly itemized, to both the county board and the local commissioners.

I might say, in passing, that the Board of Supervisors of Lee County has made the special committee for any county aid bridge consist of the Superintendent of Highways, the Supervisor for the Town, and the Highway Commissioner or Commissioners. The local interests are thus quite a large factor in the work, and are in cooperation with the superintendent.

Appeals from the decision of the commissioners to that of the superintendent introduce still other relations between them. My first was on a petition for narrowing a road to 40 feet. The commissioners had refused to grant the petition. This gave the right of appeal. But, at the hearing, I sustained the action of the commissioners.

Another appeal arose when the commissioners of a town were petitioned to vacate a certain road. They granted the prayer of the petitioners, and the superintendent felicitated himself that this case could not come before him, an appeal to the superintendent lying, by the terms of the law, only in case the petition is refused. But lo! When proceedings had advanced their long and wearisome course, as prescribed, to the stage of the "Final Order," it was found that appeal could now at last be taken. And it was so taken, and the decision was, after all, up to the superintendent. Much to my satisfaction, I was able to decide this appeal, also, in such way as to sustain the commissioners.

Moreover, where the commissioners of adjoining towns are unable to agree upon the proper division of the town-line road between the two towns, for the purpose of its maintenance, they are to leave the decision of the matter to the superintendent. Such a case has recently arisen in my county.

(b) We have thus far discussed relations arising from the county superintendent's statutory duties. A second class of relations develops from special duties assigned him by the State Highway Department as its deputy, and in conformity with the law.

Before the State office did any field work for the State aid roads, instructions were sent the county superintendent to look up the lines and corner stones, measure to the nearest corporation line, investigate the stone quarries and gravel pits near at hand, and do divers such things—a work that involved the employment of help.

Having no fund at his disposal for doing this, the writer took it up with the nearest highway commissioner of the town in which the road was to be laid, and secured him as an assistant. The idea was that the town in which the improvement was to be made could well afford to pay the bill of the assistant.

Other work that has been assigned by the head office creates the same situation. Such is that of gathering material for the township road maps, and for the annual reports on highways and bridges. My best solution, here as before, is in securing my help from the commissioners, who are to be paid by their towns.

Some counties, I understand, provide help for their superintendents in such cases, but there must be more, that like Lee County, have not done so. I wish there were a provision in the law, covering this occasional need of the superintendent, and putting him on surer ground in such matters.

(c) A third class of the county superintendent's duties, with consequent relations to the highway commissioners, is inferable from the general spirit of the road law, and from the provision that the superintendent shall:

"Advise and direct the highway commissioners of the several towns or districts in his county as to the best methods of repair, maintenance, and improvement of highways and bridges."

In the light of such instruction, the superintendent should hold himself in readiness to do things for the commissioners. He should be to them an ever present help in time of trouble. He should do cheerfully what they may find for his hand to do. If it is a new road to be laid out, tell the commissioners what legal steps to take, and if you are a surveyor, lay the road out for them. If they are having trouble with road drainage, ours is just the office to give them not only advice, but the necessary data as to levels. If farmers are troubling them by setting fences out into the highway, how can I, as a surveyor, better serve them or the public than by tracing up the lines and showing all parties exactly where the fences should be built?

If we can't do *all* such things, let us do as many of them as we can.

Not only may the superintendent consider himself an assistant to his highway commissioners, in laying out, improving and maintaining the roads, but he will find the commissioners coming to him for legal advice, also. The superintendent, himself, as an official of the county, has an adviser in the State's Attorney. But the State's Attorney is in no way bound to give gratuitous advice to the officials of a township. Their legal advice, consequently, has heretofore cost their town good money. If you and I are able to save the town some of this outlay, why is it not a privilege of the office, if not a duty, to do so?

It has been my experience, I think, to be asked two questions about the road law where I have been asked one about practical road construction. It would seem to me we need a P. J. Lucey in every county and that he should hold the appointment of superintendent

of highways therein. Under such circumstances it behooves us, I think, to heed the injunction of the psalmist, and upon the law meditate day and night.

It will be well if the superintendent is prepared to give an answer almost offhand to a hundred or so questions.

What are the steps necessary to be taken in the laying out of a new road?

What course of action is necessary in entering upon adjacent lands to cut a ditch for draining the highway?

How fill out and properly itemize commissioners' orders on the town treasurer?

May or may not a commissioner employ his own team, engine, etc., in road work at public expense?

What is the advisable road and bridge levy to make in any given town, and just how shall it be made?

How shall the offender be proceeded against who sets his fence out into the highway? Etc.

Then there are practical matters of road work upon which it will be well for the superintendent to have clear ideas, by no means forgetting, however, that the commissioners may have some good ideas of their own. In this case, the exchange of views may be interesting and helpful.

Some such matters might be:

The dragging of roads—the proper time, the proper drag, and the best arrangement for getting such dragging done.

The road machinery of the town—its housing and care, maintaining an inventory of the same.

The location and erection of guideposts.

Putting in requests for penitentiary stone for use on the roads.

I suppose every superintendent could add such suggestions to my list.

(d) I will close with a word as to some methods of communication between superintendent and commissioners.

Thus far we have discussed the casual meetings that occur in the routine of necessary road and bridge work.

Meetings called occasionally of the commissioners and other road men—one, two or three in a year—may be the source of much good. These should be in accessible places, at well-chosen times, and with some good talent as a drawing card. Hear from your own commissioners who have made a noticeable success along some line or other. Draw on the neighboring county superintendents and get the advantage of their ideas.

Use the county papers for your announcements and recommendations. Everywhere they are showing themselves more than willing to cooperate in all good roads work. If the superintendent's time admits, an occasional newspaper column under his name may furnish means of reaching the commissioners and getting the ideas of the superintendent into circulation.

I belive it would be a good idea for the superintendent to have stated office days, when road men of the county may be sure of finding him in. In counties of the first class I assume that few of the superintendents will have assistants who can keep the office open in the absence of the superintendent; so for the superintendents who are not provided with assistants,

I should think that keeping open office on, say, Saturday, might go far for the good of the cause.

Moreover, no superintendent will forget that he has the use of the mails as a means of communication with the commissioners, or that in this age of the world, men that are public-spirited enough to make good commissioners of highways have telephones in their homes, and that in this way they can ordinarily be reached at mealtime, at least, or in the evenings from seven o'clock on to bedtime.

If I had the necessary influence with the "powers that be" at Springfield, I'd see that the edition of "Illinois Highways," as they appear, should be large enough that every commissioner in Lee County would have his copy, and have it mailed to him direct from the publisher.

(e) Keep in touch with the commissioners. Call them up when wanting their help or wanting information from their locality. Help them as freely in return. Make the county superintendent so indispensable to them that they will wonder how they got along before they had one.

THE KANE COUNTY ROAD BUILDING OUTFITS.

By G. N. LAMB,
County Superintendent of Highways, Kane County.

The Forty-ninth General Assembly placed a law on the Statutes of Illinois, approved June 29, 1915, authorizing the county boards of supervisors to purchase machinery to enable counties to assist the respective townships in improving, repairing and maintaining township or district roads.

Twenty-four days after this date the supervisors of Kane County made an appropriation of $20,000 "for the purchase and necessary supervision of machinery for the building of township roads. The said machinery to operate under the direction of the county superintendent of highways and to be leased or loaned to the various townships under such rules and regulations as the road and bridge committee may devise."

Prior to this time a campaign had been conducted by the road and bridge committee of the county board and the county superintendent of highways to show the advantage to the road improvement throughout the county, of owning and operating such machinery.

Early in the year the county superintendent of highways recommended this step to the road and bridge committee with whom the scheme at once met with hearty endorsement. At the March, 1915, meeting of the supervisors he appeared before the whole board and outlined the policy to them. A short time later the road and bridge committee made a trip to Indiana to look at some road construction by machinery such as was being considered suitable for the Kane County work. It was next decided to build a demonstration half-mile of roadway near the central part of the county, and to accept the offer of certain companies to furnish the free use of their machinery for its construction. This road was built, and when near completion, the county board, acting as a committee of the whole, visited the demonstration and there voted to make the appropriation; which action was later sustained by the whole board by a vote of 30 to 6.

SELECTION OF MACHINERY.

With the fund at the disposal of the road and bridge committee, the problem then presented itself of selecting the machinery that was adapted to doing the particular work which this county most needed. It was found that 79 per cent of the roads of Kane County had been surfaced with various sorts of materials, ranging from cinders through gravel and crushed stone, to concrete or brick; and that 75 per cent of the entire road mileage was gravel. To be of the most assistance to the townships then, the solution of the problem was to furnish the machinery which would be useful in building better gravel roads than were possible under the old system, and at the same time to cheapen the entire cost of construction. The machinery selected therefore, was adapted to the production of gravel properly sized, graded or crushed; to the economic transportation of gravel over county roads of all descriptions, and to the proper formation of the road including the subgrade as well as the finished surface.

APPARATUS FOR PRODUCING ROAD METAL.

It was decided to do all hauling by means of motor trucks. To do this it became necessary to design a portable gravel producing plant which had a capacity exceeding 200 cubic yards per day, and which in loading the trucks would cause the least possible delay.

A 15-cubic-yard bin was designed so as to allow the truck to drive underneath and receive its load direct from the bottom of the hopper. The bin is also designed so that in transportation it may be lowered on to the truck, the lower part of the supports first being removed and placed in the body of the truck.

On account of the unusual height of bin designed to meet motor truck requirements and to avoid having an apparatus too top-heavy for transportation it was found not advisable to have the screen at its usual place at the top of the bin. The screen itself was made portable and performs the following functions: First, it separates the

THE PORTABLE GRAVEL-PRODUCING PLANT.

excess fine material, such as dirt and sand less than one-eighth inch in size; which is conveyed to a waste pile by a 12-inch by 30-foot conveyor-belt; second, the gravel less than 1½ inches in size is spouted to the elevator leading to the bin; third, the gravel exceeding 1½ inch in size is directed through the crusher and then into the same elevator which carries the finer gravel. The screen and elevator are driven from the crusher, and the crusher in turn by a gasoline tractor. An 18-inch by 40-foot conveyor-belt carries the gravel to the screen from a hopper, which is kept supplied from the pit by means of teams with slip scrapers.

The material fed into the plant, may be any grade of gravel or stone up to 9 or 10 inches in size. The finished product is a mixture of uncrushed gravel ⅛ inch to 1¼ inches in size, and the entire run of the crusher set to crush to 1½ inches. It is found that this product possesses excellent bonding as well as wearing qualities.

The maximum or minimum size of the entire product may be regulated by varying the size of openings in the screen and crusher.

TRANSPORTATION.

A 5-cubic-yard motor truck is provided for the hauling. The truck has steel tires 10 inches wide in front and 20 inches wide in the rear. This makes a very suitable arrangement for hauling over the extremely soft ground such as was encountered in the past season's work.

A 5-ton trailer also forms a part of the outfit and is suitable for use where the hauls are long and the roads are in condition to sustain the heavy loads.

SPREADING.

The load on the truck is discharged from the rear. The storage body is first tilted, then as the truck moves forward the endgate is swung open and the gravel is evenly distributed along the subgrade. The trailer has a bottom dump arrangement operated by means of a lever and the spreading is accomplished by pulling the trailer ahead as the gravel is discharged.

All the operations of discharging the truck and distributing the load are accomplished from the driver's seat. An extra man is required to discharge the trailer. When both vehicles are used, the trailer is discharged first, then detached; the truck is then discharged and after turning around, hitches again to the trailer at the reverse end.

ROLLING.

The rolling is accomplished by the steel tires of the motor truck. The combined weight of the truck with a load of 5 cubic yards is about 28,500 pounds with 70 per cent on the rear wheels. This gives about 500 pounds for each inch of rear tire width. The wheels are tapered; that is, the surfaces are pitched 1¼ inches so as to allow for properly crowning the road surface. The hauling is

all done over the road metal as the depositing progresses and thus no extra cost or labor is required for the rolling. The driver must see to it that as the hauling is done, all portions of the road are thoroughly rolled.

It has been found advisable to deposit the material in two layers so that any unevenness which developes after the first rolling may be remedied when the second course is applied.

In addition to the advantages to the road construction, it may be added here that the earth or gravel roads over which the hauling is done may be markedly improved or "ironed out" by the judicious driving of the steel tired truck.

GRADING.

The grading outfit consists of a 80 horse-power gasoline tractor, a scarifier and a 12-foot blade grader. This machinery may be used for preparing the roadbed for the gravel surface, or it may be used independently for the improvement of earth roads. In this capacity, some excellent results were secured during the three months in which it was in operation. It was found that the tractor not only has power to pull the 3½-ton 12-foot grader but that a second grader might be attached and thereby increase the efficiency of the outfit.

As an auxiliary to the grading outfit, the motor truck has been used successfully as the tractive power for both scarifier and grader in tearing up old gravel roads and reshaping the subgrade prior to resurfacing with gravel.

ADMINISTRATION.

No rental is charged to the townships for the use of the machinery, they being required to pay merely the operating expenses. The men operating the machines are regarded as county employees and work under instructions from the county superintendent of highways. The men are paid weekly from a fund deposited in a local bank at the county seat in the name of "Kane County Highway Department." The fuel, oil and supplies are also supplied by the same fund.

At the end of each week a statement is sent to the township showing an itemized account of the week's expenditures by the county department for labor, gasoline, oil and other supplies. As the remittances are received from the townships the fund at the bank is replenished. The weekly statements do not include such items of labor, teams or supplies as are furnished directly by the township.

In order to keep a correct record of all cost data, daily postal card reports are made out by the man in charge of his outfit and mailed to the office of the county superintendent of highways. The card shows the distribution of labor and other expense of the total day's work including men, teams, etc., furnished by the township.

The data on the cards is transferred to a book of cost data and the cards filed for future reference.

COSTS.

The outfits have not been long enough in use to enable us to give accurate cost data.

In one township the cost of grading 1.6 miles of road amounted to $43.25 per mile.

The cost of loading, screening and crushing gravel in one location was about $8.90 per day or 45 cents per cubic yard. In another location it amounted to about $17.87 per day or 26 cents per cubic yard; the variation being due to the length of haul. The cost of hauling gravel with the truck in one location amounted to about $7.00 per day or 51 cents per cubic yard which, when computing the distance hauled (5 miles) was 10 cents per yard-mile or 7 cents per ton-mile. In another location it amounted to $7.99 per day or 11 cents per cubic yard, which when computing the distance (1 mile) was 11 cents per yard-mile or 7 cents per ton-mile.

The various machines were secured from the following manufactures: The gas tractor from the Avery Company, Peoria; the motor truck from the White Company, Cleveland; the 5-ton trailer from the Troy Wagon Works Company, Troy, Ohio; the grader, scarifier, sprinkler-wagon and crusher from the Austin Western Co., Chicago, and the Gravel-handling machinery from the Stephens-Adamson Company, Aurora.

COUNTY SUPERINTENDENTS OF HIGHWAYS.

COUNTY.	NAME.	ADDRESS.
Adams	Lewis L. Boyer	Quincy, Ill.
Alexander	W. N. Moyers	Mound City, Ill.
Bond	R. O. Young	Sorento, Ill.
Boone	Thos. W. Humphrey	Belvidere, Ill.
Brown	W. O. Grover	Mt. Sterling, Ill.
Bureau	Frank R. Bryant	Princeton, Ill.
Calhoun	Jno. A. Earley	Batchtown, Ill.
Carroll	S. C. Campbell	Mt. Carroll, Ill.
Cass	John Goodell	Beardstown, Ill.
Champaign	Geo. C. Fairclo	Court House, Urbana, Ill.
Christian	C. A. Penington	Taylorville, Ill.
Clark	Zane Arbuckle	Marshall, Ill.
Clay	Howard Anderson	Louisville, Ill.
Clinton	Jno. T. Goldsmith	R. F. D. No. 3. Carlyle, Ill.
Coles	Harry Shinn	Mattoon, Ill.
Cook	Geo. A. Quinlan	Chicago, Ill.
Crawford	J. P. Lyon	Robinson, Ill.
Cumberland	Jno. A. Decker	Toledo, Ill.
DeKalb	Wm. C. Miller	Sycamore, Ill.
DeWitt	Melvin Tuggle	Clinton, Ill.
Douglas	L. O. Hackett	Tuscola, Ill.
DuPage	Eugene L. Gates	Wheaton, Ill.
Edgar	Karl J. Barr	Paris, Ill.
Edwards	Chas. C. Rice	Albion, Ill.
Effingham	Geo. T. Austin	Effingham, Ill.
Fayette	J. V. Waddell	Vandalia, Ill.
Ford	S. E. Wells	Piper City, Ill.
Franklin	Geo. F. Hampton	Benton, Ill.
Fulton	E. F. Motsinger	Canton, Ill.
Gallatin	Victor Pearce	Equality, Ill.
Greene	Irving Wetzel	Carrollton, Ill.
Grundy	Fred W. Stine	Morris, Ill.
Hamilton	Gregg Garrison	Garrison, Ill.
Hancock	Wm. Burgner	Carthage, Ill.
Hardin	W. M. Ball	Elizabethtown, Ill.
Henderson	C. R. A. Marshall	Stronghurst, Ill.
Henry	Jas. H. Reed	Cambridge, Ill.
Iroquois	Benj. Jordan	Watseka, Ill.
Jackson	Thos. G. Dunn	Gorham, Ill.
Jasper	S. A. Conner	Newton, Ill.
Jefferson	Tony C. Pitchford	Mt. Vernon, Ill.
Jersey	Chas. E. Warren	Jerseyville, Ill.
JoDaviess	Geo. E. Schroeder	Stockton, Ill.
Johnson	Chas. A. Hook	Vienna, Ill.
Kane	Geo. N. Lamb	St. Charles, Ill.
Kankakee	Frank M. Enos	Kankakee, Ill.
Kendall	Jno. D. Russell	Oswego, Ill.
Knox	Harley M. Butt	Galesburg, Ill.
Lake	Chas. E. Russell	Waukegan, Ill.
LaSalle	Geo. Farnsworth	Ottawa, Ill.
Lawerence	R. J. Benefield	Lawrenceville, Ill.
Lee	L. B. Neighbour	Dixon, Ill.
Livingston	R. W. Osborn	Pontiac, Ill.
Logan	Thos. S. Davy	Lincoln, Ill.
McDonough	W. M. Bonham	Macomb, Ill.
McHenry	C. L. Tryon	Woodstock, Ill.
McLean	Ralph O. Edwards	Bellflower, Ill.
Macon	Preston T. Hicks	Decatur, Ill.
Macoupin	O. B. Conlee	Carlinville, Ill.
Madison	W. E. Howden	Edwardsville, Ill.
Marion	Lee S. Trainor	Salem, Ill.
Marshall	L. H. Eldridge	Lacon, Ill.
Mason	H. V. Schoonover	Bishop, Ill.
Massac	J. Thrift Corlis	Metropolis, Ill.
Menard	C. M. Buckley	Petersburg, Ill.
Mercer	J. E. Russell	Aledo, Ill.
Monroe	Albert R. Gardner	Waterloo, Ill.
Montgomery	P. M. Bandy	Hillsboro, Ill.
Morgan	Lawrence V. Baldwin	Jacksonville, Ill.
Moultrie	T. C. Fleming	Sullivan, Ill.
Ogle	Alex Anderson	Polo, Ill.
Peoria	W. E. Emery	512 N. Glendale av., Peoria, Ill
Perry	Frank House	St. Johns, Ill.
Piatt	Thos. J. Anderson	Monticello, Ill.
Pike	H. H. Hardy	Hull, Ill.
Pope	W. T. S. Hopkins	Dixon Springs, Ill.
Pulaski	W. N. Moyers	Mound City, Ill.
Putnam	Mason Wilson	McNabb, Ill.
Randolph	Henry I. Barbeau	Prairie du Rocher, Ill.
Richland	G. W. Low	Olney, Ill.
Rock Island	Wallace Treichler	Rock Island, Ill.
St. Clair	David O. Thomas	Belleville, Ill.
Saline	Jno. P. Upchurch	Harrisburg, Ill.
Sangamon	Edwin White	Springfield, Ill.
Schuyler	W. S. Henderson	Rushville, Ill.
Scott	Geo. H. Vannier	Bluffs, Ill.
Shelby	N. A. Baxter	Shelbyville, Ill.
Stark	Wm. Slater	Wyoming, Ill.
Stephenson	O. G. Hively	Freeport, Ill.
Tazewell	Frank S. Cook	Mackinaw, Ill.
Union	Jos. F. Howenstein	Anna, Ill.
Vermilion	Wm. S. Dillon	Danville, Ill.
Wabash	Guy W. Courter	Mt. Carmel, Ill.
Warren	C. L. McClanahan	Monmouth, Ill.
Washington	Jno. A. Davenport, Jr	Nashville, Ill.
Wayne	Griff Koontz	Fairfield, Ill.
White	Geo. H. Brown	Carmi, Ill.
Whiteside	V. N. Taggett	Morrison, Ill.
Will	Will H. Smith	Joliet, Ill.
Williamson	P. B. Wilson	Marion, Ill.
Winnebago	Albertus R. Carter	Rockford, Ill.
Woodford	A. B. Hurd	El Paso, Ill.

SCHNEPP & BARNES, PRINTERS, SPRINGFIELD, ILL.

ILLINOIS HIGHWAYS

[Printed by authority of the State of Illinois.]

OFFICIAL PUBLICATION OF THE

STATE HIGHWAY DEPARTMENT

| VOL. III | SPRINGFIELD, ILLINOIS, JANUARY-FEBRUARY, 1916 | Nos. 1 and 2 |

THE OLD BERNADOTTE BRIDGE.

This old wooden truss bridge was built across the Spoon River, in Bernadotte Township, Fulton County, in 1845. Early in 1915 it was damaged by floods and it was decided to replace it with a modern structure. In the above picture note the temporary suspension span, put up after the bridge was damaged.

THE NEW BERNADOTTE BRIDGE.

The State Aid Bridge which takes the place of the old wooden structure shown above. Completed and accepted January 12, 1916.

THE BURLINGTON WAY

By CARL H. WEBER, Secretary-Treasurer of Burlington Good Roads Association

One of the pioneer organizations in the Central West for the fostering and crystalizing of good roads sentiment is the Burlington Way Good Roads Association of Illinois and Iowa.

Five years ago this association was founded by a band of better road enthusiasts in the central part of Illinois who had for many years struggled with the impassable Illinois roads and who decided to unite with the slogan "Pull Illinois Out of The Mud," as their motto.

Realizing the truth of the old adage that "Example is more forceful than precept" the association decided to build a stretch of model road that would serve as an example of what intelligent effort in the matter of road building could do with the ordinary earth roads.

This lead to the establishment of an automobile route from St. Louis, Missouri, through the central part of Illinois to Burlington, Iowa, and was the parent trial of what is now the Great Burlington Way Auto Trial.

The total mileage of the route at present, including its various divisions, is 790 miles, and the organization of the association has been carried out to the point where it has become one of the most powerful factors in the State for the molding of good roads sentiment.

The name "Burlington Way" was adopted because the parent trail followed very closely the right of way of the Burlington Railroad, and from the immense amount of local and tourist traffic on the trial each year, the cities through which the trail passes have come to look upon it, as, in fact, an auxiliary railroad, having many of the commercial advantages of the steel rail routes.

The official registered markings of the trail are a 6-inch band of orange flanked by two 6-inch bands of white, and every telephone pole on the entire route is carefully and distinctively banded in this manner. In addition official mileage signs are erected one mile either side of each village, town and city, along the trail giving the exact distance between adjoining places and also other interesting information.

Special red danger signs are erected at each dangerous turn and hill along the route warning the traveler of the need of caution, and specially designed and constructed warning signs are placed 300 feet either side of all railroad crossings on the trail, thus giving the driver ample notice of these dangerous places.

Particular attention is paid to the approaches of the railroad crossings in order to make them as safe as possible, and to do away with the bumps and jolts usually encountered in crossing the tracks with a car or other vehicle. Spaces between the ties are either permanently filled with crushed stone and cinders or heavy oak planking is used for the purpose of making a smooth and finished surface.

Every mile of the trail is under the personal supervision of an officer of the association who takes a special pride in the upkeep of the road, markings, and railroad crossings within his designated territory.

The parent trail, now extends from St. Louis, Mo., to Cedar Rapids, Iowa, and is divided into three divisions namely, the Southern Illinois Division from St. Louis to Beardstown, Illinois, the Northern Illinois Division from Beardstown to Burlington, Iowa; and the Iowa Division from Burlington to Cedar Rapids. Each division is placed under a supervisor who has general charge of the trail on his division.

Local "Burlington Way Booster Clubs" are organized in each village, town and city on the route and the presidents of these clubs by virtue of their office are annually elected as vice presidents of the association and have special supervision of the trail within a prescribed radius from their home city.

The home offices of the association for the year 1916 are maintained in Jacksonville, Illinois, where reside the president, Mr. W. J. Brady, and the secretary-treasurer, Mr. Carl H. Weber. Here all communications are attended to and the general policy of the association is outlined and executed.

Mr. Geo. F. Kuhlman of Beardstown is chairman of the legislative committee and lends the influence of the association to all measures affecting the road building policy of the State, which have been endorsed by the association or which are in accord with its accepted plans.

The inspection and promotion department is headed by Mr. H. C. Wilhite of Greenfield, Illinois, one of the pioneer good road boosters of Greene County, and the original promotor of the Burlington Way.

The association is officered throughout by men of recognized standing as good roads advocates and authorities, and the rank and file of the membership is composed of genuine community "boosters," who are actuated in their efforts solely by a desire to promote the cause of better roads for the welfare of their own community, and to maintain the splendid reputation of the Burlington Way as a great National highway. All service is rendered gratuitously, there being no salaried officers or employees, and thousands of dollars are contributed annually by the officers and the membership at large for furthering the work of the association.

During the past year, in response to an insistent demand, several new divisions have been established in accordance with the official rules of the association.

The Springfield Division extending from the parent trail at Greenfield; is completed by way of the capital city of Illinois, Springfield, as far as Bloomington and in the spring will be continued to Chicago, the great metropolis of the Central West.

The Beardstown-Rock Island Division connection with the parent trail at Frederick, Illinois, is designed to carry a heavy traffic and to serve a populous territory in the northwestern part of the State. This divi... divides at Astoria, one route running to Rock Isl... via Bushnell and Monmouth and the other rou... ing the same terminus by way of Lewiston, Ca... Galesburg. From Rock Island the route exten... Witt, Iowa, where a junction is made with th... Highway. The officials of Peoria County ha... appropriated $13,000 to connect with the tra... ington. This money will be expended on th... tween Peoria and Farmington.

The Burlington Way crosses several pr... east and west highways, which afford direct con... with the various large cities throughout the ...est. Junctions are made with the Big Four T... Alton and Greenfield. The Pike's Peak Ocean-t... High-way is crossed at Jacksonville and S... ; the

Cannon Ball Route at Macomb, Bushnell and Galesburg and the Lincoln Highway is intercepted at Cedar Rapids and DeWitt, Iowa.

The trail keeps well back from the Illinois River, running on the higher levels of the State, thus avoiding the danger of washouts and marshy roads, and runs through what is probably the richest farming districts in the world; the official centers of the farming industry in the United States in the various items of improvement, yield and valuation being a few miles south of Jacksonville.

The attractive and well-kept homes of the prosperous farmers bordered by waving fields of grain, presents a picture that is pleasing to the eye of the tourist and makes a trip along this highway one of great enjoyment. The farmers living along the route take a marked pride in keeping the roadway in excellent condition, and in addition are always willing to extend to the traveler every hospitality possible.

From the southern portion of the trail at St. Louis and Alton, where the autoist bowls along over a smooth roadbed on the high wooded bluffs overlooking the majestic Mississippi River, in all its grandeur; to the northern section where the "Father of Waters" is again crossed at Fort Madison a few miles north of man's wonderful achievement, the great Keokuk Dam, where the beauties of Lake Cooper, spread themselves out before the admiring gaze of the traveler, the "Way" is full of pleasing and startling scenic surprises.

In response to a growing demand, a side trip is being arranged from East Fort Madison, Illinois, along the east bank of the Mississippi through the quaint old Mormon village of Nauvoo, to the Keokuk Dam, returning to the trail on the west bluffs of the river, over a magnificent stretch of hard road to Fort Madison, Iowa. The scenery along this route is most wonderful and enchanting and several hours can be spent very profitably in viewing the great dam and power house, which indeed rank among the modern wonders of the world.

In addition to the scenic advantages many points of marked historical interest lie along the trial. Among these may be mentioned the old Cass County courthouse in Beardstown, where Lincoln as a young lawyer won the famous Armstrong murder trial; and the Lovejoy Hill, one mile below Rockbridge, Illinois. Here Owen P. Lovejoy, made his remarkable anti-slavery speech before twenty-five thousand people on the anniversary of the murder of his brother Elijah P. Lovejoy, several years before at Alton for his ceaseless opposition to slavery. Twenty-four sheep and seven cattle were barbequed at this tremendous gathering and it is conceded by authorities that this spot marks the birthplace of the Republican party, as fully five thousand votes were changed that day by Lovejoy's fiery oratory. The spot is marked by a large memorial sign, and in the city of Alton, stands an imposing monument erected to the memory of Elijah P. Lovejoy by the citizens of Illinois.

The large State institutions at Alton, Jacksonville and Lincoln should receive the attention of the traveler as well as the arsenal at Rock Island and the I. O. O. F. Orphans' Home at Lincoln; the stately capitol building and the monument and tomb of Lincoln are among the many interesting points in Springfield.

Many noted colleges and schools are located in the various cities on the trail, among them being the oldest college in the west, Illinois College; and the largest woman's college in the west, the Illinois Woman's College; both located at Jacksonville. A handsome pagoda, also at Jacksonville, marks the spot where work was commenced on the first steam railroad laid in the State of Illinois. This was known as the Northern Cross Railroad and ran from Jacksonville to Meredosia, later being extended to Springfield.

Other points of interest are covered by the 1916 official guide of the Burlington Way which is now in the hands of the printers and which will be issued shortly. This guide contains the revised maps and other items of information with regard to the "Way" and will be mailed to any address by the secretary of the association upon receipt of two 2-cent stamps to cover postage.

Almost the entire mileage of the trail in the State of Illinois has been designated as State Aid Road and during the coming spring many miles will be permanently paved with brick and concrete, while several hundred miles will be permanently graded and oiled under the supervision of the various State and county engineers.

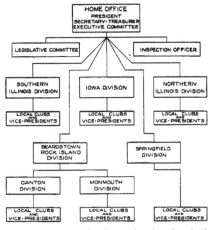

ORGANIZATION
OF
BURLINGTON WAY
GOOD ROADS ASSOCIATION

Among the powerful factors in advancing the interests of the association are the annual conventions held in August of each year and the various division "round-ups" and officers' gatherings.

The division "round-ups" are held at various times throughout the year and are largely attended by the officers and visiting delegations who make the trip in gaily decorated automobiles with quartettes and brass bands to add to the enjoyment and enthusiasm of the occasion. Division "round-ups" for 1915 were held at Greenfield, White Hall, Astoria (2), Medora, and Lincoln and were attended by thousands of people. Banquets and officers' conferences were held at Jacksonville, Springfield, Galesburg, Rock Island, and Burlington, Iowa.

It is predicted by the officials of the highway that the fifth annual convention which will be held this year in Jacksonville will be the greatest good roads gathering held in Illinois.

(Continued on Page 10.)

ROAD MAKING MACHINERY, ITS USE AND MAINTENANCE.

 By T. R. AGG, Professor of Highway Engineering, Iowa State College, Ames, Iowa.

Road making machinery has undergone important changes during the past decade and particularly during the past five years. The requirements of machinery for constructing the modern surfaced road, and for performing the earth work incidental to it, has been met by machinery manufacturers who have modified old types of machinery or have developed entirely new designs to meet the new conditions.

Many of the changes have been primarily changes in size and capacity, or merely changes in details of construction that were necessary to adapt the machinery to the modified working conditions. It is not a mere coincidence that many of the improvements were brought about by the exigencies of contract highway construction. Experience seems to indicate very conclusively that many of the changes in types and capacities of road machinery would never have been made had road work continued on a day labor or force account basis. The pressure of competitive bidding, together with the lessons contractors have learned by more or less costly experience, has led them to seek reductions in costs and consequently greater profits by securing more efficient types of machinery. As a result we find that modern road making machinery is each year becoming better adapting for the work it is to perform, is made of better materials than formerly and is being better cared for and more efficiently used.

THE TREND IN ROAD MAKING MACHINERY.

The trend in road making machinery is toward greater capacity and the elimination of common labor, and to a considerable extent the elimination of horse-drawn types of equipment. A study of cost records shows the reason. Formerly the item of labor constituted about 50 per cent of the cost of road construction and obviously it will for a long time be a very large factor, as it is in other kinds of engineering construction. Nevertheless the elimination of an appreciable amount of muscular labor is often a step toward cheapening the cost of construction and therefore, reducing to some extent the financial burden involved in the construction of permanent roads.

Many of the types of machinery formerly employed in railroad construction and in those other kinds of construction involving the handling of large quantities of coarse materials such as earth, stone or concrete aggregates, have been modified to meet the needs of the road builder, and these constitute by far the larger part of the available equipment for road building.

Another significant change that has taken place has been in the capacity of the old types of road making machinery. The blade grader, designed to be drawn by six or eight horses, is a toy beside the heavy graders now designated for traction hauling.

These changes have brought about a new set of operating conditions which are often little appreciated, and frequently neglected or disregarded.

INCREASE IN INVESTMENT FOR ROAD MACHINERY.

Obviously the heavy types of equipment are more expensive than are those formerly used, and this increased investment can only be justified by a corresponding increase in output. This necessitates the systematic and intelligent operation of the equipment under intelligent supervision. Not only must this expensive equipment be used under skilled supervision but it must also be handled by expert operators. Expensive machinery in the hands of the unskilled, the careless or indifferent operator deteriorates with fearful rapidity. Many instances have been brought to our attention where high-grade and expensive machinery has deteriorated 50 per cent in one season, due wholly to the lack of intelligent care in the operation. In many instances county and township boards have been forced to employ unskilled operators and train them for the work. As time goes by there will be available a better supply of skilled labor for the operation of tractors, rollers, graders, shovels, concrete mixers, bituminous mixing plants, oil distributors and similar modern road-making machinery. Until such a supply is available the taxpayers of the various commonwealths must pay a heavy price for the training of these men. This will show as an excessive depreciation of the road-making machinery. There is much reason to believe that in the long run the commonwealth would profit by doing a considerable part of its construction work by contract, where expensive machinery is being employed, letting the contractor stand the depreciation of equipment. It may be said that in the last analysis the community will pay the depreciation through the medium of the price paid for contract work. This is true to only a limited extent because under a system of competitive bidding they will pay only the depreciation charged by the most proficient contractors and those who are experienced enough to know that it is economy to maintain good operators and therefore have a minimum depreciation on machinery. Public officials might well take cognizance of the same fact.

VOLUME OF WORK NECESSARY FOR MODERN MACHINERY.

With the older types of machinery, which were of moderate cost and of small capacity, economy was possible in their use even though a relatively small amount of work was available in a season, but with the use of modern machinery of large capacity, economy can only be secured when the equipment can be kept busy throughout the construction season. There must be available a large enough volume of work to insure continuous operation. This is a condition that is not encountered in every community nor is its importance properly appreciated by public officials. The fixed charges on expensive machinery are high and must be distributed over a large volume of work in order to show reasonable unit prices.

An illustration of this point may be pertinent here. A certain Iowa county, which had a number of heavy grades to reduce, purchased a traction steam shovel and the necessary dump wagons for hauling material. It was possible to show on paper that this investment was fully justified by the conditions in the county and by the amount of work to be done. After a year's use it now becomes apparent that the unit cost for handling earth with this equipment is considerably higher than the contract prices for similar work which is done with the elevating grader and dump wagons or with wheelers.

The reason is not difficult to find. The machinery was operated by unskilled men, and work was not laid out enough in advance to insure continuity of operation. The shovel was moved from place to place in the county without regard to the cost of such moving and apparently with little thought as to where it would work next. The result has been that the cost of moving, the delays in moving, and the low operating efficiency has more than compensated for the inherent efficiency of the method. The average cost for moving earth with a 500-ft. haul was 25 cents per cu. yd., while the average contract price for the same haul is 20 cents.

MAINTENANCE OF EQUIPMENT.

The more expensive and complicated equipment becomes, the more expensive maintenance becomes. If an ordinary blade grader breaks down the replacement of a few bolts or at the most a few hours work by a blacksmith will put it in work order again, but if the more expensive machinery, such as the heavy tractor, breaks down, it frequently means that repair parts must be ordered from the factory and that considerable time will be lost while waiting for the parts to arrive, and that considerable additional time will be required for replacing the broken parts and readjusting the mechanism. Inability on the part of the average operator to make the finer adjustments frequently results in repeated breakdowns which could be avoided if expert mechanics could make the adjustments. On one piece of road work during the past summer five days were lost on account of the inability of the local machinist to properly babbit and adjust the bearings on the pump shaft of a heavy tractor. This delay was not only expensive in that the pay for several "straight time" men went on while the work was at a stand still but also because when the machine was back in commission unfavorable weather developed resulting in additional delay, and damage to partly completed work. This would have been avoided and the work would have been in condition to withstand wet weather had it been possible to carry out the earth work as originally planned. Adequate maintenance of the machinery is necessary not only from the standpoint of efficiency in carrying on the construction work dependent on the machinery but also for the sake of the machinery itself. Repairs must be made promptly and properly or the apparatus will suffer serious damage and abnormal depreciation.

It frequently happens that some one machine is the nucleus about which the entire construction organization is built and if for any reason this equipment is temporarily out of commission the whole organism is disrupted with a consequent loss of time which on construction in our middle western climate often means a serious loss of money.

LOST TIME AS A FACTOR IN COST.

There is a tendency to make too small an allowance for lost time in the operation of road machinery, particularly under the climatic conditions encountered in the Middle West.

One year ago a study was made of a number of macadam road outfits which indicated that under ordinary conditions the machinery could be operated at full capacity for only about 60 per cent of the time during the construction season which, as I recall it, was from June 1 to November 1. This study also showed that the mechanical equipment for hauling road materials could, under average conditions, work only about 50 per cent of the time during the construction season.

(Continued on Page 10.)

FUNDS MUST BE SET ASIDE FOR ROAD DRAGGING.

The attention of all commissioners of highways is called to Sections 62 and 107 of the Revised Road and Bridge Law, which provides for the setting aside of a definite sum of money to be used for dragging the roads in the township or district and also confer authority upon the commissioners of highways to have such roads dragged.

These sections read as follows:

62. ROAD AND BRIDGE MONEY—HOW USED.] All road and bridge moneys of any town or road district shall be held by the treasurer of the road and bridge fund subject to the order of the commissioners of highways: Provided, that not less than three ($3.00) dollars nor more than five ($5.00) dollars per mile per annum shall be taken and appropriated from the road and bridge fund of each township, or district to be known as a road drag fund to pay for the work of dragging earth roads in the township or district as provided in section 107 hereof, and that the enforcement of the law as to what roads in the township or district shall be dragged and as to how often the same shall be dragged, shall be lodged in the hands of the commissioners or commissioner of highways. [Amended by Act approved June 24, 1915.

107. ROAD DRAGS—AUTHORITY AND USE.] (A) The commissioners or commissioner of highways of their respective townships or district in the several counties of this State are hereby authorized to have earth roads dragged at all seasons of the year whenever the surface of the roads become rough so they will not properly shed the water which falls upon them.

It shall be the duty of the commissioners or commissioner of highways to designate from time to time what roads in the township or district shall be dragged. He shall cause the work to be done by giving the parties contracted with for the performance of such services such notice as shall be deemed sufficient; he shall on or before the 15th day of September in each year contract with as many suitable persons as he deems necessary to drag the roads in the townhip or district for that year, but shall not apportion the dragging of more than six miles of road to any one person. The commissioners or commissioner of highways may at any time cancel such contract or contracts for dragging the roads when the stipulations herein contained have not been properly complied with or when the work is not done in a satisfactory manner: Provided, however, that in making contracts for road dragging such contracts shall not be let for a sum exceeding one dollar ($1.00) per mile for each time dragged: Provided, further, that the width required to be dragged shall be not less than 14 feet, if the width of the roadway will permit.

(B) OBSTRUCTING DRAINAGE.] It shall be unlawful for any person or persons to place loose earth, weeds, sods, or other vegetable matter on the portion of a road which has been dragged and so maintained in good condition, or to place any material in such a manner as to interfere with the free flow of water from the dragged portion of the road to the side gutters or ditches: Provided, that this restriction shall not apply to deposits of earth or other material that may be made by the authority of the proper road officials, if necessary for filling or raising the elevation of a given section of road or other necessary construction work.

(C) TRAVEL REGULATED.] It shall also be unlawful for any person or persons to drive or cause to be driven a vehicle of any description in or upon any portion of the highway immediately after the same has been dragged and before such portion of the highway shall have partially dried out or frozen: Provided, that nothing in this section shall apply in those instances where it is impossible to drive with safety at one side of said dragged portion of the road, or where a vehicle does not make a rut on such dragged portion of the road, injurious to the work accomplished by use of the road drag or where a vehicle does not make a rut nearer than nine (9) feet from the center of the dragged portion of the road.

(D) Any violation of any of the provisions of this section by the commissioners or commissioner of highways or any person or persons who may be required under contract to drag district roads or neglect on the part of any township clerk to set aside the funds required by Section 62 of this Act shall, on conviction thereof, subject the offender to be fined not less than ten dollars ($10.00) nor more than twenty-five ($25.00) for the first offense, and for each subsequent offense shall be

(Continued on Page 12.)

Short Course in Highway Engineering
HELD AT THE UNIVERSITY OF ILLINOIS

The first short course in highway engineering was held at the University of Illinois in 1914, and was arranged for the purpose of affording to road officials and workers and all others interested in road improvement an opportunity for discussion and instruction concerning highway work.

The purpose of such a course is well described by the announcement made by the university, which reads:

"This course is intended to help men who are interested in the building and maintenance of roads. It has for its object the diffusion of information concerning the principles and the discussion of the latest improvements in this important work for the public benefit. It is hoped to bring together some of the men who have been doing things, and to make available, to all persons who can attend, the results of the latest and best experience in road building. The course is open to all persons whether engineers or not. It should be of particular interest and value to county superintendents of highways, township highway commissioners, city engineers, contractors, and others who in their official duties or private practice have to plan or work upon county or city roads. It is intended also to disseminate information concerning the construction and maintenance of bridges, culverts, drains, and similar structures which are necessary for the best use of the highways. The addresses and demonstrations will be of value to all persons who have occasion to build or repair roads whether as engineer, contractor, or foreman. All who are interested in road improvement are invited.

"It is not expected that the product of the short course will be experienced, efficient road engineers; but it is believed that even experienced civil engineers who have not made a specialty of road engineering may receive valuable help. It is believed also that men without experience in general engineering or in road work may receive important suggestions concerning road and bridge construction."

The first short course, though occupying but two weeks' time, resulted in so much good and was so enthusiastically received by those in attendance, county superintendents of highways, highway commissioners, contractors, etc., that it was decided to make the course an annual affair.

Last year the course had to be abandoned at the last moment because of the fear of spreading the dread foot and mouth disease which was so prevalent at that time.

This year the course was held at the University of Illinois at Urbana from January 10 to 21. The university adopted this year a plan somewhat different from that followed during the previous course.

The mornings were devoted to what might be termed regular classes in road and bridge work. Those in attendance were divided into two sections, designated section A and section B. These two sections alternated with each other in the mornings for an hour and a half discussion of roads and then an hour and a half discussion of bridge work; the class work in roads being in direct charge of Mr. C. C. Wiley, and the work in bridges under Mr. N. B. Gaver, both of the civil engineering department. This morning work followed a prearranged schedule, as will be noted from the program below. The men in charge of these sections each morning encouraged the "scholars" to discuss many of their problems and in this manner much light was thrown on the various details of the work.

The afternoon sessions of the course consisted of talks and lectures concerning matters of timely interest to road builders.

The evening programs were made up of lectures more "popular" in subject than the rather technical work of the morning and afternoon.

Probably one of the greatest benefits that comes from a meeting or course of this kind is the opportunity

ENGINEERING BUILDING, UNIVERSITY OF ILLINOIS.

it affords for an interchange of ideas and experiences on various phases of road work.

The road builder, from the very nature of his work, must necessarily draw from the experience of others in the performance of many of his duties. He is constantly being confronted by new problems and any opportunity which is afforded him to find out what problems are being met and how they are being met by others in his field is a benefit to him, having a value which is much greater than is ordinarily thought.

An opportunity for such discussion was afforded by the morning sessions on road and bridge work. As the program was followed through, many questions of practice were brought up and discussed. Those in attendance were enthusiastic in their praises of these class periods.

Other departments of the university cooperated with the civil engineering department in making this course a success, and the university as a whole is to be highly commended for their earnest efforts in aiding the road builders of the State.

Special credit is due to Professor F. H. Newell, head of the civil engineering department who arranged for, and was in charge of the course, and to Mr. C. C. Wiley and Mr. N. B. Garver of the civil engineering department who were in charge of the morning class work in roads and bridges.

The program of the course is given below. It will be noted that it is well balanced and is handled by men who are experts in their chosen field.

PROGRAM.

Room 221, Engineering Building.

MONDAY, JANUARY 10, 1916.

Afternoon Session.

2:00 P. M. Registration.
3:00 P. M. Address of Welcome........................
    Edmund Janes James, LL. D., Ph. D.,
        President of the University.
    W. F. M. Goss, D. Eng'g.,
        Dean of the College of Engineering.
4:00 P. M. Social Hour.

Evening Session.

7:30 P. M. U. S. Reclamation Service and Highways (Lecture illustrated by colored lantern slides)
    ....Dr. F. H. Newell,
Professor of Civil Engineering and Former Director of U. S. Reclamation Service.

TUESDAY, JANUARY 11, 1916.

Morning Session.

Roads—Surveys, Drawings and Records.
Bridges—Surveys for Bridges.

Afternoon Session.

1:00 P. M. Maintenance of Earth Roads......W. S. Gearhart,
    State Engineer of Kansas.
2:00 P. M. The Specifications of the State Highway Department......................H. E. Bilger,
    Road Engineer, Illinois Highway Department.
3:00 P. M. Oiling Clay, Gumbo and Sand Roads......
    ....W. S. Gearhart,
    State Engineer of Kansas.

Evening Session.

7:30 P. M. Effect of Roads upon Rural Life............
    ....Dr. R. E. Hieronymus,
Community Adviser, University of Illinois.

WEDNESDAY, JANUARY 12, 1916.

Morning Session.

Roads—Earth Roads and Sub-Grades.
Bridges—Area of Waterway.

Afternoon Session.

1:00 P. M. Oiling of Earth Roads.........B. H. Piepmeier,
    Maintenance Engineer, Illinois Highway Department.
2:00 P. M. Road Management...............Dr. L. I. Hewes,
    Chief of Economics and Maintenance, U. S. Office of Public Roads and Rural Engineering, Washington, D. C.

Evening Session.

7:30 P. M. Illustrated Lecture: Construction of Macadam Roads.................Dr. L. I. Hewes,
    Chief of Economics and Maintenance, U. S. Office of Public Roads and Rural Engineering, Washington, D. C.

THURSDAY, JANUARY 13, 1916.

Morning Session.

Roads—Maintenance of Earth Roads.
Bridges—Location of Bridges and Economics of Bridge Design.

Afternoon Session.

1:00 P. M. The Roads of Indiana.......Prof. G. E. Martin,
    Purdue University.
2:00 P. M. Oiled Earth Roads.............B. H. Piepmeier,
    Maintenance Engineer, Illinois Highway Department.
2:00 P. M. General Discussion:
    (a) Success of Road Day;
    (b) Cooperation of Chambers of Commerce, Automobile Clubs, etc., in Road Building;
    (c) Stimulating Interest in Better Roads.

Evening Session.

7:30 P. M. Asphaltic Highway Construction (Lecture Illustrated with moving pictures)........
    ....W. P. Blackwood,
    Barber Asphalt Paving Co.

FRIDAY, JANUARY 14, 1916.

Morning Session.

Roads—Oiled Earth Roads.
Bridge—Bridge Failures and Their Causes.

Afternoon Session.

1:00 P. M. Road Making Machinery—Its Use and Maintenance.........................T. R. Agg,
    Professor of Highway Engineering, State College, Ames, Iowa.
2:00 P. M. General Discussion. Safety First in Highway Structures: Railway and Highway Grade Crossings, Road Signs, Guard Rails, etc.
3:00 P. M. Choice of Type of Road and Principles of Design................................T. R. Agg,
    Professor of Highway Engineering, State College, Ames, Iowa.

Evening Session.

7:30 P. M. Use of Petroleum Products in Road Work..
    (Lecture illustrated with samples of oil)..
    ....James A. Cannon,
    National Refining Co., Cleveland, Ohio.

SATURDAY, JANUARY 15, 1916.

Morning Session.

8:00 A. M. Economics of Bridge Floors.......Clifford Older
    Bridge Engineer, Illinois Highway Department.
9:00 A. M. Shall the County Buy Road Building Machinery.........................G. N. Lamb,
    Superintendent of Highways, Kane County.
10:00 A. M. Laboratory Demonstrations:
    Sec. A, in Road Laboratory. Rattler Test of Paving Brick and Tests of Road Stone.
        R. L. Bowling,
        Assistant in Road Laboratory.
        C. C. Wiley,
        Instructor in Highway Engineering.
    Sec. B, in Room 221. Tests of Sand and Gravel.........................N. B. Garver,
    Instructor in Highway Bridge Engineering.

(Continued on Page 11.)

ILLINOIS HIGHWAYS.

Published Monthly by the
State Highway Department,
Springfield, Illinois.

ILLINOIS HIGHWAY COMMISSION.

A. D. GASH, *President.*
S. E. BRADT, *Secretary.*
JAMES P. WILSON.

WM. W. MARR, *Chief State Highway Engineer.*

BUREAU OF ROADS.

H. E. BILGER, *Road Engineer.*
M. W. WATSON, *Assistant Road Engineer.*
C. M. HATHAWAY, *Office Engineer.*
L. P. SCOTT, *Chief Draftsman.*

BUREAU OF BRIDGES.

CLIFFORD OLDER, *Bridge Engineer.*
G. F. BURCH, *Assistant Bridge Engineer.*
A. W. CONSOER, *Office Engineer.*

BUREAU OF MAINTENANCE.

B. H. PIEPMEIER, *Maintenance Engineer.*
F. T. SHEETS, *Assistant Maintenance Engineer.*

BUREAU OF TESTS.

F. L. ROMAN, *Testing Engineer.*
W. C. ADAMS, *Chemist.*

BUREAU OF AUDITS.

J. M. McCOY, *Chief Clerk.*
T. W. DIECKMANN, *Department Editor.*
R. R. McLEOD, *General Bookkeeper.*
G. E. HOPKINS, *Property Clerk.*

DIVISION ENGINEERS.

R. L. Bell, Buchanan-Link Bldg., Paris, Ill.
H. B. Bushnell, 144 Fox St., Aurora, Ill.
J. E. Huber, Wise Building, Mt. Vernon, Ill.
A. H. Hunter, 302 Apollo Theater Bldg., Peoria, Ill.
C. M. Slaymaker, 510 Metropolitan Bldg., E. St. Louis, Ill.
H. E. Surman, 614 People's Bank Bldg., Moline, Ill.
Fred Tarrant, State Highway Department, Springfield, Ill.

Address all communications in regard to "Illinois Highways," to State Highway Department, Springfield, Illinois.

CONTENTS.

Now is a good time to put that road drag to work.

* * *

Remember that a road that is well drained is easily maintained.

* * *

The University of Illinois is conducting some tests on monolithic brick pavement slabs.

* * *

The Peru Business Men's Association recently purchased 200 roads signs which will be placed along the highways leading into Peru. The signs are 16 by 20 inches, with black letters on a yellow background. They show the direction and distance to the city.

* * *

The Harris Trust and Savings and the First Trust and Savings Banks of Chicago bought a million dollars worth of the Vermilion County road bonds, paying $983,400 for them.

* * *

Are you a good roads booster? If not, why not?

* * *

"The Corn Belt Highway" is the name which the Bloomington Association of Commerce has given the preferred route from Chicago to St. Louis. Steps will be taken to mark the trail from Bloomington to Chicago.

* * *

Commissioner Albert J. Hale of Canton Township, Brown County, recently distributed about twenty road drags in the township. Those who use them will be paid $1 a mile.

* * *

A community is judged by its roads. What impression would your roads give a stranger?

* * *

F. H. Clapp, a well known good roads booster of Mazon, Illinois, has been elected president of the Grundy County Good Roads Association. Other officers are: John Trotter, Coal City, first vice president; H. C. Gorham, Vienna, second vice president; Thor Tesdall, Nettle Creek, third vice president; H. P. Dwyer, Aux Sable, treasurer; Ray Holderman, Morris, secretary.

* * *

Fulton County has come into line with other progressive counties of the State and has organized a county good roads association. H. H. Atherton of Lewiston is president; J. W. Strong of Canton, secretary; Jerome Lawson of Fairview, first vice president; J. P. Lingenfelter of Buckheart Township, treasurer.

* * *

Don't forget that the testing laboratory of the State Highway Department is available for the testing of all materials which are to be used on the roads. There are no charges made and only two conditions to be met: Send the material to be tested *prepaid.* Mark the package plainly, showing where it is from and who sent it.

* * *

If your township or county is going to do any oiling this year, better request us to send you a copy of our Bulletin No. 11 "Surface Oiling of Earth Roads." It tells a lot about oiling roads and how to get the best results. It's free.

* * *

But remember, oiling is a maintenance proposition only; and, as C. C. Wiley of the University of Illinois recently said:

"When we have oiled ten thousand years
    Our roads where'er they run,
We've no less days to oil these ways
    Than when we first begun!"

The association of county superintendents at a meeting held at Urbana during the time of the short course in highway engineering adopted a resolution, thanking and commending the university for giving this course. The following are the officers who were elected to serve this association for the coming year: President, R. W. Osborn, Pontiac; vice president, H. B. Wilson, Marion; secretary-treasurer, W. E. Emery, Peoria.

* * *

The fifth report of the State Highway Department is now being prepared. This report will cover the work of the department for the years 1913-14-15.

* * *

The work of the State Highway Department will be done this year under a set of new specifications which have just been completed. These specifications represent not only the knowledge and experience of the men of the highway department, but they are a composite product, containing suggestions and ideas received from other engineers, material men and contractors. These suggestions were received by sending the original draft of the specifications to these men, asking for their criticism and then finally revising the specifications embodying in the revision the best points brought out by such criticisms.

* * *

How much is our "mud" tax? This will give you an idea of it. Governor Capper of Kansas recently watched an actual test made to determine the difference in the cost of hauling grain on good and bad roads. On a hard road there had been delivered eleven tons of grain in one trip by one team, using five wagons. On the mud road two tons was all that could be delivered by a single team. The haul was four miles in each case. The teams could make three trips a day or twenty-four miles, team travel. On the mud road the team delivered six tons a day at a cost of $4.50 per team and wagon, or 75 cents a ton for the haul. On the hard road thirty-three (33) tons were delivered during the day. The cost was $4.50 for the team and wagon, or a cost of 19.7 cents a ton for the four-mile haul. The difference in this case was 55 cents a ton in favor of good roads. There were 450 tons to be delivered in this particular instance and the saving effected by the hard roads figured on the basis of the time required, was $264.

* * *

Again we say it: Are you a good roads booster? If not, why not?

* * *

Assisting counties which are contemplating bond issues for road improvement has been no small part of the work of the State Highway Department for the past five or six months. Assistance has been given the following counties in working up plans for a complete county system of roads to be improved by means of a bond issue: Stephenson, Winnebago, Lake, Dekalb, Kane, Dupage, Cook, LaSalle, Will, Livingston, Kankakee, Iroquois, Adams, Sangamon, Vermilion, Madison, Edgar, Clark, Marion, St. Clair, Edwards, Jackson, Williamson, White, Gallatin.

* * *

What are good roads worth? Read the following statements by Chas. P. Root concerning the famous concrete roads of Wayne County, Michigan, and see what these roads have done for that county:

"Bearing the burden of experiment, Wayne County, Michigan, has set the pace, in the matter of building permanent hard roads. It has been discovered that money spent in road improvement of the right sort has made a profit of 125 per cent a year for the county.

"The county spent $2,000,000 on construction and maintenance in the eight years from 1906 to 1914, inclusive, and in this period the assessed valuation of property in the county, outside of the city of Detroit, increased from $62,707,000 to $114,548,120, or 82 per cent.

"Of this increase 35 per cent, or $22,000,000, is credited to road improvement, because the assessed valuation of Detroit increased only 47.7 per cent. The increase in county valuation above the rate of increase in the city was eleven times the cost of road work, or 100 per cent profit in eight years on the total investment in improved roads.

"More than 125 miles of concrete road have been put down by the Wayne County commissioners since the system was adopted in 1906, and the roads built with the $2,000,000 bond issue are still in good condition and give promise of more than outliving the bonds. The commissioners state in their report for last year that they never have had to take up and replace a single twenty-five foot section since they have been developing this type of road, although some of the roads have been down more than seven years.

"Every mile of durable road laid is cutting down the cost of upkeep. Last year the commissioners had forty-five miles more roadway to care for than the year before, yet, they spent $5,178 less for maintenance, notwithstanding they have supervision over 1,245 miles of other type of road, such as macadam and gravel, outside of incorporated cities and villages.

"It is estimated that 90 per cent of the traffic in the county is carried on 20 per cent of the road mileage and that concrete construction should be continued until there are about 350 miles of such roads."

DO YOU KNOW?—THAT IN ILLINOIS THERE ARE 2 AUTOS FOR EACH MILE OF ROAD—THAT AUTO FEES IN 1915 WERE $924.905.—THAT ALL AUTO FEES COLLECTED ARE GIVEN BACK AS STATE AID.

LIGHTS ON ALL VEHICLES.

By JAMES H. REED,
County Superintendent of Highways, Henry County.

A few years ago a bill was introduced in our State Legislature requiring all vehicles to be equipped with lights. Much objection was raised on the ground that on wagons and private conveyances lights would be a trouble and expense not worth while, and, in the end, the bill was defeated. That lights on vehicles are some trouble and expense can not be denied. But are they not worth while?

Even before automobiles came into use, there was more or less danger of collision on the roads at night. It was not as great as now because horse-drawn vehicles are slower than automobiles and because horses have good sight and hearing. Nevertheless, we sometimes heard of locked wheels, one rig running into the other and worse accidents.

With the number of automobiles now in use the danger of collision with buggies and wagons without lights is greatly enhanced. Most vehicles are dark colored and frequently can not be seen by the driver of an automobile more than a short distance, even if directly in the rays of his headlights. At a fair rate of speed a car covers in a few seconds the distance its headlights illuminate the road. It often happens that a buggy in front of a car will not be in the direct rays of the headlights and can not be seen until the motor is uncomfortably close. Has it not happened in your experience?

If an automobile and an unlighted rig are approaching a corner in the dark, from different directions, the unlighted vehicle can not be seen until directly in front of the car. The writer distinctly remembers one time when an unlighted buggy suddenly came out of a dark side road and turned directly in front of an approaching car.

When an automobile turns a corner its lights can not reveal a rig on the road into which it is turning until it has completed the turn, no matter how close the rig is to the corner. The driver of the unlighted rig is then entirely helpless to avoid a collision.

Enough has been said to show that there is danger in driving at night without lights. In the judgment of the writer it would be well worth while to carry them.

A head-on collision which recently happened between a buggy and an automobile might easily have been avoided by having lights on the buggy.

Neither the bother nor the expense of the lights is great. Many buggies and carriages are equipped with them and it is not difficult to attach them to a wagon. Few automobile owners complain at being required to carry tail lights. As a protection, either when standing still or in motion, their value is appreciated.

Let us face the fact that driving at night without lights is unsafe and that he who does it endangers not only himself, but all others who use the roads. Let us carry lights and let us have a law requiring lights on all vehicles.

THE BURLINGTON WAY.

(Continued From Page 3.)

The program for this convention is now in preparation and will consist of the annual business meeting and election of officers to take place in the morning, and a public mass meeting with addresses and band concerts in the afternoon. The evening will be devoted to the annual banquet closing with a strong program of musical numbers and toasts.

It is to such organizations as the Burlington Way Good Roads Association, that is due the credit for creating the sentiment which is rapidly bringing Illinois to the front as a commonwealth whose roads will not suffer in comparison with the boasted highways of the eastern states.

Too long, has "Old Illinois" been famous for her bad roads and it is an evident fact that the rapidly cystalizing sentiment will soon bring the citizens in the various counties to a full realization of the necessity of the intelligent expenditure of money and labor on the country road.

RULES OF THE BURLINGTON WAY GOOD ROADS ASSOCIATION.

1. Each telephone pole on the entire route must be marked with the official registered markings of the association, viz., a 6-inch orange band flanked by two 6-inch white bands.

2. Official registered Burlington Way Signs must be erected on the trail one mile either side of every town, village or city, through which the trail passes, giving the distance to and from adjoining places.

3. Official red, metal danger signs must be erected at all dangerous turns, points and hills warning of same.

4. Official red metal danger signs must be erected three hundred feet each side of every railroad crossing reading thus, "DANGER! Railroad crossing, 300 ft."

5. All grade railroad crossings shall be on a level with the roadway, having no abrupt approaches. The space between the ties and rails shall be carefully and permanently filled with crushed stone, approximately 2½ inches in diameter, with the spaces between the stones filled with sand or cinders.

6. All earth roads shall be dragged immediately after each rain, if the condition of the roads warrant same. Roads shall be kept properly graded, crowned, and drained.

7. Each supervisor shall have general oversight of the condition of the roads on his division and each vice president shall be held responsible for the condition of the roads, signs and markings within his designated territory.

8. The local vice president of the trail shall by virtue of his office be president of the local Burlington Way Good Roads Club of his city and shall cause to be paid into the general treasury of the association the sum of $5.00 annually, from the dues of the local club. Meetings shall be called by him as often as is necessary to promote the general welfare of the trail.

9. Each division of the trail shall hold a yearly convention for the purpose of considering ways and means of bettering the condition of the trail under its jurisdiction.

10. The annual convention of the Burlington Way Good Roads Association shall be held yearly in August at which time the election of officers shall be held and the convention city selected for the coming year. The convention shall consist of (1) a business meeting open to the public, at which only accredited delegates shall be entitled to vote; (2) a public mass meeting in the interest of good roads in general and the Burlington Way in particular consisting of addresses by good roads authorities and music by bands or orchestra; (3) the annual Burlington Way banquet concluding with a program of toasts on the influence of the Burlington Way in crystalizing good roads sentiment.

ROAD MACHINERY, ITS USE AND MAINTENANCE.

(Continued From Page 5.)

In Iowa the heavy tractor grading outfits operated by the various counties work about 100 days during the season In some counties the average for several years has been about 75 working days. The amount of lost time will vary somewhat with the type of equipment and this is a factor which should be taken into consideration in showing road building machinery.

The elevating grader drawn by horses is more expensive to operate than is the same machine drawn by a tractor, but its efficiency during the season is much greater because of the large number of working days.

Some of the types of equipment used for hauling road materials can be used for a much larger percentage of the working season than can other types. Team hauling, of course, can be carried on under any except the very worst weather conditions, but this method of hauling is obsolete for large amounts of material to be moved long distances although it has demonstrated its efficiency for short hauls.

The industrial railroad can also be used under all except the very worst weather conditions, and is suitable for hauls of any length. The tractor hauling outfits are considerably hampered by soft or slippery roads and the motor truck is also handicapped by the same conditions. It becomes then, exceedingly important to take account of these facts in buying the types of machinery to be used for special kinds of work.

MAINTENANCE COSTS.

The data available on the cost of maintaining road machinery are exceedingly diversified in character and much of it has little value because of erroneous methods of estimating maintenance factors. It is possible from records that have been published to make either a good or bad showing for any one of a number of classes of equipment.

IDEAL CONDITIONS OF OPERATION.

Having discussed briefly some of the factors that enter into the effective operation or various types of road machinery it seems desirable to summarize the conditions under which expensive road building machinery can be expected to operate economically and to do work at a cost which will justify the necessary expenditure.

1. *The machinery must in every case be adapted to the use to which it is put.* Many useful machines are purchased for work entirely unsuited to them, the result being that the user is disappointed in the showing made by the machine and the public money expended brings no adequate return. In Illinois, where there is a superintendent of highways in each county, it should be possible to secure the consensus of opinion in regard to the types and sizes of road machinery that will eventually eliminate the unfit.

2. *For most types of modern road-making machinery it is absolutely necessary to provide a large volume of work each season if the equipment is to show efficiency.* This work must not be in small units widely scattered necessitating frequent moves. The season's work should be definitely planned ahead so that the equipment can operate continuously with a minimum of lost motion in shifting from place to place.

3. *Expert supervision:* It is almost axiomatic that unless expert supervision is available, modern road-building machinery can not be operated by public boards at anywhere near the cost of similar operation by private contract. Road work by day labor is on trial in the United States. It has shown efficiency in some states but in many states it has cost much more than similar work done by contract. The result is that it is being looked upon with more or less disfavor by the public and it behooves those of us who are responsible for such work to put every ounce of energy we can into systematizing the construction work under our supervision.

4. *Expert operation:* That expert operators for expensive machinery are a necessity needs no argument and such operators can not be secured without adequate compensation. They must be had, however, if economical operation of equipment is to be secured.

5. *Systematic maintenance* of machinery is also a necessity that admits of no argument. The official body

that is not in position or not willng to provide for expert and systematic maintenance of its machinery can not hope to secure economical results.

6. *Systematic cost data* must be kept on all work in which the equipment is used if the ultimate efficient and economic results are to be known. Start out with a comprehensive and well thought out system of accounting and check up on the equipment from time to time to determine whether or not it is working effectively.

7. *Cooperation* between the supervising officials, the technical experts and the ordinary workmen is the keynote of the successful operation of modern road-making machinery. The superintendent who can secure cordial and intelligent team work on the part of all of those in his employ or under his direction, is the one who will be able to show economical results when the season's record is published.

SHORT COURSE IN HIGHWAY ENGINEERING.

(Continued from Page 7.)

Afternoon Session.

Inspection of the University.

1:30 P. M. Test of Monolithic Brick Pavement Slabs, in T. and A. M. Laboratory.

2:00 P. M. Engineering Buildings.

3:00 P. M. Natural History Building.

3:15 P. M. Agricultural Group.

3:30 P. M. Work of the College of Agriculture, Morrow Hall, Agricultural Building.

MONDAY, JANUARY 17, 1916.

Morning Session.

Roads—Gravel and Macadam Roads.
Bridges—Inspection of Old Steel Bridges.

Afternoon Session.

1:00 P. M. Relation of the County Superintendent of Highways to the Township Road Commissioners...................L. B. Neighbour, *County Superintendent of Highways, Lee County.*

3:00 P. M. Laboratory Demonstrations:
    Sec. A, in Room 221. Tests of Tars, Asphalts and oils.............W. C. Adams, *Chemist, Illinois Highway Department.*
    Sec. B, in Mechanical Engineering Lecture Room. Tests of Portland Cement...... B. L. Bowling, *Assistant in Cement Laboratory.* C. C. Wiley, *Instructor in Highway Engineering.*

3:30 P. M. Laboratory Demonstrations:
    Sec. A, Mechanical Engineering Lecture Room. Tests of Cement.............. B. L. Bowling, *Assistant in Cement Laboratory.* C. C. Wiley, *Instructor in Highway Engineering.*
    Sec. B, in Room 221. Tests of Tars, Asphalts and oils.............W. C. Adams, *Chemist, Illinois Highway Department.*

Evening Session.

7:30 P. M. Highways and Waterways. (Lecture illustrated with colored lantern slides).......
...........................Dr. F. H. Newell, *Professor of Civil Engineering.*

TUESDAY, JANUARY 18, 1916.

Morning Session.

Roads—Bituminous Roads.
Bridges—Field Inspection of New Steel Bridges.

Afternoon Session.

1:00 P. M. Wisconsin Highway Standards......A. R. Hirst, *State Highway Engineer of Wisconsin.*

2:00 P. M. Creosoted Timber in Highway Construction.
....................................A. L. Keuhn, *General Superintendent American Creosoting Company.*

3:00 P. M. Road and Bridge Construction in Wisconsin.
(Illustrated lecture)..............A. R. Hirst,
State Highway Engineer of Wisconsin.

Evening Session.

7:30 P. M. Use of Coal Tar in Highways. (Illustrated by moving pictures)........Philip P. Sharples,
Barrett Manufacturing Co., New York.

WEDNESDAY, JANUARY 19, 1916.

Morning Session.

Roads—Concrete Pavements.
Bridges—Inspection of New Concrete Bridges.

Afternoon Session.

1:00 P. M. Standard Highway Construction in Iowa....
.....................T. H. MacDonald,
State Highway Engineer of Iowa.

2:00 P. M. General Discussion. Safety First in Highway Traffic; Speed Regulations, Hedges, Super-elevation on curves, Color of paint on bridges, Vehicle lights, etc.

3:00 P. M. Road and Bridge Construction in Iowa. (Illustrated by moving pictures). T. H. MacDonald,
State Highway Engineer of Iowa.

Evening Session.

7:30 P. M. Concrete Road Construction. (Illustrated Lecture).......................C. M. Powell,
Assistant Engineer Universal Portland Cement Co.

THURSDAY, JANUARY 20, 1916.

Morning Session.

Roads—Brick Pavements.
Bridges—Estimating the Cost of a Concrete Culvert.

Afternoon Session.

1:00 P. M. Importance of Minor Details in Concrete Work.......................C. M. Powell,
Assistant Engineer Universal Portland Cement Co.

2:00 P. M. Some Things Learned in Building Brick Pavements.......................J. W. Stipes,
Contractor, Champaign, Illinois.

3:00 P. M. Laboratory Demonstrations:
Sec. A, Room 221. Tests of Sand - and Gravel.......................N. B. Garver,
Instructor in Highway Bridges.
Sec. B, Road Laboratory. Rattler Tests of Paving Brick and Tests of Road Stone.
B. L. Bowling,
Assistant in Road Laboratory.
C. C. Wiley,
Instructor in Highway Engineering.

Evening Session.

7:30 P. M. The Manufacture and Properties of Paving Brick.......................A. V. Bleininger,
Professor of Ceramic Engineering.

FRIDAY, JANUARY 21, 1916.

Morning Session.

Roads—Road Design.
Bridges—Estimating the Cost of a Steel Bridge.

Afternoon Session.

1:00 P. M. Machinery for Building Stone Roads........
.......................G. A. Quinlan,
Superintendent of Highways, Cook County.

2:00 P. M. Work of the Illinois Highway Commission..
.......................A. D. Gash,
President State Highway Commission.

3:00 P. M. Design of a County System of Roads.......
.......................Wm. W. Marr
Chief State Highway Engineer.

Evening Session.

6:00 P. M. Social in Parlor.
6:30 P. M. Banquet.
7:45 P. M. Financing Road Improvements......S. E. Bradt,
Secretary Illinois Highway Commission.

8:30 P. M. Financing Road Improvements in Williamson County.......................P. B. Wilson,
Superintendent of Highways, Williamson County.

8:45 P. M. Financing Road Improvements in Cook County.......................Geo. A. Quinlan.
Superintendent of Highways, Cook County.

9:00 P. M. Roads and Rural Credit............R. F. Harris,
President First National Bank, Champaign.

TRACTION ENGINE GOES THROUGH BRIDGE.

The failure of a stirrup, which held up a floor beam, caused two panels of a bridge over the Spoon River in Persifer Township, Knox County, to drop while a traction engine was crossing the bridge, precipitating the engine into the river, 22 feet below.

Two men who were on the engine at the time were seriously injured.

The 12-ton engine pulling a tank wagon and corn sheller had just started to cross the bridge. The rear

wheels of the engine were almost over the second panel when the stirrup gave way, dropping the engine and attached machinery into five feet of water below.

The temperature was about 10° above zero and the river was covered with about six inches of ice. The bridge, which had been repaired and painted three years ago, was supposedly in good shape. This same engine had crossed it several times before. It is presumed that the cold weather had weakened the stirrup to such an extent that it snapped when the sudden strain, caused by the weight of the engine, came upon it.

FUNDS MUST BE SET ASIDE FOR ROAD DRAGGING.

(Continued from Page 5.)

fined not less than twenty-five dollars ($25.00) nor more than fifty dollars ($50.00). [Amended by Act approved June 28, 1915.

The above sections were passed by the Forty-ninth General Assembly and became effective July 1, 1916.

All money derived from a 1914 tax levied for road and bridge purposes, having been paid to the township officials prior to the time the law became effective, no money could be set aside from this levy. The money that is now being paid into the Road and Bridge Fund from the 1915 tax levy affords the highway commissioners their first opportunity of setting aside the funds as stipulated in Section 62.

It should be noted that this matter is obligatory on the part of the commissioners and a failure to do so will subject them to the penalty as provided for in "Subdivision D" of Section 107.

CORRESPONDENCE COURSE IN ROAD BUILDING.

When the short course in highway engineering was in session at the University of Illinois, a suggestion was made that a correspondence course be carried on during the interim between the sessions of the short course. The suggestion met with favor among those in attendance, and many expressed their interest in it.

It seemed to be the consensus of opinion that such a course should be elementary in theory and highly practical in all its phases; that both the subjects of roads and bridges should be discussed, but that the most urgent need was for the exposition of methods by which the old bridges could be investigated and their safety determined under present traffic conditions.

In response to the demand as outlined above the civil engineering department of the university has considered the feasibility of offering such a course and presents the first installment herewith.

This first lesson covers the definition of terms used and includes some simple problems involving their use. The discussions are elementary. It is assumed that any one taking this course has, or will have in his possession a copy of Cambria Steel Handbook or Carnegie's Pocket Companion. The Illinois Highway Department's specifications for bridges are often referred to and the student should have a copy.

A set of problems is given at the close of the discussion in order that the student may apply the principles for his own enlightenment. If he so desires, he may solve them carefully, mail the solutions to the civil engineering department of the university, and the work will be looked over and mistakes noted. The corrected papers will be returned to the author if postage is provided.

The above course is open without charge to any one interested in highway construction or maintenance. All papers sent in will be corrected as expeditiously as possible.

It is requested that all papers sent in be typewritten, if possible.

LESSON 1.

DEFINITION OF TERMS.

Since many of the terms used in the design of highway structures are somewhat technical, it was thought best to define those which are in common use.

The following definitions, while they apply in a general way to all kinds of structural design, are intended primarily to explain the meaning and use as pertaining to highway structures. It has not been the intention to make them so broad as to include all conditions.

Dead Load—The dead load on a bridge is the weight of the bridge itself, and any other permanent loads that may be superimposed.

Live Load—The live loads on a bridge consist of any variable or moving loads that may come upon it, such as a crowd of people, wagons, automobiles, motor trucks, traction engines, etc.

Snow Load—Snow load is seldom considered in the design of highway bridges because a crowd of people or a number of heavy vehicles are not likely to come upon a bridge when it has a maximum snow load.

Wind Load—Wind loads need not be considered in the design of beam bridges, but for girders and trusses these loads should be taken into account as required by the specifications.

Impact—The stresses produced by moving loads are greater than those produced by fixed or stationary loads of the same magnitude. This difference of stress is called impact.

Reactions—The forces acting upon a structure must be in equilibrium in order that the structure may remain stationary. Therefore, there must be forces acting at the supports which are equal and opposite in direction to those produced by the dead and live loads. These forces are called reactions. The reaction at one end of a beam is obtained by dividing the moment of the loads on the beam about the other end by the span length.

Tension—When two forces applied to a member are acting away from each other, tending to pull the member in two, the member is said to be in tension and the stress is a tensile stress.

Compression—When two forces applied to a member are acting towards each other, tending to crush the member, the member is said to be in compression and the stress is a compressive stress.

Unit Stress—Unit stress is the stress produced on a unit of area and is usually expressed in pounds per square inch.

Ultimate Stress—Ultimate stress is the greatest stress which a member will carry before it fails.

Working Stress—The working stress for any material is that unit stress which it has been found by experience is a safe stress to use in properly designed structures. It is usually about one-third to one-fourth of the ultimate stress.

Factor of Safety—The factor of safety is the ratio of the ultimate stress to the working stress, and as just stated is about 3 to 4.

Shear—*"Consider the forces acting on a beam to be resolved into horizontal and vertical components. Then the shear at any section is the algebraic sum of the vertical forces acting on either side of the section and is the force by which the part of the beam on one side of the section tends to slide by the part on the other side. This tendency is opposed by the resistance of the material to transverse shearing." As for example, if two plates are lapped and riveted together and a pull is applied to each plate, the rivets will have a tendency to shear (one part slide past the other) on the line between the plates.

Bending Moment—The moment of a force about a point is the product of the force and the perpendicular distance from the point to the line of action of the force.

*"The bending moment (or moments) at any section of a beam is the algebraic sum of the moments of the forces acting on either side of the section about an axis through the center of gravity of the section and is the moment which measures the tendency of the outer forces to cause the portion of the beam lying on one side of the section to rotate about the section. This tendency to bend is opposed by internal fiber stresses of tension and compression." In other words, it is the tendency of the beam to change shape or position under load, which tendency is resisted by the stresses developed in the beam.

Moment of Inertia—The moment of inertia of an area is the sum of the products arising from multiplying each elementary area by the square of its distance from an axis. Thus, the area of a cross section of an I-beam may be considered to consist of a great number of small areas, and the moment of inertia of the beam may be obtained as above.

---
* Elements of Structures, Hool.

The moment of inertia of a plane figure always consists of four dimensions of length—the area which is the product of two dimensions, and the square of the distance to the axis, or

$I = Ad^2$, in which

I = moment of inertia

A = area (length times breadth)

A = distance of area A from axis, (to be multiplied twice, or squared).

Radius of Gyration—The radius of gyration is the radial distance from the axis at which all the elementary areas might be concentrated and the moment of inertia remain the same.

If $I = Ad^2$

$$d = \sqrt{\frac{I}{A}},$$ which is the radius of gyration of a plane area.

Section Modulus—The section modulus is the quotient arising from dividing the moment of inertia of any member by the distance from the axis about which the moment of inertia is computed to the most distant point on the cross section.

Neutral Axis—When loads are applied to beams the beams become slightly curved. The fibers on the concave side are in compression and the fibers on the convex side are in tension. The neutral surface is the surface which lies between the compressive and tensile sides of the beam and has zero stress. The neutral axis is represented as a line which traces out or indicates this plane on the longitudinal section of the beam. The steel handbooks give the locations of the neutral axes for all the standard rolled shapes.

PROBLEMS.

1. What are the live loads specified by the Illinois Highway Department for a steel beam bridge of 20-foot span? What should be the maximum space between beams? What part of the concentrated load is assumed to be carried by one joist if a wooden floor is used? If a concrete floor is used?

2. If the ultimate strength of steel is 63,000 pounds per square inch and the unit working stress is 16,000 pounds, what is the factor of safety? Why is a factor of safety used?

3. Find the reactions for the beam shown in Fig. 1. Find the shear on section a-a. Find the bending moment at section b-b.

4. The moment of inertia of a beam with a rectangular cross section is,

$I = 1/12 \; bd^2$, in which

b = breadth of beam.

d = depth of beam.

What is the moment of inertia, radius of gyration, and section modulus of a 6 by 12-inch wooden beam 16 feet long? Of a 4 by 16-inch wooden beam 16 feet long? Which is the stronger if they are set on edge? Which if they are laid flatwise? Which will cost the more?

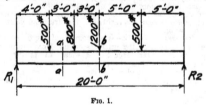

FIG. 1.

TOWNSHIP ROAD CONSTRUCTION.

The following tables give an accurate record of the cost of construction of several township roads which have been built under the supervision of the State Highway Department:

COST OF MACADAM AND GRAVEL ROADS.

MURPHYSBORO-GRAND TOWER ROAD—SAND RIDGE TOWNSHIP—JACKSON COUNTY.

CONDITIONS.

The following figures exclude contractor's profit and overhead expenses:

Total length of road constructed 19,625 ft.; width 10 ft.; total square yards of road constructed 21,805.5; kind of material used, crushed limestone; kind of aggregate used, 2½-inch stone and screenings; average thickness of material, 10 inches; average length of haul on materials, 2¾ miles; cost of material f. o. b. siding, 25c per ton freight; general condition of weather, floods in spring and summer; fall fair; rate of pay; labor $1.50 per day; teams 35 and 40 cts. per hour; road work started May 1, 1915; completed December 10, 1915.

ITEMIZED COST OF WORK.	Total cost.	Cost per sq. yd.
Engineering and general supervision	[1]	[1] .....
Superintendence and inspection....	$1,125 08	$0.0516
Excavation	898 59	0.0412
Stone 7,224 cu. yds. @ 25c ton f. o. b. siding	2,274 00	0.1042
Hauling stone	4,167 10	0.1911
Shaping and rolling subgrade and side roads	1,064 17	0.0488
Spreading stone and screenings....	310 89	0.0143
Rolling and sprinkling............	689 61	0.0316
Freight on equipment............	53 25	0.0024
Depreciation on equipment........	[1]	
Cost of culverts and bridges.......	861 53	0.0395
Total cost	$11,444 22	$0.5247
Cost, excluding excavation, culverts and end protections............	$9,684 10	$0.4440

[1] Indicates paid or furnished by the State Highway Department.

FINAL REPORT ON BITUMINOUS MACADAM ROAD.

S. I. N. U. ROAD—CARBONDALE TOWNSHIP—JACKSON COUNTY.

CONDITIONS.

No allowance for contractor's profit or overhead charges.

Amount of pavement laid 1,500 ft.; 3,500 sq. yds.; amount of pavement treated with asphalt 3,500 sq. yds.; amount of pavement treated with tar 1,600 sq. yds.; width of road between curbs 21.0 ft.; total length of curb and gutter 1,760 ft.; curb only 262 ft.; gutter only 774 ft.; average length of haul ½ mile; rate of pay: labor 25c; teams 50c per hour; amount of bituminous material used per sq. yd. 2.54 gallons; work begun September 29; completed November 25, 1915.

TOTAL COST OF LABOR AND SUPPLIES.	Total cost.	Cost per sq. yd.
Engineering and general supervision.	[1]	[1] ....
Superintendent (salary and expenses)	$270 00	$0.077
Excavation 737 cu. yds. @ 35c (contracted)	257 95	.074
Stone (2½") 803 tons @ 92½c f. o. b. siding	742 77	.212

	Total cost.	Cost per sq. yd.
Stone 750 tons @ freight 60c, $1.14-$1.28	760 64	.217
Chips (¾") 240 tons @ 92½c f. o. b. siding	222 00	.063
Chats 88 tons @ 85c f. o. b. siding..	74 80	.021
Hauling stone, chips and chats 1,881 tons	734 16	.210
Spreading stone, chips and chats 1,881 tons	203 05	.058
Shaping and rolling subgrade.......	149 17	.043
Constructing curb and gutter complete (contract)	1,279 55	.366
Asphalt (texaco No. 96) 1,400 gallons @ $.114	160 03	
6,800 gallons @ .076c............	518 48	.216
Tar (Tarvia "X") 800 gallons @ 10c	80 00	
Heating and applying bituminous material, coal, labor, etc.........	210 07	.060
Rolling, coal, water, labor..........	135 82	.039
Freight on equipment...............	27 00	.008
Incidental expense, repairs, tools, demurrage, etc.	65 21	.019
Total $5,890 70		$1.683
Cost, excluding excavation and curb and gutter $4,353 20		$1.243

¹ Indicates paid or furnished by the State Highway Department.

FINAL COST REPORT ON CONCRETE ROADS.

CONCRETE ROAD—BLAIRSVILLE TOWNSHIP—WILLIAMSON COUNTY.

CONDITIONS.

Excluding contractor's profit and overhead charges. Amount of pavement laid 3,355 ft., 3,720 sq. yds.; width of pavement 10 ft.; length of pavement constructed without transverse joints, none; spacing of transverse joints in 3,355 ft. of pavement, 100 ft.; length of haul for materials 0.52 miles; cost of cement per bbl. f. o. b. siding $1.29 net; cost of sand per cu. yd. f. o. b. siding $1.35; cost of stone per cu. yd. f. o. b. siding $1.35; amount of cement used per sq. yd. of pavement 0.29 bbls.; rate of pay: for labor, 22½c; teams 40c per hour; road started October 1; completed November 27, 1915.

COST OF LABOR AND SUPPLIES.	Total cost.	Cost per sq. yd.
Engineering and general supervision. ¹.......	¹.....	
Superintendence and inspection.....	¹$234 44	¹$.063
Insurance	46 00	.012
Excavation	841 58	.226
Stone 546 cu. yds. @ $1.35 f. o. b. siding	737 69	.198
Unloading to storage or loading sand and stone direct................	140 00	.038
Hauling stone or gravel............	279 43	.075
Sand, 323 cu. yds. @ $1.35 f. o. b. siding	436 18	.117
Hauling sand	163 50	.044
Cement 1,080 bbls. @ $1.29........	1,393 20	.375
Hauling cement	89 10	.024
Incidental hauling	10 40	.003
Clearing right of way.............	....	.....
Shaping and rolling subgrade and side roads	795 44	.214
Mixing and placing concrete handling forms and joints................	669 58	.180

	Total cost.	Cost per sq. yd.
Covering, seasoning and cleaning concrete	94 70	.025
Cost of culverts and bridges.........	23 50	.006
Freight on equipment and unloading same	137 48	.037
Depreciation or rental on equipment.	102 97	.028
Total cost $6,195 19		$1.665
Cost, excluding excavation, culverts and bridges $5,330 11		$1.433

¹ Indicates paid by the State Highway Department.

OPINIONS OF THE ATTORNEY GENERAL.

WOMEN VOTE FOR BOND ISSUE—HOW STATE AID ALLOTMENTS ARE APPLIED TO BOND ISSUE.

February 8, 1916.

STATE HIGHWAY DEPARTMENT, *Springfield, Illinois.*

GENTLEMEN: I am in receipt of your favor of the 31st ultimo, submitting several propositions relative to the revised Road and Bridge act, in substance as follows:

(1) Whether women may vote upon the question of issuing bonds for improving highways, when such question is submitted to the voters of the county, either under the road law or under the law authorizing county boards to call an election to vote upon the question of a bond issue.

(2) Where a county, as provided by section 15d, has issued bonds for the purpose of advancing the entire cost of constructing State aid roads, and desires to use its allotment of State aid funds toward the payment of such bonds, whether it is necessary for the county board to accept such allotment and provide an equal amount as provided by section 15b of said act.

In connection with this you submit the further inquiry as follows:

"If * * * it shall be necessary only for the county to accept the allotment, will it then be proper for the State Highway Commission to request the State Auditor to issue a voucher to some officer of the county (and if so, to whom) to be used in liquidating the bonds of said county? Under such a procedure what should the State Highway Commission require as evidence of the fact that the money was used in paying off said bonds?"

(3) In case a county issues bonds covering a twenty-year series, same being used in improving State aid roads, and the county's allotment of State aid funds during such twenty-year period will not aggregate an amount equal to one-half the cost of such improvement, whether the county board would have the right to receive future allotments and place the same in the county treasury for county purposes as a reimbursement for the amount paid out by the county upon the one-half of the cost of such improvement which the State is supposed to pay.

Noting your first inquiry relative to whether women may vote upon the question of issuing bonds for road purposes, I will say paragraph 546, being section 1 of an act approved June 26, 1913, granting women the right to vote, chapter 46, Hurd's Revised Statute, 1913, provides as follows:

"That all women, citizens of the United States, above the age of 21 years, having resided in the State one year, in the county ninety days, and in the election district thirty days next preceding any election therein, shall be allowed to vote at such election for presidential electors, member of the State Board of Equalization, clerk of the appellate court, county collector, county surveyor, members of board of assessors, members of board of review, sanitary district trustees, and for all officers of cities, villages and towns (except police magistrates), and upon all questions or propositions submitted to a vote of the electors of such municipalities or other political divisions of this State."

It will be noted that the above paragraph confers upon women, who are qualified voters, the right to vote upon all questions or propositions submitted to a vote of the electors of such municipalities or other political divisions of the State.

It is the holding of this department that a proposition to issue bonds for road purposes is a proposition that comes within the terms of said paragraph.

However, the right of women to vote upon the question of such bond issue must be considered with reference to various provisions of the constitution concerning the collection of an annual tax for the payment of an indebtedness incurred and the rate of taxes that a county may levy.

Section 12 of article 9 of the constitution provides in part:

"No county, city, township, school district, or other municipal corporation shall be allowed to become indebted in any manner or for any purpose, to an amount, including existing indebtedness, in the aggregate exceeding five per centum on the value of the taxable property therein, to be ascertained by the last assessment for State and county taxes, previous to the incurring of such indebtedness. Any county, city, school district, or other municipal corporation incurring any indebtedness as aforesaid, shall before or at the time of doing so, provide for the collection of a direct annual tax sufficient to pay the interest on such debt as it falls due, and also to pay and discharge the principal thereof within twenty years from the time of contracting the same."

Section 6 of said article 9 of the constitution provides:

"County authorities shall never assess taxes, the aggregate of which shall exceed seventy-five cents per $100 valuation, except for the payment of indebtedness existing at the adoption of this constitution, unless authorized by a vote of the people of the county."

A referendum vote to authorize the levy of a county tax in excess of seventy-five cents on the hundred dollars' valuation is a referendum vote in pursuance of the constitution.

The Supreme Court of this State in the case of *Scown v. Czarnecki*, 264 Ill., 305, holds, in substance, that the provision of the Woman's Suffrage act of 1913, permitting women to vote on "all questions or propositions submitted to a vote of the electors of such municipalities or other political divisions of the State" covers every referendum election, including those provided for in the constitution, and in so far as it includes referendum elections provided for in the constitution the act is invalid, but that its invalidity is confined to that matter alone; and that the act is valid in so far as it applies to elections on propositions provided for by statute alone. It would seem, therefore, that where at the time of submitting to a vote of the county a proposition to incur an indebtedness, it was necessary at the same time to submit to a vote the question of levying a tax in excess of seventy-five cents on the hundred dollars' valuation, in pursuance of section 8 of article 9 of the constitution, women would not be qualified to vote on such proposition; but that in cases where a vote on a proposition to incur an indebtedness does not at the same time involve a referendum vote under the constitution to authorize the levy of a tax, women who possess the qualifications prescribed by the Woman's Suffrage act of 1913 would be qualified voters. The right of women to vote on such proposition would not be affected, whether submitted by highway authorities or by the county board.

Concerning your second proposition relative to whether it is necessary that a county should accept the allotment of State aid funds, and provide an equal amount as provided by section 15b of the revised Road and Bridge act, where the county has, as provided by section 15d of said act, advanced the entire costs of constructing State aid roads, I will say said section 15d is a new section added to said act, by an act approved June 28, 1915, (Sess. L. 1915, p. 599,) and provides in part as follows:

"If any county desires, more rapidly than its allotments of State aid road moneys will permit, to construct a State aid road along any one or more of its highways that have been selected and designated, under the provisions of this Act, as State aid roads, such county is hereby authorized to advance, out of any county funds available from any source, or which may become available from any source, for such purpose, the entire cost of constructing such State aid roads and to make such improvement at any time. Such county shall, in such case, have the right to use any allotment of money made to it by the State Highway Commission, to defray one-half the cost of constructing new State aid roads, in the county, under the provisions of this Act, or to apply the money on the payment of any bonds or other obligations which have been or may be issued by such county, under any law of this State, to meet the cost of the construction of any

State aid road or roads constructed by county at its own expense: *Provided, however*, that the allotments made by the State shall not be used to cover more than one-half the cost of the construction of such State aid roads: *And, provided, also*, that such State aid roads shall have been constructed under, and in accordance with, plans, specifications, estimates of cost and contracts approved by the State Highway Commission and which roads shall have been found, upon inspection of the State Highway Engineer, to have been completed as provided for in said contracts. All highways constructed or improved in any county under the provisions of this section shall be known as State aid roads and shall thereafter be repaired and maintained under, and in accordance with, the provisions of section 32 of this Act.

"If any county desires so to advance money for the purpose of the construction or improvement of its State aid roads, its county board is hereby vested with full power and authority to take all necessary steps in such case and such county board may, out of any funds in the county treasury, not required for other purposes, appropriate therefrom sufficient moneys to meet the cost of constructing or improving such State aid roads, and may also, in any manner provided by law for issuing county bonds, issue bonds of the county for the purpose of constructing or improving such State aid roads: *Provided*, that the question of issuing such county bonds shall first be submitted to the legal voters of such county at any general election or at a special election which the county board is hereby authorized to call for such purpose: * * * ."

Where a county, as provided by said section, has advanced the entire cost of constructing State aid roads, either by an appropriation of funds from the county treasury, or by issuing bonds, such county has already met its allotment of State aid funds, as to the cost of the construction of such roads, in advance; and it would not be necessary for such county to take further action under section 15b, to provide a fund to meet the allotment of State aid funds.

It will be noted that State aid roads, where the entire cost of construction is advanced by the county, are to be constructed under, and in accordance with, plans, specifications, estimates of cost, and contracts approved by the State Highway Commission, and subject to inspection by the State Highway Engineer.

You will note, too, that section 15d expressly provides that where a county has advanced the entire cost of constructing State aid roads, that such county shall have the right to use any allotment of money made to it by the State Highway Commission, to defray one-half the cost of constructing new roads, as provided by said act, or it may apply such allotment on the payment of bonds issued by the county to pay the cost of roads constructed. Where such roads have been constructed upon plans, specifications, estimates of cost, and contracts approved by the State Highway Commission, and have been found by the State Highway Engineer to have been completed as provided in said contracts, the county would be entitled to its allotment of money by the State and your commission should issue a voucher to the Auditor of Public Accounts, who should then issue a State warrant payable to the county and when countersigned by the State Treasurer deliver the same to the county treasurer.

Where a county issues bonds in order to advance the entire cost of constructing State aid roads, there is no provision of the statute which requires such county to furnish evidence to the State Highway Commission that its allotment of State aid funds will be applied on the payment of such bonds. As noted, the county may, at its option, apply such allotment on payment of bonds, or in constructing other roads. Such bonds are a liability against the county which issues them; they do not constitute any liability against the State.

Relative to your third proposition, will say said section 15d does not fix any limitation of time within which a county may reimburse itself from allotments of State aid funds, to cover the State's portion of the cost of State aid roads, where the county has advanced the entire cost of such construction. The allotment of money by the State is not limited to the twenty-year period in which the bonds must be paid.

Very respectfully,

P. J. LUCEY,
Attorney General.

SCHNEPP & BARNES, STATE PRINTERS SPRINGFIELD, ILL. 1916.

Engineering Library

ILLINOIS HIGHWAYS

[Printed by authority of the State of Illinois.]

OFFICIAL PUBLICATION OF THE

STATE HIGHWAY DEPARTMENT

| VOL. III | SPRINGFIELD, ILLINOIS, MARCH-APRIL, 1916 | Nos. 3 and 4 |

GOOD ROADS MEAN A READY MARKET FOR THE FARMER.
The man in the above picture drove to town at a trot, with 180 bushels of corn.

A TYPICAL MARCH MUD SCENE.

VERMILION COUNTY BOND ROADS
BY P. C. McARDLE, SUPERINTENDING ENGINEER FOR VERMILION COUNTY.

At the time of the passage of the Tice Law in July, 1913, Vermilion County, so far as roads were concerned, was like every other county in Illinois, short on mileage of hard-surfaced roads; 10 miles of brick roads, 156 miles of so-called gravel roads, perhaps 10 miles of waterbound macadam roads constituted the total of her improved roads out of a total of 1,600 miles of dedicated roads. Her commissioners of highways had been struggling for years to metal some of their roads with bank gravel in imitation of their more successful neighbors across the state line in Indiana, and most of these roads were adjacent to the county seat. Road building up to that time had not been considered a county duty, but the Tice law gave county boards concurrent jurisdiction or vested in them the same powers for constructing, repairing and maintaining gravel, rock, macadam, or other hard roads in their respective counties as the commissioners of highways, and authorized the appointment of county superintendent of highways in each county.

Committees representing a large body of taxpayers, after having investigated the records of township expenditure for road purposes, found that for the ten years 1904-1913, Vermilion County had paid for its roads and bridges the astounding figure of $1,726,406.56 exclusive of road tax worked out (see table 1) and had practically nothing permanent to show for this expenditure. They found also that besides ordinary county expenses, and within the 75c per $100 of assessed valuation the county could issue bonds for $1,500,000.00 and retire them with interest in 20 years and build with the proceeds within three years a system of hard roads reaching every city and village in the county. These committees presented a petition to the county board of supervisors on September 11, 1913, as follows:

To the Board of Supervisors of the County of Vermilion and State of Illinois:

The undersigned committees, representing a large number of taxpayers of Vermilion County, Illinois, respectfully request your honorable body to give due consideration to the following plan for building good, hard roads in this county, to wit:

"That this board, at the next general election, submit to the voters of this county, the question of issuing twenty-year 4 or 5 per cent bonds of the county to the amount of $1,500,000, or such an amount as this board may find necessary, for the purpose of building enough good, hard roads, on highways to be selected by this board, to connect every city and village in the county with the county seat, and with each other.

"And we further request that action be taken thereon by this board at this or an early subsequent meeting."

The county board at a meeting on March 12, 1914, by appropriated action named a committee of the board to consider the whole question of road improvement naming its duties as follows:

"To consult with the Illinois State Highway Commission and its engineers, relative to the building of said system of roads; to select the roads required to complete such a system; to go over the proposed routes with such engineers in order to

determine the most available kinds and character, and the approximate cost of the roads proposed to be built, and to inspect the old bridges to ascertain how many of them can be utilized, and to divide up all of said road mileage into convenient sections to permit construction to be carried on in the different townships at the same time, and thereby, to expedite the final completion of the entire system; to estimate the amount of the twenty-year bond issue required to build such proposed roads; to fix

MAP SHOWING ROUTES WHICH WILL BE IMPROVED.
Courtesy of Engineering News.

the rate of interest that the bonds will bear and the amount of the annual payments; to take any other steps necessary to carry out the purpose of this resolution; and then to prepare for submission at the next April or June meeting of this board, a report setting forth the proposed hard road county bond issue plan in shape for submission to the voters of this county at the first opportunity"

The committee was composed of five members of the board, besides the chairman of the board and the county superintendent of highways, who were added as ex-officio members of the committee

The committee called upon the State Highway Commission and requested that the State Highway Engineer visit Vermilion County and consult with the committee. He accordingly came to Danville and went over the whole matter with the committee.

After several months' consideration, the committee brought in a report which was adopted by the board on June 10, 1914, which provided among other matters:

That the question of issuing county bonds for road building be submitted to a vote of the people at the general election in November, 1914.

That the amount of the issue be fixed at $1,500,000.

That the rate of interest on such bonds be fixed at 4 per cent, payable annually.

That said bonds be divided into twenty annual installments, one-twentieth due each year.

That a direct annual tax be levied each year to pay off the bonds and interest in twenty years. One-third of said bonds to be dated June 1, 1915; one-third June 1, 1916; and one-third June 1, 1917.

That the annual amounts required to pay off the principal and interest of such bonds in twenty years be fixed as shown in table 2.

That the roads shown on map, herewith attached, be constructed 10 feet wide of concrete or brick with gravel or rock shoulders 3 feet wide on each side.

That these roads be improved according to plans and specifications approved by the Illinois State Highway Commission.

In accordance with this resolution of the board of supervisors, an election was duly called by the county clerk and was held at the time of the general election November 3, 1914.

The form of ballot prescribed by said section 40, as hereinabove set out, was used at said general election to vote on said question of issuing said county bonds and said ballot was as follows:

(Road Improvement Ballot.)

For County Bonds............................	
Against County Bonds....................	

This ballot is for the purpose of voting upon the question of issuing bonds of the county of Vermilion, in the State of Illinois, in the sum of One Million Five Hundred Thousand Dollars ($1,500,000), for the purpose of aiding in the construction of roads and bridges in said county, the total amount of said bonds to be divided into twenty equal installments; that one installment fall due each year; that one-third of said bonds be dated June 1, A. D. 1915; one-third June 1, A. D. 1916; and one-third June 1, A. D. 1917; that the rate of interest on said bonds be fixed at 4 per centum per annum, interest payable annually; all as contemplated by a resolution or order of the board of supervisors of said county, made and entered of record on Wednesday, the 10th day of June, A. D. 1914.

A total of 20,779 votes was cast at the election and a total of 19,437 on the proposition of which 10,459 were for county bonds and 8,978 against. This majority authorized the county to issue bonds; and the board at its session on December 9, 1914, authorized its Road Improvement Committee to advertise the road bonds voted by the people, and to prepare the necessary organization to make surveys, plans, specifications, etc., in the following resolution then passed by the board:

RESOLUTION.
ROAD IMPROVEMENT.

WHEREAS, the question of issuing county bonds of the county of Vermilion, in the State of Illinois, in the sum of $1,500,000, for the purpose of aiding in the construction of roads and bridges in said county, was duly submitted to the legal voters of said county at the general election held on Tuesday, the 3d day of November, A. D. 1914; and

WHEREAS, a majority of the votes cast at such election on said question was "For County Bonds," such vote for said bonds being also a clear majority of all votes cast at said election; and

WHEREAS, it now becomes, and is, the duty of this board of supervisors to carry out the will of the people, as expressed by said vote, by issuing said bonds and constructing said system of permanent hard roads in strict accordance with the provisions and the intent of duly adopted resolutions and committee report of this board; and

WHEREAS, it is the desire of all concerned that said system of roads be very carefully and properly constructed without delay, therefore, be it

Resolved, that a committee, consisting of five members of the board be appointed by the chairman; that, in addition to said five members, the chairman of the board and the county superintendent of highways be ex officio members of said committee; that the name of said committee be "Road Improvement Committee"; and that the powers and duties of said committee shall be:

To consult with the Illinois State Highway Commission and its engineers with reference to the building of said system of permanent hard roads in said county;

To make arrangements to begin at once, and to complete a careful survey of said system of roads;

To employ a competent civil engineer, who has had practical road building experience, to superintend the field and construction work of surveying and building said system of roads;

To employ other competent civil engineers who have had practical road building experience, and necessary chainmen and assistants to form the surveying crews which will be required to complete said survey of said system of roads in time to have plans and specifications prepared for submission to this board at its March, A. D. 1915, meeting, in order that the actual work of constructing said roads may be started as soon as weather conditions will permit in 1915;

To cause to be prepared plans and specifications for each section of the roads to be improved, making separate provisions for concrete centers and brick centers, said plans and specifications to be the same in general detail, except where changes may be necessary in order to make said separate provisions, all of which plans and specifications shall meet with the approval of the Illinois State Highway Commission;

To show in said plans and specifications for each section the parts, if any, of such section, in which the gravel or stone in the old roads is to be used;

To include in such plans and specifications, wherever a bridge is necessary and there is no old bridge that can be used, plans and specifications for a new one;

To employ thoroughly competent and reliable inspectors, and such other help as may be necessary to carry on said work in a proper and expeditious manner;

To act with the county clerk of this county in getting out advertisements for the sale of said bonds and instructions to bond bidders;

To prepare printed blanks on which prospective bond buyers shall make their bids;

To act with said county clerk in the preparation of a duly certified transcript of the proceedings leading up to and authorizing the issuing of said bonds;

To prepare statements for the information of bidders for said bonds;

To have said transcript and said statements printed in pamphlet form for distribution among prospective bond buyers;

To act with said county clerk in getting out advertisements for the letting of contracts for the construction of said roads and the instructions to bidders for said contracts;

To prepare the form of contract and bond that successful contractors will be required to enter into;

To take, when this board is not in session, such action as may be necessary to carry on said work without delay until the next meeting of this board;

To take any other steps which may be necessary to carry out the will of the people as expressed by their said vote; and be it further

Resolved, that the county clerk and said committee be, and they are hereby, authorized to have done any printing necessary to carry out the purpose of this Resolution, and be it further

Resolved, that the county clerk and said committee be, and they are hereby, authorized, empowered and directed to advertise, over the official signature of said county clerk, that sealed bids for said bonds will be received by said county clerk in his official capacity, until 2 o'clock p. m., on

(Continued on page 26.)

The Construction of Gravel Roads by the Feather-Edge Method.*

By H. E. BILGER, Road Engineer, State Highway Department, Springfield, Illinois.

During the last 10 years several new types of road improvement have been developed and certain features of the older types have been more or less modified in consequence of the needs created by the changed traffic conditions. These road type developments have been prompted by considerations looking to greater ultimate economy, and as such they may be said to have been successful to a degree.

THE ALIGNMENT.

Quite aside from the road types themselves, however, there are other features of the highway equally deserving of the attention of engineers and of road officials in general. These features relate primarily to the alignment of the improvement and to such other matters as have to do with the general safety of the traveling public. The alignment that 15 years ago satisfactorily met the requirements of a maximum speed of some 8 or 10 miles per hour can not now suffice, with any reasonable degree of safety, for the present traffic conditions that impose upon the highway a speed of some 20 to 40 miles per hour. Present conditions are such as to urge that in all highway improvement this matter be given serious consideration, and in view of the increasing density of this high speed traffic, it becomes even advisable that due consideration be given to probable future traffic developments.

Without in any way interfering with the economics of highway location, there can be effected even in the details of the work such marked improvement as will tend greatly toward the general comfort and safety of the traveling public. For example, at all abrupt angles in the right-of-way, and particularly those approaching 90 degreees, an improvement in the interest of the safety of travel can be brought about by simply procuring the necessary additional right-of-way so as to permit moving the inner fence corner a distance of some 75 feet or more. By so doing the radius of the curve can be considerably lengthened and a much better view provided, to the end that public travel is benefited out of all proportion to the cost of the little triangle of land. In order that this additional right-of-way at the corner may be utilized to the utmost, it is necessary that all vegetation be kept down and that the signboards, if any, be transferred elsewhere.

At all crossroads additional land should be provided by moving the fences back to include within the limits of the right-of-way the four triangles at the corners. This greatly benefits the view in all directions by bringing the control of the corners within the authority of the road officials and thereby arresting the growth of vegetation that obstructs the view of highway travel.

In the vicinity of railroad crossings the improvement of the highway should be such as to provide an unobstructed view along the track for a distance of at least 1,000 feet each way, and this view should be enjoyed along a length of the highway extending for a distance of at least 300 feet on each side of the crossing. At these crossings it is particularly important that there be provided accommodations for two vehicles to pass with entire comfort and safety, requiring never less than 18

*Paper presented at Conference in Highway Engineering at Kansas State Agricultural College, Manhattan, Kansas, March 4, 1918.

feet, and the highway for a distance of some 50 feet or more on each side of the crossing should be practically level or should at least have a very easy grade, say not steeper than about 2 per cent. Much destruction of both life and property is caused by motor vehicles taking a run on the steep grades up to the crossing and then killing the engine right on the track. Occasionally two vehicles will make a run from opposite sides of the crossing, and upon reaching same will find that the highway does not have sufficient width for passing in the immediate vicinity of the crossing. In these days conditions of this character are next to intolerable, yet a large percentage of railway crossings present just such accommodations for the public highway traveler.

Where there is an angle greater than some 45 degrees in the alignment of the highway and the improvement at this place is on an embankment higher than say 4 feet, there should be provided on the outside of the curve a substantial looking guardrail painted white. These rails serve more as a warning to traffic than as an obstruction, and consequently, it is not anticipated that they should be built to insure positively their actual stopping of the traffic.

The proper vertical alignment for any type of road is so dependent upon such local conditions as topographic features, available funds, etc., that general recommendations might be wholly a misfit when applied to a particular road. It might be said, however, that grades should be kept reasonably consistent with the general topography of the neighboring country, but aside from this there is little justification for expenses incurred in order to obtain grades lower than some 3 per cent. However, the practicability of economic maintenance must be considered in establishing grades, as well as the construction cost and the serviceability of the road. Whatever grades may be warranted for a particular case, the well-established principles relating to earthwork for both permanency of construction and adequacy of drainage should be adhered to strictly, for herein is the basis upon which the efficiency of the whole work will be largely measured.

THE GRAVEL.

As a rule, gravel road construction is not attended by an advance preparation of the gravel and then its transportation for some distance as is done with material for macadam roads; but rather, the use of gravel for road improvement is prompted by the very nearness of the supply, and, consequently, by the lower construction cost of these roads. This being the case it is not at all practicable, or even possible, to write a rational gravel road specification for general use as is done for the construction of macadam roads the materials for which are made to order from a rock whose properties are known. In gravel road construction as in no other type, is there the necessity for deferring the preparation of the specifications for the work until after the supplies of material for the particular job in question have been thoroughly examined and tested.

In general it might be said, however, that each supply, load or application of gravel should be rather uniformly graded from fine material to the largest size, which size should preferably just pass through about a 2½- or 3-inch ring. Should the gravel contain many pieces too large to pass through this ring, it may still be a highly economical material for the particular road. These larger pieces might be broken by hand, or as the material is spread they might be raked until they come in immediate contact with the subgrade. It would be well to have at least 25 per cent of the total volume of gravel of such size as to be retained on a 1-inch ring, and at least 75 per cent of it, exclusive of clay, should be retained on a one-eighth inch square mesh.

of some 8 to 15 per cent, dry weight, of the total volume of gravel. On the other hand, if the gravel pebbles consist largely of stones of sedimentary origin, such as chert, novaculite, limestone, dolomite, etc., having comparatively high cementing properties, it may be found that by keeping the road properly shaped for some six months after construction the traffic will have ground up a sufficient quantity of this stone to form the necessary bonding material.

This matter is dependent also upon the character of traffic to which the road is to be subjected. It is evident that if the road is to be used primarily for heavy team traffic the pebbles would be ground to a

**FIFTEEN FOOT ROAD FEATHER-EDGE CONSTRUCTION
DESIGNED FOR NARROW RIGHT OF WAY IN LEVEL COUNTRY**

The gravel should be of hard, sound and durable material, containing from about 8 to 15 per cent dry weight, of clay, but not more than about 4 per cent of organic matter. If the bonding clay in the gravel is in any way deficient, there should be added such quantity as might be necessary. Excellent gravel roads can be constructed with material that differs greatly from these suggested general specifications for gravel. In fact, for any reasonably satisfactory supply of gravel not far from the site of the work, there should be made such modifications from the standard methods of construction as will permit of getting the highest possible service out of the local gravel supply.

Gravel for road construction is locally known as either bank gravel or river gravel, depending upon whether the supply is from a natural bank or pit, or from a river or other body of water. As a rule, bank gravel is preferable for road construction owing to its gradation being better, and also due to the fact that in general it contains a sufficient quantity of satisfactory bonding material, usually clay of some character. Very many bank gravels in their natural condition comply with the best specifications for gravel road construction. Where such gravel is available, road construction is greatly simplified and consists essentially of properly placing, distributing, harrowing and rolling the gravel. The bank gravel may contain a quantity of bonding clay somewhat deficient, or in excess of the quantity desired. This matter is not at all serious and can usually be remedied by a little extra care when the gravel is being loaded or distributed in seeing that about the proper amount of clay is provided for the upper 4 or 5 inches of the road.

River gravels are usually deficient in clay content, and in fact are often sufficiently clean to be entirely satisfactory for concrete aggregate. The amount of clay that must be added to river gravel depends largely upon the character of the stone making up the gravel, and also upon the length of time after the road is constructed that it should be thoroughly cemented together. If the pebbles making up the gravel consist essentially of granite or similar igneous stone having a very low cementing property, it will usually be found necessary to add a bonding clay to the amount

bonding dust in a very much shorter time than would be the case were the horse traffic very light. If the traffic were almost entirely of the motor type it would be with extreme difficulty and with probably a year's work after construction, that the gravel would become consolidated sufficiently to make a satisfactory road surface. These matters must be attended to for each individual road for it is utterly impossible to prescribe, in a general way, the advisable procedure in order to get the best results from a particular gravel whose analysis has not been made.

When gravel is deficient in bonding material there is often added thereto what is called a bonding gravel. This bonding gravel should consist of hard pebbles, sand and clay and should be well graded from fine material to a size that would just pass through about a ¾-inch ring. It should contain at least 40 per cent by volume, of pebbles that would be retained on a ⅛-inch square mesh and from about 15 to 25 per cent, dry weight, of clay, and preferably not more than about 5 per cent of organic matter. The use of bonding gravel of this quality will make possible the construction of an entirely satisfactory gravel road with the use of a gravel so clean and consisting of such hard pebbles that its use for road purposes without such a binder would be almost out of the question.

TRENCH AND FEATHER-EDGE METHODS COMPARED.

There are two general methods of gravel road construction, namely, the trench method and the feather-edge method. Certain combinations of conditions prompt the use of these respective methods, and it is necessary that a thorough study of these conditions be made before the particular method of construction is adopted.

The trench method naturally lends itself to dry weather conditions, and also to soils of such character as will not readily mix up into a mud when brought in contact with a little water, as gravelly or sandy soils, and even certain loose clay soils. For the successful use of the trench method there should be provided entirely adequate facilities for surface drainage during the construction of the road. If this is not done the excavated trench becomes in wet weather a virtual stream bed which is practically worthless so far as supporting the gravel is concerned. There is also some relation between the character of the gravel to be used and the method of construction, whether of the trench or the feather-edge. Weather and soil conditions being favorable, the trench method can be used with greater satisfaction with bank gravel than with river gravel. The reason for this is that the bank gravel will become consolidated and form a practically impervious surface to shed water from the subgrade in a much shorter time than will be the case with river gravel. The trench method is the more expensive method of construction, however, and unless conditions are strongly in its favor, it is believed that better results will be obtained eventually by the use of the feather-edge method.

The conditions that encourage the use of the feather-edge method are practically the opposite from those that encourage the trench method. If traffic conditions must be contended with during the construction of the road it will usually be found that other things being equal the feather-edge method is preferable. This method will now be considered in some detail.

FEATHER-EDGE METHOD.

The Roadbed.—Before any gravel is hauled on to the road, the cross section of the road should be brought to the requirements of the plans and the entire width of the graded roadway should be thoroughly rolled until it is of practically a uniform density at all places. At least the portion of this roadway that is to form the subgrade for the gravel should be dry, compact, almost perfectly smooth, and should have such cross slope as may be necessary to shed readily any surface water that might fall thereon. The rolling should preferably be done with a three-wheel self-propelling roller weighing from about 300 to 400 pounds per inch of width of tread on each rear wheel. If such a roller is not readily available, a tractor of similar design and having approximately the same weight will usually answer the purpose very well. During the process of rolling it will often appear to be entirely unnecessary and in fact it frequently is, but the purpose of the rolling is quite as much to detect the location of soft and yielding spots as it is to consolidate the roadbed generally. It is essential that these spots be detected before gravel is placed upon the road. When they are detected additional material should be added until the yielding ceases, and it may even be discovered that water pockets some distance beneath the ground surface will need to be released to an open channel. There should not be left on the graded roadway at any time berms of earth or other material that would interfere with the immediate drainage of its surface.

The work of placing the gravel upon the roadbed might begin at either end of the road, but it should be carried on continuously to the other end. During the process of construction and before any particular section of the road is completed the gravel might be subjected to the traffic of the vehicles used in further construction. Should such traffic rut or displace the gravel, the same should be reshaped and rerolled before further work is done toward the completion of the road.

TWO COURSE CONSTRUCTION.

When the bonding material in the gravel is not entirely satisfactory with respect to both quality and quantity, it is usually advisable that two course construction be adopted. Whether or not the work is to be done by contract, it is important that there be used some positive and accurate method of determing the volume of gravel delivered upon the roadbed. There are several methods

by which this can be accomplished, but experience seems to indicate that by the use of temporary sideboard forms the desired results can be assured and this method is not uneconomical.

Upon the satisfactory completion of the roadbed there should be set thereon, true to line and grade, temporary side forms having a width equal to the depth of the loose gravel which should be shown on the plans. These boards should be held in place by stakes at such intervals as will prevent lateral deflection greater than about 3 inches from the true alignment. Whether the gravel is to be hauled by wagons, motor trucks, industrial railways, or other vehicles, it might be dumped directly upon the subgrade. After there has been placed upon the subgrade a sufficient quantity of gravel for the lower half of the road, it should be distributed to a uniform depth by the use of a bladegrader, drag scraper, or otherwise. While this course is being spread, all the larger stones should be raked or otherwise placed directly in contact with the subgrade. Upon this course of gravel there should be placed such an amount of bonding clay as may be necessary in order that the gravel will comply with the specifications. After the gravel has been spread it should be thoroughly harrowed several times over until the cores formed by dumping it have been entirely loosened up to a density equal to that in the other portions of the gravel. The importance of this thorough harrowing can scarcely be overestimated for in order to secure the best results it is essential that the voids in the gravel be reduced to a minimum, which means that a maximum density of material must be obtained, and this density is closely approached by harrowing until the pebbles of the several sizes become so placed as to occupy the spaces between those of a large size. The cost of this harrowing as compared with the results obtained is practically negligible, and if necessary it would actually be more advisable to do away with the rolling and retain the harrowing than to do away with the harrowing and retain the rolling. The harrow should be of the stiff tooth type, and should have metal teeth at least 1 inch in diameter extending about 6 inches below the frame. The spacing of the teeth should be such as will admit of the free passage of the stones between them, and yet so displace them as to produce the density desired. The design of the harrow should provide a weight of from 8 to 12 pounds upon each tooth.

After the second course of gravel has been placed, it should be spread until its upper surface comes flush with the top of the side forms and its cross section conforms to that shown on the plans for loose gravel. The forms should then be removed and the gravel allowed to take its natural position. Upon this second course there should be distributed the necessary quantity of bonding clay. It should then be thoroughly harrowed several times over, as before, until the cores formed by dumping the gravel have been entirely loosened up and the clay has been uniformly distributed throughout. The harrowing should continue until a uniform density of material is obtained throughout the upper course.

Having done this, the earth shoulders should be shaped by the necessary cutting and filling until the cross section conforms approximately to the finished work as the plans provide. Material other than the natural earth should not be used in forming these shoulders, and all vegetable matter should be strictly prohibited from entering into the work. Upon having shaped the shoulders, the graded roadway over the entire width should be rolled several times over until it is thoroughly compacted,

(Continued on page 26.)

Purchase Prices of State Aid Roads in Illinois
(January 1 to June 30, 1915).   By M. W. WATSON, Assistant Road Engineer, State Highway Department.

July 1, 1913, marked the beginning of a new era in the history of road building in Illinois, being the date when the Revised Road and Bridge Law became effective. This law not only changed the manner of administration of township and county road affairs, but it inaugurated in this State for the first time the method of construction of permanent roads by an equal distribution of cost between the county and the State. This method, known as State aid road improvement, bids fair to place Illinois in her proper rank among the states as to the condition of her rural highways.

As in all other radical changes, considerable time was required to effect the proper organization and to comply with all the requirements of the law, before any attempt could be made to start the actual construction of any of these roads. Every step taken by the State Highway Commission required suitable action by the various county boards and as regular sessions of the county boards of supervisors usually occur only once every three months, it was impossible to obtain suitable action on any of the plans and estimates until the spring of 1914. For the foregoing reasons, coupled with the delay encountered awaiting a favorable opinion from the Supreme Court confirming the constitutionality of the Act, the date of awarding the first State aid contract was delayed until July 1, 1914, exactly one year after the law became effective. On this date State Aid Contract No. 1, was awarded for Section A, Ogle County, for the sum of $21,400, exclusive of the price of cement. This section consisted of a brick pavement, 8,500 feet in length and 10 feet in width.

Between this date and January 1, 1915, contracts were awarded for 74 sections of road, or a total of 91.27 miles. The total contract price of this work was $1,116,952 (which includes the estimated value of cement), or a total average cost of $12,240 per mile of improved road. This price, however, does not include the value of various extra items usually required throughout the course of construction.

The bulk of the State aid contracts for the two fiscal years ending June 30, 1915, should have been awarded prior to April 1, 1915, in order that the construction could have been completed during the 1915 construction season, but owing to the late beginning and to the inability of the various county boards to harmonize on the matter of State aid work, formulate plans for their State aid systems and to lay out the work they intended to do throughout the fiscal year, it was found on the first day of April, 1915, that a considerable number of the counties had not made suitable provision for the expenditure of the State aid money allotted to them. In many cases it was found necessary to award contracts at the last possible date which was June 30, the end of the fiscal year. In the lapse of time between January 1, and June 30, 1915, there were awarded contracts for 46.89 miles of State aid construction and 3 miles of bituminous resurfacing. This mileage of State aid roads as given, includes the construction of the necessary earthwork for 0.49 miles of State aid road known as Section B, Vermilion County, preparatory to the construction of the pavement at some future time when the heavy fills have had sufficient opportunity for settlement.

A summary of the contracts and the itemized contract prices for sections of State aid road work awarded from July 1, 1914, to January 1, 1915, will be found in Volume 1, No. 8, the November, 1914, edition of Illinois Highways on pages 147, 148 and 149, under the heading of "Contract Prices on State Aid Road Work." In making comparisons these prices will be termed the 1914 work and we will endeavor not to repeat the contents of this article to any considerable extent.

The total contract price for State aid road work during 1915, up to and including June 30, was $466,271. The itemized contract prices shown in the accompanying table were derived by a process of computations. Contracts were awarded on the lump sum basis, therefore no unit prices were indicated on the bids for this work. After contracts were awarded for these sections, the itemized contract price was obtained by taking the same percentage of the engineer's detailed estimated cost of the work as the contract price as awarded bore to the original total engineer's estimate exclusive of cement. These detailed prices, although probably not the exact contract price of the work as the contractor may have placed his bid, furnish more information for estimating purposes than would be obtained if unit prices were shown on the proposal, due to the tendency of bidders to present radical bids on particular items.

The cement for this work was purchased by the State Highway Commission and furnished to the contractor f. o. b. cars at the nearest steam railroad siding in the county. For this reason, the price of cement was not included in the contract and the value given in the accompanying table was obtained by using the prices in accordance with the contract between the State Highway Commission and the various cement companies.

The price of earthwork can furnish no comparative value, unless all the governing points were shown in detail, as varying conditions are encountered on each and every section of work owing to the topography of the land. It can be readily seen, however, that the earthwork on these roads was comparatively light, averaging about 5,560 cubic yards per mile of road; and that the average cost of excavation per mile of road was about $1,608 or a cost of about 28.9 cents per cubic yard. Bridge and culvert work depends entirely on the drainage conditions and offers no comparative values.

Macadam shoulders which were a popular type of construction during 1914, appear to be gradually losing favor, especially since a 15-foot width of pavement for brick or concrete construction has been approved as a standard width. The 15-foot pavement serves as a double-track road where light traffic is encountered and has none of the disagreeable construction and maintenance features which attend the macadam shoulders. Six sections of macadam shoulders were awarded during the 1915 period at an average cost of 48 cents per square yard of macadam. The price compares favorably with the price per square yard of the macadam road sections that were awarded during the same period.

It is after the value of all such items as earthwork, culverts, bridges, macadam and earth shoulders and all miscellaneous items have been deducted and the square

(Continued on page 27.)

ILLINOIS HIGHWAYS.

Published Monthly by the
State Highway Department,
Springfield, Illinois.

ILLINOIS HIGHWAY COMMISSION.

A. D. Gash, *President.*
S. E. Bradt, *Secretary.*
James P. Wilson.

Wm. W. Marr, *Chief State Highway Engineer.*

BUREAU OF ROADS.

H. E. Bilger, *Road Engineer.*
M. W. Watson, *Assistant Road Engineer.*
C. M. Hathaway, *Office Engineer.*
L. P. Scott, *Chief Draftsman.*

BUREAU OF BRIDGES.

Clifford Older, *Bridge Engineer.*
G. F. Burch, *Assistant Bridge Engineer.*
A. W. Consoer, *Office Engineer.*

BUREAU OF MAINTENANCE.

B. H. Piepmeier, *Maintenance Engineer.*
F. T. Sheets, *Assistant Maintenance Engineer.*

BUREAU OF TESTS.

F. L. Roman, *Testing Engineer.*
W. C. Adams, *Chemist.*

BUREAU OF AUDITS.

J. M. McCoy, *Chief Clerk.*
T. W. Dieckmann, *Department Editor.*
R. R. McLeod, *General Bookkeeper.*
G. E. Hopkins, *Property Clerk.*

DIVISION ENGINEERS.

R. L. Bell, Buchanan-Link Bldg., Paris, Ill.
H. B. Bushnell, 144 Fox St., Aurora, Ill.
J. E. Huber, Wise Building, Mt. Vernon, Ill.
A. H. Hunter, 302 Apollo Theater Bldg., Peoria, Ill.
C. M. Slaymaker, 510 Metropolitan Bldg., E. St. Louis, Ill.
H. E. Surman, 614 People's Bank Bldg., Moline, Ill.
Fred Tarrant, State Highway Department, Springfield, Ill.

Address all communications in regard to "Illinois Highways," to State Highway Department, Springfield, Illinois.

CONTENTS.

Young America Township, Edgar County, sold the $65,000 worth of road improvement bonds, voted to improve 22 miles of road in the township, to the Toledo Trust and Savings Bank of Toledo, Ohio.

* * *

An item about the cost of bad roads taken from the *Galesburg Evening Mail* says:

"A farmer living 7 miles from Galesburg had about 2,000 bushels of oats to sell. The latter part of December he sold 500 bushels for January delivery at 40 cents a bushel. While delivering them last January he could have sold the balance at 40 cents, but he had such bad luck hauling the 500 bushels already sold, breaking three wagons, because the roads were in such bad shape, that he did not dare undertake to deliver the other 1,500 bushels within the next 30 days. So he did not sell. When the roads were in shape so that delivery could be made, the price had dropped to 37 cents, or a loss to this farmer of 9 cents a bushel. His total loss was $134."

* * *

$40,000 is the amount of bonds voted by Byron Township, Winnebago County, to improve some of their main roads.

* * *

The *Rockford Star* is helping to stimulate and promote the good roads movement in Winnebago County by offering eight cash prizes for the eight best essays from the children of the district schools of the county on the subject "Good Roads in Winnebago County."

* * *

The State Association of Highway Commissioners and Town Clerks is planning to hold three meetings for highway commissioners for discussion of the various phases of work connected with road and bridge construction and maintenance. The first one of these meetings will be held at Salem, beginning May 23. The second one will be at Peoria beginning May 30 and the third one will be held at Dixon or Sterling.

* * *

A grader, a tractor, and an oiler constitute the additional road. machinery recently authorized by the county board of Lake County.

* * *

A vote on the proposition to levy a tax of 40 cents on each $100 assessed valuation for the next three years in Marion Township, Lee County, carried by a good majority.

* * *

A "centrifuge" for testing paints is the latest addition to the equipment of the laboratory of the State Highway Department.

* * *

Mr. B. H. Piepmeier, Maintenance Engineer, recently spent two weeks in investigating the organization and methods of the highway maintenance departments of some of the eastern states.

* * *

A total of $153,500 in bonds has been voted by five townships of Ogle County for road building. Leaf Township being the most recent with an issue of $28,000.

* * *

"The Adams County Golden Rule Good Roads Association" is the name of the organization just formed to pull for better roads in Adams County. The officers are: President, J. H. Paxton, North East Township; vice president, John Seibel, Clayton Township; secretary, Clem Hawkins, Golden; treasurer, H. G. Henry, Camp Point.

C. H. Balchowsky, a good roads booster of Frankfort, Will County, has been busy lately painting the markers along the Joilet-Valparaiso Highway. The markers have a white background with initials J-V painted on in black.

* * *

Bonding themselves for the purpose of constructing oiled earth roads did not appeal to the voters of Chatsworth Township, Livingston County, who voted down an issue of $7,000 proposed for this purpose.

* * *

A determination of the road mileage of Winnebago County recently made by County Superintendent A. R. Carter, shows a total mileage of 911.9 for the county.

* * *

The good roads committee of the Greater Moline, Association intend to locate road signs on the highways leading into Moline. It is hoped to have all the markers posted by the first week in June.

* * *

By the will of Byron Kendall, a prominent resident of Canoe Creek Township, Rock Island County, who died March 30, $1,000 is to be set aside from his estate as a trust fund, the interest from which is to be applied to bettering the roads of the township.

* * *

Evidently the value of the road drag has been realized by the farmers of Bureau County for Mr. Joe S. Cowley, a mail carrier out of Princeton, wrote the following statements for the *Princeton Record*:

"Never before have the farmers taken so much interest in the roads as they have this spring. In every neighborhood you will find a road drag. The commissioners furnish some, but most of them are made by the farmers themselves. On the 28 miles that I travel daily, every foot of it was dragged this spring, and most of the dragging is done free. The farmers now days, are sure up to date. When I started on Route No. 2 out of Princeton 14 years ago, the only man that ever touched the road was the commissioner himself, and he would only go to the main roads once a year and had a hard time to get a farmer to put a team on to help him. The road drag was a thing never heard of. The rural route has been one of the great helps in good road work, as the carriers keep the commissioners posted on the bad places."

During a violent windstorm recently in Iroquois County, a 60-foot steel bridge was lifted clear of the abutments without disturbing a single stone, and dropped upside down, 10 feet away.

VERMILION COUNTY BOND ROADS.

(Continued from page 19.)

Tuesday, the 9th day of March, A. D. 1915, when said bids will be opened and declared in open session of this board; that such advertisement be made by publishing same for at least two successive weeks before the date fixed for opening said bids, in both of the daily papers in the city of Danville and in the Chicago *Herald*, published in the city of Chicago, and one in the magazine called *"The Bond Buyer,"* published in the city of New York, the first publication in said Danville newspapers to be at least fifteen days before said date fixed for opening said bids; that said bids shall be made in strict accordance with the terms of said advertisement and with requirements which are hereby prescribed by this board and which requirements are attached hereto and made a part of this resolution by this express reference; that said requirements shall be expressly referred to in said advertisement; and be it further

Resolved, that, until money from the sale of said bonds becomes available, the necessary expenses in connection with the issuing of said bonds and the construction of said system of roads be, and are hereby, ordered paid out of any general funds of the county which may be available; and be it further

Resolved, that a direct annual tax sufficient to pay the interest on said bonds as it falls due, and also to pay and discharge the principal of said bonds within twenty years from June 1, A. D. 1915, the date of the first issue of said bonds, be, and such direct annual tax is hereby levied upon all of the taxable property in said county; that the county clerk of said county be, and he is hereby, authorized, empowered and directed to add each year to the tax rate required to raise taxes for other purposes for that year, the tax rate required to produce the direct annual tax hereinabove provided for; such direct annual tax must each year be sufficient to pay the following amounts, which include both principal and interest due in the respective years, that is to say:

Table 2.

For the year, 1915	$ 95,000
For the year, 1916	112,000
For the year, 1917	129,000
For the year, 1918	126,000
For the year, 1919	123,000
For the year, 1920	120,000
For the year, 1921	117,000
For the year, 1922	114,000
For the year, 1923	111,000
For the year, 1924	108,000
For the year, 1925	105,000
For the year, 1926	102,000
For the year, 1927	99,000
For the year, 1928	96,000
For the year, 1929	93,000
For the year, 1930	90,000
For the year, 1931	87,000
For the year, 1932	84,000
For the year, 1933	81,000
For the year, 1934	78,000

That said county clerk be, and he is hereby, authorized, empowered and directed to extend such direct annual tax for the payment of the principal and interest of said bonds at maturity on the tax books of said county; that such direct annual tax, so extended by said county clerk, is hereby ordered to be collected at the same time and in the same manner as other taxes of said county are collected; that when said direct annual tax has been collected such money shall be used solely for the purpose of paying said bonds and the interest thereon as said bonds and interest, respectively, mature.

Surveys were begun about January, 1915, and the entire system cross-sectioned, and plans were started. Bonds were advertised, but before the date set for the letting, suit was begun to determine the validity of the issue. This suit was finally determined on December 22, 1915, in favor of the bonds, by the State Supreme Court. The bonds were again advertised after the decision of the courts and $1,000,000 worth were sold at a price of $98.34, on January 20, 1916. Specifications were approved by the State Highway Commission on January 6, and by the county board on February 3. The work was ordered advertised on March 14, 15 and 16, 1916.

The bond issue was voted under sections 40 and 56 of an act to revise the law in relation to counties, approved and in force March 31, 1874, with all amendments, thereto. The Supreme Court decided that the county board had the right to issue bonds for road purposes since 1851.

The county bond roads as laid out were divided into nine divisions of approximately 19 miles each, as shown by cut, for construction purposes, and bids are asked on each of these as a separate contract, although bidders may bid on as many divisions as they like.

THE CONSTRUCTION OF GRAVEL ROADS BY THE FEATHER-EDGE METHOD.

(Continued from page 22.)

forming a firm, smooth surface, free from waves and according to the requirements of the plans. The rolling should begin at the extreme outer edges of the shoulders and should work toward the center, at each rolling of the gravel allowing an overlap of one-half of the width of one of the rear wheels, and each wheel should cover the entire gravel surface.

Should the condition of the gravel or its bonding material be such as not to compact readily under the action of the roller, sprinkling or other means should be employed to compact the gravel as the engineer may direct. The speed of the roller should not exceed about 100 feet per minute. It is quite probable that after rolling there will appear either on the shoulders or the gravel certain depressions and other irregularities. To correct these defects suitable material should be added or removed and they should then be rerolled. The finished surface should conform to the cross section shown on the plan and should present a smooth and even appearance. Should the gravel, with its natural or artificial mixture of bonding clay, for the upper 4 inches of the road, be of such a character that it will not insure a satisfactory wearing surface with a dense body and uniform texture, a 1-inch coating of bonding gravel should be applied uniformly over the entire surface of the gravel road. This bonding gravel should then be raked and rolled into the road surface until all the interstices are filled and the surface is smooth, of a uniform texture and free from waves.

ONE COURSE CONSTRUCTION.

When the conditions and materials are reasonably suitable, there can be built with one-course construction a gravel road that will in all respects prove equally satisfactory with one built by the two-course process. If the gravel contains naturally a sufficient quantity of satisfactory bonding material, one-course construction will generally prove the more economical. When so employed the gravel might be dumped upon the roadbed and then be spread with a blade grader, drag scraper, hand rakes, or otherwise until the material at the edges comes flush with the temporary forms. The forms should then be removed and the gravel thoroughly harrowed several times over until the cores formed by dumping the gravel have been entirely loosened up and the upper 4 inches has a uniform density. Otherwise the process for two-course work would apply also to the one-course.

SPECIAL FEATURES OF GRAVEL ROADS.

Unlike most types of roads, the gravel road is not yet completed when it might appear that all work has been done. Satisfactory gravel road construction being distinctly a process, it is seldom an operation that can be completed within a given period of time, however much skill and energy may be devoted to the work.

Aside from the usual maintenance required for all types of roads, there is required in addition for the gravel road that it receive attention at times for a period of some three to six months from the date of supposed completion.

When the gravel road is compared with the waterbound macadam it is evident why this additional care must be given to the gravel road. The bond in a waterbound macadam road is both mechanical and chemical. It is mechanical in the sense that the angular pieces of stone interlock with one another and become firmly keyed together under the action of the roller. The bond is also chemical as a result of the action set up by the presence of water in contact with the fine material in the stone. As contrasted with this it is evident that the mechanical bond is lacking in gravel roads. In the first place, the gravel pebbles are approximately round, and in addition their surface has been worn almost perfectly smooth by the action of water. Clean and smooth gravel pebbles simply act like so many marbles in tending to roll over one another and being slow to consolidate. It is clear, then, that the bond in a gravel road is almost entirely chemical and comes about from the clay content and also from the crushing of the gravel into finer particles under the action of the roller and the traffic. Inasmuch, as the gravel pebbles are usually from a rather hard stone as compared with limestone, there is required considerable team traffic on gravel roads before any of the pebbles become sufficiently pulverized to supply the bonding material corresponding to screenings in macadam roads.

After having become thoroughly consolidated gravel roads as a rule are more serviceable and more satisfactory than limestone waterbound macadam roads. As for comfort of travel the gravel road more nearly approaches that of an earth road in perfect condition than does the macadam road. The bonding clay content of the gravel road makes it somewhat more resilient, and consequently more desirable for travel than a rigid road. In dry or windy weather, gravel roads seldom become as dusty as macadam roads, and so from this point of view also they are more satisfactory. Gravel roads can withstand the ravages of a long spell of dry weather much better than can macadam roads.

For gravel road construction there is not required the skill or experience necessary for the other types. In fact, as regards both construction and maintenance, the very nature of the road itself is such as to be more nearly in harmony with the conditions, customs, practices, etc., prevailing in rural territory than all other types of roads except the earth road. For ordinary traffic conditions gravel road maintenance scarcely ever need consist of anything more than the addition of a little more gravel and the dragging of the road with an ordinary drag just as earth roads are cared for. This simple process with a simple equipment makes the gravel road highly adaptable to conditions that are strictly rural.

PURCHASE PRICES OF STATE AID ROADS.

(Continued from page 23.)

yard prices for the pavement proper are obtained, that the greatest value of such a tabulation as this is reached.

The price per square yard of pavement can be compared very logically in all cases, when the length of haul, price of labor and the availability of materials have been considered. When taking into account the price of the pavement proper, we can obtain various comparisons in these two tables; one is between the contract prices for the different widths of the same type of pavement, one between the contract prices of work during 1914, and the

prices for the same class of work during 1915 and another between the contract prices for the various types, both during the same and different periods.

From the 13 sections of 10-foot concrete roads awarded during the 1915 period, we find that the average price of pavement per mile of road is $7,106, while the average contract price per square yard of pavement was $1.21. For the same type of road during 1914, we find that the average contract price per mile of road was $7,250 while the average price per square yard of pavement was $1.23. Thus it can be seen that the price for a 10-foot concrete roadway has not varied materially during the two years.

As no 15-foot concrete road sections were awarded in 1914, no comparison can be obtained from the costs of this type of pavement for these two years.

From the six sections of 18-foot concrete roadway awarded during 1915, we find that the price of pavement per mile of road was $12,700 or $1.20 per square yard of paved roadway while during 1914, the average cost per mile was $12,010 and the cost per square yard, $1.14. It can scarcely be said that the price per square yard has increased for this width of pavement, as the amount of 18-foot concrete pavement awarded during 1915 was only about one-fourth of that awarded during 1914.

When the various widths of concrete pavements are considered in comparison, one with another, it would appear from these prices that the 15-foot width could be obtained at the lowest price per square yard, but we would be scarcely justified in accepting these figures as definite conclusion, as the number of sections of 15-foot pavement do not equal the number of the other two types awarded, but we are warranted in stating that either a 15-foot or an 18-foot width can be constructed at less cost per square yard than can the narrower 10-foot pavement. This, from a construction standpoint, is explained by the centralization of the work on the wider sections, while on the narrow width the same amount of work is drawn out over a greater distance and with a lateral confinement which tends to increase the cost of handling materials.

The 1915 contracts show that the average cost of 10-foot brick pavements was $11,000 per mile or $1.88 per square yard while in 1914 the price was $11,880 per mile or $2.02 per square yard which would indicate that the price for this width of brick pavement has somewhat decreased.

The price for 18-foot brick pavements is shown to have been $19,500 per mile, or $1.85 per square yard in 1915, and from the one section awarded to have been $21,430 per mile or $2.03 per square yard in 1914. These figures can scarcely be styled a comparison owing to the fact that there were so few sections awarded in either case.

A difference in price per square yard for different widths of pavement does not appear to exist in brick as it does in concrete, but the price appears to be very nearly uniform, and from these tables it appears that there is a difference in price between the concrete and brick pavements of from 70 cents to 80 cents per square yard, dependent upon governing conditions. The prices for concrete pavement seem to indicate that the cost is remaining practically stationary while the prices for brick seem to be gradually decreasing.

Owing to the small amount of work under contract for gavel and macadam pavements, very little comparative value exists but a general uniformity seems apparent in these sections of work.

(Continued on page 29.)

PURCHASE PRICES ON STATE AID ROAD WORK, JANUARY 1 TO JUNE 30, 1915.

CONCRETE AND BRICK ROADS.																		
Jo Daviess	B	1	2,850	3,187	$1,348	$5,173	$6,581	$10,440	3,978	$1,567	$126		$149			$8,713	$6,880	$1 17
Peoria	B	1	450 9,558 900	500 19,104 1,800	7,665	$4,745	$8,300	16,380	8,565	2,758	1,761		628			25,744 3,505	11,810 13,180 20,560	1 08 1 94 1 86
Totals except as noted	B	4	18,758	24,571	$8,998	$29,918	$38,911	$814,930	11,934	$4,825	$1,960		$771		Concrete Brick	$7,457 4,469	$11,680 17,490	$1 22 1 94
RESURFACING BITUMINOUS MACADAM ROADS.																		
Ogle	B	2&5	15,840	33,400		$1,500	$1,500	$500								$1,500	$500	$0 04
MACADAM ROADS.																		
Calhoun	A	1	1,020	2,560		$2,000 3,050 1,725	$2,000 3,050 1,725	$5,495 7,340	1,005 675 336	$578 775 170	$327 203		$49			$1,123 2,055	$3,187 4,096	$0 45 0 56
Union	A	1	2,300	3,067								$1,556						
Jackson	A	4	3,100															
Totals except as noted	A		7,520	6,227	$342	$6,775	$6,775	$90,474	4,976	$1,517	$449	$1,555	$49			$3,305	$4,110	$0 51
10-FOOT GRAVEL ROADS.																		
White	A	11	11,746	19,354		$13,600	$13,942	$5,263	12,769	$3,437	$2,003		$418			$8,025	$3,510	$0 41
15-FOOT GRAVEL ROADS.																		
Alexander	A	1	5,100	8,500		$5,448	$5,448	$5,640	5,430	$1,570			$117			$8,478 1,933	$3,601 4,883	$0 41 0 55
Edwards	A	1	2,100	3,500		2,794	2,794	6,850	2,617	674			117					
Totals except as noted	A		7,900	12,000		$8,172	$8,172	$5,996	8,047	$1,944			$117			$5,411	$3,964	$0 45
COMBINATION WIDTHS GRAVEL ROADS.																		
Wabash	A	3	8,980	8,880	a	$6,300	$6,300	$1,754	5,293	$1,508	$342		$573	$700		$4,077	$2,430	$0 46
Totals all gravel roads	A		27,826	40,414	$342	$28,072	$28,414	$15,382	25,100	$5,889	$1,404		$906	$700		$17,513	$3,323	$90 43
EARTH WORK AND CULVERTS.																		
Vermilion	B	2	9,550		$251	$7,064	$7,315	$15,150	34,634	$6,479	$838			$700				

NOTE.—All averages computed on the basis of total cost, mileage and yardage.
NOTE.—The prorated contract price, abbreviated to pro-con. price, is the probable contract price of the given item, based on the Department estimate and the contract price of the work.

* Concrete shoulders.
† Average.
‡ Figures include macadam shoulders only.
a Furnished by contractor.

Besides the features brought out in this article, these tables offer quite an opportunity for comparison and study and are especially valuable owing to the fact that they are the actual purchasing price and not an estimated cost, nor a cost to the contractor based on data taken during construction, which are usually given in a table of this kind. These prices, therefore, should prove of interest not only to engineers and contractors, but to any taxpayer who desires information as to what he actually pays for his roads.

TOWNSHIP ORGANIZATION OF GOOD ROADS ASSOCIATIONS.

By E. F. MOTSINGER,
County Superintendent of Highways, Fulton County.

The question of good roads, their maintenance and construction is rapidly absorbing other similar questions affecting the interests of the public. Therefore, it is essentially necessary that the public in general be not only informed but made a part of this great movement for better roads.

In years past, perhaps one official in a county was able to handle the work of the publicity side of road building, but in this twentieth century, where politics are running rampant it is vitally necessary that all the people be informed as to what is going on, not only in their county, but likewise in their township.

The demand for better roads, better methods of construction, more attention by officials in office, necessitated the formation of a county good roads associaion. The work of this association is vast and far reaching and should prove a power for better roads. But not all the people have the time or inclination to study and work for results with the county as a unit, and consequently the need of township organizations have become apparent.

Fulton County has started forming good road associations in each township, with the view of uniting the people of each community so that they may be of some force in the different policies before the people.

The principal purpose of the township association is to disseminate knowledge to all interested persons of what is being done on the roads and bridges in their township, and to solicit their opinion in the management of township affairs.

The membership of the association is open to all who fulfill the requirements of the constitution, viz: They shall be a resident of the township and pay a certain sum of money per year.

The officers shall consist of a president, vice president, secretary and treasurer. The committees shall be as follows: Membership, press, and legislative.

The duties of the various officers and committees shall be similar to those of other societies. It is probable that the membership committee will be composed of one man from each school district.

It is the purpose of the township association to send at least three men as delegates to the meetings of the county association. In this manner, the township will have sufficient representation at the county meeting to endorse and bring before that body matters of interest to the individual township.

I feel that the township organization has an opportunity to accomplish much in that it should be able to come in close contact with those interested in highway work in a territory 6 miles square. This association may assist the various township officials in the performance of their duties and in general become the local center of all activities of road work in the township.

Correspondence Course in Road Building
CONDUCTED BY UNIVERSITY OF ILLINOIS.

Lesson 2—Steel Beam Bridges With Wood Plank Floors.

Rolled steel beams may be used to support bridge floors for spans not to exceed 35 feet in length.

The standard sizes of beams are 6, 7, 8, 9, 10, 12, 15, 18, 20, and 24 inches in depth, with varying weights per lineal foot as shown in the tables of sizes given in Cambria Steel Handbook or in Carnegie's Pocket Companion.

The allowable safe bending stress on rolled beams as given in the specifications of the Illinois Highway Department is 16,000 pounds per square inch. This allowable stress may be exceeded as much as 50 per cent occasionally if the beam is in first-class condition; but it should not be exceeded at all if the beam is rusted to any appreciable extent.

When investigating the strength of old beam bridges, the weights of the beams per lineal foot, and all other necessary information concerning the beam, may be determined by measuring its depth, the width of the flange and the thickness of the web. Then, by turning to the steel handbook the beam which has these dimensions may be found. This table will give the weight per lineal foot, the moment of inertia (I), the radius of gyration (r), and the section modulus (S). (See Cambria Steel, page 158, Edition 1912) (Carnegie's Pocket Companion, page 142).

In the investigation of old beam bridges the character and stability of the supports should be looked into very carefully to see that they will support the load carried by the beams.

DISTRIBUTION OF FLOOR LOADS BY WOOD PLANK.

UNIFORM LIVE LOAD.

For uniformly distributed loads on a plank floor it is assumed that each steel beam carries the load on a width equal to the distance between joists. The joists should not be spaced farther apart than 2 ft. 6 in.

The total load will include the weight of the joists, the flooring, and the wearing surface and any live load that may be imposed. The Illinois Highway Department specifies a uniform live load of 125 pounds per square foot for spans less than 50 feet in length.

Example 1.

(a) Longitudinal Section

(b) Cross Section

Figure 1.

A span will be assumed as shown in Fig. 1.

The length of the span is 18 ft. The spacing of joists is 2 ft. Each joist must carry a strip of floor 2 ft. wide, and a uniform live load of 125 lb. per square foot

on a strip 2 ft. wide. Seasoned oak plank weigh about 4½ pounds per foot board measure. The weight of the floor per lineal foot of joist is,

$$2 \times 3 \times 4\frac{1}{2} = 27 \text{ pounds}$$

The live load per lineal foot of joist is,

$$2 \times 125 = 250 \text{ pounds},$$

The total load per lineal foot of joist is 277 pounds.

The weight of the joist itself is not usually considered in computing the load on the joist.

CONCENTRATED LIVE LOAD.

The joists should not be spaced farther apart than 2 ft. 6 in. It has been determined by experiment that, with a maximum joist spacing of 2 ft. 6 in. and a 3-inch plank floor, one joist will not receive more than 50 per cent of the total concentrated load.

The Illinois Highway Department specifies (Art. 92) that, "All floor systems shall be designed to sustain, in addition to the dead load, a concentrated live load of not less than 15 tons, which shall be considered as supported on two axles, spaced 10 feet apart, the rear axle to carry 10 tons and the forward axle 5 tons." (See also Art. 94 of the same specifications).

If the load on the rear axle is 10 tons the load on one rear wheel is 5 tons, or 10,000 pounds, and the load from the rear wheel which is carried by one joist is 5,000 pounds. Likewise the load from the front wheel which is carried by one joist is 2,500 pounds.

The concentrated live loads will produce higher unit stress than uniformly distributed live loads on all beam bridges, therefore, in the investigation of steel beam bridges, always use the concentrated loads if the bridge is required to carry the usual highway traffic.

Example 2.

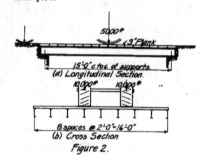
(a) Longitudinal Section

(b) Cross Section

Figure 2.

A span will be assumed as shown in Fig. 2.

The weight of the floor is the same as in Example 1, and is 27 pounds per lineal foot of joist. The concentrated load is 5,000 pounds and is applied at the center of the span in this case, to produce maximum stress.

The heavy wheel of the engine should be placed at the center of the span for spans 18 ft. 2 in. or less in length in order to get the maximum stress in the beam.

Or, if the span is greater than 18 ft. 2 in. the engine should be placed as shown in Fig. 3.

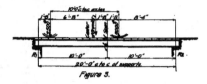

Figure 3.

The following criterion holds true for fixing the position of two concentrated loads on a beam in order to produce maximum bending moment:

The heavy load should be placed as far from one end of the beam as the center of gravity of the two loads is from the other end.

(To be continued in May issue.)

MEETING OF COUNTY SUPERINTENDENTS OF THIRD DIVISION.

The last meeting of the county superintendent of the third division was held in the office of County Superintendent of Highways, W. E. Emery, at Peoria, Illinois, on February 28, 1916.

There were present, Division Engineer, A. H. Hunter; L. H. Eldridge, county superintendent of highways, Marshall County; W. E. Emery, county superintendent of highways, Peoria, Illinois; E. F. Motsinger, county superintendent of highways, Fulton County; W. M. Bonham, county superintendent of highways, McDonough County; Frank S. Cook, county superintendent of highways, Tazewell County; R. O. Edwards, county superintendent of highways, McLean County; R. W. Osborn, county superintendent of highways, Livingston County; A. B. Hurd, county superintendent of highways, Woodford County.

The subject of oiling township roads was taken up and after considerable discussion the following conclusions were reached:

First—That the grading for oiled earth should be under the supervision of the county superintendent of highways, or his authorized assistant.

Second—That the oil should not be applied upon the road until approval had been given by the county superintendent of highways.

Third—The oil should be distributed uniformly over the width of road to be specified by the county superintendent of highways and should be applied by a pressure distributor.

Fourth—The width to be oiled should be covered by one, two or more equal strips, without overlapping. The sense of the meeting was that a strip 12 feet wide should be oiled; that the oil should be put on in two applications and that the total quantity of oil to be used, per square yard, should be left to the judgment of the county superintendent of highways.

Fifth—The road should be kept closed to public travel from the time of the first application until the oil has thoroughly penetrated the surface of the road.

Sixth—All road oil used should conform to the specifications "A," "B" or "C" of the State Highway Department, the one used being dependent upon conditions.

The county superintendent of highways should insist that a sample of the oil to be used be taken from each tank-car and sent, for analysis, to the testing laboratory of the State Highway Department or the State University, or some reliable private chemist, as designated by the county superintendent of highways.

A sample form of order blank to be used in purchasing road oils was drawn up. A copy of this will be sent to each county superintendent of the third division. An urgent request was made that this form of order be required on all purchases of this material, which had to be approved by the superintendents. In this way it is believed that a more uniform grade of oil can be obtained for use.

The question of road oilers was taken up and it was uniformly decided that an oil distributor should have:

First—A uniform spread of material.

Second—A minimum flow of one pint and a maximum of one-half gallon per square yard of surface.

Third—Should be capable of maintaining a uniform temperature.

Fourth—That they should be of the pressure type, capable of maintaining a uniform pressure.

Fifth—That the capacity of the tank should be not less than 600 gallons.

The question was discussed of pumping the oil from the tank cars by various means.

The following firms were mentioned as being able to furnish rotary pumps for pumping the oil: James B. Clow & Co., Chicago, Illinois; The Gould Pump Co., Seneca Falls, N. Y.; Fairbank-Morris Co., Chicago, Illinois.

A request was made by Mr. Hunter that a detailed report concerning all road equipment and machinery purchases approved by the county superintendents be made to him. These reports will be kept on file and will be available to the county superintendents at any time they desire to make use of them.

An assessment of fifty cents (50¢) per member was made to carry on the clerical work of the organization.

Mr. Osborn explained the uniform system of accounting of the township road and bridge funds, which has been adopted in Livingston County and offered his assistance to any county wishing to put in a similar system. Several of the county superintendents expressed themselves as favorably impressed with the system described by Mr. Osborn and invited him to attend their next county board meeting and explain there this system which is being used in Livingston County. On motion by Mr. Osborn, seconded by Mr. Cook a resolution was adopted calling for the meeting of the third division to be held on the last Monday in the months of February, April, June, August, October and December; that the place of meeting be determined from time to time.

ROAD OIL AGREEMENT
With

.................Township.................County, Illinois.

and

....
(Name and address of firm to whom order is given.)

.............................1916.

GENTLEMEN: Please ship to............................
at................county of...............State of Illinois,
on or about.................day of.................191.....
by the following route.............................gallons
of road oil, for the use of.........................Township
on the following conditions:

That a 1-quart sample of the oil taken by the county superintendent of highways, or his representative, from each car immediately upon the arrival of same at destination and test-ed at the testing laboratory of the State Highway Depart-ment, Springfield, Illinois, or some reliable chemical firm to be designated by the county superintendent of highways, shall conform in every respect to the "State Highway's Spec-ifications..............for light oil to be used in the surface treatment of earth roads." Upon the report of a satisfactory test, the highway commissioners agree to pay..............

....

(Name of firm to whom order is given.)

or order.............cents per gallon, f. o. b. at.....Illinois. As follows: ....dollars ($......) in cash and to give a Township order for............dollars ($......) due April 1, 19........

If the above mentioned oil does not conform to the spec-ifications, it is understood that the firm to whom order was given will be notified that oil is not accepted and that the above mentioned firm will receive no payment for same and in addition will be required to pay for all demurrage and other charges, and the said car of oil, or parts thereof, that are rejected, will be at their disposal.

                    Highway Commissioners
                              of
APPROVED.   ....Township
                    ....County

....

County Superintendent of Highways

Three copies of this order must be filled out. One for the town clerk, one for the salesman and one for the county superintendent of highways. All three orders must bear ap-proval of county superintendent of highways.

SPECIFICATIONS FOR ROAD OILERS.

To be 600 gallons pressure oil distributers.

Said machines must develop the work hereinafter speci-fied to the entire satisfaction of the .... committee before final acceptance will be made.

Said machines must be able to produce a uniform spread 6 ft. in width a minimum of 1 pint per square yard, and a maximum of one-half gallon per square yard of an oil con-taining 40 per cent asphaltum at a temperature of 70° F.

Said machines must also produce a uniform spread of 6 ft. in width at a minimum of 1 pint per square yard and a maximum of one-half gallon per square yard of an oil con-taining 60 per cent asphaltum at a temperature of 200° F.

Said machines must also be equipped with a pressure pump that is able to maintain a pressure of 15 lb. per square inch upon the discharge lines.

Said machines must be supplied with a heating device sufficient of maintaining a temperature of 200° F. when oil is being applied at a distance of 5 miles from loading point

All bids must be f. o. b. cars, ... Illinois, or any other shipping point in county.

OPINIONS OF THE ATTORNEY GENERAL.

A VOTE HAD BY A TOWN IN 1914 TO ABOLISH THE POLL TAX PROVIDED FOR UNDER SECTION 55 WHICH WENT INTO EFFECT JULY 1, 1913, WOULD NOT HAVE THE EFFECT TO ABOLISH A POLL TAX PROVIDED FOR BY AN ACT WHICH WENT INTO EFFECT JULY 1, 1915.

November 1, 1915.

MR. L. C. DICK,
    Town Clerk, DeLand, Illinois.

DEAR SIR: I am in receipt of your favor of the 29th instant, from which it appears that your town voted at the town election in April, 1914, to abolish payment of the poll tax,

assessment of which by the highway commissioners was pro-vided for by section 55 of the revised Road and Bridge Act of 1913. You inquire in substance whether the vote had in 1914 to abolish payment of a poll tax has the effect to abolish payment of such tax which highway commissioners are re-quired to assess under an act passed by the last legislature.

Section 55 of the Road and Bridge Act, which went into effect July 1, 1913, made it the duty of the highway commis-sioners at their annual meeting held on the second Tuesday after the annual town meeting, to assess a poll tax of not less than one nor more than three dollars against all able-bodied men; said section provided, however, that the poll tax assessed by highway commissioners should not apply to persons who resided in cities and incorporated villages; and provides, also, that upon a petition as therein prescribed the question of abolishing the poll tax might be submitted at an annual town election and that if a majority of all the votes cast were against the payment of a poll tax, that a poll tax should not be assessed in such town.

The Supreme Court, in the case of *Town of Dixon* v. *Seymour Ide,* 267 Ill. 445, held said section 55 of the act which went into effect July 1, 1913, to be unconstitutional. The basis of the court's opinion was that the clause in said section which exempted residents of cities and incorporated villages from the payment of the poll tax assessed by highway commissioners was contrary to the provision of section 9 of article 9 of the Constitution, which requires that taxes levied by municipal corporations for corporate purposes shall be uniform in respect to persons and property within the juris-diction of the body imposing such tax; the holding of the court in effect being that a statute imposing a poll tax must, in order to be valid, apply to all taxable persons within the township, including persons residing in cities and incor-porated villages.

The Supreme Court in the case of *Highway Commissioners* v. *Bloomington,* 253 Ill. 164, holds in effect that where a statute is declared unconstitutional, the situation in legal contem-plation is as though no statute had ever been passed. It follows, therefore, that the opinion of the Supreme Court holding section 55 of the act, which went into force July 1, 1913, unconstitutional, had the same effect as though said act contained no provision for the levy of a poll tax.

The legislature, with a view of meeting the objections which the court found to section 55 of the act of 1913, passed an act of 1915 which provides for the assessment of a poll tax by highway commissioners which applies to residents of cities and incorporated villages within the town as well as to persons who reside in the town outside of cities and villages. Said act also provides in what manner a vote may be had to abolish payment of such tax. A vote had by a town in 1914 to abolish the poll tax provided for under said section 55 which went into force July 1, 1913, would not have the effect to abolish a poll tax provided for by an act which went into effect in July, 1915. A vote to abolish a tax provided for under an existing statute does not have the effect to abolish the same kind of a tax which a later statute requires to be assessed. Under the act of 1915, which creates a new section 55 of the Road and Bridge Act, it becomes the duty of highway commissioners at their annual meeting to be held the second Tuesday after the annual town meeting in April, 1916, to assess a poll tax as by said act provided, unless upon a peti-tion as therein prescribed the voters at the town meeting to be held on the first Tuesday of April, 1916, vote to abolish the payment of such tax.

Very respectfully,

                    P. J. LUCEY, *Attorney General.*

On April 1 there were more than 2,500,000 automo-biles registered in the United States. During the year it is estimated that these cars will use over 12,000,000 tires, burn 1,500,000,000 gallons of gasoline, and con-sume 75,000,000 gallons of lubricating oil. It is said that in one month, now, automobile makers are turning out more cars than were built during the entire year of 1908. No wonder this is called the gasoline age.

SCHNEPP & BARNES, STATE PRINTERS SPRINGFIELD, ILL. 1916.

ILLINOIS HIGHWAYS

[Printed by authority of the State of Illinois.]

OFFICIAL PUBLICATION OF THE

STATE HIGHWAY DEPARTMENT

| VOL. III | SPRINGFIELD, ILLINOIS, MAY, 1916 | No. 5 |

Proclamation
To The People of Illinois

Three years ago there was inaugurated in Illinois the custom of dedicating one day in the year to the worthy cause of highway improvement, and so now, again this year, it becomes both my duty and my pleasure to designate such a day.

Since the enactment of the Tice Road Law, in 1913, public sentiment for better roads has grown so rapidly that to-day it is not confined to one locality only, but is State-wide in its scope.

It is no longer necessary to call your attention to the need of improving our public highways. That need you have already realized, and the realization is slowly but surely pulling Illinois out of the mud. Apathy toward road improvement has given way to enthusiasm and well-directed efforts toward the culmination of the ideal which we have placed before us—better roads for Illinois.

Our State Highway Commission, created by the law of 1913, have been steadily working on the construction of the State aid system of roads which the law contemplates. To-day they report that 150 miles of this system has been completed and that the plans call for the construction of some 470 miles during this year. Add to these facts, the enthusiasm with which many counties, townships and districts are advocating bond issues for road-building purposes and you can begin to realize to what proportions the good roads movement has grown.

Now that this movement is so splendidly started, we should not sit by content and think that it will perpetuate itself. We must keep awake if we desire to see it continue to grow in strength and popularity. Nothing will serve better to keep this problem before our eyes than a day set aside for actual constructive work on our highways.

I respectfully ask that the activities of the day, consisting of grading, draining, dragging, hauling and placing gravel and other materials, be carried out under the direction of the local highway commissioners, county superintendents of highways, good roads associations and automobile clubs, so that the effort expended will be along practical and systematic channels.

It is also to be recommended that the schools of the State, in harmony with the spirit of the day, arrange for a "Good Roads" program, which should embrace the reading of this proclamation, together with other appropriate good roads literature, and, if possible, arrange for an address on "Good Roads" to be delivered by some one who is competent to talk upon the subject.

Now, therefore, I, Edward F. Dunne, Governor of the State of Illinois, do hereby proclaim Friday, May 19, 1916, as Good Roads Day—not as a holiday, but as a hard work day, and I respectfully urge that on this day the entire commonwealth will cooperate for the improvement of the highways of Illinois.

IN WITNESS WHEREOF, I, Edward F. Dunne, do hereunto set my hand and cause to be affixed the Great Seal of the State, this twenty-fifth day of April, A. D. 1916.

Governor.

By the Governor,

Secretary of State.

GOOD ROADS DAY

Governor Dunne has proclaimed Friday, May 19, as Good Roads Day in Illinois. The date is well set, as it comes at a time when there is more than an even chance that the weather will be good and also at a time when the farmers will not be so busy but what they can spare the day from their work.

The custom of designating one day in the year for the purpose of fostering a spirit of cooperation and enthusiasm for better roads was inaugurated three years ago, and since then the day has become an annual affair.

In his proclamation Governor Dunne calls attention to the fact that Good Roads Day is to be a day of work, to be participated in by as many as possible. The amount of actual constructive work accomplished on this occasion is of secondary consideration. The most important function of Good Roads Day is to se-

forded. We can't stay at home and simply talk about this day and make it a success. United and well-concerted action, together with systematic planning and organization are the factors upon which depends success.

The activities of the day will be a subject worthy of the attention of all community organizations, such as chambers of commerce, good roads associations, automobile clubs, civic improvement leagues, etc., as well as the attention of all road officials. The individual should cooperate with the organization. It is an affair in which all are concerned and accordingly should receive hearty support.

The women also can do much toward the affair an enjoyable one by providing for a lunch to be served to the workers. This could readily take the form of a community picnic and the gathering together of the workers at this time would furnish an admirable occa-

Governor Dunne Addressing a "Road Day" Gathering.

cure the united approval and cooperation of the State as a whole for the better roads movement.

Our road problem is necessarily a community problem, and as such deserves the attention of every public-spirited citizen. We can never hope to have better roads until there is a better and truer understanding by each individual as to just what the roads mean to him or her, personally. It is by such occasions as a Good Roads Day that the attention of the public is being turned to a thoughtful and careful study of our road conditions and of the steps to be taken to improve them.

The value to be derived from this occasion will depend entirely upon the amount of cooperation af-

sion for a short talk on good roads to be made by some competent person.

In arranging for the work of the day, the plans made will depend entirely upon local conditions, and no definite rules can be laid down which would be applicable to all counties. A few general suggestions however, might be in order, so as to furnish an outline of a plan to be developed for a particular county.

The bulk of the work will consist of course of grading, draining, dragging and hauling and placing material. Accordingly every piece of road working machinery should be made available, and plans should be made ahead of time for the assignment of particular equipment for particular work.

Road Day Workers at Dinner.

Road Day in Kane County. (1914)

A careful survey of the situation should be made, and the work to be done gotten carefully in mind. Special attention should be given to remedying places in the roads that are particularly notorious or dangerous. Such actions as draining and filling a bad mud-hole, or grading out the abrupt approach at a dangerous grade crossing, bettering the view of the traveller at a dangerous crossing or turn by removing what-

porting the men to and from the places of work. An automobile owner will appreciate better than the average person what it means to improve a bad stretch of road.

During the entire day, however, the fact should not be lost sight of that Good Roads Day while it occurs but once a year, is an occasion which should be in the minds of the people the remaining 364 days

The True Road Day Spirit.

ever obstructs the view, etc., are well worth the careful consideration of all. An effort should be made to solicit aid from every one. From those who can not give their time and labor, it might be advisable to ask a cash donation, equivalent in value to a day's labor.

The owners of automobiles should be glad to donate the use of their machines for the purpose of trans-

of the year. The question of our roads is a big problem; it will take a lot of study before it is solved. But the more we think about it and study about it the sooner the solution will be available. Good Roads Day is the best means we have for promoting such thought and study. Let us all do our part in seeing that the day shall be remembered.

WHAT HAS BEEN DONE ON FORMER "ROADS DAYS."

In order to give an idea as to the character and amount of the work which has been done on previous "Roads Days," there are printed below reports from several county superintendents of highways concerning the work done in their counties on this occasion.

DEKALB COUNTY.

[By W. C. Miller, Superintendent of Highways.]

A few days prior to "Road Day" I requested that all township highway commissioners meet at the courthouse for the purpose of formulating plans for the work to be done on the roads and bridges on the above date.

The meeting was well attended, considering the time of the year, and all seemed enthusiastic. S. E. Bradt, State Highway Commissioner, J. W. Corkings, counsel for the Illinois division of the Lincoln Highway, and myself, all made addresses. Co-operation among all the road officials was practically emphasized in these talks. I requested that a report of all the work done on "Road Day" be sent in by each commissioner. I was rewarded in this. In order to avoid unnecessary details, I have summarized all the work done in as brief a manner as possible, namely:

(1) Throughout the county we were able to engage gratis twenty-four (24) traction engines and as many road graders. About ninety (90) miles of road were graded in this manner.

(2) Lincoln Highway was dragged and graded across the county for a distance of fifteen (15) miles. This was done as the Governor's party traveled over this portion on "Road Day."

(3) About three hundred and fifty (350) miles of dirt road were dragged with the common road drag.

(4) A total of one (1) mile of crushed stone was laid.

(5) A total of five (5) miles of washed gravel was laid.

(6) Two miles of 8-inch drainage tiles were started and are now completed.

(7) About thirty (30) miles of bank-run gravel were put down and are now completed.

In numerous places, where it was deemed necessary, pikes were built or cut down as conditions warranted. Many bridge floors were replaced and abutments for a 70-foot steel bridge were staked out over Coon Creek in Genoa Township.

FULTON COUNTY.

[By E. F. Motsinger, County Superintendent of Highways.]

I beg to submit the following report of the work done in Fulton County on "Good Roads Day."

"Good Roads Day" was generally observed in this county. As officials were changing in all townships and with the introduction of the single highway commissioner, a problem was presented which proved a handicap.

In one township what work was done by the farmers, they not only working on that day but continued for a week. They succeeded in cutting down a hill and filling up a low place which had been a public nuisance for years. I feel that the improvement of this particular hill is worth hundreds of dollars to the travelers on that road.

(Continued on page 41.)

EARTH ROADS

By B. H. PIEPMEIER,
Maintenance Engineer.

A great many inquiries have been made concerning earth road construction and maintenance. It would hardly seem possible that such inquiries should be made on a subject that we are or should all be, more or less familiar with. However, it is perhaps for this reason that so many are willing to offer their views concerning the construction and maintenance of earth roads. If the road builder would listen to all freely expressed views on such work, he would be working the road differently every day.

About 90 per cent of the roads in Illinois are earth roads and will likely remain as earth roads for a great many years. The greatest problem, particularly that of the township or road district, is to properly construct and maintain the existing earth roads.

While the construction and the maintenance of earth roads are comparatively simple, yet because of this simplicity, the fundamentals of the work are often neglected. In view of the tremendous amount of earth road work that is to be done it is quite important that every effort be directed along lines that will accomplish the best results with the money expended, with the plan in mind that at any future time when further improvement of the road is demanded because of increased traffic, that the preliminary work of grading and draining will not need to be repeated.

It must be held in mind that the larger per cent of work done in constructing earth roads is permanent. If the grade is properly established, the cross section properly designed, the drainage properly taken care of, etc., the work will not have to be done over or altered for future improvements. This being true, it can readily be seen that earth road construction is just as important as brick or concrete road construction and that just as much engineering skill is required to insure the best results.

A great many earth roads are constructed in a haphazard way and with very little regard for any future improvement. Such work is to be severely criticised as the time and money spent are practically wasted. Improperly worked earth roads result in a greater loss than the time and money that is put on them. Many roads are worse after working than before and the loss to the public in their use can not be measured in a monetary sense. Improper construction often puts the earth road in such shape that a very large portion of the best soil is washed away by heavy rains resulting in a serious loss to the road.

The greatest fault that could be offered against the bulk of township road construction to-day, is that the road and bridge money is spread out over all the roads in the township each year and there are but very few roads that receive the proper amount of time and money needed to put them in first-class condition. The bulk of the road and bridge money is really spent in maintenance work on the existing earth roads, when a large per cent of such roads have never been properly constructed. This means an excessive maintenance charge.

A majority of the townships have sufficient income to maintain the earth roads if they were once put into proper condition for effective maintenance. The most economic work that could be undertaken by a great many townships would be to finance some scheme that would permit all the earth roads in the township to be properly graded and drained and the necessary culverts and bridges constructed so as to be permanent. After the

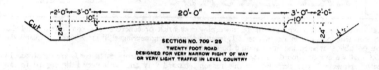

SECTION NO. 709 - 25
TWENTY FOOT ROAD
DESIGNED FOR VERY NARROW RIGHT OF WAY
OR VERY LIGHT TRAFFIC IN LEVEL COUNTRY

SECTION NO. 709 - 26
TWENTY-TWO FOOT ROAD
DESIGNED FOR VERY NARROW RIGHT OF WAY
OR VERY LIGHT TRAFFIC ON HEAVY FILLS

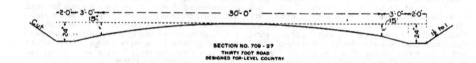

SECTION NO. 709 - 27
THIRTY FOOT ROAD
DESIGNED FOR LEVEL COUNTRY

SECTION NO. 709 - 28
THIRTY-TWO FOOT ROAD
DESIGNED FOR HEAVY FILLS

SECTION NO. 709 - 29
FIFTEEN FOOT ROAD
DESIGNED FOR VERY LIGHT TRAFFIC
FOR HEAVY CUTS

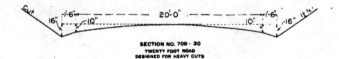

SECTION NO. 709 - 30
TWENTY FOOT ROAD
DESIGNED FOR HEAVY CUTS

Suggested Cross Sections for Earth Roads.

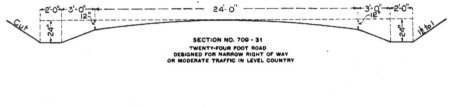

SECTION NO. 709 - 31
TWENTY-FOUR FOOT ROAD
DESIGNED FOR NARROW RIGHT OF WAY
OR MODERATE TRAFFIC IN LEVEL COUNTRY

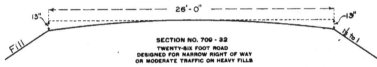

SECTION NO. 709 - 32
TWENTY-SIX FOOT ROAD
DESIGNED FOR NARROW RIGHT OF WAY
OR MODERATE TRAFFIC ON HEAVY FILLS

majority of roads Were once put in first-class condition, many of them could easily be maintained under good management by dragging and oiling, with the money that is available.

On earth roads which are properly constructed, the road drag and oil will materially improve them and permit them to serve the needs of a majority of the local traffic for a number of years. The improving and maintaining of good earth roads in a community will serve all the taxpayers alike, and will be a means of getting their support in improving, with some hard surfacing material, some of the heaviest traveled or through connecting roads.

The main principles which make for efficiency in earth roads are proper drainage and maintenance. There is no material so easily affected by improper drainage as earth. When dry, it will readily support the heaviest concentrated loads of traffic, that will be imposed upon it. The same material, when thoroughly saturated with water, will not support even a slight load. The secret, therefore, in constructing and maintaining such roads, is to utilize all possible schemes for keeping them dry.

A prominent farmer in Illinois made the remark, if he just had a roof over his earth road from the farm to the market, he would not ask for anything better. This farmer knew what the earth road needed, but his experience was limited as to how such results could be accomplished.

The skilled road builder can, with the most modern methods of construction and maintenance, drain earth roads by removing the underground seep water and treating the earth surface so that the road will be practically dry the greater part of the year and in such condition that it will serve moderate traffic economically.

The first step in the construction of an earth road is to have it surveyed and a permanent grade line and cross section established. The grade line should be established so that it will provide for the necessary drainage to the natural water courses. It should also provide for cutting down the grades and filling the hollows so there will be a permanent road bed that will not have to be disturbed for further improvement. The cross section for the road will depend somewhat upon the drainage and whether it is a first, second or third class road. The sections shown have been suggested for various classes referred to. Special attention should be given to side ditches to insure that they will provide for all surface water and remove it rapidly. Many wide

ditches .on long steep grades should be paved with concrete, riprap, or similar material to prevent serious erosion.

All culverts and bridges should be constructed of as permanent a material as can be conveniently secured. They should be of such size that they will readily provide for all surface water.

Drain tile should be laid at joints that have underground seepage and on flat swampy roads when the water has no chance to flow readily in the side ditches. Drain tile should be used only when absolutely necessary. The open side ditches properly constructed and maintained, will give better satisfaction where there is sufficient fall for the water to flow.

Earth roads can usually be constructed at a very low cost; however, they require constant maintenance, which on many very heavily traveled roads, becomes a rather heavy burden. The earth roads require constant maintenance and should never be neglected. A road, low in first cost, with high maintenance expense is often just as economical as a road of high first cost with practically no maintenance. The main purpose of a road is to satisfy the requirements of traffic. The earth road in some sections may do this as well as brick pavements in other sections. If this is kept in mind, more attention will be given to the earth roads and the money spent on them will not be thought of as lost.

After earth roads are once constructed, maintenance should begin at once. It is neglect that makes earth roads bad and causes two dollars to be spent where one would have done the work. On account of the necessity of giving earth roads constant attention it is important that every township arrange for a patrol system of maintenance or some similar form, where someone can give his entire time to a section of roads and be held reponsible for their condition.

Earth roads should be maintained by keeping a good crown on the road, keeping side ditches opened and the surface smooth so the water will readily drain to the side ditches and so traffic will be distributed over the entire surface. The distribution of traffic will keep the road uniformly compacted and free from ruts.

The systematic use of the road drag on a road that has been properly graded, will show better results, for the amount of money spent, than anything else that can be done to the road. It has been shown that systematic dragging can be done for a cost of from $10 to $15 per

(Continued on page 42.)

ILLINOIS HIGHWAYS.

Published Monthly by the
State Highway Department,
Springfield, Illinois.

ILLINOIS HIGHWAY COMMISSION.

A. D. Gash, *President.*
S. E. Bradt, *Secretary.*
James P. Wilson.

Wm. W. Marr, *Chief State Highway Engineer.*

BUREAU OF ROADS.

H. E. Bilger, *Road Engineer.*
M. W. Watson, *Assistant Road Engineer.*
C. M. Hathaway, *Office Engineer.*
L. P. Scott, *Chief Draftsman.*

BUREAU OF BRIDGES.

Clifford Older, *Bridge Engineer.*
G. F. Burch, *Assistant Bridge Engineer.*
A. W. Consoer, *Office Engineer.*

BUREAU OF MAINTENANCE.

B. H. Piepmeier, *Maintenance Engineer.*
F. T. Sheets, *Assistant Maintenance Engineer.*

BUREAU OF TESTS.

F. L. Roman, *Testing Engineer.*
W. C. Adams, *Chemist.*

BUREAU OF AUDITS.

J. M. McCoy, *Chief Clerk.*
T. W. Dieckmann, *Department Editor.*
R. R. McLeod, *General Bookkeeper.*
G. E. Hopkins, *Property Clerk.*

DIVISION ENGINEERS.

R. L. Bell, Buchanan-Link Bldg., Paris, Ill.
H. B. Bushnell, 144 Fox St., Aurora, Ill.
J. E. Huber, Wise Building, Mt. Vernon, Ill.
A. H. Hunter, 302 Apollo Theater Bldg., Peoria, Ill.
C. M. Slaymaker, 510 Metropolitan Bldg., E. St. Louis, Ill.
H. E. Surman, 614 People's Bank Bldg., Moline, Ill.
Fred Tarrant, State Highway Department, Springfield, Ill.

Address all communications in regard to "Illinois Highways," to State Highway Department, Springfield, Illinois.

CONTENTS.

Good Roads are the order of the Day.

* * *

A. M. Fitchie, of Plato, was elected secretary of the Kane County Highway Commissioners Association. The commissioners recently held their annual meeting at Geneva. These meetings afford a good chance for the commissioners to get together and exchange ideas about the different phases of their work.

* * *

Work on Vermilion County's Bond roads has started in earnest. Two contractors already have industrial railways partly constructed. The Eclipse Construction Company which has the contract for Division No. 4 have been at work for some time and expect to begin pouring concrete immediately. They estimate that on their division they will complete 1 mile a week when the work is under way.

* * *

Woodford County is to have three miles of brick road as a gift from Mr. B. M. Stoddard of Minonk, he having contributed $30,000 for this purpose. The improvement will begin one mile inside the limits of Minonk Township, and will extend 2 miles into Clayton Township.

* * *

A special Committee of the Peoria Association of Commerce recently purchased $100 worth of road signs to be used on the Delavan road through East Peoria. The markers are to be 3-inch plank boards bearing the word "Peoria" and an arrow indicating the correct route.

* * *

The hard roads' bonds of Seven Hickory Township, in Coles County, to the sum of $40,000 have been sold at full par value to Matheny Dickson & Company of Springfield, the purchasers bearing the expenses of printing, registering of bonds, attorney's fees, etc., so the township will realize the full $40,000 from the bonds.

* * *

The Medora Good Roads and Commercial Club has reorganized. A. L. Carter was elected president; E. B. Simmons, treasurer; W. B. Tietsort, Secretary.

* * *

County Superintendent Boyer of Adams County classes the roads of Keene Township among the best in the county. On a recent inspection he failed to find a single mudhole or bad place.

* * *

Vermilion County certainly believes in Good Roads. On top of their county bond issue of $1,500,000, four individual townships voted a total of $87,000 in 10-year bonds for road work: Vance Township voting $15,000; Sidell, $25,000; Catlin, $22,000 and Carroll $25,000.

* * *

Mattoon Township, Coles County, has voted $120,000 in bonds with which to build some 10 or 12 miles of brick road.

* * *

Ballard County, Kentucky, just south of Massac and Pulaski Counties in Illinois, has just voted a county bond issue of $300,000 for roads.

* * *

The following item is taken from the *Galesburg Republican Register:*

The director of public roads of the United States says it costs 275 millions of dollars for the farmer to market his crops over the earth roads each year and that a system of hard roads would reduce this cost over one-half, thereby adding about 150 million dollars, annually, to the farmers' bank account. As there are 6,351,502 farms in the United States, it would mean an average of $23.61 for each farmer.

During the fiscal year ending June 30, 1910, there originated along the railroads of this country 968,464,009 tons of freight, two-thirds of which was delivered over earth roads at a cost of $1,600,000,000. A hard roads system would have reduced this cost over one-half, making a saving of $8 for every man, woman and child in the United States and her posses-

sions. The generally accepted cost of hauling a ton of freight 1 mile over our roads is 23 cents, and the average haul is said to be a fraction over 9 miles, making a cost of $2.07 for the average haul of 1 ton.

* * *

Speaking of the cost of haulage, Dr. J. H. Waters, President of the Kansas State Agricultural College says it costs Kansas Farmers, alone, $18,750,000 to haul their tonnage to market.

* - * *

A combination grader and scarifier has just been purchased by the Highway Commissioners of Dixon Township, Lee County.

WHAT HAS BEEN DONE ON FORMER "ROADS DAYS."

(Continued from page 36.)

From the reports I have received, I would say that 200 miles of road were dragged on "Good Roads Day."

Three pipe culverts were installed and the necessary grading done to the same.

Two large hills were cut down and placed in low places. The grades were reduced in the places mentioned from grades 5 per cent and higher to 2 per cent.

A large number of road signs were placed by the several chambers of commerce.

I personally inspected 50 miles of the principal roads in six townships on "Good Roads Day."

While this county did not observe "Good Roads Day" as I had anticipated, still I feel that much has been done and accomplished toward the education of the public along the line of good earth roads.

MARION COUNTY.

[By Lee S. Trainor, County Superintendent of Highways.]

At Centralia with the assistance and cooperation of the Centralia Commercial Club and the city administration, a working force of 200 men and 27 teams was organized and put to work on Lincoln Boulevard (the main thoroughfare to the city cemetery) were about one and one-half miles of very poor earth roadway was completely transformed and converted into a very respectable road by constructing ditches, opening culverts and drains, crowning roadway etc. All the chuck and mudholes were filled with cinders donated by the Centralia Gas & Electric Co. After all the hand work had been completed the street was given the finishing touches with the grader, followed by several rounds with the drags and it stands to-day a fitting example of what can be done and I am told that the general appearance and improvement is ample payment for the many aching backs and blisters incurred in its construction.

The working force was composed of a jolly bunch of business and professional men and the work was made much lighter by an occasional trip to the "grub box" that was provided by the ladies and there was the long-to-be-remembered "buttermilk wagon" with its ample supply of that invigorating fluid provided by the Centralia Creamery Company.

In addition to the work on Lincoln Boulevard several strips of road leading into the city were dragged; in all approximately 10 miles of road received attention in Centralia township during the day.

The pupils of the city schools were organized into "clean-up" squads and set about cleaning up the campus and the streets leading to the school, planting shrubs, flowers, grass, etc., and made a very creditable showing, for which Superintendent S. H. Bohn deserves due credit.

At Salem the day was given over principally to the demonstration of several power road-working machines, and as a result of the demonstration Marion County has about 16 miles of very fine earth roads.

The International Harvester Co., the Hart-Parr Tractor Co., the Aultman-Taylor Mfg. Co., entered 30-60 gas tractors in the demonstration; N. S. Monroe & Sons, a Jumbo leveler, Breese Mfg. Co., Uncle Jim leveler, J. D. Adams & Co., a Giant King grader and a Square Deal grader, and the Austin Western Machine Mfg. Co., a Little Western grader, all of which made a favorable showing.

All of these machines and tools were busy making roads on Wednesday and again on Thursday, giving all the interested parties an opportunity to see them at work under home conditions and many of the highway commissioners of this and adjoining counties witnessed the demonstration, and Marion County reaped the benefit.

Through some misunderstanding the Mayor of Salem announced April 25 as "Road Day" for that section, and as it was too late to recall the announcements, the Salem Commercial Club took the matter up and arranged for a Road Drag Day to be held on the same date, offering several prizes and arranged for a banquet for all of the contestants together with a program for their entertainment during the afternoon. At this time I can not say what the results will be, but this I know—the Salem people are preparing to entertain a good big bunch of road boosters on the 25th.

At Sandoval a working force of about forty men was recruited, together with several teams, and about two miles of very bad road were put in shape by hauling and spreading cinders and coal mine refuse donated for that purpose by the Chicago-Sandoval Coal Co., in addition to its approximately six miles of road were dragged in the township.

In most of the other townships of the country little or no work was done on account of the farmers being so behind with

their oats planting and other farm work, making it practically impossible for them to get out on the road.

About a week prior to "Road Day" a letter from this office was addressed to all the postmasters of the county calling their attention to the Governor's proclamation and asking that they get in touch with the various rural carriers out of their offices and request them to submit a report on road improvements that might well be undertaken on Road Day and in nearly every case a very comprehensive and detailed schedule was submitted to this office which in turn was submitted to the highway commissioners in the various communities for attention. Through this and similar sources I expect to keep in touch with road conditions over the county at all times.

While we did not accomplish all the things undertaken for the day, the results attained were satisfactory and of very material assistance to the local road authorities, and I am of the opinion that another such call in the near future would result in an increased mileage of passable roads and be a great help in our getting the season's work done, as most of the townships in this county are without funds for road purposes this season, and we must, to a great extent, depend on donations of labor and material.

LEE COUNTY.

[By L. B. Neighbor, County Superintendent of Highways.]

The plans for the celebration of "Road Day" in Lee County were laid with reference to the fact that it was also "Governor's Day." The route of the Lincoln Highway crosses our county, and the Governor and his party were to traverse this highway from Chicago to Sterling by autos in the course of the day.

Realizing that wide-awake road men would want to see the Governor and his distinguished party and to catch some of the inspiration of such an occasion, I called a "get acquainted" meeting of our highway commissioners for the day.

The men of the Dixon Citizens' Association rose to the occasion, tendering a free dinner to the roadmakers, themselves attending the dinner at 50 cents per plate. The county superintendent of highways presided. Mayor W. B. Brinton gave a welcoming talk, and the Rev. A. B. Whitcombe, Lee County consul for the Lincoln Highway, stirred up enthusiasm for his favorite project.

The road officials held two sessions—a brief one in the forenoon for registry and introductions, and an all-afternoon one for discussion of the many problems confronting the commissioners and the county superintendent.

One question treated, and which would probably be of general interest, was this: No provision having been made in Lee County for assistance for the county superintendent in his field work in the various townships, the resolution was proposed and unanimously carried that it would be proper for the highway commissioners, upon his call, to assist him in such work, presenting their bills to the township as for any other highway service.

Inquiry was made as to whether such service should be paid for from the road and bridge fund of the township, or from the general fund. County Attorney Edwards gave his opinion that it would be proper to pay them from the general fund. This has the effect of not crippling the road and bridge work.

The Governor's proclamation for a general observance of "Road Day" has been spread broadcast. The county superintendent of highways had a call in all the papers of the county, and the county superintendent of schools had appealed for a suitable observance of the day by the schools. I think there was really much general interest.

Still the actual work was, as would be expected, principally done by the commissioners, and since they were called to the county seat on road duty for the day, I have thought it only justice to them to report the road improvement made the week of "Road Day."

Reports from the commissioners indicate the putting into order of many culverts, the purchase of materials for and the construction of drags, and the arrangement for their systematic use. About 250 miles of road was dragged, shaped up with such machines as the "Jumbo" or "Uncle Jim," or cleaned with rake and shovel and team.

In honor of the Governor's visit, the commissioners along the Lincoln Highway took especial pains to have it presentable. Brooklyn Township, with its "Jumbo" put over forty miles into fine condition and earned a place in the front rank of the townships.

With the attention given them, and with the dry weather now prevailing, our roads are in as good condition as they usually are in August.

EARTH ROADS.

(Continued from page 39.)

year per mile of road, after the road has once been properly graded and the drainage adequately cared for.

There has been a great deal of discussion as to how a road should be leveled or dragged. Many claim that it can be done very efficiently and effectively with a tractor and large leveler, others claim that the light 2-horse drag is more economical. There is no question but that both have proven satisfactory in different places. The most economic scheme depends a great deal upon the local conditions. It is not so much the method as the results that count. The most essential point to be observed are to keep the surface of the road perfectly smooth, well crowned, and to keep the ditches clean.

DIVISION OFFICES OF STATE HIGHWAY DEPARTMENT.

The State Highway Department divides the State of Illinois into seven divisions, as shown by the map

below. To each one of these divisions is assigned a division engineer, who has a permanent office in his division, and who has general supervision of the work done in the division by the State Highway Department. The division offices are located as follows:

Division No. 1—Aurora.
Division No. 2—Moline.
Division No. 3—Peoria.
Division No. 4—Paris.
Division No. 5—Springfield.
Division No. 6—East St. Louis.
Division No. 7—Mt. Vernon.

HIGHWAY ENGINEERING COURSE AT UNIVERSITY OF ILLINOIS.

[By F. H. NEWELL, Professor of Civil Engineering and Head of Department, University of Illinois.]

The demand for young men educated in engineering and qualified to advance in highway work is being met at the University of Illinois by a 4-year course in the Department of Civil Engineering, or to put the matter a little more accurately, there is provided in the civil engineering course an option for those students who intend to go into highway work.

At the present time there is perhaps a larger demand for properly trained young men in this field than in almost any other line of engineering. This is due to the fact that at present a large amount of money is being spent in the construction of roads and bridges —far more than during any previous period in the history of the country. Coincident with this also is the fact that few investments are being made in new railroads and in the extension of older systems, and very little is being done in water power development or irrigation. The rapidly increasing use of the automobile and the larger appreciation on the part of the public of the necessity of good highways, both in he cities and in the country, has tended to make this work come to the front in engineering enterprises.

The peculiar condition exists that while many otherwise well-informed people believe that the roads of the country are already built and that road building in general is a simple matter, yet the fact that we are in the youth of the permanent highway construction. Although roads are as old as civilization and many built by the Romans have endured through centuries, yet we are just beginning to understand the underlying principles and to develop methods of efficiency and economy, especially in the use of materials which have formerly been neglected. Thus while in popular opinion any one is competent to build a road, yet the appreciation is increasing that in this apparently simple operation there is needed the widest obtainable knowledge, skill and experience to obtain the best results.

Because of these conditions, the highway course in the engineering college has been made coordinate with the courses in structural enginnering, railroad engineering and other branches in which every one agrees that a thorough education is essential. Beginning with the freshman year and continuing through the sophomore year the "would be" road engineers receive the same training. In the third or junior year they approach the more technical side of the subject and in the senior year give special attention to such matters as highway bridge design, road construction and administration, the use of asphalt, tar, etc. In the Road Laboratory standard tests are taught and work is done along the lines which have been found necessary in practice for testing materials offered by the contractor. Opportunity is given for the inspection of roads under construction and especial attention devoted to causes of failure of the older bridges and road surfaces, pointing out the things which are to be avoided as shown by the experience in the past.

Even though a young man may not continue in highway construction throughout his professional career, yet the education obtained in this practical line has a distinct value and may be of more importance to him in later life than the more scholastic courses offered in related colleges. No man can make a mistake in taking up this work, even though ultimately he may go into industrial or commercial lines. The highway leads on to the great unknown and branches in all directions offer facilities to reach any desired goal. In the same way the highway instruction leads on and on with infinite possibilities to the student.

 # COOPERATION

By WM. BURGNER, County Superintendent of Highways, Hancock County, Carthage, Illinois

Some Good Thoughts For Good Roads Day

I can hardly hope to bring you any new thought on this old subject, for I know it has been threshed threadbare in the discussion of all classes of subjects, yet it will not down, and as long as men are striving for results in any field of work, cooperation will bob up as the key to the situation.

The Bible tells us that a long time ago the human family all lived in one country and spoke one language. One summer they all took a journey eastward, and when they reached the beautiful fields of Shinar, they resolved to settle there. One day a man said, "Let us build here a great city and erect in it a tower the top of which shall reach heaven," and they all cried out, "Good, let us go to it," and at it they went, every one of them. There was not a loafer, not a kicker, not a knocker in the whole crowd. Every man was a worker and a booster. The Lord at first smiled at their foolish plans, but they kept on working, everyone of them, until God began to get scared for fear they would accomplish their task and let old sinners climb up the tower and get into heaven by the way of the back door. So the Lord said He would go down and look into the matter, and when He reached the city and looked over the work, He uttered these wonderful words, "Behold this people is one, they have one language, and they have begun this work, and they are so determined and so united that nothing can restrain them from doing it." This is the greatest example of cooperation in history. In order to prevent them from doing the impossible, God, Himself, had to invent a number of languages and compel the people to learn them. Since that time a perfect cooperation seems to be difficult. There is no force on earth greater than the combined efforts of men. History is full of instances where the seemingly impossible has been achieved. Mountains have been removed, rivers and lakes have been made, the hills that God made have been torn down and cast into the valleys; the whole face of the earth has been changed.

The resolution of the men on the plains of Shinar to build a tower that should reach to the heavens was a foolish notion, or God would not have stopped it. The determination of men to-day to make a good road wherever men travel is not a foolish notion, but a wise one, but we have a large country and there are, must of necessity be, millions of miles of roads made before our task is finished. The building of the tower of Babel was a small undertaking compared with ours; the making of the Panama Canal, the greatest achievement of man, is a small undertaking compared with ours; but the work has begun; the battle is on. With cooperation as our lever, and a concrete block for a fulcrum, we will be able to lift this old world out of the mud, and that before long. When I think of the great task before us, just here in Illinois; when I look over our prairie farms with their deep, black gumbo soils, and much of it many miles away from rock or sand or gravel; I sometimes wonder if this task has been assigned to Hercules as one of his labors, if he would have had the courage to undertake it; but it must be done; the task must be accomplished. All things are possible, where men will it and unite their efforts to bring it about. Good roads is the live, burning question of the hour, and will be until we get them. Without a hearty cooperation of all of our efforts and forces, however, progress will be slow. Up to this date, we have not had the cooperation necessary to achieve the greatest results, but public opinion is ripening, and day by day the people are getting closer together in their beliefs along this line, and the outlook is good.

What we need now is to combine the forces and resources of the National government, the State government, the county government, the city government and the township government, and when this has been done with the approval of the individual, no power on earth can stop the advance. When thoroughly organized these forces will be irresistible.

With my whole heart I believe in law enforcement, not capriciously, nor with the harshness of a tyrant but an even, consistent, clean, manly, fearless and impartial enforcement. The law is not a whimsical tyrant, actuated by revenge, to-day one thing and to-morrow another, but it is a kindly nursing father and can be administered so as to win the respect of every rightthinking man.

We complain too much. Would we have done better had we been in charge? We complain of legislative acts. We complain of extravagance at the time when the State needed every dollar of its revenue for pressing needs and useful ends. There is no use trying to place the blame on some one else, but let us do our whole duty first, look within ourselves, examine the complicated movements of our hearts, modify that which needs change and rectify every irregular motion and we will feel better and the World will be better by us living in it.

Hancock County has caught the vision of progressiveness and her able board of supervisors see the advantage of cooperation and it is their intention with all whom they may come in contact to bring them to higher planes of usefulness in the building of better roads.

WHAT GOOD DOES THE ROAD DRAG DO?

Our ears have become so accustomed to hearing that phrase "Drag the roads" that we are perhaps beginning to lose sight of its importance. Notwithstanding the fact that we have had road dragging preached to us from the local papers, lectured and bulletined to us by the State Highway Departments and United State Office of Public Roads, and finally rammed down our throats by the State Legislature, we are still far from a true understanding of the value that results from an intelligent use of the road drag.

At the present time, approximately 90 per cent of our entire road mileage consists of earth roads (and 90 per cent is rather a conservative estimate), yet we seem to give no consideration to the fact that there is no other single feature, which will do more towards keeping this 90 per cent of our road-mileage in good condition than the homely plank or split-log drag.

In our enthusiasm for improved highways, we seem to have overlooked the fact that the drag, intelligently used, is the most efficient and economical road-working machine we have. Now "intelligently used" doesn't mean using the drag once in a while, when there is nothing else to be done. It means the constant and consistent use of the drag each and every time that the conditions are right for the work. Dragging at the wrong time is simply a waste of work and energy and may result in more harm than good.

The Legislature has realized the value of the road drag and has made it compulsory that there be set aside, each year, from a true road and bridge money of the township, a sum of $3 to $5 for each mile of road in the township to be used solely for the purpose of dragging these roads. The commissioners of highways are authorized by the law to make contracts for dragging and to designate what roads are to be dragged and the time for such dragging.

This is a good start in the right direction but it provides scarcely enough money to maintain the roads as well as it is possible to

A Road that is Maintained With the Drag.

maintain them by dragging. If there could be brought about an appreciation of the true value of road dragging and if our road funds were expended so as to provide for the proper amount of such work we should see that our abused earth roads could be brought into much better shape and made to serve us in a far better way than we ever thought possible.

Much has been said and written about the road drag, yet despite the large amount of information that

has been made available, there is a surprising lack of knowledge on the part of the average person as to just what can be expected from the drag and why such results can be expected.

The road drag must be understood before we get the maximum benefit of the energy we spend in dragging.

Too many people have the idea that the drag is an automatic device and all that is necessary is to have it pulled over the road in any manner just as long as it scratches the surface in some fashion or other. On the contrary, however, the road drag must be intelligently experimented with before an operator can get the best results. No set rules can be laid down for this work. Experience alone will show the interested operator how to get the desired results from the use of such a contrivance.

There are illustrated here the forms of drags which have proved themselves best suited to do the work. They are neither expensive nor difficult to make and if substantially constructed will last for a number of years. The drag should be made light, not heavy and should preferably be constructed of a wood which will resist decay. The front runner of the split log, or plank drag, should be shod on the cutting end and with an iron or steel strip to avoid excessive wear. This will do much towards prolonging the life of the drag.

The good that a road drag does is fivefold.

First—It seals the pores of the surface of the road and thus prevents the absorption of water by the spongy earth.

Second—It will maintain the crown of the road if properly and skillfully used, which will result in better drainage for the surface of the road.

Third—It will plane down all irregularities and small humps in the road and by transferring the material from high places to the hollows will fill up the latter and so destroy what may be the germ of a bad mudhole.

Fourth—Used immediately after a rain it will squeeze the water from the small puddles and thus make the road dry much more quickly.

Fifth—During the winter, the greatest advantage of the drag comes from its use just before a freeze. A well-dragged road that is solidly frozen is practically as good as a brick or concrete pavement.

Of these five results the first is possibly the most important and the least understood by the average person.

Take a handful of mud, such as we find on our roads, and examine it closely. You will note that it is porous. Supposing it would dry in this condition, it is readily understood that there would result an earthy sponge which would absorb a great deal of water if given the opportunity.' Now smear your finger along this chunk of mud and notice carefully the mark you make. You will see you have closed the small openings, or pores, and at the same time have brought to the surface the water with which they were filled. If the mud were to dry now, the portion which you smeared with your finger would be sealed shut and it would take a rather heavy rain to wash away the sealing coat and open up the pores again. A drag accomplishes this sealing of the pores of the road surface on a large scale. It slicks over the mud so that when dry the surface of the roadbed is effectively closed against the entrance of any moisture. At the same time the drag squeezes out the water from these pores and brings it to the surface where it can dry rapidly. Roads properly dragged will dry out weeks earlier in the spring than a road not so maintained and when dried out will be smooth and in excellent condition.

A Road That Was Not Maintained With a Drag.

wasted. It has often been stated that the right time to drag a road, at least roads such as we have generally over this State, is when it is wet and muddy and the muddier the better. If the mud is extremely bad and deep, it is possible that the lap drag, as illustrated here, can be employed advantageously. In the summer time and early fall, dragging should be done while it is actually raining, for, unless the rain is especially heavy and long continued, the water at this season of the year will penetrate the roadbed so fast that the surface will be comparatively dry after the rain has stopped with the result that the surface will work up under the drag into small lumps or clods. When this happens it is always a sign that the road is too dry for dragging. The greatest improvement in dragging roads is produced when it is possible to spread and slick the mud over the road, much in the same way as a mason works mortar with a trowel.

Don't drag a dry road. The only result that you will get will be dust, which will be turned into mud at the first rain, holding the water on the surface of the

The Split Log Drag in Use.

The Slicker or Lap Plank Drag.

It must not be expected that the drag will make a road. It is not a road builder but simply a contrivance to maintain roads that are already constructed. The repeated use of the drag, if used properly will gradually crown a road, but it should be remembered that it is not expected that it will make a road.

It is highly important that the dragging be done at the proper time, otherwise the work will be practically

road, just exactly what you want to avoid. The following pointers for dragging have been given many times before, but they should be repeated over and over again until we are all familiar with them:

Make a light drag.
Drive the team at a walk.
Don't drag a dry road.
Ride on the drag. Don't walk.

Drag when the road is muddy.

Drag, if possible, immediately before a freeze.

Begin at one side of the road, returning on the opposite side. Always drag a little earth towards the center of the road until it is raised 10 inches or twelve inches above the side of the roadway.

Do not attempt to move very much material at one time with a drag.

If the drag cuts in too much, shorten the hitch. The amount of earth the drag will carry can be regulated by the driver accurately if he stands near the cutting edge or say away from it.

When the roads are first dragged, after a very heavy muddy spell, wagons should drive, if possible, to one side until the road has had a chance to freeze or partially dry out.

The exercise of a very little care on the part of the users of the road will do quite as much as the drag towards securing a smoother road.

Use the entire surface of the road. Concentrated traffic will produce ruts.

Remember that there is a law prohibiting driving on a freshly dragged road, which reads as follows:

It shall also be unlawful for any person, or persons, to drive or cause to be driven a vehicle of any description in or upon any portion of the highway immediately after the same has been dragged and before such portion of the highway shall have partially dried out or frozen: *Provided*, that nothing in this section shall apply in those instances where it is impossible to drive with safety at one side of said dragged portion of the road, or where a vehicle does not make a rut on such dragged portion of the road, injurious to the work accomplished by use of the road drag or where a vehicle does not make a rut nearer than nine (9) feet from the center of the dragged portion of the road. (I. R. & B. law, paragraph 107C.)

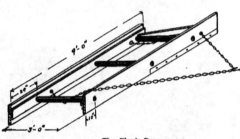

The Plank Drag.

TOWNSHIP ROAD WORK.

The following figures give the detailed cost of Township road work done under the supervision of the State Highway Department:

FINAL COST REPORT ON CONCRETE ROADS.

10-FT. BRICK ROAD—E. ELDORADO TOWNSHIP—SALINE COUNTY.

CONDITIONS.

The following figures do not include contractor's profit or overhead expenses:

Amount of pavement laid 3,100 ft.; total square yards of road completed, including curb, 3,444.4 sq. yds.; width of pavement laid, including curb, 10 ft.; width of shoulders 7 ft. 6 in.; length of pavement constructed without transverse joints 3,100 ft.; length of haul for sand and cement 1,900 ft.; length of haul for gravel and

brick 1,900 ft.; cost of cement per barrel, f. o. b. siding $1.29 net; cost of sand per cubic yard, f. o. b. siding $1.27; cost of stone per cubic yard, f. o. b. siding $1.10 per ton or $1.485 per yd.; cost of brick per square yard, f. o. b. siding $0.67; cost of labor per hour: 20c except for brick work at 25c; cost of teams 40c per hour. Amount of cement used per square yard of pavement 0.18 bbl.; work started July 10, 1915; completed September 25, 1915.

ITEMIZED COST OF WORK.	Total cost.	Cost per sq. yd.
Engineering, inspection and superintendence	[1]$246 22	[1]$0.0714
Excavation	417 37	0.121
Hauling gravel	145 10	0.042
Hauling sand	181 83	0.0527
Hauling cement	19 40	0.0056
Hauling brick	267 79	0.0776
Gravel, 365 cu. yds. @ $1.485 f. o. b. siding	542 03	0.1574
Sand, 465 cu. yds. @ $1.27 f. o. b. siding	591 20	0.1712
Cement, 623 bbls. @ $1.29 f. o. b. siding	803 38	0.2330
Shaping and rolling subgrade and side roads	422 26	0.1223
Mixing and placing concrete, handling forms and joints	547 12	0.1586
Cost of culverts and bridges	1,467 53	0.4250
Brick, 3,100 sq. yds. @ 67c per sq. yd.	2,077 00	0.6030
Laying brick 3,100 sq. yds. @ $0.0803 per sq. yd.	248 67	0.0723
Grouting brick 3,100 sq. yds. @ $0.0587 per sq yd.	182 41	0.0530
Constructing curb 6,200 ft. @ $0.0104 per ft.	64 50	0.0187
Loading and unloading machinery	49 28	0.0143
Incidentals (insurance, contract, right of way, elastic, lumber car-service, small tools)	533 69	0.1550
Total cost	$8,806 78	02.5536
Total cost, excluding excavators and culverts	$6,921 88	$2.0076

[1] Indicates paid or furnished by the State Highway Department.

COST OF APPLYING BITUMINOUS SURFACES ON MACADAM ROADS.

MACADAM ROAD—BLAIRSVILLE TOWNSHIP—WILLIAMSON COUNTY.

CONDITIONS.

The following figures do not include contractor's profit or overhead expenses:

Total length of road treated 12,022 ft.; total square yards of road treated 16,029 sq. yds.; condition of old macadam road, fair, generally, one place poor; kind of bituminous material used "Tarvia B"; amount of bituminous material used ½ gallon per sq. yd.; amount of sand 1 cu. yd. per 200 sq. yds. of surface; average length of haul on materials 1 mile; general condition of weather, good; rate of pay for labor 22½c per hour: teams 40c per hour.

(Continued on page 48.)

Correspondence Course in Road Building
CONDUCTED BY UNIVERSITY OF ILLINOIS.
Lesson 2—(Continued from April.)

METHODS FOR DETERMINING SAFE LOADS ON STEEL BEAM BRIDGES.

The stresses in the joists of a steel beam bridge are determined by the following method:

The size of the beam and its weight per lineal foot are first determined. The following data may then be secured from the handbook—The moment of inertia (I) about the neutral axis perpendicular to the web of the beam; the radius of gyration (r) about the same axis; and the section modulus (S).

The live load on the beam must be placed in such position on the floor that it will give the maximum moment (M) on the beam. For uniform loads, the load must cover the entire length of the beam. For concentrated loads follow the directions as given above and as shown in Figures 2 and 3.

Example 4.

UNIFORM LOAD.

Suppose the joists in the span shown in Fig 1 are 7 in. 15-lb. I-beams.

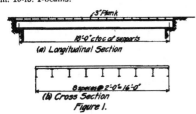

(a) Longitudinal Section

(b) Cross Section

Figure 1.

The dead load per lineal foot is 27 pounds.

The maximum moment produced by the dead load is found by the formula,

$M = \frac{1}{8} w l^2$ in which

$M =$ moment

$w =$ load per lineal foot

$l =$ length in feet.

The dead load moment is,

$$M = \frac{27 \times 18 \times 18}{8}$$

$= 1,094$ foot pounds

The live load moment is

$$M = \frac{250 \times 18 \times 18}{8}$$

$= 10,125$ foot pounds.

The total moment is

dead load	=	1,094 foot pounds
live load	=	10,125 foot pounds
impact 25 per cent of live load	=	2,531 foot pounds

Total ....13,750 foot pounds

$13,750 \times 12 = 165,000$ inch pounds.

The impact is added to take care of the stresses produced by the vibration and shock of a moving load.

It is only used in computing stresses in bridges which have plank floors.

The maximum unit stress is found by the formula

$$f = \frac{M}{S}$$ in which

$f =$ unit stress

$M =$ moment, as above

$S =$ section modulus as obtained from the handbook

The unit stress is

$$f = \frac{165,000}{10.4}$$

$= 15,865$ pounds per square inch.

The safe allowable stress is 16,000 pounds per square inch, therefore the beam is safe.

CONCENTRATED LOAD.

Example 5.

Suppose the joists in the span shown in Fig. 2 are 8-in. 18-lb. I-beams.

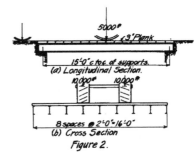

(a) Longitudinal Section.

(b) Cross Section

Figure 2.

The uniform load is 27 pounds per lineal foot, and the concentrated load is 5,000 pounds applied at the middle of the span.

The maximum moment produced by the uniform load is

$$M = \frac{27 \times 15 \times 15}{8}$$

$= 760$ foot pounds.

The maximum moment produced by the concentrated load is found by the formula.

$M = \frac{1}{4} P l$, in which,

$M =$ moment

$P =$ the concentrated load

$l =$ length in feet.

The live load moment is,

$$M = \frac{5,000 \times 15}{4}$$

$= 18,750$ foot pounds.

The total moment is,

dead load	=	760 foot pounds
live load	=	18,750 foot pounds
impact 25 per cent		
of live load	=	4,690 foot pounds

Total........24,200 foot pounds

$24,200 \times 12 = 290,400$ inch pounds.

The maximum stress is

$$f = \frac{290,400}{14.2}$$

$= 20,450$ pounds per square inch.

This stress is 25 per cent more than the allowable and would be safe only in case the structure is in first-class condition.

EXAMPLE 6. CONCENTRATED LOAD.

Suppose the joist in Figure 3, is a 9-in. 21-lb. I-beam and the span length is 20 ft. The spacing of the joists is 2 ft. 4 in. center to center. What is the maximum stress?

Figure 3.

The weight of the floor per lineal foot of beam is

$2\frac{1}{3} \times 3 \times 4\frac{1}{2} = 31\frac{1}{2}$ pounds

The moment produced by the floor is

$$M = \frac{31\frac{1}{2} \times 20 \times 20}{8}$$

$= 1,575$ foot pounds

In order to get the moment produced by the concentrated loads, the reaction at the right support must first be obtained. Multiply each load by its distance from the left support, and divide by the span length, or

$$R_2 = \frac{(1\frac{2}{3} \times 2,500) + (11\frac{2}{3} \times 5,000)}{20}$$

$= 3,125$ lb.

The maximum moment occurs under the heavy wheel and is equal to the reaction (R_2) multiplied by its distance from the heavy wheel, or

$M = 3,125 \times 8\frac{1}{3}$

$= 26,042$ foot pounds

The total moment is

dead load	=	1,575 foot pounds
live load	=	26,042 foot pounds
impact, 25 per		
cent of live load	=	6,510 foot pounds

Total ....34,127 foot pounds

$34,127 \times 12 = 409,524$ inch pounds

The maximum unit stress is

$$f = \frac{409,524}{18.9}$$

$= 21,670$ pounds per square inch

As in Example 5, this structure is safe only on the condition that it is in good shape and the steel is not rusted so as to materially affect its strength.

PROBLEMS.

1. A steel beam bridge has a span of 12 ft. The joists are 6-in. 12¼-lb. I-beams, spaced 2 ft. 6 in. c to c. The floor is 3-inch oak plank. Is the bridge safe for the loads specified by the Illinois Highway Department?

2. A steel beam bridge has a span of 18 ft. The joists are 8-in. 18-lb. I-beams, spaced 2 ft. c. to c. The floor is 2-inch oak plank. Is the bridge safe for the loads specified by the Illinois Highway Department?

3. A steel beam bridge has a span of 24 ft. The joists are 10-in. 25-lb. I-beams, spaced 2 ft. 3 in., c. to c. The floor is 3-inch yellow pine plank. Is the bridge safe for the loads specified by the Illinois Highway Department?

4. A steel beam bridge has a span of 30 ft. The width of roadway is 16 feet and there are five 12-in. 31½-lb. I-beams and two 12-in. 20½-lb. channels to support the floor. The floor is 3-inch oak plank. Is it safe under the Illinois Highway Department specifications?

5. A steel beam bridge has a span of 20 ft. The joists are 8-in. 18-lb. I-beams spaced 2 ft. 6 in., and are in good condition. The floor is 2-inch oak plank. The abutments are good. How would you strengthen this bridge to make it safe?

REFERENCES.

1. Data on the Distribution of Loads on Highway Bridges with Wooden Floors. Engineering and Contracting, January 26, 1916, p. 92.

2. Data concerning Highway Bridges in Illinois. Engineering and Contracting, October 27, 1915, p. 332.

3. Inspection and Maintenance of Highway Bridges. Engineering News, September 23, 1915, p. 604.

4. Steel Highway Bridge Failure. Engineering Record, February 28, 1914, p. 245.

TOWNSHIP ROAD WORK.
(Continued from page 46.)

ITEMIZED COST OF WORK.

	Total cost.	Cost per sq. yd.
Engineering and inspection...........[1]......	......	
Superintendence, salary and expenses..$104 22		$.0065
Bituminous material 8,000 gal. @ .05 f. o. b. siding.....................	400 00	.0250
Torpedo gravel and sand 80 cu. yds. @ $1.23 f. o. b. siding.............	98 59	.0061
Hauling bituminous material.........	......	......
Hauling torpedo gravel and sand.....	56 83	.0035
Heating and applying bituminous material, demurrage, etc................	93 35	.0058
Spreading gravel and sand...........	23 85	.0014
Sweeping and cleaning old road......	8 40	.0005
Depreciation on equipment...........[1]......		......
Freight on equipment................	36 68	.0023
Incidental expense	7 95	.0005
Total cost $829 87		$.0516

[1] Indicates paid or furnished by the State Highway Department.

FINAL COST REPORT.

Resurfacing Sand Ridge–Grimsby Road.

Length of road repaired 4100 feet; 170 cu. yds. material used. About 800 ft. was covered with about 4 inches of new stone; total cost $278.58; total sq. yds. 4550; total cost per sq. yd. $0.0612.

SCHNEPP & BARNES, STATE PRINTERS SPRINGFIELD, ILL. 1916.

ILLINOIS HIGHWAYS

[Printed by authority of the State of Illinois.]

OFFICIAL PUBLICATION OF THE

STATE HIGHWAY DEPARTMENT

| VOL. III | SPRINGFIELD, ILLINOIS, JUNE, 1916 | No. 6 |

ROAD DAY SCENES AT FLORA, CLAY COUNTY.

Some Notes on Brick Road Construction*

By H. E. BILGER, Road Engineer, Illinois State Highway Department

During the last five or six years much progress has been made in the further development of the vitrified paving block, as well as in the methods of assembling the various materials in the construction of brick roads. To the taxpaying public the results of this progress mean that for a smaller construction cost than has heretofore been paid there will be obtained a smoother, and, consequently, a much more serviceable brick road than was practicable to build by the old method. An attempt will be made to discuss in detail some particular features of modern brick-road construction.

It will be assumed that the details of both the horizontal and the vertical alignment, as well as the location of the proposed improvement, have been cared for in a manner strictly commensurate with the high type of the surfacing material. Needless to say that the more rigid and more costly the surfacing material for highway improvement, the more nearly should the improved alignment aproach a level tangent. This need not be interpreted to mean that in brick-road construction excessive cuts and fills are warranted in order to reduce the grades below some 3 or 4 per cent, but rather, that the term realignment is merely a relative one, and under similar conditions a greater expense for grading is warranted for the construction of a brick road than for an earth, gravel, macadam or any kind of a bituminous road.

THE SUBGRADE.

It seems hardly necessary to state that the subgrade upon which is to be placed the artificial foundation for the brick surface should be dry, smooth, uniformly compacted, and conform strictly with the requirements of the plans. A subgrade not uniformly compacted might be tolerated for a very resilient type of improvement, such as gravel, or macadam, for as it yields in places the surfacing material will adjust itself accordingly without appreciable damage and oftentimes even without detection. The success of such rigid types of improvement as the brick road, however, require either that there be no settlement of the subgrade whatever, or that the settlement be uniformly distributed, which is a treacherous matter to depend upon.

A safe procedure is to provide adequately for underground drainage where necessary, and then to compact thoroly the subgrade with a roller of such design as to exert a pressure of at least 300 pounds per inch of width of tread on one wheel. Every experience indicates that a properly drained subgrade compacted by such a roller is able to sustain safely a 7-inch rigid slab, as concrete or brick, carrying any load now traveling upon the rural highways of Illinois. Mathematical calculations are of but little avail when applied to the design of an economic pavement slab. The amount of load to be carried, as well as its manner of application and distribution, are such indefinite factors that nothing but correspondingly indefinite results can be obtained by their use as data for designing the economic slab.

In sections of the country where gravel, rock or similar material can be placed upon the road at a lower cost per unit volume than sand or almost any character of earth, there can arise conditions that warrant the use

*Paper presented at Conference in Highway Engineering at Kansas State Agricultural College, Manhattan, Kansas, March 4, 1916.

of an artificial mineral sub-base, such as the Telford, in order to support properly the concrete or other foundation upon which the brick surface is placed. Conditions that frequently encourage the use of a Telford sub-base are in reality but matters of drainage, for the primary function of such a base is to float or bridge the upper base over an earth sub-grade that has not been provided with adequate drainage. The Telford base merely serves to distribute the load over a larger area, this distribution being necessitated by the very fact of the presence of moisture.

STATE AID ROAD 4 MILES NORTHEAST OF SPRINGFIELD, ILL. PAVEMENT TO BE 18 FT. WIDE, 9 FEET OF BRICK WITH 4½-FT. CONCRETE SHOULDERS. CONCRETE BASE AND SHOULDERS BUILT MONOLITHIC. MIX FOR BASE 1-3½-6; FOR SHOULDERS 1-1¾-3. CONCRETE IN FOREGROUND BEING CURED UNDER ONE INCH COVERING OF SAND.

If found, there have not yet been reported in the State of Illinois any conditions that can warrant, economically, the use of a Telford or similar sub-base in addition to the base proper that carries the brick-wearing surface. The entire matter is one of drainage, for our experience has invariably proven that any properly prepared sand or earth subgrade can support safely a 7-inch rigid slab carrying the heaviest loads being encountered. If gravel or rock were cheaper in Illinois than earth and drain tile, there is little question but what the Telford base would have long ago found its way into the makeup of road improvement. Necessity having again proven to be the mother of invention, we have been driven to the problem of draining adequately the subgrade so as to carry directly thereon the rigid slab without the use of any mineral sub-base.

USE OF OLD FOUNDATIONS.

While old gravel and macadam roads can be used to great advantage as foundations for new brick surfaces, yet where such roads do not exist it seems more advisable that the foundation be of Portland cement concrete rather than either gravel or macadam, even though of a 2-inch greater depth than the concrete. To utilize economically a gravel or macadam road as the base for a brick surface, there is required greater skill than where all the work is to be new. The establishment of the grade line is a delicate matter, inasmuch as a variation of only 1 inch may require either undue scarifying of the old surface or the unwarranted addition of new gravel or stone which should be united with the old.

In order to establish this grade line properly it is frequently necessary to cross section the old road at intervals of 50 feet, this depending of course upon the condition of the surface and the regularity of its profile. After having worked out the economic position of the grade line for each station along the line of the improvement, it is usually found necessary that the old surface be scarified to some extent in order that the higher places may be removed to make room for a sufficient quantity of the bed for the brick, and that the lower places may be filled up with fresh gravel or stone to avoid an excessive depth of this bed. The scarified, reshaped and rolled surface should conform, with a permissible variation either way of one-half inch, to the contour of the finished brick surface. This rolling should be done with the roller used for the subgrade work, and the compaction of the material should be most thorough.

The curb or edging, if used, may be built of concrete, having a width of from 4 to 6 inches at the top and from 6 to 8 inches at the bottom, the total height of the edging being from 12 to 15 inches. While the edging is not really necessary as a pavement feature, yet its use is recommended because of the great convenience it offers as a guide for the template used to locate to a nicety the areas to be scarified. The edging would be constructed, of course, before any of the road is scarified. With the edgings completed the road can be scarified and easily reshaped and rolled to the proper cross section and to an alignment conforming strictly with that of the edgings. Where edgings are not used it is necessary that there be set up true to line and grade temporary side forms that will carry the template used as a guide for reshaping the old road. From the expense of furnishing, setting up and later removing these temporary side forms there is added nothing of value to the completed pavement. In view of this fact, and also in view of the precision of alignment furnished by the concrete edgings, it will be appreciated why the edgings are generally used, and more particularly when it is considered that the top width of each edging acts simply as a substitute for a corresponding width of brick surface. Upon having thus prepared the old road to serve as a base, it is ready to receive the bedding course upon which the brick are set.

NEW CONCRETE FOUNDATION.

While there may be found conditions that would warrant the construction of a new gravel or macadam foundation to carry a brick surface, yet these conditions are rare. The Portland cement concrete foundation constitutes the best that has yet been devised for brick roads. For the heaviest rural highway traffic in Illinois the fact seems demonstrated by experience that for an 18-foot road a 4½-inch concrete base is entirely satisfactory, and for a 10-foot one, 4 inches will suffice. These dimensions have been used under various soil and traffic conditions, and from every indication they are well on the side of safety.

It has further been demonstrated that the mixture for these bases need not be richer than 1-3½-6. This mixture has been used extensively with various qualities of aggregates. With reasonably satisfactory inspection of the work it is uneconomical to require that the fine and the coarse aggregates be used separately. The use of mixed aggregates, usually termed unscreened gravel, should be permitted with the restriction that one part by volume of cement shall be used to each 3½ parts of fine aggregate contained in the gravel, and that the ratio of the fine to the coarse aggregate shall be not less than 3½ to 6, nor greater than 7 to 6. With the fine aggregate

ratio running at the permissible high figure, the value of the additional cement required would be about 7 cents per square yard of base. It has been learned from specific cases that where unscreened gravel was shipped by rail for long distances the saving in the purchase and the transportation of the unscreened material as against separated aggregates amounted to more than 7 cents per square yard of base. These were extreme cases in transporting materials a long distance, so under conditions where local materials are available the saving by the use of unscreened gravel would be still more. In the construction of country roads, usually having a width of from 10 to 18 feet, there is not conveniently available on the prepared subgrade a sufficient space to pile and use the aggregates separately. In street work the situation is entirely different for there is abundant space to store the separated materials.

The consistency with which the concrete for the base should be mixed depends upon whether the road is to be constructed monolithic, or with a cushion or bed of some substantial thickness between the base and the brick. If the latter method is to be followed the concrete can be of a rather wet consistency in order to keep down the cost of the work, but of course the consistency should not be such as would permit the separation of the aggregates. If the monolithic method is to be followed a comparatively dry consistency is required in order that the brick may be placed upon the concrete almost immediately. For monolithic work it is essential that the consistency of the concrete be uniform in order that local depressions may not develop due to the weight of the brick and the process of rolling.

SIDE FORMS, MORTAR BED, ETC.

For the construction of a brick road having a sand-cement bed wood forms are permitted, inasmuch as these forms must remain in place until at least 24 hours after the pavement is grouted, which means about two weeks after the concrete base is laid. The expense of providing a sufficient length of steel forms to remain in place for two weeks would not be warranted by the advantages gained. For monolithic work, however, steel forms should be required, for the precision of alignment needed to harmonize with the smoothness of the pavement can usually be gotten only by their use.

The specifications of the Illinois Highway Department, edition of March, 1916, provide for both methods of constructing brick roads. By one method the brick are bedded upon a ¾-inch layer of dry mortar of a 1 to 4 mix, and by the other they are built monolithic with the base, a 3/16-inch layer of dry mortar of 1 to 3 mix being placed on the wet base as it is struck off. The use of the sand cushion as such has been abandoned.

By the monolithic method, the order of procedure is practically identical with that in which a sand cushion is used, except that for any particular days' work only such a length of the base is covered by the mortar as can be covered with brick the same day. All of the brick laid on any particular day should be rolled on that day, even though the grouting may not be done until a day or so later. It is essential that the brick not be allowed to remain on the mortar bed over night without being rolled to a true and uniform surface, for if the mortar bed becomes moistened and sets, no reasonable amount of rolling can produce the smoothness desired.

By the monolithic method with concrete base, the mortar bed and the brick are all placed at practically the same time, or so nearly at the same time that within a period of from 5 to 15 minutes after the subgrade has been covered with concrete, the brick are set to place. Usually not more than 10 or 15 linear feet of the base is ever exposed without being covered with brick.

Immediately upon placing the concrete on the subgrade it is roughly leveled off with shovels to the approx-

MONOLITHIC CONSTRUCTION. VIEW SHOWING TEMPLATE USED. NOTE HOW THE WORK IS CONCENTRATED.

imate thickness desired as determined by a light wood template used as a guage. For the success of the monolithic construction the use of a rigid steel template to strike off the base is essential. The template thus far used has been of the multiple type, consisting of a 6-inch I-beam in front and a 6-inch channel behind the two being spaced 2 feet apart and riding on four rollers which are supported by the steel side forms. The lower or cutting edge of the front template is located three-sixteenths of an inch below the corresponding edge of the rear template. When a 4-inch brick is used the lower edge of the rear template is set exactly 4 inches below the top of the steel forms. The space between the two templates is kept filled with dry mortar consisting of one part cement to three parts sand. As the template is drawn forward by a cable attached to the mixer the base

MONOLITHIC CONSTRUCTION. A STRIP OF THE CONCRETE BASE COVERED WITH A THIN FILM OF DRY MORTAR. NOTE THE PLANK THAT IS USED BY THE CARRIERS TO WALK UPON AS THEY COME ONTO THE PAVEMENT. THE MAN WHO IS DOING THE BATTING IS SEEN ABOUT 6 FEET IN THE REAR OF THE BRICK LAYERS.

is struck off to a smooth surface and a 3/16-inch layer of the dry mortar is distributed evenly over the wet concrete.

After the greater portion of the culling of the brick is done at the pile at the side of the road, the acceptable brick are carried to the setters on pallets and placed in stacks upon the brick pavement with the lugs all in one direction. Inasmuch as the final rolling of the brick should be done within 30 minutes from the time the concrete is laid, it is important that the culling after their having been laid in the pavement be kept to a minimum. The brick are then set upon the mortar by men standing on the brick already laid. The rolling of the brick is usually done with two-section 800-pound roller, about 24 inches in diameter and about 30 inches long. One man can readily operate the roller.

Just before the grouting begins the surface of the brick is sprinkled with water to avoid absorption from the grout. The grout filler consists of a one to one mix of cement and sand, the sand not containing more than 3 per cent by weight of organic matter and clay combined, nor more than one-half of 1 per cent of organic matter. The sand should be rather uniformly graded from the finest to the coarsest particles, and it should all be such size as to pass through a 1/16-inch square mesh sieve. Not more than 30 per cent by volume, however, should pass a sieve having 50 meshes to the inch.

MONOLITHIC CONSTRUCTION. VIEW SHOWING EDGE OF ROAD. NOTE THAT THE GROUT FILLER EXTENDS TO THE BOTTOM OF THE BRICK.

The process of grouting the brick must be done by at least two, and usually by three applications. The grout for the first application is mixed extremely thin so as to assure that it will find its way entirely to the bottom of the brick and into all spaces and recesses around each individual brick. At this application the joints are completely filled, but within a short time the grout will settle down a distance of a half-inch or more below the surface of the brick. For the second application the grout is mixed to about the consistency of thick cream. The behavior of the grout while setting must be watched very closely in order that the joints may be kept entirely full and be struck off by the squeegee flush with the surface of the brick.

While working the squeegee at an angle of about 45 degrees with the pavement the grout filler is cleaned from off the surface of the brick and the joints are entirely filled, leaving no unequalities at the edges of the brick to break down under the action of traffic. The next day after grouting the brick the steel forms are taken down and moved forward for the work of the following day.

The curing of the pavement consists of covering it with about a 3/4-inch layer of earth and keeping the earth moist for some four or five days. After at least

MONOLITHIC CONSTRUCTION. PAVEMENT READY FOR GROUTING. NOTE ALSO THE ROLLER THAT IS USED.

one week from the time the pavement is grouted the grading of the side roads immediately adjacent to the brick can begin, and within three weeks after the grouting the pavement is in proper condition for traffic.

SOME ADVANTAGES OF THE MONOLITHIC TYPE.

The greatest advantage in the monolithic method of brick road construction consists of the high degree of assurance that all of the features contemplated by the specifications will actually be realized in the completed pavement. Practically all of the hazards inherent in the very use of the sand cushion are entirely eliminated, and the method offers a straightforward and definite process in the construction of the pavement. Because of the mortar bed remaining in place the grout filler finds its way entirely to the bottom of the brick. The completed surface is smoother and more uniform than is practicable to get on a commercial scale by the use of a sand cushion. The inconvenience of constructing a curb or edging is entirely done away with, and the brick themselves extend entirely to the edges of the pavement. Practically all of the rumbling characteristic of brick pavements on a sand cushion is eliminated, and about the only noise is the sharp click of the horses' shoes.

Under normal conditions the construction cost by the monolithic method is reduced by some 10 to 15 cents per square yard. This reduction is due primarily to the fact that the work of the entire force of about 25 men is confined within a radius of about 30 feet. A much greater efficiency can be obtained under these conditions than where a part of the force is one-half of a mile down the road placing the concrete base, another part half the distance away placing the sand cushion, a third part in some other place setting the brick, and a fourth part back the other way grouting the brick. It is evident that with the labor force scattered in this manner it is not possible to carry on road construction at as low a cost as when the entire force is brought practically shoulder to shoulder with one another and the whole work is directed by one foreman.

POINTERS ON THE ROAD DRAG LAW

Sections 62 and 107 of the Revised Road and Bridge Law provide, respectively, as follows:

SECTION 62. ROAD AND BRIDGE MONEY—HOW USED.] All road and bridge moneys of any town or road district shall be held by the treasurer of the road and bridge fund subject to the order of the commissioners of highways: *Provided*, that not less than three ($3.00) dollars nor more than five ($5.00) dollars per mile per annum shall be taken and appropriated from the road and bridge fund of each township, or district to be known as a road-drag fund to pay for the work of dragging earth roads in the township or district as provided in section 107 hereof, and that the enforcement of the law as to what roads in the township or district shall be dragged and as to how often the same shall be dragged, shall be lodged in the hands of the commissioners or commissioner of highways. (Amended by Act approved June 24, 1915.)

SEC. 107. ROAD DRAGS—AUTHORITY AND USE.] (a) The commissioners or commissioner of highways of their respective townships or district in the several counties of this State are hereby authorized to have earth roads dragged at all seasons of the year whenever the surface of the roads become rough so they will not properly shed the water which falls upon them.

It shall be the duty of the commissioners or commissioner of highways to designate from time to time what roads in the township or district shall be dragged. He shall cause the work to be done by giving the parties contracted with for the performance of such services such notice as shall be deemed sufficient; he shall on or before the 15th day of September in each year contract with as many suitable persons as he deems necessary to drag the roads in the township or district for that year, but shall not apportion the dragging of more than six miles of road to any one person. The commissioners or commissioner of highways may at any time cancel such contract or contracts for dragging the roads when the stipulations herein contained have not been properly complied with or when the work is not done in a satis-

factory manner: *Provided, however,* that in making contracts for road dragging such contracts shall not be let for a sum exceeding one dollar ($1.00) per mile for each time dragged: *Provided, further,* that the width required to be dragged shall be not less than 14 feet, if the width of the roadway will permit.

(b) OBSTRUCTING DRAINAGE.] It shall be unlawful for any person or persons to place loose earth, weeds, sods, or other vegetable matter on the portion of a road which has been dragged and so maintained in good condition, or to place any material in such a manner as to interfere with the free flow of water from the dragged portion of the road to the side gutters or ditches: *Provided,* that this restriction shall not apply to deposits of earth or other material that may be made by the authority of the proper road officials, if necessary for filling or raising the elevation of a given section of road or other necessary construction work.

(c) TRAVEL REGULATED.] It shall also be unlawful for any person or persons to drive or cause to be driven a vehicle of any description in or upon any portion of the highway immediately after the same has been dragged and before such portion of the highway shall have partially dried out or frozen: *Provided,* that nothing in this section shall apply in those instances where it is impossible to drive with safety at one side of said dragged portion of the road, or where a vehicle does not make a rut on such dragged portion of the road, injurious to the work accomplished by use of the road drag or where a vehicle does not make a rut nearer than nine (9) feet from the center of the dragged portion of the road.

(d) Any violation of any of the provisions of this section by the commissioners or commissioner of highways or any person or persons who may be required under contract to drag district roads or neglect on the part of any township clerk to set aside the funds required by section 62 of this act shall, on conviction thereof, subject the offender to be fined not less than ten dollars ($10.00) nor more than twenty-five ($25.00) for the first offense, and for each subsequent offense shall be fined not less than twenty-five dollars ($25.00) nor more than fifty dollars ($50.00). (Amended by Act approved June 28, 1915.

To secure efficiency and to conform to the law the following points should be considered:

1. Do it now.
2. Select the roads to be dragged at once.
3. Interview parties desirable as contractors for dragging.
4. Select competent men and close contracts at once.
5. The letting of contracts must be at a regular meeting of the commissioners.
6. September 15 is the latest day for closing contracts for current year. Don't wait until then.
7. Don't contract with any one party for dragging more than six miles of road.
8. Do not pay more than $1.00 per mile of road for each time dragged.
9. See that the right kind of a drag is used.
10. If possible drag at least twelve times per year.
11. Supply each contractor with instructions as to how to drag.

HOW TO DRAG.

Make a light drag.
Drive the team at a walk.
Don't drag a dry road.
Ride on the drag. Don't walk.

Drag when the road is muddy or at least moist.

Drag, if possible, immediately before a freeze.

Begin at one side of the road, returning on the opposite side. Always drag a little earth towards the center of the road until it is raised 10 or 12 inches above the side of the roadway.

Do not attempt to move very much material at one time with a drag.

If the drag cuts in too much, shorten the hitch. The amount of earth the drag will carry can be regulated by the driver accurately if he stands near the cutting edge or away from it.

When the roads are first dragged, after a very heavy muddy spell, wagons should drive, is possible, to one side until the road has had a chance to freeze or partially dry out.

The exercise of a very little care on the part of the users of the road will do quite as much as the drag towards securing a smoother road.

Always drag so as to induce traffic to use the center portion of the road.

CONTRACT.

The following form of contract has been approved by the State Highway Commission and is recommended for use by the township and road district commissioners throughout the State:

CONTRACT FOR ROAD DRAGGING.

THIS AGREEMENT, made and concluded this ...... day of ......, 19.., between the Commissioners of Highways of the { Town of / Road District } .... , County of ......, Illinois, known as party of the first part, and ....

....

known as party of the second part.

WITNESSETH, That for and in consideration of the sum of $...... per mile of road, for each time dragged, the party of the second part agrees to drag the public highway designated herein, when directed to do so by the party of the first part, and to perform such other labor as specified herein, all in accordance with the directions hereinafter stated.

The highway considered in this contract shall begin at .... and end at .... being

.... miles in all.

The party of the second part shall ride the drag used, shall carry a shovel and make any small repairs at culverts and bridges as may be necessary to secure proper drainage and convenience to traffic, and shall eliminate all bumps and chuck holes in said road. Said party shall drag the road so that the side slope of the dragged portion of the highway shall not exceed one (1) inch per foot. No loose material shall be dragged to the center so as to leave a ridge which would in any way interfere with traffic. The dragged portion shall be not less than 14 feet wide and the edges shall be left so that water will flow freely to the side ditches.

It is further understood and agreed that if the party of the second part shall neglect to drag the road, when called upon to do so by the party of the first part, or their authorized representative, the party of the second part shall forfeit the sum of 50 cents per mile of said highway neglected, and it is further understood that should this neglect occur at three specific times, this contract shall become void. Unless invalidated according to these aforementioned conditions this contract shall remain in force for one year from the date of this agreement.

IN WITNESS WHEREOF, The parties hereto have set their hands, on the date herein named.

The Commissioners of Highways of the { Town of / Road District } ...., County of ....

....

....

....
(Party of the First Part.)

and

....

....
(Party of the Second Part.)

(Continued on page 61.)

The Influence of the Engineer and the Architect in Promoting an Appreciation of the Beautiful*

By CLIFFORD OLDER, Bridge Engineer

It seems to me highly probable that the works of the great artists have less influence on a nation's sense of the beautiful than the efforts of engineers and architects. The works of Michael Angelo, Rembrandt, Ruebens and other old masters of oil painting and those of Sargent, Whistler and others of the modern painters have never been seen by more than an insignificant number of our one hundred million American people and it is probably true that few of the one hundred million would really appreciate them even if they were provided with the opportunity.

note of what is there to be seen. The American child is inquisitive and you may be sure he sees as much of the alleys and backyards as he does of the lawns and parkings in front. Can he be blamed then, if he grows up with an idea that things of beauty are but for show and not a just heritage of life.

It is practically impossible, in the daytime, to get out of sight of an engineering or architectural structure. Engineers and architects are constantly striving to improve the appearance of the structures which they are called upon to design. Their task is, however, one of

MONTGOMERY BRIDGE—KANE COUNTY. DESIGNED BY STATE HIGHWAY DEPARTMENT. BUILT UNDER DIRECTION OF G. N. LAMB, COUNTY SUPERINTENDENT OF HIGHWAYS, KANE COUNTY.

On the other hand, the American public is confronted at every turn with belching smokestacks, forests of poles carrying wire entanglements, hideous, rusted steel bridges, monstrous barn-like factory buildings, freakish sky-scrappers, dirty streets, unpardonable alleys and abominable ruts or bottomless roads for county highways. Seeing unlovely things so constantly dulls our sense of the beautiful.

Our front yards are generally well kept, but it is an education to explore a few of the alleys, even of some of the best residence sections of our cities, and make

great difficulty. A bridge may be pleasing in appearance, unobtrusive or even abominally ugly, depending largely upon the cost limit set by the owner. As a rule, the engineer and the architect must fight for every dollar they may need to make their structures pleasing in appearance. An architect may be so limited as to the cost of the structure he designs, perhaps under protest, as to preclude the possibility of an harmonious and pleasing appearance, and yet one such example may be copied hundreds of times by unknowing builders.

In many cases, unduly costly features of design are insisted upon because of an unjustified prejudice on the

(Continued on page 59.)

* Paper delivered at a meeting of Springfield Engineers' Club Springfield Association of Architects and Springfield Art Club.

PERHAPS NO RECENT WORK OF THE ILLINOIS STATE HIGHWAY DEPARTMENT REPRESENTS SO CLEARLY THE CONSTANT IMPROVEMENT THAT IS BEING MADE IN OUR BRIDGES AS THE BERNADOTTE BRIDGE IN FULTON COUNTY. THE VIEW OF THE OLD BRIDGE WAS TAKEN THE TWENTY-FIRST OF APRIL 1915, THE ONE OF THE NEW STRUCTURE THE FOURTEENTH OF DECEMBER, 1915.

ORGANIZATION OF TOWNSHIP GOOD ROADS ASSOCIATIONS IN McDONOUGH COUNTY.

[By W. M. Bonham, *County Superintendent of Highways.*]

At the present time I am formulating plans for the organization of Good Roads Associations in McDonough County. My plans provide for the formation along the lines as herein outlined.

There will be an association for good roads purposes in each township; the officers to consist of the regulation officers with the addition that there will be a vice president from each school district. The imme- is also my intention to have the people so interested that each year they will take up some road in the township and get a little better work done than is being done now on the average road. It will cost to do this but in the end we will have covered a township by a system of better roads. One main object of the township organization will be to get the people together so that we will be able to get the roads dragged at the proper time. As it is now you can not depend on getting the men out when you want them. This winter I expect to start out with the intention of making the people see that the need of better roads is imperative. Too many of them are under the impression that the roads are good enough. While this county is not a hard-road county many of us

AN APPEAL TO THE MOTORIST.

Good roads advocates owe a tremendous debt to the automobile owners. The increasing use of motor cars has brought about more enthusiasm for better roads than any other one factor. For pleasure riding or touring the primary requisites are good roads for the finest car made is practically useless when the roads are hub-deep with mud and there is no enjoyment to be gained from riding when the jolts and jars of an uneven roadway are unpleasantly noticeable.

Motor car owners early realized their dependence upon the character and condition of the roads, and consequently the automobilist has ever been an ardent advocate of road improvement. True in many cases such support may have been occasioned by purely selfish desire for the direct benefit which would result to the motorists themselves, but notwithstanding this fact, we must acknowledge that automobiles have rendered a splendid service by bringing about a desire for better roads.

The increase in the number of motor cars has been enormous. At the close of last December there had been registered in Illinois some hundred and eighty thousand motor vehicles. The increasing use of the automobile is heartily welcomed by those of us who are working to give our State better roads for it means more enthusiasm and more support for the movement in which we are so interested.

A problem, however, is presenting itself which may have a very sinister bearing upon the future relationship between the automobilists and the good roads workers. This problem which so concerns us is the recklessness and carelessness exhibited by some motor car drivers and their seeming utter disregard for the rights or safety of the other users of the road. The attitude assumed by some motorists who consider the rights of their car supreme is doing much to bring disfavor upon many innocent drivers and to draw suspicion to the efforts of those who are earnestly working for the improvement of our highways for the benefit of all.

Accidents inevitably happen if a stretch of improved road is considered as a speedway where fast and recklessly driven machines assume the right of way. Accidents have frequently occurred in which an innocent party has suffered injury, or at best, narrow escape from it. In such cases many of those who advocated and sponsored the improvement of the particular thoroughfare upon which the accident happened, have questioned themselves as to the advisability of working for better roads if the safety of the public is to the endangered by some irresponsible or reckless drivers.

Happily the number of persons who are wont to usurp for themselves all right to the road is a small proportion of the total number who travel our highways, and we can not help but feel that with the help and cooperation of the vast majority, our roads can be made to serve all in the manner which is intended. We all wish to see the automobile continue as an ally and not become an enemy of the good roads movement. Cooperation will do much, personal consideration of the rights of others will do more.

Will you, Mr. Motor Car Owner, do you part? Let us have improved highways, but let us use them with due regard for the rights of others.

STATE HIGHWAY COMMISSION,
By A. D. GASH,
President.

diate duty of such vice president will be to keep in touch with the road problem in their individual district and bring to the notice of this office or to the township commissioners any matters that appear to them to need attention. The object of the township organization will be to create a feeling for the need of better roads and to have a place and time where such can be discussed. It feel that we are going to have to do something besides spending our State allotment each year. It is going to be a hard matter to get the people aroused to the fact that there is a better way of doing it than has been done in the past. A few men interested in each township will help me out a great deal in this work and I believe that I can get more men interested sooner by getting them directly interested in their own locality than I can in any other way.

After I have gotten the township organizations together I shall start on the formation of a county association which will have the same general object in view as the township organization and which will include the entire county. Each township will have a representative on the official board of the county organization whose work will be to bring the needs of their township before the public through the county association.

McDonough County is far behind many of the counties in Illinois in her road work. The reason for this is that she has never done anything as a county to further good roads themselves. She has confined all her energies to bridges and she has plenty of them. This year though we are starting on State aid road work and several propositions are coming up at the special meeting of the board in regard to other roads, besides those of the State work.

Our main purpose of the county association will be to foster this idea of the county getting into the road work itself.

INFLUENCE OF THE ENGINEER.

(Continued from page 55.)

part of the owner. Frequently, the advice of engineers and architects, if more freely accepted, would result in economies which would release sufficient funds for ornamental purposes.

For instance the smoke nuisance practically disappears with the installation of scientifically designed furnaces and the saving in fuel consumption pays good interest on the investment needed for the furnace and for a new stack of pleasing proportions, if such a one does not already exist. Painting steel structures repays the cost many times over. Sanitary streets and alleys and the sanitary disposal of waste, repays bountifully in health, even when the benefit is reduced to dollars and cents. Improved county highways repay in counteracting the enhanced cost of living. Poles may be eliminated from our streets and all wires placed underground as soon as the public is willing to pay a little additional cost for service.

These are but a few of the things that may be improved at a profit, or at but slight additional expense.

For nearly ten years, the Illinois Highway Department and its engineers have striven to create an appreciation of aesthetic, as well as service improvement of our country highways. The results may be seen in the present widespread demand for better roads and bridges. That utility is not now, as formerly, the only consideration given rural highway improvements may be illustrated by one of the many examples which might be cited. Recently, the highway officials of a certain Illinois county chose to pay $20,000 for a bridge of pleasing appearance, rather than $17,000 for a structure designed for utility only.

Can there be any question that when all our dreams come true, we will be a more prosperous and happy people?

 # How Good Roads Day Was Observed

TOUR OF GOVERNOR DUNNE.

Following out his established policy Governor Dunne in recognition of Good Roads Day, devoted his time on May 19 to promoting the cause of highway improvement. Accompanied by the State Highway Commission, the Chief State Highway Engineer, and the officers and directors of the Ivy Trail, the Governor traversed the Ivy Trail from Peoria to Joliet, making along the way many speeches for the cause of good roads. The schedule of the day was:

6.00 a. m.—Leave Peoria.
7.10 a. m.—Chillicothe, 30 minutes stop, with breakfast, under auspices of Peoria Automobile Club.
7.50 a. m.—Sparland, 10 minutes stop.
8.10 a. m.—Lacon, 10 minutes stop.
9.00 a. m.—Henry, 15 minutes stop.
9.25 a. m.—Putnam, 5 minutes stop.
10.00 a. m.—Bureau, 10 minutes stop.
10.35 a. m.—Depue, 15 minutes stop.
11.10 a. m.—Spring Valley, 15 minutes stop.
11.35 a. m.—Peru, 15 minutes stop.
12.00 m.—LaSalle, 20 minutes stop.
2.00 p. m.—Starved Rock State Park, 1 hour 30 minutes stop, with luncheon under the auspices of the Ottawa Rotary Club.
2.55 p. m.—Ottawa, 15 minutes stop.
3.30 p. m.—Marseilles, 10 minutes stop.
3.50 p. m.—Seneca, 10 minutes stop.
4.35 p. m.—Morris, 15 minutes stop.
5.00 p. m.—Channahon.
5.45 p. m.—Reach Joliet. Dinner served under the auspices of the Will County Automobile and Good Roads Association.

The *Peoria Star* gives an account of the trip as follows:

If aught were needed to stimulate the activity of Illinois' chief executive, members of the State Highway Commission, the Illinois Valley Trail promoters and party of boosters that accompanied them it was provided in the experiences of the 140-mile run over the proposed trail from Peoria to Joliet yesterday.

Here and there long stretches of good roads were found and in contrast to them were loads of the bump-the-bumps order, roads that were seas of sand, dust and dirt only negotiated by reason of the five big cars being of the most powerful eight and twelve cylinder make.

BAD ROAD CAUSE OF ACCIDENT.

The first real demonstration of bad road work came just above Putnam. The road parallels a deep cut of the Rock Island railroad, turns to the right in a sharp angle over a bridge above the tracks, then sharp to the left again. Forty minutes ahead of the governor's party, Fred C. Batchelder, an auto salesman of Chicago, was running in a big 7-passenger White car. With him was another salesman in another car. At the turn at the bridge, a wagon load of dirt had been dumped by some highway commissioner in the past and had been allowed to remain, forming a vicious "hump." Going over this, Batchelder's hands were jerked from the steering wheel and the car crashed through the railing, plunging end over end, 30 feet, to the bottom of the cut. Batchelder was taken to a Henry hospital, the Masons of Putnam taking charge of him. He was thrown free of the car and it is feared he is internally hurt. The accident was caused by the bump on the turn to the bridge. That was experience No. 1.

Experience No. 2 came a few miles further on, where a culvert gave way under the weight of the Packard car of W. E. Hull in which the Governor and Commissioner Jas. P. Wilson of Polo, were riding. The drop was only a foot and no damage resulted.

FORDED DU PAGE RIVER.

Experience No. 3 came at the crossing of the DuPage river between Morris and Joliet. An iron bridge was washed out last January. President A. D. Gash, Chicago; and S. E. Bradt, DeKalb, of the State Highway Commission, S. L. Nelson, Peoria, L. E. Fisher and the *Star* correspondent, were in a powerful Cadillac eight, driven by Rollin Travis of this city. They were leading the way and had come for miles over a good road at 45 miles an hour. Brush headed across the road gave warning of the bridge out and Travis swung his car down the bank of the stream to a place that looked fordable. It was—for the amphibious Cadillac. The water came half way up on the hood and the fan sent it over the engine in a flood. The bed of the stream was rocks as big as peck and bushel baskets. But the Cadillac went through—the first automobile, the natives averred, that ever accomplished the feat. The other machines made a detour of several miles.

CROWDS AND BIG ENTHUSIASM.

Governor Dunne spoke to crowds of 300 to 3,000 people, talking 30 times during the day. By the time Starved Rock was reached he was hoarse but game. He figured at the rock in a motion picture. The Essanay Company is making a drama called "Power" and Miss Nell Craig is the charming heroine. The Governor was no sooner out of his car than Miss Craig engaged him in animated conversation, the Governor, hat off, linen duster and hair blowing in the wind, gallantly responded. "Got 150 feet," commented the machine operator.

At the towns along the way at every country schoolhouse, the school children were out. The Governor was especially pleased at the Standard School above Putnam where the children sang a song about "Three Cheers for Governor Dunne" and "Three Cheers for the Ivy Trail." It was out in the timber but the party stopped.

Farmhouses, schools and towns all along the way were gorgeous with flags, some had processions and brass bands.

DISTINGUISHED MEMBERS OF PARTY.

Making the 140-mile tour with the State executive were A. D. Gash, of Chicago; James P. Wilson, of Polo; and S. E. Bradt, of DeKalb, members of the State Highway Commission; W. W. Marr, of Springfield, State Highway Engineer; Homer J. Tice, father of the State Aid Road Bill; United States District Attorney Charles Clyne, of Chicago, and J. R. Blackhall, of Joliet, president of the Illinois Valley Way association, W. E. Hull, and other road enthusiasts.

Five automobiles made the complete trip from Peoria, but at various points en route the motorcade was increased in numbers by the cars of escorting parties.

The *Chicago Tribune* and *Peoria Star* were the only papers with representatives with the distinguished party.

The entertainment ended with a dinner at the Woodruff Inn in Joliet, given by the Will County Automobile Club. Thirty members of the Rotary club of Ottawa met the party at Starved Rock.

CLAY COUNTY

[*By* I. E. SCOTT, *Assistant Engineer, State Highway Department.*]

[One of the places where much work was done and a tremendous amount of enthusiasm created on Good Roads Day was Flora, Clay County, Illinois.

When the plans were being formulated by the Flora Commercial Club, who assumed the leadership in the work of the day, it was thought advisable by the committee in charge that an engineer from the State Highway Department have general supervision of the work. The committee got in touch with the department and Mr. I. E. Scott, assistant engineer, was detailed to direct the efforts of the "road day" workers.

Mr. Scott describes the work of the day in the following article.—EDITOR.]

Fox Creek Bottoms, 2½ miles west of Flora, Clay County, Illinois, is known throughout the entire community as the worst stretch of road on the Midland Trail between East St. Louis, Illinois, and Vincennes, Indiana. The need for improving this particular place has been very apparent for a long time, yet because of the amount of work involved it has been put off from time to time awaiting a favorable opportunity. "Good Roads Day" this year seemed to the Flora Commercial Club the favorable opportunity which had been waited for and they

accordingly began to make plans to improve, on this day, this particular stretch of road. Under the able direction of Mr. W. D. Scuddamore, president and M. J. Bauman, secretary, of the Flora Chamber of Commerce arrangements were perfected, which resulted in the calling together of scores of "Good Roads Enthusiasts" for the avowed purpose of doing away with the treacherous con-

ROAD DAY AT FLORA, ILL.

dition of this road, which for so long a time had been a stigma upon the community.

These men brought with them 50 teams with plows, harrows, wheel and slip scrapers and wagons to be used on the work. One hundred and fifty men kept these teams and equipment busy the entire day. A traction grader and road machine were also employed, grading the road between the Fox Creek bottoms and the city of Flora. On the day previous to May 19, dynamite had been used to loosen up the surface of the Fox Creek Hill in order that it could be easily worked and the following day the hill was cut down and the road widened considerably, the earth being carried both ways and placed in the roadway to fill up washed places and to raise the grade. Permission was obtained to set back a

ROAD DAY AT FLORA, ILL.

fence in order that additional earth might be obtained along the right of way at the foot of a hill, for raising the grade. Three culverts were also eliminated and three others were relocated.

As the noon hour of "Good Roads Day" approached, women and children to the number of about 100 began to gather in Brown's Grove near the scene of activities with heavily laden baskets and proceeded to set out a bountiful picnic dinner, which it is needless to say was joyously received by the laborers. Supplementing the dinner there was lemonade, ice cream and cigars, furnished by the committee in charge.

Regardless of the fact that many of the men who were on the job were unaccustomed to such hard, manual labor as the work of the day made necessary, the amount of permanent good accomplished was far in excess of what had been anticipated and was the cause of much satisfaction to all.

The committee in charge had expected to get only a good start and to have the job finished by the highway commissioners, yet such good headway was made and so much enthusiasm created that plans were made on the spot for another similar "Good Roads Day" for the first of June and before night the use of 30 teams had been pledged for the work, which the committee hope can be practically completed the second day.

CHRISTIAN COUNTY.

[By C. A. PENINGTON, *County Superintendent Highways.*]

"Good Roads Day" was only observed in Taylorville Township for the reason that the farmers were very busy putting in their crops. In Taylorville, the Retail Merchants Association, the Chamber of Commerce and the Good Roads Committee joined in getting the business places to close at noon for three and one-half hours. In the morning some road dragging was done and a few men were put to work to refill a tile trench alongside the road. The band turned out for a few selections. At noon the picnic dinner was enjoyed at Manners Park followed by a very pointy speech delivered by B. H. Piepmeier, maintenance engineer of the State Highway Department, and also a very interesting talk by our Dr. J. N. Nelms was greatly enjoyed. Both speakers were very strong in their pleas for more dragging of our roads.

This is the first time that "Good Roads Day" has been observed in this township and only in one other township in the county for the last three years. I am sure more interest will be taken next year and more townships will observe the day.

DEKALB COUNTY.

The Good Roads Day observance in DeKalb will consist of the work of the business men who will go out to-morrow morning from DeKalb and nail up mileage signs telling the distance to DeKalb. H. G. Wright chairman of the committee from the Commercial Club made his last announcement of plans at the dinner to-day and made general invitation to the citizens of DeKalb, asking each and every one who can get away to come and take part in this work.

The start will be made at 8 o'clock from the corner of Third and Lincoln Highway and everyone who is going is expected to bring along hammer or hatchet, not for knocking purposes but with which to nail up the signs. Those who have cars and want to go along will surely be welcome.

The army which will go out from DeKalb to-morrow morning in automobiles from DeKalb to the furthermost corner of the county and in some cases over into adjoining counties for the purpose of putting up mileage signs is all ready for mobilization.

The two hundred fine signs which have been provided by the commercial club of DeKalb for the purpose are also ready. These signs, which are done in yellow with black lettering, will be apportioned out among the different parties according to the number needed as shown by the survey made last week.

About twenty-five cars will be used to carry the signs and the business men who are going to nail them up. The start will be made about 8 o'clock and if the weather is good and the roads are not rained on to-night the work will be completed and the parties will be back by about noon.—*DeKalb Chronicle.* (Issue of May 18.)

STEPHENSON COUNTY.

"Good Roads Day," Friday, was observed in many parts of the County, following the proclamation of Governor Dunne that the citizens of the State unite in making improvements along the public highways. Where the work was done in this community there was a large force of men out, according to reports from persons who were driving into the several sections of the county.

(Continued on page 62.)

ROAD DRAGGING.

(Continued from page 54.)

The following illustrations show the form of drags which have proved most serviceable. The drag should not be too heavy. A light drag is much more preferable to a heavy one.

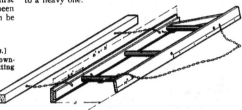

PLANK DRAG.

This drag is made from two pieces of ten or twelve-inch plank, two or three inches thick and eight or nine feet long, reinforced by a two by six-inch strip. The cross braces are four-inch sticks shaped to fit into a two-inch hole. A board platform, not shown in the cut, is laid on the cross pieces for the driver to stand upon. A trailing log may or may not be used. It serves to smooth the surface and distribute the mud that may pass by the drag.

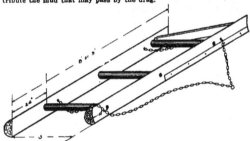

SPLIT LOG DRAG.

This drag is made from a ten or twelve-inch log, eight or nine feet long. The cross braces are four-inch sticks shaped to fit into a two-inch hole. A board platform, not shown in the cut, is laid on the cross pieces for the driver to stand upon.

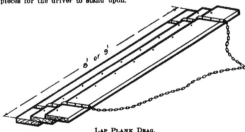

LAP PLANK DRAG.

This form of drag has proved effective for smoothing the surface.

HOW GOOD ROADS DAY WAS OBSERVED.

(Continued from page 61.)

It was noticeable, too, that all were not farmers, the people residing in the towns and villages uniting in the work. It was not an unusual sight to see men in white shirts and pressed trousers working along with the sturdy tillers of the soil.

All in all, the effort was well worth the while, many of the highways being placed in a much better condition.

Several communities which did not observe good roads day at this time will do so a week hence.—*Freeport Bulletin.*

ST. CLAIR COUNTY.

Scores of farmers with teams, graders, picks, shovels and scrapers worked on the Mascoutah road Thursday in response to the appeal of the St. Clair-Wabash Trail Association, through its local vice president, Charles Kutterer of Mascoutah.

Similar work was being done Thursday or will be done Friday all along the road through Illinois. The trail extends west through Illinois from Mt. Carmel to the Indiana line.

Crews under Louis Krauss improved that section of the road from New Memphis to Rayhill's slough; Nick Friedrich from the slough to Mascoutah; Charles Perrottet from the Silver Creek Bottoms to Rentchler; Otto Wetsel from Rentchler to the L. & N. tracks, and the remainder of the distance was in charge of Dan Dietz.

Mr. Dietz's work Thursday was for the township, but he proposed to hold another good roads day Saturday.

Vice President Kutterer said the work Thursday was the first united effort in St. Clair county to better such long strip of road.—*Belleville News Democrat.*

LAKE COUNTY.

Grant Township, that hustling town in western Lake County has started another stunt—it is to have a real Good Roads day on the 19th of May. And it promises to be some day at that.

It is expected that fully 50 or more teams are to turn out on that day to assist in hauling gravel to the stretches of road that need working. The work is to go ahead in a systematic manner, not a hit-and-miss plan. Instead of concentrating their efforts on one spot at one time, the work will be done from three different angles.

The Consumers' Ice Company has donated all the gravel which the people who will work that day can use. The plan now is to send two carloads to Ingleside, two to Long Lake and then the teams will haul all they can direct from the pit at Fox Lake. In this way many of the bad pieces of roads in the town will be cared for.

Residents are enthusiastic over the plan and indications are that the turnout will be big and instead of 50 teams and men there may be double that number.

The stunt is put over by the Fox Lake Commercial Club, an organization which is doing things for the village and the township as well.—*Waukegan Sun.*

THE ROAD DRAG.

The road drag is a simple thing
   Made from a log of wood
But a wonderful contrivance
   For making bad roads good.

It gives the road a needed crown
   A thing that must be had
To drain the water from the road
   Lest it will make it bad.

It smooths out all the ruts and bumps
   I know you will agree
That this part is a feature
   That appeals to you and me.

A drag that follows up a rain
   Helps quite a lot; and why?
By spreading out the puddles
   It helps the road to dry.

It smears the mud pores over
   And seals them tightly shut
And keeps out all the water
   (Water makes a good road rut).

Now don't dispute the points I've made
   And say I'm but a brag,
But go and do as others do
   And make-yourself a drag.

And when conditions are just right
   Just drag a mile or two
And when you see the good results
   You'll be a booster too.

Correspondence Course in Road Building
CONDUCTED BY UNIVERSITY OF ILLINOIS.

Lesson 3.—Steel Beam Bridges With Concrete Floors.

The tendency in recent years in all kinds of highway construction is toward a more permanent type than that used formerly. One of the developments growing out of this change is the use of concrete floors on steel bridges. There are several different types of these floors as shown in Figures 1 to 4. Some are made of plain concrete and some are reinforced with steel bars.

Figure 1 illustrates a concrete floor which consists of a 4-inch subfloor and a 4-inch wearing surface, placed in separate courses. This type of floor has the advantage that the wear on the surface does not affect the strength of the slab which carries the loads. If at any time the wearing surface should break or wear through, that fact alone would give warning that the floor should be repaired. Where the floor is constructed of one course of concrete it is a difficult matter to tell just when repairs are necessary, and it is also a difficult matter to make repairs in such cases.

Figure 2 illustrates a concrete subfloor with a wood block wearing surface. This type has the advantage that the wood block is much lighter than brick or concrete, thus materially reducing the dead load on the structure. The wood block may also be used with a treated, wooden plank subfloor, which would further reduce the dead load.

Figure 3 illustrates a type of reinforced concrete floor in which the steel joists are entirely incased in concrete. This is an excellent idea since it protects the steel beams from corrosion. The chief objection to it is that the cost of form work is materially increased.

Figure 4 illustrates a plain concrete floor in which corrugated iron is arched between the floor joists and serves to support the concrete until it has had time to set. This type is not economical because it requires a considerable mass of concrete which makes a heavy dead load on the structure. Its use would be at least partially justified if it completely covered the steel joists, but since it does not, there is little excuse for using it.

IMPACT ON STEEL BRIDGES WITH CONCRETE SLAB FLOORS.

The University of Illinois in conjuction with the Illinois Highway Department carried on experiments for several years to determine, if possible, to what extent impact should influence the design of steel highway bridges.

It was found from these tests that the impact varied with the speed, the class of floor, the weight of the load, and the construction and position of the member. However, on the bridges with reinforced concrete floors there was practically

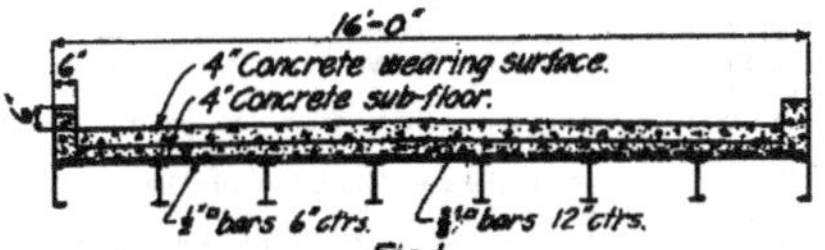

Fig. 1.

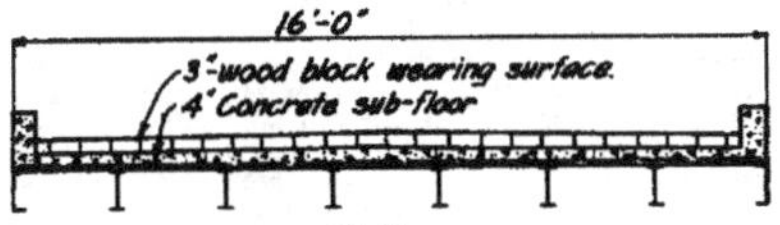

Fig. 2

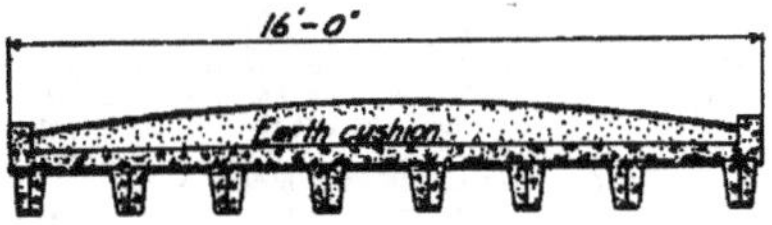

Fig. 3.

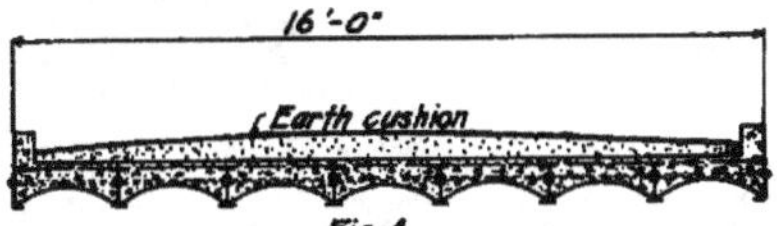

Fig. 4.

no impact, so that in the design of bridges with floors of this type, impact may be neglected.

For a detailed description of the above mentioned tests, read Reference 1.

Distribution of Concentrated Loads by Concrete Slab Floor. In the tests mentioned above information was also secured with regard to the distribution of concentrated wheel loads to the joists by the concrete floor. The conclusion drawn from a study of the results of these tests is, that the Illinois Highway Department specifications as given in article 94 are conservatively safe. This article reads as follows: "Stringers arranged parallel to the axis of the roadway shall be spaced not more than 2½ feet apart and each stringer shall be designed to carry not less than 20 per cent of the rear axle load indicated above (Art. 92) considered as concentrated at the center of the stringer span when a concrete subfloor is used, and not less than 25 per cent of the rear axle load when a timber floor is used."

Methods for Determining Safe Loads.

Uniform Live Load.

The method used to determine the safe uniform live load is exactly the same as explained for the uniform load in Lesson 2 except that no impact is added. Concrete is assumed to weigh 150 pounds per cubic foot, and earth 100 pounds per cubic foot.

Concentrated Live Load.

The method used to determine the safe concentrated live load will be illustrated by an example.

Example 1. A span is assumed as shown in Figure 5.

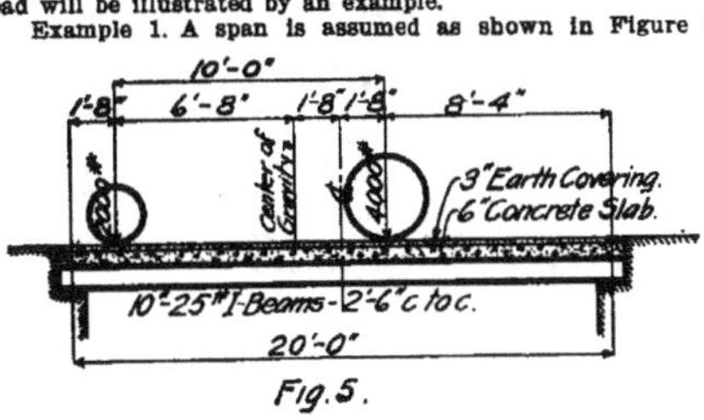

Fig. 5.

The live load is that specified in Article 92 of the Illinois Highway Department specifications. The steel is in good condition. Is the structure safe?

The dead load is,

concrete slab $=2\frac{1}{2}\times\frac{1}{2}\times150=187.5$ lb. per lin. ft.
earth covering $=2\frac{1}{2}\times\frac{1}{4}\times100=62.5$ lb. per lin. ft.
Total $=250.0$ lb. per lin. ft.

The dead load moment is,

$$M=\frac{1}{8}Wl^2=\frac{250\times20\times20}{8}$$
$$=12{,}500 \text{ ft. lb.}$$

To determine the live load moment the right reaction must first be found

$$R_2=\frac{1\frac{2}{3}\times2000+11\frac{2}{3}\times4000}{20}=2500 \text{ lb.}$$

The maximum moment occurs under the heavy wheel and is,

$$M=8\tfrac{1}{3}\times2500=20833 \text{ ft. lb.}$$

The total moment is,

dead load $=12500$ ft. lb.
live load $=20833$ ft. lb.
Total $=33333$ ft. lb.
Or $33333\times12=400{,}000$ in. lb.

The maximum stress in the joist is,

$$f=\frac{M}{S}=\frac{400{,}000}{24.4}$$
$$=16{,}400 \text{ lb. per sq. in.}$$

The bridge is safe.

Table I gives the sizes of steel beams for various spans to carry a 15-ton engine with safety. The maximum stress occurs in the flanges of the beams near the center of the span. The sizes of the beams given in the table do not take account of any reduction of area of the flanges, therefore they are not safe if holes are punched in the flanges near the center of the span.

The sizes of beams given in the table are safe for either wood or concrete floors. The impact added to the live load stresses where wood floors are used is practically equal to the stresses produced by the greater weight of the concrete floor.

A 16-foot roadway requires 6 I-beams and 2 channels. Add one I-beam for each additional 2 feet of width of roadway.

Table I.

Span in feet.	16-foot roadway.	
	6 I-beams.	2 channels.
10	8-in. 18 lb.	8-in. 13¾ lb.
12	8-in. 18 lb.	8-in. 13¾ lb.
14	9-in. 21 lb.	9-in. 15 lb.
16	9-in. 21 lb.	9-in. 15 lb.
18	10-in. 25 lb.	10-in. 20 lb.
20	10-in. 25 lb.	10-in. 20 lb.
22	12-in. 31½ lb.	12-in. 20½ lb.
24	12-in. 31½ lb.	12-in. 20½ lb.
26	12-in. 31½ lb.	12-in. 20½ lb.
28	12-in. 35 lb.	12-in. 25 lb.
30	15-in. 42 lb.	15-in. 33 lb.
32	15-in. 42 lb.	15-in. 33 lb.
34	15-in. 42 lb.	15-in. 33 lb.

PROBLEMS.

1. A steel beam bridge has a 4-inch concrete subfloor with a 4-inch concrete wearing surface. The span is 16 feet. Seven 8-inch, 18-lb. I-beams and two 8-inch, 11¼-lb. channels are used for an 18-foot roadway. Is the bridge safe for a 15-ton engine?

2. A steel beam bridge has a 5-inch concrete floor with a 6-inch earth covering. The span is 20 feet. The beams are 10-inch, 25-lb. I-beams spaced 2 ft. 4 inches c. to c. Is the bridge safe for a 20-ton engine with 14 tons on the rear axle and 6 tons on the front axle?

3. A steel beam bridge has a 4-inch concrete subfloor and a 3-inch brick wearing surface. The span is 24 feet. The beams are 12-inch, 31½-lb. I-beams spaced 2 ft. 0 inches c. to c. Is the bridge safe for a 20-ton engine with the loads distributed as in Problem 2?

4. Design the beams for a steel beam bridge with a concrete floor. The span is 28 feet. The loads are those specified by the Illinois Highway Department.

REFERENCES.

1. Impact on Highway Bridges. Journal of the Western Society of Engineers, June, 1913.

2. Tests Show How Loads Are Distributed on Reinforced Concrete Slab Floors. Engineering Record, November 6, 1915, page 578.

3. Concerning the Use of Steel Highway Bridges in Iowa. Engineering and Contracting, December 29, 1915, page 493.

4. Floors for Steel Bridges. Engineering and Contracting, January 6, 1915, page 8.

5. Wood Block Bridge Floors. Engineering Record, March 6, 1915, page 300.

6. A Discussion of the Administrative and Design Features of Highway Bridge and Culvert Work. Engineering and Contracting, December 23, 1914.

OPINIONS OF THE ATTORNEY GENERAL.

PETITION FOR VOTE ON BOND ISSUE UNDER SECTION 112 NEED NOT DESCRIBE ROADS.

May 18, 1916.

HON. GEORGE A. FALDER,
  State's Attorney, Macomb, Illinois.

DEAR SIR: I am in receipt of your favor of the 17th instant, in which you inquire in substance whether it is necessary that a petition for a vote on a proposition to issue bonds for the purpose of constructing hard roads, under section 112 of the revised Road and Bridge act, chapter 121, Hurd's Statutes, 1913, should describe the roads to be improved and the kind of road to be constructed. It appears that you are inclined to the opinion that the provisions of section 108 of said chapter, as amended by an act approved June 25, 1915 (Sess. L. 1915, p. 603) which requires a petition for a vote on a proposition to levy a special tax to describe the roads to be improved and the kind of improvement, apply to a petition for a vote on a proposition to issue bonds under said section 112.

Said sections 108 and 112 of the act of 1913 are similar to paragraphs 245 and 245a, sections 1 and 4a of the Hard Roads act of 1883, chapter 121, Hurd's Statutes, 1911. The Supreme Court in construing said sections 1 and 4a of the act of 1883, in the case of *People* v. *T. P. & W. Ry. Co.*, 248 Ill., 105, holds in substance that said sections provided two different and distinct methods of raising money for the construction of hard roads, one by a special levy under said section 1, the other by a bond issue under said section 4a; that while it was necessary that a petition for a vote on the question of levying a special tax under said section 1 should describe the roads to be improved and the character of improvement, it was not necessary that a petition for a vote on the question of issuing bonds under said section 4a should describe either the roads to be improved or the kind of improvement. It will be noted that both section 1 of the act of 1883, and section 108 of the act of 1913, provide that a petition for a vote on the question of levying a special tax shall describe the roads to be improved and the kind of road to be constructed, while neither section 4a of the act of 1883, nor section 112 of the revised act contain such a provision regarding a petition for a vote on the question of a bond issue. In view of the similarity between said sections 1 and 4a of the act of 1883, and sections 108 and 112 of the revised act, I am of the opinion that the construction of the court in the above cited case is applicable to sections 108 and 112 of the revised act; and that it is not necessary that a petition for a vote on the question of issuing bonds under section 112 should describe the roads to be improved or the specific kind of improvement.

Very respectfully,

P. J. LUCEY, *Attorney General.*

HIGHWAY COMMISSIONER CAN NOT EMPLOY HIS OWN SON—POLL TAX.

May 17, 1916.

MR. R. J. GRAHAM,
  Road District Clerk, Sparta, Illinois.

DEAR SIR: I am in receipt of your favor of the 15th instant, submitting several propositions relating to various provisions of the revised Road and Bridge act, in substance as follows:

(1) Whether it is legal for a highway commissioner to employ his own son, who is a minor, and team in doing road labor;

(2) Whether the failure of highway commissioners to deliver the poll tax list to the treasurer by the first day of May will defeat the collection of a poll tax;

(3) Whether highway commissioners can be held personally liable for the poll tax in case of neglect to provide for its collection;

(4) What persons are exempt from the payment of a poll tax;

(5) Can the commissioners determine whether or not a person is able-bodied?

(6) Whether the treasurer of the road and bridge fund is required to pay one-half of the poll tax collected from persons residing within an incorporated town or village to the treasurer of such town or village.

Noting your first proposition, I will call your attention to section 72 of the revised Road and Bridge act, chapter 121, Hurd's Statutes, 1913, which expressly prohibits highway commissioners from having, directly or indirectly, any personal pecuniary interest in labor done on the public roads. It would seem that said section would prohibit a commissioner from employing his own son, who is a minor, and team, in doing work upon the roads.

Relative to whether the failure of the highway commissioners to deliver the poll tax list to the treasurer by the first day of May will affect the right to collect such tax, I will say the act passed by the 49th General Assembly (Sess. L. 1915, p. 593) amending section 55 of said chapter 121, provides in part that the poll tax list shall be delivered to the treasurer on or before the first day of May; however, I am of the opinion that said provision is directory and not mandatory, for the reason that the failure to deliver such list to the treasurer by the time specified in the statute does not affect the merits of such tax; and consequently the failure to deliver such list to the treasurer on or before the first day of May does not affect the right to collect same. The Supreme Court, in the case of *People ex rel.* v. *Hulin*, 237 Ill., 122, holds that an irregularity not affecting the substantial justice of a tax will not defeat its collection.

Noting your third inquiry, I will say there is no provision of the statute that makes the highway commissioners personally responsible for the poll tax, for failure or neglect on their part to provide for the collection of such tax.

I construe your fourth inquiry to mean, what persons come within the provision which exempts from the payment of a poll tax persons who are not able-bodied? Said amendatory act of 1915 makes it the duty of highway commissioners to make a list of able-bodied men in their town or district, between the ages of twenty-one and fifty years, and assess against the persons on such list a poll tax of not less than one nor more than three dollars to be paid in cash. It is provided, however, that paupers, idiots, lunatics, and such others as are exempt by law, shall not be compelled to pay such tax. Said act does not define what constitutes an able-bodied person, and this department does not prescribe any rules for determining who are and who are not able-bodied within the terms of the statute. The question as to whether one is able-bodied is a question of fact, to be determined from all the facts and circumstances in each particular case. No rule applicable to all cases can be laid down. Highway commissioners are charged with the duty of making the poll tax list, and they are to exercise a reasonable discretion in determining what persons come within the terms of the statute as being able-bodied. The Appellate Court, in the case of *Sherrick* v. *Town of Houston*, 29 Ill. App., 381, holds that one who is ordinarily physically able to perform the labor usually performed by able-bodied men on the public roads is not exempt from liability for a poll tax. What is said in answer to your fourth inquiry, relative to the discretion to be exercised by highway commissioners in making the poll tax list, furnishes a sufficient answer to your fifth proposition.

Relative to whether the treasurer is required to pay one-half of the poll tax collected from residents of an incorporated town or village, to the treasurer of such town or village, I will say that said amendatory act of 1915, in addition to amending said section 55, also amends section 59 of said chapter 121, to provide that one-half of the poll tax collected from residents of an incorporated town or village shall be paid to the treasurer of such town or village.

I herewith enclose a pamphlet prepared by this department which explains said amendatory act of 1915, and also mail you under separate cover a pamphlet copy of the revised Road and Bridge act of 1913, as amended by various acts of the 49th General Assembly.

Very respectfully,

P. J. LUCEY, *Attorney General.*

SCHNEPP & BARNES, STATE PRINTERS SPRINGFIELD, ILL. 1916.

ILLINOIS HIGHWAYS

[Printed by authority of the State of Illinois.]

OFFICIAL PUBLICATION OF THE

STATE HIGHWAY DEPARTMENT

| VOL. III | SPRINGFIELD, ILLINOIS, JULY, 1916 | No. 7 |

SECTION F, ROUTE 1, KANE COUNTY—ALGONQUIN HILL.

Algonquin Hill, the Scene of Many Hard-Fought Automobile Hill-Climbing Contests, Has at Last Succumbed to the Advance of the Road Builder. A Relocation Involving 24,000 cu. yd. of Excavation in a Quarter of a Mile Reduced the Heavy Grade, Which Varied From 8 to 14 Per Cent, to 3.5 Per Cent. A Hard Surface Will Not Be Placed on This Road Until It Has Had Sufficient Time to Settle Thoroughly.

THROUGH RIBBED ARCH BRIDGE.

Under Construction at Carmi, Illinois, Over Little Wabash River, Three 90-Foot Spans, 18-Foot Roadway.

A SYMPOSIUM ON GOOD ROADS

INTRODUCTION

By Wm. W. Marr, Chief State Highway Engineer.

Any opposition which now remains to a proper development of the rural highways in Illinois is due more to a lack of knowledge of the actual facts as to the costs and benefits than to any other cause.

Well-informed people in every walk of life unite in saying that the benefits derived from road improvement are universal and that the cost of the improvement is very small compared with the good which results.

But too often those who have not given proper thought to the subject regard the benefits of road improvement as class benefits, accruing to only a certain class or group. The city man may believe that the farmers get all the good resulting from highway improvement, while on the other hand, many rural residents firmly insist that good roads are for the city people and the automobilists. The thought that the benefits of good roads are shared unequally by those who pay for them does much to impede the work of those who are endeavoring to improve the highways, not for one class or group, but for the public at large.

Good roads are a benefit to the farmer and to the automobilist, and they are likewise a benefit to all others; true, in some cases the benefits may not be so evident or direct, but nevertheless, study will always show that there is no person or group of persons who are not benefited by highway improvement in a far larger proportion than their share of the cost of the work.

In order to get different ideas on this subject, we recently requested several people who have had much to do with public work to state briefly their opinion as to the true value of road improvement and its economic importance on public welfare. These opinions were asked from men of various callings, statesmen, educators, lawyers, road experts, farmers, bankers, and so on, and as the positions occupied by these men put them in close touch with the public, their opinions as regards any public improvement must carry much weight. These men agree that the benefits of good roads are universal, and that any steps taken toward the systematic improvement of our highways should have the earnest support of everyone.

Let us get away from the idea of class benefits from road improvement and look for the larger economic importance of the movement for better highways.

PRESIDENT WOODROW WILSON.

The efforts which are now being made in most of the states for the adequate improvement of public roads should have the earnest support of every man who has the development of the states and of our Nation at heart. I am deeply interested in the movement for better roads. I realize that good roads are essential for a better agriculture, for the satisfactory marketing of farm products, for improvement in our rural schools, and the making of rural life more interesting and attractive socially. The improvement of rural conditions in these directions is a matter of concern not only to people living in rural districts but also to urban people.

The problem of road construction and maintenance are so difficult as to require the highest order of ability on the part of road officials, and I, therefore, note with much satisfaction the increasing disposition of the states to establish expert state highway departments.

GOVERNOR E. F. DUNNE.

No movement is so vital and important to the people of the State of Illinois as the improvement of its waterways and highways.

This great State of ours, while first in railway development and agricultural wealth, is woefully behind in the improvement of its roadways, being twenty-third among the states in that regard. The improvement of the highways will enhance, in my judgment, the value of all farm property in the State ten-fold the cost of building good, substantial roads throughout the State.

I am pleased to note with what enthusiasm the people of the State are taking up this vitally important matter. Every-where I have gone throughout the State I find "good roads" enthusiasm. This enthusiasm should be maintained.

Pull Illinois "out of the mud" and place her where she belongs, in the first rank of the states in the development of her highways.

J. R. BLACKHALL.

[General Manager, Chicago & Joliet Electric Railway Company, Joliet, Illinois.]

"Good Roads" or the improvement of the highways, has become the subject of such vast economic importance in the development and progress of the Nation, that it is receiving the earnest attention of people in all walks of life. Affecting vitally, as it does, the prosperity of every community and the welfare and comfort of such a large proportion of the citizens, makes it imperative that our highways be improved as expeditiously as possible.

The great financial loss resulting from transportation over unimproved mud roads, and the enormous waste of money through inefficient, out-of-date methods in road construction and maintenance still prevailing under the small unit system in many states, is appalling to those who have given the subject any study.

It is gratifying, however, to know that the people of the great commonwealth of Illinois have at last awakened to the fact that road improvement in a substantial way is necessary if we are to keep up with the progress being made in this direction by some of the other states of the Union.

To that end, comprehensive constructive laws have been enacted and a State Highway Department created and equipped with an efficient and competent staff of officers and engineers, who only need the deserving support of the people, to furnish us with a system of "good roads" in a few years, that will be unequalled in any state in the Union.

S. E. BRADT.

[Secretary of Illinois State Highway Commission.]

All people recognize the saving which will come to the actual users of the roads through their improvement. There are, however, certain economic advantages that are broader and more far reaching than this benefit.

The cost of living is determined by three factors, production, distribution and consumption.

It will be admitted, without argument, that the haul from the farm to the point of shipment is as much a factor in distribution as the haul from the point of shipment to the markets of the world, and if improved roads will decrease the cost of that primary haul, then good roads are an important factor in the cost of living. The office of Public Roads estimates the cost of hauling the average annual crop of the United States from the farm to the railroad station at not less than $500,000,000 and that this cost would be reduced one-half by the proper improvement of our road system, thus saving $250,000,000 annually. Therefore, from the standpoint of distribution improved roads would be of great economic benefit.

How will production be affected by road improvement?

The business of the farmer, in its importance, stands out separate and distinct from every other occupation for the reason that the farmer determines our food supply. Anything that tends to increase the number or efficiency of our farmers tends to increase production.

To bring about an increase in the number of farmers the educational and social advantages of the farm must be made equal to the educational and social advantages of the city. Only through the improvement of our highways can this absolutely necessary condition be brought about. Through education will come increased farm efficiency which means larger profits to the farmer and better home conditions. Hence improved roads must be the first step in increasing production

Thus, as having a direct influence upon both production and distribution, road improvement is of the greatest economic importance to every individual, regardless of occupation or locality, and regardless of whether he is personally a user of the roads or not.

FRANCIS G. BLAIR.
[SUPERINTENDENT OF PUBLIC INSTRUCTION, STATE OF ILLINOIS.]

Perhaps no other State institution feels the need of good roads more keenly than the public schools. Those located in our villages, towns and cities are not affected, but the 10,632 one-room country schools, the 14 consolidated rural schools and the 236 township high schools face this question every day of the school year. We enroll in these rural schools over 300,000 children. To get to the schools these children must travel all the way from 1 to 10 miles. Every mile of good road laid down adds to the regularity of attendance, and, therefore, to the progress along educational lines of these 300,000 children. No branch of the work of the State of Illinois would be more greatly benefited by a State-wide highway improvement than the public schools.

EDMUND J. JAMES.
[PRESIDENT OF THE UNIVERSITY OF ILLINOIS.]

The civilization of a people may be determined and judged from many points of view, from their literature, their buildings, their art, etc. The ability of a nation to construct an adequate highway system is one of the best evidences of its fitness to play a large part in the history of civilization extending over a great territory. The Greeks, of course, made few highways because their life was largely upon the sea. But the Romans, who mastered the world, accomplished that great feat quite as much because they were good road builders as because they were good fighters and constructive statesmen. The American people are the greatest road builders of modern times, as evidenced by the mileage of their railways. Now that we are beginning to develop our wagon roads and automobile roads, not merely as a mere supplement to the railway system but as, in a considerable degree, independent of, though exceedingly helpful to, a system of railway transportation, I have no doubt that we are going to rank with the Romans and with the French and the Germans and the English as builders of a network of improved highways which will change the face of our civilization.

A. D. GASH.
[PRESIDENT ILLINOIS STATE HIGHWAY COMMISSION.]

Benefits, because of good roads, are universal. Every legitimate business is of vital importance. Necessities of life, except those produced on our respective places, must go over the highways. Therefore the question, "Who is most benefited by highway improvement?" is impossible of solution. While it profits the producer to haul two tons as quickly and cheaply on good roads as one ton on bad roads, it correspondingly benefits the consumer by reducing the price.

O. M. JONES.
[SUPERVISOR, VERMILION COUNTY.]

One of the most important questions for the consideration of members of the boards of supervisors, in Illinois, at the present time, is that of better roads. Good roads are a benefit to all classes of citizens. Good roads give character to a community. Good roads lead to better conditions physically and morally with as much certainty as the building of good schools, good churches and other public buildings. Good roads attract attention to the locality where they are built. They make it more desirable as a place in which to live. People are attracted to such a locality; naturally they prefer to invest there. This results in an increased demand for property, increased values, increased comforts and better conditions generally. Such results, if they can be had with any reasonable effort, should be obtained. Things so desirable are worthy of the attention of members of the boards of supervisors. Money expended on temporary road improvements is largely a waste of public money; whereas, on the other hand, money expended for permanent road improvements is a splendid investment. It can be demonstrated mathematically that it will cost less, covering a term of years, to build a permanent good road than it will to keep a heavy traffic road in reasonable repair by temporary improvements. A county board of supervisors has the power to levy taxes for the purpose of aiding in the construction of roads and bridges in any part of the county. This power is very broad and is only limited by the reasonable discretion of the board. This power has existed for many years but until recently very little use has been made of it. In June, 1915, the Legislature, by an amendment to the Tice Road Law, provided that in case any county sees fit to advance the money, either by ordinary taxation or by issuing bonds, to improve the highways within the county, under the supervision and approval of the State Highway Commission, such roads, when so improved, will thereafter be maintained by the State Highway Commission, and the county is given the right to repay itself to the extent of one-half the cost of such improvement out of the allotments for State aid roads. This is a long stride in the right direction, and an additional inducement for permanent road improvements in Illinois. Boards of supervisors throughout the State would do well to give it their most careful and thoughtful consideration. If the boards of supervisors throughout the State will use the power they have in a *united* effort, under a plan worked out by the State Highway Commission and its engineers, much will be accomplished for better roads in Illinois.

W. H. JOESTING.
[MANAGER, ALTON BOARD OF TRADE.]

The development of sentiment for the issuance of county bonds for road building has brought to the surface many questions which require careful consideration and demand clearly-stated and convincing replies. Of these, the one recurring most frequently in our experience is: "What advantage lies in a bond issue for the farmer who lives several miles from one of the improved roads?"

At first glance it would seem that the man living directly upon the improved road obtains the greatest benefit, but careful analysis proves that the greatest gain over present conditions is to the man on the side road. With the limited road and bridge funds available in any township and the necessity of keeping the main highways in at least passable condition, little or nothing has been left for work upon the less traveled roads. As the highways to be improved under a bond issue will be immediately taken over by the State and maintained, the road and bridge funds formerly spent on these roads will be released for use upon the side roads.

In addition, money spent upon these side roads will go five times as far, or do five times as much work, as when it was spent upon the roads where heavy travel quickly wiped out every trace of the improvement. A reasonable amount of road and bridge money used in ditching and dragging side roads will place them in condition to carry the comparatively light traffic that passes over them to the main highway and the man on the side road will have, in place of a continuous haul through the mud from farm to town, a much-improved surface from farm to the main highway and a highly improved road, maintained without expense to the township or county, the remainder of the way to his town or market.

The greatest benefit from a system of roads improved by county and State aid will be derived by the man who lives from 1 to 5 miles from the main highway. A thorough understanding of the truth of this will make many friends and votes for a county bond issue.

EUGENE DAVENPORT.
[DEAN OF THE COLLEGE OF AGRICULTURE, UNIVERSITY OF ILLINOIS.]

The time has come in the development of Illinois when transportation problems must be attacked and solved. More and more people desire to move rapidly from place to place and at all seasons. Schools require the transportation of large numbers of people twice a day through nine or ten months of the year. Besides this, a heavy tonnage of crops is being moved, preferably at times when farmers are not engaged with the business of production. All these things call for better roads than we have yet developed in most parts of the State. Bad roads are partly a matter of loss, partly a matter of inconvenience, very much a matter of arrest of civilization.

JAMES P. WILSON.
[MEMBER OF ILLINOIS STATE HIGHWAY COMMISSION.]

A tax upon the farms for the improvement of the highways is an investment ranking in importance with the buying of live stock or the purchase of machinery. The expense of the transportation of farm products to the railroad station is an essential factor in computing the cost of production. The price of all farm commodities is fixed f. o. b. station.

Over the highways these products must travel. Improved roads will cheapen the trip, because one can increase the load and shorten the time; besides they are accessible every day in the year. The saving in the delivery of 1,200 bushels of corn from each quarter section in Illinois over a period of 20 years will furnish sufficient money to improve all the designated State roads. This will connect city and county. It will move the farmer nearer to the city, giving him the benefit of social and educational opportunities, which to-day he does not enjoy.

We are confident that a careful study of the situation in this State will soon unite the farmers of Illinois in an earnest demand for better roads.

B. F. HARRIS.

[CHAIRMAN OF THE AGRICULTURAL COMMISSION OF THE AMERICAN BANKERS' ASSOCIATION. PRESIDENT OF FIRST NATIONAL BANK, CHAMPAIGN, ILLINOIS.]

After a number of years' study and work in many phases of public welfare, I am convinced that of all her needs, Illinois' greatest need is a State-wide system of permanent roads.

Year-around roads will help solve many of our rural problems; will work wonders in social and marketing conditions, and bring a greater direct and indirect return than any investment we can make.

Why should we continue to pay the frightful cost of mud roads, holding back the development of the State and our people—with almost every other first-class state leading us in road organization and good road mileage?

Verily this generation must act or be derelict in its duty.

HOMER J. TICE.

[CHAIRMAN COMMITTEE ON ROADS AND BRIDGES, FORTY-NINTH GENERAL ASSEMBLY.]

Because of the conditions of the public roads of Illinois, it will cost the farmers of the State 18c per ton per mile for an average haul of five miles, which is 2.15c per bushel, for delivering the surplus corn, wheat and oats of the 1915 crop. This cost will be in the aggregate $5,921,765 or double the cost of a like service in countries and states having their main lines of travel permanently improved. This is an overcost or loss of 20¼c per acre on the corn ground, 23⅜c and 14¼c per acre on wheat and oats ground.

Permanently improved roads increase the value of land from $9 to $12 per acre.

Road conditions affect the business of the banker, merchant, liveryman and all other occupations.

Improved roads make better schools and larger attendance in rural communities. The same with attendance on church services.

The ratio of illiteracy in rural communities having indifferently improved roads is 18 to 1, compared with communities having permanently improved roads.

There is more than double the percentage of illiteracy found in rural communities of the United States as compared with cities.

The last Federal census shows a decrease in population in communities whose roads are unimproved and a heavy increase in localities having improved roads.

The bettering of home and community life, the educating and elevating of our citizens, the prosperity and advancement of our State all depend, in a large degree, upon the public roads—the means of transportation and communication.

L. Y. SHERMAN,

UNITED STATES SENATOR FROM ILLINOIS.

Highways are for the general public. Easy communication between distant localities and persons is of the first importance in production, distribution, social and political life. A highway is not merely a local benefit. It comes a part of a general system of travel. It being so, in order that the roads may be convenient in location and fit for use, cooperation is indispensable. Every road that is part of a through system of travel or that communicates with a through system is not restricted to those adjacent to it but is a link in the entire line of travel. No more important improvement now concerns the states and the General Government than the betterment of our roads.

 ## Sugar Island Bridge Between Kankakee and Iroquois Counties Damaged by Tornado.

By CLIFFORD OLDER, Bridge Engineer, Illinois Highway Department.

A destructive storm passed over a portion of northeastern Illinois on March 21, 1916. Trees and farm buildings suffered considerable damage. This storm caused the destruction of a steel bridge in Iroquois County, the wreck of which was illustrated on page 25 of *Illinois Highways,* issue of March-April, 1916. During the same storm a steel bridge, which crosses the Kankakee River near the line between Kankakee and Iroquois Counties, known as the Sugar Island Bridge, was considerably distorted.

In the case of the Iroquois County bridge, but little information could be gained in regard to the weakness which actually led to the failure, as the final twisted condition of the structure was no doubt due largely to the fall from the foundations to the stream bed.

The Sugar Island Bridge, however, was left by this storm in such condition that the effect of the wind pressure could plainly be traced, and the weak features, which were evidently close to the point of failure, could easily be distinguished.

The bridge consists of two spans, each 185 feet long, center to center of end pins. The distance, center to center of trusses, is 17 feet 2 inches and the height of trusses 26 feet.

The exact date this bridge was erected could not be determined at the time the examination was made. It was probably about fifteen to twenty years ago. The general character of the design and the type of details, which are quite well shown by the accompanying illus-

FIG. 1. VIEW SHOWING INCLINATION OF WEST SPAN.

trations, are typical of highway bridge construction of about fifteen years ago.

EFFECT OF WIND LOAD ON UPPER LATERAL SYSTEM.

Figure 1, taken looking west, shows the trusses of the west span leaning decidedly towards the north. The east span was not so badly damaged, but it also has an inclination in the same direction. It is evident that during the storm, the wind was blowing in a northerly direction.

FIG. 2. NOTE DAMAGED CONDITION OF PORTAL.

Fig. 1, 2, 3 and 4 show plainly the light character of the upper lateral system. No intermediate sway bracing was used and the top lateral struts were too light and shallow to cause any of the top chord wind load to be transmitted through the vertical posts to the lower lateral system. The top chords, although displaced laterally, were found to be in perfect alignment. The top lateral struts and diagonals were found to be practically undamaged. From these facts and the condition of the portals, it is evident that the top lateral system served, as intended in the design, to carry the wind load to the portals. The portals, however, proved to be too weak to transmit, without damage, the accumulated top chord wind load down the end posts to the foundations.

FIG. 3. A CLOSE VIEW OF THE WEST PORTAL.

The condition of the west portal of the west span is shown in Fig. 2 and 3 and the east portal of the same span in Fig. 4. Some distortion of the west portal of the east span may also be seen in Fig. 4. It is interesting to note that the distortion of the portals occurred largely in the portion not affected by the knee braces. The lacing bars, which were "flats" and connected by one rivet at each intersection, were buckled in the compression system and some of the bars in the tension system were pulled in two.

It seems evident that, providing a no more serious weakness developed elsewhere, a complete failure of the portals would have been caused by a slightly greater wind load and the tipping over of the trusses and complete collapse of the spans would have followed the failure of the portals.

EFFECT OF WIND LOAD ON LOWER LATERAL SYSTEM.

A partial failure of the lower lateral system of each span occurred also. In the case of the west span, even had the portals and top lateral system held firm, complete failure, because of the weakness of the lower lateral system, was imminent.

FIG. 4. SHOWING EAST PORTAL OF WEST SPAN AND WEST PORTAL OF EAST SPAN.

The lower chords of the trusses, as well as the floor beams and lateral rods, are of course, essential parts of the lower lateral system. The lower chords of the Sugar Island Bridge are composed of eye bars throughout the entire length of each span. The lateral rods are "rounds," passed through holes near the ends of the floor beams and also through holes in bent plates, riveted to the floor-beam webs on the far side. The ends of the rods are threaded and provided with nuts. Fig. 5 shows the end of one of the diagonals, which, because of its position in the lower lateral system, was subject to compression during this storm. Not being intended to take compression, it simply pushed through the holes in the floor beam and connecting plates until the nut was an inch or more away from the bent plate.

As in the case of the upper laterals, the tension diagonals of the lower systems did not fail, although the bent plates were somewhat distorted by the pressure of the nuts and the rods were probably somewhat over-stressed.

Fig. 5. A Diagonal Which Was Subjected to Compression.

The partial failure of the lower lateral systems occurred because of the reversal of the dead-load stress in the lower chord bars on the windward side of the bridge. The lower chords, although displaced laterally, were found to be in perfect alignment from the second panel point at one end to the second panel point at the opposite end of each truss.

Fig. 6. Showing Effect on Lower Chords.

From this fact, it does not necessarily follow, how-ever, that the dead-load stress in these panels of the lower chord was not temporarily reversed. As complete failure did not occur, a partial recovery of alignment of the lower chord after the wind load was released would be expected.

Fig. 7. Showing How Pipe Rail Was Displaced.

The alignment of the pipe rail, Fig. 7, shows fairly well that the final displacement of the lower chord was parallel to its original position, except near the ends of the span.

Probable Wind Pressure.

It is evident that the wind force brought to the shoes, in excess of that necessary to overcome the horizontal component of the dead-load thrust of the end posts, would have a tendency to pull the shoes off the founda-tions.

That this excess stress was considerable may be judged by the displacement of the stones on which the shoes rest at the pier. This is shown in Fig. 8. The movement of the upper ends of the end posts would also tend to rotate the shoes in a horizontal plane and this no doubt aided the displacement of the stones. It is doubtful if much uplift occurred, because of the lack of sway bracing and the failure of the portals. No hinged bolsters were provided, but rollers were in place under the pier shoes. This expansion device appears to have been sufficiently serviceable to have permitted a recovery movement of the lower end of the end posts when the wind load was released. This movement was limited, however, by the length of the slotted holes, through which the anchor bolts passed. The final posi-tion of one of the anchor bolts with respect to the slotted hole in the shoe is shown in Fig. 8.

It may be seen from the cuts that the horizontal component of the dead-load stress in the end posts was not sufficient to push the shoes back to place after the wind subsided. Neglecting uplift, this would lead to the conclusion that the total wind force applied to the shoes during the storm must have been more than double the horizontal component of the dead-load stress in the end posts.

It is difficult to determine just what wind load would produce a longitudinal force at the shoes equal to this amount, owing to the complicated action of the lower lateral system, following a wind load great enough to cause a reversal of the dead-load stress in some of the panels of the lower chord. Approximate computations seem to indicate, however, that the wind pressure per

FIG. 8. LOOKING DOWN THE END POSTS AT PIER, SHOWING SHOES AND BROKEN STONE.

linear foot of lower chord must have been in excess of 220 lb.

DESIGNING PRACTICE OF ILLINOIS HIGHWAY DEPARTMENT.

The specifications of the Illinois Highway Department require that a wind load of 300 lb. per foot be provided for in the plane of the lower chord and 150 lb. per foot in the plane of the upper chord of through truss bridges. In addition, it is required that when head room permits, intermediate transverse frames be introduced and designed to transfer seven-tenths of the top chord wind load, through the vertical posts to the plane of the lower chord. The lower chords, as well as all other members, are composed of shapes capable of resisting compression, as well as tension.

The continuous concrete floors used on all standard designs of the department also offer a most effectual lateral resistance in the plane of the lower chord. These features which may be distinguished in Fig. 9 are believed to be ample to take care of the maximum wind load which may be expected.

Stephenson County will vote on November 7, 1916. for a bond issue of $850,000 to build roads. The board of supervisors by a unanimous vote at their June session ordered the election. The scheme contemplates the construction of 160 miles of road of various types. Brick and concrete being used on the heaviest traveled roads. County Superintendent O. G. Hiveley and a committee of five from the board of supervisors, viz: D. G. Manus, Howard Price, Dave Felts, O. E. Stine, and Mahlon Hutmacher have been working on this scheme since December, 1915.

The Stephenson County Good Roads Association has been organized and is under the supervision of the farmers of the county. A vice president is elected from each township. A representative campaign committee of all classes of people has been appointed, and they are now at their strenuous duties. The Stephenson County Medical Society will devote all of their leisure moments to the success of the issue.

Practically all organizations and societies and a large number of farmers are in favor of the bond issue, and good roads, and that the old saying, "Dodge Stephenson County Roads," will soon be a by-gone fact, is hoped for. Here is "Success to Stephenson County."

FIG. 9. CONSTRUCTION FEATURES SUCH AS ARE SHOWN HERE ARE AMPLY SUFFICIENT TO CARE FOR HEAVY WIND LOADS.

ILLINOIS HIGHWAYS.

Published Monthly by the
State Highway Department,
Springfield, Illinois.

ILLINOIS HIGHWAY COMMISSION.

A. D. GASH, *President.*
S. E. BRADT, *Secretary.*
JAMES P. WILSON.

WM. W. MARR, *Chief State Highway Engineer.*

BUREAU OF ROADS.

H. E. BILGER, *Road Engineer.*
M. W. WATSON, *Assistant Road Engineer.*
C. M. HATHAWAY, *Office Engineer.*
L. P. SCOTT, *Chief Draftsman.*

BUREAU OF BRIDGES.

CLIFFORD OLDER, *Bridge Engineer.*
G. F. BURCH, *Assistant Bridge Engineer.*
A. W. CONSOER, *Office Engineer.*

BUREAU OF MAINTENANCE.

B. H. PIEPMEIER, *Maintenance Engineer.*
F. T. SHEETS, *Assistant Maintenance Engineer.*

BUREAU OF TESTS.

F. L. ROMAN, *Testing Engineer.*
W. C. ADAMS, *Chemist.*

BUREAU OF AUDITS.

J. M. McCOY, *Chief Clerk.*
T. W. DIECKMANN, *Department Editor.*
R. R. McLEOD, *General Bookkeeper.*
G. E. HOPKINS, *Property Clerk.*

DIVISION ENGINEERS.

R. L. Bell, Buchanan-Link Bldg., Paris, Ill.
H. B. Bushnell, 144 Fox St., Aurora, Ill.
J. E. Huber, Wise Building, Mt. Vernon, Ill.
A. H. Hunter, 302 Apollo Theater Bldg., Peoria, Ill.
C. M. Slaymaker, 510 Metropolitan Bldg., E. St. Louis, Ill.
H. E. Surman, 614 People's Bank Bldg., Moline, Ill.
Fred Tarrant, State Highway Department, Springfield, Ill.

Address all communications in regard to "Illinois Highways," to State Highway Department, Springfield, Illinois.

CONTENTS.

The county board of Cook County voted to sell $200,000 worth of the $2,000,000 bonds recently authorized for good roads. It is expected to devote this sum of $200,000 to the improvement of 12 miles of Western Avenue from Blue Island to the county line, and 3 miles of Archer Avenue, north of Lamont.

* * *

The membership of the Mason County Good Roads Association has been increased considerably in Havana Township through the efforts of Frank Keest, township representative of the association.

* * *

Good Roads Day came this year at a time when the farmers of Beaver Township, Iroquois County were busy. They accordingly postponed road day activities until June 1, and on this date 8 car loads of gravel which came from Lafayette were put on a stretch of road. The gravel was hauled from the cars by 42 teams, and there were 75 extra helpers. The value of the labor which was donated was estimated at about $300. At noon the women served dinner to the workers, thus aiding mightily in the undertaking.

* * *

Better Roads and Streets rightly says that Senator Harding of Ohio certainly hit the nail on the head when, speaking before the United States Senate he said: "The biggest question of the whole road problem is that of maintenance, and the biggest crime in public affairs today is the wanton waste resulting from lack of proper maintenance of roads which cost millions to build."

* * *

Bond County is to assist several townships of the county in repainting some steel bridges, according to a report made by County Superintendent Young, who says: "While on the way to Greenville to attend a meeting of the county board in company with Mr. Albert Wade, who was at that time chairman of the county board, we crossed several large steel bridges. Mr. Wade said it would be a very desirable thing if the county could in some way have them painted, as the townships were hardly able to do it. At the June meeting just passed, the question was brought before the board and they instructed the county superintendent to purchase paint at the expense of the county and to furnish it to the various townships, the paint to be applied at the cost of the townships. The township commissioners have expressed themselves as being heartily in favor of the proposition and are making arrangements to apply the paint as soon as possible. This is a step in the right direction, as there are quite a number of bridges in Bond County, the rebuilding of which would involve county aid. It seems only right for the county to keep in close touch with the townships and help maintain such bridges."

* * *

A special election is to be called shortly in South Fork Township, Christian County, to decide on the question of issuing bonds to the amount of $7,000 to provide funds for building three bridges over the south fork of the Sangamon River.

* * *

By a unanimous vote, the board of supervisors of Stephenson County decided to submit to the voters at the fall election the proposition of issuing bonds to the amount of $850,000 to provide funds for the construction of permanent hard roads in Stephenson County, the total mileage to be improved being 160.

County Superintendent Jordan, of Iroquois County, says that the good roads movement in his county is on the boom, and to substantiate his statements he puts forward the following facts:

"The board of supervisors at the June meeting, by a vote of 19 to 6, passed a resolution authorizing the chairman to appoint a committee of seven, including himself, to lay out a system of roads to be improved under a county bond issue, and to prepare all the necessary plans, etc., for submitting the proposition to a vote of the people.

"At a special election held in Stockland Township on June 12, the proposition to vote township bonds to the amount of $50,000 for building brick roads was carried by a vote of 153 to 77.

"At the April election, Ash Grove, Pigeon Grove and Fountain Creek Townships voted a special tax of 40c to 50c for five years to be used in oiling earth roads. This money will not be available until next year. In the meantime they are using as much of the general road and bridge funds as they can spare for this purpose.

"The county board of supervisors ordered six, 1,000-gallon Austin pressure oil distributors for the use of any township in the county that desired to oil its roads. Three of the machines have been delivered and tried out.

It was found that the 4-inch tires with which they were equipped were too narrow for the load they had to carry. Arrangements were made to have the others furnished with 8-inch tires, and if they work all right, the first three will be changed to 8-inch.

"Unusually rainy weather has seriously interfered with the work of oiling the roads. Fountain Creek Township had some of its roads oiled in excellent shape about the middle of May, but since then it has been impossible to get the roads in proper condition for oiling between rains."

* * *

The Will County Automobile and Good Roads Association is not satisfied with its present membership of about 300. They think that double that number would make a much better showing for the county. President Lem Northam intends to start a campaign immediately to increase the membership.

* * *

County Superintendent Davy says that he has been testing gravel beds in Logan County, and thus far has located two very good beds. One lies in Kickapoo Bottom on the Fifth Street State aid road and comprises more than 60 acres of very good gravel. The other is located on Deer Creek along the Mount Pulaski State aid road and contains about 50 acres of the best gravel yet located in the county. Mr. Davy is now testing the gravel on the Broadwell State aid road. Atlanta is also asking for tests to be made, and there is every reason to believe

there are many gravel beds in the county which can be made to yield a good supply of road-building material.

Also the Logan County Automobile Club is getting busy in and around Lincoln this year, and its activity is resulting in the building of good approaches to the State aid roads leading into Lincoln. They have under construction eight-tenths of a mile of gravel road on the Nicholson Road north of Lincoln and the citizens along the Seventeenth Street road are organizing to build out that way. The club intends to see to it that all the roads entering Lincoln will be put in fine condition.

Reporting further on good road activities in Logan County, Superintendent Davy says:

"The progressive farmers along the line of the North Beason road have gotten busy and laid out five miles of gravel road to be built the present summer. They raised $9,500 by popular subscription and then asked the county of Logan to contribute $1,000 which was promptly allowed, thus assuring that the road will be built. Such hustlers as Carl Shepler and William Schauneur made this road a go and demonstrated that they are not only first class citizens but progressive citizens also.

"This road begins at the eastern limit of the city of Lincoln, and ends at the Oran Township line, going through East Lincoln Township, in Logan County. The village of New Holland will build one mile of gravel road along the Burlington Way this year. Atlanta Township citizens will not be left out and they propose to construct two miles of gravel road south of Atlanta.

"Atlanta, Orville, Elkhart, Laenna, West Lincoln and Prairie Creek Townships all have large mogul tractors and a complete outfit for grading their roads, and these outfits have all more than made good. Mt. Pulaski Township bought a new tractor last year and Single Commissioner Keck is a live wire in the county. Any one passing through Logan County can tell which townships have first-class grading outfits by the way the roads are kept. The roads in Logan County are 25 per cent better now than they were previous to the passing of the Tice Road Law. Road improvement and bridge building moves steadily onward in Logan County and much improvement is in evidence."

* * *

County superintendent Conlee, of Macoupin County, has called our attention to some work which was done last year about 2½ miles east of Palmyra. It seems that a hill there had always been quite objectionable to travelers. The local people finally determined that they would

get together and stay on the job until they cut down the hill. They did, too, although it took six days and resulted in many aching backs and blistered hands. There were 15 teams donated by the farmers, and the business men of Palmyra also were on hand and did their share of the work.

MARKED THROUGH ROUTES IN ILLINOIS*
By F. T. SHEETS, Assistant Maintenance Engineer.

A few years ago such a thing as a route definitely named and marked for the guidance of the traveling public was unknown. Roads were known locally, and were considered only from the local standpoint. The possibility of a road having a relation to other states or to the country at large was not realized. Consequently, the conditions of the roads in various communities have depended upon the enterprise and progressiveness of those communities alone. Since the era of the automobile, with the attending promotion of marked through routes, a great impetus has been given to the improved roads movement. The organized interests of the through route associations have assisted isolated communities and have induced them to improve their roads. This has resulted in definite action being taken by each individual locality in such a manner as to carry out one general policy as outlined by the association promoting the route.

Practically all of the marked routes have been financed and promoted by perfected organizations of interested men and women. Men of national reputation, together with the most humble person along the route, have been closely identified with this movement. The combination of the efforts of all the interested people between these two extremes has resulted in a movement which has awakened the whole country to a realization of the fact that the time for definite action concerning the road problem is at hand. Strength always results from organization, and the strength obtained by uniting the interest of the general public far surpasses any possessed by State and county officials or isolated road legislation.

A large amount of enthusiasm has been displayed by automobile users. From the standpoint of the automobile tourist the through routes marked at frequent intervals by some conspicuous sign are very desirable. Traveling is much more pleasant when there is no danger of losing the way. Likewise hotel and garage accommodations are much better for the tourist if the bulk of the traffic proceeds along one route.

Through routes have also received the support of the automobile manufacturers. Aside from the general standpoint of public welfare, such producers have been able to advance their own interests by cooperating with the various highway associations. Through routes mean better roads, better roads mean more tourists, more tourists mean more automobiles, more automobiles mean more business.

The results obtained by such important organizations as the Dixie Highway Association, Lincoln Highway Association or the National Highway Association, far surpass the expectations of even the most optimistic promoters. The roads have been dragged and graded, permanent culverts and bridges built, and in many places the roads have been improved with some form of hard wearing surface. Local officials have cooperated with the promoters of these highways so that a large part of the money spent locally has been used on these routes. Naturally this has hastened the improvement far beyond the rate which would have prevailed if hit-or-miss methods were followed without any definite object in view.

* This article appeared in the *Motor Age*, issue of July 6, and is reprinted here through the courtesy of the publishers of that magazine.

The marking signs used so far on the through routes have consisted largely of various colored bands and symbols, painted on telephone poles or other roadside structures. This system of marking might be generally improved in the future if some more permanent marker were used. This idea might be carried out as the route became constructed of the more permanent types of pavement. In this manner the improved stretches might be honored by the more permanent marking system while the unimproved portions would be simply designated by blazing a trail of colors on the telephone poles.

The fundamental purpose of the State aid law in Illinois is to obtain a network of through roads. The policy of the State administration, the State Highway Commission and the Chief State Highway Engineer has been to bend every effort toward a State-wide system of roads which will serve local, State and through traffic. The influence of the department has been used in all cases to secure the type of road which suited the traffic conditions, and to require proper construction and maintenance of the types chosen. All matters pertaining to State aid roads have been administered in such a manner as to benefit the system as a whole rather than to cater to any narrow local prejudices.

It is plain that this policy has met with popular approval. This approval has been manifested by the formation of the various associations promoting through routes. These promoters are demanding in an unofficial way the same through system as is advocated by the State law and the State Highway Department. The cooperation of these official and unofficial interests naturally proves beneficial to the road system.

The State Highway Department is heartily in sympathy with the movement to establish marked through routes because in this manner the cause of better roads is served. In order to assist this movement, a map has been prepared by the department showing the through routes established up to date. It is believed that proper publicity may be given these routes in this manner and that their importance may be more apparent if official recognition is given. Figure 1 shows the map of marked through routes in the State. There may be some small errors in the minor routes, and in some cases incomplete information prohibited showing a route in full. The information shown, however, is believed to be correct. A glance at this map shows the magnitude of the work which has been done in Illinois alone.

A map of Illinois prepared by the State Highway Department showing the State aid roads was published in *Illinois Highways*, issue of September, 1914. It will be noted that the through routes closely follow the State aid routes. As a general rule it may be said that the State aid roads which follow the through routes are the most important ones. In addition to local traffic they accommodate fast-moving traffic, which might be compared to that carried by the main passenger lines on a railroad. The remaining State aid roads may well be compared to the spur lines which carry local passenger traffic and freight. In designing the State aid system this fact should be taken into account, and a width and type chosen which will best accommodate the conditions. In general the State aid roads which serve through traffic as well

(Continued on Page 80)

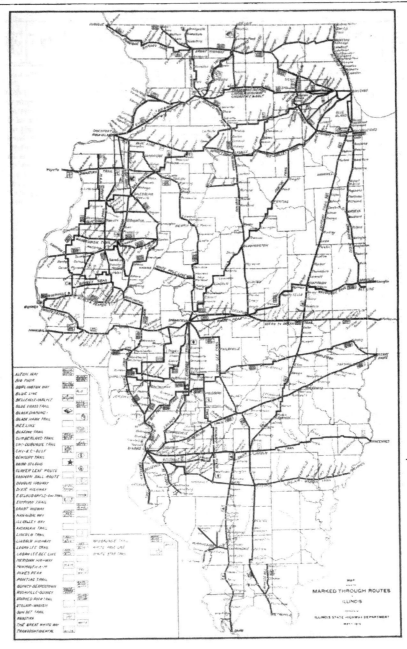

MAP
MARKED THROUGH ROUTES
ILLINOIS

ILLINOIS STATE HIGHWAY DEPARTMENT

Types of Roads, Construction and Durability
By W. W. MARR, Chief State Highway Engineer.

Counties contemplating bond issues for constructing roads along designated State aid lines frequently find it difficult to distinguish between the merits of the various types of construction now being employed.

Under the method of building roads in short lengths and without any apparent system as regards the connecting of main lines of travel between townships, cities and counties, it is inevitable that many of the roads are of such character and placed in such locations that they fail to meet with the requirements and, for this reason, a great many really good roads have failed because of being overburdened or because they were improperly constructed in some minor particular and a great many other roads failed because of the method adopted in making them. Thus, it appears that no very clear idea of what may be expected from many of the popular types now used exists among the people who are advocating good roads or a betterment of present conditions.

In the construction of State aid roads a comprehensive system has been designated, which connects all the main trading points of the county and adjoining counties. This is a decided step in the right direction but, owing to the limited amount of money provided for the building of these roads, it frequently happens that the location designated by the county board for the use of State aid allotment does not represent the most pressing need. There are several reasons for this, principal among them being that those who pay the taxes feel entitled to their part of the returns as rapidly as possible and it is difficult to prove to them that other sections of the county are entitled to any prior consideration.

As the success of a road depends not only on having a type which will meet the requirements of traffic, but also on the minimum cost necessary to meet the requirements, it follows that different types of road which will sustain different amounts and characters of traffic must necessarily be employed to meet both the principal conditions.

Fundamentally the purpose of road building is to attain a smooth surface at the least cost. Where the traffic is light, a light type of road will be as good as a heavier type, so far as all practical considerations are concerned and if we consider economy of construction at all, it is absolute waste to build a more expensive type than is necessary.

A great deal of confusion exists as to how the various types of road will be built with State aid money, or with the proceeds of county bond issues, light and heavy traffic being only relative terms: What one considers light traffic another may consider heavy, and vice versa. Each type of road is capable of sustaining some particular amount of traffic and while we may not know exactly how much traffic any particular road will accommodate satisfactorily, we do know, approximately, how much more traffic one type of road will stand than another. It therefore follows that if we proportion the type to the amount of traffic, the result will be economy in its truest sense, being independent of the service rendered, as each type will give equally good service if properly selected for the location in which it is used.

EARTH ROADS.

Earth roads have been built in this State for many years and it is common knowledge that when an earth road is in good condition it is very satisfactory to use. It is also pretty well understood that certain parts of almost any earth road are very much better than other parts. There is always a reason for this, improper drainage, grading, or other features of construction account for most of the bad spots. It is the purpose of the State Highway Commission, in building earth roads with State aid, or in county systems of roads through bond issues, to build them in a first-class manner in every respect. The grading of the road surface will be 20 to 30 feet in width and the culverts will be of proper width to correspond. The draining, shaping of ditches and construction of bridges will be done just as thoroughly and carefully as for more durable types. In this manner the class of service can be materially improved and the earth roads maintained at a high standard of serviceability, at a remarkably lower cost than through any of the older methods. When earth roads have been properly built, the money spent on them results in practically permanent construction and, if these roads are treated with oil, the dust nuisance is abated and the oil which serves as a waterproofing agent, will keep the road dry and free from mud.

GRAVEL ROADS.

Gravel road construction, under small units of authority has been so much abused that many people believe the type really worthless and a waste of money under any conditions. There is no greater mistake. Gravel roads, in the State of Illinois, have a very large field of usefulness which should not, in the interest of true economy, be overlooked. The great trouble with gravel roads seems to be that they were either improperly constructed, improperly maintained or seriously overburdened with traffic. Only an expert can determine, with any reasonable degree of accuracy, just how a gravel road should be maintained or located. Due respect for many features, the proper selection of type, location, etc., are necessary in order that the best results may be obtained. In general, the gravel roads to be built by the State Highway Department either with State aid allotment, or with the proceeds of county bond issues for building State aid roads, will be constructed by the best-known methods and maintained in an efficient and economical manner. The roadbed will be prepared as in earth road construction; the gravel applied and rolled into place in layers, using plenty of water and binding material to solidify the mass and using local materials as far as they may be economically employed and the whole construction finished in as perfect a manner as roads of any type are built.

MACADAM ROADS.

Macadam roads also have their sphere of usefulness and where materials for their construction are available, at a less cost than the material for gravel roads, macadam construction will be used and the methods employed will be the same as in the construction of gravel roads with the provision, of course, that the type is suitable to the location in which it is proposed to use it.

BITUMINOUS MACADAM OR GRAVEL ROADS.

The term bituminous as used in connection with road improvement refers to the use of either tar or asphalt as a binder (or cement) for gravel or broken stones. It is applied either to the stone or gravel in place on the road, in which case a bituminous macadam results, or it is mechanically mixed with the stone or gravel in a concrete mixer, spread upon the road, and rolled while hot. In the latter case we have what is called bituminous concrete construction.

PORTLAND CEMENT CONCRETE ROADS.

In recent years the Portland cement concrete road has become the most popular type of construction for heavy traffic rural roads. It is composed of stone or gravel, sand and cement mixed in such proportion that the result will be a very dense, hard and durable surface. This type properly constructed will sustain almost an unlimited amount of automobile traffic and a reasonably heavy horse-drawn traffic. It is easily maintained in the early part of its life and is an ideal foundation for resurfacing when this becomes necessary. It is not expensive when the amount of traffic justifies its use and the only objection to it seems to be the development of cracks due mostly to temperature changes. These cracks, however, are easily repaired at small cost and when properly maintained are of little consequence and do not materially affect the durability of the pavement.

BRICK ROADS.

Probably the greatest recent advance in methods of construction has been made in brick roads. Brick is usually laid on a concrete base though it is an ideal material for resurfacing old gravel and macadam roads. Until lately it was customary to spread a sand cushion or bed over the concrete base on which to lay the brick. Now, however, we are tending rapidly to the substitution of a mortar bed or to the elimination of the bed entirely and laying the brick directly on the fresh concrete base. The proper application of the cement grout filler is the most important part of brick construction and with careful attention to this detail very satisfactory results may be obtained even with the use of poor brick. A good brick pavement will sustain the maximum amount of traffic coming on the main highways and is probably the highest type of construction now in general use on country roads.

DURABILITY.

The question of durability is so intimately connected with the amount and character of traffic, the quality of material and workmanship and the intelligent and consistent maintenance given, that it is impossible to make a definite statement as to the life of any type of road surface for the reason that the life varies widely with changes in any of the above mentioned factors determining it.

In general it may be said, however, that we may maintain any type of road to a satisfactory standard regardless of other conditions if we are willing to pay the price. The question is, then, purely a matter of dollars and cents.

The cost of service is the first cost, plus maintenance cost, plus the interest on the money divided by the number of users; and, therefore, if the type is properly adapted to the traffic, the cost of service is approximately the same on all types.

Governor Dunne has taken special interest in the question of good roads in Illinois and has kept in close cooperation with the Highway Commission, with the result that all of the work done with State aid money, or with the proceeds of county bond issues, will be built in the best-known manner and so far as is practicable will be as permanent, one as another. In all types, the grading, drainage, bridges and culverts will be truly permanent and so constructed that none of the work will have to be repeated when a new wearing surface, or a new type becomes necessary. Where roads have already been improved to some extent, an effort will be made to use as much of the existing improvement as is practicable and only such changes as are necessary through faulty drainage, grading or location, will be made. The metalled surface will be used, if possible, in the new construction and roads which have good gravel or macadamized surfaces, may be treated with some additional material of the same class, or resurfaced with some bituminous compound, thus saving as far as possible what has been done in the past and prolonging the life of the road and generally improving the conditions.

WHAT DEKALB COUNTY IS DOING.

[By W. C. MILLER, *County Superintendent of Highways, DeKalb County.*]

1. The county board, at its last session granted aid to Kingston, Squaw Grove and Cortland Townships for three "county aid" bridges, totaling $9,000.

2. The contract for the Schule Bridge, "county aid," was awarded to H. S. Wetherell, June 13, 1916. Contract is for $1,250 with piles extra at 65c per lineal foot.

3. Three miles of macadam road, 12 feet wide and 8 inches deep, to be laid in two courses and rolled, are now being constructed in Somonauk Township. The survey was made by the county superintendent of highways and Mr. Wenger of the division engineer's office.

4. Pierce Township is getting ready to construct one mile of macadam road and is contemplating the purchase of a Galion 8-foot grader, which has been shipped for trial.

5. The township road and bridge maps have at last been completed by this office and prints have been sent to supervisors, highway commissioners and town clerks.

6. The county board, at its session this month, made provision for furnishing an assistant to the county superintendent.

7. Township purchase blanks, by which means the town boards request the approval of the superintendent, have been used in this county for the last six months. They help solve the question of asking for the approval of the superintendent in purchases exceeding $200, better than anything that has yet been attempted.

8. Throughout DeKalb County about 150 small bridges and small reinforced concrete culverts and bridges will be built the coming season. Plans are being prepared in the superintendent's office for about 90 such structures.

9. Paw Paw, Sycamore, Malta, Dekalb, Sandwich and Somonauk Townships have all their bridges, practically completed. Most of them are constructed of reinforced concrete; hardly a steel-leg bridge exists in any of the above townships.

10. Throughout DeKalb County, it is estimated that about 30 miles of gravel road will be constructed during 1916.

11. The superintendent of highways has been allowed larger quarters in the county building for an office. More furnishings, such as book cabinets, filing cabinets, chairs and a typewriter have been added.

12. DeKalb Township has purchased and is using an Austin-Western oiler with heater attachment and a 10-foot Austin-Western grader. This township also has contracted for 30,000 gallons of No. 5 standard oil at $0.0498 per gallon, f. o. b. DeKalb. The grader and

(Continued on Page 80)

WILL GIVE THE ROAD DRAG A CHANCE.

Through the efforts of the Springfield Automobile Club and the Springfield Commercial Association approximately $1,300 has been made available for dragging the main roads leading into Springfield. It is expected that a total of about 45 miles of road will be dragged 25 times. A systematic plan has been worked out and there is every reason to believe that it will be demonstrated by this undertaking just what can be done by dragging.

At a recent banquet given by the Springfield Automobile club mention was made of the fact that many of the roads leading into Springfield were in very poor condition, and the question was raised as to what could be done to improve them. County Superintendent Edwin H. White explained frankly that there was no money available at the present time with which to improve these roads, and also that the motorists themselves were, in some measure, largely responsible for the poor condition of the highways, as many times automobiles had driven over freshly dragged roads in such a way as to practically destroy the effect of the drag.

He gave as his opinion that the best way to put these roads into good shape was to raise a fund by popular subscription for the purpose of dragging, and to have a definite system whereby the dragging should continue throughout the entire year. The idea was at once taken up by the automobile club and the Springfield Commercial Association and proposed to the board of supervisors, who expressed themselves as willing to put up an amount equal to the donations received. The committee which solicited subscriptions to this fund realized about $650. This, together with the promised amount from the county, will give about $1,300 for the work.

Practically all of the work has been contracted for, the contracts on the average calling for a width of 28 feet to be dragged; the work is to be done directly under the supervision of County Superintendent White, who will notify the different parties at just what times he wishes the dragging called for in their contract to be done. When the work has been done accordingly, he will be notified by postal card that his orders have been carried out.

This plan furnishes an excellent idea for other cities which, like Springfield, are afflicted with poor roads leading into town. At the present time it is impossible to give any cost data on the work but it is hoped that by next month this information can be presented together with pictures showing some of the roads before and after dragging.

A UNIFORM ACCOUNTING SYSTEM FOR HIGHWAY OFFICIALS.

One of the provisions of the Revised Road and Bridge Law stipulates that the State Highway Commission shall "prescribe a system of auditing and

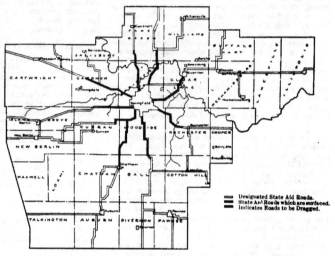

MAP OF SANGAMON COUNTY SHOWING ROADS WHICH WILL BE DRAGGED.

accounting for all road and bridge moneys for use of all highway officials, which system shall be as nearly uniform as practically possible."

When it is considered that the road and bridge taxes amount up annually to millions of dollars—for 1915 the total road and bridge tax in Illinois was $8,332,119—and that there has been probably a different system of accounting in practically every county and in many counties a different system in each township, the wiseness of this provision of the law is very apparent.

The State Highway Commission, before making up a uniform accounting system, consulted with numerous highway officials, and the forms as finally approved and recommended for use, embody many ideas gained from the experience of such officials. Mr. J. M. McCoy, chief clerk of the department, had active supervision of the preparation of this system, and incorporated in it the points which years of experience with township accounts had shown to be necessary.

The principal idea in formulating this system has been to make it as simple as possible and at the same time broad and elastic enough to meet all the needs.

The plan contemplates that each highway commissioner shall indicate each day on a statement form, the work which has been done under his direction and supervision. A separate statement being kept for each man employed, and the items of work and their cost shown in detail. These statements are then

(Continued on Page 79)

Correspondence Course in Road Building
CONDUCTED BY UNIVERSITY OF ILLINOIS.
Lesson 4.—Wooden Beam Bridges.

While wooden beam bridges are no longer considered either permanent or economical in most sections of the United States, there are many of them in existence, and there will continue to be for some time to come. It is just as necessary to examine these structures and be assured of their safety as of any other type.

It is the purpose in this lesson to give methods for computing stresses and information concerning safe stresses on wood so that the wooden beam bridges may be examined and their safety determined intelligently. It is true here, as with other types of bridges, that the individual who makes the examination of the structure must use judgment and common sense.

Before discussing the question of loads and methods of figuring stresses it will be necessary to discuss briefly some of the terms used, and some of the properties peculiar to wood as they pertain to its use in structures.

DEFINITION OF TERMS.

Nominal Size. This term is used to indicate the approximate breadth and depth of an unfinished timber. For example, a 2 by 6 is a timber which is approximately 2 in. by 6 in. in cross section before it is finished.

Actual Size. This is the actual size of the timber whether finished or unfinished. S1S1E indicates that the timber is dressed on one side and one edge. S4S indicates that the timber is dressed on four sides.

The actual size of undressed, green lumber should be very close to the nominal size.

Sap Wood. Sap wood is a cylinder of wood next to the bark and is of lighter color than the wood within.

Spring Wood. Spring wood is the inner part of the annual ring and is formed in the earlier part of the season. It often contains vessels or pores.

Summer Wood. Summer wood is the outer part of the annual ring and is formed later in the season. It is usually dense in structure and without conspicuous pores.

Defects in lumber are knots, knot holes, seasoning cracks, shakes, wanes, rotten streaks, wormholes, pitch pockets and defects in manufacturing.

Knots are classified as pin, standard and large, as to size; and round and spike as to form; and sound, loose, encased, pith and rotten as to quality.

Pitch pockets are openings between the grain of the wood containing more or less pitch or bark. These shall be classified as small, standard and large pitch pockets.

Wane is bark, or the lack of wood from any cause, on the edges of timbers.

Shakes are splits or checks in timbers which usually cause a separation of the wood between annual rings.

Rot, dote and red heart are defects which may appear as a dark red discoloration not found in the sound wood, or as white or red rotten spots.

MECHANICAL PROPERTIES.

The mechanical properties of timber beams are dependent upon the quality of wood irrespective of defects and the character and location of defects.

The mechanical properties of wood free from defects vary directly with its dry weight. The relative properties of any species may also be approximated by a comparison of the proportion of summer wood.

The most serious defects which affect the strength of timber beams are knots and cross grains occurring where fibre stresses are greatest. Timbers which have knots near the center of their lengths should not be used as joists or stringers.

SPECIFICATIONS.[1]

General Requirements. All timber shall be sound, sawed to standard size, square cornered and straight; close grained and free from defects such as injurious ring shakes and cross-grain, unsound or loose knots, knots in groups, decay, or other defects that will materially impair its strength.

[1]Manual, Am. Ry. Engineering Association.
[2]Abstracted from Proceedings of the American Railway Engineering Association, Vol. 10, Part 1, 1909.

Standard Size. "Rough timbers sawed to standard size" means that they shall not be over ¼ inch scant from the actual size specified. For instance, a 12 by 12 inch timber shall measure not less than 11¾ by 11¾ inches.

Standard Dressing. Standard dressing means that not more than ¼ inch shall be allowed for dressing each surface. For instance, a 12 by 12 inch timber, after being dressed on four sides, shall measure not less than 11½ by 11½ inches.

Stringers. Stringers shall show not less than 85 per cent heart on the girth anywhere in the length of the piece; *provided, however,* that if the minimum amount of sap is shown on either narrow face of the stringer, the average depth of sap shall not exceed one-half inch. Knots greater than 1½ inches in diameter will not be permitted at any section within 4 inches of the edge of the piece, but knots shall in no case exceed 4 inches in their largest diameter.

TREATED TIMBER.

The treating of timbers to prevent or delay decay has been practiced for many years. As the price of lumber has increased the demand for some economical and effective method for the preservation of wood has also increased.

There are many problems in the treating of timber which have not been solved. For example, the effect of the preservative treatment of wood upon its strength has not been fully determined. However, it is known that more depends upon the method of treatment than upon the kind of preservative used.

Steaming at high pressure or for too long a period will weaken the wood. The indications are that zinc chloride makes the wood more brittle and for that reason it does not withstand impact so readily. If the solution is too strong it will decompose the wood.

Soaking in creosote oil causes wood to swell, which decreases the strength accordingly, but not nearly so much as soaking in water.

Properly treated wood will last from 20 to 25 years under average conditions. All framing should be done before the timber is treated.

(To Be Continued.)

A UNIFORM ACCOUNTING SYSTEM FOR HIGHWAY OFFICIALS.

(Continued from Page 78)

certified to by the commissioner and presented at a meeting of the board of commissioners, who make an order on the town treasurer for the payment, detailing on the order the exact items for which the money was spent as is shown on the statement. From this order, the treasurer can determine the distribution of the sum expended. The original statement is retained by the clerk, who each month, furnishes the county superintendent of highways a detailed summary sheet, showing all receipts and expenditures of the township. The county superintendent in turn records all this information in condensed form in his own book, so that any time he may ascertain the exact financial status of the township. This feature will be a great aid to the county superintendent when called upon to approve orders or contracts in excess of $200, as he may determine immediately just what condition the finances of the township are in.

Among other forms provided in this system are an inventory form to be made up the 1st day of May, a copy of which is furnished the county superintendent of highways for his information and an approval form which is attached to all contracts and purchase orders in excess of $200 and which must be signed by the county superintendent before the order becomes valid.

The contract or purchase order is made up in triplicate and the county superintendent approves all three copies, retaining one for his own information and furnishing one to the treasurer that he may know all requirements of the law have been complied with, and one to the town clerk for his files.

Another feature of this accounting system is a record book for use by the town clerk in recording the minutes and orders of the highway commissioners. Much confusion has arisen in the past by a failure of the town clerk to obtain a proper record of the orders of the highway commissioners, but by the use of this book such confusion will be obviated. Space is also given in this book for several township maps on which may be recorded any notations regarding any certain work which is ordered in any particular section.

The State Highway Department has furnished each county a sufficient number of sample sets of these forms, together with letters explaining their use, for distribution to the individual townships or districts of each county. It is sincerely hoped that the counties will avail themselves of this opportunity and vote to install this accounting system which is sure to result in an increased efficiency in the use of all road and bridge money.

MARKED THROUGH ROUTES IN ILLINOIS.

(Continued from Page 74)

as local traffic should be constructed first. The types and widths chosen for through roads should be such as will carry fast-moving automobile traffic. By handling this work in the manner outlined, the purpose of both State aid roads and through routes will have been fulfilled, and the most people will have been served.

It is to be hoped that the extensive plans which the various through highway associations have under way will be carried to a successful conclusion, and that the praiseworthy effort of these organizations will be strengthened and honored by the support of the public at large.

WHAT DEKALB COUNTY IS DOING.

(Continued from Page 77)

heater combined cost $1,175. This includes engineer's hitch, an extra blade, and steerable tongue.

13. Malta Township has contracted for 12,000 gallons of No. 5 standard road oil, to be applied by the heater from DeKalb, which this township contemplates renting. The oil will cost 4½c per gallon f. o. b. Whiting, Indiana.

14. Cortland Township has recently finished the construction of an 8 by 8 foot reinforced box culvert, 20-foot roadway. F. O. Larson, Sycamore, Illinois, was awarded the contract at $628.

15. Kingston Township has purchased an Austin-Western road oiler with heater attachment, and has contracted for a large quantity of road oil for application on the road. This township has also ordered 10,000 F. B. M. creosoted lumber for reflooring bridges. The lumber is to cost $50 per thousand ft. Kingston, Illinois. Contracts have recently been made for three small reinforced concrete bridges for $1,483. F. O. Larson, contractor, Sycamore, Illinois.

OPINIONS OF THE ATTORNEY GENERAL.

COMMISSIONERS MAY CLOSE DANGEROUS ROAD— LIABILITY OF COMMISSIONERS FOR ACCIDENTS.

May 29, 1916.

Hon. CLIFFORD OLDER,
    Bridge Engineer, State Highway Department,
    Springfield, Illinois.

DEAR SIR: Under date of the 27th instant you submit the following propositions:

"From time to time we have received a number of inquiries in regard to the right of highway commissioners in case a piece of road is in dangerous condition and the commissioners have, to the best of their ability, used all of the available road and bridge fund for the repair of the roads and bridges under their jurisdiction, to erect barricades and close the road to public travel. We would be glad to have you advise us in regard to this matter."

"We would also like to know if the commissioners would be considered negligent of their duties, providing a bridge or other part of a road is in dangerous condition, and the road and bridge fund of the township is exhausted, unless they arrange to call a special election for a bond issue to cover the cost of making the road safe for public travel."

In reply to the first proposition, I will say that item 6 of subdivision (b) of paragraph 50 of chapter 121, Hurd's Revised Statutes, 1915, provides that the highway commissioners of each town or road district shall have general charge of the roads and bridges of their town or district and must keep the same in repair and improve them so far as practicable.

Paragraph 132 of said chapter 121 provides that the highway officials are authorized to keep carriages and vehicles of every kind off the public highways whenever necessary to properly repair the same.

In view of the powers mentioned above that are given to highway commissioners by statute, and from a consideration of the whole set, it being apparent that it is the duty of the highway commissioners of every town or road district in this State to perform all acts within their official capacity to protect the public against injury while traveling upon the highways in their respective townships or road districts, it necessarily follows that when public safety so demands, highway commissioners may erect barricades and close a road to public travel, when the exigencies of the case so require.

In reply to the second proposition, I will say that it has frequently been held in this State that highway commissioners can only be held personally liable for damages to persons or property with respect to the performance of their official duties when under the guise or pretense of performing a duty, they perform some ministerial duty in a wrongful and negligent manner, or where they corruptly, wilfully or negligently fail to perform some mandatory duty. *Van Middlesworth* v. *Hill,* 161 Ill., App., 592.

Item 6 of section 50 of the Road and Bridge Act, provides that the highway commissioners shall have charge of the roads and bridges of their respective towns or districts, to keep the same in repair and to improve them so far as practicable.

In the case of *Hotz* v. *Hoyt,* 135 Ill., 388, the Supreme Court held that they are clothed with the discretion as to the practicability of making improvements and as to the best methods to be employed.

In the case of *Nagle* v. *Wakey* et al., 161 Ill., 387, it was held that commissioners of highways who have in good faith, and to the best of their ability, expended the means at their command upon the roads and bridges of their town are not liable for an injury to one, who was thrown with his team and wagon from a bridge, because of the alleged negligence of the commissioners in failing to provide such bridge with railings.

Funds that may be raised by a bond issue are certainly not such funds that are at the command of highway commissioners in the sense that they may be held liable for a failure to arrange a special election for a bond issue. It is not within the power of the highway commissioners to affirmatively decide such a special election.

Very respectfully,

        P. J. LUCEY, *Attorney General.*

The township of Roscoe, Winnebago County, has voted $7,000 in bonds to be used in building 15 bridges and culverts in the township. This will mean an expenditure of about $12,000, as several of the bridges will be county aid work. The township has also purchased a portable rock-crushing outfit from the Good Roads Machinery Company for $1,940.

OCT 11 1916

ILLINOIS HIGHWAYS

[Printed by authority of the State of Illinois.]

OFFICIAL PUBLICATION OF THE

STATE HIGHWAY DEPARTMENT

| VOL. III | SPRINGFIELD, ILLINOIS, AUGUST, 1916 | No. 8 |

THE DEDICATION OF THE FIRST BOND ISSUE ROAD IN ILLINOIS.
Miss Delores Williams (center) christened the pavement after Governor Dunne (right center) had removed the last of the earth covering.

ILLINOIS' FIRST BOND ISSUE ROAD.
The first section of road to be built with Vermilion County's bond issue of $1,500,000. The above section is a 10-ft. concrete road, connecting Bismarck with Alvin. It was dedicated July 20, with impressive ceremonies; the importance of the occasion being emphasized by the presence of Governor Dunne.

FIRST SECTION OF COUNTY BOND ISSUE ROAD IN ILLINOIS DEDICATED

July 20, 1916, will always be regarded as an important date in the road building history of Illinois, for on this day there was dedicated at the little village of Bismarck, in Newell Township, Vermilion County, the first section of road ever built in the State with funds realized from a county bond issue.

The section which was dedicated is a 3-mile strip of concrete road connecting Alvin with Bismark and is the first section of Vermilion County's bond issue roads to be completed.

More than 4,000 people attended the exercises, which commenced at 11 o'clock in the morning and continued throughout the day and the importance of the occasion was emphasized by the presence of Governor Dunne and members of the State Highway Commission.

The activities of the morning commenced when Miss Marie Phillips, a Bismark girl, clipped the ribbon across the road at Bismark, thereby opening it to traffic and to the long line of automobiles which were waiting to make the trip from Bismark to Alvin. There were probably 500 cars in line, many of which were gaily decorated in honor of the occasion. Butler Township, with 30 cars, had the largest representation.

At noon, an old-fashioned picnic dinner was enjoyed in the grove just north of Bismark, as the majority of those who came to attend the exercises came with the intention of giving up the entire day to the celebration.

The afternoon was given over to a program of speeches by Governor Dunne, members of the State Highway Commission and others who had been instrumental in securing Vermilion County's system of good roads.

The speakers praised the spirit shown by the people of Vermilion County not only in getting a system of roads that will meet requirements of farmers, as well as motorists, but in making it possible for other counties to reap the benefit of the experience of Vermilion County and secure a comprehensive system of permanent highways.

It was a great day for good roads and the people who, a few years ago, scoffed and joked at the idea of bonding Vermilion County for $1,500,000 to improve the highways, were as enthusiastic as the most ardent good roads advocate.

The actual dedication of the highway occurred about 3 o'clock in the afternoon, when Governor Dunne, using a small silver shovel, cleared away the last bit of earth covering which remained on the road, and, when the surface was thus cleared Miss Dolores Williams broke a bottle of spring water on the road saying as she did so: "I hereby christen thee the first Bond Issue Road in the State of Illinois."

Governor Dunne in his talk complimented Vermilion County highly on their progressiveness and enterprise, which culminated in the bond issue of $1,500,000 for good roads. He said in part: "My friends the event we are celebrating to-day is of more than local importance. It inaugurates for Vermilion County an era of greater comfort and greater profit; it means that be-cause of good roads, replacing those which were impassable often and wasteful always, your farm lands will be worth more and your lives more worth living.

"But it is not alone in Vermilion County that this meeting is significant. The whole State should have its eyes upon what you are doing here, because what one county has done another can do. It means that the machinery of our government has achieved efficiency in this important and too long neglected department, and that we are learning as a people to conduct our public affairs as intelligently, as economically, as honestly, as scientifically as we do our private affairs.

"What has been accomplished in good roads building in the last four years? Everybody knows what Illinois highways have been. The deep, rich soil that has grown record-breaking corn crops makes a most unfavorable foundation for highway construction. It presented a problem which needed not only money, but expert management to solve. We were not stingy in money; a good sum each year was expended; but we lacked expert management; a large proportion of the money was wasted.

"When I ran for governor in 1912 the centers of business and gathering places of men and women were separated from country life by almost impassable barriers.

"In my inaugural message in January, 1913, I devoted space to as strong a presentation of this subject as was within my power. The recommendation of the message touched the legislative heart and the present good road law was the result. You are all familiar with its salient features. No subject has been so much discussed or is better understood. The last General Assembly remedied defects which a little experience had uncovered in the original, and amplified its terms to make it more elastic to meet the varying conditions and ideas prevailing in different sections of our State.

"The responsibility of putting the road law into effect was placed squarely upon my shoulders as governor, and I am now rendering you a report of how well that trust has been observed. The enactment of the new road law, found no adequate machinery in existence with which to carry out its provisions; it was necessary to construct new machinery. Immediately after the enactment of the law this task was undertaken. Commissioners were appointed and the selection of their staff was begun. I am proud and Illinois may well be proud of the result.

"The best road and bridge engineering which money can buy is entering into the construction of our State highways, the best materials are being used and the best systems which good business brains can devise are employed in the supervision of work and in the keeping of records and accounts.

"Up to the present time there has been built approximately 150 miles of State aid road and it is planned to construct about 450 miles this year so that in 1917 we will have made a start of nearly 600 miles toward the complete system of 16,000 miles of State highways which the plans of the commission contemplate.

"The people of Vermilion County must have had confidence in their government, when they voted $1,500,000 in bonds to build immediately their system of State aid roads. This is a proceeding which I wish to recommend to all counties. The advantage of it is that the people get the benefit of a system of good roads at once, rather than by piece-meal, and the difference in cost is the interest on the bonds. For instance, a county, let me say, has 100 miles of designated State aid road, the total cost of construction which would be one million dollars. Its annual allowance from the State distribution fund is, we will say, $20,000, to which you add, under the provisions of the law, a like amount, giving you $40,000. At $10,000 a mile you could therefore build 4 miles of road in a year, or the full 100 miles in 25 years.

"The bond plan permits you, by approval of the people, to issue one million dollars of bonds with which

At spring election this year, more than a million dollars' worth of such bonds were voted, and it is estimated that there will be more than 350 miles of road improved from such issues.

"Happily the fear that hard roads are going to bankrupt us is fast disappearing, because we have been able to demonstrate by practical experience and by undeniable statistics that such a disaster is impossible.

"The pioneering has been done," said the Governor in a dramatic tone of voice, in closing. "Opposition based on fear and ignorance has given place to satisfaction and interest. We have a law that is elastic and comprehensive. Our theory of State aid is correct in principle and workable in practice. In ten years our position in the matter of public highways will be of fame rather than of notoriety."

Governor Dunne clears away the last of the earth covering from the pavement. At the Governor's left are Mr. Wilson and Mr. Gash, of the Illinois Highway Commission.

to construct the 100 miles of State aid roads at once. It's all done and finished in one job and you will be able to enjoy and get the benefit of the whole system. Each year thereafter you will get your share of the State funds, or $20,000. You add $20,000 to it and apply $40,000 to the debt. In 25 years the entire issue will have been cancelled. During that time you will have enjoyed and profited by the 100 miles of road.

"Vermilion has voted $1,500,000 for 175 miles of road. Cook County has voted $2,000,000. Thirty counties are either ready to vote upon bond issues or are seriously agitating it, the proposed aggregate being twenty million dollars.

"Another important phase of this bond issue question is the enthusiasm with which individual townships and districts of some counties are voting bonds for the purpose of improving their township and district roads.

SPEECH BY HOMER J. TICE.

Homer J. Tice, the author of the Tice Road Law, in his talk made a strong argument for the betterment of the roads and called attention to the fact that the development of the State is dependent upon the development of the highways. He spoke in part as follows:

"Supply and demand, producer and consumer, each dependent upon the other, constitute and embrace every element of the business of a nation, a state or a community.

"The public road is the only practical route which the world has yet discovered for reaching the originating point of the producer's commodities and over which the producer must travel to reach the consumer and the market.

"We who are living in the first years of the twentieth century take it as a matter of no very great acclaim that a 20-hour train plies between New York and Chicago, but in talking over family history with our children one of the historic incidents related is that our grandfathers, who left New York State or old Virginia about the 1st of April made very good time, that they were able to celebrate their arrival in Illinois on the following 4th of July.

"Then, as now, the horizon of our growth was limited by the extent of our transportation facilities. The next fifty years will be marked as an era of public highway development.

"The advocacy of better roads is neither a fanciful fad nor the scheme of some selfish interest. On the other hand it is a proposition involving the financial, social, educational and religious interests of the community and the State and reaches directly the welfare of each and every individual person.

"Illinois is a great agricultural State and will forever remain so. The chief products of our farms of the central part are corn, wheat and oats—of the north, dairy products—and of the south, the rapidly developing orchards and fruit industries.

The parade over the new pavement.

"There were owned and run in Illinois, according to the records of the Secretary of State's office, 131,140 automobiles in 1914, and 180,754 in 1915—an increase in one year of 49,614 cars. Figuring the loss in tire service on the 1915 cars, we find it to be $3,506,727.60.

"By comparison, there should be more than 200,000 cars in use in Illinois in 1916 which means a tire service loss of $3,880,000 for the current year because of the present condition of our public roads.

"We have 32,522,880 acres of actual farm lands in Illinois. There are approximately 510,000 individual persons actually engaged in farming this land. The total value of all farm property and agricultural interests is $3,905,321,075 or that much invested capital. The gross annual value of all farm products produced by it from this capital stock is $597,022,581.

"The manufacturing industries of the State represent a value of $1,548,171,000. There are 561,044 individual persons actually engaged in these industries. The gross annual value of all manufactured products of the State is $1,919,277,000.

"These are startling figures and emphasize more than can mere words the need on the part of the farmer, of conservation of resources, time and labor and more efficiency in every department of his business. All around efficiency is the thing that counts. Efficiency can not be increased when time and human energy are wasted.

"Strange as it may seem, we farmers have been the last and the slowest to realize that conservation in every

phase of our business is imperative. The loss, because of public road conditions, of from 8 to 10 millions of dollars per year in the one item of transportation of our products is one of our heaviest handicaps—not only because of this specific loss, but because of its far-reaching influence on the efficiency of every other part of the industry.

"The churches and schools of a community are its greatest moral educational and social forces. And I say to you no state or nation ever has or ever will attain to the greatest greatness or achieve permanency unless the foundation stones of the structure be the church and the school. Education is the pilot and pathfinder for civilization. The standard of civilization is measured by the degree of educated Christian citizenship. That great statesman, Charles Sumner, once said, 'The road and the schoolmaster are the two most important agencies in the advancement of civilization.'

"If the public schools are to have a maximum efficiency in training and instruction, the children must be afforded facilities for reaching the schools. To do this the road from the home to the schoolhouse door must be one that can be traveled with reasonable certainty every day of the year. The most startling information obtained from the last Federal census was that showing the relation of the public road to the public school.

"Whatever builds up and sustains a community or state and brings to it broader and superior advantages, greater and more diversified pleasures, creates a love and respect for its institutions and inspires patriotic thought and sustaining purpose.

"If our purpose be, and I know it is, the elevating of our citizenship to an ever higher and higher plane and the continual advancement of our people morally and intellectually and through these agencies the establishing of a permanency that will be a sure defense for all time, and if our National ideal be the strength of justice, the charity of power and the friendship of human brotherhood, we must educate and train the mind of the child and through the child the heart and the soul and conscience of the man."

The motorists were also enthusiastic.

REVIEW OF BOND ISSUE CAMPAIGN.

It might be well to go back and review shortly the campaign which brought about this first county bond issue in Illinois for good roads.

It was less than three years ago that the subject of building a county system of roads was first given serious thought in Vermilion County. Possibly the first definite step looking toward such a bond issue was a discussion between Mr. O. M. Jones, a well-known attorney and supervisor in Vermilion County, who had just returned

(Continued on Page 90)

CONCRETE PAVEMENTS*

By B. H. PIEPMEIER, Maintenance Engineer, Illinois State Highway Department

Concrete pavements for city streets and for rural highway improvement are becoming very popular. This may be evidenced by the statement that over 1,600 miles of concrete pavement were laid during 1915. Figures indicate that more concrete pavements have been constructed during the past three years than any other of the modern types of roads. It seems, therefore, due time that engineers direct more attention to studying the various phases of concrete pavement construction in order that it may be developed to its highest efficiency.

Concrete pavement construction has been advanced during recent years on account of necessity or demand for some type of improvement that will withstand the rapidly increasing modern traffic. Ten or fifteen years ago, gravel and macadam roads were recognized almost exclusively, as the most practical and economic type of improved road. Heavy combined auto and horse-drawn traffic of recent years, however, has rapidly disintegrated the surface of such roads forming a dust nuisance, dangerous ruts and unsightly depressions that require constant and expensive maintenance. The rapid change in traffic conditions, therefore, has made it necessary in a great many instances to devise some form of pavement that would better resist this traffic, be low in first cost, free from dust and reasonable in upkeep.

Concrete pavements have been low in initial cost: First, on account of the reasonably low cost of portland cement; second, on account of the use of local materials for the aggregate; third, on account of the utilization of local unskilled labor; fourth, because of the rapidity with which the material could be mixed and placed. All of these conditions have tended to make concrete a desirable and economical material for pavement construction.

Concrete pavements which have been constructed of hard, clean aggregates and finished perfectly smooth are practically dustless under even the most severe traffic. This is due: First, to the hardness of the material, and second, to the smoothness of the finished pavement. This smooth surface of the monolithic concrete road in contrast with the block pavement contains no regular joints which tend to retain dust. This smooth and dustless surface is very desirable for rapidly moving modern traffic.

The maintenance or upkeep on concrete pavements has not been definitely determined on account of the recent development of this type of road. Cost figures to date have indicated, however, that the maintenance of the pavement proper, for the first five years, will not exceed about one-half cent per square yard per year under the average traffic conditions in Illinois. This figure does not furnish definite information concerning the maintenance of such pavements over a longer period, but indications are that the cost of maintenance of such pavements is not going to be excessive providing that the maintenance work is effectively performed.

The maintenance of concrete pavements consists chiefly in filling cracks and joints in the pavement with a suitable bituminous material. It is usually necessary and sufficient to fill all such cracks once each year; how-

ever, under heavy traffic, an occasional patching is necessary the second time. On a few pavements, it becomes necessary to cover slight depressions, pit holes and similar imperfections, with a bituminous compound to prevent disintegration. This is not done very often, and when it is necessary it affords sure proof of improper construction.

The practice in constructing concrete pavements has been to place joints at regular intervals to control or regulate the cracks. The work involved in constructing a pavement with joints at defined intervals, in filling these joints with a compound that would readily contract and expand with the pavement, together with armoring the edges of the joints with steel plates becomes expensive and in a great many cases the results are unsatisfactory. Road engineers are now questioning this item of expense and are giving preference to a monolithic or continuous slab with a careful system of maintenance on all cracks as they form. At any rate, experience is indicating that on rural highway pavements, at least, that satisfactory results may be secured by eliminating entirely all expansion or contraction joints. The expense of installing joints in the original construction of a pavement is usually sufficient to maintain the pavement surface for a period of ten to fifteen years. If more attention is given to proportioning, mixing, finishing and curing of the concrete pavement, better results may be secured and at the same or less expense.

In recent years a great deal of attention has been given to reinforcing concrete pavements to eliminate cracking and to prevent the cracks from opening up. The reinforcing steel does not always prevent concrete pavements from cracking, but a wire mesh or steel bar imbedded in the concrete does aid in preventing the cracks from opening up to any serious extent. Reinforcing steel is used more extensively on wide city streets where the cracks should be eliminated or concealed as much as possible for a matter of general appearance. Reinforcement is quite often used in 2-course concrete pavement, and in such cases is usually placed between the two courses or about 2½ inches from the wearing surface. The added expense of 15 or 20 cents per square yard of surface required for reinforcement is, however, a questionable expenditure from the economic standpoint, particularly for rural highway pavements.

There are a great many materials or compounds on the market that are highly recommended as an aid to cement in concrete pavements. The addition of various compounds which are supposed to fill the voids in concrete, thereby making it more dense and more impervious to moisture, is supposed to prevent the pavements from cracking and to assist it in resisting wear. There have been a number of experimental sections of pavements built with the addition of various compounds, but their value to date is still very questionable.

Experience clearly indicates that while there are perhaps a few conditions that justify special treatment such as having the pavement marked or cut into regular sections by means of joints and having these joints armored with soft steel plates to protect their edges, and reinforcing the pavement with wire mesh or steel bars and even adding some of the hardening or filler
(Continued on Page 90)

*Presented before the *Short Course in Concrete* for manual training and vocational teachers at the Lewis Institute, Chicago, June 27, 1916.

Federal Aid for Good Roads Work

The sum of $85,000,000 of Federal funds is made available for the construction of rural roads by the passage of the Federal Aid road bill which became a law July 11. Of this sum, $75,000,000 is to be expended for the construction of rural post roads under cooperative arrangements with the highway departments of the various states and $10,000,000 is to be expended for roads and trails within or partly within the National forests. The act limits the Federal Government's share in road work in cooperation with the states to 50 per cent of the estimated cost of construction. Federal aid may

be extended to the construction of any rural post road, excluding all streets or roads in towns having a population of 2,500 or more except the portions of such streets or roads on which the houses are, on an average, more than 200 feet apart.

Five million dollars is made available for expenditure during the fiscal year ending June 30, 1917, and thereafter the appropriation is increased at the rate of $5,000,000 a year until 1921, when the sum provided is $25,000,000, making a total of $75,000,000. In addition, an appropriation of $1,000,000 a year for 10 years, a

State.	Area as of 1910 United States census.		Population as of 1910 United States census.		Star and rural routes shown by certificate of Postmaster General as of June 30, 1916.		Percentage apportionment.	Sum apportioned.
	Square miles.	Percentage.	Population	Percentage.	Miles.	Percentage.		
Alabama	51,998	1.71796	2,138,093	2.33311	29,615	2.39111	2.14740	$104,148 90
Arizona	113,956	3.76500	204,354	.22299	3,096	.24997	1.41265	68,513 52
Arkansas	53,335	1.76214	1,574,449	1.71806	20,245	1.63458	1.70493	82,689 10
California	158,297	5.22999	2,377,549	2.59441	18,823	1.51976	3.11472	151,063 92
Colorado	103,948	3.43435	799,024	.87191	10,781	.87045	1.72557	83,690 14
Connecticut	4,965	.16404	1,114,756	1.21644	6,721	.54265	.64104	31,090 44
Delaware	2,370	.07830	202,322	.22078	2,566	.20718	.16875	8,184 37
Florida	58,666	1.93827	752,619	.82127	8,706	.70292	1.15415	55,976 27
Georgia	59,265	1.95806	2,609,121	2.84711	43,397	3.50386	2.76968	134,329 48
Idaho	83,888	2.77158	325,594	.35529	7,594	.61314	1.24667	60,463 50
Illinois	56,665	1.87216	5,638,591	6.15290	69,860	5.64048	4.55518	220,926 23
Indiana	36,354	1.20110	2,700,876	2.94723	52,619	4.24844	2.79892	135,747 62
Iowa	56,147	1.85505	2,224,771	2.42770	58,943	4.75904	3.01393	146,175 60
Kansas	82,158	2.71442	1,690,949	1.84518	53,240	4.29858	2.95273	143,207 40
Kentucky	40,598	1.34132	2,289,905	2.49877	27,113	2.18910	2.00973	97,471 91
Louisiana	48,506	1.60259	1,656,388	1.80747	9,458	.76364	1.39123	67,474 66
Maine	33,040	1.09161	742,371	.81008	13,566	1.09531	.99900	48,451 50
Maryland	12,327	.40727	1,295,346	1.41350	11,194	.90380	.90819	44,047 22
Massachusetts	8,266	.27310	3,366,416	3.67347	7,698	.62153	1.52270	73,850 95
Michigan	57,980	1.91561	2,810,173	3.06650	49,981	4.03545	3.00585	145,783 72
Minnesota	84,682	2.79782	2,075,708	2.26504	46,384	3.74503	2.93596	142,394 06
Mississippi	46,865	1.54838	1,797,114	1.96103	24,646	1.98991	1.83311	88,905 54
Missouri	69,420	2.29357	3,293,335	3.59373	57,108	4.61088	3.49993	169,720 41
Montana	146,997	4.85664	376,053	.41035	10,065	.81264	2.02654	98,287 19
Nebraska	77,520	2.56119	1,192,214	1.30096	33,964	2.74224	2.20146	106,770 81
Nevada	110,690	3.65710	81,875	.08934	2,935	.23697	1.32780	64,398 30
New Hampshire	9,341	.30862	430,572	.46985	6,444	.52029	.43292	20,996 62
New Jersey	8,224	.27171	2,537,167	2.76859	7,708	.62234	1.22088	59,212 68
New Mexico	122,634	4.05171	327,301	.35715	5,716	.46151	1.62346	78,737 81
New York	49,204	1.62565	9,113,614	9.94489	48,773	3.93792	5.16949	250,720 27
North Carolina	52,426	1.73211	2,206,287	2.40753	36,358	2.93553	2.35839	114,331 92
North Dakota	70,837	2.34039	577,056	.62969	21,548	1.73978	1.56996	76,143 06
Ohio	41,040	1.35592	4,767,121	5.20194	61,968	5.00328	3.85372	186,905 42
Oklahoma	70,057	2.31462	1,657,155	1.80831	37,145	2.99908	2.37400	115,139 00
Oregon	96,699	3.19485	672,765	.73413	11,621	.93828	1.62242	78,687 37
Pennsylvania	45,126	1.49092	7,665,111	8.36426	54,638	4.41146	4.75555	230,644 17
Rhode Island	1,248	.04123	542,610	.59210	1,093	.08825	.24053	11,665 71
South Carolina	30,989	1.02385	1,515,400	1.65362	21,851	1.76424	1.48057	71,807 64
South Dakota	77,615	2.56433	583,888	.63715	22,362	1.80550	1.66899	80,946 02
Tennessee	42,022	1.38837	2,184,789	2.38407	40,731	3.28861	2.35368	114,153 48
Texas	265,896	8.78496	3,896,542	4.25195	62,161	5.02048	6.01913	291,927 81
Utah	84,990	2.80799	373,351	.40740	3,806	.30730	1.17423	56,950 15
Vermont	9,564	.31599	355,956	.38842	8,777	.70865	.47102	22,844 47
Virginia	42,627	1.40836	2,061,612	2.24966	31,045	2.50656	2.05486	99,660 71
Washington	69,127	2.28389	1,141,990	1.24615	11,350	.91640	1.48215	71,881 28
West Virginia	24,170	.79855	1,221,119	1.33250	14,417	1.16402	1.09836	53,270 46
Wisconsin	56,066	1.85237	2,333,860	2.54674	43,854	3.54076	2.64662	128,361 05
Wyoming	97,914	3.23499	145,965	.15928	4,844	.39110	1.26179	61,196 82
Total	3,026,719	100.00000	91,641,197	100.00000	1,238,548	100.00000	100.00000	$4,850,000 00

total of $10,000,000 is made available for the development of roads and trails wholly or partly within the National forests.

DIVISION OF FUNDS.

The class of roads to be built and the method of construction are to be mutually agreed upon by the Secretary of Agriculture and the State Highway Departments.

The act provides that after making necessary deductions for administering its provisions—not to exceed 3 per cent of the appropriation for any one fiscal year—the Secretary of Agriculture shall apportion the remainder of each year's appropriation.

One-third in the ratio which the area of each state bears to the total area of all the states.

One-third in the ratio which the population of each state bears to the total population of all the states.

One-third in the ratio which the mileage of rural delivery routes and star routes in each state bears to the total mileage of rural delivery routes and star routes in all the states.

Project statements setting forth the proposed construction of any rural post roads or roads in a state are to be submitted by the State Highway Department to the Secretary of Agriculture and upon approval by the Secretary all necessary surveys, plans, specifications and estimates must be furnished. The roads projected must be of a substantial character, and items covering engineering, inspection, and unforeseen contingencies are not to exceed 10 per cent of the total estimated cost of the work.

SECRETARY'S APPROVAL.

Upon completion of the work as approved by the secretary, the amount set aside for the project is to be paid to the proper state official. The Secretary of Agriculture is given authority in his discretion to make partial payments as the work progresses, but not in excess of the Federal Government's pro rata share of the labor and material which have been actually put into construction work, nor in excess of $10,000 per mile, exclusive of the cost of bridges of more than 20 feet clear span. All construction work is subject to the inspection and approval of the Secretary of Agriculture.

The various states securing aid under the provisions of the act are charged with the making of needed repairs, and the preservation of a reasonably smooth surface, considering the type of the road, but are not obligated to make extraordinary repairs or undertake reconstruction. If, after due notice, a state fails to maintain a federally aided road properly, the Secretary is required to refuse further aid until the road has been properly repaired at state expense.

The factors of apportionment of $4,850,000 and the amounts apportioned to each state for the fiscal year 1917 are set forth in the foregoing table.

THE PROBLEM OF MAINTENANCE.

(Prepared by American Highway Association.)

When Woodrow Wilson was president of Princeton a man asked him: "Man, why don't you leave something alone and let it stay the way it is?" The president of Princeton was always trying to do something and he answered: "If you will guarantee to me that it will stay the way it is, I will let it alone; but if you knew anything, you would know that if you leave a live thing alone it will not stay where it is. It will develop and rather go in the wrong direction or decay." The president of Princeton then reminded his interrogator of what the Englishman writer said: "If you want to keep a white post white you can not let it alone. It will get black. You have to keep doing something to it. You have got to keep painting it white, and you have got to paint it white very frequently in order to keep it white, because there are forces at work that will get the better of you. Not only will it turn black, but the forces of moisture and other forces of nature will penetrate the white paint and get at the fibre of the wood and decay will set in and the next time you try to paint it you will find that there is nothing but punk to paint."

There never was a truer thing said by anybody than that and it was said to the National Press Club in Washington by the former president of Princeton, now President of the United States, to impress the men of the noble craft of journalism with the necessity of keeping abreast, if not a little ahead, of the constructive thought of the day so that what there is left of great initiative and saving grace may be turned to good account. If the President had been making a speech to the road builders of the country upon their opportunity and obligation to the public he could not have hit the nail more squarely on the head. The upkeep of the public highways is second only to their construction; indeed, it would be a useless waste of public money to build good roads without making adequate provision for their maintenance. White posts get black unless they are frequently painted white; good roads get bad unless they are constantly repaired. It is the same way with wagons and automobiles and clothes. Horses have to be reshod, harness has to be patched, tires have to be renewed, and it costs almost as much to keep a house in good livable condition as it does to pay rent when the landlord makes the repairs. Nothing lasts in this world; nothing but the blood and life are gone. There is down in the National Museum in Washington the skeleton of a sea reptile, which was digged up down at Coca, Alabama, about the time the Cosca River—which Senator Bankhead told the Rivers and Harbors Congress is one of the oldest rivers in this country—was digging its channel to the sea. The people who lived and voted in Alabama at that remote period and their commerce and their highways have all perished and only the bones from this river of doubt remain, just as in the ancient Roman Empire only here and there are to be found to-day the broken and worn-out highways over which the legions of Caesar marched in their conquest of the World. The cities have perished, the commerce has departed, the fields are forsaken and only the written story of the glory of the brave days of old remains as prophetic of the fate that will surely overtake any people or civilization that neglects to care for the highways, which, like the arteries in the human body, hold communities and states and nations together.

Whether it was thought out in precisely this way by the members of Congress in providing in the good roads act for the maintenance of the public roads to be built with Federal aid it does not matter; but one of the most important provisions of this law is that no part of the money shall be paid out by the Secretary

(Continued on Page 91)

ILLINOIS HIGHWAYS.

Published Monthly by the
State Highway Department,
Springfield, Illinois.

ILLINOIS HIGHWAY COMMISSION.

A. D. GASH, *President.*
S. E. BRADT, *Secretary.*
JAMES P. WILSON.

WM. W. MARR, *Chief State Highway Engineer.*

BUREAU OF ROADS.

H. E. BILGER, *Road Engineer.*
M. W. WATSON, *Assistant Road Engineer.*
C. M. HATHAWAY, *Office Engineer.*
L. P. SCOTT, *Chief Draftsman.*

BUREAU OF BRIDGES.

CLIFFORD OLDER, *Bridge Engineer.*
G. F. BURCH, *Assistant Bridge Engineer.*
A. W. CONSOER, *Office Engineer.*

BUREAU OF MAINTENANCE.

B. H. PIEPMEIER, *Maintenance Engineer.*
F. T. SHEETS, *Assistant Maintenance Engineer.*

BUREAU OF TESTS.

F. L. ROMAN, *Testing Engineer.*
W. C. ADAMS, *Chemist.*

BUREAU OF AUDITS.

J. M. McCOY, *Chief Clerk.*
T. W. DIECKMANN, *Department Editor.*
R. R. McLEOD, *General Bookkeeper.*
G. E. HOPKINS, *Property Clerk.*

DIVISION ENGINEERS.

R. L. Bell, Buchanan-Link Bldg., Paris, Ill.
H. B. Bushnell, 144 Fox St., Aurora, Ill.
J. E. Huber, Wise Building, Mt. Vernon, Ill.
A. H. Hunter, 302 Apollo Theater Bldg., Peoria, Ill.
C. M. Slaymaker, 510 Metropolitan Bldg., E. St. Louis, Ill.
H. E. Surman, 614 People's Bank Bldg., Moline, Ill.
Fred Tarrant, State Highway Department, Springfield, Ill.

Address all communications in regard to "Illinois Highways," to State Highway Department, Springfield, Illinois.

CONTENTS.

Champaign County's Good Roads Association was organized during the early part of July, and is devoting its energies to a campaign to secure permanent, all-the-year roads, connecting practically all the cities and villages within the county. The association will endeavor to secure the organization of a good roads association in each town or community. Officers of the county organization are, President, C. A. Kiler, Champaign; Vice President, H. M. Smoot, Homer; Secretary, C. W. Murphy, Champaign; Treasurer, J. C. Thompson.

* * *

George Fitch, the late well-known humorist, had the following to say in *Colliers Weekly* about the roads of Illinois:

"Illinois is making every effort to improve its roads. After trying every known method it now proposes to roof them over, thus allowing traffic to ride over them instead of through them.

"This is a peculiarly ungrateful proceeding on the part of Illinois, because she owes her early greatness to her famous mucilaginous mud highways. A century ago the tide of immigration set westward from Ohio and points east. It got as far as Illinois and then stopped because it couldn't get any farther. Thousands of hardy pioneers, tugged, dragged, pried and otherwise coerced their moving wagons into the bosom of Illinois—the soft, yielding gulley, gurgly bosom then gave up in despair and raised a crop. That settled it. When they found how useful the Illinois mud was except for road-making purposes they stayed on and became rich and prosperous. Lincoln's folks struggled knee deep through Illinois as far as Decatur and then settled down to wait for good roads. While they were waiting Lincoln grew up and was elected President. If Illinois roads had been navigable in the twenties of the last century, Lincoln might have been given to the Nation by Iowa or Missouri —but the soil held on to him with such desperate energy that he never got west of Springfield.

"However, not even history and early service can save the rare old three-dimension Illinois gumbo road. The State desires thoroughfares which will not climb affectionately onto the floundered automobile and creep into the watch pocket of the traveler. More Americans are traveling by automobile now than ever journeyed by stage coach in the brave old days when a city on a good postroad became a metropolis because of the traffic which passed through it, and the State which meets these travelers at its borders with a chuck hole and a one-horse team is not wise."

* * *

The last markers on the Springfield-Peoria division of the Burlington Way and the Logan-Lee Highway have been placed in position. The route lies out of Springfield on the old Peoria road passing through Fancy Prairie, Middletown, New Holland, Delavan, Dillon, Groveland and East Peoria, a distance of 69.3 miles.

* * *

The Knox County Good Roads Association has just been permanently organized with 125 members. The *Galesburg Mail* says the association discussed hard roads and the sentiment was general that with a proper campaign of education, the people of the county could be made to see the merit and practicability of building such roads. The officers of the association are Alonzo F. Paden, of Galesburg, president, and M. B. Wolsey, also of Galesburg, secretary.

Several thousand persons from St. Clair and Monroe Counties attended the good roads picnic held at Millstadt, St. Clair County, July 17. During the afternoon Homer J. Tice, gave an address on the need of improved highways. Other talks were made by Wm. N. Baltz and Mayor Marxer, both of Millstadt. All the speakers boosted the $1,500,000 bond issue of St. Clair County which will be submitted at the November election.

* * *

August 7 to 12 was "Good Roads Week" in Adams County. County Superintendent Boyer, in making preparation for the work, sent out the following appeal to the farmers:

"Come out and help us put your road in better condition. We can't do it alone and we feel that you want better roads. Every one is crying better roads and we can have them if you will help us.

"Set apart one day at least in the week designated and get your neighbors out to fix that bad place or that poor piece of road. If you have no bad places near your place then clean up your fence rows along the highway and show the traveling public that your community has progressiveness at heart.

"The commissioners of Adams County are going to tour the county at their own expense shortly after road week, and we feel that you will want your roads as good as can be found.

"Report your work to L. L. Boyer, superintendent of highways, with the estimated value of the work and help with the culvert which will be given the township doing the most and best work. Last year we had about $1,500 in work done free of charge and we should have at least two or three times that amount this year.

"The Chamber of Commerce is donating a concrete culvert to the township doing the most and best road work during the week and they have expressed a desire to help any township who asks the members providing their dinner is furnished. All put your shoulder to the wheel and help make Adams County one of the best in the State for good roads. It can and will be done if you will help.

* * *

The dust nuisance is again receiving considerable attention. The State Highway Department has on hand quite a number of copies of Bulletin No. 6 "Dust Prevention," and a copy will be gladly mailed to anyone who is interested in the subject.

* * *

Sharp turns and intersecting roads are always danger points for the traveler if he comes upon them without warning, and the efforts of road officials should be constantly directed toward warning the public of the "hair-pin" turn, the blind cross roads, and the sudden descent under the railroad culvert.

In this connection it might be well to call attention to the commendable action of the Lovell-McConnell Manufacturing Company of Newark, New Jersey, who are furnishing to automobile clubs, good roads associations, etc., without any charges whatever warning signs to be erected at dangerous points along the roads. These signs are attractive, and are practically indestructible, being made of ⅞-inch dovetailed pine and are 18 by 24 inches in size. The background is red, and in white letters appear the words "DANGER—SOUND KLAXON." Space is also provided at the top for the name of the organization erecting the signs, which is filled in by the Lovell-McConnell Company. These signs

are sent prepaid with the necessary screws for erecting them, the only obligation to be met is to see that the signs are properly placed at suitable danger points.

Showing danger sign which is furnished free by Lovell-McConnell Co.

The county superintendent's office of DeKalb County has recently completed a large scale map of the county and is having a zinc plate made of same for the county's use. Large maps of the county showing correctly all roads and also State aid roads are also being made. The county board, at its last session has made provision to accept the next allotment from the State for the purpose of constructing State aid roads. Clinton Township has offered to give $1,000 a mile for each mile of such road built with the next allotment in that township. At present three miles of State aid roads are being constructed in Afton Township. The Aetna Paving Construction Company of Chicago are the contractors. With the completion of the State aid roads built with this year's allotment, DeKalb County will have 11 miles of concrete road.

The first State aid road to be completed in St. Clair County was recently dedicated.

VERMILION COUNTY BOND ROADS.

(Continued from Page 84.)

from a trip to California and his friend, Mr. A. R. Hall, also an attorney of Vermilion County. Mr. Jones had become very much interested in the roads of California and the methods of building them and the question he put forth was, "If they do it in California, why not here in Illinois as well?" and with this in mind Mr. Hall started to figure out a plan whereby Vermilion County could replace her deplorable highways with good substantial roads. Mr. Hall made up his mind to compute the cost of 150 miles of permanent roads for Vermilion County and in a subsequent conversation with Mr. Jones told him that the most feasible scheme was to bond the county for $1,500,000. This idea, at the time, was something that was unheard of and it was regarded as more or less of a joke—the proposition of bonding a county for $1,500,000 to build roads. However, a plan was worked up whereby the issue could be spread over a period of 20 years and it was shown that the cost to each individual would be so small that there could be no valid objection on that score.

HISTORICAL FACTS ABOUT VERMILION COUNTY'S BOND ISSUE ROADS.

Good road petition filed............Sept. 11, 1913	
Special investigating committee appointed ....Mar. 12, 1914	
Favorable report of committee......June 10, 1914	
Adoption of bond issue by popular vote ....Nov. 3, 1914	
Total votes cast for bonds.........	10,459
Total votes cast against bonds.......	8,978
Women voting for bond issue.......	2,749
Women voting against bond issue...	1,670
When first strip of road was completed ....June 18, 1916	
Date first payment on bond issue of $1,500,000 ....June 1, 1915	
Date of last payment on bond issue..June 1, 1934	

At the time this question was being agitated there was no provision in the road and bridge law which enabled the county to issue bonds for the purpose of constructing roads but one of the provisions in the act in relation to counties gave the county boards the power to submit to the voters the question of issuing county bonds to enable the county board to perform the duties imposed upon it by law, and one of the duties imposed upon the board was the appropriation of funds to aid in the construction of roads and bridges in any part of the county whenever a majority of the board deemed expedient. A petition was filed before the board of supervisors on September 11, 1913, asking that the proposition of issuing $1,500,000 in county bonds be submitted to the people at the next general election, the bonds to run for 20 years, with interest at 4 per cent, payable annually. The supervisors were favorably inclined towards the proposition of calling for a vote and adopted a resolution on March 11, 1914, providing that a committee of five consult with the State Highway Commission relative to bonding the roads, to attend to all the details and to obtain all information possible for the benefit of the public so that the people themselves could see exactly what was being done. This board submitted a

report at a meeting of the supervisors on June 10, which indicated that the time was ripe for Vermilion County to vote on such a question and they recommended that the question be voted on at the election in November, 1914, and that a direct annual tax be levied each year for 20 years to pay off such bonds and interest thereon. The board of supervisors immediately passed a resolution calling for a vote on such a proposition and the matter was placed before the voters at the fall election. The proposition carried by a good majority and steps were immediately taken towards the issuing of the bonds. However, before these bonds could be sold and the work started, their legality had to be determined by a decision from the Supreme Court. A favorable decision having been rendered, the contracts were let in March, 1916; the work being divided into nine sections of about 17 miles each and the completion of this first section between Bismark and Alvin marks the starting point of the object which was in the minds of those who three years ago first advocated such a bond issue—good permanent roads for Vermilion County.

CONCRETE PAVEMENTS.

(Continued from Page 85.)

compounds, all of which are beneficial under certain conditions; yet it seems that under the majority of conditions existing in Illinois, the road engineer is more justified in giving a thorough study to the proper proportioning and mixing of the concrete aggregates and the finishing and curing of the concrete pavement surface.

The tendency in concrete road construction in many places seems to be to devise machinery and means of laying more concrete pavements and reducing its first cost at the expense of the quality of the concrete. This practice is proving to be only a detriment to such pavements. This can be evidenced by a careful inspection of a number of roads that have been in service.

Most specifications for concrete road construction merely specify the mixture of cement, sand and coarse aggregate by a proportion of 1:2:3 or 1:2:3½ without specifications covering the most effective gradation and quality of the aggregates. It is evident that 1 part of cement with 2 parts of ordinary building sand mixed with 3 or 3½ parts of gravel or stone selected without regard to gradation will not give as dense or strong a mixture as when the materials are all graded so as to obtain the maximum density.

Maximum density and quality of concrete are essential points in the construction of a concrete pavement. Maximum density can be secured by careful gradation of all material which can only be accomplished by specifying the amount of material that shall pass various sizes of screens. Inasmuch as the wearing qualities of a pavement depend almost entirely upon the quality of the aggregates, it is very important that all aggregates be tested for abrasion and compression. It is quite common to specify the French coefficient of wear on the coarse aggregate that enters into a pavement, but rarely does a specification cover a coefficient of wear on the sand. The claim is often made that the coarse aggregate in a pavement takes all the wear on a concrete pavement; however, inspection shows that the cement mortar does take considerable wear and at the same time regulates the wear on the coarse aggregate. It would seem, therefore, that a more rigid test on concrete sand should be specified. The usual test on sand is to make cement briquettes and test for tensile strength when it would seem that compression tests and some form of abrasion test would more nearly represent the condition that exists in a pavement and which would serve as a comparison with various materials just as well as the tensile strength.

The maximum density of a mixture does not always determine the strength of concrete. All tests and experiments show that the materials should be more thoroughly mixed before placing than is done on the average paving job. It is true that specifications requiring a more thorough mix will increase the cost, but at the same time such requirements will add materially to the strength of the pavement. In order to maintain the efficiency of the construction forces and to secure a more thorough mix of the aggregates, it seems that there is still a great opportunity for the machine companies or inventors to devise a mixer which by mechanical means will more thoroughly mix the materials in the same time that is now alloted by specifications on concrete pavement construction.

One of the most important operations connected with constructing a concrete pavement is that of finishing and curing the surface so as to insure smoothness and uniformity. A great many pavements which have been constructed of good material, properly mixed, are now defective on account of poorly finished surfaces. The public is always the first to condemn a pavement and a road is often condemned on account of a wavy and nonuniform surface even though the quality of the material in it may be of the highest grade. An inspection of various construction jobs will often reveal the fact that there is a wide variance in the requirements for finishing concrete pavements, many require the final finish to be made with wood floats, and some with steel floats, another omitting the floats and using only a strike board. Some engineers require the freshly laid concrete to be floated immediately behind the strikeboard. Others require floating or finishing at considerable distance behind the mixer, or when the concrete begins to get firm just prior to the initial set. The main desire in both cases is to secure a uniform and dense surface. It seems therefore that more attention should be given to devising some practical, mechanical device for striking and finishing a concrete pavement that will make it more dense and uniform than the usual method of hand floating.

A careful inspection of concrete pavements that have been in use for a number of years indicates that a well-constructed and cured concrete pavement wears very slowly even under the heaviest traffic of Illinois. The wear that has been chiefly noticeable is the result of a nonuniform surface, caused from poor floating and improper curing of the surface in the original construction. The use of any machinery or methods, therefore, that will aid in securing a uniform wearing surface will result in a better wearing and more satisfactory pavement.

The selection of a type of pavement is not always based on its economy alone, but where economy is the main consideration there is a great field for the well-constructed concrete pavement.

THE PROBLEM OF MAINTENANCE.

(Continued from Page 87.)

of Agriculture for the construction of public roads without satisfactory assurance that the roads built with the help of the United States shall be maintained after construction by the states or districts through

which they run and which they are designed to serve and save.

STATE AID ALLOTMENTS.

The following statement shows the amount of money which has been apportioned to the counties for State aid road work for the fiscal year ending June 30, 1917.

The appropriation of the Legislature in 1915 for the following biennium was two million dollars, one million of which became available and was allotted July 1, 1915.

The State Highway Commission has set aside $10,000 as a maintenance fund, and has allotted the remaining $990,000 to the counties in the ratio which the road and bridge tax raised in the individual counties bears to the total road and bridge tax of the State, with the exception of Cook County, which, as it contributes more than 40 per cent of the total automobile fees collected in the State, receive as its share of the State aid allotment, 25 per cent of the amount so collected in the county.

The tax figures used in determining the apportionment are, by law, those shown in the last published report of the State Auditor.

Counties.	Allotment 1916-17.	Counties.	Allotment 1916-17.
Adams	$ 9,591	Livingston	15,880
Alexander	10,390	Logan	10,936
Bond	4,334	Macon	16,683
Boone	5,808	Macoupin	11,027
Brown	2,799	Madison	15,469
Bureau	19,764	Marion	6,042
Calhoun	1,596	Marshall	6,118
Carroll	7,407	Mason	5,336
Cass	6,893	Massac	1,552
Champaign	20,676	McDonough	7,987
Christian	12,912	McHenry	12,966
Clark	5,446	McLean	24,196
Clay	3,487	Menard	3,657
Clinton	4,851	Mercer	9,085
Coles	8,905	Monroe	2,896
Cook	108,994	Montgomery	10,818
Crawford	4,904	Morgan	9,304
Cumberland	3,220	Moultrie	5,626
DeKalb	15,482	Ogle	12,949
DeWitt	7,920	Peoria	21,744
Douglas	7,951	Perry	2,618
Dupage	11,266	Piatt	7,223
Edgar	13,529	Pike	8,664
Edwards	1,552	Pope	1,243
Effingham	3,904	Pulaski	1,987
Fayette	7,253	Putnam	2,585
Ford	8,503	Randolph	3,615
Franklin	6,185	Richland	3,337
Fulton	11,811	Rock Island	6,285
Gallatin	2,267	Saline	8,462
Greene	7,049	Sangamon	17,010
Grundy	8,841	Schuyler	4,587
Hamilton	3,489	Scott	3,370
Hancock	9,719	Shelby	11,904
Hardin	661	Stark	5,097
Henderson	5,107	St. Clair	10,085
Henry	13,027	Stephenson	10,348
Iroquois	19,294	Tazewell	9,240
Jackson	7,880	Union	2,526
Jasper	4,052	Vermilion	29,482
Jefferson	5,124	Wabash	2,846
Jersey	3,808	Warren	9,069
JoDaviess	6,285	Washington	4,356
Johnson	984	Wayne	5,844
Kane	23,582	White	4,531
Kankakee	10,394	Whiteside	13,741
Kendall	6,050	Will	17,772
Knox	11,624	Williamson	5,440
Lake	11,953	Winnebago	14,042
LaSalle	28,384	Woodford	8,415
Lawrence	6,647		
Lee	10,461	Total	$990,000

Correspondence Course in Road Building
CONDUCTED BY UNIVERSITY OF ILLINOIS.
Lesson 4.—Wooden Beam Bridges—Continued.

TABLE I.—ALLOWABLE STRESSES.

| Kind of timber. | Bending. | | | | Shearing. | | | | Compression. | | | | | | For columns under 15 diams. Safe stress. | Formulae for safe stress in long columns over 15 diameters. |
| | Extreme fibre stress. | | Parallel to grain. | | Longitudinal shear in beams. | | Perpendicular to grain. | | Parallel to grain. | | | | | | | |
	Ultimate strength av.	Safe stress.	Ultimate strength av.	Safe stress.	Ultimate strength av.	Safe stress.	Elastic limit.	Safe stress.	Ultimate strength av.	Safe stress.						
Douglas Fir........	6,100	1,500	690	215	270	140	630	390	3,600	1,500	1,125	$1,500 (1 - \dfrac{l}{60d})$
Longleaf Pine.....	6,500	1,600	720	225	300	150	520	325	3,800	1,600	1,225	$1,600 (1 - \dfrac{l}{60d})$
Shortleaf Pine.....	5,600	1,400	710	215	330	175	340	210	3,400	1,400	1,050	$1,350 (1 - \dfrac{l}{60d})$
White Pine	4,400	1,150	400	125	180	90	290	185	3,000	1,250	950	$1,250 (1 - \dfrac{l}{60d})$
Spruce	4,800	1,250	600	180	170	90	370	225	3,200	1,400	1,050	$1,350 (1 - \dfrac{l}{60d})$
Norway Pine.......	4,200	1,000	590	160	250	125	....	185	¹2,600	1,000	750	$1,000 (1 - \dfrac{l}{60d})$
Tamarack.	4,600	1,150	670	215	260	125	....	275	¹3,200	1,230	950	$1,250 (1 - \dfrac{l}{60d})$
Western Hemlock.	5,800	1,400	630	200	¹270	125	440	275	3,500	1,300	1,125	$1,500 (1 - \dfrac{l}{60d})$
Redwood..........	5,000	1,150	300	100	......	....	340	185	3,300	1,125	850	$1,125 (1 - \dfrac{l}{60d})$
Bald Cypress.......	4,800	1,150	500	150	....	....	340	210	3,900	1,400	1,050	$1,350 (1 - \dfrac{l}{60d})$
Red Cedar.........	4,200	1,000	.....	....	....	....	470	285	2,800	1,125	850	$1,125 (1 - \dfrac{l}{60d})$
White Oak.........	5,700	1,100	840	260	270	140	920	550	3,500	1,600	1,225	$1,600 (1 - \dfrac{l}{60d})$

¹ Partially air-dry.
Adapted from American Railway Engineering Association Specifications.
These stresses are to be used without impact for live load.

l = length in inches.
d = least side in inches.

TABLE II.—MOMENTS OF INERTIA AND SECTION MODULI OF RECTANGULAR BEAMS.

| Depth in inches. | Width in inches. | | | | | | | | | |
| | 2 | | 4 | | 6 | | 8 | | 10 | |
	I	S	I	S	I	S	I	S	I	S
2	1.33	1.33	2.66	2.66	4.00	4.00	5.33	5.33	6.66	6.66
4	10.66	5.33	21.33	10.66	32.00	16.00	42.66	21.33	53.33	26.66
6	36.00	12.00	72.00	24.00	108.00	36.00	144.00	48.00	180.00	60.00
8	85.33	21.33	170.66	42.66	256.00	64.00	341.33	85.33	426.66	106.66
10	166.66	33.33	333.33	66.66	500.00	100.00	666.66	133 33	833.33	166.66
12	288.00	48.00	576.00	96.00	864.00	144.00	1152.00	192.00	1440.00	240.00
14	457.33	65.33	914.66	130 66	1372.00	196.00	1829.33	261.33	2286.66	326.66
16	682.66	85.33	1365.33	170.66	2048 00	256.00	2730.66	341.33	3413.33	426.66

I—Moment of inertia. S—Section modulus.

TABLE III.—ACTUAL SIZES, SECTIONAL AREAS AND SECTION MODULI FOR COMMERCIAL LUMBER SURFACED ONE SIDE AND ONE EDGE.

Nominal depth.		Nominal width.					
		2	4	6	8	10	12
2	S Sec. Modulus.......		1.60	2.48	3.30	4.18	5.06
4	Size...............	1⅝x3⅝	3⅝x3⅝				
	Area...............	5.89	13.14	20.39	27.64	34.89	42.14
	Sec. Modulus.......	3.56	7.94	12.32	16.70	21.08	25.46
6	Size...............	1⅝x5⅝	3⅝x3⅝	5⅝x5⅝			
	Area...............	9.14	20.39	31.64	44.56	56.06	67.56
	Sec. Modulus.......	8.57	19.12	29.66	42.70	53.72	64.74
8	Size...............	1⅝x7½	3⅝x7⅝	5⅝x7⅝	7⅝x7⅝		
	Area...............	12.19	27.64	44.56	60.06	75.56	91.06
	Sec. Modulus.......	15.24	35.12	57.56	77.58	97.60	117.60
10	Size...............	1⅝x9½	3⅝x9⅝	5⅝x9⅝	7⅝x9⅝	9⅝x9⅝	
	Area...............	15.44	34.89	56.06	75.56	95.06	114.6
	Sec. Modulus.......	24.44	55.97	91.10	121.8	154.50	186.2
12	Size...............	1⅝x11½	3⅝x11⅝	5⅝x11⅝	7⅝x11⅝	9⅝x11⅝	11⅝x11⅝
	Area...............	18.69	42.14	67.56	91.06	114.6	138.1
	Sec. Modulus.......	35.80	81.65	123.3	178.3	224.3	270.4

TABLE IV.—ACTUAL SIZES, SECTIONAL AREAS, AND SECTION MODULI FOR COMMERCIAL LUMBER SURFACED ON FOUR SIDES.

Nominal depth.		Nominal width.					
		2	4	6	8	10	12
2	Sec. Modulus S.....		1.32	2.06	2.81	3.56	4.32
4	Size...............	1½x3½	3½x3½				
	Area...............	5.25	12.25	19.25	26.25	33.25	40.25
	Sec. Modulus S.....	3.06	7.14	11.22	15.30	19.38	23.40
6	Size...............	1½x5½	3½x5½	5½x5½			
	Area...............	8.25	19.25	30.25	41.25	52.25	63.25
	Sec. Modulus S.....	7.58	17.70	27.76	37.85	47.95	58.00
8	Size...............	1½x7½	3½x7½	5½x7½	7½x7½		
	Area...............	11.06	26.25	41.25	56.25	71.25	86.25
	Sec. Modulus S.....	13.6	32.85	51.60	70.40	89.10	107.80
10	Size...............	1½x9½	3½x9½	5½x9½	7½x9½	9½x9½	
	Area...............	14.06	33.25	52.25	71.25	90.25	109.25
	Sec. Modulus S.....	21.95	52.60	82.70	112.35	142.80	172.80
12	Size...............	1½x11½	3½x11½	5½x11½	7½x11½	9½x11½	11½x11½
	Area...............	17.06	40.25	63.25	86.25	109.25	132.25
	Sec. Modulus S.....	32.35	77.2	121.40	165.50	209.00	253.70

EXAMINATION OF WOODEN STRUCTURES.

In the examination of old wood bridges prepatory to determining their safety it is necessary to inspect the parts that are most difficult to get at. Timber is most apt to rot at the most inaccessible points, or, where there is not the free circulation of air and where moisture is retained.

Quite frequently wooden timbers appear on the outside to be well preserved but are badly decayed inside. For that reason it may be necessary to bore holes in the timbers in order to examine the interior. These holes should be bored with a small auger and at points in the timber where it will not materially affect its strength. They should not be bored in the bottom of joists, but in the sides a few inches from the bottom.

Where beams have rotted to any appreciable extent the size of beam used in computing stresses should only include that part of the cross section which is sound wood. For example, if a 2 by 10 has 2 inches of rotten wood on the upper edge, the stresses should be computed for a 2 by 8 timber.

After wooden beams have become too rotten to hold spikes on the upper edge they should *not* be turned over with the rotten edge on the bottom. Rotten wood has no strength whatever in tension.

METHODS FOR DETERMINING SAFE LOADS ON WOODEN BEAM BRIDGES.

The loads, both uniform and concentrated, are applied in exactly the same manner as for steel beam bridges with wood plank floors.

The allowable unit stresses will be those given in Table I. The stresses must be computed for crossbending, and for shear along the grain, or longitudinal shear.

The method of computing stresses in the beams will be illustrated by an example.

EXAMPLE 1. A wooden beam bridge of 12-foot span has 4 by 12 longleaf pine joists spaced 18 inches on centers. The floor is 3-inch wooden plank. Is this bridge safe for a 15-ton engine as specified by the Illinois Highway Department?

Assurance must first be had as to the actual size of the joists. It will be assumed in this case that the beams are actually 4" by 12" in size.

The dead load for each joist is:

floor—1½ × 3 × 4½ = 20¼ lb.
beam—1 × 4 × 4½   = 18   lb.

Total............38¼ lb.

The dead load moment is:

$$M = \frac{1}{8} wl^2 = \frac{38 \times 12 \times 12}{8}$$

$$= 684 \text{ ft. lb.}$$

The maximum live load stress is produced by placing the heavy wheel of the engine at the middle of the span. The live load carried by one joist is 5,000 lb., as explained in Lesson 2.

The live load moment is:

$$M = \frac{1}{4} Pl = \frac{5000 \times 12}{4}$$

$$= 15000 \text{ ft. lb.}$$

The total moment is:

dead load= 684 ft. lb.
live load= 1500 ft. lb.
Total =15684 ft. lb.
or 15684x12=188,208 inch lb.

No impact is added in this case because the allowable unit stresses given in TABLE I, provide for impact.

The maximum unit stress in the beam due to bending is:

$$f = \frac{M}{S} = \frac{188,208}{96}$$

$$= 1960 \text{ lb. per. sq. in.}$$

This exceeds the allowable unit stress by about 22 per cent.

The longitudinal unit shear, or the unit shear along the grain is obtained from the formula:

$$v = \frac{V}{\frac{2}{3} bd}, \text{ in which}$$

v = unit shear,
V = maximum total shear = end reaction
b = breadth of beam
d = depth of beam.

In this case the unit shear is,

$$v = \frac{1728}{\frac{2}{3} x 4 x 12} = 48 \text{ lb. per sq. in.}$$

This is well within the allowable unit stress.

This bridge would be safe if new and well constructed. If decayed to any appreciable extent, or poorly constructed, it would not be safe.

PROBLEMS.

1. A wooden beam bridge span of 15'—0" has 4 by 12" white oak stringers spaced 2'–0" c. to c. The flooring is 3" white oak plank. Is this bridge safe for a 15-ton engine if it is in good condition?

2. A wooden beam bridge of 15-foot span has 2 by 12 stringers spaced 2'–0" c. to c. The stringers have 2 inches of rotten wood on the upper edge. What would you do with this bridge to make it safe?

3. If you were building a wooden beam bridge of 10-foot span, what size and spacing of stringers would you use? What kind of abutments would you build?

4. If you were inspecting timbers for a wooden beam bridge what would you look for?

5. Under what circumstances would it be justifiable to build wooden beam bridges in place of concrete or steel? Are wooden bridges ever economical?

REFERENCES.

1. The Inspection and Maintenance of Bridges and Allied Structures, *Engineering News*. Vol. 57, p. 482.

In the Chattanooga preparedness parade, one forcible illustration of our national unpreparedness was presented in the form of a float, illustrating the need of improved roads.

2. Mechanical Properties of Wood. Samuel J. Record, New York, 1914.

3. Manual of the American Railway Engineering Association, 1911.

4. Tests of Longleaf Pine Bridge Timbers. Bulletin 149, American Railway Engineering Association, September, 1912. *Engineering News*, December 12, 1912.

5. Strength Values for Structural Timber. Circular 189, Forest Service.

6. Structural Details or Elements of Design in Heavy Framing. H. S. Jacoby, New York, 1909.

7. A Manual of Standard Wood Construction by Arthur T. North, 1913. From Southern Pine Association, New Orleans.

OPINIONS OF THE ATTORNEY GENERAL.

HARD ROADS—LEVIES FOR.

Mr. John A. MacNeil,
Attorney at Law, Olney, Illinois.

Dear Sir: I am in receipt of your favor of the 18th instant, as attorney for commissioners of highways of the town of Olney, and note statement of facts to the effect that on March 16, 1912, a petition was filed with the clerk of the town of Olney for a vote on the proposition to levy a hard road tax of one dollar on the hundred dollars valuation for a period of five years; that in accordance with such petition an election was held on the 2d day of April, 1912, at which the proposition to levy such tax carried; that the highway commissioners, at their meeting on the first Tuesday in September, 1912, levied such tax for a period of five years and filed a certificate of such levy with the town clerk, and that the town clerk certified the same to the county clerk; that thereafter the county clerk extended such tax in accordance with such certificate, including the year 1914.

You inquire, in substance, whether, under the revised Road and Bridge Act of 1913, it is the duty of the highway commissioners to make an annual levy of the tax voted in 1912 and certify such levy to the county clerk in accordance with section 110 of the revised act. I note the cases cited by you in the 265 and 266 Illinois reports, which you seem to think conflicting.

It will be noted that the Hard Roads Act of 1883, with a few minor changes relating principally to the manner of certifying the levy, is written into the revised act of 1913, and the holding of the Supreme Court in the case of *The People* v. *The Cleveland, Cincinnati, Chicago and St. Louis R. R. Co.*, 266 Ill. 101, is to the effect that under sections 2 and 4 of chapter 131 all rights accruing under the act of 1883 are saved; holding, in substance, the "Hard Roads" provision of the revised act of 1913 to be a continuation of the Hard Roads Act of 1883.

The court in the case of *The People* v. *The Illinois Central R. R. Co.*, 237 Ill. 154, held, where the proposition to levy a hard road tax for five years was adopted, that the commissioners of highways might make one levy to cover the entire period and certify the same to the town clerk who in turn could certify such levy to the county clerk, and that it was not necessary to make such levies and certificates annually during the period for which such tax was voted; and in the case of *The People* v. *Robeson et al.*, 253 Ill. 456, the court held, in substance, that a hard road tax voted under the act of 1883 might be by one levy for the full period, or that the highway commissioners might make an annual levy of such tax.

In the case of *People* v. *The Cairo, Vincennes and Chicago Ry. Co.*, 266 Ill. 561, the objection urged against the levy of the hard road tax for the town of East Eldorado for the year 1913 was that the highway commissioners did not certify a levy of such tax to the county clerk as required by section 110 of the revised act of 1913. The court, pages 561, 562, says:

"A tax of one dollar on each $100 of taxable property for the term of five years was voted by the electors at the town meeting on April 1, 1913, and on April 15, 1913, the commissioners levied the tax for the whole period and filed a certificate of levy in the office of the town clerk. The town clerk filed a certified copy of the certificate with the county clerk, in compliance with the law then in force. It was not necessary that new levies and certificates should be made annually during the five years, (*People* v. *Illinois Central Railroad Co.*, 237 Ill. 154) the highway commissioners having a right to immediately levy the tax, and having done so, it became the duty of the county clerk to extend the portion of the tax due each year upon the tax books for the year upon which they fell due."

It would seem to be clear that the holding of the court is that where a town voted to levy a hard road tax under the act of 1883, such tax having been voted and a levy thereof having been made by the highway commissioners and certified by them to the town clerk, who in accordance with such act certified the same to the county clerk, all prior to the time the act of 1913 went into effect, it became the duty of the county clerk to annually extend such tax on the tax books without any further levy or certificate.

The case of *The People* v. *The Cairo, Vincennes and Chicago Railway Co.*, 265 Ill. 634, was a case where the town of Wabash voted at a town meeting on the first day of April, 1913, to levy a tax of one dollar on the hundred for hard roads, but such tax was extended by the county clerk upon a certificate of the town clerk dated September 2, 1913. There is nothing in the case that discloses when the highway commissioners certified the tax to the town clerk, whether before or after the revised act went into effect. However, a levy certified by the highway commissioners to the town clerk, under the act of 1883, did not become a levy until certified by the town clerk to the county clerk. After the taking effect of the revised act on July 1, 1913, the town clerk could not make a legal certificate of a levy of a hard road tax. If in that case the town clerk had certified the tax to the county clerk prior to the first day of July, 1913, then, according to the holding of the court in the case of *People* v. *Cairo, Vincennes and Chicago Railway Co.*, 266 Ill., above cited, the extension of such tax by the county clerk on the tax books would have been a valid extension. The court, page 637, holds that the vote of the town of Wabash on April 1, 1913, under the act of 1883, was binding under the revised act which went into effect July 1, 1913, and was sufficient authority for a levy by the highway commissioners; but that such levy could not be certified to the county clerk by the town clerk after the revised act went into effect; and the reasoning of the court in the cases of *The People* v. *Chicago, Burlington and Quincy R. R. Co.*, 266 Ill. 68, and *People* v. *The Cleveland, Cincinnati, Chicago and St. Louis Ry. Co.*, id. 101, is along the line of the court's holdings in the case of *People* v. *The Cairo, Vincennes and Chicago Ry. Co.*, *supra.* The distinction is that where a hard road tax was voted under the act of 1883 and the commissioners certified a levy of such tax for the full period to the town clerk who in turn certified such levy to the county clerk prior to July 1, 1913, it becomes the duty of the county clerk, under such certificate, to extend such tax annually during the period upon the tax books. Where, however, a town voted a hard road tax under the act of 1883, but the levy of such tax was not certified by the town clerk to the county clerk in accordance with said act prior to July 1, 1913, then such levy must be certified by the highway commissioners to the county clerk as provided by section 110 of the revised act.

Upon the statement of facts in your letter it appears that the tax voted by the town of Olney on April 2, 1912, was levied by the highway commissioners for the full period of five years at their meeting in September, 1912, and certified by the town clerk to the county clerk. You do not give the date on which the town clerk certified such levy to the county clerk. Assuming that the town clerk certified such levy to the county clerk prior to the time the revised act went into effect July 1, 1913, the tax voted by the town of Olney would come within the rule announced by the court in the case of *People* v. *Cairo, Vincennes and Chicago Ry. Co.*, 266 Ill. 561.

Very respectfully,

P. J. Lucey, *Attorney General.*

BRIDGES WITHIN EIGHTY RODS OF COUNTY LINES TO BE BUILT BY ADJOINING COUNTIES.

State Highway Department,
Springfield, Illinois.

Gentlemen: I am in receipt of your favor of the 11th inst., transmitting to this Department a letter of Mr. Alex. Anderson, county superintendent of highways of Ogle County, with the request that this office render an opinion on the proposition submitted.

It appears from the letter of Mr. Anderson that it is necessary to build a bridge on a county line road between the counties of Ogle and Stephenson; that said road also forms part of the boundary line running east and west between the counties of Ogle and Winnebago; that the point at which said bridge is to be built between the counties of Ogle and Stephenson is within sixty rods of the county line running north and south between the counties of Stephenson and Winnebago, and the county line running east and west between the counties of Ogle and Winnebago. His inquiry is, whether under section 36 of the Road and Bridge Act, the cost of said bridge is to be borne by the counties of Ogle and Stephenson, or whether Winnebago County may be required to contribute to the cost of same, and, if so, in what proportion such cost should be borne by the three counties.

Section 36 of the revised Road and Bridge Act provides:

"Bridges over streams which divide counties, and bridges on roads on county lines, and bridges within eighty rods of county lines, shall be built and repaired at the expense of such counties. And all such bridges over streams which form the boundary line between two counties, and all such bridges within eighty rods of such boundary line between such county and another county, equal or exceed $5,000, and the county desiring to construct such bridge has appropriated its share of the cost of such boundary line, and the cost of such bridge will constructing such bridge. And when any county desires to build any such bridge across any stream which is the boundary line, when the cost of constructing the same respectively in the proportion that the taxable property shall be $5,000 or over, shall be built by such counties in each county respectively bears to each other according to its assessed value as equalized at the time of or desires to build any such bridge within eighty rods of constructing the same, then it shall be the duty of such other county to make an appropriation for its proportion of the cost of said bridge on the basis of the assessed value of the property, real and personal, of each of said counties according to the last preceding assessment thereof as equalized, and if such other county fails or refuses to make an appropriation for its proper proportion of the cost of constructing such bridge, any court of competent jurisdiction shall issue an order to compel such county to make such appropriation upon a proper petition for that purpose, and the cost and expense of maintaining and keeping the same in repair after the same is built and constructed shall be borne in the proportion of the assessed value of the property in each of said counties according to the latest equalized assessment thereof: *Provided*, that for the building and maintaining of bridges over streams near county lines in which both are interested and where the cost thereof is less than $5,000, the expense of building and maintaining any such bridge shall be borne by both counties in such portion as shall be just and equitable between the counties, taking into consideration the taxable property in each, the location of the bridge, and the advantage of each, to be determined by the commissioner in making contracts for the same, as provided for in Section 37 of this Act."

It will be noted that this section expressly provides that bridges over streams which divide counties, and bridges on county line roads, and bridges within eighty rods of county lines, shall be built and repaired at the expense of such counties. And in case the cost of construction is $5,000 or over, such cost is to be apportioned between the counties liable in the proportion that the taxable property in each bears to the cost of construction; if the cost of construction is less than $5,000, it is to be equitably apportioned between the counties liable, taking into consideration the taxable property in each county, the location of such bridge, and the advantage that each county will derive from same, to be determined by the commissioners in making contract for such bridge.

In case where, as under the facts stated in Mr. Anderson's letter, it becomes necessary to build a bridge on a county line road between two counties, at a point within eighty rods of the county lines of a third county, it would seem under the statute above quoted that such third county would be liable for its proportionate share of the cost of such bridge, to be ascertained as the statute provides. Take .for example, a case where four counties corner; under this statute, each may be liable for its portion of the costs of a bridge built on a county line road within eighty rods of the line of each of said four counties.

Upon statement of facts in Mr. Anderson's letter, I am of the opinion that the cost of the bridge in question should be borne by the three counties of Ogle, Stephenson and Winnebago, to be ascertained in the manner the statute provides.

I herewith return letter of Mr. Anderson, as requested.

Very respectfully,

P. J. LUCEY, *Attorney General.*

DUTY OF DRAINAGE COMMISSIONERS TO BUILD BRIDGE OVER DITCH CUT ACROSS PUBLIC ROAD.

Mr. M. W. SHOOK,
  Highway Commissioner, Keenes, Illinois.

DEAR SIR: I am in receipt of your favor of the 9th instant, which may be summarized as follows:

1. Whether adjoining counties, or adjoining towns are required to construct small bridges on county lines.

2. Whether it is the duty of drainage commissioners to construct bridges over ditches cut across public roads.

3. Whether the town clerk has the right to charge a fee of ten cents each for orders which he writes out against the road fund.

Noting the first proposition, section 36 of the revised Road and Bridge Act provides in part as follows:

"Bridges over streams which divide counties and bridges on roads on county lines, and bridges within eighty rods of county lines, shall be built and repaired at the expense of such counties. And all such bridges over streams which form the boundary line between two counties, and all such bridges within eighty rods of such boundary line, when the cost of constructing the same shall be $5,000 or over, shall be built by such counties respectively in the proportion that the taxable property in each county respectively bears to each other according to its assessed value as equalized at the time of constructing such bridge. * * * * * * * * *

"*Provided*, that for the building and maintaining of bridges over streams near county lines in which both are interested and where the cost thereof is less than $5,000, the expense of building and maintaining any such bridge shall be borne by both counties in such portion as shall be just and equitable between the counties, taking into consideration the taxable property in each, the location of the bridge, and the advantage to each to be determined by the commissioner in making contracts for the same, as provided for in section 37 of this Act."

It would seem that the cost of bridges built on county lines it to be borne by the adjoining counties whether the cost of such bridge be great or small. In case, however, the cost of such bridge is less than $5,000, such cost is to be apportioned between the adjoining counties in the manner specified in the proviso above quoted.

Relative to bridges over ditches cut across public roads, the Supreme Court, in the case of *Highway Commissioners* v. *Drainage Commissioners*, 246 Ill. 388, holds, in effect, that where drainage commissioners cut a ditch across a public highway, it is the duty of the drainage commissioners to build a bridge over such ditch at the cost of the drainage district.

Relative to the right of the town clerk to charge a fee of ten cents for each order written out by him against the road fund, will say the town clerk is entitled only to such fees, for his services when acting as clerk of the board of highway commissioners, as are allowed him under section 53 of the Road and Bridge Act. There is no provision of the act which allows the clerk to charge a fee of ten cents for orders made out by him against the road and bridge fund.

Very respectfully,

P. J. LUCEY, *Attorney General.*

ILLINOIS HIGHWAYS

[Printed by authority of the State of Illinois.]

OFFICIAL PUBLICATION OF THE

STATE HIGHWAY DEPARTMENT

| VOL. III | SPRINGFIELD, ILLINOIS, SEPTEMBER, 1916 | No. 9 |

STATE AID ROAD, KANE COUNTY—SECTION D, ROUTE 1.

The Above View Shows a Section of This Road Where the Width Was Increased From 18 Feet as Originally Planned to 25 Feet, the Extra Work Being Requested and Paid For by Owners of Adjacent Property.

CONTRAST THESE TWO STRUCTURES.

The Old Bridge is Typical of Construction 40 Years Ago. Compare it With the Safety and Permanency Represented in the New Structure.

The Light of God Highway

[By H. E. HOPKINS.]

Copyright 1916 Road-Maker Publishing Company.

[The highway that begins at Columbus, N. M., for hundreds of miles winds its way down into the heart of Old Mexico. As train after train of army trucks thundered by, laden with necessities for our troops, an old woman, bereft of home and children, was asked by a newspaper correspondent what she thought it all meant. "'Tis the light of God coming to our poor land along this highway."]

ALL the long day on the Mexican trail
The motor trucks thunder and creak and wail
On a road that winds its tortuous way
Through canyons, o'er hilltops, in sand and in clay.
'Tis the trail that starts at Columbus town
And for hundreds of miles—now up, now down—
Till at length it reaches Mexico's heart
Where, some day, Peace cometh and War will depart.

"'TIS the light of God coming to our poor land!"
Cried a bent old crone, "'Tis the dear God's hand
That is guiding your soldiers who bring us aid;
Who will succor our people from bandit raid,
From outrage and pillage, from murder and greed.
This help that you bring us in our dire need
Gives us the breath of life, lightens our load—
'Tis God's light that is casting its rays on this road!"

LIGHT of God's Highway! It reaches *your* town.
Your little ones travel it up and down,
Winter and summer, to school and to play—
No storm-riven roadways to say them nay;
No doctor in need is kept from *your* door
While grief and despair tear at your heart's core,
And seconds seem hours of wait and delay;
Oft' this is their plight who won't pave their way.

LIGHT of God's Highway! There's one near your farm!
Then friends can draw near in evening's calm;
And joy's in your heart when a neighbor's hand
Welcomes your visit. Oh, you understand!
You know your life's real, and happily spent,
Not lonely and empty, nor sordidly bent.
Say, brother, it's strange that most folks can't see
What good roads have wrought for you and for me!

LIGHT of God's Highway! It's traveled by all
Who are quick to give heed to Prosperity's call.
Our country's defense, its progress, its weal,
Depend on good highways. Where is *your* zeal?
What are *you* doing? How high is *your* aim?
And what have *you* builded that's worthy the name?
Light of God Highway! How long must it plead
To make one and all of us see its great need?

(Reprinted from July, 1916, *Road-Maker*, Moline, Ill.)

Tentative Rules for Federal Aid Act Drafted by State Highway Officials.

By W. W. MARR,
Chief State Highway Engineer.

Many inquiries have come to the State Highway Department with reference to the work of the American Association of State Highway Officials, which met August 15, in the Raleigh Hotel in Washington, D. C.

Representatives of twenty-six states were present. Discussion which took place had for its purpose the bringing out of a correct interpretation of certain of the regulations, and on the first day, the 15th, changes were proposed. On the following day, thirty-five states were represented. The meeting was addressed by Secretary of Agriculture Houston, who, under the Federal Aid Act, is authorized to adopt the regulations.

The tentative draft of the rules and regulations as adopted by the state officials is as follows:

Regulation 1. Definitions.

For the purposes of these regulations, the following terms shall be construed, respectively, to mean:

SECTION 1. The Federal Aid Road Act, or the Act. An act of congress entitled "An Act to provide that the United States shall aid the states in the construction of rural post roads, and for other purposes," approved July 11, 1916. (Public—No. 156—Sixty-fourth Congress).

SEC. 2. The Secretary. The Secretary of Agriculture of the United States.

SEC. 3. Office of Public Roads. The Office of Public Roads and Rural Engineering of the United States Department of Agriculture.

SEC. 4. Ten per cent fund. Items for engineering, inspection and unforeseen contingencies, not exceeding 10 per cent of the total estimated cost of the work.

Regulation 2. Application of Regulations.

SECTION 1. These regulations apply to all provisions, except section 8 of the act and shall not be applied to section 8 unless hereafter authorized or required by order of the secretary.

SEC. 2. If a state can not constitutionally engage in any work of internal improvements, and any number of its counties shall appropriate or provide the proportion or share needed to be raised in order to entitle such state to its part of the appropriation apportioned to it, these regulations shall apply as fully as in the case of a state whose constitution does not prohibit it from engaging in any work of internal improvements.

Regulation 3. Information for the Secretary.

SECTION 1. Before an agreement is made upon any road or roads to be constructed in a state, or the character and method of construction, upon request of the secretary there shall be furnished to him, by or on behalf of the state, general information as to its laws affecting roads and the authority of state and local officials in reference to the construction and maintenance of roads; as to schemes for future construction; and as to provisions made, or to be made, for constructing and maintaining roads upon which it is contemplated that the expenditure of money appropriated by or under the act will be proposed. The information furnished shall be sufficient to enable the secretary to determine whether it is likely that the money apportioned to the state will be expended, and the roads constructed by the aid of the money will be properly maintained, in accordance with the terms of the act.

SEC. 2. Such information as may be requested by the Secretary or his authorized representative, relating to the maintenance of roads constructed under the provisions of the act, shall be furnished, from time to time, by the State Highway Departments, on forms supplied by the Office of Public Roads.

SEC. 3. Data furnished by or on behalf of a state shall be supplemented by such reports of the Office of Public Roads as the secretary may from time to time require before he decides whether the state has complied with the terms of the act or has presented a project statement which should be approved.

Regulation 4. Project Statements.

SECTION 1. A project statement shall contain all information necessary to enable the secretary to ascertain (a) whether the project conforms to the requirements of the act; (b) whether adequate funds, or their equivalent, are or will be available by or on behalf of the state for construction; (c) what purpose the project will serve and how it correlates with other highway work of the state; (d) the administrative control of, and responsibility for, the project; (e) the practicability and economy of the project from an engineering and construction standpoint; (f) the adequacy of the plans and provisions for proper maintenance of roads; and (g) the approximate amount of Federal aid desired.

SEC. 2. Suitable forms for project statements will be supplied by the Office of Public Roads.

SEC. 3. Project statements for any fiscal year may be submitted at any time after the apportionment for that year shall have been made.

SEC. 4. Projects will be deemed preferred, and recommended for approval, by the State Highway Department in the order in which the project statements are submitted, unless it be otherwise specified in writing; but the secretary may, in his discretion, consider the projects in a different order.

SEC. 5. Each project statement shall be accompanied by a sketch map, showing the location of the proposed project and all main contiguous transportation features.

SEC. 6. Suitable samples of materials suggested for use in the construction of a project shall be submitted to the Office of Public Roads, whenever requested by it, for examination prior to the secretary's decision on the project statement.

SEC. 7. Where any part of the cost of a project is to be furnished by a county or other local subdivision or subdivisions of a state, the project statement shall be accompanied by certified copy of each resolution or order, if any, of the appropriate local officials affecting the funds which are or will be made available for the supervision of the construction of the road and of the expenditure of the money provided or to be provided for paying such cost.

Regulation 5. Surveys, Plans, Specifications and Estimates.

SECTION 1. Surveys and plans shall show, in convenient form and sufficient detail, according to accepted engineering practice, necessary data, in connection with the specifications and estimates, to enable the secretary to ascertain and pass upon location, grades, drainage, bridges, other structures, special and unusual features, the work to be performed, and the probable cost thereof.

SEC. 2. Specifications shall set forth the proposed method of construction, type of construction, materials to be used and other essentials, in such detail as to afford complete knowledge of all steps to be taken in the construction of the project.

SEC. 3. The estimate for each project shall show the estimated quantity and cost of each item of construction in detail and, separately, the 10 per cent fund, and shall not include any expense of advertising.

SEC. 4. Rights-of-way and incidental damages to adjoining lands, necessary for any project shall be provided by or on behalf of the state, and the expense thereof shall not be included in the estimate or paid in any part, directly or indirectly, by the Federal Government.

SEC. 5. Grade crossings shall be avoided where practicable. The estimated cost of eliminating a grade crossing shall not include any amount the state, county or other civil subdivision has received, is to receive, or is entitled to receive, directly or indirectly, as reimbursement or payment from the owner of a public utility, for or on account of such elimination.

SEC. 6. No part of the expense of making preliminary surveys, plans, specifications or estimates prior to the acceptance of the project by the secretary, by or on behalf of the state, shall be included in the estimate or paid by the Federal Government.

SEC. 7. When plans, specifications and estimates have been approved by the secretary, no alteration thereof shall be made without his approval or that of his representative.

(Continued on page 106.)

Gravel Testing

By CLIFFORD OLDER,
Bridge Engineer, Illinois State Highway Department.

The following article is an extract from Bulletin No. 10 of the State Highway Department, "Bridge Manual for County Superintendents of Highways, Resident Engineers, and Inspectors," prepared by Clifford Older.

CLASSES OF GRAVEL DEFINED.

Unscreened gravel may be divided into three general classes. It should be understood, however, that the three classes of gravel have no reference to classes of concrete.

Gravel of the First Class Defined. The ratio of stone to sand volumes, in any natural gravel, may be less than the maximum permitted by the specifications, or in other words, the gravel may contain an excess of sand. This condition applies to perhaps 95 per cent of all natural gravels.

Gravel of the Second Class Defined. The ratio of stone to sand in a natural gravel may be exactly equal to the maximum provided by the specifications. This condition is very rare indeed.

Gravel of the Third Class Defined. The ratio of stone to sand volumes may be greater than the maximum permitted. In all such cases sand must be added in proper proportion. This condition applies to a small per cent of natural gravels.

A very convenient gravel testing outfit is shown in the accompanying cut. The testing can, which is made of galvanized iron is provided with a close fitting telescopic cover, and serves as a convenient carrying case when provided with a shawl strap as shown. The testing can is about 4 inches in diameter and 10 inches deep inside.

The scale is 10 inches long and is graduated to inches and tenths of inches.

The screens provided with the outfit have ½-, ¼- and ⅛-inch meshes.

The ¼-inch screen is used to determine the ratio of the volume of separated sand to the volume of unscreened gravel. The ⅛- and ½-inch screens are used to check the gradation of the sand and stone respectively. The can of small diameter is used as a protector in which to pack the glass graduate and for washing sand in making the clay test.

The 200 c. c. glass graduate is used for measuring volumes of sand and sediment in making the water settlement test for clay.

DETERMINATION OF PROPORTIONS—FIRST METHOD.

The following method may be used to determine the proper proportions for unscreened gravel concrete.

Procedure. The large can of the gravel tester, previously described, may be used, or if this is not available, any convenient receptacle may be substituted. Fill the receptacle level full with the gravel to be tested and then separate the sand from the stone by means of the ¼-inch screen. Repeat the process, keeping account of the number of measures of gravel used, until the number of measures of either sand or stone, given in the specifications for the class of concrete under consideration have been obtained.

Gravel of the First Class. If the number of parts of sand, required by the specifications, are obtained before the number of parts of stone, it is evident that sand is in excess, and either stone must be added or cement must be used in proportion to the sand contained in the gravel.

Cement Required. It is evident, that if such gravel is to be used without modification, 1 part of cement must be used to the number of parts of gravel screened in making the test.

In all cases it should be remembered that one bag of cement contains but 0.95 cu. ft.

EXAMPLE.—Assume that 1-2½-4 (Class A) concrete is to be used and that when 4 measures of gravel have been screened, there are 2½ measures of sand and 2 measures of stone; the ratio of stone to sand $\left(\dfrac{2}{2.5} = 0.80\right)$ is considerably less than the maximum permitted, $\left(\dfrac{4}{2.5} = 1.6\right)$. The gravel, therefore, is of the first class and may be used in its natural state, if desired, or stone may be added in order to reduce the amount of cement needed.

If no stone is to be added and as the test shows that 4 parts of gravel contains 2½ parts of sand, it is evident 1 part of cement must be used to 4 parts of the natural gravel.

If it is desired to add stone, the amount required is that which will increase the number of parts of stone found in the natural gravel, to the number of parts stated as a maximum in the specifications for the class of concrete under consideration. In the example given, this would equal 4 (the maximum permitted) less 2 (the amount contained in the natural gravel), or 2. The concrete should then be mixed in the proportions of 1 of cement 4 of gravel and 2 of stone. The same unit of measure must of course be used for cement, gravel and stone. For example, if it is desired to mix a 1-bag batch of concrete of the above proportions, 1 bag of cement (0.95 cu. ft.) should be used with 0.95 × 4 = 3.80 cu. ft. of gravel and 0.95 × 2 = 1.9 cu. ft. of stone.

Gravel of the Second Class. If upon screening a sample of gravel, it is found that a definite number of measures of gravel produce the exact number of measures of sand, and also of stone required by the specifications, for the class of concrete under consideration, it is evident that the gravel is of the second class. It is also evident that no modification of the natural gravel is necessary or desirable, providing of course that the gradation and quality of the sand and stone are satisfactory.

Cement Required. It is evident, that, as a certain number of measures of gravel produce exactly the required number of measures of sand and of stone, 1 part of cement is to be used to the number of measures of gravel screened in making the test.

EXAMPLE. If 5½ measures of gravel produce, when screened, 2½ measures of sand and 4 measures of stone, when Class A concrete is to be used, then 1 part of cement should be used to 5½ parts of gravel.

Gravel of the Third Class. If upon screening a sample of gravel, the number of parts of stone required are obtained before the number of parts of sand, it is evident that the gravel is of the third class and stone is in excess.

If used without modification, such a gravel would produce a porous, unsatisfactory concrete, and if cement should be added in proportion to the sand contained in the natural gravel only, insufficient cement would also be used. In all such cases, therefore, sufficient sand must be added to decrease the ratio of stone to sand to that provided in the specifications.

Sand Required. The amount of sand required is evidently that which will increase the number of parts of sand screened out, to the number required for the given class of concrete.

EXAMPLE. Suppose Class A concrete (1-2½-4) is to be used and when 5 measures of gravel have been screened it is found there are 4 measures of stone and 1.5 measures of sand. The ratio of stone to sand is $\dfrac{4}{1.5}$

$= 2.7$ which is greater than $\dfrac{4}{2.5} = 1.6$ the maximum

permitted in the specifications. Stone is therefore in excess and the amount of sand to add to 5 measures of gravel is 2.5 (the parts required), less 1.5 (the parts contained in the gravel), or 1. One part of sand must therefore be added to each 5 parts of the natural gravel.

Cement. When this is done, it is evident that 2½ and 4 represent the parts of volume of sand and stone in the modified gravel and one part by volume of cement must be used to 5 parts of gravel and 1 part of sand.

Limitations of First Method. The above method is practical and easily understood. In practice it does not often occur that a given number of full measures of gravel produce the required number of measures of sand or stone. It is necessary therefore, to use considerable care to avoid screening more gravel than is necessary.

When the sand or stone pile approaches the amount required, small amounts of gravel only should be placed on the screen, in order that the exact amount of gravel used may be known.

It is also necessary to screen a number of measures of gravel for each test.

Methods will now be described which, at first sight seem more complicated, but are simple when understood, more elastic and involve the screening of but one measure of gravel for each test.

DETERMINATION OF PROPORTIONS—SECOND METHOD.

Method General. It will be assumed that one of the testing outfits previously described is at hand. The nota-

tion and formulae hereafter given, however, are general and do not require special apparatus to permit their use.

Testing the Gravel. Fill the testing can level full with the gravel to be tested and then separate the sand and stone by means of the ¼ inch screen. The sand and stone may be caught on newspapers and poured back separately into the testing can for measurement. As the can is cylindrical in form and one-tenth inch on the scale represents one-hundredth of the depth of the can, the reading of the scale, when placed in the can zero and up, represents to the nearest one-hundredth, the ratio of the volume of either material contained in the can, to the volume of the gravel. The sand measurement then represents the ratio of sand to original gravel, and the stone measurement, the ratio of the stone to original gravel.

The amount of sand or stone in any given volume of gravel may be found by applying these ratios.

GRAVEL TESTING OUTFIT.

Convenient formulae may be written for determining proportions.

Notation. $x =$ ratio of volume of separated sand to volume of unscreened gravel.

$y =$ ratio of separated stone to unscreened gravel.

(For well graded gravel $x + y$ will be from about 1.10 to 1.25.)

$a =$ ratio of sand to cement required by the specifications.

(For Class A concrete, proportions 1-2½-4; $a = 2½$.)

$b =$ maximum ratio of stone to sand permitted by the specifications.

(For Class A concrete, $b = \dfrac{4}{2.5} = 1.6$)

$b' =$ ratio of stone to sand in any natural or unscreened gravel $= \dfrac{y}{x}$

$A =$ bags of cement required per cubic foot of natural gravel of the first or second class.

$B =$ cubic feet of natural gravel of the first or second class to use with one bag of cement.

$C =$ amount of stone to add to one cubic foot of gravel of the first class, in order that the ratio of stone to sand (b') in the resulting mixture may be increased to b.

D = Amount of stone to add to a 1-bag batch of gravel of the first class, so that the ratio of stone to sand in the resulting mixture may equal b.

E = Amount of sand to add to a cubic foot of gravel of the third class, in order that the ratio of stone to sand (b') in the resulting mixture may be decreased to "b."

F = Bags of cement required per cubic foot of natural gravel of the third class.

G = Cubic feet of natural gravel of the third class to use with one bag of cement.

H = Amount of sand to add to a 1-bag batch of gravel of the third class, in order that the ratio of stone to sand (b') in the resulting mixture may be decreased to b.

Rules for Quick Determination of Class. In general, if the test shows x to be greater than about 0.47, the gravel is practically sure to be of the first class, although in rare cases x may be slightly greater than this for gravel of the first class.

If the value of x is between 0.36 and 0.47, the gravel may be either of the first, second or third class, depending upon the gradation.

If the value of x is less than 0.36, the gravel is of the third class.

Positive Determination of Class of Gravel. As x and y may be taken to represent volumes of sand and stone as well as ratios, it follows from the definition of b' that

$$b' = \frac{y}{x}.$$

Gravel of the First Class. If the results of a test show that b' is less than b, then the gravel contains an excess of sand, the gravel is of the first class, and according to the specifications, stone must be added or the cement proportioned to the sand content of the unscreened gravel.

Gravel of the Second Class. If b' and b are equal it is evident, that the natural gravel contains sand and stone in proper proportions, and the gravel is of the second class. No modification of the natural gravel is necessary or desirable.

Gravel of the Third Class. If b' is greater than b, it is evident that stone is in excess and before the gravel may be used, sand must be added.

FORMULAE FOR PROPORTIONS—SECOND METHOD.

Gravel of the First Class—Formula for Cement (A). To find the number of bags of cement required per cubic foot of unscreened gravel:

The amount of sand in a cubic foot of gravel equals 1 times $x = x$ cubic feet, and as the required ratio of sand to cement equals a: then $\frac{x}{a}$ equals the cubic feet of cement to use with one cubic foot of gravel. One bag of cement, however, contains but 0.95 cu. ft. so that the number of bags of cement to use per cubic foot of gravel equals the number of cubic feet divided by 0.95 or

$$A = \frac{x}{a} \div 0.95 = \frac{x}{0.95a} \dots\dots\dots\dots\dots\dots (A).$$

To 6 cubic feet of gravel would then be required $6\left(\frac{x}{0.95a}\right)$ bags of cement; to 1 cu. yd. of gravel (27 cu. ft.) would be required $27\left(\frac{x}{0.95a}\right) = 28.4 \frac{x}{a}$ bags of cement, etc.

Gravel of the First Class—Formula for Gravel (B). To find the number of cubic feet of gravel to use with one bag of cement:

If "A" bags of cement must be used to one cubic foot of gravel then $\frac{1}{A}$ cubic feet of gravel would be required per bag of cement. As $A = \frac{x}{0.95a}$ then $\frac{1}{A} = \frac{0.95a}{x} =$ cubic feet of gravel per bag of cement $= \dots\dots\dots (B).$

Gravel of the First Class—Formula for Addition of Stone (C). To find the amount of stone to add to a cubic foot of gravel of the first class, when the addition of stone seems desirable to reduce the cost of cement:

By definition C equals the number of cubic feet of stone necessary to add to the natural stone content (y) of a cubic foot of gravel, so that the ratio of total stone to sand $\frac{x}{}$ in the mixture may equal b: Then,

$$b = \frac{y+C}{x} \text{ from which } C = bx - y \dots\dots\dots\dots(C).$$

Gravel of the First Class—Formula for Stone (D). It is frequently convenient to know how much stone would be required in case a 1- or 2-bag batch of gravel concrete is to be mixed. The amount of stone required for a 1-bag batch may be obtained by multiplying the result found by formula (B) by that found by formula (C), or the result may be found by a formula for D derived from formulae (B) and (C) as follows:

$$D = B \text{ times } C = \frac{0.95a(bx-y)}{x} = 0.95a\left(b-\frac{y}{x}\right) = 0.95a(b-b')\dots\dots\dots\dots\dots\dots(D).$$

Gravel of the Second Class. As gravel of the second class contains sand and stone in proper proportions, no modification by adding stone or sand is necessary. In all gravel concrete, however, the cement must be proportioned with respect to the sand content of the gravel. Either formula (A) or formula (B) may therefore be used.

Gravel of the Third Class—Formula for Sand (E). If b' is greater than b, stone is in excess, and before the gravel may be used, sand must be added. As previously stated, this condition is not common.

To find the amount of sand to add to a cubic foot of natural gravel when stone is in excess:

By definition, E equals the amount of sand which, when added to the sand contained in one cubic foot of the natural gravel, will make a ratio of stone to total sand equal b. Then $b = \frac{y}{x+E}$ from which $E + x = \frac{y}{b}$ and $E = \frac{y}{b} - x \dots\dots\dots\dots\dots\dots\dots\dots(E).$

Gravel of the Third Class—Formula for Cement (F). This formula determines the amount of cement to use with one cubic foot of gravel, and E cubic feet of sand. As the cement must be in proportion to the total sand, which in this case equals $x + E$, then A in formula (A) becomes F when $x + E$ is substituted for x.

$$\text{Then } F = \frac{x+E}{0.95a} = \frac{x+\left(\frac{y}{b}-x\right)}{0.95a} = \frac{y}{0.95ab} \dots\dots(F).$$

(Continued on page 106.)

CONVICT LABOR AT AVA

By B. H. Piepmeier, Maintenance Engineer State Highway Department, Springfield.

"The Old Devil's Washboard" is the name by which has been known for years an 8-mile strip of road leading south from Ava, Illinois, to the rich and fertile river bottoms of the Mississippi. The old road, or trail as it might well be called, justly deserved its name. It had been laid out according to the usual custom, along the section line, and it faithfully followed this line regardless of hills and hollows, except in some cases where it deviated in order to reach some particular farm.

Much money had to be spent on this road each year to keep up the numerous bridges and to fill the washes that followed nearly every rain. It had, for a long time, been apparent that if this road, which was impassable for a great portion of the year owing to inadequate grading and lack of drainage, could be im-

Convict Camp, Ava, Illinois. Fifty Convicts Spent the Winter in This Camp Working on a New Road From Ava to the Mississippi River Bottom.

proved the improvement would mean a boom, not only to the city of Ava, but to the farmers who desired to cultivate a great undeveloped area of some of the most fertile soil of this State.

The need of the improvement was very apparent, yet means to be used to secure it were not so evident until some progressive business men of Ava got together and communicated with the State Highway Commission and the Chief State Highway Engineer, asking for advice and assistance.

Building a 32-Foot Span Bridge. Timbers Hewn From Trees Cut From the Right-of-Way on the New Location.

The writer was subsequently assigned the task of investigating the conditions and to report as to the most feasible plan for making the improvement.

During the month of September the writer, assisted by Division Engineer J. E. Huber, spent several days in carefully going over the road and devising various plans and methods for doing the work in the most

Straightening a Stream on the New Location.

economical and feasible manner. Careful study showed that a well-constructed earth road, properly graded and drained, would economically serve the traffic requirements. Such a road could best be built by relocating a large portion of the old road and by providing the necessary grading and drainage for the entire route. The relocation was necessary in order to eliminate the various grades on the old route and to take advantage of the general topography of the country. After several days of reconnaisance an apparent location was found and although it varied in places from an eighth to a full mile from the old road, the proposed location actually shortened the route a full mile.

Cutting Down a Hill From 15 Per Cent Grade to 5 Per Cent on New Location.

Following the selection of this proposed route a mass meeting was called at Ava for the purpose of arranging the financing of the project. At this meeting committees were appointed for arousing the enthusiasm of all interested parties and for the purpose of soliciting

(Continued on page 108.)

ILLINOIS HIGHWAYS.

Published Monthly by the
State Highway Department,
Springfield, Illinois.

ILLINOIS HIGHWAY COMMISSION.

A. D. GASH, *President.*
S. E. BRADT, *Secretary.*
JAMES P. WILSON.

WM. W. MARR, *Chief State Highway Engineer.*

BUREAU OF ROADS.

H. E. BILGER, *Road Engineer.*
M. W. WATSON, *Assistant Road Engineer.*
C. M. HATHAWAY, *Office Engineer.*

BUREAU OF BRIDGES.

CLIFFORD OLDER, *Bridge Engineer.*
G. F. BURCH, *Assistant Bridge Engineer.*
A. W. CONSOER, *Office Engineer.*

BUREAU OF MAINTENANCE.

B. H. PIEPMEIER, *Maintenance Engineer.*
F. T. SHEETS, *Assistant Maintenance Engineer.*

BUREAU OF TESTS.

F. L. ROMAN, *Testing Engineer.*
W. C. ADAMS, *Chemist.*

BUREAU OF AUDITS.

J. M. McCOY, *Chief Clerk.*
EARL B. SEARCY, *Department Editor.*
R. R. McLEOD, *General Bookkeeper.*
G. E. HOPKINS, *Property Clerk.*

DIVISION ENGINEERS.

R. L. Bell, Buchanan-Link Bldg., Paris, Ill.
H. B. Bushnell, 144 Fox St., Aurora, Ill.
J. E. Huber, Wise Building, Mt. Vernon, Ill.
A. H. Hunter, 302 Apollo Theater Bldg., Peoria, Ill.
C. M. Slaymaker, 510 Metropolitan Bldg., E. St. Louis, Ill.
H. E. Surman, 614 People's Bank Bldg., Moline, Ill.
Fred Tarrant, State Highway Department, Springfield, Ill.

Address all communications in regard to "Illinois Highways," to State Highway Department, Springfield, Illinois.

CONTENTS.

A $900 contract has been awarded for the construction of a reinforced concrete bridge across Gillespie Branch, east of Checkrow, Illinois.

* * *

Approximately 3,000 feet of the proposed new 8,000-foot State gravel road at Montgomery and Geneseo have been completed.

* * *

County highway engineers from the northwest district, in their annual meeting early in September, at Galesburg, elected Alex Anderson, of Ogle County, president, and Harley Butt, of Knox County, secretary and treasurer. Bond issues for road building formed one of the important topics.

* * *

The Grafton Hard Road Improvement Association, in September, promoted a big dance, the revenues from which were applied to a road fund.

* * *

The Fargo Run concrete bridge, a mile north of the village of Kickapoo, has been completed at a cost of $3,695. Radnor Township, Peoria County, bore the expense.

* * *

Work is under way on the new "Clark Approach" concrete viaduct, 700 feet long, in Peoria. The structure will cost $120,000. It will span railroad trackage.

* * *

A contract has been awarded for a new $500 steel and concrete bridge over a slough at Volle's Corner, in Laenna Township, Logan County.

* * *

A bridge over Walbridge Creek, between Ottawa and Marseilles, is to be built at a cost of $2,470. It will be of concrete. The contract has been awarded.

* * *

The cost of construction of macadam State road in Winnebago County has been found to approximate $5,000 per mile. It was thought macadam could be laid down there for $2,000 and gravel for $3,000 a mile; but contracts let in Durand Township recently call for an expenditure of $5,125.62 a mile, or at that rate.

* * *

An auxiliary to the Community Club of upper Rock Island County has been formed for the purpose of promoting the "Good Luck" highway, from the quad-cities to Chicago. Improvement of a part of the road will be undertaken at once.

* * *

The St. Louis Bridge Company, owners of the Eads Bridge, in a recent assessment proceeding at Belleville, declared that the half of the big span which lies in St. Clair County and Illinois, is worth $2,500,000. The assessor had placed the value at a million dollars higher.

EARTH ROADS.

[By H. G. SHIRLEY, Chief Highway Engineer of Maryland.]

It will be many years before the earth road will be in the minority, and in many places it will neither be economical nor will the taxable resources justify the construction of a higher type.

The earth road has often been maintained by the most ignorant men, in fact it has not been maintained at all. It has been generally believed that it would take care of itself, requiring no work except, perhaps, the cutting away of bushes and possibly shaping with a road machine in the spring to give it better drainage to the side ditches. I know of no other type that has been so abused or has received the careless and inefficient maintenance to which the earth road has been subjected. There is no type upon which so much money is being wasted as the earth road, primarily through ignorance and neglect.

I have seen instances where a soft place existed in a hollow badly underdrained. Year after year a large amount of stone was hauled to this place and dumped on it, where it disappeared by the close of spring. Nevertheless this procedure would be steadily adhered to every successive year until the stone finally formed a compact mass. But the moisture in the earth made a mudhole at each end, and the same performance had to be repeated at each end the next year until a large

In maintaining earth roads we find that after the road has been properly shaped, the ditches opened, and the road given the proper cross section, a patrolman with a split-log drag can keep from five to eight miles in good condition for at least ten months in the year. The patrolman drags the road after each rain, when the earth is in a moist and damp condition, and thus the road is kept smooth and has the proper cross section. A description of the method of making and using such a drag can be obtained without charge from the U. S. Office of Public Roads and Rural Engineering at Washington.

When the road is dry and the surface is in good condition, the patrolman spends his time in opening up the gutters, filling any small washes that may occur in the shoulders, and if there are any spots in the road where the earth is soft and of such a nature that it will not bear the traffic, he digs it out and replaces it with

Maintenance of thousands of miles of improved roads has been seriously neglected.

As a result, improvements that cost millions of dollars to build have gone to ruin.

Ignorance on the part of an indifferent public has been largely to blame.

No financial oversight can be more disastrous to public welfare than failure to provide maintenance money for improved highways.

The character and volume of traffic determine the type of road to build, provided adequate maintenance is assured.

Economy, therefore, in road systems can be had only when proper maintenance is guaranteed.

No part of road work requires more skillful supervision than maintenance.

An inefficient method of maintenance will ruin the best of roads.

Nowhere is there a greater field for application of sound, business principles than in public highway maintenance.

Constant attention to detail, combined with cost study, produces efficiency.

Efficient maintenance—the secret of public highway success!

quantity of stone finally displaced the mud. This is expensive road building.

Earth roads should be worked in the early spring. If the roadbed is rutted, in bad condition, and flat, without the proper cross section, it should be plowed from gutter to gutter, shaped with a road machine until it has the proper cross section, and then kept constantly dragged until it is properly consolidated. After the road has been given this attention, then with a little constant care, it can be kept in good condition until the freezing and thawing are at hand, when it is necessary to dig it up again just as soon as the frost leaves the ground.

good material. In places where there are wet spots, owing to the lack of proper under drainage, the patrolman digs them out and fills them with stone or logs, making blind drains. I have found that by first putting down a layer of field stone, next placing three logs so as to form a kind of trough, and then filling in over the logs with stone, an efficient underdrain can be made to eliminate a wet spot.

To maintain a mile of earth road properly will cost from $40 to $100 a year, depending largely upon the character of soil upon which the road is built as well as upon the amount and kind of traffic.

TENTATIVE RULES FOR FEDERAL AID ACT DRAFTED BY STATE HIGHWAY OFFICIALS.

(Continued from page 99.)

Sec. 3. For all projects for which statements are submitted after December 31, 1916, standards governing the form and arrangement of plans, specifications and estimates will be hereafter prescribed and promulgated by the secretary.

Regulation 6. Project Agreements.

Sec. 1. A project agreement between the State Highway Department and the secretary shall be executed, in triplicate, on a form furnished by him, previous to commencement of the construction of the project.

Regulation 7. Contracts.

Sec. 1. Prior to the approval of the first project in a state, copies of the forms of the contracts, together with all documents referred to therein or made part thereof, and of the contractor's bonds proposed to be used under the act shall be submitted to the secretary. No alteration of such forms shall be made until it is approved by the secretary.

Sec. 2. Before work is begun on any project, adequate means must be adopted, either by advertising or by other devices appropriate for the purpose, to make certain that the Federal money set aside for the project is spent in the most economical and practical way to accomplish the objects for which it was appropriated.

Sec. 3. Immediately on publication of advertisements copies thereof shall be furnished to the Office of Public Roads.

Sec. 4. Bids shall be in such form that the unit prices at which the various services are to be performed, and the various materials furnished, will be clearly shown.

Sec. 5. Copy of the tabulated bid prices, showing the unit prices and the totals of each bid for every project, shall be furnished promptly to the Office of Public Roads.

Sec. 6. In advance of the acceptance of any bid, sufficient notice of the time and place the contract is to be awarded shall be given to the Office of Public Roads to enable it, if it so desire, to have a representative present. When a bid has been accepted prompt notice thereof shall be given to the Office of Public Roads.

Sec. 7 If the contract be awarded to any other than the lowest responsible bidder, the Federal Government shall not pay more than its pro rata share of the lowest responsible bid, unless it be satisfactorily shown that it was advantageous to the work to accept the higher bid.

Sec. 8. A copy of each contract as executed shall be immediately certified by the State Highway Department and furnished to the Office of Public Roads.

Sec. 9. The specifications and plans shall be made a part of the contract.

Sec. 10. No alteration in such contract shall be made without the approval of the secretary.

Regulation 8. Construction Work and Labor.

Section 1. Suitable samples of materials to be used in construction work shall be submitted, by or on behalf of the State Highway Department, to the Office of Public Roads whenever requested.

Sec. 2. Unless otherwise stipulated in writing by the secretary or his authorized representative, materials for the construction of any project shall, prior to use, be tested for conformity with specifications, according to methods prescribed, or approved, by the Office of Public Roads.

Sec. 3. Unless otherwise specifically stipulated in the project agreement, bridges, viaducts and underpasses shall have clear width of roadway of not less than 16 feet, and clear head room of not less than 14 feet for a width of 8 feet at the center.

Sec. 4. No part of the money apportioned under the act shall be used, directly or indirectly, to pay, or to reimburse a state, county or local subdivision for the payment of, any premium or royalty on any patented or proprietary material, specification, process, or type of construction, unless the work is open to actual competitive bidding.

Sec. 5. The supervision of each project by the State Highway Department shall include adequate inspection throughout the course of construction, to be paid out of the 10 per cent fund.

Sec. 6. Written notice of commencement and completion of construction work on any project shall be given promptly by the State Highway Department to the Office of Public Roads.

Sec. 7. Reports of the progress of construction, showing force employed and work done, shall be furnished, from time to time, whenever requested by the secretary or his authorized representative.

Sec. 8. Labor, teams, materials and equipment furnished, in lieu of money, by or on behalf of the State Highway Department on construction work shall be used only on such terms and conditions as are set forth in the project agreement, unless amended to meet changed conditions.

Regulation 9. Records and Cost Keeping.

Section 1. A separate account for each project shall be kept by or under the direction of the State Highway Department. The account shall be kept in such way as to enable the secretary, or his authorized representative, to ascertain at any time the expenditures on and the liabilities against the project and, separately, the condition of the 10 per cent fund.

Sec. 2. Such other records of contract and force account work, and of inspections and tests by or on behalf of the state, shall be kept, by or under the direction of the State Highway Department, as will enable the secretary, or his authorized representative, at any time to determine the condition of the construction and maintenance of, and the cost of the construction work and labor done on, any project, to the State and Federal Government.

Sec. 3. The accounts and records, together with all supporting documents, shall be open, at all times, to the inspection of the secretary, or his authorized representative, and copies thereof shall be furnished when requested.

Sec. 4. Certified copies of pay rolls on force account work and of all vouchers for other expenditures shall be furnished, whenever requested by the secretary or his authorized representative.

Sec. 5. Unit costs to the State and Federal Government on any project shall be kept, on forms furnished by the Office of Public Roads, whenever requested by the Secretary or his authorized representative.

Regulation 10. Payments.

Section 1. Vouchers, in the form provided by the secretary and certified as therein prescribed, showing amounts expended on any project and amount claimed to be due from the Federal Government on account thereof, shall be submitted by the State Highway Department to the Office of Public Roads, either after completion of construction of the project or, if the secretary has determined to make payments as the construction progresses, at intervals of not less than one month.

Regulation 11. Office of Public Roads.

Section 1. Papers and documents required by the act or these regulations to be submitted to the secretary may be delivered to the Office of Public Roads and from the date of such delivery shall be deemed submitted.

Sec. 2. The Director of the Office of Public Roads, and such other officials and employees thereof as the director, from time to time, may designate for the purpose, shall be deemed the authorized representatives of the secretary within the meaning of that phrase as used in these regulations.

GRAVEL TESTING.

(Continued from page 102.)

Gravel of the Third Class—Formula for Gravel (G).
The amount of gravel to use for a 1-bag batch may be found from "F" as follows:

If F bags of cement are required per cubic foot of gravel $\dfrac{1}{F}$ = cubic feet of gravel to use with one bag of cement

$$\text{cement} = 1 \div \frac{y}{0.95ab} = \frac{0.95ab}{y} = \dots\dots\dots\dots(G).$$

Gravel of the Third Class—Formula for Sand (H).
As the number of cubic feet of gravel required for a 1-bag batch = "G," and the amount of sand per cubic foot of gravel = E, then $H = G \times E = \dfrac{0.95ab}{y} \times$

$$(\frac{y}{b} - x) = \frac{0.95ab\left(\frac{y}{b} - x\right)}{y} = \frac{0.95a\,(y - bx)}{y} =$$

$$0.95a \times (1 - \frac{bx}{y}) = 0.95a\,(1 - \frac{b}{b'}) \dots\dots\dots (H).$$

GENERAL AND SIMPLIFIED FORMULAE FOR DETERMINATION OF PROPORTION.

Class of concrete.	Proportions	Required ratio of sand to cement.	Maximum ratio of stone to sand.	Bags of cement required per cu. ft. of gravel of the first or second class.	Cu. ft. of the first or second class gravel per bag of cement.	Maximum number of cu. ft. of stone which may be added per cu. ft. of gravel of the first class.	Maximum number of cu. ft. of stone which may be added per cu. ft. of gravel of the first class.	Cu. ft. of sand which must be added per cu. ft. of gravel of the third class.	Bags of cement per cu. ft. of gravel of the third class.	Cu. ft. of gravel of the third class per bag of cement.	Cu. ft. of sand required per bag batch of gravel of the third class.
		a	b	$A = \dfrac{x}{0.95a}$	$B = \dfrac{0.95a}{x}$	$C = bx - y$	$D = 0.95a\,(b - b')$	$E = \dfrac{y}{b} - x$	$F = \dfrac{y}{0.95ab}$	$G = \dfrac{0.95ab}{y}$	$H = 0.95a\left(1 - \dfrac{b}{b'}\right)$
X	1-2-3½	2	1.75	$0.53x$	$\dfrac{1.9}{x}$	$1.75x - y$	$3.33 - 1.9b'$	$0.57y - x$	$0.30y$	$\dfrac{3.33}{y}$	$1.90 - \dfrac{3.33}{b'}$
A	1-2½-4	2.5	1.60	$0.42x$	$\dfrac{2.38}{x}$	$1.60x - y$	$3.80 - 2.38b'$	$0.63y - x$	$0.26y$	$\dfrac{3.80}{y}$	$2.38 - \dfrac{3.80}{b'}$
B	1-3-5	3	1.67	$0.35x$	$\dfrac{2.85}{x}$	$1.67x - y$	$4.75 - 2.85b'$	$0.60y - x$	$0.21y$	$\dfrac{4.75}{y}$	$2.85 - \dfrac{4.75}{b'}$

a = required ratio of sand to cement.
b = maximum ratio of stone to sand.
x = ratio of sand to gravel.
y = ratio of stone to gravel.

$b' = \dfrac{y}{x}$

b' is less than b for gravel for the first class.
b' equals b for gravel of the second class.
b' is greater than b for gravel of the third class.

Simplified Formulae. As the specifications provide but three classes of concrete, the various formulae heretofore given may be simplified by the substitution of the actual values of a and b in each formula for each class of concrete. A tabulation of the general and simplified formulae is given in the above table.

THE ROAD DRAGGING SYSTEM IN SANGAMON COUNTY.

County Superintendent of Highways Edwin H. White, of Sangamon County, is watching with satisfaction the successful operation of an original plan for the systematic dragging of roads within the county.

The county board of supervisors was prevailed upon to appropriate $600 for the dragging; business men of Springfield raised another $600. This brought the total of the fund to $1,200, which the county highway superintendent says will carry the work through the current fall and winter season.

RANDOM PICTURE OF A MAIN ROAD LEADING INTO SPRINGFIELD. ONE OF THE SEVERAL HIGHWAYS UNDER COUNTY SUPERINTENDENT WHITE'S CARE.

Initiated by Mr. White, the plan was promoted by the Springfield Motor Club, under the auspices of the Springfield Commercial Association. The business men's half of the fund was raised chiefly by the motor club members.

In using this table it should be held in mind that the various formulae for finding the amount of cement required, are based on the natural or pit-run gravel and not on the modified gravel aggregate, when stone or sand has been added.

Nine main road arteries lead out from Springfield. The combined mileage which is under drag in the White system, is approximately 45 miles. Up to the last of September, 256 miles of dragging had been done, and the men to whom the dragging contracts were let were engaged in carrying their work into the late fall. Results have brought satisfaction to both the county officials and to those who have used the roads.

In awarding contracts for dragging, Mr. White gets the best figures he can, then places an individual contractor in complete charge of a given main road stretch. These sections run from four to seven miles each in length. For the proper, timely and efficient dragging of his road stretch, each contractor is held absolutely responsible. The county superintendent, of course, checks up on his work, and at all times is in touch with what is going on, both through personal inspection and through reports.

The contractor must drag 24 feet wide. Instructions which the county superintendent of highways issues to him are plain, easy to understand and comprehensive. The man who drags knows what is expected of him and when to do his work. Since the scheme was inaugurated in July, not a complaint of the results has been heard.

Of course, with a fund of only $1,200, all the roads of the county can not be treated. But the main roads are being taken care of, and, moreover, the plan is having a decidedly beneficial effect in that township commissioners, seeing the main road results, are loath to have their own minor stretches of highway go untouched. The "moral effect" is good, therefore.

When a stretch of road has been dragged, of course, the good work is not complete. Drivers of automobiles and wagons must drive in such a way as not to undo the work of the drag. This fact is realized by County Highway Superintendent White, who has succeeded in getting first-class cooperation from the users of cars and vehicles of all kinds.

CONVICT LABOR AT AVA.

(Continued from page 103.)

both money and labor, the cash donations to go for establishing a convict camp and the labor donations, consisting of the free use of teams, etc., to be used in the actual construction work after the organization of the road camp.

The development of the plans for the work at Ava finally reached a point where it was necessary to make the arrangements for establishing a convict camp and accordingly the proposition was put before, and acted upon, by the proper authorities.

On November 12, twenty-five automobiles in a parade drove into Menard, the Southern Illinois penitentiary, and carried back to Ava the fifty convicts, whom Warden Choisser had chosen to make up the proposed road camp. The interest and spirit of the men was remarkable. Although they were to start upon work which meant real labor, yet the opportunity offered them to get out into the open and once more get a little breath of freedom, even if it was under the restrictions of camp rules, seemed to cheer the men up wonderfully and the parade of automobiles had the appearance of a pleasure outing rather than that of a group of convicts on their way to hard labor. Captain McAfee, of the Southern Illinois penitentiary, was in direct charge of the men and he organized them, in accordance with their ability, into groups for the performance of particular work in establishing the camp. Everything moved along like clockwork and it was but 24 hours after the arrival of the men at the selected location that everything was seemingly in good order and the men ready to start the actual work of road construction.

LAYING A DRY STONE WALL DIVIDING A STREAM, AND PROTECTING
THE ROAD ON A NEW LOCATION.

Mr. D. S. James, an experienced road builder from the State Highway Department, was placed in immediate charge of the construction work. All forces were at once set to work under his direction in clearing and grading the right-of-way, building bridges, placing stones, and excavating and draining the road. Two weeks after the camp had been established, the work had progressed so nicely that the new location had begun to take on the appearance of a real road and it is very apparent that if the proposition undertaken is finally completed with the same success as has attended its beginning, it will go a long ways towards proving the theory of the State that convict camps established for the purpose of constructing roads for the public good are an ideal medium for constructing many roads and keeping the convicts

AT WORK ON THE NEW LOCATION.

busy and interested, and preventing some of the objectionable features of ordinary prison life.

In this particular camp at Ava the interest that was taken by the men in their work was noticeable even to a casual observer. Many of the convicts had never been accustomed to outdoor and muscular work and the many little diversions connected with the activities of this camp furnished them numerous topics for conversation and discussion, resulting in broadening their knowledge of men and affairs.

The success of this camp is perhaps largely due, first to the character of the men selected, and, second, to the careful direction given by those in charge. It did not take long for all the men to become very efficient in their work, due primarily to the interest which they took in it. Another point which might well be mentioned here is that comments were heard from many taxpayers of the community to the effect that a convict camp, established and directed as this one was, is as desirable for the community as the ordinary contractor's camp. The reason is that the penitentiary authorities select the highest type of men. This together with the restrictions and supervision given makes convict labor camps very efficient for the ordinary road work.

MODEL OF REINFORCED CONCRETE THROUGH GIRDER BRIDGE.

[By A. W. CONSOER, Office Engineer, Bureau of Bridges.]

The State Highway Department some time ago decided to have prepared a number of road and bridge models for exhibition purposes.

The U. S. Bureau of Public Roads has used similar models and it has been noticeable that they convey to the layman more information as to various construction features than can be shown by any other method. At the Illinois State Fair last year the State Highway Department in their exhibit displayed a model which was loaned by a material company, showing the various steps of concrete road construction and it was noticeable that this one feature created more interest and more comment than any other part of the exhibit. The department, therefore, took steps to secure for itself such models as might prove of the most use. The first of these models has been completed and is now on exhibition in the offices of the State Highway Commission at Springfield. It represents the various steps in the construction of a reinforced concrete through girder bridge. The model is sufficiently large to show the minutest details of construction. The falsework bents are shown in position resting on piles and supporting the forms for the girders and floor slab. At the left the girder forms are shown in position. The manner of bracing the girder forms is clearly shown. The next section shows the reinforcing bars for the girder and floor slab in position. The last section shows the finished concrete girder as it appears after the girder forms have been removed. A portion of the abutment at the right has been removed to show the end rocker bearing of the girder, which is a necessary feature of this form of construction. Near the bottom of this abutment

another portion of the wing wall has been removed to show the position of the reinforcing bars in the wing wall and footing. The back fill is shown in position and the model clearly shows how the wing walls are designed to properly restrain the back fill slopes from obstructing the waterway of the bridge.

While the model is not accurate in regard to a few technical and construction details, it is an excellent representation of this form of bridge construction and will add to the interest of future exhibits made by the Illinois State Highway Department.

 # ILLINOIS HIGHWAY PROGRESS SHOWN IN STATE FAIR EXHIBIT.

The Illinois State Highway Department exhibit at the State fair, September 15 to 23, served not only to instruct thousands of citizens in the science of State road building, to a degree, but also brought satisfaction to the Governor and other officials of Illinois and particularly to the State Highway Department members, whose earnest policies and efforts for road improvement were, in a measure, illustrated in the models, pictures and the maps which made up the display.

Occupying a prominent position along the east side of Machinery Hall, the highway exhibit was easily accessible. The big banner sign, which surmounted the whole display, attracted the attention of everyone who passed through the hall. Consequently, the list of callers was exceptionally large.

One of the first features of the exhibit which held the eye was the highway commission's large map, showing proposed State-aid routes and the amount of road in each case which had been completed. The kinds of roads diagrammed were earth, oiled earth, macadam or gravel, oiled macadam or gravel and concrete or brick. Each route in the map is so marked as to identify the type of construction.

Another of the features was the artistic and instructive picture group, in colors, loaned for the display

by the Barrett Manufacturing Company. Thirty views made up the collection. All were mounted in a cabinet and were shown in transparency, by means of illumination. The group comprised views of bituminous roads in construction.

Five road and three bridge models, which were shown, served to convey to the public a facsimile idea of construction in those lines. E. H. J. Lorenz of Madison, Wis., is the maker of the models displayed. There was the reinforced concrete slab bridge, with brick rails, with exposed sections to show details. Then, there was the reinforced concrete culvert, with exposed cross section showing details. A little grader model, setting upon a graded road model, and a form showing a reinforced concrete through girder bridge, were included in the collection. The road forms exhibited were those showing construction of bituminous macadam, brick, gravel, bituminous concrete and concrete road.

Owners and drivers of automobiles who thronged the exhibit found genuine pleasure in sitting, many of them for a long time, and studying the "motorists' map," which portrayed, in enlarged form, all the automobile routes and trails in Illinois, marked so as to show the colors for each.

(Continued on page 111.)

Correspondence Course in Road Building
CONDUCTED BY UNIVERSITY OF ILLINOIS.
Lesson 5.—Grades and Vertical Curves.

Grades are required on a road to reach points of different elevation. The rate of slope or gradient is expressed in per cents of the horizontal distance. Thus a slope of 1 foot in 100 feet (horizontal) is said to be a 1 per cent grade, or a 5 per cent grade is one which rises 5 feet in 100.

MINIMUM GRADES.

As far as traffic or the road surface is concerned a level grade or 0 per cent gradient can be used. The side ditches, however, must have some fall and if the road surface is level this must be obtained by deepening the ditch thus changing the cross-section. It is therefore more usual to give both the surface and the ditches the same slope which should not be less than 0.1 per cent and preferably should be at least 0.2 per cent. Occasionally however it is necessary to give the ditches a different slope from that of the surface, even to the extent of having opposite slopes, as for example at bridge approaches. In choosing a grade line care must be taken that the ditches receive the necessary slope for perfect drainage and that the road surface is kept well above the ditch level.

MAXIMUM GRADES.

The maximum gradient for a ditch is fixed by the tendency of the soil to wash. If the gradient can not be made flat enough to prevent wash, it may be necessary to pave the ditch, line it with concrete, or use tile.

The maximum gradient for a road surface is fixed by traffic requirements, and the maximum gradient and character of road surface are closely related.

Tractive resistance. Every road surface exerts a resistance to the movement of a vehicle and is expressed as the number of pounds of direct pull required for each ton of load. The load which a given motive power can pull on a given level road therefore depends on the kind and condition of the surface. Thus if we assume that a horse weighs 1,500 lb. and his normal pull is one-tenth of his weight, the total load (including the vehicle) he can pull on a level road having a resistance of 50 lb. per ton is

$$\frac{1,500 \times 1/10}{50} = 3 \text{ tons,}$$

or if the road resistance is 100 lb.-ton the load is 1½ tons.

Grade Resistance. A grade offers a resistance to a load since it is an inclined plane and the action of gravity tends to pull a load down a grade or resist its movement up the grade with a force which depends on the angle of slope. This force, for all practical purposes, is found to be 20 lb. per ton for each per cent of the grade. Thus the grade resistance to 2 tons on a 5 per cent grade is $2 \times 5 \times 20 = 200$ lb.

The maximum grade up which a load can be pulled depends on how much the motive power can increase its normal effort. Taking the example above and assuming that the horse can double his effort the grade up which he can pull the 3-ton load is

$$\frac{150}{3 \times 20} = 2.5 \text{ per cent}$$

while the grade up which he can pull the 1½-ton load is

$$\frac{150}{1\frac{1}{2} \times 20} = 5 \text{ per cent.}$$

It is therefore seen that the smoother the road the greater the effect of grade and the less must be the maximum grade on the smooth road if the full benefit of the smooth road is to be obtained.

Exactly the same principles apply to motor vehicles so far as maximum grades are concerned. Taking into consideration these factors and the speed of motor traffic about 6 per cent is the desirable maximum, although considerably steeper grades may be used under special conditions. On long, steep grades horses may become fatigued and provision for rest should be made by introducing short stretches of flat gradient at convenient intervals. Such spaces are also of use to motor vehicles in case of tire trouble or accidents to the machinery.

VERTICAL CURVES.

Where two different gradients meet, the abrupt change of slope will round itself off to some extent, but if the change of gradient is greater than about 2 per cent a regular vertical curve should be introduced.

These curves should have a length of not less than 15 feet for each per cent change in grade, and as much longer than this as conditions will permit. Very short curves may be used where space is cramped and traffic must move slowly. At the crest of sharp grades, especially where traffic from either direction may move rapidly, the curves should be lengthened as much as possible so that approaching drivers may see each other over the crest in ample time to pass safely. Long easy vertical curves are also material aids in reducing expansion troubles on concrete and brick roads.

A vertical curve is staked out the same as any other part of the grade line by determining the elevation of convenient points and driving grade stakes to these elevations. Stakes are usually placed 25 feet apart on the curves and therefore for convenience the total length of vertical curves should be some *even* multiple of 25, as 50, 100, 150, etc.

There are several methods of computing a vertical curve, but the following one is perhaps the clearest and easiest to follow and hence less liable to mistake for the person who computes them infrequently. A sketch is always of material aid in making the computations.

The curve used is a parabola and only two things are necessary to remember to compute the elevations: First, that the offsets from the tangents (corrections from the straight grade lines) vary with the *square* of the distance from the point of tangency (end of curve). Second, a method to find any one offset, from which the others can be computed.

In the accompanying figure, grade g_1 meets grade g_2 at the point K whose elevation is known.

Compute the elevations of A, H, J, L, M, G, which are the points on the straight grades corresponding to the desired points on the vertical curve.

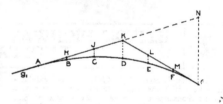

Extend grade g_1 beyond K to N, one-half of the length of the curve and compute the elevation of N. The difference in elevation of N and G is the offset NG.

Then
$$HB : NG :: AH^2 : AN^2$$
$$JC : NG :: AJ^2 : AN^2$$
etc.

If the distances AH, AJ, AN, etc., are taken in units of 25 feet instead of feet it simplifies the squaring of the numbers as the succeeding ordinates will be in the ratio to each other of 1^2, 2^2, 3^2, etc. Whence if the first ordinate HB is found the others can be found by multiplying it by 4, 9, 16, etc. It is unnecessary to compute ordinates beyond the middle of the curve since $MF = HB$, $LE = JC$, etc.

Knowing these offsets the elevations of the points B, C, D, E and F, are easily determined.

For example, assume that $g_1 = +2.0$ per cent (up grade) meets $g_2 = -2.8$ per cent (down grade) at an elevation of 520.50 and a vertical curve 150 ft. (6 units of 25 ft.) long is to be used.

Elev. $A = 520.50 - 0.75 \times 2.0 = 519.00$
Elev. $H = 520.50 - 0.50 \times 2.0 = 519.50$
Elev. $J = 520.50 - 0.25 \times 2.0 = 520.00$
Elev. $L = 520.50 - 0.25 \times 2.8 = 519.80$
Elev. $M = 520.50 - 0.50 \times 2.8 = 519.10$
Elev. $G = 520.50 - 0.75 \times 2.8 = 518.40$
Elev. $N = 520.50 + 0.75 \times 2.0 = 522.00$

Ord. $NG = 522.00 - 518.40 = 3.60$

Ord. $HB = MF = \dfrac{1^2 \times 3.60}{6^2} = 0.10$

Ord. $JC = LE = \dfrac{2^2 \times 3.60}{6^2} = 0.40 = 4 \times HB$

Ord. $KD = \dfrac{3^2 \times 3.60}{6^2} = 0.90 = 9 \times HB$

The elevations on the curve are then:

Elev. $A =$	519.00
Elev. $B = 519.50 - 0.10 =$	519.40
Elev. $C = 520.00 - 0.40 =$	519.60
Elev. $D = 520.50 - 0.90 =$	519.60
Elev. $E = 519.80 - 0.40 =$	519.40
Elev. $M = 519.10 - 0.10 =$	519.00
Elev. $G =$	518.40

ILLINOIS HIGHWAY PROGRESS SHOWN IN STATE FAIR EXHIBIT.

(Continued from page 109.)

Numerous requests were left with those in charge of the exhibit for copies of the big map, and scores of callers took away with them copies of the July ILLINOIS HIGHWAYS, the official publication of the department. which contained a reduced, though adequate, reproduction of the big, original map. The "motorists' map" occupied a position in the north end of the exhibit.

An important feature of the exhibit was the collection of photographs, showing maintenance methods as actually pursued under the supervision of the State Highway Department. These pictures covered the east wall of the exhibit space.

The visitor, looking at this interesting gallery, was brought face to face with work on sections B and C, in Vermilion County, in which work in relocating an important road involved the excavating of over 50,000

cubic yards of earth within a little over half a mile. The picture showed work on a big hill and cut.

An interesting comparison was shown in a picture taken in McDonough County. A new steel bridge had been erected alongside the old wooden structure. The modern idea of safe bridge building was contrasted strikingly with the antiquated notion of wood construction.

Algonquin Hill, a famous—or infamous—grade in Kane County was shown, in one of the pictures, as it looks to-day after having been trimmed down under the supervision of the State Highway Department. Formerly, this dreaded hill attained a maximum grade of approximately 14 per cent. After many weeks of strenuous work, the grade was reduced to the welcome average of $3\frac{1}{2}$ per cent—a marked improvement.

Governor Dunne and State Highway Commissioners Gash, Bradt and Wilson, with experts from the State Highway Department, are shown in one of the pictures at the scene of very recent improvements on the Jacksonville road, two miles west of Springfield. New concrete was being laid and the official party had been there to learn, first hand, what was being done. This was only one of their many visits to Illinois highways, either in process of improvement or in need of it.

Another of the striking pictures was that of a deep cut in LaSalle County, $1\frac{3}{4}$ miles south of Utica, showing extensive work which has been done on Section A of that county.

The State Highway Exhibit, while espoused and authoribed by the State Highway Commissioners themselves, was in immediate charge of a squad of department men, headed by A. W. Consoer, N. L. Bunn, V. J. Flanagan and W. S. Todd, all of the Bureau of Bridges.

 # PERMANENT ROADS WILL SAVE FULTON COUNTY BIG SUM.

That the county of Fulton will be able to save forty thousand dollars a year, and, at the same time, have the complete use of a system of permanent roads, in the event a million dollar bond issue should be voted, is the declaration of Mr. W. M. Fike, a land value expert. Mr. Fike has prepared a statement which, taken from *The Fulton County News*, published at Lewistown, is reproduced in part herewith:

The plain figures are here for your inspection, showing just what is being expended by the county as a whole and by each individual township, and every one knows that there is nothing to show for this vast expenditure of money for roads outside of Canton township except some bridges which have recently been built with the money. Knox and Peoria Counties are sure to vote bond issues for this purpose and unless Fulton County acts promptly she will be left far in the rear in development. The fact that it really saves money should be sufficient reason to support such a proposition, but there will be some who will endeavor to be consistent by continuing their opposition to what they term "hard" roads.

But Mr. Fike has entirely omitted one point in his calculation and which is a most important one, as many will object to a system of roads in view of the fact that "there will be other roads to keep up." Fulton County would be entitled to the maximum of State aid

money under this plan and this amount would not only be sufficient to pay interest on this million dollar bond issue, but at the same time if the county so chose it would take care of all the intersecting roads that would not be included in a system of highways for the county.

Taking the cost of such work in other counties as a criterion it may be safely estimated that from 120 to 150 miles of permanent road could be constructed with this million dollars, according to the material selected and the width of the road decided upon. Experience has proven that length of road is far better than a short road of great width as there is never any congestion on a good road where traffic moves along smoothly. Very rarely is over 9 feet of roadway actually used except for a short distance into the more populous communities. A plan of this sort would build a perfect network of roads and would be assurance that no one in Fulton County could live more than four miles off an improved road and that every village would be reached by the system.

Vermilion County recently let nine contracts for the building of its million and a half dollar system of roads, each one being started at the outskirts of the county and the county itself is physically much rougher than is Fulton. It is estimated that it will be three years before the 164 miles contracted for of brick and concrete will be completed, during which time of course the use of only a portion of the bond money will be required so that the full amount of this obligation will not be reached till the end of the three years or the completion of the work, which will make a nice little offset on the total expense.

A permanent system of roads means more prosperity all around. It means that the farmer can get to town any day in the year, can market his crops when the market is the highest, regardless of the season, and can move them over the roads at a minimum expense of horsepower, instead of literally killing his animals as was the case in more than one instance during the many months of impassable roads the past winter and spring. It means that the towns will become more prosperous as the people can get to town easier and oftener to do their trading and farm supplies will be plentiful for the villager, an experience which is not to be had for months at a time under present conditions. It means increased values, increased improvements and extensive developments—it means that Fulton County will quit building up the country in the southwest and west where thousands of her best citizens have gone during the past two generations, a loss which no county can sustain without vitally affecting its progress.

Here are the plain figures without comment as collated by Mr. Fike for the information of the people of Fulton County:

An estimated cost of a $1,000,000, bond issue payable in 20 equal annual installments, together with interest thereon, to wit:

One-twentieth part of $1,000,000.........$50,000
Approximate average annual interest per
   year 22,500

      Total annual principal and interest....$72,500
Total amount paid on principal of bonds in 20
   years $1,000,000
Total amount paid on interest of bonds in 20
   years 450,000

      Total paid $1,450,000
Total value of property for year 1915, in
   Fulton County, upon which taxes were
   extended $18,139,619

Eighty acres of land worth $12,000, assessed at $4,000, would be taxed approximately annually about .004 or $16, or 20c per acre.

The party with a home worth $1,500, assessed at $500, would pay $2 per annum, in order to raise the $72,500 per annum.

For the year 1914, the amount paid to Road and Bridge Fund was $104,579.71.

For the year 1915, the amount paid to Road and Bridge Fund was $114,520.01.

Just a glance will show anyone, that there is a fund of almost $100,000—$89,158 to be exact—which is available for one year's expenditures on the highways in Fulton, Knox and Peoria Counties.

Shall this money be spent in piecemeal fashion, or shall it be spent with the idea of making a connected system of permanent highways? Are the people more anxious for a few bridges scattered about in isolated places than they are for a general system of permanent highways? Shall we continue living in the present, or shall we make our highway ideas conform to our business ideas, and look to the future with our road work?

In all matters pertaining to our business, whether it be running a store, conducting a factory or operating a farm, we look to the future in our buildings and the general conduct of our business. Why not have the same ideas and carry out those ideas in the making of roads?

Farmington Township taxpayers helped to build some of Canton Township's permanent roads. There may be no immediate benefit to us personally, but if those roads become a part of a county system we are bound to get our share of the benefit. Let's all do our share to lift Illinois out of the mud, a mud that is rich in crop-producing qualities, and rich in the production of cuss words when you try to haul those same crops to market through it—through it, not over it.—*Farmington Bugle.*

The following is a copy of the records showing the amount of tax extended for road and bridge purposes for the various townships in Fulton County, for a term of ten years from 1906 to 1915, both inclusive, but which does not show the separate amounts for each township paid by the railroad companies and other corporations, nor does it show the separate amounts for each township paid out by Fulton County to road and bridge fund, but does show the total amount paid by the two latter accounts, together with the aggregate amount paid in from all sources to road and bridge fund for said term of ten years, to wit:

Astoria...............................	$ 26,162 13
Vermont..............................	27,657 04
Farmers..............................	22,330 17
Harris...............................	13,108 78
Lee..................................	23,552 28
Union................................	32,957 32
Woodland.............................	21,018 67
Pleasant.............................	23,307 64
Bernadotte...........................	18,594 04
Cass.................................	18,426 60
Deerfield............................	21,171 82
Ellisville...........................	10,199 27
Young Hickory........................	16,961 87
Kerton...............................	8,466 47
Isabel...............................	14,117 03
Waterford............................	4,444 93
Lewistown............................	44,741 70
Putman...............................	32,999 73
Joshua...............................	35,298 51
Fairview.............................	40,819 53
Liverpool............................	18,496 51
Buckheart............................	25,982 04
Canton...............................	102,563 84
Farmington...........................	56,149 24
Banner...............................	14,243 74
Orion................................	17,337 51
Total...............................	$691,108 41

ILLINOIS HIGHWAYS

[Printed by authority of the State of Illinois.]

OFFICIAL PUBLICATION OF THE

STATE HIGHWAY DEPARTMENT

| VOL. III | SPRINGFIELD, ILLINOIS, OCTOBER, 1916 | No. 10 |

SOLUTION

of the Problem of Safety upon our highways lies with You, the Individual. Look to the well-being of Yourself, as you travel the roads that link our Communites; see to it that You exercise the care you ought to in efforts to eliminate Hazard for your fellow travelers, and you will become at once a potent factor and Aid in the cause which we present at this time as our Appeal—

SAFETY FIRST

MY earnest sympathies and endeavors are emphatically with the man or woman who seeks to promote and carry out the idea of "Safety First" in the things that we do. Too often we are careless, and our indifference to the welfare of self in many cases spells disaster to our fellows.

SELF-protection, and the safeguarding of the physical interests of others are embodied in the great principle of "Safety First," as it should apply to our public highways. We are building good roads in Illinois. Let us conserve the lives of those who travel them, whether in automobiles, horse-drawn conveyances, or afoot.

I lend my hearty endorsement to any plan that elevates the value of human life. It is sacred, and nothing can condone the thoughtlessness of man which prompts him to jeopardize the well-being of himself and of those who travel with him.

WE want the best of highways, the most efficient in roads that man can build. Let us now strive for the safest that can be had in the way of travel. Let each individual put up to himself the problem of safety, and make its solution a personal responsibility. If he takes care of himself while using the highways, his fellow travelers are pretty apt to share his immunity from danger.

GOD speed the day when Illinois shall travel from the northern line to Cairo, free from mud; but in so doing, let her people escape the shame of peril from careless and inexcusable desecration of the rights of the roads. It is time lost that is temporarily saved at the risk of life and limb, unless the emergency itself be a question so vital that haste must needs be employed.

> Edward F. Dunne,
> Governor of Illinois.

The Hazard of the Roads; What Are You Doing to Remove It?

"Safety First!"

Is there anyone who has not heard this phrase, or slogan? Sometimes it applies as a warning against possible danger, sometimes as an alibi of one afraid to dare, and then again we sometimes are forced to listen to the strange variety of individual who would redicule the saying. Anyway, we all have heard it. It is a *bona fide*, legitimate, modern piece of word structure, this phrase; and it is intended to convey that there is merit in the conservation of human, as well as natural, resources.

ILLINOIS HIGHWAYS has access to a quantity of reports, in which county highway superintendents, the last year or so, have delineated accidents and have narrated causes thereof, upon roads which lie within their jurisdiction. The aggregate story these reports tell is pitiful.

We wonder that men and women, supposed to have at least the ordinary, instinctive impulse for self-protection, indulge the practices that lead to these county reports of causalties, disasters and tragedies.

"Safety First!"

You glance at this and immediately conclude that, in order to make the slogan operative, you must look to the way you cross a street crowded with pedestrians and vehicles; or that you must sweep both ways a railroad right-of-way before you start over the track; or, again, that you must exercise, perhaps, the rule of "hands off" when near machinery that offers a possible hazard.

While the State Highway Department sympathizes with and cooperates, so far as possible, with all lines of "safety first" advancement, its chief interest lies in the highways of Illinois, and the hazards, if any, that they present.

To return to the county reports. The story they tell is, as we said, pitiful. They sense a combination of misfortune, negligence, bad luck and indifference to personal safety. They reveal statute violation, and an utter defiance of both human and civil laws. Rules of the road, courtesies among tourists, simple principles of travel etiquette—all are sacrified by those whose misdirected energies are translated by sudden mishap, into awful penalties.

We harbor no desire to burden the reader with "horrible examples." They are numerous enough, to be sure, but, the question whether they really serve as object lessons, is debatable. Yet, in all sincerity, it seems apropos and expedient to acquaint our friends with a few of the reports, in essence, which have come into the department, and attempts made in them to ascribe causes for the accidents. Here, in substance, are a few of the county superintendents' reports:

An automobile party, familiar with an interurban crossing obscured partly by an orchard, failed to approach the intersection with due caution. In the crash which followed, four were injured.

In eastern Illinois, recently, a party were driving too fast. The car skidded, overturned, and three were hurt.

A case from northern Illinois. A driver tried to make a corner at a high rate of speed. Two were injured in the accident that followed.

Two drivers in southern Illinois approached cross roads at a high rate of speed. Both were familiar with the interesection. They met at a right angle and one was hurt.

Here is one that you will say was absolutely inexcusable. Two cars were passing, going in opposite directions, on a wide road. They crowded each other, collided, and one person was hurt.

In another disaster, the auto driver carelessly ran into a farm wagon he was attempting to pass, and a life snuffed out paid the penalty.

Due to reckless auto driving, a head-on collision occurred between the car and a horse and buggy and one person was injured, another report says.

Here is a type of casualty which presents a menace to the entire driving public. Two men, highly intoxicated, were running a car. They were topping all speed limits when the automobile struck a corner curbstone. Both, of course, were hurt. Fortunately, the accident occurred before the men had time to hit someone else.

Another report says that a car was driven upon a sharp turn in the road at too great a speed. It skidded, turned turtle and was burned. The driver was intoxicated. The county superintendent, in his indignation, suggests that the speed "be legislated out of cars"; that motors be made with a maximum capacity of 30 miles an hour.

Here is one that is hard to account for. A driver, unfamiliar with the road, was running 25 miles an hour in a fog. The car slipped off the road, turned over, and four paid the penalty with severe injuries.

In another report, the county highway superintendent says it was a case of "too much speed for the quality of road." The car skidded, lost a wheel and two were hurt.

Still another car, running too fast for safety, fouled a tree and three were hurt.

* * *

There is scarcely a limit to the number of reports which come into official hands and which bespeak criminal negligence and carelessness. Not all accidents, of course, are avoidable. But, many are.

How far-reaching will be the results of this "safety first" evangelism be? It depends, we think, upon the extent to which each individual applies the principle to himself. Proceed on the theory that the other fellow isn't safe; that you have to be. Let every driver on every road in Illinois do this, and we will wager the accident list will dwindle.

In a recent issue of *American Motorist*, a striking article from the pen of Frank Farrington appears under the caption, "The Menace of the Road." Lack of space prevents use of the article in full. However, we take the liberty of quoting sections of it. The writer, in part, says:

"It is a simple statement to make that our highways are becoming unsafe. It is a statement that we expect will be made by old fogies who never owned a motor car and who never rode faster than old Dobbin would amble. But there is not a level-headed motorist, who will admit the things he knows are true, who does not know that the risk of accident on any main highway nowadays is vastly more than a trifle. * * *

"The manufacturers of automobiles must realize that theirs is a business that should not be put on the basis of 'a short life and a merry one.' They are in business to make money next year, the year after, ten years from now. The safety of travelers on our highways is the one thing they should demand as the best step that can be taken for the protection of their industry and of its growth.

"Our roads can not be made appreciably wider. With our vast mileage we can not afford to build wide enough to give the speed maniacs an open path. We can not sacrifice more miles to more speed, more miles for the many to more speed for the few.

"The only way to make the roads safer is to make them safer. Legislation may help if we can find anyone to enforce the laws. There are laws enough now if they were obeyed.

"Some crimes are eliminated best by public sentiment. There are laws against wife-beating, but the sentiment of people against a man's beating his wife does more to keep him from doing it, or at least from getting caught at it, than all the laws on the statute books.

"Let us see that our present laws along the line of fast driving are obeyed. Let us take the stand that the man who is guilty shall be punished regardless of who or what he may be.

"Let us strive to create such a public sentiment against recklessness on the highway as will make a man ashamed to take advantage the strong take over the weak by failing to give the other fellow a fair chance. Any careful driver will give the roadhog more than half the road when he sees the latter come rushing at him, though one does regret at times that it is impossible to stand one's ground and give the other fellow what he deserves without getting worse in return. * * *

"The time has come for the automobile manufacturers to call on their customers to be careful. Otherwise many thousands of excellent prospects who have the money for cars are not going to take the chance.

"The time has come for automobile clubs to call on their members to observe all restrictions as a matter of course, but particularly to get acquainted with the meaning of 'Safety First.'

"The time has come for chambers of commerce and boards of trade and commercial clubs to take up the matter of the safety of the highways and make it their business to see that in their territory the farmer can send his family to town in carriage or motor car and feel assured that no reckless driver running amuck will annihilate them on their way.

A RECKLESS DRIVER, RUNNING A CAR AT FIFTY MILES AN HOUR, STRUCK THIS BRIDGE. IN ADDITION TO THE DAMAGE SHOWN, THE MAN WAS HURT AND THE CAR DEMOLISHED.

"The development of local retail business calls for safe highways. The development of big business demands observance of the rights of the folks who are careful. The welfare of the country requires that no class of people, reckless automobile drivers or others, be allowed to ignore and trample upon the rights of people who have less money but perhaps more of other desirable possessions."

 # AFTER THE CARELESS CHAUFFEUR.
An Illinois Official Takes a Hand.

In view of the fact that modified State laws and the nature of the duties of the office have linked inseparably the interests of the Secretary of State's department in Illinois with the institution of chauffeurdom and automobiling, it is interesting, as well as gratifying to advocates of the idea, to note progress which the department has made in direct promotion of the "Safety First" movement.

Secretary of State Lewis G. Stevenson, almost as soon as he assumed control of affairs of his office, put into operation his "Safety First" principles. He set about to gain the cooperation, first, of the Illinois Legislature; and, secondly, of chambers of commerce, commercial associations, local city and village authorities and others having to do with law administration. He succeeded.

The motor vehicle law was amended, due to the secretary's initiative. Mr. Stevenson was authorized to enlist a staff of automobile investigators. The names of three to ten men in each given community were submitted to him, through the assistance and cooperation of business men's organizations, and from each list were chosen the men of dependence and reliability to assist in the great "Safety First" and law-enforcement work.

Results of this plan have been signally important. Activities of the alert investigators have resulted in the cancellation of many licenses of chauffeurs addicted to drunkenness or carelessness.

Experience of the Secretary of State's office has led to the conclusion that most "speeding" on our highways has been done by thoughtless boys. To check this, the investigators have made occasional arrests, and the results have been wholesome. That scores of lives have been saved through the operation of these and other "safety first" methods of the department is undoubted.

Chauffeurs, these days, are not passed into possession of licenses with a song, so to speak. Thorough examinations are given. The applicants must submit to oral and written tests, and, in addition, they are given "road tests," calculated to reveal what they really know of the mechanism of cars and the safe and proper ways of driving them. In this manner, the standard of chauffeurs has been elevated to a marked degree.

A short time ago, *The Chicago Herald* asked Secretary of State Stevenson for a brief article on policies of his department, as relating to the advancement of the "safety first" movement. It was impossible to go into the subject exhaustively, yet, in his brief resume, the secretary tells interestingly of some of the things his department has done. We reproduce the article as follows:

"Seven hundred killed and 8,000 wounded!

"No, this is not the casualty report of the fight at Verdun or the result of a week's bombardment along the Ypres. It is the number who, it is estimated, will have been killed and hurt in Illinois by motor-driven vehicles during 1916, most of them due to a lack or failure to display common sense.

"In Cook County alone last year 254 persons were killed and 3,200 hurt by avoidable automobile and motor-cycle accidents. This county registers about 45 per cent of the entire State's registration. Its toll of dead probable will reach 325.

"The pity of it all is that most of these lives could have been saved had proper caution been observed. The appalling list last year prompted the General Assembly to try to prevent some of the wanton waste. At my instigation a statute was provided authorizing me to appoint automobile investigators as my special representatives to aid in enforcing the law.

"Strict law enforcement, I believe, will reduce to a minimum the toll of death and injury. So I have sought the cooperation of motor vehicle owners themselves to this end. It is a source of much pleasure here to relate that I found them eager to cooperate in any movement designed to make motor traffic more safe alike for owner and pedestrian.

"To date some 500 carefully selected persons have been appointed, all serving without compensation. The personnel includes citizens high in the professions and in the world of business.

"Each is provided with a badge of office, certificate of appointment and book of instructions. He is especially cautioned to perform his duties with discretion and impartiality and to work constantly in harmony with the State's attorney and the local authorities of his county.

"The splendid results accomplished through the activity of the investigators have exceeded my most sanguine expectations. The mere knowledge that persons in every community had been appointed to enforce the' law caused owners to manifest a stricter regard for it.

"The influence of the investigators was felt in a marked way in our automobile department. Applications for registration from persons who had been slow to register for 1916 began to pour in, in such great numbers that at the end of April, 1916, more than 165,000 applications had been received, as against 118,770 for the corresponding months of 1915. In the first four months of 1916, $842,669 was collected in fees, which is $223,000 greater that for the similar period of last year.

"The ways in which their usefulness has been manifested are many and various. Through their vigilance the drunken chauffeur has come to grief. The Secretary of State is given the power of revoking the license of any chauffeur who operates a motor vehicle while intoxicated.

"The restraint of reckless and irresponsible drivers is a valuable and effective service being rendered. In dealing with the speed fiend, where flagrant offenses make it seem advisable to institute a prosecution, the effect on lawless drivers is wholesome.

"Three times as many licenses have been issued to chauffeurs during the first four months of 1916, as were issued during the corresponding period of the preceding year.

"This increase in the State revenue is not the only desirable result of the investigators' activity.

"Not the least valuable service rendered by the investigators is their influence in promoting the "safety first" campaign, which my department is maintaining. The fact that carelessness in some form or other is responsible for most, if not all, of the accidents caused by motor vehicles, is not open to argument. Therefore, the remedy is to supplant carelessness with caution.

"The inculcation of a spirit of "safety first," the development of a fixed habit of care and caution, will prevent the cruel waste of life now occasioned by that utter carelessness which might be said to be a national trait.

A LITTLE CARE MAY SAVE YOUR LIFE AT A CROSSING LIKE THIS.

"The driver who has the "safety first" habit never violates the law. "Safety first" and law observance are synonymous.

"All the influence of this department is being exerted in behalf of this "safety first" propaganda. Supplementing the efforts of the investigators, we are sending out with every registration certificate a printed slip containing "safety first" suggestions. More than 50,000 copies have already been distributed in this manner and without additional expense."

BRIDGES BUILT BY COUNTY AID.

Mr. W. M. Bonham, County Superintendent of Highways,

Macomb, Illinois.

DEAR SIR: I am in receipt of your favor of the 26th instant, in which you inquire in substance whether section 34 of the Road and Bridge act, chapter 121, Hurd's Statutes, 1916, authorizes a petition by highway commissioners for county aid in the construction of bridges.

In reply I will say that said section has no application to the matter of granting county aid upon the petition of highway commissioners. Highway commissioners are authorized to petition county aid only as provided and upon the conditions prescribed in section 35. Section 34 applies to cases where the county board determines to build a bridge at the entire expense of the county. However, under the holding of the Supreme Court in the case of *Goodwine* v. *County of Vermilion,* 271, Ill., 126, the county board may, under paragraph 57, chapter 34, appropriate funds to aid in the construction of roads and bridges; and such aid may be granted irrespective of the conditions prescribed by section 35 of the Road and Bridge act. Where highway commissioners petition aid as provided by section 35, the statute makes the granting of such aid by the county board mandatory. The granting of county aid under paragraph 57 of chapter 34 is a matter entirely within the discretion of the board.

Very respectfully,

ATTORNEY GENERAL.

The Automobile and Grade Crossings.

By F. G. Ewald, Chief of Railroad Division, Illinois State Public Utilities Commission.

It is the railroad division of the State Public Utilities Commission of Illinois which has for one of its duties the investigation of accidents. It shall be my endeavor to present this article couched in homely terms, free from technical verbiage, so that those who may have occasion to cross the tracks of railroads in automobiles or other vehicles, may realize their danger if they do so in heedless fashion.

As I begin this article, a telegram from a railroad company is laid on my desk, reading as follows:

"———— *October 3, 1916.*
"State Public Utilities Commission, Springfield, Ill.

"Southbound passenger train No. ————, struck automobile, private road crossing, one mile north of ————, 11.30 this a. m., killing Cory Baber, Exie Baber and Lena Baber and seriously injuring Edith Baber and Ralph Baber."

The information contained in this telegram represents, perhaps, a whole family, the majority of whom have been killed outright. Is it necessary to witness such accidents to realize the horror? Need we have a personal knowledge of the relatives left behind to understand the anguish of their hearts?

A MENACE LIKE THIS CALLS BUT FOR ONE COURSE; STOP AND MAKE SURE YOU ARE SAFE.

Yesterday we received notice of a shocking accident to a party of three, crossing the tracks of a railroad, in which one was instantly killed and the other two were seriously injured. We do not know enough of the details of the accident first quoted to comment on it. So far as our informal investigation has proceeded with reference to the second accident, it would appear that the automobile was approaching the railroad crossing under a high rate of speed, and that the driver of the automobile was largely, if not wholly, to blame for this unfortunate accident.

The gradual and steady growth in the use of the automobile would seem to be responsible for the large increase in the number of accidents as compared with the use of horse-drawn vehicles. Naturally the increased use of the automobile brings with it inexperienced and incompetent drivers. Oftentimes, through incompetence, the engine of a machine is "killed" and the car is stalled on the crossing for the oncoming train to

destroy it and its occupants. It is not an uncommon thing for the driver of an automobile to drive into the side of a passing train. When the horse was the sole motive power, it was not possible, nor did it seem to be necessary to speed over the crossings; nor was it necessary to apply force in order to mount a steep grade. With the use of a horse it was a steady pull until it reached the summit, and if a stop were necessary in the face of approaching danger, it was easily made.

AN OBSCURED CROSSING. APPROACH IT SLOWLY IF YOU WOULD BE SAFE.

Not only inexperienced, but experienced drivers get into trouble through carelessness and inattention to duty. Not long ago we had occasion to investigate an accident which occurred to a locomotive engineer and his son while driving their automobile over country roads to their home. The locomotive engineer had occasion to cross the tracks of the very railroad which employs him in pulling fast passenger trains. He was

YOU ARE SAFE FROM THE RAILROAD, BUT AN OBSCURED TURNOFF (ON THE RIGHT) CALLS FOR EXTREME CAUTION.

well aware of the dangers connected with railroad operation and the accidents which occur at grade crossings. Inexperienced drivers of automobiles explain many accidents. But it would seem to be difficult to understand the psychological effect on the minds of experienced and competent drivers, including the locomotive engineer just referred to, when we consider the careless and reckless manner in which railroad crossings are approached. Speed mania, of course, is responsible for many accidents.

In crossing accidents investigated where automobiles were involved, we find from experience that about 90 per cent are due entirely to inattention to duty or to the carelessness of the automobile driver. During the year ending June 30, 1916, there were 42 persons killed and 109 injured crossing steam railroads in automobiles, an increase of 16.7 per cent and 13.5 per cent respectively over the year previous. The total number of casualties to persons crossing the tracks of steam and interurban railroads in automobiles during the year ending June 30, 1916, was 51 persons killed and 158 persons injured, an increase of 30.8 per cent and 17.0 per cent respectively, for the year previous. Is anything more needed than these comparative figures to show that there is need for greater precaution?

The railroads are gradually making improvements at many of their grade crossings in the way of widening and lengthening approaches and fully planking the crossing between the track rails so that there will be as little obstruction to the movement of automobiles as possible. Also in many cases the berm banks on the right-of-way are being lowered and other obstructions removed, in order to improve the view of approaching trains. At the more dangerous crossings flagmen, automatic crossing bells or gates are being installed. But we must remember that the flagmen, or the operator of the gates and the men required to maintain the automatic crossing bells represent the human equation, which is not infallible. The flagman occasionally is inattentive to duty; and the gates and crossing bells occasionally get out of order.

There is nothing more precious than human life. Do not sacrifice yours, or those under your care. My appeal to those using grade crossings, especially the grade crossings formed by interurban and steam railroads, would be not to depend wholly on flagmen, gates or other devices. Remember that the whir or noise of the machinery in the car you are driving is oftentimes enough to offset the noise made by an approaching train. Avoid being led into a trap. Know for yourself that the way is clear. Unless you have an unobstructed view of approaching trains—stop, look and listen.

DANGER!

THE MOST DANGEROUS TYPE OF GRADE CROSSING KNOWN. HERE, A WATCHMAN IS MAINTAINED; YET THAT DOES NOT ELIMINATE THE HAZARD. THIS PICTURE WAS TAKEN 40 FEET BACK FROM THE TRACK. THE APPROACH FROM THE OPPOSITE SIDE IS EQUALLY BAD. EMBANKMENTS RISE FROM EVERY SIDE, AND THE CROSSING IS AT THE TOP OF A HILL. THE SANE MOTORIST HAS ONE RECOURSE; STOP AND MAKE CERTAIN THERE IS NO TRAIN NEAR.

Safety first!

* * *

Stop, look, listen—then, go ahead!

* * *

Better wait at a grade crossing than in a doctor's office!

If in doubt, stop!

* * *

Danger lurkes at every railroad crossing—for the careless driver!

* * *

Play safe!

ILLINOIS HIGHWAYS.

Published Monthly by the
State Highway Department,
Springfield, Illinois.

ILLINOIS HIGHWAY COMMISSION.

A. D. GASH, *President.*
S. E. BRADT, *Secretary.*
JAMES P. WILSON.

WM. W. MARR, *Chief State Highway Engineer.*

BUREAU OF ROADS.

H. E. BILGER, *Road Engineer.*
M. W. WATSON, *Assistant Road Engineer.*
C. M. HATHAWAY, *Office Engineer.*

BUREAU OF BRIDGES.

CLIFFORD OLDER, *Bridge Engineer.*
G. F. BURCH, *Assistant Bridge Engineer.*
A. W. CONSOER, *Office Engineer.*

BUREAU OF MAINTENANCE.

B. H. PIEPMEIER, *Maintenance Engineer.*
F. T. SHEETS, *Assistant Maintenance Engineer.*

BUREAU OF TESTS.

F. L. ROMAN, *Testing Engineer.*
W. C. ADAMS, *Chemist.*

BUREAU OF AUDITS.

J. M. McCOY, *Chief Clerk.*
EARL B. SEARCY, *Department Editor.*
R. R. McLEOD, *General Bookkeeper.*
G. E. HOPKINS, *Property Clerk.*

DIVISION ENGINEERS.

R. L. Bell, Buchanan-Link Bldg., Paris, Ill.
H. B. Bushnell, 144 Fox St., Aurora, Ill.
J. E. Huber, Wise Building, Mt. Vernon, Ill.
A. H. Hunter, 302 Apollo Theater Bldg., Peoria, Ill.
C. M. Slaymaker, 510 Metropolitan Bldg., E. St. Louis, Ill.
H. E. Surman, 614 People's Bank Bldg., Moline, Ill.
Fred Tarrant, 730 Reisch Bldg., Springfield, Ill.

Address all communications in regard to "Illinois Highways," to Earl B. Searcy, Department Editor, State Highway Department, Springfield, Illinois.

CONTENTS.

Safety—the best rule of the road!

* * *

Eighty-nine thousand dollars worth of construction has been authorized by the Cook County board on the 147th Street and the Midlothian roads, leading out of Chicago. Four miles, all told, will be improved.

* * *

The new County Home bridge, near County Home, Stephenson County, has been completed at a cost of $1,333, and has been officially accepted by County Highway Superintendent Hiveley. It is of steel construction.

* * *

A contract has been awarded for the construction of the Johns bridge in Payson Township, Adams County. The cost will be $635. The Middleburg bridge in Gilmer Township, Adams County, will be built at a cost of $890.

* * *

Gravel coating will be placed on the Preston, Morris and Asher roads, near Paris. The work will cost $7,349.

* * *

It takes less than ten seconds to slow down at a railroad crossing and make sure that it is safe. Is your life worth ten seconds?

* * *

The Salisbury and the Ball Township bridges, in Sangamon County, have been accepted by County Highway Superintendent Edwin H. White.

* * *

The supervisors of Adams County have accepted two new bridges, one in Missouri Township, the other in Versailles. The bridges are of concrete.

* * *

Vermilion County supervisors, who have made a record in road building, have provided $62,000 out of the regular county road fund for three new bridges south and southeast of Georgetown. The two larger spans, in Georgetown and Kendree Townships, will cost $53,000; and a smaller bridge will cost the remaining $9,000. The improvements were needed to make the new bond issue road standard.

* * *

A macadamized road is being constructed from Dupage into Lockport.

* * *

The sum of $26,000 has been appropriated by the Henry County supervisors for the purpose of repairing the road leading from Kewanee to Cambridge, in Henry County. The road is not seriously out of repair so the fund is expected to suffice.

* * *

In Tazewell County, the sum of $109,973.74 has been levied for road and bridge purposes in the sixteen townships of the county. The greatest amount levied by any one township is $16,000; the smallest, $3,000.

* * *

Word of the recent appointment of two new county highway superintendents in Illinois counties has reached the department. One of them is S. E. Wells, just named in Ford County; the other is O. C. Rabbenneck, the new incumbent in Washington County.

* * *

The best highway in the State can be your death-trap—if you are careless!

* * *

Recklessness can not be legislated out of existence. It is up to *you* to eradicate it!

The Relation of Maintenance to Construction on Public Highways in Illinois.

By B. H. Piepmeier, Maintenance Engineer., Illinois State Highway Department.

The economy of any type of road depends almost entirely upon its proper maintenance. A careful study of money expended and the results obtained in the maintenance of the public highways in Illinois indicates that considerable more thought and consideration should be given to this important part of road improvement. The present trend to public thought in road matters seems directed almost entirely to means and methods of securing more improved roads, only few officials giving proper consideration to the maintenance of existing roads or of roads contemplated for improvement.

A great many different types of roads have been condemned in the eyes of the public chiefly on account of the lack of proper maintenance. It it not uncommon to hear the layman say that certain types of roads are very unsatisfactory, as they go to pieces rapidly under even ordinary traffic. It is evident that if proper maintenance had been given such roads, they would not be condemned but on the contrary would be recommended for use in many places.

The value of a public highway depends almost entirely upon the condition of its surface throughout the year. The traveling public is not usually concerned in regard to the type of the road so long as the condition of the surface of the road is such that it satisfies all requirements of traffic during all seasons of the year. It is apparent that if proper maintenance would be given to many of the cheaper types of roads, they could be kept in a condition that would virtually satisfy the traffic in a great many localities.

A FINISHED CAREER.

No one will dispute the economy of a brick pavement on an extremely heavily traveled road or the economy of the well-kept earth road for light farm traffic. With these two extreme conditions satisfied, it is evident that if proper maintenance is given, that there must be economy in some of the numerous other types of improvements for roads which have traffic conditions varying between the limits of traffic that warrants a well-kept earth road and traffic that justifies a brick-wearing surface.

It is evident that the average layman does not consider all advantages of the various types of improvements when selecting a type of road. Very often, the public is prejudiced against certain types of roads on account of their lack of knowledge of their first cost and the cost of upkeep. Again, they may be prejudiced

PREPARING A ROAD BASE.

against certain types by published information that is not authentic. It has been proven without question, however, that the *principal cause for prejudice is dissatisfaction, which results from improper maintenance.*

It is not uncommon to see many different types of roads constructed, and then after they begin to show signs of slight wear to have them neglected entirely or some means of repair or maintenance imposed that has been

LAYING THE BRICK.

found, by long practice, to be defective. For example, it is common to see mudholes in earth roads filled with riprap, crushed stone, cinders, etc., paying an enormous price for the material when it is apparent that proper drainage, with all holes filled with earth from the side road is more satisfactory and economical. Old gravel and macadam roads are often repaired by filling ruts and depressions with inferior material that is readily displaced by traffic or ground to dust. Bituminous surfaces are often patched, if patched at all, by loose stone or gravel and in some cases concrete. A number of streets and roads have been inspected where brick was used to patch concrete surfaces, and concrete used to patch brick surfaces. Such careless methods used for the maintenance of public highways and streets not only makes many types of roads unsatisfactory and uneconomical, but tends to discourage road improvement, particularly the cheaper types of improvement which are

annual maintenance. The general feeling seems to be that when a road surface requires some annual maintenance to keep it in good shape, it is an expensive type and should be avoided; when, if the difference in the original cost plus the interest on the investment, plus the repairs, were taken into consideration, the cheaper type of surface would in many cases be more economical.

It is evident that the average layman does not consider all divisions of cost when selecting a type of improved road. Quite often the high first cost of a pavement is overshadowed by its low maintenance cost. Again, it is not hard to find localities that utterly overlook maintenance cost and give preference to that type

INSPECTING A NEW ROAD UNDER CONSTRUCTION.

LEFT TO RIGHT—GOVERNOR EDWARD F. DUNNE, STATE HIGHWAY COMMISSIONERS GASH, WILSON AND BRADT, ROAD ENGINEER H. E. BILGER, CHIEF STATE HIGHWAY ENGINEER WM. W. MARR, WM. BRETZ, INSPECTOR K. N. EVANS AND CONTRACTOR JOHN E. BRETZ.

in many localities the more economical if properly maintained.

The proper maintenance of many improved roads and streets is neglected on account of the inability of the road officials, in a great many cases, to assess a tax that is sufficient to do the work which they realize should be done. By special assessments, most any kind of improvement may be undertaken, but to provide a fund and an effective method of supervision for maintenance purposes is quite a different problem and one that has not been properly met in many localities.

The tendency in promoting a system of improved roads is to select types of roads which require very little

of road with which they may be familiar or that type which will give the greatest mileage. In comparing different types of roads, there are three things which must be taken into consideration, namely, the first or original cost of the improvement, the interest on the money invested in the improvement and the total upkeep cost. When all of these factors are taken into consideration, it is evident that many of the cheaper types of roads are more economical on account of their low first cost.

In selecting a type of road on the three principles set forth above, it is very essential that provision be made for proper and efficient maintenance. If by reason of local conditions, or circumstances that might delay or prevent proper maintenance, preference should be given to the types of pavements that may require only a small amount of maintenance or be serviceable even under neglect of maintenance. Neglecting proper maintenance for but one year on many types of roads is very much more serious than the amount of money involved represents. One season's neglect of maintenance or improper maintenance often results in complete destruction of some of the cheaper types of road surfaces.

There are very few men experienced in the maintenance of various types of roads. There seems to be a tendency to shun this phase of road work in preference for construction. This may probably be explained by the so-called "fussy methods" that must necessarily accompany much maintenance work. Again, the usual plan for making repairs on a road is to wait until it becomes almost impassable and then hurriedly secure the services of the first man available for doing the work with very little thought in regard to his experience. A good maintenance or repair man can not be trained in a day or one season, nor can a road be effectively maintained by only occasional consideration. Effective and efficient maintenance is accomplished only by constant attention of the experienced man that will give personal attention to all details of the work.

It is the utter neglect of maintenance and improper methods followed by many road officials that have molded the sentiment of the masses of people against such work. The neglect of maintenance has not only served to destroy many useful and economical roads, but in so many cases have molded sentiment to have no faith in any type of road that requires annual maintenance. This neglect and inefficiency on the part of many road officials has led road promoters to disregard the type of road which in many cases would be most economical for a community.

WATCH AFTER THE BRIDGES!

Apropos of "safety first," maintenance and of other progressive policies which the State Highway Commission of Illinois and ILLINOIS HIGHWAYS are advocating, we quote the following from an exchange:

"No matter how good the surface of a road may be, if the bridges are weak and the culverts poor, the highway is far from satisfactory. The annual record of bridge failures under threshing machines and other heavy loads makes a long list, and the cost of repairing

TESTING A BRIDGE.

the annual damage to poor culverts is a large sum. In progressive communities, therefore, strong steel and concrete bridges and well-built culverts are being constructed before expensive road surfacing is done. This work is often paid for out of the annual tax levy for road and bridge construction, and adsorbs such a large part of the funds that too little money is left for grading and surfacing.

Good bridges and culverts are permanent structures, and the Deputy Minister of Highways of Ontario, Hon. W. A. McLean, has advised the taxpayers of that province to pay for them by a bond issue where the total expenditure for the purpose is large. In such a case he suggests compiling a complete list of the bridges and culverts needed, preparing plans and estimates for their construction, and then financing the work so that its cost will be equitably distributed over a period of years rather than be concentrated on the taxpayers of a few years. Where there are few of these structures and none is expensive, the policy of paying for them out of the annual tax levy can not be criticized, in his opinion, for it does not interfere appreciably with satisfactory progress in grading, drainage, surfacing, and maintenance."

HANDBOOK FOR HIGHWAY ENGINEERS.

[Reviewed by C. M. HATHAWAY, Office Engineer, Illinois State Highway Department.]

Authors: Wilson G. Harger, Civil Engineer, First Assistant Engineer New York State Department of Highways; Edmond A. Bonney, Supervising Engineer New York State Department of Highways.

Second Edition, Limp leather 4½ inches by 7 inches, 609 pages illustrated.

McGraw-Hill Book Company, Inc., $3 net.

The second edition recently published brings the first edition up-to-date and adds a great deal of new and interesting subject matter.

This is especially true of the chapters on "Top Courses," "Construction" and "Specifications," each of which has been nearly doubled. Concrete road construction is extensively dealt with in this edition and given due consideration.

The book as a whole seems strictly up-to-date and covers practically every phase of highway construction and design. Although based to a great extent on the writers' local conditions, its general features can almost always be adapted to one's specific case by using a little judgment, and taking into account the local conditions. It is excellent for an office reference book and should be especially useful as a handbook for the field man, as the latter generally has very little chance to carry many technical books with him, nor does he usually have access to them locally. The book is handy to carry and in a very compact form contains information touching practically every feature of the work which a highway field man might need information on. The usual mathematical tables are included.

The book may be outlined by chapters as follows:

Chapter 1. A discussion on grades and traffic resistance with a number of tables showing ruling grades in several states.

Chapter 2. A discussion and many sketches of cross sections of the various roads and pavements. Very complete and valuable.

Chapter 3. Discusses with a number of tables small culverts, runoff and under drainage. Also gives tables showing properties and quantities of materials for same.

Chapter 4. Foundations for roads dealing especially with broken stone or gravel.

Chapter 5. A complete discussion of the modern types of pavements, giving general methods of construction, adaptability, cost and comparative values; also treats of maintenance and cost.

Chapter 6. Brief discussion and cuts of guard fences, gutters, curbs, retaining walls, etc.

Chapter 7. Describes the various road-building materials with tests for same. Contains a number of excellent tables.

Chapter 8. Treats of the proper making of road surveys. Numerous tables, problems on running curves, adjustments, etc.

Chapter 9. Deals of office practice from plotting of plans to making of the estimate. Numerous tables and a great amount of information bearing on the figuring of estimates.

Chapter 10. An excellent chapter giving construction cost data and organization for the various types of construction. Very complete and although based strictly on local consideration, may be readily adapted to serve as a guide for a specific case.

Chapter 11. Covers the main features of all types of construction.

Chapter 12. This chapter on specifications is drawn up largely on New York state practice, but is very complete as to both materials and construction for roads and pavements of all kinds.

The usual logarithm and other mathematical tables, etc., cover about 125 pages. Appendix "A" cites the traffic regulations of the state of Ohio, also for section of New York state.

 # A Traffic Census, And What It Shows.

That a traffic census can be utilized for purposes of determining the type of roads needed along certain highways is demonstrated, in an interesting way, in a report which has come in from Rockford.

Nine main roads lead out from the city of Rockford, and late in June and early in July, the number of passing vehicles, motor and horse-drawn, was counted daily for a week. Highway commissioners had been confronted with a serious problem of maintenance, in view of the fact that motor car and truck traffic especially had grown to such a great extent; so the census was taken. Reading of it will reveal how definitely the census has told the story of traffic along each of the nine roads.

The census was taken under the direction of County Superintendent of Highways A. R. Carter, of Winnebago County. In his letter to ILLINOIS HIGHWAYS, he states that the township of Rockford has approximately 87 miles of roadways, built of water-bound macadam.

Due to the large increase in motor traffic and in the number of motor trucks, the problem of maintenance has become an urgent one. The roads have been treated on the surface with Tarvia B, or asphalt oils, which agencies have in a measure helped solve the problem. This season, the township is using approximately 60,000 gallons of Tarvia B, and 10,000 gallons of liquid Aztec.

"We are getting good results from this work, and where our road is in proper condition, I believe this method will help to solve the problem for maintenance of our water-bound macadam roads," Mr. Carter writes.

Although the accompanying table is self-explanatory, it is interesting to note the ratios of motor vehicles to horse-drawn, on the various roads. Traffic on the South Main Street road, as the table indicates, was heaviest during the census week. In the seven days, 14,704 conveyances of all kinds passed in the course of the hours during which the observations were taken. On that road, there were 4⅖ times more motor vehicles than horse-drawn.

The North Second Street road shows even a larger per cent than that. In all, a total of 11,803 vehicles were recorded as passing, and the motor outnumbered the horse-drawn conveyances, seven to one.

The census indicates, strikingly, which roads ought to be improved with a view of permanency and which ought to be maintained for the purpose of accommodating lighter traffic. Obviously, the South Main Street, the North Second Street and the Kishwaukee Street roads are the ones over which travel is heaviest.

Such barometers of travel serve highway officials everywhere as valuable guides.

ROCKFORD TOWNSHIP HIGHWAY TRAFFIC REPORT, 1916.

Station.	June 29th.		June 30th.		July 1st.		July 2d.		July 3d.		July 5th.		July 6th.		Total horse drawn.	
	Horse drawn.	Motor.	Horse drawn.	Motor.	Horse drawn.	Motor.	Horse drawn.	Motor.	Horse drawn.	Motor.	Horse drawn.	Motor.	Horse drawn.	Motor.		
W. State St.	105	565	117	425	122	597	69	980	116	481	102	475	116	476	762	
Kilburn Ave.	210	367	231	350	304	479	133	708	334	341	264	323	242	347	1,718	
N. Main St.	128	313	103	311	117	353	37	389	145	350	110	331	89	300	729	2,277
N. Second St.	155	1,059	209	1,096	250	1,440	146	2,555	284	1,384	201	1,442	188	1,366	1,456	10,347
Charles St.	16	576	15	47	180	466	158	665	162	394	130	376	96	113	766	2,684
Kishwaukee St.	680	1,027	730	1,024	635	1,227	166	1,189	464	1,138	556	979	595	1,035	3,667	7,619
S. Main St.	352	1,766	421	1,457	388	1,778	209	2,473	429	1,678	338	1,355	400	1,680	2,597	
Montague.	95	319	131	260	161	490	112	543	168	289	144	312	156	304		
Cunningham.	55	144	55	128	72	141	72	276								

Census taken from 7 a. m. until 9 p. m.   *Bridge out after this date.

REPORT OF THE BUREAU OF BRIDGES FOR SEPTEMBER.

During the month of September plans, estimates and specifications for sixty-five (65) concrete bridges and sixteen (16) steel bridges were prepared and sent out to county superintendents of highways. The total estimated cost of these bridges is $125,021.

According to reports received, contracts were awarded during the month on plans prepared for county superintendents of highways for sixty-seven (67) concrete bridges and six (6) steel bridges, at an average cost of 95.4 per cent of the estimates. The total estimated cost of this work amounts to $91,656.

Contract was awarded on alternate plans for one bridge; the estimated cost for this work on State plans amounts to $1,660.

Plans, estimates and specifications for five (5) sections of State aid bridge work, including twelve (12) bridges were completed and sent out to the respective county boards. The total estimated cost of this work is $8,779.50.

Contracts were awarded during September by the State Highway Commission for three (3) sections of State aid bridge work, including eight (8) bridges, at an average cost of 94.4 per cent of the estimates. The total estimated cost of this work amounts to $8,321.80.

Plans and estimates for bridge and culvert work to be built in connection with State aid road contracts were prepared for sixteen (16) sections of State aid road work, including 277 bridges and culverts, the total estimated cost of which equals $21,500.

Summing up, plans were prepared for 370 bridges and culverts, the total estimated cost of which equals $155,300.50.

Fourteen (14) bridge and culvert plans prepared by county superintendents of highways were checked and approved.

The following outlines briefly the status of the work in the bridge office on October 5, 1916:

There were on hand ready for work eight (8) bridge inspection reports; three (3) bridge plans had been prepared but not checked on that date; twenty-eight (28) bridge plans had been completed, together with the estimates, and were practically ready to be sent out.

The total pay roll in the Bureau of Bridges for the month of September amounts to $1,725. If we charge this entire amount against the preparation of plans and specifications and make an allowance of ten (10) per cent for overhead; the cost of preparing plans and specifications during the month amounts to 1.23 per cent of the total estimated cost of the work completed during the month.

GOVERNOR DUNNE AND "SAFETY FIRST."

Governor Edward F. Dunne is an outspoken disciple of the "Safety First" evangelism. He is familiar with the ways of the road, has traversed every known kind of

MANY SUCH BRIDGES IN ILLINOIS. THE DRIVER IS SAFE IF HE USES ORDINARY CARE.

railroad crossing, dangerous and otherwise, and is therefore rated as one calculated to know whereof he speaks.

Three years ago, the Governor took his first official step toward eliminating what he—and in his opinion the general public as well—regards as dangerous crossings. Since then, he has overlooked no opportunity to cooperate with State highway and township highway commissioners, and railroad officials, in the interest of the "safety first" movement.

A HIDDEN THOROUGHFARE SUCH AS THIS CALLS FOR EXTREME CAUTION ON THE PART OF THE TRAVELER.

The executive called a large number of railroad and other officials into conference with him. He placed before them his ideas. He told them he wanted cooperation to the end that, in Illinois, three kinds of railroad crossings be eliminated: the "hogback" crossing, the "diagonal" and the "obscured" crossing.

The "hogback" crossing, in which the railroad grade rises abruptly from the road approach on either side, presents a serious menace to motorists because it is on such crossings that automobile engines are most easily "killed." The Governor recommended that, to remedy this evil, the road on either side be filled to a distance back of 50 to 75 feet, in order to "meet" the railroad grade and thus eliminate the sharp and dangerous abruptness.

In recommending the removal of diagonal crossings, where at all possible, Governor Dunne urged that the rectangular crossing be substituted. On a diagonal, the driver may be able to see the track ahead of him, but with extreme difficulty back of him. Necessarily, the diagonal crossing road, in a measure, parallels the track. The Governor urged that, at a suitable point, the road be diverted, and run across the track at a right angle with it, thus giving the motorist an equal chance on both sides to see an approaching train.

Further, the Governor urged that the "obscured" crossing be discarded. Where sheds, weeds or other obstructions cut off the view, the executive urged that clearances be made at least a hundred feet back, thus giving the traveler an opportunity to see the track.

Since that conference three years ago, in which the Governor urged the cooperation of railroad and highway officials, results for the better have been evident. Railroads, the Governor believes, are doing their utmost to protect and safeguard their crossings; and many motorists are profiting from the "safety first" idea, as applied by them to themselves. The menace of the reckless driver still exists, however; and this, the Governor deplores.

NEWS FROM ABROAD.

A scenic highway across the continental divide was opened through Wolf Creek Pass, Colorado, in August. The road is a 30-mile connecting link in a 600-mile state highway across the state. The portion of the road on the eastern side of the divide is about 16 miles long, and that on the western side about 14. Grades were kept down to 6½ per cent except in a few cases where that had to be exceeded. The topography governed the alignment of most of the road and there are many deep cuts, heavy fills, sharp curves, and bridges. As a rule the road is 14 feet wide, including the ditch, although on some sections where the grading was unusually heavy, it was built only 10 feet wide. The roadbed is flat and slopes toward the bank side where there is a drainage ditch. Log culverts are used throughout the length of the road, and the bridges are also of logs. These bridges are queen post structures, 20 feet wide, and of spans up to 40 feet. A little more than half the road is surfaced with rock obtained on the ground. The remainder is to be surfaced later with disintegrated granite. The road was paid for by the state, the work being done under the supervision of a joint board representing the counties interested. All plans were approved by the State Highway Commission. The average cost to the state was about $3,000 per mile.

* * *

The Southwest Trail Association, which is marking a highway from Kansas City to Chicago, will extend its trail through La Salle County over the route of the Illinois Valley Way, providing the cities along the route see fit to mark the trail. It was first contemplated to construct this highway through Illinois, extending from Davenport, Iowa, along the route taken by the Lincoln Highway, but this route is longer than the Illinois Valley Way, and this is one of the inducements that has suggested the change.

* * *

Marking the Illinois Valley Way, the thoroughfare between Chicago and Peoria, following the Desplaines and Illinois Rivers, along its 170 miles of road will be probably completed this fall. The route was dedicated recently by members of the State Highway Commission and a number of good roads boosters. The marker adopted by the "I. V. Way" association is unique in road-marking in this section of the country. It will be a 12-foot concrete post with a concrete target at the top bearing the name of the way in its shortened form—"I. V. Way."

COMING MEETINGS.

November 23-25—National Municipal League—Annual convention, Springfield, Mass. secretary, Clinton Rogers Woodruff, 705 North American Building, Philadelphia, Pa.

December 5-7—American Association of State Highway Officials—Annual meeting, St. Louis, Mo. Secretary, Dr. Joseph Hyde Pratt, Chapel Hill, N. C.

December 7-8—Third Annual meeting of Northwestern Road Congress at Hotel Sherman, Chicago, Ill.

January 20, 1917—Western Paving Brick Manufacturers' Association—Meeting, Kansas City, Mo. Secretary, G. W. Thurston, 416 Dwight Building, Kansas City, Mo.

February 5-9, 1917—American Road Builders' Association—Fourteenth Annual Convention ; Seventh American Good Roads Congress under the auspices of the A.

R. B. A., and Eighth National Good Roads Show of Machinery and Materials, Mechanics' Hall, Boston, Mass. Secretary, E. L. Powers, 150 Nassau street, New York, N. Y.

February 7-15, 1917—Tenth Chicago Cement Show—Coliseum, Chicago, Ill. Secretary, Robert F. Hall, 210 South La Salle Street, Chicago, Ill.

HIGHWAYS TO HAVE COMFORT STATIONS.

A nation-wide campaign has been launched by the Public Comfort Station bureau, 261 Broadway, New York, backed by the American Automobile Association, National Highways Association, National Old Trails Road Association, and other national organizations, to provide roadside stations in cities along all highways like passenger stations along the right-of-way of a railway.

The plan was called forth by the urgent needs for public comfort stations, and the almost criminal lack of them in this country, which is far behind Europe in that respect. Railways have taken care of their passengers by providing toilet accommodations in the stations and on the trains, but no provision has been made by the public for the public. The entire motor-traveling public is dependent on private kindness for their accommodations, in spite of the fact that more people now travel by motor than by train.

These national associations purpose using their joint influence to have erected in every city through which a main highway runs, one or more public comfort stations, provided with a comfortable waiting room, equipped with sanitary toilet accommodations for men and women, containing pure and wholesome drinking water and in hardware localities having a small water-softening apparatus to supply soft water for automobile radiators. The stations are to be equipped with telephones so that wherever located, the traveler will always be in touch with the outside world. Other necessary electrical equipment will likewise be provided. The waiting room can be used, too, as an emergency hospital in case of accidents along the road, while telephones connecting the various stations along the line will tend to prevent crime or check the escape of criminals along the highways.

In the western part of the country, where cities are rather far apart, they plan to have counties or townships put up community buildings along the line of travel, containing auditoriums where lectures can be delivered, halls where dances can be held, and rural companies of state militia or national guards organized, drilled and quartered.

It is found in the European war that the automobile and motor truck play as important parts as the railways. The aeroplane has created for itself possibly a more important place in warfare. A system of good roads criss-crossing the country like a spider web, and dotted with automobile and aeroplane stations, would, therefore, prove valuable from a military standpoint.

So that all the features of value in war times will be incorporated in the buildings, the War Department has detailed Major Carl F. Hartmann to cooperate in the work.

To build a public comfort station such as this plan calls for will cost approximately $10,000. For the small towns and cities, a less expensive building is contemplated, but which contains all of the elements found necessary to make a station safe and sanitary. By the clever working out of this plan, these stations will be not
(Concluded on page 127.)

SWAMP ROADS.

By GEORGE W. COOLEY.

Road superintendents sometimes fail to provide the elaborate drainage necessary to obtain a proper foundation, because expensive drainage work reduces the funds available for surfacing. This applies particularly to the great mileage of main rural roads on which there is an insistent demand by road users for surfacing, with impatience at any delay made to provide proper foundations.

In undeveloped swamp country, the most permanent work is obtained by building the roadway embankment of material obtained by dredging a ditch on the upstream side of the road, with an auxiliary road ditch on the other side.

The top soil from the ditches is first spread over the roadway and the dredge then excavates enough firm material to provide a substantial foundation when deposited on the top soil. The ditches are dug with practically vertical sides, in order to obtain the largest amount of firm material, usually found at the bottom. The ditches must be of sufficient size to provide the necessary drainage after they have become contracted by the breaking down of the slopes. The low points in the ditch, excavated to secure material, will become filled with sediment after a year or two.

OVERCOMING A SWAMPY STRETCH.

It sometimes appears extravagant to make such large ditches on road work, but in new country lateral drainage is always carried to the road ditches and should be provided in advance. There is not much difference in cost, however, between small ditches by hand and a large dredged ditch, on account of the lower cost of machine work per cubic yard.

After drainage is secured, the important work is to eliminate all vegetable or perishable matter and to build up the foundation uniformly. Dragging and planing the subgrade as it is being built will prevent the wavyness of surface which develops occasionally after the completion of a road, and it is advisable to specify such work. Surfacing with gravel constitutes the final work on the main rural roads in many parts of the country, and a great deal of money is wasted in not preparing the foundation properly for this surfacing. Until it is compacted, the coat of gravel acts like a sponge, holding water until the foundation becomes so soft that traffic

drives some of the gravel into the underlying material. This causes not only a loss of gravel but also an uneven surface.

A hard foundation for gravel can be obtained where the soil is clay by spreading two or three inches of sand or gravel over the clay, mixing them together, and rolling until a smooth surface is obtained. With a sandy subsoil, clay is required to make a firm foundation. Where no clay is available, success has been attained by spreading about four inches of loose straw over the sand, but care must be exercised to prevent the straw from becoming mixed with the gravel. Muskeg or pulverized peat has also been used to advantage under like conditions.

HIGHWAYS TO HAVE COMFORT STATIONS.

(Concluded from page 126.)

only be self-supporting, but will pay for the cost of construction within ten years. That means that a city builds a station, owns it outright, and out of the receipts from the pay privileges pays back the loan to itself. It is not a charge upon the community, but a good paying investment in dollars, decency and health.

J. J. Cosgrove is director of the public comfort station bureau. The campaign for public comfort stations belongs to no one, however, but is a great general uprising for conveniences so long needed and equally long denied. Societies and individuals are invited to cooperate in the work.—*The Road-Maker.*

HIGHWAY IMPROVEMENT IN KENTUCKY.

[Extract from Article by RODMAN WILEY.*]

Kentucky was one of the first states in the union to have a highway commission, such an organization having been in existence as early as 1810. Some very fine roads were built under the direction of those early engineers. Many of the roads were provided with telford bases of widths up to 18 feet with light grades and easy curves, and with drainage structures up to those of moderate spans built of dry masonry. With the advent of the railroads in the 30's there came a decrease in the attention paid to the building of roads, and for about 75 years road work was carried on in a very haphazard manner.

Realizing that road building was an engineering problem and that millions of dollars were being wasted through inefficient management, the state legislature at the 1912 session established a highway commission and appropriated $25,000 to pay its expenses. Provision was also made for a road fund to be obtained from the sale of automobile licenses. The duties of the department, as defined by this act, were largely advisory. So much work was done wherever the engineering advice of the commission was accepted and so much interest was aroused in the road problem, that at the 1914 session of the legislature a state aid law was adopted and an inter-county seat road system was established. The financing of the work was taken care of by the levying of a 5-cent tax on every $100 worth of taxable property, and this with the automobile license fund which had been accumulating since 1912, brought the state aid fund during 1915 to approximately $750,000. The work was started late and was carried on with considerable difficulty because few of the counties understood how to operate under the new law. But in spite of these hindrances about 800 miles of roads were surveyed and let by contract, and about 450 miles of the roads were completed at a cost of something like $1,350,000.

*Commissioner of Public Roads of Kentucky.

ILLINOIS NOTES.

Contracts were recently awarded at Springfield for three State-aid roads in LaSalle County; a 1-mile road out of Seneca, which is of brick and concrete construction; two miles of macadam road out of Earlville, and two miles of concrete road out of Lostant.

Approving maps of a comprehensive network of hard, smooth highways connecting Will County cities and villages, a special good roads bond committee of the board of supervisors plans to urge at the annual October meeting legislation, which will submit to the people the question of a $1,500,000 bond issue. The contact has been awarded for constructing three miles of waterbound macadam highway in Reading Township at $12,300. This work will complete the hard roads laid out in that township several years ago. The commissioners are prepar-

ing to surface four miles of the waterbound macadam constructed by convicts.

The committee having in charge the laying out of the system of hard roads for Pike County has completed its labors, and the designated roads were so selected that all the towns will be connected by one continuous system.

The contract has been awarded for the construction of six and one-quarter miles of monolithic brick pavement in Stockland Township, Iroquois County, the bid being $56,252.52. Work will begin at once. The new pavements are to be 9 feet in width, 1 foot less than the Vermilion County bond roads. Earth shoulders are to be constructed, and the road will be graded and put in good shape. The contract calls for constructing brick roads north and south from Stockland for a mile and west to the Milford Township line.

COUNTY SUPERINTENDENTS OF HIGHWAYS.

COUNTY.	NAME.	ADDRESS.
Adams	Lewis L. Boyer	Quincy, Ill.
Alexander	W. N. Moyers	Mound City, Ill.
Bond	R. O. Young	Sorento, Ill.
Boone	Thos. W. Humphrey	Belvidere, Ill.
Brown	W. O. Grover	Mt. Sterling, Ill.
Bureau	Frank R. Bryant	Princeton, Ill.
Calhoun	Jno. A. Earley	Batchtown, Ill.
Carroll	S. C. Campbell	Mt. Carroll, Ill.
Cass	John Goodell	Beardstown, Ill.
Champaign	Geo. C. Fairclo	Court House, Urbana, Ill.
Christian	C. A. Penington	Taylorville, Ill.
Clark	Zane Arbuckle	Marshall, Ill.
Clay	Howard Anderson	Louisville, Ill.
Clinton	Jno. T. Goldsmith	R. F. D. No. 3. Carlyle, Ill.
Coles	Harry Shinn	Mattoon, Ill.
Cook	Geo. A. Quinlan	Chicago, Ill.
Crawford	J. P. Lyon	Robinson, Ill.
Cumberland	Jno. A. Decker	Toledo, Ill.
DeKalb	Wm. C. Miller	Sycamore, Ill.
DeWitt	Melvin Tuggle	Clinton, Ill.
Douglas	L. O. Hackett	Tuscola, Ill.
DuPage	Eugene L. Gates	Wheaton, Ill.
Edgar	Karl J. Barr	Paris, Ill.
Edwards	Chas. C. Rice	Albion, Ill.
Effingham	Geo. T. Austin	Effingham, Ill.
Fayette	J. V. Waddell	Vandalia, Ill.
Ford	S. E. Wells	Piper City, Ill.
Franklin	Geo. F. Hampton	Benton, Ill.
Fulton	E. F. Motsinger	Canton, Ill.
Gallatin	Victor Pearce	Equality, Ill.
Greene	Irving Wetzel	Carrollton, Ill.
Grundy	Fred W. Stine	Morris, Ill.
Hamilton	Gregg Garrison	Garrison, Ill.
Hancock	Wm. Burgner	Carthage, Ill.
Hardin	W. M. Ball	Elizabethtown, Ill.
Henderson	C. R. A. Marshall	Stronghurst, Ill.
Henry	Jas. H. Reed	Cambridge, Ill.
Iroquois	Benj. Jordan	Watseka, Ill.
Jackson	Thos. G. Dunn	Gorham, Ill.
Jasper	S. A. Conner	Newton, Ill.
Jefferson	Tony C. Pitchford	Mt. Vernon, Ill.
Jersey	Chas. E. Warren	Jerseyville, Ill.
JoDaviess	Geo. E. Schroeder	Stockton, Ill.
Johnson	John H. Sharp	Cypress, Ill.
Kane	Geo. N. Lamb	Geneva, Ill.
Kankakee	Frank M. Enos	Kankakee, Ill.
Kendall	Jno. D. Russell	Oswego, Ill.
Knox	Harley M. Butt	Galesburg, Ill.
Lake	Chas. E. Russell	Waukegan, Ill.
LaSalle	Geo. Farnsworth	Ottawa, Ill.

COUNTY.	NAME.	ADDRESS.
Lawrence	R. J. Benefield	Lawrenceville, Ill.
Lee	L. B. Neighbour	Dixon, Ill.
Livingston	R. W. Osborn	Pontiac, Ill.
Logan	Thos. S. Davy	Lincoln, Ill.
McDonough	W. M. Bonham	Macomb, Ill.
McHenry	C. L. Tryon	Woodstock, Ill.
McLean	Ralph O. Edwards	Bellflower, Ill.
Macon	Preston T. Hicks	Decatur, Ill.
Macoupin	O. B. Coniee	Carlinville, Ill.
Madison	W. E. Howden	Edwardsville, Ill.
Marion	Lee S. Trainor	Salem, Ill.
Marshall	L. H. Eldridge	Lacon, Ill.
Mason	H. V. Schoonover	Bishop, Ill.
Massac	J. Thrift Corlis	Metropolis, Ill.
Menard	C. M. Buckley	Petersburg, Ill.
Mercer	J. E. Russell	Aledo, Ill.
Monroe	Albert R. Gardner	Waterloo, Ill.
Montgomery	P. M. Bandy	Hillsboro, Ill.
Morgan	Lawrence V. Baldwin	Jacksonville, Ill.
Moultrie	T. C. Fleming	Sullivan, Ill.
Ogle	Alex Anderson	Polo, Ill.
Peoria	W. E. Emery	512 N. Glendale av., Peoria, Ill
Piatt	Thos. J. Anderson	Monticello, Ill.
Pike	H. H. Hardy	Hull, Ill.
Pope	W. T. S. Hopkins	Dixon Springs, Ill.
Pulaski	W. N. Moyers	Mound City, Ill.
Putnam	Mason Wilson	McNabb, Ill.
Randolph	Henry I. Barbeau	Prairie du Rocher, Ill.
Richland	G. W. Low	Olney, Ill.
Rock Island	Wallace Treichler	Rock Island, Ill.
St. Clair	David O. Thomas	Belleville, Ill.
Saline	Jno. P. Upchurch	Harrisburg, Ill.
Sangamon	Edwin White	Springfield, Ill.
Schuyler	W. S. Henderson	Rushville, Ill.
Scott	Geo. H. Vannier	Bluffs, Ill.
Shelby	N. A. Baxter	Shelbyville, Ill.
Stark	Wm. Slater	Wyoming, Ill.
Stephenson	O. G. Hively	Freeport, Ill.
Tazewell	Frank S. Cook	Mackinaw, Ill.
Union	Jos. F. Howenstein	Anna, Ill.
Vermilion	Wm. S. Dillon	Danville, Ill.
Wabash	Guy W. Courter	Mt. Carmel, Ill.
Warren	C. L. McClanahan	Monmouth, Ill.
Washington	O. C. Rabbeneck	Nashville, Ill.
Wayne	Griff Koontz	Fairfield, Ill.
White	Geo. H. Brown	Carmi, Ill.
Whiteside	V. N. Taggett	Morrison, Ill.
Will	Will H. Smith	Joliet, Ill.
Williamson	P. B. Wilson	Marion, Ill.
Winnebago	Albertus R. Carter	Rockford, Ill.
Woodford	A. B. Hurd	El Paso, Ill.

ILLINOIS HIGHWAYS

[Printed by authority of the State of Illinois.]

OFFICIAL PUBLICATION OF THE

STATE HIGHWAY DEPARTMENT

| VOL. III | SPRINGFIELD, ILLINOIS, NOVEMBER, 1916 | No. 11 |

*A Road Well Built, then Maintained—
the Most Faithful of Public Servants.*

A GLIMPSE OF ILLINOIS IN HER EARLY HIGHWAY INFANCY

Whatever value a backward look may have as a source of inspiration for the future, it remains an undisputed fact that very often, by means of comparison, we gain ideas which serve to assist us in guaging progress.

Illinois has had road laws for many years. Set alongside the elaborate and scientific road statute plan of to-day, the original mandates governing highway interests would seem inadequate and ridiculous. Yet, the system had to have a beginning, and the bit of early history which we shall endeavor to present in this article will throw an interesting light upon road extension in its infancy in this State.

We have had loaned to us, for reference, a copy of the first report, made to the Governor and the General Assembly, of the original "Illinois Good Roads Commission." The report is the property of Mr. Fred C. Dodds, of Springfield, who assisted in compiling and writing it. The Commission was created in an act approved May 15, 1903, and its report was issued, after two years of research and investigation, under date of January 25, 1905, to the Forty-fourth General Assembly which convened in that year. The personnel of the first commission included DeWitt W. Smith, chairman; H. U. Wallace, and E. A. Mitchell.

When the Illinois Good Roads Commission of 1903 set out to perform the tasks with which it was charged, it went at the thing definitely and exhaustively. Its business was to ascertain the condition of roads in the State at that time. Boards of highway commissioners throughout Illinois were appealed to as the sources of information.

The Commission sought information as to the mileage of wagon roads in the numerous townships, the amount of hard surfacing that had been done, materials used and the cost per mile, tiled ditches and other means of drainage, taxes, bridges, cost of law administration, character of soil, machinery used, and many other questions which entered into the road situation of those days.

Eight hundred and thirteen of the total 1,567 townships in the State at that time, reported back a combined mileage of 52,423. With 64.48 miles per township as an average, it was estimated, in the report, that the State had a total of 101,040 miles of wagon roads, exclusive of streets in cities and villages. The aggregate road and bridge tax, in townships, in 1903 was $3,792,080.66. Twelve years later, this tax had jumped to $8,332,119.

Handicaps under which township highway officials worked were recognized by the original commission. It was declared in the report that, through the operation of inadequate laws, a large part of the road and bridge tax was wasted, and the results for which it was intended never realized. Good faith of the officials themselves was not questioned, as the report, at one point, declares:

"Given a proper system, the present highway officials can, we are sure, administer the same and achieve better results than under the present one."

When the report was made, there was much speculation as to Illinois' production of road-building materials. The geological survey, which had been started in 1859 and completed in 1889, was not an up-to-date guide; and the Commissioners were more or less at a loss to know what to report, in this respect. Reference was made to deposits of naturally crushed and broken stone, found in certain southern counties, and known as "novaculite." Gravel, stone, limestone and sandstone were to be found, of course. In the main, however, accurate information was lacking, and the report naively suggests, in lieu of earlier investigation, the biblical injunction, "Seek and ye shall find."

Sixty-five counties had reported 3,916 miles of tile, used in underground drainage of roads. The tile system had been found to be satisfactory, especially where the line of drainage had been laid along one or the other sides of the road, instead of down the center.

The "hard roads" section of this first report is about as caustic as it is brief and striking. Here is the paragraph which summed up the situation:

"Thirteen counties in the State report a total of 26¼ miles of hard roads built under the provisions of the present Hard Road law. Some of these reports are favorable to the law; others are not favorable. On the whole, we may safely say that a system which has been in force 22 years, and under which only 26¼ miles of road have been built, has not proven satisfactory to the people of the State."

This was between the years 1903 and 1905, and Illinois had less than 30 miles of hard road to show for 22 years of so-called hard roads administration. Contrast this with 600 miles of modern improved roadway, built or contracted for since 1913, when the present law went into effect!

The report avers that "road building in Illinois is as yet in a primitive state," and, further, that "we have made but little progress since pioneer days." It is admitted, however, that, in Illinois, "there have been many extenuating excuses." Early native soil fertility, and the ease with which returns were had from the land, are blamed in part for lack of attention to the roads. The report contains this paragraph of what might be termed "road philosophy."

"Of all the States of the Union, Illinois is the best supplied with fertile soil, and has the most meagre distribution of road surfacing material. But surfacing material does not make the road. It simply finishes or covers it, just as a roof finishes or covers a house. No amount of surfacing can make a permanently good road if its foundations and sides are defective and weak. Neither can good foundations and sides compensate for a leaky roof. A structure, to be good, must be all good, just as a chain, to be strong, must be strong in all of its links. Of no structure is this more true than a wagon road."

In the 25 years preceding 1903, the people of Illinois spent approximately $75,000,000 on wagon roads, and the Commission, in its report, laments that, as a whole, road conditions in 1903 and 1904 were little better than a quarter of a century before. The $75,000,000 referred to was paid in direct taxes.

Mud roads are ranked, in the report, as "luxuries." There is something refreshing in the statement that "the

(Continued on Page 132.)

TO MAKE AN EARTH ROAD GOOD, YOU MUST MAINTAIN IT

By B. H. PIEPMEIER, Maintenance Engineer, State Highway Department

Many inquiries are made concerning earth road construction and maintenance. It would seem hardly possible that such inquiries should be made on a subject that we are or should all be, more or less familiar with. However, it is perhaps for this reason that so many are willing to offer their views. If the road builder would listen to all freely expressed ideas on such work, he would be working the road differently every day.

DITCHES CLEAN; TRAFFIC IN CENTER.

About 90 per cent of the roads in Illinois are earth, and will likely remain as earth roads for a great many years. The greatest problem, particularly that of the township or road district, is properly to construct and maintain the existing earth roads. In view of the tremendous amount of earth road work that is to be done and of money to be spent for such work, it is quite important that every effort be directed along lines that will accomplish the best results and that will be a part of further improvement.

It must be kept in mind that the larger per cent of work done in constructing earth roads is permanent. If the grade is properly established, the cross section, the drainage, etc., it will not have to be done over or altered for future improvements. This being true, it can readily be seen that earth road construction is just as important as brick or concrete road construction and just as much engineering skill is required to insure the best results.

A great many earth roads are constructed in a haphazard way and with very little regard for any future improvement. Such work can only be severely criticised, as the time and money spent is practically wasted. Improperly worked earth roads result in a greater loss than the time and money that is wasted. Many roads are worse after working than before, and the loss to the public in the use of same can not be measured in dollars. Improper construction often puts the earth road in such shape that a very large per cent of the best soil is washed away by heavy rains and this is a serious loss to the road.

The greatest fault that could be offered against the bulk of township road construction to-day, is that the road and bridge money is spread out over all the roads in the township each year and there are but very few roads that receive the proper amount of time and money to put them in first-class condition. The bulk of the road and bridge money is really spent in maintenance work on the existing earth roads, when a large per cent of such roads need constructing before any money is spent in maintenance.

A majority of the townships have sufficient income to maintain the earth roads if they were once put into proper condition for effective maintenance. The most economic work that could be undertaken by a great many townships would be to finance some scheme that would permit all the earth roads in the township to be properly graded and drained and the necessary culverts and bridges constructed of a permanent material. After the majority of roads were once put in first-class condition, many of them could easily be maintained under good management by dragging and oiling, with the money that is available.

Earth roads properly maintained by use of the road drag and oil will be materially improved, and will serve the needs of a majority of the local traffic for a number of years. The improving and maintaining of good earth roads in a community will serve all the taxpayers alike, and will be a means of getting their support in improving, with some hard surfacing material, some of the heaviest traveled, or through connecting roads.

The main principles, making for efficiency in earth roads, are proper drainage and maintenance. There is no material so easily affected by improper drainage, as earth. When dry, it will readily support the heaviest concentrated loads of traffic, that will be imposed upon it. The same material when thoroughly saturated with water, will not support the slightest load. The secret, therefore, in constructing and maintaining such roads, is to utilize all possible schemes for keeping them dry.

A prominent farmer in Illinois remarked that if he just had a roof over his earth road from the farm to the market, he would not ask for anything better. This farmer knew what the earth roads needed, but his experience was limited as to how such results could be accomplished.

A NOVEMBER OILED EARTH ROAD.

The skilled road builder can, with the most modern methods of construction and maintenance, drain earth roads by removing the underground seep water and treating the earth surface so that the road is practically dry the greater part of the year and in such condition that it will serve moderate traffic economically.

The first step in the construction of an earth road is to have it surveyed and a permanent grade line and cross section established. The grade line should be established so that it will provide for the necessary drainage to the natural water courses. It should also provide for cutting down the grades and filling the hollows so there will be a permanent roadbed that will not have to be disturbed for further improvement. The cross section for the road will depend somewhat upon the drainage and whether it is a first-, second- or third-class road. Special attention should be given to side ditches to insure that they will provide for all surface water and remove it rapidly. Many side ditches on long, steep grades should be paved with concrete, riprap or similar material to prevent serious erosion.

All culverts and bridges should be constructed of as permanent a material as can be conveniently secured. They should be of such size that they will readily provide for all surface water.

Drain tile should be laid at points that have underground seepage and on flat, swampy roads, when the water has no chance to flow readily in the side ditches. Drain tile should be used only when absolutely necessary. The open side ditches properly constructed and kept clean, will give better satisfaction where there is sufficient fall for the water to flow.

A WINTER ROAD CAN BE LIKE THIS.

Earth roads can usually be constructed at a very low cost; however, they require constant maintenance which on many very heavily traveled roads, becomes expensive. The earth roads require maintenance and should not be neglected. A low first cost road with high maintenance expense is often just as economical as a high first cost road with practically no maintenance. The main purpose of a road is to satisfy the requirements of traffic. The earth road in some sections may do this as well as brick pavements in other sections. If this is kept in mind, more attention will be given to the earth roads and the money spent on them will not be thought of as lost.

After earth roads are once constructed, maintenance should begin at once. It is neglect that makes earth roads bad and causes $2 to be spent where $1 would have done the work. On account of the necessity of giving earth roads constant attention, it is important that every township arrange for a patrol system of maintenance or similar form, where someone can give his entire time to a section of roads and be held responsible for their condition.

Earth roads should be maintained by keeping a good crown in the road, keeping side ditches opened and the surface smooth so the water will readily drain to the side ditches and so traffic will be distributed over the entire surface. The distribution of traffic will keep the road uniformly compacted and free from ruts.

The systematic use of the road drag on a road that has been properly graded, will show better results, for the amount of money spent, than anything else that can be done to the road. It has been shown that systematic dragging can be done for a cost of from $10 to $15 per year per mile of road, after the road has once been properly graded and the drainage adequately cared for.

There has been a great deal of discussion as to how a road should be leveled or dragged. Many claim that it can be done very efficiently and effectively with a tractor and large leveler; others claim that the light 2-horse drag is more economical. There is no question but that both have proven satisfactory in different places. The most economic scheme depends a great deal upon the local conditions. It is not so much the method as the results that count. The main thing is to keep the surface of the road perfectly smooth, well crowned and the ditches clean.

A GLIMPSE OF ILLINOIS IN HER EARLY HIGHWAY INFANCY.

(Continued from Page 130.)

American farmer is the only one in the civilized world who is rich enough to afford the luxury of mud roads." The paradoxical nature of the observation would lead the reader to conclude, either, that the American farmer was a model of enterprise and a world-wide example in thrift, or, that America trailed, in lamentable fashion, the other countries of the globe in road construction.

Of the three original "Illinois Good Roads Commissioners," Mr. Smith, of Springfield, had had extensive experience as a highway commissioner; Mr. Mitchell was a business man of Chillicothe, and Mr. Wallace was chief of the engineering department of the Illinois Central Railroad at Chicago.

NATIONAL GOOD ROADS SHOW.

The eighth National Good Roads Show, under the auspices of the American Road Builders' Association, will be held in Mechanics Building, Boston, Mass., on February 5, 6, 7, 8 and 9, 1917, in connection with the fourteenth annual convention of the association. This exposition will include exhibits by leading manufacturers of machinery and materials used in road and street construction and maintenance.

The program for the convention proper is now in course of preparation and will include papers and discussions on subjects connected with road and bridge building and street paving by men who are recognized as authorities on the subjects with which they will deal.

The National Good Roads Show, which for a number of years has been a feature of the conventions of the American Road Builders' Association, has increased in size and importance year after year. The coming exhibition takes on added importance on account of the great amount of road work planned for next year in view of the funds appropriated under the recently enacted Federal Aid law and the additional large sums to be expended by the various states and smaller units of government.

A contract has been let for the construction of a new bridge across Kiser Creek near New Canton, in Pike County. The cost will be $9,343. The bridge will be 150 feet long and of reinforced concrete.

A MONOLITHIC PROCESS DEMONSTRA-TION

Paris, one of the active road-building centers of Illinois, was the mecca on October 6, of several hundred visitors, whose interest in the processes of monolithic brick paving construction led them to gather at the Edgar County seat from across the Indiana line and from many sections of the State and county.

VIEW OF THE CROWD AT PARIS.

It was a demonstration—staged along with regular township work on the Chicago Road—essentially for the benefit of delegates to the annual meeting of the National Paving Brick Manufacturers Association at Terre Haute, Ind., October 5 and 6.

Interest in the event was not confined, however, to the several hundred delegates. Road men who could get to Paris on the 6th made the trip; experts in the various lines of construction were there. Two of the State Highway Commissioners, Mr. Bradt and Mr. Wilson, the Chief State Highway Engineer, Mr. Marr, and the division engineers, with one exception, mingled with others of the unique and interesting assemblage. Alan Joy Parrish, of Paris, is the con-

COMMISSIONERS, CHIEF STATE HIGHWAY ENGINEER AND DEPARTMENT MEN AT THE DEMONSTRATION.

tractor whose work was viewed. W. T. Blackburn headed the committee of Paris business men who acted as hosts to the visitors, the Illinois highway officials assisting in the reception of those who came from over the State line.

Hospitality was one of the prime keynotes of the day. The main body of visiting delegates arrived in Paris from Terre Haute at 10 o'clock in the morning, and, after detraining from their special cars, were received by the Paris business men with automobiles, in which they were driven without delay to the 1,100-foot stretch of new road construction at the north edge of the city. Mr. Parrish, the contractor, was there to receive the crowd of several hundred convention delegates and to answer their questions relative to the work which they found proceeding at top speed. For nearly two hours, the men—and a few women—swarmed about the new road and the machinery with which it was being put down. Shortly after noon, the visitors were summoned to West Park, nearby, to enjoy the festivities and substantial eating which only a barbecue can supply. In the afternoon, the guests were taken for an automobile drive over Paris roads, including the first and original stretch of monolithic

COMPLETING THE BASE. DRAWING THE TEMPLATE EVENLY FROM DRUM OF BIG MIXER.

brick paving—400 feet constructed in March, 1915. At 4 o'clock, the convention people departed for Terre Haute where, in the evening, they concluded their annual meeting with a large banquet.

Demonstration of the actual laying of the new monolithic—one-piece or one-slab—road could not have been had under more favorable circumstances. Atmospherically, the day was perfect; the mechanism which Contractor Parrish had on the job, operated without a hitch; his men were keyed up to a degree of enthusiasm which only an audience of interested spectators can inspire, and every condition was right and in keeping with a successful showing.

Briefly, the method, or stages, which Mr. Parrish demonstrated to the visitors were these:

Preparation of a perfect subgrade. Width of road, 16 feet.

Setting of forms to true line and grade.

Laying of base of 4 inches of concrete, uniformly mixed, distributed and compacted.

Application on base of thin sheet of sand and cement, mixed dry, with the aid of the monolithic template. The template was designed by Mr. Parrish himself.

Immediate laying of the 4-inch brick behind the template.

Rolling of the brick by hand, using a 700-lb. roller.

Application of filler with grouting machine, leaving the pavement to set.

Though it is new and has not yet had time to undergo the test of time, the monolithic form of improved hard road apparently has a brilliant future. The finished monolithic pavement on a country road makes one of the smoothest thoroughfares known, and, experts believe, one of the most permanent.

CLOSE VIEW OF TEMPLATE.

Thoroughly solidified and set, the monolithic pavement presents, to all intents and purposes, a single piece of construction. As soon as the brick is laid, capillary attraction takes place between the thin covering of sand and cement, and the base. The rolling, which is done diagonally over the freshly laid brick, serves as an aid to the process of capillary attraction, and makes a free mortar of the sand and cement coating, thus helping to bind the brick to the base. The moisture works up from the base, which is freshly put down, thus affecting the thin coating upon which the brick are laid.

LAYING THE BRICK, JUST BEHIND TEMPLATE.

The grouting is, of course, vitally important. The filler which is spread evenly over the freshly laid brick by a modern machine, made for the purpose, settles between the lugs, making it possible for the entire layer of pavement to "cure" as one piece and one body.

Hence the name, monolithic. The "curing" process requires about two weeks.

Mr. Parrish, who is as well posted on the monolithic method as any contractor in the country, has studied exhaustively his favorite type of construction. As yet, he has found no material defect in the monolithic paving. Last winter, he subjected it to tests. It emerged from all of them successfully. The contractor is of the opinion that monolithic pavement can be made cheaper than other forms, although varying conditions have made this year's work unfavorable for the computing of cost.

ROLLING THE BRICK DIAGONALLY, JUST AFTER LAYING.

A 4-inch standard brick is used by Mr. Parrish in all of his work. He believes the 3-inch brick is not satisfactory, partly because of the apparent inability to make a commercial success of it. In applying the filler, he mixes one part cement and one part sand, using two coats. The Marsh-Capron grouter, which accommodates especially the needs of the monolithic form, is used in distributing the filler. With it, Mr. Parrish has succeeded in reducing filler troubles to a minimum.

Discussion among the hundreds of visitors who watched the processes with intense interest covered every phase of the work. Many asked about the wis-

GROUTING MACHINE AT WORK.

dom of laying brick upon concrete. Mr. Parrish discouraged this, saying the finished surface, in such cases, usually was not so smooth. Authorities who watched the processes agreed that best results were gained by wetting the mass *ahead* of the filler.

The kind of template used, and its operation, furnished a basis for much speculation. Mr. Parrish yields to no one in his judgment in this particular item. He has made several templates of his own, and on them holds his own patents. The one which he showed in operation at Paris was his new 16-foot machine, with wider rollers than have marked former templates. As it moves down the steel frame track—the frames or molds serving as the "rails"—the template is drawn by a chain attached to the drum of the big mixer, thus insuring uniform movement and, consequently, a perfectly smooth film of dry sand and cement on top of the base.

The new road which the visitors saw in process of laying will be paid for by Paris Township. The immediate stretch is 1,100 feet long, connecting with a monolithic pavement to the north, in Chicago Road, which was laid a short time ago.

BRICK MANUFACTURERS MEET.

Terre Haute, Ind., was the convention city of delegates to the thirteenth annual meeting of the National Paving Brick Manufacturers' Association, October 5 and 6. President C. C. Blair, of Youngstown, Ohio, presided at the business sessions, which were held in the Deming hotel, at Terre Haute.

The program for the first day included the address of the president, a report on the association work by Will P. Blair, secretary, and a report on the publicity work of the organization by H. H. Macdonald, assistant secretary.

All of the officers were reelected, as follows: C. C. Blair, Youngstown, Ohio, President; J. W. Robb, Clinton, Ind., Vice President; Will P. Blair, Cleveland, Ohio, secretary; C. C. Barr, Streator, Ill., treasurer; H. H. Macdonald, Cleveland, Ohio, assistant secretary.

The new directors are: J. B. Wilcox, Alliance, Ohio; Eb Rodgers, Alton, Ill.; W. N. Alderman, Athens, Ohio; C. C. Barr, Streator, Ill.; C. C. Blair, Youngstown, Ohio; G. O. French, Canton, Ohio; R. C. Burton, Zanesville, Ohio; Will P. Blair, Cleveland, Ohio; J. W. Robb, Clinton, Ind.; C. J. Deckman, Cleveland, Ohio; J. G. Barbour, Canton, Ohio; F. L. Manning, Portsmouth, Ohio; J. L. Murphy, Nelsonville, Ohio; John Kline, Wickliffe, Ohio; R. A. Doan, Nelsonville, Ohio; G. E. Carlyle, Portsmouth, Ohio; J. R. Zmunt, Cleveland, Ohio; C. P. Mayer, Bridgeville, Pa.; H. C. Adams, Danville, Ill.; G. H. Francis, Greensburg, Pa.; F. W. Lucke, Chicago, Ill.; D. R. Potter, Clarksburg, W. Va.; J. H. Simpson, Dayton, Ohio; E. M. Grant, Morgantown, W. Va.; and S. R. Strong, Seattle, Wash.

On October 6 there was an inspection of the brick pavements of Terre Haute, after which those attending the meeting went to Paris, Ill., to witness the demonstration of brick highway construction under the recently adopted specifications.

Engineers and manufacturers from almost every part of the country were present. Among the men who took long trips to attend the convention and the Paris demonstration were C. L. Costello, San Francisco, Cal.; S. W. Hume, New York; L. S. Smith, Madison, Wis.; D. P. Walter, Clarksburg, W. Va.; J. T. Voshell, Washington, D. C.; James J. Tucker, University of Oklahoma, Norman, Okla.; C. W. Denniston, Rochester, N. Y.; Floyd W. Allen, Seattle, Wash. Past President C. J. Deekman was in attendance also.

Authorities on paving who were present included: Prof. Lawson, Rensselaer polytechnic institute; W. A.

Alsdorf, Columbus, Ohio, author Ohio road law and secretary good roads federation; Frank Rogers, highway commissioner of Michigan; I. O. Baker, University of Illinois, author of a standard work on roads and pavements; Prof. L. Smith, University of Wisconsin; Henry Metzel, chief engineer of Columbus, Ohio, and chairman paving committee of American Association of Municipal Improvement; Prof. Benjamin, dean of college of engineering at Purdue, and Prof. Tucker, University of Oklahoma.

ROAD AND BRIDGE EXPENDITURES.

Statistics for the calendar year 1915 recently compiled by the Office of Public Roads and Rural Engineering of the U. S. Department of Agriculture, show that the total length of public roads in the United States outside the limits of incorporated towns and cities was about 2,452,000 miles on January 1, 1916. Of this, about 277,000 miles, or 11.3 per cent were improved with some form of surfacing. The mileage of surfaced roads has been increasing at the rate of about 16,000 miles a year, and in 1915 approximately one-half of this increase was made under the supervision of state highway departments. In addition, these departments supervised the maintenance of nearly 52,000 miles of main and trunkline roads.

The increase in expenditures for road and bridge work in the United States has been approximately $80,000,000 per year in 1904 to about $282,000,000 in 1915, an increase of more than 250 per cent. The expenditure of state funds during this same period increased from about $2,550,000 to more than $53,000,000. In addition, more than $27,000,000 of local funds was spent under state supervision in 1915, bringing the total road and bridge expenditures managed by the states to $80,514,699. This amount is greater than the total expenditures for roads and bridges from all sources in 1904.

The growth in importance of the state highway departments has been rapid. The first of these agencies was created in 1891 in New Jersey, and now some form of highway department exists in every state except Indiana, South Carolina, and Texas. These departments had expended since their inception to January 1, 1916, an aggregate of $265,350,825 in state funds for road and bridge construction, maintenance, and administration. They had constructed over 50,000 miles of roads in cooperation with the states. More than 40,000 miles of these roads were surfaced.

The falling off in the value of road work performed by statute and convict labor was from $20,000,000 in 1904 when the total road expenditures were $80,000,000, to about $15,000,000 in 1915 when the total expenditures had grown to $282,000,000. This was a reduction from 25 per cent of the total in the former year to less than 5½ per cent of the total in 1915.

The cash road and bridge expenditures of the United States averaged only $28 per mile of rural roads in 1904. In 1915 this average had grown to $109 per mile. New Jersey led all other states both in 1904 and in 1915 with $221 and $475 per mile respectively. Nevada made the least expenditure in both years—$3.72 per mile in 1904 and $17 per mile in 1915.

A new concrete 40-foot bridge over French Creek, on the line of Peoria and Knox Counties, has been contracted for. It will cost $2,554.

ILLINOIS HIGHWAYS.

Published Monthly by the
State Highway Department,
Springfield, Illinois.

ILLINOIS HIGHWAY COMMISSION.
A. D. GASH, *President.*
S. E. BRADT, *Secretary.*
JAMES P. WILSON.

WM. W. MARR, *Chief State Highway Engineer.*

BUREAU OF ROADS.
H. E. BILGER, *Road Engineer.*
M. W. WATSON, *Assistant Road Engineer.*
C. M. HATHAWAY, *Office Engineer.*

BUREAU OF BRIDGES.
CLIFFORD OLDER, *Bridge Engineer.*
G. F. BURCH, *Assistant Bridge Engineer.*
A. W. CONSOER, *Office Engineer.*

BUREAU OF MAINTENANCE.
B. H. PIEPMEIER, *Maintenance Engineer.*
F. T. SHEETS, *Assistant Maintenance Engineer.*

BUREAU OF TESTS.
F. L. ROMAN, *Testing Engineer.*
W. C. ADAMS, *Chemist.*

BUREAU OF AUDITS.
J. M. McCOY, *Chief Clerk.*
EARL B. SEARCY, *Department Editor.*
R. R. McLEOD, *General Bookkeeper.*
G. E. HOPKINS, *Property Clerk.*

DIVISION ENGINEERS.
R. L. Bell, Buchanan-Link Bldg., Paris, Ill.
H. B. Bushnell, 144 Fox St., Aurora, Ill.
J. E. Huber, Wise Building, Mt. Vernon, Ill.
A. H. Hunter, 302 Apollo Theater Bldg., Peoria, Ill.
C. M. Slaymaker, 510 Metropolitan Bldg., E. St. Louis, Ill.
H. E. Surman, 614 People's Bank Bldg., Moline, Ill.
Fred Tarrant, 730 Reisch Bldg., Springfield, Ill.

Address all communications in regard to "Illinois Highways," to Earl B. Searcy, Department Editor, State Highway Department, Springfield, Illinois.

CONTENTS.

After having been closed for several weeks because of the installation of a new bridge, the road between Tuscola and Arcola has been reopened.

* * *

Coles County will accept State aid for its highways this year. The county board has appropriated $8,905 and an equal amount will be given by the State.

* * *

A unique method was employed a few weeks ago in tearing down the old Locust Street bridge across the Chicago & Alton Railroad tracks at Bloomington. A wrecking outfit was hitched to the span, which had been loosened from its approaches, and the entire structure was pulled down. Then it was cut up into small pieces and the debris hauled away. A new bridge will replace the old one.

* * *

A 50-foot pile bridge is to be built across a swampy stretch on the county line between Portland Township, Whiteside County, and Phenix Township, Henry County.

* * *

R. A. Cullen, of Pekin, has been awarded a contract for the construction of the Bernhausen bridge in Cincinnati Township, Tazewell County. The Cullen bid was $1,819.

* * *

The Northeast Conference of County Highway Superintendents held its meeting recently in Kankakee. The delegates were guests of the Kankakee supervisors, County Highway Superintendent Frank M. Enos and the Woman's Relief Corps. Next year's annual meeting will be held in Rockford.

* * *

Cornelius Knipers, residing near Lansing, Cook County, has been named highway commssioner to succeed William Krause, of Glenwood, who is unable to serve longer as commissioner because of his duties as postmaster at Glenwood.

* * *

The Burlington Way has been marked through North Central Illinois. From Peoria to Rockford, the route will be through Peoria, Tazewell, Woodford, Marshall and La Salle Counties, and through the towns of East Peoria, Washington, Metamora, Roanoke, Benson, Minonk, Rutland, Wenona, Lostant, Tonica, La Salle, Oglesby, and thence to Ottawa via the State Park at Starved Rock.

* * *

The *Quincy Herald* recently published a road map of Adams County, showing routes in use and those proposed for improvement. The map will serve as a valuable guide for travelers through the county.

* * *

Fondulac Township, in Peoria County, has accepted the proposal of the Holt Manufacturing Company to build a gravel road, known as the "Caterpillar Trail" from East Peoria to the upper free bridge in Fondulac Township.

* * *

Six new bridges on the State aid road in Washington Township, Peoria County, are to be built. The contract has been awarded to Smith Brothers of Washington. The work will cost a little less than $2,800.

* * *

A contract has been let to L. V. Wallingford & Sons, of Prophetstown, for the construction of five reinforced concrete bridges along the county line between Whiteside and Carroll Counties. The work will cost $3,359. It is to be completed by December 1.

ILLIN

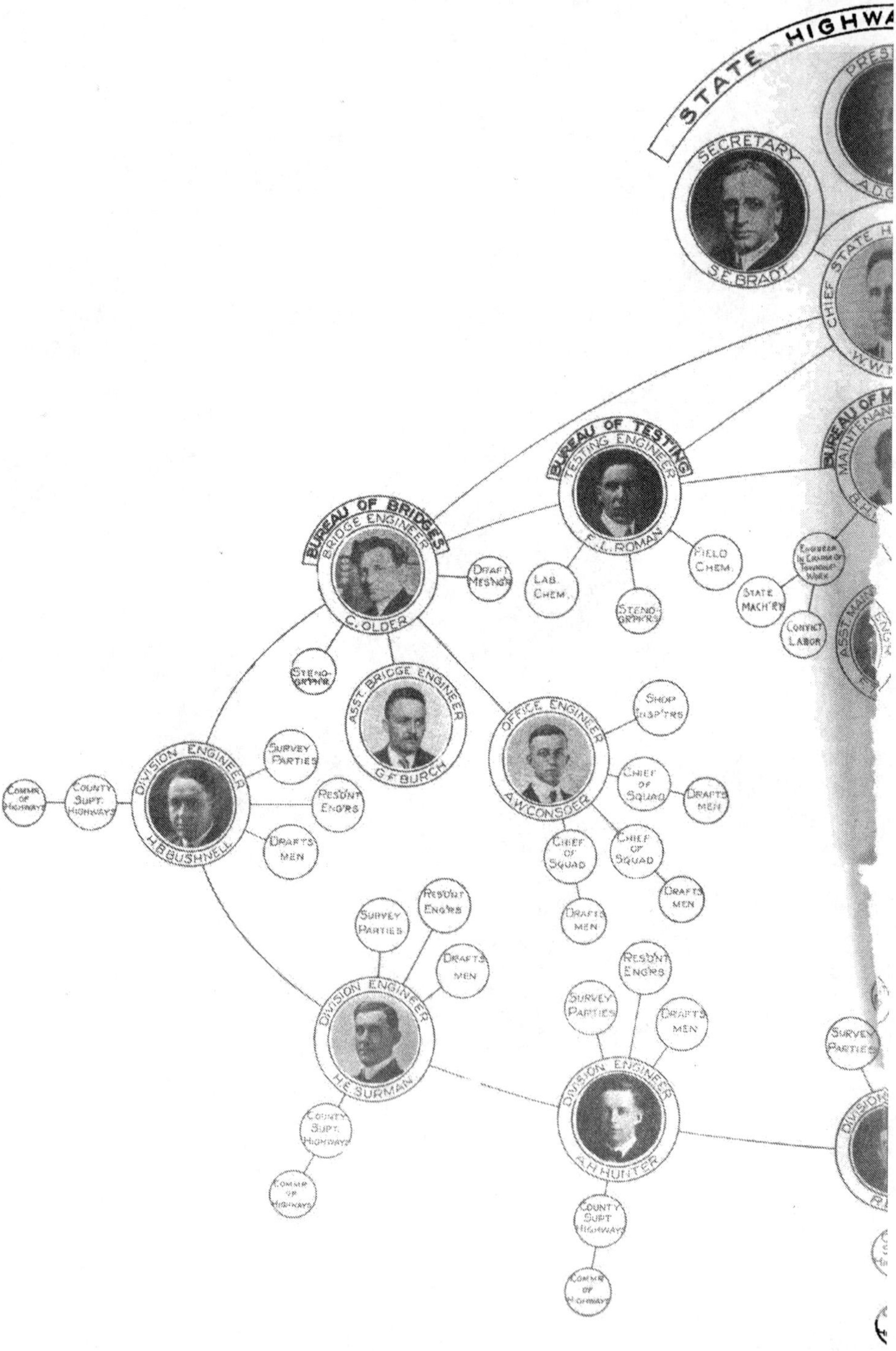

PRES

SECRETARY
S.E.BRADT

A.D.G

CHIEF STATE H
W.W.

BUREAU OF TESTING
TESTING ENGINEER
F.L.ROMAN

BUREAU OF M
MAINTENAN

FIELD
CHEM.

BUREAU OF BRIDGES
BRIDGE ENGINEER
C.OLDER

DRAFT
MESN'GR

LAB.
CHEM.

ENGINEER
IN CHARGE OF
TOWNSHIP
WORK

STATE
MACH'RY

STENO
GRAPHERS

CONVICT
LABOR

STENO
GRPHR

ASST
MAI

ASST BRIDGE ENGINEER
G.F.BURCH

SHOP
INSP'TRS

OFFICE ENGINEER
A.W.CONSOER

SURVEY
PARTIES

CHIEF
OF
SQUAD

DRAFTS
MEN

COMM'R
OF
HIGHWAYS

COUNTY
SUPT.
HIGHWAYS

DIVISION ENGINEER
H.B.BUSHNELL

RESID'NT
ENGR'S

CHIEF
OF
SQUAD

CHIEF
OF
SQUAD

DRAFTS
MEN

DRAFTS
MEN

DRAFTS
MEN

RESID'NT
ENGR'S

RESID'NT
ENGR'S

SURVEY
PARTIES

DRAFTS
MEN

SURVEY
PARTIES

DRAFTS
MEN

SURVEY
PARTIES

DIVISION ENGINEER
H.E.SURMAN

DIVISION ENGINEER
A.H.HUNTER

DIVISIO
E
R

COUNTY
SUPT.
HIGHWAYS

COUNTY
SUPT
HIGHWAYS

COMM'R
OF
HIGHWAYS

COMM'R
OF
HIGHWAYS

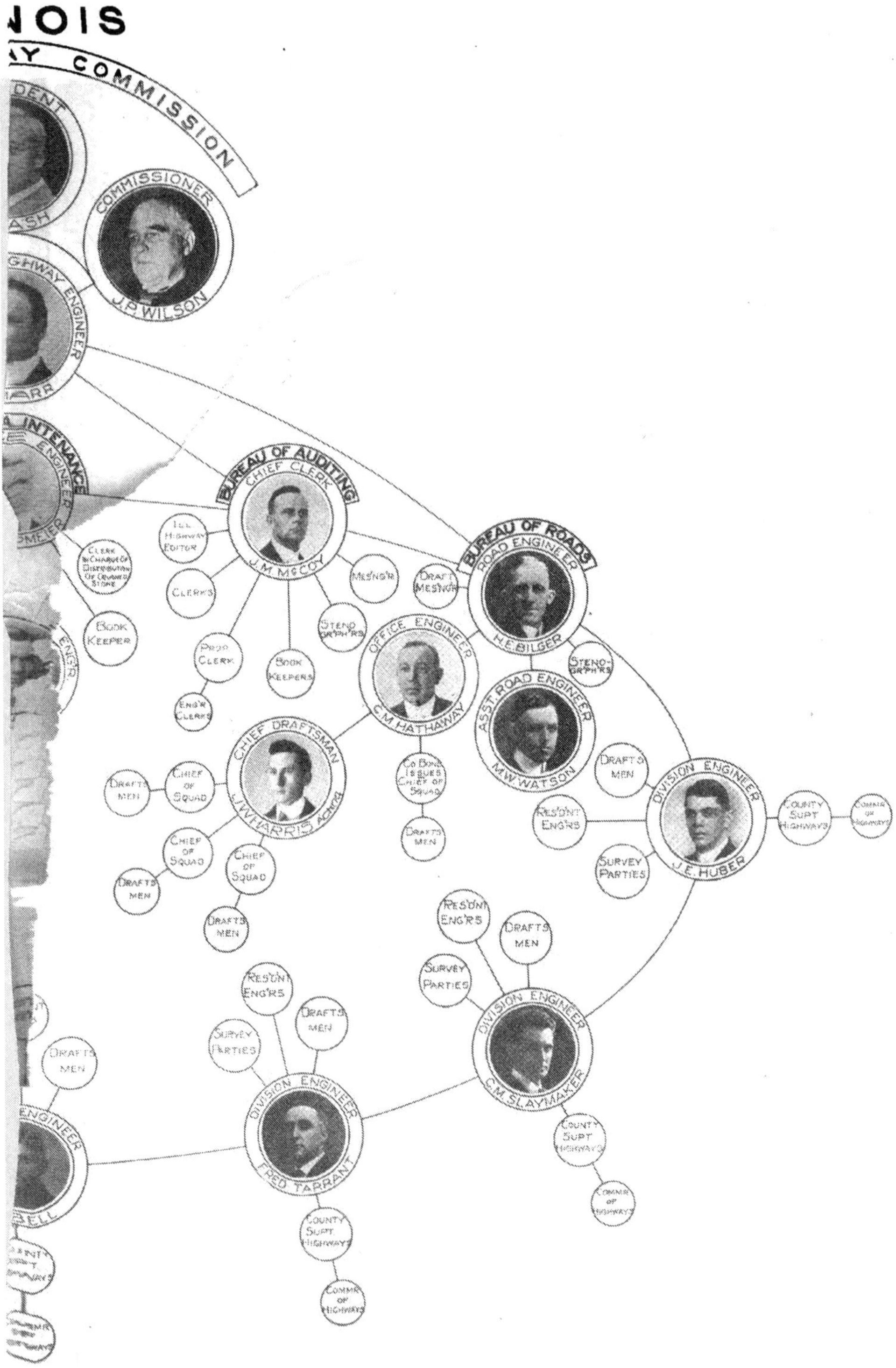

DENT

ASH

COMMISSIONER
J.P. WILSON

GHWAY ENGINEER

ARR

MAINTENANCE
ENGINEER

MEIER

CLERK IN CHARGE OF DISTRIBUTION OF CRUSHED STONE

CLERKS

BOOK KEEPER

BUREAU OF AUDITING
CHIEF CLERK
J.M. McCOY

ILL HIGHWAY EDITOR

MES'NG'R

DRAFT MES'NGR

PROO CLERK

BOOK KEEPERS

STEND DR'PH'RS

ENG'R CLERKS

BUREAU OF ROADS
ROAD ENGINEER
H.E. BILGER

STENO-DR'PH'RS

OFFICE ENGINEER
C.M. HATHAWAY

ASST ROAD ENGINEER
M.W. WATSON

DRAFTS MEN

CHIEF DRAFTSMAN
J.W. HARRIS ACHD

DRAFTS MEN

CHIEF OF SQUAD

CHIEF OF SQUAD

DRAFTS MEN

CHIEF OF SQUAD

DRAFTS MEN

CO.BNDS ISSUES CHIEF OF SQUAD

DRAFTS MEN

RES'DNT ENG'RS

SURVEY PARTIES

DIVISION ENGINEER
J.E. HUBER

COUNTY SUPT HIGHWAYS

COMM'R OF HIGHWAYS

RES'DNT ENG'RS

DRAFTS MEN

SURVEY PARTIES

DIVISION ENGINEER
C.M. SLAYMAKER

COUNTY SUPT HIGHWAYS

COMM'R OF HIGHWAYS

RES'DNT ENG'RS

DRAFTS MEN

SURVEY PARTIES

DIVISION ENGINEER
FRED TARRANT

COUNTY SUPT HIGHWAYS

COMM'R OF HIGHWAYS

ENGINEER

BELL

DRAFTS MEN

JUNT UPT HWAYS

COMM'R HWAYS

The Organization of the State Highway Department

By Wm. W. MARR, Chief State Highway Engineer.

In 1913 the Legislature passed a law revising the statutes of Illinois in relation to roads and bridges and creating a State Highway Department with new powers and duties.

A State Highway Commission of three members was provided to be appointed by the Governor and to have general control of the department. A State Highway Engineer, appointed by the Governor, was also provided, to be the executive officer of the commission. Such employes as were necessary to carry on the work of the department were to be appointed through competitive civil service examinations.

The work of the department has grown by leaps and bounds and it has recently been necessary to reorganize the force along permanent lines. The accompanying chart (insert) will illustrate perhaps as clearly as possible the organization as it has been adopted. The work of the department has been divided into five character divisions or bureaus with a bureau chief in charge of each of the five main divisions. These are respectively: The Bureau of Bridges, Bureau of Testing, Bureau of Maintenance, Bureau of Auditing and Bureau of Roads. The various bureau chiefs have responsible charge of all the work of the department of the particular character to which they are assigned.

The work is further subdivided along territorial lines into seven districts, each under the direction of a division engineer, who is in direct responsible charge of all work in his district. The division engineers report to the respective bureau chiefs in accordance with the character of the work involved. Each division engineer is located in a permanent office in his division and has an independent organization of his own, reporting directly to him in all matters.

In addition to the division engineers, each bureau chief has reporting to him an independent office force for which he is directly responsible. There is in the organization no conflict of authority or division of responsibility. It will be noted from an inspection of the chart that no member of the department reports to or receives orders from more than one superior. The various assistants' report to their immediate superior and whenever an assistant has a specific branch of work assigned to him, his subordinates report only to himself.

On the other hand, no member of the department is authorized to issue instructions to any but the immediate subordinates, which operates clearly and definitely to define authority and responsibility in all cases and to obviate the confusion which naturally results when a superior officer attempts to direct work over the heads of intermediate officials.

Owing to the vast territory in which the department operates and the scattered condition of the work, the overhead and engineering cost have been comparatively high in the past, but due to the establishment of division engineers in permanent quarters and otherwise perfecting the present organization, the cost of engineering has been greatly reduced and the efficiency of our men has been materially increased.

Probably the greatest factor in the work of the department at the present time is the phenomenal growth of sentiment for the construction of systems of roads by counties. This is a very different problem from the piece-meal construction of short stretches of road at widely separated points, by means of State aid. The construction of one road is simple in comparison to improving a comprehensive system of roads in a county.

Approximately thirty counties in the State are now contemplating bond issues for the improvement of State aid roads in the respective counties and from present indications upwards of $20,000,000 in bonds for road construction will have been involved in elections by the end of the year. This has at times taxed to the limit our facilities for making preliminary plans and investigations.

The department furnishes to counties contemplating bond issues, a number of different tentative plans for a comprehensive system of county roads on designated State aid lines for their consideration. County boards then take up the matter, usually through a committee which investigates and recommends some particular plan. If the action of the county board is favorable, the question of issuing bonds is submitted to the people at a special election called for the purpose. The amount of money which a county may raise in this manner is limited by the Constitution to 5 per cent of the assessed valuation of all property in the county less any outstanding county bond indebtedness. This is usually sufficient in any county to build a complete system of roads composed of various types adapted to the amount and character of traffic on each particular road.

STATE BREVITIES.

The condition of the highway bridge over the Vandalia line near Atlanta, Logan County, has been pronounced unsafe.

* * *

County Superintendent Thomas of St. Clair County, has reported that the county has between 1,000 and 1,100 miles of county and State road.

* * *

The Rossville-Paxton Hard Road Association was formed at a recent meeting in Rossville. George Merritt is president, and Glen Prillamen, secretary-treasurer.

* * *

The highway commissioners of Schuyler County have levied $44,960 for road purposes next year.

The Decatur Bridge Company has been awarded the contract to build a new steel and concrete bridge over Salt Creek, in McLean County, at a cost of $11,600. The structure will be in Broadwell Township.

* * *

A new $2,420 bridge, of concrete construction, is to be erected over the Whitechurch Slough on the Tennessee Prairie Road, three miles east of Higgins, Illinois. The structure will take the place of three old bridges which have spanned the place.

* * *

The McLean County board of supervisors visited Vermilion County in a body, recently, to inspect the road system which is rapidly making the border county famous.

Concrete Bridge Construction and the Economy of it as Emphasized by War Prices

By A. W. CONSOER, Engineer, Bureau of Bridges

From the time of its organization in 1913, the Illinois State Highway Department has encouraged the construction of reinforced concrete bridges, inasmuch as such practice is ordinarily more economical than the construction of steel bridges which, though they might sometimes be cheaper as regards the cost of construction, yet, because of excessive maintenance and renewal charges, would prove more expensive when ultimate cost is considered.

However, since December, 1914, we have witnessed an unprecedented rise in the cost of structural steel. The price of structural steel at the mills in Pittsburgh increased from $1.10 per 100 pounds in December, 1914, to $2.60—$2.75 per 100 pounds in October, 1916. These war prices have resulted in a marked increase in the cost of steel bridge construction. The cost of concrete bridge construction has also increased somewhat because of higher prices for reinforcing steel, but the increased price of steel has not been as important an element in the cost of concrete bridges as in the cost of steel bridges. Another factor in the increased cost of steel bridge work has been the difficulty in securing prompt mill shipments, and the necessity of securing structural material from warehouses at prices considerably higher than the mill rates. Both classes of construction have been increased in cost by increases in the cost of other structural materials, machinery and labor and higher interest rates.

The result has been, that the construction cost of steel bridge work has advanced more rapidly than the construction cost of concrete bridge work. The accompanying table is interesting in that it shows, both by the bids actually submitted, as well as by the comparative estimates prepared, the decided economy of concrete bridges in a number of cases for which alternate plans for both steel and concrete bridges were prepared.

These plans were prepared by the Bureau of Bridges during the years 1914-1916. They cover only those cases where there was some doubt as to whether a concrete or steel bridge would prove more economical for the site in question. For the majority of bridge sites, the advantage of the one type of bridge construction over the other is apparent from the comparative estimates for a concrete and a steel bridge.

An examination of the table shows that the advantage of building concrete bridges applies not only to single short-span bridges, but also to the construction of bridges over comparatively wide streams where it is

TABLE SHOWING COMPARISON BETWEEN COSTS OF STEEL AND CONCRETE BRIDGES.

Name of Bridge.	Location.	Total span (feet.)	Estimated Costs. Steel.	Estimated Costs. Concrete.	Low bids received. Steel.	Low bids received. Concrete.
Sneakout...........	Cave Township, Franklin County..........	50	$ 1,930	$ 2,160	$1,863 00	¹ $1,869 60
Bluff City..........	Woodland and Hickory Townships, Fulton and Schuyler Counties..................	60	2,580	3,250	2,699 00	¹ 2,989 00
Burtons...........	Nunda Township, McHenry County........	400	15,300	17,000	13,705 00	14,000 00
Mt. Moriah Church..	LaGrange and E. Fork Townships, Bond and Montgomery Counties	60	3,180	3,210	¹ 2,552 50	2,900 00
Brady.............	Pea Ridge Township, Brown County........	60	2,855	3,660	¹ 2,422 00	3,229 00
Popham...........	Pleasant Grove Township, Coles County....	50	2,240	2,050	1,760 00	¹ 1,840 00
Pond Creek........	Frankfort and Lake Creek Townships, Franklin and Williamson Counties.....	30	1,335	1,500	¹ 947 00	No returns. Not included in totals.
Pinney.............	Bolo Township, Washington County........	30	1,300	1,445	¹ 1,250 00	1,250 00
Corrigan...........	Amity Township, Livingston County.......	150	7,950	7,550	7,200 00	7,600 00
Troumbower.......	Buckhart and Mt. Auburn Townships, Christian County	50	1,970	2,000	1,224 00	1,499 00
Kellogg...........	Clintonia Township, DeWitt County........	50	2,275	2,360	2,350 00	No returns. Not included in totals.
Dunn Prairie.......	Ewing Township, Franklin County........	55	2,000	2,125	1,948 00	¹ 1,913 00
Grassy Creek.......	Saline Township, Williamson County.......	30	985	1,125	No returns	¹ 1,098 00 Not included in totals.
Sedgwick..........	Lisbon Township, Kendall County.........	36	1,595	1,730	1,690 00	¹ 1,685 40
Watson............	Cherry Valley and Monroe Townships, Winnebago and Ogle Counties..............	150	7,620	6,640	6,855 00	¹ 5,999 00
Richards..........	Sheridan Township, Logan County........	30	1,272	1,208	No returns	¹ 1,200 00 Not included in totals.
Stuhan...........	Sheridan and W. Lincoln Townships, Logan County	30	1,520	1,445	No returns	¹ 1,400 00 Not included in totals.
New Canton........	Pleasant Vale Township, Pike County.....	150	11,220	9,680	11,800 00	¹ 9,343 00
Melton County Line.	Westfield and Kansas Townships, Clark and Edgar Counties	50	3,350	3,310	2,897 00	¹ 2,680 00
No. 1 Centennial....	Douglas Township, Iroquois County.......	120	7,560	10,410	¹ 9,300 00	9,980 00
McCue............	Greenwood Township, McHenry County....	50	2,415	2,515	¹ 2,680 00	2,423 00
	Totals	1,691	$82,852	$86,373	....	....
		1,521	....	....	$71,745 50	$71,200 00

NOTE: ¹ Denotes the award of the contract.

necessary to use a number of concrete spans. The last eight bridges in the table were contracted for in 1916, and in a number of these cases both the estimates and low bids received indicate that a concrete bridge is cheaper in first cost than a steel bridge. The one notable exception, the No. 1 Centennial bridge in Douglas Township, Iroquois County, is explained by the fact that a concrete bridge for this site involved the construction of a long central pier about 22 feet high, built on a skew. In the case of the Centennial No. 1 bridge, however, it would have been possible to justify the selection of a concrete bridge on the basis of cheaper ultimate cost.

The difference in the low bids for a steel and a concrete bridge amounts to $680. At 5 per cent, the interest charges on this sum amount to $34 per annum. To keep the steel bridge in first-class condition, it should be painted at least once in five years. The cost of cleaning and painting the bridge will be about $200, or an annual charge of about $40. It is evident that painting the steel alone would more than make up for the difference in the first costs.

For the majority of stream crossings in Illinois, however, the head room is considerably less and the cost of constructing piers is low enough to result in more decided economy in the construction of multiple span concrete bridges.

There is no indication of a break in the steel market at present, and it seems evident that the very marked economy of concrete bridge construction will continue for some time to come.

WHY AUTOMOBILE ACCIDENTS OCCUR

By Dr. LEONARD KEENE HIRSHBERG, A. B., M. A., M. D.

From October American Motorist

There are more than 3,000,000 motor cars in use in these United States and Canada. There are only 15,000,000 voters in the country and perhaps the same number of families.

This means that one family in every four or five owns a motor car.

Scientists and experienced shop foremen in machine shops and factories estimate that not one person in forty can properly guide and control a simple motor in a store or factory.

The average man is not clear in his vision, his hearing, his other common senses, or in his muscular control. His muscle sense is particularly defective, incomplete, and ineffective from lack of use in childhood and youth.

These statistics explain in a fashion, why it is often suicidal for some people to drive or to ride in automobiles, and, together with other things, accounts for the fact that over 200 automobile accidents occur each week day and three times as many on Sundays and holidays.

Fortunately of the 600 motor car mishaps which occur in the United States on Sundays, only one-tenth involve injuries to the occupants if the data collected by doctor of engineering, George Greenfield, M. D., is correct..

That is to say, collisions between machines are ten times more frequent than injuries to their occupants.

In other words the percentage of risk to your life and health in a moving automobile is about the same as having typhoid fever. One person in each group of ten, ill with typhoid, has dangerous and possible fatal complications. One car in every ten that is wrecked has its occupants thus exposed to mortal risks.

The technical investigation upon which my facts are founded contains many interesting lessons for the auto rider, and chauffeur who wishes to live and learn, as well as to learn to live.

WHERE AUTO ACCIDENTS OCCUR.

Thus it has been discovered that 23 out of every 24 accidents to automobiles take place at the intersections of crossroads, highways where one driveway leads at right angles into another, and where one street crosses another.

These unhappy accidents do not commonly occur, as is usually supposed, at places of congested, down-town traffic. Indeed, motor cars seldom collide in shopping districts or where machines are most numerous. The catastrophes usually happen, not at rush hours, at noon, at work-quitting times, but in clear streets and less busy intervals.

The reason for this, in view of these statistical researches, is obvious. Where congestion is thickest, hours busiest, and danger imminent, drivers are less heedless of caution. Were there even no traffic policemen and signals of warning at such places and times —and there generally is one or the other—there would still be less likelihood of calamity then.

Though men are naturally inclined "to take a reckless chance"—to be careless, negligent, or, in their egotism imagine they can outplay the average against them on the highways as well as the highroads of auto life—in crowded districts they key themselves up and act with sanity and discretion.

Not so, however, when an open stretch of street or driveway is before them. With a weakness and disregard for the law of averages and an egotistic expectation that they can "get away with it," they "open her up" and race along parkways, county roads, and drives with intersections every third of a mile or less.

WHEN FOLLY MEETS FOLLY.

The upshot of all this is the inevitable. Soon or late that car and that driver will meet his counterpart coming at right angles or from some acute turn at a common point and then, of course, hell breaks loose, cars are smashed and one time in ten the occupants of both cars killed or seriously banged about.

Yesterday was Sunday. It was a cloudy, partially rainy day. There were, therefore, fewer cars on the roads and in the parks than might have been there on a brilliant summer holiday. Yet the usual thing happened. Around New York City there were twenty odd motor catastrophes, ten in Philadelphia, seven in Baltimore. No doubt the same percentage elsewhere.

Of these 37 records at hand, 33 happened at street intersections or where one highway crossed another. There were 180 persons in the 60 automobiles concerned, or an average of nearly 3 to the car. Of the 180, twenty were bruised, burned, hurt internally, or with enough damage to be taken to hospitals. Two were killed.

As far as my researches go, two-thirds report that there were no horns, bells, or other warning signals heard from each other as they approached the crossings. Practically all, no doubt, disregarded the plain commands of caution and intelligence, to wit, to slow down at turns, crossings, and intersections of streets.

It is all very well in the open country on a fine stretch of level road with no trees or hills to hide a cross street or other road, to occasionally take a brief spin of 30 or 40 miles an hour.

This, however, is worse than the acme of folly on wet, hilly, treelined, or precipitous roads with high hills on either side concealing what is ahead from sight.

A speed as slow as 10 or 15 miles an hour is enough for most travel and brings the tourist to his destination just as quickly, as a rule, as a breakneck velocity. Indeed, the old fable of the tortoise and the rabbit is more than ever applicable to automobile touring.

Another most instructive series of facts brought out by these eminently necessary investigations is that 90 of every 100 warning signals on automobiles do not penetrate far enough into space and can not be heard far enough or around corners.

Experiments conducted in a psychological laboratory with ten different devices for making warning noises yielded strange results. The old-time horns with rubber bulbs, and the deep basso Klaxons, were the ones that could best be heard around corners for any great distance at right angles to the source of the sound.

In brief, these tests prove that most of the warning signals used on cars are woefully inadequate insofar as sanity and common sense information is needed to tell of the approach of motor cars when going over 20 miles an hour.

WHAT A PSYCHOLOGIST FOUND.

Obviously, another important factor is also involved in these intersection accidents. A woman psychologist at work recently on the normal human eye—at the point not quite near the centre of the back wall of the eye is a spot without vision—found that the most alert and sharpest eyed person in the world may fail even to see a giant truck coming from the side some distance ahead Briefly, this means that at a certain vital moment, when the auto driver should see the approach of another car at right angles, and slow down to 10 miles an hour when going 30, the object falls on the blind spot of his eyes and he misses it. This also accounts for some calamities at street crossings.

Such observations as are here reported, if studied, remembered, and applied to driving motor cars, should serve to reduce the ever-growing number of automobile mishaps. Experienced chauffeurs and those who have driven cars for two or more years will at once recognize the practical value of the information here brought to light. Beginners and new drivers, like the child that must be burned before it fears the fire, will likely not heed the words and the experience thus gained. They must, like the burnt child, suffer first themselves perhaps before they will take these discoveries to heart.

[EDITOR's NOTE.—The foregoing article, which we take the liberty of borrowing from *American Motorist* is applicable, in nearly everything which Dr. Hirshberg writes, to Illinois. This department is interested primarily in the construction and maintenance of roads; but when students of highways and their problems undertake to delineate wholesome theories of safety upon our lanes of travel, we can not help but affix our stamp of approval.]

TRADE FOLLOWS THE BEST ROUTE.

In a recent issue, *The Farmers' Review*, in pursuance of its series of articles on "Community Development," contains the following treatise on the subject, "Transportation":

"Commercial necessity has been a mighty factor in man's development.

"Through this impelling force man has overcome many of the barriers to commercial and social intercourse.

"He has taken advantage of the winds and tides. He has dug canals, tunneled mountains, widened and deepened rivers and harbors and harnessed steam and electricity to bring about his ends in business.

"Railroads have been built from ocean to ocean, affording easy highways for transportation.

"The importance of easy communciation from state to state, from big city to big city, has long been recognized. And yet, the importance of easy highways in our own smaller community development has been sometimes overlooked.

"The small towns that dot the map of Illinois have individual transportation problems to solve. Each town must see to it that it is easy of access. Not alone for trade, for man's intelligence finds it most effective evidence in the social side. So let us have good roads leading into each town, not alone for the business they bring, but for the social development also.

"The question of good wagon roads is a vital business and social question. It has been demonstrated that it costs more to move a ton of hay or a bushel of wheat 10 miles over an ordinary country road than to haul it 500 miles by rail or 2,000 miles by water. The price of some staple crop is often due to inability to market it on account of conditions of country roads. Each year at certain seasons trade in small towns is dull, and collections slow, because of impassable roads.

"Good roads are open to everybody—everywhere. They are needed not alone for heavy hauling, for many of the trips the farmer makes over the roads are with light loads, or with no loads at all. Time is a factor and the distance from towns or school or neighbors is an important matter and enters into our every-day life, so time may be saved and greater social opportunities may be enjoyed.

"Good roads are not alone a town asset, but a community asset as well. They are just as essential to the progress of communities as good homes, good churches, good schools and good markets. It is important that people who live in towns and cities get out into the country, just as important as it is that the people who live in the country shall get into town.

"Of course, the automobile is helping in the good roads movement, but that the automobile may be fully efficient as a social factor let us have good roads leading into our small towns.

"Other things being equal, trade follows the easiest and best route."

A novel demonstration took place at the Illinois-Wisconsin State line on the Sheridan Road, September 26, to mark the inauguration of a movement to improve the Chicago-Milwaukee Road. Governor Philipp of Wisconsin and a representative for Governor Dunne of Illinois were present and took part in the ceremony.

The Road Roller and Scarifier; their Use in Building and Maintaining Macadam, Gravel and Earth Roads

With the present day enthusiasm for better roads, there is being given more thought to the good which can be accomplished by means of the road roller and scarifier in building and keeping in repair, not only macadam and gravel roads, but also our humble, much maligned, earth roads.

This realization has brought about a desire on the part of many individual townships to own for themselves a roller and scarifier.

USE ON GRAVEL AND MACADAM ROADS.

The advantages resulting from the use of a roller in constructing either gravel or macadam roads make it almost necessary that a roller be employed in building such roads. With a roller, it is possible to get the road in much better condition when it is being constructed, compacting the foundation and surface thoroughly, and as a result the road can be opened to traffic very much earlier than would have been possible had the roller not been used. .

If the foundation and wearing surface of a gravel or macadam road has been thoroughly compacted by a roller before the road is opened to traffic, the road will not rut or disintegrate nearly as rapidly as if the surface had been left to be compacted by the traffic. Also the proper rolling of the surfaces of gravel and macadam roads will make them much more uniform and will thereby eliminate considerable maintenance expense.

Maintaining gravel and macadam roads by means of a scarifier and roller necessitates an accurate knowledge of just what results are to be secured and the best methods to be used to secure such results.

In many cases it will be found that macadam and gravel roads have been maintained for a number of years by the addition of new surface material, and as a result, the road has been built up to such an extent that it is actually dangerous for travel. An investigation of the condition of a gravel or macadam road, which is in need of repairs, may often show that it is a useless expense to add additional material to fill the depressions and ruts and that it will be much more economical to scarify the surface to a depth of some 2 to 4 inches, then reshape the material by means of a scraper or drag and reroll with a roller. The result will very closely approximate a road as good as new and the cost when there is no new material added, will be only from about 4 to 10c per square yard, a very nominal sum when compared with the results obtained.

In maintenance work of this kind the scarifier does not disturb the foundation course but merely loosens the wearing surface so that it can be reshaped to its original cross section. In such work as this, the roller can be used to pull the scarifier and by such a procedure the total cost of scarifiying and rerolling a mile of road will be found very slight. In case the surface of a road is not too badly rutted it can often be brought back to a smooth condition by the use of the roller alone. This can best be done in the spring before the ground is thoroughly settled or when the surface is wet after heavy rains. If, however, the surface is too uneven or too hard to respond to the roller, it will be necessary to scarify as suggested above.

THE ROLLER ON EARTH ROADS.

While considerable attention has been given to the matter of the use of the roller on gravel or macadam roads, it has many times been overlooked that the roller can be made to play a very important part in the construction of the ordinary earth road.

Water, of course, is the natural enemy of the earth road and anything we can do to facilitate the drainage of the road will result in a better road a larger percentage of the time. .

An earth road will absorb water in proportion to the density of the surface and the slope of the crown. The slope of the crown of a road is, of course, limited by the safety and convenience of the travelers, that is to say, a road which has too much crown is both dangerous and unpleasant to travel upon by reason of the tilting or slipping of the vehicle. On the other hand, however, there is no such limit to the amount the surface can be compacted and it therefore stands to reason that after we have secured the maximum allowable crown for the road our attention should be turned to the thorough compaction of the surface.

This can be secured by a roller better than by any other means and a thorough rolling will do much toward securing a dense surface, which will retard the absorption of moisture.

The percentage of time that an earth road is in use depends largely on the water content of the earth forming the roadway (this applies of course to all ordinary soils, except sand). If the water is concentrated or localized, the result is an ordinary mudhole and the entire stretch of road will be useless as long as this one mudhole presents a barrier to traffic. However, if the water is not concentrated or localized, but is distributed uniformly, we will have, true enough, a muddy road but one which is more or less passable, depending on the depth of penetration of the water. It, therefore, follows that any steps that are taken to shed water more rapidly from the surface of the road or to prevent the saturation of the road, will increase the service of the particular road correspondingly.

Accordingly, the use of the road roller on an earth road by compacting the surface, justifies the expense by doing away with soft, yielding spots in the surface, which absorb so much water that even a slight rain produces a bad mudhole, destroying the value of the road until this one particular mudhole is passable.

It must not be thought that a road roller will keep an earth road from becoming muddy or will keep it in shape every day in the year. It will, however, by making the surface of the road uniformly compacted, produce a highway which, when one portion of it is suitable for traffic, all portions are likewise suitable.

The question comes up as to the economy of the township's purchasing such equipment for its own use. Any township which has had sufficient money to build 10 to 20 miles of gravel and macadam roads can ordinarily afford to own a scarifier and roller, and their proper use will prove to be economical as well as a great help in maintaining a smooth-surfaced road. In townships where less money is available it probably would not be practical to purchase such an outfit alone, but we would recommend that two or more contiguous townships join together in the ownership of a roller at least, the scarifier being necessary only where there are gravel or macadam roads to maintain.

A number of county boards are becoming interested in the amount of good that can be done by the use of such equipment and appreciating the fact that the township with a small mileage to care for is not justified in purchasing for itself such equipment, are purchasing such outfits in the name of the county and renting them at a nominal charge to those townships which can not economically afford to own such an outfit. In such cases, it is entirely possible to arrange for expert supervision for such construction gangs and to provide for experienced operators and in this way the work is done more economically and the machinery is busy during the entire season of work, which naturally results in a lower cost.

STATE HIGHWAY DEPARTMENT IN NEW OFFICES.

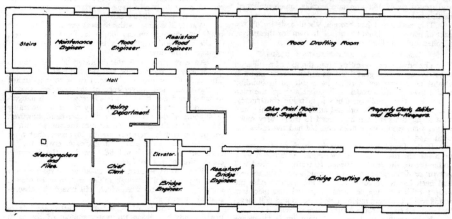

SIXTH FLOOR PLAN.

It is gratifying to the State Highway Department, and doubtless of some interest to the public, to announce that the department has a home of its own again in the capitol building.

After removal from the west wing, second floor, the offices of the department were distributed, where rooms were found to be vacant, throughout the third floor. For a year, it was thus established in committee quarters back of the House and Senate chambers. Even wardroom space was occupied.

It is a more pleasant habitat, however, that lately has sprung into existence as department headquarters. The fifth and sixth floors in the south wing—converted into suites as the result of legislative appropriations made two years ago—greet the visitor now as finished offices. The chart illustration which accompanies, explains the arrangement of the new department rooms.

On the fifth floor are the administrative offices, including the rooms of the commissioners and the Chief State Highway Engineer. There is also the auditorium, and space which may be devoted to contract letting and to other purposes of the department.

The sixth floor contains the "mechanism" of the department. The chief clerk is given a room whence he directs the work of the departments under him, and the other divisions, including the road, bridge, blue print, clerical, editorial, bookkeeping, stenographic and engineering departments have quarters on this floor.

Both the newly finished floors, under the roof of the south wing, are accessible by elevator. First floor entrance to the elevator is found in the south end of

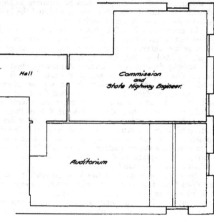

FIFTH FLOOR PLAN.

the south wing, west side, opposite the door to the Adjutant General's office.

Occupancy of the new department offices suggests a bit of evolution in the utility of the State capitol building. When the structure was erected, no provision was anticipated for office needs above the third floor.

COUNTRY ROADS PROTECTED CHEAPLY FROM SCOUR.

[By George E. Schaefer, *County Superintendent of Highways, Geneseo, N. Y.*]

(From *Engineering Record*.)

Country highways of to-day are the outgrowth of old Indian trails. As the course of the original trail followed the line of least resistance, so to-day, and particularly in the region of mountain streams and tributaries of great velocity and fall, we still find many sections of road too close to waterways, and seriously susceptible to scour and wash.

A large mileage in such locations can not be changed and must, of necessity, be as adequately safeguarded for traffic as the funds of the community will permit. The prevalence of rugged territory usually typifies a decreased population and therefore a correspondingly lessened assessed valuation of property and a minimum amount of highway funds. And furthermore, for a number of reasons these streams frequently change their courses, and where bank protection was necessary before, it becomes useless unless the stream returns to its former channel. Finally, for financial reasons and otherwise, the more expensive construction, such as concrete and steel sheeting, is eliminated and only cheap local materials utilized.

Where the subsoil is of rock a good type of construction for bank protection and to prevent scour is of tree trunks or logs laid in horizontal layers parallel to the stream, with laterals running at right angles to them back into the roadway at distances of 5 or 6 ft. These are bolted or dovetailed to the stream logs, and are locked securely under the highway with deadmen or with dowels. A heavy fill of brush and stone is then placed back of the sheeting. This type is very economical where logs and rock are abundant.

In unstable soils good results have been obtained by driving piling along the bank, preferably staggered, and filling in between the piles with green brush and stone in alternate layers. The brush should not be thrown in haphazard, but placed evenly, and the more the better. It should skew with the stream—that is, be at an angle of about 45° downstream. Care should be taken to procure green brush and have enough rock on top to hold it down.

Piling in straight lines sheeted with planking has not given as good results in this county as that staggered with brush and stone, for the reason that the planking cost is excessive and the earth back of the sheeting invariably washed out from underneath, with resultant caving in of the roadway. Where the velocity of the stream is very great, and large quantities of debris come down, it is sometimes necessary to wire piling together and also to wire it under the highway.

Good bank protection can also be acquired with brush and stone alone, skewed downstream and placed in alternate layers as with piling. Willow brush should be used if possible, and large rock. In a great many cases the willow takes root, eventually forming a natural protection.

Another type giving good results is practically of corduroy construction, layers of logs bound together and lying at right angles to the stream, or better, pointing slightly downstream. These should also be interspersed with brush and well weighted down above the water line.

Baffle dams or water breaks of piles, brush and rock are also used at curves in the stream and just above weak spots in the bank. They jut out into the stream on a downstream skew to about the center, and by driving the water to the opposite side tend to protect the bank at the curve or at the weak spot.

Many roads in this section are protected in this manner, and at very low cost, due to the most of the materials being acquired gratis. If well built, they answer the same purpose as concrete or steel sheeting.

POUNDING CONCRETE SUPERIOR.

"Wherever concrete can be cured by pounding, that method is to be preferred over all others," says the Portland Cement Association. California was, we believe, the first state to practice the flooding of the finished concrete pavement with a view to keeping moisture present, to enable the concrete to acquire strength and hardness under proper conditions.

Showing Longitudinal Dike in Concrete Flooding.

"Even where water is obtainable for use in this manner it is, of course, desirable to prevent unnecessary loss. This is particularly true in hot climates, where evaporation is rapid and where scarcity of water more often prevails.

"The original method of diking roads in California has been improved upon by adding an additional longitudinal dike near the edge of the concrete, as shown in an accompanying view. This prevents unnecessary loss of water and gives double assurance that concrete will be covered at the crown of the pavement as well as the sides. These two precautions are very essential and the added dike seems to make the desired ends more certain."

"THE STREATOR WAY" MARKED.

The route of "The Streator Way" has been marked to Starved Rock, according to announcement which has come to the department. The work was done under the auspices of The Streator Way Association, of which John R. Fornof is president, and Arthur Van Loon secretary.

Signs which have been used are steel, with white lettering on a red background, reading, "The Streator Way—To Starved Rock." "Turn right" and "turn left" signs have been so placed that the tourist can easily negotiate them. The marking of the way extends from Peoria to Streator, from Bloomington to Streator, from Dwight to Streator and from Streator to Starved Rock. The plan contemplates Streator as the southern gateway to Starved Rock.

COUNTY AID BRIDGE QUESTIONS ANSWERED.

Several interesting questions pertaining to road and bridge construction are answered in an opinion, given the department late last month by Attorney General Lucey. The text of the opinion, which we can recommend to county officials for careful study, follows:

State Highway Department, Springfield, Illinois.

GENTLEMEN: I am in receipt of your favor of the 20th instant (October), and note statement to the effect that the question frequently arises in connection with the construction of new bridges concerning the disposal of the material in the old structures, which, in some cases, is of considerable value.

You submit several inquiries in substance as follows:

(1) Where a bridge built at the expense of a township is replaced by one built with county aid, is the salvage of the old structure the property of the township, or should it be divided between the township and the county?

(2) In the case a bridge built originally with county aid, would the salvage belong to the township, or should it be divided between the township and the county?

(3) Where a bridge on a county line road, built at the expense of adjoining townships, is replaced by one built by the adjoining counties, is the salvage of the old structure the property of such adjoining townships, or of the counties?

(4) In the case of bridges on highways that are being improved as State aid roads, which were built at the cost of one or more townships, or by a township with county aid, to whom does the salvage in the old structures belong?

In reply I will say there is no provision of the Road and Bridge act which applies specifically to either of the above propositions, nor have I been able to find any decision by the Supreme Court, or by the Appellate Courts of this State, which passes upon the matter.

Paragraph 39 of the Township Organization act, chapter 139, Hurd's Statutes, 1916, confers upon townships the power to acquire by purchase, and to hold property both real and personal, for the use of the inhabitants, and to sell and convey the same; and a similar power is conferred upon counties by paragraph 24 of chapter 34.

The Appellate Court, in the case of *Brockhausen v. Boehland*, 36 Ill. App., 224, holds in substance that where a highway has been abandoned, an injunction will not lie to prevent the highway commissioners from removing a bridge thereon, such bridge being the property of the township. Property in a bridge may be in a single township, or in adjoining townships, or in a single county, or in adjoining counties. In the case of a bridge built at the expense of a township, the bridge is the property of the township, and the fact that it is replaced with a bridge built by county aid would not affect the town's right of property in the old bridge.

Relative to bridges that were built by county aid, I will say that paragraph 19 of the Road and Bridge act of 1883, chapter 121, Hurd's Statutes' 1911, made it the duty of the county board, upon certain conditions therein specified, to pay one-half the cost of a bridge necessary to be built in a township; and the like duty is imposed upon counties by section 35 of the revised act, chapter 121, Hurd's Statutes, 1916. Neither under paragraph 19 of the act of 1883, nor under section 35 of the revised act, can the amount contributed by the county board be said to be a voluntary donation. It was contributed by force of statute, because the statute made it the duty of the county to contribute; and the duty is such that a writ of mandamus would lie to compel compliance. The county has no right of action against the township for the amount contributed. I am of the opinion that a bridge built by county aid becomes the property of the township, and that the county has no property rights therein.

In the case of a bridge built by adjoining townships, the right of property would be in the townships.

In the case of a bridge on a county line road built by adjoining counties, the right of property therein would vest in the counties.

Very respectfully,

P. J. LUCEY, *Attorney General.*

Shelby County supervisors have rejected State aid for road building this year. About $11,000 was available for all purposes.

Townships in LaSalle County in which State aid roads are to be constructed will include Waltham, Eagle, Groveland, Manlius, Grand Rapids and Peru. New bridges are to be built over Badger Creek, in Otter Creek Township, and two in Ophir Township. Two are to be constructed, also between Woodford and La Salle Counties.

According to a recent report there are now under construction in the state of Arkansas, a total of 916.13 miles of roads in various counties at a cost of $4,193,-994. In addition to this work, the construction of approximately 1,200 miles of roads is in contemplation, the plan being to complete this supplementary work during the remainder of this year and the early part of 1917.

Road bonds aggregating $13,685,500 have been voted by 34 counties in Florida. Several other counties will vote shortly on additional bond issues. The work on the roads to be built under these bond issues has already been started and includes sand-clay, brick and rock construction. A large per cent of the rock roads is being oiled.

STOP, LOOK AND LISTEN!

From two widely separated sources the need of attention at crossings of railways and highways has been recently shown ephatically. The Iowa Highway Commission reports that in July out of a total of 36 fatalities on the roads of the state, 15 were due to trains striking vehicles, and in addition 17 persons were injured. And from the Southern Pacific Company comes the statement that of 33,500 automobile drivers observed at grade crossings, 53 per cent did not look either way before crossing the tracks and 8 per cent looked only one way. Only 0.52 of 1 per cent stopped their machines before crossing.

Trains must run on tracks and on time; their engineers have no choice of routes. The automobilist can choose his route and regulate his rate of speed, but many grade crossings can not be seen until just before they are reached, when the driver has little time to slacken speed. Road authorities should therefore see that warning signs are placed far enough from every grade crossing to make it certain that if an accident occurs on the crossing it is the fault of the driver, through his negligence to exercise proper care after ample warning.

Our Thanksgiving wish in essence: Better highways than ever before throughout Illinois, and prosperity to the worthy people who travel them.

ILLINOIS HIGHWAYS

[Printed by authority of the State of Illinois.]

OFFICIAL PUBLICATION OF THE

STATE HIGHWAY DEPARTMENT

VOL. III	SPRINGFIELD, ILLINOIS, DECEMBER, 1916	No. 12

A Christmas Lay for every Ear:
May roads like These
'Spite frost and freeze
Ere long well please
All Illinois throughout the Year!

—Christian County. Illinois.

THE PROBLEM OF MATERIALS
By Wm. W. MARR, Chief State Highway Engineer

Any discussion of the relative merits of materials for construction leads invariably to delicate, or even perilous situations. Especially is this true when disinterested observers have the temerity to press their views or opinions on a well-informed audience, among whom might be found some strong partisans. I, therefore, approach the subject with great timidity, not that I fear offense may be taken where none is meant, but rather that I seriously doubt my ability to express my thought.

We are of one accord—all of us—in demanding results and theories as but a means to an end. But Oh! how difficult it is to produce results—satisfactory results—"to deliver the goods"! There are so many factors involved that it seems as if there were always a slip somewhere. We are not usually judged, however, with due consideration for the difficulties we have encountered, but on the contrary we are in the final analysis credited with success or failure, according to the manner in which the bare facts impress those who pass sentence. This discussion must not become pessimistic however, for the viewpoint of the writer is exactly the opposite.

Right here it may be well to say a word regarding the wonderful progress made by the material interests of our State in promoting the use of their products. I refer particularly to the methods employed and note with growing satisfaction and approval that the strong tendency is away from the old practice of advocating the use of a particular material to meet all requirements, regardless of its suitability, and only because its sale brings profits to its promotor. The day of the "best pavement" has passed. This is now frankly admitted by the most selfish and shortsighted of our producers. I say shortsighted because there is nothing to my mind which in the past has been a greater drawback to road improvment than the confusion created in the public mind by the unscrupulous tactics of promotors who devoted the greater part of their energy to villifying their competitors. There was some excuse for this, however, in that competitors very generally used common weapons, but I am glad to say that I do not know of any large interest using the old methods. They have, by common consent, as it were, abandoned such practices and have come to realize that to meet the demands for materials suitably selected economically and satisfactorily to fullfill their purpose will tax them all to their full capacity.

In harmony with the "eternal fitness of things" it has come to pass that while the material producers in the past were themselves largely responsible for the slow development of road improvement, they are now a most potent factor in promoting the cause. The reason for their success is simple. It is because the public, greatly through their efforts, is now being informed of the facts. They are conducting great educational campaigns and adding much weight to their arguments by subordinating or eliminating the directly selfish notions and concentrating their efforts on teaching the need of better highways. They employ large forces of the best available men to preach the doctrine of better roads, to study their products, to improve their value and to see that a word once stated is done as well as it can be done with the present knowledge of the subject.

The inspectors employed by producers are instructed to investigate the methods of construction involving the use of their material in any particular work and to report back any fault found in order that it may be corrected through proper officials. Notwithstanding the fact that engineers realize to a greater or less extent their own limitations, criticism of their work is seldom welcomed and is often resented as an affront to either their knowledge, ability or integrity. Correcting bad practice is a difficult task and should for the benefit of all interested be entrusted only to those especially qualified through experience, tact and knowledge of human nature to handle it.

Many disinterested persons will unhesitatingly say that the determination of the type of improvement should be left to the engineer and yet when their own pocketbooks are affected, will immediately distrust either his ability or sincerity. The reasons for this are many. In the first place, experience teaches that we must look after our own pocketbooks. Then more or less conflicting data are always to be had, and this naturally confuses us. We think or attempt to think, and in our futile effort to grasp in a moment what would take years to learn, it is small wonder that we jump to conclusions. After all, ours is a government by representation and in view of the admitted success of this form, it would appear that the power to determine the type of a public improvement should be as it is vested in representatives duly elected. Let them secure such information and advice as they will, and on the whole we will have little cause for complaint.

The engineer, in a broad sense, is a director of effort and a scientific expert in the knowledge of the use and abuse of materials, their value, quality and limitations. His function is, I take it, to present, in a fair and impartial way, his acquired knowledge of actual facts to those who have to construe these facts and who, in the light of other factors which may enter the proper solution and of which they presumably have knowledge, have power to act.

It strikes me that it is unbecoming of an engineer, as such, to urge the use of a material of construction. To illustrate, let us take for example a city pavement. What engineer is as well qualified to determine the significance of noise, for instance, as a factor entering into the selection of the proper type of pavement for a given street, or to determine the relation between cost and benefit to the property assessed, as the representative of the district? In a locality where materials for construction are produced is it not often good business to use the home products providing the cost is commensurate with the value of the resulting pavement?

Of course the country road furnishes a very different problem from that of the city street. Fewer factors enter the determination of the proper type of pavement in the former than in the latter. It would seem that the type of country road is almost purely a commercial problem and such factors as noise and aesthetic features are given scant consideration while minimum cost of service under conditions obtaining is of the most vital importance.

(Continued on Page 149.)

THE CARE OF EARTH ROADS IN WINTER

By FRANK T. SHEETS, Assistant Maintenance Engineer

One of the most vital and most important problems in highway work in Illinois is that of maintaining the 80,000 miles of earth roads to the maximum possible efficiency.

The earth surface can be kept smooth and serviceable for traffic with comparative ease during nine months of the year, if sufficient care and the principles of common sense are used. However, during the three winter months, the action of rain and snow, freezing and thawing, combined with the destructive forces of traffic, render the maintenance of a smooth surface a task not easily accomplished. As a result the big highway problem in Illinois at present is the care of earth roads in winter.

The conditions which have existed in past years can be largely eliminated if a concentrated effort is made on the part of the people as a whole. The impassable roads during the winter months are largely caused by neglect. This neglect is costing the taxpayers thousands of dollars more than it would cost to remedy conditions.

The first way to care for an earth road in winter is to prepare it for this care by intelligent work in the summer, paradoxical though the statement may seem. No one should expect or permit an earth road to enter upon the winter period in a flat, undrained condition. The road should be well crowned, adequate side ditches should be provided, underdrainage should be placed wherever necessary. To be brief, the earth road should be constructed in summer. We have already been too long spending good money maintaining what we have called an earth road but which in reality never was anything but a flat strip of Illinois soil bounded by two fences.

In winter it is essential that the ditches, drains and culverts be watched and all obstructions to drainage removed. A few minutes' use of a shovel may eliminate a saturated roadbed, or a stopped up culvert.

Keep the ditches and culverts clean. Then when rain falls or snow and ice melt, far less damage will result.

When drainage has been maintained, the problem of surface maintenance presents itself. It is unavoidable that the surface should cut up under traffic during a thaw or during a rainy spell. Yet no one can say it is necessary to let this surface freeze in such a condition. Nothing more unpleasant can be experienced than traveling over a rough, rutted and frozen surface.

The road drag comes to the rescue of the earth road in winter with the same efficiency as in summer. If rough, cut up road is dragged before a freeze and then frozen in the smooth condition, a boulevard is enjoyed until the next thaw. If a wet surface is dragged and then dried, a good road is also enjoyed.

It is not necessary to say how the dragging shall be done; the important thing is to get some one to use the drag.

Common sense will soon teach how to perform the work. A study of weather predictions and a corresponding use of the drag at opportune times will work wonders with Illinois earth roads.

Many people are prone to criticize road conditions, yet are unwilling to inconvenience themselves to better the conditions they are bewailing. Witness the individual who drives up the middle of a dragged road before it is dried or frozen. A public-spirited attitude and cooperation on the part of the individual citizen plus an intelligent use of the road drag together with the expenditure of a little cash will work wonders with winter road conditions in Illinois.

HOME MATERIALS FOR ROAD BUILDING.

When a competent engineer is engaged to look after road building and maintenance, one of the first economies he makes in many cases is the utilization of local materials previously neglected or undiscovered. Sometimes plans for road building are prepared without proper investigation of local materials supposed to be abundant, and after the work has commenced it is discovered the plans must be changed because the quantity or quality of the materials was overestimated. Gravel and crushed stone are very heavy and their transportation is costly, and every endeavor should be made to ascertain whether suitable materials can be obtained locally before they are imported at heavy expense.

The surfacing of a road costs more than most people believe. In the case of 87 gravel roads, the grading and drainage averaged 41 per cent and the surfacing 59 per cent of the total cost, in 104 waterbound macadam roads, the grading and drainage cost 35 per cent and the surfacing 65 per cent. In 53 bituminous macadam roads, these proportions were 27 and 73 per cent. These figures show that more than half the cost of a surfaced road is generally spent for the materials and labor employed in surfacing the graded and drained roadbed.

The good judgment that comes to an intelligent highway engineer through experience will often show him that instead of using local materials exclusively, as originally proposed before he was employed, the annual cost of the road to the taxpayers will be reduced by bringing in some material by rail. What he can accomplish in this way will depend on the knowledge of local materials which he can acquire. Usually he is too busy to do much searching himself, but he can obtain much assistance if the local authorities will make systematic endeavor to ascertain the location of all ledges, sand banks and gravel beds in their neighborhood. These are public resources of real importance, and should be a matter of record.

In some communities school children have been encouraged to search for them, and in many places local amateur geologists and mineralogists have done a public service while riding their hobbies. There can be no question that the lack of complete knowledge of this nature is needlessly increasing the cost of road construction and maintenance in many parts of the country.

WHAT A CHRISTIAN COUNTY TOWN-SHIP HAS DONE

Buckhart Township, Christian County, Illinois, has a system of road improvement all its own. The revenues from a five-year tax which has been voted, the enthusiastic and up-to-the-minute cooperation of township road officials, and an inspiring supply of energy, interest and enterprise all figure about equally in the success of the Buckhart plan, as far as it has gone.

In starting to work out the scheme by which it is proposed, ultimately, 'to boulevard the township with a network of 365-day main roads, the people of the enterprising little unit voted the tax for five years which has been alluded to. That was in August 1915.

The specific purpose of this tax was to enable the township officials to grade, drain and oil treat 32 miles of highways. The first tax money was collected this year. It amounted to $7,016.26, or 50 cents in the $100.

actual oiling, therefore, were the best that could have been attained.

The necessary contracts were awarded in July. They were let to the Mound City Oil and Supply Company of St. Louis, Mo., for furnishing 75,000 gallons or more of road oil for the sum of 3.65 cents a gallon, f. o. b. Edinburg, Illinois; and to Elbert Wanack of Edinburg, Illinois, for applying oil, the sum of 1 cent per gallon. The oil was put on with an Austin-Western pressure distributor with heater attachment.

THE OILER USED. PRESSURE DISTRIBUTOR WITH HEATER ATTACHMENT.

The cost of oil and application of three coats of one quart each was as follows:

109,113 gallons of oil f. o. b. Edinburg, Ill.,
@ 3.65c $3,982 62
8,049 gallons of oil f. o. b. Edinburg, Ill.,
@ 3.60c 289 76
117,162 gallons of oil applied @ 1c.......... 1,171 62

Total $5,444 00

ONE OF THE IMPROVED STRETCHES. HILLS LIKE THESE HOLD NO TERRORS FOR THE TRAVELER.

Grading was commenced early last spring. It was planned that all preliminary work be finished two or three months before the application of the oil in order to allow traffic to pack down all loose earth in the center of the road.

Then, the roads which were to be oiled were surveyed, grades established and plans gotten out and filed with the township clerk. The ditches and roadbed were again gone over and constructed with a view to providing proper drainage. Tile was laid where needed and inlets placed about two feet away from the ditches in order not to be damaged by grading which might follow.

When the roads were graded, the crown was made somewhat higher than required for sufficient drainage in order that it might be "shaved" off slightly when the oil was applied, thus insuring a hard, smooth surface upon which to put the oil. Loose earth that might have accumulated was also done away with. Conditions for the

LEFT TO RIGHT—TOWNSHIP HIGHWAY COMMISSIONERS, FRED BAUGHMAN, D. B. WILSON, FRANK RALPH, AND COUNTY HIGHWAY SUPERINTENDENT C. A. PENINGTON.

The number of miles oiled was nearly 16, making an average of $340.25 per mile. The work was superintended by Frank Ralph, D. B. Wilson, and Fred Baughman, commissioners of highways for the township, and C. A. Penington, county superintendent of highways, with office at Taylorville.

If the reader doubt the virtues of the plan and its results as practiced in Buckhart Township, he need but to visit that enterprising section of Christian County and drive for a time over the oiled roads.

The other day the writer was standing off to the side of one of the best finished stretches when a farmer passed, driving a team hitched to one load of corn and leading, from the back end of the wagon on which he was riding, another team which drew the second of two of the biggest loads of Illinois' staple crop one ever saw. Nearly one hundred dollars' worth of white and yellow grain passed by, and the marketing of it was facilitated a hundred-fold by the character of highways over which the farmer had to drive. That prosperous harvester, we'll venture a guess, placed his unqualified stamp of approval upon the floor-like surface that stretched ahead of and behind him.

Of course. the road officials of the township are not done. It is their plan to keep the roads already improved well dragged this winter, then in the spring or summer, or as soon as the weather is practicable, to apply another coat of oil.

The commissioners of Buckhart Township are a little disappointed at present over a matter which they hope later to see fixed up to their satisfaction. From the township line north, on the western-most road which has been oiled, is a stretch of unoiled highway, extending through another township for a distance of about 2¾ miles. This unimproved link lies between the oiled roads of Buckhart Township and the long oiled stretch leading out from Springfield east through Rochester. Were it oiled, it would connect the Buckhart Township roads with the one farther north, thus making a continuous line of oil from Springfield to Edinburg and, a little later, to Taylorville.

Buckhart Township citizens are proud of their roads, and well they may be. Half of the proposed 32 miles have had their first three coats; more will be treated the coming year. It is not probable the entire remaining 16 miles will be oiled by the close of 1917, for maintenance of the mileage already improved must be attended to.

Notwithstanding, an unusually worth-while showing has been made in the start.

THE PROBLEM OF MATERIALS.

(Concluded, from Page 146.)

By cost of service I mean the unit cost per vehicle per mile per year, or some similar basis. This cost is divided into first cost, interest cost and maintenance cost. One is as important as another. It may be noted here that the problem of life of pavement disappears for State aid roads in Illinois as the law now stands. This law provides for maintaining a satisfactory surface regardless of type and all there is of interest remaining is cost of service. Who cares about the type as long as the surface is smooth, satisfactory and serviceable? What road traveler will not enthuse over the merits of any type which serves his purpose and which he finds in good condition for an appreciable distance? How many drivers of all sorts of vehicles will abandon a paved surface for an earth road in good condition? As long

as a satisfactory surface is maintained it is well nigh impossible to arouse any public interest in either types or cost of service. It, therefore, behooves us to give maintenance the consideration it merits.

I have little to say concerning the relative merits of concrete and brick highways. I don't know much to say. I confess I have never since known half as much as I did the day I received my degree in college. I do not say this in an idle attempt to occupy neutral ground or in a futile endeavor to straddle the question, but rather because I realize perhaps more keenly by reason of intimate association with the work the immense possibilities that are still in store for us. I do know, however, that while there is much unlearned or yet unknown about either type that there have recently been improvements and developments in each that is little short of marvelous. I do know that there are many examples of good and bad pavements of any type —notable successes and miserable failures. I do know that many of the failures can not be satisfactorily explained or rather that there are many plausible explanations for any one case and that neither concrete nor brick pavements are by any means fool proof.

Concrete pavements are enjoying a most remarkable popularity and have been in use long enough to demonstrate beyond question their value in the scheme of road improvement. I do not share the misgivings of those who point to the cracking of concrete roads and believe that with the providing of reasonable maintenance, the cracks are of comparatively little significance.

Brick pavements have always been popular and are more popular now than ever before. The new type of monolithic brick is receiving material favor and seems to offer immense possibilities. I regard proper grouting of the brick as of prime importance and believe, with a well-drained and settled road bed, that the thickness of concrete base for brick pavements is of little significance. Heavy loads do not make an appreciable impression on ordinary dry earth roads and from this I take it that the earth itself sustains the load, provided it is settled and dry. The problem then seems to be to keep the earth under the brick pavement in a dry condition after it has once settled by properly waterproofing it. This is accomplished by a perfect grout filler. Perfection is also necessary to insure stability in the structure.

In choosing between concrete and brick, I should consider carefully the availability of materials, the relative costs and the character and amount of traffic the road might be expected to bear.

[Editor's Note.—Mr. Marr was asked to prepare a paper on the subject, "Ceramic Materials in Highway Construction," and to present it as part of the program which marked the dedication at the University of Illinois a short time ago of the new Ceramic Engineering Building. The foregoing was his contribution. We feel that it will appeal to "Illinois Highways" readers as ethical, conservative and sound and that, in "tone," it is in keeping with the elevating policies which the Department would foster, not only in the production of ceramic, but all other materials as well.]

At the general election November 7, the measure in California, which provided for an appropriation of $15,000,000 for state road work was approved by a large majority. The new appropriation includes $12,000,000 for completing the system now under way and $3,000,000 for a county and cooperative plan under which eight additional extensions will be undertaken. The present highway organization will be continued, and the new work is to be started at once. Several counties in California have also voted independent bond issues. Among them are Sacramento County, with an issue of $1,700,000, and Stanislaus County, with a $1,500,000 issue.

Evils of an Inadequate Township System and the Need of Reform

By B. H. PIEPMEIER, Maintenance Engineer, State Highway Department

One of the greatest detriments to our country roads can undoubtedly be charged to methods which have been followed in supervising the work.

The blame can not fairly be attached to the highway commissioner. He is forced, by local sentiment, to do many things contrary to his own views, and to standard practices heretofore established. The highway commissioner who is not willing to yield to the suggestion of a majority of taxpayers is forced to terminate his services at the next election.

The highway commissioner, with practical ideas and with definite plans in view, is frequently beaten at the polls on account of the system and on account of failure of the voters to understand many of the fundamental principles that govern road construction and maintenance. The result, therefore, is the changing of road officials every few years. The new official has new ideas, new obligations, and the public highways suffer the results. Again, an incompetent highway commissioner may be able to secure the necessary votes to hold him in office for a great many years. Quite often a highway commissioner may be found whose entire ambition is to hold office or beat the other candidate at the election. Such public officials have very little regard for the betterment of the public highways.

Again it is optional with the voters whether they want three highway commissioners or one highway commissioner to oversee the road work in each township or road district. Here again, the voters may be influenced for or against the three-highway-commissioners system. They may be against the single-highway-commissioner system because they are not familiar with its advantages. They may be against it on account of the fear of some incompetent candidate who is sure to control the majority of votes. It is evident that one incompetent highway commissioner with the control he has of public funds, is worse than taking chances on three.

The single-highway-commissioner system, has, without question, many advantages over the system using three, provided a township is successful in securing the services of a competent man. However, under the present system of electing commissioners by popular vote every three years, regardless of their ability, the efficiency of even the single-commissioner system is very materially reduced.

In view of existing conditions, it seems necessary that some scheme other than electing the highway commissioners by popular vote, involving possibly a modification of the present system, must be developed to insure more economic results on the public highways. The big corporations and business men of to-day are looking for trained men to handle their various divisions of work. It is evident that the railroad companies and business corporations could not exist if the heads of the various departments, or the men that do things, were given their places by popular vote of the people. Yet much of the public work is trying to exist under such conditions.

The time is not far distant when the majority of taxpayers will see the fallacy of the old method and will demand that our public road work be handled in a more efficient and business-like way.

The most advanced and efficient work of to-day is handled by trained men. It seems evident therefore, that some scheme should be devised that will insure that all road officials are especially fitted for their work before being placed in office, and after they are once in office, that their term be not less than six years. To determine the fitness of candidates for the office of highway commissioner they should meet certain qualifications that should be prescribed by the Chief State Highway Engineer through the county superintendent of highways. The qualifications ought to have the approval of the State Highway Department so as to make them as near uniform throughout the State as conditions will permit. The candidates who have passed or who meet the prescribed qualifications may then be voted on at a regular township election. The man receiving the highest number of votes should be the highway commissioner of the township or road district.

Business organizations or corporations of any kind always subject their candidates for employment to a rigid examination before employing. The examination may consist of a personal interview where the candidate is required to give a complete outline of his experience together with references as may be required, or a written examination where similar information may be demanded. The method of examining may depend upon the nature of the work. The main thing to note is that corporations do require that their employees be qualified for the position they hold. Another point is that practically all employees of a business concern or corporation are responsible to someone above them. These are points that make for efficiency and, without question, would prove to be of benefit to township organization if they could be established.

Under the present system of township or road district organization, the commissioners are not responsible to anyone, and the results are diversified opinions and methods concerning road work. Centralization of responsibility and authority insures efficiency. It would seem, therefore, that the men doing the actual road work in a township or road district should report direct to a single highway commissioner, he in turn to the county superintendent of highways and the county superintendent of highways to the Chief State Highway Engineer.

The Galena Good Roads Association has been organized. Improvement of the condition of all roads in the Galena vicinity will be the immediate object of the organization. The officers are: President, E. A. Fitch; vice president, Paul Kerz; treasurer, F. F. Dunnebeck; secretary, W. L. Miller; directors, B. A. Hoskins, T. M. Harney, J. H. Billingsley, J. J. Eulberg, S. J. Hughlett, F. E. Owens.

The naming of all highways in Kane County has been suggested. The roads will be named after well-known good road enthusiasts of the county, it is said, if the plan is carried out.

NEWS FROM THE COUNTIES

County Highway Superintendent F. M. Enos, of Kankakee County has reported that, at a meeting a short time ago of the county board of supervisors, the board voted to hold an election on January 17, 1917, on the proposition of issuing bonds for $750,000. Much campaigning for the issue is about to be inaugurated.

* * *

Scarcity of labor and difficulty in securing materials have contributed toward delays in the State aid work in Lake County, according to a report made by County Highway Superintendent Charles E. Russell. In a letter, Mr. Russell reports the following progress from his county:

"We have operated two county outfits, one consisting of a roller and scarifying outfit and the other a tractor grading outfit. Both have been the means of improving a considerable mileage of road and seem to have received the general approval of the public and local township officials with whom we cooperated.

"The townships have constructed about 10 miles of stone road and about an equal mileage of gravel road. Owing to inexperience of some of the township officials, but more especially the lack of proper labor-saving machinery, some of this work has not been of the most satisfactory character, but probably up to the general standard of township work. A considerable number of small concrete bridges and culverts have been constructed with county aid and are pleasing and permanent improvements. If our road work could be done on the same basis we believe it would make for better roads and more general satisfaction."

* * *

Piatt County has made progress. County Highway Superintendent T. J. Anderson, briefly reviewing the work in his territory since last year, reports the following:

"Since the spring of 1915, Piatt County has built 4½ miles of concrete-brick pavement out of the village of Mansfield, 9-foot brick with 3-foot concrete shoulders, making a total road width of 15 feet.

"In 1916, we have built a 9-foot monolithic brick pavement, 3½ miles in length, leading out of the city of Monticello. The contract has been let also for a 1¼ miles stretch of monolithic brick pavement, 10 feet wide, extending out from the village of Bement. This work is to be completed next spring. The foregoing is State aid work.

"Three of our townships have done considerable oiling of earth roads. This work includes Blue Ridge Township, in which 10 miles have been oiled, Willow Branch Township, in which 11 miles have been oil treated, and Bement, in which 3½ miles have been oiled. Two other townships will do some oiling next spring.

"We have built a 200-foot and a 100-foot modern bridge by county aid, also a number of spans from 20- to 100-foot lengths on our county lines."

* * *

Logan County is making ready to set a mark in 1917, for all future time, as regards road improvement. In a letter to the department, County Highway Superintendent Thomas S. Davy, of Lincoln, writes as follows:

"The County of Logan is getting ready for a large amount of work next year. We now have 10 miles of gravel road surveyed and have 10 more miles which we are getting ready to gravel. We have been making some geological researches by testing out several gravel beds where very good deposits of gravel have been found. The man in charge of this work is Mr. L. H. Holland of Lincoln, who has had success in taking out gravel and other substances from below the ground. Mr. Holland has proven himself the best man in Central Illinois for testing out underground work with a 6-inch pipe. He has located, to date, four very good gravel beds, lying where we can have easy access to our roads, which we intend to improve. We will locate gravel near Atlanta, Middletown and New Holland and in Eminence Township, in our county.

"In addition to fine gravel deposits we have also located two very good limestone rock deposits, where we can get the best rock for crushed-rock work. Our State aid road committee with O. E. Reiterman as chairman is doing much toward handling the road proposition in a "big way" and the prospect for next year is that a county-wide gravel road system will be adopted for graveling every road in the county. The next year now promises therefore to be a very busy one.

"A bond issue is contemplated in order to get the work done quickly for the county. A petition will be prepared asking the county board to give the voters light in the matter."

* * *

The following interesting synopsis of work done in Williamson County has been received from County Highway Superintendent P. B. Wilson of Marion:

"Between June 2d and August 18th, Williamson County awarded contracts for 20.2 miles of improved roads, all of which with the exception of 5.6 miles are to be concrete and the remaining 5.6 miles to be bituminous macadam.

"All work for both types is being built under Illinois State Highway specifications. On 12.9 miles the slab is 10 feet in width and on the remaining 1.7 miles of concrete road the slab is 15 feet in width.

"The work is divided into eleven contracts and is being constructed in five different townships. The roads selected for this improvement are all designated State aid Roads and when the work is completed the four largest towns in the county will be practically connected with a modern highway.

"Some difficulty was experienced in getting contractors to bid on this work and it was necessary to readvertise several contracts. Labor has been scarce and owing to a shortage of cars and the unprecedented demand for road building materials in this section of the State, great difficulty has been experienced in securing materials. On account of these conditions 50 per cent of the contracts will not be completed this season. However, the grading work has been practically completed and the contractors will be able to rush work through in the spring if materials can be furnished.

"Three of the contracts were awarded to Johnson & Flodin of Chicago, Illinois, five to Dunlap-Dippold Co. of Edwardsville, Illinois, and three to Wm. Lough & Son of Marion, Illinois.

"The total estimated cost of these roads including cement is $237,213.14."

ILLINOIS HIGHWAYS.

Published Monthly by the
State Highway Department,
Springfield, Illinois.

▬▬11

ILLINOIS HIGHWAY COMMISSION.
A. D. GASH, *President.*
S. E. BRADT, *Secretary.*
JAMES P. WILSON.

WM. W. MARR, *Chief State Highway Engineer.*

BUREAU OF ROADS.
H. E. BILGER, *Road Engineer.*
M. W. WATSON, *Assistant Road Engineer.*
C. M. HATHAWAY, *Office Engineer.*

BUREAU OF BRIDGES.
CLIFFORD OLDER, *Bridge Engineer.*
G. F. BURCH, *Assistant Bridge Engineer.*
A. W. CONSOER, *Office Engineer.*

BUREAU OF MAINTENANCE.
B. H. PIEPMEIER, *Maintenance Engineer.*
F. T. SHEETS, *Assistant Maintenance Engineer.*

BUREAU OF TESTS.
F. L. ROMAN, *Testing Engineer.*
F. L. SPERRY, *Assistant Testing Engineer.*
W. C. ADAMS, *Chemist.*

BUREAU OF AUDITS.
J. M. McCOY, *Chief Clerk.*
EARL B. SEARCY, *Department Editor.*
R. R. McLEOD, *General Bookkeeper.*
G. E. HOPKINS, *Property Clerk.*

DIVISION ENGINEERS.
R. L. Bell, Buchanan-Link Bldg., Paris, Ill.
H. B. Bushnell, 138 Fox St., Aurora Ill.
J. E. Huber, Wise Building, Mt. Vernon, Ill.
A. H. Hunter, 302 Apollo Theater Bldg., Peoria, Ill.
C. M. Slaymaker, 510 Metropolitan Bldg., E. St. Louis, Ill.
H. E. Surman, 614 People's Bank Bldg., Moline, Ill.
Fred Tarrant, 730 Reisch Bldg., Springfield, Ill.

Address all communications in regard to "Illinois Highways," to Earl B. Searcy, Department Editor, State Highway Department, Springfield, Illinois.

CONTENTS.

STATE BREVITIES.

M. R. Vanhouten of Canton has been awarded a contract to build a new concrete bridge in Banner Township, Fulton County. The cost will be $388.

* * *

The first monolithic road for Peoria and vicinity is being laid on a 1,300-foot stretch leading west from East Peoria along the foot of the bluff.

* * *

Commissioners of highways of Ridott Township, Stephenson County, and County Highway Superintendent Hiveley have accepted 14 reinforced concrete culverts, the aggregate cost of which was $2,700. W. A. Liljequist of Freeport was the contractor. W. A. Daughenbaugh has been awarded a contract to paint every steel bridge in the township. Officials estimate that failure to paint all bridges in the county has netted a loss of $5,000 to $10,000 a year.

* * *

Hadley Creek bridge in Barry Township, Pike County, is to be repaired at a cost of $650. William Hoos has been given the contract.

* * *

A new bridge is to be constructed 2½ miles east of Bushnell, at a contract cost of $522. The Weigert Construction Company will do the work.

* * *

Roseville, this fall and winter, is experimenting with late road oiling. Six thousand gallons will be spread, the property owners believing the season is not too late for profitable results.

* * *

Completion of three sections of new road in Vermilion County has been certified as follows: Alvin-Bismarck road, 2.73 miles long, costing $22,870.57; Ridgefarm south to county line, one-half mile in length, costing $3,915.75; Tilton-Catlin road, 3.15 miles long, costing $39,347.93.

* * *

Eight business men of Harvard, each subscribing $200, have started a fund with which to improve the roads leading into their city.

* * *

The Commercial Club of Mt. Sterling is engaged in an effort to have all roads leading into the city graded and put into first-class condition before bad weather sets in.

* * *

Twenty-five miles of roads in Logan County are slated for improvement by graveling next spring. Work will be commenced as soon as weather conditions permit.

* * *

The Ottawa-Belvidere section of the Burlington Way was organized at a meeting in Ottawa recently. The vice presidents chosen to represent the towns between Ottawa and Belvidere are as follows: Ottawa, A. Richards; Leland, H. W. Watts; Baker, A. J. Kirkhus; Waterman, Thomas Roberts; DeKalb, J. H. Jarboe; Sycamore, C. M. Kugler; Genoa, George Loptien; Belvidere, A. G. White. General Superintendent Peoria-Belvidere Division, J. F. Richardson, Jr., Ottawa.

* * *

Farmers of Rice Township, Jo Daviess County, have organized the Rice Indian Head Trail Association. The officers are: President, J. B. Schuler; secretary, R. B. White; directors, F. Bautsch, D. S. Gray and William Beadle.

SIXTH DIVISION PROGRESSES

With a total of 12⅗ miles of improved roadway, complete or in the making, and 32 bridges of all kinds to its credit, Division No. 6, in which Division Engineer C. M. Slaymaker has jurisdiction, is conservatively exploiting the progress which State aid is making in some of the more difficult sections of Illinois.

In his office in East St. Louis a few days ago, Mr. Slaymaker reviewed, for ILLINOIS HIGHWAYS, the work which has been done and is now going forward.

CONVICTS AT WORK ON A FILL, ST. LOUIS-KASKASKIA ROAD, NORTH OF MENARD.

At the present time, there is no township work in the division. Two pieces of oiled earth road were accepted a short time ago—sections B and C in Clinton County. Both are 24-foot roadways and each has a 15-foot oil strip. Convicts from the Southern Illinois penitentiary are at work on an interesting stretch of the St. Louis-Kaskaskia road, north of Menard. Operations have extended something like 3 miles north of Menard, toward St. Louis. The construction can not, perhaps, be said to be wholly technical, yet the work is effective, and the laborers are converting the roughest and crudest trail into a finished highway in pretty smart fashion.

Bond County has the only monolithic paving in the division. This work extends a little over half a mile on section C. The pavement is being laid 10 feet wide, with earth shoulders. On this stretch, first use is being made of the new 90-degree turn, with parabolic curve, as designed by Road Engineer H. E. Bilger of the State Highway Department.

A summary of the status of State aid work in the various counties of the division at the middle of November will serve to inform readers of progress there, to wit:

Bond—Section C, route 3, monolithic; delay caused recently because of slow shipment of brick.

Calhoun—Section B, route 1, macadam; work slow.

Effingham—No contracts awarded.

Fayette—Section B, route 10, macadam. Contract let, rough grading half done, machinery and stone slow.

Greene—Sections B, C and D, routes 1, 3 and 1, respectively, oiled earth. C not started, B half done, though no oil will be applied this year; D well along.

Jersey—Section D, route 6, oiled earth. Complete except for application of oil.

Madison—Section B, concrete, work started in October; sections B, bituminous macadam, work not started.

Monroe—Section B, concrete, work not started; section C, plain earth; practically complete.

Montgomery—Sections C, D and E, all plain earth; D complete, C and E not started.

Scott—Sections C, D and E, plain earth; C done except drainage; D and E not started.

St. Clair—Sections B, C and D, all plain earth. B nearly complete, C and D to be completed this month.

On State aid bridges, work is going forward at the present time in Clinton, Jersey and Macoupin Counties.

Division Engineer Slaymaker has emphasized, during his incumbency in the sixth division, the importance and efficiency of the State aid plan and its operation in his territory. It is gratifying to highway officials to know that there was not one of the 16 counties in the division which did not make at least some slight use of the money accruing from the first two years' allotment.

The following will summarize the State aid work, in roads and bridges, which has been commenced or completed in the sixth division since the present system became operative:

ROADS.

Fayette—7,410 feet, macadam; Jersey—3,100 feet, earth; Macoupin—12,200 feet, macadam; Monroe—2,650 feet, earth; Madison—11,539 feet, earth; St. Clair—10,764 feet, concrete; Bond—2,700 feet, brick; Calhoun—1,920 feet, earth; Clinton—6,050 feet, concrete; Effingham—8,394 feet, concrete. Total roads of all kinds, 66,727 feet, or approximately 12.6 miles.

BRIDGES.

Greene—4 concrete, 1 steel; Jersey—4 concrete; Montgomery—8 concrete; Perry—1 concrete, 1 steel; Randolph—4 concrete; Scott—2 reinforced concrete, 1 culvert; Washington—6 reinforced concrete. Total, 30 concrete, 2 steel.

EXETER BRIDGE, SCOTT COUNTY, 45-FOOT SPAN AND 18-FOOT ROADWAY. RECENT COMPLETION.

The counties in Mr. Slaymaker's division are Randolph, Perry, Washington, St. Clair, Monroe, Clinton, Madison, Bond, Fayette, Effingham, Montgomery, Macoupin, Jersey, Greene, Scott and Calhoun.

At Metamora, Ill., a Good Roads Club has been formed for the purpose of promoting improvement of all roads within Metamora Township.

SOUTHERN ILLINOIS COMING

Down in southern Illinois, where rains are said to turn the earth's surface into "soup," they are making real progress toward an ultimate system of good roads. Not only State aid, but county and township work as well are giving the highways in several communities of division No. 7 a distinctly modern aspect.

This is Division Engineer J. E. Huber's territory. In administering unto the needs of his district, Mr. Huber finds his problems as numerous as the moods of April weather.

NINE-FOOT GRAVEL ROAD IN WABASH COUNTY. PICTURE TAKEN TWO MONTHS AFTER COMPLETION. NOTE TIGHT SURFACE AND ABSENCE OF RUTS.

An even score of counties make up division No. 7. They are Alexander, Pulaski, Massac, Union, Johnson, Pope, Hardin, Jackson, Williamson, Saline, Gallatin, Franklin, Hamilton, White, Wabash, Edwards, Wayne, Jefferson, Marion and Clay. Mr. Huber's office is at Mt. Vernon, the seat of the division.

Up to and including last month, State aid work had progressed in the division as follows:

Alexander—Section B, gravel; to be completed about January 1. Car shortage has held up shipments of road gravel. Work well along despite handicap. 13,120 feet.

Edwards—Section B, brick; practically complete. 1,125 feet.

DRAWING THE TEMPLATE BY HAND ON EDWARDS COUNTY MONOLITHIC ROAD. FIRST-CLASS RESULTS WERE OBTAINED.

Franklin—Section C, concrete; finished November 8. 6,416 feet.

Jackson—Section C, earth; work delayed. Will be completed next spring. 12,600 feet.

THE GROUTING PROCESS. NOT ELABORATE, BUT IT WAS EFFECTIVE, JUST THE SAME.

Jefferson—Section B, earth; slow. Due for completion this month. 15,700 feet.

Marion—Section D, earth; slow work on bridges and culverts. 22,460 feet.

Massac—Section B, earth; rough grading done, drainage slow on account of delay in shipment of concrete materials. 5,370 feet.

Union—Section B, earth; tardy shipment of concrete materials has prevented completion of work before now. 1,790 feet. Section C, earth; due for completion this month. 4,500 feet.

FRANKLIN COUNTY CONCRETE ROAD, FINISHED A SHORT TIME AGO. A MILE AND A QUARTER IN LENGTH.

Clay—Section B, concrete; work not started. 1,875 feet; section C, earth; work not started. 2,550 feet.

Williamson—Section E, concrete; work not started. 3,674 feet.

Pulaski—Section B, gravel; work not started. 4,600 feet.

State Aid bridge work is progressing in Gallatin, Hardin, Pope and Pulaski Counties.

Two pieces of work were completed recently. In Wabash County, 3,820 feet of gravel were finished early

(Concluded on page 156.)

THE USE OF A BELT IN SURFACING CONCRETE PAVEMENTS

By H. B. Bushnell, First Division Engineer

Some experiments were made in Michigan recently with the purpose in view of improving upon the ordinary methods used in surfacing concrete pavements.

The most common, present-day practice specifies that the surface shall be finished with a wood float. Engineers differ as to when this floating should be done; some specify that the floating shall take place very soon after the concrete has been leveled off by the strike board while others require that the floating be done just prior to the time at which the concrete takes its initial set.

The first method invites water and stone pockets and a film coating of cement and the lighter impurities in the aggregate, on the surface of the pavement.

Late floating insures a better wearing mortar surface and greater freedom from stony pockets, but it is often difficult to insure that the floating is done at just the right time. At the end of a day's run the floater is generally permitted to work close to the strike board in order to avoid finishing after dark. After noon hour, in hot weather, the concrete often is found too stiff to

FIGURE 1. SHOWING GENERAL OPERATION OF BELT.

float well. A sudden shower may make it impossible to get over the surface even hurriedly with the hand float before it is necessary to cover the pavement with canvas.

Good finishers are scarce. Even with the most experienced men there is a tendency to float spots that are low and flat, due principally to the fact that the finisher concentrates his efforts over a very small area.

As the wearing surface, the most noticeable and one of the most important points in the pavement, is left to an ordinary workman for the finishing touches, the personal equation of this workman is of vital importance to a satisfactory product.

As to the origin of this new process, the writer is informed that on a contract job in Michigan a short time ago, the finishers struck and left the contractor with a large surface of pavement that had been struck off but not floated. In an effort to save this concrete by getting it smoothed off before it set, the contractor tore some strips from his tent and dragged these across the pavement with surprisingly good results. He then conceived the idea of doing away with his finishers entirely and floating the surface by means of a canvas belt. The writer heard of this incident and was greatly impressed with the possibilities of belt floating.

The matter was immediately taken up with the Illinois Hydraulic Stone and Construction Company of Elgin, Illinois, contractors for Section H, Kane County State aid road, and they agreed to try out the belt. Two belts were secured; one 3-ply 8-inch canvas belt and one 5-ply 10-inch belt, both having a composition rubber

FIGURE 2. BELT POSITION IN FIRST FLOATING.

covering. The concrete was mixed at such consistency that when deposited in a pile it would tend to flatten but would not run at the edges. The concrete was struck off in the usual manner and after the surplus water disappeared from the surface of the concrete the 8-in. belt was dragged back and forth over the pavement with practically the same motion as used for the strike board.

FIGURE 3. THE EFFECT OF BELTING.

Figure 1 shows the general operation of the belt and its relative position to the strikeboard for average conditions.

Figure 2 shows the position of the belt during the first floating. The left half of the picture shows the surface after the strikeboard has been used and the right half shows the surface after having been gone over once with the belt. Ridges in the mortar are very noticeable after this first floating.

Just prior to the concrete taking its initial set the pavement is gone over a second time with the belt. This second floating grinds down all the ridges left after the first floating. The right half of the view of Figure 3 shows the surface after the first floating and the left half shows the surface after the second floating.

The second floating leaves a gritty, granular mortar surface entirely free from ridges, flat spots, or pockets. It was found that better results could be secured by the use of a 10-nch belt for the second floating because of its greater weight, but if the heavier belt was used for the first floating it had a tendency to flatten the crown in the soft concrete and to dig into the surface.

During the past few weeks eight other contractors on State aid work in northeastern Illinois have commenced to use these belts. Some of them have purchased new canvas belts and have had considerable difficulty, due to the stiffness of the material. This defect can readily be remedied by shipping the belt enough to limber it up. The plain canvas belt pulls harder than when covered with rubber, but not to such an extent as to be objectionable.

In Kane County the contractor is placing from 600 to 800 sq. yds. of 18-foot concrete pavement per day and has no finisher on the pay roll. The strikeboard men handle the belt and do the edging. Where armored joints are used it is necessary to do a small amount of hand floating around the joint, but this is done by the men who place the joints.

This construction feature appeals to the contractor as it saves him money and the worry of keeping a good finisher on the job; and it appeals to the engineer because of the superior surface and the fact that its operation is nearly "foolproof."

SOUTHERN ILLINOIS COMING.

(Concluded from page 154.)

in August; in Franklin County, 6,416 feet of concrete were completed early in November.

The various road types and the length of each in Mr. Huber's district which have been built, or for which contracts have been awarded for completion this year or early in 1917 follow:

Earth, 79,240 feet; gravel, 21,540 feet; concrete, 11,965 feet; brick, 1,125 feet. Total, 113,870 feet, or approximately 21 miles. All of this work except 12,699 feet is under construction.

Five townships in Williamson County have shown enterprise as well as interest in the improved road movement. They issued bonds, in the aggregate, for approximately $300,000, then turned the money over to the county board which, pursuant to section 15-D of the State road and bridge law, is expending the money for road building according to terms of an agreement with the commissioners of the five townships.

Division No. 7 has approximately 250 miles of improved highways. Upward of 100 miles of these roads lie in Wabash County, where gravel has been used in vast quantities.

A new steel and concrete bridge is to be erected over Kickapoo Creek in Logan County at a cost of $4,865. The span will be 85 feet long and 18 feet wide.

BUREAU OF BRIDGES REPORT FOR OCTOBER.

During the month of October plans, estimates and specifications for 69 concrete bridges and 10 steel bridges were prepared and sent out to county superintendents of highways. The total estimated cost of these bridges is $101,459.

Plans, estimates and specifications for two sections of State aid bridge work in Wayne County, including 17 bridges, were completed and sent out to the county board. The total estimated cost of this work amounts to $10,030.

Plans and estimates for bridge and culvert work to be built in connection with State aid road contracts were prepared for three sections of State aid road work, including 13 bridges, the total estimated cost of which equals $1,730.

Summing up, plans were prepared for 109 bridges and culverts, the total estimated cost of which equals $113,219.

Plans for 123 bridges and culverts prepared by county superintendents of highways were checked and approved.

According to reports received, contracts were awarded during the month on plans prepared for county superintendents of highways for one concrete bridge and nine steel bridges at an average cost of 106.6 per cent of the estimates. The total estimated cost of this work amounts to $30,880. The unusual condition indicated by the percentage given above was probably due partly to the unsettled condition of the steel market, and partly to the fact that in a number of cases the time of completion set in the contract was somewhat unreasonable.

Contract was awarded during October by the State Highway Commission for one section of State aid bridge work in Fulton County, including two bridges at the estimated cost of $955.

A number of new bridge and culvert standards were completed. These include the standard plans for abutments for slab bridges with cantilever wing walls, plain concrete abutments for slab and girder bridges, box culverts with plain concrete side walls and head walls, and revised standard plans for private entrances. The zinc etchings of these standard plans are now in the hands of the printer and the standards will be ready for use within a few weeks.

The following outlines briefly the status of the work in the Bureau of Bridges on November 1, 1916. There were on hand ready for work 23 bridge inspection reports; 3 bridge plans had been prepared but not checked and 6 bridge plans had been completed, together with the estimates and were practically ready to be sent out. The bridge office is in a position at the present time to handle requests for the preparation of plans and specifications for bridge work expeditiously.—*Compiled by A. W. Consoer, Office Engineer.*

The employment of Louisiana prisoners upon the public roads is being agitated by the New Orleans Association of Commerce. Louisiana prisoners were employed with some success on the public roads from 1909 to 1911, but were withdrawn in order that their labor might be used in building levees to protect low-lying lands from floods. The State has taken a progressive attitude in regard to convict labor, the constitution prohibiting the leasing of convict labor and prisoners working only upon public works and farms.

HOW A KENTUCKY COUNTY OBTAINED GOOD ROADS

By the Kentucky Department of Highways

In a preliminary examination of the roads in the several counties under supervision, the earth roads of Hopkins County attracted attention because of their generally good condition, which investigation showed to be due to the installation of a system of maintenance by split-log drags.

Previous to 1911, the county roads were in charge of a road supervisor, who authorized the expenditure of a county road fund. Seven or eight grader outfits were employed for eight or nine months during the year. County warrants were issued, with no method of adequate bookkeeping to show the expenditures, and as a result the road fund was overdrawn yearly and the deficiency taken from other county funds. With a change of county officials it was found that while the county road fund amounted to about $32,000, over $39,000 had actually been expended on approximately 250 miles of roads, the amount of work done being the smallest for which the citizens would stand and yet pay the bills.

The new county officers, appreciating the high cost for the small amount of work rendered, published these conditions, which resulted in the formation of the Hopkins County Good Roads Association, with the object of securing better county roads and a knowledge of the items of expenditure on roads. The first action of the association was to require the approval of the fiscal court before payment of any claim against the county. In 1912 a county engineer was appointed, replacing the road supervisor. The county roads were measured under his supervision and 2-mile sections designated, and in January, 1913, drags were started on about 100 miles of the county roads. This original contract was only for dragging the roads, which work was to be done four times between January 1, and April 1, at a cost of $10 to $12 per mile. As the sections dragged were not continuous, the citizens at once appreciated the difference between the maintained road and that which was not maintained. Consequently the next contract, which called for dragging and also for cleaning the ditches for six months, until November, 1913, resulted in contracts for 150 miles of road at a reduced cost.

In November, 1913, a contract substantially like that now in use was adopted and the time of the contract was for one year, or until November, 1914. Over 200 miles were maintained this year at an average cost of $28 per year per mile. For the year from November, 1914, to November, 1915, the benefit of the maintained roads was so well understood by the citizens that 560 miles were under contract at an average cost of $24.35 per mile per year.

In November, 1915, a 2-year contract was entered into, which the county may revoke for nonperformance of the obligation at the end of the first year. About 520 miles are now under contract, at prices ranging from $12 to $40 per mile per year, the average being $22.10. It is expected this mileage will soon be increased. Originally a contractor was allowed to have charge of 8 miles, but now he is not allowed to contract for more than 4 miles of road.

Under the 1915 contracts the contractor must trim the branches which overhang and interfere with travel on the roadway; keep the roadway between ditches free from shrubbery and weeds; keep the ditches clean, free from obstructions, and at all times capable of carrying the water. "He shall by June 1, each year, grade the roads with dump scraper, grader, drag and ditcher, or in any way he may see fit, so that the center of the roadway shall be crowned so that the water will flow from the center of the road to the side ditches, and at no place will the water stand on the road or run down the road. The road shall be dragged from ditch to ditch at each dragging, when the road is wet, but not sticky."

A record of the number of draggings is kept by the county engineer on cards which, before mailing by the contractor, are countersigned by the rural carrier or a reliable citizen. The contractor also hauls material and constructs all culverts and bridges of 10-foot span or under, and keeps the approaches to and the floors and abutments of all bridges and culverts on his road in good traveling condition. The ditcher and split-log drag used are described in the U. S. Department of Agriculture's Farmers' Bulletin No. 321.

An analysis of these contracts shows that where the contract has been faithfully executed there is a decrease each year in the cost per mile, mainly because the farmer contractor has learned from experience that continuous maintenance makes a lower cost of time and labor each succeeding year.

The benefits of this system are great improvements in the traveled ways, and, at a reasonable cost, the repairing of all the roads throughout the county at practically the same time. The work is done by the farmer at a time when he could not be busy on the farm. The low first cost of the equipment, which is usually made by the farmer-contractor, makes the work attractive to him, and this is increased by the payment for his labor in November, just before his taxes are due. Each contract is usually adjoining the contractor's farm, so he has a personal interest in having his section well kept.

The officials are beginning to appreciate the need of data regarding the width of surface maintained and the amount of traffic borne by the different roads, and no doubt in the near future will institute changes in the contract, based on the width of surface and traffic conditions, which will again reduce the cost of maintenance and at the same time pay the contractor a more equitable price when compared with what the contractor on another road is doing for the payment made to him.

The Commercial Association of Kankakee has undertaken to raise $1,500 with which to assist in financing the county campaign for the proposed $750,000 bond issue for roads. The election will be held in January.

The Colquitt Bridge in Concord Township, Adams County, has been accepted by the road officials. Work is going forward on other bridges in the county.

STATE AID ROAD SIGN PICKED.

The official State aid road sign for Illinois has been chosen. The design for it was submitted by W. H. Lienesch, chief engineer for the Universal Concrete Products Company, 208 South LaSalle Street, Chicago.

Competition for the prize which the State Highway Department posted in an announcement last June, brought designs from about 75 competitors throughout the United States, from California to Massachusetts. It was stipulated that the drawings should illustrate the proposed type of sign, to be erected along all State aid roads.

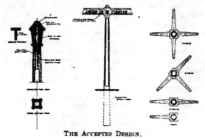

THE ACCEPTED DESIGN.

The accompanying illustration shows Mr. Lienesch's design. It was selected by the State Highway Commission, the Chief State Highway Engineer and approved by Governor Dunne because of its simplicity and durability, and its evident ability to serve the purpose to which it will be put. The sign is of concrete construction.

ENGINEERING SHORT COURSE AT STATE UNIVERSITY.

The Department of Civil Engineering of the University of Illinois announces that in cooperation with the State Highway Department the fourth annual Short Course in Highway Engineering will be held at the University on January 8 to 19, 1917.

The program is now in course of preparation. It is planned to interest those engaged in the development of country roads, the administration of municipal affairs, and contracting. . Each subject will be handled by a specialist. The program will include men well known in the field of highway engineering.

It is intended that the course shall be a continuation of the work of last year for those who have attended previously, but courses will be arranged for those coming for the first time. The subjects treated will include social, economic, and financial problems of road improvement, road laws and their administration, and the various technical problems of road and bridge construction. Special attention will be given matters related to bond issues and the development of county-road systems.

The course is open to any one interested in highway problems without examinaton or other prerequisite, and no fee will be charged.

Tazewell County has reported 112 miles of oiled roads. Eight more miles are scheduled for oiling, it is stated.

From Chicago Heights comes the report that the drinking fountain, presented by members of the Arche Club of Chicago, located at the intersection of the Dixie and Lincoln Highways, was recently dedicated. W. G. Edens, Chicago consul of the Lincoln Highway Association, accepted the gift on behalf of the National Association.

Under the auspices of the Goodrich National Touring Bureau of Akron, Ohio, the Goodrich Company has made a guide post sign, as shown in the illustration. In a letter to ILLINOIS HIGHWAYS, the company says:

"We are willing to furnish any of the county commissioners with our GUIDE POST signs to erect on the main highways of the county at confusing crossroads and forks, furnishing these signs gratis, the county to pay for the cost of the four-inch post and the labor in erecting same."

Announcement has been made that the Meridian Highway between Pana and Maroa has been marked. A stretch of 30 miles between Maroa and Bloomington yet remains to be marked, thus completing the line from Pana to Beloit. Work is progressing in the marking of the way from Beloit to Madison, Wis.

A contract has been awarded to John Brogen of Eldred, Ill., for the construction of Section G, State aid road, Macoupin County. It is to be oiled earth, and will extend 20,244 feet out from Mt. Olive. The contract price is $7,277.

Five new bridges in Rock Grove Township, Stephenson County, have been accepted. The bridges were built at a cost of $2,079.

DIXON BRICKS LINCOLN HIGHWAY
By L. B. NEIGHBOR, Highway Superintendent of Lee County, Illinois

(From November *Dependable Highways*.)

The expenditure by a township of $82,500 in a single year for highway purposes is noteworthy even in a State so imbued with good road progress as Illinois. This is the record made by Dixon Township, Lee County, Illinois, located almost exactly 100 miles west of Chicago. It is further to the credit of Dixon Township that she is resurfacing her main highways most durably with brick.

The highways chosen for improvement are known locally as the Franklin Grove, Palmyra and Colony Roads. The first two are, in fact, one highway and constitute the Lincoln highway in its east and west approaches, respectively, to the city of Dixon, which is the county seat of Lee County. This portion of the improvement is 17 feet 3 inches in width and the lengths are the 1.75 miles for the Franklin Grove road and 1.3 miles for the Palmyra road.

A different design has been chosen for the Colony road, due to the fact that the center of the highway is occupied by an interurban car track. There will be two brick driveways of 10 feet in width each, while the central 10 feet, including the track, will be filled with crushed stone. This improvement extends a little more than a mile. The contract prices are, respectively, $28,300, $25,000 and $28,000, but such is the importance of these highways to local trade and traffic that there is practically unanimous approval of the expenditure.

All three roads will greatly facilitate haulage to and from the adjacent farming country, stimulating mercantile operations of varied character. The Colony road also leads to the Country Club and to Dixon's splendid 200-acre Lowell park. Franklin Grove and Palmyra roads, being parts of the Lincoln highway, will carry a heavy tourist traffic, which can be made a source of both profit and advertising when accommodated on the new scale of comfort and satisfaction.

The work east of Dixon is now complete and that north of town practically so. The grading and most of the curbing has been completed west of town.

The specifications for the brick pavement on all three jobs were substantially the same. The old road in each case was worn out macadam. Sufficient stone was added to make a foundation six inches deep after rolling. Upon the stone base the brick were laid on a two-inch sand cushion and grouted with cement filler. When possible, the old macadam in place was used intact, except where condition required the addition of fresh stone in order to give the full depth of six inches to the base.

The brick are retained on Palmyra road by a concrete edging 5 by 12 inches, on Colony road by a combined concrete curb and gutter on the outside of each paved stretch and a 6 by 11-inch curb next to the car track.

Messrs. F. W. Fisher, T. F. Rosbrook, W. H. Lennox are the Highway Commissioners in charge of the expenditure on these roads.

Work on the Lincoln Highway divisions is in charge of Engineer H. T. Shaw.

The writer, as Lee County Superintendent of Highways, has general direction of all engineering and construction. Messrs. Duffy and Hubbard are the contractors on Palmyra and Colony roads, and Messrs. Rink and Schnell were awarded the contract for the improvement of Franklin Grove road.

Location for $10,500 worth of State aid work in 1917 was selected by the supervisors at their September meeting. It will be placed in Palmyra Township, west of Dixon, and there is an expectation that Palmyra will bond itself for $60,000 to continue the road to the county line. A 10-foot brick roadway with 4-foot shoulders of broken stone is the approved form of construction. Brick roads, well built, are certainly in good repute here.

The Central Illinois Auto Trails Association has been formed. Its purpose is to make Peoria the hub of 20 marked automobile trails before the 1917 season opens. Eugene Brown is president, John Winzeler vice president and George Alfs secretary-treasurer of the Association. Other good roads organizations have been dissolved in order to give impetus to the Central Association.

County Highway Superintendent Frank R. Bryant of Bureau County has tendered his resignation from the superintendency, effective February 1. Mr. Bryant was elected county surveyor in November, hence his action. He will see that all pending road improvement contracts are complete before quitting his position.

NEW MAP SHOWING

HIGHWAY ENGINEERING DIVISIONS OF
ILLINOIS

Divisions of the Engineers: First—Bushnell; Second—Surman;
Third—Hunter; Fourth—Bell; Fifth—Tarrant;
Sixth—Slaymaker; Seventh—Huber.

UNIVERSITY OF ILLINOIS

FEB 6 1917

ENGINEERING LIBRARY

ILLINOIS HIGHWAYS

[Printed by authority of the State of Illinois.]

OFFICIAL PUBLICATION OF THE

STATE HIGHWAY DEPARTMENT

VOL. IV	SPRINGFIELD, ILLINOIS, JANUARY, 1917	No. 1

—Kane County (Concrete).

THE

N E W YEAR'S

GREETING

—Jackson County (Brick).

ILLINOIS
and Road Types That Beautify Her Two Extremities.

A HIGHWAY EPOCH FINISHED, AND A SEASON'S GREETING

The close of a year, fiscal or calendar, ever since the organization of business, has conveyed the idea of a fit and appropriate time for reckoning; a period suitable for retrospect and a look toward the future.

Obviously, we are concerned particularly with the business of making and maintaining roads. The State Highway Commission has devoted its time to this cause; the highway department has executed the policies of the commission—all to the end that the close of 1916 and the beginning of this, the new year of 1917, might witness a meritorious progress in highway improvement.

Illinois, the fertility of whose soil is legend, has been the scene of endeavor.

Were we to report upon the things done only in the year just closed, however, we scarcely would do justice to a department which has barely broken in a new piece of legal and statute machinery.

May we, then, devote a little attention, not so much to the year 1916, but to the two preceding years as well? Indeed, let us date what we have to say from 1913, when the Illinois Legislature, recognizing the growing needs of the great commonwealth sadly lacking in improved roads, extended and revised the laws pertaining to them, and gave to a new State Highway Commission a new set of statutes with which to begin to work out the highway destinies of the State after an entirely new plan. The *tout ensemble* carried with it a revamped interest, a modified enthusiasm and a "drive" which could not have been had under former conditions.

Illinois, in her time, has been a pretty busy State. Her people have occupied themselves with agriculture and the industries. Her agrarian pusuits have given her especial recognition from sister states. Garden spots abound. In many localities we reflect with pride upon the fact that rich loam is measured, not in inches, but feet. Corn, oats, wheat, alfalfa, fruits and truck grow with facility and success. The soil aids husbandry in all its phases and makes it prosperous.

The establishing of this agricultural reputation has kept the commonwealth occupied. So thoroughly busy has been Illinois in this partial development of her rich

BUILDING GRAVEL ROAD IN WABASH COUNTY.

resources that, until very recent years, she has paid comparatively little heed to the development, after a systematic plan, of the arteries and lanes of highway travel and commerce which really give the land its intrinsic value.

So much by way of preface. We turn now, briefly, to efforts which have been expended in the last three years toward establishing in Illinois a system of improved roads which will stand the test of passability 365 days of the year.

In 1913, the road and bridge laws of Illinois were codified, revised and amended. The State Legislature created the present State Highway Department, supplanting the preceding organization, and vested in it broader powers and duties than obtained before. Three State highway commissioners, a chief State highway engineer and their subordinates comprise the department of to-day.

A 1916 BRIDGE IN RANDOLPH COUNTY.

Broadly, the law gives the commission general supervision over highways and bridges which are constructed, improved and maintained in whole or in part by the aid of State moneys, an advisory relationship with county highway superintendents and a great deal of detailed duty in connection with the drafting of plans and estimates for proposed roads and bridges, the letting of State aid contracts, etc. The term "State aid" was defined by the law as applying to all bridge and highway work, done at the joint expense of the State and county.

The early months of this new epoch constituted a time largely of preparations. Visible results began to make their appearance, however, by the following year. In 1914 and 1915, the commission awarded contracts for 172.21 miles of State aid road. Most of the construction was of concrete.

Until October 21, in 1916, 265.48 miles of State aid road had been contracted for, making a total mileage to that time, under the new plan, of 437.69. The 1916 work was largely earth and oiled earth improvement.

Illinois road types, as included in the State aid contracts, embrace concrete, brick, macadam, gravel, bituminous macadam, earth, oiled earth and bituminous concrete. It may be said in all fairness that seasons in Illinois, in the last two years, have not been favorable to construction. Consequently, there is an overlapping of contracts.

Many changes have come in construction methods in the last two years. Brick road building especially has been all but revolutionized. The old sand-cushion type of brick road is giving way, in many instances, to the new monolithic and sand-cement formation. The former carries a curbing; the latter does not.

(Concluded on Page 9.)

v.4 #7 last no. published

BOND ISSUE BY STATE IS ASKED IN SUM OF SIXTY MILLION DOLLARS

Officers and members of the Illinois Highway Improvement Association, in their fifth annual meeting at Danville December 19, registered the first official sanction by a State road body of the proposed issuance by Illinois of bonds for a systematic improvement of the commonwealth's highways. A bond issue of $60,000,000 was recommended by the association.

In the resolutions which were unanimously adopted, the following propositions were endorsed and urged as worthy of attention and enactment by the General Assembly:

1. A proposed $60,000,000 State bond issue; the Legislature to vote at the current session to submit the proposition to the people of Illinois for an election to be held in November, 1918. The resolution recommended that the bonds be serial, carry interest of 3½ to 4 per cent, and mature in 20 years. It was proposed that the State Highway Commissioin have supervision over the construction of roads improved from the funds accruing from the bonds, and in a general way, the suggested routes of improved roads, as illustrated in a tentative may drawn by the State Highway Department, were approved. It was proposed to start work on the approximate 4,000 miles of suggested roads at about the same time. Where roads contemplated in the State system are coextensive with county bond improvement roads, it is proposed in the resolution that a fair value of such overlapping stretches be determined, and that a corresponding amount be paid by the State to the county either on the retirement of its bonds or for application on further work.

2. Increase of automobile license fees, all funds accruing therefrom to be expended in highway improvement.

3. Action by the Illinois General Assembly which will enable the State to avail itself of its apportionments of Federal aid road improvement money.

This, in substance, was the work of the association. Its president, Mr. W. G. Edens of Chicago, pronounced the action "the most important move since Illinois was admitted to the Union."

The business session of the annual meeting was held in the Elks' Club. Fifty-one counties of the State were represented. Delegates were entertained by the chamber of commerce of Danville at lunch at the Elks Club and on the excursion to the State line where, in the midst of a blizzard, that part of the Dixie Highway lying in Vermilion County was dedicated. It had been planned to make an elaborate feature of the dedication, but suddenly inclement weather made it difficult to procure more than a few cars with which to make the trip.

Conferences of the delegates to the annual meeting were held informally on the evening before the convention and on the morning of convention day. The proposed State bond issue, automobile licenses and Federal aid were discussed.

One of the speakers of the day was Speaker David E. Shanahan of Chicago. Mr. Shanahan, who has been a close student of Illinois finances in the Illinois Legislature for a score of years, advised that, should there be a State bond issue, it ought to be made "a wise and conservative investment." He also impressed the delegates with his assertion that improved roads, when built, ought to "start somewhere and end somewhere." His statement, in the minds of the delegates, voiced the appeal of many taxpayers of the State who, if they are to spend their money for road improvement, wish to see the improvement done after a systematic and effective plan.

Secretary S. E. Bradt of the Illinois State Highway Commission sketched verbally the issues which confronted the delegates. He explained that $3,300,000 of Federal aid money will be available by Illinois in the coming five years, provided of course the State appropriates a like amount. Mr. Bradt advocated a State bond issue and declared the bonds should be serial in form. He compared the $3 to $10 automobile license scale in Illinois with fees in other states, ranging from 50 cents per horsepower to $40 a car.

Chief State Highway Engineer W. W. Marr emphasized the importance of maintenance in bringing about a system of improved State roads. Chairman A. D. Gash of the commission and James P. Wilson, also of the commission, were called upon for talks. They predicted the ultimate improvement of Illinois roads after a systematic plan. Former State Senator Dunlap of Savoy, in a short talk declared that road improvement progress could best be made through concentrated efforts.

The association elected officers for the ensuing year as follows:

President—W. G. Edens, Chicago.

Vice Presidents—R. J. Finnegan, Chicago; J. A. Logan, Elgin; C. A. Kiler, Champaign; W. F. Crossley, Cairo; Arthur R. Hall, Danville.

Treasurer—Thomas Sudduth, Springfield.

Secretary—R. W. Dunn, Chicago.

Directors—W. E. Hull, Peoria; L. H. Bissell, Effingham; Eugene Funk, Bloomington; E. H. Hilker, Granite City; C. H. Way, East St. Louis; Fred W. Jencks, Elgin; Henry Paulman, Chicago; E. D. Landroehn, Shermerville; W. E. Taylor, Moline; O. M. Jones, Danville; W. P. Graham, Rochelle; F. W. Cushing, Highland Park; H. G. Wright, DeKalb.

DIXIE HIGHWAY DEDICATED.

Snow which fell with unabated fury marred, but did not prevent the dedication near Danville on December 19 of the portion of the Dixie Highway lying in Vermilion County. The ceremony which had been planned for the occasion was carried out speedily though interestingly.

At the christening of the highway, three girls played the important roles. They were Miss Elizabeth Bell of Danville (Miss Danville), Miss Hazel Leigh (Miss Dixie) and Miss Margaret West (Miss Chicago) of Chicago. John H. Harrison of Danville presided. The trio of girls, typifying their respective

(Concluded on Page 4.)

REPORT FROM THE FIRST DIVISION

In mileage, the progress which the first engineering division in Illinois has made in State aid road construction in the last year has been substantial. Division Engineer H. B. Bushnell has charge of the territory constituting the division.

A little over 60 miles of improved roadways have been built. More than 23 miles additional have been contracted for, but at the close of 1916 were not completed. Operations in the division therefore have extended to between 83 and 84 miles of new road.

Mr. Bushnell, who has closed his construction season, has had much difficulty along the line of labor questions. Contractors who have entered upon contracts with equipment and in good faith have been seriously handicapped. All possible consideration has been extended to them and in spite of conditions, work has been pushed along with exceptional results.

Twelve counties make up the district. We believe it would be of interest to review the work which has been done in each of them. In the following summary, we give the completed jobs:

Boone County—Section B, 10-foot concrete, 4,600 feet; C, 15-foot concrete, 2,700 feet.

Cook County—Section A, 18-foot concrete, 2,623 feet; B, 18-foot concrete, 7,111 feet; C, 18-foot concrete, 24,000 feet; D, 18-foot concrete, 16,235 feet; E, 18-foot concrete, 19,443 feet; F, 18-foot concrete, 9,940 feet; G, 18-foot concrete, 12,957 feet; H, 18- and 24-foot concrete, 8,145 feet; J, 18-foot concrete, 7,314 feet; K, 18-foot concrete, 7,560 feet; N, 18-foot concrete, 2,607 feet.

DeKalb County—Section A, 10-foot concrete, 6,009 feet; C, 10-foot concrete, 17,879 feet.

DuPage County—Section A, 18-foot concrete, 10,800 feet; B, 18-foot concrete, 2,225 feet; C, 18-foot bituminous macadam, 7,200 feet.

Grundy County—Section A, 10-foot concrete, macadam shoulders, 9,400 feet; B, 10-foot concrete with macadam shoulders and 10-foot bituminous macadam, 3,100 feet; C, 10- and 15-foot bituminous macadam, 6,280 feet.

Kane County—Section A, 18-foot concrete, 17,665 feet; B, 50-foot bridge, concrete, with 200 feet of pavement; C, 18- and 24-foot concrete, 3,220 feet; D, 18- and 25-foot concrete, 4,828 feet; E, 18-foot monolithic brick, 972 feet; F, 30-foot earth, 3,390 feet; G, 18-foot concrete, 7,400 feet.

Kankakee County—Section A, 10-foot concrete, macadam shoulders, 9,450 feet; B, 10-foot concrete, macadam shoulders, 1,200 feet; C, 10-foot concrete, macadam shoulders, 3,581 feet; D, 15-foot concrete, 5,310 feet; E, 20-foot brick, 1,341 feet; F, 18-foot monolithic brick, 5,280 feet; G, 15-foot macadam, 5,280 feet.

Kendall County—Section A, 15-foot concrete, 8,200 feet.

Lake County—Section A, 10- and 15-foot concrete, macadam shoulders, 13,825 feet.

McHenry County—Section A, 10-foot concrete, macadam shoulders, 2,600 feet; B, 10-foot concrete, macadam shoulders, 1,500 feet; C, 15-foot concrete, 1,080 feet; D, 15-foot concrete, 2,640 feet; E, 15-foot concrete, 2,640 feet; F, 15-foot concrete, 2,640 feet.

Will County—Section A, 10-foot concrete, macadam shoulders, 9,900 feet; B, 18-foot concrete, 11,150 feet.

Winnebago County—Section A, 18-foot concrete, 7,680 feet; B, 10-foot concrete, macadam shoulders, 8,350 feet; C, 18-foot concrete, 10,150 feet.

KOPPEL CAR TRAIN, USED IN ROAD BUILDING IN NORTHERN ILLINOIS.

Work which is under contract and construction, but which at the close of 1916 was incomplete is summarized in the division as follows:

Boone County—Section D, 10-foot concrete, 800 feet; E, 10-foot concrete, 3,514 feet; F, 10-foot macadam, 8,000 feet.

Cook County—Section I, 18-foot concrete, 14,077 feet; L, 18-foot concrete, 6,011 feet; M, 36-foot monolithic brick, 20 feet State aid, and 18-foot concrete, aggregate, 9,364 feet; O, 18- and 30-foot asphaltic concrete, 7,981 feet.

DeKalb County—Section D, 10-foot concrete, 18,990 feet.

Kane County—Section H, 18-foot concrete, 15,500 feet.

Lake County—Section B, 15-foot concrete, 5,040 feet; C, 18-foot concrete, 2,275 feet.

McHenry County—Section G, 10-foot gravel, 10,500 feet; H, 10-foot gravel, 10,500 feet.

Will County—Section C, 18-foot concrete, 9,000 feet.

DIXIE HIGHWAY DEDICATED.

(Concluded from Page 3.)

interests carried out the christening and formally turned over to the public the link of road which will connect the Chicago-to-Florida highway.

A few automobiles were procured for the trip to the scene of the dedication, near the State line southeast of Danville. Exceedingly bad weather seriously interfered with what was intended to have been an elaborate ceremony.

After the dedication, those who participated returned to the city and enjoyed with the Illinois Highway Improvement Association delegates the luncheon at the Elks' Club.

Alignment and Drainage of Rural Highways

By H. E. BILGER, Road Engineer, State Highway Department

[SYNOPSIS.—Description of small details essential to successful highway construction, but frequently neglected. Simple means of rendering grade crossings less dangerous, and the essentials of alignment to insure surface drainage.]

The really permanent part of the entire improvement of a rural highway is its alignment, both horizontal and vertical. Hence the alignment merits attention before greater expenditures are made for surfacing work, which at best is of but a relatively temporary character. This statement applies particularly to the level prairie states of the Middle West, where to superficial appearances there seems little choice in the matter of alignment.

In the prairie states the general features of highway alignment as originally established, in most cases, will meet satisfactorily the requirements of modern traffic. These highways as a rule follow the section lines east and west, and north and south, and are straight.

Because of the unusually favorable conditions afforded by the topography and because also of the fact that practically all parts of the country could be utilized for agricultural purposes, a very large mileage of highways was laid out in the states of the Mississippi Valley.

The State of Illinois, for example, has 1.69 miles of rural roads for each square mile of land area. Likewise Richland County, Illinois, has a corresponding figure of 2.27, the greatest in the State; while Pope County has 0.95 miles, the least in the State.

In view of this large mileage of intersecting roads on grades that invite high speed and on a soil that yields its best crops with the worst mud, it is evident that close attention should be paid to all details of highway alignment and particularly to those involving drainage.

SMALL DETAILS OF HORIZONTAL ALIGNMENT OFTEN NEGLECTED.

Marked improvement can be effected in small details that will tend greatly toward the general safety and comfort of the traveling public. For example, at all abrupt angles in the right-of-way, and particularly those approaching 90°, greater safety of travel can be brought about by simply procuring enough additional right-of-way to permit moving the inner fence corner a distance of only 30 or 40 feet. By so doing, the radius of the curve can be considerably lengthened and a much better view provided. Travel is benefited out of all proportion to the cost of the little piece of land. In order that this additional right-of-way at the corner may be utilized to the utmost, it is necessary that all vegetation be kept down and that signboards, if any, be transferred elsewhere.

A typical 90° angle in a highway is shown in the accompanying sketch, similar to which there must be more than 100,000 in Illinois alone. To keep the improvement at the corner within the 50-foot right-of-way lines would require a curve having only a 52.9-foot radius, and the clear sight provided for the traveler would be only 70 feet.

As contrasted with this, notice the advantages afforded by acquiring the piece of land *KLMN* (see sketch), which contains 0.055 acres and would cost, at the rate of $300 per acre, only $16.50. The longer curve provides an outlook of 142 feet, as against the 70 feet for

the other. At the same time it shortens the pavement from *a* to *b* by an amount sufficient to save 40.6 square yards for a 15-foot pavement—about $70 on a brick pavement and $50 on one of concrete, which is about three times a reasonable price for the land.

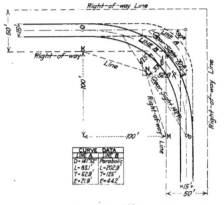

RECOMMENDED CURVE FOR 90° TURNS, ILLINOIS HIGHWAYS.

In addition to this, the right-of-way is not contracted at the corner as it is by the shorter radius curve, so that the 17.5-foot margin between the inner edge of the pavement and the property line is preserved for use as an earth road around the corner as well as on tangents. Moreover the land *KLMN* because of its corner location, is practically valueless for agricultural purposes.

At all crossroads additional land should be provided by moving the fences back to include the land at the four corners within the limits of the right-of-way, as proposed in the sketch. This brings the control of the corners within the authority of the road officials, who can have removed all vegetation that obstructs the view of the approaches.

Where there is an angle greater than 45° in the alignment and the improvement at this place is on an embankment higher than, say, four feet, there should be provided on the outside of the curve a substantial-looking guardrail painted white, to serve as a warning to traffic.

IMPROVEMENTS AT RAILWAY GRADE CROSSINGS.

In the State of Illinois there are 95,696 miles of rural highways and 13,198 miles of steam railroads. As practically all the highways have been located on the section lines, their directions are north and south, and east and west. With comparatively few exceptions the general directions of the railways are also north and south, and east and west, so it becomes at once apparent what a relatively large number of crossings are formed by the railroads and the highways; and considering the practically level topography it is readily seen why 87 per cent, or 17,119, of these crossings are at grade.

Economic conditions do not exist that will at this time warrant the separation of grades on as many as 10 per cent of these crossings in the rural parts of Illinois. Nevertheless, every effort should be made to improve these crossings in a manner that will minimize the accident hazard.

In the vicinity of crossings the improvement should be such as to provide an unobstructed view along the track for a distance of at least 1,000 feet each way, and this view should be enjoyed along a length of highway extending a distance of at least 300 feet on each side of the crossing.

It is particularly important that there be provided accommodations for two vehicles to pass with entire safety and comfort at the crossing, requiring never less than 18 feet; and the highway for a distance of 50 feet or more on each side of the crossing should be practically level or should at least have a very easy grade, say not steeper than about 2 per cent.

Much destruction of both life and property is caused by motor vehicles taking a run on the steep grades up to the crossing and then stalling the engine on the track. Occasionally two vehicles will make a run from opposite sides of the crossing and upon reaching it find that the highway does not have sufficient width for passing.

VERTICAL ALIGNMENT AND DRAINAGE.

In establishing the general vertical alignment of the highway there must be carefully considered the construction cost, the serviceability of the road and the practicability of economic maintenance. These three factors will assume varying degrees of importance, dependent largely upon the development of the country contiguous to the road improvement.

The proper alignment for any road is so closely related to such local conditions as topographic features, available funds, etc., that general recommendations might be wholly a misfit when applied to a particular case. It can be safely said, however, that grades should be kept reasonably consistent and closely in harmony with the general topography of the neighboring country, but aside from this there is little justification for expenses incurred in order to obtain grades lower than some 3 or 4 per cent.

To design highway improvements according to a limiting grade fixed for a geographical area even as large as 15,000 square miles is not warranted either by the nature of or by any factors of the highway problem. The whole matter is more of a local issue as regards both the factors of construction and the use of the roads, but in order to make the most out of a given combination of conditions a broad experience in road building is required.

THE MOST ESSENTIAL ELEMENT IN SURFACE DRAINAGE.

The particular feature of a large percentage of the Illinois road work commanding attention is the necessity for positive surface drainage of the roadbed by elevating it above the level of the adjacent fields. In order to maintain satisfactorily a road surface in practically level country on other than a sandy soil it is generally absolutely necessary to forestall capillarity by elevating the roadbed.

It is probably true that on more than one-half of the mileage of the roads in the State the traveled way is lower than the general elevation of the adjacent fields, and in a large percentage of these cases the practicable gradient of the side ditches is not sufficient to carry off surface water. This condition is due to the simple fact that formerly highway construction consisted chiefly of fencing off a right-of-way across the prairie without attention to the matter of surface drainage.

In connection with tilling the land for agricultural purposes the under-drainage of the road has been given more consideration than the surface drainage. It has not been fully appreciated that underground drains are primarily for the removal of underground water and that for the removal of surface water these drains can not be depended upon as more than a 20 per cent substitute for complete surface drainage.

CLASSIFICATION OF SOILS IN FACILITY OF DRAINAGE.

With respect to their properties of shedding or absorbing surface water all characters of soil encountered in Illinois road work may be assigned to one of the three following classes:

Class 1. Impervious soils, such as the prevailing gumbo throughout the corn belt, or any dense clay or other soil through which surface water will not readily penetrate.

Class 2. Semipervious soils, those soils of an intermediate character that evidently are not assignable to either Class 1 or Class 3.

Class 3. Very porous soils, including sand, gravel or loose stone; soils through which surface water will readily penetrate.

In case of doubt as to whether a particular soil should be assigned to Class 1 or Class 2 it should be assigned to the former, and for doubt between Classes 2 and 3 the assignment should be made to Class 2.

HOW TO DEAL WITH EACH CLASS OF SOIL.

Class 1. No matter whether on an elevated table-land or on a low bottom, where the obtainable side-ditch grade is less than 0.4 per cent, not more than 800 feet of road in one stretch should have the crown of its subgrade (finished crown for earth roads) less than 12 inches above the general elevation of the adjacent land without the limits of the right-of-way, notwithstanding the size of the side ditches.

Exceptions to this rule would be where the highway follows a practically level ridge and the adjacent land drains away from the road on both sides; also, where the highway follows along land that all drains one way. In the latter case, needless to say, cross-culverts should be placed at suitable intervals to carry the water from the higher ditch to natural outlets.

Class 2. Same as Class 1, except that 0.2 per cent should be substituted for 0.4 per cent.

Class 3. The crown of the subgrade should be at least 6 inches above the general elevation of the adjacent land without the limits of the right-of-way.

Notwithstanding the character of soil, where the grade of the side ditches is from 0.4 per cent to 1 per cent an endeavor should be made to keep the crown of the subgrade at least six inches above the general elevation of the adjacent fields. With a nonporous soil and an open-ditch gradient of less than 0.4 per cent it is difficult to provide surface road drainage by seeking natural channels located at considerable distances apart. A more effective and more positive practice is to elevate the roadbed by filling from borrow pits to an elevation above the accumulated water level, which under the conditions assumed is the general level of the adjacent fields.

REDUCE SPEEDING HAZARDS ON VERTICAL CURVES.

The speed of motor vehicle traffic requires that other details of vertical alignment be given full consider-

(Concluded on Page 10.)

NEWS FROM THE COUNTIES

The "Kankakee County Highway Improvement Association" has been formed. Members for the most part are farmers, though interest in the movement extends to men of all trades and professions. In addition to the officers, an executive committee will be named to include a supervisor and the highway commissioners from each township. The elected officers are:

President, Walter Lowe, Aroma Park; vice president, Vern Beedy, Manteno; secretary, F. M. Enos, Kankakee; treasurer, William Miller, Otto.

Secretary Enos is the highway superintendent of Kankakee County.

* * *

From Peoria County issues the report of a novel means of getting results as related to the dragging of public roads. A number of small drags were purchased a short time ago, it is said, and were placed along the side of roads where dragging was desired. Passing automobilists then were invited to "hook up" and drag a few miles. The aggregate of the results thus obtained was said to be surprisingly large. It is hinted that other counties, the coming season, may adopt the plan.

* * *

Organization of the "McDonough County Good Roads Association" took place at a meeting held recently at Macomb. The movement represents success of efforts of County Highway Superintendent W. M. Bonham, who for some time has promoted the county association idea.

The association expects to bring about the construction of 12 to 15 miles of State aid earth roads the coming season. Officers elected are:

President, John T. Lockett, of Tennessee Township; vice president, James Derry, Adair; secretary and treasurer, Eric Leander; board of directors, J. A. Long and W. L. Yeast of Macomb and George B. Huston of Blandinsville; publicity committee, Bruce Bailey of Blandinsville, Charles Wallace of Tennessee and Superintendent W. M. Bonham, Macomb.

* * *

Highway Superintendent L. B. Neighbour of Lee County, in a summary of work prepared for ILLINOIS HIGHWAYS, notes that due to the scarcity of labor and high cost of materials, bridge construction in Lee County has been kept to the lowest possible minimum the last year. Mr. Neighbour summarizes the work done in his county in the season just closed as follows:

Earth roads graded (for the most part without survey), 118 miles; brick road constructed, 40,000 square yards; macadamized, 16 miles; graveled, 2 miles; macadam resurfaced, 6 miles; sand covered with clay, 2 miles; macadam road oiled, 14.5 miles; earth road oiled, 34 miles; new road laid out and improved, 0.75 mile; tile laid for highway drainage, 1.75 miles; new bridges constructed, 14; bridges permanently repaired, 54; concrete culverts constructed, 55.

* * *

A report from F. W. Stine, superintendent of highways in Grundy County, gives an interesting conception of work which has been done in his territory.

Grundy County has 2 miles of concrete road with 4-foot shoulders of crushed stone, and 1¼ miles of bituminous bound macadam, all built by State aid in the last two years.

The county has many small bridges and culverts of concrete, under construction; also many floors on small bridges of 4-inch reinforced concrete, applied after bridges had been stiffened to the required sustaining capacity with I beams and truss rods. In December, a large bridge, comprised of two 75-foot spans, was built by the Joliet Bridge and Iron Company. The contract price was $8,900.

County Superintendent Stine closes his report to ILLINOIS HIGHWAYS with the statement:

"I consider the use of the road drag as of greater benefit to a greater number of persons, for the least expenditure of money, than any other one improvement agency in this county."

* * *

County Superintendents of Highways of Division Number 6, D. O. Thomas, chairman, met in the Commercial Club rooms at East St. Louis, Illinois, on Tuesday, December 5, 1916. There were present R. O. Young of Bond County, John A. Earley of Calhoun, John T. Goldsmith of Clinton, J. V. Waddell of Fayette, Irving Wetzel of Greene, W. E. Howden of Madison, H. I. Barbeau of Randolph, D. O. Thomas of St. Clair, George H. Vannier of Scott, and O. C. Rabenneck of Washington County. Mr. Moore, representing the State Highway Department, and C. M. Slaymaker, division engineer, were also present.

The morning was spent in an informal discussion of road affairs, and in the afternoon the following program, with a discussion of each paper, was carried out:

1. "The Building of Hard Roads by Townships," W. E. Howden, Madison County.

2. "The Proper Cross Section for Roads," J. T. Goldsmith, Clinton County.

3. "County Road Machinery Outfits," Geo. H. Vannier, Scott County.

4. "Bond Issues for Road Improvement," D. O. Thomas, St. Clair County.

The meeting then adjourned to meet again in March, 1917, at East St. Louis.

MICHIGAN OFFICIAL MAKES VISIT.

Among the visitors to the State Highway Department in December was Leroy C. Smith of Lansing, Mich., first civil engineer deputy of Michigan. He was here on Thursday, Dec. 7, while on his way north from St. Louis, where he attended the meeting of the American Association of State Highway Officials. His stop-off was purely informal. While here he was driven over stretches of 1913, 1914 and 1915 hard roads near Springfield.

Mr. Smith stated that 60 per cent of the improved roads in Michigan are gravel. The county bond issue plan is a bit slow of progress there, he said, though six or eight counties have adopted it. He expressed himself as keenly interested in and complimentary of the general road plan in Illinois.

Frank F. Rogers is the Michigan State Highway Commissioner.

ILLINOIS HIGHWAYS.

Published Monthly by the
State Highway Department,
Springfield, Illinois.

◀━━ll

Address all communications in regard to "Illinois Highways," to Earl B. Searcy, Department Editor, State Highway Department, Springfield, Illinois.

CONTENTS.

MAKE WIDE THE CULVERTS.

That wide culverts play not only a theoretical but a practical part of wisdom is attested by Highway Superintendent Edwin H. White of Sangamon County.

In his "Bridge Manual," issued recently as Bulletin No. 10, Bridge Engineer Clifford Older of the State Highway Department advocates a culvert at least wide enough to accommodate both shoulders of a road. Apropos of this argument, County Highway Superintendent White sent Mr. Older a letter a short time ago in which he narrated a chain of incidents happening within his territory which seemed proof conclusive of the wisdom of culverts of width, instead of a narrow type. He wrote as follows:

"In speaking of the cost of wide concrete culverts on our highways I would like to relate some incidents to which my attention was called during last State fair week.

"Small culverts should be made long enough to accommodate the full shoulder to shoulder width of the road. The cost of such culverts per foot of length is insignificant. For instance the average cost for 10 feet of a two by two concrete box culvert is about $24.00. It evidently would not pay to restrict the side roads shown above to save this amount."—From Bulletin No. 10, the "Bridge Manual."

"On one of our main highways leading south from Springfield we had an 8-foot span, 14-foot roadway, I beam bridge of the bedstead type, over a small draw that crossed the road. The bridge was set on the center line of the road which is 66 feet wide. This road is what is known as a 2-track road, both sides being used for driving.

"During fair week the dust was bad, and owing to the great amount of travel during that week it was kept pretty well stirred up at all times, making it impossible to see very far ahead. However, as there were two smooth tracks, one on each side, a fair speed could be maintained without danger of collision.

"At the bridge site, however, we had four accidents, one automobile striking the guard rail so hard that it broke a 5-inch channel. The other cars, which were lighter, did less damage to the bridge, but more to the autos.

"The point I wish to bring out is that the cost of repairing these cars would build three concrete culverts of sufficient width for this particular place, to say nothing about the number of lives that were endangered. All of these victims were taxpayers in Sangamon County.

"The draw drains about 180 acres and the bridge has finally been replaced by a 3½ by 5 by 34 foot box with 9 by 14 by 1 foot headers."

A HIGHWAY EPOCH FINISHED AND A SEASON'S GREETING.

(Concluded from Page 2.)

Maintenance is a feature which the Illinois Highway Department emphasizes both in theory and practice. The Bureau of Maintenance was organized by Chief State Highway Engineer Wm. W. Marr in 1915, prior to which time maintenance was handled as township work by the engineer in charge.

AN ILLINOIS GRAVEL ROAD.

Recognizing that the highest degree of efficiency under the extended laws could be had only with the best possible form of organization, the commission early authorized the formation of departments in such a way that the work of the State might go forward after the most efficient and methodical plan that could be devised.

Maintenance is effectively carried on through the operation of the department's organization. The State is divided into seven divisions, each constituting the jurisdiction of a division engineer. All field maintenance is directly under the respective division engineers. Superintendents in charge of actual maintenance report direct to the division engineer, he to the chief of the Bureau of Maintenance and the bureau chief, in turn, to the Chief State Highway engineer.

In 1915, 100 miles of State aid road were maintained, at a total cost of $10,266.98. In Illinois, the average expense of filling cracks and joints in concrete pavements has been $0.004 per square yard of pave-

VERMILION COUNTY BRICK ROAD.

ment. A large portion of the maintenance expense has been in the upkeep of side roads, ditches, repairing of bridges, etc.

Bridge building in Illinois comprises a busy little industry of its own. Naturally, its supervision has in-

volved important attention from the department. In 1914 and 1915—no work having been attempted under State supervision in 1913—contracts were let for 2 steel and 311 concrete bridges, at a total contract cost of ·$182,842.65. Plans had been drawn for a total of 356 spans of all kinds, but only 313 were undertaken.

Township and county bridge work from January 1, 1913 to January 1, 1916 forms an interesting item. Plans were prepared by the department in 1913 for 238 bridges, in 1914 for 243 and in 1915 for 381. Contracts were actually awarded in the three years, respectively, for 139, 109 and 252 bridges, at a total aggregate contract price of $744,292.88. The contracts came to $76,650.12 less than the costs as estimated.

In 1916, a total of 4,890 bridge plans were prepared by the department. The month of April brought the greatest number of demands for specifications, 1,447. The estimated cost of the work, as contemplated in the plans, will be $1,608,960. This embraces both State aid and township and county bridge work.

Under the Illinois law, counties that desire to proceed with road building more rapidly than State aid funds will permit, may issue bonds, through the county board, after the question has been first passed upon affirmatively by the people at an election. Cook County now has operative a bond issue of $2,000,000 and Vermilion County one of $1,500,000. In Cook, approximately 40 miles of new, modern road were contracted for the last year. In Vermilion, approximately 170

CENTRAL ILLINOIS OILED ROAD.

miles are under improvement, or contract to be improved. The bond question is an issue in several other counties of the State.

That the work of the Department, under the new order of things, has been heavy and varied is obvious. That a creditable start has been made along the right direction, the department believes, is also obvious.

There is no disposition to count the great work as other than merely begun. Illinois highway development, after methods which will insure general results and permanency, is in its infancy.

Five hundred miles of permanently improved road to-day may appear meager alongside the advances which will be made in the next quarter of a century.

Yet, can one gainsay the progress of recent years when he stops to think that, in the 25 years preceding the organization of the first State Highway Department in 1905, Illinois built but 26 miles of hard road— a fraction over a mile a year?

The year to which we have just bidden farewell brought interesting results. May the New Year, with its incentive to extend a cordial season's greeting to ILLINOIS HIGHWAYS readers, serve as another link in the chain of progress toward the State's ultimate position of highway supremacy.

ALIGNMENT AND DRAINAGE OF RURAL HIGHWAYS.

(Concluded from Page 6.)

ation. For the most rigid types of Illinois roads, as brick and concrete, parabolic vertical curves should always be used when the rate of change from one grade to another is as much as 1 per cent, and for the more resilient types of roads when the rate of change is as much as 2 per cent. Both the safety and the comfort of travel require these vertical curves, though their proper lengths are dependent upon factors that necessarily must be assumed.

It would be only reasonable to assume that in rural territory automobiles frequently ascend short grades up to 10 per cent at a rate of from 15 to 25 miles per hour. To come from this speed to a full stop, there should be provided at least 150 feet. If it is assumed that on ascending grades two automobiles are approaching one another, each at the rate of, say, 20 miles per hour, the vertical curve at the summit should be of such length as to enable the drivers to see one another when they are at least 300 feet apart.

With the eyes of the drivers five feet above the road surface no vertical curve is required to meet this condition when the change in the rates of the grades is not more than 6.67 per cent. When this change is 10 per cent, however, the curve should never be less than 200 feet long. Likewise, changes of 13 and 16 per cent would require minimum curves of 292 feet and 360 feet, respectively. Practical considerations would commonly suggest the use of vertical curves before they would be required to meet this condition, but nevertheless it is well to have in mind reasonable limits within which ordinary practice should be confined.

While the search for the ideal road-surfacing material and the battle for supremacy of certain material interests go on, the local road-building authorities can not do better than confine their activities to the fundamentals of the highway problem—namely, the establishment of a drainage practice similar to that of the railways and the production of a highway alignment that will properly fit *all* the purposes for which it exists.

[EDITOR'S NOTE.—The foregoing article was written for and is reproduced from *Engineering News*, issue of November 9. In addition to the prominent space given Mr. Bilger's contribution editorial mention as well was made. Consent to reprint the article was kindly given ILLINOIS HIGHWAYS by *Engineering News*.]

JUNIOR HIGHWAY ENGINEER TEST WILL BE GIVEN.

Information which will be of interest to every prospective candidate for a position as junior highway engineer in Illinois is contained in a letter, which Secretary Ward R. Robinson of the State Civil Service Commission has addressed to the State Highway Commission, and which explains the manner of conduct of an examination which is to be held under the commission's auspices February 3, next. It will be obvious that ample time remains for those who wish to enter this examination.

The letter from the secretary and chief examiner of the Civil Service Commission reads, with reference to the examination, as follows:

"In accordance with the recommendations of your engineers, the commission has decided to alter its plans and will make this examination an unassembled one. This means that there will be no technical examination of the usual written kind, but that on February 3 a set of questions dealing with the applicant's education and experience will be mailed to each applicant. He will then fill out his replies carefully and send the information to the commission where it will be checked over by persons competent to pass upon the comparative worth of the education and experience of the applicants. Those persons who make passing grades will be placed on tentative eligible lists and all of their statements concerning their experience and their records as employees will be carefully investigated. Those whose records appear satisfactory will be placed on the eligible lists which will be used in making certifications to the highway department for the filling of vacancies occurring during the construction seasons of 1917 and other years, so long as the list may be in existence.

"This plan will probably bring much better results than the commission has been able to secure in its written examinations, in the past. While many applications are received from residents of Illinois, most of them come from persons who have not finished their college work but are taking the examination with a view of taking up highway work upon graduation in June. This means that a large portion of the eligible list is not available for the use of the highway department until long after the construction season.

"There are always many persons throughout the country who are interested in these examinations and who would like to be connected with the Illinois State Highway Department but who can not take the necessary steps to qualify because of the expense of coming to Illinois for examination and the uncertainty of employment.

"This new plan does away with all these objections. Since the examination is open to nonresidents of Illinois, persons residing in any part of the United States can take the examination on equal terms with persons living in Springfield, and without going to any expense, can know just what the chances are for employment. The commission feels certain that applications will be received from a large number of very well qualified applicants.

"This position pays the usual starting salary of $75 a month with possibility of an increase to $120. The examination is open to citizens of the United States who are 21 years old. In general the duties of the position involve the preparation of plans for road and highway bridge construction; inspection of such construction; education equivalent to graduation from a school of civil engineering of recognized standing required, with particular knowledge of highway construction suitable to conditions in Illinois, and of the design and construction of plain and reinforced concrete and simple steel bridges. Good physical condition required."

THE EDITORIAL VIEWPOINT

[EDITOR'S NOTE.—ILLINOIS HIGHWAYS is in receipt daily of newspaper clippings pertaining in subject matter to about every general phase of road construction. Now and then an editorial is commixed with the news reports of work done or contemplated. Sometimes these editorial expressions commend, sometimes they condemn, the proposition at issue. ILLINOIS HIGHWAYS, in its effort to enlighten, feels that very often these editorials reflect a popular conception which even technical road builders might profitably know. In this belief, we take pleasure in presenting to our readers this month a brief symposium which, though relating in some instances to questions purely local, represent interesting viewpoints toward the great general highway problem as it exists in the State and county.]

A GOOD EXAMPLE.

The State Highway Department has just issued orders to clear the State aid roads of all billboards and signs. This is a movement which has been advocated by The Star's Country Life department for years. That the State is realizing what a menace these are to the beauty of the open country, is indeed encouraging. They really do little good for the advertiser who takes such a method of calling attention to his wares, as the average farmer resents the liberty that is taken with his property. Instead of being attracted to a store that is advertised in gaudy type on some tree that otherwise would present a beautiful appearance, country folk are more likely to feel bitter toward its management. The proper place for advertising is in the columns of the daily newspaper. This now reaches every country home and is capable of conveying just as strong a message as can a billboard which mutilates a beautiful landscape. Now that the movement is started by the State, our local rural societies would do well to take up the matter and make it known that their members appreciate the beauty of God's open country.—Rockford, Ill., *Star.*

GOOD ROADS.

When a permanent road is constructed, the present generation builds for the future. Its children and its grandchildren will have the use and benefit of the road. Generations to come will enjoy it.

For that reason, the cost of the road's construction should not fall wholly on the present generation. Those who are to make use of it after the builders have passed on should be required to pay something for the privilege and the benefit.

Everyone wants permanent roads and wants them now. To build a complete system at once, and pay for it out of current revenues would, however, be too great a burden. This is why Vermilion County voted to issue bonds, covering a period of years, for the construction of permanent roads. Sangamon County should do the same thing.—Springfield, Ill., *State Journal.*

GOOD ROADS AID FARMER.

It is often difficult to make farmers believe that good roads are of financial value to them. They agree that good roads are desirable as a means of making rural life less narrow. They agree that good roads make it easier for children to go to school, for the doctor to reach the farm, and for all hands to meet for religious and social purposes. But many of them say that it is mere "theory" to claim any direct financial results from road improvements. Now "theory," if true, is just as helpful as are facts, and in this case it is easy to show how facts support theory. The facts can be obtained with the help of officials of the railways shipping farm products out of a district before its roads were improved and after the improvement.

A specific case in Virginia may be taken as an illustration. The figures were collected by George P. Coleman, state highway commissioner. Before the roads in one of the counties of that state had been improved, the largest amount of farm and forest products shipped out of the county in any one year was 49,000 tons. In 1909, the amount of dairy products shipped was 115,000 pounds. During that year 40 miles of road were improved at an expense of $100,000. In 1911, two years after the improvement, 71,000 tons of farm and forest products and 273,000 pounds of dairy products were shipped. The increase was 45 and 140 per cent respectively in these two classes of products. The increase in wheat shipments was 59 per cent, in tobacco 31 per cent and in lumber and other farm products 48 per cent over the best records made before the roads were improved. This is by no means all of the direct result of having good roads for marketing. Careful studies of traffic in the county were made by Commissioner Coleman for two years, which showed that it cost at least 20 cents to haul a ton a mile on unimproved roads and 12 cents a ton a mile on improved roads. The records showed that the average haul of 65,000 tons of products was eight miles. Consequently the improvement of the roads over which the hauling was done saved the farmers $41,600 in marketing 65,000 tons of products. This sum saved in only two years is more than two-fifths of the cost of the road work which effected it.—Boston, Mass., *Transcript.*

ROAD TAXES, NOT TALK.

The good roads movement in Illinois needs the support of taxes, not talk. Too long this public necessity has been put off to another day. As the Association of Commerce has well said, until Illinois is known for its good roads it can not claim to be abreast of its opportunities as a state.

The trouble is that taxes have not kept pace with talk. Good roads have been excellent oratorical topics, but appropriations have not been as popular. The Pacific coast states, the Atlantic coast states and much of the Central West have surpassed Illinois in handling this essential need. Yet no State has a greater opportunity.

With farm lands as rich as any on the globe, with a congeries of cities accounting for one of the great world centers of population, with natural environment which might be the play places of hundreds of thousands, the State has been content to move very slowly.

Conditions, it is true, are not so bad as they were when the Illinois farmers had practically to dig themselves in at the approach of cold weather and to await in loneliness the coming of spring. But they are bad enough. We are not to be compared with New York or California so far as good roads are concerned. In fact, we seem to belong to another highway epoch.

Illinois has, however, the nucleus of effective good roads machinery in the State Highway Commission. The Tice bill, which created that commission, may well be strengthened and expanded. An extensive system of State roads should be built. State aid, not only in money but in engineering guidance, should be made more easily attainable by the counties. The Federal good roads aid should be utilized. An organization for maintaining in good repair roads already built should be developed.

But most of all Illinois should appropriate generously for this great purpose. It ought not to be necessary to add that the money authorized should be expended with a tender regard for the rights of the taxpayers—not in the loose and easy fashion of certain street building in Chicago. The time is at hand for a great stride forward.—Chicago, Ill., *Herald*.

WHAT EAGLE GROVE DID.

It is not likely that more than a small percentage of the people of this country ever heard of Eagle Grove, an Iowa town of about 4,500 population. Although small it is reached by several railways and is the marketing place of a flourishing rural district. Some of the enterprising citizens decided it ought to have still more trade, and that the best way to develop such trade was to improve the main roads leading into the country. So about eighteen months ago they organized a good roads committee, which raised more than $10,000 in cash and secured promises of labor of equal value from farmers. A grader, scrapers, drags, and the necessary tools were bought and 35 miles of gravel roads were built. The really important fact is that the business men and farmers realized from the outset that building the roads was merely the first step necessary for good highway transportation. So they organized a system of patrol-maintenance for the new roads, the funds being furnished by the business men of the city. While it is true that road work ought to be under public officials, it is also true that well-managed construction and maintenance at private expense is often of high educational value and prepares the way for proper public administration. Often public officials have to be shown that it is possible to do it, how to do it, and that the community is willing to pay for it if good work is done. It should not be forgotten, in this connection, that even in wealthy cities like New York and Chicago, such important work as good street cleaning was not well organized until merchant associations carried it on better than public departments had done and thus demonstrated its practicability and desirability.—Moline, Ill., *Dispatch*.

GOOD ROADS.

The *News-Record* as an enthusiastic believer in the issuing of bonds for the construction of a highway system in Sangamon County, commends the Springfield Motor Club for its advocacy of the submission of a bond issue proposition to a vote of the people.

The matter was agitated last spring, but some of the leading farmers, who above all others should favor good roads, opposed the plan and it was dropped.

Vermilion County is building a system of highways under a bond issue of $1,500,000, and it will be the banner county of the State in highway improvement as a result. Other counties have voted bonds or are preparing to do so. The farmers are among the most enthusiastic supporters of the bond issue plan in these counties.

Under a bond issue, the State aid money given the county is used in paying off the bonds. The upkeep of the roads is greatly decreased. And the public has the benefit of the roads while they are being paid for, instead of taking twenty years to build them and having to keep up dirt roads in the meantime.

What is needed is a campaign of education. That is the way Vermilion County did it. Once the taxpayers get the right view of the proposition, they will support

the bond issue. To submit it to a vote before they get the fullest information on the subject would be to invite defeat.—Springfield, Ill., *News-Record*.

GOOD ROADS STILL AN ISSUE.

A majority of the voters of Will County recently registered a protest against a proposed $1,500,000 bond issue for the purpose of constructing permanent highway pavements in this county.

This does not mean that the good roads issue is to be shelved during the next few years. On the contrary, there is a growing belief that the sentiment recorded in the ballots was not so much against the project of having good roads as it was against the methods that were to be employed.

Men of good judgment who made a study of the bond issue idea declare it was the most feasible plan that could be devised, and the good road boosters are willing to stand by that plea. Nevertheless, it is possible a second campaign for good roads might iron out the differences over methods and bring under one banner enough voters to get Will County started on this most important work.

When all objections have been analyzed, it will be found that good highways are one of the most important factors in city and country development that can be listed. The question of good or bad roads enters into the cost of living and has much to do with the abnormal prices that are now being levied upon the people. Possibly, direct connection on this point can not be made in local territory, but in many of the states the movement of grain and other food products depends in a large measure on the condition of the country highways.

This is but one of many elements supporting the cause of good roads. The city business man will find this a fruitful field for enthusiasm. With passable highways between the country and the city all the year through, city trade will expand by at least 50 per cent, according to those who have watched the experiment. On this selfish basis alone, the merchant could afford to back a good roads movement, financially and in other ways.

But there are other good reasons not so selfish. Good country highways mean the development of the country and city school privileges and a broadening of our educational resources. More of the right kind of knowledge will make the boys and girls better fitted for the duties of citizenship, and in this manner the whole community is benefited.

Good roads are vitally essential and are bound to come. The only argument is with regard to the best method to bring the improvements about.

That is the talking point for the next campaign, and if it is conducted fairly, the chances of success will be greatly enhanced.—Joliet, Ill., *Herald-News*.

Officers and directors of the Illinois Highway Improvement Association, at a meeting held recently in Chicago, went on record as favoring Illinois' acceptance of its full quota of Federal aid money, which will amount to $3,300,000 in the next five years. The State is required, under the Federal statute, to appropriate a like amount.

County Highway Superintendent Edwin H. White of Sangamon County has accepted four new bridges. They are in Gardner and Maxwell Townships and on the county line, northeast of Illiopolis.

Bituminous Surface for a Defective Concrete Pavement

By B. H. Piepmeier, Maintenance Engineer

The highway commissioners of Deerfield Township, Lake County, constructed a concrete pavement on the Green Bay Road in 1912. The concrete road was about one-half mile long and 18 feet wide. It was built under very poor conditions and very late in the season. It was evident from the beginning that the pavement, as constructed, would not withstand the excessively heavy traffic.

DEFECTIVE SECTION, BEFORE TREATMENT.

However, poor as the concrete surface was recognized as being, it remained in very serviceable condition until the last year.

The concrete surface, in the past two years, had shown signs of rapid disintegration. There were a number of sections that tended to ravel as if the concrete had been frozen before thoroughly hardening. Many of the sections were badly cracked and numerous spots showed up wet for a number of days following a light rain, indicating that the concrete was very porous in places.

The road was in such condition that the first impression would lead one to decide that the surest way to repair it would be to rebuild entirely or resurface with brick or bituminous concrete, or possibly four inches of additional cement concrete. Finances would not permit reconstruction or resurfacing, and, too, the grade of the pavement was such that it was not desirable to raise the wearing surface 4 or 5 inches.

After careful examination by Charles E. Russell, county superintendent of highways, and the writer, it was decided to apply a bituminous surface over the entire defective area. There were a number of sections of the pavement that were apparently in good condition but for sake of appearance and uniformity, the entire pavement was treated alike.

The tar surface was applied as follows: The entire pavement was first thoroughly cleaned with a rotary broom. The surface was then treated with Tarvia B at the rate of one-fourth gallon per square yard, applied under pressure from the Barrett truck, which delivered the material direct from the Chicago plant.

The Tarvia B was applied first to act as a primer and to absorb any surplus dust and to penetrate and waterproof the porous spots. Tarvia X at 225° F. was then used to fill all cracks and large depressions. In connection with the Tarvia X the necessary sand, chips and stone were used to bring the surface to a true cross section. Tarvia A at the rate of about one-half gallon

APPLYING THE SURFACE.

per square yard was then applied under pressure from the oil truck at a temperature of about 200° F.

Immediately following the application of Tarvia A the necessary torpedo gravel (size ⅛″ to ¼″) was spread over the surface to hold the bituminous material, prevent it from sticking and to insure a more uniform wearing surface.

The resulting pavement presents an appearance a great deal like a bituminous concrete road. It is not expected that surfaces of this kind will be permanent, yet if the necessary precautions are taken in cleaning the pavement and applying the bituminous material, very satisfactory results may be expected.

It is probable that such a surface occasionally will need a very light application of tar covered with torpedo gravel. Such treatments if carefully constructed and maintained will restore faulty sections of concrete pavements to a very serviceable condition and at very reasonable cost. The following shows the total cost and cost per square yard on the work referred to in the foregoing:

Total square yards in defective pavement	6,000
Total square yards new pavement treated with Tarvia B	1,000
Total amount of Tarvia B used, 1,495 gal. or 0.21 gal. per sq. yd.	
Total amount of Tarvia A used, 3,009 gal. or 0.50 gal. per sq. yd.	
Total amount of Tarvia X used, 1,510 gal. or 0.25 gal. per sq. yd.	
Tarvia A, B and X, 6,014 gal. at average price of 11½c per gal. delivered =	$692.83 or $0.115 per sq. yd.
Torpedo gravel and stone 172 cu. yds. at $1.85 =	318.07 or 0.053 per sq. yd.
Labor	100.00 or 0.017 per sq. yd.
Total	$1,110.90 or $0.185 per sq. yd.

FINISHED PAVEMENT, AFTER TREATMENT.

NEW AUTO TRAILS MARKED.

Highway promotion of an active variety is reported in a news story which the Association of Commerce of Sterling, Ill., has contributed to ILLINOIS HIGHWAYS. Completion of new brick roads and the marking of new auto trails are narrated as follows:

The recent completion and opening for travel of three miles of brick paving just east of city of Sterling, Illinois, makes a 7-mile stretch of brick traversed by Lincoln Highway through Sterling Township. The brick paving done by Dixon Township this year completes another 7-mile stretch of brick along the Highway, Dixon Township, now being paved with brick from one end to the other. Between Sterling and Dixon Townships is the township of Palmyra, in Lee County, in which about one and a half miles of brick is to be built by State aid in 1917, in continuation of the Dixon Township brick. The remainder of the highway to the Sterling brick is to be improved with gravel by the township authorities. Also in this vicinity three more miles of the Lincoln Highway, in Hopkins Township, in Whiteside County, just west of Sterling, are to be rebuilt by State aid in 1917. Gravel and stone are the materials to be used.

Sterling and Rock Falls have recently become the center of two new well-marked auto trails that promise to become important feeders for the Lincoln Highway, the Indian Head and Diamond Trails.

The Indian Head Trail goes northwest from Sterling to Milledgeville, Chadwick, Mt. Carroll, Savanna, Hanover, Galena and is expected soon to be marked to La Crosse, Wis., and Minneapolis. South, this trail goes through Stones, Van Petten, Walnut, Princeton, Tiskilwa, Whitehead Corners, Chillicothe, Peoria.

The Diamond Trail goes north from Sterling to Polo, Forreston, Baileyville, Freeport; southwest, to Prophetstown, Springhill, Geneseo, Cambridge, Andover, Woodhull, Galesburg. Considerable State aid and township bond issue road work is to be done on both these trails next summer.

Early next spring the Black Hawk Trail Association, of which Governor Frank O. Lowden is president, is to mark its route, which extends along beautiful Rock River, from Sterling, via Dixon, Grand Detour, Oregon, Byron, Rockford, Rockton, to Beloit, Wis. This trail is named after the famous Indian warrior, Black Hawk, whose majestic statue overlooks Rock river at Oregon, Illinois. The Indian Head Trail secures its name from the great stone Indian head wrought by nature, at Savanna, Illinois, which stands as a sentinel along the scenic route north of that city, and overlooking the Mississippi River.

MUST TAKE AWAY SIGN BOARDS.

In the belief that ungainly and unsightly signs of an advertising nature along public highways mar the beauty of the road itself and of the contiguous landscape, the Illinois Highway Commission has directed that all such advertising signs be removed from along all State aid roads.

The order came in a letter directed from Chief State Highway Engineer W. W. Marr for the commission to all advertisers. Other communications sought the co-operation of county highway superintendents and, through them, of township officials as well, to the end that the antisign campaign may be carried to a beneficial conclusion.

The State Highway Commission desires, first of all of course, to conserve the interests of the State aid roads. The placing of signs has become such a universal practice that it has come to amount to nothing less than a nuisance, in the opinion of the commission. Moreover, the commission believes such staring objects as the majority of sign boards of to-day do not really advertise; that, in many instances, they repel instead of attract the favor of travelers.

The order is expected to help bring Illinois' chain of State aid roads up to the top notch of taste and natural beauty.

NOVEMBER REPORT, BUREAU OF BRIDGES.

During the month of November, 1916, plans, estimates and specifications for sixteen concrete bridges and four steel bridges were prepared and sent out to county superintendents of highways. The total estimated cost of these bridges is $39,665.

Plans, estimates and specifications for three concrete bridges to be built as extra work on State aid bridge contracts were prepared. The total estimated cost of this work amounts to $737.70.

Plans and estimates for bridge and culvert work to be built in connection with State aid road contracts were prepared for two sections of State aid road work, including forty-one bridges and culverts, the total estimated cost of which equals $3,450.

Summing up, plans were prepared for 64 bridges and culverts, the total estimated cost of which equals $43,852.70.

Plans for nine bridges and culverts prepared by county superintendents of highways were checked and approved. One alternate plan was checked and disapproved.

According to reports received, contracts were awarded during the month on plans prepared for county superintendents of highways for ten concrete bridges at an average cost of 86.8 per cent of the estimates, and for five steel bridges at an average cost of 95.1 per cent of the estimates. The total estimated cost of this work amounts to $19,415.

The prints of the new standard plans for abutments for slab bridges with cantilever wing walls were received and are now in use.

The following outlines briefly the status of the work in the Bureau of Bridges on December 1, 1916:

There were on hand ready for work three bridge inspection reports; five bridge plans had been prepared but not checked, and 25 bridge plans had been completed, together with the estimates, and were practically ready to be sent out.

The bridge office at the present time is in a position to give prompt attention to requests for the preparation of plans and specifications for bridge work.—*Compiled by* A. W. CONSOER, *Office Engineer.*

AN IMPROVEMENT VISUALIZED!

First Division Engineer H. B. Bushnell of Aurora, the other day, mailed in two pictures which serve to illustrate graphically the "before" and "after" of a typical Illinois highway improvement. Typical, that is, so far as the degree of change is concerned.

."BEFORE."

The pictures were taken of section "G," in Kankakee County. The contrast presented is all the more striking for the reason that the two views were "snapped" from the same point of focus.

"AFTER."

This is a 15-foot water-bound macadam road, very recently completed. It is rated as a splendid piece of work. The old road was of very fine sand, making traffic in dry weather an exceedingly difficult matter. Often it was all but impassable.

At the meeting of the Northwestern Road Congress, held in December in Chicago, Chairman A. D. Gash of the Illinois State Highway Commission was elected president of the congress. Secretary S. A. Bradt of the Illinois Commission was elected one of the directors of the congress. T. R. Agg, former road engineer of the State Highway Department of Illinois, is secretary-treasurer of the organization. Mr. Agg is now with Ames University.

William Hoos of Pittsfield has been given the contract to construct a number of bridges in Atlas Township, Pike County, at an aggregate price of over $8,000.

AN ANNOUNCEMENT

THE MAILING LIST OF "ILLINOIS HIGHWAYS" HAS GROWN WITH SUCH STRIDES IN THE LAST FEW MONTHS THAT WE ARE COMPELLED AT LAST TO TAKE STEPS TO KEEP IT WITHIN THE DESIRED PUBLICATION LIMIT.

IN NOVEMBER. EVERY COPY, EXCEPT THE FEW RETAINED FOR OFFICE FILES, WAS MAILED OUT. LAST MONTH, THE SITUATION WAS LITTLE BETTER.

WE HAVE BEEN PUBLISHING SEVERAL THOUSAND COPIES OF EACH MONTH'S ISSUE, AND BECAUSE OF THE HIGH COST OF PAPER AND PRINTING, DO NOT DESIRE TO EXCEED OUR PRESENT LIMIT. YET, WE WANT "ILLINOIS HIGHWAYS" IN THE HANDS EVERY MONTH OF THOSE INTERESTED IN THE WORK OF THE STATE HIGHWAY DEPARTMENT, OF WHICH THE PUBLICATION IS THE OFFICIAL ORGAN.

IN THIS MONTH'S ISSUE, YOU WILL FIND A CARD. IF YOU DESIRE TO CONTINUE TO RECEIVE "ILLINOIS HIGHWAYS," KINDLY FILL IT OUT, AFFIX A STAMP AND MAIL IT IN, NOT LATER THAN FEB. 1, 1917. YOU ARE MORE THAN WELCOME EITHER TO CONTINUE READING THIS MAGAZINE, OR TO BE- COME A NEW READER. IT IS SENT FREE OF ALL COST TO YOU.

WE WISH SIMPLY TO REVISE OUR MAILING FILE, WITH THE PURPOSE OF ELIMINATING ANY DEAD LIST THAT MAY EXIST.   **—The Editor.**

ILLINOIS HIGHWAYS

[Printed by authority of the State of Illinois.]

OFFICIAL PUBLICATION OF THE

STATE HIGHWAY DEPARTMENT

| VOL. IV | SPRINGFIELD, ILLINOIS, FEBRUARY, 1917 | No. 2 |

Monolithic Brick, Platt County, Built 1916.

Good Roads.

"Good roads are a good investment, but a comprehensive system of good roads must wait for a generation, unless bonds are issued to defray the cost.

"Motor vehicles are rapidly supplanting horse-drawn vehicles. When good roads have become the rule, and not the exception as now, auto trucks will likely take the place of horses and wagons in the transportation of the products of the farm. With good roads, the upkeep and maintenance of motor vehicles would be largely reduced. The license fees now paid are only a trifling percentage of the cost of operation. If good roads were assured, the owners of motor vehicles could pay a much larger license fee and still be the gainers.

"I believe it is possible to work out some plan by which the principal and interest of a bond issue sufficient for this purpose could be largely, if not entirely, paid from the receipts of such license fees."

Hon. Frank O. Lowden,
Governor of Illinois.

(Extract from inaugural address delivered by Governor Lowden on January 8, 1917, before the Fiftieth General Assembly)

Earth Roads and the Central Illinois Farmer
By A. H. HUNTER, Division Engineer, Third Division, State Highway Department

It was my good fortune to be present at an open meeting of the road and bridge committee of our General Assembly held in the House of Representatives at Springfield, Illinois, about the first of April, 1915. At this meeting representatives of various organizations throughout the State presented their views concerning the changes and amendments which they deemed advisable to have incorporated in the State Road Law. One or two speakers, I remember in particular, made mention of what they termed "permanent earth roads." At several times since this meeting, I have heard humorous comments concerning those remarks. It might be humorous in its way, but as a matter of fact the State Aid law is so amended and so worded that the statement "permanent earth roads" is incorporated and made part of our Road and Bridge law.

Perhaps many of those who made such humorous remarks pertaining to the matter of earth roads looked at it in a different attitude from what we might expect. It occurs to me, since giving this subject some attention, that the expression "permanent earth roads" might be considered correct. The greater portion of our present road system in this State is earth roads and probably will be earth roads for years to come. According to the best information available, which information by the way was secured from measurements from the best available maps, it is found that the total road mileage of the State of Illinois is approximately 96,676 miles. The amount of earth roads involved in this comprises practically all of the mileage mentioned. Even when we add the mileage improved by State aid within the last two years together with the miles of existing gravel or macadam that was in place, we find that still approximately 95 per cent of the total mileage of the State remains as earth roads. It is my opinion that these earth roads if properly crowned, graded and drained should permanently and economically exist on from 70 to 80 per cent of our rural highways.

Within the last few years, we have had considerable interest shown in dragging, grading, and maintaining these earth roads. In addition, oil has been found to be an important element in the proposition of maintenance or improving the condition of the surface. At this writing, several sections of the State have been interested in the proposition to such an extent that they have purchased considerable machinery and oil in large quantities which they expect to have applied upon the road surface. In one county near Peoria, the officials saw fit to purchase about 200,000 gallons of oil for this season's use.

Along these same lines, our department has been requested to prepare plans and specifications for more than 100 miles of oiled earth roads. At this writing there are under construction, two sections of oiled earth road in this division and the continuation of this work is expressed in resolutions passed by several county boards. It is probable that our department alone will construct perhaps 50 or 60 miles of this type of road in Central Illinois next season.

According to the best information available—the State Auditor's report of 1914—I found that the amount of money levied for road and bridge purposes throughout the State of Illinois was in excess of eight millions of dollars. As those figures were based on the tax levy of September 1913, I am led to believe that this figure is perhaps exceeded at this writing and feel I would not be far wrong if the figures nine millions of dollars were used. Assume that the above sum of money was available, and assume the mileage of roads which would be provided for, you can see at once that the amount of money with which township officials are provided to maintain the earth roads in their vicinity is slightly less than $100 a mile. Should we be able to go through roughly and remove all moneys that were expanded in the construction of hard roads or bridges you would find that the maintenance of the earth roads would be about $40 or $50 per mile.

In a report furnished by the state officials of Iowa, statement is made that the amount of money available for the maintenance of the earth roads in that particular state is about $40 a mile. As Illinois and Iowa are sister states and very similar in industry and soil conditions, it seems likely that the above approximation that I have made is reasonably near correct.

In many places the townships do not obtain much in excess of $2,000 per year for the construction and maintenance of their road system. With work of this kind it is very difficult to secure low unit prices. The work is comparatively small and so distributed that it is impossible to secure contractors that will do the work at a reasonable figure. In many instances the township can not afford to own a tractor or grader outfit and consequently do the major portion of the work with horse-drawn machinery. In some instances where it is found desirable to purchase a tractor or grading outfit you are confronted with the proposition of cost. It has frequently been called to my attention that some townships have spent more in one year for the purchase of grading machinery than the entire tax levy available in that particular year. This again confronts you with the matter of finances with which you have not been adequately provided.

On this basis it is apparent that it is impossible to keep all roads in satisfactory condition with the funds available. If you township commissioners concentrate the funds on the main traveled roads, the people living on the less traveled highways will kick. If you try to please every one by spreading the money used over the entire system, all the roads are in bad shape and everybody kicks. It would seem that no matter what you endeavor to do you will be criticized from some standpoint and you are sure to have half if not all the community dissatisfied with your work. For all this responsibility and blame, you are compensated with the magnificent salary of $2 a day, if you are located in a township which has three commissioners. In case your community works under the single commission system, the official has a little better opportunity to receive reasonable compensation for his services. If it were possible to double or perhaps treble the present taxes for road maintenance, wouldn't you still have a pretty difficult time in making improvements of any consequences? Apparently, looking at the situation from a distance, this system of road administration is about as unsatisfactory as the road.

The growing interest in highway improvement resulted in 1913, in the passing of the State Aid Road law. This revised law, which has since been amended and is frequently referred to as the Tice Road Law, has as its most important feature a comprehensive plan of the rural highways called State aid. It was intended that this law should assist the farmer in his transportation problem. On the other hand it would assist every township commissioner by eventually relieving him of the maintenance of from 15 to 20 per cent of the total road mileage.

The law made it the duty of the county board of supervisors to designate on the map, furnished by the State Highway Department, a system of main traveled roads extending throughout the county. It was the intent that a complete system be laid out connecting the larger cities and an effort made to place these roads so as to benefit the larger cities and the largest number of people. It was expressed, however, that these State aid roads were not to comprise more than 15 per cent of the total road mileage in counties of the first class, 20 per cent of the total road mileage in counties of the second class and 25 per cent of the total road mileage in counties of the third class. There is only one third-class county in the State. This is Cook County. A careful investigation of county roads resulted in finding that from 70 to 80 per cent and not infrequently more, of the total traffic in a county is carried on the main roads. It was the intention that these roads should be designated as the State Aid, and when approved by the county board and by the commission was to be placed on file in the office of the county clerk and a copy retained in our Springfield office. This portion of the law has been complied with, and each county has now in its possession a map showing the system of highways designated for future improvement.

The Legislature has seen fit from time to time to make allotments to the various counties for State improvement of these systems. Up to the present, practically all money allotted has been obtained from the automobile tax. The following allotments have been made.

July 1, 1913 to July 1, 1914................ $ 400,000
July 1, 1914 to July 1, 1915................   700,000
July 1, 1915 to July 1, 1916................ 1,000,000
July 1, 1916 to July 1, 1917................ 1,000,000

In the above allotments the only fund that has been raised by general taxation is the first one of $400,000. All other allotments have been made from funds secured by assessing the tax upon the motor vehicles.

The allotments are proportioned to the counties in the same ratio as the road and bridge tax bears to the total road and bridge tax of the State, provided that counties in which more than 40 per cent of the total amount appropriated by the General Assembly for building roads is collected, including any amount collected for automobiles or kindred licenses there shall be allotted to that county only 25 per cent. It was found that Cook County paid 42.72 per cent of all road and bridge tax and 42.76 per cent of all moneys collected from automobile and kindred licenses. This difference between approximately 43 per cent and 25 per cent is reallotted to the other counties in proportion to their road and bridge tax compared to that of the entire State exclusive of Cook County.

In order for each county to avail itself of these allotments, it was necessary for it to raise an equal amount, the combined sum to be spent on the improvement of such section of State aid roads as the county board sees fit to designate. The type of construction is determined by the county board from the following list: Brick, concrete, macadam, gravel, any combination of the above or permanent earth improvement.

It has been suggested that each county should receive the direct benefits of its own automobile tax. Or in other words, that the moneys collected from automobile fees and kindred licenses should be returned directly to the county. If this were the case your allotment would be smaller than under the present system. As an example we find that Peoria County received on July 1, 1915, an allotment of $21,744, while the records in the office of the Secretary of State show Peoria County collected only $18,827.86. By this comparison you can see that this county would be the loser of approximately $3,000 if this system was adopted. Do not lose sight of this either, that Peoria County contains the second largest city in the State, is densely populated and in all probability contributes more to the automobile fund than most of the adjoining agricultural communities.

The present allotment available July 1, 1916, was entirely from funds obtained from automobile licenses. This automobile fund collected in the State treasury can not be expended for any other purpose than road improvement. All money that is paid in by the car owners to the Secretary of State is deposited at the treasury and allotted at the will of the State Legislature. All charges for license numbers and incidental work necessary to handle this department is provided for in appropriation paid to the Secretary of State. In other words all money that is collected from this source is deposited in the State treasury and is available for road construction.

There has been a large increase in the number of cars in this State and recently I was advised that the number of automobile licenses issued this season had exceeded 250,000. In view of this fact it seems certain that there will be sufficient funds in the State treasury to provide for other allotments in considerable excess of one million dollars. It seems logical to predict that our present working of the State aid road law will continue with the prospect of much larger appropriations than in the past.

One of the best provisions of the Tice Road Law is that of maintenance. This one item of good road making has received less attention than any other and the neglect of it has caused more loss of public money than you can imagine. It is my opinion that the present demand for brick or concrete pavements for rural communities is due much to neglect of maintenance on sections of previously constructed earth, gravel, or macadam. In fact, most of our gravel or macadam roads have not received any attention for so long a time that repairs could be made only by replacing the entire surface. There is, or should be, maintenance on every form of construction, no matter what type, width or thickness. Did it ever occur to you what an appearance and depreciation in value would result if you left your own home without any attention for a period of five or six years, yet that is exactly what has been done in many instances with our highways. On our roads we have presented a sur-

(Concluded on Page 23.)

WITH THE COUNTY SUPERINTENDENTS

ILLINOIS HIGHWAYS always welcomes letters, reports or tidings of any kind, pertaining to road and bridge work, from county highway superintendents throughout the State.

We believe publicity such as is secured through the medium of a publication like this serves the double purpose of benefiting localities where work is going on, and of creating an inspiration for other communities which may hear of good deeds elsewhere.

County highway superintendents are in a position, if they chose to avail themselves of its advantage, to do their counties invaluable good by letting the other sections of the State know what's doing within their respective territories.

It does not always follow that superintendents may have statistics or specific road building progress to report. There are peculiar conditions that would do no harm to publish, little odds and ends directly or indirectly connected with the road construction problem. At any time the superintendents may have information of any interesting character whatsoever, ILLINOIS HIGHWAYS is ready and anxious to give it space.

A few letters were received last month.

A WINNEBAGO ODDITY.

The Winnebago County superintendent of highways, A. R. Carter, writing from Rockford, says:

"I believe we have a condition in Winnebago County that does not exist in any other place in Illinois. At the 1916 spring election, the town of New Milford and town of Rockford voted on the proposition of uniting, which was carried by both townships. They were formally united by the action of the board of supervisors at the June session. The law states that all town officers shall hold their respective offices until the next spring election, so we have the following conditions:

The town of Rockford has 2 supervisors, 17 assistant supervisors, 2 town clerks, 4 highway commissioners, (the town of New Milford being under the single commissioner system), 77 square miles of area, 153 miles of road, of which 60 per cent are improved with macadam or gravel. The total valuation of the township, including the city of Rockford, is $25,031,761. Total amount available for roads and bridges during the season of 1917 equals one-half the city tax or $58,958."

FOR OIL IN M'DONOUGH.

Initial steps toward independent work are reported in a letter from W. M. Bonham of Macomb, highway superintendent of McDonough County.

"At the December meeting of the board of supervisors, the board appropriated $3,000 for the buying of road oil. This is the first time the county has ever done anything with the road question, except the State aid work.

This money will be apportioned among the various townships according to the ratio of the road and bridge tax in that township to the total tax in the county for that purpose. A township, to get aid, will have to put up a like amount. If any township does not accept the allotment, it will revert back to the fund to be reallotted to those that have accepted their share.

The proportions to the various townships will run from $79.44 to $261.99. There will be certain restrictions in regard to this work, which, though practically assured, have not been approved as yet by the road committee of supervisors.

"By having this appropriation to work with, and having the assistance of a county good roads association which I recently organized, I believe that in a short time McDonough will be in the front ranks of the counties that are staying by the earth road."

SYSTEM IN CLAY.

We can not help but admire the conciseness and the comprehensiveness of the financial report which Highway Superintendent Howard M. Anderson of Clay County made to the county board of supervisors at its final meeting of 1916, last month at Louisville, the county seat.

Mr. Anderson transmitted a copy of his report to ILLINOIS HIGHWAYS. It is brief and interesting, and we take pleasure in publishing it herewith. It covers receipts and expenditures in the county on highway projects for the fiscal year ending September 5, 1916, showing figures from the individual townships as well as the aggregate amounts.

Broadly, the receipts for the year from all sources were $28,610.60 and the expenditures for road purposes $24,763.29, showing a county balance on the date named of $3,921.18. Only two townships showed deficits.

The tabulated report follows:

CLAY COUNTY HIGHWAY RECEIPTS AND EXPENDITURES IN 1916.

Townships.	Balance Sept. 7, 1915.	From town collector.	From county collector.	Poll tax.	Other sources.	Total receipts.	Grading.	Dragging.	Bridges and culverts.	Bridge and culvert repairs.	Machinery.	Machinery repairs.	Damages.	Miscellaneous.*	Total expended.	Balance Sept. 5, 1916.	Deficit.
Xenia	$ 156 44	$1,016 61	$ 394 85	$ 60 00	$ 6 00	$1,627 87	$ 212 10	$ 90 00	$ 296 40	$ 90 13	$312 70		$100 00	$ 29 00	$1,690 33		$62 46
Songer	39 97	1,235 82	112 78	170 00		1,564 37	297 85	21 50	959 96	17 50	100 00	$ 4 25		28 96	1,426 32	$ 138 05	
Oskaloosa	284 11	1,015 32	373 49	381 00	10 60	2,064 52	467 12	29 75	1,304 29	51 11		18 95		94 68	2,055 88	8 64	
Larkinsburg	14 21	1,049 96	383 56	257 00		1,705 39	778 39	28 11	473 03	110 44	200 00			96 84	1,686 81	18 58	
Harter	608 36	2,440 09	1,237 90	906 00	90 00	5,367 35	1,134 75	54 00	2,133 13	25 00	435 70	68 62		572 50	4,417 70	942 65	
Louisville	858 58	1,126 16	498 81	98 00	148 31	2,723 86	941 66	53 50	965 66	214 43		4 00		482 12	2,660 36	63 50	
Blair	15 75	1,068 36	170 58	18 00		1,414 52	533 08	18 88	612 23	72 28		6 50	6 25	76 98	1,318 15	96 37	
Stanford	968 62	1,606 94	374 89	177 50	401 20	3,471 25	749 04	21 23	945 70	280 47	238 50	15 82		737 29	2,989 05	482 20	
Hoosier	41 40	1,136 75	246 07	100 75		1,564 97	673 46		486 16		278 90	23 25	154 61		1,576 38		11 41
Bible Grove	20 97	1,330 15	97 21	318 00		1,766 33	458 65	154 20	868 79	37 25		20 90		15 21	1,599 27	167 06	
Clay City	1,128 10	1,149 87	411 91	274 00		2,963 88	671 58	69 60	504 31			15 03		1 50	1,262 04	1,701 84	
Pixley	177 33	1,551 73	135 28	385 50	126 35	2,376 29	419 42	184 05	1,160 48	4 65	338 85	7 60		72 95	2,088 00	288 29	
Totals	$4,514 64	$15,749 56	$4,477 53	$3,086 65	$782 46	$28,610 60	$7,329 05	$823 82	$11,496 44	$833 35	$1,916 82	$164 91	$260 86	$2,208 01	$24,763 29	$3,921 18	$73 86

*NOTE—Old unclassified orders received by treasurers are included in "Miscellaneous" column.

ONCE A THICK BASE, ALWAYS?

Much interest attaches to the building in Iroquois County of a stretch of monolithic brick road, in which a 1-inch concrete base is being used in the construction.

There are students and authorities—so far as authorities on a type of road a year and a half old can be said to exist—who insist that a 1-inch base in a monolithic road is sufficient, provided of course the grout is of the right mix and is properly applied. Alan J. Parrish, a well-known contractor of Paris, Ill., builds his monolithic roads with a 4-inch base. He is Illinois' pioneer, so far as construction of the particular type in question goes.

A few months ago when several hundred delegates to the annual meeting of the National Paving Brick Manufacturers' Association went from Terre Haute, Ind., to Paris to see Mr. Parrish's road-building methods demonstrated, the base was one of the chief features of the work under discussion among the men.

In its designs for monolithic roads, the Illinois State Highway Department requires 4 inches as the minimum thickness of the concrete base. Even though monolithic construction is in its infancy and has yet to stand the test of time before judgment can be passed upon it, it looks as if a 4-inch base would certainly insure a slab permanent enough for every purpose to which the road would be put. A thinner base naturally means some decrease in cost, hence the growing question:

Can the monolithic brick road be built upon a base substantially thinner, with permanency and satisfactory service of the road resulting?

The base promises to have devoted to it a vast amount of study and experiment in the coming years on the part of contractors and of students of road building. There are advocates of a 1-inch base; there are others who declare that 2 or 2½ inches marks the ragged edge limit of safety.

Whatever the results may or may not be, they are giving the 1-inch base a chance in Iroquois County to assert its qualities. It will be no mean trial, for the stretch of road is to be five miles long. *Engineering Record* tells of the work in the following article:

In accordance with the theory that a dry, compacted earth roadbed without any material depth of foundation will, by itself, sustain any county traffic, Stockland Township, Iroquois County, Illinois, is building five miles of monolithic brick road nine feet wide, on a concrete base 1 inch thick. Carried to the limit from the structural standpoint, no base would be used, for the compacted soil is counted upon to take the load, and the brick is to act simply as a surfacing material, keeping the earth foundation dry. This means extraordinary pains to insure deep side ditches. The purpose of the thin layer of concrete, which can hardly be termed a base or foundation, is not to hold the brick nor to bear weight, but to make a smooth surface on which to lay the brick and one on which the grout will stop.

As in the Vermilion County brick roads, wire-cut lug brick are laid directly on the wet concrete within 20 feet of the mixer. A 1:2½:4 mixture is used, the large material being roofing gravel passing a one-half inch screen and remaining on a one-fourth inch screen. The moisture consistency is considered of the greatest importance. It is such that the mix will just run down a 30° grade of the Boss mixer spout. It is then struck off with a hand template which is cut back 8 to 10 inches to permit a zigzag motion. The base is so thin and the mixture so granular that if the water content is right the bricks are easily sustained, thus giving a smooth surface.

An Anyweight water roller weighing 25 pounds to the linear inch is used within 6 to 8 feet of the brick layers to take out any small irregularities. The roller is pushed transversely across the brick rather than lengthwise, because it is considered that the sidewise rolling is like sliding two straight-edges together to produce a straight line. In other words, as the roller approaches the end of one row of bricks it rests on the center of adjacent rows. In the lengthwise rolling the roller jumps over the joints from one row of bricks to another, thus tending to rock the individual brick.

The grouting was done with a small Marsh-Capron mixer, using practically the same procedure as was followed in the Vermilion County work. A 1:1 mix of cement, fine plaster and sand, of the consistency of cream, is spread directly from the mixer into the joints with a brush. The second coat is applied from wheelbarrows as soon as the first coat is settled but not set up. The third coat should be the filler left on top of the bricks from the other two coats and squeezed into the joints to fill them flush with the top. It is the aim to keep the grouting operation within from 100 to 200 feet of the brick layers.

Some of the construction advantages noted on this work are the small mixer required for the foundation work and the small amount of aggregate needed, the latter materially reducing the teaming item.

The work is being carried out for the township by Bishop & Liddell, contractors, Danville, Ill.

FARMERS USE THE SIDE ROADS.

Many persons living off the "main road" think they derive no benefits from its improvement. That this impression is wrong, however, is indicated by the accompanying view showing common practice on one of California's concrete paved highways.

Farmers living on unimproved roads off the "main line" use two, three or more teams to haul their produce to the concrete pavement and there transfer it to motor trucks and trailers, or reduce the number of teams, because they can haul greater loads in less time over the concrete highway to their market town.

A transfer of produce.

This view is on one of California's highways, otherwise known as the Bakersfield Road, near Grape Vine Creek, Cal.—*Press note, Portland Cement Association.*

* * *

Sangamon and Christian Counties have awarded a contract for the repair of Illiopolis Slough bridge, which spans the North Fork of the Sangamon River in Mosquito Township, Christian County. The bridge is 300 feet long.

EARTH ROADS AND THE FARMER.

(Concluded from Page 20.)

face open to the combined action of the elements and traffic and positively neglected it for years.

Upon completion of any State aid road it becomes the duty of the State Highway Department to maintain it. You, as township commissioners, are relieved from this burden and will have time and funds to devote to the repair or construction of other work. The law states, however, that it is the duty of the county to pay the entire expense of maintenance on earth roads, one-half the maintenance on gravel or macadam. All other types of pavement shall be maintained by the State without any cost to the county whatsoever.

It is apparent that if allotments are continued at the present rate, the present system of State aid roads will not be completed until after most of us will be dead and gone. If we are to receive any benefit from highway improvements we must have means of immediate construction. This is provided for in the new law by a bond arrangement, such bonds to be issued to mature in not less than 10 nor more than 20 annual series, the last series to mature not more than 20 years from the date of issue. The total amount of bonds shall not exceed 5 per cent of the assessed valuation of property in any county and deductions are to be made for any outstanding debts or obligations. Counties, such as Peoria, Fulton, Livingston, or LaSalle, could raise by this means funds ranging from $1,000,000 to $1,750,000 depending entirely upon their assessed valuation. Vermillion County recently voted for issuing $1,500,000 worth of bonds and last spring awarded contracts for the construction of 166 miles of road.

To carry successfully a bond issue in any county, it will be necessary for you, or those individuals connected with it to inform every voter of the plain facts of the case. In general, the Central Illinois farmer treats a bond in much the same manner as he would a mortgage on his farm. He does not like a debt and you can not blame him, and before you can convince him it will be necessary to give a detailed explanation of the cost and workings of a bond issue.

The average assessed valuation of an acre of improved farm land of Central Illinois is about $25; the highest average figures given in the reports of the State Auditor show $31 while many counties are found in which the assessed valuation does not exceed $20 per acre. With these figures as a basis you can determine what a bond issue will cost the farmer on the average. Assuming the assessed valuation of $25 per acre, you will find that the bond issue will cost the farmer from 8 to 9 cents per acre per year. Assuming that the farmer has a farm of 160 acres his average yearly outlay in taxes due to bonds would amount to approximately $14.40. The bond argument is frequently enlivened by claims that the interest on the bonds is too great a debt to hand to our next generation. The average interest per acre of land slightly exceeds 2 cents per year. On the basis of 160-acre farm the owner would pay the large sum of $3.20 for the advantages of a good road that could be used every day out of the 365.

On roads constructed by bond issue the same method of procedure in the maintenance is carried out as on the ordinary State aid road. It is required, however, that all contracts and constructed portions of road are in accordance with the standards of the State Highway Department. If the county so desires, it can apply the allotments which come in the future to the payment of bonds or interest, it being understood, however, that the State

will not pay more than one-half the total cost of construction.

To make road building a success in Central Illinois, it will be necessary for all, county and State and township, to inform themselves as to the proper type of construction, the best methods of construction and the proper means of maintenance. This information once secured, it should be a common duty to advise the farmer. My experience has been that the Illinois farmer is a broadminded man, who until recently, has opposed road improvement for the reason that he was not informed. Acquaint him with the advantages of good highways and his assistance will be assured.

The farmer has acquired his property by a process of saving. He did not get rich by stock and bond investments or board of trade operations. He detests a spendthrift, and we should give him the best possible return for his investment if we expect him to assist us in the united effort we are making to advance this State in the character of her road improvement.

[EDITOR'S NOTE.—The foregoing paper was presented by Division Engineer Hunter at the recent meeting in Peoria of the Illinois Society of Highway Commissioners and Town Clerks. It contains earth road information which we believe will interest not only township highway officials, but farmers in Illinois as well. It is with pleasure therefore that we present it in full in this month's issue of ILLINOIS HIGHWAYS.

[The term "permanent" as the law uses it in qualifying the earth type, applies more particularly to the grading and drainage work, which may be of such a permanent nature that it will not depreciate in value or have to be built over when a hard surface is later added.]

SURVEYING CONCRETE PAVEMENTS.

The maintenance survey of concrete pavements in the United States recently undertaken by field engineers of the Portland Cement Association, is progressing satisfactorily. According to late reports, nearly 20,000,000 of the 70,000,000 square yards of such pavements have been examined and reported upon and it is expected the work will be completed during the course of the next month. Over 100 engineers stationed in various parts of the country are making this inspection.

Solving a drainage problem, Cook County. It was necessary to dig this ditch a mile long.

One of the objects of this survey is to secure data based on actual experience so that methods of construction and maintenance that have produced the best results may be definitely determined with a view to raising the standards of practice in concrete pavement construction generally. When this work is completed, the Portland Cement Association will have a complete history of all concrete pavement in the United States—roads, streets and alleys.

ILLINOIS HIGHWAYS.

Published Monthly by the
State Highway Department,
Springfield, Illinois.

ILLINOIS HIGHWAY COMMISSION.

A. D. GASH, *President.*
S. E. BRADT, *Secretary.*
JAMES P. WILSON.

WM. W. MARR, *Chief State Highway Engineer.*

BUREAU OF ROADS.

H. E. BILGER, *Road Engineer.*
M. W. WATSON, *Assistant Road Engineer.*
C. M. HATHAWAY, *Office Engineer.*

BUREAU OF BRIDGES.

CLIFFORD OLDER, *Bridge Engineer.*
G. F. BURCH, *Assistant Bridge Engineer.*
A. W. CONBOER, *Office Engineer.*

BUREAU OF MAINTENANCE.

B. H. PIEPMEIER, *Maintenance Engineer.*
F. T. SHEETS, *Assistant Maintenance Engineer.*

BUREAU OF TESTS.

F. L. ROMAN, *Testing Engineer.*
F. L. SPERRY, *Assistant Testing Engineer.*
W. C. ADAMS, *Chemist.*

BUREAU OF AUDITS.

J. M. McCOY, *Chief Clerk.*
EARL B. SEARCY, *Department Editor.*
R. R. McLEOD, *General Bookkeeper.*
G. E. HOPKINS, *Property Clerk.*

DIVISION ENGINEERS.

R. L. Bell, Buchanan-Link Bldg., Paris, Ill.
H. B. Bushnell, 138 Fox St., Aurora Ill.
J. E. Huber, Wise Building, Mt. Vernon, Ill.
A. H. Hunter, 302 Apollo Theater Bldg., Peoria, Ill.
C. M. Slaymaker, 510 Metropolitan Bldg., E. St. Louis, Ill.
H. E. Surman, 614 People's Bank Bldg., Moline, Ill.
Fred Tarrant, 730 Reisch Bldg., Springfield, Ill.

Address all communications in regard to "Illinois Highways," to Earl B. Searcy, Department Editor, State Highway Department, Springfield, Illinois.

CONTENTS.

"BURLINGTON WAY" DIVISIONS.

ILLINOIS HIGHWAYS is in receipt of the listed divisions, and the cities and towns touched therein, which make up "The Burlington Way," one of the automobile trails of the Middle West. Receipt is due to the courtesy of Mr. A. E. Nissen of Iowa City, Iowa, who is engaged in trail organizing.

The "Burlington" trail covers the following territory:

Parent Trail—St. Louis to Burlington, Cedar Rapids and St. Paul. St. Louis, Venice, Granite City, Nameoki, Mitchell, Wood River, Alton, Godfrey, Brighton, Piasa, Medora, Kemper, Rockbridge, Greenfield, Berdan, White Hall, Roodhouse, Manchester, Murrayville, Woodson, Jacksonville, Concord, Arenzville, Beardstown, Fredrick, Rushville, Littleton, Industry, Macomb, Blandinsville, LaHarpe, Dallas City, Pontoosuc, Niota (all in Illinois), Fort Madison, Weaver, Burlington, Dodgeville, Roscoe, Morning Sun, Columbus, Junction, Conesville, Lone Tree, Iowa City, North Liberty, Curtis, Shueyville, Cedar Rapids, Sylvia, Center Point, Walker, Rowley, Independence, Bryantsburg, Hazelton, Oelwein, Hawkeye, Alpha, Waucoma, Jackson Junction, Protivin, Cresco, Bonair, Lime Springs, Chester (all in Iowa), Spring Valley, Racine, Stewartsville, Rochester, Zumbrota, Pine Island, Cannon Falls, Hampton, St. Paul.

Greenfield and Springfield Division—Greenfield, Burns Station, Waller, Palmyra, Modesto, Rohrer, Waverly, New Berlin, Springfield.

Springfield-Bloomington-Joliet and Chicago—Springfield, Sherman, Williamsville, Elkhart, Broadwell, Griggs, Lincoln, Athol, Kruger, Longdale, McLean, Funk's Grove, Shirley, Bloomington, Normal, Towanda, Lexington, Chenoa, Ocoya, Pontiac, Odel, Dwight, Gardner, Braceville, Braidwood, Wilmington, Elwood, Joliet, Lockport, Lemont, Spring Forest, Justice, Argo, Chicago.

Springfield-Peoria Division—Springfield, Sherman, Fancy Prairie, Middletown, New Holland, Delavan, Dillon, Groveland, East Peoria, Peoria.

Peoria-Ottawa and Belvidere Division—Peoria, East Peoria, Washington, Metamora, Roanoke, Benson, Minonk, Rutland, Wenona, Lostant, Tonica, Lowell, Starved Rock, Ottawa, Baker, Leland, Waterman, Sycamore, Genoa, Belvidere.

Peoria-Farmington Division—Peoria, Hanna City, Eden, Tripoli, Farmington.

Beardstown-Galesburg and Rock Island Division—Beardstown, Fredrick, Browning, Bader, Astoria, Ipava, Duncan Mills, Lewistown, Bryant, St. David, Canton, Norris, Farmington, Union Town, Maquon, Knoxville, Galesburg, Henderson, Rio, Alpha, New Windsor, Milan, Rock Island.

Astoria-Monmouth and Rock Island Division—Astoria, Vermont, Table Grove, Adair, Epperson, Bushnell, Walnut Grove, Youngstown, Roseville, Larchland, Monmouth, Gerlaw, Alexis, Viola, Milan, Rock Island.

Rock Island-Dubuque and Cresco Division—Rock Island, Davenport, DeWitt, Welton, Delmar, Maquoketa, Huntsville, Fulton, Zwingle, Dubuque, Durango, Rickardsville, Holy Cross, Luxemberg, Millville, Guttenburg, Clayton, McGregor, North McGregor, Monona, Rossville, Waukon, Decorah, Ridgeway, Cresco. (There connecting with the Parent Trail to Rochester and St. Paul.)

St. Louis-Litchfield and Springfield Division— (Organized at Litchfield, January 22.)

St. Louis and Cairo Division—(To be organized during February 1917.)

Peoria-Freeport and Madison Division and Belvidere and Milwaukee Division—(To be organized in March. 1917.)

NEW CLUBS AND OTHER NOTES

Associated road organizations of Chicago and Cook County met at the Lexington Hotel in Chicago recently and registered endorsement of the action of the Illinois Highway Improvement Association in recommending a $60,000,000 State bond issue for road improvement. Other acts of the association also were given unanimous O. K. Robert F. Farr of the Chicago Real Estate Board was elected secretary and committees were appointed. These committees will cooperate with Cook County highway officials in the carrying out of this year's road improvement program.

* * *

The Congerville Diagonal Trail and Good Roads Club was organized by citizens of Congerville, Woodford County, at a recent meeting.

Leslie Reel was elected president of the club, Sam Amsbury, vice president and Charles Stephens, secretary and treasurer.

Committee chairmen are: Membership, Willis Nutty; good roads, Carl Irons; legislative. Ed. Kaiser; finance, S. L. Lantz; publicity, Simon E. Lantz; entertainment, C. A. Daniel.

* * *

Another Diagonal Trail and Good Roads Club has been organized at Deer Creek, Tazewell County. By-laws adopted by all such trail organizations were embraced in this club's governing rules.

Officers elected were: President, J. A. Danforth; vice president, F. L. Belsly; secretary, L. M. Norris; treasurer, Dr. L. M. Chapman.

Chairmen of committees were as follows: Membership, J. E. Garver; finance, Benjamin A. Danforth; legislative, J. M. Davis; good roads, John King; publicity, Joseph Hexamer.

The committee chairmen and the officers compose the executive committee.

Fifty-seven charter members were enrolled.

* * *

Still another Diagonal Trail and Good Roads Club, formed to promote the interests of the trail after which it is named, has been formed at Morton, Tazewell County.

DECEMBER REPORT—BUREAU OF BRIDGES.

During the month of December, 1916, plans, estimates and specifications for 36 concrete bridges and 7 steel bridges were prepared and sent out to county superintendents of highways. The total estimated cost of these bridges is $81,750.

Plans and estimate for one concrete bridge to be built as extra work on a State aid road contract were prepared. The estimate for the work is $1,060.

Summing up, plans were prepared for 44 bridges, the total estimated cost of which equals $82,810.

Plans for 7 bridges and culverts prepared by county superintendents of highways were checked and approved.

According to reports received, contracts were awarded during the month on plans prepared for county superintendents of highways for 4 concrete bridges at an average cost of 91.2 per cent of the estimates. The total estimated cost of this work amounts to $5,345.

Officers named at Morton are: G. T. Kiblinger, president; B. F. Schmallenberger, vice president; Jacob Grieder, secretary; J. C. Ackerman, treasurer.

The chairmen of committees are: Finance, Fred Reuling; membership, W. Walz; legislature, Dr. H. L. Yoder; publicity, F. B. Mills; good roads, Lewis Welk.

* * *

Citizens of Liberty Township, Adams County, at a meeting held recently at the home of Mr. and Mrs. Albert Fenton, organized the Liberty Farm and Good Roads Club, designed to promote agricultural and highway interests of the community. Clay Hayden was elected president, D. K. Kiser, vice president, and Mrs. Maude Hayden, secretary and treasurer.

* * *

The Federated Road Associations was formally organized at a meeting at the Missouri Atheletic Association's Club in St. Louis, Mo., recently and $9,500 subscribed as the nucleus of a fund which will be used to promote the building of good county, state and National highways in Missouri and in those portions of Illinois which are tributary to St. Louis.

Organizations represented at the meeting were the Business Men's League, Associated Retailers, St. Louis Clearing House Association, Automobile Club of St. Louis and the Automobile Dealers' and Manufacturers' Association.

The following officers were elected:

Daniel C. Nugent, president; Edward M. Flesh, first vice president; Harry B. Hawes, second vice president; Allan W. Clark, third vice president: F. W. A. Vesper,, fourth vice president; Samuel Plant, fifth vice president; Paul J. Fisher, temporary secretary, and Festus J. Wade, treasurer.

* * *

The good roads committee of the Hamilton Club, Chicago, has endorsed the platform of the Illinois Highway Improvement Association recommending the proposed $60,000,000 Illinois bond issue for road improvement.

New standard plans for abutments for girder bridges with cantilever wing walls were completed and are now in the hands of the engraver.

The following outlines briefly the status of the work in the Bureau of Bridges on January 1, 1917.

There were on hand ready for work 4 bridge inspection reports; 5 bridge plans had been prepared but not checked; and 9 bridge plans had been completed, together with the estimates, and were practically ready to be sent out.—Compiled by A. W. Conseer, *Office Engineer.*

Supervisors of Pike County have reelected County Highway Superintendent H. H. Hardy for the coming year.

* * *

Peoria County will vote on a $1,700,000 bond issue proposition April 3. The county board has submitted the question.

THE COOK COUNTY SYSTEM

Cook County is fast becoming proud of her road progress. She has, exclusive of Chicago City pavements, 13 miles of State aid road, 40 miles of county bond road contracted for and due for completion the coming

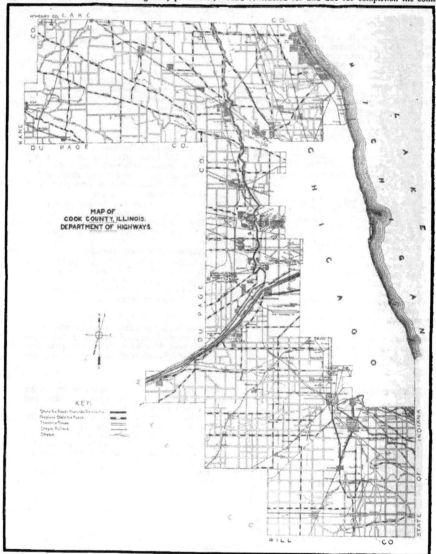

The comprehensive road plan in Cook.

spring, and plans laid, the consummation of which will realize to the county some 135 or more miles of first-class concrete by the close of this year.

County Highway Superintendent George A. Quinlan, himself an enthusiast, and head of an energetic highway force, is bending every effort toward a remarkable showing in the next ten months.

The system which is being carried out in Cook County will contemplate an improved main highway every direction from the Chicago corporate limits to the county boundary.

Cook County is one of the two counties of the State which is operating under a recent bond issue. Her issue was for $2,000,000. More than half a million dollars were expended last year on work.

Not only will most of the improved road work involve concrete construction, but practically every highway will be wide, 18 feet being the width commonly built to. The county board is cooperating with the county highway superintendent to the end that the Cook County road system shall be second to none.

The bridge and culvert work of the county highway superintendent the last year formed an important feature of the department's duties. In the twelve months ending November 30, 1916, Mr. Quinlan's department inspected 720 bridges and culverts, designed 471 at an estimated cost of $149,767.26; let contracts for 407, at a cost of $117,028.92, supervised the completion of 246, costing $81,575.59. The number remaining uncompleted at the close of the season was 178.

The accompanying chart shows graphically the Cook County proposed system of road improvement.

Sheridan Road Link Is Completed.

Sheridan Road is one link nearer completion as a continuous improved route through north shore towns. The latest step was the completion and opening to traffic of the concrete pavement between the north village limits of Wilmette and the south village limits of Kenilworth. This stretch is outside of either village and was built through the cooperation of New Trier Township, the county, the Sanitary District, the Sheridan Road Improvement Association and abutting property owners. This new pavement also makes available the concrete pavement on Sheridan Road in Kenilworth completed last summer.

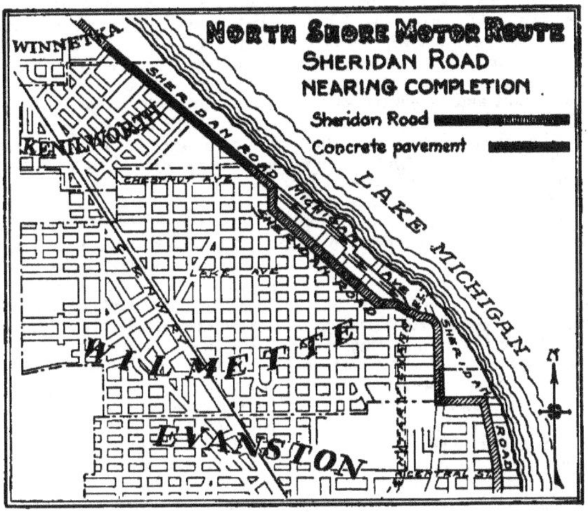

NORTH SHORE MOTOR ROUTE
SHERIDAN ROAD
NEARING COMPLETION.

Sheridan Road ▬▬▬▬
Concrete pavement ▬▬▬▬

Motorists who in the last two or three years have tried to find desirable routes through north shore towns will welcome the new, permanently-paved direct route. The completion of this stretch of concrete pavement on the road marks a further step in the linking of Chicago and Milwaukee by means of a good highway—the aim of the Sheridan Road Improvement Association.

The ultimate completion of the Sheridan Road project, with its superior mileage and its interstate identification, will give not only northern Illinois and southern Wisconsin a unique distinction, but the Middle West as well.

A part of the brick improvement on Sheridan Road through Wilmette is not yet ready to be opened, but a few weeks of fair weather will see it completed. In the meantime, a good through route is provided on Sheridan Road in connection with Michigan Avenue, the first street to the east.

Promotors already have gained a vast deal of satisfaction from contemplations of the scheme. Those familiar with the drive from Chicago do not have to stretch their imaginations far to gain a mental picture of the finished improvement and all that it will mean.

The firm of Miller & Husband of Springfield, has completed the construction of the new 100-foot span Kessner Bridge, in Orion Township, Fulton County. The contract price was $7,860. The superstructure is steel, the floor concrete and the span is 18 feet wide.

A contract to build the Rapp Bridge on the line between Whiteside and Henry Counties has been awarded to T. O. Nules & Brother of Galesburg. The contract price is $2,350.20. The bridge will be a 50-foot span, 16 feet wide.

THE EDITORIAL VIEWPOINT

[EDITOR'S NOTE.—ILLINOIS HIGHWAYS is in receipt daily of newspaper clippings pertaining in subject matter to about every general phase of road construction. Now and then an editorial is commixed with the news reports of work done or contemplated. Sometimes these editorial expressions commend, sometimes they condemn, the proposition at issue. ILLINOIS HIGHWAYS, in its effort to enlighten, feels that very often these editorials reflect a popular conception which even technical road builders might profitably know. In this belief, we take pleasure in presenting again to our readers a brief symposium which, though relating in some instances to questions purely local, represent interesting viewpoints toward the great general highway problem as it exists in the State and county.]

BUILDING ROADS.

To finance the building of roads by issuing bonds is justified only by good roads. The life of the roads must be as long as the life of the bonds. They should be longer. Otherwise we are burdening the future with payment which does not serve it.

Illinois needs roads. Its roads do not compare with those of surrounding states. It is noted for bad roads. Dozens of organizations have been shouting these facts for several years but little has been done. Where roads have been built they have in many cases gone to pieces. Maintenance and repair of roads are familiar to us only as phrases.

Illinois must have better roads, and if a bond issue is required to build them we should issue bonds. There are, however, several things which must be kept in mind. Vehicles are increasing in weight and in speed. Where roads were required ten years ago to carry farm wagons they are now required to support automobile trucks and heavy tractors. The amount of traffic is increasing enormously. Roads will have to be wider. Experience has shown that few of the older and cheaper methods of road building will stand this new kind of traffic. In and about Cleveland roads made of vitrified brick on a concrete base are proving themselves durable and satisfactory. That is the kind of road Illinois needs.—Chicago, Illinois, *Tribune*.

* * *

A STATE HIGHWAY SYSTEM.

Two years ago, when a State bond issue for the construction of an Illinois highway system was suggested, the people refused to take it seriously. A great deal has been accomplished since that time, however, and the proposal of the Illinois Highway Improvement Association at Danville that the State shall issue $60,000,000 in bonds for road building is not an impossible one.

Many counties are coming to the conclusion that it is better to issue bonds for the construction of county highway systems than to spend twenty years building roads under the State aid act. Vermilion County is completing a system which cost $1,500,000, and the people are delighted with it. Other counties have voted to follow this example.

If this is good for counties, it also would be good for the State.

Sixty million dollars would build 4,000 miles of hard road, connecting practically all cities of 2,000 population. The tax for the interest and liquidation of the bond issue would extend over a period of twenty years and would amount to only 4½ cents an acre. This would not be burdensome.

Such a system would place Illinois in the front rank in highway improvement.—Springfield, Illinois, *News-Record*.

THOSE ROADS.

The paving of country roads has many virtues aside from those which may appear to the average man. The fact that bumps and mudholes have been done away with is evident to anybody. The fact, also, that dust is lessened in the summer, is very evident. Automobiles and teams travel with greater satisfaction, speed and with greater pleasure. Grain and other farm produce may be brought to market at a less expense and in less time than when poor roads are allowed to exist.

But there are other advantages which paved country roads have.

Public school attendance in one county in North Dakota has increased 20 per cent, since good roads have been provided in that county. This is the report of the superintendent of the county schools. The good roads have also made possible the consolidation of several of the smaller schools in this county. The number of automobiles in one county in New York was doubled as a direct result of improved country roads. Local lines of transportation, resembling a form of street car service, have been started by automobiles since these roads were improved. That land values increase with improved roads is very apparent in any state. With improved roads there is a lessening of the hardships which inclement weather usually inflicts on a community.

Thus is it seen that the value of good, permanent country roads is not generally recognized in full. Peoria County, with infamously poor country roads, would be benefited in scores of different ways if the county adopted a definite system of road improvement.—Peoria, Illinois, *Journal*.

* * *

ROAD BONDS.

The recommendation of the Illinois Highway Improvement association that the Legislature submit to popular vote the question of bonding the State for $60,000,000 for building the State roads, carries more weight than would ordinarily be the case, owing to the character of the association and the conservative steps which preceded that action. The association itself was a representative body, having a large attendance of farmers, members of county boards, business men, highway officials and delegated members coming from about 52 counties; the leading counties being strongly represented. The plan and scope of the proposed bonding was carefully worked out in advance, by men familiar with financing large undertakings and well informed on measures which carry weight in the bond market and have standing with business men.—Rockford, Illinois, *Register-Gazette*.

* * *

THE GOOD ROADS QUESTION.

If it be argued that the newspapers dwell too much upon the good roads question, the answer is as ready, to quote Shakespeare, as a borrower's cap. "Good roads are a vital necessity." And good roads are coming, because they are a natural part of the economic development of the country. The railroad was the first relief afforded a transportationless world. China has no roads worthy of the name, and China stands where it stood 6,000 years ago. Without the railroads and the telephone and the telegraph the world would stand still. Good roads and the automobile bring to every community the advantages of the railroad and the interurban. It is as idle, therefore, to oppose them as it was for the Japanese to oppose, 60 years ago, the advent of western ideas and western progress. They may suffer temporary defeat here and there, but good roads are coming, and the community which welcomes them quickest will reap the benefits first.—Peoria, Illinois, *Star*.

* * *

HIGHWAYS TOO NARROW.

In discussing the building of public highways an exchange insists that a number of accidents have been due to the narrowness of the highways, where cars have either come together or one has been forced over the edge in an endeavor to avoid collision.

No roadway should be constructed that is less than 16 feet in width, and 18 would be a still greater factor for safety; and where the improved part is 16 feet or even 18, there should be an apron on either side whose width is at least 3 feet.

Built in this manner, there can be little danger of a car turning turtle, no matter how fast it is going if it is forced to turn off the improved part. Besides the great traffic that such improved highways bring is alone a necessity for their being wide as well as to take care of future traffic conditions.—Sterling, Illinois, *Gazette*.

A GOOD ROADS INSPIRATION.

Concrete with macadam shoulders. A stretch on Kankakee River in Kankakee County.

SHORT COURSE AIDS ROAD MEN.

Approximately 100 men, including nearly 50 county highway superintendents, supervisors and others interested in the road building problem, assembled at the University of Illinois and followed daily the class sessions, the lectures and the discussions which marked the highway engineering short course, held January 8 to 19, inclusive.

Professors in the university gave their time to the short course and promoted classroom work after much the fashion of student study. Time was given, of course, for informal discussion of subjects as they were suggested by speakers, or by the men who were in attendance at the course.

The time was spent in the study of road and bridge subjects. Half of the class sessions were devoted to purely technical or semitechnical study. The remainder were put in in round-table style, with the professor in charge directing the discussions along stated lines.

On Thursday, January 18, "Illinois Better Road Day" was observed, with the engineering and the agricultural short courses thrown together.

Speakers at the short course included officials, members of the Illinois State Highway Department, county highway superintendents and other authorities. State Highway Commissioner Wilson and Chief State Highway Engineer Marr attended and took part

in some of the sessions. Chairman Gash and Secretary Bradt were both prevented from attending on account of illness.

STATE BREVITIES.

Highway superintendents from five north central counties met at Peoria recently in a discussion of road problems. In the meeting were W. E. Emery of Peoria County, R. W. Osborn of Livingston, A. B. Hurd of Woodford, Ralph O. Edwards of McLean and L. H. Eldridge of Marshall.

* * *

The new bridge over Whitechurch Slough, three miles east of Centralia, has been completed and is in use. The contract price was $2,420.

* * *

The Illinois Highway Improvement Association which, in its annual meeting recently at Danville endorsed a proposed $60,000,000 bond issue in Illinois, has opened campaign and good roads headquarters in the Lexington Hotel at Chicago.

* * *

One and one-fourth miles of brick road, State aid, east of Urbana, in Champaign County, have been completed. C. A. Michaels was the contractor in charge.

COUNTY REPORTS ECHO PROGRESS

There is a vast deal of satisfaction, as well as interesting data, to be gained from such comprehensive reports of work done in 1916, as have been issued by the superintendents of highways of some of the counties, as reported up to this time to ILLINOIS HIGHWAYS.

Among the counties in question are Vermilion, where progress has attracted attention from the entire middle west; Winnebago, where operations have been active, and Kane, the scene of fruitful endeavors.

William S. Dillon of Danville, the Vermilion County superintendent, has issued in attractive booklet form his third annual report. It reviews, in a newsy, interesting way, the work of the year 1916, and tabulates both State aid and bridge construction progress in a form which is readily understandable by any who read.

The following extracts from Mr. Dillon's report serve to illustrate the manner in which the resume of Vermilion County operations during 1916 have been prepared for and presented to the public:

STATE AID ROADS.

"In the report of last December, the superintendent of highways gave a summary of the State aid roads completed and the cost of the same to that date. Since then, the road to Moore's Corner has been completed, with the exception of 2,221 feet, which is now under construction and is to be built of stone, and will soon be ready for traffic. The total cost of this brick road completed from the city limits to Moore's Corner, including a $11,883.00 bridge, is $136,174.23, and the distance is 7.15 miles, 1.15 miles being 18 feet wide.

"Since then, Contract 'E' has been let to the Eclipse Construction Company of Winnetka, Illinois, for the sum of $49,445.25 and extends from Moore's Corner north a distance of 2.28 miles. The estimated cost of cement is $4,220.97, making a total of $53,666.22. The grading for this work is practically completed.

"Upon the completion of Contract 'E,' the State aid allotments of $93,097.00, will be expended. The allotments for 1917-18 will not be known until after the Legislature meets this winter.

Section A, Route 2—16,100 feet.

Original contract	$48,171 10	
Extra work	779 68	
Cement	5,915 04	
Total, Route A		$54,865 82

Section B, Route 2—2,550 feet.

Original contract	7,063 78	

Section B, Route 2—1,343 feet.

Extra work	4,908 80	
Cement	246 96	
Total, Route B		12,219 54

Section C—160 feet.

Steel bridge	11,883 00	
Total, Route C		11,883 00

Section D—15,600 feet.

Original contract	39,966 39	
Estimated cement	5,060 48	
Total, Route D		45,026 87

Total distance, 37,765 feet.		
Cost of macadam, estimated		12,179 00
Total cost to Moore's Corner		$136,174 23

Section E.

Original contract	$49,445 25	
Estimated cement	4,220 97	
		$53,666 22
Less macadam		12,179 00
		$41,487 22

Total State aid	$177,661 45
To date amount available	8,451 71
Amount	$186,113 16

TOWNSHIP BOND ROADS.

"Since the Tice Law went into effect, the following townships have voted on a bond issue for hard roads:

Township.	Amount voted.
Georgetown	$ 65,000 00
Elwood	38,000 00
Catlin	22,000 00
Sidell	20,000 00
Grant	5,000 00
Carroll	25,000 00
Danville	106,000 00
Newell	80,000 00
A total of	$361,000 00

"The length of the roads to be improved by these bond issues amount to about 50 miles. The contract in Georgetown Township was let for a 20-foot concrete road, and is about half completed; in Ridgefarm, for a 16-foot monolithic brick pavement, which is half completed; in Catlin for a 20-foot monolithic brick pavement, half completed; and in Grant Township a 5-foot concrete pavement to be built jointly with the county bond road. Work has been started on the last mentioned road. In Sidell Township the contract has been let for one mile of 16-foot concrete pavement. Work will commence on this in the spring. In Danville and Newell, the bond issue was defeated. In Vance, it carried by one vote, but the proceedings were irregular and it has been apparently dropped. In Carroll Township, the bond issue carried by a good vote, but on account of some flaw it has to be voted on again, which will be in a short time. Georgetown voted twice; Sidell, twice; Carroll, Danville and Newell will vote again.

"In Catlin, Georgetown and Ridgefarm, the villages have expended about $60,000 additional to the bond issue, in widening the roads that go through these towns. Ross, Butler, Blount and McKendree, are all talking bond issue, and it will not be long until a majority of the 18 townships in Vermilion County will have permanent roads.

MR. CARTER'S REPORT.

In the opening paragraphs of his annual report, County Highway Superintendent A. R. Carter of Winnebago voices some keynote sentiments with reference to improved road construction. He has this to say:

"During the fiscal year ending December 15, 1916, the routine office and field work connected with the office of the superintendent of highways has been carried on as in previous years. The systematic inspection of all roads and bridges in the county having been completed previously, this particular portion of the superintendent's duties has been considerably lessened. On account of the busy season, the results of these inspections have not been tabulated, but rather kept on loose leaves, indexed and classified by townships.

"The severe weather and high water of the spring months was very destructive to our roads and bridges, and I believe I say authoritatively that the roads in Winnebago County are in much worse condition this season than last. The rapid increase in traffic has also been a very destructive agent, especially to the macadam roads in the vicinity of the city of Rockford. This latter condition alone has forced the commissioners of the town of Rockford to surface treat the main roads in the township with Tarvia or asphalts at a rather large cost, although the results are in most cases well worth the money expended.

"The present methods for building and maintaining roads by the townships will not suffice for our present and ever-changing traffic conditions. The traffic on our highways is no longer a local matter, but rather a county and State problem, and the problem of financing the construction and maintenance of the heavily traveled roads must be assumed by a larger unit."

Mr. Carter embraces in his report the following paragraphs with reference to State aid work:

"Like all construction work during the season, the progress on our State aid road construction was rather slow, due to the unusual labor conditions and shortage of material. The road has been completed, however, and I believe we have an excellent job.

"The following gives the cost of the road, including extensions:

Section.	Distance, original contract.	Total distance improved.	Contractor.	Amount, original contract.	Total amount, contract including extension and extra work.	Total cost of cement.	Total cost of road.
C	9,150'	10,350'	W. S. Hubbard & Co.	$15,935 56	$18,023 86	$9,010 29	$27,034 15

"The total cost of this road per mile, 18 feet wide, would then be $13,781.00.

"One of the peculiar features of road construction was encountered on this work. On account of the level country, it was impossible to get drainage for the surface water without going to the necessary large expense of laying a storm sewer. Even had it been possible to carry the water in side ditches, a large cost of the work then should have been used in building many private entrance culverts, as this road extends through the suburban population adjacent to the city of Rockford. In order to take care of the surface drainage, catch basins were built wherever necessary, consisting of digging a hole 2 feet by 4 feet by 5 feet deep until the layer of gravel was reached, which underlies this section of the country. These catch basins were then filled with large gravel stones varying from above 2-inch to 3-inch stones and covered over the top with a finer stone. The contract price of these basins was $4 apiece and the total number required was 68, so you can readily see that the drainage problem on this road was rather inexpensive. It might well be added that so far, these catch basins have worked successfully.

"I find that the sentiment in the board of supervisors and in the county as well, especially among the highway commissioners, is rapidly changing in favor of the more permanent type of road. We can well afford to spend more money in the original investment and thereby reduce the high maintenance cost, and by building concrete or brick roads, eliminate the maintenance cost entirely from the county, as in the latter case, this maintenance will be entirely assumed by the State of Illinois."

MR. LAMB'S REPORT.

George N. Lamb of Geneva, highway superintendent of Lake County, has sent in a copy of his annual report. It reviews interestingly the work covered in the year 1916. Extracts from it follow:

"The weather conditions during the months of February and March, 1916, were especially severe on our rural highways. While it is true that 75 per cent of the roads of this county are surfaced with gravel and 5 per cent with other hard materials the soft weather early in the season caused the gravel in many places to break through and become full of chuck holes. The rapid increase in heavy traffic has also had a very destructive effect, and owing to these two agencies it is believed that in spite of extensive repairs made during the season the roads throughout the county as a whole are not in as good condition to-day as they were a year ago.

"The present problem of maintaining highways is greater than most of us realize. In this county, motor traffic alone in the five years ending December 31, 1915, increased 778 per cent (it is believed that the increase during the past year has broken all the preceding records) while the increase in township revenues for road purposes during the same period of years was only 29 per cent. In other words the township funds to provide for the additional traffic have increased only 3.7 per cent as fast as the traffic itself—an uneven race, to say the least.

"The common methods of road construction in use five years ago will not suffice for our present conditions. Traffic is no longer a local matter and the problems of financing road improvements are now too great for the local township. The State Aid Road Law is designed to relieve this strain on the townships but under present conditions many years must elapse before they can all receive material benefit. A number of counties in northeast Illinois, in addition to the State aid, have provided outfits of road-building machinery which are loaned to the townships to enable them to use their limited funds to the best possible advantage. * * *

"The past season has been exceedingly unfavorable to State aid road construction. Contracts with the Cameron, Joyce Co., for Section 'F' Dundee township and with the Grohne Construction Co., for Section 'G' in St. Charles township were both completed several months after the specified time. The contract with the Illinois Hydraulic Stone and Construction Co., for Section 'H' in St. Charles township is about 35 per cent completed and an extension of the time limit on the contract has been granted. The unusual labor conditions and the difficulty of securing materials are responsible for the delays.

"Bridge building in a few of our townships is even now practically at an end. This is because the concrete bridge or culvert, when properly designed and constructed, is considered permanent. The commissioners of highways in general have heartily cooperated with this department in adopting this type. In building a permanent bridge the question of width of roadway and capacity of waterway should receive more careful consideration than for the more temporary structures. The waterway should be ample but not excessive, while the width of roadway and the carrying capacity of the bridge should provide for future traffic as well as for our present traffic."

PREVAILED AGAINST BY FLOODS.

This is part of a section of concrete road built in 1914, east from Mt. Vernon, Jefferson County. The picture was taken half a mile east, looking toward the city. Since its construction, the road has not been maintained, except for the more or less regular rebuilding of the shoulders.

Taken last month, this picture shows what happens to the Mt. Vernon road about three times a year. The area shown is the same as that in the above picture, looking east instead of west. Division Engineer J. E. Huber, in whose territory this problematical road stretch lies, thinks it little wonder that the shoulders fail to survive the aquatic onslaughts. It is probably fortunate that the original road is still intact and in better than average condition, so far as smoothness is concerned.

ILLINOIS HIGHWAYS

[Printed by authority of the State of Illinois.]

OFFICIAL PUBLICATION OF THE

STATE HIGHWAY DEPARTMENT

| VOL. IV | SPRINGFIELD, ILLINOIS, MARCH-APRIL, 1917 | Nos. 3-4 |

—Concrete Road near Coleman Illinois.

DEPARTMENT MERGER CARRIES

Governor Lowden's Plan, a Radical Reform, to Become Effective July 1.

A governmental reform, embracing a consolidation of departments, commissions, etc., and the concentration of authority with a view of promoting a greater efficiency, will become operative in Illinois on July 1, 1917.

This radical change from the governmental plan which has been followed in Illinois since its incorporation as a State in 1818, comes as a Centennial marker of progress and an evidence of the study which modern students of political systems have devoted to movements calculated to be of benefit to commonwealths such as ours.

The new law, the effectiveness of which will bring the change, is known as "The Civil Administrative Code of Illinois." Popularly known as "The Consolidation Bill," it was passed by the Fiftieth General Assembly March 1, 1917, and a few days later received the signature of Governor Frank O. Lowden, author of the new plan.

Broadly, this new system of State government reduces the number of departments and commissions, and vests in the directing heads of the new divisions a concentrated authority. Departmental heads will be held responsible for the performance of duties of their respective divisions, and at all times their departments will bear a directly communicable relationship to the Governor, the executive head of the State.

Out of the existing 126 boards, departments, commissions, etc., nine general departments are formed under the new law. They are the departments of—

Finance;
Agriculture;
Labor;
Mines and Minerals;
Public Works and Buildings;
Public Welfare;
Public Health;
Trade and Commerce;
Registation and Education.

At the head of each department will be a director. Under him will be an assistant director and such other employees of the State as shall be necessary to the economical and efficient conduct of the State's business. Specific provision has been made in the new code for the taking over of employees now in the classified service who shall be needed under the new regime, thus insuring an uninterrupted administration of civil service. There will be no employment of men and women now on pay rolls, of course, where their services are not needed in the new organization of departments.

Except for the immediate staffs and forces connected with the departments of elective officers, the new code abolishes bodily all existing commissions, boards, departments and the executive and administrative officers thereof. It seeks emphatically to put Illinois' government under one roof, and so far as possible physically, to concentrate the entire plant of governmental machinery at Springfield. Branches will be established elsewhere in the State when necessary, but the administrative

heads will be resident in Springfield, and at all times in personal charge of their departments.

Powers of the several departments under the new code are indicated generally by the titles. The finance division will devise a uniform system of bookkeeping, accounting, etc., and will maintain a constant check upon the expenditure of all State moneys. Funds collected by other departments will be turned over to the State treasury promptly, and provision has been made in the new law for systematic publicity, not only of the financial side of the State's business, but of the work of the government generally.

Salaries of the new departmental heads will grade from $7,000 downward. A tremendous saving of salary money paid to executive officers will be one of the features of the new code.

Since our interests lie especially in the work of what, under existing laws, is and has been the State Highway Department, we desire to convey to readers of ILLINOIS HIGHWAYS what the new law will bring to us in the way of changes.

The State Highway Department, as it is now, will automatically of course cease to exist, along with the other departments of the State. The highway division has been included in the general department of Public Works and Buildings. In the new order, it will constitute an important section. Instead of a commission and a Chief State Highway Engineer, as at present, there will be—under the Director of Public Works and Buildings—a Superintendent of Highways, and a Chief Highway Engineer, who will have sole charge of the highway work of the State. Where four men administered the affairs of the department in the past, two will do it in the future.

The Department of Public Works absorbs not only the present State Highway Department, but a number of other commissions and boards as well. It will have control of State printing, contracts for supplies, public buildings and grounds and numerous other matters pertaining to the government.

In addition to the immediate officers of the various new departments, the code provides for several boards, the members of which shall serve in an advisory capacity, purely, to the departments with which they are connected. None of these advisory boards carries a salaried officer, their labors for the State being free. It is Governor Lowden's aim that these boards shall perform exactly the functions which their titles imply— of advising and counseling with the department officers upon questions which from time to time may arise.

In addition to the directors of departments, the following executive and administrative officers, boards and commissions, which said officers, boards and commissions in the respective departments, shall hold offices created and designated in the new code as follows:

Department of Finance:

Assistant director of finance;
Administrative auditor;

Superintendent of budget;
Superintendent of department reports.

Department of Agriculture:
Assistant director of agriculture;
General manager of the State fair;
Superintendent of foods and dairies;
Superintendent of animal industry;
Superintendent of plant industry;
Chief veterinarian;
Chief game and fish warden;
The food standard commission, which shall consist of the superintendent of foods and dairies and two officers designated as food standard officers.

Department of Labor:
Assistant director of labor;
Chief factory inspector;
Superintendent of free employment offices;
Chief inspector of private employment agencies;
The industrial commission which shall consist of five officers designated industrial officers.

Department of Mines and Minerals:
Assistant director of mines and minerals;
The mining board, which shall consist of four officers designated as mine officers and the director of the department of mines and minerals;
The miners' examining board, which shall consist of four officers, designated miners' examining officers.

Department of Public Works and Buildings:
Assistant director of public works and buildings;
Superintendent of highways;
Chief highway engineer;
Supervising architect;
Supervising engineer;
Superintendent of waterways;
Superintendent of printing;
Superintendent of purchases and supplies;
Superintendent of parks.

Department of Public Welfare:
Assistant director of public welfare;
Alienist;
Criminologist;
Fiscal supervisor;
Superintendent of charities;
Superintendent of prisons;
Superintendent of pardons and paroles.

Department of Public Health:
Assistant director of public health;
Superintendent of lodging house inspection.

Department of Trade and Commerce:
Assistant director of trade and commerce;
Superintendent of insurance;
Fire marshal;
Superintendent of standards;
Chief grain inspector;
The public utilities commission, which shall consist of five officers designated public utility commissioners;
Secretary of the Public Utilities Commission.

Department of Registration and Education:
Assistant director of registration and education;
Superintendent of registration;
The normal school board, which shall consist of nine officers, together with the director of the department and the superintendent of public instruction.

Advisory and nonexecutive boards, in the respective departments, (to serve without salary) are created as follows:

Department of Agriculture:
A board of agricultural advisors, composed of fifteen persons, and a board of State fair advisors consisting of nine persons, not more than three of whom shall be appointed from any one county.

Department of Labor:
A board of Illinois free employment office advisors, composed of five persons;
A board of local Illinois free employment office advisors, for each free employment office, composed of five persons on each local board.

Department of Public Works:
A board of art advisors, composed of eight persons;
A board of water resource advisors, composed of five persons;
A board of highway advisors, composed of five persons;
A board of parks and buildings advisors, composed of five persons.

Department of Public Welfare:
A board of public welfare commissioners, composed of five persons.

Department of Public Health:
A board of public health advisors, composed of five persons.

Department of Registration and Education:
A board of natural resources and conservation advisors, composed of seven persons;
A board of State museum advisors, composed of five persons.

The new Illinois code will bring practically under one head—the Governor—the whole of the governmental machinery of the State outside the duties which attach to the immediate departments of the other five elective officers.

When Governor Lowden espoused the plan, long before his election, he foresaw it as a means of concentration of authority and, consequently, of a keener efficiency. Scattered as it was, the old government, with its fragments, was regarded as inadequate. Authority was too remotely distributed. The work of the departments could be too easily neglected.

Governor Lowden believed the public was not getting the sort of government it was paying for. So he launched the proposed change as a campaign issue, and the Illinois electorate commended and approved with an overwhelming vote for his election last November. Loyal support and immediate cooperation by the Illinois General Assembly as soon as it convened made it possible for the Governor to realize his official wishes.

NEW MAGAZINE.

It is with pleasure, and congratulations, that we welcome to our exchange file the January issue, No. 1, Vol. I, of *Concrete Highway Magazine.*

This new publication, the first number of which is most attractive in design and subject matter, is to be issued monthly by the Portland Cement Association, general offices of which are in Chicago. The lead article of the initial issue was contributed by A. N. Johnson, consulting highway engineer of the association. Following it are more than twenty pages of handsomely illustrated sketches, dealing with various phases of concrete highway construction.

In its scope, the new magazine will be national. Concrete construction and problems from every part of the country will be treated in the publication.

1917 ALLOTMENTS ESTIMATED

It will be of interest to ILLINOIS HIGHWAYS readers to know what the probable allotment of State aid money will be this year to counties in Illinois, if the Legislature appropriates the full amount collected in 1916.

During last year, the former Secretary of State's office did not itemize the automobile license fee receipts by counties. Estimating on the basis of a general increase over the State of an average of 34½ per cent, however, this department, with the assistance of Secretary of State Emmerson's staff, has arrived at what probably was not far from the exact total from each county. With such a computation furnished, this department has proceeded with figuring out the probable allotment which will be made to the various counties this year.

The table covering this information follows:

	Estimated amount of automobile fees paid in by counties in 1916, computed on the basis of the 34½ increase over the entire State.	Amount which would be allotted to each county in 1917, on basis of total amount collected in 1916.
Adams	$ 11,833 24	$ 12,220 00
Alexander	2,343 61	5,820 00
Bond	1,914 62	4,920 00
Boone	4,656 86	7,610 00
Brown	1,964 84	3,709 00
Bureau	15,500 92	21,750 00
Calhoun	1,174 52	2,461 00
Carroll	7,769 65	9,070 00
Cass	4,242 26	7,590 00
Champaign	20,545 55	26,018 00
Christian	7,875 51	16,310 00
Clark	4,022 11	6,610 00
Clay	1,629 74	3,885 00
Clinton	2,744 00	5,810 00
Coles	6,184 40	10,440 00
Cook	470,610 91	119,533 00
Crawford	7,377 73	7,170 00
Cumberland	1,268 74	4,255 00
DeKalb	14,536 72	18,900 00
DeWitt	5,574 08	8,530 00
Douglas	5,716 81	9,220 00
DuPage	9,175 63	14,610 00
Edgar	7,302 87	12,720 00
Edwards	1,076 78	2,310 00
Effingham	2,430 35	5,870 00
Fayette	2,130 95	7,720 00
Ford	6,888 55	11,180 00
Franklin	3,505 14	7,370 00
Fulton	11,131 08	15,420 00
Gallatin	1,027 98	2,440 00
Greene	3,135 80	8,730 00
Grundy	6,691 44	9,740 00
Hamilton	534 37	3,600 00
Hancock	9,063 05	12,550 00
Hardin	214 46	1,271 00
Henderson	2,030 00	6,750 00
Henry	16,404 10	17,900 00
Iroquois	14,340 56	25,380 00
Jackson	3,161 76	7,300 00
Jasper	1,661 14	5,160 00
Jefferson	1,636 26	5,690 00
Jersey	1,653 77	4,400 00
JoDaviess	6,159 70	9,460 00
Johnson	520 92	2,710 00
Kane	26,779 92	29,650 00
Kankakee	14,453 56	15,720 00
Kendall	4,783 57	6,990 00
Knox	10,773 96	13,920 00
Lake	13,266 53	19,410 00
LaSalle	32,160 20	33,200 00
Lawrence	$ 7,190 30	$ 7,660 00
Lee	13,420 24	16,300 00
Livingston	17,385 67	24,450 00
Logan	9,243 66	15,230 00
Macon	14,084 19	21,450 00
Macoupin	5,290 16	13,660 00
Madison	10,479 63	20,860 00
Marion	3,970 17	7,030 00
Marshall	5,643 34	8,230 00
Mason	5,074 89	7,620 00
Massac	1,047 04	3,152 00
McDonough	8,592 16	11,800 00
McHenry	12,355 43	15,800 00
McLean	24,775 36	31,700 00
Menard	3,086 51	6,130 00
Mercer	7,702 26	11,060 00
Monroe	1,616 35	3,710 00
Montgomery	6,923 05	13,620 00
Morgan	6,291 57	13,090 00
Moultrie	2,846 22	6,920 00
Ogle	12,610 38	18,220 00
Peoria	25,323 47	27,300 00
Perry	1,873 32	4,580 00
Piatt	6,396 62	10,300 00
Pike	3,977 78	10,920 00
Pope	318 56	1,770 00
Pulaski	891 33	2,419 00
Putnam	1,741 77	3,050 00
Randolph	2,513 97	6,900 00
Richland	1,960 47	3,755 00
Rock Island	20,053 24	7,300 00
Saline	2,335 46	5,332 00
Sangamon	16,591 05	20,680 00
Schuyler	2,707 28	5,430 00
Scott	1,499 94	4,690 00
Shelby	4,868 25	11,500 00
Stark	5,123 52	6,720 00
St. Clair	14,718 71	14,880 00
Stephenson	13,825 05	15,550 00
Tazewell	10,014 63	16,350 00
Union	1,771 42	4,532 00
Vermilion	18,701 63	27,150 00
Wabash	2,234 52	2,710 00
Warren	7,641 56	12,940 00
Washington	1,787 71	4,780 00
Wayne	1,907 82	5,890 00
White	2,230 08	5,430 00
Whiteside	14,887 27	15,910 00
Will	19,503 52	29,620 00
Williamson	4,592 66	7,280 00
Winnebago	20,626 99	23,500 00
Woodford	9,662 41	9,630 00
Miscellaneous	1,175 80	
Total	$1,236,556 35	$1,236,566 00

ILLINOIS LICENSE SCALE LOW.

Much is being said these days about automobile license fees in Illinois as compared with fees collected from motorists and motor vehicle owners in other states.

The State Highway Department, for the information of the General Assembly and of others who may be studying the question, has obtained and compiled, in tabular form, reports from the leading automobile states which serve to contrast Illinois' comparatively low scale with the fee rates charged elsewhere.

One of the proposed measures advocated in connection with the State road bond issue is an increase in motor vehicle fees. The department has arranged a chart showing other states' fees ranging as high as $40 a year. In the cases of two states, a set fee of $5 a year is charged.

The scale of fees, as shown in the new department chart, follows:

(Concluded on page 39.)

WORK IN FIFTH DIVISION

 State aid work last year was given an effectual boost in the fifth engineering division of Illinois, in which Fred Tarrant, with headquarters and offices at Springfield, is the division engineer.

Approximately 10 miles of State aid road were completed at the close of the year and a large mileage was in course of construction. Operations were general throughout the division with the coming of spring.

The counties in Division Engineer Tarrant's territory are Hancock, Adams, Pike, Schuyler, Brown, Morgan, Cass, Mason, Menard, Sangamon, Logan, Christian, Dewitt, Macon, Piatt and Shelby.

State aid does not, of course, constitute all, by any means, of the work in the district. In a few of the counties, townships have done notable improving.

Division Engineer Tarrant has supplied ILLINOIS HIGHWAYS with the following summary of the status of State aid work in the various counties at the beginning of this year:

ADAMS.

Section B, Route 5.

Contractor—Rees Brothers, Quincy, Ill.
Type and width—15-foot waterbound macadam.
Length—6,910 feet.
Contract price—$12,985.23.
Cement—$400.33 (not included in contract price).

NOTE.—At the present date the macadam roadway is practically complete while the earth shoulders are only about 90 per cent complete. Owing to the fact that this contract was so nearly completed, the contractor deposited a check for nine hundred dollars guaranteeing the completion of this work according to the plans and specifications. This work will be re-dressed and placed in good shape in the spring.

BROWN.

Section D, Route 7.

Contractor—C. A. Weaver & Son, Clayton, Ill.
Type and width—24-foot earth road.
Length—6,985 feet.
Contract price—$2,699.88.
NOTE.—This work was completed in 1915.

CASS.

Section C, Route 5.

Contractor—John A. Sarff, Virginia, Ill.
Type and width—12-foot bituminous macadam resurfacing.
Length—6,900 feet.
Contract price—$3,163.

Section C, Route 15.

NOTE.—About 40 per cent of this work was completed this season but owing to the lateness of the season, work was closed down for the winter.

Section D, Route 7.

Contractor—John A. Sarff, Virginia, Ill.
Type and width—12-foot bituminous macadam resurfacing.
Length—5,435 feet.
Contract price—$2,009.

NOTE.—The rough grading on this section of work was practically completed. No bituminous work was placed this fall. However, the work was closed down until spring.

Section E, Route 8.

Contractor—Beardstown Construction Company, Beardstown, Ill.

Type and width—10-foot concrete.
Length—4,281 feet.
Contract price—$6,147.
Cement—$1,917.54 (in addition to contract price).
NOTE.—This section was completed and accepted last fall.

CHRISTIAN.

Section A, Route 9.

Contractor—Hannan-McDonald Company, Chicago, Ill.

Type and width—24-foot oiled earth.
Length—102 stations.
Contract price—$8,146.91.

NOTE.—Owing to the heavy grading through the flat branch bottom, the grading on this section ran extremely high. The section was changed from a 30-foot roadway to a 24-foot roadway, which reduced the yardage on this section about 1,650 yards. The money saved on this section due to this change was placed in a slab bridge. The culvert work and the excavation on this section of road has been completed. However, there has been no shaping of the roadway and no oil applied on this section. Work was closed down for the winter.

Section B, Route 15.

Contractor—Hannan-McDonald Company, Chicago, Ill.

Type and width—24-foot oiled earth.
Length—18,600 feet.
Contract price (original)—$8,247.18.

NOTE.—The actual improvement on this road calls for 22,156 feet. An omission was made at the Wabash Railroad crossing and also the new bridge across South Fork, making a total omission of 644 feet in the 22,800 lineal feet improved. The amount of cement on this section contracted for was $460.16. The original contract from station 0 to station 180 was completed. The rough grading and culvert on the authorized extension on this section were completed. However, no reshaping or oiling was done on this section. Work was closed down for the winter.

Section C, Route 12.

Contractor—Hannan-McDonald Company, Chicago, Ill.

Type and width—24-foot oiled earth (reduced from 30 feet).
Length—2,800 feet.
Contract price—9,262.46.
Cement—$428.80.

NOTE.—This section of road was originally figured for a 30-foot roadway but was reduced to a 24-foot roadway, thus making a saving sufficient to extend this section 2,400 feet and also build a 24-foot slab bridge. Very little has been done on the extension of this work—the same being closed down for the winter.

HANCOCK.

Section A, Route 1.

Contractor—Siens Brothers, Dallas City, Ill.
Type and width—24-foot earth road.
Length—9,000 feet (including extension on this work).
Contract price—$4,309.39.
Cement—$373.85.

NOTE.—About 95 per cent of this section was completed. Work will be resumed in the spring. This improvement extends from the south city limits of Dallas City in a southerly direction.

Section B, Route 4.

Contractor—J. W. McConnell, Carthage, Ill.
Type and width—24-foot earth road.
Length—13,700 feet.
Contract price—$4,569.68.
Cement—$196.98.
NOTE.—The drainage structures are about 35 per cent completed while the grading is about 75 per cent completed.

Section C, Route 9.

Contractor—Augusta Road Improvement Association.

-Type and width—Earth.

Length—12,800 feet.

Contract price—$4,416.83.

Cement—$412.90.

NOTE.—The work on this section is about 90 per cent completed.

Section D, Route 14.

Contractor—W. O. Kunkel, Carthage, Ill.

Type and width—24-foot earth.

Length—16,945 feet.

Contract price—$4,551.51 (cement furnished by contractor).

NOTE.—This improvement starts at the west city limits of Carthage and extends in a westerly direction. This section is about 75 per cent completed.

MACON.

Section A. Route 1.

Contractor—Benj. Harrison, Decatur, Ill.

Type and width—24-foot oiled earth.

Length—62,215 feet.

Contract price—$27,581.87.

Cement—$1,132.98.

NOTE.—This section of road starts at the north city limits of Decatur and extends in a northerly direction to the DeWitt County line. This contract price does not include the deduction made for culverts and grading, nor does it include the contract price of additional work which consists of two 40-foot girders. The grading on this section is about 98 per cent completed, while the oiling is about 60 per cent completed.

Section B, Route 12.

Contractor—Benj. Harrison, Decatur, Ill.

Type and width—Oiled earth 24-foot and 30-foot.

Length—61,989 feet.

Contract price—$23,446.28.

Cement—$1,112.28.

NOTE.—This section of road starts at the city limits of Decatur and extends in a westerly direction. Very little work was done on this section during 1916. The only work done was the placing of about a mile of 12-inch tile.

MASON.

Section A, Route 1.

Contractor—Jansen & Zoller, Pekin, Ill.

Type and width—Oiled earth.

Length—34,900 feet.

Contract price—$9,972.62.

NOTE.—This improvement starts at the east city limits of Havana and extends in an easterly direction. Grading on this section is about 85 per cent completed. Owing to the extreme difficulty having arisen in connection with the sandy soil, arrangements were made with the highway commission and the county board to place a layer of clay on this section of road before oiling same. However, no clay or oil was placed on this section during 1916. The work was closed down for the winter.

MENARD.

Section C, Route 2.

Contractor—E. E. Brass, Petersburg, Ill.

Width and Type—15-foot concrete.

Length—1,400 feet.

Contract price—$5,266.80.

Cement—$1,063.98.

NOTE.—There is extremely heavy cutting on this hill. Nothing was done on this section of work during 1916. Contractor intends to start work early in the spring.

MORGAN.

Section B, Route 11.

Contractor—Cocking Cement Co., Jacksonville, Ill.

Width and Type—Oiled earth.

Length—39,376 feet.

Contract price—$17,600.

NOTE.—This improvement starts at the west city limits of Jacksonville and extends in a westerly direction for 39,376 feet. Grading on this section is about 90 per cent completed, while no finishing or oiling has been done at all. This will be completed in the early spring of 1917.

PIATT.

Section B, Route 6.

Contractor—C. A. Michael, Mattoon, Ill.

Width and Type—9-foot monolithic brick.

Length—18,620 feet.

Contract price—$39,602.09 (includes cement).

NOTE.—This construction was placed on the side of the road. The original contract on this section of work called for $28,250. However, sufficient funds were available to place a county and State extension and also a county extension and a private extension on this work. The amount of this contract was approximately $39,602.09, and was a continuous improvement from station 0+00 to station 186+20. This contract was awarded in 1915 and completed in December, 1916.

Section C, Route 1,

Contractor—W. F. Lodge, Monticello, Ill.

Width and type—10-foot monolithic brick.

Length—6,100 feet.

Contract price—$11,387.12.

Cement—$1,725.00.

NOTE.—This improvement starts at the north city limits of Momence, paralleling the I. T. S. for a distance of 6,100 feet. However, there will be sufficient money available for a considerable extension on this section of work. The contract for this work was awarded late last fall and nothing has been done on same. Work will start early in the spring.

PIKE.

Section B, Route 4.

Contractor—Cameron, Joyce & Co., Keokuk, Iowa.

Type and width—15-foot waterbound macadam.

Length—12,930 feet.

Contract price—$32,875.21.

Cement—$382.73.

NOTE.—This improvement starts at the south city limits of Perry, Illinois and extends in a southerly direction for 12,930 feet. Owing to the extreme heavy grading through the bottoms, this work was very expensive. Rough grading is approximately 90 per cent completed while the macadam is about 50 per cent completed. Work on this section was laid over until spring.

SANGAMON.

Section G, Route 2.

Contractor—Cameron, Joyce & Co., Keokuk, Iowa.

Type and width—9-foot brick with 4½-inch concrete shoulders.

Length—4,140 feet.

Contract price—$13,673.00.

NOTE.—Owing to 8-foot or 9-foot embankments placed through the Sangamon River bottom, this improvement was very expensive. This work has been completed.

Section H, Route 5.

Contractor—Henry Nelch & Son, Springfield, Ill.

Type and width—18-foot sand-cement cushion.

Length—3,625 feet.

Contract price—$13,238.86.

Cement—$2,061.72.

NOTE.—This section of work was completed in the fall of 1916.

Section I, Route 8.

Contractor—John E. Bretz, Springfield, Ill.

Type and width—18-foot sand-cement brick type of construction.

Length—3,880 feet.

Contract price—$13,691.68.

Cement—$2,100.00.

NOTE.—This improvement starts at the west city limits of Springfield and extends in a westerly direction. This section was completed in the fall of 1916.

Section J, Route 3.

Contractor—John E. Bretz, Springfield, Ill.

Type and width—Sand-cement brick type of construction (18-foot.)

Length—3,825 feet.

Contract price—$13,162.95.

Cement—$2,206.62.

NOTE.—This extension begins at the northeast city limits of Springfield and extends in an easterly direction. This section is approximately 90 per cent completed. The completion on this section was delayed until spring.

SCHUYLER.
Section C, Route 5.

Contractor—Cameron, Joyce & Co., Keokuk, Iowa.
Type and width—10-foot concrete.
Length—3,750 feet.
Contract price—$7,218.22.
Cement—$1,794.26.

NOTE.—This improvement starts at the far end of section A in this county and extends in a northerly direction. This section of work was completed in December, 1916.

(Concluded from page 36.)

Alabama	$7.50 to $20.00	per annum
Arizona	5.00 to 15.00	per annum
California	4.00 to 25.00	per annum
Connecticut	5.00 to 35.00	per annum
Illinois	3.00 to 10.00	per annum
Indiana	5.00 to 20.00	per annum
Iowa	8.00 to 25.00	per annum
Kentucky	6.00 to 20.00	per annum
Maine	5.00 to 15.00	per annum
Maryland	5.00 to 35.00	per annum
Massachusetts	5.00 to 25.00	per annum
Michigan	5.00 to 35.00	per annum
New Hampshire	10.00 to 40.00	per annum
New Jersey	4.00 to 15.00	per annum
New York	5.00 to 25.00	per annum
Ohio	5.00 set fee,	per annum
Pennsylvania	5.00 to 20.00	per annum
Rhode Island	5.00 to 25.00	per annum
Virginia	4.00 to 25.00	per annum
Wisconsin	5.00 set fee,	per annum

TO ARMS!

Captain Bilger!
Sergeant Hopkins!

Erstwhile road engineer of the State Highway Department, H. E. Bilger, residing at 714 South State Street, received notification from the War Department a short time ago of his appointment to captaincy in the Engineer Officers' Reserve Corps of the United States Army.

Captain—Road Engineer—Bilger took the examination for qualification at St. Louis January 10. The commission which has come to him in recognition of merit has a life of five years at the end of which time it will be renewable, with the approval of the Secretary of War and in conformity with other army regulations.

In his new role, Captain Bilger stands liable to call for actual service with the United States Army at any time the war department may deem the services of the engineers as needed.

Another of the State Highway Department donned the khaki early. He is First Duty Sergeant, Gene E. Hopkins of Company C, Fifth Infantry, Illinois National Guard, whose rendezvous is Springfield.

Sergeant Hopkins was called out of bed at an early hour Monday morning, March 26, and was directed, pursuant to orders from the Adjutant General's department, to assist in mobilizing his company at the State Armory in Springfield. He worked until 8.30 a. m., when he reported to the State Highway Department, in khaki clad, and as soon as temporary arrangements could be made for handling his work as property clerk, he hastened away in obedience to War Department orders to be ready, at a moment's notice, to go whither he was sent.

When the war call comes, someone has to assume the burden. To such patriots as Captain Bilger—who is ready—and to Sergeant Hopkins—who is in service—may we extend the wish of good luck.

Whether they wear bars, stripes, or even stars or eagles, we'll venture the forecast that the State Highway Department boys won't let anyone show them up!

MAKES EFFICIENCY CHART.

Robert R. McLeod, general bookkeeper and accountant in the State Highway Department, has designed an original charting of office work and duties, calculated to insure a systematic form of procedure and a higher degree of efficiency.

Mr. McLeod's chart shows, first, the duties of an accountant. Secondly, it sets forth, according to the nature of the work, whether these duties are daily, weekly or monthly. Extended lines show at a glance when the work in each instance is to be performed. Provision is made in the chart, also, for annual and semiannual reports.

The chart, with its bird's-eye view, lists the checking and recording of cement invoices, recording of claims, the posting of the purchase journal, etc., which constitute the daily tasks; the weekly recording and posting, and the monthly taking of trial balances, preparation of reports, etc.

Mr. McLeod is ready to attest the value of his plan because he is using it to-day in his work in this department. *Concrete Highway Magazine* learned of his chart and requested an article from its originator, which appeared in the February issue of the magazine. In the course of this article, Accountant McLeod says:

"The work of an accountant in a State Highway Department presents many complex and varied problems, owing to the nature of the work and the manner in which it must be performed; therefore a man in charge of the accounts covering road and bridge construction and maintenance, must, above all, if he would escape criticism and perform his work efficiently, have a thoroughly systematic program for conducting his work."

NEW CONTRACTS AWARDED.

The following State aid contracts were awarded by the State Highway Commission, February 14, 1917:

County.	Sec.	Type.	Contractor.	Amount.
Alexander.	C	Novaculite Macadam.	H. L. Wedding, Cairo, Illinois	$17,970 84
Franklin..	D	Concrete ...	H. R. Cawood, Mt. Vernon, Illinois	8,905 59
Jasper....	E	Earth	Jas. Benefiel, Newton, Illinois	6,191 64
Madison...	C	Bituminous Macadam Resurfacing	Powell & Gauen, Collinsville, Illinois	5,374 05
Massac....	C	Bridge	J. R. Sleeter, Metropolis, Illinois	700 00
Mercer....	F	Earth	E. A. Lord Constr. Co., Monmouth, Illinois	4,109 81
Mercer....	H	Earth	E. A. Lord Constr. Co., Monmouth, Illinois	4,346 60

ILLINOIS HIGHWAYS.

Published Monthly by the
State Highway Department,
Springfield. Illinois.

ILLINOIS HIGHWAY COMMISSION.

A. D. Gash, *President.*
S. E. Bradt, *Secretary.*
James P. Wilson.

Wm. W. Marr, *Chief State Highway Engineer.*

BUREAU OF ROADS.

H. E. Bilger, *Road Engineer.*
M. W. Watson, *Assistant Road Engineer.*
C. M. Hathaway, *Office Engineer.*

BUREAU OF BRIDGES.

Clifford Older, *Bridge Engineer.*
G. F. Burch, *Assistant Bridge Engineer.*
A. W. Conroe, *Office Engineer.*

BUREAU OF MAINTENANCE.

B. H. Piepmeier, *Maintenance Engineer.*
F. T. Sheets, *Assistant Maintenance Engineer.*

BUREAU OF TESTS.

F. L. Roman, *Testing Engineer.*
F. L. Sperry, *Assistant Testing Engineer.*
W. C. Adams, *Chemist.*

BUREAU OF AUDITS.

J. M. McCoy, *Chief Clerk.*
Earl B. Searcy, *Department Editor.*
R. R. McLeod, *General Bookkeeper.*
G. E. Hopkins, *Property Clerk.*

DIVISION ENGINEERS.

R. L. Bell, Buchanan-Link Bldg., Paris, Ill.
H. B. Bushnell, 135 Fox St., Aurora Ill.
J. E. Huber, Wise Building, Mt. Vernon, Ill.
A. H. Hunter, 302 Apollo Theater Bldg., Peoria, Ill.
C. M. Slaymaker, 510 Metropolitan Bldg., E. St. Louis, Ill.
H. E. Surman, 614 People's Bank Bldg., Moline, Ill.
Fred Tarrant, 730 Reisch Bldg., Springfield, Ill.

Address all communications in regard to "Illinois Highways," to Earl B. Searcy, Department Editor, State Highway Department, Springfield, Illinois.

CONTENTS.

AN EXPLANATION.

We deplore the fact that this issue appears as the "March-April" number. ILLINOIS HIGHWAYS would much rather never use the hyphen. We like to get our magazine out each month as a separate entity, with subject matter relating to the work and seasonble activities of that particular month.

State finances, or the lack of them, however, has made the consolidation of numbers necessary. State funds out of which comes the cost of printing this publication, along with many others, suffered a state of exhaustion. The Superintendent of Printing felt obliged to suspend, temporarily, the publishing of all State printed matter, except that which was imperatively necessary.

The March issue would have been out early in the month except for the delay which came from causes given in the foregoing. We consolidate in order not to interfere with the regularity of publishing in the future.

NOTICE.

Readers of ILLINOIS HIGHWAYS will remember that in the January issue we announced a revision of the mailing list as about to take place. We enclosed cards for return, these cards to permit of expression by readers whether they wished to continue to receive this publication.

Several thousands of these cards and personal letters came back at once. The mailing list revision, therefore, was begun without delay, and has been completed.

As we stated in January, we want ILLINOIS HIGHWAYS the official publication of this department, in the hands each month of all who are interested in reading it. We do not, however, want a single copy of the magazine wasted. Paper and the cost of printing approach too near an altitude record to warrant an idle expenditure of State money.

The magazine is sent, if at all, free of all charge to you, the reader. Therefore, we shall expect, if you receive it, that you read it. If you do not care to, kindly be courteous enough to notify us of your lack of interest, and we will appreciate it as a genuine favor. We want to eliminate from our mailing list every name which does not stand for a monthly reader of our publication.

It would be well for persons receiving several or more copies of ILLINOIS HIGHWAYS each month to check up closely and be certain that the magazine is remailed to none but those who want to familiarize themselves with its contents.

* * *

The new concrete road in South Ottawa Township, LaSalle County, has been opened for traffic. It is one mile long, and marks the beginning of a hard-surfaced road from Ottawa to La Salle along the south bank of the Illinois River. The F. E. Ball Company did the work, which is State aid.

Egyptian Obstacles, or Road Problems in Southern Illinois

By J. E. Huber, Division Engineer, Seventh Division.

Illinois is a large State. Conditions throughout differ greatly—more than one who is not familiar with all sections of the State may realize. In fact, it seems sometimes that in southern Illinois alone there is a wide enough variation to suffice for several states.

It is extremely difficult therefore to enact laws, prescribe rules, or draft specifications for road improvements that will meet the requirements of all parts of the State; and it is only natural that we should judge any innovation pertaining to this line of work by the degree to which we anticipate the change will fit the conditions of the locality we represent. Hence, a better understanding of the divers conditions in the State may have a broadening influence on our future judgment.

It may be well to state at the outset that my remarks are intended to be very general, and refer to no particular county, for fear that a few of the county superintendents of highways from the wealthier counties of southern Illinois, having in mind only the counties they represent, may think my statement of conditions too severe; and likewise the county superintendents from the poorer counties of central and northern Illinois may think I am too optimistic concerning their conditions.

Good roads should be considered an investment returning enormous dividends—paying for themselves in a short time; but the improvement of a system of roads necessitates a large inital outlay, and not until the general public reaches a full appreciation of the advantages to be derived from road improvement, and is willing to authorize the necessary expenditure, can there be much prospect of road improvement on a large scale. The problem of arousing the public from its lethargy and creating a demand for road improvement is common to nearly all parts of the country, and probably nowhere in Illinois is this problem more difficult of solution than in the southern part.

Southern Illinois, as a whole, has been very slow in taking up the good roads movement, and in this respect, it may likely remain several years behind other parts of the State, though its final awakening is certain.

I would not, however, have you infer that this section of the State is entirely destitute of good roads. There are several communities in which considerable road improvement has been done, and much progress made in this line of work. Neither is it my intention to emphasize the poverty and conservatism of this territory, except by so doing to disclose some of the adverse conditions encountered, and cause others to realize that the successful achievement of road improvement in southern Illinois oftentimes requires greater effort and personal sacrifice from the small group of progressive citizens, who usually act as sponsors for such projects, than is usually requisite in other parts of the State.

Some of the more important factors entering into the road problem of southern Illinois, and those which give it a more serious aspect than in other parts of the State, are the extremely poor condition of both roads and bridges at the present time, the difficulty of maintaining the roads from the destroying influences of the elements, rather than from traffic, and, most important of all, the difficulty of securing sufficient funds

for adequate road improvement without imposing burdensome taxation upon the assessable property.

Generally speaking, the rural highways of southern Illinois are the worst to be found in the State. The roads have been sadly neglected in past years, and owing to soil and topographic conditions, these roads deteriorate more rapidly when neglected than those in any other portion of the State. Clay soil is encountered throughout the entire southern territory. In some localities this clay is very dense and compact, and retains water very readily. In other places, the soil is of a very light, loose nature, having no body whatever, and pulverizes into dust very easily. Both kinds, however, are readily subject to erosion, and when saturated, flow almost like water. It is not at all uncommon to see what was originally a small ditch, no larger than a plow furrow, develop within a short time into a stream measuring 20 feet or more from bank to bank.

In no portion of the State can there be found as great a variation in topographic conditions as in southern Illinois. A considerable portion of this territory, commonly known as the "Southern Illinois Ozarks," is extremely rough and rugged, while both north and south of this range of hills there is much flat country, a large portion of which is swampy and subject to frequent overflows. This was the first part of the State settled, and, partly due to the unfavorable topographic conditions which were encountered, the highways, in a considerable portion of this territory, were not located on section lines; but were laid out to connect the early settlements, with as little hill climbing as possible, and with no regard to the distance traversed. While the original locations of many of these roads may have been wisely chosen, yet through neglect and lack of maintenance, hundreds of miles of road have literally washed away, and now serve more as watercourses for draining adjacent land than for road purposes, making a complete relocation of a considerable portion of the road mileage both desirable and economical.

The causes for the disastrous neglect of these roads in past years have been both lack of sufficient funds for maintenance, and wasteful disbursement of the funds at hand. It may be truthfully stated that the average farmer in southern Illinois is less progressive and has had less experience in methodical business dealings than the central or northern Illinois farmer, and that the opportunities for intellectual development have not been as great as they have been in other parts of the State. For these reasons, it has been comparatively easy for the occasional unscrupulous highway commissioner to misappropriate public funds without detection, and likewise, since many highway commissioners have been very lax in keeping their records and accounts the townships have been, in many cases, easily defrauded in the purchase of machinery and materials.

As a result of these conditions, a large percentage of the townships in southern Illinois were found to be very badly in debt at the time the Revised Road and Bridge Laws became effective, and it has been no small part of the work of some county superintendents of highways to help these townships gain a better financial standing. This has been done only by strict economy and close attention to accounts, and a number of the county superintendents deserve considerable credit for their valuable help in these matters.

In an attempt to make clear some of the governing conditions in the different parts of the State, I have chosen for the purpose of comparison, 20 counties in the northern part, 20 in the central part, and 20 in the southern part of the State. The counties in the central and northern parts were chosen at random, and with the exception of leaving Cook County out of consideration, no attempt was made to select the richest or poorest counties. The 20 counties in southern Illinois are those which comprise Division No. 7, and are the ones with which I am most familiar. These counties compare very closely with the others in what may be properly termed southern Illinois, after eliminating St. Clair County from consideration. The total area, population, mileage of rural highways and assessed valuation of each group of counties were obtained, and comparisons of these totals discloses some interesting information.

To summarize: The miles of highway per unit of area in the three territories are very nearly the same, the central portion being slightly in the lead, having 1.8 miles per square mile, there being, however, a wide variation in the several counties in each group. Neither does the population per mile of road differ greatly in the three territories, the northern group having 42 persons; the central group, 34 and the southern group, 33 persons per mile of rural road. These figures are based on the total population, and when we consider that in the southern district there are only two cities having more than 10,000 inhabitants, and that the largest has a population of less than 15,000, while in the northern and central portions there are such cites as Rockford, Aurora, Joliet, Peoria, Springfield, Quincy and Decatur, it is safe to state that the rural population per mile of road in southern Illinois greatly exceeds that in central Illinois and at least equals that in northern Illinois.

Local conditions may exert a modifying influence, yet it is generally assumed that the volume of traffic on country highways is approximately proportional to the density of the rural population. The density of rural population probably affords a better means of comparison of traffic than does the total population, since all country people are users of the highways, while there are hundreds of persons residing in the large cities already mentioned who do not venture upon the country highways, on the average, once in six months.

It may be pertinently stated here that the automobile traffic on southern Illinois highways is by no means as great as will be found in other parts of the State. One of the main reasons for this is the poor condition of the roads and the consequent difficulty of operating automobiles in this section; but with comprehensive road improvements the automobile traffic is certain to increase at a rapid rate.

The urgent need of a comprehensive road improvement program in southern Illinois is further emphasized by an investigation of railroad facilities, both steam and electric. The interurbans, which farmers and residents in small towns in other parts of the State have found so indispensable for quick and dependable communication, are almost unknown in southern Illinois, except in the immediate vicinity of St. Louis. The northern group of counties has 490 miles of electric railway; the central group, 380 miles, while the southern group has a total of only 34 miles, and but little prospect of additional mileage.

Though the mileage of steam railroads per unit of area in southern Illinois is not far below that in other sections, the passenger service is unspeakably bad in comparison. I speak with authority on this subject, as I have spent many hours in futile attempts to make desired train connections, such attempts usually resulting in all-night stops at some crossroad. As a result of these poor facilities for travel, the southern Illinois farmer, finding a trip over the country highways expedient during a portion of each winter, has but three options. He may walk, ride a mule, or stay at home.

These comparisons show that the need of good roads is as urgent, if, indeed, not greater in southern Illinois than in any other section of the State for the proper development of its resources. To anyone familiar with conditions, it is also apparent that improved through routes, or roads for automobile touring, while highly desirable, are not as greatly needed in southern Illinois as are systems of improved roads radiating from the important trading centers. As these market roads are improved, and the people realize their advantages, they will also realize that the benefits of the improvement are directly proportional to the extent of the system, and an insistent demand for improved through routes will necessarily follow.

Next, we shall discuss the most difficult problem —that of financing road improvements. Comparisons of the wealth of the groups of counties previously referred to show an assessed valuation of $19,650 per mile of country highway in the northern group, $17,100 per mile in the central group, and but $8,100 per mile in the group of Southern counties—or to make the comparison more apparent, it may be stated that the valuation per mile in the southern territory is only 47 per cent of that in the central and 41 per cent of that in the northern part of the State. It is thus apparent that less than half the amount of money may be spent in improving southern Illinois roads per mile that may be expended in other parts of the State, if the property is to be assessed at the same rate; yet it is reasonable to expect that these roads will be subjected to a traffic almost as great, if not quite so destructive, as will be found in other territories, while the damage done to southern Illinois roads by rains, overflows and erosion is immeasurably greater than that done to roads in any other section.

A study of the comparative costs of road improvement in different parts of the State shows the cost in southern Illinois to be relatively high. The initial cost of an improvement is governed by the cost of materials and labor, and also by the condition of the road at the time the improvement is made. Prices of materials depend largely upon availability, and in this respect, northern Illinois has great advantages over other portions of the State. Both central and southern Illinois have, at this time, very little good road building material readily available. There are, however, in the southern section a few natural deposits of material suitable for road surfacing, but owing to the small demand for it, little development work has been done. The most notable deposit is that of novaculite or chert gravel, existing in great quantities in the bluffs along the lower Mississippi River, but owing to unfavorable freight rates, this material is now used in only a very small territory in Illinois.

It is generally assumed that labor is much cheaper in the southern part than elsewhere in the State, but this is not true to any great extent. Hauling costs may be somewhat lower, due to cheaper team hire, but manual labor is considerably less efficient and dependable and thereby offsets the difference in the rate of pay.

After considering the adverse conditions already enumerated, even the most enthusiastic good roads advocate is forced to admit that a comprehensive system of hard surfaced roads throughout southern Illinois can not be realized for several years to come. This statement introduces the problem of expending the available funds in such a manner that the greatest benefit will be derived therefrom, and a discussion of this problem can not proceed far without involving the selection of the type of road.

There are many who believe that the roads designated for improvement should be provided, in so far as the funds will permit, with surfacing of a high class, enduring type, so that maintenance costs will be minimized. A great many others favor the use of cheaper types of surfacing in order that the improvement may be extended as far as possible. Considered solely from an engineering standpoint, the first course seems the proper one in many instances; but considering present conditions in southern Illinois, it is probable that expediency demands the pursuance of the latter course, with but few exceptions, especially where satisfactory provisions for maintenance are assured. This procedure provides for giving immediate service to the greatest number of people, and is therefore most instrumental in creating sentiment for better roads and a demand for additional improvements.

Illustrative of the greater service often given by the cheaper types of improvement, I shall mention the recent State aid work in a certain southern Illinois county. A road was designated for improvement. It has been overflowed several times each year by back water from the Ohio River, often preventing the people residing in that part of the county from reaching the county seat and principal trading center. The amount of money available was so small that had this improvement consisted of a road surfaced with concrete or brick, it would have been impossible to improve more than one-third of the required distance, and while such a road would have been greatly appreciated, it would not have possessed, by far, the utility afforded by the earth fill which was constructed entirely across the lowland overflowed. In fact, the manner in which the money was expended met with such general approval that before the contract was hardly completed an excellent gravel wearing surface was placed on this fill entirely by donation labor.

In this connection, it may be stated that the recent amendment of the Road and Bridge Laws, whereby County Boards may designate the types of State aid improvements, has been more beneficial to southern Illinois than to any other portion of the State.

In dealing with road improvement in southern Illinois a greater number of puzzling and vexatious construction problems, requiring careful study and special treatment, are met than are usually encountered in other sections. The details of the construction of roads and pavements in comparatively level and rolling territories where roads follow section lines, are becoming more and more standardized each year, there being certain materials, methods and dimensions, the use of which is generally accepted as standard practice; and these are departed from mainly for the purpose of experiment. The proper adjustment of horizontal and vertical alignment and dimensions and locations of ditches for roads in rough country can not, however, follow any certain set of rules, each improvement having its own distinctive features and demanding special consideration in order to reduce the cost of construction and maintenance to a minimum. Especially is this true of improvements crossing overflow bottoms, and in such cases, thorough knowledge of all governing conditions is essential before one is competent to decide upon proper designs. Even then, unless one is considerably inclined to over-design such improvements, he is likely to register occasional failures among his successes to remind him that the "hindsight" is vastly superior to the foresight.

I might continue pointing out the difficulties of road work in southern Illinois indefinitely, but for fear of being termed a confirmed pessimist, I shall endeavor to enumerate some of the more encouraging features. It is gratifying to be able to state that every county in this section of the State has taken up the State aid proposition, even though considerable coaxing was required in some instances, and that there is little doubt but that all counties expect to proceed with State aid work in future. Of course, the few roads that may be improved each year by means of State allotments will not go far toward satisfying the immediate needs of this part of the State, but the work done thus far has had a remarkable influence in promoting other work and in attracting attention to the great need of extensive improvement.

These few improvements have undoubtedly introduced better types and methods of construction than formerly prevailed in most localities, and for this reason alone, are well worth their cost; but it is probable that the greatest indirect benefit from State aid work will result from the few sections of earth roads improved this year. If by a demonstration of what may be accomplished by proper maintenance of a well drained earth road, the township officials can be induced to employ similar methods on the roads in their care, great good undoubtedly will result.

It has been quite general so far for the county boards to designate for State aid improvement roads which were notoriously the worst in the counties, and the wonderful improvements over the existing old trails effected by the new construction have been the source of much gratification to those connected with the work, as well as the users of the road.

It has been amusing to observe the attitude of the local people in regard to many of the improvements. Frequently they are at first very dubious concerning the feasibility of the work; then as the construction proceeds they become very critical and discover many defects, it being very common to hear such objections to the work as "It's too wide" or "too narrow," "too high" or "too low," "too thick" or "too thin"; but shortly after the road is completed and opened to traffic the public discovers the one remaining important "defect" and forgets all of the others—for on every hand is heard the cry: "The thing is too blamed short."

Another encouraging feature is the rapidly changing attitude of the boards of supervisors of several southern Illinois counties toward the road question. Some of the boards, which a few years ago were reactionary and remarkably antagonistic toward these improvements, are now openly enthusiastic on the same propositions, and it is improbable that the people of any southern Illinois county, desiring in the future to vote on the question of issuing county bonds for road improvements, will be denied this privilege through any lack of action by the county boards.

My intention has been to present a few of the principal features of the road problem of southern Illinois without attempting a solution of this problem, but before closing I desire to direct attention to a financial difficulty, the removal of which may tend to expedite road improvements in this section of the State. Probably the most effective instrument available for instituting road work on a large scale is the county bond issue proposition, only recently made feasible, but the State Constitution limits the outstanding bonded indebtedness to 5 per cent of the assessed valuation within the county.

On account of the very low valuation it is found extremely difficult in many of the southern counties to propose for improvement a system of roads of sufficient extent to secure the interest and support of enough voters to carry the proposition. The opinion has been expressed by several well-informed men in southern Illinois that it would be little, if any, more difficult to carry a bond issue proposition for 10 per cent than one for 5 per cent of the assessed valuation. They maintain, and I think rightly, that to secure the support of the farmer it is necessary to assure him of the improvement of a road reasonably close to his home, and for this reason it often requires a greater amount than may be realized from a 5 per cent bond issue to secure the support of a majority of the farmers.

These men also believe that the doubling of the tax likely will not diminish the enthusiasm of many of those now in favor of a 5 per cent bond issue, while most of those who now oppose this proposition are so constituted that they would likely oppose a bond issue if for only one-half of 1 per cent. The proposed constitutional convention may afford an opportunity for the raising of this limit, and such a change would no doubt be beneficial.

If, perhaps, this cursory statement of the road problems of southern Illinois will help to explain why some of the county superintendents of highways from that section are unable to come before you and point with pride to a long list of successful accomplishments in the way of road improvements; if some of the superintendents from other parts of the State who have thought their lot hard to bear, and have sometimes imagined that, compared with themselves, Job was a "lucky dog," can go back to their work encouraged by the thought that others are in worse predicaments than they, then the discussion of this problem has not been without results.

[EDITOR'S NOTE.—The foregoing article by Division Engineer Huber of the Seventh District, with headquarters at Mt. Vernon, was presented as one of the special features of the State University engineering short course at Urbana in January. It is a frank discussion of conditions as he has to meet them in his territory. It does not seek to heap blame; merely to state facts, in order that the rest of the State may appreciate what southern Illinois must face in the fight for better roads.]

ATTORNEY GENERAL'S OPINION DEFINES PURCHASING LIMITATIONS.

A short time ago, Chief State Highway Engineer William W. Marr asked Attorney General Edward J. Brundage for an opinion defining the exact limitations of township highway commissioners in proceeding with road or bridge repair work, the cost of which exceeded $200. The State law, as the Attorney General interprets it, clearly vests in county superintendents of highways the duty of approving such expenditures on the part of commissioners when the sum total exceeds $200.

Mr. Brundage's opinion, which will interest directly every county superintendent and every road commissioner in Illinois, was transmitted to Mr. Marr as follows:

You call my attention to that part of the revised Road and Bridge law, which provides that contracts entered into by commissioners of highways, for the construction and repair of roads and bridges, if the cost thereof exceeds $200, must be approved by the county superintendent of highways, and request that I advise you as to the proper construction which should be placed upon said provision. This provision of the law is clause 5, subdivision (b), paragraph 50, chapter 121, Hurd's Revised Statutes, 1916, page 2269, and provides that the highway commissioners of each town or road district shall have power, and it shall be their duty:

"To direct the construction and repair of roads and bridges within the town or district, to let contracts, employ labor and purchase material and machinery therefor, subject to the limitations herein provided: *Provided, however*, that no contract shall be let for the construction or repair of any road or bridge or part thereof in excess of the amount of $200, nor shall any machinery or other appliances to be used in road construction in excess of such amount 'be purchased without the approval of the county superintendent of highways."

It is also provided by clause 5, division (d), paragraph 8, chapter 121, Hurd's Revised Statutes, page 2253, with reference to the powers and duties of the county superintendent of highways, that he shall—

"Keep a record of all contracts or purchases of materials, machinery or apparatus to be used in road construction in excess of two hundred dollars ($200) approved by him in any town or district as hereinafter provided."

These two provisions of the statute govern the powers and duties of the county superintendent of highways and the commissioners of highways, with reference to the manner of letting contracts for the construction or repair of roads and bridges, and purchases of machinery or other appliances to be used in road work. County superintendents of highways and commissioners of highways are statutory officers, and their powers and duties are limited to those expressly given by statute or necessarily implied therefrom.

The language used by the Legislature in clause 5, *supra*, with reference to the commissioners of highways, is explicit, and the only question which can arise thereunder is as to the meaning and scope of the word "contract," as used in said clause. In this connection, it must be understood that the word "contract" includes not only written, but also oral contracts.

In the determination of that question, I also refer to another proposition submitted by you in your letter, in which you inquire if the commissioners of highways are authorized to construct or repair highway bridges, by day labor, when the cost of labor and materials exceeds $200 although the cost of the materials alone would not exceed $200. In a case of that character "contract," as used in said statute, includes the construction of the bridge—not only the purchase of materials, but also the employment of labor. The contract, in such case, may not be separated so as to constitute one contract for the materials and another contract for labor or employment of labor. To give the provisions of the statute any other construction would place in the hands of the commissioners of highways the power to let a contract for the construction of a bridge, where the amount involved is in excess of $200, by dividing the work in such manner that the stone, steel, wood work, labor, excavation, etc., would each cost less than $200, but the whole would cost more than $200. This would be contrary to not only the letter but also the spirit of the statute.

I am therefore clearly of the opinion that commissioners of highways may not purchase materials and employ laborers in the construction or repair of roads or bridges, or any part thereof, nor purchase machinery, without the approval of the county superintendent of highways, when the sum total of all the proposed expenditures concerning an entire scheme or plan of construction or repair or purchase exceeds $200.

A CONFERENCE AT WORK
The Northeast Section Starts the New Year.

County highway superintendents who form the membership of the Northeast Conference of County Superintendents of Highways of Illinois met in Chicago in the office of George A. Quinlan, the Cook County superintendent, on Tuesday, February 13. Every member was present.

It was the first meeting of the year, 1917. Mr. Quinlan crowded the twelve superintendents, together with two officials from the division engineer's office at Aurora and invited guests, into his private office room in the Cook County courthouse and from 10 o'clock in the morning until 5 o'clock in the afternoon—with an hour and a half out for a sociable lunch—the men discussed road and bridge problems in what they all agreed was the best meeting of its sort within their recollection.

The superintendents present from the twelve counties in the conference district, which is coextensive with the territory of Division Engineer H. B. Bushnell of the first State Highway Department division, were the following:

George N. Lamb, Kane, chairman of the conference; Charles E. Russel, Lake, secretary of the conference; George A. Quinlan, Cook; A. R. Carter, Winnebago; Fred W. Stine, Grundy; Thomas W. Humphrey, Boone; John D. Russell, Kendall; Will H. Smith, Will; Frank M. Enos, Kankakee; E. L. Gates, DuPage; W. C. Miller, DeKalb, and C. L. Tryon, McHenry.

There were also present Division Engineer Bushnell, his assistant engineer, L. P. Scott; C. L. Hanson, assistant to County Superintendent Lamb of Kane, and Earl B. Searcy, department editor, State Highway Department. The meeting was closed to all others.

The discussion of road subjects occupied the morning. In the afternoon, the time was given over to bridges. A set program was followed in both sessions, though discussions assumed an informality which yielded profitable talks. Ideas were freely exchanged. Everybody was at home, and no one withheld expressions which he regarded as at all worth disseminating.

In the road session, papers were read by County Superintendents Gates and Tryon and Division Engineer Bushnell. The discussions were led by Superintendents Humphrey, Charles E. Russell and John D. Russell. Mr. Gates treated the subject, "Relations between highway commissioners and county superintendents of highways," Mr. Tryon took up the subject, "Gravel road construction in McHenry County," and Mr. Bushnell talked on "Some causes for cracks in concrete pavements."

The luncheon hour was one of the bright spots in the day's program. Mr. Quinlan of Cook, already host to the extent of turning over his office use to the conference, insisted on being the good fellow still further, so as his invited guests he took the delegates to the Hotel Sherman, where lunch was served in one of the private dining rooms. After luncheon was served, Mr. Bushnell assumed the chairmanship as toastmaster and toasts were responded to by Chairman Lamb and Secretary Russell of the conference. In the course of the informal program, Mr. Quinlan and Mr. Searcy also were called upon for short talks.

Returning to Mr. Quinlan's office, the superintendents at 2 o'clock opened their afternoon program, with the discussion of bridge problems the feature.

The afternoon speakers were Mr. Quinlan, who discussed with the aid of personally prepared sheets the subject, "Calculation sheets for the design of reinforced concrete bridges;" Mr. Hanson, who read a paper on "Bridges in Kane County;" Mr. Carter, who read a paper on "Bridge foundations," and Mr. Stine, who spoke informally on "Culverts for poorly drained roads." The afternoon discussions were led by Messrs. Miller, Scott, Enos and Smith.

In featuring the Northeast Conference in this issue of ILLINOIS HIGHWAYS, we are pleased to reproduce the papers which were read. All were short. Messrs. Quinlan and Stine spoke without manuscripts. The other five papers, together with the original poem-toast which Mr. Lamb recited at the luncheon, follow:

RELATIONSHIPS.

[By E. L. GATES.]

In writing this paper on "The Relation Between the Highway Commissioners and the County Superintendent of Highways," I am going to compare the different persons with a great tree, whose fruit should be the best variety of hard roads.

This fruit should not only be hard and sound, but should have a touch of beauty as well.

In raising this fruit, everything that enters into the making of it, from the highway commissioners to the State Highway Commission, has some part, and the fruit will not be well matured if each does not perform his duty well.

The general public has the use of this fruit, and the great tree which furnishes it should be kept in a healthy state, for fear the public might become sick of it and cut it down and destroy it.

The tree standing in the northeast part of the great State of Illinois is known as Tree No. 1, and its roots extend into 12 counties. One root shooting off to the northwest into Winnebago County, known as the "Carter" root, is fed by other roots coming from 15 townships. These township roots are made up of 33 supervisors and 41 road commissioners. The Carter root is long and slim, so its relation to the feeding roots must be wrong, or it would grow into another shape.

The Boone County root, known as the "Humphrey" root, is fed from 8 townships, and is supported by 10 supervisors and 20 road commissioners, so this, the smallest county, has a good deal of surplus energy, and the Humphrey root looks healthy and fat, and likes an argument. This relation is also wrong, for, although the proportion of highway commissioners in proportion to what they could have—that is, three to every township, is the smallest in the 12 counties, yet it is not small enough.

The McHenry County root, known as the "Tryon" root, is also slim, for, with 17 townships, 49 road commissioners and 17 supervisors, as you can see, the relation must be wrong.

The Lake County root, known as the "Russell" root, with its 17 townships, 47 road commissioners and 37 supervisors, furnishes a good deal of moisture to the tree, but I am afraid it is growing too fast, for it is climbing into other fields.

The Cook County root, known as the "Quinlan" root, with 25 townships, 75 road commissioners and 25 supervisors, is, as you see, completely out of relation, but it is furnishing fruit of the best variety. It has other feeders bonded onto it, which forces its fruit ahead of the rest, and therefore the relation is not correct.

The Du Page County root, known as the "Gates" root, with 9 townships, 25 road commissioners and 13 supervisors, is, as you can see, in fine shape, and is ready at the present time to add some of the bonded roots, so that it may be able to protect itself from the Kane and Cook County roots, which have already grown up to the county line and are trying to squeeze the life out of it—at least they are knocking the stuffing out of its roads.

The Kane County root, known as the "Lamb" root, is not soft and woolly, as the name might indicate, but with its full share of road commissioners—3 to each of its 16 townships and 41 supervisors—it is adding extra machinery to force the fruit out of the ground, and is delivering it in the modern way—by motor truck.

The De Kalb County root, described as the "Miller" root, with 19 townships, 23 supervisors and 51 road commissioners, is in the same shape as Du Page County in reference to bonded roots, only it wants to run out a few feeders in the shape of rollers and county equipment to make its relation to the other counties and to the highway commission correct.

Kendall County's root, known as the "Russell" root—but not of the same variety that you will find in Lake County—is, they tell me, in the right relationship, with 9 townships, 9 supervisors and 27 road commissioners. We all know that this variety of "Russell's sprouts" would please any one, and are glad to see the good results.

Will County's root, known as the "Smith" root, made up of 24 townships, 44 supervisors and 72 road commissioners—more county officers than any other of the 12 counties—is helping feed the main root by its promotion of good roads. The county is a large one, and the Smith root has a very large territory to cover. It will take some time to get the ground in suitable condition, but by constant treatment it will surely bear its part in the great work.

Grundy County, with its "Stine" root, is also, with its 17 townships, 19 supervisors and 49 road commissioners, furnishing the right stuff to bring the tree to bearing.

Last, but not least, Kankakee County, with its "Enos" root, is waiting, like Du Page County, for a little more fertilizer to push out its bonded roots. Its 17 townhips, with 23 supervisors and 43 road commissioners, are working in harmony for a larger variety and a better grade of fruit, and we all hope to visit there again, as we know the ladies and the supervisors know how to meet the needs of these poor, suffering roots.

As you can see by adding the various figures given, there are 193 townships, 284 supervisors and 547 road commissioners aiding in the construction of this tree.

Mr. Bushnell, our honored division forester, has a task on his hands in keeping the different branches pruned and in the right relation one with another, and only by supporting him with the best we have in the separate counties can we hope to sustain the tree that the public is so anxiously watching.

One main root in a county could not hope to bring results without the assistance of the other roots which are really the life of the tree, but there is such a thing as getting too many roots and have all roots and suckers without a main trunk and a system which brings results.

The county superintendent, or the main root of the county, should bear such relation to the roots, which, according to the present laws, are the life of the township, so as to show results. He should not favor one above another, and he should not fail to use the pruning knife if it is necessary. A root allowed to grow of its own free will will follow the easiest channel and will curl into all sorts of shapes, similar to our roads of to-day.

The county superintendent should remember that he is not greater than the tree, nor greater than the feeder roots that are supporting him, but simply holds a position where he can direct and help in bringing into fruition one of the greatest and most neglected crops of the State of Illinois.

CRACKS IN CONCRETE ROADS.

[By Division Engineer Bushnell.]

The man who attempts to tell by a superficial examination the causes for all the cracks that one can reasonably expect to appear in the average concrete road after a life of several years, has undertaken a task of no mean proportions.

The road and paving engineers of to-day know that such factors as contraction, expansion, condition of sub-grade, lack of drainage, frost and traffic, or a combination of these factors, may cause cracks but there are very few engineers who would ever attempt to analyze a pavement and draw conclusions as to the exact cause of each individual crack. The man with very limited experience is occasionally prone to jump at conclusions, based upon the results of one or two short sections of road. One man may have built a road that developed cracks in the fill section and was free from cracks in the cut sections. Another may find these conditions reversed. Subdrainage by stone drains or tile may be used, and the resulting pavement be reasonably free from cracks. Inexperience might lead to the conclusion that tile drainage is necessary in all cases.

About two years ago, a mile of 18-foot concrete road was built north of Chicago in which a number of experiments were tried. This road was constructed with an average thickness of 7 inches, and with a mixture of 1 part cement, 2 parts sand and 3½ parts stone. In one section hydrated lime was added to the mix, in another woven wire mesh reinforcement was used, and in the third part the plain 1-2-3½ mixture was used without the addition of either lime or reinforcement. After a few months' service the plain section showed the fewest cracks, the section where lime was used ranked second, and the section that was reinforced had the greatest number of cracks. Inexperience might lead one to conclude from this experimental section that hydrated lime and reinforcing steel not only were of no benefit to a pavement but were actually a detriment.

It is not the purpose or intention in this paper to attempt to explain all the causes of cracks in concrete pavements, nor to enter into a mathematical discussion of the stresses set up in the pavement bv the various forces that might be exerted. The scope of the paper will be limited to a brief general discussion of the most common causes of cracks that have come under the observation of the writer.

Contraction. Contraction due to temperature changes probably accounts for more transverse cracks than any other one factor. This is especially true on roads where the joints are spaced far apart or entirely eliminated. Construction during the autumn months, when the days are hot and the nights cool, is especially susceptible to contraction cracks. These early contraction cracks, that occur before the pavement is opened to traffic, are practically all transverse, but later on they may develop as a resultant of a contraction force and some other force, and form either a transverse or a diagonal crack.

Shrinkage. Shrinkage is a form of contraction caused by a reduction in the water content of the concrete. To guard against these cracks, most specifications provide that the green concrete shall be kept covered and moist for ten days to two weeks. Pavement placed during extremely hot weather, or when the wind is blowing hard, must be carefully protected to keep the surface from becoming crazed.

Expansion. Where joints are placed from 25 to 35 feet apart, very few cracks should be occasioned by expansion or contraction, providing the joints are properly installed and are of sufficient size to provide free movement. Where joints are not constructed normal to the surface of the pavement, the force of expansion often causes one slab to lift over the one adjacent to it. This is especially true where the joints are over 50 feet apart. Where plain felt joints are used great care must be exercised to insure that the joint is normal, as a very few degrees either way from a plane normal to the surface of the pavement is liable to result in the slabs riding one another.

When a very hot spell follows immediately after a protracted rainy season, the expansion in the pavement is greatly increased. Experiments show that the volume of concrete is influenced as much or more from its water content, as from the average temperature range. Pavement placed late in the fall and subjected to very hot weather early in the spring before the concrete has dried out probably presents the most extreme case liable to occur. The lifting of the slabs develops stresses that may cause transverse, diagonal or longitudinal cracks. In many cases the slabs are lifted clear of the subgrade for several feet back of the joint. While in this condition they are very susceptible to transverse or diagonal cracks caused by heavy traffic.

A few years ago several miles of concrete road were built with the joints at an angle of 75 degrees with the center line of the pavement. In a number of instances when the pavement expanded the slabs had a tendency to slide laterally. In some cases a movement of 2 inches was noted. Where this movement was free and unobstructed, very little cracking resulted, but where one end of the slab bound, and the other end moved, transverse cracks appeared. Where one corner bound diagonal and longitudinal cracks resulted.

Subgrade. Volumes have been written about the necessity of a smooth hard subgrade, but the writer believes that a uniform subgrade is much more essential than a hard one. Concrete roads have been laid upon new fills and upon uniformly weak foundations with very fair results. The writer does not mean to imply that every effort should not be made to secure a hard subgrade, but he believes that where such is impossible or impracticable, a uniform subgrade of more or less yielding character may successfully support a concrete pavement.

In many of the country roads the old pike is very narrow, and the old metaled surface of gravel or macadam even narrower. In constructing concrete pavements on these narrow pikes especially where it is necessary to straighten out the alignment, it is very difficult to secure a subgrade of uniform hardness. In such cases it is quite customary to provide that the entire road bed be scarified, reshaped and rolled in an effort to secure a uniform foundation. Unless some such practice is followed, some portions of the subgrade are certain to be much harder than others and longitudinal cracks are almost certain to develop. A rough subgrade retards the movement of the pavement in expansion and contraction, and may tend to develop transverse cracks.

Frost. The effect of frost action upon roads and pavements depends almost entirely upon drainage. Uniformity of drainage is as essential as uniformity of subgrade. The writer has made observations on a number of roads where the elevation of the pavement during the winter was from 1 inch to 2 inches higher than during the warm seasons. Needless to say, where the drainage was poorest, the heaving was greatest. In some cases the heaving was uniform over a distance of several hundred feet and in such cases practically no cracks appeared in the pavement.

In the design of concrete roads for country highways an earth shoulder is nearly always provided. This shoulder may be designed with ample slope to take the water away from the pavement into the ditch and thence to some outlet, yet the entire design may be upset unless the ruts in the shoulder are kept filled. For example a heavy vehicle turns out on the shoulder during a rain just preceding a freeze. Water stands in the rut and saturates a portion of the subgrade, causing excessive frost action. This nonuniform heaving and settling accounts for some of the longitudinal and diagonal cracks. It is not uncommon during the winter months to see the corner of one slab lower than the adjacent one, and the layman nearly always attributes this to settlement. In nearly every case, however, it is not settlement at all but heaving of the high slab caused by frost action.

The writer recalls one case where a road piked up about 4 feet above the surrounding country, and with apparently perfect drainage, developed a longitudinal crack several hundred feet in length, due entirely to frost action. During a late winter freshet, a small creek flooded all the land adjacent to the road. The water raised to a point about 6 inches below the pavement. One side of the fill was saturated. The other side was not subject to this saturation, as an interurban railway occupied that side of the highway and the railroad fill was as high as the pavement. This kept the water away from the pavement on that side. Shortly after the freshet there was a hard freeze. The side of the fill that was saturated, heaved and later, when the frost went out of the ground, settled. This unequal movement of the opposite sides of the pavement caused a very large longitudinal crack.

Poor Joints and Surface. Poor joints and surface cause impact from vehicles. With the heavy fast moving trucks that are common to-day, the necessity for a smooth surface should not be overlooked. A joint where the two slabs are not of exactly the same elevation causes a certain amount of impact from every load passing over the pavement. If we add to this, a soft or weak point in the subgrade, every opportunity is offered for a rupture in the pavement. The appearance of cracks in a concrete road or pavement has been advanced by some as a sign of absolute failure, but experience with this type of road is rapidly educating the public to the belief that these cracks are not serious if properly maintained. There are many who now believe that transverse cracks are no more harmful than contraction joints, and no more costly to maintain, where systematic maintenance is possible. This belief has led to the construction of monolithic pavements on many miles of road in this and other states. The fact that the cracks that usually occur in a well-constructed concrete road or pavement are not considered to seriously effect its efficiency should not, however, be interpreted to mean that we can, therefore, slight the details of design and construction for it is very probable that under those conditions the utility of the pavement would seriously suffer.

GRAVEL CONSTRUCTION IN McHENRY.

[By C. L. Tryon.]

McHenry County has about 1,006 miles of public highways. All of the main traveled roads between cities and villages have been graveled at least once, and how many more times I have been unable to learn. One highway commissioner told me that he had graveled a certain road four times during the last 24 years. This road is built through a swampy country. Another road was graveled 15 years ago and has greater traffic than the former. The only work done on this road has been to shape up the surface with a grader each spring. The natural drainage is good.

It would be of little use to know, except in a general way, just how many times the roads have been graveled, because the drainage, grading and traffic are not uniform. Each road and portion thereof is a problem in itself.

Roughly, about 85 per cent of the roads in McHenry County have a gravel-wearing surface. The grading and drainage have not been taken care of in a proper manner, and it is now difficult to correct the faults of grading because the present roadbed would be destroyed.

Gravel is plentiful and cheap, costing from 7c to 25c per load of a yard and a quarter at the pit. The pits are so located that the average haul for 75 per cent of the county is about 1½ miles; for the other portion about 2½ miles.

The usual method of construction has been to dump three loads of gravel to each two rods of road, along the center of the traveled way, then level the tops of the piles of gravel by drawing a blade grader over the road once. If possible the traffic avoids getting on the gravel until it has passed through the winter and spring rains. If the gravel contained coarse stones, part of them were thrown out at the pit and from year to year others were raked out of the road as they worked to the surface. It was believed that a profuse use of gravel, which was cheap, would take care of most of the evils of improper drainage and grading. And it did make a much better road than the natural surface and was fairly satisfactory for horse-drawn wagons for a greater portion of the year.

Since the automobile has become so generally used, we find that in dry weather the binder is blown out of the gravel and in wet weather, the gravel is thrown to the sides of the road and ruts and holes are formed, which collect water and make the road rough, and so go from bad to worse. Each spring the roads are gone over with a light grader and the gravel is pushed back into the holes and ruts. But it does not stay in place. If we attempt to run the blade of the grade low enough to cut down to the bottoms of the holes and ruts, the grader will slide over the surface and loosen the stones, intead of cutting to a smooth surface. Thus the roads are left rough and wavy.

Last fall, the highway commissioners of our richest township bought a 10-ton gas roller with an Austin Western attached scarifier, which is operated by compressed air pressure. By means of this scarifier, the top few inches of the surface is loosened so that the grader can cut to a smooth surface and then the loose material rolls down nicely. Only a few short stretches of road have as yet been repaired with this outfit, but they show excellent results. The working speed is two miles per hour. In some places it is necessary to run the scarifier over the same portion of the road twice before the surface is sufficiently loosened to grade well. The machine will not pull the grader and scarifier at the same time. I doubt the economy of using the roller for the light grading needed. One man has run the machine, however. Better results may be obtained by having one extra man to raise and lower the scarifier, as you may desire to cut deeper in some places than others. It has seven teeth and will tear up a strip about 4 feet wide. The cost of the attached scarifier was $450.

Realizing that the best part of the road metal is being removed when the cobblestones and boulders are thrown out at the pit, or raked out of the gravel on the roads, three townships now crush a portion of the gravel for their main roads. The material consolidates quickly and the wagons and autos will at once drive on the road and it soon packs down smoothly. This crushed gravel stays in place much better than pit-run material. But after a time on account of all vehicles driving in the same track, ruts are formed, and it is found that the roadway is so hard that the grader has little effect and the road must be scarified and reshaped. It costs about 35 cents per cubic yard to crush gravel, which together with a cost of 10 cents per yard for the material makes a cost of 45 cents per cubic yard on the wagons. This is the cost of about four yards of pit-run gravel, and many doubt the economy of crushing. However, the teamsters are able to haul about three more loads per day on an average haul of one mile on account of the speed of loading and saving of time from not having to pick out the stones. And, after all, it is the hauling that is the larger item of cost. The surface of the road is so much better and compacts so much more quickly that the road users are enthusiastic over the crushed gravel roads.

The State aid roads were built of crushed gravel last year. They are 10 feet wide, and the gravel was placed 12 inches thick, between 12-inch boards held in place by iron stakes. Gravel was then dragged with a spiketooth harrow. The surface packed down in a short time. The contract is not yet completed, although the roads are in use and the only objection heard is that the crown is too high. This will doubtless be remedied when the shoulders are finished. The cost, including culverts, was $6,000 per mile, which is one-half the cost of our concrete sections per mile.

TOAST TO THE NORTHEAST CONFERENCE.

[With apologies to A. D. Gash.]

I

The Northeast Conference is an amicable bunch,
  Just ordinary men of affairs.
We're not found stampeding the souphouses for lunch,
  Nor aspire we to be millionaires.

II

We are ginks who have entered the road-building game
  And found that they're major league stunts;
No tables in Trautwine could compass our aims,
  So we fashioned the said conference.

III

In north Illinois, to the right of the vane,
  Does this conf'rence of road-builders meet;
Twelve counties we are, with out problems akin,
  Better roads we must guard from defeat.

IV

Yet in these same counties, the roads are our shame,
  They're the "weighed-in-the-balances" kind,
Where tire-raveled highways disfigure the plain
  And puncture the car driver's mind.

V

Long suff'ring have been these brave stokers of gas,
  As mudholes and dust they've defied;
(They're as numerous as hoppers that live in the grass,
  And as rapidly multiplied).

VI

'Tis relief they now ask from the ruts and the jolts,
  And the pebbles that eat up their tires,
And the bumpity-bumps that loosen their bolts
  And the rubber-smeared tape from their wires.

VII

Not alone do these mahouts of buzz wagons cuss;
  But the drivers of horses and mules,
And the tossers of corn; they all make a fuss,
  They'll all swear we road builders are fools.

VIII

But roads are not builded by raising a din,
  Nor by sland'ring the road builder's "rep";
Ye who want boulevards, come across with the tin,
  Boost the road game with zeal and more pep.

IX

Oh, to ape Billy Sunday in raising the dough!
  For mud roads tax us heavier than good;
Through these channels of commerce our produce must flow,
  If we'd shackle the high cost of food.

X

Who'll chasten the knocker, and set his path right,
  And enlighten his militant wife?
No license they carry our progress to blight,
  Or to oust all the joy out o' life.

XI

Give ear, Northeast Conference; make our purposes stancher,
  Endow us with wisdom and grit,
For rural transportation'll be on the hummer
  Till our roads for all traffic are fit.

—Written and delivered by Chairman Lamb at the Hotel Sherman luncheon.

KANE COUNTY BRIDGES.

[By C. L. Hanson.]

A survey made of the roads and bridges during the season of 1916 showed that there were 1,900 bridges and culverts in Kane County on the township roads outside of the cities and villages. This gives an average of 2.3 bridges or culverts per mile of road or an opening of 10.9 feet per mile of road in the county. Of this total of 1,900 bridges and culverts, 517 are built wholly or partly of wood or steel; the balance are made of either concrete or stone, or other material of a permanent nature. Most of these 517 more or less temporary bridges must be replaced during the next few years with more permanent structures. At the present rate of building it will take 20 years or more to furnish Kane County completely with permanent bridges.

A bridge built of concrete is considered a permanent structure if properly designed and constructed. Already there are a few townships in the county in which bridge building is practically at an end because the commissioners of highways have constructed nothing but permanent bridges during the last few years. The commissioners of highways in general have cooperated with the county highway department in adopting the concrete type of bridge or culvert. Most of the plans for the larger culverts and bridges that have been built in the county during the last two years have been furnished by the highway department and the bridges have been built under the supervision of the county superintendent of highways.

In the last three years the county highway department has prepared 33 standard plans for bridges and culverts to be used in the townships and county bridge work. There have been prepared 12 standard plans for reinforced concrete box culverts ranging in span from 2 feet to 10 feet; 9 plans have been prepared for flat slab superstructures ranging in span from 12 feet to 30 feet; and 9 standard abutment plans have also been made for use with both slab and girder superstructure.

On the standard plans the width of roadway is not shown. For each different width of roadway a new bill of material must be figured, so the bill of material table is blank in a number of places. These blank spaces are filled in with a soft pencil directly on the tracing before printing, for each width of roadway as required.

To facilitate the work a quantity sheet has been worked up from which the missing dimensions and quantities for the standards can be procured. For each standard the different missing dimensions and quantities are given for a number of different widths of roadways. By the use of this sheet or table a plan can be made ready in a very short time for any standard size culvert for any width of roadway.

The county highway department standard plans are made with the idea of having the bridges in this county have somewhat of a uniform appearance. When special plans are made the rails and other parts of the bridge that are visible to the traveler are made to conform with the standard plans as nearly as can be done. On all bridges built under the supervision of the department, the railings have a pebble dash finish with the exception of the panels which are smooth. There has been no trouble encountered, where the work has been done by contract, to get the general appearance of the rails uniform; but in cases where the commissioners of highways have constructed the bridges the work has not been done very satisfactorily. There have been but very few cases in Kane County where the commissioners of highways have built their own bridges when the span required has been over 2 or 3 feet.

When the commissioners of highways of any township desire to have plans for a bridge or culvert prepared by the county highway department a meeting is usually held at the site of the proposed bridge by the commissioners and the county superintendent of highways and a bridge survey report filled out and signed. This blank report is filled out by the county superintendent of highways and signed by the commissioners. The numbers of the bridge, road and section are given on this blank so that it can be located on the map in the office and filed accordingly. This bridge survey gives all the necessary information needed in order to design a bridge for this particular site. These reports can be filed away and during the winter months the plans and special provisions be prepared so that there will be no delay in starting the construction early in the next season. It is sometimes hard to get the commissioners of highways to plan that far ahead in their bridge work.

The contracts for bridge work are let in the usual way by the highway commissioners and the contract sent to the county superintendent of highways for his approval. In Kane County there are only two or three contractors who compete in the bridge work for the townships, so that the department does not have much trouble in "breaking in" new contractors for each job. The county furnishes inspection on all bridge work for which plans have been prepared in the office of the county highway department.

In the last three years the county highway department has prepared plans and furnished supervision for the construction of a total number of 58 concrete bridges or culverts costing in the aggregate $37,000. A larger number of small concrete and vitrified pipe culverts have been constructed directly by the highway commissioners themselves.

During this three-year period the county has built one 40-foot through girder span with a 24-foot roadway between the counties of DeKalb and Kane, and repaired one 50-foot steel span bridge on the same county line. The cost of the construction and repair of these two bridges was borne jointly by the two counties. A steel beam bridge on reinforced concrete abutments was built on the McHenry-Kane County line by Kane County alone. This particular bridge was constructed over a drainage ditch through which a dredge will have to be run in a few years. The bridge was built in a location where it was not deemed justifiable in spending money for a permanent structure.

Under State and county supervision the township of Aurora built a bridge across the Fox River at Montgomery during the year 1914 at a cost of about $13,000. This bridge has a total length of 308 feet with four 65-foot arches and has a roadway of 25 feet.

The State Highway Department has constructed a number of small culverts on the State aid roads of Kane County during the last two years, but only one of any size has been built and that is a 40-foot deck girder with a 24-foot roadway. On the State aid road north of St. Charles the State is now constructing a 50-foot deck girder bridge.

At the present time plans are being drawn and estimates made for over $40,000 worth of concrete bridge work for the coming year. One of these proposed bridges is to be built across the Fox river at Dundee, Illinois. This plan calls for a bridge 240 feet long, four 55-foot deck girder spans, and with a 60-foot roadway. These plans are completed and have been sent to the State Highway Department for approval.

From the outlook at the present time there will be plenty of bridges to construct in Kane County for a number of years to come. Not only will new bridges have to be built, but there will also have to be much work done on widening present bridges and culverts to take care of the increasing traffic on our roads.

BRIDGE FOUNDATIONS.

[By A. R. Carter.]

It is not the intent of this paper to go into the different classes of foundations for bridge work nor into the design of footings, but rather into the construction of the same. Realizing that in the construction of reinforced concrete bridges, the part of the work that generally gives us the most difficulty is the placing of concrete footings when there is water present, it became necessary to devise a system of drainage to be installed in the bottom of the excavation to take care of the water in order that the same would not be forced up through the fresh concrete carrying away with it a large amount of cement.

During the season of 1916 it became necessary to rebuild one of the abutments to the Roscoe River bridge in Roscoe Township, Winnebago County. This bridge consists of two main river spans of wrought iron, and a pony steel truss at either end. The abutment on the west end of the bridge was badly cracked. The mortar was practically all out of the joints and one wing was cracked completely away from the abutment, and there was great danger of the same overturning. In fact, the top of the wing was out about 8 inches beyond the face of the abutment.

It was originally planned to rebuild one wing of reinforced concrete, and point up the abutment and other wing, but, after the beginning of the work, it was found that the abutment and other wing were in poor condition, due to the fact that they were constructed with thin facing stone and backed up with loose rubble, so a new design was made for a complete new abutment and wing.

The total height of the bridge from bottom of the footings to the top of the finished roadway was about 20 feet. This necessitated a width of footings under the wing which were designed as cantilevers of 8 feet, and the width of the abutment footings was also made the same.

The excavation was carried through a sandy loam soil until within about 5 feet of the bottom of the footing. This latter 5 feet consisted of coarse clean gravel, ranging from pea gravel to about 1¼ inches in diameter with very little sand present. From the time gravel was encountered, water began to flow in very freely. At first the water was kept down sufficiently by the use of a diaphragm pump to enable the men to excavate and get the cribbing in place.

As soon as this was accomplished, a pump pit was dug at the end of the wing which was the width of the footing and about 5 feet long. This pit was excavated about 18 inches below the remainder of the footing and then a 4-inch by 3-inch submerged centrifugal pump was installed, as shown in the accompanying photograph. This pump was operated by a 7 horsepower gasoline engine. As soon as the pump was put into operation, the excavation was carried down rapidly. The pump pit was kept at all times from 1 foot to 18 inches below the remainder of the excavation. The cribbing, which consisted of 3-inch T. P. plank with 4-inch by 4-inch T. P. posts and braces, was worked down with little difficulty as the excavation progressed.

After the excavation was completed to the desired depth and all piling had been driven it became necessary to devise some means of carrying the water to the pump pit while the process of concreting was taking place.

It was finally decided to construct a drainage system of 1-inch boards. These drains were made of various widths ranging from 4 inches wide to 3 inches high inside to about 8 inches wide and 3 inches high inside. Then several holes were cut inside of these boxes and small laterals were connected up to the main boxes. Then in turn, small holes were cut in these laterals and in the main drains, and gravel stones varying from 1¼ inches to 2½ inches were placed around the holes to prevent the concrete from flowing into the drains.

As practically all of this water came from the bottom, it became necessary to cover the entire bottom of the footing with a good grade of tarred building felt just preceding the placing of the concrete. The plan of the footings called for a depth of 2 feet of concrete with reinforcing bars placed horizontally 6 inches from the bottom.

In order to get sufficient concrete over the drainage boxes, the top of the footings were raised 3 inches above that shown on the plans, making a total thickness of footing of 27 inches. Concreting was then commenced at the end opposite the pumping pit and a 9-inch layer was carried over the entire length, approximately 60 feet at one operation. Then the horizontal and vertical steel was placed and a second layer of 15-inch thickness was carried through when the second set of horizontal bars were placed, and then the remaining 3 inches of concreting was completed.

This system worked out very successfully, and after placing the first 9 inches of concrete over the entire footing, at no place was there any indication of water coming up through the concrete. The tarred felt forced all water into the drainage system, and when the first layer was in place, the boxes were running full of water. The pump was operated continuously from the time the concreting was begun until completed. When it was shut down the water was allowed to raise up over the concrete.

The writer supervised the placing of several bridge footings similar to the above during the season of 1916 with equally good results, and I am positively convinced that there is no necessity whatever of placing concrete in bridge footings in water or allowing water to come up through the concrete, washing a large per cent of the cement out of the aggregate.

Care must be exercised in this class of construction that the width of the footings is not reduced to such an extent by the drainage system as to increase a bearing on the soil beyond the allowable loads. It may become necessary to increase the width of footings to obtain the required area of soil footing.

During the excavation, it became necessary to shut down the centrifugal pump for a moment while the same was being lowered, and to prevent the water from rising too rapidly, a small diaphragm pump was started.

The value of good equipment was fully demonstrated in this work, not only as a paying investment to the contractor, but from the standpoint of the excellent results obtained in placing concrete in bridge footings.

SOUTHERN CONFERENCE HELD.

Ten county highway superintendents of Division No. 7 assembled at Mt. Vernon on Thursday, March 22, in the first superintendents' conference of the year for that district.

The division contains twenty counties. Railroad facilites are such however, compared with those of other parts of the State, that the representation of ten county highway officials was regarded as good. Division Engineer J. E. Huber of Mt. Vernon cooperated in the meeting which was held in the Jefferson County courthouse.

An informal program was followed during the morning and afternoon though the meeting, more than anything else, was a round table discussion of problems which the superintendents of southern Illinois face.

The superintendents posted themselves upon many features of road construction and administration, and imparted among themselves the results of their work in the far down-state section. In addition to Division Engineer Huber, Road Engineer H. E. Bilger of the State Highway Department was present and took an active part in the discussions. Earl B. Searcy, department editor, also attended the meeting. The next conference will be held at Fairfield, in Wayne County, on June 6. It is planned to have a special program at that time.

Those present at Mt. Vernon included G. H. Brown of White County, president of the conference; Gregg Garrison of Hamilton County, secretary; W. T. S. Hopkins, Pope; James F. Howenstein, Union; Griff Koontz, Wayne; W. N. Mayers, Pulaski; Tony C. Pitchford, Jefferson; C. C. Rice, Edwards; John H. Sharp, Johnson; John P. Upchurch, Saline.

Members of the conference voiced their desire to have representation upon the new board of highway advisors, with five members, which will cooperate as an advisory adjunct to the officials of the new Public Works Department after July 1, who will administer highway affairs in Illinois. President Brown of the conference was strongly recommended for one of the five places. The members of this board will serve without pay.

ILLINOIS · HIGHWAYS

[Printed by authority of the State of Illinois.]

OFFICIAL PUBLICATION OF THE

STATE HIGHWAY DEPARTMENT

| VOL. IV | SPRINGFIELD, ILLINOIS, MAY-JUNE, 1917 | Nos. 5-6 |

Most of this road consists of 5 to 6½ per cent grades Baffle walk protection for gutters.

STATE AID ROADS IN HENRY COUNTY
Concrete.

A modern country home. It graces the only comparatively level spot in this 3½-mile
stretch of scenic highway.

Virtues of the Single Commissioner Plan of Township Highway Administration

By FRANK T. SHEETS, *Assistant Maintenance Engineer*

For years Illinois has been spending about $7,000,000 annually for township roads and bridges. A survey of past experience with the old three-commissioner plan of township highway administration reveals irrefutably the fact that the results obtained in road and bridge work have not been commensurate with the money expended. This, in most instances, has not been caused by dishonest or corrupt road officials or by a desire on the part of these men to neglect their duties. The cause for the past failures is that the system is fundamentally unsound.

The law provides that, when there are three township commissioners, their salary shall be $2 per 'day for every day they are employed on road work. It is obvious that no successful farmer or business man can afford to neglect his business to direct road work for that insignificant sum. Again it is true that most of our commissioners are farmers. When it is a good time to work the roads, it is a good time to farm and as a result the farming is done and the roads suffer. Yet it is the successful farmer or business man that must be used as a commissioner if the old three-commissioner plan is to be bearable. So often we see an incompetent individual placed in the office merely because he needs the money. If a man can't handle his own private affairs with success, he certainly should not be placed in a position to handle public business and public funds.

Much dissatisfaction has arisen in the past on account of the fact that under the three-commissioner plan, no one is personally responsible for road conditions. The blame for mistakes or neglect has been readily shifted from one to the other. Oftentimes the efforts of the progressive member have been squelched by the conservative or incompetent element. Chaotic conditions have been the result.

The experience of business corporations the world over has been that economical and satisfactory results can be obtained only by having one executive in direct charge of work upon whom all responsibility is centered. There may be advisory committees galore, but one trained competent man should be placed in direct charge of the specific piece of work. The Legislature comprehended the fact that the same principles which govern private business should also be applied in public affairs when in 1913 they passed the law which enables a township to adopt the single commissioner system of road administration.

The single commissioner system has many good features. In the first place the compensation provided in the law is sufficient to enable a competent man to be secured. The position of highway commissioner is then his business and not a side line. All his time can be spent on road work and thus the work is done at the right time.

The single commissioner can keep in touch with the highway developments of the day, learn new methods and become thoroughly familiar with current highway engineering practice. He can become skilled in the operation of various kinds of road machinery and so avoid the "hit or miss" methods which have been in vogue.

Furthermore, the single commissioner is wholly responsible to the taxpayers for results. If work is neglected or improperly done the responsibility can not be evaded.

Township business may be greatly expedited under this system. Instead of waiting until a meeting of three commissioners can be held to settle certain trivial details of the work, the single commissioner makes the decision and settles the matter forthwith. Much of the expense, which now occurs for holding meetings to settle such affairs, may be eliminated. In the case of business requiring an official meeting for its transaction much more prompt action can be obtained as only the town clerk and the commissioner are required.

The large saving to the township will come, however, in the increased efficiency in the handling of work, and the same expenditure of funds will produce far greater results.

Since the new law was passed, many townships throughout the State have taken advantage of their opportunity to adopt the single commissioner system. The results which have been obtained are most gratifying. Road and bridge work has proceeded more satisfactorily, better business methods have been adopted, and the public confidence won. In only a few cases has there been any dissatisfaction where the new plan was tried. An investigation of these show that the cause was in the voters' choice of a man for the job and not in the system itself. The most striking evidence in favor of this single commissioner plan is that practically all townships which have tried it are satisfied, and refuse to turn back.

[EDITOR's NOTE.—Many inquiries come to the department for information and opinions relative to the growing problem of township road law administration. In view of this fact, Mr. Sheets has written the foregoing article which we publish as an able and concise appeal for greater efficiency in the township—this efficiency to be gained through the adoption of the single, concentrated, one-commissioner plan.]

STATE BREVITIES.

The big Vermilion bridge, built in 1914, on a State aid road near La Salle, is cited by Bridge Engineer Clifford Older of the State Highway Department as an example of the utility of reinforced concrete in a special article contributed by Mr. Older to the February number of *Concrete Highway Magazine*. Plans for the structure were prepared by the department. The bridge has an 18-foot roadway and consists of four reinforced concrete through girder approach spans and one 224-foot steel channel span with a 4-inch reinforced concrete subfloor.

* * *

R. A. Culligan, of Tremont, Ill., has been given the contract to build bridge No. 13 in Stockland Township, Iroquois County. The contract price is $2.054. The bridge will be 40 feet long, will have an 18-foot roadway and will be of reinforced concrete.

* * *

The firm of Donica & Ault, of Tuscola, has been awarded a contract to build a 100-foot bridge on the line between Piatt and Douglas Counties for $1,949.

SALVAGING A CONCRETE BRIDGE

By L. P. SCOTT, *Maintenance Engineer*, Division No. 1

On one of the State aid routes in Boone County, Illinois, is a reinforced concrete girder bridge consisting of two 30-foot spans. The bridge was built by the townships with plans prepared by the State Highway Department. Although piles were recommended by the highway department, the local officials in building the bridge omitted them thinking the foundation material sufficiently good to justify their omission. Some months later the State took this bridge over for maintenance in connection with the building of the State aid road, having first been assured by the local officials that the foundation material upon which pier and abutments rested was good blue clay.

In the spring of 1916 during extreme high water the center pier was undermined allowing pier and superstructure to settle as is shown in the accompanying illustra-

View of bridge after settlement.

tion. The maximum settlement was 21 inches, on the down-stream side. The settlement caused several cracks in the girders, extending in a diagonal direction from the top to the floor. These cracks were similar to the well-known shear cracks in a failing concrete beam.

A careful examination of the superstructure indicated that the same might be salvaged by jacking it up, removing the old pier, and replacing it by a new one supported on concrete piles cast in place in the blue clay. Accordingly plans were prepared and a contract for the repair was let.

The first problem in the construction was to eliminate the water from the hole scoured out beneath the bridge. Lack of clearance and the depth of the water under the

General view of job.

bridge made a cofferdam impracticable and as a substitute an earth dam was thrown up entirely across the stream above the bridge and this tapped by a wooden flume to carry the ordinary stream flow to a point below

the bridge. A 4-inch centrifugal pump was then installed to pump out the pond. This arrangement proved very satisfactory, the only inconvenience experienced being due to an occasional overflow, in which case the work was delayed until the stream flow had subsided to the capacity of the flume and the pond could be pumped out.

Upon first removing the water it was discovered that the old pier footing was loose from the main body of the

Method of filling the form.

pier for two-thirds of its length from the lower end, was broken, and had settled to one side. Instead of blue clay, as was anticipated, gravel and sand was found for a depth of two feet below the old foundation. Casting concrete piles in place was therefore abandoned.

With the idea of securing adequate support for the new pier and for the jacks, as well, six concrete pedestals 3 by 3 by 6 feet deep were cast, three on each side and as close to the old pier as possible. The four corner pedestals were placed directly under the girders, and upon these were arranged sills, posts, caps, and jacks. The superstructure weighing some 22 tons to the corner

Finished pier. False work still supporting superstucture.

was then slowly lifted to a few inches above its original position. The old pier was utilized to block from while rearranging the jacks and building falsework.

The only false work used was eight green oak posts 10 inches in diameter and cut to a length that would extend from sills on the outside edge of the aforesaid pedestals to a 6 by 16 inch cap extending from one girder to the other. The inside half of the pedestals

(Concluded on Page 57.)

ANSWERING THE WAR CALL

It seems more than likely that some of the highway department men will be among those who carry the stars and stripes in battle line to France.

At the time of writing, we haven't witnessed the possible inroads from conscription. As we peruse the list, nevertheless, our attention is fastened upon the names of men of the department whom we well know, who are serving in Uncle Sam's army, who are in training at Fort Sheridan and elsewhere; others who have qualified as eligible for training and still others who are anxious—and who intend if possible—to go.

Department men didn't exactly go ramping to the recruiting stations and, to the last man, beg enlistment. We don't ordinarily do things here by the "ramps" method. Yet, when men enough to compose 20 per cent of the total number of department employees are moved to enter service, qualify for it, or express their immediate desire to be in it—when one-fifth of us do this upon our own spontaneous initiation, we don't feel as if we had missed a stampede very far.

Briefly, the State Highway Department—exclusive of service the draft may impose upon our members—has made this showing:

Six men are in service or training; 11 have qualified for training; 13 have applied, but have received no notification; 3, at least, expect to try for commissions. This makes a total of 33 men. The total number of department employees, including the men in the field is about 150.

The date of writing is May 24. We can not presage the future, therefore must confine our statements to conditions as they are.

Reiterating to a limited degree, let us recall that Gene Hopkins, the department property clerk, is a regular army man, serving somewhere in Illinois with his command, Company C, Fifth Infantry, Illinois National Guard. Hopkins' command has been Federalized, which makes him and his compatriots liable for service anywhere in the world. Office Engineer Arthur W. Consoer and Junior Engineer Vincent Flanagan, of the bridge department, are in training at Fort Sheridan, trying for commissions as first and second lieutenants, respectively. Road Engineer H. E. Bilger has received a commission as captain in the Engineers' Reserve Corps, but has not yet been summoned; and Earl B. Searcy, the department editor, qualified for the officers' reserve training, but was not called for the first encampment at Fort Sheridan because of crowded conditions. That suffices for the immediate office force. When conscription gets in its work, the showing may be greatly amplified, for all of these named, except Mr. Bilger, and, of course, Sergeant Hopkins, are liable under the draft act.

ILLINOIS HIGHWAYS has compiled a census of "war candidates" from among the employees in the various engineering divisions. Letters from the division engineers show the following status:

First—Men who have qualified for commissions in the Engineers' Officers' Reserve Corps are Division Engineer H. B. Bushnell, Junior Engineers Lloyd Schwartz, C. J. Johnson, J. H. Long, H. C. Peterson, R. E. Thomas. One or two others were to make application.

Second—Junior Engineers M. M. Small and J. R. Burner have made application for appointment to the Engineers' Officers' Reserve Corps.

Third—No enlistments, but A. K. Fogg, located at Bloomington, expects to take the examination for assistant civil engineer in the U. S. Navy.

Fourth—Don M. Forester, with a commission as second lieutenant in the Engineers' Officers' Reserve Corps, reported for duty at Fort Logan H. Roots, Arkansas, on May 8. Engineers of the division who are eligible under the conscription act and who will register on June 5, are P. F. Jervis, F. C. Feutz, H. B. Sennott, George H. Baker, Harold Andrew, G. A. Somerville, Oscar E. Silbermann, C. H. Apple and R. L. Stover.

Fifth—Junior Engineer C. S. McArdle, candidate for first lieutenant's commission, is in training at Fort Sheridan. Applications for admission to training have been made by Assistant Engineer K. N. Evans and Junior Engineers George Shopmeyer and Kirk McFarland.

Sixth—Junior Engineer J. V. Curnutte left May 14, for training at Fort Benjamin Harrison, Indiana. Junior engineers have made application for admission to the Engineers' Officers' Reserve Corps as follows: C. I. Buggraf, B. C. McCurdy, S. F. Wilson, T. L. Flatt and Lisle Hunt.

Seventh—E. A. Kane, H. A. Sawyer and G. J. Cornett have passed the examination for commissions with the Engineers' Officers' Reserve Corps; and Division Engineer J. E. Huber, T. E. Fieweger and Carl R. French have applied for commissions. R. P. Devine, who left the service of the department a few weeks ago, also has made application.

Nathan T. Ashkins, until a year ago a junior engineer in the road department, was served with instructions the middle of May to be prepared to sail in early June with Canadian troops for France. Mr. Ashkins, who the last year has traveled, with headquarters in Louisville, Ky., owes Canadian allegiance, hence the source of his orders.

There is not a man among these named, or others whom conscription may usher under arms, who would willingly rend the flesh of a brother with bayonet or bullet; yet, we venture the assertion, there's not a man in the entire department who would hesitate, should the common cause of liberty require, to take up both bayonet and the smaller death-dealing implements, if need be, to aid and abet the confronting national duty.

The present war, to the sorrow of the world, computes its combatants and its dead and wounded in seven and eight figures; not in five or six. The few whom this department may sacrifice won't merit any vast identity so far as numbers go; yet, the credit for a just cause won will be theirs the same as any one's else.

Our "boys" understand — from fundamentals learned in Illinois road work—that a "relocation" of a Teutonic enemy's governmental aims and policies must come. The opposing force has traveled the "highway" of military absolutism too long. We hope, with our governmental leaders at Washington, that "bridging" of the chasm which separates world war from a world peace will not involve a "span" of fighting, cruel bloodshed and suffering of great length; but, on the other hand, that the right, as we interpret it, shall soon prevail.

Bituminous Surfaces for Highway Bridge Floors

By B. H. PIEPMEIER, Maintenance Engineer,
Illinois State Highway Department

The constant reflooring of old steel highway bridges is one of the greatest maintenance expenses connected with highway work.

There are numerous steel bridges in use on which it is necessary to maintain wood floors primarily on account of the light flimsy structures that have been built. The modern highway bridge is designed to carry a heavy floor and one that will withstand ordinary traffic for a number of years. The typical plank floor of the old steel bridge, however, is subject to decay, which requires it to be replaced about every five years and when it is subjected to heavy traffic it is necessary to replace it every one to three years on account of wear.

On account of the poor quality of present bridge timber together with its advance in price, engineers have been led to devise some form of light and yet durable reflooring material. Creosoted bridge plank have proven

Fig. I. Showing bituminous mixture as it is placed on old bridge floor. Mixture should cover entire floor to prevent decay of lumber.

very economical on isolated bridges where traffic was light and did not wear out the flooring. The creosoting prevented decay and therefore permitted such floors to remain in use a great many years. The wear, however, is the most serious on the average highway bridge floor, hence, some form of treatment seemed necessary to prevent excessive wear.

In Illinois a number of old bridge floors have been replaced with creosoted subplank and then surface treated with a bituminous material in connection with stone chips or torpedo gravel. The bituminous mixture was maintained so as to resist the wear of traffic. It has been found that such bituminous surfaces can be maintained at less expense than the continual repairs and renewals that are necessary where the ordinary plank flooring is used.

The expense connected with securing creosoted bridge plank together with the delays and inconvenience of applying the usual bituminous wearing surface, discouraged the average road official in placing such floors on the numerous short spans that are scattered in all parts of his district.

In view of this condition, it seemed necessary to develop some method of treatment that would preserve the ordinary plank flooring and at the same time relieve it from excessive wear. The writer, therefore, made several investigations with different materials and mixtures with an idea of finding a product that was low in

first cost and could be used by the average road official with little trouble.

The material that has proven most successful is a mixture of stone chips (three-fourths of an inch down to dust, with the dust removed) and an emulsified asphalt that could be readily mixed with the aggregate without either being heated.

The advantages of the emulsified asphalt are that it can be used cold, can be thinned with water, can be used on a wet day, and will permit thorough cleaning of plank with water prior to its application. The use of such a bituminous product insures a thorough coating of the aggregate and at the same time will not permit a surplus of the material that might cause creeping, bleeding a leakage through small cracks that may exist in the sub-flooring. The dense mixture of stone chips and sand that becomes thoroughly coated with a film of asphalt readily packs under traffic and forms a mat that resists in a measure the wear of traffic. It also waterproofs the surface so that when properly maintained will ordinarily prevent the untreated floor from decay until the old bridge will be replaced with a more permanent structure.

Bridge floors should have a crown of from 2 to 4 inches, the plank fitted as close together as possible and all cracks filled with wood strips prior to the application of the bituminous mixture. The plank should be thoroughly cleaned with water, after which the mixture should be evenly spread over the entire surface to a thickness of 1 to 1½ inches. The surface should then be sanded lightly and then tamped or rolled. Where tamping or rolling is not convenient the surface should be carefully watched during the first few days to see that it is not displaced by traffic. It is not necessary to close the bridge from traffic while the mixture is being applied or during the time it is setting.

The bituminous mixture should be made up by mixing about 1 gallon of emulsified asphalt with 1 cubic

Fig. II. After a few months' use. The material, when properly applied, irons out perfectly smooth and can be maintained by surface treatments the same as an ordinary bituminous road.

foot of aggregate. The bituminous compound should be thoroughly stirred and in some cases a slight amount of water added to make it liquid before it is mixed with the aggregate. The materials may be mixed by machine or by hand until all stones are thoroughly coated before being applied on the floor.

(Concluded on Page 57.)

LEE COUNTY AND HER PIONEER TRAILS

By L. B. NEIGHBOUR, County Highway Superintendent.

All Illinois could not furnish a locality with more interesting and historic trails than those of Lee County. They were surveyed, or gained recognition by travel, three-quarters of a century ago. Gone now are the first settlers, who made and used them. It is a question whether among their descendants there are still numbered any whose memory goes back to the day of the ox-hauled "prairie schooner," and of the "flying stage coach," that required "only 48 hours" for the trip from Dixon on east across the prairies to Chicago, or south to Peoria.

Along the same "cattering" lines first followed, or moved in a later day to the section lines nearest and most nearly parallel, these roads are many of them serving the needs of the public to-day. Others, though are little more than a map. Here a diagonal road showing on the map; further on another running in the same general course, indicates a line of old-time travel. Along it the pioneer galloped his riding pony or guided his ox-team. These roads led from one settlement or settler's cabin to the next, or to the mill, to the lead mines, or to the market.

Natural conditions determined the location both of the settler's cabin and his trail. He established his home in some grove. He built his mill where there was water power. The trails were the connecting arteries. But these had also to be adapted to the lay of the land. Particularly they had to intersect the sloughs and streams at the shallowest and firmest bottoms for fording.

What were the conditions of Lee County in a state of nature? The white man found the land within our present borders to consist principally of two valleys. One was that of Rock River, carrying to the Father of Waters through the northwesterly part of the county, and draining about one-fourth its area. The remaining three-fourths was for the most part the drainage basin of the great "Inlet" and "Winnebago" swamps—the region which now, since it has been drained into a continuous channel, we are coming to designate as the "Green River" country.

At the coming of the settler, this vast expanse of swamp was thought of only as a hunting ground. It was the home and breeding place of wild fowl to an extent almost beyond present-day conception.

The stream of civilization had scarcely more than well started in this direction, when came that thrilling chapter of Illinois history, made by the "Bandits of the Prairie." This chain of houes thieves, horse thieves, highway robbers and murderers upon occasion, lived and operated along the great swamp, all the way from the Mississippi River and up to the headwaters of our low country. No need to go into history here, save to say that their exploits were in many cases identified with the early Lee County trails. And their haunts and burial places are yet pointed out along these highways.

Except for Rock River and its slopes, Lee County at that time lay a vast shallow lake, green in the summer, spreading out townships in extent, with a fringe of upland prairie, freely dotted with groves. In Lee County this low country took somewhat the shape of

a dumbbell. Near the center, the borders of the swamp approached each other. The water narrowed to a running stream, and the bottom was more or less rock and gravel. In the stretch of many miles across the State this neck was almost the only part of the swamp at which travel could make a crossing. The easterly limit was "Inlet" and the westerly limit, so far as used for crossing at any rate, was in the Welty and Brewster neighborhood, some fifteen miles down stream. All through this stretch of country the land was wooded down to the stream's edge. It was somewhere within this fifteen miles that all travel between the Rock River country and that south and east of the swamps must pass.

Already—this was in the 30's—trade centers had sprung up in the north end of the State and were creating important cross-country commerce. To the east lay Chicago, terminus of lake navigation, an outfitting point for the great west country. To the northwest, on the Mississippi, Galena was turning out lead for the needs of civilization. A hundred miles south from Lee County, at the upper end of effective navigation on the Illinois, stood Peoria, then an active trade competitor of Chicago; and still farther up the river, and bidding for trade, was Peru. Chicago, Peru and Peoria all sought lines of travel to Galena.

"Inlet" being the farthest east that the Green River country could be crossed, became the objective point from Chicago, and grew into a well-known settlement on the Chicago-Galena route.

The Welty crossing, almost due north from Peoria, determined the direction of the trail from that point to Rock River. These two main routes, heading for Galena, intersected at the land of Rock River.

Here Father Dixon, then living in Peoria, and carrying the mails between Peoria and Galena, induced the half-breed Ogee to establish a ferry, later to be taken over by Father Dixon himself, and to become known as Dixon's Ferry, and ultimately as Dixon.

Thence on, Dixon is to be thought of not as a mere ferrying point, but as a center of importance, as regards both trade and early history.

We have named some principal objective points. There were other and smaller centers which also must be considered. Up Rock River half a dozen miles, at the "Grand Detour" there had been a French trading post before Father Dixon arrived here. The name "Grand Detour" remains and shows its French origin. The post was near the river, on the farm now owned by Gene Harrington. Down the river, at its mouth, were Davenport and Rock Island.

Minor settlements lying outside our present boundaries were Buffalo Grove (now Polo), Oregon City, Hickory Grove (afterwards Lane Station, and now Rochelle) Shabbona's Grove, Ottawa, Mendota, Princeton and Sterling. The three towns last named were not, I think, so early centers as the others.

Within the county were Gap Grove, and Sugar Grove, of Palmyra; Franklin Grove, of China; Brush Grove, at the north border of Reynolds; Allen's, Smith's and Twin Groves, of Willow Creek; Paw Paw and Four-Mile Groves, of Wyoming; the Malugins, Big and Little, of Brooklyn and Viola; Inlet Grove, of Lee Center; Knox Grove, of southeast Sublette; Perkins Grove, on the boundary of Sublette and over in Bureau; East Grove, from which the present East Grove Township takes its name; "Dad Joe's" Grove, on the hill just over into Bureau County; and Palestine Grove, skirting Green River from the Welty crossing all the way up to Amboy.

From its strategic position at the ferry, Dixon came naturally to be the intersecting point of all the principal trails. To the north ran the Galena trail, with the branch at Drew's Corners, leading to Sterling, and the Woosung road, leading to Polo. The Pine Creek road came later.

To the northeast, on the south side of the river, are the Grand DeTour and Daysville roads. To the east, the Franklin Grove road. To the southeast, the Inlet and Chicago road, and the Peru road, this latter closely following, and often using the old Illinois Central grade. To the south, the Peoria road, by the way of the Welty crossing, the corduroy toll road, and Dad Joe's tavern; also later, the Pump Factory road to Ohio and Princeton. To the southwest, the Rock Island road, laid out in the 40's as a State road. It was to "start at a point on the north boundary of the public square, in Rock Island and to end at the Pecatonica." It passes through Rock Falls and Grand DeTour, as well as Dixon.

Of these many trails, the "Chicago," the "Peru" and the "Peoria" converging at Dixon, and becoming the "Galena" trail, were of the greatest importance. Abram Ackert, Esq., of Dixon, tells of picking up mineral near Woosung that had evidently been dropped from old freighters, long ago carrying ore from the Galena mines to the smelting works at Peru.

Along all the trails, besides the post stations, there were roadside taverns. But out of Dixon, toward Galena the first regular stop of the stage was at Buffalo Grove, or Polo. On the Peoria road the first was at Dad Joe's house. On the Peru road, the first was at Rocky Ford. On the Chicago road, the first was at Inlet.

At Rocky Ford, where the Peru road crosses Green River, ran on intersecting east and west trail from Prophetstown to Inlet. Main Street, Amboy, and the high road thence down to Binghampton, perpetuates this trail, which now at least, ends at Lee Center. For this village, after the days of the banditti, took on the importance held before that by the hamlet of Inlet, and largely robbed it of its population.

From Lee Center there runs an old trail southerly through the town of Sublette to LaMoille. Also from LaMoille a road runs northeasterly to Knox Grove. It crosses the Illinois Central north of Henkel Station by the high bridge, and is locally known as the "old Chicago road."

Also from Lee Center there ran an important trail a little west of north. Two or three miles out it forked. The easterly fork ran up to Franklin Grove. The westerly bore up to Grand DeTour, with its famous plow shops, passing through the Stiles and Harrington farms, and near the site of the old French trading post already mentioned.

Leaving Franklin Grove off a mile to its west, and traveled to this day from the Mong schoolhouse to the county line, there was a trail leading nearly due north from the Inlet country to bitter old time rival of Dixon's Ferry, then rather ambitiously known as Oregon City.

The old Emmert (later Schulz) Flouring Mill on Franklin Creek, in Nachusa Township, was also reached by trails from all four directions.

In the northeast corner of the county, up out of Alto and Reynolds towns, run old trails, converging at Rochelle.

Through eastern Sublette and Lee Center towns are old trails, with a general course north of west, from Mendota to the Inlet. They are largely fenced off the original lines now, however, and no longer the thoroughfares they once were.

From Malugin, on the Chicago road, there was a trail heading northeasterly into the "Little Malugin" country.

The principal trail center yet demanding notice is Paw Paw. It is on the famous old Chicago stage road, the third stop out from Dixon. To the southwest there ran an old diagonal trail to Princeton, now locally known as the Mendota road. North ran the trail to Smith's Grove, the Willow Creek country, and Rochelle. While to the south and southeast are the roads to South Paw Paw and Ottawa.

Study any map of the county, and the roads that you see following diagonal or crooked lines may safely be assumed to be trails of long ago.

With the coming of the railroads, in the 50's and the consequent establishment of new trading centers; with the fencing in of the farms and removal of the roads to the section lines; and with the carrying through of that most important measure that ever marked the history of Lee County—I refer to the drainage of the Swamps—have come vastly different road locations.

The operations of the new road law also gives us new main arteries of travel. These are doubtless to be the great roads of the future. Hereafter it is with them that we must deal.

But the old "diagonal" road has a place in history, along with the pioneer. We can not lose our interest in either of them, nor scarcely think of one apart from the other.

On the eve of an opening, mighty era of road improvement, it seems only fitting that we take this backward look over the "Trails" which brought us hither.

In closing this article, the writer begs to acknowledge the debt he owes a good friend, Frank E. Stevens, in his excellent "History of Lee County," for no little of the historical data herein contained.

WAR AID PLEDGED.

The American Association of State Highway Officials has tendered its services to the Secretary of War, and on March 22 the executive committee of the Association met with Colonel Winslow at the War Department and worked out a plan by which the association can serve the War Department by furnishing engineers, making available road machinery, and cooperating in the construction of roads that will be of strategic value as military roads.

At the same meeting, the executive committee decided to hold the 1917 meeting of the association at Richmond, Virginia, December 4 to 7. Invitations for this meeting were received from the following cities: Chicago, Ill.; Grand Rapids, Mich.; Toledo, Ohio; Buffalo, N. Y.; New York City, N. Y.; New Haven, Conn.; Asbury Park, N. J.; Washington, D. C.; Richmond, Va.; Norfolk, Va.; Raleigh, N. C.; Pinehurst, N. C.; and Jacksonville, Florida.

ILLINOIS HIGHWAYS.

Published Monthly by the
State Highway Department,
Springfield, Illinois.

P5304—7,500M ◄━━━11

ILLINOIS HIGHWAY COMMISSION.
A. D. GASH, *President.*
S. E. BRADT, *Secretary.*
JAMES P. WILSON.

WM. W. MARR, *Chief State Highway Engineer.*

BUREAU OF ROADS.
H. E. BILGER, *Road Engineer.*
M. W. WATSON, *Assistant Road Engineer.*
C. M. HATHAWAY, *Office Engineer.*

BUREAU OF BRIDGES.
CLIFFORD OLDER, *Bridge Engineer.*
G. F. BURCH, *Assistant Bridge Engineer.*
A. W. CONSOER, *Office Engineer.*

BUREAU OF MAINTENANCE.
B. H. PIEPMEIER, *Maintenance Engineer.*
F. T. SHEETS, *Assistant Maintenance Engineer.*

BUREAU OF TESTS.
F. L. ROMAN, *Testing Engineer.*
F. L. SPERRY, *Assistant Testing Engineer.*
W. C. ADAMS, *Chemist.*

BUREAU OF AUDITS.
J. M. McCOY, *Chief Clerk.*
EARL B. SEARCY, *Department Editor.*
R. R. McLEOD, *General Bookkeeper.*
G. E. HOPKINS, *Property Clerk.*

DIVISION ENGINEERS.
R. L. Bell, Buchanan-Link Bldg., Paris, Ill.
H. B. Bushnell, 138 Fox St., Aurora, Ill.
J. E. Huber, Wise Building, Mt. Vernon, Ill.
A. H. Hunter, 302 Apollo Theater Bldg., Peoria, Ill.
C. M. Slaymaker, 510 Metropolitan Bldg., E. St. Louis, Ill.
H. E. Surman, 614 People's Bank Bldg., Moline, Ill.
Fred Tarrant, 730 Reisch Bldg., Springfield, Ill.

Address all communications in regard to "Illinois Highways," to Earl B. Searcy, Department Editor, State Highway Department, Springfield, Illinois.

CONTENTS.

WE THANK YOU!

We are human, the same as anyone else.

When our readers praise us, we smile. Satisfaction overspreads our countenance. When other folks like the things we do, we are pleased. We feel, naturally, that some one has appreciated our effort to perform our duty, fulfill our mission.

A few weeks ago, when the editor of ILLINOIS HIGHWAYS was receiving hundreds of cards and letters telling of the wishes of the senders to remain on our revised mailing list, some of the readers made the best of an opportunity to inscribe opinions and sentiments, without any sort of invitation. Noting that the number was growing appreciable the editor, human like, culled out these expressions of spontaneity and saved them. They range from monosyllables to sentences.

We are herewith producing some of them. If you are not interested in knowing what others think of us, dear reader, let this introduction serve you as a time-saver. If you'll bear with us in our vanity this time, however, we'll let you read them.

Going right down through the stack of cards, we find the following said in appreciation of ILLINOIS HIGHWAYS and of the courtesy of this department in sending it to readers gratis:

"I get much good from it."

"Your's for success."

"Many thanks for the past."

"Thanks."

"Thank you."

"Am very much interested in ILLINOIS HIGHWAYS."

"Thanks for mailing it thus far."

"Thanks in advance."

"I appreciate your courtesy and enjoy your magazine."

"Anxious to have it."

"I have complete file and use it for reference."

"It is the best little booster for good roads that comes to me."

"Thanks."

"Thank you."

"You have a very useful magazine."

"Thank you kindly."

"Thank you."

———

A good roads association was formed recently at Cramer, Peoria County. Officers elected are as follows: President, James Wasson; secretary, Thomas Higgs; committee, Ed Smith, Ollie Wasson and Mr. Gillard, all of the Elmwood Township; Ed Kessler and Lewis Switzer of Cramer; O. P. Rice and William Lane of the Brunswick Township.

———

Thurston County, Washington, is the first county in that state to receive Federal aid in hard surfacing its county roads. The county will receive $28,000 and is now completing surveys for 4 miles of concrete pavement 20 feet wide.

———

The M. & P. Contract Company was awarded the contract recently to build the Warner bridge on the Will and Kankakee County line. The contracting firm is of Hatfield, Ind. The contract price is $47,569.

———

Daniel Alford, of Cuba, Ill., has been awarded contracts to build a county aid bridge (Fulton County) over Put Creek, in Cass Township, cost $1,237, and a bridge near Geeseman, cost $910.

Big Mileage for Fifth Division This Year

The fifth engineering division this year may witness the completion of more than 130 miles of State aid road. Part of this work is unfinished from 1916; part of it new.

Division Engineer Fred Tarrant, who is in charge of the territory, a short time ago furnished ILLINOIS HIGHWAYS a report on work in his district as it stood March 1. The division is made up of 16 counties in the central and western part of the State. In every one of them, State aid work is being done.

The synopsis of work from the division follows:

County.	Section.	Route.	Type.	Mileage.	Cont— Estimate.	Remarks.
Adams......	C	5	15" W. B. mac.	2.36	$35,004 20	
Brown......	E		Bridge	......	3,008 58	
Cass........	C	5	Resurfacing Bit. mac....	1.32	3,165 00	1916 contract.
Cass........	D	7	Resurfacing Bit. mac....	1.04	2,011 00	1916 contract.
Cass........	F	3	10" and 15" mon. brick.	0.29	4,858 60	
Cass........	G	7	10" bit. mac...	0.66	6,715 00	
Cass........	H	3	10" concrete.	0.19	1,711 76	
Christian ...	A	9	Oiled earth...	1.98	8,154 00	80% completed. 1916 contract.
Christian ...	B	15	Oiled earth...	4.32	8,076 00	1916 contract.
Christian ..	C	12	Oiled earth...	5.52	1,865 91	Extension 90%
					8,104 00	1916 contract.
Christian ...	D	9	Oiled earth...	1.23	1,951 29	Extension 90%
					5,090 00	
Christian ...	E	15	Oiled earth...	1.04	4,538 00	
Christian ...	F	12&23	Oiled earth...	1.39	4,541 00	
Christian ...	G	20	Oiled earth...	1.21	4,869 70	
Christian ...	H	3	Oiled earth...	1.61	4,974 50	
DeWitt......	A	1	Earth........	3.81	7,568 40	
DeWitt......	B	1	Earth........	1.80	3,420 00	
DeWitt......	C	2	Earth........	1.39	2,654 00	
DeWitt......	D	7	Earth........	4.74	8,156 34	
DeWitt......	E	9	Earth........	4.38	8,080 34	
Hancock....	A	1	Earth........	1.70	4,131 00	1916 contract.
					680 38	Extension 96%.
Hancock....	B	4	Earth........	2.60	3,848 73	1916 contract.
					906 88	Extension 90%.
Hancock....	C	9	Earth........	2.42	2,376 00	1916 contract.
					2,191 33	Extension 99%.
Hancock....	D	14	Earth........	3.22	2,776 00	1916 contract.
					1,781 51	Extension 96%.
Hancock....	E	1	Earth........	1.33	4,674 00	
Hancock....	F	1	Earth........	1.95	3,066 08	
Hancock....	G	9	Earth........	2.56	4,486 00	
Hancock....	H	14	Earth........	2.79	4,309 08	
Logan.......	E	3	15" gravel....	1.83	8,073 00	
Logan.......	G	13	15" gravel....	1.85	8,008 00	
Logan.......	G	11	15" gravel....	1.76	8,143 12	
Logan.......	H	7	15" gravel....	1.87	8,199 00	
Logan.......	I	3	15" gravel....	1.71	8,086 00	
Logan.......	J	5	15" gravel resurface..	0.80	1,983 00	
Macon......	A	1	Oiled earth...	12.71	31,251 00	1916 contract.
					1,815 15	Extension 80%.
Macon......	B	12	Oiled earth...	18.75	25,816 00	
Mason.......	A	1	Oiled earth...	6.61	10,160 00	1916 contract.
					5,308 32	Change 70%.
Menard ...	C	2	15" concrete..	0.26	6,330 78	
Menard ...	D	6	15" concrete..	0.46	7,008 60	
Morgan....	B	11	Oiled earth...	7.49	18,053 43	1916 contract.
					3,058 43	Extension 85%.
Morgan....	C	7	Oiled earth...	6.69	14,737 00	
Piatt........	C	1	10" mon. brick	1.15	13,953 68	
Pike........	B	4	15" W. B. mac.	1.38	16,559 00	1916 contract 9%.
Pike........	H	4	15" W. B. mac.	1.09	17,388 44	1916 contract 30%.
Sangamon..	I	2	15" resurface concrete....	1.54	1,795 88	
Sangamon..	M	5	15" resurface bit. mac....	0.83	1,394 00	
Schuyler....	D	1	10" concrete..	0.38	4,327 96	
Schuyler....	E	2	10" concrete..	0.28	4,481 32	
Shelby......	E	5	Earth........	2.06	3,553 00	
Shelby......	F	1	Earth........	2.48	3,553 00	
Shelby......	G	15	Earth........	2.76	4,013 00	
Shelby......	H	11	Earth........	2.16	4,651 00	
Total mileage				130.2	$406,008 99	

Totals.

Type.	Mileage.	Estimate.
Brick	1.44	$ 18,792 25
Concrete	1.57	33,935 42
Bit. Macadam......................	0.68	6,715 00
W. B. Macadam.....................	4.83	58,951 64
Gravel	8.52	40,503 12
Oiled Earth	63.50	161,537 26
Earth	44.14	82,266 81

Resurfacing Work.

Concrete	1.54	$1,795 88
Bit. Macadam........................	3.19	6,570 00
W. B. Macadam.....................	0.80	1,983 00

Bridge Work.

Brown	1	$3,008 58

SALVAGING A CONCRETE BRIDGE.

(Concluded from Page 51.)

was then utilized as bearing for the jacks while transfering the load from the pier to the false work.

After the jacks had been removed the old pier was destroyed with dynamite. Holes were drilled through the bridge floor and into the pier by means of a steam drill. The holes averaged about 2 feet in depth and were loaded with from one-half to one stick of 40 per cent dynamite. This loading proved to be just about right as no damage was done to the false work and the concrete was shattered just enough to make it easily handled. The shattered concrete was removed and later used for riprap.

The new pier was built upon a reinforced concrete footing cast entirely over the old footing and the inside half of the concrete pedestals. The reinforced footing was designed to transfer the entire load to the six pedestals. The concrete for the pier proper was mixed upon the bridge and poured directly from the mixer over the rail into the form where it was shoveled and pushed back until flush with the top. Cast iron rockers and plates under each girder were installed with the placing of the last concrete.

It is interesting to note that the cracks in the girders due to the settlement of the bridge closed almost entirely when the superstructure was brought back to its original position. A feature of the repair was the fact that traffic over the bridge was never delayed for more than five minutes at any one time.

BITUMINOUS SURFACES FOR HIGHWAY BRIDGE FLOORS.

(Concluded from Page 53.)

Under ordinary conditions, such treatment can be applied at a cost of 25 to 30c per square yard, including labor and materials, but excluding the bridge timbers. This is about one-half the cost of the mastic surfaces that have been applied where it was necessary to heat the bituminous material and build up a wearing surface by successive layers of bituminous material and stone chips or torpedo gravel, and about one-fourth as much as renewing the bridge floor with ordinary hardwood lumber. So it is readily seen that such treatment may be used to a great advantage in highway bridge work as it will reduce the maintenance cost and at the same time make old structures much more serviceable. The reduction of impact, caused by the smooth surface, compensates for the slight additional dead load.

The above experiment and investigation has been carried out for the State Highway Department, with the consent and authorization of William W. Marr, Chief State Highway Engineer.—From January 11, 1917, issue of *Engineering News*.

FEMININE ROAD BUILDERS!

Our faithful stenographic staff. Chief State Highway Engineer Marr was induced to leave his busy office long enough to face the camera, flanked about by the girls who write the Department's letters. Left to right—Erma Black, Nell L. Keeler, Cleta L. Abbott (back), Sara Schwartz, Mrs. Margaret M. Vernor, Katherine F. Mahoney, Mr. Marr, Mrs. Margaret Dawes, Lulu Flure, Esther G. Broverman, Anna Hartter, Marie Purcell. Bonnie Grace Neher, bridge department typist, was on her vacation, hence was not in the picture.

IROQUOIS REPORT IS MADE.

The annual report of Highway Superintendent Benjamin Jordan of Iroquois County, submitted late in February to the supervisors of his county, tells briefly of the work in 1916, and hints also at some of the contract troubles which were faced in that section of the State.

Mr. Jordan, in his report, states 13 county aid bridges, and 5 township bridges were constructed in the course of the year. A fraction over 101 miles of road were oiled once, and 37½ miles were oiled twice, 354,307 gallons having been used. With reference to the letting of contracts, County Superintendent Jordan says:

"Last summer bridge contracts were hard to dispose of. On August 21, we advertised for bids on six county aid and two township bridges. No bids were received for four of the county aid jobs, and only one each for the township bridges. After readvertising, on September 4, we managed to let contracts for three of the jobs by begging some local concrete men to take them at their own figures, which were considerably higher than the estimates. The fourth one we had to let go over until next year, and, after advertising the third time we succeeded in letting it along with three new county aid bridges on the eighth of February, this year."

In Stockland Township, the people voted bonds aggregating $50,000 for the building of 6.4 miles of brick roads. Over two miles had been completed at the close of the year.

Four townships in Whiteside County this year will spend nearly $70,000 for the building of hard roads. Jordan Township will spend $20,000, Genesee over $25,000, Sterling $15,000 and Erie $7,500.

CORN BELT ROUTE ORGANIZED.

Announcement has been made of the partial organization of the Illinois Corn Belt Association which plans to extend a trail, well improved, from Effner, Iroquois County, on the eastern Illinois line, through Peoria and to Burlington, Iowa—almost a straight line across the corn belt of north central Illinois.

ILLINOIS HIGHWAYS was in receipt a short time ago of information relative to this new trail from Secretary-treasurer G. R. Curtiss of El Paso. The organization meeting of the Peoria-Chenoa division was held in El Paso on February 6, at which time officers were elected as follows:

President—A. B. Hurd, El Paso; secretary-treasurer, G. R. Curtiss, El Paso; supervisor Peoria-Chenoa division—L. J. Schultze, Chenoa.

Directors—George Alfs, Peoria; J. E. Millard, East Peoria; Paul R. Goddard, Washington; Benjamin Kaufman, Cruger; Frank B. Stumpf, Eureka; H. R. Brown, Secor; J. F. Schofield, El Paso; Mark Fruin, Enright; Ward Hiserodt, Gridley; J. H. Andrews, Meadows; Victor F. Nicol, Chenoa.

By-laws were adopted at this meeting. The official marker will be a yellow ear of corn against a white background. The route will pass over designated State aid roads so far as possible and will connect with many prominent trails. The Peoria-Burlington division was organized in March.

A bill has been introduced in the Wyoming legislature providing for a State Highway Department. The primary object in introducing this bill is to place Wyoming in a position to benefit under the distribution of funds for roads, authorized by the Federal Aid Act.

KEEP YOUR ORIGINAL BRIDGE CONSTRUCTION RECORDS.

The Bureau of Bridges is frequently called upon to undertake the investigation of old steel bridges to determine their serviceability under present day traffic requirements, or their suitability for a heavier loading than they are carrying at the present time.

In making such investigations, it is always desirable to have at hand the original shop drawings from which the structure was fabricated and erected, but it is very seldom that these drawings are available. Even in the case of large bridges, such as those spanning the Illinois River, it is almost always impossible to obtain a copy of the original plans and a record of the construction operations.

Recently while preparing plans for the reconstruction of a large bridge, information was desired by the Bureau of Bridges concerning the elevation of the bottom of footings of the stone masonry piers. No information on this point was available, and it was necessary to drill holes down through the centers of the stone piers to secure the necessary information. The cost of the drilling operations amounted to over $300.

In the investigation of old metal bridges it is necessary to know whether the material used in fabrication was strucurtal steel or weaker wrought iron, the use of which for bridge work was discontinued about 1890. It is practically impossible to determine the character of the metal by a superficial examination, and it sometimes becomes necessary to cut out a test piece of metal from the bridge in question, and to have tests made to determine the character of the material at considerable expense.

These are but two of many examples that could be cited to illustrate the inconvenience and needless expenses which frequently result from the lack of bridge construction records.

The importance of keeping an accurate and complete record of all bridge construction work can not be over-emphasized, and this matter is worthy of painstaking attention by all highway officials in charge of bridge work. The records filed for possible future reference should be records of the actual construction operations. For example, if piles were used in the foundation, the number, size and penetration of the piles used should be indicated. The record blue prints should show any changes from the original plans, such as modifications of the foundation plans, particularly changes in the elevations of the bottom of footings. It is desirable, also, to incorporate in the records infomation concerning the character of the subsoil underlying the foundations.

The importance of such construction records in the case of bridges which are well designed for what appears to be a conservative estimate of future loadings and are properly constructed under competent supervision may not be obvious. It is not likely that the loadings assumed in the design of reinforced concrete bridges under the specifications of the State Highway Department will be realized for many years to come, and yet, special conditions involving unusual traffic requirements may arise, which will make a good set of construction records of great value. For example, it is entirely possible that some of the highway bridges, adjacent to cities, may at some future time be used to carry a street car loading.

Recently the Bureau of Bridges received a request for the investigation of a steel bridge. The highway commissioners were contemplating granting a franchise to a certain manufacturing company to lay tracks and operate an industrial railway over the bridge, and wished to know whether the bridge could be used with safety for the traffic imposed by the heavily loaded trains of cars.

The time and labor involved in securing adequate construction records is negligible, when compared to the value such records may possess at some time in the future. In the case of bridges built after plans and specifications prepared by the Illinois State Highway Department, in addition to keeping records of the construction in their own files, county superintendents of highways should submit information regarding alterations and additions to the original plans to the Bureau of Bridges, in order that the records on file there may be an exact construction record of the bridge as actually built.

WATSON GOES TO KANSAS.

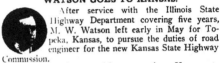

After service with the Illinois State Highway Department covering five years, M. W. Watson left early in May for Topeka, Kansas, to pursue the duties of road engineer for the new Kansas State Highway Commission.

Mr. Watson's removal is a promotion. He came to this department May 31, 1912. During the last two years, he had been assistant road engineer. Prior to that time, he had served in an engineer's capacity.

Before coming to Illinois, Mr. Watson had been in the employment of the United States Engineers, War Department, in Ohio River improvement, working out of Louisville, Ky. He had assisted also in various engineering projects in Ohio, West Virginia and Kentucky.

Mr. Watson's resignation was effective May 7, last. He was one of the valued bureau chief assistants, and his removal to Kansas carries with it the belief on the part of his friends that the recently created Kansas commission, in Mr. Watson, has annexed a capable man and one who will measure up to requirements. His elevation came by virtue of appointment.

C. M. Hathaway, office engineer in the road department, is performing the duties of assistant road engineer, succeeding Mr. Watson; and J. W. Harris, chief draftsman, is filling the position of office engineer.

Organization of the Peoria, Pekin, Havana and Jacksonville trail took place recently in a meeting at Havana. It was voted to leave the selection of the official colors to the State Highway Commission.

The officers elected were as follows:

President, L. R. Craig, Jacksonville; vice president, Louis Heckman, Manito; secretary-treasurer, to be selected by Havana Commercial Association; directors, Pekin, Walter Conover; Manito, E. E. Ethel; Forest City, J. J. Gilmore; Bath, Mr. Travis; Chandlerville, Dr. Franklin; Virginia, M. C. Petfish; Literberry, S. H. Crum.

The directors for Peoria, Havana and Jacksonville to be selected by the Commercial organizations of their respective cities.

The Vincennes Bridge Company was awarded the contract to build the Handly bridge, one mile west of Oliver, Edgar County, a short time ago, for the contract price of $5,609.

A STATEMENT.

(Compiled by State Highway Department.)

TOTAL ILLINOIS STATE AID MILAGE AWARDED FROM JULY 1, 1914, TO JANUARY 1, 1917, INCLUDING EXTENSIONS.

Type.	Length. Feet.	Miles.	Per cent completed.
Brick	311,005	58.90	88
Concrete	860,089	162.91	94
Bit. Concrete	7,981	1.51	5
Bit. Macadam	63,392	12.00	82
W. B. Macadam	70,218	13.30	73
Gravel	129,542	24.53	82
Oiled Earth	653,360	123.74	46
Plain Earth	399,257	75.61	82
Bit. Mac. Resurfacing	31,501	5.96	84
Total	2,526,345	478.46	

SUMMARY OF STATE AID BRIDGES AWARDED, EXCLUSIVE OF BRIDGES CONTAINED IN STATE AID ROAD CONTRACTS PREVIOUS TO JANUARY 1, 1917.

County.	Number of bridges.	Total. cost.
Clinton	2	$ 5,261 16
Cumberland	53	9,872 94
Franklin	6	1,366 00
Fulton	10	17,372 62
Gallatin	11	4,466 00
Greene	5	5,645 10
Hamilton	16	8,267 35
Hardin	2	2,262 80
Jasper	29	6,705 00
Jersey	10	4,421 00
Johnson	7	2,516 78
Kane	1	2,749 07
Knox	3	4,071 75
McDonough	26	20,466 44
Macoupin	15	21,985 85
Marion	2	6,666 50
Marshall	18	6,077 53
Massac	5	3,069 85
Menard	1	805 00
Mercer	10	21,224 53
Montgomery	25	9,978 61
Perry	2	4,882 50
Pope	27	4,549 12
Pulaski	5	2,956 96
Putnam	19	8,590 00
Randolph	4	4,925 15
Richland	3	2,943 00
Saline	2	1,785 25
Schuyler	1	1,269 20
Scott	2	4,626 07
Shelby	32	9,820 70
Stark	23	12,326 00
Stephenson	4	2,128 80
Tazewell	6	2,489 00
Vermilion	1	11,804 00
Washington	6	3,194 00
Wayne	10	7,739 83
Williamson	3	740 00
Woodford	7	1,520 00
Total	414	$253,541 46

Percentage of work completed equals 94.5 per cent.

New Contracts Awarded.

(State Aid.)

County.	Sec.	Route.	Type.	Contractor.	Amount.
FEBRUARY 28, 1917.					
McDonough	F	1	Earth	D. E. Shively, Cerro Gordo	$ 2,513 22
McDonough	G	2	Earth	D. E. Shively	2,297 83
McDonough	H	4A-4	Earth	D. E. Shively	2,182 68
McDonough	I	5	Earth	D. E. Shively	2,054 45

NEW CONTRACTS AWARDED—Concluded.

County.	Sec.	Route.	Type.	Contractor.	Amount.
MARCH 28, 1917.					
Bureau	I	3A and 3	Concrete	Trompeter & Sons, Peru.	8,567 79
Cass	F	3	Brick	J. G. Pratt, Virginia	4,135 00
Cass	E	2	Concrete	J. G. Pratt, Virginia	1,154 00
Champaign	E	2	Brick	} C. A. Michael, Mattoon.	36,900 00
Champaign	G	4	Brick		
Champaign	J	6	Brick		
Hancock	F	1	Earth	A. O. McCoy, Versailles.	4,673 00
Hancock	F	4	Earth	J. W. McConnell, Carthage	3,346 76
Hancock	G	9	Earth	A. O. McCoy, Versailles.	4,495 06
Hancock	H	14	Earth	J. W. McConnell, Carthage	3,704 53
Jo Daviess	F	1	Concrete	} R. F. Conlon. Cuba City.	8,691 00
Jo Daviess	E	1	Concrete		
McLean	A	15-16	Earth		
McLean	B	7	Earth	Cameron, Joyce & Co., Keokuk, Iowa.	36,800 00
McLean	C	7	Earth		
Marion	E	2	Earth	G. K. Carver, Mt. Vernon.	5,170 32
Marion	F	2	Earth	G. K. Carver, Mt. Vernon.	4,674 72
Menard	D	6	Concrete	E. E. Brass, Petersburg.	4,890 05
Monroe	B	1	Concrete	H. H. Hall Construction Co., Murphy Bldg. E. St. Louis.	3,844 48
Moultrie	C	2	Concrete	Mink & Sizemore, Paris.	8,112 98
Moultrie	D	5	Concrete	Mink & Sizemore	6,974 16
St. Clair	E	10	Waterbound macadam resurfacing	C. H. Degenhardt, Alton.	19,976 00
Washington	B	1	Earth	White & Braley, Litchfield	7,358 84
Winnebago	D	11	Waterbound macadam	Fred K. Carrice, Rockford	2,386 80
Winnebago	E	6	Concrete	Hart & Page, Rockford	21,358 15
APRIL 11, 1917.					
Christian	D	9	Oiled earth		
Christian	E	15	Oiled earth	} Buis & Olson. St. Joseph. Mo.	22,113 00
Christian	F	12-23	Oiled earth		
Christian	G	20	Oiled earth		
Christian	H	7	Oiled earth		
Coles	C	N	Brick	A. C. Loomis Co., Mattoon	15,256 04
DeWitt	A	1	Earth		
DeWitt	B	6	Earth	W. C. Meneely. Frankfort, Ind.	26,250 00
DeWitt	C	2-11	Earth		
DeWitt	D	7	Earth		
DeWitt	E	9	Earth		
Edwards	C	5	Brick	J. C. Carlyle, Albion	2,602 03
Fulton	F	20	Bridges	Illinois Steel Bridge Co., Jacksonville	14,675 00
Kendall	B	1	Concrete	J. Hinden & Son, Pana	13,906 36
Kendall	C	1	Concrete	J. Hinden & Son, Pana	4,330 01
Lee	C	5	Bituminous macadam resurfacing	Duffy & Hubbard, Dixon.	9,985 49
Lee	E	5A	Gravel	H. P. Johnson, Sterling.	7,297 16
McDonough	J	1	Earth		
McDonough	K	2	Earth	} Buis & Olson, St. Joseph. Mo.	11,890 00
McDonough	M	8	Earth		
Massac	A	4	Earth	Arch Shelton, Metropolis.	1,301 00
Monroe	D	1	Waterbound macadam	H. C. Wolf, Waterloo.	2,465 00
Morgan	C	7	Oiled earth	Cocking Cement Co. Jacksonville	14,121 11
Rock Island	D	3	Concrete	S. D. Hicks, Construction Co., Moline	9,289 03
Sangamon	L	2	Concrete resurfacing and repairing	John E. Bretz, Springfield	1,444 40
Sangamon	M	5	Bituminous macadam surface treatment and resurfacing.	H. Nelch & Son, Springfield	1,398 22
Schuyler	D	1	Concrete	Beardstown Concrete Construct'n Co., Beardstown	3,217 87
Schuyler	E	2	Concrete	Beardstown Concrete Construct'n Co., Beardstown	3,471 48
Union	E	7	Earth	Howenstein Bros. Anna.	2,594 33
Whiteside	F	1	Gravel	N. B. Ridge, Sterling	12,039 60
Whiteside	G	3	Gravel	N. B. Ridge, Sterling	12,950 17
MAY 2, 1917.					
Lake	C	6	Concrete	C. P. Moran, Waukegan	21,459 72
Tazewell	H	2	Concrete	Smith Bros', Concrete Co., Washington	5,325 89
MAY 9, 1917.					
Adams	C	5	Waterbound macadam	Cameron, Joyce & Co., Keokuk, Iowa	34,494 00
Bond	D	2	Brick	Van Deusen & Baumberger, Greenville	7,553 15
Clinton	F	4	Concrete	Weber & Williams Construction Co., 6349 Washington ave., St. Louis.Mo.	3,219 18
Fulton	I	1	Concrete	Public Service Construction Co., Omaha, Nebr.	6,531 60
Effingham	E	1	Concrete	A. C. Loomis, Mattoon	5,600 00
Macon	C	10	Oiled earth	Wm. Amman, Decatur	10,322 35
Wayne	C	3-4-5 9A-12	Bridges	Vincennes Bridge Co., Vincennes, Ind.	5,374 00
Wayne	D	1-16-18	Bridges	M. Frazier, Louisville	4,374 00

' (Spec. D).

NOTE.—Where states are not given contracting firms are of Illinois cities.

IN AND OUT OF THE STATE

Highway Superintendent J. A. Decker, of Cumberland County, makes special mention, in a recent issue of *The Toledo Democrat*, of the enterprise of Highway Commissioner Z. S. Haskett, of Neoga Township. The one-commissioner plan obtains there and Haskett is demonstrating its superiority over the three-commissioners system. In Mr. Haskett's township are 114 miles of highway, 72 of which were carefully graded last season. The cost was $1,132.56, or an average outlay of $15.73 per mile. Much work was done also on bridges.

* * *

New State Highway Commissions have been organized in Missouri and South Carolina. The Texas legisalture recently passed a bill creating a State Highway Department.

An administration bill, providing for the raising of $15,000,000 in five years through the levy of a 1 mill tax, has been passed and signed by the governor in New Jersey. The money is to be raised for road improvement. The State Highway Department also is reorganized.

* * *

A plan is being evolved for marking the trail of the old circuit traveled by Abraham Lincoln in Illinois when he was a practicing lawyer. The movement is under the auspices of the Illinois Daughters of the American Revolution. It is estimated $10,000 will be required to perform the task. Lincoln's travel lay among the counties of what was the old eighth judicial circuit. He resided in Springfield and rode horseback through the counties of the circuit, including Sangamon, Christian, Morgan, Menard, Mason, Tazewell, McLean, Macon, Champaign, Vermilion, Coles, Douglas, Moultrie, Shelby, Woodford, Macoupin and Peoria.

* * *

County highway superintendents of the third engineering division met February 26 in Peoria. All but two of the eleven superintendents of the district were present. A. B. Hurd of El Paso, Woodford County, was elected secretary of the conference for the coming year, and R. W. Osborn of Pontiac, Livingston County, was elected director. Division Engineer A. H. Hunter was present and took part in the program which was said to have been among the best in the history of the organization. Sessions were held in the courthouse.

* * *

Highway Superintendent G. H. Brown, of White County, has called our attention to a statement in a recently contributed article, which ran, as published, thus: "The allotments (referring to automobile license fee allotments for State aid roads in Illinois) are proportioned to the counties in the same ratio as the road and bridge tax bears to the total road and bridge tax of the State, provided that in the case of a county in which more than 40 per cent of the total amount appropriated by the General Assembly for building roads is collected, including any amount collected for automobiles or kindred licenses, there shall be alloted to that county only 25 per cent."

Mr. Brown suggests that, in order to make it clear, there should have been added to the last line the words, "of the amount so collected in such county."

This situation, of course, applies to Cook County, which does pay into the State treasury about 43 per cent of all automobile license fees collected. Mr. Brown is correct. Assuming that in the State $1,000,000 is paid in auto license fees, and Cook County pays 43 per cent of that amount, Cook would receive back as an allotment not one-fourth of the entire amount, $250,000, but one-fourth of her per cent of fees, or only about $107,500. Mr. Brown aptly adds:

"Get the Illinois farmer to see that 75 per cent of the automobile tax collected in Cook County is spent on roads outside of Cook County, and you will make boosters of many who now are knockers."

To our mind, the last thing in the world the Illinois farmer could object to is the share which Cook County pays of road building funds. It might be further enlightening to say that, under the $60,000,000 State road bond issue plan, with automobile license fees paying the total bill, Cook County will pay a proportionately large part of the total sum which is intended for the improvement of 4,000 miles of highways.

* * *

The Illinois Supreme Court, in a decision handed down last December, reverses a former decision and in so doing decides that it is the duty of drainage commissioners to restore highways after the commissioners have found it necessary to cut ditches across natural watercourses. This settles the question of who shall rebuild bridges over dredge ditches which cross public highways. A clause of the law which placed the responsibility upon highway officials was found by the court to be unconstitutional.

AUTOISTS OF STATE ORGANIZE.

At the most representative gathering of delegates from motor clubs, good roads and trails associations ever assembled in Illinois, the "Illinois State Auto and Good Roads Association" was formed at a meeting in Springfield on March 7.

The objects of the new organization were defined in the by-laws in the following words:

To promote and maintain a State organization of motor clubs and trail associations; to advocate reasonable and non-discriminating regulations of the use of motor vehicles; to encourage construction and maintenance of permanent roads and improvements of all highways; to protect the motorists against unjust legislation; to encourage a fraternal feeling among all who ride in autos with due regard to the safety of all others using public highways.

The association early in its meeting endorsed the proposed $60,000,000 bond issue project. Officers were named to direct the work of the new State body as follows:

President, Clarence J. Root, Springfield; vice president, George Alfs, Peoria; treasurer, Henry Paulman, Chicago; directors, one year, Dr. I. A. Lumpken, Mattoon; J. W. Grapes, Bloomington; two years, M. K. Guyton, Aurora; Thomas Sudduth, Springfield; and L. H. Bissell, Effingham. The secretary is to be employed.

The single highway commissioner plan was adopted in the February eltction by voters in Victoria and Galesburg Townships, Knox County.

FEDERAL AID FOR THIS YEAR.

A statement of Federal aid apportionments among the various states, as appropriated by Congress, doubtless will be of interest to readers.

The following table gives the appropriations which will be available during the present fiscal year, ending June 30, 1917. In order to avail itself of this government money, any state must vote to expend a corresponding amount. The State Highway Department then submits plans for such roads to the Secretary of Agriculture for his approval. The Federal cooperation includes in its plan supervision of roads by the highway department of a state which adopts the system.

The amount allotted to each state this year is as follows:

Alabama	$104,148 90
Arizona	65,513 52
Arkansas	82,689 10
California	151,063 92
Colorado	83,690 14
Connecticut	31,090 44
Delaware	8,184 37
Florida	55,976 27
Georgia	134,329 48
Idaho	60,463 50
Illinois	220,926 23
Indiana	135,747 62
Iowa	146,175 60
Kansas	143,207 40
Kentucky	97,471 91
Louisiana	67,474 66
Maine	48,451 50
Maryland	44,047 22
Massachusetts	73,850 95
Michigan	145,783 72
Minnesota	142,394 06
Mississippi	88,905 84
Missouri	169,720 41
Montana	98,287 19
Nebraska	106,770 81
Nevada	64,398 30
New Hampshire	20,996 62
New Jersey	59,212 68
New Mexico	78,737 81
New York	250,720 27
North Carolina	114,381 92
North Dakota	76,143 06
Ohio	186,905 42
Oklahoma	115,139 00
Oregon	78,687 37
Pennsylvania	230,644 17
Rhode Island	11,665 71
South Carolina	71,807 64
South Dakota	80,946 02
Tennessee	114,153 48
Texas	291,927 81
Utah	56,950 15
Vermont	22,844 47
Virginia	99,660 71
Washington	71,884 28
West Virginia	53,270 46
Wisconsin	128,361 07
Wyoming	61,196 82

CLUBS AND THEIR WORK.

A good roads and community club has been formed by the citizens of Forrest City. Organization of this new body took place in the interests of the P. P. H. & J. trail (Peoria to Jacksonville) and business men and farmers generally are interested in it. Officers elected were: W. R. Barnes, president; H. A. Keefer, vice president; John Pemberton, secretary; P. S. Ingersoll, treasurer.

* * *

The Danvers Good Roads club has been organized. Several trails lead through the Danvers district. One of the club's purposes will be to see that a long mileage of oil is put down. Officers of the club were elected as follows: Philip Ehrman, president; Dr. Ziegler, vice president; H. L. Stuckey, secretary-treasurer; J. W. Habecker, William Berman, F. A. Vance, J. W. Thrush, Walter Resser and Cory Yoder, directors.

* * *

The Mason County Good Roads association, in a recent meeting, elected officers for the coming year. Those named were: President, Dr. E. J. List, Havana; vice president, Adolph Schill, Havana; secretary, J. H. Heberling, Mason City; treasurer, W. E. Ainsworth, Mason City; directors, John M. Henninger, Havana; D. K. Behrends, Quiver; Frank Martin, Bath; Harry Blessmann, Lynchburg; John Prief, Kilbourne; H. J. Lewis, Crane Creek; Charles Shipp, Sherman; John Gilmore, Forest City; John Gay, Manito; C. C. Patterson, Jr., Salt Creek; L. W. Cross, Mason City; H. D. Fink, Pennsylvania; Isaac Reed, Allen's Grove. One director was elected from each township in the county.

* * *

A "safety first" sign suggestion. Photo taken on an Illinois road.

The Booster club of Versailles, Ill., has begun a good roads campaign which promises results. It is proposed to put a banquet at stake, those making the poorest showing in the improvement of roads leading into Versailles, to pay the cost. Two inspections of the road, one before work is begun and another in September, after the work is finished, will be a part of the program.

Members of the Washington Township Good Roads association, Tazewell County, reorganized their association recently and in so doing elected the following officers to serve during the coming year: President, Jos. Morris; vice president, John White; treasurer, Geo. M. Stimson; secretary, Clayton Roehm. The association will make active efforts in the future to bring about better road conditions in and near Washington Township.

The Sterling Association of Commerce has given its approval of the proposed $60,000,000 State bond issue for roads. Governor Lowden was formally notified of the Association's action.

APRIL REPORT, BUREAU OF BRIDGES.

During April, 1917, plans, estimates and specifications for 1 steel bridge and 15 concrete bridges were prepared and sent out to county superintendents of highways. The total estimated cost of these bridges is $21,430.

Plans, estimates and specifications for two sections of State aid bridge work, including 1 steel bridge and 8 concrete bridges, were prepared, the total estimated cost of which is $16,970.

Plans and estimates for 10 bridges and culverts to be built in connection with State aid road work were completed. The total estimated cost of this work equals $15,020.

Summing up, plans were prepared for 35 bridges and culverts, the total estimated cost of which equals $53,420.

In addition to the plans for drainage structures on State aid road contracts prepared by the Bureau of Bridges, plans for 157 such bridges and culverts were prepared in the division offices. The total estimated cost of this work amounts to $18,612.

During the month 18 bridge plans prepared by county superintendents of highways were checked and approved, and 3 sets of shop drawings for steel bridges were checked and approved. The designs of 7 existing bridges were investigated and reported on.

According to reports received, contracts were awarded on plans prepared for county superintendents of highways for 48 concrete bridges and 4 steel bridges at an average cost of 98.1 per cent of the estimates. The total estimated cost of this work amounts to $60,985.

Contracts were awarded on alternative plans for 4 bridges at a total cost of $7,400.

Contracts were awarded by the State Highway Commission for 4 sections of State aid bridge work, including 1 steel bridge and 11 concrete bridges at an average cost of 99.4 per cent of the estimates. The total estimated cost was $23,988.40.

On May 1, there were on hand ready for work 17 bridge inspection reports. All other requests for the preparation of bridge plans had been complied with.— Complied by A. W. Consoer, *Office Engineer.*

"INDIAN HEAD TRAIL" FORMED.

A marked and well-improved highway through Illinois, Wisconsin and Minnesota is now in the making—the "Indian Head Trail." This organization is backed by commercial clubs of all the towns through which is passes. The present southern terminal is Peoria, Illinois, and it extends through from Princeton, Sterling, northwest to Savanna, thence north through Winona to Minneapolis.

Officers of the association are nonsalaried and are located at Savanna, Illinois. For the purpose of carrying on the work of the association the officers are asking that each locality be represented by a commercial club and if the cities are without such an organization, urge the immediate organization of such a club to carry on the work. As a result commercial clubs have been organized in the cities of Princeton, Walnut, Rock Falls, Milledgeville, Chadwick, Shannon, Lanark, Hanover and Galena in Illinois; Hazel Green, Cuba City, Platteville, Lancaster and Prairie du Chien in Wisconsin, and in Sabula, Miles and Preston, in Iowa.

Cities located on this trail as well as farming communities are notified that it is not merely a marked highway that this association is seeking but an improved highway for interstate automobile travel as well as local travel and as a result of these demands upon communities, the following improvements have been authorized in Illinois:

One mile of brick road in Sterling Township, Whiteside County, costing $10,000;

One and one-half miles of gravel road in Harmon Township, Lee County, costing $6,000;

One mile of concrete road in Coloma Township, Whiteside County, costing $8,500;

Two miles of concrete road in Carroll County, costing $16,000;

One mile of gravel road in Mt. Carroll Township, Carroll County donated by public subscription and built last fall, costing $5,000;

Six hundred days of labor donated by residents of Hanover, in Jo Daviess County;

Cash subscriptions given by the business men of Galena, $5,000.

The Savanna chamber of commerce inaugurated a movement asking the board of supervisors of Carroll County to pass a resolution to investigate the best method of improving all of the roads of Carroll County and in this resolution requested the Carroll County supervisors to investigate thoroughly the plan of first grading and draining all of the roads of Carroll County and building of bridges and culverts after which the county could take up the subject of permanent roads. The Indian Head Trail Association everywhere is advocating that the permanent part of the highway is the foundation. The commercial clubs of Sterling, Illinois, in Whiteside County, and of Galena, in Jo Daviess County, have also endorsed this plan of road building.

Improvements authorized in Wisconsin as a result of efforts of this Trail Association consist of $36,000 worth of road surfacing by the Zinc Mining Companies of Cuba City and Platteville and the erection of a $60,000 bridge over the Wisconsin River at Prairie du Chien, to be built by donations.

The plan of the organization is to stir up community spirit but not community antagonism; to bring into communities higher ideals of road building, road managing and take with it thoughts of better schools, better parks and general road conditions.

The officers of this organization are located in Savanna, Ill., as follows:

President, John Acker; vice president, W. P. Hacker, Milledgeville; secretary, W. F. Miller; treasurer, J. B. Schreiter.

AUTOMOBILE COMPETITION.

The automobile, running on highways built largely at the expense of the railroads, has become a transportation factor which can not be ignored. There are registered and in use in the United States more than 3,000,000 passenger automobiles which it is estimated cover an average distance of 5,000 miles each per year. Assuming that the average number of passengers is three, we must credit the automobiles with 45,000,000,000 passenger miles, which at 2 cents per mile are worth $900,000,000. On this basis the automobiles render a passenger service worth nearly $200,000,000 per year more than that of all the railroads and only about $300,400,000 less than that of all the railroads, electric railways and street car lines put together. Of course, all of this vast sum by no means represents revenue lost to the railroads. Nevertheless the increasing competition must be felt keenly.— *Earth Mover.*

WORK IN CHRISTIAN COUNTY.

A synopsis of work in Christian County, according to the status in early April, has been given in the following letter from County Highway Superintendent C. A. Penington, of Taylorville:

"On April 3, a special tax was voted in Taylorville and Mt. Auburn Townships for grading, draining, dragging and oil treating roads. The rate in Taylorville Township was 30c and in Mt. Auburn Township 72c on each $100 assessed valuation, raising about $5,000 a year for five years in the former township and about $6,000 a year for three years in the latter.

"On March 15, a contract was let by the commissioners of highways of the towns of Buckhart and Mt. Auburn for a 50-foot reinforced concrete girder bridge for the sum of $2,218.90 to J. A. Brown, of Palmer, Illinois. The commissioners of highways of the town of Stonington and the undersigned let the contract at Taylorville for a 30-foot I-beam bridge in the town of Stonington on April 16.

"A bond issue for $12,000 to build bridges in the town of May was defeated on April 3.

"The town of Buckhart will re-oil 16 miles of roads and put the first coat on 7 miles additional from a special tax."

A MERITORIOUS CONTRAST.

The crossing last fall.

Last October, ILLINOIS HIGHWAYS ran a cut, the one at the top, as illustrative of the most dangerous type of railroad crossing known. The picture was taken from a distance of about 40 feet, showing the crossing, in a depression at the top of a hill, virtually hidden from view, and constituting a menace to the public which even a vigilant watchman could not entirely remove. The picture appeared in our "Safety First" edition which readers will remember.

The scene now is entirely changed. We have, instead of the view as shown in the picture above, the

As it looked this spring.

radical application of remedy — the subway — which will never fail to wipe out the menace of the grade crossing. These two pictures speak for themselves. The crossing is on the main line of the C. P. & St. L. Railroad, West Washington Street road, Springfield. The camera was positioned in almost exactly the same relative point of focus for both pictures. The photographer was looking east from about 40 feet west of the track. The improvement was not quite finished in the second picture.

ILLINOIS HIGHWAYS

[Printed by authority of the State of Illinois.]

OFFICIAL PUBLICATION OF THE

STATE HIGHWAY DIVISION

VOL. IV	SPRINGFIELD, ILLINOIS, JULY, 1917	No. 7

AN ILLINOIS "MILITARY ROAD."
A Company of Artillery drilling on Milwaukee Avenue, an 18-foot Cook County concrete road.

The New Code Operative; Era of Activity Opens

Illinois has passed under the new form of government provided in Governor Lowden's Civil Administrative Code. The change took place July 1.

ILLINOIS HIGHWAYS is concerned especially with the extent to which the new order of things will affect the Division of Highways, now a part of the general department of Public Works and Buildings.

Though it is impossible at this time to impart to our readers all the changes of policy which may be adopted with reference to the conduct of highway affairs in Illinois, it is certain that the new era now opening will be characterized, so far as this division is concerned, with the greatest activity in its history.

We make this statement for specific reasons. First, the appropriations for the coming two years for road improvement in the State are the largest that a General Assembly ever has set aside. Secondly, the proposed State bond issue of $60,000,000 has been given the O. K. of the Legislature, has been signed by the Governor, and in November, 1918—a date within the coming biennium —will be put up to the people of Illinois for a vote. With double the possible road work and the bond issue the chief tasks, there will be little rest for the division.

Newly appointed officers of our general department, that of Public Works and Buildings, as well as of our own immediate division, have been too busy with initial details of organization to give much time as yet to permanent policies for the future.

Judge Leslie D. Puterbaugh of Peoria is director of the general department, following his appointment by the Governor. Thomas Vennum, of Watseka, is the assistant director. Both men are of high type, and they have plunged heart and soul into the gigantic task of organizing one of the biggest and most important departments in the State government.

Under the new code, as we have explained in a preceding issue, there is no highway commission. That body passed into history, and in its stead is the Superintendent of Highways, who will administer the highway laws and interests as did the old commission. Intimately identified with the Superintendent is the Chief Highway Engineer, whose status from that which obtained under the old regime is little changed. We are happy to state that for the office of Superintendent of Highways the Governor has appointed S. E. Bradt of DeKalb, former member and secretary of the commission; and for the office of Chief Highway Engineer, William W. Marr of Chicago, who has served in the same capacity during the last three years. Both men are students of and technical authorities on road questions in Illinois. They were named because of their preeminent qualifications.

The division has also a board of highway advisors, whose duty it shall be, under the code, to "advise relative to the construction, improvement and maintenance of State highways." This board, announced July 12 by the Governor, consists of the following prominently known men:

Homer J. Tice, Greenview;
William G. Edens, Chicago;
Robert D. Clarke, Peoria;
Joseph M. Page, Jerseyville;
A. R. Hall, Danville.

This completes the official personnel of our division. No material changes are anticipated in the staff of engineers, etc., because the new law provides for the retention of all employees under civil service, who are qualified to remain and who are competent.

As we have declared before, there is a busy biennium ahead of the division of highways. Elsewhere in this issue readers will find a financial statement by Superintendent of Highways Bradt. It shows the larger available fund for road building.

Not only is the State aid for the coming two years to be administered, but the Federal aid as well. Illinois' apportionment of the Federal fund for the year ending June 30, last, was $220,000. For the year ending June 30, next, it is $440,000, giving a combined total of $660,-000—or, to be exact, $663,000—and the Illinois Legislature appropriated a like sum to meet this. The grand total, as the reader will readily see, is $1,326,000. This money is to be spent under the supervision of our division, and little time will be wasted in letting contracts.

The Legislature appropriated anew the sum of $1,200,000 for road work and other allied purposes. At least $950,000 of this amount will go into State aid contracts. Add this to the Federal appropriation and you have the total of $2,276,000 which will be available for new contracts. Over and above this, the General Assembly reappropriated the unexpended balance of $1,-173,979.07, to pay for road work already under contract.

ROAD IMPROVEMENT APPROPRIATIONS LARGER THAN FORMERLY.

[*Statement by S. E. BRADT, State Highway Superintendent.*]

The appropriations made by the Fiftieth General Assembly for road improvement are as follows:

Unexpended balance	$1,173,979
To meet Federal allotment	1,326,000
For State aid work	1,200,000
Total	**$3,699,979**

Amount appropriated and to be appropriated by Federal Government and the counties of Illinois	3,699,979
Total available for expenditures for road improvement in Illinois during 1917 and 1918	**$7,399,958**

Appropriation by Forty-ninth General Assembly for road improvement—	
Unexpended balance	$ 600,000
State aid roads	2,000,000
Total	**$2,600,000**

Excess appropriations in 1917 over 1915	$1,099,979

It was not deemed wise to appropriate at this time any further sums for road improvement because of the high price of material and labor, as well as the scarcity of labor and the possible inability of contractors to ob-

(Concluded on page 69)

Four Thousand Miles of Hard Road; Not One Cent of Taxes

Sixty million dollars' worth of hard road without a penny's worth of taxation—this is what is proposed under the provisions of the State Bond Issue law, which Governor Lowden fostered in the beginning, and which he signed June 23, after the General Assembly had made of it a measure which he regarded as wise and equitable.

That is to say:

The people of Illinois, in November 1918, will be privileged to vote on the proposition of issuing $60,000,000 in State bonds, said bonds to pay 3½ per cent to buyers, the total bill of interest and principal to be footed by men and women in Illinois who own automobiles.

Not one cent in taxes is contemplated. Land will not be molested. Automobile license fees, however, will be doubled—but the item scarcely will be noticed by the individual.

The State Bond Issue plan was something of a surprise even to its intimate advocates. Good roads leaders throughout Illinois had vaguely talked it for some time, and at the Danville meeting of the Highway Improvement Association last December, the delegates adopted a resolution favoring the issue, and declaring in favor of an increase in auto license fees.

Even then, however, the thing had not taken form. Governor Lowden was consulted. He declared himself emphatically in favor of the plan as a whole; but he suggested—and later demanded—that not a part, but all, of the bill be paid through the medium of the license fee increase. Advocates of the measure, surprised, began to figure anew—and it finished with the discovery that automobile drivers could pay it all in the coming twenty years without being hurt, and that there existed no occasion whatever for extending taxes against real estate.

The plan provides for the construction of approximately 4,000 miles of hard surfaced roads. The map on another page shows where these roads will lie, and the points which they will connect.

The routes were selected by members of the former State Highway Commission. They entertained the purpose solely of accommodating the greatest number of population centers in the State. They had to figure within marked limitations, for a mileage such as sixty millions would pay for represented barely 4 per cent of the total highway mileage of the State. Problems of construction also had to be taken into consideration, and the distribution of cost, as well as the matter of reaching the greatest population possible.

It was a hazardous job, that of picking routes for this proposed gigantic, yet wonderfully important, undertaking. Members of the Legislature debated the routes, made a few minor changes, but in the main passed on the original draft to Governor Lowden with their assurance that it was the best that could be done.

Bear in mind that this proposed State Bond Issue system is a through system. Creators of the plan would like to see every hamlet and village in the State touched by this chain of modern roads—but finances, or the lack of them, can not be made to meet this wish. The billion and a half or more which would be required to surface every mile of rural highway in Illinois would vie, in enormity, with war expenditures. So, it must be a gradual process, and framers of this plan had in mind

the *State*, not the local community. It could not be otherwise, and succeed.

Adoption of the State plan will not interfere with county work. In the first place, granted the plan is voted on affirmatively by the people in November of next year, it will be 1920 before contracts can be let and actual work commenced. The job is a stupendous one. Meanwhile, State aid will be in operation, and the counties will be availing themselves of the chance to continue building, the same as in the past.

Nor will township work be stopped. These smaller units in the counties may proceed to raise funds, according as they are able, for their own short stretches of road. It is a mutually reciprocal, yet "dove-tailing," process which will be in operation from the United States Government on down the line. The Federal aid will be expended by the states, with Federal approval, for roads that make for national benefits; the State, by means of its bond issue, will be able to build roads which will constitute a wonderful chain for the good of the State as a State; counties, through State aid, and their own endeavors, will be expected to continue to build highways

A scenic stretch in Central Illinois. Brick road with concrete shoulders.

—to connect with the State system; and the townships will fill in their links, to connect with the county systems.

To those who may feel as if they have been skimped in the State plan, let us say that such is not their plight. You regard your home town merchant as an important business personage in proportion to his ability to handle a line of goods which will serve vast numbers. If he kept only such articles as you yourself had use of, his business would never merit important mention. The wider the community to which he is able to adapt his dealings, the bigger business man he is and, consequently, the prouder you are of him and his establishment.

It is this very community feature of the proposed State system which will make it a success. The start must be made somewhere. The map in this issue represents the best scope, the most representative, that could be devised. The scheme isn't a chain of 102 county systems; it's one State system. The counties are not going to pay the bill. Motorists who live in the length and breadth of Illinois, and who travel the State, are the ones against whom the cost is going to be taxed. The plan constitutes a wonderful opportunity for the people of

ILLINOIS
STATE BOND ISSUE
ROAD SYSTEM

Illinois, at the expense of a single class, to build a system of modern roads which will bring money benefits to every class, and which will advance Illinois to a position of international conspicuity.

In the accompanying table, arranged by Chief Highway Engineer Marr, is shown the operation of the bond issue plan in tabular form.

Issuance of the bonds will start in the year 1920. At that time, and annually thereafter for five years, there will be put out an issue of $10,000,000 each, making in all the sixty millions. With the aid of Secretary of State Emmerson and his staff, this division has arrived

at what it estimates will be a very conservative collection of motor license fees each year. This scale is shown in the first column of the table. These collections are figured up to 1944, by which time at the latest, it is estimated not only can all interest on the bonds be paid, but the aggregate principal retired, as well, thus wiping out the State obligation. Meanwhile, contracts will be awarded in 1920, and as soon as the work can be done, contractors will rush the 4,000 miles of modern highway to completion. The table shows clearly the sequence proposed in the issuance of the bonds, the payment of interest and principal and the manner of their maturity.

TABLE SHOWING ESTIMATED AMOUNT OF MOTOR FEES REMAINING FOR STATE AID AND MAINTENANCE WORK AFTER PAYING THE ANNUAL COST OF BOND ISSUE—ESTIMATE BASED ON A 100% INCREASE IN FEES AND A GRADED INCREASE IN CARS TO A TOTAL OF 600,000.

Year.	Estimated motor fee collections.	Payment on principal.	Interest.	Total payment principal and interest.	Available for State aid allotments (including maintenance)	Outstanding bonds	First maturity.	Second maturity.	Third maturity.	Fourth maturity.	Fifth maturity	Sixth maturity
1920	$4,800,000	$2,400,000	$350,000	$2,750,000	$2,050,000	$10,000,000	$2,400,000					
1921	5,200,000	2,400,000	616,000	3,016,000	2,184,000	17,600,000	400,000	$2,000,000				
1922	5,500,000	2,400,000	892,000	3,292,000	2,218,000	25,200,000	400,000	400,000	$1,600,000			
1923	5,800,000	2,400,000	1,118,000	3,518,000	2,252,000	32,800,000	400,000	400,000	400,000	$1,600,000		
1924	6,000,000	2,400,000	1,414,000	3,814,000	2,186,000	40,100,000	400,000	400,000	400,000	400,000	$400,000	
1925	8,000,000	2,400,000	1,680,000	4,080,000	1,920,000	48,000,000	100,000	400,000	100,000	400,000	400,000	$400,000
1926	6,000,000	2,400,000	1,506,000	3,906,000	2,104,000	45,600,000	100,000	100,000	100,000	100,000	400,000	400,000
1927	6,000,000	2,400,000	1,512,000	3,912,000	2,168,000	43,200,000	400,000	400,000	400,000	400,000	400,000	400,000
1928	6,000,000	2,400,000	1,428,000	3,828,000	2,172,000	40,800,000	400,000	400,000	400,000	400,000	400,000	100,000
1929	6,000,000	2,400,000	1,344,000	3,744,000	2,256,000	38,400,000	100,000	400,000	400,000	400,000	400,000	400,000
1930	6,000,000	2,400,000	1,260,000	3,660,000	2,340,000	36,000,000	400,000	400,000	400,000	400,000	400,000	400,000
1931	6,000,000	2,400,000	1,176,000	3,576,000	2,424,000	33,600,000	400,000	400,000	400,000	400,000	400,000	400,000
1932	6,000,000	2,400,000	1,092,000	3,492,000	2,508,000	31,200,000	400,000	400,000	400,000	400,000	400,000	400,000
1933	6,000,000	2,400,000	1,008,000	3,408,000	2,592,000	28,800,000	400,000	400,000	400,000	400,000	400,000	400,000
1934	6,000,000	2,400,000	924,000	3,324,000	2,676,000	26,400,000	400,000	400,000	400,000	400,000	400,000	400,000
1935	6,000,000	2,400,000	840,000	3,240,000	2,760,000	24,000,000	400,000	400,000	400,000	400,000	400,000	400,000
1936	6,000,000	2,400,000	756,000	3,156,000	2,844,000	21,600,000	400,000	400,000	400,000	400,000	400,000	400,000
1937	6,000,000	2,400,000	672,000	3,072,000	2,928,000	19,200,000	400,000	400,000	400,000	400,000	400,000	400,000
1938	6,000,000	2,400,000	588,000	2,988,000	3,012,000	16,800,000	400,000	400,000	400,000	400,000	400,000	400,000
1939	6,000,000	2,400,000	504,000	2,904,000	3,096,000	14,400,000	400,000	400,000	400,000	400,000	400,000	400,000
1940	6,000,000	2,400,000	420,000	2,820,000	3,180,000	12,000,000				400,000	400,000	400,000
1941	6,000,000	2,400,000	396,000	2,796,000	3,204,000	9,600,000			1,200,000	400,000	400,000	400,000
1942	6,000,000	2,400,000	252,000	2,652,000	3,348,000	7,200,000				1,600,000	400,000	400,000
1943	6,000,000	2,400,000	168,000	2,568,000	3,432,000	4,800,000					2,000,000	400,000
1944	6,000,000	2,400,000	81,000	2,481,000	3,510,000	2,400,000						2,400,000
Totals	$147,400,000	$60,000,000	$22,050,000	$82,050,000	$65,350,000		$10,000,000	$10,000,000	$10,000,000	$10,000,000	$10,000,000	$10,000,000

SINGLE COMMISSIONER LAW.

There have been many inquiries as to when the new highway commissioner law goes into effect, or rather as to when the three highway commissioners go out of office and are succeeded by one man. An opinion has been rendered to the effect that the law went into effect July 1, this year, but the single commissioner will not be elected until the township election next spring and the three commissioners will continue to hold office until the new man is elected and qualifies.

It is believed that greatly increased efficiency will come as a result of the new law. The one commissioner will receive $4 per day. Heretofore the three commissioners have received $2 per day each. They were paid only for the time they put in at the work.

NEW ERA OPENS.
(Concluded from page 66.)

tain material owing to the shortage of cars in which to ship such material.

It is understood, however, that in the event conditions are such as to allow the expenditure of a reasonable proportion of the amount appropriated as above for State aid work by September 1918, that county boards will then be advised to provide funds by levy to meet an additional allotment to be made available by the Fifty-first General Assembly on April 1, 1919, through an emergency appropriation of $1,000,000.

The entire amount appropriated for road improvement aggregating $3,699,979 will be paid out of the fund derived from motor license fees, which have been collected for that purpose only—hence these appropriations in no way add to the general taxes of the State.

NEW MOTOR LAW SIGNED.

The New Motor Law provides for the following rates to take effect January 1, 1918, and January 1, 1920:

	1917	1918	1920
10 hp. and less	$ 3 00	$ 4 50	$ 6 00
25 hp. and more than 10	4 00	6 00	8 00
35 hp. and more than 25	6 00	9 00	12 00
50 hp. and more than 35	8 00	16 00	20 00
More than 50 hp	10 00	20 00	25 00
Motor bicycle	2 00	3 00	4 00
Electric vehicles to and including 2 tons	5 00	10 00	12 00
Electric vehicles over 2 tons	10 00	20 00	25 00

This law further provides that the fund thus created known as the "road fund" can be used only for two purposes, viz: First, for the payment of the principal and interest of any bonded indebtedness incurred by the State of Illinois for road construction and second, for the improvement of the highways of the State.

It will thus be seen that both purposes are primarily the improvement of our roads and that this money constitutes a special fund paid in and set aside for that specific purpose.

Northwest Conference Wants Building to Continue

It's a sort of epoch-making situation when county highway superintendents, in a meeting designed to furnish an opportunity merely to exchange road and bridge building ideas, have to take war into consideration in the major part of their discussions.

Such was the case, however, at Rock Island on June 7, where superintendents of the Northwest Division gathered in their first meeting this year. They will meet again on Thursday, September 6, at Oregon, and if the second meeting is as interesting as was the first, the superintendents who do not attend will be unfortunate indeed.

At the Rock Island meeting, there were present the following: County Highway Superintendents Alex Anderson, Ogle, chairman of the conference; H. M. Butt, Knox, secretary; C. R. A. Marshal, Henderson; L. B. Neighbour, Lee; V. N. Taggett, Whiteside; J. E. Russell, Mercer; Wallace Treichler, Rock Island, the host during the day; and Division Engineer Hugo E. Surman, Road Engineer H. E. Bilger and Department Editor Earl B. Searcy, of the State Highway Department. Sessions were held in the supervisors' room in the Rock Island County courthouse.

The formal program, if such it may be called, occupied only the morning. In the afternoon, the visitors went in automobiles to the new Colona bridge, in course

Second Division Superintendents at Colona bridge.

of construction across the Rock River a mile west of Colona, where they enjoyed a detailed inspection of the imposing new structure, now nearly complete.

County Superintendent Butt, secretary of the conference, was the first speaker at the morning meeting. His subject was, "My experience in maintaining State aid earth roads in Knox County." Mr. Butt devoted most of his talk to road dragging, the most potent means of earth road maintenance. In another column further detail as to methods he has employed.

The prize discussion of the morning came when the next topic was introduced. Its subject was, "Should we continue to improve our highways and construct bridges during the war or should we call a halt and do only the work that is absolutely necessary?" Chairman Anderson and Mr. Taggett were booked for the discussion of this question. Mr. Anderson expressed the opinion that counties of the State ought to proceed conservatively, in view of the war, but that at least a reasonable amount of work

ought to be carried on. Mr. Taggett said counties ought to avoid false economy, yet should guard their expenditures. Necessary building ought to go on, he declared, yet there should be no extravagances. This seemed to be the view of a majority of the seven superintendents present.

Mr. Treichler of Rock Island, the host, however, entertained some less conservative notions about the matter, and while the assemblage listened with keen interest, he gave expression to them.

"Build as extensively as possible," was Mr. Treichler's advice. He admitted that prices of materials had soared, yet high prices, he said, are pretty equally distributed; and wages and other channels of expenditure

Dredge at work on fill leading to Colona bridge, Rock Island County side.

have kept pace with costs. Mr. Treichler's work lies largely in the city of Rock Island, where the greatest paving program in the city's history is to be carried out this year. He declared he knew of only one objector to building improvements; and that individual was one who had disapproved of better roads and streets for the last thirty years, regardless of whether the country was at war or enjoying peace. It was the Rock Island super-intendent's belief that time limits ought to be waived in contracts, but that, except for this modification, con-tracts should be let for as much work and under condi-tions as nearly normal as possible. In any event, he said, high prices ought not to interfere with the work of building.

Mr. Neighbour of Lee County addressed the super-intendents on the subject, "What reports should be made by a superintendent of highways to the County Board?"

"Make these reports full of ideas, propaganda and the like," advised Mr. Neighbour. The Lee County superintendent voiced his belief that, in addition to the regular reports to the county boards, information relative to road building and development within the counties ought to be supplied to interested newspapers, thus en-abling the public at large to become familiar with what was going on.

Division Engineer Surman, speaking on the subject, "What investigation should be made in order to deter-mine the span of a culvert or bridge?" gave technical di-rections for determining spans. His talk was followed by a brief discussion, in the course of which he answered questions and volunteered the use of his tables for the benefit of the superintendents.

In extending an invitation to the conference to meet in special session September 6, in Ogle County, Chairman Anderson stated that visiting delegates would find it profitable not only to meet in Oregon, but to arrange also to visit Grand Detour and other points in the picturesque county. After determining the meeting date in Septem-ber, the delegates to the conference session went to the Harms hotel where, as Mr. Treichler's guests, they en-joyed lunch.

The Colona bridge, which the superintendents visited in the afternoon, will stand as a monument to the memory of able and earnest hands and brains which had to do with its building.

Stretching from the wooded reserves on the Rock Island County side of the Rock River, a few hundred yards below the main line bridge of the Rock Island rail-road, to the foliage bordered shores of Henry County, this new bridge looks as if it would accomodate highway, and even interurban traffic for all time to come. Its alignment is perfect, and every one of the eleven spans of 69 feet each in length spells stalwart support, perma-nency and beauty.

The total length of the bridge proper is approxi-mately 755 feet. Leading up to it on the Rock Island County side will be a fill 4,000 feet in length. On the Henry County side, there will be a fill approach about 1,000 feet in length. The total approximate cost of the bridge will be $62,000 and of the fills combined, $18,000. The bridge is being built at inter-county expense and un-der State supervision. It is on the Rock Island-Moline-Chicago Road, and lies on one of the routes included in the proposed State bond issue road system. The struc-ture is of concrete throughout, with brick rails. The Gould Construction Company of Davenport, Iowa, is building the bridge, and the Charles Stevens Company of Geneseo is building the fills. On June 7, the bridge was 70 per cent finished. It was expected that it, with the fills, would be ready for public traffic some time in Sep-tember.

Following the visit to the Colona bridge, the super-intendents returned to Moline and Rock Island where they took trains for their various homes.

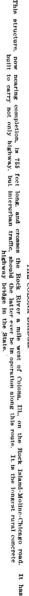

This structure, now nearing completion, is 755 feet long, and crosses the Rock River a mile west of Colona, Ill., on the Rock Island-Moline-Chicago road. It has been built to carry not only highway, but interurban traffic, should the latter ever be in operation along this route. It is the longest rural concrete highway bridge in the State.

THE COLONA BRIDGE.

ILLINOIS HIGHWAYS.

Published by authority

State of Illinois.

P5813—7,500 ◄━━► 11

DEPARTMENT OF PUBLIC WORKS AND BUILDINGS.

DIVISION OF HIGHWAYS.

SPRINGFIELD, ILLINOIS.

PUBLIC WORKS AND BUILDINGS.

LESLIE D. PUTERBAUGH, *Director.*
THOMAS VENNUM, *Assistant Director.*

DIVISION OF HIGHWAYS.

S. E. BRADT, *Superintendent.*
WM. W. MARR, *Chief Highway Engineer.*

BUREAU OF ROADS.

H. E. BILGER, *Road Engineer.*
C. M. HATHAWAY, *Assistant Road Engineer.*
J. W. HARRIS, *Office Engineer.*

BUREAU OF BRIDGES.

CLIFFORD OLDER, *Bridge Engineer.*
G. F BURCH, *Assistant Bridge Engineer.*
NIXON L. BUNN, *Office Engineer.*

BUREAU OF MAINTENANCE.

B. H. PIEPMEIER, *Maintenance Engineer.*
F. T. SHEETS, *Assistant Maintenance Engineer.*

BUREAU OF TESTS.

F. L. ROMAN, *Testing Engineer.*
F. L. SPERRY, *Assistant Testing Engineer.*

BUREAU OF AUDITS.

J. M. McCoy, *Chief Clerk.*
R. R. McLEOD, *General Bookkeeper.*
EARL B. SEARCY, *Editor.*

DIVISION ENGINEERS.

SEVEN DIVISIONS.

1st —H. B. BUSHNELL, 138 Fox St., Aurora.
2d —H. E., SURMAN, 614 Peoples Bank Bldg., Moline.
3d —A. H. HUNTER, 302 Appollo Theatre Bldg., Peoria.
4th—R. L. BELL, Buchanan-Link Bldg., Paris.
5th—FRED TARRANT, 730 Reisch Bldg., Springfield.
6th—C. M. SLAYMAKER, 510 Metropolitan Bldg., East St. Louis.
7th—J. E. HUBER, Wise Bldg., Mt. Vernon. .

CONTENTS.

WE DEPART, SMILING.

ILLINOIS HIGHWAYS appears this issue for the last time.

Readers with whom this little magazine has become a familiar document doubtless will feel a bit of regret at the announcement. We can not help but look back, and know that HIGHWAYS has done some good, has made the official highway department of Illinois friends, and in the aggregate, has served a worthy purpose.

But, these are progressive days, and progress brings changes. When the State Highway Department of the last four years passed out of existence at midnight June 30, its policies died with it. A new governmental aim came into being; new points of perspective were ushered into the foreground, and a different administrative organization was launched.

The aim of things from now on is concentration. Authority must be attracted inward, instead of diffused outward. The same figurative principle holds with reference to a major portion of what heretofore has been our valued publicity matter. Instead of letting each department pursue an independent publicity course of its own, as in the past, it is probable the future will devolve some sort of a centralized plan, whereby the various departmental publications will be welded into one. Thus will ILLINOIS HIGHWAYS, or its withering spirit, be absorbed.

Born in April, 1914, ILLINOIS HIGHWAYS peacefully succumbs in this, the month of July, 1917, at the age of three years and three months; secure in the belief that if succeeding publications of its kind are successful in proportion to the scope of departmental territory covered, readers of whatever our descendant may be will feel the same pulsating interest in our State government that HIGHWAYS readers of the past have felt in highway activities in Illinois.

"ILLINOIS HIGHWAYS" bids it loyal readers, each and all, an affectionate farewell upon this, its final appearance.

QUARRIES IN SOUTHERN ILLINOIS.

A discussion of southern Illinois road problems, contained in a special article contributed last month, resulted unfortunately in a misinterpretation on the part of a valued reader.

It was feared, in the criticism of the article which reached ILLINOIS HIGHWAYS, that readers might have gained the impression that the southern part of the State is devoid of natural road building materials, consequently has no producing industries. This is not the case, as anyone at all posted, knows.

Southern Illinois prides herself in possession of several stone quarries, samples from which have been analyzed by the State chemist and have passed the required test. Not only that, but the stone has been used in large quantities in construction work.

Quarries lying in the southern belt include the following: Columbia Quarry Company, St. Louis, Mo., quarry at Columbia, Monroe County; Charles Stone Company, Marion, quarry at White Hill, Johnson County; Casper Stolle Quarry Company, East St. Louis, quarry at Ill Falling Springs, St. Claire County; East St. Louis Quarry Company, quarry at Ill Falling Springs; and the Massey Stone Company, Anna; quarry at Añna.

With complete or partial destruction of from 20 to 30 bridges in Fulton County from recent floods, damage to bridges alone in that county, it has been estimated, will reach near $150,000. Not only large bridges, but culverts as well, have suffered.

Department Directors Take Charge

Directors of the nine general departments under the Civil Administrative Code of Illinois assumed their duties Monday morning, July 2, and, with the aid of their assistants, set in operation the machinery of Illinois' new governmental plan.

Governor Lowden named the following department directors who now are at work in their efforts to concentrate authority and increase the efficiency of the various branches:

Department of Finance—Omar H. Wright, Belvidere.

Department of Agriculture—Charles Adkins, Bement.

Department of Labor—Barney Cohen, Chicago.

Department of Public Works and Buildings—Judge Leslie Puterbaugh, Peoria.

Department of Mines and Minerals—Evan D. John, Carbondale.

Department of Public Welfare—Charles Thorne, Winnetka.

Department of Health—Dr. C. St. Clair Drake, Springfield.

Department of Trade and Commerce—William H. Stead, Ottawa.

Department of Registration and Education—Francis W. Shepherdson, Chicago.

Appropriations made to meet all needs of State government for the coming two years, as approved by the Governor, reached the total of $50,581,101. In connection with the action of the executive on appropriation bills, the following statement was issued from the Governor's office:

The Fiftieth General Assembly passed 74 appropriation bills carrying a total of $51,581,344. The majority of these bills reached the Governor in the closing of the session. He vetoed bills and items aggregating $1,070,243. This left the net appropriations for the entire session $50,581,101.

To obtain a fair comparison of appropriations this year the increase in appropriations in other states should be shown along with Illinois. The following table fairly illustrates the immense increase in cost of government during war times:

State.	1915–17	1917–19
Illinois	$47,791,971	$50,581,101
Ohio	33,408,588	49,919,249
Michigan	14,713,266	17,416,580
California	19,047,260	27,291,845
	1915–16	1917–18
Massachusetts	¹$19,024,547	$25,604,644

¹ One year.

In contrasting the appropriations of the Fiftieth General Assembly with those of the Forty-ninth General Assembly, conditions and certain items should be taken into consideration. For instance, under the civil administrative code passed during this session, consolidating all boards and commissions into nine departments, all funds paid into the treasuries of State institutions (other than the University of Illinois) must hereafter be paid immediately into the State treasury. In the past it has been the custom for many of these institutions to use the moneys paid to them which were not included in the appropriations and the public generally knew nothing of them.

A large item of the increase in appropriations this year is found, for instance, in the industrial funds appropriated as working capital for the penal and reformatory institutions, the normal schools and the Illinois and Michigan canal. These appropriations aggregate $1,214,786.

Then there were deficiency appropriations necessary because of large expenditures during the last two years which made it necessary for the Legislature to pass twenty measures for relief of the different departments and boards, appropriating in all to them $1,354,234.

In previous sessions it had been the custom for legislatures to appropriate "unexpended balances" of previous appropriations. These balances were not itemized. This year it was held necessary to state the exact amount of the reappropriations. They aggregated $1,578,605.

In addition to increasing the cost of commodities the war made additional military appropriations necessary. The Fiftieth General Assembly appropriated $800,000 for this purpose.

Still another item should be considered. For the first time it was necessary for the State to make an appropriation of $663,000 per annum from the general fund to meet a like amount appropriated by the Federal Government for the construction of public highways. These appropriations for the two years appear for the first time, and total $1,324,000.

New Contracts Awarded.

County.	Sec.	Route.	Type.	Contractor.	mount
MAY 23, 1917.					
Carroll....	C	8	Earth....	Gund-Graham Co., Freeport.	$13,207 74
Putnam ...	E	4	Gravel....	Concrete Building & Products Co., Granville........	5,288 82
JUNE 13, 1917.					
Ford........	C	5	Concrete.	Public Service Construction Co., Omaha, Nebr	9,341 00
Grundy......	D	3	Concrete.	Booth, Nicholson & Gilchrist Gardner.................	14,109 70
Peoria......	E	2	Concrete.	Canterbury Bros., Peoria, Ill.	30,282 68
JUNE 20, 1917					
DeKalb.....	E	9	Concrete.	Public Service Construction Co., Omaha, Nebr	19,576 78
DeKalb.....	F	1	Concrete.	Public Service Construction Co., Omaha, Nebr	8,706 00
Hardin......	C	2	Bridges..	Wallace Harlan, Greenville.	1,240 00
Jackson*....	D	3	Blt. Mac'm	Bland & Ferguson, Cairo....	11,987 88
Jackson*....	E	3	Blt. Mac'm	Bland & Ferguson, Cairo....	5,633 44
Jackson*....	F	11	Blt. Mac'm	Bland & Ferguson, Cairo....	5,929 72
Jackson*....	G	13	Blt. Mac'm	Bland & Ferguson, Cairo....	4,491 51
JUNE 27, 1917.					
Clay........	D	4	Earth....	L. V. Chesrown, Olney......	2,606 12
Fulton......	J	15	Earth....	A. O. McCoy, Versailles.....	2,094 04
Fulton......	Q	13	Earth....	A. O. McCoy, Versailles.....	3,795 49
Johnson	1-8-4-9	Bridges..	Ed. M. Heaton. Marion......	3,119 48
Madison ...	B	2	Concrete.	A. Fabrig, Edwardsville....	9,965 15
Madison ...	E	1	Concrete.	G. R. Hyten, Edwardsville..	8,809 92
Madison ...	F	9	Concrete.	Jos. Kesl. Edwardsville.....	9,822 35
Madison ...	G	8	Concrete.	Hug Lumber & Construction Co., Highland...........	10,427 46
Perry......	C	1	Bridges..	The Parham Construction Co., East St. Louis........	2,109 00
Randolph ..	C	7-1-9-3	Bridges..	The Parham Construction Co., East St. Louis........	5,097 00
Richland ...	D-E-F	9-3-6-7	Bridges..	L. N. Chesrown, Olney......	5,700 00
Union	D	1	Earth.....	White & Braley, Litchfield..	2,133 32
Warren.....	I	3	Concrete.	E. A. Lord Construction Co.. Monmouth.............	14,837 00
White.......	B	2	Gravel....	Arkansas Construction Co., Mt. Vernon. Ind.........	7,516 38
White.......	C	3	Gravel....	Arkansas Construction Co.. Mt. Vernon. Ind.........	6,976 99
JULY 5, 1917.					
Cook	P	1	Concrete.	Chicago Heights Coal Co. Chicago Heights..........	70,068 14
Cook	Q	5	Concrete	Connelly & Dunning, 138 W. Washington st., Chicago....	50,968 30
Mercer...	J	7	Earth.....	Buis & Olson. St. Joseph. Mo.	5,092 30
Mercer...	K	3	Earth.....	Cameron&Joyce.Keokuk.Ia.	9,172 90
Knox.	½F	11	} Earth...	} Cameron&Joyce.Keokuk.Ia.	12 827 94
	G	16			

* These sections awarded under specifications "A."

The Chicago division of the newly organized Touring Club of America has been formed. Headquarters of the parent organization will be in Chicago. Promotion of good roads and of travel upon them will be the objects of the body. Officers of the Chicago division as chosen are: President, William G. Edens; first vice president, William F. Grower; second vice president, Arnold Joerns; secretary, Joseph E. Callender; treasurer, Lucius Teter.

NEW ILLINOIS ROAD LAWS

Although the State Bond Issue bill was the measure of prime importance, so far as proposed money involved is concerned, the Fiftieth General Assembly, which adjourned in June, gave much of its time to other important road and bridge measures now a part of the Illinois statutes.

It was difficult for a time to assemble a trustworthy summary of bills which passed, and which either were signed by the Governor or became laws without his signature. ILLINOIS HIGHWAYS, however, has dug into the records and as a result presents herewith a list of the measures which passed the Senate and House, and which on July 1, became law.

As our inquiry revealed, the measures are as follows:

SENATE.

31. Dunlap. Providing on State aid routes through towns of 2,500 or less, for a wider road through the municipality, said city or village to pay the cost of the excess width.

200 Dunlap. Providing that any three petitioners, whose names are on a petition for alterations in a road, may appeal to the county highway superintendent. Formerly all the petitioners had to make the appeal.

409. Dunlap. Highway commissioners must relocate roads, if necessary, where grades have been ordered separated or abolished by the Public Utilities Commission at railroad crossings.

487. Kessinger. Providing that any association organized to promote the improvement of highways may register its name and marking design with the Department of Public Works and Buildings, and fixing a penalty for infringement.

545. Canaday. Provides that cities, except Chicago, may levy an additional tax not exceeding 3 mills on the dollar, annually, for the purpose of oiling streets within the municipality.

159. Glackin. Permitting the employment of convicts in the State institutions in the preparation of road building material.

HOUSE

852. Volz. Authorizes upon majority vote at a town meeting, the transfer of surplus town funds to other town funds or to the general road and bridge fund.

377. Scanlan. Legalizing all elections held under the road and bridge act of 1913, where such elections were held and conducted at the place of the last annual meeting in any such town or district and any bonds which have been or may be issued in pursuance of such action.

148—E. Walter Green. Validating bonds issued for road improvement purposes when receiving a majority vote at an annual or special town meeting after a majority of the voters voting in an election have authorized such issue.

116. Watson. Confers upon county boards authority to issue bonds for highway improvement after their authorization in an election held for the purpose and validating same.

906. Lacy. Requiring highway commissioners to mail notices of poll tax, also to post notices of same in ten most conspicuous places in township.

212. Dieterich. Enables cities of 10,000, instead of 5,000 as formerly, to collect toll from bridges for purpose of paying interest and principal of bonds. Amends 1907 act.

246. Watson. Amends 1913 law by taking, from the total amount levied for roads in cities less than 15,000, the amount required as damages incurred in drainage construction.

378. Baker. Provides for one commissioner of highways in townships instead of three; term, two years; pay, $4 per diem for all necessary time put in.

559. Meents. State Bond Issue bill.

578. Meents. Federal aid appropriation of $663,000 per annum.

635. Pace. Legalizes bonds in townships or road districts to pay debts incurred by highway commissioners in repairing roads and bridges.

645. Rowe. Permits highway commissioners to reduce the width of roads, except State aid roads, which require written consent of the Department of Public Works.

1006. Bancroft. Provides for register of all highway bonds in county clerk's office.

The foregoing synopsis does not attempt to include the major appropriation measures. They are given in other columns of this issue.

THE SUPERINTENDENT OF HIGHWAYS.

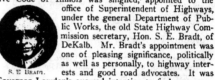

Governor Lowden, soon after the Civil Administrative Code of Illinois was signed, appointed to the office of Superintendent of Highways, under the general Department of Public Works, the old State Highway Commission secretary, Hon. S. E. Bradt, of DeKalb. Mr. Bradt's appointment was one of pleasing significance, politically as well as personally, to highway interests and good road advocates. It was Governor Lowden's avowed intention to find men commensurate, in point of ability, with the offices created under the new and efficient code.

S. E. BRADT.

The man who, under the new regime, will have in his hands the administration of Illinois' highway affairs —Mr. Bradt—is a banker of prominence, has been a student of road problems for many years, and is a man of several years' experience in the handling of State highway duties.

As minority member of the State Highway Commission which went out of being June 30, Mr. Bradt, to whom was entrusted the duties of secretary, was active, keenly intelligent, full of initiative and an invaluable adviser of his fellow commissioners. Governor Lowden recognized in him a man and an official thoroughly competent to undertake the vast and difficult duties which necessarily lie ahead in adapting highway policies and interests to the State governmental reform.

Promotion of the State bond issue plan, in itself an immense undertaking which will require not only highway knowledge but financial genius as well, comprises one of the big duties of the new Highway Department. Mr. Bradt's experience in helping to shape the bond plan, coupled with service he has done the State in other capacities in the past, was guarantee enough to the Governor that, under Mr. Bradt's superintendency, the highway affairs of Illinois during this administration will be taken care of efficiently and economically.

Politically, Mr. Bradt is a Republican. He is identified prominently with banking and financial interests in his home county, and not only has studied highway problems for years, but has served highway interests as well. He is popularly known throughout the entire State.

MR. MARR REMAINS IN OFFICE.

Governor Lowden, toward the last of June, completed the appointment of the two executive officers of the Division of Highways with the retention of William W. Marr, of Chicago, as Chief Highway Engineer. This means that the division, in the hands of Superintendent Bradt and of Chief Highway Engineer Marr, will be under the direction of competent men, familiar with Illinois road conditions, and with the work attending their control.

Mr. Marr, like Mr. Bradt, is familiarly known to good road advocates throughout the State. He has put in four years as Chief State Highway Engineer, was mainly responsible for the efficient departmental organization which obtained during the last administration, and is in a position to go ahead with the State bond issue, and with the road building program of the future.

Mr. Marr has the sincere friendship and the best cooperative spirit of all who work with him, and is the sort of an official who commands confidence and who gets results.

THOMAS NOW A LIEUTENANT.

Robert E. Thomas of Rockford, formerly a junior engineer in the road division of the State Highway Department, and until very recently the resident engineer on section E, route 6, Winnebago County, Division Engineer Bushnell's district, has received a signal promotion, carrying with it a lieutenancy in the United States navy.

Lieutenant Thomas' work will consist of designing and construction of all naval work on shore, such as piers, wharves, quaywalls, dry docks, navy yards, gun factories, gun testing grounds, etc. His duties will come immediately under the supervision of the Bureau of Yards and Docks, U. S. N.

Men picked for this work are civil or assistant civil engineers, and the comparatively few selected were chosen only after a most exacting examination, covering several days. Employment in this bureau has been tendered in the past only to the two honor men from Annapolis each year. The bureau has been small. War contingencies, however, have made it necessary to enlarge the department.

Examinations were held in Washington, D. C., in May. The written portion occupied four days and the oral, physical, etc., three days. The number of men who started in to take the tests was 190. Six vacancies were announced originally, but it has been authoritatively stated that about 15 will be appointed. Mr. Thomas will be one of the fifteen. Late in June, he received notice to regard himself as under orders, and to arrange personal affairs accordingly. Consequently, he resigned from his work in connection with the State Highway Department, and made ready to await word to report to Annapolis for 30 days' training before permanent assignment to a navy yard.

Carrying with it the rank of lieutenant, the position pays $2,552 per annum, and the commission is permanent, conditioned, of course, on satisfactory service.

Lieutenant Thomas is married. Mrs. Thomas formerly was Miss Helen Lloyd, of Springfield, and earlier, of Indian Head, Md.

Word has been received that A. K. Fogg, of Division Engineer Hunter's office, also has passed this examination, and is expecting to be commissioned.

MAY REPORT, BUREAU OF BRIDGES.

During May, 1917, plans, estimates and specifications for 50 concrete bridges were prepared and sent out to county superintendents of highways. The total estimated cost of these bridges is $58,110.

Plans, estimates and specifications for four sections of State aid bridge work, including 31 concrete bridges, were prepared, the total estimated cost of which is $11,488.40.

Plans and estimates for 5 bridges and culverts to be built in connection with State aid road work were completed. The total estimated cost of this work equals $3,120.

Summing up, plans were prepared for 86 bridges and culverts, the total estimated cost of which equals $72,718.40.

In addition to the plans for drainage structures on State aid road contracts prepared by the Bureau of Bridges, plans for 275 such bridges and culverts were prepared in the division offices. The total estimated cost of this work amounts to $34,305.92.

During the month, 60 bridge plans prepared by county superintendents of highways were checked and approved, and 5 sets of shop drawings for steel bridges were checked and approved. The designs of 3 existing steel bridges were investigated and reported on. Alternative plans for 5 bridges were checked and approved. One shop inspection of a steel bridge was made.

According to reports received, contracts were awarded on plans prepared for county superintendents of highways for 31 concrete bridges and culverts, 1 steel bridge and the repairs to 1 existing steel bridge at an average cost of 99.8 per cent of the estimates. The total estimated cost of this work amounts to $36,360.70.

Contracts were awarded by the State Highway Commission for 2 sections of State aid bridge work, including 17 concrete bridges at an average cost of 97.2 per cent of the estimates. The total estimated cost was $10,030.

On June 1, there were on hand 3 inspection reports ready for work; 1 bridge plan checked, but not estimated; and 19 bridge plans completed, together with the estimates and practically ready to be sent out.—*Compiled by N. L. BUNN, Office Engineer.*

A Morgan County State aid road, taken in February of this year. It had just been dragged, preparatory to oiling. Courtesy of Cocking Cement Co., contractors.

SECOND DIVISION AFTER 109 MILES

The second Illinois district, over which Division Engineer H. E. Surman has supervision, is endeavoring to make a noteworthy showing before the close of the present construction season.

The tables which follow were furnished on June 16 to ILLINOIS HIGHWAYS by Division Engineer Surman.

They show a total of 43 miles of modern, improved road finished in the last two years, and 65.9 miles under construction in June, with a view to finishing the grand total of approximately 109 miles by fall.

Tabulated reports are given on work in the second division which has been completed and which is under construction respectively, in the tables as follows:

WORK COMPLETED IN SECOND DIVISION.

County.	Sec.	Route.	Type.	Width.	Length in feet.	Cost.	Year comp.	Location.	Contractor.
Bureau	A	7	Concrete. Hillsidebrick.	15 15	4,140 746	$10,853 97	1915	West city limits of Princeton on Cannon Ball Trail.	Grohne Contracting Co., Joliet.
Bureau	B	4	Concrete.	15&18	4,847.6	7,762 58	1915	South city l'ts of Princeton, Tiskilward rd	Grohne Contracting Co., Joliet.
Bureau	C	3	Concrete.	15	5,600	8,982 14	1915	East city limits of Princeton on Cannon Ball Trail.	C. W. Jensen, Chicago.
Bureau	D	1	Concrete.	15	5,357	7,747 54	1915	North city l'ts of Princeton on Dixon rd.	C. W. Jensen, Chicago.
Carroll	A	2	Concrete.	10	8,840	13,351 20	1915	1 mile w. of Mt. Carroll on Lanark rd.	Gund-Graham Co., Freeport.
Carroll	B	2	Gravel.	15	10,230	14,731 41	1916	On Lanark rd. at end of conc'te Sec.A.	Gund-Graham Co., Freeport.
Henderson	A	2	Gravel.	15	2,700	4,315 10	1916	E.city l'ts of Oquawka on Monmouthrd.	E. A. Lord Constr. Co., Monmouth.
Henry	AaB	1	Concrete.	15	12,750	34,563 63	1916	Ne. limits of Cambridge on Geneseo rd.	Grohne Constr. Co., Joliet.
JoDaviess	A	1	Concrete.	10	4,700	6,801 36	1915	Nw. city l'ts of Galena, Grant Highway	Empire Constr. Co., Des Moines, Ia.
JoDaviess	B	1	Hillside brick.	10	450		1915	Southeast city limits of Elizabeth on the Grant Highway.	Empire Constr. Co., Des Moines, Ia.
			Concrete.	10	3,550	6,374 84			
JoDaviess	C	1	Concrete.	10	2,595	4,688 33	1916	1 mile northwest of city limits of Galena on the Grant Highway.	R. F. Conlon. Cuba City, Wis.
Knox	A	8 & 11C.	3conc'te b'dg's	30'-24'-30'	10'-16'-30'	4,071 75	1916	Bridges known as Appleton, Harshberger and Meek.	Farmington Cmt. Co., Farmington.
Knox	B	1 & 2	Earth.	15'-24'-30'	57,834	23,236 51	1916	N.city l'ts of Galesburg, Burlington Way	Cameron, Joyce & Co., Keokuk. Ia.
Lee	A	5	Concrete.	10	11,310	21,256 58	1915	5 m. se. city l'ts of Dixon on Chicago rd.	Edw. M. Laing Co., Highland Park.
Mercer	C	3, 4, 5, 6A.	3conc'te b'dg's			5,449 53	1916	Bridges known as Monson culvert, Parker-Robinson bridge. Volk culvert, Hall bridge. Parker bridge.	Connelly & Dunning, Chicago.
Mercer	D	1	Steel bridge.		130' span	7,740 00	1916	Bridge known as Sugar Grove bridge.	Porter McCully, Mackinaw.
Mercer	E	1, 2, 7 & 8	4conc'te b'dg's			8,035 00	1915	Bridges known as Gowdy bridge. Attic b'dge.Braught b'dge and German b'dge	Porter McCully, Mackinaw.
Ogle	A	3	Brick.	9	10,300	29,700 83	1915	2 miles east of city limits of Oregon on the Oregon-Rochelle road.	Gund-Graham Co., Freeport.
Ogle	B	2 & 5	Bit.macadam.	17	16,222	3,496 96	1915	East city limits of Oregon, extends east and south to Stinnistippi Farm.	E. F. Davis, Oregon.
Rock Island	A	11	Concrete.	10	4,969	7,355 13	1915	West city limits Taylor Ridge and extends west on Edgington road.	McCarthy Impr. Co., Davenport. Ia.
Rock Island	B	3	Concrete.	10	3,000	4,882 90	1915	4 miles s. w. of Hillsdale and extends west on Watertown-Hillsdale road.	McCarthy Impr. Co., Davenport. Ia.
Stark	B	1,2,3,3A&5	14 R. C.					Bridges known as Mike Colgan, Steaser, Freidman. Haggerty. Spier culvert. Hall and McCormack.	Connelly & Dunning, Chicago.
			Culvs.&b'dg's.	30&24		6,897 80	1916	Colgar. Jefferson. Merria. Schaad, Jordan. Leadley, Foster.	
Stark	C	1, 5, 7 & 8	8conc'te b'dg's			5,428 20	1916	Bridges known as Code. House, Davis, Downend. Sorrensen, Galbraith, Turnbull. Winnens. McKeighen's.	Connelly & Dunning, Chicago.
Stephenson	A	9	Brick.	18	3,386	13,905 78	1915	Se. limits of Freeport. Grant Highway	Gund-Graham Co., Freeport.
Stephenson	B	7, 14, 6 & N	4conc'te b'dg's			2,128 30	1916	Bridges known as McConnell, Hershey, Pope and Althoff.	W. H. Shons, Freeport.
Stephenson	C	13	Brick. Concrete.	Double. 10	475 2,215	6,404 82	1915	West city limits of Freeport, extending west on Grant Highway.	Gund-Graham Co., Freeport.
Warren	A	7	Brick.	10	3,500	13,162 68	1915	1 m. s. city of Monmouth. Roseville rd.	Merrifield Constr. Co., Monmouth.
Warren	B	12	Brick	10	4,904	12,503 24	1915	1 m. w.city l'ts Monmouth.Oquawka rd.	Merrifield Constr. Co., Monmouth.
Warren	C	12	Brick.	10	20,095	5,778 40	1915	West city limits of Monmouth to section B on Oquawka rd.	E. A. Lord Constr. Co., Monmouth.
Warren	D	7	Concrete.	10	5,350	11,756 45	1916	At end of section A, 1½ miles south of city limits of Monmouth. Roseville rd.	E. A. Lord Constr. Co., Monmouth.
Whiteside	A	6	Concrete.	10	3,100	8,090 56	1914	Beginning 2 miles south of city of Morrison on the Morrison-Prophetstown rd.	Shugart & Munsen. Nevada. Iowa.
Whiteside	B	1	Concrete.	15&18 with gutters.	4,900	10,112 97	1915	Beginning 1½ mile east of city limits of Morrison, thence east on Lincoln Highway.	Walter & Windes. Glencoe.
Whiteside	C	1	Concrete.	15	3,500	6,587 06	1915	West city limits of Morrison. on the Morrison-Fulton road.	Walter & Windes. Glencoe.
Whiteside	D	8	Gravel.	10	14,125	13,914 94	1916	East city limits of Coleta on Sterling rd.	H. P. Johnson. Sterling.
Whiteside	E	9	Gravel.	10	8,015	12,823 66	1916	South city limits of Rock Falls on the Sterling-Deer Grove road.	H. P. Johnson. Sterling.

NOTE.—Where states are not given, contracting firms are of Illinois towns.

SUMMARY.

Total for concrete roads	17.2 miles.	Total for earth roads	10.9 miles.
Total for brick roads	5 3 miles.		
Total for bituminous macadam roads	3.1 miles.	Total mileage, all types.	43.0
Total for gravel roads	6 5 miles.	Total number of bridges, 38 concrete and 1 steel.	

BUTT MAKES DRAGGING RECORDS.

Highway Superintendent Butt, of Knox County, who addressed the Rock Island meeting June 7, on road dragging, presented an interesting table of expenditures, hours put in in dragging, etc., which he said would serve him as a basis for contracts for future dragging.

This table, which is produced herewith for reference of superintendents elsewhere who may find the system practicable, was based on the actual work of five different men, four of them operating horses and one of them a tractor. The cost per mile for the dragging, the time put in and other facts are established.

The work of the tractor, Mr. Butt said, had been as efficient as that done by horses. Superintendents present at the meeting, however, were inclined to the belief that too many tractors would be required for average dragging, in order to get it done when it should be. Overhead cost, they believed, would be too greatly increased.

Mr. Butt's records, as given at the meeting, follow:

C. E. Rafferty.

Date.	Horses.	Rounds.	Miles traveled.	Size.	Time— hours.
March 19.........	4	2	4	7	3
March 26.........	4	3	6	7	3½
April 2.........	4	2½	21	7	6
April 7.........	4	2	17	7	5½
April 12.........	4	2	17	7	6
May 2.........	4	6	27	7	11
May 7.........	4	5	22½	7	8
May 11.........	4	3	25½	7	7½
			140		50½

Average speed per hour—2.77 miles.
Total cost—$37.88.
Cost per mile traveled—27 cents.

E. L. Haines.

Date.	Horses.	Rounds.	Miles traveled.	Size.	Time— hours.
March 28.........	4	2	10	7	4
May 2.........	4	2	10	7	3½
May 5.........	4	2½	12½	7	4½
			32½		12

Average speed per hour—2.71 miles.
Total cost—$9.00.
Cost per mile traveled—27.7 cents.

Milton Deatherage.

Date.	Rounds.	Miles traveled.	Size.	Time— hours.
March 29......... Tractor	1	24	2 drags	10
April 22......... Tractor	1	24	2 drags	15

Average speed per hour—1.92 miles.
Cost—$25.
Cost per mile traveled—50.2 cents.

Arthur Robertson.

Date.	Horses.	Rounds.	Miles traveled.	Size.	Time— hours.
March 24.........	4	1½	16	7	5
March 26.........	4	3	30	7	8¾
April 3.........	4	3	16	7	7½
April 6.........	4	2	12	7	4½
April 7.........	4	2	8	7	3½
April 10.........	4	2	12	7	4
April 21.........	4	2	12	7	4
April 26.........	4	2	14	8	5
May 2.........	4	3	27	8	9¼
May 5.........	4	1½	13½	8	5
May 14.........	4	3	28	8	10
			188½		66½

Average speed per hour—2.83 miles.
Total cost—$49.88.
Cost per mile traveled—26½ cents.

H. L. Alton.

Date.	Horses.	Rounds.	Miles traveled.	Size.	Time— hours.
March 21.........	3	2	10	7	6
March 26.........	3	1½	14	7	6
April 2.........	4	2	8	7	5
April 3.........	4	2	12	7	5
April 7.........	4	2	16	7	5
April 10.........	4	1½	5	7	3
April 12.........	4	2	16	7	6
May 2.........	4	3	28	7	10
May 6.........	4	3	28	7	11
			137		57

Average speed per hour—2.40 miles.
Total cost—$40.95.
Cost per mile traveled—29.8 cents.

WORK UNDER CONTRACT IN SECOND DIVISION. JUNE 16, 1917.

County.	Sec.	Route.	Type.	Width feet.	Length feet.	Contract price.	Per cent completed.	Location.	Contractor.
Bureau.......	I	3 & 3A	Concrete.	15	4,550	$ 8,557 79	2.5	South city limits of Ladd.	Trompeter & Sons, Peru.
Carroll........	C	8	Drainage str. and earth.	30, 24	19,000	13,207 74	Not strtd.	Southwest city limits of Mt. Carroll, Mt. Carroll to Savanna.	Gund-Graham Construction Co., Freeport.
Henry	C	1	Oiled earth.	24	40,119	23,711 58	40%	3½ miles from Cambridge on the Geneseo road.	Cameron & Joyce Construction Co., Keokuk, Iowa.
Henry	D	6	Oiled earth.	24	50,016	23,215 28	5%	Northwest of Kewanee.	Cameron, Joyce & Co., Keokuk, Ia.
Joe Daviess..	D	1	Earth and concrete.	21	1,006	5,522 67	30%	1 mile east of Elizabeth.	R. F. Conlon, Cuba City, Wis.
Joe Daviess..	E	1	Concrete.	10	3,150	4,621 15	5%	3 miles west of Galena.	R. F. Conlon, Cuba City, Wis.
Joe Daviess..	F	1	Concrete.	10	2,475	4,282 73	5%	2 miles east of Elizabeth.	R. F. Conlon, Cuba City, Wis.
Knox.......	C	3	Earth.	30	2,290	6,587 03	97%	Galesburg Wataga road.	Cameron, Joyce & Co.
Knox.......	D	10	Earth.	24	24,176	3,705 96	45%	Galesburg to Knoxville.	Cameron, Joyce & Co.
Knox.......	E	11	Earth.	30	14,980	4,474 07	65%	Knoxville east.	Cameron, Joyce & Co.
Lee..........	B	5 A	Gravel.	15	15,985	7,919 02	85%	North city limits of Amboy.	Gund-Graham Co., Freeport.
Lee..........	C	5	Bit. mac.R&S.	15	5,960	9,865 49	Not strtd.	1¼ miles southeast of Dixon.	Duffy & Hubbard, Dixon.
Lee..........	E	5 A	Gravel.	15	6,150	12,513 64	Not strtd.	1½ miles north of Amboy.	Henry & Johnson, Sterling.
Mercer......	F	7	Earth.	24	7,507	4,109 31	5%	Aledo to Joy, west city l'ts of Aledo.	E. A. Lord Const. Co., Monmouth.
Mercer......	G	2 & 2 A	Earth.	24	16,041.1	4,302 00	30%	South of Reynolds.	E. A. Lord Const. Co., Monmouth.
Mercer......	H	6 & 6 B	Earth.	24	14,985.3	4,346 50	97%	3½ miles east of Seaton.	E. A. Lord Const. Co., Monmouth.
Mercer......	I	8	Earth.	24	15,361.6	3,930 00	40%	North city limits of Joy.	E. A. Lord Const. Co., Monmouth.
Ogle........	C	1	Concrete.	10	7,080	19,532 27	80%	Oregon-Byron road, 2 miles north of Oregon.	Gund-Graham Co., Freeport.
Rock Island..	C	9	Concrete.	10	4,475	9,276 58	Not strtd.	Rock Island-Andalusia road.	S. D. Hicks Const. Co., Moline.
Rock Island..	D	3	Concrete.	10	4,450	9,280 03	35%	1½ miles northeast of Watertown.	S. D. Hicks Const. Co., Moline.
Stark.........	D&E	5	Earth.	24	47,125	18,914 34	40%	East of Lafayette and east of Toulon.	Cameron, Joyce & Co., Keokuk, Ia.
Stephenson..	D	1	Waterbound macadam.	15	5,600	11,989 33	80%	Freeport-Cedarville road.	Gund-Graham Co., Freeport.
Stephenson..	E	6	Brick with 8' conc. shoul.	4' shoul.	6,000	18,146 73	25%	Northwest city limits of Freeport.	Gund-Graham Co.
Whiteside ..	F	1	Gravel.	15	8,778	12,689 60	5%	On Lincoln highway, ½ mile north from Agnew.	N. B. Ridge.
Whiteside ...	G	3	Gravel.	10	13,800	12,950 17	40%	West city limits of Prophetstown.	N. B. Ridge.

NOTE.—Where states are not given, contracting firms are of Illinois cities.

SUMMARY.

Total for concrete roads...................... 5.3 miles.	Total for oiled earth roads....................... 17.1 miles.
Total for brick roads...................... 1.1 miles.	Total for plain earth roads....................... 33.2 miles.
Total for bituminous macadam roads.......... 1.2 miles.	
Total for waterbound macadam roads.......... 1.1 miles.	Total mileage all types....................... 65.9
Total for gravel roads...................... 6.9 miles.	

At the time of compilation, contracts were later to have been let for work in the second division as follows:

Three and one-half miles of concrete road in Bureau County, ⅝ mile of brick road in Lee County, 1 mile of concrete or brick in Warren County, 1¼ miles of concrete road in Ogle County and 7½ miles of earth road in Mercer County.

·IN WAR TIMES, BUILD!

It is almost a shame to have to advocate a cause which of its own innate self—superficially, internally, externally, and in every other way—is so manifestly worthy.

We refer to the principle comprehended in the title of this article.

Yet, who hasn't heard the plaint: "We ought to go ahead with improvements, but the war——?"

That's as far as they get, most of those who preface an apology for inactivity with these words, or similar. They are honest in that, often, they don't try to force or manufacture any additional excuses. Still, the doubt is father to inertia, and the tendency toward a chronic case of cold feet—chronic so long as the war lasts, at least—persistently wends its way.

It's too bad, this war time scare in its relation to building projects. Thank heaven it isn't general, but the seed of morbid suspicion has been so deeply rooted in many localities and in many minds that only a miracle, we suspect, will kill the "fear plant" before it attains a dangerous maturity.

We laud with all the enthusiasm that is in us the efforts of magazine and newspaper editors to allay the "building in war times" dread and dismay. It is an artificial, unfounded, unworthy weakness: and regarding it as such, we join hands with the patriots who just now are expending honest time and effort to clamp upon it a summary quietus.

Our particular interest lies in the highways of our State, yet the principle we apply to them will hold in the case of any legitimate building or improvement enterprise.

Creeks and rivers in Illinois during the next few years are going to continue to flow. Their channels will broaden a little each twelve months, and they will present the same barriers to traffic that they constitute to-day. It's going to take bridges to get across them a few years from now the same as it requires spans to-day. We'll not be able to fly. or wish ourselves our automobiles, rigs, and horses, across.

Illinois roads are not going to be improved unless we look after their surfaces. The mud is going to be just as deep five years from now on unimproved roads as it is to-day. Heavy tires on auto wheels will slip or mire down then the same as now. There isn't a chance in the world for transformation—unless money, plenty of it, and materials, vast quantities of them, are blended together and, with the aid of labor, molded into permanent traffic surfaces.

How utterly wrong even to think of a cessation of road, bridge and other building, just because the country is at war. War! The most pertinent and sailent reason in all our history for a stimulated progress. Not an artificial progress. That isn't the idea. Don't misunderstand us. But a steady energetic reasonable and industrious activity in all lines of business. We've got to maintain such a status. If we don't, we might as well ask ourselves the sober question, "After the war, what National fate will we suffer?"

We can not endorse hysteria in any form. That applies to frenzied editorials as. well as paroxysms of fear with reference to industry and· its status during the war. We are endeavoring, therefore, to weigh our words. War time, of all times, precludes the policy of "easing up" on building. We've got to preserve the potential value of our country. Without it, we are weakened—and more liable to fall a prey to an invading enemy. With a nation hustling and bristling with an "as usual" air, in all its avenues of business, we are a thousand times more apt to prove invincible, financially and in man power.

A number of editorials have attracted our interest of late by their earnest advocacy of the "keep on building" policy. None of them advises an artificial prosperity. They all, however, decry the ill advice of individuals who, because the country is at war, would have the Nation crawl into a hole and pull the hole in after it. We are glad to reproduce a few of these editorials, which follow:

Feather-edge gravel, 10-foot, in Wabash County, 1916.

BUILDING IN WAR TIMES.

The Illinois Legislature has abandoned its plans for extensive building operations in the State departments and institutions, and with the ear of faith we already hear applause the country over. Bravo! Let cities, commonwealths, and the Federal Government follow suit!

To which impending outbursts we reply, "Be orthodox, brethren, but don't be more orthodox than His Holiness the Pope." Paris has not suspended public building operations because of the war. Neither has Berlin. To curtail such operations, if by curtailment you mean putting a check on wild and wanton extravagance, is doubtless advisable. Self-confessed pork barrel expenditures must halt, and there are other pork barrels besides the celebrated cask of iniquity at Washington. Pork kegs, we might term them. States and cities have each their own. Away with such! But not with the long projected and long needed improvements that have an incontestable value. Just because we are no longer in a position to throw money about, it does not follow that we must scrimp or perish. Neither does it follow that scrimping will prevent our perishing. It may even help us to.

As we look at it, a quietus clapped on legitimate public building enterprises would rank with the mania for private economy that is now impoverishing milliners and dressmakers and many a distressed tailor. Fine—is it not?—to see her ladyship economize by starving her modiste! Inspiring to see her husband economize by skinning his tailor! For that is what it comes to. And they call it patriotism.

Patriotism! Ye gods and little fishes! One plain duty of patriotism in war time is to keep the pot a-boiling. Waste is wicked, but legitimate spending a virtue. Within the bounds of reason, go on spending. It promotes "business as usual." It steadies the State. And what applies to the individual applies equally to municipalities, commonwealths, and the Federal Government. Let there be no havoc wrought in the building trade and its half dozen allied industries in the name of patriotic economy. To put a peremptory quietus on legitimate and sorely needed public building projects is to sow disorder, unrest, and distress at the very time when such calamities would work a maximum of mischief. Let us keep our hair on. In avoiding waste, let us also avoid the economy that in the end spells extravagance.

—*Chicago (Ill.) Tribune.*

LET'S BUILD WHILE WE FIGHT.

Americans have a habit of quitting work and crowding around when an accident occurs. The case in point is the world's "accident" in Europe:

We are in danger of losing our heads and stopping work while the conflict is on. This would be a serious happening but, happily, every American can help to prevent it without adding to the noise and confusion of going to war.

The only thing necessary is to go quietly on in attending to our own business.

While our naval and military forces are hastening to the front to destroy agencies and obstacles that seek to impede our growth, it is essential that we redouble our constructive efforts at home.

We can both build and fight and we ought to seize upon this advantage as the greatest opportunity created by the war.

Let both public and private useful building construction proceed. Production and handling of building materials and public and private construction work are fundamental industries of the country. Any tendency to suspend or postpone building projects is inconsistent with maintaining our prosperity. The country is prosperous. Building investors should not hesitate to go ahead with their plans. Railroads should spare no effort to supply the building industry with the cars needed to transport materials. Government, state, county, and municipal authorities should encourage the continuance of all kinds of building. Road and street improvements in particular should go on unabated. Bad roads and streets are factors of first importance in the present high cost of foodstuffs. Never before was the improvement of highways so essential.

The lumber, brick, cement, lime, sand, gravel, stone, and other building materials industries are basic. Neither Government regulations nor railroad restrictions should be unnecessarily imposed to interfere with them. If any action is taken which results in the prostration of so fundamentally important industries, there is real danger of a surplus of unemployed labor, a surplus of railroad cars and a crippling of business that will seriously embarrass the Government in financing the war.

Let us build while we fight.!

—*Portland Cement Association.*

AUTOISTS ON THE HIGHWAYS.

Every motorist should know something of the law which controls his use of the public highway, says *Milestones.* He should understand his rights and his liabilities. The roads are for the use of the general public, and a member of the public has a right to utilize them in any proper way, and driving over them in an automobile is a proper use.

When the automobile first appeared this was not easily conceded. An early law in England required that every automobile be preceded by a man on foot carrying a red flag. In America is was sought to bar the motor car from the highways, but it is now thoroughly established that the automobile is a proper vehicle to use upon a public way.

Having a right to go upon the road, the motorist is not responsible if, merely because of the automobile's presence, a horse becomes frightened and causes injury. But if the motorist is careless and because of this injury results, he will be legally responsible.

Turn to the right is the familiar rule of the road known to all who drive. While the law requires that you turn to the right on meeting another machine, it does more—it requires that the other driver use due care to avoid collisions, and if he does not, merely turning to the right will not excuse him before the courts.

Further, a lighter vehicle is expected to avoid a heavier one as far as possible. This does not relieve the heavier vehicle from all responsibility of turning out, but it need only turn out as far as is reasonable under the circumstances.

The motorist and the pedestrian have equal rights in the road, and neither has a right of way over the other. Each must take care to avoid the other and keep out of his way.

If another motorist stops his car in the road to view the scenery, or a farmer pulls up with his load of hay to gossip with a friend, thus blocking the road, you have a right to be angry about it and demand that they clear the way for travel.

The roads are open to the public for the purpose of travel, and no one has a right to use them for other purposes to the detriment of others.

Legal responsibility for accidents along the road is placed upon the party who was negligent.

Sangamon County brick road, showing wide, modern culvert.

Directory of County Highway Superintendents in Illinois.

Corrected to Date and Listed According to Division Engineering Districts.

FIRST DIVISION.
(TWELVE COUNTIES.)

County.	Superintendent.	Address.
Boone	Thos. W. Humphrey	Belvidere.
Cook	R. P. V. Marquardsen	Chicago.
	(Temporary.)	
DuPage	Eugene Gates	Wheaton.
Grundy	Fred W. Stine	Morris.
DeKalb	Wm. C. Miller	Sycamore.
Kane	Geo. N. Lamb	Geneva.
Kankakee	Frank M. Enos	Kankakee.
Kendall	John D. Russell	Oswego.
Lake	Chas. E. Russell	Waukegan.
McHenry	C. L. Tryon	Woodstock.
Will	Will H. Smith	Joliet.
Winnebago	A. R. Carter	Rockford.

SECOND DIVISION.
(FOURTEEN COUNTIES.)

County.	Superintendent.	Address.
Bureau	John E. Johnson	Princeton.
Carroll	S. C. Campbell	Mt. Carroll.
Henderson	C. R. A. Marshall	Stronghurst.
Henry	James H. Reed	Cambridge.
Jo Daviess	Geo. E. Schroeder	Stockton.
Knox	Harley M. Butt	Galesburg.
Lee	L. B. Neighbour	Dixon.
Mercer	J. E. Russell	Viola.
Ogle	Alex Anderson	Polo.
Rock Island	Wallace Treichler	Rock Island.
Stark	Wm. Slater	Wyoming.
Stephenson	O. G. Hively	Freeport.
Warren	C. L. McClanahan	Monmouth.
Whiteside	V. N. Taggett	Morrison.

THIRD DIVISION.
(ELEVEN COUNTIES.)

County.	Superintendent.	Address.
Ford	S. E. Wells	Piper City.
Fulton	E. F. Motsinger	Canton.
LaSalle	Geo. L. Farnsworth	Ottawa.
Livingston	R. W. Osborn	Pontiac.
McLean	R. O. Edwards	Bellflower.
McDonough	W. M. Bonham	Macomb.
Marshall	L. H. Eldridge	Lacon.
Peoria	W. E. Emery	Peoria.
Putnam	Mason Wilson	McNabb.
Tazewell	F. S. Cook	Mackinaw.
Woodford	A. B. Hurd	El Paso.

FOURTH DIVISION.
(THIRTEEN COUNTIES.)

County.	Superintendent.	Address.
Champaign	Geo. C. Fairclo	Urbana.
Clark	Zane Arbuckle	Marshall.
Coles	Harry Shinn	Mattoon.
Crawford	J. P. Lyon	Robinson.
Cumberland	Jno. A. Decker	Toledo.
Douglas	L. O. Hackett	Tuscola.
Edgar	Karl J. Barr	Paris.
Iroquois	Benj. F. Jordan	Watseka.
Jasper	S. A. Connor	Newton.
Lawrence	R. J. Benefiel	Lawrenceville.
Moultrie	T. C. Fleming	Sullivan.
Richland	G. W. Low	Olney.
Vermilion	Wm. S. Dillon	Danville.

FIFTH DIVISION.
(SIXTEEN COUNTIES.)

County.	Superintendent.	Address.
Adams	Lewis L. Boyer	Quincy.
Brown	W. O. Grover	Mt. Sterling.
Cass	John Goodell	Beardstown.
Christian	C. A. Pennington	Taylorville.
DeWitt	Melvin Tuggle	Clinton.
Hancock	Wm. Burgner	Carthage.
Logan	Thos. S. Davy	Lincoln.
Macon	Preston T. Hicks	Decatur.
Mason	H. V. Schoonover	Bishop.
Menard	C. M. Buckley	Petersburg.
Morgan	L. V. Baldwin	Jacksonville.
Piatt	Thos. J. Anderson	Monticello.
Pike	H. H. Hardy	Pittsfield.
Sangamon	Edwin White	Springfield.
Schuyler	W. S. Henderson	Rushville.
Shelby	N. A. Baxter	Shelbyville.

SIXTH DIVISION.
(SIXTEEN COUNTIES.)

County.	Superintendent.	Address.
Bond	R. O. Young	Sorento.
Calhoun	Jno. A. Earley	Batchtown.
Clinton	Jno. T. Goldsmith	Carlyle.
Effingham	Geo. T. Austin	Effingham.
Fayette	J. V. Waddell	Vandalia.
Jersey	Chas. E. Warren	Jerseyville.
Macoupin	O. B. Conlee	Carlinville.
Madison	W. E. Howden	Edwardsville.
Monroe	Albert R. Gardner	Waterloo.
Montgomery	P. M. Bandy	Hillsboro.
Randolph	Henry I. Barbeau	Prairie du Rocher.
St. Clair	David O. Thomas	Belleville.
Scott	Geo. H. Vannier	Bluffs.
Washington	O. C. Rabbeneck	Nashville.
Perry	Frank House	St. Johns.
Greene	Irving Wetzel	Carrolton.

SEVENTH DIVISION.
(TWENTY COUNTIES.)

County.	Superintendent.	Address.
Alexander	W. N. Moyers	Mound City.
Clay	H. M. Anderson	Louisville.
Edwards	C. C. Rice	Albion.
Franklin	George F. Hampton	Benton.
Gallatin	Victor Pearce	Equality.
Hamilton	Gregg Garrison	Garrison.
Hardin	W. M. Ball	Elizabethtown.
Jackson	Thos. G. Dunn	Gorham.
Jefferson	Tony G. Pitchford	Mt. Vernon.
Johnson	John H. Sharp	Cypress.
Marion	Lee S. Trainor	Salem.
Massac	J. Thrift Corlis	Metropolis.
Pope	W. T. S. Hopkins	Dixon Springs.
Pulaski	W. N. Moyers	Mound City.
Saline	John P. Upchurch	Harrisburg.
Union	Jos. F. Howenstein	Anna.
Wabash	Guy W. Courter	Mt. Carmel.
Wayne	Griff Koontz	Fairfield.
White	George H. Brown	Carmi.
Williamson	P. B. Wilson	Marion.

CPSIA information can be obtained
at www.ICGtesting.com
Printed in the USA
LVHW081134080722
723042LV00001B/25